Macromedia® Flash® Professional 8 Beyond the Basics
Hands-On Training

By Shane Rebenschied

lynda.com/books | Peachpit Press
1249 Eighth Street • Berkeley, CA • 94710
800.283.9444 • 510.524.2178 • 510.524.2221(fax)
http://www.lynda.com/books
http://www.peachpit.com

lynda.com/books is published
in association with Peachpit Press,
a division of Pearson Education
Copyright ©2006 by lynda.com

ISBN: 0-321-29387-8

0 9 8 7 6 5 4 3

Printed and bound in the
United States of America

Lynda Weinman's | Hands-On Training

Macromedia®

Flash® Professional 8
Beyond the Basics

Includes Exercise Files and Demo Movies

lynda.com

By Shane Rebenschied

H•O•T Credits

lynda.com Director of Publications: Tanya Staples

Editor: Karyn Johnson

Production Coordinator: Myrna Vladic

Compositor: David Van Ness

Copyeditor: Kimberly Wimpsett

Proofreaders: Liz Welch, Darren Meiss

Interior Design: Hot Studio, San Francisco

Cover Design: Don Barnett, Owen Wolfson

Cover Illustration: Bruce Heavin (bruce@stink.com)

Indexer: Julie Bess, JBIndexing Inc.

Video Editors and Testers: Rob Haberle, Scott Cullen, Michael Cooper, Eric Geoffroy

H•O•T Colophon

The text in *Macromedia® Flash® Professional 8 Beyond the Basics H·O·T* was set in Avenir from Adobe Systems Incorporated. The cover illustation was painted in Adobe Photoshop and Adobe Illustrator.

This book was created using QuarkXPress and Microsoft Office on an Apple Macintosh using Mac OS X. It was printed on 60 lb. Influence Matte at Courier.

Table of Contents

Introduction

A Note from Lynda Weinman

Most people buy computer books to learn, yet it's amazing how few books are written by teachers. Shane Rebenschied and I take pride that this book was written by experienced teachers, who are familiar with training students in this subject matter. In this book, you'll find carefully developed lessons and exercises to help you learn intermediate-level Flash 8 skills.

This book is targeted to Flash designers and developers who want to go beyond the basics of simple animations and button programming. It walks you through creating a real-world project including modular ActionScript code, video, sound, and interactivity. The premise of the hands-on approach is to get you up-to-speed quickly with Flash 8 while actively working through the lessons in this book. It's one thing to read about a program and another experience entirely to try the product and achieve measurable results. Our motto is, "Read the book, follow the exercises, and you'll learn the program." I have received countless testimonials, and it is our goal to make sure it remains true for all our Hands-On Training books.

This book doesn't set out to cover every single aspect of Flash 8. What we saw missing from the bookshelves was a process-oriented tutorial that teaches readers core principles, techniques, and tips in a hands-on training format.

I welcome your comments at **fl8btbhot@lynda.com**. If you run into any trouble while you're working through this book, check out the technical support link at **www.lynda.com/books/HOT/fl8btb**.

Shane Rebenschied and I hope this book will improve your skills in Flash 8. If it does, we have accomplished the job we set out to do!

—Lynda Weinman

About lynda.com

lynda.com was founded in 1995 by Lynda Weinman and Bruce Heavin in conjunction with the first publication of Lynda's revolutionary book, *Designing Web Graphics*. Since then, lynda.com has become a leader in software training for graphics and Web professionals and is recognized worldwide as a trusted educational resource.

lynda.com offers a wide range of Hands-On Training books, which guide users through a progressive learning process using real-world projects. lynda.com also offers a wide range of video-based tutorials, which are available on CD-ROM and DVD-ROM and through the **lynda.com Online Training Library**. lynda.com also owns the **Flashforward Conference and Film Festival**.

For more information about lynda.com, check out **www.lynda.com**. For more information about the Flashforward Conference and Film Festival, check out **www.flashforwardconference.com**.

Product Registration

Register your copy of *Macromedia Flash Professional 8 Beyond the Basics Hands-On Training* today and receive the following benefits:

- **FREE 24-hour pass to the lynda.com Online Training Library™** with over 10,000 professionally produced video tutorials covering over 150 topics by leading industry experts and teachers

- news, events, and special offers from lynda.com

- the lynda.com monthly newsletter

To register, visit **http://www.lynda.com/register/HOT/fl8btb**.

Additional Training Resources from lynda.com

To help you master and further develop your skills with Flash 8, Web design, and Web development, register to use the free, 24-hour pass to the **lynda.com Online Training Library™**, and check out the following training resources:

Flash Professional 8 Essential Training
with Shane Rebenschied

Flash Professional 8 New Features
with Shane Rebenschied

Flash Professional 8 Beyond the Basics
with Shane Rebenschied

Flash 8 User Experiences Best Practices
with Robert Hoekman Jr.

Flash Professional 8 and Photoshop CS2 Integration
with Michael Ninness

Studio 8 Web Workflow
with Abigail Rudner

About Shane

Shane Rebenschied graduated from the Art Center College of Design in 1998 with an emphasis on traditional and digital media. Since then, his work has appeared in the annuals of the Society of Illustrators (Los Angeles and New York) as well as in numerous national and international publications and advertising campaigns. He is a fan of old paper and stains and can often be found staring at pieces of corroded, rusted metal. Shane is a professional freelance illustrator, Macromedia Flash designer/developer/consultant, and author living somewhere in the Arizona desert. Shane is the author of the *Photoshop Elements 2 Hands-On Training* and *Macromedia Flash MX 2004 Beyond the Basics Hands-On Training* books as well as numerous video-based training titles in the lynda.com Online Training Library. He maintains an online portfolio at **www.blot.com** and is a partner in the interactive design firm Cloudforge **www.cloudforge.com**.

Acknowledgments from Shane Rebenschied

I'd like to devote a small amount of ink and paper to those people who I couldn't do without:

My wife and kids, for putting up with me even after I'd been up all night writing and could barely remember my own name in the morning. I couldn't exist without you three.

My mother. I mean, really…if you're writing acknowledgments, you *have* to give a shout out to your mom!

Tanya Staples, for patiently reviewing every word in this book, for offering to help when I'm sure you had many other things to do, and for being helpful at all hours of the day. I couldn't have done it without you.

Lynda Weinman, for the opportunity. I can't thank you enough.

Ron Haberle, **Scott Cullen**, and **Michael Cooper**, the beta testers for this book. You all did a fantastically amazing job ensuring not only that everything is correct but that it's written in the clearest way possible. Your help is invaluable to me and to every reader of this book.

Robert Hoekman, Jr., for helping to craft the initial concept, scope, and direction of this book and its predecessor, *Macromedia Flash MX 2004 Beyond the Basics Hands-On Training*.

Ryan Conlan, for doing the majority of the design work for the L.A. Eyeworks Web site built throughout this book. Check out more of Ryan's work at **www.angelplasma.net** and **www.cloudforge.com**.

Peachpit Press, specifically **Kim Wimpsett** and **Karyn Johnson**, for all your hard work and attention to detail. Without your help this book wouldn't be even half of what it is.

You, the reader, both for choosing one of the best books to learn Flash with (*nudge* *wink*) and for investing your own time and energy to bettering yourself by learning a great program like Flash 8.

How To Use This Book

This section outlines important information to help you make the most of this book.

The Formatting in This Book

This book has several components, including step-by-step exercises, commentary, notes, tips, warnings, and video tutorials. Step-by-step exercises are numbered. File names, folder names, commands, keyboard shortcuts, and URLs are in bold so they pop out easily: **filename.htm**, the **images** folder, **File > New**, **Ctrl+Click**, **www.lynda.com**.

Captions and commentary are in dark-gray text. This is commentary text.

Interface Screen Captures

Most of the screen shots in this book were taken on a Windows machine using the Windows XP operating system. The only time you'll see Mac screen shots is when the interface differs from the Windows interface. I own and use numerous Macs, so I noted important differences when they occur and took screen shots accordingly.

Opening Windows Files on a Mac

As you work with Flash 8, you might need to open, on a Mac, a file created in Windows. Therefore, I want to make sure you are aware of a glitch that can cause you some confusion. Macs have difficulty recognizing FLA files created in Windows. When you're on a Mac, you may not be able to simply double-click the FLA file created in Windows to open it. Instead, you will need to open Flash 8 and choose **File > Open**. At this point, you still may not see some of the FLA files when you use the **Browse** dialog box. You can get around this by changing the **Enable** option to **All Files**. This displays all files in the folder. You can then open and save the file on your Mac, and it should open normally when you double-click it.

What's on the HOT CD-ROM?

You'll find a number of useful resources on the HOT CD-ROM, including the following: exercise files, video tutorials, and information about product registration. Before you begin the hands-on exercises, read the following sections so you know how to set up the exercise files and video tutorials.

Exercise Files

The files required to complete the exercises are on the **HOT CD-ROM** in a folder called **exercise_files**. In Chapter 2 you'll copy the **exercise_files** folder onto your **Desktop** so you can use them to follow along with the exercises in this book. In the **exercise_files** folder you'll also find the **la_eyeworks > completed_site** folder, which contains a working, completed site that should match the site you'll end up with at the conclusion of this book. If you encounter difficulties in any of the exercises, and cannot find a solution, you can refer to the completed site files and compare them with your working files.

On Windows, when files originate from a CD-ROM, they automatically become write-protected, which means you cannot alter them. Fortunately, you can easily change this attribute. For complete instructions, read the upcoming "Making Exercise Files Editable on Windows Computers" section.

Video Tutorials

Throughout the book, you'll find references to video tutorials. In some cases, these video tutorials reinforce concepts explained in the book. In other cases, they show bonus material you'll find interesting and useful. To view the video tutorials, you must have QuickTime Player installed on your computer. If you do not have QuickTime Player, you can download it for free from Apple's Web site: **www.apple.com/quicktime**.

To view the video tutorials, copy the videos from the **HOT CD-ROM** onto your hard drive. Double-click the video you want to watch, and it will automatically open in QuickTime Player. Make sure the volume on your computer is turned up so you can hear the audio content.

If you like the video tutorials, refer to the instructions earlier in this chapter, and register to receive a free pass to the **lynda.com Online Training Library**, which is filled with more than 10,000 video tutorials covering more than 150 topics.

Making Exercise Files Editable on Windows Computers

By default when you copy files from a CD-ROM to a Windows computer, they are set to read-only (write-protected), which will cause a problem with the exercise files because you will need to edit and save many of them. You can remove the read-only property by following these steps:

1 Copy the **exercise_files** folder on the **HOT CD-ROM** to your **Desktop**.

2 Open the **exercise_files** folder you copied to your **Desktop**, and choose **Edit > Select All**.

3 Right-click one of the selected files, and choose **Properties** from the contextual menu.

4 In the **Properties** dialog box, select the **General** tab. Uncheck the **Read-Only** option to disable the read-only properties for the selected files and folders in the **exercise_files** folder.

Making File Extensions Visible on Windows Computers

By default, you cannot see file extensions, such as .htm, .fla, .swf, .jpg, gif, or .psd, on Windows computers. Fortunately, you can change this setting easily. Here's how:

1 Double-click the **My Computer** icon on your **Desktop**.

Note: If you (or someone else) changed the name, it will not say **My Computer**.

2 Select **Tools > Folder Options** to open the **Folder Options** dialog box. Click the **View** tab.

3 Uncheck the **Hide extensions for known file types** option to make all file extensions visible.

Flash Professional 8 System Requirements

Windows

- 800 MHz Intel Pentium III processor (or equivalent) and later

- Windows 2000, Windows XP

- 256 MB RAM (1 GB recommended to run more than one Studio 8 product simultaneously)

- 1024 x 768, 16-bit display (32-bit recommended)

- 710 MB available disk space

Mac

- 600 MHz PowerPC G3 and later

- Mac OS X 10.3, 10.4

- 256 MB RAM (1 GB recommended to run more than one Studio 8 product simultaneously)

- 1024 x 768, thousands of colors display (millions of colors recommended)

- 360 MB available disk space

Getting Demo Versions of the Software

If you'd like to try demo versions of the software used in this book, you can download demo versions from the following Web page:

www.macromedia.com/downloads/

1

Background

Right now, you're probably standing in a small, cramped bookstore aisle trying to decide whether you should buy this book. You're probably thinking to yourself, "What is this book going to teach me? Do I *want* to learn what this book is teaching? *Can* I learn what's in this book? How much of Macromedia Flash do I really want or need to know?" These are all perfectly valid questions, but they're questions I most assuredly can't answer in this first paragraph. So bear with me, and read a little more of this first chapter as I outline the topics this book will cover, what you will be learning, and how you will go about doing it. You may want to find a place to sit down first, though.

What Is This Book?

In its barest essence, the goal of this book is to teach you intermediate-level Flash. (See the next section for more about the definition of *intermediate*.) Expanding upon that goal, this book aims to teach you intermediate-level Flash in the context of building *things*. In this book, you will learn how to use Flash Professional 8 (you can also use Flash Basic 8 to complete the majority of the exercises) to do the following:

- Construct scrolling text (text loaded into Flash from an external text file) and modify its appearance using CSS (**C**ascading **S**tyle **S**heets)

- Build a dynamic slideshow (from external JPEG files loaded into your Flash movie)

- Create a feedback form

- Construct an MP3 jukebox

- Build a streaming video player

- Build a navigation menu

- Construct a preloader

- Create a Flash Player 8 detector

To learn how to build these features (and much, much more), you should already be comfortable with basic Flash concepts such as its tools, the animation techniques of motion and shape tweening, the various types of symbols and their differences. Also, you should have *at least* basic ActionScript knowledge, such as what `stop`, `play`, `goto`, and `loadMovie` do and what variables are. For a good idea of what this book assumes your Flash 8 knowledge base is, check out the following

Hands-On Training book, also available from lynda.com:

Macromedia Flash Professional 8 Hands-On-Training
by James Gonzalez,
developed with Lynda Weinman
lynda.com/books and Peachpit Press
ISBN: 0321293886

Or, sign up to use the free 24-hour pass to the **lynda.com Online Training Library** provided in the introduction of this book, and check out the following video training resource:

Flash Professional 8 Essential Training
with Shane Rebenschied

Scan through the table of contents of either resource, and make sure you are familiar with the topics covered. From a skill-level perspective, this book starts where those resources leave off and ends where an "advanced" Flash 8 resource would pick up.

By the end of this book, you will know how to take all these separate pieces (an MP3 jukebox, a streaming video player, and so forth) and integrate them into a unified, cohesive Web site. This book focuses on "modular" Flash 8 construction—that is, I emphasize constructing your Flash 8 content in a way where you can treat the separate pieces of a Web site as individual *modules*. A module can play and function by itself, or you can easily plug it into a Web site for added functionality. As I'll describe later in this chapter, this gives you—a Flash 8 designer/developer—great freedom when creating your content because you can reuse it for multiple purposes.

What Is "Beyond the Basics"?

The term *Beyond the Basics* applies to the next level of education after the basic Hands-On Training series. What does that mean? Essentially, the *Beyond the Basics* moniker covers intermediate-level techniques whereas the basic Hands-On Training series targets beginners. To get the most from this book, you should have a firm grasp of beginner-level Flash development. You should already know the Flash interface, including how to do the following tasks:

- Access the panels

- Use the drawing tools

- Animate using motion and shape tweens

- Work with and create the different types of symbols, as well as understand how the symbols differ from each other

- Import assets (vectors, bitmaps, and so forth) into your project

- Work with text and the different types of text fields

- Create basic ActionScript such as **stop**, **play**, **goto**, and **loadMovie**

- Work with variables

- Work with sound and video

- Publish movies

Having a solid grasp of these beginner-level Flash 8 concepts will allow you to absorb the information in this book as best as possible.

One of the most overlooked areas of Flash 8 training is the intermediate level. If you look in bookstores for other Flash 8 training books, you'll see a plethora of material covering beginner-level and advanced-level Flash 8 techniques, but a vast desert exists where the intermediate Flash 8 training should be. Did I say *desert*? Heck, I meant Death Valley. Very, very little material allows the average Flash 8 student to gracefully navigate the chasm between introductory-level and advanced-level Flash 8. I have designed this book specifically to bridge this gap by teaching you not only intermediate-level Flash 8 techniques but also best development practices, modular thinking, and site development.

So, if you're not quite ready to enter the "advanced" Flash 8 realm where you learn about arrays, data binding, and the like, but you're ready to move past the basics and into more challenging Flash 8 design and development, calmly rise from your seat, and advance slowly (walk, don't run) to the checkout counter with this book in hand.

Modular, Modular, Modular

Picture this: You design and build a Web site for some clients. You build for them a slideshow to show off their products, create some scrolling text about the company and the products they sell, build a video player so they have a forum to talk directly to visitors, make a menu system so the viewer can navigate the site, and even add a little music player to play some tunes. Then, a month later, imagine another company sees the previous site you created and now wants you to build a site for them. This potential client would also like similar features—slideshow, video player, menu, music, and so forth—but is in a real hurry and needs the site done yesterday. Taking a deep breath, you calmly explain to the client that Flash sites are complex, can't be done overnight, and require lots of ActionScript programming to customize their features. You thank the client for complimenting you on the site you previously built but clarify to them that building a new Web site—even though the features are similar—would still take a lot of time to construct because everything needs to be customized. Or does it?

In this book, the focus is not only on showing you intermediate-level ActionScript and how to build a Flash 8–based Web site but also on how to do it in a *modular* fashion. Instead of building a customized Web site where everything is tied together and reliant upon each other, you'll learn how to break the Web site up into logical, stand-alone modules. These modules will work the same in one site as they could in another, and they could even be removed from a Web site and played by themselves (for instance, on a PDA [**P**ersonal **D**igital **A**ssistant] device such as a Pocket PC), or even burned onto a CD-ROM or attached to an email. This provides you with an extraordinary amount of freedom because it allows you to *design a module once and then reuse it for multiple purposes*.

This comes at a price, however. Constructing a modular Web site takes a little extra planning when building those modules so they will function the same *in* a Web site as they would *outside* it. But in exchange for extra planning, you gain the satisfaction of turning to the aforementioned hypothetical client and saying, "Sure, I can have something for you by tomorrow."

What's New in Flash 8?

As with any product upgrade, Flash 8 introduced a huge list of improvements, modifications, and additions. Like Flash MX 2004, Flash 8 is split into two "flavors": Flash Basic 8 and Flash Professional 8. In essence, they are the same product. (When purchasing Flash, everyone receives the same program. But if you purchase and then enter a "professional" serial number, you then "unlock" the professional features.) The following table describes a few of the new features and whether those features are available only in the professional version:

New Features			
Feature	Description	Flash Basic 8	Flash Professional 8
Filters (graphic effects)	You can now add Adobe Photoshop–like filters to your Flash graphics! These include filters, such as Drop Shadow, Blur, Glow, Bevel, and more.		✓
Blend modes	Blend modes—a feature commonly offered in image-editing programs such as Photoshop and Macromedia Fireworks—are now available in Flash! Blend modes allow you to define how the hues and values in one image are affected by the hues and values in the images underneath it. This allows Flash designers to better merge images to create interesting effects. Artists rejoice!		✓
Advanced easing control	Precisely control your tweens with the new advanced easing control feature. Advanced easing allows you to accurately define the easing of objects in an animation.		✓
Object-based drawing mode	In previous versions of Flash, drawn objects could affect other overlapping shapes in, sometimes, unintentional ways. Object-based drawing mode allows you to draw shapes that will not interfere with one another.	✓	✓
FlashType text rendering	A new font-rendering engine, called *FlashType*, is available in Flash 8. This new method of rendering allows type to remain clear and readable, even when reduced to small sizes.	✓	✓
Text custom anti-aliasing	In addition to FlashType, Flash Professional 8 also now gives you the ability to precisely control the anti-aliasing of your text.		✓

continues on next page

	New Features *(continued)*		
Feature	Description	Flash Basic 8	Flash Professional 8
Gradient enhancements	Gradients can now use up to 16 colors and additionally provide support for adjusting the focal point of a gradient.	✓	✓
Script Assist	For those of you familiar with Flash MX or prior, remember working with ActionScript in Normal Mode? It's back, but it's now called *Script Assist*. Script Assist assists Flash users in authoring ActionScript without requiring detailed knowledge of ActionScript.	✓	✓
Document tabs for Mac users	Flash MX 2004 introduced a tabbed document window for Windows users, allowing Flash users to easily switch between opened Flash files. Sadly, Mac users were not also given this feature. This has changed in Flash 8, and now Mac users can appreciate the workflow benefits that document tabs provide.	✓	✓
Single Library panel	In Flash MX 2004 and prior, each opened FLA file would have its own, free-floating Library panel. This could make working with the libraries of multiple FLA files somewhat confusing. Flash 8 now consolidates the multiple library panels into a single panel displaying the library for the current, foremost FLA file.	✓	✓
Object-level undo	Instead of Flash keeping track of undos on a document-wide level, the new object-level undo allows you to track undos on a per-object basis.	✓	✓
Bitmap smoothing	Bitmap images scaled up or down now look much better because of the new bitmap smoothing feature.		✓
Run-time bitmap caching	This new feature allows you to specify a static movie clip or button symbol to be cached at run time. This has the effect of optimizing playback performance because caching a movie clip or button as a bitmap prevents the Flash Player from having to continually redraw the graphics on the Stage.		✓
New video codec	Flash 8 now uses a new video encoder by On2 called the *On2 VP6 video codec*. This new codec	✓	✓

continues on next page

New Features *(continued)*

Feature	Description	Flash Basic 8	Flash Professional 8
New video codec *(continued)*	provides better-quality video at a smaller file size than the Sorenson Spark codec offered in Flash MX 2004. Additionally, importing, compressing, and skinning video for playback has been *greatly* optimized, allowing video to be easily and quickly added to your Flash content. You can now also add *cue points* to your video, which allows you to script events to be triggered by those cue points.		
New video encoder	Flash Professional 8 also ships with the *Flash 8 Video Encoder*, a stand-alone application allowing you to easily encode a single video file or even batch compress multiple files.		✓
File upload	A new ActionScript class called `FileReferenceList` gives you the ability to select one or more files to upload.	✓	✓
GIF and PNG support with the loadMovie action and the MovieClipLoader class	In previous versions of Flash, only JPEG and SWF files were capable of being dynamically loaded into a SWF file (using the `loadMovie` action or the `MovieClipLoader` class), but Flash 8 now adds GIF and PNG files to its list of supported file types.	✓	✓
Scale 9	A new method of creating graphics for components called *Scale 9* allows graphics to more appropriately scale when the components they're used in are resized.	✓	✓
Stroke enhancements	You can now define how the end (*cap*) of a stroke appears as well as join types (what should happen where strokes join with others). Additionally, you can add gradients to strokes and ensure horizontal or vertical strokes don't get unintentionally blurry with a feature called *stroke hinting*.	✓	✓
SWF file metadata	When you publish your SWF file, you can now include metadata information within it, thereby allowing search engines to more effectively catalog the content in your Flash files.	✓	✓

This table covers just a *few* of the new features in Flash 8. For a list of many more additions and improvements, visit Macromedia's Flash 8 Features page here:

www.macromedia.com/software/flash/flashpro/productinfo/features/

Upgrading from MX 2004 to 8

Sometimes, upgrading your software from an old version to a newer one can be a steep, slippery slope. Fortunately, if you're upgrading from Flash MX 2004 to Flash 8, the process is easy. Oh sure, you need to learn a few new features and additions (as I mentioned in the previous section), but in terms of "gotchas" or caveats, you'll find the transition to be fairly seamless. The following are a few items you need to be aware of if you're upgrading from Flash MX 2004:

- It's quite easy to forget whether object-based drawing is enabled. In fact, you may begin drawing and expect shapes to interact with each other like they have in all previous versions of Flash. If your shapes aren't interfering with each other like you're expecting, or if you're seeing turquoise boxes around the shapes you draw, you may need to turn object-based drawing off.

- The unified Library panel can be somewhat confusing as you transition from Flash MX 2004 to Flash 8. Remember, you can always click **New Library Panel** (on the right side of the Library panel) to create a separate Library panel for another FLA file you may have open, thereby allowing you to drag assets from one library to another.

You can read a great article on Macromedia's Web site about migrating from Flash MX 2004 to Flash 8 here:

www.macromedia.com/software/flash/ flashpro/productinfo/upgrade/

1 | What Are You Building in this Book?

In this opening exercise, you'll examine the online L.A. Eyeworks Web site, which is the Flash project you will build throughout this book. At the beginning of each chapter, you will get to see the finished module *before* you actually start building it. That way, as you're assembling a module, you'll already have a clear understanding of what the final result looks like and how it behaves.

You first need to make sure you have the latest version of the Flash Player.

1 Open your preferred browser, and type the following URL:

www.macromedia.com/go/getflashplayer

2 Follow the instructions to download and install the latest version of the Flash Player, which will ensure you're using an up-to-date version of the Flash plug-in.

3 After you've finished installing Flash Player 8, enter the following URL in your preferred browser:

www.lynda.com/flash8btb/laeyeworks/

When the site finishes loading, you'll see quite a few features. You'll see the main menu navigation bar at the top of the page, a splash graphic in the middle, and a music player at the bottom of the page. The music is off by default so viewers aren't inundated with sound as soon as they visit the Web site. If you want to listen to music as you browse through the site, click the Play button in the lower-left corner of the site.

4 Click the **about us** option at the top of the page in the navigation bar to load the **About Us** module.

Notice the About Us module has a sub-menu and is divided into three subsections: **our history**, **our staff**, and **video**.

The **our history** and **our staff** subsections both contain scrolling text. (You can scroll the text up or down by clicking the up and down arrow buttons on the right side of the page.) One of the interesting features of this text, how-ever, is it is styled using CSS. You'll learn more about this feature in later chapters.

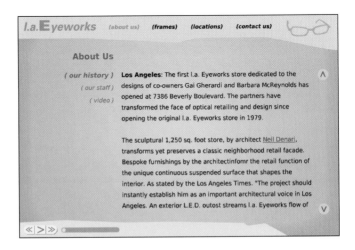

5 Click the **our staff** subsection.

Notice the two animating images integrated into the text. These are actually SWF files linked from within the **our staff** text file, much like you'd insert an image in a Web page. Neat!

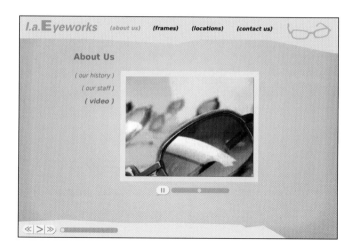

6 Click the **video** subsection button. Here you will see the video start playing. (**Note:** If you have a slow Internet connection, it will take longer for the video to start playing.)

This external FLV file (meaning, it wasn't placed in the Flash 8 movie; it's a separate FLV file existing apart from the other files) is being streamed from a Web server (no fancy server software required), using ActionScript, into the About Us module. I'll talk all about this feature, and its advantages, in Chapter 11, *"Building a Video Player."* Notice below the video is a Pause button so the viewer can pause/play the streaming video. Next to the Pause button is a progress slider displaying the playback progress of the video.

Next you'll explore some of the other sections.

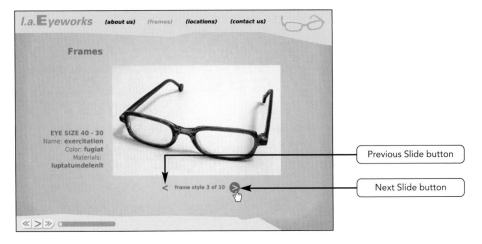

Previous Slide button

Next Slide button

7 Click the **frames** option in the navigation bar at the top to load the **frames** section, which displays an interactive slideshow allowing you to view ten frames. Click the **Next Slide** button to advance to the next image, or click the **Previous Slide** button to return to the previous image.

Notice to the left of each image is an updating description of each pair of frames. Below the frames' images are buttons to navigate backward and forward through the slideshow. Between the buttons is a bit of text informing you—out of how many frames total—which frame you're currently viewing. The interesting feature of this slideshow is each frame image is an external JPEG file, and each text description is an external TXT file (also styled using CSS). These files are dynamically loaded into the Flash SWF file and are displayed as the user clicks through the slideshow. You will learn how to build this slideshow, as well as why it is constructed in this manner, in Chapter 7, *"Building a Slideshow."*

8 Next, click the **locations** option in the navigation bar to load an interactive map. Clicking one of the stars on the map of Los Angeles (and surrounding areas) loads more information about the particular L.A. Eyeworks location. Similar to the **our staff** subsection in the **About Us** module, the location detail displays an inline, animated SWF file, accompanied by CSS-styled text.

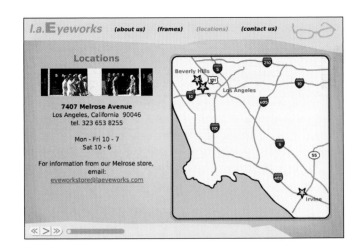

Because the Locations module simply reuses actions and techniques that you will learn in other modules, it has been prebuilt for you. You will use ActionScript to hook it into the main menu in Chapter 12, *"Building the Main Menu."*

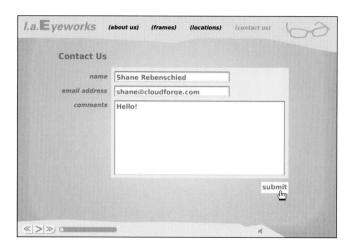

9 From the main menu navigation bar, click the **contact us** option to load a feedback form where you can enter your name, email address, and comments. Once you have entered your information in this form, click the **submit** button.

If you entered information in each field, when you click the submit button you will see the "thank you" message shown in the illustration here. Notice how your name (or whatever you entered in the name field) has been inserted into this message. When you get to this part, you'll be surprised how easy it is to do this. If you didn't enter information in each field, when you clicked the submit button, you would see an error message. This error message would politely say you forgot to fill out each field and would provide you with a back button so you could fix the error.

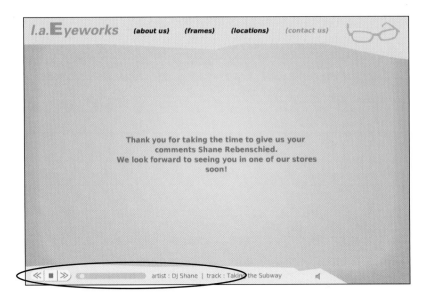

10 Last, click the **Play** button at the lower-left corner of the site window to begin downloading and playing an MP3 file. Like the video player module, this MP3 player progressively downloads an MP3 file from a Web server. Additionally, this MP3 player displays the artist and track name of the currently playing MP3 file. (This information is retrieved from the MP3's ID3 tags, which you'll learn more about in Chapter 10, "*Building an MP3 Player.*") It also allows you to change the currently playing music track by clicking the **Next Track** and **Previous Track** buttons and adjust the volume of the playing music by dragging the volume slider. This is one sexy bit of Flash 8 ActionScript to wow your neighbors and amaze your friends.

So, as you can see from this brief site tour, a lot is going on in this site. During the construction of this Web site, you'll be introduced to a wide array of topics and ideas—everything from site development techniques to workflow suggestions to a multitude of ActionScript objects (*classes*), variables (*properties*), and functions (*methods*). As you learn these new techniques and the necessary ActionScript, I'll explain each step in detail.

In the next chapter, you will begin to learn about Web site development/construction techniques as well as which file formats work best when importing graphics from various image-editing programs.

2

Where Do I Start?

As a Flash instructor for three years, recording Flash video training titles for the lynda.com Online Training Library, writing books, teaching at numerous corporations, and speaking at many Flashforward conferences in San Francisco and New York, one question follows me no matter where I go: "How do I take all of this piecemeal knowledge and build a site? Where do I start? Where does it all begin?" OK, OK...so that's three questions...but they all really fall under one question: "Where do I start?"

This chapter attempts to answer that question. Keep in mind you can take many different approaches to this process. I will outline one way to construct a site, show how to integrate all sorts of files into Flash, and offer some workflow suggestions to make your life a little easier as you begin the process of building modules and—in the end—a Web site, all inside Flash 8.

What Is the Site Construction Process?

The site construction process is unique. What follows is a general guideline of steps; if followed, these steps should help ease any bumps and bruises possibly occurring as you transition from the idea of the Web site in your head to working on actual designs, to bringing those designs into Flash, and to building the finished Web site. As you gain more experience and know-how in Flash, you can modify these steps so they are geared more toward your workflow and technique. Without further ado, here is my suggested process for constructing a Flash-based Web site.

1. Content and Target Audience

a. What Is the Content?

Before you even start *thinking* about design, come up with a solid plan of what you want to say or present and how you're going do it. What are you going to put online for the world to see? What's the subject matter?

For the L.A. Eyeworks site, the content of the Web site revolves around the company L.A. Eyeworks— the glasses, its history, its staff, its culture, its love of art, and so forth. L.A. Eyeworks, as a company, gives design a high priority, from the frames it sells to the store in which it sells them. In preparing to design the site, you should carry the same emphasis in design over into the Web site. You also know you have the following material to integrate into the site design:

- Text about the history of L.A. Eyeworks

- Information about the staff

- Video about L.A. Eyeworks

- Pictures and information about the glasses

- Maps showing where the L.A. Eyeworks stores are located

- A form where a visitor to the Web site could send feedback

- Music

This is the material you have to work with and consider as you begin to think about constructing the Web site.

b. Who Is the Target Audience?

After you've determined what the content will be, next you need to determine who will be interested in this content. Your content consumer is called your *target audience*. For example, if you're designing a Web site for a vacation villa in France, your target audience is most likely going to be 1) wealthy, and 2) have "refined" tastes. Once you can identify what the target audience is, you will have a head start on how to present the site. Using the aforementioned villa as an example, you would probably choose a color palette similar to the landscape of the area and of the villa itself (ask the client to fly you out there so you can "gather reference material" ;)), choose script fonts for decorative type and easily readable sans-serif font faces for body text, and create simple (yet elegant) navigation. As you can see, determining your target audience defines the *entire design* of the Web site and, as such, should be decided early in the site development process.

For the L.A. Eyeworks Web site, the target audience—generally—is the urban, young, hip L.A. crowd. You can gather this information by the type of person who purchases glasses from L.A. Eyeworks as well as the type of person who L.A. Eyeworks caters to. Therefore, you can ascertain using Flash 8 to build the Web site is certainly warranted, and you can "get away with" more in terms of design. You can legally (in a design sense) use more garish colors, louder music, and a less traditional user interface if you so choose. By clearly defining the target audience, you know specifically what you can and cannot use when constructing the Web site. And yes, the target audience dictates even whether you should use Flash 8.

2. Layout and Design

a. Flowchart

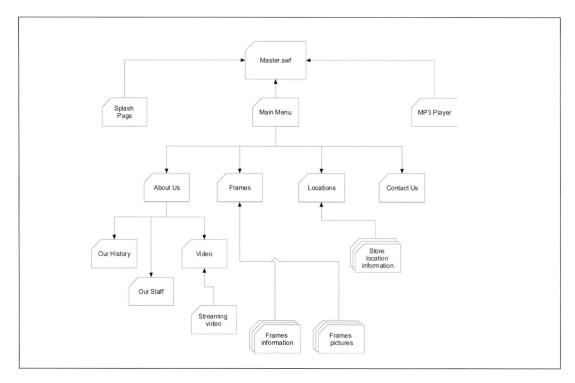

Since you've figured out your content and identified the target audience, you're ready to start creating a flowchart. A *flowchart*, as its name implies, helps you see the "flow" of your Web site. The illustration shown here is an example of a flowchart, which allows you to define the overall structure of the site and helps you begin thinking about the navigation and how the viewer will traverse through your site. It also helps you locate and remove any possible roadblocks in the navigation; that is, you can avoid visitors navigating to one section of your Web site but then getting stuck there because they have no way to navigate *away* from that page. The structure of your Web site, as laid out in the flowchart, is also commonly referred to as *tiers*. The fist tier of the site is often the main page and navigation bar. The second tier is any page linked to from the first tier, and so on, and so forth.

The illustration shown here is the flowchart for the L.A. Eyeworks Web site. As you can see, the first tier is the main "master" SWF file where the splash page, main menu, and MP3 player initially load. From the main menu, the viewer can navigate to the second tier, which includes the About Us, Frames, Locations, and Contact Us modules. In this flowchart, the third tier is really a pseudo-tier because it doesn't represent a separate "page" of information, just information being loaded into the second tier. From this flowchart you can easily and quickly see how the viewer will navigate through the L.A. Eyeworks site. This gives you a good idea of how you need to construct the navigation bar and the options comprising it.

b. Storyboard

After the flowchart comes the storyboard. The storyboard, essentially, evolves from the flowchart. Similar to the storyboards created for film and television, your storyboard could be a small sketch (you can whip out the ol' pen and paper if you'd like) defining where the main design elements would be, as well as a general estimate of the physical size of the movie. Is it going to be wide? Tall? Small? You should start to think, in general terms, about how big the movie will be. For instance, the storyboard sketch shown here represents the main L.A. Eyeworks page.

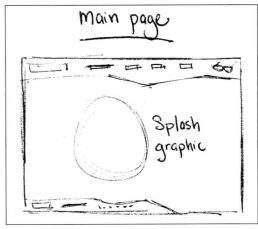

So, as you can see, the storyboard should be just a collection of quick sketches to generally block in the graphic elements of your Web site. The storyboard is where you first begin to think about the overall design of the site. From this sketch of the main L.A. Eyeworks page, you can begin to see where the main menu is located (and some of the elements contained within it), the music player, and the main splash graphic. Oftentimes the client will want to sign off on the storyboard sketches, so you might want to consider "formalizing" them (a fancy word for makin' them look polished) by creating them in a graphics program, such as Macromedia FreeHand, Macromedia Fireworks, Adobe Illustrator, Adobe Photoshop, or any other graphics-editing program you have. Also, many programs are *specifically* for creating flowcharts and diagrams. Appendix B, *"Flash Professional 8 Resources"* recommends some of these; a couple quick recommendations are Microsoft Visio (**office.microsoft.com/**) for Windows and Graffle (**www.omnigroup.com/**) for Mac users.

c. Static Mock-Ups

To further extend the storyboard, another optional step is to take the simple storyboard graphics (or site diagrams) and import them into a new Flash 8 project. You can then quickly add invisible buttons (with simple **gotoAndStop** actions assigned to them) to the navigational elements of the mock-up to create a "click-through" of the entire site. This process is a great way to bring the flowchart and storyboard together to manufacture a quick, clickable mock-up of the site navigation. This step allows you to more easily identify navigational bottlenecks as well as to give you a good understanding of the flow of the site as the viewer navigates from page to page. Building a static mock-up should minimize the possibility of discovering navigational mistakes *after* the design or construction process has begun.

d. Design

You've now done all that prep work, so it's time to start working on the design. The design of the site is often the step in the site development process producing the most questions. "Which program should I start working in? Should I start working in Flash? Fireworks? Illustrator? Photoshop?" Ahhhh! Take deep breaths. Yes, myriad design programs are on the market today, each with their own pros and cons. I'll answer these questions, in detail, in the section "What Program Do You Start In?" later in this chapter. Until then, just keep in mind designing the site comes after creating the storyboard.

For the L.A. Eyeworks Web site, I constructed some initial design concept graphics in three programs. I used Photoshop to plan some rough designs, decide on the physical size of the site, build the background graphic, and choose a color scheme. I used Illustrator to build some vector graphics, such as the vector glasses' shape and the main menu background shape. I then used Flash 8 to integrate the content, lay it out, and begin experimenting with the animated mask for the main menu, as well as a little of the interactivity. I then contracted out the remaining design work to Ryan Conlan, a designer and one of my partners at our interactive design firm, Cloudforge (**www.cloudforge.com**). Ryan worked on the designs in Photoshop. When he finished the designs, he gave the Photoshop file to me. I opened his file in Photoshop, exported each module (About Us, Frames, and so forth) as a JPEG file, imported each into a new FLA file in Flash, and then used the file as a template on which to build the finalized (and slightly modified) work. Although I had many ways to integrate graphics created in other programs (some of which integrate into Flash 8 easier than others) into a Flash 8 movie (as you'll see later), I chose Photoshop in this case.

3. Development and Implementation

a. Step 1 (Flash): Lay Out the Navigation

Of all the steps, the development/implementation step differs the most from person to person. When beginning the final design phase in Flash 8, I prefer to lay out the navigation first. Why? Well, the navigation is an *essential* element of the site. It is the main vehicle for viewers to get the content they want and then get out of there. Once you have settled the design and layout of the navigation, you will then know *exactly* how much physical space you have left over for the second- and third-level tier content.

When planning the navigation for the L.A. Eyeworks site, I knew whatever navigation layout I came up with—based on the movie size of 600 × 400 pixels—it needed to take a minimal amount of space to leave enough room for the content. Therefore, I decided to go with a long, skinny, horizontal layout spanning the length of the Web site. By being loaded into its own level, the navigation bar would be visible throughout the Web site, regardless of whichever section was currently being viewed.

b. Step 2 (Flash): Design and Implement the Main and Tertiary Content

Once you lay out the navigation, you know how much available design space is left over for tertiary content. *Tertiary content* refers to the layout, design, code, and implementation of the second- and third-tier (and so forth) pages.

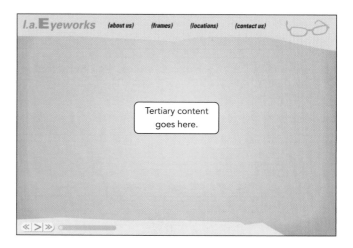

c. Step 3 (Flash): Create Navigation Interactivity

This is the last step in the construction process. By now, the designs are finished, and the content is all laid out and can be viewed and interacted with correctly. You merely have to program the main navigation menu so when the viewer clicks a button in the navigation bar, the appropriate section loads and displays. Of course, after you've programmed the navigation bar and the site is working correctly, the *last* step is to create your Flash plug-in detector, upload your content to a Web site, and begin the testing process.

4. Deployment/Upload and Testing

Lastly, you will—of course—need to deploy (upload) the finished site. Once the completed site has been fully uploaded, then you should begin the process of testing the Web site on a variety of computers using a mixture of Internet connections. Your Flash 8 project can become a completely different beast, in the blink of an eye, once it is uploaded to a Web site for testing. Once you start viewing the site as it gets streamed over the Internet, and as it plays back on a fast or slow computer, you may notice many issues you didn't notice before. Some content may load before others, some graphics might not appear, and—potentially—some content might not load at all! For the most part, if anything is going to "break" when you test the project on various computers, it will be either information (data) or text. Because you have a variety of ways to deal with text in Flash 8, you have more room for compatibility errors, font-embedding issues, and the like. Testing remains a vital step of deploying *any* Web-based content.

Flash has a built-in Simulate Download feature, which allows you to simulate how a SWF will look/perform when downloaded over Internet connections of various speeds. (You can choose on which speed to test it.) Although this is a useful feature (and one you will be using later in this book), it simulates what a SWF file would look like if downloaded at a *constant* speed. Unfortunately, downloading content on the Internet is rarely constant. Internet traffic, noise in your phone line, and so forth, can have drastic effects on *actual* download speeds. As a result, it's best to test a Web site using "real-world" Internet connections over a period of time. Using the Simulate Download feature also shows you (of course) how your movie performs only on *your* computer. Viewers on faster or slower computers may have a completely different experience when viewing your project, which is why it's always a good idea to view a Flash project on as many kinds of computers as possible. This testing should—ideally—approximate how an average Internet viewer would see your work. Usually after a round or two of testing, you'll need to modify/adjust your site so it is relatively glitch free.

When building your site and coding ActionScript, I suggest to first just get it—whatever "it" is you're working on—working and then make it pretty. As you are programming your interactivity and fixing the bugs that will inevitably crop up, it'll be easier to track down the source of a bug if you have less happening. That way, if something goes wrong, you can more easily trace a bug because you will know it could be only one or two issues causing the problems. After you have the interactivity working correctly, *then* you can slowly start making it pretty and adding to it, making sure to test it as you modify it. If you build and test in stages, it will greatly help you track down problems before they become buried under lines of code, fonts, and symbols.

For the L.A. Eyeworks Web site, because a lot of attention was given to how (from an ActionScript viewpoint) all the assets (SWF files, JPEG files, variables, and so forth) would load, it's relatively easy to program the navigational interactivity.

TIP: | **Finding Resources about Site Construction**

The subjects of Web site construction, usability, and user interface design are hot topics. If you stop by your local bookstore or library, you'll find a whole section devoted to these themes. If you want to read up before you begin your Web site planning, here are my book suggestions:

- *Don't Make Me Think: A Common Sense Approach to Web Usability* by Steve Krug. New Riders, 2000.

- *Web Navigation: Designing the User Experience* by Jennifer Fleming. O'Reilly & Associates, 1998.

- *Web ReDesign: Workflow That Works 2.0* by Kelly Goto and Emily Cotler. New Riders, 2004.

What Program Do You Start In?

So, you've got your content, figured out your target audience, created a flowchart, and even sketched out storyboards, and now you're ready to start designing your Web site. Should you just open Flash 8 and start drawing, or should you start somewhere else? If you decide to start somewhere else, then where? What program should you start designing in? The answer is, without sounding like a cop-out, use whichever program you are most comfortable using. Yes, yes…I can hear the boos and hisses now, but hear me out.

Sure, each graphics-editing program has its pros and cons. Each graphics-editing program also has *different* pros and cons when it comes to integrating with Flash 8. The question is, are those pros and cons *serious* enough to warrant switching from your graphics-editing program of choice for another one you're not so familiar with using? My answer is, no. Now what if you don't really have a "graphics-editing program of choice?" What should you do then? For those of you who aren't attached to a specific graphics-editing program, or who might consider switching for a greater ease of workflow, this section contains a detailed breakdown of several image-editing applications.

Quite a few image-editing applications are currently on the market. For this example, I'll focus on a few of the heavy hitters. When beginning to work on your designs, your choices are essentially the following:

- Macromedia Flash

- Macromedia FreeHand

- Macromedia Fireworks

- Adobe Illustrator

- Adobe Photoshop

Separating them into groups, Flash 8, FreeHand, and Illustrator are *exclusively* vector-based image-editing applications. On the other side of the graphics gamut, Fireworks and Photoshop both—primarily—work with and output graphics in a bitmap (raster) format. Without getting into the details at this point (those will be coming later in this chapter), I'll cover a few issues to keep in mind when choosing one of these programs to create your graphics.

Flash 8, being the Macromedia program it is, will obviously have slightly stronger integration capabilities with other Macromedia applications. When importing Fireworks or FreeHand graphic files into Flash 8, you will have more options to specify how Flash 8 treats those files when they are imported. Translation? Macromedia products play well with other Macromedia products. That's not to say you can't correctly import Photoshop or Illustrator graphics. In fact (as you'll see later), exporting your Illustrator designs as SWF files can yield some fantastic results when imported into Flash 8. Now obviously, if you could do all your design work directly inside Flash 8, it would greatly streamline your workflow. But Flash 8's strength is being an animation, interactivity, and programming application, not a graphics-editing application. Chances are, you (or other designers working with you) will need to do a decent portion of your design work elsewhere. In the next exercise, I will show you the options you're given when importing graphics from numerous sources.

With Flash 8's improved support for high-quality PDF and EPS importing, coupled with the capability for Illustrator to export great SWF files, your choice for which image-editing program to do the majority of your design work in should really come down to whichever one you're most comfortable using. Everything else is just details.

NOTE:

Learning Fireworks, Illustrator, and Photoshop

In this chapter, you'll learn how to effectively work with Flash and other graphics programs, such as Fireworks, Illustrator, and Photoshop. If you're interested in learning more about how to use these programs, sign up to use the free 24-hour pass to the lynda.com Online Training Library provided in the introduction of this book, and then check out the following video-based training resources:

Macromedia Fireworks Essential Training
with Abigail Rudner

Adobe Illustrator CS2 Essential Training
with Jeff van West

Adobe Photoshop CS2 Essential Training
with Michael Ninness

Adobe Photoshop CS2 for the Web Essential Training
with Tanya Staples

Or, check out the following Hands-On Training books, also available from lynda.com:

Adobe Illustrator CS Hands-On Training
by Jeff van West, with Lynda Weinman
lynda.com/books and Peachpit Press
ISBN: 0321203038

Adobe Photoshop CS2 for the Web Hands-On Training
by Tanya Staples, with Lynda Weinman
lynda.com/books and Peachpit Press
ISBN: 0321331710

1 | Installing the Site Font

In this exercise, you'll install the free, cross-platform, open source font Bitstream Vera to use throughout the creation of the L.A. Eyeworks site content. The font is included on the HOT CD-ROM, so all you have to do is follow the steps in this exercise to install the font on your computer.

You can also download and read more about the Bitstream Vera font on the Gnome Web at **www.gnome.org/fonts/**.

---

1 Quit Flash 8 if you have it open. When installing fonts, it's best if you have your applications closed first.

---

2 Open the **la_eyeworks** folder in the **exercise_files** folder on the **HOT CD-ROM**, and then navigate to the **exercise_files > resources > font > ttf-bitstream-vera-1.10** folder. Within the **ttf-bitstream-vera-1.10** folder are all the faces of the Vera font. Install all the faces of the Vera font onto your computer. If you need more information about installing fonts for your particular operating system, here are some resources to help you:

- Visit **docs.info.apple.com/article.html?artnum=106417** for Mac OS X v10.2 and earlier.

- If you're running Mac OS X 10.3 (Panther) or later, simply double-click the font faces you want to install. This launches Font Book and gives you the option to install the font.

- Visit **support.microsoft.com/default.aspx?scid=kb;en-us;314960** for Windows 95/98/2000/NT/ME/XP.

In the next exercise, you will learn how to import a graphic (created in another graphics-editing program such as Fireworks or Illustrator, for example) into a Flash 8 movie. As a Flash 8 designer or developer, you will most likely be working with graphics (provided by co-workers or freelance designers) created in various programs. You will learn which file formats import into Flash 8 with the least amount of difficulty in the next exercise.

Integrating with Fireworks, Illustrator, and Photoshop

It's a rare Flash 8 Web site designer who can create all the graphics needed for a Web site by using Flash 8 alone. However, as the drawing and typography tools gain more features and flexibility with each release of Flash, you might start to see more designers using Flash alone to create the majority of their graphics. Until then, however, it's actually quite common as a designer to develop the Web site graphics in *multiple* graphics programs and then assemble them all into one cohesive project—in the end—in Flash. Trying to get programs to play well with each other's files has never been a dauntless task, however. In this exercise, you'll learn which file formats you can import into a Flash 8 movie with the *least* amount of trouble. You'll start by creating an empty FLA file in Flash 8 and then importing a layout of the navigation menu for the L.A. Eyeworks Web site, all created with different image-editing programs. This will allow you to see the options you have when importing images of various file types into Flash 8, as well as which file types translate better when imported into Flash 8. By the end of this exercise, you should have a much stronger understanding of which file formats you can rely on and, conversely, which ones you should avoid when building graphics for your Flash 8 Web site.

---

1 In the **exercise_files > la_eyeworks** folder on the **HOT CD-ROM**, you'll see a **file_types** folder containing the various image files you will use for this exercise. Copy this folder, and its contents, onto your **Desktop**.

---

2 Open Flash 8, and press **Ctrl+Alt+N** (Windows) or **Cmd+Opt+N** (Mac) to create a new, blank document. Or, just click **Flash Document** under the **Create New** header in the **Start Page**.

Next, you'll change the Stage dimensions to better fit the size of the graphics you will be importing.

---

3 Press **Ctrl+J** (Windows) or **Cmd+J** (Mac) to open the **Document Properties** dialog box. (You can also open the **Document Properties** dialog box by clicking the **Size** button in the **Property Inspector**.)

---

4 Type **600 px** in the **(width)** field, and click **OK**.

This gives you more horizontal space to fit the graphics you will be importing.

You'll first import the navigation bar graphic created with Fireworks 8.

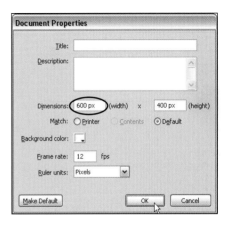

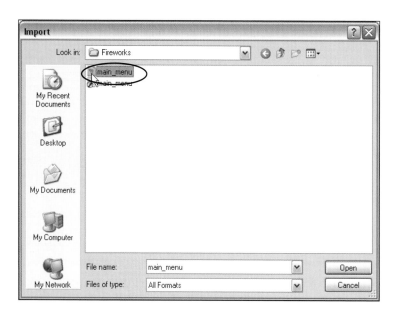

5 Choose **File > Import > Import to Stage**. From the **Import** dialog box, navigate to the **file_types** folder you copied to your **Desktop**. Then, navigate to the **Fireworks** folder, and double-click the file **main_menu.png**. (Depending on your operating system, you might not see the **.png** extension.)

This is a native PNG graphic saved from Fireworks 8.

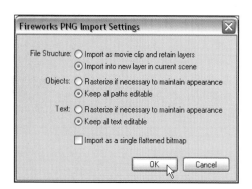

6 Flash 8, recognizing you're attempting to import a Fireworks 8 PNG file, will open the **Fireworks PNG Import Settings** dialog box, which allows you to specify *how* you want the graphic to be translated when it's imported into Flash 8. As you can see by reading the options, you can choose whether you want the graphic to be imported into a movie clip symbol or into a new layer. You can also choose whether you want to leave the text and objects editable or—to maintain their closest appearance to the original graphic—to rasterize the images, thereby making them uneditable. Select **Import into new layer in current scene**, **Keep all paths editable**, and **Keep all text editable**. Make sure **Import as a single flattened bitmap** is unchecked, and then click **OK**.

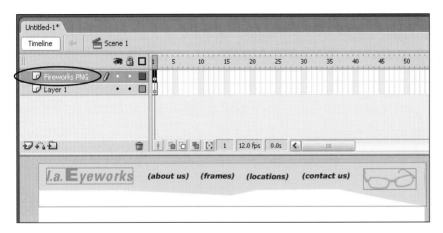

The navigation bar created in Fireworks 8 then imports into Flash 8, complete with graphics and text, into its own new layer, Fireworks PNG.

In Step 6, if you had chosen **Import as movie clip and retain layers**, Flash 8 would have automatically created a movie clip symbol, imported the Macromedia Fireworks 8 PNG file into that movie clip, and sorted the various parts of the image into named layers corresponding to the named layers in the Fireworks 8 file. Neat! This has the benefit of 1) retaining the layer naming/separation you set up in the Macromedia Fireworks 8 file, and 2) keeping the scene Timeline nice and clutter free because the Fireworks 8 graphics are imported into a new movie clip. Also, if you had created any symbols in the Fireworks 8 file, when you import the PNG file into Flash 8, it would retain those symbols! It unfortunately doesn't keep the symbol names you defined in Fireworks 8, however.

7 Deselect the selected graphics by pressing **Esc**. Then, double-click the **about us** navigation option.

Notice how the text is still editable, here inside Flash 8!

---

8 Close this FLA file, don't save the changes, and create a new, blank FLA file. Using the techniques you learned in Steps 3 and 4, change the movie dimensions to **600 px** wide.

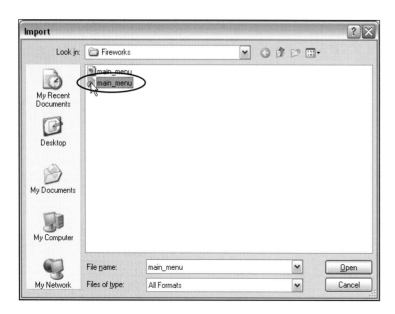

9 Choose **File > Import > Import to Stage**. From the **Import** dialog box, navigate to your **Desktop > file_types > Fireworks** folder, and double-click the **main_menu.swf** file. This is a SWF file exported from Fireworks 8.

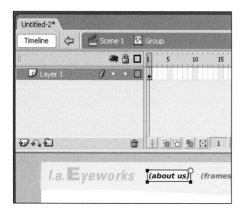

Notice how it looks like the Fireworks 8 PNG file you imported previously.

---

10 Double-click the **about us** navigation option.

This time, however, notice how the text **about us** has been placed within a group. Within the group, however, the text still remains editable. The only difference, in this case, between a Fireworks 8–created PNG file and an exported SWF file is the text is directly editable from the PNG file import, but the SWF file import groups the editable text. All in all, Flash 8 likes both Fireworks 8 PNG and SWF files, with minor differences between the imported graphics and text and the original Fireworks 8 graphic.

Next you'll import a graphic created with FreeHand.

---

11 Close this FLA file, don't save the changes, and create a new, blank FLA file. Using the techniques you learned in Steps 3 and 4, change the **Stage** dimensions to **600 px** wide.

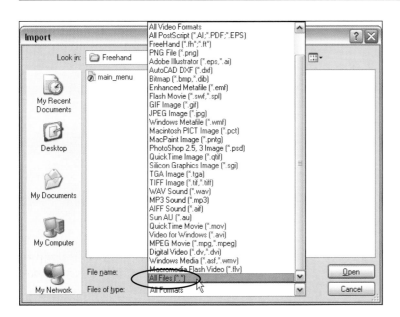

12 Press **Ctrl+R** (Windows) or **Cmd+R** (Mac). From the **Import** dialog box, navigate to your **Desktop > file_types > Freehand** folder. If you don't have FreeHand installed on your computer, you'll most likely see only one file, **main_menu.swf**. If you don't see the FreeHand file **main_menu**, click the **Files of type** pop-up menu, and choose **All Files**. This shows you all the files in the current folder, regardless of whether Flash 8 thinks it can import them.

13 Double-click the FreeHand file **main_menu** to import it into your Flash 8 movie.

14 Flash 8, understanding you're importing a FreeHand file, opens the **FreeHand Import** dialog box. Modify your options so they match the ones in the illustration shown here, and then click **OK**.

The Freehand Import dialog box lets you specify a few options to modify how Flash 8 will treat various aspects of this file as it imports it. You can specify what the FreeHand pages and layers will be translated to when they are imported, as well as which FreeHand pages you want to import, whether invisible and background layers are included, and whether Flash 8 should maintain the editable text blocks.

As you can see, new layers have been automatically created for you. These layers, and their names, correspond to the layering in the original FreeHand document! However, because of how the graphics were set up in the original FreeHand document, only one of the layers, Fireworks 1, actually contains the graphics.

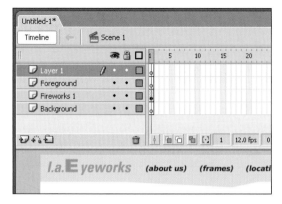

15 Double-click the navigation text **about us**. Just like the imported Fireworks 8 file, the text is editable! Strangely, the text blocks for text imported from a FreeHand document are all fixed-size text blocks (as represented by the square at the top-right corner of an editable text block). To convert a fixed-size text block into a "stretchy" text block (which resizes to fit the text you type within it), double-click the square at the top-right corner of the text block.

Also, you'll notice the FreeHand file translates nicely when imported into the Flash 8 movie. The graphics look great, and the text is still editable.

You've now seen how the two flagship Macromedia image-creation applications—FreeHand and Fireworks—fare when working with Flash 8, so it would be irresponsible of me to *not* show how Adobe's image-creation apps stack up.

16 Close this FLA file, don't save the changes, and create a new, blank FLA file. Using the techniques you learned in Steps 3 and 4, change the **Stage** dimensions to **600 px** wide.

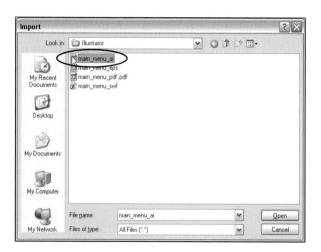

17 Import a file to your **Stage** by pressing **Ctrl+R** (Windows) or **Cmd+R** (Mac). From the **Import** dialog box, navigate to your **Desktop > file_types > Illustrator** folder. Then, locate the file **main_menu_ai.ai**, and double-click it.

This is the same navigation layout graphic you've seen in this exercise, except the graphics were created and saved in Illustrator CS2.

---

18 The **Import Options** dialog box appears, allowing you to choose how you want Flash 8 to deal with various aspects of importing the Illustrator file. The options here are identical to the ones when importing a FreeHand file. Modify your options so they match the illustration shown here, and then click **OK**.

As you can see when the file finishes importing, Flash 8 didn't do the greatest job (in this case) of translating the navigation bar text. The green background, the vector L.A. Eyeworks logo, and the vector glasses all translated fine. But the text is a mess. If you peek at the library, you'll notice Flash 8 also created a new folder called **Clip Paths** and inserted a couple of automatically created symbols into it.

You might also notice a Missing Font Warning dialog box appear saying you're missing a font used in the file. In actuality, the font—Bitstream Vera Sans Bold Oblique—used in the Illustrator file is the same as you installed earlier. In this case, a miscommunication is taking place between the Illustrator file type and Flash 8, which prevents the type from being displayed with the correct font. If you see this dialog box appear, just click **Use Default**. Alternately, you can click **Choose Substitute**, view the missing font(s), and choose a font installed on your computer to use as a substitution.

So, native Illustrator CS2 files fared moderately, but what about Illustrator CS2–created EPS files?

---

19 Close this FLA file, don't save the changes, and create a new, blank FLA file. Using the techniques you learned in Steps 3 and 4, change the movie dimensions to **600 px** wide.

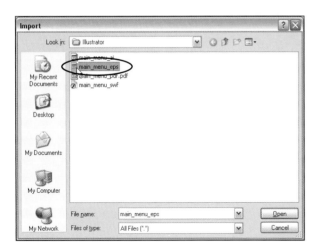

20 Import a file to your **Stage** by pressing **Ctrl+R** (Windows) or **Cmd+R** (Mac). From the **Import** dialog box, navigate to your **Desktop > file_types > Illustrator** folder. Then, locate the file **main_menu_eps.eps**, and double-click it.

21 The **Import Options** dialog box appears. Because you're already familiar with the choices it offers, modify your options so they match the ones in the illustration shown here, and then click **OK**.

Once the file has finished importing, you'll most likely notice a color shift. The L.A. Eyeworks logo, in particular, has shifted to a rather garish, '80s, florescent green. The navigation bar text has also been turned into one giant text block. Whereas, in the original file, the navigation options were each separate text blocks, now they have been combined into one text block. Additionally, some of the text spacing has been changed, and extra kerning has inadvertently been added. Barring those inconsistencies, the Illustrator CS–created EPS file fared better than did the actual Illustrator file (AI).

You've now seen importing AI and EPS files; what about PDF files?

22 Close this FLA file, don't save the changes, and create a new, blank FLA file. Using the techniques you learned in Steps 3 and 4, change the movie dimensions to **600 px** wide.

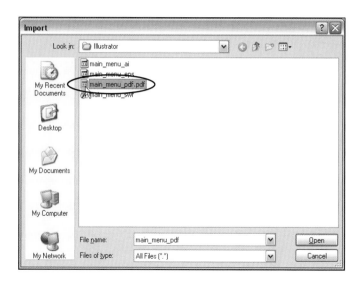

23 Import a file to your **Stage** by pressing **Ctrl+R** (Windows) or **Cmd+R** (Mac). From the **Import** dialog box, navigate to your **Desktop > file_types > Illustrator** folder. Then, locate the file **main_menu_pdf.pdf**, and double-click it.

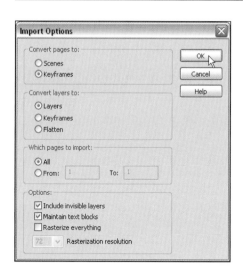

24 The **Import Options** dialog box appears. Because you're already familiar with the choices it offers you, modify your options so they match the illustration shown here, and then click **OK**.

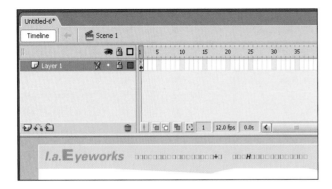

25 Once the file has finished importing, the results you're greeted with are the same as the results you achieved when importing the actual Illustrator CS2 file.

Illustrator can also export its images as Macromedia SWF files. Next, you'll import a SWF file generated by Illustrator CS2 and observe the results.

---

26 Close this FLA file, don't save the changes, and create a new, blank FLA file. Using the techniques you learned in Steps 3 and 4, change the movie dimensions to **600 px** wide.

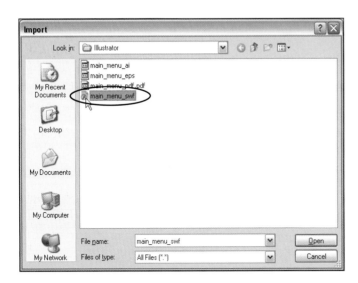

27 Import a file to your **Stage** by pressing **Ctrl+R** (Windows) or **Cmd+R** (Mac). From the **Import** dialog box, navigate to your **Desktop > file_types > Illustrator** folder. Then, locate the file **main_menu_swf.swf**, and double-click it.

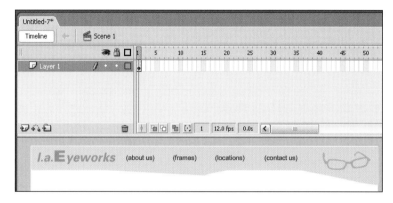

When the file finishes importing, you'll notice the results you've achieved with this imported SWF file are roughly the same as the results of importing the EPS file. One big difference, however, is evident if you double-click one of the navigation options. You'll see the navigation option is grouped, but the text within the group is an editable text block. Unlike the imported EPS file, the textual navigation options *haven't* all been clumped together into one large text block.

The final results give the edge to exporting a SWF file from an Illustrator design. The colors, designs, and even the editable type all translate into Flash 8 with minimal difficulty. However, for complex designs using Illustrator-specific techniques, the results might vary. It's best to export/save your Illustrator designs as a variety of formats and then import those into Flash, keeping whichever one gives you the best results.

Although Photoshop is not a vector-based program, like Illustrator, FreeHand, and Fireworks, it still remains the image-editing choice for a large number of creative professionals. In addition, it offers some vector-based tools, specifically shapes and type. The next part of this exercise will show you how to save your Photoshop designs to achieve the best results when importing them into your Flash 8 projects.

---

28 Close this FLA file, don't save the changes, and create a new, blank FLA file. Using the techniques you learned in Steps 3 and 4, change the movie dimensions to **600 px** wide.

---

29 Import a file to your **Stage** by pressing **Ctrl+R** (Windows) or **Cmd+R** (Mac). From the **Import** dialog box, navigate to your **Desktop > file_types > Photoshop** folder. Then, locate the file **main_menu_psd.psd**, and double-click it.

This is the original PSD document natively saved by Photoshop CS2.

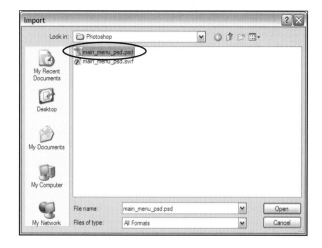

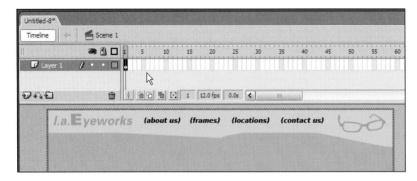

After the file has finished being translated/imported, you'll notice—as usual—the graphic looks great but is one large, uneditable raster graphic. If you open the library for this FLA file, you'll notice just one bitmap graphic: **main_menu_psd**.

Photoshop CS2 ships with a separate application called Adobe ImageReady CS2, which is designed specifically for creating Web graphics. Like Illustrator CS2, ImageReady CS2 lets you export SWF files, which you can then import into Flash 8.

---

30 Close this FLA file, don't save the changes, and create a new, blank FLA file. Using the techniques you learned in Steps 3 and 4, change the movie dimensions to **600 px** wide.

31 Import a file to your **Stage** by pressing **Ctrl+R** (Windows) or **Cmd+R** (Mac). From the **Import** dialog box, navigate to your **Desktop > file_types > Photoshop** folder. Then, locate the file **main_menu_psd.swf**, and double-click it.

This exports the SWF file from ImageReady CS2.

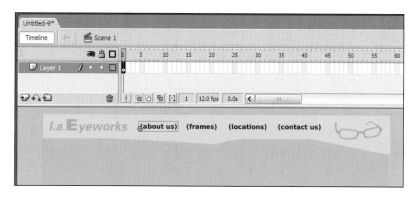

After the file has finished being translated/imported, you'll notice the results are similar to when you imported a SWF file created in Illustrator CS2. The navigation buttons are separate, editable text blocks, and the vector-based shape (in this case the glasses) is fully editable in Flash 8.

The final word: In this exercise, you imported quite a few files created with a variety of image-editing programs. You've imported files created in Fireworks 8, FreeHand, Illustrator CS2, and Photoshop CS2. All in all, each program was able to create at least one file format that could be imported into Flash 8 with workable results. Some files, however, were more "workable" than others.

---

32 Close the FLA file (and don't save the changes) you imported the PSD file into—you won't be needing it again in this chapter.

NOTE:

Leaning More about Photoshop CS2 and Flash 8 Integration

To learn more about Photoshop CS2 and Flash 8 integration, specifically about how to import content from Photoshop CS2 into Flash 8 with the best results, sign up to use the free 24-hour pass to the lynda.com Online Training Library, and check out the following video-based training resource:

Photoshop CS2 and Flash 8 Integration
with Michael Ninness

Improving Your Workflow

Since you've seen various ways to import artwork created in other graphics-editing programs, here are a few workflow suggestions:

- If you're working in a team, use shared libraries. As you'll see in this book, shared libraries are a great way to share graphics, fonts, and anything else you can import into your Flash 8 library with the rest of your team. That way, if you need to change an asset, all you have to do is open the shared library FLA file, make your changes, and publish the SWF file. Everyone else on your team using that SWF file will now have access to those updated graphics. How about that?

- Split one project up into multiple pieces (FLA files). If you're working in a team environment, this is a great way to delegate different parts of a single project to different people on your team. You can then bring all the separate pieces together again by using the `MovieClipLoader` (or its predecessor, `LoadMovie`) to load all the SWF files into one unified project. I hate to sound like a broken record, but yeah, you'll be doing this in the book as well.

In the next chapter, you'll get your hands dirty by creating the "master" FLA file, which will contain much of the reusable ActionScript you will use throughout the L.A. Eyeworks Web site. You will also begin to write some of the reusable ActionScript by creating the `MovieClipLoader` script to control all the loading of external SWF and JPEG files. Lastly, you will create and precache a shared library to contain elements you can easily reuse throughout all the modules in the Web site.

3

Getting Started

In the previous two chapters, you learned the basics of Macromedia Flash 8 Web site construction, and here is where you will begin to put those concepts into practice. In this chapter, you will create the "master" SWF file that will hold all the other SWF files for the sample Web site, as well as store many reusable ActionScripts. You will also write the main ActionScript that controls the loading of *all* the SWF, JPEG, PNG, and GIF files that will be used throughout the Web site. You will additionally learn about—and create—a shared library to store assets (such as font faces) that will be reused throughout the site. This is quite a large chapter covering many new and important topics, so if you're reading this late at night and thinking, "I'll just finish this chapter before I head to bed," I strongly suggest waiting until you've had a good night's rest before continuing…unless you want to have really weird dreams of being chased by giant MovieClipLoaders with large, gnashing fangs.

What Is a "Master" SWF File?

Unless you've been living in a cave since 1954, you're probably aware of J.R.R. Tolkien's books, now a three-part movie series, *The Lord of the Rings*. In today's omnipresent media, I'm sure you've heard the movie tagline "One ring to rule them all" in reference to a magically crafted omnipotent ring that has the power to control the many other magical rings. In the upcoming exercise you'll create the "one ring" of the sample Web site. This master SWF will act as the container into which all other SWF files will load. It also will hold some ActionScripts that you will use and reuse throughout the Web site, such as the ActionScript to load assets (the `MovieClipLoader`), the ActionScript to load variables (`LoadVars`), and the ActionScript to load and apply style sheets (`TextField.StyleSheet`). By creating this master SWF and using it to store ActionScript variables and functions that you will frequently refer to from the other SWF files comprising this Web site, you will accomplish two major goals:

- You centralize your commonly used ActionScript code. This allows you to easily

modify your ActionScript code one time, in one, centralized location. Because the other SWF files all refer to this central code, they will automatically utilize any changes you make to that ActionScript. Instead, if you had written this commonly used ActionScript directly in each SWF that needed it, when you wanted to make a change (or fix a mistake) to that script, you would have to make that modification *multiple* times for each SWF file in which the code resided. As you will see, keeping your ActionScripts centralized can *greatly* improve your workflow.

- By centralizing your ActionScript, you reduce the file size of your Web site. If you were to insert this repeatedly used ActionScript into each SWF file, you could add quite a lot to the overall file size of the project. But by keeping the common, frequently used code in one place, and just *referring* to it from other SWF files whenever you need it, you're cutting down on the overall file size of the Web site by not repeating identical code.

What Are Classes, Objects, Methods, and Properties?

As you begin to write the ActionScript code to make this Web site functional, you will run into some unfamiliar terminology. This section briefly describes the ActionScript language definitions for classes, objects, methods, and properties. I'm a big believer in using analogies to help in the learning process. To help you better understand these complex topics, I'll use a dog in my explanations. Although some of this terminology may initially sound confusing to you, you will become much more familiar with these terms as you complete the exercises throughout this book.

- **Classes:** Classes are the blueprints defining a group of objects. For example, a dog would fall under a class of animal. All animals have certain characteristics a dog shares. You can think of a class as, simply, a category of objects. From a Flash 8 viewpoint, movie clips and buttons are classes. Both movie clips and buttons have methods and properties making up their classes and defining what they can and cannot do when you use them in your projects.

- **Objects:** Objects, essentially, are instances of classes. Just like you can have an instance of a graphic symbol on your Stage, an object (from an ActionScript standpoint) is an instance of a class. An object, such as a dog, is just a collection of methods and properties (more on methods and properties next) inherited from its class. Also, like dogs, objects are unique because each can have a distinctive name and can be referred to by that name. Within Flash 8, for example, instances of movie clips and button symbols are objects because they are instances of their respective classes.

- **Methods:** Methods are the behaviors of an object. The behaviors (methods) of a dog object would be it barks, pants, slobbers, pees on your furniture, and chews up your shoes. In terms of Flash 8 ActionScript, classes have their own built-in methods that you can use, or you can even create your own methods by assigning them to a function (more on functions later in this chapter). Analogously, a dog inherently barks (its built-in method), but if you so desired, you could add a behavior allowing the dog to levitate cats and fly them around a room (an added method). A movie clip object, for example, has methods such as play, stop, next frame, and so forth.

- **Properties:** Properties are attributes defining an object. For instance, all dogs (well...most, anyway) have four legs, two eyes, a tail, a mouth, and bad breath. A movie clip object, for example, has properties such as its visibility (`_visible`), alpha (`_alpha`), rotation (`_rotation`), and so forth.

You'll encounter a few of these terms in the first exercise in this chapter.

NOTE:

What Are Variables?

You'll see variables used frequently throughout this book. A *variable*, in essence, is a container—created with ActionScript—for storing data or references to object instances or even for assigning to objects you've created. You can think of a variable as similar to a symbol; but where a symbol is a container to hold something visual—a graphic, some text, and so forth—a variable is a container to hold data such as a name, some numbers, and so on. In this book, you'll get plenty of experience creating variables. You'll use variables as containers to hold numbers (such as the running time of your music tracks), as containers to hold strings (such as the name of the visitor who is sending you comments using your feedback form), and as containers to hold ActionScript objects (such as the `MovieClipLoader` object you'll be building later in this chapter.

Variables are an invaluable keystone for working inside Flash 8, and as such, you'll get a ton of experience using variables to accomplish various tasks.

What Is Strict Typing?

As you write ActionScript during the course of this book, you'll notice something you probably haven't seen. As you are writing actions and creating variables, you'll include a little extra text after the variable name. This bit of additional text immediately following a variable is called *strict typing*, which essentially allows you to specify what kind of data type the value of that variable will be. If this initially sounds confusing, keep in mind you will gain more confidence and experience with strict typing as you use it within the exercises in this and other chapters. For your reference, here is a sample of strict typing:

```
var myVar:String = "Here is a string of text.";
var myVar2:Number = 1234;
```

See how after **myVar** it says **:String** and after **myVar2** it says **:Number**? These circled identifiers are two examples of strict typing tags. When adding strict typing to your own actions, you simply type them immediately following a variable. As mentioned, the purpose of strict typing tags is to specify the value of the variable; so, in this example, **myVar** contains data of the String type, and **myVar2** contains data of the Number type. Using strict typing when writing your ActionScript has some advantages, but as an intermediate-level Flash 8 user, you should be aware of three details:

- Strict typing allows you to explicitly state what sort of data is being entered into a variable. Strict typing also allows you to *change* the data type within a variable. In other words, if a number is being entered into a variable but you want the data type to be a string, you can specify that by using strict typing. *Why* would you want to do something like that? Well, if you were performing some calculations with numbers (division, multiplication, and so forth), you would want those numbers to be handled as the Number data type, *not* as the String data type. Trying to perform mathematical calculations (as you will be doing to create progress bars and pre-loaders) on a String data type will yield only errors.

- It's considered good ActionScript 2.0 coding practice to use strictly typed variables and objects, because by using strict typing, you're explicitly specifying the data type (String, Number, and so forth) of a variable or an object. By unequivocally letting Flash 8 know what the data type of a variable is, you help reduce potential errors in your movie.

- Strictly typing variables will help you write ActionScript faster, since the Actions panel will supply code hints and autocompletion for built-in classes (objects) as you're writing them.

Strict typing is not mandatory when writing your ActionScript, and for that matter, it is supported only when publishing a SWF file using ActionScript 2.0 (the default ActionScript version when you create a new FLA file in Flash 8). If you don't use strict typing, in most cases your actions will work just fine, but I wanted to point it out early in the book as something new to ActionScript 2.0. My goal in this book is to teach you correct ActionScript practices; also, if you choose to learn more about advanced-level Flash 8 ActionScript, you'll already understand what some of these terms and best practices are.

What Is a Function?

You can think of a symbol as a container for holding graphics. You can reuse a symbol multiple times without adding a significant amount to the file size of your SWF file. A function is similar in that respect, but a function doesn't hold graphics; it holds ActionScript. Therefore, you can think of a *function* as a container for holding ActionScript code for reuse throughout your project. Functions are *extremely* useful when you have a block of ActionScript code that needs to be repeated during your movie. As an example, say you have a series of buttons, such as in the navigation bar on a Web site. And when the viewer clicks any of those buttons, you want an animation in a movie clip to start playing, you want the background music to stop, and you want some text to appear in a Dynamic text field on the Stage. Without using a function, you would have to put all those same actions on *each button instance*. Then, when you wanted to make a change to those actions, you would have to make the same ActionScript changes on every button instance! What if you had 50 buttons? That's a recipe for insanity if I have ever seen one. Instead, you could create a function that contains the ActionScript code to perform the same three actions (start movie clip playing, stop background music, and display message) and then just add one line of ActionScript code to each button instance telling the function to execute the actions contained within it. Then, if you ever needed to make changes to your ActionScript, you wouldn't have to make those changes on each button instance. Instead, you just change the ActionScript in the function, and you're all done. So you can see what a function looks like, here is a sample:

```
function buttonClick () {
  myMC.play();
  myMusic.stop();
  myMessage.text = "You clicked on a button.
  Congratulations!";
}
```

In this sample, **buttonClick** is the name this function was given. (It can be any name you want,

as long as it doesn't begin with a number, have spaces in the name, or contain any special characters [?, *, %, and so forth].) Indented between the brackets ({ }) are the actions you want performed when the function is called. To get the actions contained within the function to execute, you simply type the function name (making sure you specify the path to the function if it resides on a different Timeline) and add the function's call operator like so:

```
buttonClick();
```

And, yes, ActionScript 2.0 syntax *is* case sensitive, so if you wrote

```
buttonclick();
```

the function would not be executed.

Another nicety functions offer is that you can pass parameters to a function. In other words, you can pass commands to the function from wherever the function is being triggered. (In the aforementioned example, the function is being triggered from a button.) For example, using the same function in the previous sample, what if you wanted the message to be different depending upon which button the viewer clicked? Right now, that message is "hard-coded" into the function, meaning the same message will be displayed no matter which button the viewer clicks. In that case, you could assign a parameter to the function and then, from the button the viewer clicks, send a string of text to the function parameter. If it sounds like I'm speaking Greek, maybe an example will help. Here's what the same function would look like with a parameter assigned to the message:

```
function buttonClick (msg) {
  myMC.play();
  myMusic.stop();
  myMessage.text = msg;
}
```

As you can see, after the **buttonClick** function name, between the parentheses, it now says **msg**. And, no, that doesn't refer to the taste-enhancing food additive; it's just a name I assigned it, and it's short for "message." If you look at the last action within that function, you'll also see the same `msg` parameter repeated after `myMessage.text =`. The parameter `msg` essentially just acts like a place-holder for whatever you send it when you trigger the function. For example, when someone clicks a button in the navigation bar titled Our Products, and you want the aforementioned function to be executed but the message to display **We have lots of stuff. Check it out.**, then this is the action you would assign to the Our Products button:

```
on (release) {
  buttonClick ("We have lots of stuff. Check it
  out.");
}
```

The **We have lots of stuff. Check it out.** text is the function parameter that gets passed to the func-tion when the viewer clicks the button. The mes-sage gets inserted where you added the parameter placeholder **msg**, and *voila*, your Dynamic text field on the Stage will display unique text when the viewer clicks that particular button.

A *function parameter* is essentially just a local vari-able. By "local," I mean as soon as the function is executed, the parameter (local variable) is destroyed to conserve memory. You can even cre-ate variables with the same name as the function parameter, and the two will not conflict.

The function used in the previous examples is a function you create with ActionScript. In addition to being able to create your own functions, objects have built-in functions called *methods* (as you'll see when you build the **MovieClipLoader** later in this chapter).

Although I'm sure you still have many questions about functions and how you can use them, you'll learn more about top-level functions and methods throughout this book.

What Is the MovieClipLoader, and How Does It Differ from loadMovie?

`loadMovie` allows you to load a SWF, JPEG, PNG, or GIF file into another SWF file. This is an awe-some feature because it allows you to break up one large project into multiple, smaller pieces, thereby allowing you to load those other SWF files whenever the viewer requests them. It's also a great way to reduce the download time of your Flash 8–based Web sites because it allows you to have only the *basic* information (such as the navi-gation menu) initially be downloaded and dis-played on viewers' computers. Then, when viewers request it, they can download other sec-tions of the Web site piecemeal.

As nice as `loadMovie` is, shortcomings in `loadMovie` left many Flash developers wanting more, such as better procedures for constructing a preloader, for managing errors, and so forth. Because of these reasons, Macromedia—in Flash MX 2004— introduced a new (and improved) way to load external assets such as SWF, JPEG, PNG, and GIF files. This action is the `MovieClipLoader`.

The `MovieClipLoader`, in effect, performs the same tasks `loadMovie` did—it allows you to load SWF, JPEG, PNG, and GIF files into another SWF file's movie clips or levels. The big difference, however, between `loadMovie` and the `MovieClipLoader` is that the `MovieClipLoader` is much more sophisticated and offers many more options for loading—and dealing with—SWF, JPEG, PNG, and GIF files.

The `MovieClipLoader` is its own class to which you assign *listeners*, which (as their name implies) sim-ply listen to what the `MovieClipLoader` is doing. Then, when a particular event occurs, they do whatever you tell them to do. For example, if you use the `MovieClipLoader` to load an external JPEG file and the file doesn't exist, you can have the

onLoadError listener return an error to the viewer. In the past, when using **loadMovie** to load assets, if you wanted to create a preloader to show the pre-loading progress of the loading file, you would have to create some kind of loop to continually trigger your preloader ActionScript code. But now, the **MovieClipLoader** has its own built-in loop capabilities in another listener called **onLoadProgress**. In many respects, the **MovieClipLoader** is much easier to use, and it gives you more options for handling the loading of external SWF, JPEG, PNG, and GIF files. For your reference, the following table describes the various **MovieClipLoader** listeners and what they do:

MovieClipLoader Listeners

Listener	Description
onLoadComplete	This listener (and all the actions within this listener function) is triggered when the loading asset has been completely downloaded.
onLoadError	This listener (and its associated actions) is triggered if the loading asset fails to load for one reason or another.
onLoadInit	Similar to **onLoadComplete**, this listener (and its associated actions) is triggered when the loading asset has been completely downloaded and the first frame of the loaded clip has been executed. In some ways, this is preferred over **onLoadComplete** because by the time **onLoadInit** is triggered, you know the loaded clip is completely loaded and ready to go.
onLoadProgress	This listener (and its associated actions) is triggered every time loaded content is written to disk. In other words, every time any bit of information is downloaded from the clip you are loading, the **onLoadProgress** listener is triggered. **onLoadProgress** is—essentially—your ActionScript loop that continually gets triggered as your content is downloading. Within the **onLoadProgress** method is where you would write your preloader ActionScript code (as you'll see in Chapter 7, "*Building a Slideshow*").
onLoadStart	This listener (and its associated actions) is triggered when your asset begins to download.

As you can see (but probably not fully comprehend just yet), the **MovieClipLoader** is a powerful tool to incorporate into your projects. You will be writing your first **MovieClipLoader** in the next section.

Creating the Master SWF and Setting Up the MovieClipLoader

In this exercise, you will begin constructing the first piece of the L.A. Eyeworks site by designing the master SWF file. As you read in the section "What Is a 'Master' SWF File?" the **master.swf** file will act as the container into which the other SWF modules (Music, Frames, About Us, and so forth) will load. It will also be the container for some ActionScript code you will be reusing frequently. By keeping the frequently used actions in a central location, you reduce production time because you don't have to repeat the code wherever you need it, and you'll have a *much* easier time making changes to the script later. In this exercise, you will also write the `MovieClipLoader` script that will do *all* the loading of SWF, JPEG, PNG, and GIF files throughout the entire site.

You'll learn quite a lot in this exercise, so if you need to take a break or jog around the block, now is the time to do so.

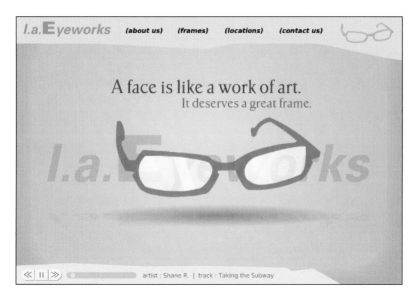

1 Open your preferred browser, and type the following URL:

www.lynda.com/flash8btb/laeyeworks/

This opens the completed site in your browser. Depending on the speed of your Internet connection, it may load fast, or it may take a minute. When the completed L.A. Eyeworks Web site first loads, you'll see the navigation bar appear at the top, the music player appear at the bottom, and an animated splash graphic appear in the middle. These three elements are actually all separate SWF files: **main_menu.swf**, **music.swf**, and **splash.swf**, respectively. These three SWF files all automatically load into the **master.swf** container file when the Web site first loads.

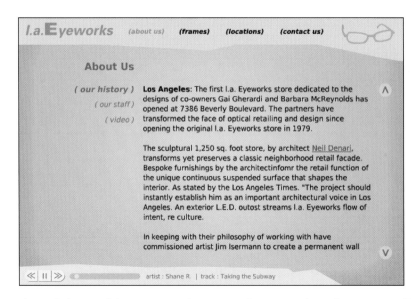

If you click one of the navigation buttons at the top, such as **about us**, you'll see the splash graphic disappear, and in its place loads the About Us module (another SWF file). The same holds true if you click any of the other navigation buttons. The center content is essentially an interchangeable module that swaps out whenever the viewer clicks a navigation button. All this content is loaded—and contained within—the **master.swf** file you will be constructing next. When the viewer clicks one of the navigation buttons, it instructs the `MovieClipLoader` instance in the **master.swf** file to load a particular SWF, JPEG, PNG, or GIF file. Sound pretty simple? Straightforward? In essence, it is. Of course, it takes a bit of elbow grease, hard work, and some well-thought-out ActionScript to make it look this simple, but that's why you're reading this book, to learn how to do all that, right?

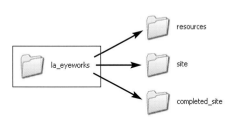

2 The **la_eyeworks** folder on the **HOT CD-ROM** contains all the files you will be working with throughout this book. Copy this folder, and its contents, onto your **Desktop**.

You'll be referring to the files within this folder frequently, so make sure you know *exactly* where it resides on your computer. This folder also acts as the root site folder for the L.A. Eyeworks site. In other words, the **la_eyeworks** folder you just copied onto your **Desktop** is where you will save all the files you work with throughout this book.

Note: If you're currently working in Windows, follow the instructions in the Introduction to make the folder and files within it read/writable.

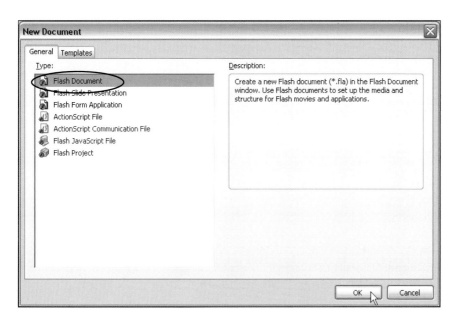

3 Launch Flash 8. Choose **File > New**, and from the **New Document** dialog box, select **Flash Document**. Click **OK**.

Note: Some windows in Flash 8 will have slightly different appearances depending on whether you are using Flash Professional 8 or Flash Basic 8. For example, the professional version's Start Page is slightly different from the basic version's Start Page. The New Document dialog box (pictured previously) is another one of those places. In Flash Professional 8, the General and Templates tabs have more options than are available in the standard version. Although differences occur depending on which version of Flash you're using, the exercises in this book cover processes that will work in both versions of the program.

When one SWF file loads into another, the base SWF file defines the frame rate of all the other SWF files loaded into it, which means the **master.swf** file (which you just created but haven't yet saved) determines the frame for *all* the SWF files loaded into it. For the L.A. Eyeworks Web site, so that the splash graphic and main menu animations play smoothly, you should set the frame rate to 21 fps. Although the frame rate setting is a contentious issue among Flash designers, 20 fps or 21 fps is a fast enough frame rate to make your animations play smoothly. (Lower frame rates tend to make animations stutter.) It's also not too taxing on the viewers' computer processors. (The faster the frame rate you set, the harder it is for the viewers' computers to keep up with that frame rate.)

4 Open the **Document Properties** dialog box by pressing **Ctrl+J** (Windows) or **Cmd+J** (Mac). Set **Dimensions** to **600 px** wide by **400 px** high. Set **Background color** to the hexadecimal color **#B4CCE5** (you can do this by clicking the **Background color** swatch and, from the color picker that appears, typing the hexadecimal color value in the field to the right of the color swatch). (This color value was taken from the original Adobe Photoshop site mock-up.) Set **Frame rate** to **21** fps. Click **OK**.

Tip: If you click **Make Default**, Flash 8 will use the settings you've just specified as the base settings for all new documents you create.

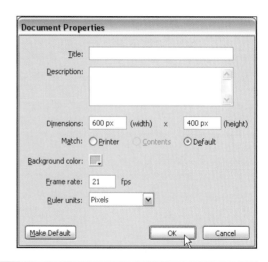

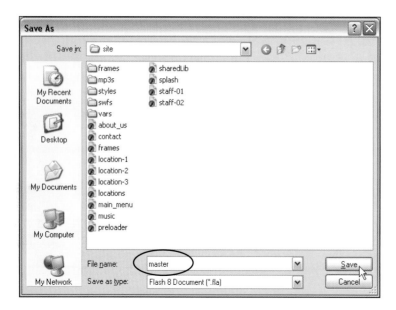

5 Choose **File > Save** to save this FLA file. In the **Save As** dialog box, navigate to your **Desktop**, navigate into the **la_eyeworks** folder you copied there at the beginning of this exercise, and navigate then into the **site** folder. Name your file "**master**," and click **Save**.

Note: If you're on a Mac, you should also add the three-letter extension **.fla** at the end of the file name. This will help the Windows operating system—should you ever give your FLA file to someone using Windows—to better recognize which program the file belongs.

Another element common to all the loaded SWF files is the background. The same image is visible in the background, no matter at which SWF file the viewer is currently looking. In the next step, you will add the background image to the **master.fla** file.

6 Rename **Layer 1** to "**bg**," create a new layer, and rename it to "**a**." The **a** layer is where you will write your ActionScript code, and the **bg** layer is—yep, you guessed it—where the background image will go. Make sure you have the **bg** layer selected before continuing to the next step.

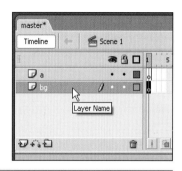

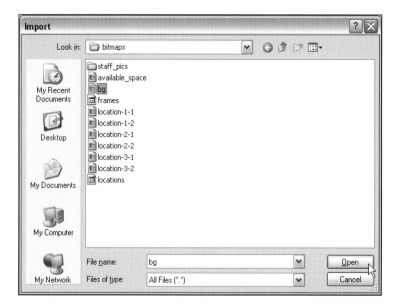

7 Press **Ctrl+R** (Windows) or **Cmd+R** (Mac) to import an item to the **Stage**. In the **Import** dialog box, navigate to your **Desktop**, navigate into the **la_eyeworks** folder, navigate into the **resources** folder, and then navigate into the **bitmaps** folder. Select the bitmap graphic **bg**, and click **Open** (Windows) or **Import** (Mac) to import the selected bitmap graphic to the **Stage**.

The **bg** bitmap graphic (which is the same physical size as the Stage—600 x 400) should automatically place itself so that it is aligned on top of the Stage. You can verify this by opening the **Info** panel (**Ctrl+I** [Windows] or **Cmd+I** [Mac]) and making sure the **Symbol Position** registration point is set to the top-left point and the x and y coordinates are both set to **0**.

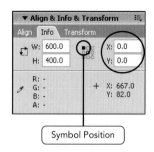

8 Lock the **bg** layer, and single-click the first keyframe in the **a** layer. Open the **Actions** panel by pressing **F9** (Windows) or **Opt+F9** (Mac OS X 10.3 or later.)

Before you can use the `MovieClipLoader`, you first have to create it with ActionScript. Just like if you wanted to use an image in your Flash 8 movie, you'd first need to create the image, convert it to a symbol, and place it on the **Stage**. The `MovieClipLoader` needs to be set up the same way essentially. Using ActionScript, you first need to create an instance (called an *object*) of the `MovieClipLoader` class before you can use it, which is what you will do next.

---

9 In the **Actions** panel, type

`var myMCL`

In simple English, this instructs Flash 8 to create a variable called **myMCL**. The text *var* in ActionScript is short for "variable." (It also determines the variable scope, which is a little too advanced for this book.) So when you see *var* preceding a name (in this case, **myMCL**), it means create a variable and assign the following name to it. Although preceding a variable name with the text *var* isn't required in all cases, it is recommended to adhere to good ActionScript practices, and it is needed when assigning a data type to a variable (as you will see next). In the next step, you'll assign a `MovieClipLoader` object to the **myMCL** variable. That way, whenever you need to tell the `MovieClipLoader` object to do anything, you just refer to it by its variable name, **myMCL**.

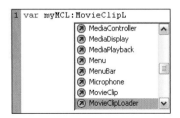

10 After `var myMCL`, type

`:MovieClipLoader`

As you type `:MovieClipLoader,` a scrollable box appears with various options. If you'd like, without typing the rest of `:MovieClipLoader`, you can simply select it from this list and then press **Enter** (Windows) or **Return** (Mac). Flash 8 then inserts it into your code for you! This scrollable box is one example of *code hinting*—Flash 8's way of trying to be helpful. Based on what you're typing, Flash 8 sees you're using strict typing (denoted by the colon) to set the data type of the variable you just created, **myMCL**. In this case, you're using strict typing to tell Flash 8 the variable **myMCL** is of the type `MovieClipLoader`. If you omitted the strict typing statement, `:MovieClipLoader`, your ActionScript would still work. But with the introduction of ActionScript 2.0 in Flash MX 2004, using strict typing is recommended because it complies with ActionScript 2.0 specifications. In other words, Macromedia recommends using strict typing in order to follow good ActionScript programming practices, which is primarily why you will be using it throughout the exercises in this book.

```
1  var myMCL:MovieClipLoader = new MovieClipLoader();
```

11 After `var myMCL:MovieClipLoader`, type

`= new MovieClipLoader();`

In essence, this tells Flash 8 to create a new instance of the `MovieClipLoader` object and place it within the variable `myMCL`. In the future, when you want to tell this particular `MovieClipLoader` instance to do anything, you can simply refer to it by using the variable you assigned the reference to, `myMCL`.

Congratulations! You just created a new `MovieClipLoader` object that you will soon be able to use to load SWF, JPEG, PNG, and GIF files to your heart's content. Without knowing it, you just added quite a lot of functionality to your Flash 8 project. Much like adding a movie clip to your project automatically gives you the ability to use ActionScript to modify its methods and properties such as visibility, alpha, rotation, and so forth, adding the `MovieClipLoader` object to your project allows you to use its built-in methods and listeners to load SWF, JPEG, PNG, and GIF files, get progress reports on their downloading progress, and so forth. Writing just one line of code actually adds a lot more than you realize. You'll see more of the functionality of the `MovieClipLoader` in later exercises throughout this book.

Now, even though you've created a new `MovieClipLoader` object, you still need a few more lines of ActionScript to make it work. Once the `MovieClipLoader` is complete and fully scripted, you will be able to tell it to perform tasks such as load a SWF file. But if you want it to report details of the loading process—such as how much of the file has been loaded, what to do after the file has been fully downloaded, and so forth—don't ask the `MovieClipLoader`, because it doesn't know. To get information about what the `MovieClipLoader` is doing, you need to assign a listener to the `MovieClipLoader`. The listener will then respond to different events the `MovieClipLoader` sends it. For example, when you tell the `MovieClipLoader` object to load a SWF file, the `MovieClipLoader` begins loading that SWF file. When it's finished, it sends a parameter (success) to the `onLoadComplete` method of the listener object, if you assigned one. You can then write a script within the `onLoadComplete` method to specify what should happen when the SWF file is completely loaded.

```
1  var myMCL:MovieClipLoader = new MovieClipLoader();
2  var myListener:Object = new Object();
```

12 Click at the end of the first line of code you just wrote, and press **Enter** (Windows) or **Return** (Mac) to create a new line. Then type

`var myListener:Object = new Object();`

In essence, this tells Flash 8 to create a new variable called `myListener` (which is strict typed to specify the value of the variable will be an object) and to place a new, generic object within that variable. Up to this point, the variable `myListener` is just a variable with a generic object assigned to it. It is not yet *listening* to the events being passed from the `MovieClipLoader`. You will do that next.

```
1  var myMCL:MovieClipLoader = new MovieClipLoader();
2  var myListener:Object = new Object();
3
4  myMCL.addListener(myListener);
```

13 Click after the second line of code, and press **Enter** (Windows) or **Return** (Mac) a couple times. (Flash 8 ignores empty breaks, so you could have one line break or 50; it doesn't matter.) Then, type

`myMCL.addListener(myListener);`

This takes the generic object you created called **myListener** and assigns it as a listener to the **MovieClipLoader** object called **myMCL**. Now, whenever the **MovieClipLoader** (**myMCL**) sends an event (when it starts loading a file, when it stops, and so forth), you can assign a listener to perform some script when the event occurs.

Note: You can add as many listeners as you want to respond to events fired from this object. You'll see a few of these in this and upcoming chapters.

Congratulations! You just created your first **MovieClipLoader** script! As you will see, the **MovieClipLoader** can do so much more. To prevent you from bursting too many brain cells all at once, you'll add functionality to the **MovieClipLoader** piecemeal. In Chapter 8, *"Building a Preloader,"* you will give the **MovieClipLoader** more functionality by building a preloader into it. But for now, this simple **MovieClipLoader** will load whichever SWF, JPEG, PNG, or GIF file you tell it to load. In the next step, you'll do just that.

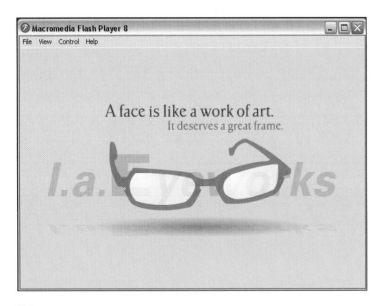

14 Minimize (Windows) or hide (Mac) Flash 8. Then, open the **la_eyeworks** folder you copied onto your **Desktop** at the beginning of this exercise. Now, open the **site** folder, and double-click the file **splash.swf**. (Your operating system might not show the file extension.) This should automatically open the animated **splash.swf** file in the stand-alone Flash Player 8, which is provided with the Flash 8 install. In the next step, you'll write one line of code instructing your new **MovieClipLoader** in the **master.fla** file to load this **splash.swf** file.

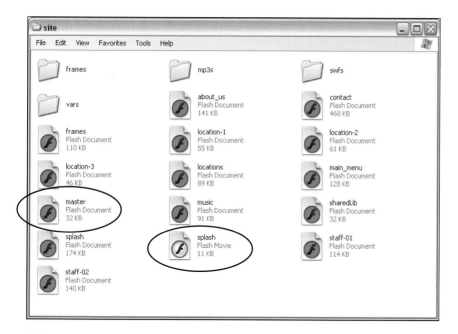

15 Close the **splash.swf** file, and look at the **site** folder again.

Notice how the **splash.swf** file is in the same folder your **master.fla** file (where the `MovieClipLoader` script resides) is.

When loading assets into Flash 8 projects, it's important to understand where the assets are located in relation to the file doing the loading.

---

16 In Flash 8, make sure you still have **Keyframe 1** in the a layer selected and the **Actions** panel is open. Then, click after the last line of code, and press **Enter** (Windows) or **Return** (Mac) on your keyboard a couple times to create a few line breaks. (This just gives you a little visual space between the important parts of your script.)

```
1 var myMCL:MovieClipLoader = new MovieClipLoader();
2 var myListener:Object = new Object();
3
4 myMCL.addListener(myListener);
5
6 myMCL.loadClip("splash.swf", 5);
```

17 Type the following:

```
myMCL.loadClip("splash.swf", 5);
```

Simply, this instructs your `MovieClipLoader` (`myMCL`) to load the SWF file **splash.swf** into Level 5. By this point, you most likely know you have two choices for a destination when loading one SWF (or JPEG, PNG, or GIF) file into another SWF file: You can load the SWF/JPEG/PNG/GIF file into a movie clip, or you can load the SWF/JPEG/PNG/GIF file into a level. A *level* is essentially an invisible layer that floats above the movie doing the loading. Loading content into a level also gives you the ability to set the visual stacking order of the loaded content. In this case, you're loading the **splash.swf** file into Level 5. Level 2 is above Level 1, Level 3 is above Level 2, so on, and so forth. The movie doing all the loading (in your case, **master.swf**) is referred to as Level 0 (or, in ActionScript terms, `_level0`).

Note: When loading assets (SWF files, JPEG files, and so forth) into a level, you can load them into any level starting with 0, all the way to the incredibly ridiculous high number of 2,130,706,429 (yes, that's two *billion* and change). So, as you can see, you have plenty of room to load assets into any level you choose.

NOTE:

MovieClipLoader Backward Compatibility

One point to keep in mind is the `MovieClipLoader` you just constructed is *not* backward compatible with viewers who are looking at your content with version 6 (or prior) of the Flash plug-in. The `MovieClipLoader` will work correctly *only* for viewers who are using version 7 or 8 of the Flash Player. In Chapter 13, *"Getting It Ready for the World,"* you will learn how to create a Flash plug-in detector to identify visitors who are using earlier versions of the Flash plug-in. Once you have identified those visitors, you can inform them that their plug-in is out of date and provide them with a link where they can update it. This will prevent visitors from entering your site and discovering a Flash 8 movie that isn't compatible with their older plug-ins.

If you (or your client) *require* backward compatibility with earlier versions of the Flash plug-in (such as version 5 or 6), you need to use the ActionScript command `loadMovie` (or `loadMovieNum`), which is compatible with older plug-in versions. Because this book is about learning the latest version of Flash and the features it provides, obviously many features used in this book aren't compatible with earlier versions. However, because the `MovieClipLoader` is such an integral part of this method of site construction, you should be aware of its lack of backward compatibility.

NOTE:

Security Policy

Flash 8 introduces a new security policy regarding how Flash content communicates both over the Internet and on your local hard drive (called the *local sandbox*). In previous versions of Flash, when you tested your Flash content on your computer's hard drive (local), the content could communicate over the Internet. Additionally, when you tested your Flash work on a remote Web server, the Flash content could communicate with your local computer. The new Flash 8 security policy restricts those kinds of communications and essentially acts as a firewall to prevent unauthorized material from leaving your computer in addition to entering it. For the most part, this new security policy probably will not affect the work you do in Flash. However, you can read more about the policy, as well as what steps you should take if Flash prompts you to modify these security settings, at the following URL:

www.macromedia.com/devnet/flash/articles/fplayer8_security.html

In later chapters, you may need to slightly adjust the local security policy to preview your work. Refer to the previous URL if you need to adjust your local security settings.

Cross-Domain Policy File

Introduced with Flash Player 7 was a new security policy that restricts any kind of data (variables, XML [EXtensible Markup Language] content, and so forth) from being loading into a SWF file if that data resides outside the domain name on which the SWF file resides. In other words, if you have a SWF file located at **www.mydomain.com** and you are attempting to load data on another server accessible at **www.myotherdomain.com**, it won't work. If you need to load data located outside the exact domain name where your SWF file is located (the SWF file doing the loading), you need to create something called a *cross-domain policy file*, which is essentially a simple XML file (named **crossdomain.xml**) stored at the root level of the server. Within that XML file is a list of URLs *allowed* to access the data on that server. An example of the **crossdomain.xml** file looks like this:

```
<?xml version="1.0"?>
<!DOCTYPE cross-domain-policy SYSTEM "http://www.macromedia.com/xml/dtds/
cross-domain-policy.dtd">
<cross-domain-policy>
   <allow-access-from domain="www.company.com" />
</cross-domain-policy>
```

If you are trying to load data into your Flash 8 project located under a different domain name and you are *not* using a cross-domain policy file, when visitors view your Flash 8 content, they will be presented with a warning dialog box asking them whether they are willing to accept the loading of content from another server. Obviously, as a Flash 8 designer/developer, this is not something you would like the viewer of your Web site to see.

For more information about the specifics of the Flash 8 plug-in security policy and the cross-domain policy file, visit Macromedia's Web page about this issue:

www.macromedia.com/cfusion/knowledgebase/index.cfm?id=tn_14213

Note: Starting with Flash Player 7.0.r19, a new action has been added (`System.security.loadPolicyFile`) to allow the cross-domain policy files to be placed in other locations on the hosting Web server. You can read more about these cross-domain policy file changes here:

www.macromedia.com/devnet/mx/flash/articles/fplayer_security.html

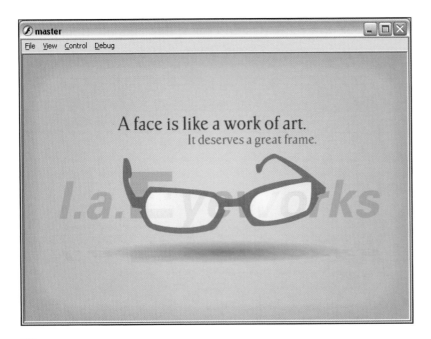

18 Test your movie by choosing **Control > Test Movie**.

As you can see, the **splash.swf** file loads perfectly into the **master.swf** file (where your `MovieClipLoader` script is located). When you load a SWF or JPEG file into a level, the top-left corner of the asset (x:0, y:0) is aligned with the top-left corner of the base SWF file (also x:0, y:0); therefore, the **splash.swf** file is positioned perfectly aligned with the **master.swf** file. This is because both the splash and master SWF files were created with the same Stage size. So, when designing content in the asset files (**splash.fla**, **music.fla**, **about_us.fla**, and so forth), you know—relative to the Stage—how everything is going to be positioned when it loads into the container master.swf.

Now, I know the four lines of ActionScript code you wrote in this exercise may seem somewhat excessive to load just one SWF file into another. Keep in mind, however, this `MovieClipLoader` code will be controlling the loading of *all* the SWF, JPEG, PNG, and GIF files throughout the *entire* L.A. Eyeworks site. Also, you should already understand all the advantages the `MovieClipLoader` has over the quasi-deprecated `loadMovie`. (See the earlier section "What Is the MovieClipLoader, and How Does It Differ from loadMovie?" for more detailed information on the major differences.)

There you have it—your first, working example of the new `MovieClipLoader`!

19 Save your **master.fla** file by choosing **File > Save**.

In the next exercise, you'll learn how to use the incredibly useful, file-saving awesomeness that is the shared library. A *shared library* is essentially a SWF file with a bunch of assets in it—symbols, fonts, and so forth—to use within *any* of your other SWF files. It's almost the same concept as a symbol (a reusable element), except this is essentially an *entire library* of reusable elements for sharing across multiple SWF files.

What Is a Shared Library?

You've seen how you can use symbols (graphic symbols, movie clip symbols, and so forth) to reduce the file size of your Flash 8 movie when reusing identical elements. But what if you've broken your Flash 8–based Web site into multiple pieces, are loading them into another SWF file using `loadMovie` or the `MovieClipLoader` (as you are doing in this book), and you have a symbol you want to use in every SWF file? Even more typical, what if you had a common font you were using across all those SWF files? Traditionally, you would simply duplicate the symbol within each SWF file, or in the case of fonts, you would just embed the font face in each SWF file where you're using it. This adds to the overall file size of your project because you are causing the user to download the same symbol multiple times for each SWF file where it's used *and* causing them to download the same font multiple times! But what can you do? You can't have one symbol or font being used *across* multiple SWF files, right? Wrong. By using something called a *shared library*, you can.

A shared library, by itself, is unglamorous. Essentially, it is just an FLA whose library you populate with symbols, fonts, and so forth. The difference between a plain FLA file and an FLA file with a shared library starts when you assign a linkage ID name (a unique name, much like an instance name you assign to a symbol instance) to each of the items you want to be available for sharing in other SWF files. You'll learn to do this in the upcoming exercise. When you want to share one of those items in another FLA file, you simply drag the item from your shared library to the library in another FLA file where you want to use that item. Flash 8 automatically makes a link to that shared element (which is essentially just an alias to the item in the shared library), and you can then use it in your project. You can share those elements in as many files as you want.

A shared library element is not actually embedded in the file into which you dragged it. It still resides in the shared library FLA file. The shared element in the host FLA file is, basically, an alias to the original item in the shared library! It's just like the concept behind symbols (reusable elements), except taken to the level of being able to reuse items (nearly anything you can import into a library) *across* SWF files. How incredibly powerful is that?

In this exercise, you will create the shared library. The shared library will contain the shared elements you will use to complete the exercises throughout this book.

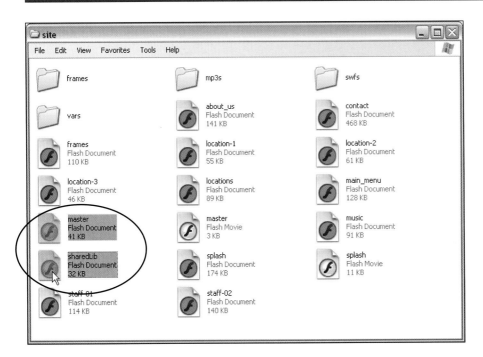

1 Open **master.fla** (which you created in the last exercise), if you accidentally closed it, *and* **sharedLib.fla**. These files are both located in the **site** folder, which is in the **la_eyeworks** folder on your **Desktop**.

2 In the **sharedLib.fla** file, open its library. In it, you'll notice only one file, a button symbol called **btn. arrow**.

Don't worry, though—you'll flesh out that shared library in just a minute.

The intended use of a shared library is to share assets across multiple SWF files. If an asset is being used only once, in one SWF file, you really have no reason to include it in a shared library.

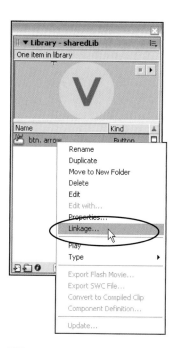

3 **Right-click** (Windows) or **Ctrl+click** (Mac) the **btn. arrow** symbol in the **sharedLib** library, and from the contextual menu, choose **Linkage**.

4 This opens the **Linkage Properties** dialog box, which is where you specify how this library item can be shared and what its name will be. First, click the **Export for ActionScript** check box. This automatically checks the **Export in first frame** box as well. Then, in the **Identifier** field, type **arrowBtn**. This name can be anything you'd like. But just like when you name a symbol instance, do not begin the name with numbers or use spaces or special characters such as ?, *, and so forth. Finally, click the **Export for runtime sharing** check box. This also automatically fills the **URL** field with the name this SWF file will have when published, **sharedLib.swf**.

Here's further explanation of what the various fields and check boxes are:

Linkage Properties

Option	Description
Identifier	This is a unique name you need to assign each library element you want to share. This name can be whatever you want, but you should avoid spaces in the name, numbers at the beginning of the name, and special characters such as $, #, and so forth.
AS 2.0 Class	This is the name of the ActionScript 2.0 class you want to assign to this shared library symbol.
Export for ActionScript	This lets shared library elements be manipulated with ActionScript.
Export for runtime sharing	This lets the shared library element be used during run time. *Run time* refers to when the SWF file is playing (running). If you do not click this check box, your shared library element will not appear in its destination document when playing.
Import for runtime sharing	This check box is available when choosing Linkage on the shared library item in the *destination* document. Leaving this box unchecked will disallow that shared library element from being displayed during run time.
Export in first frame	This exports this shared library element so it is accessible in the first frame. If you *do not* click this check box, place an instance of your shared library item on the Stage in the frame where it is first needed.
URL	This is the URL where this shared library SWF file will be located. Flash 8 automatically enters the name of the SWF file in which the shared library element resides, in this case, **sharedLib.swf**.

5 Click **OK**. That symbol is now sharable and can be dragged into the library of other FLA files.

Next, you need to create a new font symbol to share in your other SWF files!

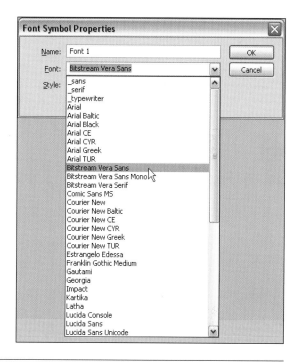

6 Click the **Library Preferences** button, and from the pop-up menu, choose **New Font** to open the **Font Symbol Properties** dialog box.

From here, you choose the font symbol you want to create and what name you want to give it (the name appearing in the library). From the **Font** pop-up menu, you should see the Bitstream fonts you installed in Chapter 2, *"Deciding Where to Start."* On Mac OS X, you should see more Bitstream Vera fonts than the ones listed in the illustration shown here. The Windows operating system groups the various font face styles, but on a Mac the face styles are *not* grouped, which means Windows and Mac users will have to follow a slightly different procedure which, you can be sure, I will note in the following steps.

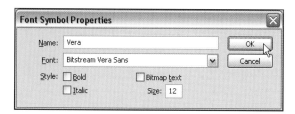

7 Both in Windows and on a Mac, select **Bitstream Vera Sans** from the **Font** pop-up menu. In the **Name** field, type **Vera**. Make sure **Bold**, **Italic**, and **Bitmap text** are all unchecked. The **Size** option is irrelevant with how you're using fonts in this book, so leave **Size** set to whatever it is currently. Click **OK**.

Great! You just created a symbol in your library, except this symbol is an entire font face! Pretty cool. Next, you need to add three other Vera faces you will be using throughout the L.A. Eyeworks site.

(Windows XP)

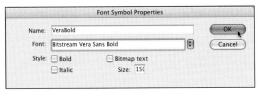
(Mac OS X)

8 Repeat Step 7, but in Windows, select the font **Bitstream Vera Sans**, and then click the **Bold** check box. On a Mac, select the font **Bitstream Vera Sans Bold**. On a Mac, you *do not* need to click the **Bold** check box. Both in Windows and on a Mac, in the **Name** field type **VeraBold**. Click **OK**.

(Windows XP)

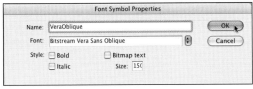
(Mac OS X)

9 Repeat Step 7 again, but in Windows, select the font **Bitstream Vera Sans**, and then click the **Bold** and **Italic** check boxes. On a Mac, select the font **Bitstream Vera Sans Bold Oblique**. On a Mac, you *do not* need to click the **Bold** and **Italic** check boxes. Both in Windows and on a Mac, in the **Name** field type **VeraBoldOblique**. Click **OK**.

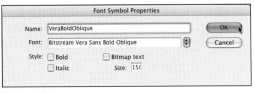
(Windows XP)

(Mac OS X)

10 Repeat Step 7 once more, but in Windows, select the font **Bitstream Vera Sans**, and then click the **Italic** check box. On a Mac, select the font **Bitstream Vera Sans Oblique**. On a Mac, you *do not* need to click the **Italic** check box. Both in Windows and on a Mac, in the **Name** field type **VeraOblique**. Click **OK**.

Fantabuloso! If you look at your **sharedLib.fla** library, you'll notice you have the original shared button symbol, **btn. arrow**, but now you also have four font symbols in there, too: **Vera**, **VeraBold**, **VeraBoldOblique**, and **VeraOblique**. Next, you need to set the linkage options for each font symbol (just as you did for the **btn. arrow** symbol in Steps 3 and 4) so you can share them with your other SWF files.

11 In the **sharedLib** library, **right-click** (Windows) or **Ctrl+click** (Mac) the font symbol **Vera**, and from the contextual menu choose **Linkage**. In the **Linkage Properties** dialog box, click the **Export for ActionScript** check box (which also automatically checks the **Export in first frame** box) and the **Export for runtime sharing** check box. Also make sure the **Identifier** field automatically sets itself to **Vera** (the same name you gave the font symbol when you created it) and the **URL** field automatically sets itself to **sharedLib.swf**. Click **OK**.

12 Repeat Step 11 for the remaining three font symbols. All the settings should be the same as the settings in Step 11, with the following exceptions: for the font symbol **VeraBold**, make sure **Identifier** is set to **VeraBold**; for the font symbol **VeraBoldOblique**, make sure **Identifier** is set to **VeraBoldOblique**; and for the font symbol **VeraOblique**, make sure **Identifier** is set to **VeraOblique**. Whew!

Because you've enabled linkage for those font symbols, you can use them in as many SWF files as you'd like. (You'll see how to do that in the next chapter.) The huge benefit of using a shared library is the font outlines for these four Vera faces are embedded only in this **sharedLib.swf** file. All the other SWF files comprising the L.A. Eyeworks site, which *also* use these shared Vera font faces, will *not* have the font outlines embedded in their SWF files. They just reference the font faces embedded in this **sharedLib.swf** file. Using a shared library to share fonts across SWF files (as you just set up in this exercise) can *greatly* reduce the overall size of your Flash 8 project because the same font outlines are not being embedded in every SWF file in which they're used. Huzzah!

The last item of business is to perform a little shared library trickery. Before you start, however, you should first understand why you have to perform these extra steps. In the next chapter, you will use some of the shared fonts from the shared library you just created within another SWF file. When a visitor first comes to your Web site and starts viewing your content, the first time a shared library element is requested from another SWF, Flash 8 starts downloading the *entire* shared library SWF file. Flash 8 will not simply download the one item it needs from the shared library (unfortunately). Instead, when the first item within a shared library is requested, it will trigger the downloading of the entire shared library SWF file. Although this is fine and workable, depending on the size of the shared library SWF, it could bring the playback of your Flash 8 movie to a grinding halt. It would, of course, be best to be able to load the **sharedLib.swf** file in a controlled manner so the viewer knows what's happening.

The problem, however, is simply preloading the **sharedLib.swf** file doesn't do the trick (even though you'd think it would work, logically). Flash 8 simply re-downloads the **sharedLib.swf** file when the first shared element is used. Instead, you'll create a "trigger" SWF whose job it is, essentially, to trigger the downloading of the **sharedLib.swf** file at a point in the movie where you can control its downloading. All this trigger SWF file will be comprised of is one of the shared library elements on its Stage. This **trigger.swf** file will then load using the `MovieClipLoader` at the beginning of the project. When the **trigger.swf** file loads, since it uses a shared library element, it triggers the loading of the **sharedLib.swf** file, and from that point on, any of the shared library elements can be used—instantly—in any SWF file in the Web site.

You first need to create the triggerman, **trigger.fla**, which will simply use one of the shared library elements and will trigger the downloading of the **sharedLib.swf** file.

13 Save your **sharedLib.fla** file by choosing **File > Save**, and then choose **File > Publish** to publish a SWF file in the same directory where the **sharedLib.fla** file resides (**Desktop > la_eyeworks > site**).

---

14 Close the **sharedLib.fla** file.

---

15 Create a new, blank FLA by pressing **Ctrl+Alt+N** (Windows) or **Cmd+Opt+N** (Mac).

You don't need to be concerned with the dimensions or background color of this FLA file because all it's being used for is to trigger the loading of the shared library. The viewer will never even know this file has loaded. Once the shared library loads, the **splash.swf** file will replace the loaded **trigger.swf** file.

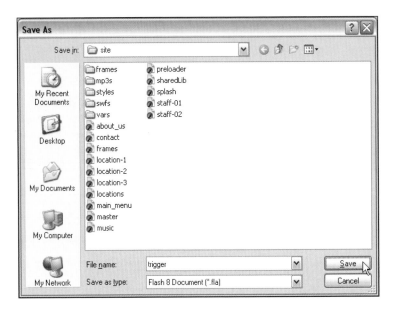

16 First, save this new FLA by choosing **File > Save As**. Save it in your **Desktop > la_eyeworks > site** folder, and name it "**trigger**." Click **Save**.

---

17 Open the **sharedLib Library** window by choosing **File > Import > Open External Library**. In the **Open as Library** dialog box, double-click **sharedLib**. This will open *just the library* of the **sharedLib.fla** file.

The trigger file needs only one symbol from the shared library. As soon as the **master.swf** file loads the **trigger.swf** file and sees a shared element on the Stage, it will immediately start downloading (and caching) the entire **sharedLib.swf** shared library!

---

18 Drag **btn. arrow** to the work area (the gray area around the outside of the white **Stage** area) of **trigger.fla**. You want this button symbol to be on the work area because you do not want it to be visible on the **Stage** when the **trigger.swf** file gets loaded into **master.swf**.

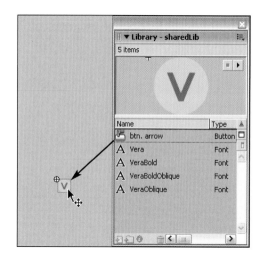

Unfortunately, with how the **master.fla** Timeline is currently set up, the loading of *all* the SWF files occurs on Keyframe 1. Now that you've created a file that will trigger the loading of the shared library SWF file, you obviously want that to happen *before* the **splash.swf** file loads. The shared library, because it is such an essential piece of this Web site (after all, it contains the fonts used throughout nearly all the SWF files), needs to load *first*. Therefore, you will start spacing out the loading of the various SWF files throughout the **master.swf** Timeline. The initial content (**trigger.swf**, **sharedLib.swf**, and so forth) will load right away on Keyframe 1, and then once the content has been loaded, the playhead will proceed to Keyframe 10 where the next piece will load, the splash graphic **splash.swf**. You will build on that same layout—spacing the loading of the various site sections throughout the **master.swf** Timeline—in later chapters in this book. For now, however, you need to add an action to trigger the **master.swf** Timeline to start playing once the **trigger.swf** file has been loaded and has also completely loaded the shared library, **sharedLib.swf**.

---

19 Rename **Layer 1** to "**shared lib asset**." Then create a new layer, and rename it to "**a**."

---

20 Select the first keyframe in the **a** layer, and open the **Actions** panel (by pressing **F9** [Windows] or **Opt+F9** [Mac]).

```
_level0.play();
```

21 Write an action to instruct the **master.swf** Timeline to play by clicking in the **Actions** panel and typing

_level0.play();

This instructs the **master.swf** Timeline (**_level0**) to play. This action will get triggered, obviously, once **trigger.swf** has been completely downloaded. But because **trigger.swf** also has on its Stage a shared library element, which thereby triggers the downloading of **sharedLib.swf**, the **_level0.play();** action won't execute until *both* **trigger.swf** and **sharedLib.swf** have been completely downloaded. Whew!

Now you just need to save the changes to this **trigger.fla** file and publish a SWF file.

To avoid cluttering your site folder, you should instruct this FLA file not to create the extraneous HTML file when you publish it.

22 Choose **File > Publish Settings**. In the **Publish Settings** dialog box, uncheck **HTML**. This prevents a **trigger.html** file from being created when you publish this FLA file. Because the **trigger.swf** file will load into the **master.swf** file, the HTML file is unnecessary.

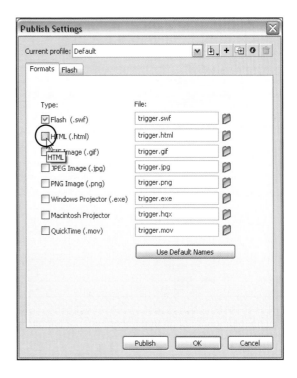

23 Click **Publish**. This will publish a **trigger.swf** file in the **site** folder (the same location where the **trigger.fla** is saved). Then click **OK** to close the **Publish Settings** dialog box.

24 Save your **trigger.fla** file by choosing **File > Save**. Once you've saved the changes, close **trigger.fla** by choosing **File > Close**. (You can also use the keyboard shortcut **Ctrl+W** [Windows] or **Cmd+W** [Mac] to close a file.)

Meanwhile, on the **master.fla** Timeline, all the actions are still bundled together on Keyframe 1. In the next few steps, you'll need to move the loading of the **splash.swf** file so it happens further down the Timeline of **master.swf**. You'll also instruct the **MovieClipLoader** on **master.fla** to load **trigger.swf**. **Trigger.swf**, of course, will trigger the loading of the shared library because it uses a shared library item on its Stage. Lastly, you'll need to create some sort of loading message so the viewer isn't just left staring at a blank page while **trigger.swf** and **sharedLib.swf** are downloaded behind the scenes.

25 Make sure you are in the **master.fla** file. (If you closed it, you can open it by navigating to your **Desktop > la_eyeworks > site** folder and double-clicking **master.fla**.) Select Keyframe 1 in the **a** layer, and open the **Actions** panel.

```
1  var myMCL:MovieClipLoader = new MovieClipLoader();
2  var myListener:Object = new Object();
3
4  myMCL.addListener(myListener);
5
6  myMCL.loadClip("splash.swf", 5);
7  myMCL.loadClip("trigger.swf", 5);
```

26 Click after the `myMCL.loadClip("splash.swf", 5);` line, and press **Enter** (Windows) or **Return** (Mac) to create a new line break. Then, load the **trigger.swf** file into **Level 5** by typing

`myMCL.loadClip("trigger.swf", 5);`

Because the **trigger.swf** file doesn't have any items visible on the Stage—only the one shared library button on the work area—you won't see anything visual on the **master.swf** Stage when the **trigger.swf** file loads. Once the **trigger.swf** file is loaded, and the Flash Player 8 sees it is referencing a shared library item, it will begin downloading (and caching) all the items in the shared library (**sharedLib.swf**). Once the **sharedLib.swf** file has been completely downloaded, you will be able to instantly use any shared items from within any loaded SWF file. Neat-o!

You probably have also noticed that **trigger.swf** is loading into the same level as **splash.swf**, `_level5`. This is because all **trigger.swf** is needed for is to (as its name implies) trigger the downloading of the shared library. But once **trigger.swf** has done its job, then it is not needed anymore. Therefore, **splash.swf** will simply load into its place, kicking **trigger.swf** out in the process. Although having both **trigger.swf** and **splash.swf** load into the same level is not a problem, having them load into the same level at the *same time* is. With the way the script is currently set up, **splash.swf** will start to load but will get immediately unloaded and replaced with **trigger.swf**. In this setup, the viewer would never get to see **splash.swf**. Instead, you want **splash.swf** to load *after* **trigger.swf** has loaded and has done its job and *after* the shared library has loaded. You will be reorganizing the loading order in the next few steps.

---

27 Click **Frame 10** in the **a** layer, and add a new keyframe by pressing **F6**. Then, so the **bg** layer is also visible out to **Frame 10**, select **Frame 10** in the **bg** layer, and add frames to that point by pressing **F5**.

Keyframe 10 in the **a** layer is where you will insert the action to trigger the **splash.swf** file to load. One of the reasons why you're triggering **splash.swf** to load from Frame 10 is because you want **splash.swf** to load *after* **trigger.swf** has been loaded (which occurs on Frame 1) and to trigger the downloading of the shared library (**sharedLib.swf**). Once both **trigger.swf** and **sharedLib.swf** have been completely downloaded, the `_level10.play();` action you assigned to the first keyframe of **trigger.swf** will be executed, and **master.swf** will play to Frame 10. Of course, you need **master.swf** to be paused on the first keyframe to begin with, so you will be writing a Stop action to do just that in the next few steps. In Chapter 12, *"Building the Main Menu,"* you will see another reason why having the action trigger the loading of **splash.swf** on Frame 10 is beneficial.

```
1  var myMCL:MovieClipLoader = new MovieClipLoader();
2  var myListener:Object = new Object();
3
4  myMCL.addListener(myListener);
5
6  myMCL.loadClip("splash.swf", 5);
7  myMCL.loadClip("trigger.swf", 5
```

28 Click **Keyframe 1** in the **a** layer, and open the **Actions** panel (**F9** [Windows] or **Opt+F9** [Mac]). Then, select the `myMCL.loadClip("splash.swf", 5);` line by dragging over it, and **right-click** (Windows) or **Ctrl+click** (Mac) it. From the contextual menu that appears, choose **Cut**. This cuts the action from **Keyframe 1** and stores it in the computer's clipboard, to be pasted elsewhere.

29 Select **Keyframe 10** in the **a** layer (which you added in Step 27), and in the **Actions** panel, **right-click** (Windows) or **Ctrl+click** (Mac). From the contextual menu that appears, choose **Paste**. This pastes the `myMCL.loadClip("splash.swf", 5);` action you cut from **Keyframe 1** into **Keyframe 10**.

Because you do not want these actions to be continually executed as the playhead loops through the Timeline, you need to add a **stop()** action to Keyframe 10.

```
1  stop();
2  myMCL.loadClip("splash.swf", 5);
```

30 Click to the left of the `myMCL.loadClip("splash.swf", 5);` line, and press **Enter** (Windows) or **Return** (Mac) to create a line break *above* that action. Then, click the top, empty line in the **Actions** panel, and write a **stop()** action by typing

`stop();`

When the playhead encounters Keyframe 10, it will stop. The `MovieClipLoader` will then load **splash.swf** into Level 5, thereby unloading and replacing **trigger.swf**, which was loaded in Keyframe 1. So **master.swf** doesn't initially start playing by itself (you want it to wait on the first keyframe until **trigger.swf** and **sharedLib.swf** have been completely downloaded), you need to add another **stop()** action to Keyframe 1.

```
1  stop();
2  var myMCL:MovieClipLoader = new MovieClipLoader();
3  var myListener:Object = new Object();
4
5  myMCL.addListener(myListener);
6
7  myMCL.loadClip("trigger.swf", 5);
```

31 Single-click **Keyframe 1** in the **a** layer. Then, in the **Actions** panel, click before the top line of code, `var myMCL:MovieClipLoader = new MovieClipLoader();`, and press **Enter** (Windows) or **Return** (Mac) to create a line break. Click the new line break you just created, and add a **stop()** action by typing

stop();

Now the **master.swf** Timeline will be paused until **trigger.swf** and **sharedLib.swf** have both been completely downloaded, thereby triggering the action telling **master.swf** it is OK to play: `_level0.play();`.

Even though you are not quite finished yet, this is a good point to stop and test your work thus far.

---

32 Save your **master.fla** file by choosing **File > Save**. Then, test your movie by choosing **Control > Test Movie**.

When the Preview window appears, you should see (within half a second), the splash graphic appear. Although it's great to see it is, at least, loading and working correctly, you don't really know whether the shared library has loaded correctly and whether the **trigger.swf** file has done its job properly. To get more information about the loading process, as well as what a viewer on a slow modem would see, you'll use the Bandwidth Profiler in conjunction with Simulate Download (prior to Flash MX 2004, Simulate Download was referred to as *show streaming*).

---

33 While you're still viewing the preview of **master.swf**, choose **View > Bandwidth Profiler**. This will divide your **Preview** window in half. The bottom half contains the viewable SWF file, and the top half contains the **Bandwidth Profiler**.

The Bandwidth Profiler, as you probably know, tracks how much data would be sent, for each frame, if a SWF file were being viewed by someone over the Internet. It also allows you to preview how a SWF would perform when downloading, using a variety of Internet connection speeds. When using `loadMovie` or—as in your case—the `MovieClipLoader`, the Bandwidth Profiler will also show you which assets are being downloaded and will simulate how long those assets would take to download over different Internet connection speeds.

First, you need to give the Bandwidth Profiler pane, which displays the loading information, more room so you can see everything.

---

34 First, make the entire **Preview** window as tall as your monitor will allow. Then, drag the moveable horizontal bar down so you can still see the SWF file but are using the majority of the space to see what's going on in the **Bandwidth Profiler**. Lastly, drag the moveable vertical bar as far to the right as possible. Essentially, you're reshuffling the three panes of the **Bandwidth Profiler** so the statistics portion gets the most available space. This area is where you will see which assets are being loaded and their progress as they are being downloaded.

Now that you've set up your Preview window, you need to choose a modem speed for the test.

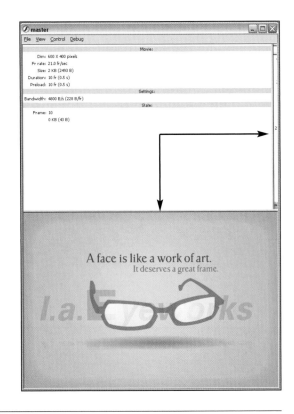

35 Choose **View > Download Settings > 56k (4.7 KB/s)**. As you can see from this list, you can choose from quite a few Internet connection speeds to test, or you can even create your own by choosing **Customize**. However, you've chosen the most common nonbroadband connection speed: a 56K modem. Next, when you tell Flash 8 to play this SWF file, it will play it as if it were being accessed over the Internet using a 56K modem. Neat!

36 Choose **View > Simulate Download**.

Watch the Bandwidth Profiler as it shows you which assets are loading and their progress. You'll notice how, almost instantly, the **sharedLib.swf** file begins to download. Once it has finished downloading, you'll see—under the State section—the frame quickly advance to 10, and then the **splash.swf** file will download and display. *Magnifique!* The only problem with how this is currently set up is the viewer gets the unfortunate experience of having to sit there and look at a blank screen while the **sharedLib.swf** file gets downloaded in the background. In this case, the shared library SWF is relatively small (44 KB), but

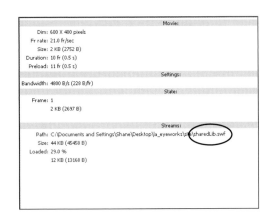

that's not always the case. So viewers know what the heck is going on, you should write a short message informing them something is actually happening and, no, the Web site isn't broken.

---

37 Close the **Preview** window.

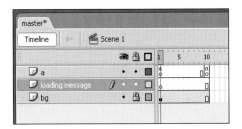

38 Click the bottom-most layer, **bg**, and add a new layer. Rename the new layer to "**loading message.**" This is the layer that will, of course, contain the text message **loading assets** on the **Stage**.

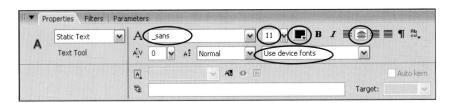

39 With the **loading message** layer still selected, select the **Text** tool. Then, in the **Property Inspector**, choose a **Static Text** type, a **Font** of **_sans** (located at the top of the font list in Windows and at the bottom of the font list on a Mac), a **Font Size** of **11** pt, and a color of **black**. Make sure **Align center** is selected as well as **Use device fonts**. These settings will allow you to type your loading message with the device font **_sans**. A device font, as you probably know, is not embedded in the published SWF file. Instead, it instructs a viewer's computer to use a font already installed on its system to display the text, much like standard text viewed on an HTML-based Web page does.

Note: Flash 8 has a bug in the Text tool. Sometimes (and I say "sometimes" because it doesn't happen consistently) when you select the Text tool, the Property Inspector will not update to show you the Text tool options. If you experience this bug, to see the text options in the **Property Inspector**, click the **Text** tool, and then click the **Stage** with the **Text** tool. Although this will create a text field based on your previous settings, it will also update the Property Inspector to display the text options. You can then simply delete that text field and set the text options in the Property Inspector.

You want to use a device font for this loading message because you want the text to display instantly, without having to download any font outlines first. Therefore, from the time this file first loads, the viewer will know exactly what's happening.

40 Click the **Stage**, and type **loading assets**. This is the brief message viewers will see as they wait for the **sharedLib.swf** file to finish downloading.

41 Press the **Esc** key to exit from type-editing mode, and open the **Align** panel (**Ctrl+K** [Windows] or **Cmd+K** [Mac]).

42 First making sure the **To Stage** button is selected, click the **Align horizontal center** and then the **Align vertical center** buttons. This will align the text block **loading assets** to the center of the **Stage**.

43 Close the **Align** panel.

You want the **loading assets** message to be displayed on the Stage only while the playhead is paused on the first keyframe. But after the playhead plays to Keyframe 10 and loads **splash.swf**, you want the loading assets message to disappear. To accomplish this, all you need to do is insert a blank keyframe on Frame 2 of the loading message layer.

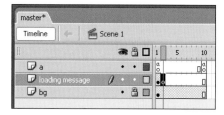

44 Single-click **Frame 2** in the **loading message** layer, and then add a blank keyframe there by pressing **F7**. Now, the **loading assets** message is visible only on **Frame 1**.

45 Lock the **loading message** and **a** layers, and then save the changes you've made to **master.fla** by choosing **File > Save**.

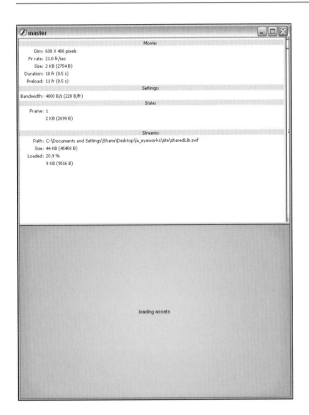

46 Test the movie again by choosing **Control > Test Movie**. Once the **Preview** window opens, choose **View > Simulate Download** to simulate the downloading of **master.swf** and the assets loading into it. You'll see your new message, **loading assets**, appear on the **Stage** while the **sharedLib.swf** file is downloading. Once the shared library SWF file has been completely downloaded, the message will disappear, and in its place the splash graphic, **splash.swf**, will load and display.

Congratulations! You've successfully created, loaded, and provided loading feedback for the shared library. It has been precached, so it can be used in any SWF file also loaded into the **master.swf** file, instantly.

In the next chapter, not only will you learn how to utilize the shared library items, but you will also learn how to populate a Dynamic text field with text from an external TXT file (using **LoadVars**), how to make the text scroll, how to modify the loaded text using a combination of HTML (**H**yper**T**ext **M**arkup **L**anguage) and CSS (**C**ascading **S**tyle **S**heets), and how to add inline SWF files within the scrolling text! The next chapter contains a *ton* of new and exciting examples, so go lock the door, and tell your significant other to go to bed without you because you have a *different* date tonight!

4

Using the LoadVars Class

In this chapter, you'll learn how to utilize the **LoadVars** class to dynami-cally load text—from an external text (TXT) file—into a text field in the About Us module. By using ActionScript to dynamically load external text into your Macromedia Flash 8 project, you open yourself—and the client—up to new possibilities. Without using dynamically loaded text, when you want to make even a simple change to the text in one of your movies, you (or the client) would have to open the FLA file, make the changes to the text, and publish an updated SWF file. But if you dynami-cally load the text into your movie using the **LoadVars** class, when you (or the client) want to make any changes to the text, you can merely open the text file in a simple text editor, make your changes, and save the file. You don't need to open the FLA file or even own a copy of Flash 8! Once you've learned how to load the external text into your movie, you will also learn how to make the text scrollable. So as you might suspect, you're going to learn about loads of new actions and techniques in this chapter. I'll wait while you go guzzle some coffee and sugar to gear yourself up.

1 | Previewing What You Are Building

In this exercise, you'll preview exactly what it is you will be building in this chapter before you start building it. That way, as you begin to learn about some of the more advanced topics, the steps will make more sense to you because you will already know how to apply the techniques to a working Web site.

1 Open your preferred browser, and navigate to the following URL:

www.lynda.com/flash8btb/laeyeworks/

2 Once the L.A. Eyeworks Web site finishes loading, click the **about us** button in the top navigation bar. This loads the **about_us.swf** file into **master.swf**, replacing the splash graphic.

The loaded/scrolling text is what you'll build in this chapter. Notice when the About Us module loads, the **our history** text displays automatically. The **our history** text, which is actually from a separate text file (**our_history.txt**), loads into the **about_us.swf** module using an ActionScript class called

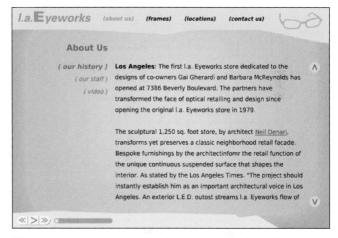

LoadVars. Also notice some of the text is bold, the text contains paragraph breaks, and a hyperlink even changes color when you hover your mouse over it! This text is styled using HTML (**H**yper**T**ext **M**arkup **L**anguage) to create the bolding, paragraph breaks, and hyperlinks and further enhanced with **C**ascading **S**tyle **S**heets (CSS) to create the hyperlink color change when the mouse hovers over it. The CSS styles are loaded in—and applied—from a separate CSS file. You will learn how to style the text using HTML and CSS in Chapter 5, *"Using HTML and CSS."*

I'm sure you've started to realize a lot of Dynamic text will be loaded and styled (using HTML and CSS) in this—and later—chapters. This might make you wonder, "Why go through all the extra effort of dynamically loading text and then styling it with a CSS file? Why not just type the darn text right into Flash 8 and be done with it?" The main reason why I'm showing you, in this book, how to dynamically load text from a separate text file comes down to one reason: it makes it easy for you (or your client) to easily update the content. By loading text inside an external TXT file, it's *very* easy to update. The client (or even yourself, for that matter) doesn't need a copy of Flash 8 to update the Web site. All your client (or you) has to do is open the text file, make any necessary changes, and upload the updated text file to the server. The next time visitors view the Web site, they will see the updated content. How spiffy is that? So, it may take a little longer to plan and construct, but—as you'll see—it's more than worth the extra time in the long run.

In this exercise, you'll incorporate the fonts from the shared library. By linking to the shared fonts, you can display text in the About Us module using those shared font outlines. Since the font information will be "borrowed" from the shared library, no font information will need to be embedded in **about_us.swf**, and the file size of the final SWF file will be greatly reduced.

---

1 Minimize (Windows) or hide (Mac) Flash 8, and then navigate to your **Desktop > la_eyeworks > site** folder. From there, open the two FLA files, **sharedLib** and **about_us**, by double-clicking them.

When you open the **about_us** FLA file, you'll notice a few items already in place for you. Probably the first item you'll notice is the background image. This image was taken from the Web site design mock-ups constructed in Adobe Photoshop, saved as a JPEG file, and then imported and placed into the **about_us.fla** file. You'll also notice the layer this image is in, **available space**, is set to a guide layer,

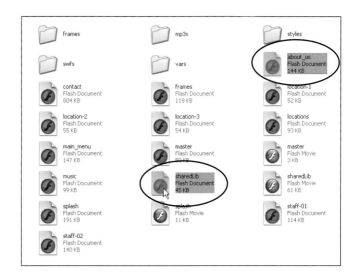

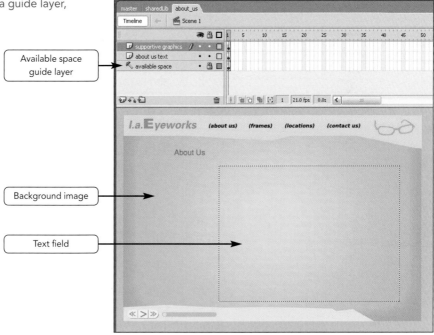

Available space guide layer

Background image

Text field

which means whatever is in the layer (in this case, the background image) will *not* be in the SWF file when it's published; it's visible only while you're working with the FLA file. The background image has been placed inside this FLA file so, as you're building the content for the About Us module, you already know *exactly* how much available design space you can use. The background image shows you where the main navigation menu is and where the MP3 player is, thereby also revealing how much space you have left. Without this background guide image, you'd be designing blind.

You'll also notice **about_us.fla** already has the Dynamic text field drawn for you (where the content will be loaded), and if you press **Ctrl+L** (Windows) or **Cmd+L** (Mac) to open the Library, you'll notice some prebuilt elements there for you to use. To conserve time, many of the FLA files and graphical elements you'll need to complete the exercises have already been created for you. You'll also find the prebuilt items are simple, such as a button or a movie clip with a text field inside it—items you should already know how to build. You, however, will add the ActionScript and fabricate the functionality as you complete the exercises in this book.

---

2 Open the **about_us** and **sharedLib** libraries, and position them so they're side by side. Then, in the **sharedLib Library**, select the four, shared **Vera** fonts you created in Chapter 3, *"Getting Started,"* by **Shift+clicking** them. After you have the four fonts selected, drag them on the **about_us Library** panel.

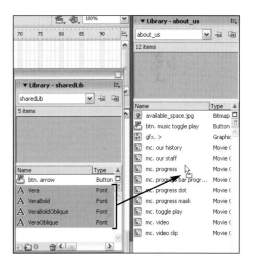

After you've dragged the four fonts on the **about_us Library**, you should see them appear there. Next, you should verify the linkage was set correctly when you dragged the shared **Vera** fonts from the **sharedLib Library** into the **about_us Library**.

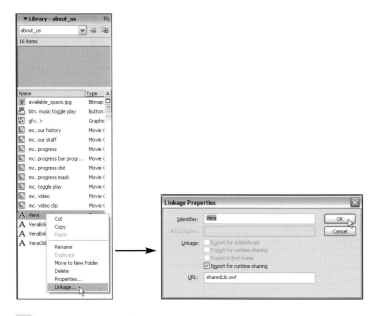

3 In the **about_us Library** panel, **right-click** (Windows) or **Ctrl+click** (Mac) the font **Vera**. From the resulting contextual menu, choose **Linkage** to open the same **Linkage Properties** dialog box you saw in Chapter 3, *"Getting Started,"* when you assigned properties to the Vera fonts in the **sharedLib Library**. However, in the **about_us** FLA file, the **Identifier** field should contain **Vera**, and only the **Import for run-time sharing** box should be checked. The **URL** field should be **sharedLib.swf**.

Note: If you expand a Library panel wide enough, you'll notice under the Linkage column it lists which library items are shared (linked) and what the identifier name of the shared item is.

Flash 8 automatically set these options when you dragged the shared fonts from the **sharedLib** Library into the **about_us** Library. As its name implies, the **Import for run-time sharing** check box is a sure sign these shared Vera fonts are being imported (from the **sharedLib.swf** file indicated in the URL field) for run-time sharing, and as such, the fonts outlines will *not* be embedded in the **about_us.swf** file when it is published. Instead, the **about_us.swf** file will simply reference the Vera font outlines in the **sharedLib.swf** file whenever it needs them.

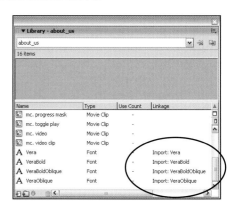

Note: If your Linkage Properties dialog box doesn't look the same as the one in the illustration, you might have incorrectly set the options for the shared Vera fonts when you created them. If your settings differ from the settings shown in the illustration, delete the four shared fonts you just dragged into the **about_us** Library, open (or bring to the foreground) the **sharedLib** FLA file, and verify you completed Steps 6 through 14 in the exercise "Creating and Precaching the Shared Library" in Chapter 3, *"Getting Started,"* correctly. Once you've verified you've completed steps correctly, repeat the steps in this exercise.

4 Once you've verified the linkage properties are correctly set, click **OK** to close the **Linkage Properties** dialog box.

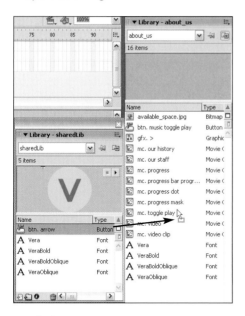

You'll also use the shared button **btn. arrow** in the About Us module to give the user a button to click to scroll through the loaded text.

---

5 In the **sharedLib Library** panel, drag the shared button symbol, **btn. arrow**, onto the **about_us Library** panel. Just like you did with the shared Vera fonts, this will make a shared link with the **btn. arrow** symbol in the **about_us Library**. You will be utilizing this button in Exercise 3.

---

6 Close the **sharedLib.fla** file—you won't need it again in this chapter. Choose **File > Save** to save **about_us.fla**.

You just created links from the shared library elements in the **sharedLib.fla** file to the About Us module. Now you can use those shared elements (the four Vera fonts and the **btn. arrow** symbol), knowing each time you use them, you're not increasing *in the least* the file size of the **about_us.swf** file. Thanks to the precaching of the shared library you constructed in Chapter 3, *"Getting Started,"* you can also use those shared elements instantly, in any SWF loaded into **master.swf**. Now, if only I could eat that extra slice of pizza without it increasing in the least *my* file size!

Adding Comments

When authoring ActionScript, sometimes you'll want to prevent a line or a block of code from being performed (when troubleshooting a script, for example). You might also want to insert messages in your ActionScript to make it easier for yourself, or your client, to understand what's going on in a script. Unless you're one of those gifted scripting geniuses, it can be difficult to look at 100+ lines of ActionScript code and immediately understand what's doing what. Luckily, you can prevent lines or blocks of actions from being performed on playback and can write messages within the ActionScript itself. You do this with something called *commenting*, which allows you to leave comments within a script. Commenting also allows you to "comment out," or prevent from being performed on playback, a line or multiple lines of ActionScript code. So you can see what commenting looks like, here is a sample of some comments in a script:

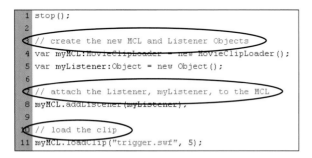

```
1  stop();
2
3  // create the new MCL and Listener Objects
4  var myMCL:MovieClipLoader = new MovieClipLoader();
5  var myListener:Object = new Object();
6
7  // attach the Listener, myListener, to the MCL
8  myMCL.addListener(myListener);
9
10 // load the clip
11 myMCL.loadClip("trigger.swf", 5);
```

This code comes from the **MovieClipLoader** script you wrote in Chapter 3, *"Getting Started,"* but with comments added so the main parts of the script include instructions. Adding comments to your scripts is highly encouraged. As you can see, you just need to type two slashes (//) before the line you want to explain (or the line of code you want to comment out). Commenting is recommended for the following reasons:

- Commenting allows you to easily scan through, and identify, the parts of a script. Commenting is especially helpful for long scripts because the comments can help you see what's happening in a complex script.

- Commenting is not only helpful while you're working on a Flash 8 project but also after you've completed a project. Take this mini-hypothetical example: You complete a Flash 8–based Web site for a client, and months later, the client returns to you, wanting to update the Web site. If you commented your scripts, you'll be able to more easily jump back in and identify the various pieces of a script after a long hiatus. It's always difficult to understand exactly what a script is doing if you aren't familiar with it or haven't seen it in awhile. Commenting can help ease the transition.

- Clients might sometimes want you (or your company) to design and program the Web site but then want to update/maintain the site themselves. Commenting can help them understand what a script is doing and even provide them with instructions for updating the actions.

- When troubleshooting buggy scripts, it's sometimes useful to prevent a line or multiple lines of code from performing. By adding a couple slashes before a line of code, you can comment the line out and prevent it from being performed on playback.

When attempting to write a large comment, or comment out a large block of ActionScript, it becomes time-consuming (to say the least) to add double slashes at the beginning of each line. Luckily, it's extremely easy to comment multiple lines. To mark the beginning of a multiline comment, simply type /*, and to mark the end of the comment, type */. Here's a sample—using the previous code example—of a multiline comment:

```
1  /*
2  Dynamic slideshow code © 2005 by Shane Rebenschied.
3  Feel free to distribute and use this code (but do not sell), but
4  if any changes or improvements are made, I'd love to hear about them!
5  comments@blot.com
6  */
7
8  //// variable initialization
9
10 // Specify how many total images there are in the slideshow here:
11 var totalItems:Number = 5;
12
13 // Specify the name of the folder that the images are in here:
14 var imageFolderName:String = "images/";
15
16 // Specify the base name (If your images are all titled
17 // "slide1.jpg", "slide2.jpg", etc.  Your "base name" would be "slide")
18 // of the images here:
19 var imageBaseName:String = "image";
20
21 var imageNum:Number = 1;
22 preloader._visible = false;
23
24 ////
```

As you can see, it's easy to comment an entire block of text or ActionScript of any length. Flash 8 also dims commented text or actions to make it clearly evident what in the Actions panel is commented and what is not. (However, you can change the color the actions and comments are displayed in using the **ActionScript** tab in **Preferences**.)

In the following steps, you will add yet more ActionScript to **master.fla**. To begin to follow good practices and to clearly mark the separate areas and functionality of the script, you will be instructed to add comments to better define those areas.

3 | Writing the LoadVars Object

In this exercise, you'll assign one of those shared Vera fonts to the Dynamic text field on the **about_us.fla** Stage and start writing the **LoadVars** object to make this whole site work. You'll find detailed tables explaining the capabilities of the **LoadVars** class after this exercise.

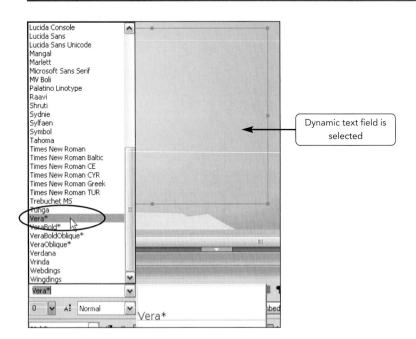

Dynamic text field is selected

Vera*

1 Make sure you're in the **about_us.fla** document, and then click the Dynamic text field on the **Stage** to select it. Once the text field is selected, click the **Font** pop-up menu in the **Property Inspector**, and from the resulting font list, choose **Vera***. Notice **Vera** has an asterisk (*) after its name (as do **VeraBold**, **VeraBoldOblique**, and **VeraOblique**, for that matter). This is how Flash 8 lets you know **Vera** is a font symbol residing in the library.

Currently, the Dynamic text field is set to display Vera at 12-point black using the (new) anti-alias method of **Anti-alias for readability**. Although these settings are fine for now, you will actually be using CSS to modify the size and color of the text later in this chapter.

You've imported and linked the shared font Vera to the Dynamic text field, so it's time to load some text. You will be accomplishing this with the **LoadVars** class. But where should you write this script? Should it be written into the Timeline of **about_us.fla** or somewhere else? The answer mostly depends on how frequently the **LoadVars** object will be used. In the context of this book's site construction, the **LoadVars** script will actually be used in every module. It will be used in the About Us module to load the **our history** and **our staff** text, in the Frames module to load the descriptive frames text, in the Locations module to load information about each store location, and even in the Contact module to potentially *send* the form variables to a CGI (**C**ommon **G**ateway **I**nterface) script to process the information. So, because of the frequency of which the **LoadVars** script will be used, it makes the most sense to write the script in a

- **;**: The semicolon (which you'll see at the end of most lines of ActionScript) tells Flash 8 this is the end of the action. (**Note:** Flash 8 will still compile your scripts without semicolons, but it is good practice to use them since other programming languages you might get into later may require them!)

So, again, this script essentially reads, "Level 5 has a text field called **loadedInfo**. I want you to take the value of the variable **info** (which was loaded into the **myLV LoadVars** object from the external text file) and insert it as HTML-formatted text." This action will be executed only if the loading variables have been completely downloaded and parsed.

Keep in mind, because this **LoadVars** script is going to be used by multiple SWF modules, whatever you tell this script to do needs to work properly across all the modules. Having said that, what should happen when all the variables have completely downloaded? Well, once the variables have been downloaded, you want to insert them in a text field and display them to the viewer (which is what you just scripted in the previous step). However, Flash 8 needs to know the exact instance name of the Dynamic text field where these variables are going to be inserted. Essentially, by specifying the exact instance name of a text field in this script, you need to make sure, as you're constructing the other modules, the text field—where the variables will load into when the **LoadVars** action is triggered—has the same instance name as the name referenced in this script. In other words, the text field (in each module) in which the variables are going to load into, needs to have the same name as the one referenced in the **LoadVars** script. Programming ActionScript to be reused by multiple SWF files takes a little extra planning, but as you work through the exercises in this book, you'll realize it's well worth the effort.

Later in this exercise, you'll write an action to specify what Flash 8 should do if the loading variables *don't* load correctly. For example, maybe the variables file wasn't named correctly, or maybe it wasn't uploaded to the correct location on the server. In that case, the variables file wouldn't load properly. If this happened, you would want some kind of error message to appear so the viewer knows something untoward has happened in the loading process. Luckily, the **LoadVars** object gives you the ability to deal with error management whereas the older **loadVariables** action does not. If you used **loadVariables** and you had a problem loading some variables, the viewer would never know it unless you wrote a bunch of extra code.

In the next step, you need to tell Flash 8 where this **if** statement (which you just wrote the previous action within) ends. If you have experience writing HTML, you know when you create a beginning anchor tag, **<a>**, you also need to specify where it ends by writing **</a>**. Writing an **if** statement (and a function, too, for that matter) in Flash 8 is similar, because you've started the **if** statement (in Step 9), and now you need to specify where it ends.

```
12  //----------------<LoadVars>--------------------\\
13  var myLV:LoadVars = new LoadVars();
14
15  myLV.onLoad = function (success) {
16      if (success) {
17          _level5.loadedInfo.htmlText = myLV.info;
18      }
```

11 Click at the end of the **_level5.loadedInfo.htmlText = myLV.info;** line, and press **Enter** (Windows) or **Return** (Mac) once to create a line break. Then, end the conditional **if** statement by typing the following:

```
}
```

This closed curly brace marks the end of the **if** statement and the action residing inside it.

You should also specify what should happen if you have a problem loading the variables file.

```
12  //-----------------<LoadVars>--------------------\\
13  var myLV:LoadVars = new LoadVars();
14
15  myLV.onLoad = function (success) {
16      if (success) {
17          _level5.loadedInfo.htmlText = myLV.info;
18      } else {
```

12 Click after the closed curly brace (**}**) you typed in Step 11, and type the following:

else {

When writing an **if** statement, you specify for certain actions to be executed *if* a statement turns out to be **true**. In this exercise, you're using **if** to see whether some variables have been successfully loaded into the **myLV LoadVars** object. But how do you tell Flash 8 to do something different if the statement is *not* true? The answer is, you use **else**. In plain English, this would essentially read, "If the variables have been loaded, insert those variables into the **loadedInfo** text field. Otherwise, do something else." The "Otherwise, do something else" part is **else**. Just like the **if** statement, under **else** you need to specify what should happen if the variables fail to load for some reason.

```
12  //-----------------<LoadVars>-------------------\\
13  var myLV:LoadVars = new LoadVars();
14
15  myLV.onLoad = function (success) {
16      if (success) {
17          _level5.loadedInfo.htmlText = myLV.info;
18      } else {
19          _level5.loadedInfo.text = "There has been an error loading the requested information. Please contact the
        Webmaster and report your error.";
```

13 Click at the end of the **}** **else {** line, press **Enter** (Windows) or **Return** (Mac) once to create a line break, and type the following:

_level5.loadedInfo.text = "There has been an error loading the requested information. Please contact the Webmaster and report your error.";

What this line (and the line prior to it) essentially says is, "If the loading of the external variable file is *not* successful, display an error message in the **loadedInfo** text field on the Stage of the SWF file loaded into Level 5." Next, you just need to end **else** and the **onLoad** function actions.

```
12  //-----------------<LoadVars>-------------------\\
13  var myLV:LoadVars = new LoadVars();
14
15  myLV.onLoad = function (success) {
16      if (success) {
17          _level15.loadedInfo.htmlText = myLV.info;
18      } else {
19          _level15.loadedInfo.text = "There has been an error loading the requested information. Please contact the
    Webmaster and report your error.";
20      }
2   }
```

14 Click at the end of the **_level15.loadedInfo.text = ...;** line, press **Enter** (Windows) or **Return** (Mac) once to create a line break, and then end **else** by typing a closed curly brace (**}**). Close the function action by pressing **Enter** (Windows) or **Return** (Mac) to create another line break and then typing another closed curly brace (**}**).

Congratulations! You just completed your first **LoadVars** script! Much like the **MovieClipLoader** script, the **LoadVars** script doesn't require much code—only eight lines in this case, including the extra (but not required) error handling. However, you get a lot of oomph for the little amount of scripting. This **LoadVars** script will handle the loading of *all* the variables used throughout *all* the modules. Your work is not quite done yet, however. You have written the **LoadVars** script, but you still need to insert the correct variable name (**info**) into the **ourHistory.txt** file, assign an instance name of **loadedInfo** to the text field into which the variables will load, and write the action telling the text file to be loaded.

As a good housekeeping chore, you should write a comment showing where the **LoadVars** script ends.

```
12  //-----------------<LoadVars>-------------------\\
13  var myLV:LoadVars = new LoadVars();
14
15  myLV.onLoad = function (success) {
16      if (success) {
17          _level15.loadedInfo.htmlText = myLV.info;
18      } else {
19          _level15.loadedInfo.text = "There has been an error loading the requested information. Please contact the
    Webmaster and report your error.";
20      }
21  }
22  //-----------------</LoadVars>-------------------\\
```

15 Click after the last closed curly brace (which you typed in Step 14), and press **Enter** (Windows) or **Return** (Mac) once to create a line break. Then, select and copy the comment

//----------------<LoadVars>------------------

and paste it underneath the bottom curly brace. Once you've pasted the comment, add a slash before the word **LoadVars**. This symbolizes the end of the **LoadVars** script. When finished, your script should look like the one in the illustration.

16 Save your **master.fla** file by choosing **File > Save**.

What Is LoadVars?

Simply put, **LoadVars** is to variables what the **MovieClipLoader** is to SWF, JPEG, PNG, and GIF files. The **MovieClipLoader**—which you constructed in Chapter 3, *"Getting Started"*—allows you to load external SWF, JPEG, PNG, and GIF files. Built into the **MovieClipLoader** class are listeners allowing you to monitor the downloading progress of an asset, detect whether an error has occurred (such as attempting to load a file that doesn't exist), and so forth. Similarly, the **LoadVars** class allows you to load external assets, as well as provides you with the ability to monitor the downloading progress and detect whether any errors have occurred. The major difference between the **MovieClipLoader** and the **LoadVars** class is the **MovieClipLoader** loads external SWF, JPEG, PNG, and GIF files whereas **LoadVars** loads *variables* from external files. Another difference is **LoadVars** also allows you to *send* variables from your Flash 8 movie to a URL of your choosing. You'll see this feature used in a later chapter to be able to send the information (variables) the viewer types in a contact form to a CGI script for processing and emailing the results. For your reference, here are the methods, properties, and event handlers for the **LoadVars** class:

Methods, Properties, and Event Handlers for the LoadVars Class	
Methods	
Method	**Description**
addRequestHeader()	Allows you to add or change the HTTP header when you send your variables using POST. An HTTP header is basically a little bit of information preceding the variable/value pairs to let the receiving server know how to deal with the information it is receiving.
getBytesLoaded()	Reports the number of bytes that have been downloaded from a file triggered using the **load()** method (see below for more on **load()**).
getBytesTotal()	Reports the total amount of bytes for a file triggered using the **load()** method.
load()	Downloads a file from a URL of your choosing.
send()	Opposite of **load()**, essentially. **send()** sends the variables (using the POST method) to a URL of your choosing.
sendAndLoad()	Performs a **send()** (sends variables to a URL, such as a CGI script) and then downloads the server's response.
toString()	Takes all the variables in a **LoadVars** instance and returns them in a URL-encoded format, like so: `myVar1=my%20value1&myVar2=my%20value2`

continues on next page

Properties

Property	Description
contentType	This property allows you to modify the MIME (**M**ultipurpose **I**nternet **M**ail **E**xtensions) type of the data being sent to the server. The default is `application/x-www-form-urlencoded`. The only time you should need to adjust the **contentType** is if the middleware (ASP, PHP, CGI, and so on) is expecting to receive the variables from a different MIME type.
loaded	Querying this property will allow you to determine whether variables you're loading using `load()` or `sendAndLoad()` have been fully loaded. This is a Boolean value (meaning, it's either **true** or **false**)—**true** if the variables have been fully loaded and **false** if they haven't or if an error occurred in the loading process.

Event Handlers

Event Handler	Description
onData	This handler (and any actions you place within it) is triggered when the data you're downloading has been *completely* downloaded from the server *or* if there's an error in the downloading process. What's the difference between the **onData** event handler and the **loaded** property? The **loaded** property will just return a **true** or **false** depending on whether the variables have been downloaded. The **onData** event handler, on the other hand, is essentially a function you can place actions within (just like a regular function). When the unparsed data has been completely downloaded from the server, the **onData** event handler (and the actions within it) is triggered.
onLoad	This is similar to **onData**, except the **onLoad** event handler is triggered *after* **onData** is triggered. Essentially, **onData** is triggered when the unparsed (raw) data has been completely downloaded, and **onLoad** is triggered when the data has been completely downloaded *and* parsed (put in a format Flash 8 [and you] can use). If you want an action to be performed after all your variables have been downloaded and are ready to use (placed in a Dynamic text field, for example), use the **onLoad** event handler instead of the **onData** event handler.

As you can see, the **LoadVars** class is a fairly robust method for loading, sending, and handling variables.

4 | Loading the "our history" Text

In this exercise, you'll utilize the **LoadVars** script—which you wrote earlier in this chapter—to load text from an external text file into a text field to form the **our history** subsection in the About Us module. You'll learn how to add the proper variable to the text file as well as how to write the action to instruct the **LoadVars** object to load the variables from a particular text file.

1 Minimize (Windows) or hide (Mac) Flash 8, and then navigate to your **Desktop > la_eyeworks > site > vars** folder.

Inside the **site** folder is a **vars** folder. The **vars** folder (short for "variables") is where you will store most of the variable files used throughout the L.A. Eyeworks Web site. Because the text files with the variables are stored in a *different* folder within the **site** folder, you need to make sure—when writing the ActionScript— to tell Flash 8 *exactly* which folder the variables are in and the name of the text file you want to load.

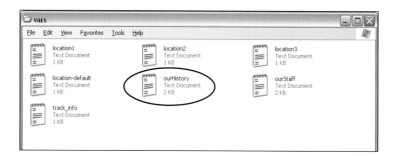

2 Within the **vars** folder, open the file **ourHistory.txt** (some operating systems, such as Windows XP, hide the file name extension) in a simple text editor. (Use Notepad if you're working in Windows, and use TextEdit or BBEdit if you're on a Mac.)

As you can see, this file is essentially a large amount of unformatted text. The goal, however, is to take all this text and use ActionScript to insert it into the Dynamic text field on the Stage in the About Us module. You've already written the **LoadVars** script, which, when triggered, will load the value of the variable **info** from this text file and place it inside a text field with the instance name **loadedInfo**. You might also notice this text file has no sign of an **info** variable. In the next step, you'll add this variable.

3 Click at the beginning of the text file, and type the following:

`info=`

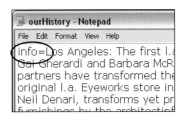

Make sure no spaces appear before or after the equals sign. When specifying variable/value pairs (also known as *key/value pairs*) in a text file that will be loaded into Flash 8 using `LoadVars.load` or `MovieClip.loadVariables`, you type the variable (in this case, it's `info`), immediately followed by an equals sign. Everything after the equals sign is the value of the variable. It's the value of the `info` variable that will actually be loaded into the `loadedInfo` text field on the Stage of the About Us module. So you can see a comparison, when you are creating a variable/value pair directly inside the **Actions** panel in Flash 8, you would type it as such:

`var info:String = "Los Angeles: The first...";`

As you can see, similarities exist between how variable/value pairs are defined in a text file and how they are defined directly inside Flash 8.

---

4 Save your **ourHistory.txt** file by choosing **File > Save**, and bring Flash 8 into the foreground again.

---

5 Bring the **about_us.fla** file into the foreground. You should still have the **about_us.fla** file open, but if you accidentally closed it, you can open it by navigating to your **Desktop > la_eyeworks > site** folder and double-clicking **about_us.fla**.

---

6 Single-click the large Dynamic text field on the **about_us.fla Stage** to select it, open the **Property Inspector** by pressing **Ctrl+F3** (Windows) or **Cmd+F3** (Mac), and type **loadedInfo** for the instance name. Make sure you capitalize the *I* in *Info*. Flash 8 is case sensitive, so if you accidentally type a lowercase *i*, the loaded variables will *not* load into this text field.

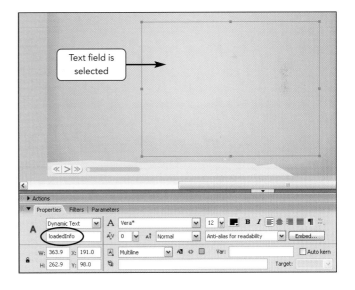

You have the `LoadVars` script all dressed up with no place to go, the variable specified in the text file, and the instance name specified for the text field the variable's value will load, so now you need to tell the About Us module from which text file to load the variables.

7 In **about_us.fla**, create a new layer, and make sure it resides above the other layers. Rename this new layer to "**a**" (for actions).

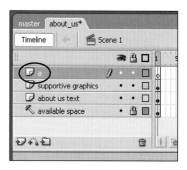

8 Click the first keyframe in the new **a** layer, and open the **Actions** panel by pressing **F9** (Windows) or **Opt+F9** (Mac).

```
1  _level0.myLV.load("vars/ourHistory.txt");
```

9 In the **Actions** panel, type the following:

_level0.myLV.load("vars/ourHistory.txt");

In simple terms, this action says, "Tell the **myLV LoadVars** object on Level 0 (the **master.swf** file) to load the variables from the text file **ourHistory.txt**, which is located in a folder called **vars**." Remember, the **LoadVars** script, which controls the loading of variables throughout the L.A. Eyeworks site, is located on the **master.fla** Timeline. The **master.fla** file is the container into which all the other SWF modules (including **about_us.swf**) will load. As such, whenever you're writing a script in one of the modules referring to something in the **master.swf** file (in this case, the **LoadVars** script), you have to tell Flash 8 to look in **_level0**, which refers to the container SWF file, **master.swf**.

Eventually, the **_level0.myLV.load("vars/ourHistory.txt");** line will be integrated into other actions you will be creating in the About Us module. For now, however, you've added it to check the **LoadVars** script and to make sure everything works the way it should. This returns to the idea of building the functionality in pieces. First, build it simply to make sure it works, and then build all the bells and whistles on top of that.

Because the About Us module refers to the master **LoadVars** script located within the **master.fla** Timeline, to test the About Us module and make sure everything works, you must load the **about_us.swf** file into the **master.swf** file (so it can refer to and use the **LoadVars** script). In the following steps, you'll add the action to make this happen.

10 Save your **about_us.fla** file by choosing **File > Save**. Then, publish a SWF file from the **about_us.fla** file by choosing **File > Publish**. The publish settings for the **about_us.fla** file have already been set up so when this movie is published, it publishes only a SWF file (instead of the default SWF and HTML combination).

If you want to see the publish settings specified for this—and the other—modules, choose **File > Publish Settings**.

11 Bring the **master.fla** file to the foreground. Single-click **Keyframe 10** in the **a** layer, and open the **Actions** panel by pressing **F9** (Windows) or **Opt+F9** (Mac).

```
1  stop();
2  // myMCL.loadClip("splash.swf", 5);
```

12 Comment out the `myMCL.loadClip("splash.swf", 5);` line by adding two slashes at the beginning of the action. As covered earlier, adding two slashes before a line of code will "comment out" that line and prevent it from being included when Flash 8 compiles the code.

Instead of loading the **splash.swf** file (which is the action you just commented out), you want to load the **about_us.swf** file into the **master.swf** file to make sure the **LoadVars** script is set up correctly and everything works.

```
1  stop();
2  // myMCL.loadClip("splash.swf", 5);
3  myMCL.loadClip("about_us.swf", 5);
```

13 Click at the end of the commented `// myMCL.loadClip("splash.swf", 5);` line, and press **Enter** (Windows) or **Return** (Mac) once to create a line break. Then, write the action to load the **about_us.swf** file into the **master.swf** file into **Level 5** (the same level the splash graphic, and all the other module SWF files, loads into) by typing the following:

`myMCL.loadClip("about_us.swf", 5);`

Just like the other `myMCL.loadClip` actions you wrote in Chapter 3, *"Getting Started,"* to load the splash and trigger SWF files, this action loads the **about_us.swf** file into Level 5.

14 Save your **master.fla** file by choosing **File > Save**, and then test the movie by choosing **Control > Test Movie**.

After you choose **Control > Test Movie**, you should see the About Us module loaded and, within it, a large block of text. The block of text is the same text in the **ourHistory.txt** file, but it has now been loaded into the **about_us.swf** file, thanks to your new **LoadVars** script! How cool is that? Now, you need to make sure the **LoadVars** error handling, which you scripted in the previous exercise, works correctly. To test the error handling, you need to locally simulate an error accessing or loading the variable file by changing the name of the **ourHistory.txt** file the script is attempting to load.

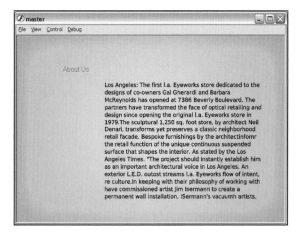

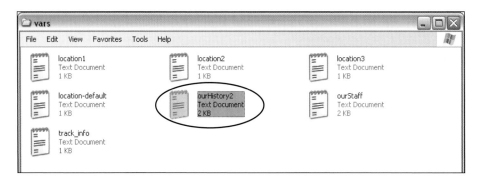

15 Minimize (Windows) or hide (Mac) Flash 8, and then navigate to your **Desktop > la_eyeworks > site > vars** folder. Within the **vars** folder, change the name of the **ourHistory.txt** file to something else, such as **ourHistory2.txt**.

16 After you have changed the name of the **ourHistory.txt** file, return to Flash 8. Make sure the **master.fla** file is in the foreground and you've saved all your changes, and then test the movie by choosing **Control > Test Movie**. When the **master.swf** file displays, in place of the **our history** text, you should now see your error message, **There has been an error loading the requested information. Please contact the Webmaster and report your error.** Fantastic!

As you can see, the error handling works like a champ. This is the message the viewer will see if they have a problem accessing or loading the variables file you're instructing Flash 8 to load. Before you call this exercise done and smack it on the butt, you need to return the **ourHistory2.txt** file to its previous, and correct, name.

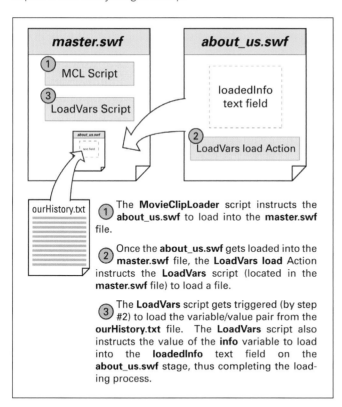

17 Minimize (Windows) or hide (Mac) Flash 8, and then navigate to your **Desktop > la_eyeworks > site > vars** folder. Change the file name **ourHistory2.txt** to its original name of **ourHistory.txt**.

Undoubtedly, you learned a lot of new techniques in this exercise. To better drive home the idea behind the **LoadVars** object and how it is integrated with the various SWF files, the following diagram visually explains how everything is set up:

In the next exercise, you'll learn how to add some actions to a couple of buttons to allow the visitor to scroll up or down through the loaded text. Now, go take a break before continuing. You deserve it after completing this exercise!

5 | Making the Text Scroll

In this exercise, you'll add a couple buttons to the About Us module to allow the viewer to scroll through the loaded text. As you will see, making text in a text field scroll is actually quite simple.

1 Bring the **about_us** FLA file to the foreground.

2 Lock the top-most layer, **a**, and create a new layer. Rename this new layer to "**scroll buttons**" and position it so it is underneath the **a** layer.

3 With the **scroll buttons** layer selected, open the **about us Library** by pressing **Ctrl+L** (Windows) or **Cmd+L** (Mac).

4 Drag the shared **btn. arrow** button symbol from the **about us Library** on the **Stage**, and position it toward the bottom-right corner of the text field. Remember, this **btn. arrow** button symbol is a symbol you brought over from the **sharedLib** shared library file. Because of this, adding this button to your movie doesn't increase the file size of the published SWF file. Yay for shared libraries!

So, now you have a button to allow the viewer to scroll down through the text, but what about allowing them to scroll up? Easy enough. All you need to do is copy the down-facing arrow button, and flip it so it's pointing up. Simple!

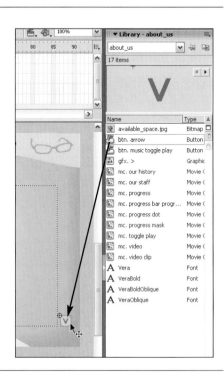

5 While pressing the **Alt+Shift** (Windows) or **Option+Shift** (Mac) keys, drag the **btn. arrow** symbol up so it's aligned with the top of the text field. The **Alt** (Windows) or **Option** (Mac) key copies the symbol as you drag it, and the **Shift** key constrains the dragging so you're assured you're dragging it straight up.

6 With the copied button symbol still selected, choose **Modify > Transform > Flip Vertical**. This… well…flips the button vertically so it is facing upward. Doing this also offsets the button alignment with the text field a little, so you'll need to reposition it.

7 Reposition the up-facing button symbol so it's aligned with the top of the text field. The easiest way to do this is by using the arrow keys on the keyboard. This allows you to fine-tune the position of whatever you have selected.

I'm sure the majority of you, by the time you've read this book, have added at least a few simple actions to button instances. When you've added actions to buttons, you've probably selected the button symbol instance on the Stage, opened the Actions panel, and began to write actions to add interactivity to the button. Well, starting with this book, you'll learn to do things a little…differently. And for many of you, this will probably be a major leap in how you think about the relationship between actions and their accompanying symbols.

You won't add actions directly to these arrow button symbol instances. In other words, you won't select the button symbol on the Stage, open the Actions panel, and add actions to the button symbol (as you're probably used to doing). Instead, you'll add your button actions to the first keyframe in the **about_us.fla** file, where all the rest of your actions will also be placed to make up the interactivity for everything (well, nearly everything) going on in the About Us module. You're probably saying to yourself, "What? How can I make my buttons interactive by adding actions to a keyframe? Furthermore, why would I want to do something as daft as that?"

You'll learn the answers to these questions by completing this exercise, but essentially it goes like this: Yes, you can script mouse events (**onRollOver**, **onRelease**, and so forth) to button and movie clip symbols from a keyframe action. The mouse event is actually attached to a function, and then the actions within the function are executed when that particular mouse event occurs (when the viewer clicks the button, for example). The reason why you'd want to do something like this goes back to one of the main points in this book, which is centralization—keeping as much content and ActionScript code as possible in one location. When you attach ActionScript directly to button symbol instances, you're essentially scattering your actions into the wind. Whenever you've needed to modify an action attached to a button symbol—nested within a couple other symbols—you'd have to manually open each nested symbol until you reach the symbol to which the actions are attached. Then you could modify the actions and retrace your steps to where you were previously.

After I show you this method of adding actions to symbols, you'll look at the method of adding actions directly to symbol instances and say to yourself, "Geez. What a pain that was." By keeping all the ActionScript code in one location, it makes it much easier to see how all the pieces interact. It's difficult to see the interconnectivity of the scripts when you're jumping from symbol to symbol and looking at each script snippet in isolation from all the others.

The first step in this process is to add instance names to the symbols to which you want to attach scripts.

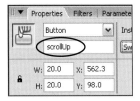

8 With the up-facing arrow on the **Stage** still selected, open the **Property Inspector**. In the **Instance Name** field, type **scrollUp**. Now the button symbol has a unique instance name, so you can add interactivity to it using ActionScript.

9 Single-click the down-facing arrow on the **Stage** to select it, and then in the **Property Inspector** type **scrollDown** in the **Instance Name** field.

Both button symbols now have instance names, so you can attach actions to them from the first keyframe.

10 Select the first (and only) keyframe in the **a** layer, and open the **Actions** panel by pressing **F9** (Windows) or **Opt+F9** (Mac).

```
1   _leve10.myLV.load("vars/ourHistory.txt");
2
3   //--------------<scroll buttons>----------------\\
4
5   //--------------</scroll buttons>----------------\\
```

11 Click at the end of the **_leve10.myLV.load("vars/ourHistory.txt");** line, press **Enter** (Windows) or **Return** (Mac) two times to create a couple of line breaks, and then add the following comment:

//----------------<scroll buttons>----------------

Then press **Enter** (Windows) or **Return** (Mac) two more times to create some space to add some script, and add the closing comment:

//----------------</scroll buttons>----------------

Now you have your commenting set up, but you still need to place the actions within them.

```
▼ Actions - Frame
  ⊹  ∅  ⊕  ✓  ≣  ⊕  ℓ℧
1   leve10 muLV lood("vars/ourHistory.txt");
         Insert a target path
2
3   //--------------<scroll buttons>----------------\\
4  |
5   //--------------</scroll buttons>----------------\\
```

12 Click between the two comment lines, and then click the **Insert Target Path** button (the small target) located at the top of the **Actions** panel.

This button opens the **Insert Target Path** dialog box, which allows you to easily find a "target" to which to assign ActionScript. Essentially, any item (movie clip/button symbol, Dynamic/Input text field, and so forth) you've given an instance name to will appear in the Insert Target Path dialog box.

13 Make sure the **Relative** radio button is selected (which means *relative* to where you're writing this script), and click the button target **scrollDown**. When you select **scrollDown**, you'll notice the path to that particular symbol instance is inserted in the path field at the top of the dialog box. The **this** preceding the button instance name **scrollDown** refers to "this" **Timeline** from which the action is being triggered. In this case, **this** refers to the main **Timeline** of the **about_us.fla** file. Once you've selected **scrollDown**, click **OK**.

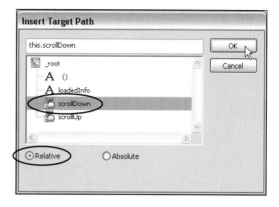

Note: If you don't see the `scrollDown` and `scrollUp` button symbols listed in the Insert Target Path dialog box, you probably forgot to assign instance names to those button symbols. Return to Steps 8 and 9, and make sure you followed them correctly.

```
3  //--------------<scroll buttons>----------------\\
4  this.scrollDown
5  //--------------</scroll buttons>---------------\\
```

After you clicked OK in the Insert Target Path dialog box, you'll be returned to the Actions panel, where you should see `this.scrollDown` inserted where you had originally clicked, between the comments.

```
3  //--------------<scroll buttons>----------------\\
4  this.scrollDown.onRelease = function() {
5  //--------------</scroll buttons>---------------\\
```

14 After `this.scrollDown`, type the following:

`.onRelease = function () {`

Don't forget to add the dot (.) between `scrollDown` and `onRelease`. Simply, this action reads, "When the `scrollDown` button is clicked...." As yet, this is only the first part of the script. When adding actions to button mouse events (as you're doing here), you must assign them to a function; hence, that's why you have the = `function () {` portion of the action. Whatever you want to happen when the viewer clicks the `scrollDown` button, you add within the function, as you're about to do. At this point, you might also be wondering what the various mouse events are (`onRelease`, `onRollOver`, and so forth). You can see the mouse events, and read a description of each one, by opening the **Help** panel (**F1**). In the **Help** panel sidebar, navigate to **ActionScript 2.0 Language Reference > ActionScript classes > Button** (and then scroll down to **Event Summary**).

```
3  //--------------<scroll buttons>----------------\\
4  this.scrollDown.onRelease = function() {
5      loadedInfo.scroll += 1;
6  //--------------</scroll buttons>---------------\\
```

15 Click at the end of the `this.scrollDown.onRelease = function () {` line, press **Enter** (Windows) or **Return** (Mac) once to create a line break, then type the following:

`loadedInfo.scroll += 1;`

A simple explanation of what this line says is "Set the `scroll` property of the `loadedInfo` text field to be whatever it currently is, but add one onto it."

`loadedInfo`, if you remember, was the instance name you gave to the text field on the Stage—the one into which the variables load.

An inherent property of a text field is **scroll**. The **scroll** property is measured in lines. So, if you added **5** onto the **scroll** property of a text field with text inside it, you would make the text jump up five lines.

The += is called an *addition assignment*. Essentially, all it does is tell Flash 8 to take the first part of the script, **loadedInfo.scroll**, add the value on the right of it (**1**), and reassign it to the variable on the left. In other words, when making text in a text field scroll, you essentially want to tell Flash 8, "Take the **scroll** property, and add **1** onto whatever the **scroll** property is currently set to." One way of writing that idea in ActionScript is to use **loadedInfo.scroll = loadedInfo.scroll + 1;**. This would simply read, "Take the **scroll** property of the **loadedInfo** text field, set it to whatever the **scroll** property of the **loadedInfo** text field *currently* is, but add **1** onto that." When setting an expression to itself, it's easier and simpler to just write +=, as you used in this script.

```
3  //--------------<scroll buttons>----------------\\
4  this.scrollDown.onRelease = function() {
5      loadedInfo.scroll += 1;
6  }
7  //--------------</scroll buttons>---------------\\
```

16 Click at the end of the **loadedInfo.scroll += 1;** line, press **Enter** (Windows) or **Return** (Mac) to create a line break, and close the function by typing the following:

```
}
```

That's it! That's all you need to do to make the text scroll down one line when the viewer clicks the **scrollDown** button. (It actually moves the text *up*, but it makes sense to think of it as scrolling down.) Now you just need to write a similar function to scroll the text upward.

Rather than write all the code from scratch again, it will save you a lot of time to copy the script you just wrote and then change the parts you need to change.

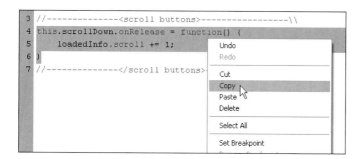

17 Select the script you just wrote (between the comment lines) by clicking and dragging. Then, **right-click** (Windows) or **Ctrl+click** (Mac) the selected code, and from the contextual menu, choose **Copy**.

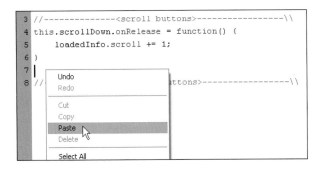

```
3  //-------------<scroll buttons>---------------\\
4  this.scrollDown.onRelease = function() {
5      loadedInfo.scroll += 1;
6  }
7  |
8  //|                        ttons>---------------\\
```

18 Click after the closed curly brace (}), press **Enter** (Windows) or **Return** (Mac) to create a line break, then **right-click** (Windows) or **Ctrl+click** (Mac) the new line break, and finally from the contextual menu that appears choose **Paste**. This pastes the script you just copied to the new line.

You now need to modify the copied script to make the text field scroll up when the viewer clicks the `scrollUp` button.

```
3   //-------------<scroll buttons>---------------\\
4   this.scrollDown.onRelease = function() {
5       loadedInfo.scroll += 1;
6   }
7   this.scrollUp.onRelease = function() {
8       loadedInfo.scroll -= 1;
9   }
10  //-------------</scroll buttons>---------------\\
```

19 In the copied script, change `scrollDown` to `scrollUp` (the instance name of the `scrollUp` button). If you can't remember the `scrollUp` button instance name, you could always click the **Insert Target Path** button to have Flash 8 insert the name and path for you, just like you did in Steps 12 and 13. Change += to –=. (You want to set the `scroll` property one line down [and hence use the negative value], not one line up.) The finished script should read like this:

```
this.scrollUp.onRelease = function () {
   loadedInfo.scroll -= 1;
}
```

Six lines of ActionScript later, and you have scrolling text! But before you start breaking out the champagne and caviar, you should test your movie to make sure everything works. Keep in mind you can view the About Us module only when it is loaded in the **master.swf** file. This is because the script needed to load the Dynamic text (variables) into the **about_us.swf** file is located within the **master.swf** file.

20 Save your **about_us.fla** file by choosing **File > Save**. Then publish an updated SWF file from this file by choosing **File > Publish**.

Note: It's important to publish a new SWF file every time you make significant changes to one of the modules and then want to preview the master FLA to view the changes you've made to those modules (About Us, and—as you'll see later—Frames, Locations, and so forth). If you make changes to one of the modules but don't publish a new SWF file from the updated FLA file, the next time you preview **master.fla**, you will be looking at outdated content.

21 Bring the **master.fla** file to the foreground.

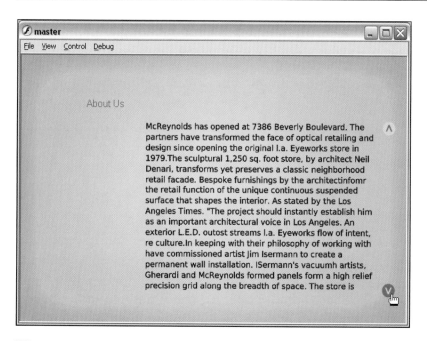

22 Preview the **master.fla** file by choosing **Control > Test Movie**. When the **master.swf** file appears, you will see the **About Us** module automatically load, and the loaded text will also automatically appear. By clicking the **scrollDown** and **scrollUp** buttons, you will be able to make the Dynamic text scroll down and up. Sweet! Each time you click the **scrollDown** or **scrollUp** buttons, the text will respectively scroll down or up one line.

VIDEO:

adv_scroller.mov

With the scrolling text you just constructed, the text will scroll only if you repeatedly click the **scrollUp/scrollDown** buttons. But what if you want the text to *continually* scroll as the viewer held their mouse button down on the **scrollUp/scrollDown** buttons? To learn more about creating this advanced type of scrollable text, check out **adv_scroller-part1.mov** and **adv_scroller-part2.mov** in the **videos** folder on the **HOT CD-ROM**.

Creating Scrolling Text with the TextArea Component

Another way to easily create scrolling text is by using one of the components in Flash 8. Components are, of course, prebuilt widgets you can easily drag and drop onto your Flash 8 movies to add functionality. One of those components is the **TextArea** component, and it essentially allows you to quickly and easily add scrollable text to your project:

1. To add the **TextArea** component to your Flash 8 movie, simply drag it from the **Components** panel and drop it on the **Stage**.

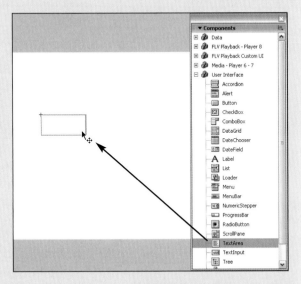

2. Then, with the **TextArea** component selected on the **Stage**, simply open the **Component Inspector** panel, click the **text** field, and type (or paste) the text you want to be displayed.

continues on next page

Creating Scrolling Text with the TextArea Component *(continued)*

3. By using the **Free Transform** tool, you can grab one of the **TextArea** component's resize handles and resize it to the size you want.

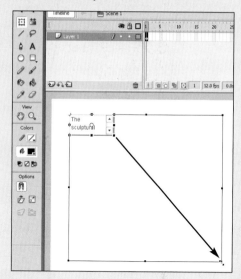

4. Choose **Control > Test Movie**, and you now have instant scrollable text, complete with a draggable slider!

Voila! Super simple, eh?

However, one of the major differences between the scrolling text you built manually in the previous exercise and the scrollable text in the **TextArea** component is by using a component, you're *significantly* increasing the overall file size of your project. For instance, just adding the **TextArea** component to your project *immediately* adds a cool 40KB to the size of a SWF file. Although the **TextArea** component provides you with a quick and easy way to add scrolling text (with a draggable scroll bar) to your project, you have to ask yourself whether it's worth the additional file size.

Once again, congratulations! In this exercise, you not only learned how to make text scroll up and down but, more important, you learned how to attach actions to a symbol from the Timeline! Again, this is a powerful technique because it allows you to keep your ActionScript centralized for easy modifications, comparisons, and references.

In Chapter 5, *"Using HTML and CSS,"* you will learn how to format and style the loaded text by using a combination of HTML and CSS. Being able to control the styling of dynamically loaded text is a valuable piece of knowledge because it allows you (or the client) to modify the text without having to deal with the FLA file or even open Flash 8. You can make changes quickly and easily by using a simple text editor. You'll learn how to utilize some of that flexibility in the next chapter.

5

Using HTML and CSS

In the previous chapter, you learned how to use the **LoadVars** class to dynamically load text from an external text file and populate a text field with the loaded text. In this chapter, you will learn how to style and modify the appearance of the loaded text using HTML (**H**yper**T**ext **M**arkup **L**anguage) and CSS (**C**ascading **S**tyle **S**heets). Not only that, but you will also learn how to use the **TextField.StyleSheet** class to dynamically load an *external* CSS file, much like you learned how to use **LoadVars** to dynamically load text from an external TXT file. By keeping the CSS file *external* to the Macromedia Flash 8 project and using ActionScript to load and utilize the file, you gain the same benefits as when loading external text. You, or your client, can easily modify how the text is styled by merely changing the external CSS file with a simple text editor or even a WYSIWYG (**W**hat **Y**ou **S**ee **I**s **W**hat **Y**ou **G**et) HTML editor, such as Macromedia Dreamweaver 8. If you're designing two versions of a Web site, one with HTML and one with Flash 8, you can even have them *share* the same CSS file. How about that for making life simpler?

1 | Previewing What You Are Building

In this exercise, you'll get to preview exactly *what* you are building *before* you start building it. Therefore, as you're working through the exercises in this chapter, you'll have a better idea of how some of the abstract ActionScript concepts fit together to create a functional piece of the L.A. Eyeworks Web site.

1 Open your preferred browser, and navigate to the following URL:

www.lynda.com/flash8btb/laeyeworks/

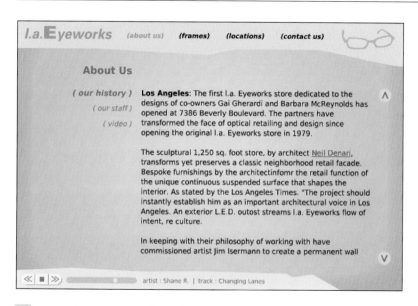

2 Once the L.A. Eyeworks Web site finishes loading, click the **about us** button in the top navigation bar. This loads the **about_us.swf** file, replacing the splash graphic.

Notice how some of the text is in bold, the text contains paragraph breaks, and a hyperlink even changes color when you hover your mouse over it! This text is styled using HTML (to create the bold, paragraph breaks, and hyperlinks) and further enhanced with CSS (in this case, to create the color change when the mouse hovers over the hyperlink). The CSS styles are also loaded in—and applied—from a separate CSS file.

3 When you're finished, close your browser.

2 | Modifying the Loaded Text Using HTML

So, you've loaded some text into your Flash 8 movie. What now? What about making it pretty? How can you change the font, color, size, and so forth, of the text loading dynamically? Up until this point, you've probably modified the look and feel of your text by clicking it with the Text tool and then changing the text settings in the Property Inspector. But with dynamic text, the text doesn't exist in the text field when you're working in the Flash 8 project. How do you go about modifying the text styles? Fortunately, Flash 8 allows you to modify the look and feel of dynamic text by adding HTML tags to the text file where the text resides! Not only that, but as you'll see in the next exercise, Macromedia introduced in Flash MX 2004 the capability to further modify the text by using CSS! In this exercise, you'll learn how to modify the dynamic text by inserting a few simple HTML tags in the **ourHistory.txt** file.

Flash 8 supports a few HTML tags for formatting your text. These tags, with short examples of each, are as follows: anchor **<a>**, bold **<b>**, font color **<font color="#FFFFFF">**, font face **<font face="Arial, Helvetica, sans-serif">**, font size **<font size="18">**, image **<img>**, italics **<i>**, list **<li>**, paragraph **<p>** (which you can use the **align** and **class** attributes with), span **<span>** (which you can use the **class** attribute with), line break **
, and underline **<u>. You can also use the following HTML attributes within a **<textformat>** tag: **leftmargin**, **rightmargin**, **blockindent**, **indent**, **tabstops**, and **leading**. So, as you can see, Flash 8 supports only a small subset of the many HTML tags modern browsers support. You can do a lot with the available tags, however. For a full description of each HTML tag Flash 8 supports, open your **Help** panel (**F1**), and from the Help "books" on the left, choose **Learning ActionScript 2.0 in Flash > Working with Text and Strings > Using HTML-formatted text > About supported HTML tags**.

Another great advantage of using HTML tags (and later, CSS) to modify the text appearance is you never need to open Flash 8. You can do all this work right inside the text file, alongside the text! In this exercise, you'll use a few of these tags to modify the appearance of the dynamic text.

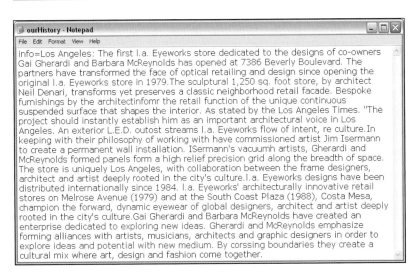

1 Minimize or hide Flash 8, navigate to your **Desktop > la_eyeworks > site > vars** folder, and open the **ourHistory.txt** file in Notepad (Windows), TextEdit (Mac), BBEdit (Mac), or an equivalent simple text editor.

This is the same text file, **ourHistory.txt**, you opened in Chapter 4, *"Using the LoadVars Class,"* and to which you added the `info` variable. Now, you'll add some HTML tags to this text file to slightly style the text. First, you'll create a few line breaks in the text so, when the viewer is scrolling through the text, it doesn't appear as one huge block of type.

To create a paragraph break, you might initially think you use the paragraph tag, **<p>**. However, in Flash 8, the **<p>** tag functions slightly differently than it does in a browser. In Flash 8, the **<p>** tag *defines* a new paragraph but does not create a paragraph *break*. In Flash 8, paragraph tags specify text alignment (**<p align="right">**) and assign CSS style classes (**<p class="body">**). To create a visual paragraph break in the text, use two **
** tags.

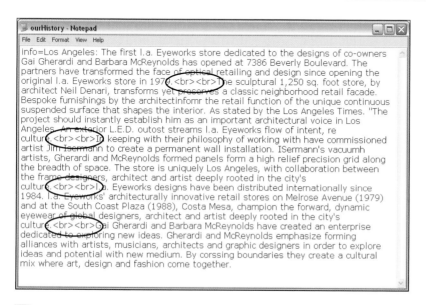

2 Type two break tags, **

**, before the following sentences: *The sculptural 1,250 sq. foot store…*; *In keeping with their philosophy…*; *I.a. Eyeworks designs have been distributed…*; and *Gai Gherardi and Barbara McReynolds have created….* To help you find those places easier, the break tags are circled in the illustration.

3 Save your **ourHistory.txt** text file by choosing **File > Save**, and bring Flash 8 into the foreground. Then, make sure **about_us.fla** is the FLA file currently in the foreground.

Even though in Chapter 4, *"Using the LoadVars Class,"* you specified the text loading into the text field should be HTML-formatted text (by typing the action `htmlText`), that's only half the job. You also need to turn on the **Render Text as HTML** option for the **about us** text field to tell Flash 8 to use (and not display) the HTML tags you're typing.

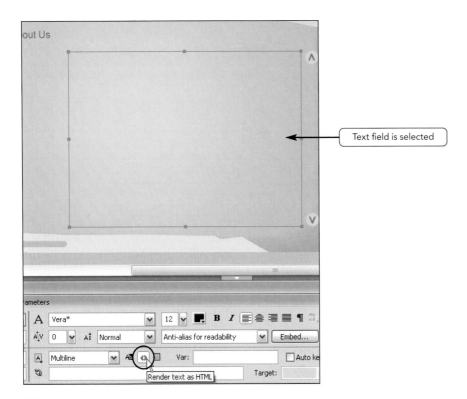

Text field is selected

4 Make sure you're in the **about_us.fla** file and have selected the `loadedInfo` text field, and then click the **Render text as HTML** button in the **Property Inspector**. Now, any text loading into the text field will utilize its HTML tags for formatting, alignment, and so forth. If you did not click the **Render text as HTML** button, the HTML tags would actually be *displayed* (rather than utilized) along with the text, which, obviously, would be a bad thing.

Since you've changed the **about_us.fla** file, you need to save your changes and publish a new SWF file.

---

5 Save your **about_us.fla** file by choosing **File > Save**. Then, publish a new SWF file by choosing **File > Publish**.

Note: After completing Step 5, if you attempt to publish your document and nothing happens, click somewhere on the Stage first and then attempt publishing again.

You've now published a new **about_us.swf** file, so you can preview the work you've done thus far by returning to the **master.fla** file and testing your movie.

---

6 Bring the **master.fla** file into the foreground. Then, test the movie by choosing **Control > Test Movie**.

When the **master.swf** preview window appears and the About Us module and **our history** text loads, you should see your line breaks. Scroll through the text to view the line breaks you added with HTML. Again, one of the great features of using HTML markup tags to style your dynamically loaded text is it makes it *very* easy for you, or your client (or both), to style the text to your liking without opening Flash 8.

Next, you'll add another HTML tag, this time to create a hyperlink with a portion of the text!

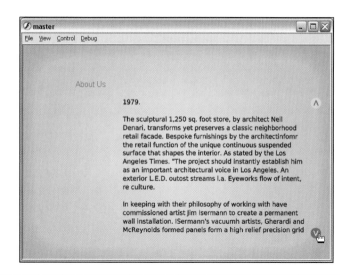

---

7 Close the **master.swf** preview window, then minimize (Windows) or hide (Mac) Flash 8, and finally open the **ourHistory.txt** file again.

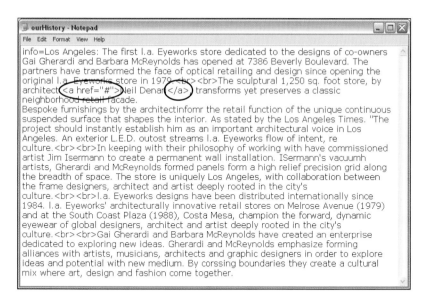

8 In the **ourHistory.txt** file, before the words *Neil Denari*, type the following:

`<a href="#">`

And, after the words *Neil Denari*, type

`</a>`

The **<a>** tag is called an *anchor tag*, and it allows you to create a hyperlink on a bit of text (just like in an HTML-based Web page). The **</a>** tag is the *closed* anchor tag. Just like when you're writing ActionScript functions and **if** statements, Flash 8 needs to know where the anchor starts and where it stops. The text between the anchor tag (**<a>**) and the closed anchor tag (**</a>**) (on the words *Neil Denari* in this example) is the hyperlink. The text between the quotation marks after **href=** is the URL where you want the visitor to be taken when they click the hyperlink. In this case, you're using a "placeholder" URL—signified by the # symbol—because Mr. Denari doesn't have a Web page of his own.

Wouldn't it also be nice to be able to specify your own *leading* (the amount of space between each line) for this text? Thankfully, you can, and it's *very* easy to do.

9 Click immediately after **info=** (located toward the beginning of the text file), and then use the **<textformat>** tag to add 7 points of leading by typing the following:

<textformat leading="7">

Just like with the other HTML tags, you also need to specify where the **<textformat>** tag ends.

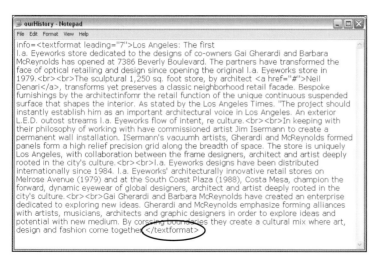

10 Click at the end of the text file, and close the **<textformat>** tag by typing the following:

</textformat>

By putting the opening **<textformat>** tag at the beginning of the text, and the closed **</textformat>** tag at the end, you apply the property of **leading="7"** to *all* the **our history** text.

Since you know your Flash 8 files are all set up to accept HTML tags in loaded text files, you don't even need to return to Flash 8 to preview the changes!

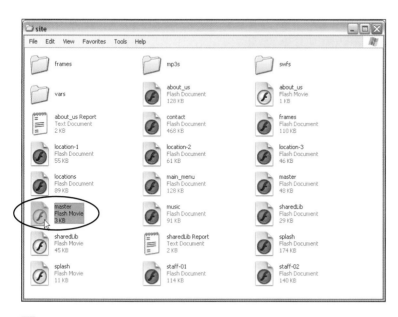

11 Save your **ourHistory.txt** file, navigate to your **Desktop > la_eyeworks > site** folder, and double-click the **master.swf** file to open it in the stand-alone Flash Player 8.

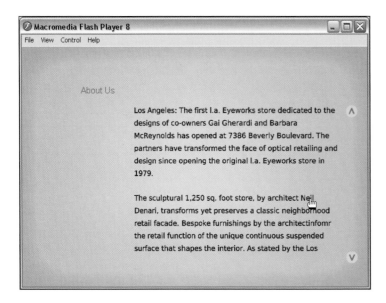

12 After you've double-clicked the **master.swf** file, you'll see the loaded text, with your custom-specified leading of 7 pixels applied to it! Within the text, however, the words *Neil Denari* won't look like the average hyperlink on a Web page, because Flash 8, by default, renders a hyperlink differently than a browser does. However, if you hover your mouse cursor over the text *Neil Denari*, you'll notice the arrow cursor turns into a Hand icon.

Even though the *Neil Denari* text doesn't *look* like a hyperlink, it still acts like one. If you were to type a real URL in the **ourHistory.txt** file in place of the URL placeholder, #, clicking the *Neil Denari* text in this SWF file would open your specified URL in a browser. You can even call JavaScript from these hyperlinks as well by using (`"javascript:myMethod('param');"` or `"asfunction:myMethod('param'))`!.

---

13 Once you have finished looking at the work you've done thus far, close the stand-alone Flash Player, and return to Flash 8.

In the next exercise, you will—among other things—make the hyperlink look and act like a "traditional" hyperlink does in a browser.

So there you have it. In this exercise, you used HTML tags to add line breaks and a hyperlink to the dynamically loaded text. Although you may not realize it yet, this is a fantastically powerful feature because it allows you to easily style dynamic text. Or more appealingly, your clients can do it themselves (or maybe not…depending on the client). For more information about the HTML tags Flash 8 supports, open the **Help** panel (**F1**), and from the Help "books" on the left, choose **Learning ActionScript 2.0 in Flash > Working with Text and Strings > Using HTML-formatted text > About supported HTML tags**.

Understanding CSS and Flash 8

Introduced with Flash MX 2004 was the ability to use CSS to modify the styling of text. Similar to HTML tag support, Flash 8 supports substantially fewer CSS properties than what a browser supports. For most uses, however, Flash 8's supported CSS properties should be sufficient. For detailed, up-to-date information about the CSS properties Flash 8 supports, open the **Help** panel (**F1**), and from the Help "books" on the left, choose **Learning ActionScript 2.0 in Flash > Working with Text and Strings > Formatting text with Cascading Style Sheets > Supported CSS properties**.

When you want to use CSS to modify the style of Dynamic text in your Flash 8 project, you have essentially two ways to do it. You can create and write the CSS styles directly in the Flash 8 project by using the Actions window. Or, you can write the CSS styles in a separate CSS file (much like you have a separate **ourHistory.txt** file to contain the **our history** text) and then dynamically *load* the CSS file and apply it to a text field when you need it. Even though creating a separate CSS file to contain the CSS styles and then dynamically loading and applying those CSS styles takes more effort (and ActionScript elbow grease), it has clear advantages over writing your CSS styles directly in the Flash 8 project. Namely, if you're loading a separate CSS file, when you want to make changes to the CSS styles, you simply have to open the CSS file with any simple text editor (or a CSS-editing program such as Dreamweaver 8, Bradsoft's Top Style, or others) and make the required changes. (For more CSS-editing program recommendations, see Appendix B, "*Flash Professional 8 Resources.*") The next time the SWF file plays, those CSS changes are automatically loaded and applied to the dynamic text. Conversely, if the CSS styles were written directly in your Flash 8 movie, the only way to edit those styles would be to open the FLA file in Flash 8, make the required changes, and then republish a new SWF file from the FLA file. By dynamically loading and applying an external CSS file, you can

also use the *same* CSS file you use for the HTML portions of a Web site. This significantly reduces production time because you don't have to use separate CSS files for the Flash 8 and HTML portions of a Web site, and by making changes to the CSS file, you're updating not only the HTML content but the Flash 8 content as well! As you can see, even though it may require a little extra effort to dynamically load and apply an external CSS file, it is a *much* better way to approach CSS integration in your Flash 8 projects.

When loading external CSS files and applying them to a text field, those styles need to be loaded and applied *before* the text is loaded into the same text field. If the text gets loaded into a text field first and *then* the styles are applied to that text field, the text will *not* utilize the CSS styles until new text loads into the same text field. So, when you load external CSS files, you need to ensure the CSS styles are applied to the text field *first*. Because of this, you *won't* be placing the ActionScript to perform the dynamic CSS loading/applying within the **master.fla** file, as you have with the other scripts used by multiple SWF files (such as the `MovieClipLoader` and `LoadVars` scripts). This is because the scripts placed on the first keyframe in the **master.fla** file execute all at the *same time* (roughly). If you put the script that loads and applies the CSS file on the first keyframe of **master.fla** with the other scripts, the `LoadVars` script (which loads the text from the external text file and inserts it into the text field) would execute at the same time as the CSS-loading script. This has the potential for the text to load into the text field *before* the CSS styles are applied to the field. As I mentioned previously, this would cause the loaded text to *not* utilize the CSS styles. Because of this potential problem, you will be writing the CSS-loading script directly in the SWF file requiring it. Although this goes against my preaching of keeping commonly used scripts centralized, from an intermediate Flash 8 perspective it's the best way around the potential problems I just outlined.

3 | Using CSS

In this exercise, you'll learn how to use ActionScript to load—and apply—an external CSS file to a text field. In addition, you'll learn how to use CSS to apply styles to text (giving you the ability to change text color, font face, font size, and so forth) and to style the way a hyperlink looks and behaves.

---

1 Minimize (Windows) or hide (Mac) Flash 8, and navigate to your **Desktop > la_eyeworks > site > styles** folder. In there, you'll find a file called **styles.css**. (Again, on some operating systems, the file might not display its three-letter **.css** extension.) Once you've located it, open the **styles.css** file.

Note: If you have Dreamweaver installed, the document opens in Dreamweaver when you double-click it. If you don't have Dreamweaver installed, you can open the **styles.css** file in a simple text editor such as Notepad (Windows), TextEdit (Mac), or BBEdit (Mac).

---

2 Once you've opened the file, you'll see it contains CSS style information. Now, because this book isn't only about CSS, I won't go over all the nitty-gritty details about working with and editing CSS. That's a whole topic unto itself. Following this exercise is a table with a quick breakdown of the CSS tags used in this **styles.css** document and what they all mean.

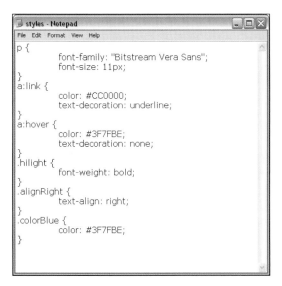

Note: When defining font families in a CSS document, if you want to use fonts from the shared library—as this example does—you need to specify the font name as you see it within the **Font Symbol Properties** dialog box in the shared library, *not* as the linkage identifier name you assigned to the font symbol.

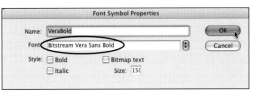

(Windows)   *(Mac)*

Warning: Here's where a glaring cross-platform difference, for the most part, stems from how the Windows and Mac operating systems treat installed fonts. Fonts installed in Windows are grouped by their font faces. In other words, the Bitstream Vera font you installed earlier was comprised of a series of faces—Vera Sans, Vera Sans Bold, Vera Sans Italic, and so forth. In Windows, those separate faces are listed as only one face, Vera Sans, with various *styles* (bold, italic, and so forth) representing the individual (grouped) font faces. A Mac, however, does *not* group the separate font faces as Windows does. This is an important detail because it affects how you specify which font face to use in the CSS file you will be loading in this exercise. The **styles.css** file you currently have open is the proper **styles.css** file for the Windows operating system—you don't need to make any changes to it if you're in Windows. But notice how, under the CSS class **.hilight**, when the bold style of Bitstream Vera Sans is needed, the CSS file just sets the font weight to bold. Because the **.hilight** class will be applied to selective bits of text within the CSS-redefined **<p>** tag, the **.hilight** class will inherit the styles applied to the **<p>** tag, namely, the font face (Bitstream Vera Sans), font size, and font color. (They're called *cascading* style sheets, because the styles flow down to one another.) So, in Windows, because the font faces are grouped, to change the font face to Bitstream Vera Sans Bold, you just have to change the font weight (a.k.a. font style) to bold.

NOTE:

Mac Users, Read This!

On a Mac, where the fonts *are not* grouped as they are in Windows, instead of **font-weight: bold** under the **.hilight** CSS class, you instead need to use the font face in which you want the text to be displayed. So, if you're currently on a Mac and you created the shared library with the shared Bitstream fonts on a Mac, you need to delete **font-weight: bold;** and replace it with **font-family: "Bitstream Vera Sans Bold";**.

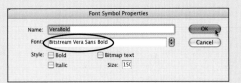

In essence, when specifying a font face in a CSS file in conjunction with a shared font in a shared library (as you are in the construction of the L.A. Eyeworks Web site), you need to use the *same CSS* font family *name* the font uses in the shared library under your operating system. This has *no* effect on what the viewers see when they visit the L.A. Eyeworks Web site. You don't need to create separate CSS files for the Mac and Windows operating systems. If you want a CSS-styled text field to use one of your shared fonts, you need to ensure the font family name you specify in the CSS file matches the font name displayed in the **Font** field in the **Font Symbol Properties** dialog box. In other words, this is only an author-time issue, not a run-time issue.

You've now seen the CSS styles, so you need to specify where those styles will be applied in the **ourHistory.txt** file.

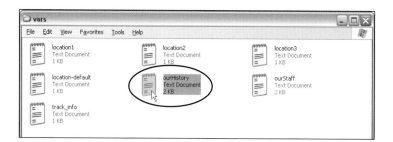

3 Navigate to your **Desktop > la_eyeworks > site > vars** folder, and open the **ourHistory.txt** file (or bring it to the foreground if you still have it open from the previous exercise) in Notepad (Windows), TextEdit (Mac), BBEdit (Mac), or an equivalent simple text editor.

Within the **ourHistory.txt** file, you want all the text to be styled using the CSS-redefined paragraph tag **<p>**. If you recall, the **styles.css** file redefined the **<p>** tag so whatever was within the **<p></p>** tags would be styled with an 11-point Bitstream Vera font. You also want the first two words of the **our history** text, *Los Angeles*, to be in bold. Luckily, a CSS class for just this purpose was precreated for you, in the **styles.css** file, called **.hilight**.

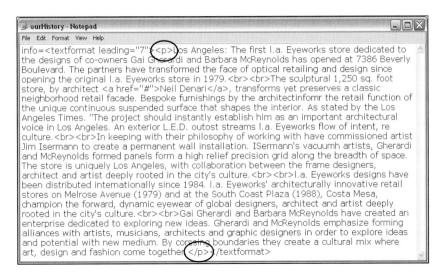

4 In the **ourHistory.txt** file, add a paragraph tag, **<p>**, between the words *Los Angeles* and the **<textformat leading="7">** tag. Then, add a closed paragraph tag, **</p>**, at the end of the text file, immediately after the last period but before the **</textformat>** tag. Since you used CSS to style everything within the paragraph tags, all the text within this document will have those styles applied to it.

Next, the text *Los Angeles* needs to appear in bold. To do this, you will apply the CSS **class** attribute to the **<span>** tag.

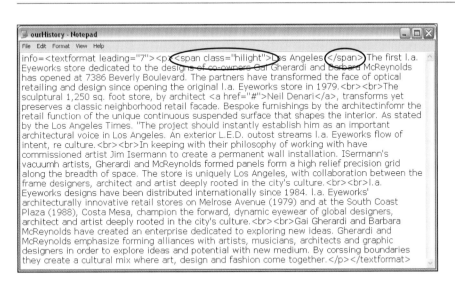

5 Click between the paragraph tag, **<p>**, and the words *Los Angeles:*, and type the following:

<span class="hilight">

Then you need to specify where the span ends. Click *after* the words *Los Angeles:*, and type the following:

</span>

6 Save your **ourHistory.txt** file by choosing **File > Save**.

Great! You've gotten a peek at what's going on "behind the scenes" in the **styles.css** file, and you've set the style tags in the **ourHistory.txt** file. Next, you need to write the script to dynamically load the **styles.css** file into your **about_us.fla** movie and apply it to the `loadedInfo` text field where the dynamically loaded text (such as the **ourHistory.txt** file) appears.

---

7 Close the **styles.css** and **ourHistory.txt** files, and bring Flash 8 to the foreground. Once you're in Flash 8, make sure the **about_us.fla** file is in the foreground. If you accidentally closed **about_us.fla**, you can easily open it again by navigating to your **Desktop > la_eyeworks > site** folder and double-clicking the **about_us.fla** file.

---

8 Select the first keyframe in the **a** layer, and open the **Actions** panel by pressing **F9** (Windows) or **Opt+F9** (Mac).

```
1  //---------------<load CSS>---------------\\
2
3  //---------------</load CSS>---------------\\
4
5  _level0.myLV.load("vars/ourHistory.txt");
```

9 In the **Actions** panel, move the top action, `_level0.myLV.load("vars/ourHistory.txt");`, down two lines by clicking to the left of the line and pressing **Enter** (Windows) or **Return** (Mac) twice. Then, click the top line in the **Actions** panel, and type the first comment:

`//---------------<load CSS>---------------\\`

After you've typed the comment, press **Enter** (Windows) or **Return** (Mac) twice to create two line breaks (and to give yourself an empty line to start writing actions), and then type the closed comment:

`//---------------</load CSS>---------------\\`

The commenting is in place, so you can start writing the script to load and apply the external CSS file.

```
1  //---------------<load CSS>---------------\\
2  var cssStyles:TextField.StyleSheet = new TextField.StyleSheet();
3  //---------------</load CSS>---------------\\
```

10 Click between the two comments you just added in the previous step, and create a new **TextField.StyleSheet** object by typing the following action:

`var cssStyles:TextField.StyleSheet = new TextField.StyleSheet ();`

Much like you saw with the `MovieClipLoader` and `LoadVars` objects, this action creates a new **TextField.StyleSheet** object within the **cssStyles** variable and strict types the data type of the variable to **TextField.StyleSheet**. Before you can load CSS styles and apply them to a text field, you must create this line, which in turn creates a new **TextField.StyleSheet** object. Then, you can tell the **TextField.StyleSheet** object which CSS file you want to load.

```
1  //----------------<load CSS>-------------------\\
2  var cssStyles:TextField.StyleSheet = new TextField.StyleSheet();
3  cssStyles.load("styles/styles.css");
4  //----------------</load CSS>------------------\\
```

11 Click at the end of the **var cssStyles:TextField.StyleSheet = new TextField.StyleSheet ();** line, press **Enter** (Windows) or **Return** (Mac) to create a line break, and then write the action to load the **styles.css** file by typing the following:

cssStyles.load ("styles/styles.css");

Just like with the **MovieClipLoader** and **LoadVars** actions, when you're telling the objects to load a file, you first type the variable name (in this case, **cssStyles**) you assigned to the object and then type **.load** and the name/location of the file you want to load. You'll also notice the CSS file you're directing the **cssStyles TextField.StyleSheet** object to load is **styles/styles.css**. You might be wondering what the slash (/) means. Remember, the **styles.css** file containing the CSS information you want to load is *not* located in the same directory as the **about_us.fla** file. Instead, it's located in a folder—within the folder where the **about_us.fla** file is—titled **styles**. If you're referencing an asset located in a different directory, you need to specify the directory path to the target file, as you have just done here by using the forward slash to separate the directory structure. Next, you need to tell the **TextField.StyleSheet** object what to do when the **styles.css** file has been completely downloaded. You will do this in the same way you did it in the **LoadVars** script—which you wrote in Chapter 4, *"Using the LoadVars Class"*—by creating an **onLoad** function.

```
1  //----------------<load CSS>-------------------\\
2  var cssStyles:TextField.StyleSheet = new TextField.StyleSheet();
3  cssStyles.load("styles/styles.css");
4  cssStyles.onLoad = function (success) {
5  //----------------</load CSS>------------------\\
```

12 Click at the end of the **cssStyles.load ("styles/styles.css");** line, press **Enter** (Windows) or **Return** (Mac) to create a line break, and then create the beginning of the **onLoad** function by typing the following:

cssStyles.onLoad = function (success) {

Like the function you wrote when you authored the **LoadVars** script in the **master.fla** file, this **onLoad** function will automatically execute when the targeted file (**styles.css** in this case) is completely downloaded. So, what should happen after the CSS file has been downloaded? Two actions need to take place in this case: The CSS styles need to be applied to the **loadedInfo** Dynamic text field, and the text needs to load into the text field. As mentioned, the CSS styles need to be applied to the text field *before* the text is loaded into the same text field. That way, the text inherits the CSS styles as it is loaded into the field. If the CSS styles are applied to the text field *after* the text is inserted into the field, the text will *not* inherit the CSS styles.

```
1  //----------------<load CSS>--------------------\\
2  var cssStyles:TextField.StyleSheet = new TextField.StyleSheet();
3  cssStyles.load("styles/styles.css");
4  cssStyles.onLoad = function (success) {
5      if (success) {
6  //----------------</load CSS>-------------------\\
```

13 Click at the end of the **cssStyles.onLoad = function (success) {** line, press **Enter** (Windows) or **Return** (Mac) to create a line break, and type the following:

 if (success) {

At this point, you're probably saying to yourself, "Gee, this seems rather…familiar." Again, the structure of this script is nearly identical to the **LoadVars** script you wrote earlier in this chapter. You're creating this conditional **if** statement within the **onLoad** function because you want to determine *if* the **styles.css** file was loaded and parsed correctly. Within this **if** statement, you will script what you want to happen *if* the styles are loaded correctly. As with the earlier **LoadVars** script, you will also specify what you want to happen if the **styles.css** file was *not* loaded and parsed correctly.

```
1  //----------------<load CSS>--------------------\\
2  var cssStyles:TextField.StyleSheet = new TextField.StyleSheet();
3  cssStyles.load("styles/styles.css");
4  cssStyles.onLoad = function (success) {
5      if (success) {
6          loadedInfo.styleSheet = cssStyles;
7  //----------------</load CSS>-------------------\\
```

14 Click at the end of the **if (success) {** line, press **Enter** (Windows) or **Return** (Mac) to create a line break, and then attach your CSS styles to the **loadedInfo** text field by typing the following:

loadedInfo.styleSheet = cssStyles;

This line essentially says, "Attach a style sheet to the **loadedInfo** text field, and the style sheet to attach is the **cssStyles TextField.StyleSheet** object (the object into which you loaded the **styles.css** file)." Since the text field has CSS styles applied to it, you can safely load the text into the field.

```
1   //----------------<load CSS>--------------------\\
2   var cssStyles:TextField.StyleSheet = new TextField.StyleSheet();
3   cssStyles.load("styles/styles.css");
4   cssStyles.onLoad = function (success) {
5       if (success) {
6           loadedInfo.styleSheet = cssStyles;
7
8   //----------</load CSS>-------------------\\
9
10  _level0.myLV.load("vars/ourHistory.txt");
11
```

15 Click at the end of the **loadedInfo.styleSheet = cssStyles;** line, and press **Enter** (Windows) or **Return** (Mac) to create a line break. Underneath the **TextField.StyleSheet** object script you're currently writing is the action—which you wrote earlier in this chapter—to load the **ourHistory.txt** file using the **myLV LoadVars**

object located in the **master.fla** file. This is the action you want to be executed after the CSS styles have been applied to the **loadedInfo** text field. So, simply select this action by dragging over it, and then drag it to the new line break you just created under the **loadedInfo.styleSheet = cssStyles;** line.

Now you just need to close the **if** statement and then script what should happen if the **styles.css** file did not load and get parsed correctly for one reason or another. Just like the **LoadVars** script you authored earlier, you'll specify an error message be inserted into the **loadedInfo** text field should an error occur.

```
1  //----------------<load CSS>------------------\\
2  var cssStyles:TextField.StyleSheet = new TextField.StyleSheet();
3  cssStyles.load("styles/styles.css");
4  cssStyles.onLoad = function (success) {
5      if (success) {
6          loadedInfo.styleSheet = cssStyles;
7          _level0.myLV.load("vars/ourHistory.txt");
8      } else {
9  //----------------</ load CSS>------------------\\
```

16 Click at the end of the **_level0.myLV.load("vars/ourHistory.txt");** line, press **Enter** (Windows) or **Return** (Mac) to create a line break, and then close the **if** statement and add an **else** by typing the following:

} else {

Here you can specify what should happen if the **styles.css** file was not downloaded and parsed successfully. The **if/else** relationship essentially reads in plain English, "If so-and-so happens, do this. Otherwise (else), do this other thing."

For this, you'll specify the same result as you specified in the **LoadVars** script. Essentially, you'll insert an error message into the **loadedInfo** text field.

```
1  //----------------<load CSS>------------------\\
2  var cssStyles:TextField.StyleSheet = new TextField.StyleSheet();
3  cssStyles.load("styles/styles.css");
4  cssStyles.onLoad = function (success) {
5      if (success) {
6          loadedInfo.styleSheet = cssStyles;
7          _level0.myLV.load("vars/ourHistory.txt");
8      } else {
9          loadedInfo.text = "There has been an error loading the requested information.
   Please contact the Webmaster and report your error.";
10 //----------------</ load CSS>------------------\\
```

17 Click at the end of the **} else {** line, press **Enter** (Windows) or **Return** (Mac) to create a line break, and then write the action to insert the error text into the **loadedInfo** text field by typing the following:

loadedInfo.text = "There has been an error loading the requested information. Please contact the Webmaster and report your error.";

There you have it—the error message in all its stunning glory. This also completes the major sections of the **TextField.StyleSheet** object script. All you have to do now is close the **else** and **onLoad** function actions by inserting a couple of closed curly braces (**}**).

```
1  //----------------<load CSS>-------------------\\
2  var cssStyles:TextField.StyleSheet = new TextField.StyleSheet();
3  cssStyles.load("styles/styles.css");
4  cssStyles.onLoad = function (success) {
5      if (success) {
6          loadedInfo.styleSheet = cssStyles;
7          _level0.myLV.load("vars/ourHistory.txt");
8      } else {
9          loadedInfo.text = "There has been an error loading the requested information.
   Please contact the Webmaster and report your error.";
10     }
11 }
12 //----------------</ load CSS>-------------------\\
```

18 Click at the end of the `loadedInfo.text = "There has been…";` line, press **Enter** (Windows) or **Return** (Mac) to create a line break, and close the `else` statement by typing a closed curly brace (**}**). Press **Enter** (Windows) or **Return** (Mac) again to create another line break, and then close the `onLoad` function by typing another closed curly brace (**}**).

You just completed the `TextField.StyleSheet` script. You've achieved quite an accomplishment, which is clearly recognizable when you sit back and look at the script you just composed. Congratulations! But before you start clapping your hands in glee and prancing around the living room, you should save and test your work to make sure everything is functioning as you expect.

---

19 Save your **about_us.fla** by choosing **File > Save**. Then, since you've changed the **about_us.fla** file, you need to publish a new SWF file incorporating those changes. You'll then preview the **about_us.swf** module through the **master.swf** file.

Note: The reason why you constantly need to publish a SWF file from the **about_us.fla** file (and from the other modules, as well, once you get there) whenever you change the FLA file is because of the way the content is structured. Remember, many of the necessary actions are located within the **master.fla** Timeline. Because of this, the site modules loaded into the **master.swf** file (About Us, Frames, Locations, and so forth) need to be viewed *through* the **master.swf** file.

---

20 Publish a new SWF file from the **about_us.fla** file by choosing **File > Publish**. This will publish an updated **about_us.swf** file in the **site** folder (where the **about_us.fla** file is located).

---

21 Minimize (Windows) or hide (Mac) Flash 8, navigate to your **Desktop > la_eyeworks > site** folder, and double-click the **master.swf** file to preview your work in the Flash Player.

Awesome! There's the **our history** text, dynamically loaded and styled using a dynamically loaded style sheet! As you can see, the text *Los Angeles* is in bold thanks to the `hilight` CSS class, and the *Neil Denari* hyperlink looks like a hyperlink you see on HTML-based Web pages. Not only that, but if you hover your mouse over the hyperlink, it will perform the `a:hover` CSS style and display the hyperlink with no underline and in a different color!

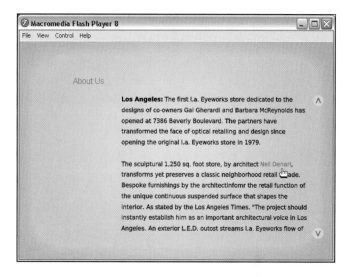

Not only have you just styled the dynamic **our history** text, but you also have made those style changes using a combination of HTML and a dynamically loaded CSS file. As I mentioned, a *huge* advantage to this setup is now, whenever you want to modify the font style, font color, or font size, you don't need to open Flash 8 to do it! You can just open the **styles.css** file in a simple text editor and make your changes there. The next time the **about_us.swf** file appears, it will automatically incorporate your changes. Über cool. Give yourself a big pat on the back!

You'd be a slack Flash 8 designer/developer if you didn't perform one last check. Remember when you wrote the **onLoad** error handling for the CSS file? You specified an error message should display in the **loadedInfo** text field if the **styles.css** file was *not* successfully loaded. The viewer will see this error message if a problem occurs while locating or loading the **styles.css** file for some reason. To test this error management, all you need to do is rename the **styles.css** file. Then, Flash 8 won't be able to load the file (because it's looking for a file named **styles.css**) and will display the error message.

22 Navigate to your **Desktop > la_eyeworks > site > styles** folder, and change the name of the **styles.css** file to something else, such as **styles2.css**.

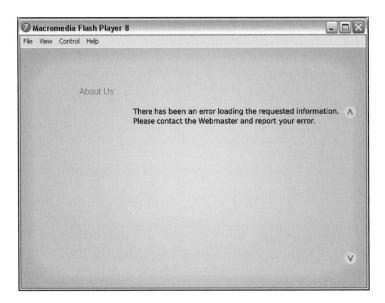

23 Navigate to your **Desktop > la_eyeworks > site** folder, and test your `TextField.StyleSheet` error management by double-clicking the **master.swf** file to play it in the Flash Player. You should see the error message appear in place of the text! This is because, back in the `TextField.StyleSheet` script, you specified within the **onLoad** function if the **styles.css** file did *not* load correctly, it should instead (else) display this error message.

You've now verified the error message works properly, so you need to return the **styles2.css** file to its proper name.

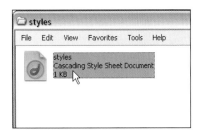

24 Close the stand-alone Flash Player, navigate to your **Desktop > la_eyeworks > site > styles** folder, and rename the **styles2.css** file to its proper name, **styles.css**. If you were to double-click the **master.swf** file again to play it, you'd notice your text is back to "normal" and displays correctly.

The following table describes the various CSS styles used in the styles.css file.

---

styles.css Properties Description

Property	Description
p	Defines the styling information of the HTML paragraph tag, **\<p>**. Whatever properties you assign to this style will affect every place you've used the **\<p>** tag. For example, this is useful when you want to specify the base styling of all the text in a text field. For the exercise you just finished, any text within the HTML tags **\<p>** and **\</p>** will be styled with the font Bitstream Vera Sans and set to 11 pixels.
a:link	Defines the styling information of any hyperlinks (hyperlinks use the HTML tag **\<a>**) in the text. For the exercise you just finished, all hyperlinks will have the hex color #CC0000 (red) applied to them with an underline.
a:hover	Defines the styling information of any hyperlinks over which the viewer's mouse is hovering. For the exercise you just finished, the **a:hover** style specifies when the viewer hovers over a hyperlink, the link will change from its **a:link** styling to a style where the text is colored using the hex color #3F7FBE (blue), with no underline under the hyperlink.
.hilight	Defines the styling information of whatever you assign this class to. For the exercise you just finished, when you assign the **.hilight** class to an HTML tag (such as **\<span>**), the displayed font will change to be set to a font weight of bold. This will, essentially, just make the text this class is applied to appear in bold. Because this class will be applied selectively within the CSS-redefined **\<p>** tag, it will inherit any styles applied to the **\<p>** tag, namely, the font face, color, and size. When this class is applied to a bit of text, it will change—in Windows—only the font to the bold style of Bitstream Vera Sans. On a Mac, you need to specify, instead of **font-weight: bold**, the name of the font face, Bitstream Vera Sans Bold, to achieve the same results.
.alignRight	Defines the styling information of whatever you assign this class to. For the exercise you just finished, when you assign this class to an HTML tag, the text will be aligned to the right side of the text field it appears within.
.colorBlue	Defines the styling information of whatever you assign this class to. For the exercise you just finished, when you assign this class to an HTML tag, the text will be colored using the hex color #3F7FBE (blue).

You learned some great new actions and techniques in this chapter! Not only did you learn how to modify the layout of dynamically loaded text using HTML tags, but you also learned how to style the text using CSS and how to dynamically load an external CSS file containing all your CSS style information. After you begin to use these techniques in your own Flash 8 projects, you'll probably start to wonder how you ever developed Web sites without them!

In the next chapter you will learn to use the **TextFormat** class to create a very, very cool interactive submenu for the About Us module. You will also learn how to incorporate nested, inline SWF files in your dynamic text! I know, I know—I'm excited, too!

6

Using the
TextFormat Class

In this chapter, you will learn how to use the `TextFormat` class to create a nifty, completely ActionScript-driven, interactive submenu for the About Us module. Once you create the submenu, you will use it to dynamically load the text for the **our staff** subsection. In the **our staff** subsection, you will also add inline (inline with the text) SWF files to the scrollable **our staff** text. Keep reading—it only gets better.

1 | Previewing What You Are Building

In this exercise, you'll preview the interactive submenu you'll be building in this chapter before you start building it. That way, as you begin learning how to create some of the advanced ActionScript functionality, the steps will make more sense to you because you will already know how to apply the techniques to a working Web site.

---

1 Open your preferred browser, and navigate to the following URL:

www.lynda.com/flash8btb/laeyeworks/

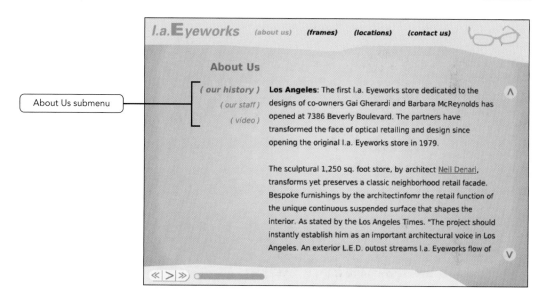

2 Once the L.A. Eyeworks Web site finishes loading, click the **about us** option in the navigation menu.

Notice how the **our history** text loads by default. You finished constructing this in Chapter 4, *"Using the LoadVars Class."* But also notice, in the submenu, how the **our history** option is bold and a point size bigger than the other options.

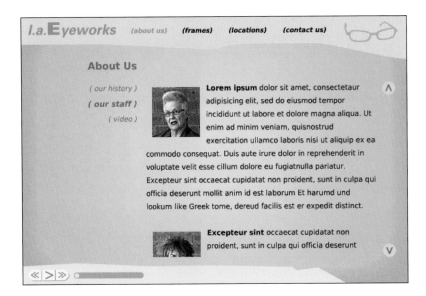

3   Click the submenu option **our staff**. When you click the **our staff** option, the **our history** option reduces a point size without bold formatting, but the **our staff** option then becomes one point size larger and bold. See a pattern here?

Essentially, the submenu behaves in the following manner:

- Whichever section the viewer is currently looking at, the submenu option corresponding to the active section becomes "disabled." The text increases by one point size, and the text becomes bold.

- When the viewer clicks another submenu option, the disabled submenu option becomes "enabled." It reduces by one point size and is no longer bold.

- Whichever section displays by default when the About Us module first loads (in this case, the **our history** section), that submenu option automatically is disabled.

- When a submenu option becomes disabled, viewers cannot interact with it. They will not see the Hand icon when they move their mousee over it, and nothing will happen when they click it.

- When a submenu option becomes re-enabled, viewers can then interact with it. They will see the text rollover effect, and clicking the option will trigger the loading of the corresponding section.

Although initially you may have taken the little submenu for granted and not really given it a second thought, I hope now you'll appreciate it a little more. Quite a lot of interactivity is happening in the submenu, and Macromedia Flash 8 doesn't build it all for you. It will take a bit of ActionScript, as well as learning some new actions, to build the submenu functionality. So go grab a cup of coffee, a cushion for your chair, and get started with the construction!

---

4   Close your browser.

What Is the TextFormat Class?

In essence, the **TextFormat** class allows you to use ActionScript to alter the text formatting of static text or text within Dynamic or Input text fields. When you want to modify text formatting by using the **TextFormat** class, you first have to create an instance (object) of the **TextFormat** class. One way to do this is by simply typing the following:

```
var myFormat:TextFormat = new TextFormat();
```

Then, you can "attach" text-formatting styles to the **myFormat** variable you assigned the **TextFormat** object to by typing the following, for example:

```
myFormat.font = "Bitstream Vera Sans";
myFormat.color = 0xFF0000;
myFormat.bold = true;
myFormat.size = 13;
```

Then, once you've defined the styling of the **myFormat TextFormat** object, you can easily apply those styles to text in a text field by typing the following, for example:

```
this.myTextField.setTextFormat(myFormat);
```

And *voila*! The text in the text field immediately takes on the text styles you defined in the **TextFormat** object. Pretty nifty, eh?

In addition to specifying the **TextFormat** class styles in the format I just outlined, you can also specify the **TextFormat** class styles in one line, as parameters of the **TextFormat** class constructor. Essentially, this allows you to reduce the amount of code it would require to specify text styles. For example, to specify the same text styles created in the previous example, you could set the same text font, size, color, and bold formatting by typing it in one line:

```
var myFormat:TextFormat = new TextFormat("Bitstream Vera Sans", 13, 0xFF0000, true);
```

As you can see, this method takes fewer lines of ActionScript code than does the previous method. However, when specifying the **TextFormat** properties in this manner, you need to specify the parameters in a specific order, as follows:

```
new TextFormat(font, size, color, bold, italic, underline, url, target, align, leftMargin, rightMargin, indent, leading);
```

When using this method, if you want to set the font, size, and bold formatting but leave the color (between the size and bold formatting) alone, you still have to set the parameter to **null**. For example:

```
new TextFormat("Bitstream Vera Sans", 13, null, true);
```

So, as I'm sure you're coming to understand, the **TextFormat** class can be a fantastic, powerful way to modify the text style through ActionScript. Based on a viewer's feedback (moving the mouse, clicking menus, and so forth), you can specify—using ActionScript—how the text in your movie changes according to the viewer's input.

You will use the **TextFormat** class in the next exercise to modify the text styling of the submenu text options as the viewer interacts with them. A table, describing the various **TextFormat** class properties, follows the next exercise.

2 | Adding the Submenu

In this exercise, you'll build the submenu to allow the viewer to navigate within the About Us module. Eventually you'll have a total of three submenu options: **our history**, **our staff**, and **video**. Although you will build the interactivity for the **video** submenu option in the exercises in this chapter, you won't create the **video** section until Chapter 11, *"Building a Video Player."*

---

1 Bring Flash 8 to the foreground. Then, make sure **about_us.fla** is the FLA file currently in the foreground.

The first task you need to do is set the **About Us** title text so it is using the appropriate Bitstream Vera Sans font.

---

2 Single-click the **About Us** static text box on the **Stage** to select it. Then, in the **Property Inspector**, click the **Font** pop-up menu, and choose the font **VeraBold***.

You'll also notice three other fonts with asterisks (*) next to their names: Vera*, VeraBoldOblique*, and VeraOblique*. The four font faces with asterisks next to their names are the shared fonts from the **sharedLib.fla** file. Whenever you have a font symbol in your library, those fonts will have asterisks next to their names in the Font pop-up menu. The names appearing in the Font pop-up menu are the names you gave the fonts' symbols when you created them in the shared library.

Note: Because of the way Windows groups font styles (as mentioned in Chapter 5, *"Using HTML and CSS"*), you'll need to perform one extra step to get this shared VeraBold font to display correctly.

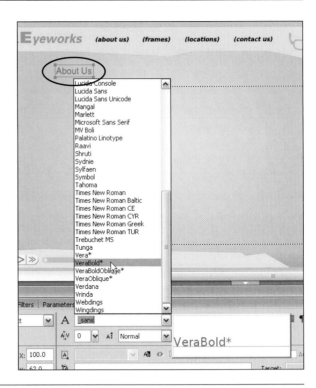

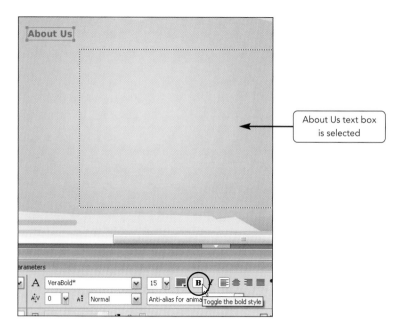

About Us text box is selected

3 If you're working in Windows, after you selected the **VeraBold*** font from the **Font** pop-up menu, you also need to click the **Bold Style** button in the **Property Inspector** to have the shared font display its bold style. Mac users *do not* need to perform this step.

To help you get started creating the submenu options, I've provided the Dynamic text fields, nested within movie clips. You may be thinking, "Text fields nested in movie clips?" The reason you'll be using Dynamic text fields nested within movie clips is because, as you saw in the submenu tour at the beginning of this exercise, the submenu options will visually change depending on the currently loaded section. To accomplish this, you'll use ActionScript to dynamically modify the appearance and interactivity of the text depending on which section is active. Since these text fields need to be clickable—as well as un-clickable when the situation calls for it—they need to be nested within MovieClips, where their precise interactivity can be controlled.

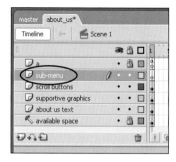

4 Select the layer underneath the **a** layer, and create a new layer. Rename this new layer to "**sub-menu**."

5 Open the **Library** window by pressing **Ctrl+L** (Windows) or **Cmd+L** (Mac).

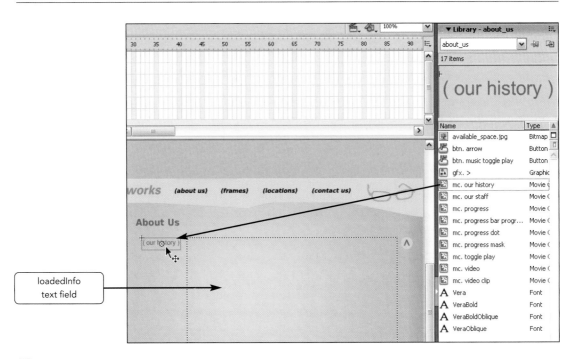

6 With the **sub-menu** layer selected, drag the symbol **mc. our history** from the **Library** window, and position it aligned to the top-left side of the `loadedInfo` text field.

Next, you should set up the **our history** submenu option so it is set at its "default" (that is, non-highlighted) style.

7 Open the **our history** movie clip by double-clicking its instance on the **Stage**. Once you're inside the **mc. our history** movie clip, select the text field on the **Stage** by clicking it once.

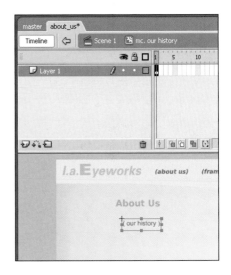

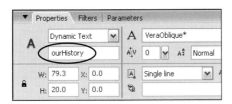

8 From the **Font** pop-up menu in the **Property Inspector**, choose **VeraOblique***. If you're in Windows, you also need to click the **Italic Style** button. The other options were already set for you when the text field was created, but if you accidentally changed the settings, you want to make sure it's a **Dynamic Text** field, the **Font Size** setting is **11**, the **Font Rendering Method** setting is **Anti-alias for readability**, and the **Color** setting is the hex value **#3F7FBE** (blue). Although you will be specifying these same text-formatting styles later using ActionScript, you're still setting these options here because it gives you a good idea of what the text will look like when it will be formatted using the `TextFormat` object. If you didn't specify these settings and just left the text at its default settings (to be styled by the `TextFormat` object upon playback), it would be difficult to approximate the final look and feel, positioning, and alignment as you position the text in this layout.

Note: When you change the font face from **_sans** to **VeraOblique***, you will notice the text become slightly larger. It might even appear to overlap the `loadedInfo` Dynamic text field you can see on Scene 1. Later in this exercise you will realign the text, so don't worry about repositioning it just yet.

Because you'll be using ActionScript to modify many aspects of this text field (font face, font size, alignment, and so forth), you also *must* give the Dynamic text field an instance name. Without an instance name, you would not be able to target this text field with ActionScript and therefore would not be able to modify it.

9 In the **Property Inspector**, type **ourHistory** in the **Instance Name** field. Now, when you want to target this text field with ActionScript, you can use the name **ourHistory**.

master about_us*

Timeline Scene 1 mc. our history

10 Return to **Scene 1** by clicking its tab at the top-left of the **Timeline**.

11 Since you changed the font face and style, once you're back in **Scene 1** you might need to adjust the alignment of the **our history** movie clip. You can do this easily and precisely using the arrow keys on the keyboard to nudge the **our history** movie clip into place.

Since you'll be targeting the `ourHistory` text field inside of the **mc. our history** movie clip, you need to give the instance of this movie clip an instance name as well. If you don't give this movie clip instance a name, you won't be able to access the text field inside it.

12 With the instance of the **mc. our history** movie clip still selected, give this movie clip instance a name by typing **ourHistoryMC** in the **Instance Name** field of the **Property Inspector**. Now, when you want to target the `ourHistory` text field inside this movie clip with ActionScript, you can simply refer to it by typing **ourHistoryMC.ourHistory**.

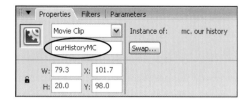

Now you just need to repeat this process for the remaining two submenu options: **our staff** and **video**.

13 Repeat Steps 6 through 12 to integrate the movie clips **mc. our staff** and **mc. video** into the submenu. When repeating those steps, here's some specific information you'll need: The **our staff** Dynamic text field should have an instance name of (yep, you guessed it) **ourStaff**, and you should give the **mc. our staff** movie clip instance containing the **ourStaff** text field an instance name of **ourStaffMC**. The **video** Dynamic text field should have an instance name of **ourVideo**, and you should give the **mc. video** movie clip instance containing the **ourVideo** text field an instance name of **ourVideoMC**.

When you're finished, the three submenu options should be all nicely aligned to their right sides and spaced evenly, slightly apart. Ahh…there's something to be said for a nicely ordered submenu.

14 Once you've completed setting up the submenu options, save your **about_us.fla** file by choosing **File > Save**.

Next, you need to set up ActionScript objects to change the text styles when the viewer interacts with the submenu options.

15 Select the first keyframe in the **a** layer, and open the **Actions** panel by pressing **F9** (Windows) or **Opt+F9** (Mac).

```
23  //--------------</scroll buttons>----------------\\
24
25  // create TextFormat Objects that define the states of the sub-menu options
```

16 Click after the closing scroll button's comment line, //-----------</scroll buttons------------\\, press **Enter** (Windows) or **Return** (Mac) twice to create a couple line breaks, and then type the following comment all on one line:

`// create TextFormat Objects that define the states of the sub-menu options`

Underneath this comment is where you will build the **TextFormat** ActionScript objects for changing the text styles. These objects will execute when viewers interact with the submenu options. (For example, when a viewer moves the mouse over the **our history** option, the **TextFormat** object defining the **rollOver** appearance will execute.) Because you will be specifying a font face to use, this process will differ depending on whether you're in Windows or on a Mac. This goes back to what I mentioned previously about how Windows groups font styles together but a Mac does not. I'll clearly mark any steps that differ.

First, you will create a **TextFormat** object to handle how the submenu text options will appear when they're disabled. A submenu option will become disabled under one of these two circumstances:

- When a subsection (**our history**, **our staff**, and so forth) is loaded, the corresponding submenu option will appear disabled.

- When a viewer moves the mouse over an active (that is, nondisabled) submenu option, the option will display the disabled style. Moving the mouse off the submenu option will cause the text to revert to the enabled style.

```
25  // create TextFormat Objects that define the states of the sub-menu options
26  var btnDisable:TextFormat = new TextFormat();
```

17 Click after the comment you typed in Step 16, press **Enter** (Windows) or **Return** (Mac) to create a line break, and then begin to create the **btnDisable TextFormat** object by typing the following:

`var btnDisable:TextFormat = new TextFormat();`

This line creates a new **TextFormat** object and assigns it to the variable **btnDisable**. Now, you just need to specify how the submenu text options will appear when they meet one of the two circumstances outlined previously. To refresh your memory, by default, the submenu text options appear as 11-point Bitstream Vera Sans Oblique. When a submenu text option appears disabled after its corresponding subsection loads, or when a viewer rolls the mouse over it, you want the style to change to 12-point Bitstream Vera Sans Bold Oblique. (Essentially, the font changes to *bold* oblique—instead of just oblique—and increases one point size.)

```
25  // create TextFormat Objects that define the states of the sub-menu options
26  var btnDisable:TextFormat = new TextFormat("Bitstream Vera Sans", 12, null, true, true);
```

(Windows)

18 If you're working in Windows, click between the parentheses after **TextFormat**, and type the following:

"Bitstream Vera Sans", 12, null, true, true

As detailed in the "What Is the TextFormat Class?" section, this sets the font to Bitstream Vera Sans, sets the font size to 12, sets the color to null (not modified), disables the bold formatting, and enables the italic formatting.

```
25  // create TextFormat Objects that define the states of the sub-menu options
26  var btnDisable:TextFormat = new TextFormat("Bitstream Vera Sans Bold Oblique", 12);
```

(Mac)

19 If you're on a Mac, click between the parentheses after **TextFormat**, and type the following:

"Bitstream Vera Sans Bold Oblique", 12

The reason why these steps differ depending on the platform goes back to Windows' grouping of font styles. Because Windows groups the Bitstream Vera Sans font styles together, you cannot refer—with ActionScript—to the font (as you have on a Mac in this case) as Bitstream Vera Sans Bold Oblique. All Windows "sees" is "Bitstream Vera Sans." So in Windows, if you want the Bitstream Vera Sans font face to appear both bold and italic, you need to add bold and italic parameters to the **TextFormat** object. A Mac does *not* group the font styles, so Mac users can refer directly to the font face Bitstream Vera Sans Bold Oblique.

Since you've specified what the submenu text options will look like when they're disabled (or rolled over), you need to specify what the submenu text options will look like when they're enabled (or rolled off).

```
25  // create TextFormat Objects that define the states of the sub-menu options
26  var btnDisable:TextFormat = new TextFormat("Bitstream Vera Sans", 12, null, true, true);
27  var btnEnable:TextFormat = new TextFormat();
```

20 Click after the **var btnDisable:TextFormat = new TextFormat…** line you created in Step 17, press **Enter** (Windows) or **Return** (Mac) to create a line break, and then begin to create the **btnEnable TextFormat** object by typing the following:

var btnEnable:TextFormat = new TextFormat();

```
25  // create TextFormat Objects that define the states of the sub-menu options
26  var btnDisable:TextFormat = new TextFormat("Bitstream Vera Sans", 12, null, true, true);
27  var btnEnable:TextFormat = new TextFormat("Bitstream Vera Sans", 11, null, false, true);
```

(Windows)

21 If you're running Windows, click between the **TextFormat** parentheses, and type the following:

"Bitstream Vera Sans", 11, null, false, true

This sets the **btnEnable TextFormat** style to (respectively) the Bitstream Vera Sans font, 11 points, no color change, no bold, and italic.

```
25  // create TextFormat Objects that define the states of the sub-menu options
26  var btnDisable:TextFormat = new TextFormat("Bitstream Vera Sans Bold Oblique", 12);
27  var btnEnable:TextFormat = new TextFormat("Bitstream Vera Sans Oblique", 11);
```

(Mac)

22 If you're on a Mac, click between the **TextFormat** parentheses, and type the following:

"Bitstream Vera Sans Oblique", 11

This, of course, sets the **btnEnable TextFormat** style to the 11-point Bitstream Vera Sans Oblique font.

That's it! You now have your two **TextFormat** objects: **btnDisable** and **btnEnable**. These two **TextFormat** objects will be used as the user interacts with the submenu options and when content is loaded into the About Us module. Next, you can test these **TextFormat** objects by instructing the submenu option—which corresponds to the automatically loaded section (**our history**)—to disable itself. Because the **our history** subsection gets automatically loaded when the About Us module loads, it stands to reason the **our history** submenu button should therefore be disabled. This also acts as a visual identifier to viewers to reinforce which subsection they're currently viewing.

```
25  // create TextFormat Objects that define the states of the sub-menu options
26  var btnDisable:TextFormat = new TextFormat("Bitstream Vera Sans", 12, null, true, true);
27  var btnEnable:TextFormat = new TextFormat("Bitstream Vera Sans", 11, null, false, true);
28
29  // disable the sub-menu option that corresponds to the currently loaded section
```

23 Click after the **var btnEnable:TextFormat = new TextFormat…** line, press **Enter** (Windows) or **Return** (Mac) twice to create a couple of line breaks, and then type the following comment:

// disable the sub-menu option that corresponds to the currently loaded section

24 Click after the comment line, and press **Enter** (Windows) or **Return** (Mac) to create a line break.

When applying a **TextFormat** object to alter the text style of some text, you need to make sure you apply it to the text field. This is why, when you dragged the submenu options onto the Stage, you gave instance names to the Dynamic text fields and the movie clip instances containing them. Fortunately, you don't have to remember the instance names you assigned to the movie clips and text fields.

25 Click the **Insert a target path** button at the top of the **Actions** panel. This opens the **Insert Target Path** dialog box.

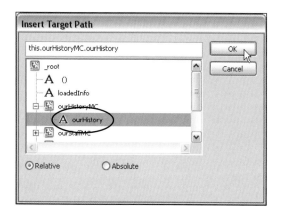

26 Open the **ourHistoryMC** movie clip by clicking the plus sign to its left (on a Mac, it's an arrow). Here you'll see the text field you gave an instance name to, **ourHistory**. Click **ourHistory** once to select it. When you do, you'll see the target path appear at the top of the dialog box. Click **OK** to insert the path in the **Actions** panel.

```
25  // create TextFormat Objects that define the states of the sub-menu options
26  var btnDisable:TextFormat = new TextFormat("Bitstream Vera Sans", 12, null, true, true);
27  var btnEnable:TextFormat = new TextFormat("Bitstream Vera Sans", 11, null, false, true);
28
29  // disable the sub-menu option that corresponds to the currently loaded section
30  this.ourHistoryMC.ourHistory.setTextFormat(btnDisable);
```

27 Click after the target path inserted in the **Actions** panel, and apply the **btnDisable TextFormat** to the **ourHistory** text field by typing the following:

.setTextFormat(btnDisable);

Don't forget to add the dot (.) between **ourHistory** and **setTextFormat**. In essence, this line says, "Apply **btnDisable TextFormat** to the **ourHistory** text field nested inside the **ourHistoryMC** movie clip." To apply a **TextFormat** object to a text field, you use the **setTextFormat** action (followed by, in parentheses, the name of the **TextFormat** object you want to apply), as you saw here.

Great! In the past few steps, you created two **TextFormat** objects to set the style formatting of the sub-menu text options, and you applied one of those objects (**btnDisable**) to the **ourHistory** text field. It's time to test your movie and make sure everything works as expected!

28 Save your **about_us.fla** file by choosing **File > Save**. Then, publish an updated SWF file from this FLA by choosing **File > Publish**.

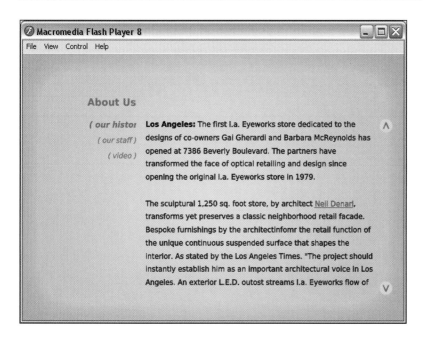

29 Minimize (Windows) or hide (Mac) Flash 8, navigate to your **Desktop > la_eyeworks > site** folder, and double-click the **master.swf** file to preview your work in the stand-alone Macromedia Flash Player 8.

If everything works as expected, you should see something looking *exactly* like the illustration. You'll see the **our history** text, nicely in bold and one point size bigger than its submenu option cousins (thanks to the **btnDisable TextFormat** object), but if you look closely, the **our history** text is cut off! It simply says *our histor*. What has happened here is, when the **btnDisable TextFormat** object was applied to the text field, it made the text bold and one point size bigger. When this happened, the text exceeded the size of the text field. Because the text field remains at the same size (it does not automatically increase in size along with the text), the text within the field appears cropped. Not only that, but also take note *how* the text resized in the field. It resized to the right. This will happen, by the way, when you add the **rollOver** ActionScript to the submenu options. Unless you tell it otherwise, when the viewer rolls over each sub-menu text option, the text will be styled with the **btnDisable TextFormat** object and will increase in size, thereby cropping the text as you currently see with *our histor*.

To prevent this from happening, you need to add an action to tell each submenu text field to auto-size itself. If you left it at that, the text field would expand to fit the text within it (even when the **btnDisable TextFormat** object changes the text formatting), but it would expand to the right. That wouldn't be a good thing because it would expand right into the **loadedInfo** text field! So, not only do you need to use ActionScript to tell the submenu text fields to auto-size, but you also need to tell them to auto-size to the *left*.

The following table describes all of the available **TextFormat** class properties:

TextFormat Class Properties

Property	Description
TextFormat.align	Allows you to specify the alignment of a paragraph. Your options are `left`, `center`, and `right` for left-aligned, center-aligned, and right-aligned, respectively.
TextFormat.blockIndent	Allows you to set the indentation, in points, of all the text.
TextFormat.bold	Indicates with a Boolean value whether you want the text to be bold (`true`) or not (`false`).
TextFormat.bullet	Indicates with a Boolean value whether the text is a bulleted list (`true`) or not (`false`). If `TextFormat.bullet` is set to `true`, the text is indented, and to the left of the first line in each paragraph a bullet (•) is displayed.
TextFormat.color	Allows you to specify the color of the text. Keep in mind although this color value is specified as a hex value (#000000 for black, #FFFFFF for white, and so forth), it's preceded with the text 0x. So, for example, if you were using the `TextFormat` color property to set the text color to black, you would write `TextFormat.color = 0x000000;`.
TextFormat.font	Allows you to specify the font face of text. For example, if you were using the `TextFormat` font property to set the text's font face, you would write `TextFormat.font = "Bitstream Vera Sans";`. Because the font name is a string, you need to make sure to enclose the font name in quotes.
TextFormat.indent	Allows you to set the indentation, in points, of the first character in each paragraph. Similar to `TextFormat.blockIndent`, but `blockIndent` sets the indentation of *all* of the text.
TextFormat.italic	Indicates with a Boolean value whether you want the text to be italic (`true`) or not (`false`).
TextFormat.kerning	Indicates with a Boolean value whether kerning is enabled (`true`) or disabled (`false`).
TextFormat.leading	Allows you to specify the leading (the space between each line of text), in points.
TextFormat.leftMargin	Allows you to specify the size of the left margin (the distance between the left edge of the text field and the text itself), in points.
TextFormat.letterSpacing	Allows you to specify how much space (in pixels) is between each letter.

continues on next page

TextFormat Class Properties *(continued)*

Property	Description
TextFormat.rightMargin	Allows you to specify the size of the right margin (the distance between the right edge of the text field and the text itself) of text, in points.
TextFormat.size	Allows you to specify, in points, the size of the text.
TextFormat.tabStops	Allows you to specify, in points, custom tab stops. Tab stops are, for example, where the text insertion point jumps to when you're typing inside an Input text field and you press the Tab key.
TextFormat.target	Allows you to specify the browser window that will be targeted when the viewer clicks some text that has been assigned a URL. (See later in this table for the `TextFormat.url` description.) If you're familiar with HTML (**H**yper**T**ext **M**arkup **L**anguage) programming, this is the same as the `target` property you can assign to an anchor tag, `<a href=http://www.myWebSite.com target="_blank">`, for example. If you do not specify a `TextFormat.target` property, the default is `_self`, which means when the viewer clicks a text link with a URL assigned to it, it will open that URL in the same browser window.
TextFormat.underline	Indicates with a Boolean value whether you want the text to be underlined (**true**) or not (**false**).
TextFormat.url	Allows you to specify a URL to which the text will link. Because the URL is a string, you need to make sure you enclose the URL in quotes.

3 | Auto-Sizing a Text Field

In this exercise, you'll create some ActionScript allowing the submenu text fields to auto-size, which will make those text fields automatically expand and contract as the text within those fields is modified by the **TextFormat** class. This will also prevent the submenu text options from getting cropped—as you saw in the previous exercise—when an option becomes disabled.

---

1 Close the Flash Player 8 window within which you were playing the **master.swf** file, and bring Flash 8 to the foreground. Then, make sure **about_us.fla** is the FLA file currently in the foreground.

---

2 Select the first keyframe in the **a** layer, and open the **Actions** panel by pressing **F9** (Windows) or **Opt+F9** (Mac).

```
25  // set the alignment of the sub-menu options to autoSize right
26
27  // create TextFormat Objects that define the states of the sub-menu options
28  var btnDisable:TextFormat = new TextFormat("Bitstream Vera Sans", 12, null, true, true);
29  var btnEnable:TextFormat = new TextFormat("Bitstream Vera Sans", 11, null, false, true);
30
31  // disable the sub-menu option that corresponds to the currently loaded section
32  this.ourHistoryMC.ourHistory.setTextFormat(btnDisable);
```

3 Click to the *left* of the **// create TextFormat Objects that define the states of the sub-menu options** comment line, press **Enter** (Windows) or **Return** (Mac) twice to create several line breaks (which will also move the comment, and everything else underneath it, down two lines), and then move your cursor up two lines. Then, create a new comment by typing the following:

// set the alignment of the sub-menu options to autoSize right

---

4 Click to the right of the comment you created in the previous step, and press **Enter** (Windows) or **Return** (Mac) to create a line break.

---

5 Click the **Insert a target path** button at the top of the **Actions** panel, and in the **Insert Target Path** dialog box expand the **ourHistoryMC** movie clip, and select **ourHistory**. When you click **ourHistory**, you'll see the path inserted at the top of the dialog box. Click **OK**.

This inserts the path to the **ourHistory** text field in the Actions panel.

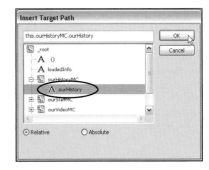

```
25  // set the alignment of the sub-menu options to autoSize right
26  this.ourHistoryMC.ourHistory.autoSize = "right";
```

6 After `this.ourHistoryMC.ourHistory`, type the following:

`.autoSize = "right";`

Don't forget the dot (.) between `ourHistory` and `autoSize`. Essentially, this action says, "Allow the `ourHistory` text field to expand to fit whatever is inside it (`autoSize`) but have it size *from* the right (so content spreads out to the left)."

Now you just need to repeat those steps to set `autoSize = "right"` for the remaining two submenu text fields, `ourStaff` and `ourVideo`.

```
25  // set the alignment of the sub-menu options to autoSize right
26  this.ourHistoryMC.ourHistory.autoSize = "right";
27  this.ourStaffMC.ourStaff.autoSize = "right";
28  this.ourVideoMC.ourVideo.autoSize = "right";
```

7 Repeat Steps 5 and 6 to set `autoSize = "right"` for the `ourStaff` and `ourVideo` text fields. Once finished, your actions should look like the ones in the illustration.

Fantabuloso! You just told the text fields in the submenu options to resize themselves (anchored at the right so they resize to the left) to fit whatever text is in the fields. You can easily test this by publishing a new SWF file from **about_us.fla**, opening **master.swf**, and observing how the **our history** submenu options appear.

8 Save your **about_us.fla** file by choosing **File > Save**. Then, publish an updated SWF file by choosing **File > Publish**.

9 Once you've published a new SWF file from **about_us.fla**, hide or minimize Flash 8, navigate to your **Desktop > la_eyeworks > site** folder, and double-click **master.swf** to open it in Flash Player 8.

You'll now notice the submenu option (**our history**) is no longer cropped! Thanks to the `autoSize = "right"` action, the `ourHistory`, `ourStaff`, and `ourVideo` text fields will now automatically resize to make room for whatever text is displayed within their fields. Not only that, but the fields will be anchored on the *right* and will expand (or contract) out (or in) to the left if need be. Sweet!

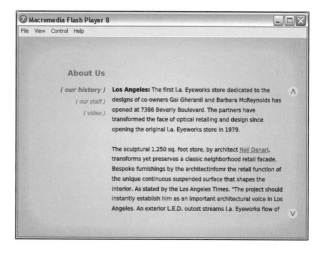

Creating the Rollover/Rollout States of the Submenu Options

In this exercise, you'll create the ActionScript to control the rollover/rollout states of the submenu options. As you saw in Chapter 4, *"Using the LoadVars Class"*—when you added the functionality to the buttons allowing the viewer to scroll the **loadedInfo** text up and down—you will *not* add ActionScript directly to the submenu options. Instead, in the spirit of keeping your scripts centralized, you will add the submenu option ActionScript to a keyframe in the **about_us.fla** Timeline.

---

1 Close the stand-alone Flash Player 8 window you were viewing the **master.swf** file with, and bring Flash 8 to the foreground. Then, make sure **about_us.fla** is the FLA file currently in the foreground.

---

2 Select the first keyframe in the **a** layer, and open the **Actions** panel by pressing **F9** (Windows) or **Opt+F9** (Mac).

```
34  // disable the sub-menu option that corresponds to the currently loaded section
35  this.ourHistoryMC.ourHistory.setTextFormat(btnDisable);
36
37  //------------------<our history option>------------------\\
```

3 Click at the end of the bottom action in the **Actions** panel, **this.ourHistoryMC.ourHistory.setTextFormat(btnDisable);**. Press **Enter** (Windows) or **Return** (Mac) twice to create a couple of line breaks, and then type the opening comment for the actions that will govern the behavior of the **our history** submenu option:

//--------------<our history option>---------------

```
37  //------------------<our history option>------------------\\
38
39  //------------------</our history option>------------------\\
```

4 Select the comment line you just created and copy it. Then, click after the comment line, press **Enter** (Windows) or **Return** (Mac) twice to create a couple of line breaks (to give yourself a little room between the comments to write some actions), and paste the comment line you just copied. Then, close the comment by typing a slash (/) before **our history**.

```
37  //--------------<our history option>---------------\\
38  this.ourHistoryMC.onRollOver = function() {
39  //--------------</our history option>---------------\\
```

5 Click between the two **our history** comment lines you just created, and write the **rollOver** function for the **our history** submenu option by typing the following:

this.ourHistoryMC.onRollOver = function () {

This line essentially says, "When a viewer rolls the mouse over the ourHistoryMC movie clip on *this* Timeline (the same Timeline this script is being authored on), perform this function...."

Now you just need to define what should happen when a viewer rolls the mouse over one of the sub-menu options. Ignore, for now, that you've already told the **our history** submenu option to be disabled when the About Us module first loads (corresponding to the **our history** text also loading automatically when the About Us module first loads). If the viewer clicks another submenu option, the **our history** option will become re-enabled, and the viewer will then be able to interact with it. So, what should happen when a viewer moves the mouse over the **our history** option? All that should happen is **TextFormat btnDisable**—which you created earlier—should be applied to the **ourHistory** text field. That way, when the viewer moves the mouse over the **our history** option, the **our history** text will become bold and one point size bigger.

Note: When you're adding ActionScript to the Timeline (as you are now) to define what happens when certain mouse events (**onRollOver**, **onRollOut**, **onRelease**, and so forth) occur, you can think of the actions you add within a function (such as the one you just created) as being within the Timeline you just targeted if the action is preceded by the keyword **this**. In other words, in the function you just wrote, you targeted the **ourHistoryMC** movie clip. Any actions you place within this function and you precede with **this.** are within the ourHistoryMC movie clip Timeline. If you leave off the **this.** keyword, the action will address the root Timeline. So, when you're writing actions within a function such as the one you just wrote, you need to be aware of how you're writing paths to variables, objects, named symbols, and the like.

```
37  //--------------<our history option>----------------\\
38  this.ourHistoryMC.onRollOver = function() {
39      this.ourHistory.setTextFormat(btnDisable);
40  //--------------</our history option>----------------\\
```

6 Click after the **this.ourHistoryMC.onRollOver = function () {** line you wrote in the previous step, press **Enter** (Windows) or **Return** (Mac) once to create a line break, and then instruct the **ourHistory** text field to set its **TextFormat** (which you created earlier) to **btnDisable** by typing the following:

this.ourHistory.setTextFormat(btnDisable);

You might be wondering why you didn't have to specify the *full path* to the **ourHistory** text field. In other words, why didn't you write **this.ourHistoryMC.ourHistory.setTextFormat(btnDisable);**? Don't you have to tell Flash 8 the **ourHistory** text field is in the **ourHistoryMC** movie clip? No. As mentioned a few paragraphs ago, when adding actions within a mouse event function (like the one you just wrote), the action(s) within the function are *inside* the target of that function. Although this description may have just seemed like gibberish, it essentially breaks down like this: The line where you define the mouse event function (which you wrote in Step 5) targets the **ourHistoryMC** movie clip, which means the actions placed within this function exist *inside* the **ourHistoryMC** movie clip's Timeline. So, if you want to refer to something inside the movie clip Timeline (such as, in this case, the **ourHistory** text field), you can just refer to it directly as you wrote in Step 6.

```
37 //--------------<our history option>---------------\\
38 this.ourHistoryMC.onRollOver = function() {
39     this.ourHistory.setTextFormat(btnDisable);
40 }
41 //--------------</our history option>---------------\\
```

7 Close this function by clicking after the `this.ourHistory.setTextFormat(btnDisable);` line you wrote in the previous step, press **Enter** (Windows) or **Return** (Mac) once to create a line break, and type a closed bracket (**}**).

Fantastic! Similarly to the **onRelease** functions you earlier added to the **loadedInfo** scrolling text buttons, this function governs what happens when a viewer rolls the mouse over the **our history** submenu option. Now, of course, you should specify what happens when a viewer rolls the mouse *off* (**onRollOut**) the **our history** option. Luckily, from an ActionScript point of view, the **onRollOut** script will be similar, which means you can just copy the **onRollOver** script you just wrote, paste the copy below it, and easily change a few simple items.

```
37 //--------------<our history option>---------------\\
38 this.ourHistoryMC.onRollOver = function() {
39     this.ourHistory.setTextFormat(btnDisable);
40 }
41
42 //--------------</our history option>---------------\\
```

8 Click after the closing function bracket you created in the previous step, and press **Enter** (Windows) or **Return** (Mac) to create a line break.

```
37 //--------------<our history option>---------------\\
38 this.ourHistoryMC.onRollOver = function() {
39     this.ourHistory.setTextFormat(btnDisable);
40 }
41 this.ourHistoryMC.onRollOver = function() {
42     this.ourHistory.setTextFormat(btnDisable);
43 }
44 //--------------</our history option>---------------\\
```

9 Select the three lines of ActionScript comprising the `this.ourHistoryMC.onRollOver` function by dragging from the top line to the closing bracket. Once you have those three lines selected, hold down **Ctrl** (Windows) or **Opt** (Mac), and drag the selected script to the line break you created in the previous step. This copies the entire **onRollOver** script, and now you can easily make a few minor adjustments to it to create an **onRollOut** function. Easy!

```
37  //-------------<our history option>----------------\\
38  this.ourHistoryMC.onRollOver = function() {
39      this.ourHistory.setTextFormat(btnDisable);
40  }
41  this.ourHistoryMC.onRollOut = function() {
42      this.ourHistory.setTextFormat(btnEnable);
43  }
44  //-------------</our history option>----------------\\
```

10 In the copied function, change **onRollOver** to **onRollOut**, and change **btnDisable** to **btnEnable** (the name of the **TextFormat** object you created earlier). That's it! The new function basically reads, "When a viewer rolls the mouse off the **our history** option, change the text format of the **ourHistory** text field to the **btnEnable TextFormat** object (Bitstream Vera Sans Oblique font face at 11 points)."

You can't test your work just yet because, by default, the **our history** submenu option is already disabled. But the remaining two submenu options also need to have the same (relatively) **onRollOver** and **onRollOut** functions assigned to them. Just like you did in Steps 9 and 10, you can select *both* the functions you just created, copy them, and modify a few items to make them work correctly for the two remaining submenu options.

```
37  //-------------<our history option>----------------\\
38  this.ourHistoryMC.onRollOver = function() {
39      this.ourHistory.setTextFormat(btnDisable);
40  }
41  this.ourHistoryMC.onRollOut = function() {
42      this.ourHistory.setTextFormat(btnEnable);
43  }
44  //-------------</our history option>----------------\\
45
46
```

11 Click after the closing **</our history option>** comment line, and press **Enter** (Windows) or **Return** (Mac) twice to create two line breaks.

```
37  //-------------<our history option>----------------\\
38  this.ourHistoryMC.onRollOver = function() {
39      this.ourHistory.setTextFormat(btnDisable);
40  }
41  this.ourHistoryMC.onRollOut = function() {
42      this.ourHistory.setTextFormat(btnEnable);
43  }
44  //-------------</our history option>----------------\\
45
46
```

12 Select both **onRollOver** and **onRollOut** functions you just created for the **our history** option—making sure to also select the comments—by dragging over the entire script.

```
37  //-------------<our history option>-------------\\
38  this.ourHistoryMC.onRollOver = function() {
39      this.ourHistory.setTextFormat(btnDisable);
40  }
41  this.ourHistoryMC.onRollOut = function() {
42      this.ourHistory.setTextFormat(btnEnable);
43  }
44  //-------------</our history option>-------------\\
45
46  //-------------<our history option>-------------\\
47  this.ourHistoryMC.onRollOver = function() {
48      this.ourHistory.setTextFormat(btnDisable);
49  }
50  this.ourHistoryMC.onRollOut = function() {
51      this.ourHistory.setTextFormat(btnEnable);
52  }
53  //-------------</our history option>-------------\\
```

13 Hold down **Ctrl** (Windows) or **Opt** (Mac), and drag the selected script to the second line break you created in Step 11. This copies the entire block of actions down to where your line break is.

Because of the way the instance names of the submenu option movie clips and text fields are structured, all you essentially have to do to make this script work for the **our staff** option is replace each occurrence of the word *History* with the word *Staff*.

```
46  //-------------<our staff option>-------------\\
47  this.ourStaffMC.onRollOver = function() {
48      this.ourStaff.setTextFormat(btnDisable);
49  }
50  this.ourStaffMC.onRollOut = function() {
51      this.ourStaff.setTextFormat(btnEnable);
52  }
53  //-------------</our staff option>-------------\\
```

14 In the copied script, replace each occurrence of the word *History* with the word *Staff*. So, for example, instead of `this.ourHistoryMC.onRollOver = function () {`, the version of this action targeting `ourStaffMC` instead reads `this.ourStaffMC.onRollOver = function () {`. Make sure to also replace the word *History* with *Staff* in the duplicated comments.

You could have, of course, created the `onRollOver` and `onRollOut` scripts from scratch if you so chose. But it's much simpler to copy the functions you already created for the **our history** option and change a few items so they apply to the **our staff** option. Because the scripts, for the most part, are nearly identical, it's much easier to copy and change them than it is to write them from scratch.

Now you can test the **our staff** submenu option script you just created.

15 Save your **about_us.fla** file by choosing **File > Save**. Then, publish an updated SWF file by choosing **File > Publish**.

---

16 Minimize (Windows) or hide (Mac) Flash 8, navigate to your **Desktop > la_eyeworks > site** folder, and double-click **master.swf** to open it in Flash Player 8.

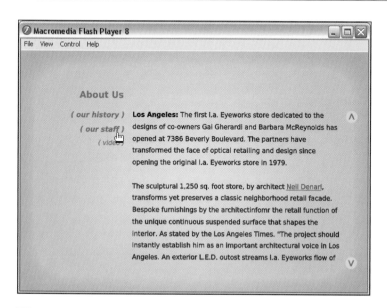

17 When the stand-alone Flash Player 8 window opens and the **About Us** module appears, move your mouse over and off the **our staff** option. The text changes as you move your mouse over and off the sub-menu option. Cool! You just created a **rollOver/rollOut** effect, *purely* with ActionScript. Congratulations!

---

18 Keep the stand-alone Flash Player 8 window open because you will need it in the next exercise.

EXERCISE

5 | Disabling Interactivity for Usability

You just saw how to use the **TextFormat** class to create an interactive submenu, but you need to finish what you started by "fixing" how the submenu options respond to user interaction. As you'll see in the first few steps in this exercise, sometimes you'll want to disable the interactivity for a particular submenu option. In this exercise, you'll learn how to create this functionality.

1 Now, before you start feeling all warm and fuzzy about what you accomplished in the previous exercise, roll your mouse over and then off the **our history** option.

Notice how when you roll your mouse over the **our history** option, you see the Hand icon appear, which represents interactivity. It means, in effect, "Hey, if you click me, something's going to happen." Because the **our history** section is already loaded, and the **our history** option is therefore already disabled, you don't want to see the Hand icon when a viewer rolls the mouse over the **our history**

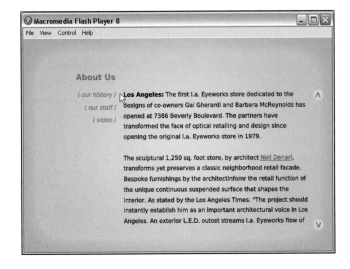

option. In fact, you don't want a viewer to see the Hand icon when moving the mouse over an option whose section is already loaded. In other words, if the **our staff** section is loaded, and thereby the **our staff** submenu option is disabled, you don't want the viewer to see the Hand icon. Why not? Well, when a section is already loaded, clicking that section's option should not do anything. What could it do? The viewer is already viewing the relevant content. Therefore, you will (later) use ActionScript to disable the interactivity of the submenu option corresponding to the currently loaded section, which means when the **our staff** section is loaded, moving your mouse over the **our staff** submenu option will not display the Hand icon. Also notice when you roll your mouse off the **our history** submenu option, the **our history** text reverts to its enabled state, which is bad, because now the submenu has no visual representation of which subsection the visitor is currently viewing. This goes back to the idea of when the viewer should see the Hand icon and when they shouldn't, and luckily this is easy to correct.

2 Close the stand-alone Flash Player 8 window, and bring Flash 8 to the foreground. Then, make sure **about_us.fla** is the FLA file currently in the foreground.

3 Select the first keyframe in the **a** layer, and open the **Actions** panel by pressing **F9** (Windows) or **Opt+F9** (Mac).

First, you'll write an action to disable the interactivity of the **our history** submenu option when the About Us module first loads.

```
34  // disable the sub-menu option that corresponds to the currently loaded section
35  this.ourHistoryMC.ourHistory.setTextFormat(btnDisable);
36  this.ourHistoryMC.enabled = false;
```

4 Click after the `this.ourHistoryMC.ourHistory.setTextFormat(btnDisable);` line, press **Enter** (Windows) or **Return** (Mac) once to create a line break, and then disable the interactivity of the **ourHistoryMC** movie clip by typing the following:

`this.ourHistoryMC.enabled = false;`

This line, in effect, reads, "Set the **enabled** property of the **ourHistoryMC** movie clip to **false**." When you set the **enabled** property of a movie clip or button symbol to **false**, you disable any interactivity the symbol has. It's almost like temporarily deleting the actions assigned to a symbol.

Because it's good practice to test work after any major changes, you should now test this addition to make sure it works.

5 Save your file by choosing **File > Save**. Then, publish an updated SWF file by choosing **File > Publish**.

6 Minimize (Windows) or hide (Mac) Flash 8, navigate to your **Desktop > la_eyeworks > site** folder, and double-click the **master.swf** file to open it in the stand-alone Flash Player 8.

7 When the stand-alone Flash Player 8 window opens and the **About Us** module loads, move your mouse over the **our history** submenu option. Notice now how you don't see the Hand icon when your mouse interacts with the **our history** option! The **.enabled** property essentially disables the interactivity of a symbol. In fact, whenever the viewer clicks *any* of the other submenu options, not only will you want to set the **TextFormat** style of that text option to **btnDisable**, but you'll also want to disable the interactivity of that option with the **.enabled** property. In a later exercise in this chapter, you'll create this functionality.

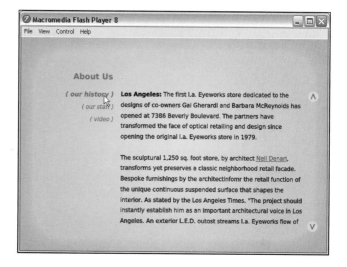

6 | Copying and Pasting Functionality

Before continuing to shape the interactivity of the submenu, you should first finish defining the **onRollOver/ onRollOut** functionality of the options in the submenu by adding ActionScript to the **video** option.

---

1 Close the stand-alone Flash Player 8 window you had open in the previous exercise, and bring Flash 8 to the foreground. Then, make sure **about_us.fla** is the FLA file currently in the foreground.

---

2 Click the first keyframe in the **a** layer, and open the **Actions** panel by pressing **F9** (Windows) or **Opt+F9** (Mac).

```
47  //-------------<our staff option>--------------\\
48  this.ourStaffMC.onRollOver = function() {
49      this.ourStaff.setTextFormat(btnDisable);
50  }
51  this.ourStaffMC.onRollOut = function() {
52      this.ourStaff.setTextFormat(btnEnable);
53  }
54  //-------------</our staff option>--------------\\
55
56
```

3 Click after the closing the **</our staff option>** comment line, and press **Enter** (Windows) or **Return** (Mac) twice to create a couple of line breaks.

```
47  //-------------<our staff option>--------------\\
48  this.ourStaffMC.onRollOver = function() {
49      this.ourStaff.setTextFormat(btnDisable);
50  }
51  this.ourStaffMC.onRollOut = function() {
52      this.ourStaff.setTextFormat(btnEnable);
53  }
54  //-------------</our staff option>--------------\\
55
56  //-------------<our staff option>--------------\\
57  this.ourStaffMC.onRollOver = function() {
58      this.ourStaff.setTextFormat(btnDisable);
59  }
60  this.ourStaffMC.onRollOut = function() {
61      this.ourStaff.setTextFormat(btnEnable);
62  }
63  //-------------</our staff option>--------------\\
```

4 Select the entire **our staff** option script (including the opening and closing comment lines) by dragging around it. Then, while holding down **Ctrl** (Windows) or **Opt** (Mac), drag the selected script to the second new line you created in Step 3. This copies the entire **our staff** option script below the original.

```
56  //--------------<our video option>----------------\\
57  this.ourVideoMC.onRollOver = function() {
58      this.ourVideo.setTextFormat(btnDisable);
59  }
60  this.ourVideoMC.onRollOut = function() {
61      this.ourVideo.setTextFormat(btnEnable);
62  }
63  //--------------</our video option>----------------\\
```

5 In the script you just copied, change every occurrence of the word *Staff* to *Video*. For example, change the line `this.ourStaffMC.onRollOver = function () {` to `this.ourVideoMC.onRollOver = function () {`.

There you have it! You just completed the `onRollOver` and `onRollOut` interactivity for the three submenu options. Congratulations! Before continuing, you should probably save, publish, and check your work once more to make sure everything works.

---

6 Save your **about_us.fla** file by choosing **File > Save**. Then, publish an updated SWF file by choosing **File > Publish**.

---

7 Minimize (Windows) or hide (Mac) Flash 8, navigate to your **Desktop > la_eyeworks > site** folder, and double-click the **master.swf** file to preview your work in the stand-alone Flash Player 8.

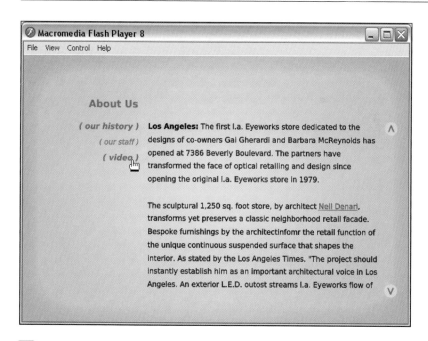

8 When the stand-alone Flash Player 8 window opens and displays the **About Us** module, make sure all the submenu options (well, except **our history**, of course) work properly when you roll your mouse over and off each text option. Neat!

---

7 | Enabling Interactivity for Usability

You've scripted what the submenu options do when a viewer rolls over/off each option, so you now need to script what should happen when a viewer *clicks* each option. In this exercise, you'll write ActionScript to specify what happens when a viewer clicks the **our history** or **our staff** options. You'll script the **video** option in Chapter 11, *"Building a Video Player."*

---

1 Close the Flash Player 8 window, and bring Flash 8 to the foreground. Then, make sure **about_us.fla** is the FLA file currently in the foreground.

---

2 Select the first keyframe in the **a** layer, and open the **Actions** panel by pressing **F9** (Windows) or **Opt+F9** (Mac).

Because the **our history** option is disabled by default, you'll first create a script to define what happens when the viewer clicks the **our staff** option.

```
47  //--------------<our staff option>---------------\\
48  this.ourStaffMC.onRollOver = function() {
49      this.ourStaff.setTextFormat(btnDisable);
50  }
51  this.ourStaffMC.onRollOut = function() {
52      this.ourStaff.setTextFormat(btnEnable);
53  }
54  this.ourStaffMC.onRelease = function() {
55  //--------------</our staff option>---------------\\
```

> Click after this bracket, and then press Enter (Windows) or Return (Mac) to create a line break to type the next action.

3 Within the **our staff** script, click after the closing **onRollOut** function bracket (**}**), press **Enter** (Windows) or **Return** (Mac) to create a line break, and then create the **onRelease** function by typing the following:

this.ourStaffMC.onRelease = function () {

Now, you must figure out exactly what should happen when a viewer clicks the **our staff** option. Later in this chapter, you'll define what content should load and how the other submenu options should behave when that happens, but for now, you need to decide what the **our staff** option will do when the viewer clicks it. In essence, when the viewer clicks the **our staff** option, it will become what the **our history** option is now. It will have **btnDisable TextFormat** applied to it (Bitstream Vera Sans Bold Oblique at one point size bigger, which is 12 points), *and* its interactivity will be disabled by setting its **enabled** property to **false**.

```
47  //-------------<our staff option>---------------\\
48  this.ourStaffMC.onRollOver = function() {
49      this.ourStaff.setTextFormat(btnDisable);
50  }
51  this.ourStaffMC.onRollOut = function() {
52      this.ourStaff.setTextFormat(btnEnable);
53  }
54  this.ourStaffMC.onRelease = function() {
55      this.ourStaff.setTextFormat(btnDisable);
56      this.enabled = false;
57  }
58  //-------------</our staff option>---------------\\
```

4 Click after the `this.ourStaffMC.onRelease = function () {` line, press **Enter** (Windows) or **Return** (Mac) once to create a line break, and type the following:

```
this.ourStaff.setTextFormat(btnDisable);
this.enabled = false;
}
```

You've seen these actions before, of course. But together they say, "First, set the **TextFormat** style of the **ourStaff** text field to be **btnDisable**. Then, disable the interactivity of the **ourStaffMC** movie clip by setting its **enabled** property to **false**."

---

5 Save your file by choosing **File > Save**. Then, publish an updated SWF by choosing **File > Publish**.

---

6 Minimize (Windows) or hide (Mac) Flash 8, navigate to your **Desktop > la_eyeworks > site** folder, and double-click the **master.swf** file to open it in the stand-alone Flash Player 8.

---

7 When the stand-alone Flash Player 8 window opens and the **About Us** module loads, click the **our staff** submenu option.

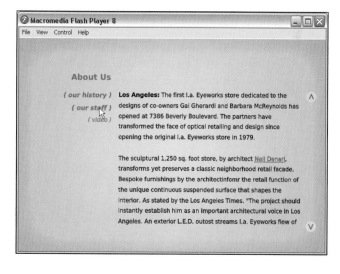

When you do that, you'll notice the **our staff** text becomes one point size bigger, the font face becomes bold, and the Hand icon is replaced with the standard cursor arrow. Great! This is exactly what you want to happen. The problem now (hee hee) is both the **our history** and **our staff** options are disabled. Instead, when the viewer clicks the **our staff** option, you want any other option currently disabled to become re-enabled. Unfortunately, from an ActionScript point of view, it's not easy to tell Flash 8 to disable all the other options *except* the one you just clicked. So, you'll take advantage of the mere milliseconds it takes Flash 8 to execute the actions you tell it to execute. You'll create a function whose sole job is to re-enable *all* the submenu options. Then, you will trigger that function each time the viewer clicks an option. You will instruct Flash 8, immediately after that function is triggered, to *then* disable the option the viewer just clicked. If—after that brief description—you're still lost, continue with the following steps as you learn to build the re-enable function and complete the scripting for the submenu. I'm sure after you complete the next steps, it'll become much clearer to you.

First, you need to create a function to enable all the submenu options. These are all actions you've seen before; you will just place them within a function so they can be easily executed when needed.

---

8 Close the stand-alone Flash Player 8, and bring Flash 8 to the foreground. Then, make sure **about_us.fla** is the FLA file currently in the foreground.

---

9 Select the first keyframe in the **a** layer, and open the **Actions** panel by pressing **F9** (Windows) or **Opt+F9** (Mac).

```
34  // disable the sub-menu option that corresponds to the currently loaded section
35  this.ourHistoryMC.ourHistory.setTextFormat(btnDisable);
36  this.ourHistoryMC.enabled = false;
37
38  |
39
40  //-----------------<our history option>-------------------\\
41  this.ourHistoryMC.onRollOver = function() {
42      this.ourHistory.setTextFormat(btnDisable);
43  }
44  this.ourHistoryMC.onRollOut = function() {
45      this.ourHistory.setTextFormat(btnEnable);
46  }
47  //-----------------</our history option>-------------------\\
```

10 Click to the *left* of the `<our history option>` comment line, press **Enter** (Windows) or **Return** (Mac) twice to create two line breaks, and then press the **up arrow** key twice to move the insertion point up two lines.

This gives you some space in the Actions panel to write the option's re-enable function.

```
38  // re-enable the sub-menu options
39  function reEnableOptions() {
40      this.ourHistoryMC.enabled = true;
41      this.ourHistoryMC.ourHistory.setTextFormat(btnEnable);
42      this.ourStaffMC.enabled = true;
43      this.ourStaffMC.ourStaff.setTextFormat(btnEnable);
44      this.ourVideoMC.enabled = true;
45      this.ourVideoMC.ourVideo.setTextFormat(btnEnable);
46  }
```

11 Create the function that, when called, will enable all the options in the submenu by typing the following:

```
// re-enable the sub-menu options
function reEnableOptions () {
  this.ourHistoryMC.enabled = true;
  this.ourHistoryMC.ourHistory.setTextFormat(btnEnable);
  this.ourStaffMC.enabled = true;
  this.ourStaffMC.ourStaff.setTextFormat(btnEnable);
  this.ourVideoMC.enabled = true;
  this.ourVideoMC.ourVideo.setTextFormat(btnEnable);
}
```

These are all actions you have seen before; this time they are just all nested within a function called **reEnableOptions**. As you can see by looking at the list of actions within the **reEnableOptions** function, what they do—together—is set the **enabled** property of each submenu option to **true** and set the text formatting of each submenu option text field to the **TextFormat** object, **btnEnable**. Therefore, when this function is triggered, each option in the submenu will be available to interact with the viewer. *After* this function is performed, another action (which you will write next) then *disables* whichever option the viewer clicked.

As you saw in Step 7, when the viewer clicked the **our staff** submenu option, the **our staff** option became disabled—as it should—but the **our history** option did not become re-enabled. You will use the **reEnableOptions** function, which you just created, to do this. When the viewer clicks a submenu option, all the submenu options will become re-enabled, and then the option the viewer clicked will become disabled.

```
57  //--------------<our staff option>----------------\\
58  this.ourStaffMC.onRollOver = function() {
59      this.ourStaff.setTextFormat(btnDisable);
60  }
61  this.ourStaffMC.onRollOut = function() {
62      this.ourStaff.setTextFormat(btnEnable);
63  }
64  this.ourStaffMC.onRelease = function() {
65      reEnableOptions();
66      this.ourStaff.setTextFormat(btnDisable);
67      this.enabled = false;
68  }
69  //--------------</our staff option>----------------\\
```

12 Within the **our staff** option script, click after the **this.ourStaffMC.onRelease = function () {** line, press **Enter** (Windows) or **Return** (Mac) to create a line break, and then trigger the **reEnableOptions** function by typing the following:

reEnableOptions();

That was relatively painless, wasn't it?

In this case, the ordering of the actions is important. Within the **onRelease** function, first comes the **reEnableOptions** function call. This action executes, and all the submenu options instantly become "active" again. *Then* come the next two lines where the option the viewer clicked, **our staff**, becomes disabled. It gets the **btnDisable TextFormat** applied to it, and its **enabled** property is set to false. *Voila!* Before writing similar **onRelease** actions for the remaining two submenu options, you should test the modifications you made to the **ourStaff** option first.

13 Save your file by choosing **File > Save**. Then, publish an updated SWF file by choosing **File > Publish**.

14 Minimize (Windows) or hide (Mac) Flash 8, navigate to your **Desktop > la_eyeworks > site** folder, and double-click the **master.swf** file.

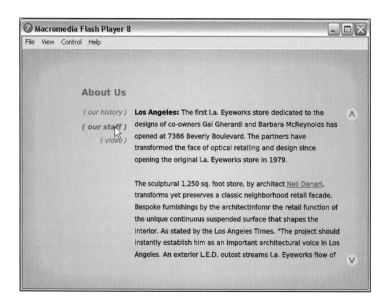

15 When the stand-alone Flash Player 8 window opens and displays the **About Us** module, click the **our staff** submenu option. When you do, **our staff** becomes disabled. (You can no longer interact with it, and it becomes bold and one point size larger.) Also, the **our history** option that *was* disabled is now enabled, and you can interact with it. Huzzah!

In the next exercise, you will duplicate the same effect for the **our history** and **video** subsection options.

8 | Finishing the Submenu

In this exercise, you'll duplicate the re-enable/disable functionality you added to the **our staff** submenu option in the previous exercise to create the same interactivity effect for the **our history** and **video** options.

---

1 Close the stand-alone Flash Player 8 you had open from the previous exercise, and bring Flash 8 to the foreground. Then, make sure **about_us.fla** is the FLA file currently in the foreground.

---

2 Select the first keyframe in the **a** layer, and open the **Actions** panel by pressing **F9** (Windows) or **Opt+F9** (Mac).

Since the **onRelease** script you completed writing for the **our staff** option in the previous exercise is nearly identical to the one required for the other two submenu options, why not simply copy the **onRelease** script on the **our staff** option and paste it for use with the remaining two options?

---

3 Select the **our staff onRelease** script, which you completed in the previous exercise, by dragging around it. Then, copy the script. You can easily copy the script by pressing the keyboard shortcut (**Ctrl+C** [Windows] or **Cmd+C** [Mac]), or you can

right-click (Windows) or **Ctrl+click** (Mac) any portion of the selected script and choose **Copy** from the resulting contextual menu (as shown in the illustration).

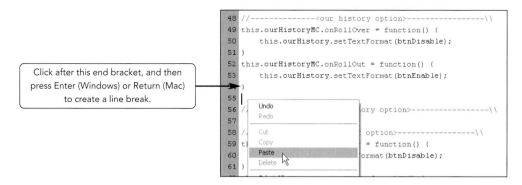

Click after this end bracket, and then press Enter (Windows) or Return (Mac) to create a line break.

4 Then, within the **our history** option actions, click after the close function bracket (**}**) after the **onRollOut** function, and press **Enter** (Windows) or **Return** (Mac) to create a line break. **Right-click** (Windows) or **Ctrl+click** (Mac) the new line break, and choose **Paste** from the resulting contextual menu. This pastes the **onRelease** script you copied from the **our staff option**, and you can now modify it to work correctly for the **our history** option.

```
48  //-------------<our history option>---------------\\
49  this.ourHistoryMC.onRollOver = function() {
50      this.ourHistory.setTextFormat(btnDisable);
51  }
52  this.ourHistoryMC.onRollOut = function() {
53      this.ourHistory.setTextFormat(btnEnable);
54  }
55  this.ourHistoryMC.onRelease = function() {
56      reEnableOptions();
57      this.ourHistory.setTextFormat(btnDisable);
58      this.enabled = false;
59  }
60  //-------------</our history option>---------------\\
```

5 Within the copied **onRelease** script, change the two occurrences of the word *Staff* to *History*.

As simple as that, this **onRelease** script will now apply to the **our history** option! Now, you need to perform these same steps to apply this **onRelease** script to the **video** option as well.

```
76  //-------------<our video option>---------------\\
77  this.ourVideoMC.onRollOver = function() {
78      this.ourVideo.setTextFormat(btnDisable);
79  }
80  this.ourVideoMC.onRollOut = function() {
81      this.ourVideo.setTextFormat(btnEnable);
82  }
83  this.ourVideoMC.onRelease = function() {
84      reEnableOptions();
85      this.ourVideo.setTextFormat(btnDisable);
86      this.enabled = false;
87  }
88  //-------------</our video option>---------------\\
```

6 Within the **our video** option script, click after the end function bracket (**}**) for the **onRollOut** function, and press **Enter** (Windows) or **Return** (Mac) once to create a line break. **Right-click** (Windows) or **Ctrl+click** (Mac) the new line break, and choose **Paste** from the resulting contextual menu. This pastes the **our staff onRelease** script, which you still have in your computer's clipboard, where you can then adjust it to work properly with the **our video** option. To make the **onRelease** script work correctly, all you have to do is replace the two occurrences of the word *Staff* with the word *Video*.

Lastly, when the viewer clicks the **our history** submenu option, not only do you want the other options to be re-enabled, and not only do you want the **our history** submenu option to become disabled, but you also want the **our history** section content to load. In the next exercise, you will create another About Us module subsection: **our staff**. By the end of the next exercise, when you click the **our staff** option, the **our staff** content will load. You need to give the viewer the ability to re-view the **our history** content, if they so choose, by adding an action to load the **our history** content when the viewer clicks the **our history** option. Nicely enough, you've already written that action. Remember how, in the previous chapter, you wrote the action to load the **our history** text when the About Us module first loads? Well, you want the same action to be performed when the viewer clicks the **our history** submenu option.

```
1  //----------------<load CSS>-------------------\\
2  var cssStyles:TextField.StyleSheet = new TextField.StyleSheet();
3  cssStyles.load("styles/styles.css");
4  cssStyles.onLoad = function (success) {
5      if (success) {
6          loadedInfo.styleSheet = cssStyles;
7          _level0.myLV.load("vars/ourHistory.txt");
8      } else {
9          loadedInfo.text = "There has been an er
   Please contact the Webmaster and report your er
10     }
11 }
```

                                        | Undo |
Redo
Cut
Copy
Paste
Delete

7 Scroll to the top of the **Actions** window, select the action
`_level0.myLV.load("vars/ourHistory.txt");`, and copy it.

```
48 //--------------<our history option>----------------\\
49 this.ourHistoryMC.onRollOver = function() {
50     this.ourHistory.setTextFormat(btnDisable);
51 }
52 this.ourHistoryMC.onRollOut = function() {
53     this.ourHistory.setTextFormat(btnEnable);
54 }
55 this.ourHistoryMC.onRelease = function() {
56     reEnableOptions();
57     this.ourHistory.setTextFormat(btnDisable);
58     this.enabled = false;
59     _level0.myLV.load("vars/ourHistory.txt");
60 }
61 //--------------</our history option>---------------\\
```

8 Scroll down the **Actions** panel until you reach the **our history** option script. Then, within the
onRelease function, click after the `this.enabled = false;` line, press **Enter** (Windows) or **Return** (Mac) to
create a line break, and paste the copied action into the new line.

Now, when the viewer clicks the **our history** submenu option, the **our history** text will load, exactly like it
does when the About Us module first loads.

Before you begin the celebratory dancing and drinking, you should save, publish, and test your work to
make sure everything works as intended.

9 Save your file by choosing **File > Save**. Then, publish an updated SWF file by choosing **File > Publish**.

10 Minimize (Windows) or hide (Mac) Flash 8, navigate to your **Desktop > la_eyeworks > site** folder,
and double-click the **master.swf** file to open it in the stand-alone Flash Player 8.

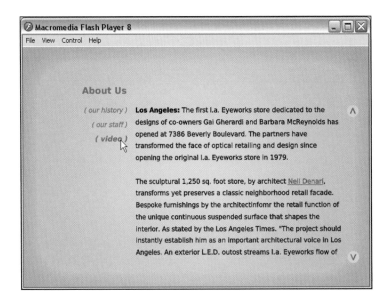

11 Whee! This is almost fun (oh, what simple pleasures we Flash developers have)! Click each submenu option. As you click an option, whichever option was previously disabled should become re-enabled. Click each submenu option to make sure this occurs.

---

12 When you're finished marveling at your genius creation, close the stand-alone Flash Player 8 window.

There you have it! Quite a few lines of code later, you have a fully interactive submenu, all created with ActionScript! Even though for some of you this exercise took all the effort you could muster, keep in mind the benefits are well worth the effort you put into creating this menu and what you learned by doing it. If you had built this submenu using beginner-level methods, you would probably have button symbols nested within movie clip symbols, and you would then instruct the playhead within the movie clip to jump around, thereby displaying the various buttons enabled and disabled. Can you imagine, however, making any significant changes to the submenu if you constructed it in this manner? It would be time-consuming to edit or work with it in any meaningful way. Conversely, with the submenu you just constructed, edits and modifications are a breeze! If you want to change the text styling of the `rollOver` states, for example, all you have to do is modify the `btnDisable TextFormat` action, and you're done. *One* action defines how every submenu button will look when a viewer moves the mouse over it. So, although building a submenu in this manner certainly has a higher learning curve than the basic method, it is well worth it in the end.

In the next and final exercise, you will make a minor edit to the **our staff** option script to allow visitors to see the **our staff** information when they click the **our staff** submenu option. Imagine that. This submenu is actually *useful* too. What a novel idea!

---

9 | Creating the "our staff" Subsection

In this exercise, you'll create the **our staff** subsection. Similar to the **our history** subsection, the **our staff** content is essentially text located in an external text file. This content will load and display when the viewer clicks the **our staff** submenu option you created earlier in this chapter. As you have seen in previous exercises in this book, the **our staff** text is styled using HTML tags and CSS (**C**ascading **S**tyle **S**heets) styles (which you load using a script you created in a previous exercise) to make it more visually appealing. (Because you already learned about them, the HTML and CSS tags have already been written into the **our staff** text file for you.) You will also learn how to integrate inline SWF files into the **our staff** text the text actually wraps around, much like an embedded image in an HTML-based Web page!

1 Minimize (Windows) or hide (Mac) Flash 8 (if you have it in the foreground), navigate to your **Desktop > la_eyeworks > site > vars** folder, and open the file **ourStaff.txt** in Notepad (Windows), TextEdit (Mac), or BBEdit (Mac).

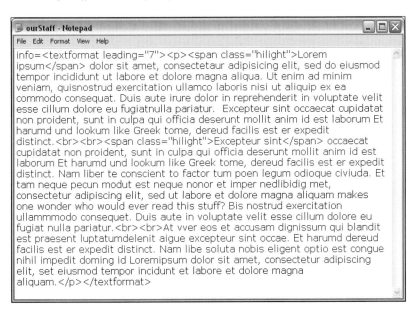

As you can see, this **our staff** section text uses *greeking* (gibberish text often used as placeholder text in design mock-ups) with identical HTML tags as the ones you learned how to utilize in the **ourHistory.txt** file in a previous exercise. Also notice the variable in this text file, **info**, has the same name as the variable in the **ourHistory.txt** file. When using the **LoadVars** script—which you created in Chapter 4, *"Using the LoadVars Class"*—to load text from an external text file, you *must* use the variable **info** within the text file. This is because the **LoadVars** script is looking for—specifically—the variable **info** and the text (the variable's value) within it to load.

First, you'll add an action to load the variables from this **ourStaff.txt** file into the **loadedInfo** text field when the viewer clicks the **our staff** submenu button in the About Us module.

2 Bring Flash 8 to the foreground. Then, make sure **about_us.fla** is the FLA file currently in the foreground.

---

3 Select the first keyframe in the **a** layer, and open the **Actions** panel by pressing **F9** (Windows) or **Opt+F9** (Mac).

Because of the extra effort you put into crafting the **LoadVars** script, loading the variables from an external text file (such as the **ourStaff.txt** file) requires only one action.

```
63  //-------------<our staff option>---------------\\
64  this.ourStaffMC.onRollOver = function() {
65      this.ourStaff.setTextFormat(btnDisable);
66  }
67  this.ourStaffMC.onRollOut = function() {
68      this.ourStaff.setTextFormat(btnEnable);
69  }
70  this.ourStaffMC.onRelease = function() {
71      reEnableOptions();
72      this.ourStaff.setTextFormat(btnDisable);
73      this.enabled = false;
74      _level0.myLV.load("vars/ourStaff.txt");
75  }
76  //-------------</our staff option>---------------\\
```

4 Locate the **our staff option** script, then under the **onRelease** function click after the **this.enabled = false;** line, and write the action (which is nearly identical to the action you wrote earlier in this chapter to load the variables from the **ourHistory.txt** file) to instruct the **LoadVars** object within the **master.swf** Timeline to load the variables from the **ourStaff.txt** file by typing the following:

_level0.myLV.load("vars/ourStaff.txt");

Simply, this action says, "Tell the **LoadVars** object called **myLV**—which is located in the **master.swf** file (**_level0**)—to load the variables from the **ourStaff.txt** file within the **vars** folder." The **LoadVars** script then takes over, loads the variables from the **ourStaff.txt** file, and inserts them into the text field called **loadedInfo** in **_level5** (the level into which the **about_us.swf** file is loaded).

Before continuing, you should test what you've done so far to make sure everything is working.

---

5 Save your file by choosing **File > Save**. Then, publish an updated SWF file by choosing **File > Publish**.

---

6 Minimize (Windows) or hide (Mac) Flash 8, navigate to your **Desktop > la_eyeworks > site** folder, and double-click the **master.swf** file to open it in the stand-alone Flash Player 8.

---

7 When the Flash Player 8 window opens, and the **About Us** module loads, you'll see the **our history** information load automatically. Then, click the **our staff** submenu option. You'll notice the **our history** information be replaced with the styled greeking text you saw in the **ourStaff.txt** file at the beginning of this exercise. Coolio! If you click the **our history** submenu option, you'll notice the **our staff** text will be replaced with the **our history** text. Then, if you click the **our staff** option, you'll notice the **our history** text be replaced with the **our staff** text, Then, if you click…well…you get the idea.

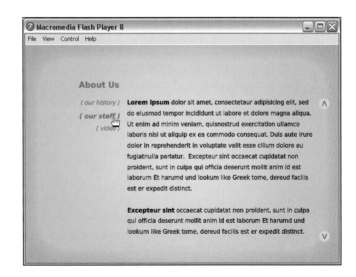

---

8 You've gotten the **our staff** text to load correctly, so you'll now learn how to embed SWF files inline in that text. Close the stand-alone Flash Player 8, and then navigate to your **Desktop > la_eyeworks > site > swfs** folder.

9 In the **swfs** folder, you'll notice a SWF file titled **staff-01.swf**. Double-click this SWF file to open it in the stand-alone Flash Player 8. Note the location of this file. Just like when you're using the **LoadVars** class to load the variables from an external TXT file, you need to know the location of this SWF file so you can write the correct path to it in the **ourStaff.txt** file.

As you'll see when the SWF file opens, it's just a series of three animated images fading into each other. Later, if you're interested in seeing the source FLA file for this SWF file, navigate to your **Desktop > la_eyeworks > site** folder, and double-click the **staff-01.fla** file.

---

10 Close the stand-alone Flash Player 8.

In the **swfs** folder, you'll also notice another SWF, in particular, titled **staff-02.swf**. **staff-01.swf** and **staff-02.swf** are the two SWF files you will place—inline—in the **ourStaff.txt** file.

---

11 Bring the **ourStaff.txt** file to the foreground. If you accidentally closed it, you can open it again by navigating to your **Desktop > la_eyeworks > site > vars** folder and opening the **ourStaff.txt** file in your text editor.

---

12 Within the **ourStaff.txt** file, add the HTML information to place the **staff-01.swf** file inline before the opening text *Lorem ipsum* by clicking *before* the HTML **<p>** tag toward the beginning of the text file and typing the following:

```
<img src="swfs/staff-01.swf" width="75" height="75" align="left" hspace="10" vspace="5">
```

Quite a lot is going on in the HTML tag, as you can see. The HTML tag itself, stripped of all its attributes, is **<img>** (short for "image," of course). **src**, short for "source," is the path to, and the name of, the SWF (or JPEG, PNG, or GIF) file to place. When writing a path to the file to place, one interesting tidbit to keep in mind is the path you want to write should *not* be written relative to the text file within which it will be placed. Instead, the path should be written relative to the SWF file into which this text will get loaded. In other words, when writing a path to a SWF/JPEG/PNG/GIF file within a text file getting loaded into another SWF file (as the **ourStaff.txt** file is doing), write it relative to where the SWF file is located (the SWF file the text gets loaded into, *not* the SWF added—inline—to the text file). This is somewhat counterintuitive, especially if you've built any HTML-based Web pages. But once you remember the text file gets loaded into a SWF file, and the path to the inline images must be written relative to that SWF file, it makes a little more sense. The other HTML attributes are fairly self-explanatory: **width** and **height** are the width and height of the SWF file in pixels. **align** is how the SWF/JPEG/PNG/GIF file will be aligned within the text field. For `align`, your options are `left` and `right`. If you don't specify an `align` attribute, the default is `left`. `hspace` and `vspace` are how large of horizontal and vertical (respectively) pixel buffers you want between the SWF/JPEG/PNG/GIF file and the text surrounding it. The HTML `<img>` tag is one of those tags you don't have to close (`</img>`).

Before writing the other **staff-02.swf** file into the **ourStaff.txt** file, you should test your changes thus far to make sure everything works correctly. Because you're making all these changes to the **ourStaff.txt** file, you don't even need to return to Flash 8 to view the changes.

---

13 Save your **ourStaff.txt** file by choosing **File > Save**. Then, minimize (Windows) or hide (Mac) your text-editing program, navigate to your **Desktop > la_eyeworks > site** folder, and double-click the **master.swf** file to view it in the stand-alone Flash Player 8.

14 When the stand-alone Flash Player 8 window opens, and the **About Us** module loads, click the **our staff** submenu option to load the **ourStaff.txt** file. When you do, you'll see the **staff-01.swf** file, inline (and animating) within the loaded text. Holy cripes, Batman! As simple as it may seem, this feature is really awesome, and it gives the designer many more design possibilities than previously available. Hurray!

Now you just need to add the HTML tag to insert the **staff-02.swf** file into the text.

---

15 Close the stand-alone Flash Player 8 window, and bring the **ourStaff.txt** file to the foreground.

Because both the **staff-01** and **staff-02** SWF files are the same size, it's easier to copy the `<img>` tag (and its attributes) you wrote in Step 12 and paste it where you need it, rather than type the long tag from scratch.

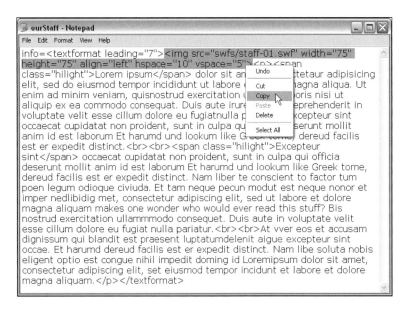

16 Select the **`<img src="swfs/staff-01.swf" width="75" height="75" align="left" hspace="10" vspace="5">`** line, and copy it.

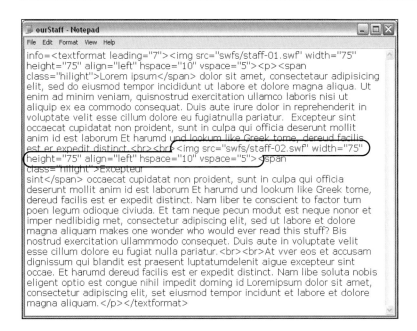

17 Toward the middle of the **ourStaff.txt** text file are two break tags (**`<br><br>`**). Click *after* those tags, and paste the **`<img>`** tag you just copied. Then, simply change the name of the SWF file from **staff-01.swf** to **staff-02.swf**.

That's it! You should verify your changes work, one last time.

18 Save your **ourStaff.txt** file by choosing **File > Save**. Then, minimize (Windows) or hide (Mac) your text-editing program, navigate to your **Desktop > la_eyeworks > site** folder, and double-click the **master.swf** file to view it in the stand-alone Flash Player 8.

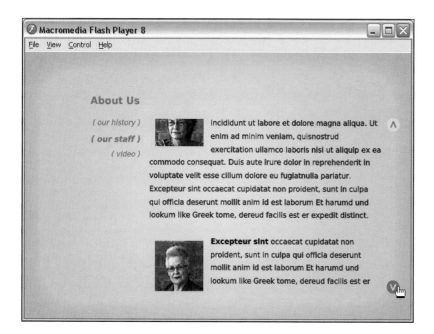

19 When the stand-alone Flash Player 8 window opens, and the **About Us** module loads, click the **our staff** submenu option to load the **ourStaff.txt** file. Inline within the loaded text are the two SWF files: **staff-01.swf** and **staff-02.swf**. Awesome! You can also scroll through the loaded text or switch to the **our history** section and scroll through the text there as well.

I certainly hope you're pleased with your progress in this book thus far because you have *definitely* come a long way. And it's only Chapter 6! In the past few chapters, you learned a *lot* of new information while constructing the About Us module. You learned how to use the `LoadVars` class to dynamically load text from an external file, how to scroll through loaded text, how to style loaded text using HTML tags written in the text file, how to further style dynamic text by using dynamically loaded (using the `TextField.StyleSheet` class) CSS files, how to build an ActionScript-controlled submenu using text options styled using the `TextFormat` class, and (as if that wasn't enough) how to embed inline SWF files in the dynamic text. You absorbed an incredible amount of content in these past few chapters, and I highly recommend taking a vacation after completing this mammoth task.

In the next chapter, you will build on what you learned in this chapter by constructing a dynamic slideshow. This slideshow will constitute the Frames module and will utilize dynamically loaded JPEG images for each frame picture and dynamically loaded information about each frame (using, of course, `LoadVars`). You will also revisit the `MovieClipLoader` and expand on it to create a graphical preloader to display the preloading progress of your content. Whew! It's a lot to cover, so you'd better get started.

7

Building a Slideshow

In this chapter, you will build the interactive slideshow that fits into the Frames module of the L.A. Eyeworks Web site. The Frames module is a simple slideshow comprising the slideshow images, a few lines of descriptive text with each image, and a small Dynamic text field displaying which image is currently being viewed out of the total number of images. What makes this slideshow interesting, however, is all the slideshow images and accompanying descriptive text will be dynamically loaded using the `MovieClipLoader` and `LoadVars` object you created in Chapter 3, *"Getting Started,"* and Chapter 4, *"Using the LoadVars Class,"* respectively. The viewer will also be able to click Next Slide and Previous Slide buttons—which you will make functional by writing the ActionScript—to navigate through the dynamic slideshow.

1 | Previewing What You Are Building

In this exercise, you'll see the finished Web site so you can get a better idea of the slideshow you will be building before you begin.

---

1 Open your preferred browser, and access the following URL:

www.lynda.com/flash8btb/laeyeworks/

---

2 When the Web site loads, click the **frames** option in the navigation bar at the top of the page.

This loads (using the `MovieClipLoader`) the Frames module. Immediately (or somewhat immediately, depending on the speed of your Internet connection) you should see the first slide in the slideshow, which is actually a JPEG image stored in a separate folder on the Web server. As you click the Next Slide (>) and Previous Slide (<) buttons below the slides, the `MovieClipLoader` loads the next and previous (respectively) slides in sequence. As each new slideshow image appears, you'll also notice the text to the left of the slide updates to describe each pair of glasses. Not only that, but below the slide image is another bit of text specifying which image is being viewed out of the total number of images.

In this exercise, you'll learn how to combine many of the scripts you constructed in previous chapters to build this slideshow. I hope you're excited, because you'll be learning some really powerful techniques as well as beginning to see—now that you've created many of the main scripts (`MovieClipLoader`, `LoadVars`, and so forth)—how easy it can be to create some fairly complex interactivity. It's not all going to be simply review, however. A major part of learning to work with Macromedia Flash 8 is learning how to combine actions in various ways to achieve different types of interactivity. Even though you'll be reusing certain actions in this and following chapters, you will be mixing those actions together and adding to them in different ways to create different types of functionality and interactivity.

---

3 When you're finished viewing the **Frames** module, close your browser.

---

2 | Setting Up

In this exercise, you'll open a prebuilt FLA file and get ready to add functionality to it. You will add some instance names to movie clips and text fields used in this module, and you'll import some elements from the shared library.

---

1 Navigate to your **Desktop > la_eyeworks > site** folder, and double-click the file **frames.fla** to open it in Flash 8.

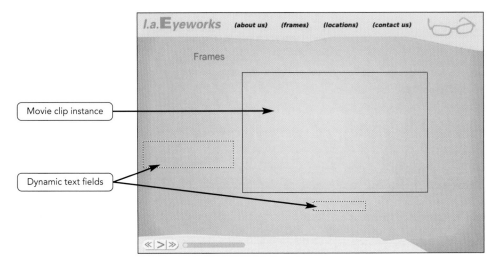

Once you have the **frames.fla** file open, you'll notice it contains two Dynamic text fields and a movie clip symbol with a box drawn in it. That box around the movie clip symbol, by the way (which is simply a stroke drawn inside the movie clip symbol), represents the physical size of the slideshow JPEG images—320 × 200 pixels—and is there merely to give you a visual representation of where the slideshow images will appear when they are dynamically loaded into the movie clip. When you're finished creating the Frames module, you will disable the stroke so it isn't published in the completed SWF file.

Because both Dynamic text fields and the movie clip instance will be targeted with ActionScript, they—of course—need to have unique instance names. The far-left Dynamic text field is where descriptive information will appear about each slideshow image. The movie clip instance is where each slide will load. Lastly, the Dynamic text field below the movie clip instance is where the slide number information will appear.

First, however, you will need to bring in some shared elements to use when constructing this module.

---

2 Make sure you *don't* have **sharedLib.fla** open. (If it *is* open, you won't be able to complete the rest of this step.) Then, choose **File > Import > Open External Library**. When the **Open as Library** dialog box opens, navigate to your **Desktop > la_eyeworks > site** folder, and double-click **sharedLib.fla**. This will open only the library of the shared library, **sharedLib.fla**.

---

3 Make sure you also have the **frames Library** window open, and then select the symbols **btn. arrow**, **Vera**, and **VeraBold** in the **sharedLib Library** window. (You can select them all by **Shift+clicking** each one in turn.) Once you've selected these symbols, drag them onto the **frames Library** window. As you've seen previously, this creates a link to the shared library items in the file.

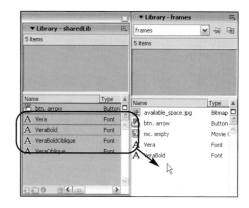

4 Close the **sharedLib Library** window. You won't need it again in this exercise.

You've linked the shared fonts (wasn't that easy?), so you can now assign them to the two premade Dynamic text fields on the **frames.fla** Stage.

5 Select the left-most Dynamic text field by single-clicking it. Then, in the **Property Inspector**, from the **Font** pop-up menu, choose the shared font symbol **Vera***. Also, set the **Font rendering method** to **Anti-alias for readability**.

Text field is selected

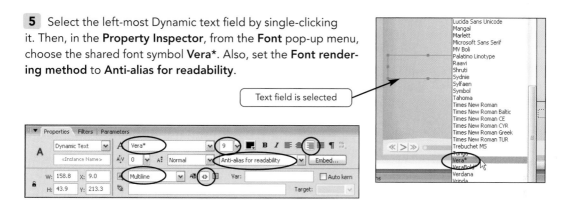

Leave the rest of the text field options the way they are. The text field should be set to a font size of **9**, an alignment of **Align right**, a line type of **Multiline**, and a font-rendering method of **Anti-alias for readability**. The **Render Text as HTML** button should already be selected. Of course, to be able to specify this text field as the target to load text into, you need to give it an instance name.

6 With the text field still selected, in the **Property Inspector** type **loadedInfo** in the **Instance Name** field.

loadedInfo is now the instance name of this text field, and you can use this name when you want to target **loadedInfo** with ActionScript. If your brain isn't mush by now, you might recall the instance name **loadedInfo** from previous exercises. **loadedInfo** is the name of the text field the **LoadVars** script (which you wrote in Chapter 4, "*Using the LoadVars Class*") will put variable values in when you load the variables from an external text file. Later, when you use the **LoadVars** script to load the slide information variable files, the values of those external variables will be inserted in this **loadedInfo** text field.

Because the remaining text field will be targeted with ActionScript, you also need to define its settings, as well as give it an instance name.

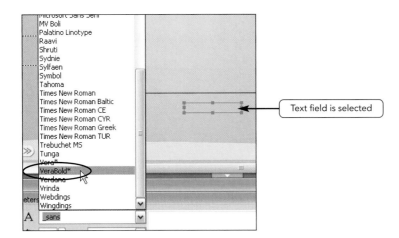

Text field is selected

7 Click the bottom-most text field once to select it. Then, in the **Property Inspector**, from the **Font** pop-up menu, choose **VeraBold***.

The font size should be **9**, the text color should be **#3F7FBE** (blue), the alignment should be **Align center**, the line type should be **Single line**, and the font-rendering method should be **Anti-alias for readability**. Additionally, **Render Text as HTML** should *not* be enabled.

Note: If you're working in Windows, click the **Bold Style** button (as is circled in the illustration). If you're on a Mac, leave **Bold Style** disabled.

8 With the lower text field still selected, click in the **Instance Name** field in the **Property Inspector**, and give this field an instance name by typing **frameNum**.

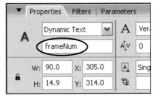

You also need to give an instance name to the movie clip instance where the slide JPEG image will dynamically load.

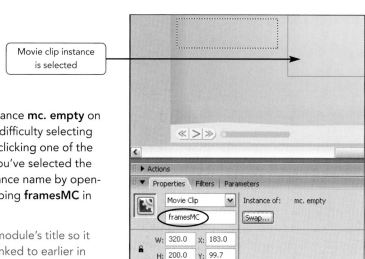

Movie clip instance is selected

9 Single-click the movie clip instance **mc. empty** on the **Stage** to select it. (If you have difficulty selecting the movie clip instance, try single-clicking one of the sides [strokes] of the box.) Once you've selected the movie clip instance, give it an instance name by opening the **Property Inspector** and typing **framesMC** in the **Instance Name** field.

Lastly, you should set the Frames module's title so it uses one of the shared fonts you linked to earlier in this exercise.

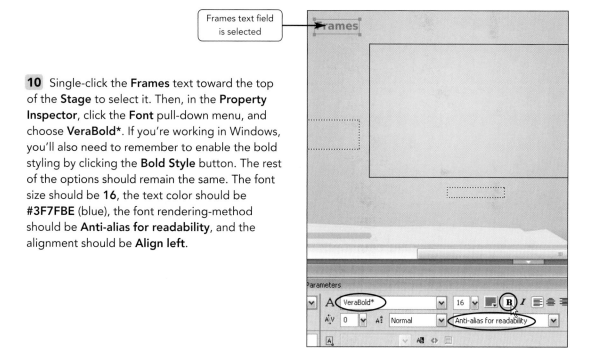

Frames text field is selected

10 Single-click the **Frames** text toward the top of the **Stage** to select it. Then, in the **Property Inspector**, click the **Font** pull-down menu, and choose **VeraBold***. If you're working in Windows, you'll also need to remember to enable the bold styling by clicking the **Bold Style** button. The rest of the options should remain the same. The font size should be **16**, the text color should be **#3F7FBE** (blue), the font rendering-method should be **Anti-alias for readability**, and the alignment should be **Align left**.

11 Save your **frames.fla** file by choosing **File > Save**.

There ya have it! This Frames module is all set up and ready for you to add the slideshow interactivity. In the next exercise, you will write some scripting to dynamically load the slideshow JPEG images into the `framesMC` movie clip instance.

NOTE:

What Is the "if" Statement?

Chapter 4, *"Using the LoadVars Class,"* briefly introduced the **if** statement, which allows you to create *conditional logic* in your Flash 8 movie. In other words, you can create a script to execute when certain circumstances occur in the Flash 8 movie, or you can even have a different script execute when *different* circumstances present themselves. The **if** statement allows your movie to react as various conditions arise. For example, if you want to check to see whether the content loading into **_level5** has finished yet and, if so, play the main Timeline, you could use an **if** statement like this:

```
if (_level5.getBytesLoaded() == _level5.getBytesTotal()) {
  _level0.play();
}
```

When the **if** statement executes, it will check to see *if* **_level5** has been loaded. (The scripting within the parentheses after **if** is called the *condition*.) After the **if** statement finds a result, it returns a Boolean value—a **true** or a **false**. If the condition is **true** (in this case, if **_level5** has completely loaded), the **if** statement executes all the actions between the curly braces (**{}**), called the *statements*. So, in this example, the **if** statement simply reads, "If the bytes loaded for **_level5** are equal to **_level5**'s total bytes (meaning **_level5** has completely downloaded), tell the main Timeline (**_level0**) to play." Pretty straightforward, eh?

But what if you want a different action to execute if the condition is *not* true? The way the script is currently set up, if the condition is not true, Flash 8 just ignores the statement(s) within the **if** statement and continues processing any other actions available. In other words, it just moves on. But, what if you want some text to be inserted into a text field on the main Timeline if the condition turns out to be false (if **_level5** hasn't completely downloaded yet)? In this situation, you can write an **else** into the **if** statement. You can use an **else** when you want some other action to happen if the condition turns out to be false. This is called *branching logic*. Here is what an **else** would look like integrated into the previous **if** statement:

```
if (_level5.getBytesLoaded() == _level5.getBytesTotal()) {
_level0.play();
} else {
  _level0.textMsg.text = "still downloading";
}
```

So, as you can see, the **else** is just tacked on after the **if** statement. Whatever you want to happen if the condition for the **if** statement turns out to be false, you place within curly braces after **else**. Those actions will execute automatically if the **if** condition is false.

if statements, as you've gotten a taste of here, are *essential* to creating many kinds of powerful interactivity inside Flash 8. They allow your movie to ask questions and to then respond appropriately based on the answers it receives. You have already used **if** statements in scripts you've written thus far, and you will continue to use them throughout other exercises in this book.

3 | Loading the First Slide

In this exercise, you'll create some ActionScript to load the first image of the slideshow into the correct location in the Frames module. The slideshow is fairly basic. What makes this slideshow interesting, however, is each image in the slideshow is an external JPEG file. As a result, **frames.swf** will be smaller in file size, and you will have the added advantage of being able to swap images without ever opening the Flash 8 project (great for clients who want to maintain the work you've done for them!). You'll start constructing this slideshow by building simple functionality. Then, over the course of the exercises in this chapter, you will add more complex interactivity, such as providing the viewer with a way to navigate through the slideshow.

1 Before you start writing the ActionScript, you should first see where the slideshow images are and what their filenames are. Navigate to your **Desktop > la_eyeworks > site** folder, which is where, of course, all your site files (including **master.swf**, **about_us.swf**, **frames.swf**, and so on) are located. Within the **site** folder, you'll notice a folder titled **frames**. Double-click the **frames** folder to open it.

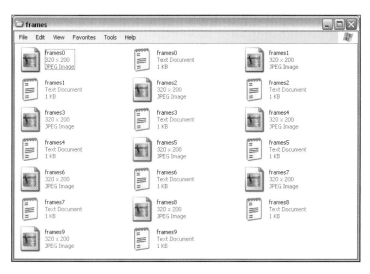

You'll notice the **frames** folder contains a series of JPEG and TXT files. But take notice of their names. If you look at the JPEG images, notice how their file names all begin with **frames** and are then followed by a number—**frames0.jpg**, **frames1.jpg**, and so forth. (The illustration here doesn't show the file extensions because that is the default behavior in Windows XP. If you would like Windows XP to show file extensions, the instructions in the Introduction will show you how to enable this feature. On the other hand, if you're on a Mac, the operating system *does* show the file extensions by default.) The associated text files also use this naming convention. These files were named this way (sequentially) on purpose. When you write the ActionScript to advance to the next slide, you'll simply tell Flash 8 to get the file starting with the word **frames** and then add a number to it one greater than the current slide.

2 Bring Flash 8 to the foreground.

3 Make sure you still are working in the **frames.fla** file. If you accidentally closed it, you can open it again by accessing your **Desktop > la_eyeworks > site** folder and double-clicking the **frames.fla** file. (You can also select **frames.fla** from the **Open a Recent Item** column on the **Start Page**.)

4 Single-click the first (and only) keyframe in the top-most layer, **a**, and open the **Actions** panel by pressing **F9** (Windows) or **Opt+F9** (Mac).

```
1
2
3   // ----------------<pre-built code for chapter 7>---------------- \\
4   /*
5   frameNum.autoSize = "center";
6   loadedInfo.autoSize = "right";
7   // ----------------<TextField.StyleSheet>---------------- \\
8   var cssStyles:TextField.StyleSheet = new TextField.StyleSheet ();
9   cssStyles.load ("styles/styles.css");
10  cssStyles.onLoad = function (success) {
11      if (success) {
12          loadedInfo.styleSheet = cssStyles;
13          loadFrame();
14      } else {
15          loadedInfo.text = "There has been an error loading the requested information.
    Please contact the Webmaster and report your error.";
16      }
17  }
18  // ----------------</TextField.StyleSheet>---------------- \\
19  */
20  // ----------------</pre-built code for chapter 7>---------------- \\
```

You'll immediately notice some prebuilt actions in the Actions panel. These actions are ones you will be utilizing later in this chapter, and they have been included with the starter file **frames.fla** because they are all actions you've already used in this book. If you look at the included actions, you'll find two **autoSize** actions (which you learned how to use in Chapter 6, *"Using the TextFormat Class,"* to auto-size the **about us** submenu text fields). You'll also notice a **TextField.StyleSheet** object (nearly identical to the one you created in Chapter 5, *"Using HTML and CSS,"* which you used to load and apply CSS [Cascading Style Sheets] styles to the **loadedInfo** text field in the About Us module). Additionally you'll find that the included actions have been commented out. That way, as you're working on the ActionScript in the first part of this chapter, the included actions won't interfere with the scripts you're writing. Later in this chapter, you will uncomment the prebuilt actions and utilize them in a few new ways, such as creating the dynamic descriptive slide text and the dynamic slide counter text.

Next, you'll write an action to load the first slideshow image—using the ubiquitous **MovieClipLoader**—into the **framesMC** movie clip instance on the Stage. However, you don't want to write an action saying, "Go load the image **frames0.jpg** into the **framesMC** movie clip." Why not? Well, you need to keep in mind this slideshow needs to be *dynamic*. When the viewer clicks the Next Slide button, you need to be able to tell Flash 8 to take whichever slide image the viewer is currently looking at and load the next one in the sequence. This is why each slideshow image is named in sequence: **frames0**, **frames1**, and so forth. Remember, the word **frames** remains consistent throughout each image; only the number at the end changes. So, what you need first is a way to keep track of the current image number. By default, the viewer will start by looking at image 0. When the user clicks the Next Slide button, Flash 8 will download and display image 1.

```
1  var curFrameNum:Number = 0;
2
3  // ----------------<pre-built code for chapter 7>---------------- \\
4  /*
5  frameNum.autoSize = "center";
6  loadedInfo.autoSize = "right";
```

5 In the **Actions** panel, click the top-most empty line break (provided for you as well) above the prewritten actions, and type the following:

var curFrameNum:Number = 0;

You've already seen everything in this action. Essentially, you're simply creating a variable called **curFrameNum**, you're strict typing it as a number, and you're then inserting 0 into the variable. The variable, **curFrameNum** (short for "current frame number"), is, of course, going to keep track of which slide the user is currently viewing. But why start at 0? Why not just start at 1 instead? You can actually start at any number you'd like when building this slideshow; you just need to incorporate the numbering scheme into the script you'll write later in this chapter. However, as mentioned previously, my goal in this book is to teach you good ActionScript practices. That way, if you decide to further your ActionScript knowledge, you'll already be a step ahead and won't have to relearn the basics of more advanced methods. So, you're starting with 0 here because more advanced actions, such as array elements and XML (**EX**tensible **M**arkup **L**anguage) nodes, start with 0. In Flash 8 ActionScript—and most other computer programming languages—0 (even though you may think of 0 as representing "nothing" and thereby simply not use it) is the first number when counting sequentially: 0, 1, 2, 3, and so forth.

In the next step, you'll incorporate the variable you just created into an action to instruct the **MovieClipLoader** object to load the first slide (**frames0.jpg**) into the **framesMC** movie clip instance.

```
1  var curFrameNum:Number = 0;
2
3  _level0.myMCL.loadClip("frames/frames" + curFrameNum + ".jpg"
```

6 Click at the end of the **var curFrameNum:Number = 0;** line, press **Enter** (Windows) or **Return** (Mac) twice to create a couple of line breaks, and then create the first part of the slide-loading action by typing the following:

_level0.myMCL.loadClip("frames/frames" + curFrameNum + ".jpg"

Although this action isn't finished yet, what you have written thus far should be fairly familiar to you. What is probably *unfamiliar* to you is the plus signs you see in this action. All the plus signs do are concatenate. Technically, the plus sign is a *symbolic operator* called *addition* (yeah, duh, eh?). When you see the plus sign, you can simply think of it as tape (the sticky kind). It takes whatever comes before it and adds it onto whatever comes after it, just like if you were adding numbers like 2 + 2. The addition operator in Flash 8, however, is much more powerful. In this action, it is adding *strings* ("frames/frames" and

".jpg") onto an *expression* (the variable **curFrameNum**). Now, when this action gets compiled when you publish your movie, the expression **curFrameNum** will be replaced with whatever the value of the variable is. As you wrote in the previous step, the value of the **curFrameNum** variable is 0. So, when this part of the action is compiled, it will read **_level0.myMCL.loadClip("frames/frames0.jpg"**. Of course, **frames** is the name of the folder storing the images, and **frames0.jpg** is the name of the first JPEG image to load. Cool! To complete this action—now that you've specified which asset to load (**frames/frames0.jpg**)—you need to write *where* the asset should load.

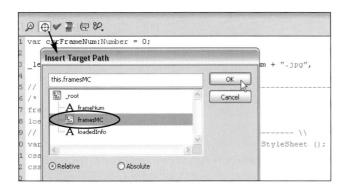

7 Click at the end of the **_level0.myMCL.loadClip("frames/frames" + curFrameNum + ".jpg"** line, and then type a comma and a space (,). Next, you need to specify the location (and the path to the location) where the slideshow image will load. Click the **Insert Target Path** button. In the resulting **Insert Target Path** dialog box, click the **Relative** radio button, select **framesMC**, and then click **OK**. **this.framesMC** (the path to where the slide images are to be loaded) will then be inserted into the action.

Alternately, if you remembered the instance name and path to what you're targeting, you could simply type it in the Actions panel by hand without ever opening the Insert Target Path dialog box. However, using the Insert Target Path dialog box is a great way to ensure you have specified both the path and the spelling correctly when writing an action.

```
1  var curFrameNum:Number = 0;
2
3  _level0.myMCL.loadClip("frames/frames" + curFrameNum + ".jpg", this.framesMC);
```

8 To end the action, make sure the insertion point (the blinking bar showing you where you're typing) is after **this.framesMC**, and then type an end parenthesis (**Shift+0**) and a semicolon (**;**).

Taken as a whole, this action simply reads, "Use the **MovieClipLoader** script (located in the **master.swf** movie [**_level0**]) to load the image located at **frames/frames0.jpg** into the **framesMC** movie clip instance."

Before continuing, it's always a good idea to test your work. As you continue, then you'll know you're building on working ActionScript. Of course, to test the Frames module, you first need to publish an updated SWF file. Then, because the Frames module uses the **MovieClipLoader** script located in **master.fla**, you need to return to **master.fla**, add an action to load the Frames module, and test **frames.swf** as it loads into **master.swf**.

9 Save your **frames.fla** file by choosing **File > Save**. Then, publish an updated SWF file by choosing **File > Publish**.

---

10 Bring **master.fla** to the foreground. If you accidentally closed it since you worked with it last, you can easily open it by navigating to your **Desktop > la_eyeworks > site** folder and double-clicking **master.fla**.

---

11 Select **Keyframe 10** in the **a** layer, and open the **Actions** panel by pressing **F9** (Windows) or **Opt+F9** (Mac).

```
1  stop();
2  // myMCL.loadClip("splash.swf", 5);
3  // myMCL.loadClip("about_us.swf", 5);
4  myMCL.loadClip("frames.swf", 5);
```

12 Comment out the `myMCL.loadClip("about_us.swf", 5);` line by adding two slashes (//) before the line. Then, click after the same line, and press **Enter** (Windows) or **Return** (Mac) to create a line break. Lastly, write the action that will load the **frames.swf** file into **_level5** by typing the following:

`myMCL.loadClip("frames.swf", 5);`

---

13 Save your **master.fla** file by choosing **File > Save**. Then, test **master.fla** by choosing **Control > Test Movie**.

When the Frames module loads into **master.swf**, you'll instantly see the first slideshow image appear. Awesome!

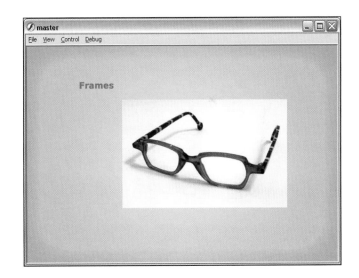

---

14 Close the preview window, and return to **frames.fla**.

You've now gotten the first slideshow image to load correctly, so over the next few exercises you'll add a script to enable users to navigate through the slides using the Next Slide and Previous Slide buttons.

---

4 | Loading the Total Slides Variable

In this exercise, you'll add the Next Slide/Previous Slide buttons the viewer will use to navigate through the slideshow. You'll also create a new **LoadVars** object to handle the loading of an external variable to keep track of the total number of slides in the slideshow. The total number of slides variable (**totalFrames**) is important because it represents the total number of images in the slideshow. By keeping track of the total number of images, you can (and later will) write an action to allow the slideshow to loop as the viewer navigates through the slideshow images.

1 Single-click the layer below the **a** layer (**frame info**), and create a new layer. Rename the new layer to "**buttons.**" This layer will hold the **Next Slide/Previous Slide** buttons.

2 Open the **frames.fla Library** by pressing **Ctrl+L** (Windows) or **Cmd+L** (Mac).

3 Drag an instance of the button symbol **btn. arrow** from the **Library** onto the **Stage**. Position the button below the **framesMC** movie clip instance and a little to the right of the **frameNum** Dynamic text field.

Currently, the arrow button is pointing down. To visually make the most sense as the Next Slide button, it should really be pointing to the right.

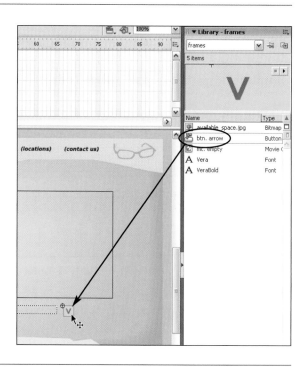

4 With the **btn. arrow** button symbol still selected, choose **Modify > Transform > Rotate 90° CCW**. This will, as the menu option implies, rotate the arrow button so it's pointing to the right. After rotating it, you will need to use the arrow keys to nudge the arrow button into place.

Next, you need a button to allow the viewer to navigate backward through the slideshow.

5 Hold down **Ctrl** (Windows) or **Opt** (Mac), and drag the **btn. arrow** button symbol instance to the left side of the **frameNum** Dynamic text field. This copies the **btn. arrow** button symbol.

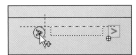

6 With the copied button symbol selected, choose **Modify > Transform > Flip Horizontal**, which flips the copied button symbol so it is pointing left instead of right. You might need to use the arrow keys to reposition the copied button arrow after you've flipped it.

As you've seen, if you want to assign ActionScript to the button symbols from a keyframe, you need to first give instance names to both button symbols.

7 With the left-facing arrow button selected, click in the **Instance Name** field in the **Property Inspector**, and type **prevSlideBtn**. This is now the instance name of the **Previous Slide** button and is the name you can use when you want to refer to it with ActionScript.

8 Select the right-facing arrow button, and type **nextSlideBtn** in the **Instance Name** field.

Since you've given a unique name to each button instance, you can begin to create the script to control the Next Slide/Previous Slide functionality. You'll start by writing the **onRelease** function you will attach to the **nextSlideBtn** button symbol. The first part of this process is identical to when you attached actions—from a keyframe to a symbol instance—previously in this book.

9 Select the first keyframe in the **a** layer, and open the **Actions** panel by pressing **F9** (Windows) or **Opt+F9** (Mac).

```
1  var curFrameNum:Number = 0;
2
3  _level0.myMCL.loadClip("frames/frames" + curFrameNum + ".jpg", this.framesMC);
4
5  // ------------------<next slide button>------------------ \\
6
7  // ------------------</next slide button>------------------ \\
```

10 Click at the end of the action you wrote in the previous exercise, **_level0.myMCL.loadClip("frames/frames" + curFrameNum + ".jpg", this.framesMC);**, and press **Enter** (Windows) or **Return** (Mac) twice to create a couple of line breaks. Then, type the opening comment:

`// ----------------<next slide button>------------------ \\`

Click at the end of that comment, press **Enter** (Windows) or **Return** (Mac) twice to create two more line breaks, and then type the closing comment:

`// ----------------</next slide button>------------------ \\`

Now you have the opening and closing comments to contain the Next Slide button's ActionScript.

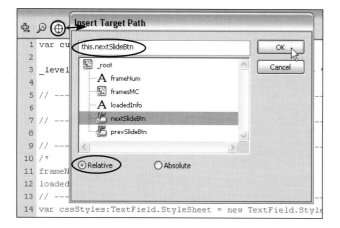

11 Click between the opening **<next slide button>** and closing **</next slide button>** comment lines, and then insert the path to the button symbol you want to target with ActionScript by clicking the **Insert a Target Path** button. In the resulting **Insert Target Path** dialog box, make sure **Relative** is selected, and then select the button symbol **nextSlideBtn**, which inserts the instance name, and the path to it, in the target field. Click **OK**.

```
5  // -------------------<next slide button>------------------ \\
6  this.nextSlideBtn.onRelease = function() {
7  // -------------------</next slide button>------------------ \\
```

12 Click after the inserted target path, `this.nextSlideBtn`, and type the following:

`.onRelease = function() {`

Make sure to type the period (**.**) between **nextSlideBtn** and **onRelease**. The first line in this function says, "When the viewer clicks (**onRelease**) **nextSlideBtn**, execute the following actions within this function."

Next, you need to create the actions to execute when the viewer clicks the Next Slide button. So, at this point as a Flash 8 designer/developer, you should be asking yourself, "OK, self, what should happen when the viewer clicks the Next Slide button? Well, I want an action to execute to tell the **MovieClipLoader** to load the next JPEG in sequence. Hmm. But what will happen if the viewer is already looking at the last slide in the sequence? What should happen then? I suppose if the viewer is already looking at the last slide and the viewer then clicks the Next Slide button, the slideshow should return to the first slide in the sequence. That way, the slideshow will continually loop as the viewer clicks through it."

The functionality you'll start to create in this exercise (and will then finish in the following exercise) will cause the slideshow to loop back to the beginning when the viewer is looking at the last slide in the slideshow and then clicks the Next Slide button. So, how would you start writing a script to take all that into account? The first fact you want to determine—when the viewer clicks the Next Slide button—is whether the viewer is currently looking at the last slide. If yes, you can then instruct your **MovieClipLoader** to load the first slide in the sequence. If not, you can then tell the **MovieClipLoader** to simply load the next slide in sequence. A key piece to this script working correctly is finding out *which* slide is the *last* slide. If you want the slideshow to loop back to the first slide when the viewer has reached the end of the slideshow, you first need a way to determine which slide is the last.

Earlier in this chapter you created a variable, **curFrameNum**, to track the current slide. Now you need another variable to keep track of the *total number* of slides. You could easily create this variable in the first keyframe of **frames.fla**. But if your clients ever wanted to add or remove slides (thereby changing the number of total slides), they would have to open **frames.fla** in Flash 8 (because Flash 8 FLA files can't be opened in previous versions of Flash) and have the know-how to change the number in the variable. As discussed earlier in this book, it's best to keep any elements (variables, images, and so forth) clients might need to change themselves *outside* the FLA file. That way, if your clients need to make a change, it's much easier for them—with much less know-how (not to mention the necessary software)—to do it themselves.

Therefore, instead of creating the variable—which keeps track of the total number of slides in the slideshow—in **frames.fla**, you'll store the variable in an external text file and use **LoadVars** to dynamically load it. Because of the way you originally set up the main **LoadVars** script in **master.fla**, you can use it only to load the descriptive text for each slideshow image. So, in order to utilize another external variable for a different purpose, you'll create a separate, slimmed-down **LoadVars** script to specifically load the variable to track the total number of slides. Although this may sound excessive, keep in mind it requires only two lines of code (and two lines of code you've seen before, at that).

You'll return to this **nextSlideBtn** script later, but first you need to write the **LoadVars** script to allow you to determine the total number of slides. You need to know this number before you can continue writing the functionality for the Next Slide and Previous Slide buttons.

```
1  var slideInfoLV:LoadVars = new LoadVars();
2
3  var curFrameNum:Number = 0;
4
5  _level0.myMCL.loadClip("frames/frames" + curFrameNum + ".jpg", this.framesMC);
6
7  // -------------------<next slide button>------------------- \\
8  this.nextSlideBtn.onRelease = function() {
9  // -------------------</next slide button>------------------- \\
```

13 Click to the left of the top-most line, **var curFrameNum:Number = 0;**, and press **Enter** (Windows) or **Return** (Mac) twice to create a couple of line breaks. This pushes the **var curFrameNum:Number = 0;** action down two lines, thereby giving you room above it to add more actions. Then, click the top-most empty line break you just created, and define a new **LoadVars** object with the instance name **slideInfoLV** by typing the following:

var slideInfoLV:LoadVars = new LoadVars();

As you saw in Chapter 4, *"Using the LoadVars Class,"* this action creates a new **LoadVars** object and assigns it the instance name of **slideInfoLV**. This **LoadVars** object loads the external variable (within a text file) to keep track of the total number of slides in the slideshow. So, what about that text file? Because you've already seen what comprises a text file containing external variables, I created the text file for you to save you some time. Before you load it into your project, however, you need to know the name of the variable in the text file, as well as *where* the text file is located.

---

14 Minimize (Windows) or hide (Mac) Flash 8, and navigate to your **Desktop > la_eyeworks > site > vars** folder.

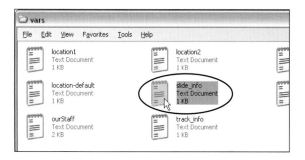

15 Within the **vars** folder is a text file titled **slide_info.txt**. Open this text file in a simple text editor such as Notepad (Windows), TextEdit (Mac), or BBEdit (Mac).

As you can see, the contents are basic. You'll see one variable, **totalFrames**, with a value of 10. Now, technically this slideshow has ten slides total. However, the last slide in the slideshow ends with 9

(**frames9.jpg**). So when using the **totalFrames** variable in a script to define which slide is the *last* slide, 10 is actually incorrect. Later, when you use **totalFrames** in a script, you will need to make sure you take into account that although the **totalFrames** variable *does* represent the total number of slides, it *does not* represent the number of the *last* slide in the slideshow (9). Again, this is because the slide show starts with 0.

The main reason why you have to jump through a few ActionScript hoops when dealing with **totalFrames** is because you (and the client) want to be able to easily update this variable. If your client ever modified the total number of slides, all they would have to do is to open this text file, update the number, save the file, and upload it to the correct location on the server. *Voila!* The client wouldn't need to open/edit the **frames.fla** file or even own a copy of Flash 8. Now that you've seen the contents of the text file and where it's located, you can load it and utilize it in the project.

---

16 Close the text file, and bring Flash 8 to the foreground. Make sure you still have **Keyframe 1** selected in the **a** layer of **frames.fla** and your **Actions** panel is open.

```
1  var slideInfoLV:LoadVars = new LoadVars();
2  slideInfoLV.load("vars/slide_info.txt");
3
4  var curFrameNum:Number = 0;
5
6  _level0.myMCL.loadClip("frames/frames" + curFrameNum + ".jpg", this.framesMC);
7
8  // -------------------<next slide button>------------------- \\
9  this.nextSlideBtn.onRelease = function() {
10 // -------------------</next slide button>------------------- \\
```

17 Click at the end of the top-most action, **var slideInfoLV:LoadVars = new LoadVars();**, press **Enter** (Windows) or **Return** (Mac) to create a line break, and then load the variables from the **slide_info.txt** file by typing the following:

slideInfoLV.load("vars/slide_info.txt");

This action uses the **LoadVars** object you just created, **slideInfoLV**, to load the variables from the **slide_info.txt** file in the **vars** folder.

You have now loaded, within the Frames module, the total number of slides in the slideshow. Whenever you need to use that number in a script, you can simply write **slideInfoLV.totalFrames**, where **slideInfoLV** is the instance name of the **LoadVars** object you created and **totalFrames** is the variable name (which contains the total number of slides [10]) located within the loaded **slide_info.txt** file. Cool!

In the next exercise, you will finish writing the script to allow the viewer to navigate (and loop) Next Slide through the slideshow.

---

5 | Adding the Next Slide Button's Functionality

In this exercise, you'll continue writing the ActionScript to allow the viewer to advance to the next image in the slideshow. You'll also write actions in this script to allow the slideshow to *loop*—that is, to return to the beginning of the slideshow if the viewer is already looking at the last slideshow image when clicking the Next Slide button.

```
 8  // ------------------<next slide button>------------------ \\
 9  this.nextSlideBtn.onRelease = function() {
10
11      if (curFrameNum < Number(slideInfoLV.totalFrames) - 1) {
12  // ------------------</next slide button>------------------ \\
```

1 Within the **Next Slide** button's script, click at the end of the `this.nextSlideBtn.onRelease = function() {` line, press **Enter** (Windows) or **Return** (Mac) twice to create two line breaks, and type the following:

```
if (curFrameNum < Number(slideInfoLV.totalFrames) - 1) {
```

What this `if` action says is, "If the slide number currently being viewed (**curFrameNum**) is less than the total number of slides (as retrieved from the external **slide_info.txt** file) minus one…." Remember, you need to subtract 1 from the **totalFrames** variable because even though the variable represents the total number of slides (10), the last slide is 9 (**frames9.jpg**).

However, what is probably not familiar to you in this action is the inclusion of **Number**, which is a built-in function to convert the expression within the parentheses after it to a number. The reason you're using **Number** in this action comes down to this: When you use **LoadVars** to load variable/value pairs from an external text file—as you did earlier in this chapter to load the total number of slideshow images—the values are loaded into the **LoadVars** object as strings. A string, as mentioned earlier, is a bit of text such as "Shane Rebenschied." Conversely, a **Number** is a number such as 1, 2, 3, and so forth. Now normally, when you're loading a number in a text file into your Flash 8 project using **LoadVars**, you can display the number in your movie, and everything will work just fine. But if you want to use the number in an equation, Flash 8 normally won't be able to use it properly.

For example, say you have a variable in an external text file called **myVariable**. And the value of the variable is 1. Your text file would look like this: **myVariable=1**. You then use a **LoadVars** object with an instance name of **myLV** to load the variable into your Flash 8 project. Then, you'd like to add 1 to the **myVariable** number. So from within your Flash 8 movie, you write **myLV.myVariable + 1;**. Because the value of **myVariable** is 1, you would expect the result of the equation to be 2. What you'd actually end up with, however, is 11. Instead of using mathematical addition to add 1 + 1, Flash 8 has concatenated 1 and 1 for a result of 11 because the loaded **myVariable** number is treated as a string (text). So, before you can use a number you've imported into your project using **LoadVars**, you need to convert the number (which is actually a string), into an actual number. In Step 1, that's what **Number(slideInfoLV.totalFrames)** does. The **Number** function converts the value of the **slideInfoLV.totalFrames** (which, if you remember, is 10) into a number. You're converting the value of the **slideInfoLV.totalFrames** variable into a number because you are using it to subtract 1 from in an equation. In more advanced ActionScript terms, this is referred to as *casting*.

Now, if the **if** action you wrote in Step 1 is true (when executed), it means the viewer is not currently looking at the last slide. If the viewer isn't looking at the last slide in the slideshow when the **nextSlideBtn** button is clicked, the next slide—in sequence—should load. How, exactly, do you go about loading the next slide in sequence? First, you need to add 1 to the variable keeping track of the current slide. Then, you can tell the MovieClipLoader to load that particular slide number. First, you need to add 1 to the current slide number (so the script can then load the next slide in sequence).

```
8  // -------------------<next slide button>------------------- \\
9  this.nextSlideBtn.onRelease = function() {
10
11     if (curFrameNum < Number(slideInfoLV.totalFrames) - 1) {
12         curFrameNum ++;
13 // -------------------</next slide button>------------------- \\
```

2 Click at the end of the **if** action, **if (curFrameNum < Number(slideInfoLV.totalFrames) – 1) {**, press **Enter** (Windows) or **Return** (Mac) once to create a line break, and then add 1 to the current slide number by typing the following:

curFrameNum++;

This simple action basically says, "Add 1 to the number in the **curFrameNum** variable." The **curFrameNum** variable, as you remember, is keeping track of which slide number is the current slide. The double plus sign (++) you see in the action is called an *increment*. It just adds 1 onto the expression. So, in this case, the **curFrameNum** variable resolves (when the Frames module is first played) to 0. When you increment the number, it changes the number to 1. The increment operator (++), in this case, simply tells Flash 8 to add 1 to the number within the **curFrameNum** variable. Nifty!

Before you write the action to actually load the slideshow images, you should first complete the **if** action by writing an **else** action to define what should happen if the **if** action turns out to be false. In other words, what should happen if the viewer *is* looking at the last slide when clicking the Next Slide button? Simply, to make the slideshow loop, you should reset the **curFrameNum** variable to 0.

```
10 // -------------------<next slide button>------------------- \\
11 this.nextSlideBtn.onRelease = function() {
12
13     if (curFrameNum < Number(slideInfoLV.totalFrames) - 1) {
14         curFrameNum ++;
15     } else {
16         curFrameNum = 0;
17     }
18 // -------------------</next slide button>------------------- \\
```

3 Click at the end of the **curFrameNum++;** line, press **Enter** (Windows) or **Return** (Mac) once to create a line break, and add the **else** action by typing the following:

} else {

Then set the **curFrameNum** variable to equal **0**, and end the **else** action by clicking at the end of the **} else {** line, pressing **Enter** (Windows) or **Return** (Mac) once, and typing the following:

curFrameNum = 0;
}

When you're finished writing the `if` and `else` actions, they should look like the ones in the illustration.

What the `if` and `else` actions say when combined is, "When the viewer clicks the Next Slide button, if the current slide number is less than the total number of slides (minus 1), then set the current slide to be one number greater than the current slide. Otherwise (if the viewer *is* looking at the last slide), just set the current slide number to 0." The combined `if` and `else` actions make the slideshow loop when the viewer gets to the end.

You've defined what number should reside in the `curFrameNum` variable, so now you need to write the action to load that particular slide number. But rather than copy the action—which you wrote earlier in this exercise—to load the slide image into the `framesMC` movie clip instance, you'll instead place that action within a function. (Remember, a function is just a container to hold actions.) Because the load slide action will be needed when the viewer clicks the Next Slide button or the Previous Slide button, it will be easier to just place the action within a function and then call that function whenever you need it instead of duplicating the action and attaching it to the Next Slide and Previous Slide buttons. Later, this function will also contain the action to load the descriptive slide text. Because those actions will need to execute from various places (from the Next Slide button and from the Previous Slide button), it's a much better workflow to place those commonly used actions in a function and simply call that function whenever it is needed.

```
 6  function loadFrame() {
 7      _level0.myMCL.loadClip("frames/frames" + curFrameNum + ".jpg", this.framesMC);
 8  }
 9
10  // ------------------<next slide button>------------------ \\
11  this.nextSlideBtn.onRelease = function() {
12
13      if (curFrameNum < Number(slideInfoLV.totalFrames) - 1) {
14          curFrameNum ++;
15      } else {
16          curFrameNum = 0;
17      }
18  // ------------------</next slide button>------------------ \\
```

4 Click at the beginning of the action that loads the current slide, `_level0.myMCL.loadClip("frames/frames" + curFrameNum + ".jpg", this.framesMC);`, and press **Enter** (Windows) or **Return** (Mac) to create a new line break *above* that line. Then, create a new function by clicking the new line and typing the following:

```
function loadFrame() {
```

5 To close the function, click at the end of the `loadClip` action, `_level0.myMCL.loadClip("frames/frames" + curFrameNum + ".jpg", this.framesMC);`, press **Enter** (Windows) or **Return** (Mac) once to create a line break, and type a closed curly brace (**}**).

The `loadClip` action should also be indented within the function (to follow proper ActionScript formatting), so click at the beginning of the `_level0.myMCL.loadClip("frames/frames" + curFrameNum + ".jpg", this.framesMC);` line, and press **Tab** once to indent the action. Great! Now when you want the `loadClip` action (and any other actions you place within that function) to execute, you can just call the function's name (and the path to the function, if you're calling the function from a different Timeline) by typing `loadFrame();`.

So, you've created a function to hold the action that loads the slideshow image, so you can call the **loadFrame** function from the **nextSlideBtn** function.

```
10  // --------------------<next slide button>-------------------- \\
11  this.nextSlideBtn.onRelease = function() {
12
13      if (curFrameNum < Number(slideInfoLV.totalFrames) - 1) {
14          curFrameNum ++;
15      } else {
16          curFrameNum = 0;
17      }
18
19      loadFrame();
20  // --------------------</next slide button>-------------------- \\
```

Click after this closed curly brace

6 Within the **Next Slide** button's script, click after the closing **else** curly brace (as circled in the illustration), press **Enter** (Windows) or **Return** (Mac) twice to create a couple of line breaks, and trigger the **loadFrame** function by typing the following:

loadFrame();

This triggers the **loadFrame** function—thereby executing all the actions within it—when the viewer clicks the Next Slide button. Because it comes *after* the **if** and **else** actions that set what the number in the **curFrameNum** variable should be, when the **loadFrame** function is triggered, it will load whichever slide corresponds with that number. Pretty slick!

As yet, however, the only action within the **loadFrame** function is the action to load the next slide JPEG file. Later in this chapter, you will place another action within that function to be triggered each time the viewer clicks the Next Slide and Previous Slide buttons.

```
10  // --------------------<next slide button>-------------------- \\
11  this.nextSlideBtn.onRelease = function() {
12
13      if (curFrameNum < Number(slideInfoLV.totalFrames) - 1) {
14          curFrameNum ++;
15      } else {
16          curFrameNum = 0;
17      }
18
19      loadFrame();
20
21  }
22  // --------------------</next slide button>-------------------- \\
```

7 Close the **nextSlideBtn** function by clicking at the end of the **loadFrame();** line, pressing **Enter** (Windows) or **Return** (Mac) twice to create a couple of line breaks, and typing a closed curly brace (**}**).

There you have it—the (nearly) completed functionality for the Next Slide button! But before you can test your movie, you need to add one last action. By moving the **loadClip** action—which loads the current slideshow image—into a function (as you did in Steps 4 and 5), it won't automatically execute when the Frames module first loads. Translation? When the Frames module first loads, the first slideshow image will not automatically load and display. To fix this, you need to call the function so the **loadClip** action *will* execute when the Frames module first loads. Later, you will incorporate this action into another action, but for now—for testing—you can just call the function outright.

```
6  function loadFrame() {
7      _level0.myMCL.loadClip("frames/frames" + curFrameNum + ".jpg", this.framesMC);
8  }
9  loadFrame();
```

8 Click after the closed curly brace for the **loadFrame** function, press **Enter** (Windows) or **Return** (Mac) once to create a line break, and trigger the **loadFrame** function by typing the following:

loadFrame();

When the **frames.swf** file first loads, this automatically executes the **loadFrame** function and all the actions within it. What does this mean in plain English? It means now, when the Frames module first loads, the first slide automatically loads.

9 Save your **frames.fla** file by choosing **File > Save**. Then, publish an updated SWF file by choosing **File > Publish**.

10 Minimize (Windows) or hide (Mac) Flash 8, navigate to your **Desktop > la_eyeworks > site** folder, and double-click **master.swf** to play it in the stand-alone Macromedia Flash Player 8.

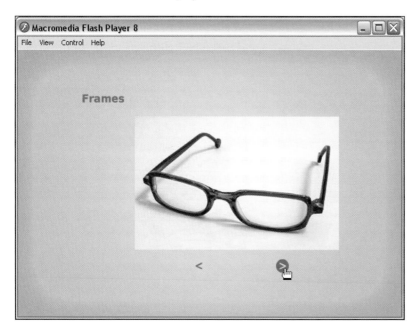

When the Frames module first loads into **master.swf**, you should see the first slideshow image load and display, just like it did before. But now, click the Next Slide button. When you click the Next Slide button, the next image in the slideshow sequence will load and display where the first image was. Stupendous! Each time you click the Next Slide button, the next slideshow image will load. (Behind the scenes, your movie is adding 1 to the `curFrameNum` variable every time you click the Next Slide button.) When the last slideshow image, **frames9.jpg**, appears, the `if` action you wrote within the `nextSlideBtn.onRelease` function is no longer true. The `curFrameNum` value is no longer less than the `totalFrames` value minus 1 (that is, 9). Since the `if` action is no longer true, the `else` action you wrote takes over and resets the `curFrameNum` variable to 0, and then the `loadFrame` function triggers, causing the slideshow to load the first slide in sequence, **frames0.jpg**. So, as you can see, you can keep clicking that Next Slide button until you grow calluses an inch thick on your finger, but the slideshow will never end. Thanks to the combination of the `if` and `else` actions, the slideshow will seamlessly loop through the images.

---

11 Close the stand-alone Flash Player 8 window, and bring Flash 8 to the foreground. Make sure **frames.fla** is still your foreground FLA file and you have the first keyframe in the **a** layer selected with the **Actions** panel open.

Now, obviously, you need to add similar—but opposite—functionality to the Previous Slide button. Luckily, the ActionScript you wrote for the Next Slide button is similar to the script needed for the Previous Slide button. How so? It means in the next exercise you can duplicate the script you just wrote for the Next Slide button and slightly modify the duplicate so it will work for the Previous Slide button. Whew!

Adding the Previous Slide Button's Functionality

In this exercise, you'll finish what you started in the previous exercises. You'll take the Next Slide button script, duplicate it, and modify it to work with the Previous Slide button. Because the functionality of the Next Slide/Previous Slide buttons is similar, it makes sense to reuse as much of the work as possible.

```
11  // -----------------<next slide button>----------------- \\
12  this.nextSlideBtn.onRelease = function() {
13
14      if (curFrameNum < Number(slideInfoLV.totalFrames) - 1) {
15          curFrameNum ++;
16      } else {
17          curFrameNum = 0;
18      }
19
20      loadFrame();
21
22  }
23  // ----------------</next slide button>-----------------
```

Undo	
Redo	
Cut	
Copy	
Paste	
Delete	
Select All	
Set Breakpoint	
Remove Breakpoint	
Remove Breakpoints in This File	

1 Select the entire **Next Slide** button's script, even the open/closed comment lines. Then, **right-click** (Windows) or **Ctrl+click** (Mac) anywhere on the selected script. From the resulting contextual menu, choose **Copy**.

```
11  // -------------------<next slide button>------------------- \\
12  this.nextSlideBtn.onRelease = function() {
13
14      if (curFrameNum < Number(slideInfoLV.totalFrames) - 1) {
15          curFrameNum ++;
16      } else {
17          curFrameNum = 0;
18      }
19
20      loadFrame();
21
22  }
23  // -------------------</next slide button>------------------- \\
24
25  |
26
27  // -----------------uilt code for chapter 7>--------------- \\
28  /*
29  fr                            ";
30  lo                          t";
31  // -----------------ield.StyleSheet>--------------- \\
```

Undo
Redo
Cut
Copy
Paste
Delete

2 Click at the end of the closing **Next Slide** button's comment, // --------------</next slide button>-------------- \\, and press **Enter** (Windows) or **Return** (Mac) twice to create a couple of line breaks. Then **right-click** (Windows) or **Ctrl+click** (Mac) the second new line you just created, and from the resulting contextual menu, choose **Paste**. This pastes a copy of the **Next Slide** button's script below the original.

```
25  // -------------------<previous slide button>------------------- \\
26  this.nextSlideBtn.onRelease = function() {
27
28      if (curFrameNum < Number(slideInfoLV.totalFrames) - 1) {
29          curFrameNum ++;
30      } else {
31          curFrameNum = 0;
32      }
33
34      loadFrame();
35
36  }
37  // -------------------</previous slide button>------------------- \\
```

3 In the copied script, start by changing the comments. Change the word *next* in the opening comment to *previous*. Do the same for the closing comment. Make sure you're making these changes to the copied script and not to the original **Next Slide** button's script.

This script applies to the Previous Slide button, so you also need to make sure you change the target of the **onRelease** function.

```
25  // -------------------<previous slide button>------------------- \\
26  this.prevSlideBtn.onRelease = function() {
27
28      if (curFrameNum < Number(slideInfoLV.totalFrames) - 1) {
29          curFrameNum ++;
30      } else {
31          curFrameNum = 0;
32      }
33
34      loadFrame();
35
36  }
37  // -------------------</previous slide button>------------------- \\
```

4 Change the targeted button symbol **nextSlideBtn** to target the **Previous Slide** button, **prevSlideBtn**.

When navigating through the slideshow backward, you obviously don't need the **if** action to check whether you're not viewing the last slideshow image. When going backward, you want the **if** action to check whether the viewer is looking at the first slide when clicking the Previous Slide button. If the viewer is already looking at the first slide, then you want the slideshow to jump to the *last* slide in the sequence. This is the same concept as the Next Slide button, just in reverse.

```
25  // ------------------<previous slide button>------------------ \\
26  this.prevSlideBtn.onRelease = function() {
27
28      if (curFrameNum == 0) {
29          curFrameNum ++;
30      } else {
31          curFrameNum = 0;
32      }
33
34      loadFrame();
35
36  }
37  // ------------------</previous slide button>------------------ \\
```

5 Within the parentheses after the **if** statement, change the condition **curFrameNum < Number (slideInfoLV.totalFrames) − 1** to instead read **curFrameNum == 0**. Again, since the viewer is navigating backward, you need to determine whether the viewer is viewing the first image in the slideshow when clicking the **Previous Slide** button. If the viewer clicks the **Previous Slide** button, you need to tell the slideshow to jump to the *end* and display the last image (thereby, making the slideshow loop).

But before continuing writing this script, you probably want to know what's with the double equals signs (==) after **curFrameNum**. Up until this point, you've seen only a single equals sign used in an action. The single equals sign is called an *assignment operator*. As you've seen in this script, it simply *assigns* the value to the right of the equals sign to what is on the left of the equals sign. In the previous script, you wrote **curFrameNum = 0**. This action *assigns* 0 to the variable **curFrameNum**. But what if—when writing an action—you wanted to check for equality? What if you wanted to check whether the content to the left of the equals sign is *equal* to what is on the right? In the modification you just made to the **if** action in the previous step, you wrote **if (curFrameNum == 0)**. Instead of assigning a value to an expression (as a single equals sign does), this **if** action will check to see whether the value of the variable **curFrameNum** is *equal* to 0. The double equals sign is an *equality operator*. It simply tests for equality between what's on the left of the equals sign and what's on the right.

So, what should happen if the slideshow image the viewer is looking at is the first slide when clicking the only button? Simply, the slideshow should jump to the last image. That way, the slideshow will loop, even as the viewer continually clicks the Previous Slide button (just like what happens—but in reverse—when the viewer continually clicks the Next Slide button).

```
25  // ------------------<previous slide button>------------------ \\
26  this.prevSlideBtn.onRelease = function() {
27
28      if (curFrameNum == 0) {
29          curFrameNum = Number(slideInfoLV.totalFrames) - 1;
30      } else {
31          curFrameNum = 0;
32      }
33
34      loadFrame();
35
36  }
37  // ------------------</previous slide button>------------------ \\
```

6 Change the line **curFrameNum++;** to instead read as follows:

curFrameNum = Number(slideInfoLV.totalFrames) - 1;

This action reads, "Set the current frame number to be whatever the total number of frames is minus 1." The `slideInfoLV.totalFrames` should be familiar—you used it in the Next Slide button script for the same purpose (to retrieve the total number of slides in the slideshow). In this case, you're using the same variable to set the current slide number variable (**curFrameNum**) to equal the total number of slideshow frames if the user clicks the Previous Slide button while viewing the first slide in the slideshow. But just like before, you're subtracting 1 from the **totalFrames** variable to arrive at the number representing the last slide in the slideshow, 9. Since the **totalFrames** variable represents the total number of slides in the slideshow, but not the *number* in the last slide of the slideshow, you need to subtract 1 to get the correct number—9—to use in this script.

You've specified what should happen if the viewer clicks the Previous Slide button when the slideshow is already on the first image, so you need to specify what should happen when the viewer clicks the Previous Slide button when the slideshow is *not* on the first slide image. Well, simply enough, the slideshow should just go to the *preceding* image.

```
25  // -------------------<previous slide button>------------------- \\
26  this.prevSlideBtn.onRelease = function() {
27
28      if (curFrameNum == 0) {
29          curFrameNum = Number(slideInfoLV.totalFrames) - 1;
30      } else {
31          curFrameNum --;
32      }
33
34      loadFrame();
35
36  }
37  // -------------------</previous slide button>------------------- \\
```

7 Within the **else** action, change the line **curFrameNum = 0;** to instead read this:

curFrameNum--;

In the Next Slide button's script, you used the action **curFrameNum++;** to add 1 to the value of the **curFrameNum** variable. This action (as I'm sure you guessed) simply does the opposite and *subtracts* 1 from the value of the **curFrameNum** variable. The double minus signs are a *decrement operator*. The double minus signs merely subtract 1 from the expression to its left. In this case, they subtract 1 from **curFrameNum** variable.

Taken all together, this Previous Slide button's script says, "When the viewer clicks the Previous Slide button, if the current slide image is 0, tell the **MovieClipLoader** script to load and display the *last* slide in the slideshow. Otherwise, just load the previous image in the slideshow."

Congratulations! You've finished adding the slideshow functionality to the Next Slide/Previous Slide buttons! But, of course, you should test your changes to make sure everything is working as it should.

8 Save your **frames.fla** file by choosing **File > Save**. Then, publish an updated SWF file by choosing **File > Publish**.

9 Minimize (Windows) or hide (Mac) Flash 8, navigate to your **Desktop > la_eyeworks > site** folder, and double-click **master.swf** to view it in the stand-alone Flash Player 8.

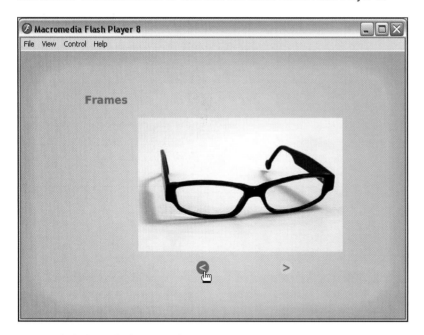

As you click through the Next Slide and Previous Slide buttons, notice how the slideshow continually loops both forward and backward. Very nice! You should give yourself a big pat on the back. You just created a slideshow that not only loops forward and backward but also dynamically loads each slide image from an external JPEG file.

---

10 When you're finished, close the stand-alone Flash Player 8 window, and bring Flash 8 to the foreground. Make sure **frames.fla** is still the foreground FLA and you have the first keyframe in the **a** layer selected with the **Actions** panel open.

---

7 | Adding the Slideshow Descriptive Text

In this exercise, you'll utilize the prebuilt **TextField.StyleSheet** object—which was included with the **frames.fla** file—to load and display the dynamic descriptive text accompanying each slide in the slideshow. With each slide (if you remember from Exercise 1) are a few lines of descriptive text that update along with the slideshow images.

1 In **frames.fla**, with the first keyframe in the **a** layer selected and the **Actions** panel open, scroll down toward the bottom of the actions.

```
39  // -----------------<pre-built code for chapter 7>---------------- \\
40  /*
41  frameNum.autoSize = "center";
42  loadedInfo.autoSize = "right";
43  // ----------------<TextField.StyleSheet>---------------- \\
44  var cssStyles:TextField.StyleSheet = new TextField.StyleSheet ();
45  cssStyles.load ("styles/styles.css");
46  cssStyles.onLoad = function (success) {
47      if (success) {
```

2 Select the following two comment lines, and delete them:

```
// ----------------<pre-built code for chapter 7>---------------- \\
/*
```

```
48          loadFrame();
49      } else {
50          loadedInfo.text = "There has been an error loading the requested information.
    Please contact the Webmaster and report your error.";
51      }
52  }
53  // ----------------</TextField.StyleSheet>---------------- \\
54  */
55  // ----------------</pre-built code for chapter 7>---------------- \\
```

3 Then select and delete the bottom two comment lines:

```
*/
// ----------------</pre-built code for chapter 7>---------------- \\
```

As mentioned earlier, the block of actions you just uncommented is pretty straightforward. The top two lines simply set the text fields **frameNum** and **loadedInfo** to allow them to resize as big as need be and to align center and align right, respectively:

```
frameNum.autoSize = "center";
loadedInfo.autoSize = "right";
```

The block of actions commented as **TextField.StyleSheet** is nearly identical to the **TextField.StyleSheet** object you authored in Chapter 5, "*Using HTML and CSS.*" This **TextField.StyleSheet** script loads the

CSS style sheet **styles.css** located in the **styles** folder, and if the loading is successful, applies those styles to the **loadedInfo** text field on the Stage, and executes the **loadFrame** function you created earlier in this chapter. If the loading of the **styles.css** file is *not* successful for one reason or another, an error message appears in the **loadedInfo** Dynamic text field.

This **TextField.StyleSheet** script is inside **frames.fla** so the descriptive text accompanying each slide can be styled using an external style sheet. That way, you (and your client) can change the styling of the descriptive text quickly and easily by modifying the **styles.css** file.

As of yet, you haven't written an action to load the descriptive slide text into the **loadedInfo** Dynamic text field. But before you start writing the action, you need to know *where* it should be located. Because the descriptive text accompanies each slide in the slideshow, it should be written alongside the action loading each JPEG file in the slideshow. Earlier in this chapter you wrote a function called **loadFrame** and placed the slide-loading action within that function. As the viewer clicks the Next Slide and Previous Slide buttons, the **loadFrame** function executes, and the next or previous slide loads. The action loading the text with each slide also appears within the **loadFrame** function, so it executes at the same time.

```
6  function loadFrame() {
7      _level0.myMCL.loadClip("frames/frames" + curFrameNum + ".jpg", this.framesMC);
8      _level0.myLV.load("frames/frames" + curFrameNum + ".txt");
9  }
```

4 Within the **loadFrame** function, click at the end of the **_level0.myMCL.loadClip("frames/frames" + curFrameNum + ".jpg", this.framesMC);** line, press **Enter** (Windows) or **Return** (Mac) once to create a line break, and type the following:

_level0.myLV.load("frames/frames" + curFrameNum + ".txt");

This action instructs the **myLV** LoadVars object—which you created in **master.fla** in Chapter 4, *"Using the LoadVars Class"*—to load the variables from the text file corresponding with the current slide number. In Exercise 3, you saw the descriptive slideshow TXT files located in the same folder as the slideshow images and with the same naming convention as the images—**frames0.txt**, **frames1.txt**, and so forth. This action simply utilizes the **curFrameNum** number to load the variables from the appropriate text file.

As you can see in the action you just wrote, it has many similarities to the action above it that loads the slideshow JPEG image. Simply, the action you just wrote says, "Tell the **myLV** LoadVars object located in **master.swf** to load the variables from a text file." Just like the **loadClip** action above it, the name of the text file to load the variables from depends on whatever number is currently in the **curFrameNum** variable. When **frames.swf** is first loaded, **curFrameNum** equals 0. This action, when first compiled, would then read **_level0.myLV.load("frames/frames0.txt");**. But every time the reader clicks the Next Slide or Previous Slide button, the **curFrameNum** number will shift one number up or down, respectively. At the same time, the **loadFrames** function—and the actions within it—will execute.

In Exercise 5, you added an action to trigger the **loadFrame** function when **frames.swf** first loads. But now the action loading the descriptive text is also within the **loadFrame** function, so you don't want it to execute right when **frames.swf** is first loaded. As mentioned in Chapter 5, *"Using HTML and CSS,"* when applying CSS styles to a text field, for the text within that field to utilize the CSS tags, the text has to load the text field *after* the styles have been applied to the same field. Simply, this means load and apply the CSS styles first, and *then* load the text. Therefore, you want the **loadFrame** function to execute only *after* the styles have finished downloading.

```
43  // -----------------<TextField.StyleSheet>--------------- \\
44  var cssStyles:TextField.StyleSheet = new TextField.StyleSheet ();
45  cssStyles.load ("styles/styles.css");
46  cssStyles.onLoad = function (success) {
47      if (success) {
48          loadedInfo.styleSheet = cssStyles;
49          loadFrame();
50      } else {
51          loadedInfo.text = "There has been an error loading the requested information.
    Please contact the Webmaster and report your error.";
52      }
53  }
54  // -----------------</TextField.StyleSheet>--------------- \\
```

Because the action triggering the **loadFrame** function has already been written in the **TextField.StyleSheet** script (see the illustration), all you need to do is delete the same **loadFrame();** action you added "in the open" in Exercise 5.

```
6   function loadFrame () {
7       _level0.myMCL.loadClip("frames/frames" + curFrameNum + ".jpg", this.framesMC);
8       _level0.myLV.load("frames/frames" + curFrameNum + ".txt");
9   }
10  loadFrame();
```

5 Scroll up in the **Actions** panel. Underneath the **loadFrame** function is the action to execute that function, **loadFrame();**. Select **loadFrame();**, and delete it.

Now the **loadFrame** function, which loads the current slide and accompanying descriptive text, will execute only after the **styles.css** file has been completely downloaded and applied to the **loadedInfo** text field, or if a Next Slide/Previous Slide button was clicked.

6 Save your **frames.fla** file by choosing **File > Save**. Then, publish an updated SWF file by choosing **File > Publish**.

7 Minimize (Windows) or hide (Mac) Flash 8, navigate to your **Desktop > la_eyeworks > site** folder, and double-click **master.swf** to open and view it in the stand-alone Flash Player 8.

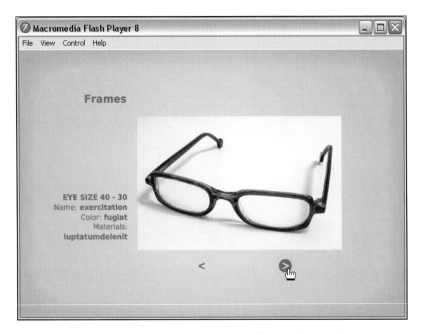

This time, when the Frames module loads, you'll see a block of styled, descriptive text next to each slide-show image. As you click the Next Slide and Previous Slide buttons, not only will the next and previous slides appear, but the descriptive text will also update accordingly!

Of course, the great feature of the descriptive text is that not only is the text all located in individual text files (for easy editing by you or the client), but the text is also *styled* using an external **styles.css** style sheet. To change the styling of the text, you can simply open the **styles.css** file, make your changes, and save the file. Keep in mind, however, the same **styles.css** file is also used in other modules. So, any changes you make to the **styles.css** file will also be incorporated into the rest of the L.A. Eyeworks Web site. If you want to modify the styling of *just* the descriptive slide text, you can create new style classes in the **styles.css** file to apply solely to the descriptive text, or you can create a separate CSS file loaded specifically for use in the slideshow.

---

8 When you're finished, close the stand-alone Flash Player 8 window, and bring Flash 8 to the foreground. Make sure **frames.fla** is still the foreground FLA file and you have the first keyframe in the **a** layer selected with the **Actions** panel open.

---

8 | Adding the Current Slide Counter

In this exercise, you'll create a counter to keep track of which slide the viewer is seeing. You will insert that number, along with a little bit of text and the total number of slides, into the **frameNum** Dynamic text field sitting between the Next Slide and Previous Slide buttons.

You need two numbers to create this counter. You need the current slide number the viewer is looking at, and you need the total number of slides. Thankfully, you already have been keeping track of those variables. The first variable you created in this chapter, **curFrameNum**, is the variable keeping track of which slide number is currently being viewed. The variable keeping track of the total number of slides is the one you imported from an external TXT file earlier in this chapter. The variable name is **totalFrames**, but because it was loaded into your project using **LoadVars**, it has to be referenced inside the **LoadVars** object. So when referring to the **totalFrames** variable, you need to write **slideInfoLV.totalFrames**.

The action you're about to create, which inserts the slide counter text into the **frameNum** text field, is an action you want to happen when any of the following occur:

- The **frames.swf** file first loads.

- The viewer clicks the Next Slide button.

- The viewer clicks the Previous Slide button.

Because the slideshow will use this action in multiple places, you should place it within a function. Then you can simply call the function whenever you need the action to execute. The function **loadFrame** you created earlier in this chapter would be a perfect place to insert the counter action you're about to create. The **loadFrame** function also gets called when **frames.swf** first loads and when the viewer clicks the Next Slide or Previous Slide button. However, because the slide counter action uses a variable located in an external TXT file (**totalFrames**), you want the action to be performed only once that variable has been completely downloaded. If you simply stuck the slide counter action wherever, then the counter text possibly would be inserted into the **frameNum** text field before the **totalFrames** variable had been completely downloaded. If that happened, the slide counter text would not display correctly.

To get the slide counter action to execute only when the **totalFrames** variable has been completely downloaded, it needs to be in a separate function. This function will then execute from an **onLoad** event handler within the **LoadVars** object. Does it sound like I'm talking gibberish again? It will become clearer as you work through the steps in this exercise.

---

1 Make sure you're in **frames.fla**, you have the first keyframe in the **a** layer selected, and you have the **Actions** panel open.

```
 6  function loadFrame() {
 7      _level0.myMCL.loadClip("frames/frames" + curFrameNum + ".jpg", this.framesMC);
 8      _level0.myLV.load("frames/frames" + curFrameNum + ".txt");
 9  }
10
11  function slideCounter() {
12
13  }
```

Click after this curly brace.

2 Click after the closed curly brace for the **loadFrame** function (circled in the illustration), press **Enter** (Windows) or **Return** (Mac) twice to create a couple of line breaks, and then create and close a new function by typing the following:

```
function slideCounter() {

}
```

Note: Don't forget to add a line break between the **function slideCounter() {** line and the closed curly brace (**}**). This gives you space where you can begin typing the next action.

```
11  function slideCounter() {
12      frameNum.text = ("frame style " + (curFrameNum + 1) + " of " + Number(slideInfoLV.totalFrames));
13  }
```

3 Click in the empty line break between the **slideCounter** function and the closed curly brace, and write the action to display the slide counter text in the **frameNum** text field by typing the following all on one line without any line breaks:

```
frameNum.text = ("frame style " + (curFrameNum + 1) + " of " + Number(slideInfoLV.totalFrames));
```

By now, you're probably saying to yourself, "What is all that…stuff?" Since there's quite a lot going on in this action—some of which you probably recognize, some of which you probably don't—here's a breakdown of the pieces of this action (from left to right):

- **frameNum.text =**: This you will recognize as the command to insert some text into a Dynamic text field with an instance name of **frameNum**. As mentioned, **frameNum** is the name of the Dynamic text field on the Stage sitting between the Next Slide and Previous Slide buttons. Everything after the equals sign is the text to be inserted into the text field.

- **"frame style "**: This tells Flash 8 you want to insert the string **"frame style"** into the text field. (Notice the space after the word *style* and before the end quote.)

- **+**: You will recognize the plus sign, used throughout this action, from previous exercises. It allows you to add (concatenate) more text after the first string, **"frame style"**.

- **(curFrameNum + 1)**: This takes the **curFrameNum** variable (whatever number it happens to be at that time; when **frames.swf** first loads, it's 0) and adds 1 to it. Why would you want to add 1 to it? If you recall, the **curFrameNum** variable, to adhere to good ActionScript practices, initially equals 0. Although it makes sense to use 0 as the starting number of the slideshow, a visitor to the L.A. Eyeworks Web site would most likely get confused if they saw the slide counter text read **frame style 0 of 9**. So to create a more logical message, you'll add 1 to the **curFrameNum** and **slideInfoLV.totalFrames** variables when they are placed into the **frameNum** text field. That way, the slide counter text will read something that makes much more sense to the viewer, **frame style 1 of 10**.

You'll also notice this is in parentheses. You've also probably noticed parentheses used throughout this action. Whenever you see a set of parentheses, it simply tells Flash 8 to execute whatever is inside the parentheses *before* executing whatever is outside the parentheses. By enclosing **curFrameNum + 1** within parentheses, you're telling Flash 8 to first get the value of the **curFrameNum** variable, add that number to 1, and then perform whatever is outside those parentheses. By using parentheses, you can control how parameters are applied to each other and can prevent other parameters from being inadvertently applied to others.

- **" of "**: This, like **"frame style "** simply instructs Flash 8 to insert the string **" of "**. (Notice the space before and after the word *of*.)

- **Number(slideInfoLV.totalFrames)**: As you saw in Exercise 5 earlier in this chapter, this simply instructs Flash 8 to retrieve the value of the loaded variable **slideInfoLV.totalFrames** and change that data type to a number.

Next, you need to instruct the function **slideCounter** to execute when the **totalFrames** variable within the **slide_info.txt** file has been completely downloaded. To do that, you can add an **onLoad** event handler to the **slideInfoLV LoadVars** object you created earlier in this chapter.

```
1  var slideInfoLV:LoadVars = new LoadVars();
2
3  slideInfoLV.onLoad = function (success) {
4  slideInfoLV.load("vars/slide_info.txt");
```

4 Click at the end of the **var slideInfoLV:LoadVars = new LoadVars();** line (at the top of the **Actions** panel), press **Enter** (Windows) or **Return** (Mac) twice to create a couple of line breaks, and type the following:

slideInfoLV.onLoad = function (success) {

This creates the **onLoad** event handler for the **slideInfoLV LoadVars** object. Next, you need to define what should occur *if* (hint, hint) the variables within **slide_info.txt** have been completely downloaded and conversely what should occur *if* there is an error accessing **slide_info.txt**.

5 Complete the **onLoad** event handler by clicking at the end of the **slideInfoLV.onLoad = function (success) {** line, pressing **Enter** (Windows) or **Return** (Mac) once to create a line break, and typing the following:

```
3  slideInfoLV.onLoad = function (success) {
4      if (success) {
5          slideCounter();
6      } else {
7          frameNum.text = "error";
8      }
9  }
```

```
if (success) {
  slideCounter();
} else {
  frameNum.text = "error";
}
}
```

As you saw in Chapter 4, *"Using the LoadVars Class,"* when you wrote the **myLV LoadVars** object in the **master.fla** Timeline, these series of actions say, "If the variables within the **slide_info.txt** file are downloaded successfully, execute the **slideCounter** function. Otherwise (**else**), insert the text *error* into the **frameNum** text field."

Learning to write ActionScript is akin to learning how to read phonetically. When learning to read, you might look at a long word such as *fantastically* and initially give up because it looks so daunting. But if you phonetically break it down, *fan-tas-tic-ally*, it will make much more sense. ActionScript can be similar—if you look at a large block of ActionScript, you might say to yourself, "Geez. There's no way I'll understand what's going on there." But if you break it down piece by piece and line by line (as I have and will continue to do throughout this book), it will become much clearer as you work through it.

Although you're not yet finished, you have enough to test the changes you've made thus far.

---

6 Save your **frames.fla** file by choosing **File > Save**. Then, publish an updated SWF file by choosing **File > Publish**.

---

7 Minimize (Windows) or hide (Mac) Flash 8, navigate to your **Desktop > la_eyeworks > site** folder, and double-click **master.swf** to open and view it in the stand-alone Flash Player 8.

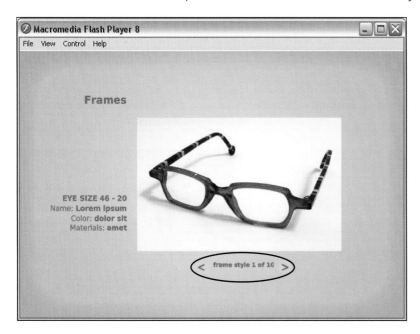

When the Frames module loads, you'll see the text **frame style 1 of 10** between the Next Slide and Previous Slide buttons. Hooray! However, you'll notice if you click either the Next Slide or Previous Slide button, the text never changes. You'll fix that next by triggering the **slideCounter** function each time the viewer clicks the slideshow navigation buttons.

---

8 When you're finished, close the stand-alone Flash Player 8 window, and bring Flash 8 to the foreground. Make sure **frames.fla** is still the foreground FLA file and you have the first keyframe in the **a** layer selected with the **Actions** panel open.

```
25  // --------------------<next slide button>-------------------- \\
26  this.nextSlideBtn.onRelease = function() {
27
28      if (curFrameNum < Number(slideInfoLV.totalFrames) - 1) {
29          curFrameNum ++;
30      } else {
31          curFrameNum = 0;
32      }
33
34      loadFrame();
35      slideCounter();
36
37  }
38  // --------------------</next slide button>-------------------- \\
```

9 Scroll down to the **Next Slide** button's script, click at the end of the `loadFrame();` line, press **Enter** (Windows) or **Return** (Mac) once to create a line break, and type the following:

`slideCounter();`

This executes the `slideCounter` function and the action within it. Within it is, of course, the action inserting the slide counter text into the **frameNum** text field. When this action executes again, it will retrieve the current values of the variables, and the **frameNum** text field on the Stage will update.

Next, you need to repeat this process for the Previous Slide button.

```
40  // --------------------<previous slide button>-------------------- \\
41  this.prevSlideBtn.onRelease = function() {
42
43      if (curFrameNum == 0) {
44          curFrameNum = Number(slideInfoLV.totalFrames) - 1;
45      } else {
46          curFrameNum --;
47      }
48
49      loadFrame();
50      slideCounter();
51
52  }
53  // --------------------</previous slide button>-------------------- \\
```

10 Scroll down to the **Previous Slide** button's script, click at the end of the `loadFrame();` line, press **Enter** (Windows) or **Return** (Mac) once to create a line break, and type the following:

`slideCounter();`

And there you have it—the `slideCounter` function now triggers when the variables within **slide_info.txt** have been completely downloaded and when the viewer clicks either the Next Slide or Previous Slide button. This will cause the **frameNum** text to update as the viewer navigates through the slideshow.

Before you start congratulating yourself, you should test your changes one last time to make sure everything is working as it should.

---

11 Save your **frames.fla** file by choosing **File > Save**.Then, publish an updated SWF file by choosing **File > Publish**.

---

12 Minimize (Windows) or hide (Mac) Flash 8, navigate to your **Desktop > la_eyeworks > site** folder, and double-click **master.swf** to open and view it in the stand-alone Flash Player 8.

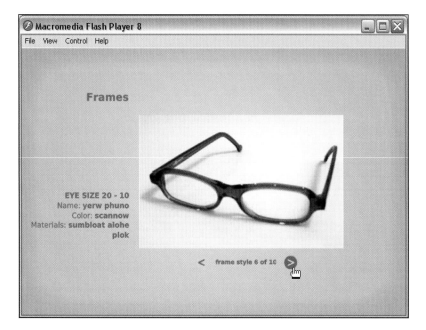

13 When the slideshow appears, click the **Next Slide** and **Previous Slide** buttons. As you do, you'll notice the text between the slideshow navigation buttons updating. Congratulations!

---

14 When you're finished, close the stand-alone Flash Player 8, bring Flash 8 to the foreground, and close **frames.fla**.

In this chapter, you learned how to create a seamlessly looping slideshow accompanied by dynamic descriptive text and a slide counter offering feedback about which slide you're currently viewing. As mentioned, one of the awesome features of this slideshow is nearly everything is dynamic and external to the Flash 8 movie. The slideshow images are external JPEG files brought in using the `myMCL MovieClipLoader` object in **master.swf**, the descriptive text comprises external TXT files loaded using the `myLV LoadVars` object (and styled with an external style sheet) also located in **master.swf**, and the slide counter text is dynamically created using variables involved in the functionality of the slideshow. By keeping the content external to the FLA file, you make it much easier for yourself or your client to update the individual pieces.

As you worked through the exercises in this chapter, I hope you were able to realize how much faster it is to create a slideshow with this level of dynamics with relatively minimal effort, thanks to the `MovieClipLoader` and `LoadVars` scripts you created—and are now repurposing for a different use—in earlier chapters.

8

Building a Preloader

In this chapter, you will learn how to build a preloader. You can construct preloaders in a variety of sizes, shapes, and designs, but their basic function remains the same. A *preloader*, essentially a graphic or small amount of text, gives the viewer feedback about the progress of whatever is currently being loaded into the Macromedia Flash 8 movie. Some preloaders display how many bytes or kilobytes have been downloaded; others just show progress bars or simply animated "loading" graphics. When the downloading asset has completely downloaded, the preloader usually disappears, and the downloaded content appears. In this chapter, you will write ActionScript to make a graphical preloader appear and function when the `MovieClipLoader` is activated to download a SWF, JPEG, PNG, or GIF asset. If you've built a preloader before, you'll be pleasantly surprised at how simple it is to create a preloader using the `MovieClipLoader` class.

1 | Previewing What You Are Building

In this exercise, you'll look at the finished L.A. Eyeworks Web site so you can see how the preloader looks and works *before* you start building it. That way, as you work through some of the abstract ActionScript concepts in this chapter, you'll have a better idea how they apply to the finished piece.

1 Open your preferred browser, and access the following URL:

www.lynda.com/flash8btb/laeyeworks/

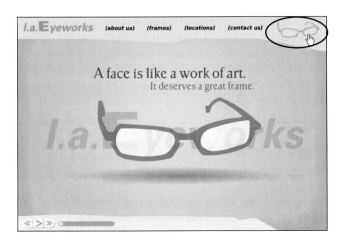

2 When the Web site finishes loading, click the **glasses** graphic at the top-right corner of the navigation bar.

This triggers a SWF file with a large JPEG image inside it to start downloading. Because the SWF file is downloading into **_level5**—the same level where the splash graphic resides—the splash graphic disappears. In its place appears a graphic of a "faded" pair of glasses. As the content is downloading, you'll see an identical graphic of glasses "wipe in" over the faded pair. Depending on the speed of your Internet connection, the downloading—and thereby the animated "reveal" of the glasses—may

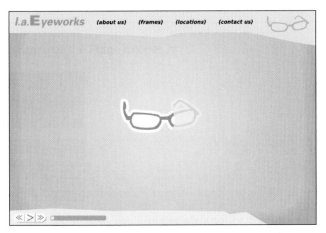

move quickly, or it may take a few minutes. As more of the SWF file downloads, you see more of the glasses. When the glasses have been completely revealed, the preloader disappears, and the downloaded SWF file appears in its place. During the course of this book, you won't add functionality to the

a layer and open the **Actions** panel, you'd notice a `stop()` action has been applied there, which means the shape-tweened animation you see in the layer beneath **a** would *not* automatically play. This animation would instead pause on the first frame. The ActionScript you will write in the next exercise will determine when and where the animation plays.

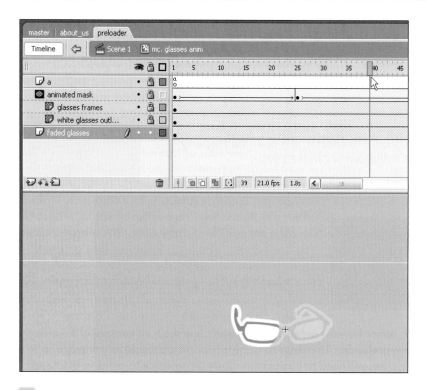

5   Drag the playhead down the **mc. glasses anim Timeline**. As you do, you'll notice a nearly identical **glasses** graphic (except this one is not faded) animate over the **faded glasses** image. This is done, as you can see in the **Timeline**, with a simple shape tween acting as a mask. As the mask animates, it reveals the glasses.

Instead of the more common linear progress bar, the L.A. Eyeworks site will use this "themed" progress bar to act as the visible side of the preloader.

6 Drag the playhead to the end of the shape-tweened mask animation. You'll notice the mask animation ends on **Frame 100**.

It ends, purposefully, on Frame 100 for the following reason: A progress bar, much like you see on your computer when you download a file from the Internet, is actually showing you the percentage of the downloaded file. Percentages, of course, go from 0 (none downloaded) to 100 (completely downloaded). In the next exercise, when you begin writing the ActionScript to create the preloader, you will—using a little math—find out what percentage of the file has been downloaded up until that point. Once you know the percentage, you can simply tell this animated preloader mask to move the playhead to the corresponding number. *Voila*! So, yes, the preloader "reveal" animation starts on Frame 1 and ends on Frame 100 for a reason: each frame of the preloader animation corresponds with a percentage downloaded of the SWF, JPEG, PNG, or GIF file.

Because you'll want the preloader to appear on top of all the other assets in the L.A. Eyeworks site (what good does the preloader do you if it appears *underneath* the slideshow, eh?), you'll need to use the `myMCL MovieClipLoader` object to load the preloader in a level above the rest of the L.A. Eyeworks content. Of course, before you can use the `MovieClipLoader` to load the preloader, you need to publish a **preloader.swf** file.

---

7 Choose **File > Publish**. This publishes a SWF file, **preloader.swf**, in the **site** folder where the rest of the L.A. Eyeworks site files are located.

---

8 Close **preloader.fla**—you won't need it again in this chapter. If you're prompted to save your changes, click **No** (Windows) or **Don't Save** (Mac).

In the next exercise, you'll write the `onLoadProgress` listener into the `MovieClipLoader` object. You will also complete the preloader by writing a few actions to control various aspects of how the preloader behaves.

---

3 | Working with onLoadProgress

In this exercise, you'll write ActionScript to make the preloader fully functional. Because the `MovieClipLoader` class has a built-in event model specifically for creating preloaders and monitoring the downloading progress of SWF, JPEG, PNG, and GIF files, it makes your job as the Flash 8 designer/developer much easier than in previous versions of Flash.

Before you can start manipulating the preloader with ActionScript, you need to use the `myMCL` `MovieClipLoader` object you created in Chapter 3, *"Getting Started,"* to load the **preloader.swf** file into a level *above* all the other loaded SWF and JPEG files.

---

1 Open **master.fla** by using the **Start Page**, by choosing **File > Open Recent**, or by navigating to your **Desktop > la_eyeworks > site** folder and then double-clicking **master.fla**.

---

2 Select the first keyframe in the **a** layer and open the **Actions** panel by pressing **F9** (Windows) or **Opt+F9** (Mac).

```
 9  // trigger the MCL to load these assets:
10  myMCL.loadClip("trigger.swf", 5);
11  myMCL.loadClip("preloader.swf", 50);
```

3 Click at the end of the `myMCL.loadClip("trigger.swf", 5);` line, press **Enter** (Windows) or **Return** (Mac) once to create a line break, and load **preloader.swf** into **Level 50** by typing the following:

`myMCL.loadClip("preloader.swf", 50);`

As you have seen, this loads **preloader.swf** into Level 50. Loading **preloader.swf** into a high level like 50 ensures it is above all the other assets and you have plenty of room underneath it to load other assets.

You've now loaded **preloader.swf** into Level 50, so you can begin to author the ActionScript to make the preloader work. To start, you'll first create the **onLoadProgress** listener.

```
 2  //---------------------<MCL>---------------------\\
 3  var myMCL:MovieClipLoader = new MovieClipLoader();
 4  var myListener:Object = new Object();
 5
 6  myMCL.addListener(myListener);
 7
 8  myListener.onLoadProgress = function() {
 9
10  }
11  //---------------------</MCL>---------------------\\
```

4 Click at the end of the **myMCL.addListener(myListener);** line, press **Enter** (Windows) or **Return** (Mac) twice to create a couple of line breaks, and create the **onLoadProgress** listener by typing the following:

```
myListener.onLoadProgress = function () {

}
```

Note: Be sure to include an extra line break between the open curly brace (**{**) and the closed curly brace (**}**). This gives you a line break within the **onLoadProgress** function where you can begin to write the pre-loader ActionScript.

If you can stretch your brain cells all the way back to Chapter 3, *"Getting Started,"* you'd remember the **onLoadProgress** listener (and the actions you create within it) executes *every time* content is downloaded using the **MovieClipLoader** class. In other words, when a SWF, JPEG, PNG, or GIF file is told to download using the **MovieClipLoader** class, every time content is written to disk the **onLoadProgress** listener—and the actions you write within it—execute.

Prior to Flash MX 2004—before **MovieClipLoader** class was introduced—building a preloader involved creating a way to continually loop through the preloader ActionScript code. Usually this involved creating some sort of ActionScript-based loop such as a **setInterval** loop or an **onClipEvent(enterFrame)** loop. However, with the introduction of the **MovieClipLoader** class, and within that the **onLoadProgress** listener, Flash 8 essentially removes the extra steps of having to write an ActionScript loop. All you have to do now is create the **onLoadProgress** listener, as you just did, and Flash 8 automatically executes the actions you place within it every time downloading content is written to disk. I can't even begin to tell you how much of a leap ahead this is from previous methods of constructing preloaders.

Now, to build a progress bar–based preloader—as you will in this chapter—you need to know two essential facts about the currently downloading SWF, JPEG, PNG, or GIF file. You need to know how many bytes have been downloaded and how many total bytes the file has. Once you know these two numbers, you can perform a little math to arrive at the *percentage* of the asset that has been downloaded up to that point. And finally, once you have the percentage, you can tell the playhead of the preloader shape-tweened animation to go to a certain frame.

In Chapter 4, *"Using the LoadVars Class,"* when you wrote the **LoadVars** script, you learned certain parameters are automatically passed from the **LoadVars** object. Specifically, you learned the **LoadVars** object sends either a **true** or **false** Boolean value for the **success** parameter, depending on whether the variables have been downloaded correctly. The **MovieClipLoader** class *also* automatically sends parameters when various events occur. Nicely enough, the **MovieClipLoader** class broadcasts **loadedBytes** and **totalBytes** parameters for the **onLoadProgress** listener to receive and utilize to build a preloader. How easy is that?

```
8    myListener.onLoadProgress = function(target_mc:MovieClip, loadedBytes:Number, totalBytes:Number) {
9
10 }
```

5 Click between the parentheses after `myListener.onLoadProgress = function` (as shown in the illustration), and enter the `onLoadProgress` function parameters by typing the following:

`target_mc:MovieClip, loadedBytes:Number, totalBytes:Number`

`loadedBytes` and `totalBytes` are, as I mentioned previously, parameters passed from the `MovieClipLoader` object. These parameters give you the loaded bytes of the currently downloading SWF, JPEG, PNG, or GIF file and the total bytes of the downloading asset, respectively. You will utilize these two parameters when writing the preloader ActionScript in the next steps. `target_mc`, another parameter passed from the `MovieClipLoader` object, gives you the name of the SWF, JPEG, PNG, or GIF asset the `MovieClipLoader` object is currently downloading. Although you won't be utilizing the `target_mc` function parameter name when constructing this preloader, you still have to enter it as a parameter of the `onLoadProgress` function, or the preloader won't work. This is because (in case you wanted to know) the SWF, JPEG, PNG, or GIF file being targeted is always the first parameter passed from the event. Without the first parameter being received by the `onLoadProgress` listener, the `loadedBytes` and `totalBytes` parameters would not be received either.

As you can also see in this step, each of the parameters has been strict typed. Since function parameters are essentially like variables, they can—and should—be strict typed as well. `target_mc` is a parameter for a movie clip, so it has been assigned a strict-type data type of `MovieClip`. `loadedBytes` and `totalBytes`, on the other hand, will be numbers, so they have been assigned the `Number` data type.

So, you now have the `onLoadProgress` listener set up correctly. The next step is to write the ActionScript to make the preloader show the progress of the currently downloading asset.

```
8    myListener.onLoadProgress = function(target_mc:MovieClip, loadedBytes:Number, totalBytes:Number) {
9        var preloadPercent:Number = Math.round((loadedBytes / totalBytes) * 100);
10 }
```

6 Click on the empty line break between the open curly brace (**{**) and the closed curly brace (**}**), as shown in the illustration, and type, all in one line with no line breaks, the following:

`var preloadPercent:Number = Math.round((loadedBytes / totalBytes) * 100);`

- The first part of this action, `var preloadPercent:Number`, should be familiar to you. You're simply creating a local variable called `preloadPercent` and strict typing it so its data type is a number. That way, you ensure the value of the variable (everything to the right of the equals sign) is a number and not another data type, such as String, which might break your script.

- `Math.round` simply rounds the value resulting from the expression in the following parentheses. In this case, `loadedBytes` is divided by `totalBytes`, and then the result is multiplied by 100. That way, if the number turns out to be 24.3, `Math.round` rounds it down to 24. If the number turns out to be 24.5, however, `Math.round` will round it *up* to 25. In other words, `Math.round` rounds the value to the nearest whole number. You need a whole number in this action because you'll use it to direct the preloader animation to the correct frame.

- **(loadedBytes / totalBytes)** merely divides **loadedBytes** and **totalBytes**. Remember, in place of these parameters, the **MovieClipLoader** object inserts the relative numbers for whatever SWF, JPEG, PNG, or GIF file it is currently downloading at the time. Because these parameters are in parentheses, they are calculated *first*, and then everything outside the parentheses executes.

- The asterisk (*) in * **100** is a multiplication operator. Just like in basic math, it multiplies the value to its left by the value to its right.

When completely executed, the number inserted in the **preloadPercent** variable is the percentage of the currently downloading SWF, JPEG, PNG, or GIF file that has been downloaded up until the time this action executes. As you can see, the math involved to calculate the percentage downloaded is fairly straightforward. You simply divide **loadedBytes** into **totalBytes** and then multiply the result by 100.

You now have the percentage of progress of the downloading SWF, JPEG, PNG, or GIF file, so you can use this number to instruct the preloader animation to go to a specific frame.

```
8   myListener.onLoadProgress = function(target_mc:MovieClip, loadedBytes:Number, totalBytes:Number) {
9       var preloadPercent:Number = Math.round((loadedBytes / totalBytes) * 100);
10      _level50.preloader.gotoAndStop(preloadPercent);
11  }
```

7 Click at the end of the `var preloadPercent:Number = Math.round((loadedBytes / totalBytes) * 100);` line, press **Enter** (Windows) or **Return** (Mac) once to create a line break, and type the following:

`_level50.preloader.gotoAndStop(preloadPercent);`

This action instructs `_level50` (the level **preloader.swf** is loaded into) to move the playhead in the **preloader** movie clip instance to the number in the **preloadPercent** variable you created in the previous step. So, in essence, whatever percentage (0 to 100) the downloading SWF, JPEG, PNG, or GIF file has completed downloading, the **preloader** movie clip in **preloader.swf** moves its playhead to the equivalent frame.

And that's the preloader! Again, if you've written a preloader before, I'm sure you're elated at how simple the construction of this preloader is.

To complete the preloader, you still need to specify when the preloader should be visible and when it shouldn't. If you don't, when an asset has been completely downloaded, the preloader will remain visible on the Stage. To hide the preloader once an asset has been fully downloaded, you will utilize another **MovieClipLoader** listener, called **onLoadComplete**.

```
 2  //-------------------<MCL>---------------------\\
 3  var myMCL:MovieClipLoader = new MovieClipLoader();
 4  var myListener:Object = new Object();
 5
 6  myMCL.addListener(myListener);
 7
 8  myListener.onLoadProgress = function(target_mc:MovieClip, loadedBytes:Number, totalBytes:Number) {
 9      var preloa⌐              ⌐Math.round((loadedBytes / totalBytes) * 100);
10      level150.p   Click after this  op(preloadPercent);
11  }              closed curly brace
12
13  myListener.onLoadComplete = function(target_mc:MovieClip) {
14      _level50._visible = false;
15  }
16  //-------------------</MCL>---------------------\\
```

8   Click after the closed curly brace of the **onLoadProgress** function, press **Enter** (Windows) or **Return** (Mac) twice to create a couple of line breaks, and then type the following:

```
myListener.onLoadComplete = function (target_mc:MovieClip) {
  _level50._visible = false;
}
```

Although you probably understand the majority of what this script is doing, you are probably not familiar with the **onLoadComplete MovieClipLoader** listener. As its name implies, the **onLoadComplete** listener executes when the downloading SWF, JPEG, PNG, or GIF file has been *completely* downloaded. Within the **onLoadComplete** function, the action **_level50._visible = false;** instructs Level 50—the level the preloader is loaded into—to turn its visibility off, which, of course, makes it invisible. So, when taken together, this script reads, "When the currently downloading SWF, JPEG, PNG, or GIF file has been *completely* downloaded, hide the preloader."

So, you've specified when the preloader should hide itself, but you need to specify when it should be visible. If you don't, once the preloader hides itself the first time, you will never see it again. That type of functionality may work well for the in-laws, but it's not a good practice to follow when constructing a preloader.

```
 8  myListener.onLoadProgress = function(target_mc:MovieClip, loadedBytes:Number, totalBytes:Number) {
 9      _level150._visible = true;
10      var preloadPercent:Number = Math.round((loadedBytes / totalBytes) * 100);
11      _level150.preloader.gotoAndStop(preloadPercent);
12  }
13
14  myListener.onLoadComplete = function(target_mc:MovieClip) {
15      _level150._visible = false;
16  }
```

9   Click at the end of the **onLoadProgress** function, **myListener.onLoadProgress = function (target_mc, loadedBytes, totalBytes) {**, press **Enter** (Windows) or **Return** (Mac) once to create a line break, and type the following:

```
_level50._visible = true;
```

Similar—but opposite—to the action you wrote in Step 8, this action instructs **preloader.swf** (loaded in Level 50) to become visible.

When the preloader ActionScript is taken all together, it reads, "Every time data is downloaded from a SWF, JPEG, PNG, or GIF file downloaded using the `MovieClipLoader` class, make the preloader visible, figure out the downloaded percentage of the asset, and move the preloader playhead to the same frame. Then, when the asset has been completely downloaded, hide the preloader."

10 Save your **master.fla** file by choosing **File > Save**.

11 Preview **master.fla** by pressing **Ctrl+Enter** (Windows) or **Cmd+Return** (Mac). When the preview window opens, show the Bandwidth Profiler by choosing **View > Bandwidth Profiler**.

To better test the preloader, you should make sure the download settings are set to a slow modem speed. That way you can better see how the preloader is working as it downloads the relatively small slideshow JPEG images.

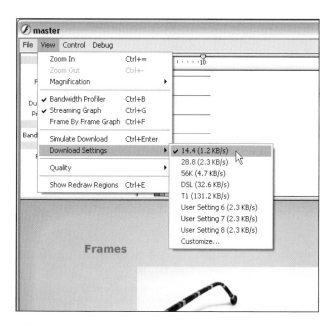

12 Choose **View > Download Settings > 14.4 (1.2 KB/s)**.

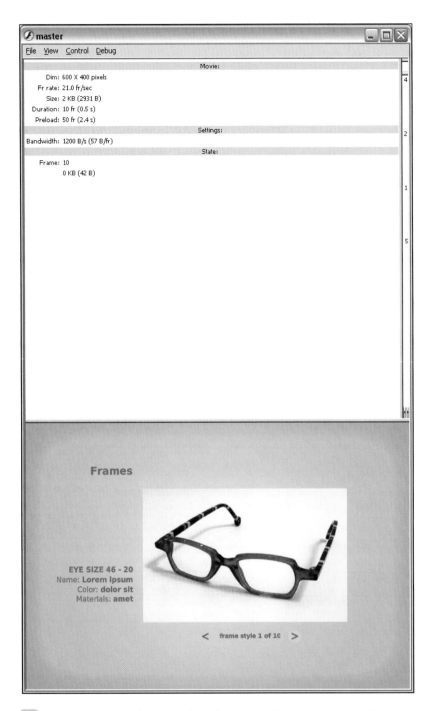

13 As you have done before, adjust the panes of your preview window—as you can see in the illustration—so you can see more information about what's being accessed and downloaded as you test your movie.

14 Test your preloader by now choosing **View > Simulate Download**. As its name implies, this tests how your movie will be downloaded by someone visiting with the modem speed you selected (a 14.4k modem).

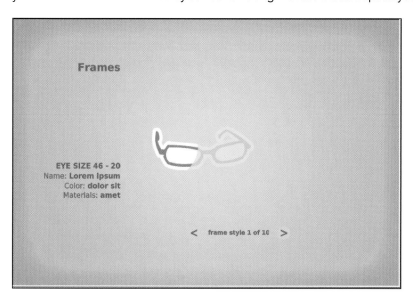

Once the shared library has been completely loaded, you will see the slideshow start to load. When it does, you will see your preloader automatically appear and show the downloading progress of the first slideshow JPEG image! Once the slide finishes downloading, the preloader graphic will automatically disappear. Additionally, each time you navigate through the slides in the slideshow by clicking the forward and backward buttons, you will see the preloader reappear to give visual feedback about the downloading progress of the preloader. How's that for only a few lines of code and a simple animation?

There you have it—a working, functional preloader! You don't need any extra actions to allow the preloader to work for all the modules in the entire L.A. Eyeworks site. Anytime any SWF, JPEG, PNG, or GIF file is downloaded using the `myMCL MovieClipLoader` object, this preloader will automatically do its thing.

VIDEO: | **detailed_preloader.mov**

To learn more about constructing a preloader to provide more feedback about the currently downloading movie, check out **detailed_preloader.mov** in the **videos** folder on the **HOT CD-ROM**. In this video, you'll learn not only how to show the downloading progress of the asset by percentage but also how to show how many kilobytes have been downloaded out of the total kilobytes.

I hope you had a nice rest in this relatively simple chapter, because you're about to jump back into ActionScript to learn how to build and script a feedback form! In the next chapter you'll learn how to use a few simple components combined with the `_global.style` declaration to create a form that allows you to use a font face, size, and color of your choosing.

Building a Form

In this chapter, you will build a form—where the visitor can leave you feedback—completely within Macromedia Flash 8. Building the form will involve using the **TextArea** and **TextInput** components and some ActionScript elbow grease. In this chapter, not only will you build the feedback form, but you will also learn what it takes to send the form results to a CGI (**C**ommon **G**ateway **I**nterface) script to be processed. (You'll learn more about what a CGI script is later in this chapter.) Although you won't actually be uploading the L.A. Eyeworks site to a remote Web server during the course of this book, I *will* address in Appendix C, *"Getting Your Work Online / Using CGIs,"* how a Flash 8–built form interfaces with a CGI script and where you can find CGI scripts online to use in conjunction with your own Web presence provider to process your Flash 8 form results.

1 | Previewing What You Are Building

Before you get started constructing the feedback form, it will help you to better understand exactly *what* you are building if you look at the final result first. In this exercise, you'll look at the finished feedback form so as you learn about some of the abstract concepts in this chapter, the form will make more sense to you because you'll already understand how the techniques fit together to create the final, working feedback form.

1 Open your preferred browser, and access the following URL:

www.lynda.com/flash8btb/laeyeworks/

2 When the Web site finishes loading, click the **contact us** button in the menu bar. This loads the **Contact Us** module, which contains a feedback form. Type something in each field in the form, and click **submit**.

After you click **submit**, you'll see some text appear on the Stage. If you read the first sentence, you'll notice your name—or whatever you typed in the **name** field—appears in the text. This is a nice way to personalize a "thank you" message like this one, and it also lets viewers know their feedback was received.

When you clicked the **submit** button, the Contact Us module—behind the scenes—nicely packaged your information and passed it to a CGI script on the remote Web server, which then arranged your comments in an email and sent it to you. Pretty slick! When you build the contact form, if you choose to connect it to your own CGI script on your Web server, you'll be able to define the email address to which the viewer's comments will be sent.

Note: If I were to check my email at this point, the email you see here would be waiting in my Inbox. The CGI script processed the form results, collected the form information, and formatted it nicely in an email for me. Nifty! If you choose to connect the feedback form to your own CGI script on your Web server, depending on the CGI script/server combination, your email might be organized differently than what you see here.

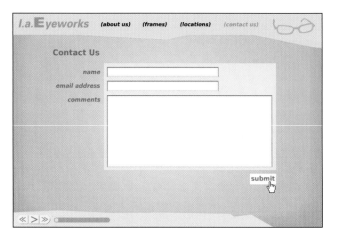

3 Return to the feedback form. (You can do this by clicking another option in the main menu and then, after that section loads, clicking the **contact us** main menu option again.) This reloads the **Contact Us** module.

4 This time, *do not* type any information in the form. Instead, just click the **submit** button.

This time you'll notice a *different* message on the Stage. This message reads, "Oops. It appears that you didn't fill the form out completely. Please go back and make sure you entered the correct information in *all* fields." Below the message is also a **< back** button, which, when clicked, will return you to the feedback form so you can type something in all the fields in the form.

In this chapter, you will write the ActionScript to create this functionality. In essence, when the viewer clicks the **submit** button, an action executes to check whether viewers typed information in *every* field. If they didn't, then upon clicking the **submit** button, they will see this error message. However, if viewers *did* type information in *every* field, then they will see the message you saw in Step 2.

All in all, this chapter is long but fairly straightforward. You'll learn how to utilize a few components to create a feed-

back form, how to create simple form validation (checking to see whether the viewer typed text in every form field), how to define tab order, and how to use a **LoadVars** object to package and send the feedback form text to a CGI script for processing. So, go splash some cold water on your face and do some jumping jacks because the following exercises cover a lot of information!

2 | Setting Up

In this exercise, you'll begin gathering all the necessary pieces to create the feedback form. Since you've already learned a few of the techniques to make the feedback form fully functional, I've included a pre-built starter file, **contact.fla**, to give you a head start. You'll start by dragging some components to the Stage to act as the fields in the form, and you'll then give unique instance names to those components—as well as a few other symbols—so you can reference them with ActionScript.

---

1 Close any other FLA files you currently have open in Flash 8.

---

2 Minimize (Windows) or hide (Mac) Flash 8. Navigate to your **Desktop > la_eyeworks > site** folder, and double-click **contact.fla**.

This is a prebuilt FLA file, complete with some assets to get you started constructing the feedback form.

First you need to import two shared fonts, Bitstream Vera Sans Bold and Bitstream Vera Sans Bold Italic.

---

3 Choose **File > Import > Open External Library**. From the resulting **Open as Library** dialog box, navigate to your **Desktop > la_eyeworks > site** folder, and double-click **sharedLib.fla**. This opens only the **sharedLib.fla Library**.

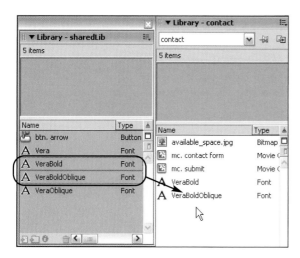

4 Position the two libraries so they're next to each other. Then in the **sharedLib Library**, select the two shared font symbols **VeraBold** and **VeraBoldOblique**, and drag them into the **contact Library** panel.

As you have seen before in this book, this imports those two shared font symbols into **contact.fla**, where you can use them without increasing the file size of the published **contact.swf** file.

---

5 Close the **sharedLib Library** panel—you won't need it again in this chapter.

Next, you will use those two shared font symbols to define the font faces of some various text blocks. Later, you will use those same font symbols when specifying the font face for the feedback form components.

6 On the **Stage** of **contact.fla** is the **Contact Us** module. Single-click it to select it.

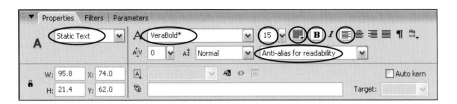

7 With the **Contact Us** text block selected, open the **Property Inspector** by pressing **Ctrl+F3** (Windows) or **Cmd+F3** (Mac). Most of the text options have been predefined for you, but you still need to set a few options. Click the **Font** pop-up menu, and from the Font list, choose **VeraBold***. This is one of the shared fonts you imported in Step 4. Then, if you're working in Windows, click the **Bold Style** button. (If you're on a Mac, *do not* click the **Bold Style** button.) Lastly, simply verify the other settings match those in the illustration shown here.

To keep the feedback form self-contained and easy to move around later, you will construct it within a movie clip.

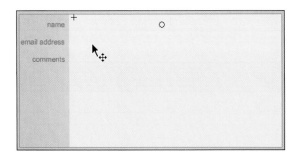

8 Single-click the light-blue box on the **Stage**. If you look at your **Property Inspector**, you'll notice it is an instance of the movie clip symbol **mc. contact form**. Along with the light-blue box, the text **name**, **email address**, and **comments**—which act as labels for the soon-to-be three components comprising the feedback form—are also nested within the **mc. contact form** movie clip.

9 Double-click the **mc. contact form** movie clip instance to open it.

Within this movie clip instance are two prebuilt layers, bg and text. The bg layer contains the light-blue background (to make it easier to see its enabled layer outline mode), and the text layer contains the text **name**, **email address**, and **comments**.

10 Select the three blocks of text: **name**, **email address**, and **comments**.

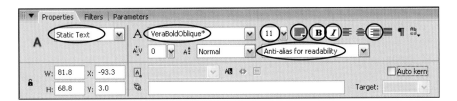

11 With the three text blocks selected, open the **Property Inspector** by pressing **Ctrl+F3** (Windows) or **Cmd+F3** (Mac). Most of the text options have been predefined for you, but you still need to set a few options. Click the **Font** pop-up menu, and from the Font list, choose **VeraBoldOblique***. This is one of the shared fonts you imported in Step 4. Then, if you're working in Windows, click the **Bold Style** and **Italic Style** buttons. (If you're on a Mac, *do not* click the **Bold Style** button or the **Italic Style** button.) Lastly, simply verify the other settings match those in the illustration shown here.

Now you just need to drag the components comprising the feedback form to the Stage and give each of them an instance name, and then you'll be ready to start writing some ActionScript to breathe interactive life into the form.

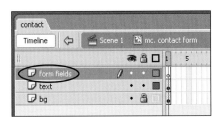

12 Create a new layer. Rename the new layer to "**form fields.**"

13 Open the **Components** panel by pressing **Ctrl+F7** (Windows) or **Cmd+F7** (Mac).

Note: The options available in the Components panel will differ depending on whether you're using Flash Basic 8 or Flash Professional 8. In both versions of Flash, however, you'll have a User Interface group.

14 Expand the **User Interface** group by clicking the **plus sign** (Windows) or **right-facing arrow** (Mac) to the left of the group. This reveals all the user interface components.

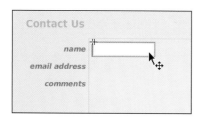

15 Drag the component **TextInput** from the **Components** panel, and place it to the right of the text block **name** but just within the yellow box (which is the vector outline of the light-blue box you saw earlier on the **Stage**).

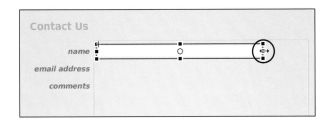

16 With the `TextInput` component on the **Stage** still selected, select the **Free Transform** tool (**Q**). Then, expand the width of the `TextInput` component by clicking the center, right-most resize handle and dragging it to the right.

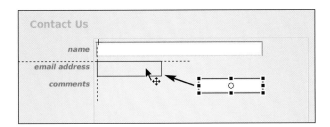

17 Drag another instance of the `TextInput` component from the **Components** panel onto the **contact.fla** file's **Stage**. Place it to the right of the text block **email address** but just underneath the `TextInput` component to the right of **name**. You can also utilize **auto-align** (shown in the illustration) to assist you with achieving precise alignment.

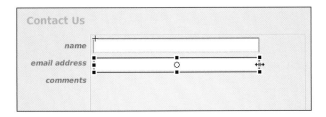

18 Using the **Free Transform** tool again, drag the center, right-most resize handle to the right until it is the same width as the `TextInput` component that's to the right of the **name** text block.

Note: If you prefer, you can use the **Info** panel—instead of the **Free Transform** tool—to make sure the components are the same size and aligned on the same x coordinates.

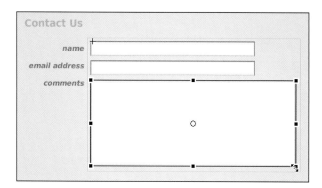

19 From the **Components** panel again, drag an instance of the `TextArea` component, placing it on the **Stage** to the right of the **comments** text block. (**Note:** Drag an instance of the `TextArea` component, *not* the `TextInput` component you utilized in the previous steps.) Then, using the **Free Transform** tool, resize the `TextArea` component so it matches what you see in the illustration.

Depending on your operating system, you may need to slightly adjust the position of the text blocks **name**, **email address**, and **comments** so they are better aligned with the components you just placed on the Stage.

The components you just dragged to the Stage will be the input fields where viewers will type their names, email addresses, and comments. But before you can continue, you need to give each component an instance name. Once each component has a unique instance name, you'll be able to target each one with ActionScript.

---

20 With the **Selection** tool selected (**V**), single-click the `TextInput` component to the right of the **name** text block.

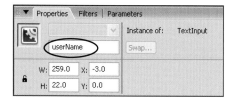

21 Open the **Property Inspector** by pressing **Ctrl+F3** (Windows) or **Cmd+F3** (Mac), and in the **Instance Name** field, type **userName**.

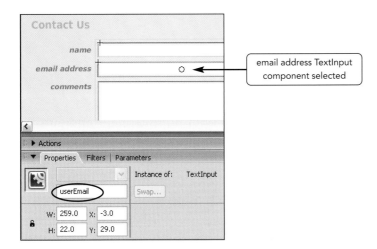

email address TextInput
component selected

22 Single-click the `TextInput` component to the right of the **email address** text block, and in the **Property Inspector**, type **userEmail** in the **Instance Name** field.

Note: By this point, you're probably wondering where these instance names come from that you're assigning to the components. Well, like variables, these instance names can be whatever you'd like. However, you still have to follow the same naming conventions when assigning instance names: no spaces, no special characters (!*&), and so forth. Later, you will write some actions to collect the information the viewer has typed into the component fields, package them, and send them to a CGI script to be processed.

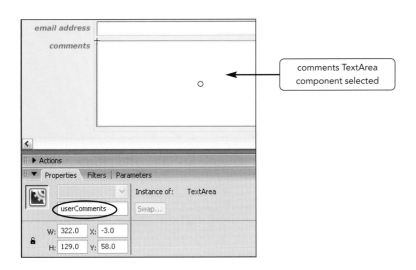

comments TextArea
component selected

23 Single-click the `TextArea` component to the right of the **comments** text block. In the **Property Inspector**, type **userComments** in the **Instance Name** field.

Great! You've given instance names to each of the form components, so you can now target each one with ActionScript. Before you start writing the ActionScript, however, you need a few more pieces in place. After viewers have typed text in the feedback form, they'll need something to click to send their comments to you.

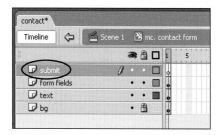

24 Create a new layer. Rename the new layer to "**submit**." This layer will contain the movie clip instance the viewer will click to submit the feedback form to a CGI script for processing.

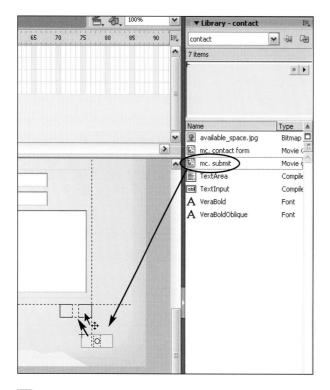

25 Open the **contact.fla Library** by pressing **Ctrl+L** (Windows) or **Cmd+L** (Mac), and drag an instance of **mc. submit** to the **Stage**. Then, reposition it so it's underneath the yellow-outlined box and their right sides are aligned.

Note: You'll notice the **mc. submit** movie clip instance you just dragged to the Stage has a Dynamic text field nested within it (represented by the dashed outline). If you were to double-click this movie clip instance, you'd also notice two frames within this symbol. On the first frame, the background rectangle is light blue, and on the second frame it's white. These two frames make up the rollover effect you will trigger later with ActionScript. The Dynamic text field within the movie clip is where you will insert text, also using ActionScript. This allows you to use this generic movie clip for a variety of uses and gives you the ability to change the text in the movie clip depending on how and where it is being used.

26 With the **mc. submit** movie clip instance still selected, open the **Property Inspector**, and type **submitBtn** in the **Instance Name** field.

mc. submit movie clip instance selected

You've created the form fields using components and have the submit button ready to go, so the last "setting up" step is to give the movie clip these elements are all nested within, **mc. contact form**, an instance name. Remember, if you want to target elements nested within a symbol using ActionScript, the parent symbol instance also needs a unique instance name.

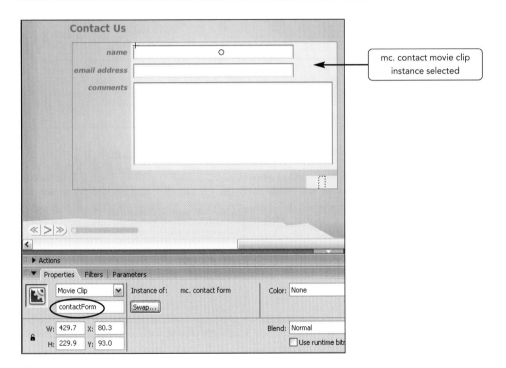

mc. contact movie clip instance selected

27 Return to the **Scene 1 Timeline** by clicking its icon above the **Timeline**. Single-click the **mc. contact form** movie clip instance. Then, open the **Property Inspector**, and type **contactForm** in the **Instance Name** field.

Now, whenever you want to use ActionScript to target, for example, the **userName** component residing in the **mc. contact form** movie clip instance, you can type (from the main, **Scene 1 Timeline**): **contactForm.userName**. Easy!

---

28 Save your **contact.fla** file by choosing **File > Save**.

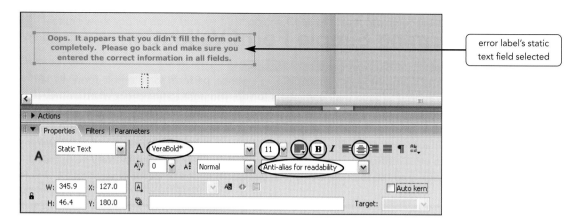

error label's static
text field selected

2 Single-click the error message's static text field on the **Stage** to select it. Then, from the **Font** pop-up menu in the **Property Inspector**, choose the shared font symbol **VeraBold***. If you're working in Windows, click the **Bold Style** button. (If you're on a Mac, you should *not* click the **Bold Style** button.) Lastly, simply verify the text options in your **Property Inspector** match those in the illustration.

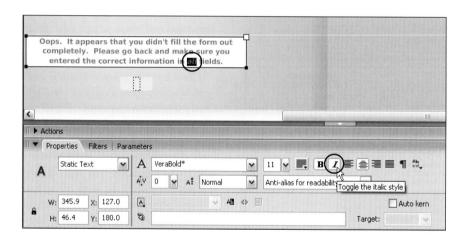

3 In the error message, make the word **all** italicized by double-clicking the text field, selecting the word **all**, and—if you're working in Windows—clicking the **Italic Style** button. If you're on a Mac, select the word **all**, and instead of clicking the **Italic Style** button, click the **Font** pop-up menu, and then choose the shared font symbol **VeraBoldOblique***.

The last "housekeeping" step before you begin to author the simple form validation script is to specify the font face for the **correct** message. You just specified the font face for the **error** label; now you need to repeat the process for the **correct** label.

4 Move the playhead so it's over the **Timeline** label **correct** on **Keyframe 20**.

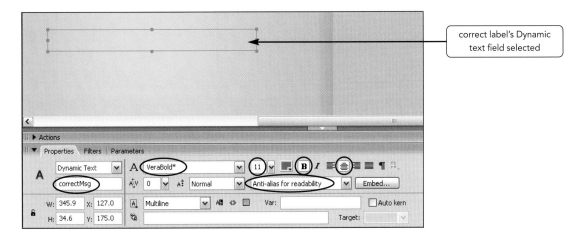

correct label's Dynamic text field selected

5 On the **Stage**, single-click the Dynamic text field to select it. Then, in the **Property Inspector**, click the **Font** pop-up menu, and choose the shared font symbol **VeraBold***. If you're currently working in Windows, click the **Bold Style** button in the **Property Inspector**. (If you're on a Mac, you *do not* need to click the **Bold Style** button.) Lastly, verify the text options in your **Property Inspector** match those in the illustration.

So, you've changed the font face of the **correctMsg** Dynamic text field, but what text is going to be displayed there?

---

6 Click **Keyframe 20** in the **a** layer, and open the **Actions** panel by pressing **F9** (Windows) or **Opt+F9** (Mac).

```
3  //-------------------<correct message AS>-------------------\\
4
5  this.correctMsg.autoSize = "center";
6  this.correctMsg.text = "Thank you for taking the time to give us your comments " + gatherForm.visitor_name + ".\n
   We look forward to seeing you in one of our stores soon!";
7
8  //-------------------</correct message AS>-------------------\\
```

You'll quickly notice some prebuilt ActionScript already exists in Keyframe 20. Like the other prebuilt ActionScripts in **contact.fla**, these actions were included because, for the most part, they are actions you've already learned. The two actions you see in Keyframe 20 instruct the **corrrectMsg** Dynamic text field on the Stage to automatically resize from the center and to insert some text within the text field.

However, you probably aren't familiar with a couple elements within the bottom-most action:

- **gatherForm.visitor_name**: At this point, you have no idea what **gatherForm.visitor_name** is. Later in this chapter, you will construct a **LoadVars** object to collect the text the viewer types in the feedback form. Once you've collected the text, you will have the option of sending it to your own CGI script to be processed. Well, **gatherForm** is the name of the **LoadVars** object. One of the variable names within the **gatherForm LoadVars** object is **visitor_name**. As you'll see later in this chapter, you will write an action to instruct Flash 8 to take whatever the viewer types in the **name** field in the feedback form and insert it into the **visitor_name** variable in the **gatherForm** object. (I'll talk about the "hows" and "whys" of doing that later in this chapter.) In the script, on Keyframe 20 in layer a, **gatherForm.visitor_name** is inserted within two strings: **Thank you for taking the time to give us your comments** and **.\n We look forward** to seeing you in one of our stores soon! If a visitor to the L.A. Eyeworks Web site were to type **Shane** in the **name** field and click **submit**, the message would read: **Thank you for taking the time to give us your comments Shane. We look forward to seeing you in one of our stores soon!**

- **\n**: The other piece you probably do not recognize is the text **\n** that's included at the beginning of the string **.\n We look forward to seeing you in one of our stores soon!** Inserting **\n** in a string of text allows you to create a line break. So instead of the two strings of text being combined with the visitor's name into one long line, the **\n** inserts a line break. The resulting text looks like this:

Thank you for taking the time to give us your comments Shane.
We look forward to seeing you in one of our stores soon!

Note: **\n** is referred to as an *escape sequence* and, as briefly mentioned, represents a new line. Escape sequences are useful, for example, if you want to insert a quotation mark within a *string* of text. If you were to just type a quotation mark within a string of text, you would get compile errors when you tried to publish your FLA file. The ActionScript compiler would interpret those quotation marks as the end or beginning of another string. Escape sequences allow you to use certain characters that cannot be represented in ActionScript otherwise. Besides **\n**, you can insert other escape sequences into strings of text. A table, listing these escape sequences, appears after this exercise for your reference.

You've now seen—and set up—the **error** and **correct** messages the viewer will see if the feedback form has been filled out incorrectly or correctly (respectively), so it's time to start writing some ActionScript. The actions you're about to write will perform some simple form validation. If the viewer has typed text in *every* form field, you'll show the viewer the **correct** message. On the other hand, if the viewer *has not* typed text in every form field, you'll show the viewer the **error** message.

---

7 To start, select the first keyframe in layer **a**, and open the **Actions** panel by pressing **F9** (Windows) or **Opt+F9** (Mac).

As you can see, Keyframe 1 has some pre-built ActionScript. Just like in previous FLA files, this ActionScript involves actions you learned earlier in this book. In this case, these actions apply to the **submit** button. Reading down the ActionScript, you'll notice it's mostly comprised of rollover and rollout actions for the **submitBtn** movie clip instance. Toward the top are two actions. One, `this.contactForm.submitBtn.btnLabel .autoSize = "center";`, allows the text field nested within the **mc.submit** movie clip to automatically resize itself from its center. The other, `this.contactForm.submitBtn`

```
1  stop();
2
3
4
5  // ---------------<pre-built code for chapter 9>---------------- \\
6  /*
7  //--------------------<submit button AS>--------------------\\
8
9  this.contactForm.submitBtn.btnLabel.autoSize = "center";
10 this.contactForm.submitBtn.btnLabel.text = "submit";
11
12 // onRollOver
13 this.contactForm.submitBtn.onRollOver = function() {
14    contactForm.submitBtn.gotoAndStop (2);
15 }
16
17 // onRollOut
18 this.contactForm.submitBtn.onRollOut = function() {
19    contactForm.submitBtn.gotoAndStop (1);
20 }
21
22 // onRelease
23 this.contactForm.submitBtn.onRelease = function() {
24
25 }
26
27 //--------------------</submit button AS>--------------------\\
28 */
29 // ---------------</pre-built code for chapter 9>--------------- \\
```

`.btnLabel.text = "submit";`, then inserts the text *submit* into that Dynamic text field. You'll also see, toward the bottom, an empty function set up for the **onRelease** behavior of the submit button. It's within the empty **onRelease** function you'll write the action to perform the simple form validation.

First you need to uncomment the provided ActionScript.

```
 5  //  ----------------<pre-built code for chapter 9>--------------  \\
 6  /*
 7  //------------------<submit button AS>--------------------\\
 8
 9  this.contactForm.submitBtn.btnLabel.autoSize = "center";
10  this.contactForm.submitBtn.btnLabel.text = "submit";
```

8 Select the top two commenting lines, as shown in the illustration, and delete them.

```
27  //--------------------</submit button AS>--------------------\\
28  */
29  //  -----------------</pre-built code for chapter 9>---------------  \\
```

9 Then, select the bottom two commenting lines, as shown in the illustration, and delete them as well.

Since you've removed these comments, the ActionScripts are ready to go.

> Click here (slightly inset) between
> the open and closed curly braces.

```
21  // onRelease
22  this.contactForm.submitBtn.onRelease = function() {
23      |   I
24  }
```

10 Click between the `this.contactForm.submitBtn.onRelease = function() {` line and the closed curly brace (}). To follow correct ActionScript formatting, click slightly inset between the two lines where a tabbed space has already been inserted for you (as shown in the illustration).

```
21  // onRelease
22  this.contactForm.submitBtn.onRelease = function() {
23      if (contactForm.userEmail.text == ""
24  }
```

11 Then, type the following:

`if (contactForm.userEmail.text == ""`

This is, of course, the beginning of an **if** statement. In essence, it reads, "If the text in the **userEmail** component (in the **contactForm** movie clip) is equal to nothing…." As you can see, after the double equals signs are two quotation marks, back to back. This symbolizes the absence of text. In other words, the viewer has *not* typed *anything* in the **userEmail** field. But remember, you need to check whether the viewer typed some information in *every* field. You need an **if** statement to essentially say, "If the viewer has *not* typed some text in the **userEmail** field, the **userName** field, *or* the **userComments** field, show the **error** message. Otherwise, show the **correct** message."

```
21  // onRelease
22  this.contactForm.submitBtn.onRelease = function() {
23      if (contactForm.userEmail.text == "" || contactForm.userName.text == "" ||
    contactForm.userComments.text == "") {
24  }
```

12 Finish the **if** statement by typing the following all on one line with no line breaks (the line break you see in the action in the illustration shown here is because the actions wrap in the **Actions** panel):

|| contactForm.userName.text == "" || contactForm.userComments.text == "") {

Note: For consistency and better readability, type a space after the action you started in Step 11 and the action you are continuing in this step.

What will strike you as new as you're typing the rest of this **if** statement are the double pipes (**||**). You can type the pipes, by the way, by pressing the **Shift+**. The double pipes—in ActionScript—are called a *logical* **OR** operator. Very simply, it means "or." So, by adding them to this **if** statement, you are now saying, "If the **userEmail** field is empty *or* if the **userName** field is empty *or* if the **userComments** field is empty…." And, obviously, the **if** statement isn't completed yet.

Now, what should happen if the **if** statement you just wrote is false? In other words, what should happen if the viewer has *not* typed text in *every* field? Yes, as you have read before in this exercise, the error message should appear.

Click after this open curly brace, and press Enter (Windows) or Return (Mac) to create a line break.

```
21  // onRelease
22  this.contactForm.submitBtn.onRelease = function() {
23      if (contactForm.userEmail.text == "" || contactForm.userName.text == "" ||
    contactForm.userComments.text == "") {
24          gotoAndStop("error");
25  }
```

13 Click after the open curly brace (circled in the illustration shown here) you finished typing at the end of Step 12, and press **Enter** (Windows) or **Return** (Mac) once to create a line break. Then, type the following:

gotoAndStop ("error");

This, of course, tells the playhead to move to the frame label **error**.

Now, you need to specify what should happen if that **if** statement is *not* true. In other words, what should happen if the viewer *did* type text in *every* field? Well, if the viewer did type text in every field, as you know, the **correct** message should appear.

```
21  // onRelease
22  this.contactForm.submitBtn.onRelease = function() {
23      if (contactForm.userEmail.text == "" || contactForm.userName.text == "" ||
    contactForm.userComments.text == "") {
24          gotoAndStop("error");
25      } else {
26          gotoAndStop("correct");
27      }
28  }
```

14 Click at the end of the **gotoAndStop ("error");** line, press **Enter** (Windows) or **Return** (Mac) once to create a line break, and type the following:

```
} else {
  gotoAndStop ("correct");
}
```

As you have seen before, this adds an **else** statement to the **if** statement. Within the **else** statement, the playhead is instructed to move to the **correct** label. Taken all together, this **if** statement reads, "If the viewer does *not* type anything in the **userEmail**, **userName**, or **userComments** fields, move the playhead to the **error** label. Otherwise, move the playhead to the **correct** label."

And there you have a simple form validation script! All it's really checking for is whether the viewer has typed *something* in *every* text field. If the viewer has, a "thank you" message appears. If not, an error message appears.

Now you just need to save your work, test the movie, cross your fingers, and make sure everything is working as you expect.

---

15 Save your **contact.fla** file by choosing **File > Save** or by pressing **Ctrl+S** (Windows) or **Cmd+S** (Mac).

---

16 Test **contact.fla** by choosing **Control > Test Movie** or pressing **Ctrl+Enter** (Windows) or **Cmd+Return** (Mac).

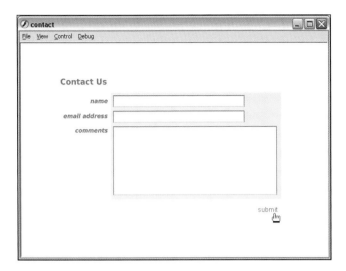

17 When the previous window appears and you see your **Contact Us** form, don't type anything in any of the fields. To test the *form validation script* (to use a fancy term for a simple **if** statement) is working correctly, just click **submit**.

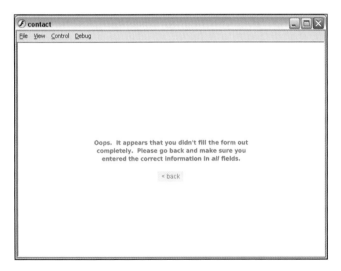

Because you didn't type text in *every* field, the **if** statement works correctly and moves the playhead to the **error** label, thereby displaying the error message. Yay!

---

18 Click **< back** to return to the **Contact Us** form (**Keyframe 1**).

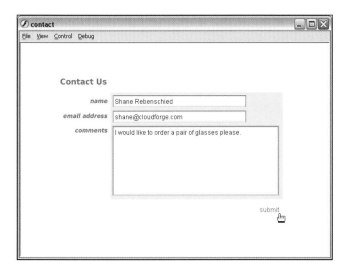

19 This time, type something in every field, and click **submit**.

Now, because you typed text in *every* field, the **if** statement is false, which causes the **else** statement within it to execute. This moves the playhead to the **correct** label, displaying the "thank you" message. If you read the "thank you" message, you'll notice in place of where your name should be (or whatever you typed in the **name** field), it instead says "undefined." Unless you actually typed **undefined** in the **name** field, you'll realize the form validation script is not actually working as intended. This is because the action used to retrieve the text typed in the **name** field references a **LoadVars** script you haven't created yet. Until then, you'll just have to take my word it will work (honest!) later in this chapter.

But, as you can see, the form validation script worked—yet again—and displayed the "thank you" message when text was typed in *all* the fields.

To be a good Flash 8 designer/developer, you should also make sure the form validation script works as intended when only one or two fields have text in them.

20 With the preview window still open, press **Ctrl+Enter** (Windows) or **Cmd+Return** (Mac) *twice*. This reloads the **contact.swf** file, and the form appears again.

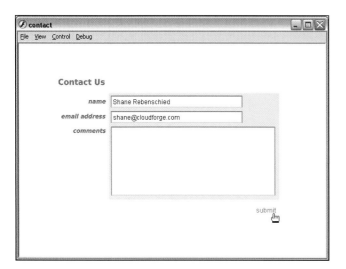

21 This time, type some text in only one or two of the fields but not all. Then, click **submit**.

You'll then see, once again, the error message.

When the viewer types something in the form and clicks the submit button, a simple **if** statement executes to make sure text has been typed in *every* field. Based on the results of the check, either an "oops" or "thank you" message will be displayed.

22 When you're finished previewing **contact.swf**, close the preview window, and return to **contact.fla**.

Congratulations! Your **Contact Us** feedback form is a raging success.

Escape Sequences	
Escape sequence	**Character**
\b	Backspace character
\f	Form-feed character
\n	Line-feed character
\r	Carriage-return character
\t	Tab character
\"	Double quotation mark
\'	Single quotation mark
\\	Backslash

VIDEO: | **tab_order.mov**

The *tab order* defines which field should be the "active" field when the viewer presses the **Tab** key. As you have seen when filling out an HTML (**H**yper**T**ext **M**arkup **L**anguage) form on a Web site, when you are typing in a form field and press the **Tab** key, the active field status will jump to another field. Well, using the **tabIndex** action, you can specify the order in which the various form fields will become active as the viewer presses the **Tab** key. To learn about how to define the tab order, and how it can be beneficial when dealing with complex form layouts, check out **tab_order.mov** in the **videos** folder on the **HOT CD-ROM**.

In this exercise, you'll build a **LoadVars** object whose job it will be to collect the text the viewer has typed in the form fields and store it. You'll also learn how Flash 8–based forms connect to CGI scripts, as well as what you'll need to modify in order to take the stored text and send it to a CGI script on your own server for processing. Initially, this process may sound somewhat daunting, but as you'll see when you start writing the ActionScript, it's actually fairly straightforward.

Before you get started, I should answer two questions possibly burning in your mind: What is a CGI script, and what does it have to do with the feedback form? The answer is actually multifaceted, and I could spend pages explaining the various aspects of CGI processing. Because this is a Flash 8 book, however, it wouldn't be prudent to ramble on about CGI scripts, middleware, and Web servers. So what follows is the condensed version.

CGI is a program residing on a Web server. A CGI script can be written in a variety of computer programming languages such as C/C++, Perl, PHP, Python, and so forth. The job of the CGI script is to act as a middleman between the Web page (in your case, the L.A. Eyeworks Contact Us form) and the Web server. The ultimate goal of the feedback form is to take what the viewer types in the form, organize it so it's easy to read (the raw output of a form is quite difficult to read by itself), and email it. Flash 8 can't perform all those tasks by itself. Flash 8 simply gathers the raw text the viewer types in the form and sends it someplace else. Flash 8 cannot organize the information in an easy-to-read format, and it can't email that content to an email address. That's where the CGI script comes in. From the Contact Us form, you'll use a **LoadVars** object to take the text the viewer types in the form, arrange it in a way to make sense to the CGI script, and then pass it to the CGI script (yes, **LoadVars** can *send* as well as *receive* variables). The CGI script will grab the text, organize it so it's easier to read by a human, and then shoot it off to the Web server with instructions to email it to an address. Because the CGI script is the middleman in this process, a CGI script is often called *middleware* (taken from the term *software*). The type of CGI script you can use depends on the type of server on which your Web site is hosted. Additionally, most Web presence providers these days offer some standard CGI scripts to process form results for you. A common one is called **FormMail**. You will learn more about locating an appropriate server and CGI scripts in Appendix C, *"Getting Your Work Online/Using CGIs"*

So, you have a little bit of an understanding of how the CGI script links to the feedback form. You're ready to start constructing a **LoadVars** script to send the form results to the CGI script for processing.

---

1 Make sure you have **contact.fla** still open, you have **Keyframe 1** in the **a** layer selected, and the **Actions** panel is open.

The first piece you need to construct is the **LoadVars** object. You've seen this a few times before, so you won't find any surprises here.

```
1  stop();
2
3  var gatherForm:LoadVars = new LoadVars();
```

2 Click between the **stop();** action at the top of the **Actions** panel and the //-------------<**submit button AS>**-------------\\ comment. Then, type the following:

var gatherForm:LoadVars = new LoadVars();

As you have seen before, this simply creates a new variable (**gatherForm**), strict types it as a **LoadVars** data type, and assigns a new **LoadVars** object to that variable.

The remaining actions—gathering the feedback results and sending them to the CGI script—need to execute only *after* the **submit** button has been clicked and *after* the simple form validation script, which you wrote in the previous exercise, has validated the form results as correct. All this means is because these next series of actions will need to execute when a specific event occurs, you'll create a function in which these actions will reside. Later, you'll trigger this function so it will execute when the form has been submitted and verified.

```
3  var gatherForm:LoadVars = new LoadVars();
4
5  function sendForm() {
```

3 Click at the end of the **var gatherForm:LoadVars = new LoadVars();** line you wrote in the previous step, press **Enter** (Windows) or **Return** (Mac) twice to create a line break, and type the following:

function sendForm() {

As you have also seen before, this simply creates a function called **sendForm**. Within this function, you will write the rest of the actions associated with preparing and sending the feedback form results to a CGI script.

```
3  var gatherForm:LoadVars = new LoadVars();
4
5  function sendForm() {
6      gatherForm.email_to = "your@email.com";
```

4 Click at the end of the **function sendForm() {** line, press **Enter** (Windows) or **Return** (Mac) once to create a line break, and type the following:

gatherForm.email_to = "your@email.com";

However, in place of **your@email.com**, type the email address where you want the form results to eventually get sent.

What this action says, in essence, is, "Create a property called **email_to** in the **gatherForm LoadVars** object. Then, assign the string **your@email.com** to the **email_to** property." As explained in Chapter 3, *"Getting Started,"* objects—like the **gatherForm LoadVars** object—consist of properties and methods. By first typing the name of the **LoadVars** object (**gatherForm**), a dot (.), and then **email_to**, you're assigning a new property called **email_to** to the **gatherForm LoadVars** object. Lastly, = **"your@email.com"** is assigning the string **your@email.com** to the **email_to** property. When this script is finished, all the properties contained within the **gatherForm** object will be sent to a CGI script to be processed. When Flash 8 sends the properties in the **gatherForm** object, they are actually sent as variables a CGI script can read and process. So, **email_to**—for example—within the FLA file is considered a property of the **gatherForm** object. But when it gets sent to the CGI script, it is sent and interpreted by the CGI script as a variable.

You know where **gatherForm** came from, but what about **email_to**? Where the heck did you get that? As mentioned previously in this chapter, a CGI script processing these form results would be expecting to receive certain variables. Some of those variables, such as **email_to**, are required. If you do not create the required variables, a CGI script will not process the form correctly. If you already have a Web presence provider and access to a form-processing CGI script, your particular CGI script will probably be expecting *different* variables. Sometimes, the CGI script programmer will insert some comments at the top of the CGI script stating which variables it needs in order to work correctly, and sometimes a CGI script you download online comes with a read-me file explaining those details. If you're having a CGI script custom-built for your needs, make sure you find out from the CGI script programmer which variables are required. That way, you'll know which properties you *must* create within the **gatherForm** object to be sent to the CGI script. Usually, the only required variable is the one defining the email address to which the form results will be emailed.

The next **gatherForm** properties you'll create are properties corresponding with the remaining fields in the feedback form.

```
3  var gatherForm:LoadVars = new LoadVars();
4
5  function sendForm() {
6      gatherForm.email_to = "your@email.com";
7      gatherForm.visitor_comments = contactForm.userComments.text;
```

5 Click at the end of the **gatherForm.email_to = "your@email.com";** line, press **Enter** (Windows) or **Return** (Mac) to create a line break, and type the following:

gatherForm.visitor_comments = contactForm.userComments.text;

Similar to the action you created in Step 4, this action creates a property called **visitor_comments** in the **gatherForm LoadVars** object. However, *unlike* in Step 4, this action takes the text in the **userComments TextInput** component in the **contactForm** movie clip symbol and inserts it into the **visitor_comments** property.

If this sounds somewhat confusing to you, here's another way to think of it: When you go to the grocery store, choose the food you need (milk, Ibuprofen, pasta, Ibuprofen, bread, Ibuprofen, and so forth), and head to the checkout clerk to pay for your items, the clerk doesn't just throw your food back into the shopping cart. The clerk—or a bagger—will take your foodstuffs, put them in bags, and then give the bags to you. That way, you can easily transport all the separate items to your car. Applying that analogy to the actions you've written in this exercise, think of the text in the feedback fields as the separate food items, the **gatherForm LoadVars** object as the grocery bag, and the CGI script as the car to get those groceries (text) home.

Now, many CGI scripts are set up so you can create as many form fields as you'd like. You just need to make sure when you're assigning the text in a particular field to a property in the **gatherForm LoadVars** object—as you just did in Step 5—that the property you're assigning the text to has a unique name. Although the behavior of some CGI scripts will differ, most CGI scripts should just take those extra variables and insert them into the email it sends.

Next you need to assign the text within the remaining two form fields to their own properties within the **gatherForm LoadVars** object.

```
3  var gatherForm:LoadVars = new LoadVars();
4
5  function sendForm() {
6      gatherForm.email_to = "your@email.com";
7      gatherForm.visitor_comments = contactForm.userComments.text;
8      gatherForm.visitor_name = contactForm.userName.text;
9      gatherForm.visitor_email = contactForm.userEmail.text;
```

6 Click at the end of the **gatherForm.visitor_comments = contactForm.userComments.text;** line, press **Enter** (Windows) or **Return** (Mac) once, and type the following:

```
gatherForm.visitor_name = contactForm.userName.text;
```

7 Then press **Enter** (Windows) or **Return** (Mac) again to create another line break, and type the following:

```
gatherForm.visitor_email = contactForm.userEmail.text;
```

And there you have it. You've now assigned the text within each of the three feedback form fields to their own unique properties within the **gatherForm LoadVars** object. Now you just need to write the action to take all the groceries out to the car…err…I mean you need to write an action to take all the properties in the **gatherForm LoadVars** object and send them to a CGI script for processing.

```
3  var gatherForm:LoadVars = new LoadVars();
4
5  function sendForm() {
6      gatherForm.email_to = "your@email.com";
7      gatherForm.visitor_comments = contactForm.userComments.text;
8      gatherForm.visitor_name = contactForm.userName.text;
9      gatherForm.visitor_email = contactForm.userEmail.text;
10
11     gatherForm.send("/cgi-sys/formmail.pl", "_blank", "POST");
```

8 Click at the end of the **gatherForm.visitor_email = contactForm.userEmail.text;** line, press **Enter** (Windows) or **Return** (Mac) twice to create a couple of line breaks, and type the following:

```
gatherForm.send("/cgi-sys/formmail.pl", "_blank", "POST");
```

This action, in essence, reads, "Send the form variables in the **gatherForm LoadVars** object to the CGI script located at **/cgi-sys/formmail.pl**. When the server responds, open its response in a new, blank window and also send the form results using the POST method." Because a few tasks are being performed in this action, here's a quick breakdown:

- **gatherForm.send()**: As outlined in Chapter 4, *"Using the LoadVars Class,"* the **LoadVars** class has a **send** method you can use to send the variables in a **LoadVars** object to a URL. **Note:** The similar **sendAndLoad** method not only sends the variables to the CGI script, but it also loads any response the CGI script generates.

- **"/cgi-sys/formmail.pl"**: This is the path on the remote server where the CGI script is located. If you're using your own CGI script on another server, the CGI script help documentation or the CGI script programmer should tell you what to type here. On most servers, CGI scripts are located in a folder named `cgi-bin`.

- **"_blank"**: Depending on the CGI script being used to process the form text, the script may send results from the server to the browser. Usually this is just a confirmation or "thank you" message to let you know the form results were received and understood successfully. In place of **_blank** (between the quotes), you can also specify a specific HTML frame name to which the results will be returned. Because the L.A. Eyeworks Web site doesn't use frames, you're using **"_blank"** to have the browser open a new, blank window to receive the server results. As mentioned a few paragraphs ago, you can also use the **sendAndLoad** method to send the form results and then load the corresponding CGI script response (if any). If you use **sendAndLoad**, instead of specifying the HTML window or frame name you want the server response sent to, you specify the ActionScript object name where the response should be sent.

- **"POST"**: This specifies how Flash 8 will format the variable/value pairs to send to a CGI script. Your two choices here are POST and GET. Most current scripts use POST.

There you have it! You just wrote the ActionScript to collect all the form text into several properties in the **gatherForm LoadVars** object and send them to a CGI script to be processed and emailed to an address of your choosing. Of course, you still need to close the **sendForm** function.

```
3   var gatherForm:LoadVars = new LoadVars();
4
5   function sendForm() {
6       gatherForm.email_to = "your@email.com";
7       gatherForm.visitor_comments = contactForm.userComments.text;
8       gatherForm.visitor_name = contactForm.userName.text;
9       gatherForm.visitor_email = contactForm.userEmail.text;
10
11      gatherForm.send("/cgi-sys/formmail.pl", "_blank", "POST");
12  }
```

9 Click at the end of the `gatherForm.send("/cgi-sys/formmail.pl", "_blank", "POST");` line, press **Enter** (Windows) or **Return** (Mac) to create a line break, then close the function by typing a closed curly brace:

```
}
```

As a last little bit of housekeeping, to better visually separate this script from the others, you should add some comments.

```
3  // ------------------<send form LoadVars>------------------ \\
4  var gatherForm:LoadVars = new LoadVars();
5
6  function sendForm() {
7      gatherForm.email_to = "your@email.com";
8      gatherForm.visitor_comments = contactForm.userComments.text;
9      gatherForm.visitor_name = contactForm.userName.text;
10     gatherForm.visitor_email = contactForm.userEmail.text;
11
12     gatherForm.send("/cgi-sys/formmail.pl", "_blank", "POST");
13 }
14 // ------------------</send form LoadVars>------------------ \\
```

10 Click at the beginning of the `var gatherForm:LoadVars = new LoadVars();` line, press **Enter** (Windows) or **Return** (Mac) once to push that action, and all others beneath it, down one line, and then click in the new empty line break you just created to type the following:

`//------------------<send form LoadVars>------------------\\`

11 Then copy that comment, click after the closed curly brace you typed in Step 9, press **Enter** (Windows) or **Return** (Mac) once to create a line break, and paste the copied comment. Slightly change the comment by adding a slash (/) before the word **send** (as shown in the illustration).

Finally, you need to specify when the **sendForm** function should execute, thereby sending the form results to a CGI script to be processed. The form results should be sent to a CGI script only when the viewer has filled out the feedback form, clicked **submit**, and the simple form validation script has verified *every* field has something in it.

```
32  // onRelease
33  this.contactForm.submitBtn.onRelease = function() {
34      if (contactForm.userEmail.text == "" || contactForm.userName.text == "" ||
    contactForm.userComments.text == "") {
35          gotoAndStop("error");
36      } else {
37          sendForm();
38          gotoAndStop("correct");
39      }
40  }
```

12 Within the `if` statement you wrote in Exercise 3 (as shown in the illustration), click at the end of the `} else {` line, press **Enter** (Windows) or **Return** (Mac) once to create a line break, and type the following:

`sendForm();`

This action, of course, executes the **sendForm** function you just wrote, thereby causing the form text to get packaged into the **gatherForm LoadVars** object and sent to a CGI script for processing. Pretty nifty, eh?

13 Save your **contact.fla** file by choosing **File > Save** or pressing **Ctrl+S** (Windows) or **Cmd+S** (Mac).

In the next exercise, you'll learn how to modify the appearance of the text viewers see when they type in the feedback form. You'll even learn how to choose a custom font for the form!

5 | Styling the Form

By now you have a *nearly* fully functional feedback form. The viewer can type information in the various fields and submit the form. If you have your own Web space and a form-processing CGI script to use, you can even slightly modify the script in the previous exercise, enabling you to send the form results to your CGI script to be processed. (Consult your Web presence provider for CGI scripts you can use and for any questions you may have about communicating with the CGI script.) However, as the viewer types text in the form fields, the form will display the text using the `TextInput` and `TextArea` component default settings. The defaults are a font family of _sans (usually displayed as Arial or Helvetica on the viewer's computer), a font size of 10, and a font color of black. In this exercise, you'll learn how to modify the default settings so you can use whichever font family, size, or color you'd like.

You have a variety of ways to modify the styling of a component. You can assign styles to individual component instances, to entire classes of a component, or even to *all* components in an entire SWF file. Because the feedback form in the L.A. Eyeworks Web site has three components—from two different component classes—it will be easier and less time-consuming to modify the styling of *all* the components in **contact.swf** with one action. You do this using the `_global.style` declaration.

For more about styling components, open the **Help** panel (**F1**), and from the Help "books" on the left, choose **Using Components > Customizing Components > Using styles to customize component color and text**.

Note: If you accidentally minimized the left side of the **Help** panel and don't know how to get it back, click the **Table of Contents** button at the top of the **Help** panel.

You'll start by specifying what font family you want to use for all the components in **contact.swf**.

```
14  // ------------------</send form LoadVars>------------------ \\
15
16  _global.style.setStyle("fontFamily", "Bitstream Vera Sans");
17
18
19  //------------------<submit button AS>--------------------\\
```
(Windows)

```
14  // ------------------</send form LoadVars>------------------ \\
15
16  _global.style.setStyle("fontFamily", "Bitstream Vera Sans Bold");
17
18
19  //------------------<submit button AS>--------------------\\
```
(Mac)

1 Click at the end of the comment //------------------</send form LoadVars>------------------\\, press **Enter** (Windows) or **Return** (Mac) twice to create a couple line breaks, and then do the following depending on your operating system:

If you're working in Windows, type the following:

```
_global.style.setStyle("fontFamily", "Bitstream Vera Sans");
```

If you're on a Mac, type the following:

```
_global.style.setStyle("fontFamily", "Bitstream Vera Sans Bold");
```

The only difference between the two operating systems is that Mac users can refer directly to Bitstream Vera Sans Bold whereas Windows users cannot. If you're working in Windows, to use the bold style of Bitstream Vera Sans, you will need to add one action. (In other words, Mac users can skip to Step 3.)

```
14  // ------------------</send form LoadVars>------------------ \\
15
16  _global.style.setStyle("fontFamily", "Bitstream Vera Sans");
17  _global.style.setStyle("fontWeight", "bold");
18
19
20  //------------------<submit button AS>--------------------\\
```

(Windows)

2 *Windows users only*: Click at the end of the `_global.style.setStyle("fontFamily", "Bitstream Vera Sans");` line, press **Enter** once to create a line break, and type this:

```
_global.style.setStyle("fontWeight", "bold");
```

`_global` is called the *global style declaration*. By using the global style declaration, as you have just done, you can easily modify the styling of *all* the components used throughout an entire SWF file. By styling all the components using the global style declaration, you can easily create a unified look and feel for all the components used in a project.

The actions (or action, if you're on a Mac) you just added instruct *all* the components in **contact.swf** to use the font Bitstream Vera Sans with bold (or the font Bitstream Vera Sans Bold, if you're on a Mac) for the text typed into them.

3 Save your **contact.fla** file by choosing **File > Save** or pressing **Ctrl+S** (Windows) or **Cmd+S** (Mac). Then preview the feedback form by choosing **Control > Test Movie** or pressing **Ctrl+Enter** (Windows) or **Cmd+Return** (Mac).

4 When the **contact.swf** preview window appears, type some text in each of the field components.

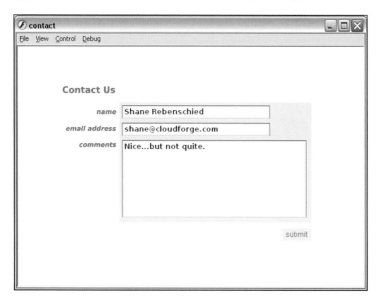

Now, you'll notice the text typed in the component fields is using the font you specified. However, if you look closely, you'll notice the text is aliased (meaning, the edges of the text is not smoothed, or *anti-aliased*). And if you were to copy **contact.swf** and **sharedLib.swf** (because **contact.swf** uses the shared fonts from the shared library) onto a computer that does *not* have the specified font installed, the text would be displayed using the default _sans font *even though you specified a shared font to use*. To have the field components use the bold Bitstream Vera Sans font (or the Bitstream Vera Sans Bold font, if they're on a Mac) even if the viewer does not have the font installed, you have to add another action to instruct Flash 8 to embed the font you've chosen for the components.

---

5 Close the preview window, and return to **contact.fla**. Then, make sure you have **Keyframe 1** in layer **a** still selected and the **Actions** panel open.

```
16  _global.style.setStyle("fontFamily", "Bitstream Vera Sans");
17  _global.style.setStyle("fontWeight", "bold");
18  _global.style.setStyle("embedFonts", true);
```
(Windows)

```
16  _global.style.setStyle("fontFamily", "Bitstream Vera Sans Bold");
17  _global.style.setStyle("embedFonts", true);
```
(Mac)

6 Click at the end of the `_global.style.setStyle("fontWeight", "bold");` line (Windows) or at the end of the `_global.style.setStyle("fontFamily", "Bitstream Vera Sans Bold");` line (Mac), press **Enter** (Windows) or **Return** (Mac) once to create a line break, and type the following:

`_global.style.setStyle("embedFonts", true);`

Some of you, upon reading the previous step, might be wondering why you have to instruct Flash 8 to embed fonts. You might be thinking, "What is the purpose of the shared fonts in the shared library if you are embedding the font outlines in **contact.swf** as well?"

You'll be happy to know, because you're using shared fonts in a shared library by writing an action to instruct Flash 8 to embed the font outlines, Flash 8 will *not* embed the font outlines a second time. Instead—because you have chosen a font you previously specified as a shared font—**contact.swf** will simply use the shared font. Setting the global style declaration of **embedFonts** to **true**—as you just did—will not only allow visitors who don't have the correct font installed on their computers to see that exact font in the component fields, but it also has the added benefit of anti-aliasing (smoothing) the text displayed in those fields.

---

7 Save your **contact.fla** file by choosing **File > Save** or pressing **Ctrl+S** (Windows) or **Cmd+S** (Mac). Then preview the feedback form by choosing **Control > Test Movie** or pressing **Ctrl+Enter** (Windows) or **Cmd+Return** (Mac).

---

8 When the **contact.swf** preview window appears, type some text in each of the field components.

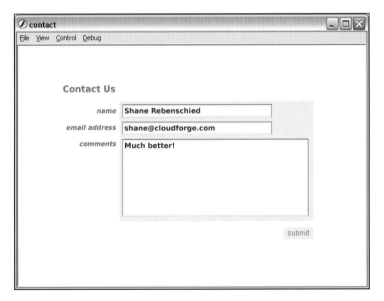

Now you'll notice when you start typing in the field components, the text appears using the font you specified (even for viewers who don't have that font installed on their computers) and is anti-aliased as well. Fantastic!

Next you'll specify the font size and font color for the text in the field components.

---

9 Close the preview window, and return to **contact.fla**. Then, make sure you have **Keyframe 1** in layer **a** still selected and the **Actions** panel open.

```
16  _global.style.setStyle("fontFamily", "Bitstream Vera Sans");
17  _global.style.setStyle("fontWeight", "bold");
18  _global.style.setStyle("embedFonts", true);
19  _global.style.setStyle("fontSize", 12);
20  _global.style.setStyle("color", 0x3F7FBE);
```

(Windows)

```
16  _global.style.setStyle("fontFamily", "Bitstream Vera Sans Bold");
17  _global.style.setStyle("embedFonts", true);
18  _global.style.setStyle("fontSize", 12);
19  _global.style.setStyle("color", 0x3F7FBE);
```

(Mac)

10 Click at the end of the `_global.style.setStyle("embedFonts", true);` line, press **Enter** (Windows) or **Return** (Mac) once to create a line break, and type the following:

`_global.style.setStyle("fontSize", 12);`

11 Then, press **Enter** (Windows) or **Return** (Mac) to again to create another line break, and type this:

`_global.style.setStyle("color", 0x3F7FBE);`

The **fontSize** style is fairly self-explanatory. It allows you to specify the size of the font displayed in the components. However, you might be a little confused about how colors are defined using the **color** style. Luckily, it's quite easy to understand. The color you specified in this step, **0x3F7FBE**, is essentially a hexadecimal number preceded by **0x**. So, when you want to choose a color to use, you can simply use the built-in Flash 8 Color Mixer panel to find the hexadecimal value of the color you want, add a **0x** to the front of it, and there's your color.

NOTE: | **Using Themes**

Flash 8 components also have built-in *themes* from which you can choose. You've probably noticed as you click in one of the component fields and press **Tab** to advance to the next field in sequence, a green "halo" appears around the outside of the field to show you it has the focus. This green halo is the default component theme called, appropriately, **haloGreen**. By using the **_global** style declaration, you can change the default theme from **haloGreen** to others such as **haloBlue** or **haloOrange**. (You have only three *default* themes to choose from.) To change a theme for all your components—to maintain a consistent appearance—you can simply type the following:

`_global.style.setStyle("themeColor", "haloBlue");`

You can even set your own halo theme color by typing this:

`_global.style.setStyle("themeColor", 0xFF0000);`

This gives you a bright red halo around all the components in a SWF file.

Before continuing, you should save and test your work.

---

12 Save your **contact.fla** file choosing **File > Save** or by pressing **Ctrl+S** (Windows) or **Cmd+S** (Mac). Then preview the feedback form by choosing **Control > Test Movie** or pressing **Ctrl+Enter** (Windows) or **Cmd+Return** (Mac).

---

13 When the **contact.swf** preview window appears, type some text in each of the field components.

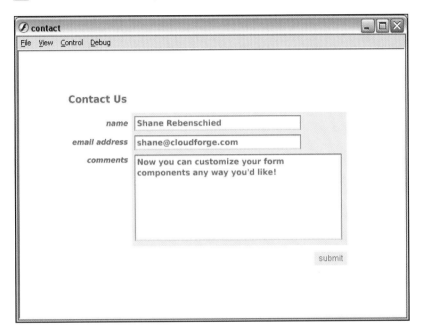

You'll immediately notice, as you start typing in the field components, that not only is the text a slightly different size, but it's now a different color. Congratulations! You've successfully used the `_global` style declaration to modify the font family, size, and color of the text within the component fields. And the font family you're using is pulled from the shared library, so you're—yet again—not increasing the file size of the finished SWF file by using a custom font face.

As the last housekeeping task to perform before you close the book (bad pun intended) on this chapter, you should specify the font face for the **submit** button.

---

14 Close the preview window, and return to **contact.fla**.

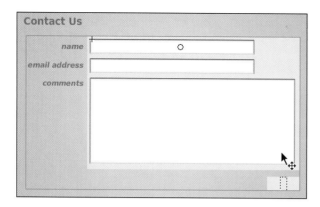

15 On the **Stage**, double-click the **contactForm** movie clip instance (the same movie clip holding the feedback form) to open it.

16 Then, double-click the **submitBtn** movie clip instance to open it.

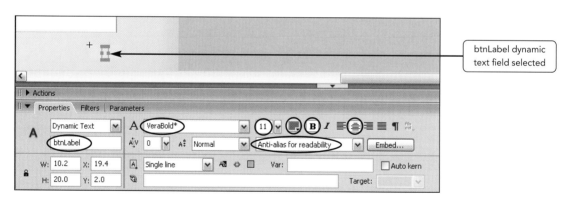

btnLabel dynamic text field selected

17 Single-click the **btnLabel** Dynamic text field to select it, and open the **Property Inspector** by pressing **Ctrl+F3** (Windows) or **Cmd+F3** (Mac). Most of the text options have been predefined for you, but you still need to set a few options. Click the **Font** pop-up menu, and choose **VeraBold***. This is one of the shared fonts you imported earlier. Then, if you're working in Windows, click the **Bold Style** button. (If you're on a Mac, *do not* click the **Bold Style** button.) Lastly, simply verify the other settings match those in the illustration.

18 Return to the **Scene 1 Timeline** by clicking its tab on the top of the **Timeline**.

---

19 Save your **contact.fla** file by choosing **File > Save** or pressing **Ctrl+S** (Windows) or **Cmd+S** (Mac). Then preview the feedback form by choosing **Control > Test Movie** or pressing **Ctrl+Enter** (Windows) or **Cmd+Return** (Mac).

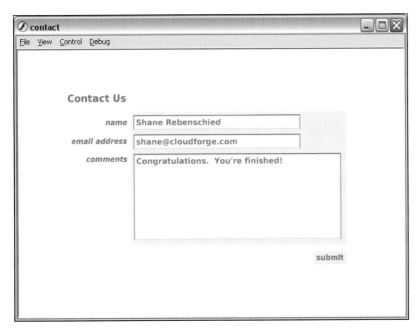

And there you have it—a nifty, functional, customized feedback form!

In the next, exciting chapter, you will learn how to use the Sound class to create an MP3 jukebox complete with a preloader, playback progress bar, and adjustable volume controls. See you there!

10

Building an MP3 Player

In this chapter, you will learn how to build a nifty, multitrack MP3 player to play MP3 files as it progressively downloads them. You'll build a small interface to allow the viewer to stop or play the MP3 file as well as skip to the next or previous track. This MP3 player will also display the artist and track name of the currently playing MP3 file using the ID3 tags built into the MP3 files themselves. (You'll learn what the ID3 tags are later in this chapter.) Lastly, you will build a slider to display the progress of the currently playing MP3 file, and you'll integrate a preloader into the progress bar. As you're probably beginning to realize, you'll be building and learning many new techniques in this chapter. If you haven't taken a break in awhile, now would probably be a good time.

1 | Previewing What You Are Building

In this exercise, you'll preview and interact with the finished MP3 player you will be building in this chapter. By first having a good understanding of what you will be building, it will help you better understand some of the more abstract ActionScript topics as you learn them.

1 Open your preferred browser, and access the following URL:

www.lynda.com/flash8btb/laeyeworks/

2 When the Web site finishes loading, click the **Play** button at the bottom left of the page. This begins downloading an MP3 music file from the Web server. You'll also notice when you click the **Play** button, it turns into a **Stop** button. This is often called a *toggle button* because it toggles back and forth between two functionalities. It's a great way of conserving screen space and is something you can see in many programs.

As soon as a small amount of the MP3 file has downloaded to your computer, you'll see two occurrences. First, you'll see a light-blue bar animate across the dark-blue bar sitting to the right of the Previous Track, Play/Stop, and Next Track buttons. This animated, light-blue bar represents how much of the MP3 file has downloaded to your computer. When the light-blue bar reaches the end of the dark-blue bar, the entire MP3 file has been downloaded. This is a preloader, much like the preloader you constructed in Chapter 8, *"Building a Preloader,"* except this preloader was constructed specifically for the MP3 player. On top of the light-blue bar is an even lighter-blue "dot," initially resting on the left side of the bar. When enough of the MP3 file has downloaded to your computer, the music automatically starts playing, and the dot starts moving. This dot represents the playback progress of the music, much like the play-head does in Flash 8, Windows Media Player, Apple QuickTime, and so forth. When the dot gets to the right side of the bar, the music track has finished playing.

Second, after a small amount of the MP3 file has downloaded to your computer, you'll see some text appear to the right of the dark-blue bar. This text states the artist name as well as the track name. As mentioned in the introduction to this chapter, the artist and track information is dynamically grabbed from ID3 tags (more on these later) from the MP3 files.

If you wait until the first track finishes downloading, you'll notice the player automatically begins downloading another—different—MP3 file. The preloader starts animating again, and once the music starts playing, the dot starts animating. The ID3 track information also updates to display information about the new track. Pretty nifty! The other way to advance to the next track, besides waiting for the current track to play all the way through, is to click the **Next Track** button. Clicking the **Previous Track** button, of course, plays the previous track in sequence.

The MP3 player streams external MP3 files dynamically in this manner because it makes it *extremely* easy to update the music. Whenever you want to add, remove, or change MP3 files, you simply make sure they're named appropriately and their ID3 tags are set correctly, drop them in the **mp3s** folder, change some variables in an external text file, and you're done.

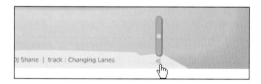

3 Lastly, click the **speaker** icon toward the bottom-right side. When you do, you'll notice a small, green slider appear above it.

If you click the light-green dot on the slider, you'll hear the volume of the music change as you drag the slider up and down. Also, you'll see a number to the right as you drag the dot representing the percentage of the volume level. As you drag the dot up and down, you'll also notice the text's alpha changes. The louder the volume, the more opaque the volume text. The quieter the volume, the more transparent the text becomes. When you release your mouse button, the percentage will disappear.

As you can see, a *lot* of functionality is crammed into the bottom portion of the L.A. Eyeworks Web site. In this chapter, you will learn how to build all this functionality using some actions you've already learned about as well as some you haven't.

What Is Progressive Downloading, and What Is Streaming?

The MP3 files the player will download from the Web server start playing *as they are downloading*. Flash 8 SWF files perform this same way. If you have a longish SWF file, when the viewer comes to your Web site to view your movie, the SWF file starts playing as soon as the first frame has been downloaded. Flash 8 downloads its content—SWF files, MP3 files, FLV (**Fl**ash **V**ideo) files, JPEG files, and so forth—using something called *progressive downloading*. As it sounds, a *progressively* down-loading file will download and play little by little from the beginning of the file to the end. Once an entire SWF, MP3, or FLV file has been downloaded to the viewer's computer, you are able to "seek" (fast-forward and rewind) through the content with no difficulties. However, if you want to seek to a point in an MP3 file—for example—that hasn't downloaded yet, you're out of luck.

An alternate way of delivering your content to Flash Player 8 is by using something called *stream-ing*, which uses RTMP (**R**eal **T**ime **M**essaging **P**rotocol). When content is *streamed* from the Web server, it is *not* saved to the viewer's com-puter hard drive, which means less memory and hard drive space is required to play the content (MP3 files, FLV files, and so forth). Also, because the content is not saved to the viewer's computer, this method is fairly *secure* as well (meaning it

would be more difficult for average computer users to take the content they just watched and use it for their own purposes). With streaming content, such as an MP3 or FLV file, for example, you can even "jump" to a portion of the content that hasn't downloaded yet; a feature a progres-sively downloading asset doesn't have. However, to truly *stream* content, you need special server software called the FCS (**F**lash **C**ommunication **S**erver). You can purchase and read more informa-tion about the FCS on Macromedia's Web site: **www.macromedia.com/software/flashcom/**.

The FCS offers a number of advantages over "tra-ditional" progressive downloading such as being able to dynamically serve different FLV files based on the viewer's Internet connection speed. If you're in charge of serving *lots* of video streams to *many* viewers, you should look into the FCS because it offers the most features and flexibility. In Appendix C, *"Getting Your Work Online/Using CGIs,"* I will list some Web presence providers offering the FCS for use.

However, because of the specialized nature and relative complexity of the FCS, this book covers accessing content using progressive download, which *does not* require any special server software or configuration.

Compressing Sound for Streaming

In the MP3 player you will be building in this chapter, the MP3 sound files will reside—external to the SWF file eventually controlling them—on the remote Web server. You will write some ActionScript to load and play one of the MP3 tracks when an event occurs. But how did the music tracks become MP3 files? How were the MP3 files compressed, and how should you com-press MP3 files to be progressively downloaded from a Web server?

You can create MP3 files using many programs. In Appendix B, *"Flash Professional 8 Resources,"* I will address the common programs you can use to convert a sound file—such as a WAV file, an AIFF file, and so forth—into an MP3 file. For now, however, if you need a good, free, cross-platform program to play and compress MP3 files, try using Apple iTunes. It's available for free at **www.apple.com/itunes/** and works on both Windows and Mac computers.

As mentioned in Chapter 2, "*Where Do I Start?*," the target audience really will be the defining factor for what level of MP3 compression you should use and even how heavily you should compress the video, as you'll see in Chapter 11, "*Building a Video Player.*" As discussed in Chapter 2, the target audience for the L.A. Eyeworks Web site is likely to have a broadband Internet connection. Therefore, you can be a little liberal with how you compress the sound files. In other words, you can sacrifice file size—to a point—in exchange for good sound fidelity. However, if most of your target audience still accesses the Internet using a slow dial-up connection, you would instead want to lower the sound quality (which means to increase the MP3 compression) in exchange for a smaller file size. In essence, the larger the file size of the MP3 file, the better the audio will sound but the longer it will take to download. Conversely, the smaller the size of the MP3 file, the worse the audio will sound but the less time it will take to download. Again, determining the target audience for the Web site (or widget) you are constructing is *crucial* to deciding what type of MP3 compression to apply to your sounds.

Without getting into the nitty-gritty details of MP3 sound compression, bit rates, sample rates, and so forth, here are three MP3 tips you should understand:

- When you have your original music file (WAV, AIFF, and so forth), make sure—in whichever sound-editing program you're using—the *sample rate* is in an increment of 11 kHz (11, 22, 44, and so forth). If you use a sample rate *not* in an increment of 11, Flash 8 will resample them when played. This might cause the MP3 file to play/behave unexpectedly. Normally, sound files have an 11 kHz incremental sample rate, so this isn't much of an issue. However, if you are integrating audio into your Flash 8 project and the audio starts sounding like it's in a different pitch, or you notice other strange anomalies, check the audio sample rate to make sure it's in an increment of 11 kHz.

- When choosing an MP3 *bit rate* to encode your sound file to, remember the bit rate corresponds to the minimum bandwidth throughput

the viewer will need to download the MP3 file at a fast enough rate so playing the sound doesn't overtake the downloading of the sound. In other words, if you encode your sound file with a bit rate of 126 kbit/sec, the viewer downloading that MP3 file will need to have an Internet connection of *at least* 12.6 k/sec or greater to download the sound as fast or faster than it is playing. As long as the viewer has a connection speed equal to or greater than the bit rate of the MP3 file, the sound will not stop or "stutter" as it is downloading. The MP3s you will be using for the L.A. Eyeworks Web site are encoded using a VBR (**v**ariable **b**it **r**ate), which means the bit rate will increase or decrease to accommodate how dynamic the sound is. Averaged out, the bit rates are approximately 103 kbit/sec, meaning the MP3 files will stream uninterrupted over a Internet connection of at least 10.3 k/sec. (The average dial-up modem speed is 5.6 k/sec. Broadband is usually *at least* ten times 10.3 k/sec.) However, Flash 8 has an action to allow you to specify how much of an MP3 file it should *buffer* (download and cache) before it begins playing the sound file. This will help to decrease the possibility of the sound playing faster than it can download, which results in the sound stopping before it reaches the end. You will learn about the action later in this chapter.

- When assigning or modifying the ID3 tags in your MP3 files, use only ID3 version 2.3 or version 2.4 tags. Version 2.2 tags *are not supported*, and ID3 version 1 tags are inserted at the *end* of the MP3 file (which means they cannot be accessed or used until the MP3 file has *completely* downloaded). ID3 version 2.3 or version 2.4 tags are stored at the *beginning* of the MP3 file and can therefore be accessed as soon as the MP3 file starts downloading. You'll learn more about ID3 tags later in this book, and Appendix B, "*Flash Professional 8 Resources,*" lists programs to view and edit MP3 ID3 tags.

Note: If you'd like to learn more about how Fraunhofer MP3 compression (the MP3 compression scheme Flash 8 supports) works, you can read about it here: **www.iis.fraunhofer.de/amm/techinf/layer3/index.html**

2 | Setting Up

In this exercise, you'll make a few modifications to the prebuilt starter **music.fla** file you'll be working with for the remainder of this chapter. Just like the previous chapters, this chapter's prebuilt FLA file includes some prebuilt elements and ActionScript to allow you to jump right into the new exercises and steps, bypassing the material you've already learned. In this exercise, you'll get a brief tour of what has been included with the provided FLA file so you have a good understanding of what you will be building on throughout the chapter.

---

1 Navigate to your **Desktop > la_eyeworks > site** folder, and double-click **music.fla** to open it in Flash 8.

2 Once the FLA file opens, look at the **Timeline**. You might need to expand the **Timeline** view a little to see all the layers.

As you can see, this FLA file has quite a lot of provided content. You'll also notice—besides the usual bg layer—two layers (volume and progress) are specified as guide layers and are locked and hidden. These layers are set like this so they will not be visible while you're working and will not be exported when you test your movie. These layers are for you to use when watching the included movies **volume_slider.mov** and **music_progress.mov**, which you'll read about later in this chapter. Until then, however, these layers are essentially disabled so they'll stay out of your way while you work on the other exercises.

---

3 Click **Keyframe 1** in layer **a**, and open the **Actions** panel by pressing **F9** (Windows) or **Opt+F9** (Mac).

```
 1
 2
 3  /*
 4  //---------------<pre-built ActionScript for Chapter 10>-------------------\\
 5
 6  //---------------<sound initialization>-------------------\\
 7  var curTrackNum:Number = 0;
 8
 9  // autosize some text fields
10  this.helpBubble.autoSize = "center";
11  this.trackInfo.autoSize = "left";
12
13  // load the track info vars
14  var myMusicLv:LoadVars = new LoadVars();
15  myMusicLv.load("vars/track_info.txt");
16
17  //---------------</sound initialization>-------------------\\
18
19  //---------------<volume control>-------------------\\
20
21  // initialize some volume control settings
```

Note: Not all the ActionScript provided with **music.fla** is pictured in the previous code. Because of the large amount of included ActionScript, it would be impractical to show it all here.

Just like a few of the previous prebuilt FLA files, you'll notice this FLA file comes with quite a lot of ActionScript already written into the first keyframe. The included actions are a testament to how much you've learned so far in this book, because the actions you see in the first keyframe are all actions you already know. If you scroll down the Actions panel, you should see lots of familiar actions. Although you probably do not immediately understand what they're all doing, you'll be pulling some of the actions from the commented area to use in various exercises throughout the remainder of this chapter.

---

4 Minimize the **Actions** panel by pressing **F9** (Windows) or **Opt+F9** (MacOS X 10.3 or later) again.

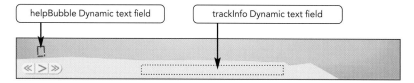

At the bottom of the Stage, you'll notice two Dynamic text fields. The small one above the Play/Stop, Next Track, and Previous Track buttons is where a small amount of descriptive text will appear when a viewer rolls the mouse over the buttons beneath it. This Dynamic text field already has an instance name of **helpBubble** applied to it. The larger Dynamic text field toward the bottom-middle of the Stage is where the MP3 ID3 tag information will appear. This field already has an instance name of **trackInfo** applied to it. As with many of the other prebuilt FLA files you've worked with in this book, in the next few steps you will import a shared font and apply it to those text fields.

---

5 Make sure you *do not* have **sharedLib.fla** open. If it is open, the next few steps will not work correctly.

6 Choose **File > Import > Open External Library**.

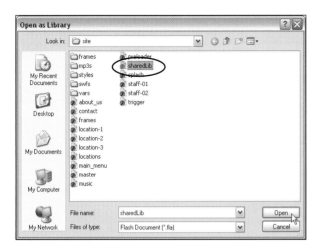

7 In the **Open as Library** dialog box, navigate to your **Desktop > la_eyeworks > site** folder, and single-click **sharedLib.fla** to select it. Click **Open** to open only the **sharedLib.fla Library**.

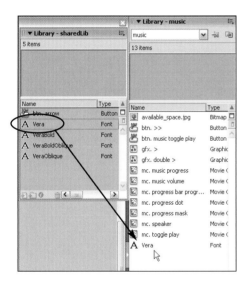

8 Open the **music.fla Library** by pressing **Ctrl+L** (Windows) or **Cmd+L** (Mac), and position the **sharedLib Library** and the **music Library** panels next to each other so you can see both simultaneously. Then, drag the shared font **Vera** from the **sharedLib Library** onto the **music Library**.

As you have done a few times in this book, you just made a link to the shared font **Bitstream Vera Sans** in **music.fla**. You don't need to drag over any other shared fonts because Vera is the only font you will use when constructing the MP3 player.

9 Close the **sharedLib Library**.

trackInfo Dynamic text field selected

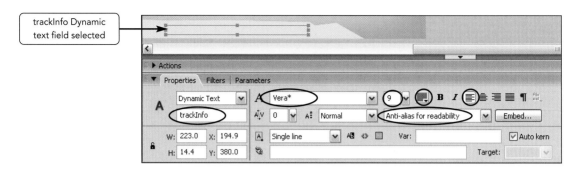

10 Next, single-click the large Dynamic text field, **trackInfo**, on the Stage. Then, in the **Property Inspector**, click the **Font** pop-up menu, and choose the shared font **Vera***. The remaining options have already been set for you, but quickly double-check your **Property Inspector** matches the one in the illustration here.

helpBubble Dynamic text field selected

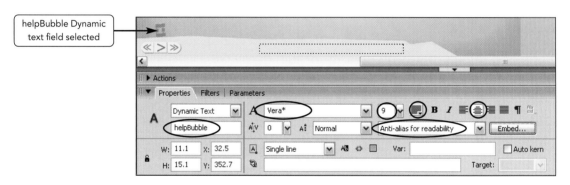

11 Repeat Step 10, but this time make sure you have the small, bottom-left Dynamic text field (**helpBubble**) selected first. Once again, verify the settings you see in the **Property Inspector** match those in the illustration here.

That's it! The symbols you see on the Stage—and even those on the locked and hidden guide layers—already have instance names applied to them to save you time and energy. Don't worry—you'll be using your saved energy later in this chapter as you write the ActionScript to construct this über cool MP3 player.

In the next exercise, you will write the ActionScript to dynamically load and play the first MP3 file.

3 | Loading the MP3 File

In this exercise, you'll write the ActionScript to load and play the first external MP3 file. As you work through the steps in this exercise, you'll see many similarities between how you write and construct this ActionScript and how you've authored some previous actions. In the following exercises in this chapter, you will learn how to give the viewer the ability to change the currently playing MP3 track, stop or play the music, observe the download and playing progress of an MP3 file, and change the volume of the music. This is simply the first—but critical—step in building the entire, fully functional MP3 player.

1 Minimize (Windows) or hide (Mac) Flash 8, and navigate to your **Desktop > la_eyeworks > site** folder.

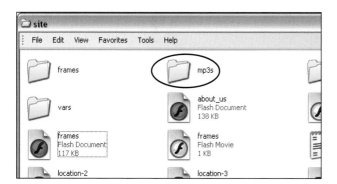

2 In the **site** folder you'll see—among other items—a folder called **mp3s**. Double-click **mp3s** to open it.

In the **mp3s** folder, you'll see two MP3s, **mp3-0.mp3** and **mp3-1.mp3**, which are the two MP3 tracks you will be loading and controlling in this chapter. Since you now know what they're named and where they're located in relation to the rest of your site files, you can write the ActionScript to load and manipulate them using the **Sound** object.

3 Close the **mp3s** folder, and return to Flash 8. Make sure **music.fla** is still the foreground FLA file.

4 Select **Keyframe 1** in the **a** layer, and open the **Actions** panel by pressing **F9** (Windows) or **Opt+F9** (Mac).

The first step is to create a **Sound** object to handle the music you will load and later control. The **Sound** object, as you will see, is similar in construction to the `MovieClipLoader` and `LoadVars` scripts you built in previous chapters.

```
1  //----------------<sound setup>-----------------\\
2  var bgMusak:Sound = new Sound();
3  //----------------</sound setup>-----------------\\
4
5  /*
6  //----------------<pre-built ActionScript for Chapter 10>-----------------\\
7
8  //----------------<sound initialization>-----------------\\
9  var curTrackNum:Number = 0;
```

5 Click the empty line break—already provided for you—at the top of the **Actions** panel above the prebuilt actions. Then, create a new **Sound** object by typing the following:

```
//----------------<sound setup>----------------\\
var bgMusak:Sound = new Sound();
//----------------</sound setup>----------------\\
```

As you have already seen with the `MovieClipLoader` and `LoadVars` objects, the action you just wrote simply creates a new **Sound** object named **bgMusak** under a commented line.

Much like the slideshow you constructed in Chapter 7, *"Building a Slideshow,"* the viewer will be able to advance forward and backward through the available MP3 tracks. However, where the slideshow had ten images, the MP3 player in this chapter uses only two tracks. As you'll see as you write the ActionScript for the MP3 player, it's easy to add or remove MP3 tracks later. Because the MP3 player allows the viewer to switch between tracks, you need to create a variable to keep track of which MP3 track is currently playing, just like you did with the **curFrameNum** variable you created for the slideshow.

Create two empty line breaks above the sound setup comment, and then click here.

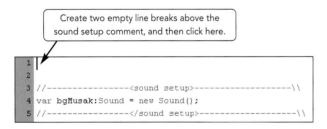

```
1  |
2
3  //----------------<sound setup>-----------------\\
4  var bgMusak:Sound = new Sound();
5  //----------------</sound setup>-----------------\\
```

6 Click at the beginning of the `//----------------<sound setup>----------------\\` comment line, and press **Enter** (Windows) or **Return** (Mac) twice to push all the actions in **Keyframe 1** down two lines. Then, click at the new, empty line at the top of the **Actions** panel.

```
 1  |
 2    ↖
 3  //----------------<sound setup>------------------\\
 4  var bgMusak:Sound = new Sound();
 5  //----------------</sound setup>------------------\\
 6
 7  /*
 8  //--------------<pre-built ActionScript for Chapter 10>------------------\\
 9
10  //----------------<sound initialization>------------------\\
11  var curTrackNum:Number = 0;
```

7 Select the following two lines of actions:

```
//----------------<sound initialization>----------------\\
var curTrackNum:Number = 0;
```

Drag them to the top-most empty line break you created in Step 6. This removes the action and comment line from the commented-out prebuilt actions included with the FLA file, thereby making them "active."

Although the comment line is self-explanatory, you probably want to know what the **var curTrackNum:Number = 0;** action does. Again, just like you used the variable **curFrameNum** in the slideshow FLA file to keep track of the current slide number, you will use the **curTrackNum** variable to keep track of the currently playing MP3. Because you will script the capability of the MP3 player to change tracks, you need to be able to keep track of *which* track is currently playing. Later, you will use the number within the **curTrackNum** variable (**0**) to specify which MP3 track should load.

```
 1  //----------------<sound initialization>------------------\\
 2  var curTrackNum:Number = 0;
 3
 4  //----------------<sound setup>------------------\\
 5  var bgMusak:Sound = new Sound();
 6  bgMusak.loadSound("mp3s/mp3-" + curTrackNum + ".mp3", true);
 7  //----------------</sound setup>------------------\\
```

8 Click at the end of the **var bgMusak:Sound = new Sound();** line, press **Enter** (Windows) or **Return** (Mac) once to create a line break, and type the following:

bgMusak.loadSound("mp3s/mp3-" + curTrackNum + ".mp3", true);

Although you may initially be somewhat confused as to what this action is doing, keep in mind this action is similar to the one you set up in Chapter 7, *"Building a Slideshow,"* to load a JPEG file into the slideshow. The action you just wrote loads an MP3 file using the **Sound** object **loadSound** event handler. The name of the MP3 it loads starts with the string **"mp3s/mp3-"** (because the MP3 name starts with **mp3-** and is in the **mp3s** folder in your **Desktop > la_eyeworks > site** folder). After that string, the script takes the number in the **curTrackNum** variable (**0**), sticks it onto the **"mp3s/mp3-"** string before it and the **".mp3"** string after it. The final result of the action is **mp3s/mp3-0.mp3**. This is, of course, the path to—and the name of—the first MP3 file that will load and play.

You'll also notice this action has **true** written into it. This Boolean value specifies whether the loading MP3 should be considered a *streaming* sound (**true**) or not (**false**). A streaming sound, as this MP3 player uses, will start playing as soon as enough of the sound has been downloaded and will continue playing as the remainder of it downloads. A nonstreaming sound is considered to be an *Event sound* and will *not* begin playing until the *entire* sound has been downloaded to the viewer's computer.

Since you have now written enough ActionScript to create a wee bit of functionality, you can test your movie!

---

9 Save your **music.fla** file by choosing **File > Save**.

---

10 Test your movie by choosing **Control > Test Movie** or pressing **Ctrl+Enter** (Windows) or **Cmd+Return** (Mac).

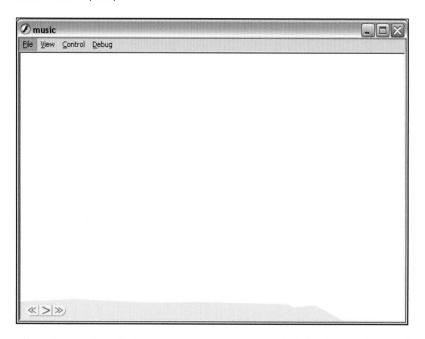

When the preview window opens, you won't see a whole lot, but you'll hear the first MP3 file (**mp3-0.mp3**) immediately start playing. When the track finishes playing, it will stop. In Exercise 5 in this chapter, you will write a script to automatically instruct the MP3 player to load and play the next MP3 file in sequence when the current MP3 file finishes playing. Congratulations! You just loaded and streamed an external MP3 file.

Lastly, you should write a small script to show the viewer an error message if an error occurs when loading an MP3 file.

---

11 Close the **music.swf** preview window, and return to **music.fla**. Make sure you have **Keyframe 1** selected in layer **a**, and make sure the **Actions** panel is open.

Insert a line break here.

```
4  //----------------<sound setup>------------------\\
5  var bgMusak:Sound = new Sound();
6
7  bgMusak.loadSound("mp3s/mp3-" + curTrackNum + ".mp3", true);
8  //----------------</sound setup>------------------\\
```

12 Click at the end of the action **var bgMusak:Sound = new Sound();**, and press **Enter** (Windows) or **Return** (Mac) to create a line break. This is where you will write a script to insert an error message into the **trackInfo** Dynamic text field if an error occurs when attempting to load an MP3 file.

```
59  //----------------</volume control>----------------\\
60
61  bgMusak.onLoad = function(success) {
62      if (!success) {
63          trackInfo.text = "Failed to load track.";
64      }
65  }
66
67  //----------------<next track>----------------\\
```

Undo
Redo
Cut
Copy
Paste
Delete

13 Scroll a little over halfway down the **Actions** panel until you get to the script you see selected in the illustration here. The script resides between the **//----------------</volume control>----------------** comment and the **//----------------<next track>----------------** comment. Select the script, and cut it from the **Actions** panel by **right-clicking** (Windows) or **Ctrl+clicking** (Mac) anywhere on the selected script and choosing **Cut** from the resulting contextual menu.

```
4   //----------------<sound setup>------------------\\
5   var bgMusak:Sound = new Sound();
6
7   b                              3-" + curTrackNum + ".mp3", true);
8   /                             setup>------------------\\
9   /
10  /
11  /                            lt ActionScript for Chapter 10>----
12  /
13
```

Undo
Redo
Cut
Copy
Paste
Delete
Select All

14 Scroll to the top of the **Actions** panel, and **right-click** (Windows) or **Ctrl+click** (Mac) in the empty line break you created in Step 12. From the resulting contextual menu, choose **Paste**. This pastes the script—which you cut in Step 13—so it comes immediately after the **var bgMusak:Sound = new Sound();** action.

It's important this pasted script comes before the **bgMusak.loadSound("mp3s/mp3-" + curTrackNum + ".mp3", true);** action. In this case, the error message won't display unless the **bgMusak.onLoad** action comes *before* the **bgMusak.loadSound** action.

The **bgMusak.onLoad** script you just cut and pasted was included for you in the provided **music.fla** file because it is nearly identical to—and has the same functionality—as the **myLV.onLoad** script you wrote in Chapter 4, *"Using the LoadVars Class."* Where the **myLV.onLoad** script showed an error message to the viewer if the variables could not be loaded from an external text file, the **bgMusak.onLoad** script shows the viewer an error message if an external MP3 cannot be loaded. The **bgMusak.onLoad** script essentially reads, "When the MP3 file loads, if it was not successful (**!success**) in its loading, insert the text *Failed to load track.* in the **trackInfo** Dynamic text field on the Stage."

Of course, you would be a slack Flash developer if you didn't now test the error handling to make sure it works correctly.

15 Minimize (Windows) or hide (Mac) Flash 8, and navigate to your **Desktop > la_eyeworks > site** folder. Then, rename the **mp3s** folder to "**mp3**." (You're just temporarily removing the *s* at the end to test your script.)

16 Then, return to Flash 8, and make sure **music.fla** is still your foreground FLA file.

17 Save your **music.fla** file by choosing **File > Save** or pressing **Ctrl+S** (Windows) or **Cmd+S** (Mac).

18 Test your movie by choosing **Control > Test Movie** or pressing **Ctrl+Enter** (Windows) or **Cmd+Return** (Mac).

When **music.swf** opens in the preview window, not only will you see the output window open with an error message (close the output window when it opens), but you'll also see the error message **Failed to load track.** in the **trackInfo** text field on the MP3 player bar at the bottom of the Stage. Who would've thought you'd be happy to see an error message, eh?

You now know the MP3 file loads and plays correctly, and you know the error message appears if a problem occurs when loading the MP3 file, so you can rename the **mp3** folder back to its *correct* name of **mp3s**.

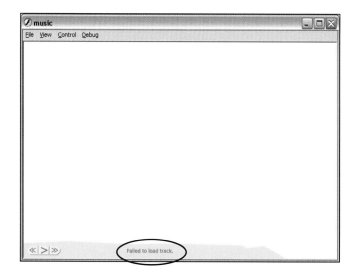

19 Close the preview window, and minimize (Windows) or hide (Mac) Flash 8.

20 Navigate to your **Desktop > la_eyeworks > site** folder, and rename the folder **mp3** to its correct name, **mp3s**.

21 Return to Flash 8, and make sure **music.fla** is the foreground FLA file.

Give yourself a big pat on the back (and maybe a stiff drink) because you just completed the loading, streaming, playing, and error handling of the first MP3 file.

In the next exercise, you will learn how to play and stop the music.

What Is the Sound Class?

The **LoadVars** class loads and sends variables, the **MovieClipLoader** class loads SWF, JPEG, PNG, and GIF files, and now you have the **Sound** class, which loads sounds. The **Sound** class can load sounds external to the SWF file by using the **Sound.loadSound()** method—which you just learned about in the previous exercise—and it can even control a sound file (with linkage turned on) in an FLA file's library using the **Sound.attachSound()** method. By using the **Sound** class, you can do the following:

- Dynamically load sounds external to the SWF file

- Monitor the downloading progress of an external sound file

- Change the volume and pan of a sound

- Start and stop a sound

- Read the ID3 tags of an MP3 file

The **Sound** class can work with the AIFF, WAV, and MP3 file formats. For the most part, however, you'll probably be working mostly with MP3 sound files because they offer a smaller file size with comparable quality. **Note:** The smaller the file size of the media you're working with, the less RAM (**R**andom **A**ccess **M**emory) is consumed on both the author's and viewer's computer.

For your reference, the following table lists the **Sound** class methods, properties, and event handlers. To read more about the **Sound** class, open the **Help** panel (**F1**), and from the Help "books" on the left, choose **ActionScript 2.0 Language Reference > ActionScript classes > Sound**. As you work through the exercises in this chapter, you'll get to use some of these when constructing the L.A. Eyeworks MP3 player.

Methods, Properties, and Event Handlers of the Sound Class

Methods

Method	Description
`attachSound()`	Allows you to specify the linkage name of a sound in the library you want to attach to a **Sound** object.
`getBytesLoaded()`	Returns the number of bytes downloaded up to that point from the currently loading sound.
`getBytesTotal()`	Returns the total number of bytes of the sound currently being downloaded.
`getPan()`	When the sound pan is set using **setPan()**, the **getPan()** method returns the last value set using **setPan()**.
`getTransform()`	Similar to **getPan()**, except **getTransform()** returns the last value set using **setTransform()**.
`getVolume()`	Similar to **getPan()** and **getTransform()**, except **getVolume()** returns the last value set using **setVolume()**.
`loadSound()`	Allows you to load an external MP3 file. The **loadSound()** method allows you to specify the path to the MP3 file you want to load as well as whether it should play while downloading (a streaming sound) or not (an Event sound).
`setPan()`	Allows you to specify the pan (left and right balance) of a sound attached or loaded into a **Sound** object.
`setTransform()`	Somewhat of a combination between **setPan()** and **setVolume()**, the **setTransform()** method not only allows you to simultaneously manipulate the panning *and* volume of a playing sound but also the level of the sound in each ear. This allows you to achieve some fairly complex panning and volume effects with your sounds.
`setVolume()`	Allows you to specify the volume of a sound attached or loaded into a **Sound** object.
`start()`	Allows you to start playing a sound. The **start()** method also allows you to specify a few parameters such as how many seconds into the sound it should start playing, as well how many times you want the sound to loop.
`stop()`	If you just use the **stop()** method with no parameters, all sounds will stop playing. But you can also specify the linkage ID name like so: **stop("myLinkedSymbol")**, which stops the playback of a single sound.

continues on next page

Methods, Properties, and Event Handlers of the Sound Class *(continued)*

Properties

Property	Description
duration	Returns the duration of a sound in milliseconds. **Warning:** If you use the **duration** property to find out the duration of a linked sound, it returns the actual duration of the sound. However, if you use the **duration** property to find out the duration of a sound currently being streamed, it returns only the duration of the sound that has been downloaded *up to that point.*
id3	Allows you to access the ID3 tag information of an MP3 file. You will learn more about this property in Exercise 4.
position	Returns the number of milliseconds a sound has been playing. You can use this property in conjunction with the **duration** property to create a playback progress bar.

Event Handlers

Event Handler	Description
onID3	Each time new ID3 tag information is available, this event handler (and any actions you place within it) executes. This is useful for triggering the population of a text field with MP3 ID3 tag information.
onLoad	Executes when a sound loads. You used this in the previous exercise to display an error message if the MP3 is unable to load correctly.
onSoundComplete	Executes when the MP3 has stopped playing. You will use this event handler in Exercise 6 to tell Flash Player 8 to automatically load the next MP3 track in sequence when the currently playing MP3 reaches the end. Similar to the **LoadVars** and **MovieClipLoader** classes, the **Sound** class offers a variety of ways to load, monitor, and control sounds. You'll be using a few of these methods, properties, and event handlers throughout this chapter.

4 | Stopping and Playing the Music

Nothing is more irritating than when you visit a Flash 8–based Web site, some music starts playing, and you can't turn it off. This shameful act doesn't seem to occur as much as it did two to four years ago, but every once and awhile I stumble across a Web site where the forgetful designer declined to give the viewer a way to turn off the looping bit of music. In this exercise, you will show pity on poor Internet surfers and build a way for them to turn your music off should it become too distracting. In case viewers change their minds once the music has been turned off, you'll also provide them with a way to turn it back on again. Tallyho!

At this point in the construction of your MP3 player, the MP3 starts playing automatically. However, in a new area of politeness, more and more Flash designers and developers are opting to have the music *off* by default. That way, viewers are not aurally bombarded when first entering your site. Then, if viewers think some music would go well with what they're looking at, they can click the Play button to begin playing the music. With your current MP3 player, the music starts automatically playing because the **bgMusak Sound** object actions controlling the playing of the music are all sitting "in the open" in Keyframe 1. An easy way to prevent those actions from automatically executing when **music.swf** first loads is to enclose them in a function. Therefore, the actions within the function will execute only when the function is explicitly called.

So, the first step in this process is to create a new function and move the **bgMusak Sound** object actions into their new function home.

```
4  //----------------<sound setup>----------------\\
5  function playMusak() {
6  var bgMusak:Sound = new Sound();
7  bgMusak.onLoad = function(success) {
8      if (!success) {
9          trackInfo.text = "Failed to load track.";
10     }
11 }
12 bgMusak.loadSound("mp3s/mp3-" + curTrackNum + ".mp3", true);
13 //----------------</sound setup>----------------\\
```

1 Click at the end of the comment //----------------**<sound setup>**----------------\\ line, press **Enter** (Windows) or **Return** (Mac) once to create a line break, and type the following:

```
function playMusak() {
```

As you have seen, this is the opening action to create a new function called **playMusak**. Next, you need to specify where the function ends.

```
 4  //----------------<sound setup>------------------\\
 5  function playMusak() {
 6  var bgMusak:Sound = new Sound();
 7  bgMusak.onLoad = function(success) {
 8      if (!success) {
 9          trackInfo.text = "Failed to load track.";
10      }
11  }
12  bgMusak.loadSound("mp3s/mp3-" + curTrackNum + ".mp3", true);
13  }
14  //----------------</sound setup>------------------\\
```

2 Click at the end of the **bgMusak.loadSound("mp3s/mp3-" + curTrackNum + ".mp3", true);** line, press **Enter** (Windows) or **Return** (Mac) once to create a line break, and type the following:

```
}
```

This closed curly brace marks the end of the **playMusak** function. All the actions between the **function playMusak() {** line and the closed curly brace you just typed are now part of the **playMusak** function. Now, a few of you might be wondering what the action **var bgMusak:Sound = new Sound();** is doing within the function. After all, the action doesn't start the music playing. It just simply creates a new **Sound** object called **bgMusak**. The reason why the action creating the **bgMusak Sound** object is contained within the **playMusak** function is because when the viewer clicks the **Next Track** or **Previous Track** button, or when the track ends and advances to the next track in sequence, you want the **bgMusak Sound** object to be re-created from scratch. By leaving the action creating the **bgMusak Sound** object in the **playMusak** function, each time the function executes, the **Sound** object will be created anew. If you *did not* do this, whenever the MP3 player switched to another track, some of the **bgMusak Sound** object's properties—such as **duration** and **position**—would get confused. In their little world, they're buzzing happily along, tracking the duration of the MP3 file and the current millisecond position it has played so far, and the duration of the MP3 suddenly changes! If you were using the **duration** and **position** properties to script a playback progress slider (as you will be building later in this chapter), since those values suddenly changed with the switching of the MP3 file, the playback slider is all messed up now, too. Drat!

By re-creating this **Sound** object each time another track loads, it will prevent the aforementioned confusion, and all the properties associated with the **Sound** object will be cleared as well.

In an attempt to follow correct ActionScript formatting, you should indent the actions within the **playMusak** function.

```
 4   //---------------<sound setup>---------------\\
 5   function playMusak() {
 6       var bgMusak:Sound = new Sound();
 7       bgMusak.onLoad = function(success) {
 8           if (!success) {
 9               trackInfo.text = "Failed to load track.";
10           }
11       }
12       bgMusak.loadSound("mp3s/mp3-" + curTrackNum + ".mp3", true);
13   }
14   //---------------</sound setup>---------------\\
```

3 Select all the actions between the `function playMusak() {` line and the curly brace ending the function (`}`). Once you've selected all those actions, press **Tab** to indent them.

However, the way the script is currently set up causes a slight problem. In Step 5 of the previous exercise, you created a new **Sound** object with `var bgMusak:Sound = new Sound();`. Then, in Steps 1 and 2 in this exercise, you moved this action, and a few others, into a function. Therefore, the **bgMusak** variable you're attaching a new **Sound** object to resides within the function **playMusak** and can therefore *be accessed only* from within the same function. Why is this bad? Well, if you are writing a script and it originates from *outside* the **playMusak** function, you can't access the **bgMusak Sound** object.

To get around this, you first need to create the **bgMusak** variable from *outside* the **playMusak** function, and then from within the function you can assign the variable to the **Sound** object. Therefore, when you need to refer to the **bgMusak** variable to which the **Sound** object is attached (to tell the sound to stop, get its duration, and so forth) from outside the **playMusak** function, you can easily do so. This is called *initializing* a variable.

```
 4   //---------------<sound setup>---------------\\
 5   function playMusak() {
 6       bgMusak = new Sound();
 7       bgMusak.onLoad = function(success) {
 8           if (!success) {
 9               trackInfo.text = "Failed to load track.";
10           }
11       }
12       bgMusak.loadSound("mp3s/mp3-" + curTrackNum + ".mp3", true);
13   }
14   //---------------</sound setup>---------------\\
```

4 Within the **playMusak** function, change the action `var bgMusak:Sound = new Sound();` so it instead reads as follows:

`bgMusak = new Sound();`

However, because you still want to set the data type of the **bgMusak** variable to a **Sound** object using strict typing, in the next step you'll initialize the variable *outside* the function. As covered previously, if you used `var bgMusak:Sound` to strict type the **bgMusak** variable from *within* the function, **bgMusak** would then reside *within* the function and would be inaccessible from *outside* it.

```
1  //---------------<sound initialization>-------------------\\
2  var curTrackNum:Number = 0;
3  var bgMusak:Sound;
4
5  //---------------<sound setup>------------------\\
6  function playMusak() {
7      bgMusak = new Sound();
8      bgMusak.onLoad = function(success) {
9          if (!success) {
10             trackInfo.text = "Failed to load track.";
11         }
12     }
13     bgMusak.loadSound("mp3s/mp3-" + curTrackNum + ".mp3", true);
14 }
15 //---------------</sound setup>------------------\\
```

5 Click at the end of the **var curTrackNum:Number = 0;** line toward the top of the **Actions** panel, press **Enter** (Windows) or **Return** (Mac) once to create a line break, and type the following:

var bgMusak:Sound;

This action creates a new variable called **bgMusak** and strict types it to a **Sound** object. So now, the **bgMusak** variable resides on **_root**, *outside* the **playMusak** function. The action within the function, **bgMusak = new Sound();**, now just assigns a new **Sound** object to the **bgMusak** variable on **_root**. Now, when you want to refer to the **bgMusak Sound** object, you can easily do so with **_root.bgMusak**, or—if the action you're authoring also resides on **_root**—with **bgMusak**.

Now the first MP3 file won't automatically start downloading and playing—because you inserted ActionScript into a function—so you can start writing the actions to play and download the music when viewers click the Play button and to stop the music when they click the Stop button.

6 On the **Stage**, double-click the instance of the **mc. toggle play** movie clip symbol. This movie clip symbol contains both the **Play** and **Stop** buttons and acts as a toggle button. (When you click the **Play** button, it advances to the next frame to show the **Stop** button. When you click the **Stop** button, it returns to the **Play** button.)

7 Once you've opened the **mc. toggle play** movie clip symbol, single-click the **Play** button on the **Stage**, and open the **Actions** panel by pressing **F9** (Windows) or **Opt+F9** (Mac).

At this point, some of you might be wondering—after all the talk of *centralizing* ActionScript code by putting it on the first keyframe—why you're selecting a button symbol and opening the **Actions** panel. Sacrilegious! The reason is, in this case, to retain simplicity. To save valued space on the Stage, the Play and Stop buttons are a toggle button. Just like the controllers for QuickTime and Windows Media Player, when you click the Play button and the media begins to play, the Play button toggles to a Stop button. Clicking the Stop button stops the media and then toggles to a Play button.

You can create toggle buttons in a few ways; putting some buttons in a movie clip symbol is only one of those ways. When using the technique of adding mouse events to button and movie clip symbols from a keyframe—what you've been using exclusively up until this point—it unfortunately breaks down when it comes to a movie clip–based toggle button. ActionScript can't instruct a symbol to do something if that symbol does not exist yet. In the case of this toggle button, the Play button is initially visible, but the Stop button is not. Simply, this messes up the way you've been writing your ActionScript up until now. Sure, you can make this work in several ways, using different techniques, while still keeping your ActionScript centralized, but in this case it's easier to go low-tech than it is to go high-tech. Rather than try to stuff more new techniques and ActionScript down your throat just to create a simple toggle button, I thought it would be best to go simple in this case. You already have enough new material to learn in this chapter.

```
1  on (rollOver) {
2      _root.helpBubble.text = "play music";
3  }
4
5  on (rollOut) {
6      _root.helpBubble.text = "";
7  }
8
9  on (release) {
10     nextFrame();
11 }
```

Upon opening the Actions panel, you'll notice the Play button already has some ActionScript assigned to it. These actions are simply saying, "When a viewer rolls the mouse over the Play button, put the text *play music* in the **helpBubble** Dynamic text field on the Stage. When a viewer rolls the mouse off the Play button, clear the text in the **helpBubble** field. Lastly, when the viewer clicks the Play button, move the play-head in this movie clip symbol to the next keyframe, thereby displaying the Stop button." The Stop button also has ActionScript already assigned to it essentially doing the opposite of what the Play button does.

Now, you need to add the action saying, "When the viewer clicks the Play button, play the music."

```
1   on (rollOver) {
2       _root.helpBubble.text = "play music";
3   }
4
5   on (rollOut) {
6       _root.helpBubble.text = "";
7   }
8
9   on (release) {
10      _root.playMusak();
11      nextFrame();
12  }
```

8 Click at the end of the **on (release) {** line, press **Enter** (Windows) or **Return** (Mac) once to create a line break, and type the following:

_root.playMusak();

This action tells the **playMusak** function—the one in which you moved all the sound-related actions into in Steps 1 and 2—on **_root** to execute. When this function executes, the first MP3 track will start downloading and playing.

Once the music has started playing, you of course want to give the viewer a way to turn it off. However, just telling the music to stop playing won't actually do the trick. The problem with simply telling the music to stop is if one of the MP3s is currently downloading when the viewer clicks the Stop button—even though you could write an action telling the music to stop and it would—the MP3 file would still continue to download. Until the track finishes its downloading, most of a visitor's available bandwidth would be consumed. This will slow down everything else the visitor tries to access/download on your Web site until the downloading file completes. So, instead of simply telling the music to stop, you'll write a quick action to delete the *entire* **bgMusak Sound** object. By deleting the **bgMusak Sound** object, not only will the sound stop playing, but if an MP3 track is currently in the process of downloading, the download will stop as well!

At this point, some of you might be saying, "Delete the **Sound** object? Uhh…don't we need it to play the MP3 files?" As a matter of fact, you do need the **bgMusak Sound** object to play the music. But remember, with the way the MP3 player is currently written, the **bgMusak Sound** object is created anew every time the Play button is clicked and every time—as you will see later—the Next Track and Previous Track buttons are clicked.

In the next few steps, you will create a function on the Scene 1 Timeline (**_root**) to delete the **bgMusak Sound** object. You're putting this sole action within a function because the Stop button as well as the Next Track and Previous Track buttons will use it.

9 Return to **Scene 1** by clicking its tab on the top-left of the **Timeline**.

10 Click **Keyframe 1** in layer **a**, and open the **Actions** panel by pressing **F9** (Windows) or **Opt+F9** (Mac).

```
5 //---------------<sound setup>-------------------\\
6 function stopMusak() {
7 function playMusak() {
8     bgMusak = new Sound();
```

11 Toward the top of the **Actions** panel, click after the comment //---------------<sound setup>------
----------\\ line, press **Enter** (Windows) or **Return** (Mac) once to create a line break, and type the first line of the function:

```
function stopMusak() {
```

```
5 //---------------<sound setup>-------------------\\
6 function stopMusak() {
7     delete bgMusak;
8 }
9 function playMusak() {
10    bgMusak = new Sound();
11    bgMusak.onLoad = function(success) {
```

12 Click at the end of the action you typed in the previous step, press **Enter** (Windows) or **Return** (Mac) once to create another line break, and type the following:

```
delete bgMusak;
}
```

And again, even though you have to type the line breaks, Flash 8 will automatically format (indent) the ActionScript for you.

Now you have a function called **stopMusak**. When called, **stopMusak** will delete the **bgMusak Sound** object. Not only will this cause the playing music to stop, but it will also halt any downloads the **bgMusak Sound** object is performing.

Warning: Because of a bug in Apple's browser Safari (prior to version 2), once you trigger the progressive downloading of an MP3 file, you have *no way to stop it.* Deleting the **Sound** object—as you just scripted—will not stop the downloading file. It will just keep downloading regardless of whether you stop the sound, load another sound into the same object, or even delete the entire **Sound** object. The only confirmed way to stop the progressive downloading of an MP3 file when using Safari is to close the browser window. Unfortunately, this is not really a "realistic" bug workaround, so you'll sadly just have to accept it as a bug (which, fortunately, has been fixed with version 2.0 and later). Therefore, when the viewer who is running Safari 1.x clicks the Play button to initiate the progressive downloading and playing of the external MP3 file, the MP3 track will continue to download even if the viewer decides halfway through the download to stop the music or to listen to the next track by clicking the appropriate button. This means until the track finishes downloading, most of the viewer's available bandwidth will be consumed. This will slow down everything else the visitor tries to access/download on your Web site until the downloading file completes. Although this is certainly unfortunate, it's even more of an impetus to try to keep the file sizes of your media down to their—realistically—smallest possible sizes. This issue doesn't affect any other browsers for Mac OS X (including Safari 2.0 and later) or Windows.

Next, you need to call the **stopMusak** function from the Stop button so the music stops when it's clicked.

13 On the **Stage**, double-click the instance of the **mc. toggle play** movie clip symbol.

14 Move the playhead to **Frame 2**. Then, on the **Stage**, single-click the **Stop** button to select it, and open the **Actions** panel by pressing **F9** (Windows) or **Opt+F9** (Mac) if it isn't already open.

```
1  on (rollOver) {
2      _root.helpBubble.text = "stop music";
3  }
4
5  on (rollOut) {
6      _root.helpBubble.text = "";
7  }
8
9  on (release) {
10      _root.stopMusak();
11      prevFrame();
12  }
```

15 Click at the end of the **on (release) {** line, press **Enter** (Windows) or **Return** (Mac) once to create a line break, and type the following:

_root.stopMusak();

This action executes the **stopMusak** function on **_root** (the Scene 1 Timeline). The **stopMusak** function deletes the **bgMusak Sound** object, which causes the playing sound to stop playing and any MP3 downloading into the **Sound** object to *stop* downloading.

Lastly, you need to test the changes you've made to make sure everything is working as it should.

16 Save your **music.fla** file by choosing **File > Save** or pressing **Ctrl+S** (Windows) or **Cmd+S** (Mac).

17 Test your movie by choosing **Control > Test Movie** or pressing **Ctrl+Enter** (Windows) or **Cmd+Return** (Mac).

18 When **music.swf** opens in the pre-view window, you won't hear the music start playing, as it did the last time you tested the movie. To start the music playing, click the **Play** button.

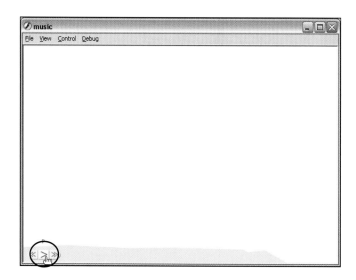

19 Once you click the **Play** button, the music will start playing, and the **Play** button will change to a **Stop** button. While the music is playing, if you click the **Stop** button, the music will stop!

So, congratulations! You just gave the viewers the ability to start and stop the background music.

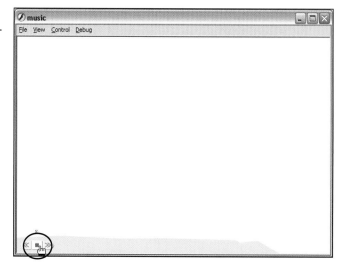

However, while you were testing your movie, you probably noticed something strange. When you moved your mouse over the Play and Stop buttons, you most likely noticed a small bit of text appear above the buttons. If you remember, the prebuilt ActionScript already applied to those buttons told a Dynamic text field—on the Stage—with an instance name of **helpBubble** to display the text *play music* and *stop music*. Well, you haven't told the **helpBubble** Dynamic text field to automatically resize itself to fit whatever text is displayed inside it. So, the small bit of text you're seeing is only the first letter or two of *play music* and *stop music*. In the next step, you'll use the **autoSize** action—which you've used previously—to instruct the **helpBubble** text field to resize itself when necessary.

20 Close the preview window to return to **music.fla**. Then, return to **Scene 1** by clicking its tab at the top-left of the **Timeline**.

21 Click **Keyframe 1** in layer **a**, and open the **Actions** panel by pressing **F9** (Windows) or **Opt+F9** (Mac).

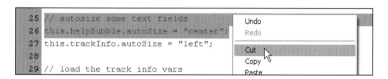

22 In the **Actions** panel, scroll down a little until you reach the commented-out, prebuilt actions for Chapter 10. Select the following actions—toward the top of the prebuilt actions:

```
// autosize some text fields
this.helpBubble.autoSize = "center";
```

23 Then, **right-click** (Windows) or **Ctrl+click** (Mac) anywhere on those selected actions. From the resulting contextual menu, choose **Cut**.

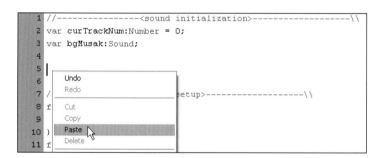

24 Scroll to the top of the **Actions** panel, and click at the end of the **var bgMusak:Sound;** action. Press **Enter** (Windows) or **Return** (Mac) twice to create a couple line breaks, and then **right-click** (Windows) or **Ctrl+click** (Mac) the second empty line break you just created. From the resulting contextual menu, choose **Paste**.

This pastes the actions you just cut from the prebuilt action set.

```
1  //--------------<sound initialization>---------------\\
2  var curTrackNum:Number = 0;
3  var bgMusak:Sound;
4
5  // autosize some text fields
6  this.helpBubble.autoSize = "center";
7
8  //--------------<sound setup>---------------\\
```

Now you have an action—just like you've created in earlier chapters—telling the **helpBubble** Dynamic text field to automatically resize itself to accommodate any text inserted into it.

---

25 Save your **music.fla** file by choosing **File > Save** or pressing **Ctrl+S** (Windows) or **Cmd+S** (Mac).

---

26 Test your movie by choosing **Control > Test Movie** or pressing **Ctrl+Enter** (Windows) or **Cmd+Return** (Mac).

27 When the **music.swf** preview window opens, move your mouse over the **Play** button. When you do, you'll notice—above the buttons—the text **play music** appears. Click the **Play** button to play the music and to toggle the **Play** button to show the **Stop** button. When your mouse is over the **Stop** button, the text should then read **stop music**.

---

28 When you're finished checking out the rollover text, close the **music.swf** preview window.

And *voila!* You just completed constructing the music player's Play and Stop buttons, as well as some descriptive text that gets inserted into a text field when the viewer rolls over these buttons.

In the next exercise, you will write a little ActionScript to pull the ID3 tag information from the currently playing MP3 and insert it into a text field on the Stage. Just when you thought it couldn't get more exciting….

---

5 | Displaying the ID3 Tag Information

As you're probably aware, the "digital music revolution" is well underway. With MP3-playing software such as Apple iTunes for your computer, portable MP3 devices such as the Apple iPod, and now boom boxes and car stereos playing MP3s, digital music is quickly becoming a technology being integrated into our daily lives. If you've ever played an MP3 file on your computer or on a portable MP3-playing device, have you ever wondered how the software or device knew you were listening to "Windowlicker" by Aphex Twin? Or which order the album tracks are supposed to be in, or even which album the songs came from? This information is actually written into each MP3 track, and the various bits of information are called *ID3 tags*. The ID3 tags keep track of a wide variety of information about each MP3 file such as the name of the artist, the name of the album, the track name, the year the song was released, which track number it is out of the total number of tracks, the genre, and more.

Starting with Flash MX, you could use a little ActionScript to have the Flash Player grab some of those ID3 version 1 (v1) tags and display them. This is useful when you want to have an MP3 player, for example, display some dynamic information about the currently playing track without having to manually type it all in your FLA file. However, the problem with ID3 v1 tags and building an MP3 player to progressively download its MP3 tracks from a remote server was that ID3 v1 tags are stored at *the end* of the MP3 file, which meant you couldn't access those ID3 tags until the MP3 had been *completely* downloaded. Obviously, when attempting to create a streaming MP3 player, having the ID3 tags at the end of the file doesn't help you much. With the introduction of Flash MX 2004—and now Flash 8—Flash Player 7 and 8 both support ID3 version 2.3 (v2.3) and 2.4 (v2.4) tags. The great feature of ID3 v2.3 and v2.4 tags is they're stored at *the beginning* of the MP3 file and can therefore be accessed as soon as the MP3 file starts downloading. So, if your MP3 player progressively downloads its tracks—as you are building it do in this chapter—you can display those ID3 tags right from the get-go.

In this exercise, you'll write some ActionScript to grab a few of those ID3 tags and display them in the **trackInfo** Dynamic text field on the Stage.

---

1 First, make sure **music.fla** is the current foreground FLA file, you have **Keyframe 1** in layer **a** selected, and you have the **Actions** panel open.

The ID3 tags appear in the long, horizontal Dynamic text field at the bottom of the Stage. Remember, that text field has an instance name of **trackInfo** already applied to it. When you use ActionScript to insert some text in that field, it will *not* automatically resize itself to fit the inserted text. Just like you did in the previous exercise, you need an action to do that for you.

```
23  /*
24  //---------------<pre-built ActionScript for Chapter 10>-------------------\\
25
26
27
28
29  this.trackInfo.autoSize = "left";        Undo
30                                           Redo
31  // load the track info vars
32  var myMusicLv:LoadVars = new Load        Cut
33  myMusicLv.load("vars/track_info.t        Copy
34                                           Paste
                                             Delete
```

2 Scroll down in the **Actions** panel a bit until you come to the action **this.trackInfo.autoSize = "left";**. Once you've located the correct action, select it, and then **right-click** (Windows) or **Ctrl+click** (Mac) it. From the resulting contextual menu, choose **Cut**.

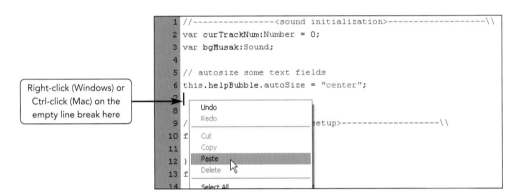

Right-click (Windows) or Ctrl-click (Mac) on the empty line break here

```
1  //---------------<sound initialization>-------------------\\
2  var curTrackNum:Number = 0;
3  var bgMusak:Sound;
4
5  // autosize some text fields
6  this.helpBubble.autoSize = "center";
7
8                    Undo
9   /                Redo              etup>-------------------\\
10  f                Cut
11                   Copy
12  }                Paste
13  f                Delete
14                   Select All
```

3 Scroll toward the top of the **Actions** panel, click at the end of the **this.helpBubble.autoSize = "center";** line, and press **Enter** (Windows) or **Return** (Mac) once to create a line break. Then, **right-click** (Windows) or **Ctrl+click** (Mac) the new, empty line break. From the resulting contextual menu, choose **Paste**.

```
5  // autosize some text fields
6  this.helpBubble.autoSize = "center";
7  this.trackInfo.autoSize = "left";
```

As you have seen a few times, you now have an action to set the **trackInfo** Dynamic text field so it will automatically resize as needed while keeping the text within it aligned to the left side of the field.

If your brain isn't jello yet, you might recall the earlier table called "Methods, Properties, and Event Handlers of the Sound Class." In that table is a **Sound** class event handler called **onID3**. The **onID3** event handler fires every time the ID3 tags change whichever sound is being loaded using the **bgMusak Sound** object. This is just the thing you need to populate a Dynamic text field with the MP3's ID3 tags! In fact, that's exactly what you'll use in the next steps.

```
 9 //---------------<sound setup>------------------\\
10 function stopMusak() {
11     delete bgMusak;
12 }
13 function playMusak() {
14     bgMusak = new Sound();
15     bgMusak.onID3 = function() {
16     bgMusak.onLoad = function(success) {
17         if (!success) {
18             trackInfo.text = "Failed to load track.";
19         }
20     }
21     bgMusak.loadSound("mp3s/mp3-" + curTrackNum + ".mp3", true);
22 }
23 //---------------</sound setup>------------------\\
```

4 In the **Actions** panel, locate the actions contained within the **<sound setup>** comments. Then, click after the **bgMusak = new Sound();** line, press **Enter** (Windows) or **Return** (Mac) once to create a line break, and type the opening action for this event handler:

bgMusak.onID3 = function() {

Just like the other **Sound** class event handlers—such as **onLoad**, which you wrote in Exercise 3—the **onID3** event handler needs to be assigned to a function. The actions you place within this function will execute each time the **onID3** event handler fires.

```
 9 //---------------<sound setup>------------------\\
10 function stopMusak() {
11     delete bgMusak;
12 }
13 function playMusak() {
14     bgMusak = new Sound();
15     bgMusak.onID3 = function() {
16         trackInfo.text = "artist : " + bgMusak.id3.TCOM + " | track : " + bgMusak.id3.TIT2;
17     bgMusak.onLoad = function(success) {
18         if (!success) {
19             trackInfo.text = "Failed to load track.";
20         }
21     }
22     bgMusak.loadSound("mp3s/mp3-" + curTrackNum + ".mp3", true);
23 }
24 //---------------</sound setup>------------------\\
```

5 Click at the end of the **bgMusak.onID3 = function() {** line, press **Enter** (Windows) or **Return** (Mac) once to create a line break, and then type—all on one line with no line breaks—the following:

trackInfo.text = "artist : " + bgMusak.id3.TCOM + " | track : " + bgMusak.id3.TIT2;

In plain English, this action reads, "Insert some text into the **trackInfo** Dynamic text field. The text to insert should be *artist* :, then the ID3 tag **TCOM** (which is the composer/artist), the text *| track* :, and then the ID3 tag **TIT2** (which is the track title)." So, if the currently loading/playing MP3 is "Windowlicker" by Aphex Twin, the final result of this action—and thereby the text to be inserted into the **trackInfo** text field—is **artist : Aphex Twin | track : Windowlicker**.

Note: To see a full list of the ID3 tags Flash 8 can access, open the **Help** panel (**F1**), and from the Help "books" on the left, choose **ActionScript 2.0 Language Reference > ActionScript classes > Sound > id3 (Sound.id3 property)**.

```
9  //---------------<sound setup>-----------------\\
10 function stopMusak() {
11     delete bgMusak;
12 }
13 function playMusak() {
14     bgMusak = new Sound();
15     bgMusak.onID3 = function() {
16         trackInfo.text = "artist : " + bgMusak.id3.TCOM + " | track : " + bgMusak.id3.TIT2;
17     }
18     bgMusak.onLoad = function(success) {
19         if (!success) {
20             trackInfo.text = "Failed to load track.";
21         }
22     }
23     bgMusak.loadSound("mp3s/mp3-" + curTrackNum + ".mp3", true);
24 }
25 //---------------</sound setup>-----------------\\
```

6 Close the **bgMusak.onID3** function by clicking at the end of the action you wrote in the previous step, pressing **Enter** (Windows) or **Return** (Mac) to create a line break, and typing the following:

```
}
```

And that's it! All this action is doing is every time the ID3 information changes for the sound being targeted by the **bgMusak Sound** object, the **onID3** event handler is triggered, and some text, along with some ID3 tags, is inserted into the **trackInfo** text field. As you saw when writing this action, when you want to get access to the ID3 tags for the MP3 file being downloaded/played, you first type the name of the **Sound** object the MP3 file is loading into (**bgMusak** in this case), **id3**, and then the name of the ID3 tag for which you want to grab the value. So, if you wanted to get access to any comments inserted into the ID3 comment tag of an MP3 file, you could simply use **bgMusak.id3.COMM**.

Quite a few programs allow you to edit the ID3 tags of MP3 files. In Appendix B, *"Flash Professional 8 Resources,"* you'll find some recommended ID3-editing programs for both Windows and Mac.

Before congratulating yourself, you should test your movie to make sure everything is working.

7 Save your **music.fla** file by choosing **File > Save** or pressing **Ctrl+S** (Windows) or **Cmd+S** (Mac).

8 Test your movie by choosing **Control > Test Movie** or pressing **Ctrl+Enter** (Windows) or **Cmd+Return** (Mac).

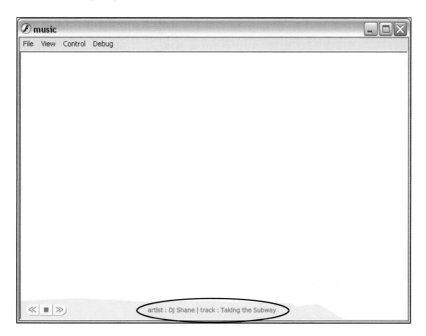

When **music.swf** appears in the preview window, click the **Play** button. As you have already seen, this will start playing the music. But when it starts playing, you'll also see some text appear in the **trackInfo** text field. It will say *artist : DJ Shane | track : Taking the Subway*. The text *artist :*, the pipe (|), and the text *track :* were all manually specified in the action you wrote in Step 5, but the text *DJ Shane* and *Taking the Subway* is the content of the ID3 tags **TCOM** and **TIT2**, respectively. Pretty darn cool!

As mentioned, any time you can use dynamic content, go for it. By incorporating the ID3 tags into the track information displayed in the **trackInfo** Dynamic text field, it makes the MP3 player so much easier to update in the future. Whenever you want to add or remove MP3s, either you or the client simply has to verify the correct ID3 tags have been set, upload the MP3s to the server, and you're done!

At this point, you might be looking at the large, blank space between the last track, the Play/Stop button, the Next Track button, and where the ID3 information is and wondering why it's there. Later in this chapter, you will be referred to watch the movie **music_progress.mov** where you will learn how to script a MP3 preloader and a playback progress slider, which is what will sit in the empty space.

---

9 When you're finished checking out the ID3 text, close the preview window, and return to **music.fla**.

In the next exercise, you'll script a way for the viewer to skip to the next track or return to the previous track. You will also script the capability for the MP3 player to automatically advance to the next MP3 track in sequence when the currently playing song reaches its end.

---

6 | Changing Tracks

What would an MP3 player jukebox be if you couldn't switch tracks, eh? In this exercise, you'll add some ActionScript to allow the viewer to advance to the next MP3 track in sequence, go to the previous MP3 track, or just wait for the currently playing MP3 to end and let the MP3 player switch to the next track automatically.

Similar to the slideshow, the MP3 player will loop through the MP3 tracks. When Track 1 finishes playing, the MP3 player advances to Track 2. When Track 2 finishes playing, the MP3 player returns to Track 1. (The player has only two MP3 tracks.) So, for the script to know whether the MP3 file it is currently playing is the *last* MP3 track in the sequence, you need to keep track of the total number of MP3 tracks. When constructing the slideshow, you used the variable `totalFrames` to keep track of the total number of slides. In this exercise, you'll create a variable named `totalTracks` to keep track of the total number of MP3 tracks. But just like you did with the slideshow, you'll keep the variable in an external text file and use a `LoadVars` object to load the variable into your SWF file. This allows you or the client to easily add or remove MP3 tracks to the MP3 player and make the required changes without even having to open Flash 8. So, the first step is to load the `totalTracks` variable.

---

1 Minimize (Windows) or hide (Mac) Flash 8, and navigate to your **Desktop > la_eyeworks > site > vars** folder.

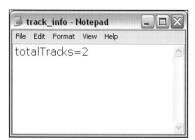

2 In the **vars** folder, open the text file **track_info.txt** in a simple text-editing program such as Notepad (Windows), TextEdit (Mac), or BBEdit (Mac). In that text file, you'll see one variable, `totalTracks`, with a value of **2**. If you—or the client—ever added or removed MP3 tracks, you'd simply have to change this value accordingly.

You've seen where the text file is, what it is named, and what's inside of it, so you can now write the `LoadVars` script to load it into **music.swf**.

---

3 Close the text file, and return to Flash 8. Then, make sure **music.fla** is the foreground FLA file, you have **Keyframe 1** selected in the **a** layer, and you have the **Actions** panel open.

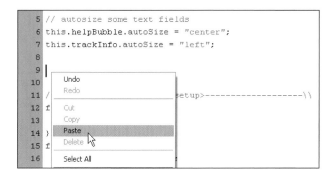

```
27  /*
28  //----------------<pre-built ActionScript for Chapter 10>------------------\\
29
30
31
32
33
34
35  // load the track info vars
36  var myMusicLv:LoadVars = new LoadVars();
37  myMusicLv.load("vars/track_info.txt");
38
39  //----------------</sound initialization>-
40
```

4 Scroll down in the **Actions** panel until you reach the following script:

```
// load the track info vars
var myMusicLv:LoadVars = new LoadVars();
myMusicLv.load("vars/track_info.txt");
```

Then, select those three lines, and **right-click** (Windows) or **Ctrl+click** (Mac) anywhere on the selected script. From the resulting contextual menu, choose **Cut**.

```
5   // autosize some text fields
6   this.helpBubble.autoSize = "center";
7   this.trackInfo.autoSize = "left";
8
9   |
10
11  /                              setup>------------------\\
12  f
13
14  }
15  f
16      Select All
```

5 Scroll to the top of the **Actions** panel, click at the end of the **this.trackInfo.autoSize = "left";** line, and press **Enter** (Windows) or **Return** (Mac) twice to create a couple line breaks. Then, **right-click** (Windows) or **Ctrl+click** (Mac) the second empty line break you just created. From the resulting contextual menu, choose **Paste**.

```
5   // autosize some text fields
6   this.helpBubble.autoSize = "center";
7   this.trackInfo.autoSize = "left";
8
9   // load the track info vars
10  var myMusicLv:LoadVars = new LoadVars();
11  myMusicLv.load("vars/track_info.txt");
```

Presto! You now have a **LoadVars** object called **myMusicLv** to load the variables from the file **track_info.txt** located in the **vars** folder. As you saw earlier, this text file contains the variable **totalTracks** with a value of **2**. So whenever you're writing an action and you need to get access to that variable/value, you can simply type **myMusicLv.totalTracks**.

Since you now know how many tracks you have, you can use this number in a script to get the MP3 player to loop through all the music tracks. In the next few steps, you'll write a script to instruct the MP3 player to advance to the next track in sequence when the currently playing track finishes. If the last track is the currently playing track, when it finishes playing, the script will automatically instruct the MP3 player to load and play the first track.

Because you will later write a script to change the track when the current track finishes playing, you need to have a way to detect when a playing track reaches its end. Fortunately, just like **onLoad** and **onID3**, Flash 8 has an event handler to fill this need. In the next few steps, you'll use the **onSoundComplete** event handler to detect when the current track has finished playing and to then advance to the next track in sequence.

```
13  //---------------<sound setup>-------------------\\
14  function stopMusak() {
15      delete bgMusak;
16  }
17  function playMusak() {
18      bgMusak = new Sound();
19      bgMusak.onSoundComplete = function() {
20      bgMusak.onID3 = function() {
21          trackInfo.text = "artist : " + bgMusak.id3.TCOM + " | track : " + bgMusak.id3.TIT2;
22      }
23      bgMusak.onLoad = function(success) {
24          if (!success) {
25              trackInfo.text = "Failed to load track.";
26          }
27      }
28      bgMusak.loadSound("mp3s/mp3-" + curTrackNum + ".mp3", true);
29  }
30  //---------------</sound setup>-------------------\\
```

6 Within the **<sound setup>** comments, click at the end of the **bgMusak = new Sound();** line, press **Enter** (Windows) or **Return** (Mac) once to create a line break, and type the following:

```
bgMusak.onSoundComplete = function() {
```

Similar to the **onLoad** and **onID3** event handlers you wrote earlier in this chapter, this line is the first step in creating the **onSoundComplete** event handler. Where the **onLoad** event handler was triggered when the sound was loaded and the **onID3** event handler was triggered when the sound's ID3 information changed, the **onSoundComplete** event handler triggers when the currently playing sound finishes (completes). So, now you just need to specify what should occur when that happens.

You first need to find out whether the currently playing track is the *last* track in sequence. If it is the last track that just finished playing, you need to tell the MP3 player to load and play the *first* track.

```
13  //----------------<sound setup>------------------\\
14  function stopMusak() {
15      delete bgMusak;
16  }
17  function playMusak() {
18      bgMusak = new Sound();
19      bgMusak.onSoundComplete = function() {
20          if (curTrackNum == (myMusicLv.totalTracks - 1)) {
```

7 Click at the end of the **bgMusak.onSoundComplete = function()** { line, press **Enter** (Windows) or **Return** (Mac) once to create a line break, and type the following:

```
if (curTrackNum == (myMusicLv.totalTracks - 1)) {
```

Simply, the beginning of this **if** statement reads, "If the track number (the number of the currently playing MP3) is equal to the total number of tracks minus 1…."

Why "the total number of tracks minus 1?" some of you might be saying. Remember, the MP3 file names start with 0 (for reasons stated in Chapter 7, "*Building a Slideshow*"), as in **mp3-0.mp3**, **mp3-1.mp3**, and so forth. So even though you have two tracks total, the last MP3 file in sequence ends with 1. Therefore, when you need to determine whether the last MP3 track is playing, you need to subtract 1 from the **totalTracks** variable. Some of you, upon hearing that explanation, might be thinking, "Well why not just put **1** in the **totalTracks** variable instead of **2**? Then you'd avoid having to do that silly subtraction stuff." And even though that would surely work, do you really want to explain to the client in charge of updating the **track_info.txt** file to subtract 1 from the total number of MP3 tracks? Because I don't exactly relish explaining details like this to the client (who has other things to worry about), it's much easier to just subtract 1 from the **totalTracks** variable in the code.

The **if** statement you just wrote essentially asks whether the currently playing track is the last track in sequence. If this statement results in the Boolean **true**, when this track finishes playing (**onSoundComplete**), the **curTrackNum** value should return to 0. As you'll see later, after the **curTrackNum** number has been set to whichever track should play next, you'll simply call the **playMusak** function, which will then play whichever MP3 track number is specified in the **curTrackNum** variable.

```
13 //---------------<sound setup>---------------\\
14 function stopMusak() {
15     delete bgMusak;
16 }
17 function playMusak() {
18     bgMusak = new Sound();
19     bgMusak.onSoundComplete = function() {
20         if (curTrackNum == (myMusicLv.totalTracks - 1))
21             curTrackNum = 0;
22         } else {
23             curTrackNum ++;
24         }
```

8 Click at the end of the action you wrote in the previous step, press **Enter** (Windows) or **Return** (Mac) once to create a line break, and type the following:

```
curTrackNum = 0;
} else {
curTrackNum ++;
}
```

Note: Although you need to create the line breaks just like as shown in the previous code, Flash 8 automatically indents the actions for you.

Taken along with the **if** statement you started writing in Step 7, this script reads, "If the currently playing track number is equal to the total number of available MP3 tracks (meaning, there aren't any more new tracks to play), set the current track number to 0 (the beginning). Otherwise, set the current track number to whichever number comes next." So, now you've set **curTrackNum** to whichever track number should be playing when the current track finishes, but you haven't (yet) instructed the MP3 player to actually *play* a specific MP3 track.

```
13 //---------------<sound setup>---------------\\
14 function stopMusak() {
15     delete bgMusak;
16 }
17 function playMusak() {
18     bgMusak = new Sound();
19     bgMusak.onSoundComplete = function() {
20         if (curTrackNum == (myMusicLv.totalTracks - 1)) {
21             curTrackNum = 0;
22         } else {
23             curTrackNum ++;
24         }
25         playMusak();
26     }
```

9 Press **Enter** (Windows) or **Return** (Mac) to create a new line break under the last closed curly brace you typed in Step 8, and type the following:

```
playMusak();
}
```

This instructs the MP3 player to execute the **playMusak** function you built earlier, which, of course, starts playing whichever track number is specified in the **curTrackNum** variable. The last line (**}**) closes the `bgMusak.onSoundComplete` function, and you now have an MP3 player that automatically and continually loops through all the MP3 tracks it has available.

Now, you just need to cross your fingers, whisper a small prayer, put on your tinfoil hat, and test your movie!

10 Save your **music.fla** file by choosing **File > Save** or pressing **Ctrl+S** (Windows) or **Cmd+S** (Mac).

11 Test your movie by choosing **Control > Test Movie** or pressing **Ctrl+Enter** (Windows) or **Cmd+Return** (Mac).

12 When **music.swf** appears in the preview window, click the **Play** button to start playing the music. Now you just need to kick back and wait for the track to reach the end to hear it automatically advance to the next track in sequence. Coolio!

When the track automatically changes to the next track, you'll see the ID3 text automatically change as well. This is because the **onID3** event handler was notified the ID3 information for the music had changed and then executed all the actions within the function to which it is attached. The actions within the **onID3** event handler function grabbed the new ID3 information from the new MP3 and displayed it in the **trackInfo** Dynamic text field. It's like a well-oiled machine!

Because the script you just wrote essentially instructs the MP3 player to play the next MP3 track in sequence—even jumping back to the first track if it needs to—the MP3 player will play continual music until the cows come home.

But what if the viewer doesn't want to wait for the currently playing track to end before listening to the next track? Maybe the viewer thinks the current track is boring and wants to hear what the next track sounds like. In that case, the viewer will click the Next Track or Previous Track button, which you've kindly given them, to jump one track ahead or one track behind in sequence. In the next steps, you'll bring all the ActionScript together to make this functionality work. Thankfully, the ActionScript to add this functionality to the Next Track and Previous Track buttons will be nearly identical to the script you just wrote.

13 Close the preview window, and return to **music.fla**. Make sure you have **Keyframe 1** selected in layer **a** and you have the **Actions** panel open.

```
 89  //----------------<next track>----------------\\
 90  this.nextTrackBtn.onRollOver = function() {
 91      helpBubble.text = "next track";
 92  }
 93
 94  this.nextTrackBtn.onRollOut = function() {
 95      helpBubble.text = "";
 96  }
 97
 98  this.nextTrackBtn.onRelease = function() {
 99  ///
100      musakToggle.gotoAndStop(2);
101  }
102
103  //----------------</next track>----------------\\
104
105  //----------------<previous track>----------------\
106
107  this.prevTrackBtn.onRollOver = function() {
108      helpBubble.text = "previous track";
109  }
110
111  this.prevTrackBtn.onRollOut = function() {
112      helpBubble.text = "";
113  }
114
115  this.prevTrackBtn.onRelease = function() {
116  ///
117      musakToggle.gotoAndStop(2);
118  }
119
120  //----------------</previous track>----------------\\
```

Contextual menu items: Undo, Redo, Cut, Copy, Paste, Delete, Select All, Set Breakpoint, Remove Breakpoint, Remove Breakpoints in This File, View Help

14 Scroll toward the bottom of the **Actions** panel, and select the giant block of code starting with the comment //----------------**<next track>**----------------\\ and ending with the comment //----------------**</previous track>**----------------\\, as shown in the illustration here. Then, **right-click** (Windows) or **Ctrl+click** (Mac) anywhere on the selected script. From the resulting contextual menu, choose **Cut**.

Although it may initially look daunting, the ActionScript you just cut is just a series of simple **onRollOver**, **onRollOut**, and **onRelease** mouse event commands for the Next Track and Previous Track buttons. After you paste this ActionScript into the correct place in the next step, you will add to the script to make it functional for the Next Track and Previous Track buttons.

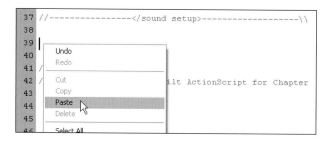

15 Scroll up in the **Actions** panel a little, click at the end of the //----------------**</sound setup>**---------------------\\ line, and press **Enter** (Windows) or **Return** (Mac) twice to create a couple of line breaks. Then, **right-click** (Windows) or **Ctrl+click** (Mac) the second empty line break you just created. From the resulting contextual menu, choose **Paste**.

This pastes all the ActionScript you just cut from the prebuilt actions area. Again, this code was provided for you because it's all stuff you've already learned. If you read the code, you'll see it's just a series of simple mouse events for the Next Track and Previous Track buttons. What you need to do now, however, is modify the **onRelease** mouse events for both the Next Track and Previous Track buttons so when the viewer clicks one those buttons, the currently playing track changes. As mentioned previously, the ActionScript to create this functionality will be nearly identical to the ActionScript you already wrote for changing the track when the currently playing song finishes. So, to save yourself some time and energy, you'll just copy some ActionScript you've already written and paste it into the **onRelease** states of the Next Track and Previous Track buttons.

```
19      bgMusak.onSoundComplete = function() {
20          if (curTrackNum == (myMusicLv.totalTracks - 1)) {
21              curTrackNum = 0;
22          } else {
23              curTrackNum ++;
24          }
25          playMusak();
26      }
27      bgMusak.onID3 = function() {
28          trackInfo.text = "artist : " + bgMusak.id3.TCOM +
```

Contextual menu: Undo / Redo / Cut / Copy / Paste / Delete / Select All / Set Breakpoint

16 Underneath the **bgMusak.onSoundComplete = function() {** line, select all the ActionScript you wrote in Steps 7 through 9, as shown in the illustration here. Then **right-click** (Windows) or **Ctrl+click** (Mac) anywhere on the selected script. From the resulting contextual menu, choose **Copy**.

```
39  //--------------<next track>--------------\\
40  this.nextTrackBtn.onRollOver = function() {
41      helpBubble.text = "next track";
42  }
43
44  this.nextTrackBtn.onRollOut = function() {
45      helpBubble.text = "";
46  }
47
48  this.nextTrackBtn.onRelease = function() {
49
50  ///
51          n                    );
52  }
53
54  //---                         k>--------------\\
55
```

Contextual menu: Undo / Redo / Cut / Copy / Paste / Delete

17 Scroll down a little in the **Actions** panel until you come to the **<next track>** comment lines. **Note:** The actions within the **<next track>** and **</next track>** comments are actions applying to the **Next Track** button on the **Stage**. Then, click at the end of the **this.nextTrackBtn.onRelease = function() {** line, and press **Enter** (Windows) or **Return** (Mac) to create a line break. **Right-click** (Windows) or **Ctrl+click** (Mac) the new line break you just made, and from the resulting contextual menu, choose **Paste**.

```
48  this.nextTrackBtn.onRelease = function() {
49          if (curTrackNum == (myMusicLv.totalTracks - 1)) {
50              curTrackNum = 0;
51          } else {
52              curTrackNum ++;
53          }
54          playMusak();
55  ///
56      musakToggle.gotoAndStop(2);
57  }
```

This pastes the **if** statement you copied from the **bgMusak.onSoundComplete** function. Now, within the **nextTrackBtn.onRelease** mouse event, the script essentially reads like this, "When the viewer clicks the Next Track button, if the currently playing track number is equal to the total number of tracks, set the track number to 0. Otherwise, set the current track number to be 1 greater than whatever it currently is. After you've set the track number to be whatever it should be, tell the music to play."

```
48  this.nextTrackBtn.onRelease = function() {
49          if (curTrackNum == (myMusicLv.totalTracks - 1)) {
50              curTrackNum = 0;
51          } else {
52              curTrackNum ++;
53          }
```

Note: Depending on how you copied and pasted the **if** statement, the first line of the **if** action might be indented one tab too many. If this happens to you, simply click right before the **if**, and press **Delete** (Windows) or **Backspace** (Mac) to remove the extra tab. When you're finished, the **if** should be aligned with the curly brace (**}**) before **else** and the curly brace (**}**) under **curTrackNum ++;**.

However, if viewers come to the L.A. Eyeworks Web site, click the Play button to start playing some music, decide they don't like the music—which is still downloading to the computer—and click the Next Track button, the next track starts downloading, but the previous track does not stop downloading. It continues to download, using up unnecessary bandwidth until it finishes its download. This would be horrible because unless the viewer is on a high-speed broadband Internet connection with bandwidth to spare, the poor Internet connection is now trying to download *two* large MP3 files *simultaneously*. Just like you did with the Stop button, you need to tell the **bgMusak** music to stop downloading whichever MP3 track it's currently downloading *before* it starts downloading another. Fortunately, you've already created the **stopMusak** function to do just that.

```
48  this.nextTrackBtn.onRelease = function() {
49          if (curTrackNum == (myMusicLv.totalTracks - 1)) {
50              curTrackNum = 0;
51          } else {
52              curTrackNum ++;
53          }
54          stopMusak();
55          playMusak();
56  ///
57      musakToggle.gotoAndStop(2);
58  }
```

18 Click at beginning of the `playMusak();` line, and press **Enter** (Windows) or **Return** (Mac) to create a line break. Then, click the new line break you just created above `playMusak();`, and type the following:

`stopMusak();`

As you used with the Stop button earlier in this chapter, the `stopMusak` function deletes the `bgMusak Sound` object. By deleting the `bgMusak Sound` object, not only does it stop the currently playing sound, but it will also stop any sound currently being downloaded into that **Sound** object as well. Then, after that has occurred, the next action `playMusak` triggers the next sound to start playing.

Next, you need to write similar functionality for the Previous Track button. However, where the `if` statement for the Next Track button was *identical* to the `if` statement you wrote earlier in the `bgMusak.onSoundComplete` event handler, the `if` statement for the Previous Track button needs to change to accommodate for going *backward* in sequence.

Currently, the `if` statement added to the Next Track button first checks to see whether the currently playing track is the last available track. However, when going backward through the MP3 player, you're not really interested if you're on the *last* track. You're more interested if you're on the *first* track. That way, if you *are* on the first track when the viewer clicks the Previous Track button, you can instruct the MP3 player to load the last track.

```
62  //---------------<previous track>-----------------\\
63
64  this.prevTrackBtn.onRollOver = function() {
65      helpBubble.text = "previous track";
66  }
67
68  this.prevTrackBtn.onRollOut = function() {
69      helpBubble.text = "";
70  }
71
72  this.prevTrackBtn.onRelease = function() {
73
74  ///
75      musakToggle.gotoAndStop(2);
76  }
77
78  //---------------</previous track>-----------------\\
```

19 Scroll down a little in the **Actions** panel until you come to the **<previous track>** comment lines. These actions within the **<previous track>** and **</previous track>** comments are actions relating to the

Previous Track button on the **Stage**. Then, click at the end of the `this.prevTrackBtn.onRelease = func-tion() {` line, and press **Enter** (Windows) or **Return** (Mac) to create a line break.

```
72  this.prevTrackBtn.onRelease = function() {
73      if (curTrackNum == 0) {
74          curTrackNum = (myMusicLv.totalTracks - 1);
75      } else {
76          curTrackNum --;
77      }
78  ///
79      musakToggle.gotoAndStop(2);
80  }
```

20 Click the new line break you created in the previous step, and type the following:

```
if (curTrackNum == 0) {
curTrackNum = (myMusicLv.totalTracks - 1);
} else {
curTrackNum --;
}
```

As usual, besides the line breaks you see in the code sample and in the illustration here, Flash 8 automatically formats the ActionScript for you as you type it. So, you don't need to worry about adding or removing tab spaces; Flash 8 will do it all for you.

Although this `if` statement script is similar to the one you added to the Next Track button, it's a wee bit different. Taken along with the **prevTrackBtn.onRelease** mouse event, this `if` statement reads in plain English, "When the viewer clicks the Previous Track button, if the currently playing track is the first track, set the current track number to be whatever the total number of tracks is. Otherwise, just set the current track number to be one number lower than whatever it currently is." In essence, the `if` statements handle the MP3 files in the same way the slideshow behaved. With the slideshow, it continually loops through the ten available slides as the viewer clicks the Next Slide and Previous Slide buttons. The MP3 player does the same, except with MP3 files instead of JPEG files.

To finish, you still need to write the action to delete the **bgMusak Sound** object and another action to start playing the correct track.

```
72  this.prevTrackBtn.onRelease = function() {
73      if (curTrackNum == 0) {
74          curTrackNum = (myMusicLv.totalTracks - 1);
75      } else {
76          curTrackNum --;
77      }
78      stopMusak();
79      playMusak();
80  ///
81      musakToggle.gotoAndStop(2);
82  }
```

21 Click after the closed curly brace you ended with in the previous step, and press **Enter** (Windows) or **Return** (Mac) to create a line break. Then, type the following:

```
stopMusak();
playMusak();
```

And—drum roll, please—there you have it! Of course, the last step is to save and test your work to make sure everything is working as it should.

---

22 Save your **music.fla** file by choosing **File > Save** or pressing **Ctrl+S** (Windows) or **Cmd+S** (Mac).

---

23 Test your movie by choosing **Control > Test Movie** or pressing **Ctrl+Enter** (Windows) or **Cmd+Return** (Mac).

---

24 When **music.swf** opens in the preview window, click the **Play** button to start playing the music.

25 When the music starts playing, click the **Next Track** button. You'll notice the MP3 player starts playing the next track and the ID3 information updates as well.

previous track

artist : DJ Shane | track : Taking the Subway

26 Once you've verified the **Next Track** button works correctly, click the **Previous Track** button. You'll notice the MP3 player plays the previous track in sequence. (However, with only two MP3 tracks, it's hard to tell if it went back a track or went forward a track. I suppose you'll just have to take my word for it!)

If you continually click the Previous Track or Next Track buttons, you'll notice the MP3 player loops continually through the available tracks.

Hooray! You just constructed a working, fully functional MP3 player complete with Stop, Play, Next Track, and Previous Track buttons, as well as a Dynamic text field that is updated with ID3 tags pulled from the MP3 files. Break out the champagne—or at least a spritzer—because you've achieved quite an accomplishment in this chapter.

VIDEO:

music_progress.mov

You can build a few pieces of functionality in one graphic element. For instance, you can build a preloader (different from the `MovieClipLoader`-based preloader you constructed in Chapter 8, "*Building a Preloader*") to monitor and display the download progress of the MP3 files. Built into that, you can also construct the ActionScript to animate a small slider across the same graphic. This slider represents the playback progress of the currently playing MP3. To learn more about how to do all this, check out **music_progress-part1.mov, music_progress-part2.mov**, and **music_progress-part3.mov** in the **videos** folder on the **HOT CD-ROM**.

artist : DJ Shane | track

You can see the results of this QuickTime movie by pointing your browser to **www.lynda.com/flash8btb/laeyeworks/**, clicking the **Play** button on the MP3 player, and watching the graphic (highlighted in the illustration here) to the right of the Play/Stop, Next Track, and Previous Track buttons.

---

volume_slider.mov

You can also adjust the volume of the music by creating a draggable slider. As you drag the slider up and down, the volume of the music will adjust accordingly. To learn more about how to do this, check out **volume_slider-part1.mov**, **volume_slider-part2.mov**, and **volume_slider-part3.mov** in the **videos** folder on the **HOT CD-ROM**.

You can see what you will be building in this video by pointing your browser to **www.lynda.com/flash8btb/laeyeworks/**, clicking the **Play** button on the MP3 player, clicking the small speaker icon toward the right side of the MP3 player bar, and dragging the light-green slider. You'll also notice, as you drag the slider, displayed to right of the slider is the volume listed as a percentage. When you stop dragging the slider, the percentage text disappears. Clicking the **speaker** icon again will hide the volume slider.

I highly recommend watching, and following along with, the two videos **music_progress.mov** and **volume_slider.mov**. Not only do they teach some new and interesting ActionScript concepts, but you'll also get to add some great functionality to the MP3 player. Treat the videos just as you would the exercises in the book.

In the next chapter, *"Building a Video Player,"* you will learn how to create a video player. When building the video player, you'll learn how to use the `NetStream` class to progressively download an FLV file from a remote server, as well as how to stop and play the video. The next chapter contains lots of new topics, so go rest up before continuing!

11

Building a Video Player

In this chapter, you will learn how to build a video player. Much like the MP3 player, this video player will progressively download an external FLV (**Fl**ash **V**ideo) file into the About Us module you worked on in Chapters 4, 5, and 6. Some of the many benefits of creating a video player that progressively downloads its video content are as follows: You can use higher-quality video, you have no limit—besides the viewer's free hard drive space—on the length of video you can use, and you don't get any performance degradation as when using video in Macromedia Flash MX. This chapter has lots of great new stuff to learn, so strap yourself to your chair, close the curtains, lock the door, and let's get to it!

1 | Previewing What You Are Building

In this exercise, you'll see the finished video player you'll be building *before* you start. That way, as you're working through the exercises in this chapter, you'll have a better idea of how some of these abstract ActionScript concepts fit together to create a functional piece of the L.A. Eyeworks Web site.

1 Open your preferred browser, and navigate to the following URL:

www.lynda.com/flash8btb/laeyeworks/

2 Once the L.A. Eyeworks Web site finishes loading, click the **about us** option in the navigation bar.

3 When the **About Us** module loads, click the **video** option, which makes the video automatically begin downloading from the remote server. As soon as five seconds of video has downloaded, the video will automatically start playing.

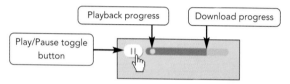

You'll also notice, as the video is downloading, a darker-blue bar animating from left to right across a lighter-blue bar. The dark-blue bar represents the downloading progress of the FLV file. When enough of the video has downloaded and the video starts playing, you'll see a lighter-blue dot animating from left to right across the darker-blue bar. The blue dot represents the playback progress of the video. Once the dot gets to the farthest-right point of the bar, the video ends. At any time during the playback progress, you can click the Play/Pause toggle button to pause or play the video.

Lastly, when the video finishes playing, you'll notice the playback progress dot jumps back to the beginning, and the Pause toggle button switches back to the Play button, which allows viewers to click it to begin playing the video again if they'd like.

---

4 When you're finished checking out the **video** section, close your browser.

In this chapter, you will build all this functionality—everything from the progressive downloading of the FLV file to the Play/Pause toggle button, to the video preloader, and to the playback progress slider. You have a lot to learn, so keep reading!

Note: Flash Professional 8 allows you to quickly and easily incorporate a prebuilt video player similar to the one you will be building in this chapter. However, rather than rely on prebuilt components and functionality, you will learn how to build one from scratch. This gives you the ability to *customize* the functionality of the video player to fit the client's needs.

---

2 | Setting Up

In this exercise, you'll collect all the pieces you need to build the video player. You will also assign instance names to a few symbols so, as you begin to write the ActionScript to make this whole thing work, you'll be all set to start scripting.

---

1 Navigate to your **Desktop > la_eyeworks > site** folder, and double-click **about_us.fla**.

As discussed in Chapter 6, *"Using the TextFormat Class,"* you'll integrate the video player into the About Us module. If you can remember all the way back to Chapter 6, when you were constructing the sub-menu, you built and scripted an option for the video section. When the viewer clicks the video option, the video will download and play directly in the About Us module.

Once **about_us.fla** finishes opening, the first piece you need is a new layer in which to place the video content.

2 Single-click the **sub-menu** layer to select it, click the **Insert Layer** button to create a new layer, and rename the new layer to "**video**."

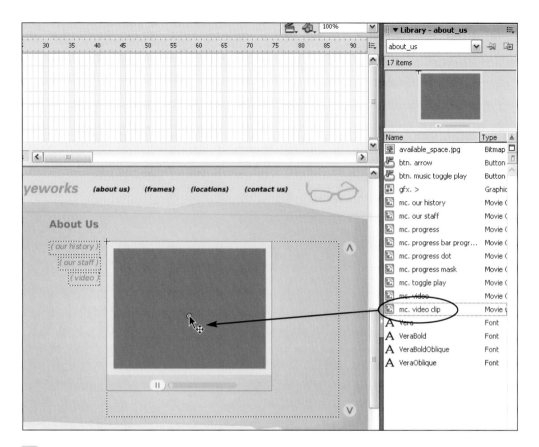

3 With the **video** layer selected, open the **about_us.fla Library** by pressing **Ctrl+L** (Windows) or **Cmd+L** (Mac). Then, locate the movie clip symbol **mc. video clip**, and drag it to the **Stage**.

This movie clip was precreated to get you started. Inside the **mc. video clip** movie clip symbol is space for the video to display, the Play/Pause toggle button to appear, and the preloader/playback progress slider to display. Although these elements have been provided for you, they lack the ActionScript to make them functional. You will write the ActionScript during the course of this chapter.

All the elements making up the video player reside in this movie clip. The reason why this one movie clip contains all these items is twofold: First, instead of cluttering up the Scene 1 Timeline with a bunch of layers relating to the video section, they're all nicely contained within this movie clip symbol. Second, as the viewer navigates to and from the video section, some ActionScript, which you'll write, will show and hide the video and all its related graphics. By keeping all of these video items within one movie clip, you can easily use one action to hide and reveal the movie clip—and the elements within it—whenever you need to do so.

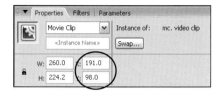

4 With the instance **mc. video clip** still selected on the **Stage**, open the **Property Inspector** by pressing **Ctrl+F3** (Windows) or **Cmd+F3** (Mac). In the **Property Inspector**, set the **X:** and **Y:** positions of the **mc. video clip** instance to **191.0** and **98.0**, respectively. This aligns the top-left of the **mc. video clip** symbol instance with the top-left of the Dynamic text field where the **our history** and **our staff** text displays.

Now, because you will be targeting this movie clip, and the items inside it, with ActionScript, you need to give this movie clip instance an instance name.

---

5 With the **mc. video clip** movie clip instance selected on the **Stage**, type **videoContainer** in the **Instance Name** field in the **Property Inspector**. Because this movie clip instance now has a unique instance name, you can target it—and control it—with ActionScript.

mc.videoclip movie clip instance selected

For the FLV file to be displayed when it begins download-ing, it needs to be attached to a video object on the Stage. In the next few steps, you'll create a new video object which you will later use ActionScript to attach the down-loading FLV file to.

---

6 Double-click the **videoContainer** movie clip instance on the **Stage** to open it.

7 Single-click the top-most layer, **progress bar**, to select it. Then, create a new layer by clicking the **Insert Layer** button. Rename the new layer to "**video object**."

---

8 Open the **about_us.fla Library** by pressing **Ctrl+L** (Windows) or **Cmd+L** (Mac).

9 Select **New Video** from the **Library options** menu located in the top-right corner of the panel.

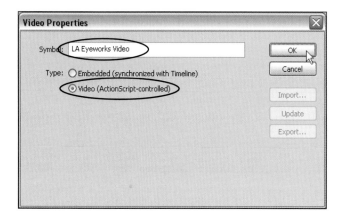

10 This opens the **Video Properties** dialog box. Make sure the radio button **Video (ActionScript-controlled)** is selected, type **LA Eyeworks Video** for its name, and click **OK**.

This inserts a new item in your library called **LA Eyeworks Video**. You might also notice it has a little video camera icon to symbolize it is a video object.

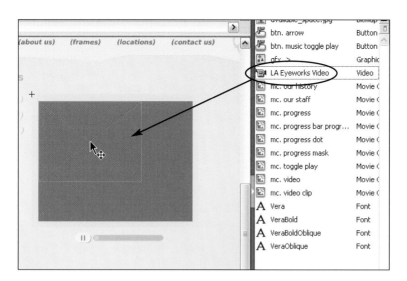

11 With the new layer **video object** still selected, drag an instance of the **LA Eyeworks Video** video object to the **Stage**.

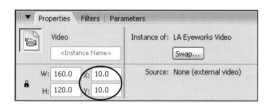

12 In the **Property Inspector**, set the **X:** and **Y:** coordinates to **10** and **10**, respectively. This aligns the video object so it's 1 pixel up and to the left of the dark-blue background in the **faux drop shadow** layer. When the progressively downloaded video plays in the video object, it will appear as if it has a slight drop shadow because of that 1 pixel offset from the dark-blue background.

However, if you want the video to play at the same size as the source video, you need to make sure the video object and the source video have the same sizes. Currently—and by default—the video object is 160 ×120 pixels. The source video, which you haven't seen yet, is actually 240 ×180 pixels. If you don't resize the video object to match, the video will be scaled to be the same size as the video object when it downloads and plays. If the video is scaled—especially if it's not scaled at the same aspect ratio as the original content—it won't look as good as it would if it was played at a one-to-one ratio. Also, if Flash 8 has to scale the video while it is playing, it will decrease the performance of your Flash project slightly. Anytime Flash has to scale content, it requires Flash to perform calculations it wouldn't have to perform if the content was not scaled. Because of those extra calculations, it can theoretically slow down the playback performance of your Flash content.

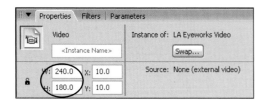

13 With the video object on the **Stage** still selected, open the **Property Inspector**, and type **240** in the **W:** field and **180** in the **H:** field. This sets the physical dimensions of the video object to be the same size as the source FLV video.

Note: If you click the lock icon to the left of the **W:** and **H:** fields in the **Property Inspector**, you'll lock the aspect ratio of your content. In other words, if you first click the lock icon, when you scale your selected content by typing a value in just the **W:** or **H:** field, it will scale the other value proportionately.

Lastly, to be able to use ActionScript to instruct the progressively downloading video to attach itself to your new video object, you first need to give it an instance name.

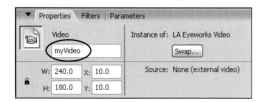

14 Type **myVideo** (paying close attention that you have the spelling and capitalization correct) in the **Instance Name** field in the **Property Inspector**.

And there you have it! Your video now has a place to be displayed. Every other item you will be targeting with ActionScript in this chapter already has its own instance name, including the Play/Pause toggle button and the playback/download progress bar, which have instance names of **togglePlay** and **vidProgBar**, respectively.

15 Save your **about_us.fla** file by choosing **File > Save**.

In the next exercise, you will start writing some ActionScript. You will begin to write the scripts to show and hide the **videoContainer** movie clip instance—where the video and all the related graphics are embedded—as the viewer navigates to and from the video section.

What Are FLV Files?

In this chapter, you will be using ActionScript to progressively download a video clip into the **about_us.swf** file. The video clip is in a format called **Fl**ash **V**ideo but is usually referred to by its acronym, FLV. By this point, you're probably wondering what the heck FLV files are. The original video content can come directly from a video camera or from a video-editing program such as Apple Final Cut Pro, Apple iMovie, Adobe Premiere, Adobe After Effects, and other programs creating video content. The objective is to take your video footage and convert it to the FLV format.

Essentially, you have five ways to create an FLV file, each with its own strengths and weaknesses: Flash 8's built-in video compressor, the FLV QuickTime Export plug-in shipping with Flash Professional 8, the Flash 8 Video Encoder also shipping with Flash Professional 8, Sorenson Squeeze 4.2 with the On2 VP6 Pro Plug-in (available for Windows only at the time of this book printing), and On2 Flix 8. What these five methods have in common is the codec they use to compress the video. *Codec*—an acronym for **co**mpression/**dec**ompression—is the method by which the video is compressed. Flash 8 introduced a new video codec, On2 VP6, to offer better quality and smaller file sizes than its predecessor (the Sorenson Spark codec), as well as supporting alpha channels in the video! Flash 8 supports video compressed with the new On2 VP6 codec and can also use video compressed with the Sorenson Spark codec introduced in Flash MX 2004. So, even though these methods compress video using the same codec, the quality of the *engine* actually doing the compressing differs between the three. The FLV file you will be using in this chapter was compressed using Sorenson Squeeze.

Note: Although the benefits of the new On2 VP6 codec are clear, you—as a Flash developer—must keep a few issues in mind when deciding which codec to use when encoding your video. When comparing On2 VP6 to Sorenson Spark, compressing your video using the On2 VP6 codec requires more time to compress the video and also consumes more processing power on the part of the viewer's computer when playing the video. Additionally, FLV files created using the new On2 VP6 codec can be viewed only by those with Flash Player 8 or higher installed. If you want to make sure your video is backward compatible with Flash Player 6 or 7, use the Sorenson Spark codec instead. So, before you commit yourself to using the latest and greatest codec, keep these issues in mind.

Flash 8's Built-in Video Compressor

Import a video into a blank FLA file in Flash 8 (standard or professional). If you have Apple QuickTime 7 or later installed on your system, you can import AVI, DV, MPG/MPEG, and MOV video file formats both in Windows and on a Mac. If you're working in Windows and you have DirectX 9 or later installed, you can also import the WMV and ASF video formats. Once you've imported the video file, go through the Import Video wizard, choose your compression settings, and let Flash 8 compress the video. Once the video has finished compressing, it will appear in the same directory on your hard drive as where you saved the FLA file. For more information about the supported video formats you can import into Flash 8, open the **Help** panel (**F1**), and from the Help "books" on the left, choose **Using Flash > Working with Video > About digital video and Flash > Supported file formats for video**.

- Pros: You don't need any additional software. You can use your existing Flash 8 software to compress the video as an FLV file.

- Cons: Other compression solutions—namely On2's Flix Pro and Sorenson Squeeze 4.2 with the On2 VP6 Pro Plug-in—offer more compression options and yield FLV files with better quality and a smaller file size.

FLV QuickTime Export plug-in

If you own Flash Professional 8, you can use the FLV QuickTime Export plug-in packaged with the Flash installer. The FLV QuickTime Export plug-in will "plug into" a variety of video-editing and video-encoding applications both in Windows and on a Mac. If you have Flash Professional 8 (the plug-in won't work if you have Flash Basic 8) and if you've installed the plug-in, you can open one of the compatible applications and export your video as an FLV file directly from that application. To read more information about the video exporter plug-in, open the **Help** panel (**F1**), and from the Help "books" on the left, choose **Using Flash > Working with Video > About digital video and Flash > About encoding video**.

- Pros: The FLV QuickTime Export plug-in allows you to export your video directly from many common video-editing applications such as Avid Xpress/Media Composer and Final Cut Pro. This helps you streamline your workflow, thereby saving you time.

- Cons: The FLV QuickTime Export plug-in comes only with the professional version of Flash 8 and doesn't offer as many compression options (including the higher-quality 2-pass encoding) as does On2's Flix Pro and Sorenson Squeeze 4.2 with the On2 VP6 Pro Plug-in.

You can read more about the FLV QuickTime Export plug-in and incorporating video into Flash projects here:
www.macromedia.com/devnet/flash/articles/flv_exporter.html

Before using the FLV QuickTime Export plug-in, it's always a good idea to check for updates first. To see whether the FLV QuickTime Export plug-in has been updated, check this URL:
www.macromedia.com/support/flash/downloads.html

Flash 8 Video Encoder

Another method to create an FLV file is using the new stand-alone application packaged with Flash Professional 8 called the *Flash 8 Video Encoder*. The Flash 8 Video Encoder offers all the same options the FLV encoder in Flash 8 does, but it also lets you batch compress video. If you have multiple videos you need compressed and don't have the additional funding to purchase a third-party video compression application, then the Flash 8 Video Encoder will fit your needs perfectly.

- Pros: Gives you the same compression options Flash 8 does but allows you to batch compress video, enabling you to effortlessly compress two videos or two hundred.

- Cons: This has the same issues as the FLV QuickTime Export plug-in: it comes only with the Professional version of Flash 8 and doesn't offer as many compression options (including the higher-quality 2-pass encoding) as does On2's Flix Pro and Sorenson Squeeze 4.2 with the On2 VP6 Pro Plug-in.

You can view a short walkthrough of using the Flash video encoder here:
www.macromedia.com/devnet/flash/articles/encoding_video_04.html

Sorenson Squeeze with the On2 VP6 Pro Plug-in

The fourth way to create FLV files is by using a third-party application by Sorenson Media called *Sorenson Squeeze*. Sorenson Squeeze—either the Sorenson Squeeze Compression Suite or Sorenson Squeeze for Flash—also allows you to compress your original video as an FLV file. While Sorenson Squeeze can compress video sources as FLV files using the Squeeze codec, Sorenson Squeeze 4.2 with the On2 VP6 Pro plug-in allows Sorenson Squeeze to compress FLVs using the new On2 VP6 codec.

- Pros: 1) Sorenson Squeeze allows you to compress video using 2-pass compression, which usually yields better-looking video with a smaller file size. 2) Sorenson Squeeze, being an application whose sole purpose in this universe is to compress video, has a great compression engine. Video compressed with Sorenson Squeeze typically looks better than video compressed with Flash 8, the FLV QuickTime Export plug-in, and the Flash 8 Video Encoder. 3) Sorenson Squeeze gives you a *ton* of options when compressing video— from allowing you to capture DV (**D**igital **V**ideo) directly in Squeeze to batch processing and to alpha-channel support with the new On2 VP6 codec. If you are in charge of getting lots of video clips into your Flash projects— or if you just want high-quality video in your SWF files—definitely check out Sorenson Squeeze. You can download a trial version of Sorenson Squeeze from the Sorenson Media Web site at **www.sorensonmedia.com**. This may sound like a sales pitch, but I can assure you I don't get anything from recommending Sorenson Squeeze to you other than making sure you get the best possible solution to meet your needs.

- Cons: You have to pay for *both* Sorenson Squeeze 4.2 (if you have Squeeze 4.0, the 4.2

upgrade is free) and the On2 VP6 Pro plug-in to compress video using the new On2 VP6 codec. After you've plopped down a chunk of change for Flash 8, you may not be willing to drop more money to buy *another* program—and a plug-in—to compress your Flash 8 video. Using Sorenson Squeeze also adds another step to your production process. With some of the other options, you can go from your video-editing program directly into Flash. But Squeeze's great options and quality comes at a price. You have to go from your video-editing application to Sorenson Squeeze and *then* to Flash.

You can read more about Sorenson Squeeze here: **www.sorensonmedia.com/**

On2 VP6 Flix 8

The last method to create an FLV file comes straight from the horse's mouth. In early 2005, On2 purchased the Flix video compression software from Wildform and revamped it to compress video using its On2 VP6 codec. The benefit of this is not only does On2 Flix 8 offer many of the same benefits Sorenson Squeeze 4.2 offers, but it also contains some of the same features available when Flix was owned by Wildform, including being able to export your video in vector format for a unique look.

- Pros: It allows you to not only compress high-quality FLV files for Flash delivery but also supports the creation of vector videos, videos automatically embedded into a SWF file (for short clips), 2-pass encoding, alpha channels, and more.

- Cons: As with Sorenson Squeeze, you have to pay for On2 Flix 8. Also, unlike when importing video into Flash 8, no easy-to-use wizard walks you through the steps. Some of the options may initially be somewhat daunting.

You can read more about On2 Flix 8 here: **www.on2.com/technology/flix-features/**

To Embed or Not to Embed

When wanting to integrate video into your Flash project, you essentially have two choices. You can either embed the video in the SWF file or keep the video (FLV) external in order to progressively download it *into* the SWF file. In this chapter, you will be using the latter option. You will be progressively downloading an external FLV for the following reasons:

- Progressively downloading and playing external FLV files is less memory intensive. Video files embedded in the SWF file are loaded into memory all at once, whereas external FLV files play using cached memory and use only small amounts of memory at a time.

- The aforementioned memory issue from which embedded video suffers also affects performance. If you have a long video clip being entirely loaded into the viewer's memory, this can greatly reduce playback performance. Because external FLV files aren't constrained by that limitation, you can easily incorporate long video files into your Flash project without the same performance degradation.

- Video files embedded in a SWF file *must play back at the same frame rate as the SWF file.* However, external FLV files can play at a differ-

ent frame rate than the SWF files in which they appear. A SWF file can have a frame rate of 21 fps (**f**rames **p**er **s**econd), but the FLV file displayed within the SWF file can play at a different frame rate such as 30 fps. Normally, when you shoot some video with a digital video camera (a.k.a. *DV cam*), you shoot it at 29.97 fps. Films you see at the movie theater, on the other hand, are shot at 24 fps. However, in terms of a Flash 8 project, a frame rate of 30 fps is quite high (more on frame rates in the nearby note). With an external FLV file, you can have the best of both worlds. You can have your SWF file play back at one frame rate—such as 21 fps—and your FLV play back at its "native" 29.97 fps. Keep in mind, however, the higher the frame rate of your FLV file, the *more frames there are per second.* The more frames per second, the larger the file size of the FLV file, since it has more frames to store. When compressing your video as an FLV file, a general guideline is to use half the rate of the original source footage. So, if you're starting with footage from a DV cam—which records at 29.97 fps—create an FLV file at 15 fps. If you're starting with footage from film—which records at 24 fps—create an FLV file at 12 fps.

NOTE:

More about Frame Rates

The following is excerpted from the book *Macromedia Flash Professional 8 Hands-On Training* by James Gonzalez (Peachpit Press/lynda.com, 2005):

When you set a frame rate in Flash 8, you're setting the maximum frame rate for your movie or how quickly the movie "tries" to play. The actual playback frame rate depends on several factors, including the download speed and processor speed of the computer used to view the movie. If the frame rate is set higher than the computer can display, the movie will play as fast as the computer's processor will allow. If you set the frame rate to 200 (which is really high), the average computer will not be able to display the movie at this rate. Also, frames with more objects, colors, or transparency than others take more time for the computer to render. Thus, the actual frame rate can vary during playback because of the rendering requirements from one frame to another.

Based on these factors, use a frame rate of at least 12 fps and not more than 25 fps so the average computer can display your movie as you intended. A frame rate of 15 to 20 fps, which is similar to the 24 fps used in motion pictures, works well most of the time.

Keeping the FLV file external allows you to load it in *only* when necessary. By using ActionScript to open an individual connection to download the FLV file and then closing that connection when the user leaves that section, you minimize the amount of unnecessary downloading that wastes bandwidth. Even saving a little bandwidth can lower the bandwidth costs for larger corporations.

It's because of these three main reasons you're using an external FLV file in this chapter. Unless you're using a simple, short video clip, I highly recommend *always* progressively downloading external FLV files whenever you need to integrate video content into your Flash projects.

Peek-a-Boo: Specifying When the Video Will Appear

You're finished setting up the **videoContainer** movie clip where the video will appear and be controlled, so now you need to specify when it should and shouldn't be visible. Currently, if you were to preview your changes, you'd notice the **videoContainer** movie clip sits directly on top of the **our history** and **our staff** content. Obviously, having a video clip sitting on top of the other sections would interfere with the viewer reading the content. In this exercise, you'll write some ActionScript to control when the **videoContainer** movie clip instance will and won't be visible.

1 Return to **Scene 1** by clicking its tab above the top-left corner of the **Timeline**.

2 Single-click **keyframe 1** in layer **a**, and open the **Actions** panel by pressing **F9** (Windows) or **Opt+F9** (Mac).

The first step is to write an action telling the **videoContainer** movie clip—where the video and all its related graphics are nested—to initially be hidden. When the viewer first arrives at the About Us module, you don't want the video content to be visible. The viewer has to click the video option to make it appear.

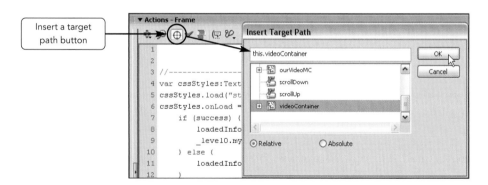

3 Scroll to the top of the **Actions** panel, and click at the beginning of the top-most line, //------------
----<load CSS>----------------\\. Press **Enter** (Windows) or **Return** (Mac) twice to create two line breaks. Then, click the new, top-most empty line break, and click the **Insert a target path** button. In the resulting **Insert Target Path** dialog box, scroll down until you find **videoContainer**, and click it to select it. Lastly, making sure the **Relative** radio button is selected, click **OK**.

This inserts the path to **videoContainer**, `this.videoContainer`. Next, you need to tell the **videoContainer** movie clip instance to turn off its visibility.

```
1  this.videoContainer._visible = false;
2
3  //-----------------<load CSS>-------------------\\
4  var cssStyles:TextField.StyleSheet = new TextField.StyleSheet();
5  cssStyles.load("styles/styles.css");
```

4 After `this.videoContainer`, type the following:

`._visible = false;`

As you have seen, `_visible` is a property you can set for text fields, buttons, movie clips, and even entire levels. In this case, you're simply instructing the `_visible` property of the **videoContainer** movie clip instance to be `false` (not visible).

Note: Don't forget to add the period (.) after `videoContainer` and before `_visible`.

Before you continue, you need to check the changes you've made up to this point to make sure everything is working properly.

---

5 Save your **about_us.fla** file by choosing **File > Save**.

Now, because the About Us module relies on `LoadVars` and `MovieClipLoader` objects residing in **master.swf**, you need to preview **about_us.swf** from *within* **master.swf**.

---

6 Publish a SWF file from **about_us.fla** by choosing **File > Publish**.

---

7 Choose **File > Open Recent**. If you see **master** in the open recent list, select it to have Flash open it for you. Otherwise, choose **File > Open**. Then, in the **Open** dialog box, navigate to your **Desktop > la_eyeworks > site** folder, and double-click **master.fla** to open it.

The last time you modified **master.fla** was in Chapter 8, *"Building a Preloader,"* when you added ActionScript to the `myMCL MovieClipLoader` object to manage the preloading of SWF and JPEG files. Prior to that, you modified some ActionScript on Keyframe 10 in **master.fla** so **frames.swf** initially loads. In doing that, you commented out an action to load **about_us.swf**. For **about_us.swf** to load, you need to comment out the action loading **frames.swf** and uncomment the action loading **about_us.swf**.

---

8 In **master.fla**, single-click **Keyframe 10** in layer **a** to select it, and open the **Actions** panel.

```
1  stop();
2  // myMCL.loadClip("splash.swf", 5);
3  myMCL.loadClip("about_us.swf", 5);
4  // myMCL.loadClip("frames.swf", 5);
```

9 Add two slashes at the beginning of the **myMCL.loadClip("frames.swf", 5);** line, and *remove* the two slashes at the beginning of the **myMCL.loadClip("about_us.swf", 5);** line.

As you have seen quite a few times, by adding two slashes before the action loading **frames.swf**, you prevent the action from being compiled, and thereby executed, when **master.swf** plays. By *removing* the two slashes before the action loading **about_us.swf**, you *allow* the action to be compiled and executed when **master.swf** runs.

10 Save your **master.fla** file by choosing **File > Save** or pressing **Ctrl+S** (Windows) or **Cmd+S** (Mac).

11 Preview **master.fla** by pressing **Ctrl+Enter** (Windows) or **Cmd+Return** (Mac).

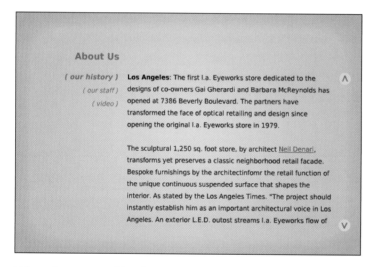

When **about_us.swf** loads into **master.swf**, you'll know you've done everything right if the **videoContainer** movie clip instance does *not* appear. However, if you click the **video** option, you'll quickly notice nothing happens.

In the rest of this exercise, you will create one function to *show* the **videoContainer** movie clip instance and another function to *hide* it. These two functions will execute when the viewer enters and leaves the video section in the About Us module.

12 Close the preview window, and close **master.fla**—you won't need it again in this chapter. In **about_us.fla**, make sure you still have **Keyframe 1** selected in layer **a** and you still have the **Actions** panel open.

The first step is to create the two functions you will need to reveal and hide the **videoContainer** movie clip instance. Why functions? Well, you want a set of actions to execute only when a certain event happens—

such as when the viewer clicks the video option or another menu option; therefore, by putting those actions within a function, those actions will not execute until you call the function. Also, you'll want to perform a group of actions multiple times. When the viewer clicks **our history** or **our staff**, you'll want the same set of actions to execute. By putting all those actions within a function, you can keep all the necessary actions in one place without having to duplicate or repeat those actions everywhere you need to use them.

```
90       this.enabled = false;
91   }
92   //-------------</our video option>---------------\\
93
94   |
```

13 Scroll down to the bottom of the **Actions** panel. Click at the end of the comment line //------------
----</our video option>----------------\\, and press **Enter** (Windows) or **Return** (Mac) twice to create two line breaks. Then, click the bottom-most line break.

```
91   }
92   //-------------</our video option>---------------\\
93
94   //-------------<video activate>---------------\\
95   function videoActivate() {
96
97   }
98   //-------------</video activate>---------------\\
```

14 Create the first function by typing the following four lines:

```
//-------------<video activate>-------------\\
function videoActivate() {

}
//-------------</video activate>-------------\\
```

When typing the ActionScript, make sure to type an additional line break between the open and closed brackets starting and ending (respectively) the function. That way, you have an empty line break to begin writing the actions to be contained within the function.

Next, create the function to eventually *deactivate* (hide) the video player.

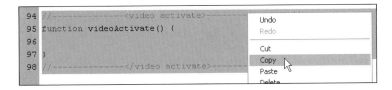

15 Select the actions you created in Step 14, **right-click** (Windows) or **Ctrl+click** (Mac) those actions, and from the resulting contextual menu, choose **Copy**.

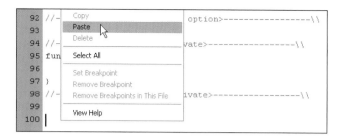

16 Click at the end of the `//-------------</video activate>-------------\\` line, and press **Enter** (Windows) or **Return** (Mac) twice to create two line breaks. Then, **right-click** (Windows) or **Ctrl+click** (Mac) the second line break you just created. From the resulting contextual menu, choose **Paste**. This pastes a copy of the `videoActivate` function—and its associated comments—two lines below the original.

```
 94 //-------------<video activate>----------------\\
 95 function videoActivate() {
 96
 97 }
 98 //-------------</video activate>----------------\\
 99
100 //-------------<video deactivate>--------------\\
101 function videoDeactivate() {
102
103 }
104 //-------------</video deactivate>--------------\\
```

17 In the copied script, change the word *activate* in the open and closed comment lines to *deactivate*. Also, make sure to change the function name to "**videoDeactivate**."

Since you now have the functions set up, you can start filling them with the appropriate actions.

Before you can start writing the actions, however, you need to figure out what you want to happen when the viewer clicks the **video** option and what should happen when the viewer clicks another option such as **our history** or **our staff**. When viewers click the **video** submenu option, they want to see the video, and therefore the following should happen: 1) The scroll down and scroll up buttons—allowing the viewer to scroll through the **our history** and **our staff** information—should disappear. 2) Any text currently being displayed in the **loadedInfo** text field should be cleared. 3) The video content (**videoContainer**) should become visible. Later, you will also add actions to specify additional event to happen—such as the video to start playing—but for now, this enables the video content to display while the content for the other sections becomes hidden.

Essentially, the opposite should happen when the viewer clicks one of the other submenu options. If the viewer clicks **our history** or **our staff**, the video content should disappear, the scroll down and scroll up buttons should reappear, and the content the viewer requested should load.

Start by writing the four actions to execute when the viewer requests the video.

```
 94 //--------------<video activate>----------------\\
 95 function videoActivate() {
 96     scrollDown._visible = false;
 97     scrollUp._visible = false;
 98     loadedInfo.text = "";
 99     videoContainer._visible = true;
100 }
101 //--------------</video activate>----------------\\
```

18 Click the empty line break between the **function videoActivate() {** line and the closed curly brace (**}**). Then, write four actions by typing the following:

```
scrollDown._visible = false;
scrollUp._visible = false;
loadedInfo.text = "";
videoContainer._visible = true;
```

As you can see, the actions are fairly straightforward. The two actions **scrollDown._visible = false;** and **scrollUp._visible = false;** just tell the scroll down and scroll up buttons to hide. **loadedInfo.text = "";** inserts nothing into the **loadedInfo** text field—where the **our history** and **our staff** text appears. By inserting nothing into the text field, it clears any text currently in the field. Lastly, **videoContainer._visible = true;** simply instructs the **videoContainer** movie clip instance, where the video content is nested, to display itself. This is the "opposite" action to the one you created in Steps 3 and 4 in this exercise.

You've specified what should happen when the viewer requests the video content, so now you should also specify what should happen when the viewer clicks one of the other options such as **our history** or **our staff**.

```
103 //--------------<video deactivate>----------------\\
104 function videoDeactivate() {
105     loadedInfo.scroll = 0;
106     scrollDown._visible = true;
107     scrollUp._visible = true;
108     videoContainer._visible = false;
109 }
110 //--------------</video deactivate>----------------\\
```

19 Click the empty line break between the **function videoDeactivate() {** line and the closed curly brace (**}**). Then, write four actions by typing the following:

```
loadedInfo.scroll = 0;
scrollDown._visible = true;
scrollUp._visible = true;
videoContainer._visible = false;
```

Three of the four actions are essentially opposites of what you just wrote in Step 18. When the viewer wants to leave the **video** section and navigate to another section such as **our history** or **our staff**, the scroll down and scroll up buttons both reappear, and the **videoContainer** movie clip then disappears. The remaining action, **loadedInfo.scroll = 0;**, instructs the **loadedInfo** text field on the **Stage** to set its **scroll** property back to **0**. This action is here because if the viewer was—for example—scrolling through the **our history** section, clicked the **video** option, and then returned to another section such as **our history** or **our staff**, the text loaded into the **loadedInfo** text field would inherit the last scroll position. In other words, if the viewer had scrolled halfway down a block of text in the **our history** section, went to the **video** section, and then returned to any other section that inserted text into the **loadedInfo** text field, that text would automatically scroll itself to the point at which the viewer left. `loadedInfo.scroll = 0;` sets the scroll property of the **loadedInfo** text field back to **0**, so if the reader returns to either **our history** or **our staff**, the text will load and display with the first line visible at the top of the field.

If you were to preview your movie at this point, you would see…nothing. Nothing would be changed from when you previewed it last. Remember, the `videoActivate` and `videoDeactivate` functions you just so lovingly crafted won't automatically execute themselves. They need to be told *when* they should perform. Well, the `videoActivate` function, which activates the video, should execute when the viewer requests the video—when the viewer clicks the **video** option. The `videoDeactivate` function, on the other hand, should execute when the viewer *leaves* the video section. So, when the viewer clicks the **our history** or **our staff** options, the video content should "deactivate."

You might also be wondering what happens if the viewer clicks one of the main menu options such as frames, locations, and so forth. "Shouldn't we specify what happens then?" you might be wondering. If you think back to how the separate sections display, you might remember that each section (about us, video, locations, and so forth) is loaded into **master.swf** into **_level5**. So, when the viewer clicks another main menu button, the entire About Us module is cleared and a new section loads into its vacated place. So no, you don't need to specify what happens when the viewer clicks one of the main menu options.

In the next few steps, you'll write the actions to specify which function executes and from where.

```
80  //-------------<our video option>----------------\\
81  this.ourVideoMC.onRollOver = function() {
82      this.ourVideo.setTextFormat(btnDisable);
83  }
84  this.ourVideoMC.onRollOut = function() {
85      this.ourVideo.setTextFormat(btnEnable);
86  }
87  this.ourVideoMC.onRelease = function() {
88      reEnableOptions();
89      this.ourVideo.setTextFormat(btnDisable);
90      this.enabled = false;
91      videoActivate();
92  }
93  //-------------</our video option>----------------\\
```

20 Within the `this.ourVideoMC.onRelease` function (shown in the illustration here), click at the end of the `this.enabled = false;` action, press **Enter** (Windows) or **Return** (Mac) once to create a line break, and type the following:

`videoActivate();`

This action simply says, "When the viewer clicks the **video** submenu option, execute the `videoActivate` function." The `videoActivate` function, of course, displays the video content and hides the other section content.

```
65  //--------------<our staff option>--------------\\
66  this.ourStaffMC.onRollOver = function() {
67      this.ourStaff.setTextFormat(btnDisable);
68  }
69  this.ourStaffMC.onRollOut = function() {
70      this.ourStaff.setTextFormat(btnEnable);
71  }
72  this.ourStaffMC.onRelease = function() {
73      reEnableOptions();
74      this.ourStaff.setTextFormat(btnDisable);
75      this.enabled = false;
76      _level0.myLV.load("vars/ourStaff.txt");
77      videoDeactivate();
78  }
79  //--------------</our staff option>--------------\\
```

21 For the **our staff** option, click at the end of the **_level0.myLV.load("vars/ourStaff.txt");** action, press **Enter** (Windows) or **Return** (Mac) to create a line break, and execute the **videoDeactivate** function by typing the following:

videoDeactivate();

When the viewer clicks the **our staff** option, the video content hides, the scroll down and scroll up buttons reappear, the **scroll** property gets reset for the **loadedInfo** text field, and the **our staff** information loads.

The last step is to execute the **videoDeactivate** function when the viewer clicks the **our history** submenu option.

```
50  //--------------<our history option>--------------\\
51  this.ourHistoryMC.onRollOver = function() {
52      this.ourHistory.setTextFormat(btnDisable);
53  }
54  this.ourHistoryMC.onRollOut = function() {
55      this.ourHistory.setTextFormat(btnEnable);
56  }
57  this.ourHistoryMC.onRelease = function() {
58      reEnableOptions();
59      this.ourHistory.setTextFormat(btnDisable);
60      this.enabled = false;
61      _level0.myLV.load("vars/ourHistory.txt");
62      videoDeactivate();
63  }
64  //--------------</our history option>--------------\\
```

22 For the **our history** submenu option, click at the end of the **_level0.myLV.load("vars/ourHistory.txt");** action, press **Enter** (Windows) or **Return** (Mac) once to create a line break, and type the following:

videoDeactivate();

You've now specified when and where the video content should and shouldn't be visible, so it's time to test your changes.

Loading and Playing the Video

In this exercise, you'll learn to use the **NetConnection** and **NetStream** classes to progressively download and play an external FLV file. Buckle up because you've gone too far to stop now!

Because you don't want the actions that load and play the external FLV file to automatically execute when **about_us.swf** first loads, you'll put them in a function.

```
110     scrollUp._visible = true;
111     videoContainer._visible = false;
112 }
113 //-------------</video deactivate>-------------\\
114
115 //-------------<video>-------------\\
116 function initializeVideo() {
117
118 }
119 //-------------</video>-------------\\
```

1 Click at the end of the bottom line, //-------------**</video deactivate>**-------------\\, press **Enter** (Windows) or **Return** (Mac) twice to create two line breaks, and type the following:

```
//-------------<video>-------------\\
function initializeVideo() {

}
//-------------</video>-------------\\
```

When typing the ActionScript, make sure to type an additional line break between the open and closed brackets starting and ending (respectively) the function. That way, you have an empty line break to begin writing the actions to be contained within the function.

You will be creating three separate objects within this function: a **NetConnection** object to provide a connection to download the FLV file, a **NetStream** object to control the playback of the FLV file (the **NetStream** object is to FLV files what the **Sound** object is to MP3 files), and a **LoadVars** object to load the variable .txt file to store the total running time of the FLV file. Because you will be using objects within a function, you will first need to instantiate the objects *outside* the function so you can target them with ActionScript. This is the identical concept you learned in Chapter 10, *"Building an MP3 Player,"* when you instantiated the **bgMusak Sound** object *outside* the **playMusak** function.

```
116 //--------------<video>--------------\\
117 var myNetConn:NetConnection;
118 var myNetStream:NetStream;
119 var videoLV:LoadVars;
```

2 Click at the end of the opening video comment line, //-------------**<video>**-------------\\, press **Enter** (Windows) or **Return** (Mac) once to create a line break, and instantiate the three objects by typing the following:

```
var myNetConn:NetConnection;
var myNetStream:NetStream;
var videoLV:LoadVars;
```

These three actions, from top to bottom, create a new **NetConnection** object with an instance name of **myNetConn**, a new **NetStream** object with an instance name of **myNetStream**, and a new **LoadVars** object with an instance name of **videoLV**. In the **initializeVideo** function, you will use all three objects to create the script to progressively download the FLV file. Make sure you also press **Enter** (Windows) or **Return** (Mac) after you type the last action to create an empty line break (for simply visual purposes) between the three actions you just wrote and the **initializeVideo** function.

Although there's a fair amount of ActionScript involved—as you are about to see—in the progressive downloading of the external FLV file as well as the loading of an external variable to track the total running time of the FLV file, the actions and their order are fairly formulaic. In other words, once you've written these actions once, you can easily copy and paste them to a completely different project and have them work with only a few minor changes.

```
115 //--------------<video>----------------\\
116 var myNetConn:NetConnection;
117 var myNetStream:NetStream;
118 var videoLV:LoadVars;
119
120 function initializeVideo() {
121     myNetConn = new NetConnection();
122 }
123 //--------------</video>----------------\\
```

3 Click the empty line break between the **function initializeVideo() {** line and the closed curly brace (**}**), and create a new **NetConnection** object by typing the following:

```
myNetConn = new NetConnection();
```

As its name implies, a **NetConnection** object instructs Flash 8 to open a new network connection. Although it sounds like you can do a lot with it, the **NetConnection** object is a specific connection for progressively downloading an FLV file locally (from your hard drive or removable media), over an HTTP (**H**yper**T**ext **T**ransfer **P**rotocol) connection (from a Web server), or streamed from an FCS (**F**lash **C**ommunication **S**erver). The **NetConnection** object was also available in Flash MX (6), but it allowed you to make a connection only to the FCS for streaming video. Since the release Flash MX 2004, you can also use the **NetConnection** and **NetStream** objects to progressively download FLV files locally or over HTTP without needing the FCS.

Once you've created a **NetConnection** object, the next step is to use the **connect** constructor to open a connection.

```
115  //-------------<video>-------------\\
116  var myNetConn:NetConnection;
117  var myNetStream:NetStream;
118  var videoLV:LoadVars;
119
120  function initializeVideo() {
121      myNetConn = new NetConnection();
122     ( myNetConn.connect(null); )
123  }
124  //-------------</video>-------------\\
```

4 Click at the end of the **myNetConn = new NetConnection();** line, press **Enter** (Windows) or **Return** (Mac) once to create a line break, and type the following:

myNetConn.connect(null);

This action simply opens a local connection for you to progressively download a local or remote FLV file. The **null** parameter you see is a required parameter. You *must* pass the **null** parameter for the **connect** constructor to work correctly. When used in conjunction with the FCS, instead of the **null** parameter, you would pass the hostname and server address as a parameter (such as **rtmp://myApplicationInstance**).

Since you've created and set up a new **NetConnection** object, now you need to create a new **NetStream** object. As briefly mentioned earlier in this exercise, the **NetStream** object is to FLV files what the **Sound** object is to MP3 files. The **NetStream** object allows you to monitor and control various aspects of a progressively downloading or streaming FLV file such as pause, play, track the downloading progress, and so forth. The **NetStream** object—which you've already assigned the instance name of **myNetStream** to— uses the **NetConnection** object to download or stream FLV files through.

The first step is to create a new **NetStream** object to which to pass the instance name of a **NetConnection** object.

```
115  //-------------<video>-------------\\
116  var myNetConn:NetConnection;
117  var myNetStream:NetStream;
118  var videoLV:LoadVars;
119
120  function initializeVideo() {
121      myNetConn = new NetConnection();
122      myNetConn.connect(null);
123     ( myNetStream = new NetStream(myNetConn); )
124  }
125  //-------------</video>-------------\\
```

5 Click at the end of the **myNetConn.connect(null);** line, press **Enter** (Windows) or **Return** (Mac) to create a line break, and type the following:

myNetStream = new NetStream(myNetConn);

Now, whenever you want to find out what your FLV file is up to, or to tell it to do something, you can refer to it by its **NetStream** object instance name, **myNetStream**.

Next, you need to tell the video object you created in Exercise 2, **myVideo**, to receive the video source from the **myNetStream NetStream** object.

```
115  //--------------<video>---------------\\
116  var myNetConn:NetConnection;
117  var myNetStream:NetStream;
118  var videoLV:LoadVars;
119
120  function initializeVideo() {
121      myNetConn = new NetConnection();
122      myNetConn.connect(null);
123      myNetStream = new NetStream(myNetConn);
124      videoContainer.myVideo.attachVideo(myNetStream);
125  }
126  //--------------</video>---------------\\
```

6 Click at the end of the `myNetStream = new NetStream(myNetConn);` line, press **Enter** (Windows) or **Return** (Mac) once to create a line break, and type the following:

`videoContainer.myVideo.attachVideo(myNetStream);`

This action instructs the video object `myVideo`—which is embedded within the `videoContainer` movie clip instance—to receive the video from the `myNetStream` `NetStream` object.

And there you have, in its barest essence, the nearly completed script to progressively download an FLV file into the `myVideo` video object. The only action left to actually begin the progressive download of an FLV file is the action instructing the `NetStream` object *which* FLV file to download. Before you write that action, though, you need to incorporate a few other actions into this script.

When an FLV file begins to progressively download into the `myVideo` video object, it will start playing as soon as one-tenth of a second of video has been downloaded. For broadband users this is great because it means they can watch the video as it is downloading. They don't have to wait for the whole video to download before they can start watching it. However, for a viewer using a slow Internet connection such as a 56k modem, even though the video will start playing as soon as one-tenth of a second of it has been downloaded, it will stop playing shortly thereafter. The problem is that a viewer using a slow Internet connection is watching the video faster than it can download. Therefore, when the video catches up to what has been downloaded, it will stop and wait for another one-tenth of a second of video to download, and then it will start playing again. Start. Stop. Start. You get the idea.

Luckily, Macromedia has provided a method allowing you to specify how many seconds of video Flash Player 8 should *buffer* (pre-download) before it begins to play. Although this buffer time is one I suggest you modify to suit your own needs, for the L.A. Eyeworks site you'll initially set the buffer to five seconds, which means the viewer has to wait until five seconds of video has been downloaded before it begins playing. By modifying the buffer to fit the specifics of your video for your own projects, you can minimize the stopping and starting that slow connections experience when viewing video content.

```
115  //---------------<video>---------------\\
116  var myNetConn:NetConnection;
117  var myNetStream:NetStream;
118  var videoLV:LoadVars;
119
120  function initializeVideo() {
121      myNetConn = new NetConnection();
122      myNetConn.connect(null);
123      myNetStream = new NetStream(myNetConn);
124      videoContainer.myVideo.attachVideo(myNetStream);
125      myNetStream.setBufferTime(5);
126  }
127  //---------------</video>---------------\\
```

7 Click at the end of the `videoContainer.myVideo.attachVideo(myNetStream);` line, press **Enter** (Windows) or **Return** (Mac) to create a line break, and type the following:

`myNetStream.setBufferTime(5);`

This action—as you can probably guess—instructs the **myNetStream NetStream** object to set its buffer time to five seconds.

At this point, you could write the simple action to load the FLV file and call it a night. However, in Exercise 6 you will be building a playback slider to animate across a bar as the video is playing. When the slider gets to the end of the bar, the video is finished. To be able to construct a playback slider like that, you need to know two facts. You need to know how much of the FLV file has played up until that point, and you need to know the total running time of the FLV file. When you have those two numbers, you can figure out everything else you need.

As you saw in the **music_progress.mov** movie in Chapter 10, *"Building an MP3 Player,"* you used the **duration** property of the **Sound** object, and a little math, to calculate the total running time of the progressively downloading MP3 file. When working with the **NetStream** object, however, you can retrieve the total duration of an FLV file a little differently but much more simply. All the FLV compression applications I mentioned earlier embed *metadata* (in this context, metadata is simply additional information about the FLV file)—including the total running time of the video—at the beginning of the FLV file. Using the **onMetaData** handler, you can retrieve this information and use it, for example, to create and animate the playback progress slider as you will build in Exercise 6.

```
121  function initializeVideo() {
122       myNetConn = new NetConnection();
123       myNetConn.connect(null);
124       myNetStream = new NetStream(myNetConn);
125       videoContainer.myVideo.attachVideo(myNetStream);
126       myNetStream.setBufferTime(5);
127
128       myNetStream.onMetaData = function(infoObject:Object) {
129
130       }
131  }
```

8 Locate the `initializeVideo` function. Within that function, click *after* the action
`myNetStream.setBufferTime(5);`, press **Enter** (Windows) or **Return** (Mac) twice to create a couple of line
breaks, and type the following:

`myNetStream.onMetaData = function(infoObject:Object) {`

`}`

Since **onMetaData** is an event of the **NetStream** object, you assign it to your **NetStream** object by typing
myNetStream.onMetaData. Just like the **onLoadProgress** event handler is assigned to a **MovieClipLoader**
object as a function (**myMCL.onLoadProgress = function() {**), you're doing the same here but with a
NetStream object instead. Like the **MovieClipLoader** object, the **NetStream** object broadcasts information
when certain events occur. The **NetStream** object has an **onMetaData** event—as you've employed here—
with which the **myNetStream** object broadcasts information (such as the video's duration, creation date,
data rates, and so forth) when it receives metadata embedded within an FLV file it is handling. It broadcasts the information to an object called **infoObject**, which you've entered as a parameter and to which
you've assigned the **onMetaData** event.

```
122  function initializeVideo() {
123       myNetConn = new NetConnection();
124       myNetConn.connect(null);
125       myNetStream = new NetStream(myNetConn);
126       videoContainer.myVideo.attachVideo(myNetStream);
127       myNetStream.setBufferTime(5);
128
129       myNetStream.onMetaData = function(infoObject:Object) {
130           videoTRT = infoObject.duration;
131       }
132  }
```

9 Click the empty line break between the open curly brace and the closed curly brace of the function
you just wrote, and type the following:

`videoTRT = infoObject.duration;`

Simply, this action reads, "Take the value of the **duration** property of the **infoObject** object, and assign it
to a variable called **videoTRT**." As I mentioned earlier, as the **NetStream** object receives metadata from an
FLV file, it broadcasts the information to the **onMetaData** handler using the **infoObject** object. Each piece
of information—duration, creation date, data rate, and so forth—is sent to the **infoObject** as a property.
So, as you've done here, to get the **duration** property, you simply type **infoObject.duration**. You might
also have noticed you didn't type **var** before the **videoTRT** variable, and you didn't strict type it, because

you will need to access the value of that variable from outside the **myNetStream** object. Therefore, as you have done before, you will need to instantiate the variable.

```
116  //--------------<video>----------------\\
117  var myNetConn:NetConnection;
118  var myNetStream:NetStream;
119  var videoLV:LoadVars;
120  var videoTRT:Number;
121
122  function initializeVideo() {
123      myNetConn = new NetConnection();
124      myNetConn.connect(null);
```

10 Click after the action **var videoLV:LoadVars;**, press **Enter** (Windows) or **Return** (Mac) to create a line break, and type the following:

var videoTRT:Number;

This both instantiates the **videoTRT** variable and strict types it to the Number data type. Now, whenever you need to access the total running time of the FLV file, you simply type **videoTRT**. Easy!

Because of the introduction of this new functionality, you should slightly rearrange the procedure for what should happen when the viewer clicks the **our video** option. Currently, the **videoActivate** function immediately executes, which just hides the other content. To rearrange the load order so everything works properly, you first want the **initializeVideo** function to execute so the **NetConnection** and **NetStream** objects are created, enabling you—as you will see later—to both find out what the loading/playing video is doing and find out *where* it should be loading. Then you want the **videoActivate** function to execute so the other content is hidden and the FLV file is instructed to load. Thankfully, this is a quick and simple procedure.

```
82  //--------------<our video option>----------------\\
83  this.ourVideoMC.onRollOver = function() {
84      this.ourVideo.setTextFormat(btnDisable);
85  }
86  this.ourVideoMC.onRollOut = function() {
87      this.ourVideo.setTextFormat(btnEnable);
88  }
89  this.ourVideoMC.onRelease = function() {
90      reEnableOptions();
91      this.ourVideo.setTextFormat(btnDisable);
92      this.enabled = false;
93      videoActivate();
94  }
95  //--------------</o      Undo              ------\\
96                          Redo
97  //--------------<vi                        -----\\
                            Cut
                            Copy
```

11 Locate the **ourVideoMC.onRelease** function. Within it, locate the **videoActivate();** action. Select that action, **right-click** (Windows) or **Ctrl+click** (Mac) it, and choose **Cut**.

```
122  function initializeVideo() {
123      myNetConn = new NetConnection();
124      myNetConn.connect(null);
125      myNetStream = new NetStream(myNetConn);
126      videoContainer.myVideo.attachVideo(myNetStream);
127      myNetStream.setBufferTime(5);
128
129      myNetStream.onMetaData = function(infoObject:Object) {
130          videoTRT = infoObject.duration;
131      }
132      videoActivate();
133  }
134  //--------------</video>---------------\\
```

12 Scroll down to the bottom of the actions, click after the closed curly brace (**}**) defining the end of the **myNetStream.onMetaData** function, press **Enter** (Windows) or **Return** (Mac) to create a line break, and paste the **videoActivate();** action in the empty line break.

Now, the **videoActivate** function, and the actions within it, won't execute until the **initializeVideo** function has executed first. Next, you just need to specify when the **initializeVideo** function executes.

```
89  this.ourVideoMC.onRelease = function() {
90      reEnableOptions();
91      this.ourVideo.setTextFormat(btnDisable);
92      this.enabled = false;
93      initializeVideo();
94  }
```

13 In the Actions panel, scroll back up until you locate the **ourVideoMC.onRelease** function where you cut the **videoActivate** action from in Step 11. Click the same empty line break where **videoActivate** used to reside (after **this.enabled = false;**), and type the following:

initializeVideo();

So now, when the viewer clicks the **video** submenu option, the **initializeVideo** function executes. The **initializeVideo** function sets up the required **NetConnection** and **NetStream** objects, uses the **onMetaData** event of the **myNetStream NetStream** object to have the FLV file's total running time stored in a variable for later use, then hides the other information, and finally shows the video content. What you're missing now is the video itself and the action instructing the **NetStream** object to load the video.

Before you attempt to test your work and load the FLV file, you should have a good idea of *where* the FLV is located.

14 Minimize (Windows) or hide (Mac) Flash 8, and then navigate to your **Desktop > la_eyeworks > resources > video** folder.

In the **video** folder you'll notice two files, **la_eyeworks_video.flv** and **LAEyeworks_480.mov**. If you'd like, you can open the MOV file in the QuickTime Player to watch the original 480 x 360 video. But the file you're really interested in is the one you will be progressively downloading into **about_us.sw**f, the **la_eyeworks_video.flv** file. As you can see in the illustration here, its file size weighs in at a fairly hefty 3.2MB. But considering this video—even though it was scaled down in size when it was compressed to an FLV file—is three minutes and sixteen seconds long, that's not a bad file size.

15 In Windows, **right-click** the **la_eyeworks_video** file, and from the resulting contextual menu, choose **Copy**. On Mac OS X, **Ctrl+click** the **la_eyeworks_video.flv** file, and from the resulting contextual menu, choose **Copy "la_eyeworks_video.flv"**.

16 Then, navigate to your **Desktop > la_eyeworks >** **site** folder. In Windows, **right-click** an empty space in the **site** folder. From the resulting contextual menu, choose **Paste**. On Mac OS X, **Ctrl+click** an empty space in the **site** folder, and from the resulting contextual menu, choose **Paste item**.

This copies the **la_eyeworks_video.flv** file into the **site** folder where the rest of the site files are.

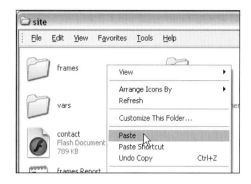

---

17 Return to **about_us.fla** in Flash. Make sure you have **Keyframe 1** selected in layer **a** and you have the **Actions** panel open.

```
97  //--------------<video activate>----------------\\
98  function videoActivate() {
99      scrollDown._visible = false;
100     scrollUp._visible = false;
101     loadedInfo.text = "";
102     videoContainer._visible = true;
103     myNetStream.play("la_eyeworks_video.flv");
104 }
105 //--------------</video activate>----------------\\
```

18 In the **Actions** panel, scroll until you find the **videoActivate** function. Then, click at the end of the **videoContainer._visible = true;** action, press **Enter** (Windows) or **Return** (Mac) to create a line break, and type the following:

myNetStream.play("la_eyeworks_video.flv");

When the **videoActivate** function executes, this action instructs the **myNetStream NetStream** object you created earlier in this exercise to begin progressively downloading and playing the FLV file **la_eyeworks_video.flv**. Because the FLV file resides in the same directory as the rest of your site SWF files, you don't need to specify a path to the FLV file; you can just type its name to load and play it. If you were building a site with more than several FLV files, you could keep your site files organized by creating a separate folder to store them.

Whew, congratulations! You just finished writing the ActionScript required to progressively download and play an external FLV file. You also utilized the **onMetaData** event of the **NetStream** object to discover the total running time of the FLV file and then store the number in a variable. In Exercise 6, you will use this number to construct the playback progress slider.

Before you continue to the next exercise, however, you should save and test your work to make sure everything is working correctly.

19 Save your **about_us.fla** file by choosing **File > Save**.

---

20 Publish an updated SWF file by choosing **File > Publish**.

---

21 Minimize (Windows) and hide (Mac) Flash 8, and navigate to your **Desktop > la_eyeworks > site** folder. Double-click **master.swf** to open it in Flash Player 8.

---

22 When the **About Us** section appears, click the **video** submenu option.

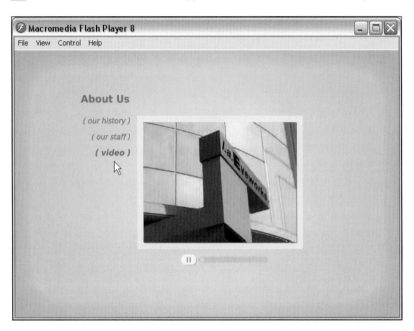

When you click **video**, you'll notice video is playing where once just a dark-blue box appeared! Thanks to a bit of ActionScript and some sweat, you just successfully loaded an external FLV file—using a `NetConnection` and `NetStream` object—into the `myVideo` video object. You'll also notice by clicking one of the other submenu options, the section will load and the video section will disappear. Clicking the **video** section will make the other section content disappear, the video content reappear, and the video start playing again. However, you might also notice when you click **our staff** or **our history**, while the new content loads in and the video disappears, you can still hear the video playing. This is because even though you've told the video to hide itself, you haven't told it to stop playing. You can fix that with one simple action.

---

23 Close the Flash Player 8 window, and return to **about_us.fla** in Flash 8. Once again, make sure you have the first keyframe selected in layer **a** and your **Actions** panel open.

```
107  //--------------<video deactivate>---------------\\
108  function videoDeactivate() {
109      loadedInfo.scroll = 0;
110      scrollDown._visible = true;
111      scrollUp._visible = true;
112      videoContainer._visible = false;
113      myNetStream.pause();
114  }
115  //--------------</video deactivate>---------------\\
```

24 Locate the `videoDeactivate` function, click *after* the `videoContainer._visible = false;` action, press **Enter** (Windows) **or Return** (Mac) to create a line break, and tell the video to pause playback by typing the following:

`myNetStream.pause();`

Now, when the viewer clicks one of the other sections in the About Us module and the `videoDeactive` function executes, not only will it hide the video but it will also pause it.

25 Once again, save your **about_us.fla** file, publish a new SWF file, hide Flash 8, navigate to **Desktop > la_eyeworks > site**, and double-click **master.swf** to open it in Flash Player 8.

26 When the **About Us** module loads, click the **our video** link. Once the video has started playing, click **our staff** or **our history**. Now, not only should the video content disappear, but you should also no longer hear it play. Hooray!

Pretty darn nifty! You're now reaping the benefits—which were covered earlier—an external FLV provides. Congratulations, once again.

27 When you're finished oohing and aahing at your magnificent creation, close the Flash Player 8 window, and return to **about_us.fla** in Flash 8.

In the next exercise, you will write a little ActionScript to enable the viewer to pause and play the video when the Play/Pause toggle button is clicked.

5 | Creating the Play/Pause Toggle

In this exercise, you'll allow the user to play and pause the FLV file. You will do this by adding a small amount of ActionScript to the Play and Pause buttons so, when clicked, they will play or pause the progressively downloading FLV file.

Just like you saw in Chapter 10, *"Building an MP3 Player,"* when adding actions to a toggle button—like this Play/Pause toggle button—you need to add the ActionScript *directly* to the button instances. As you remember, the method you've been learning—attaching ActionScript to a button or movie clip symbol via actions on keyframes—will not work correctly with this kind of toggle button. Instead, you must attach the ActionScript directly to the button instances.

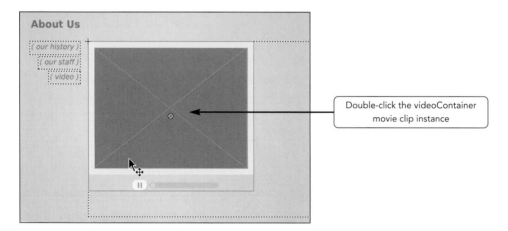

Double-click the videoContainer movie clip instance

1 On the **Stage**, double-click the **videoContainer** movie clip instance to open it.

2 Then, double-click the **togglePlay** movie clip instance—where the Play and Pause buttons reside—to open it.

3 Single-click the **musakPauseBtn** button instance on the Stage, and open the **Actions** panel by pressing **F9** (Windows) or **Opt+F9** (Mac).

```
1  on (release) {
2      nextFrame();
3  }
```

You'll notice a few simple actions assigned to the Pause button already. These actions simply move the playhead to the next frame when the viewer clicks the Pause button. In a few steps, you'll see the Play button has an action to move the playhead back to Frame 1 when the viewer clicks it, which is what makes it a "toggle" button. Now, you just need to add an action to the Pause and Play buttons to instruct the FLV file to pause and "unpause" when clicked.

```
1  on (release) {
2      _root.myNetStream.pause();
3      nextFrame();
4  }
```

4 Click at the end of the **on (release) {** line, press **Enter** (Windows) or **Return** (Mac) once to create a line break, and type the following:

_root.myNetStream.pause();

As you learned in the previous exercise, this action instructs the **myNetStream NetStream** object back on Scene 1 (**_root**) to pause the FLV file. **pause()** is a method of the **NetStream** class. You can pass a **true** or **false** (Boolean) parameter to the **NetStream** object in the **pause()** method. If you type **true** in the parentheses after **pause**, the FLV file will pause. If you type **false**, the FLV file will resume playing. However, if you don't pass any parameters in the **pause()** method—as you are doing in the action you just wrote in Step 4—it acts as a toggle pause. Each time you send the **pause()** method to the **NetStream** class, it will either play or pause the FLV file. Therefore, you can easily copy this action and apply it to the Play button without any changes. Yay! This is something simple for a change!

5 Select and copy the **_root.myNetStream.pause();** action you just wrote.

6 Move the playhead to **Frame 2**. On the **Stage**, single-click the **musakPlayBtn** button instance to select it, and open the **Actions** panel by pressing **F9** (Windows) or **Opt+F9** (Mac).

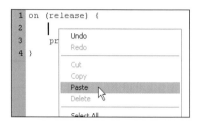

7 Click at the end of the **on (release) {** line, and press **Enter** (Windows) or **Return** (Mac) to create a line break. Then, **right-click** (Windows) or **Ctrl+click** (Mac) the new line break, and from the resulting contextual menu, choose **Paste**.

```
1  on (release) {
2      _root.myNetStream.pause();
3      prevFrame();
4  }
```

This pastes the action you created in Step 4 onto the **musakPlayBtn** toggle button.

The Pause button on Frame 1 pauses the FLV file when clicked and advances the playhead to Frame 2 where the Play button is. The Play button unpauses the FLV file—by simply executing the **pause()** method of the **NetStream** object again—and moves the playhead to Frame 1 where the Pause button is. Pretty straightforward, yes?

Now you just need to test the Play/Pause toggle button to make sure it works correctly.

8 Save your **about_us.fla** file by choosing **File > Save** or pressing **Ctrl+S** (Windows) or **Cmd+S** (Mac).

9 Publish an updated SWF file by choosing **File > Publish**.

10 Minimize (Windows) or hide (Mac) Flash 8, and navigate to your **Desktop > la_eyeworks > site** folder. Double-click **master.swf** to open it in Flash Player 8.

11 When the **About Us** module appears, click the **video** submenu option to display the video content.

12 When the video starts playing, click the Pause button. When you do, the FLV file will pause, and the Play button replaces the Pause button.

13 Click the Play button, and the FLV file resumes playing.

You now have a working Play/Pause toggle button! Pretty darn nifty.

14 Close the Flash Player 8 window, and return to **about_us.fla** in Flash 8.

In the next exercise, you will write some ActionScript to make the small, light-blue dot animate across the progress bar as the FLV file plays. The dot—as you saw when building a similar one for the MP3 player in the **music_progress.mov** movie in Chapter 10, *"Building an MP3 Player"*—represents the playback progress of the FLV file.

What Is the NetStream Class?

As mentioned earlier in this chapter, the **NetStream** class is to FLV files as the **Sound** class is to MP3 files. The **NetStream** class provides methods and properties for controlling an FLV file and for finding out what an FLV file is doing. By using a **NetStream** object, you can determine the following:

- You can find out whether the FLV file should be paused or playing.

- You can specify how many seconds of the FLV file should be preloaded before it begins playing.

- You can find out how many bytes of the FLV file have downloaded and how many bytes the FLV file is total.

- You can find out how many seconds of the FLV file have played.

You can use the **NetStream** object for quite a bit more than is listed here. For more information about the **NetStream** class, open the **Help** panel (**F1**), and from the Help "books" on the left, choose **ActionScript 2.0 Language Reference > ActionScript classes > NetStream**. For your immediate reference, this table lists the **NetStream** methods, properties, and event handlers:

Methods, Properties, and Event Handlers of the NetStream Class

Methods

Method	Description
close()	Stops playing the FLV file, resets the **time** property to **0**, and allows the **NetStream** object to be used to load another FLV file. This method also deletes the copy of the FLV file on the viewer's computer downloaded using HTTP (from a remote Web server).
pause()	Pauses or resumes the playback of an FLV file. The first time you call the **pause()** method, it pauses the FLV file. If you call it again, it resumes playing the FLV file. You can also pass a Boolean (**true** or **false**) parameter to the **NetStream** object in this method. **pause(true)** pauses the FLV file, and **pause(false)** resumes playback.
play()	Starts playing an external FLV file. Within the parentheses you specify which external FLV file you want to start playing, like so: **myNetStream.play("myFLV.flv");** .
seek()	**seek()**, as its name implies, allows you to move the playback point of the FLV file to a new point in time. You can write **NetStream.seek(30);** to move your FLV file to 30 seconds from the beginning (replacing *NetStream* with the name of your **NetStream** object, of course). This is akin to creating an action to fast-forward or rewind an FLV file.
setBufferTime()	Allows you to specify how many seconds of video need to be buffered (preloaded) before the FLV file begins to play. To use this, simply call this method and pass the buffer time amount—in seconds—like so: **NetStream.setBufferTime(15);** .

continues on next page

Properties

Property	Description
bufferLength	Returns the number of seconds of video currently in the buffer.
bufferTime	Returns the number of seconds assigned to the buffer. Unless modified with the **setBufferTime** method, the default buffer amount is one-tenth of a second (**.1**).
bytesLoaded	Returns how many bytes of the FLV file have downloaded. You can use **bytesLoaded** in conjunction with **bytesTotal** to create a preloader—as you will see later in this chapter.
bytesTotal	Returns the total number of bytes of the FLV file currently downloading.
currentFps	Returns the current value of how many frames per second at which the FLV file is playing. Monitoring this property when testing your project on different computers will help you fine-tune your FLV file optimization so you can achieve acceptable frame rates on slower computers.
time	Returns how many seconds of the FLV file have played.

Event Handlers

Event Handler	Description
onCuePoint	Triggered when a cue point, embedded in the FLV file, is reached. This allows you to listen to your FLV file play back and, when a cue point is reached, to trigger actions to be executed. For more information about the **onCuePoint** event handler, refer to your **Help** panel under **ActionScript 2.0 Language Reference > ActionScript classes > NetStream > onCuePoint**.
onMetaData	Triggered when an FLV file containing embedded metadata is played. Earlier in this chapter you saw you can use this to get the duration of the FLV file. For more information about the **onMetaData** handler, refer to your **Help** panel under **ActionScript 2.0 Language Reference > ActionScript classes > NetStream > onMetaData**.
onStatus	Triggered when the status of the FLV file changes—such as when FLV file playback starts or stops—or when an error occurs accessing the FLV file. A **NetStream** object will pass strings of text to the **info** object when certain events occur such as when an FLV file starts or stops, when a requested FLV file can't be found, and when the buffer is empty or full. The strings describing the event—which are passed to an **info** object—are called *code properties*. The status of the code properties—either **Status** or **Error**—is called a *level property*. For your reference, the following table describes the various **onStatus** event code properties. You will be using the **NetStream.Play.Stop** code property later in this chapter to reset the FLV file when it has finished playing.

NetStream onStatus Events

Code property	Level property	Description
NetStream.Buffer.Empty	Status	The buffer is empty. Once the buffer is empty, there is no more video to play, and the FLV file will therefore stop playing. As the FLV file continues downloading, it fills the buffer. Once the buffer has been completely filled, the `NetStream.Buffer.Full` message will be sent, and the FLV file will continue playing.
NetStream.Buffer.Full	Status	The buffer is full, and the FLV file will begin playing.
NetStream.Buffer.Flush	Status	The FLV file has finished streaming, and the buffer will be emptied.
NetStream.Play.Start	Status	The FLV file playback has started.
NetStream.Play.Stop	Status	The FLV file playback has stopped.
NetStream.Play.StreamNotFound	Error	The requested FLV file could not be found.
NetStream.Seek.InvalidTime	Error	When an FLV file is being progressively downloaded, this event will be utilized if the viewer has tried to seek or play the video past the point that has been downloaded.
NetStream.Seek.Notify	Status	Seeking through the FLV file is complete.

6 | Building the Playback Progress Slider

In this exercise, you'll construct the playback progress slider. The progress slider is a small, light-blue dot moving across the progress bar as the FLV file plays. Just like the playhead in other video applications such as QuickTime and Windows Media Player, this progress slider represents how much of the video has been played and how much is still left to play. When the slider reaches the farthest-right point on the bar, the video is finished. However, because of the extra ActionScript and additional complications involved, you *will not* add the functionality of a *draggable* progress slider like QuickTime and Windows Media Player have.

Building this playback slider is relatively simple and is also similar to the playback slider you built in the previous chapter. All you need to know is how many seconds of the video have played and the total running time. Once you have this information, you'll need to script a way for Flash to continually loop through and recalculate those numbers, moving the slider to the appropriate position each time.

You'll start by creating an ActionScript loop. You'll build this loop so it triggers at the same time the FLV file begins playing. If you remember, the action to start playing the FLV file resides in the `videoActivate` function.

1 Make sure you're in **Scene 1** by clicking its tab at the top-left corner, above the **Timeline**.

2 Select **Keyframe 1** in layer **a** and open the **Actions** panel by pressing **F9** (Windows) or **Opt+F9** (Mac).

In the next few steps, you'll build a way for Flash 8 to continually loop through some ActionScript. But how exactly do you go about building a loop? You can do this in a few ways. In earlier versions of Flash, developers built a "keyframe loop" where the `gotoAndPlay()` action would be employed to make the Timeline playhead continually play a series of frames. Each time the playhead looped, a series of actions would take place. However, now that Flash's programming language—ActionScript—has matured into a more robust form, you can loop through a series of actions in better ways.

You really have two main methods of looping through ActionScript. You can use the `setInterval()` function to instruct another function to continually execute at specific time intervals, or you can use the more "old-school" `onEnterFrame` event handler to loop through some ActionScript attached to a movie clip. Although `setInterval` is a little more "involved" to set up, it gives you good control over how often the loop should be performed. Conversely, an `onEnterFrame` loop is a little easier to set up, but you don't have control over how often the loop is performed (it loops at the same rate as the SWF file's frame rate).

In this exercise, you'll use the `onEnterFrame` loop event handler to create your ActionScript loop because 1) it's easier to set up, and 2) you don't need specific and ultimate control over how often the ActionScript loops. All in all, 21 fps—the same frame rate as **about_us.swf**—is plenty fast enough for what you're trying to accomplish.

```
97  //--------------<video activate>----------------\\
98  function videoActivate() {
99      scrollDown._visible = false;
100     scrollUp._visible = false;
101     loadedInfo.text = "";
102     videoContainer._visible = true;
103     myNetStream.play("la_eyeworks_video.flv");
104
105     videoContainer.vidProgBar.onEnterFrame = function() {
106
107     }
108 }
109 //--------------</video activate>----------------\\
```

3 Scroll through the **Actions** panel until you locate the **<video activate>** comment. Then, click at the end of the **myNetStream.play("la_eyeworks_video.flv");** line, press **Enter** (Windows) or **Return** (Mac) twice to create two line breaks, and type the following:

```
videoContainer.vidProgBar.onEnterFrame = function() {

}
```

Make sure to type a line break between the **videoContainer.vidProgBar.onEnterFrame = function() {** line and the closed curly brace below it. This gives you a line break where you can start typing some actions within the **onEnterFrame** function.

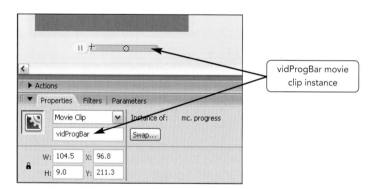

vidProgBar movie clip instance

The **videoContainer.vidProgBar** part of the action is the path to the **vidProgBar** movie clip instance. This is the movie clip where the progress bar, progress slider, and preloader mask are contained. When assigning the **onEnterFrame** event handler to a movie clip, it's best to assign it to the movie clip containing the items you will be targeting with ActionScript.

Just like when you are assigning mouse events—**onRelease**, **onRollOver**, and so forth—to a button symbol, you need to attach the **onEnterFrame** event handler to a function. The actions within this function—what you will be writing next—will execute when **onEnterFrame** triggers.

So, when the viewer clicks the video submenu option in the About Us module, the **videoActivate** function triggers, which thereby triggers this **onEnterFrame** loop to start. What actions do you want to execute 21 times a second? Well, you want a few events to happen. You want Flash to find out what percentage of the FLV file has played. Just like you learned in Chapter 10, *"Building an MP3 Player,"* in the **music_progress.mov** movie (if you didn't watch that movie, I *highly* recommend you go watch it now), to get the percentage of the FLV file played, you need to divide how much time has played up to that point by the total amount of time. Once you have the number, you multiply it by 100, which gives you the percentage-played number. The percentage-played number is the one you will use to move the playback slider to its appropriate position. Again, just like in the **music_progress.mov** movie, the progress bar is 100 pixels wide. (Actually, it's a little wider than 100 if you consider the rounded caps at the end, but where the slider will move within that bar is 100 pixels wide.) Each pixel the progress slider moves represents a percent of the FLV file that has played.

The first step is figuring out the percentage of the FLV file that has played.

```
97  //--------------<video activate>----------------\\
98  function videoActivate() {
99      scrollDown._visible = false;
100     scrollUp._visible = false;
101     loadedInfo.text = "";
102     videoContainer._visible = true;
103     myNetStream.play("la_eyeworks_video.flv");
104
105     videoContainer.vidProgBar.onEnterFrame = function() {
106         var progPos:Number = Math.round((myNetStream.time/videoTRT) * 100);
107     }
108 }
109 //--------------</video activate>----------------\\
```

4 Click the empty line break you added in Step 3 between the `videoContainer.vidProgBar.onEnterFrame = function() {` line and the closed curly brace beneath it, and type the following:

`var progPos:Number = Math.round((myNetStream.time/videoTRT) * 100);`

Most of this script should already be familiar to you since you wrote an action nearly identical to it in the **music_progress.mov** movie in Chapter 10, *"Building an MP3 Player."* But to reiterate, in this action you're creating a local variable called **progPos**, strict typing it to the Number data type, and then inserting a number into it. The number is derived from a small equation. Get how many seconds of the FLV file has played (**myNetStream.time**), divide that number by the total running time of the FLV file (**videoTRT**), multiply the result by 100, and then round that result to the closest whole number (**Math.round**).

Note: You might also be wondering why you're creating the variable **progPos** and strict typing it *within* the **onEnterFrame** function when, in the past, you've instantiated the variables *outside* a function. The reason why you take the extra step of instantiating a variable outside a function is so you can refer to the variable from other actions also outside the function. When you use **var** to create a variable within a function, it becomes a *local variable* to be referenced only from within the *same* function. In this case, because the variable **progPos** is *not* going to be referenced from anywhere else except from within the function itself, it doesn't need to be instantiated from outside the function first.

Note: Local variables (variables created within a function and preceded by the **var** statement) are removed from memory once they are no longer referenced, making your programs or Web sites run more efficiently in the long run.

Next, you need to instruct the playback slider to move to whatever percentage of the FLV file has played.

```
 97  //-------------<video activate>----------------\\
 98  function videoActivate() {
 99      scrollDown._visible = false;
100      scrollUp._visible = false;
101      loadedInfo.text = "";
102      videoContainer._visible = true;
103      myNetStream.play("la_eyeworks_video.flv");
104
105      videoContainer.vidProgBar.onEnterFrame = function() {
106          var progPos:Number = Math.round((myNetStream.time/videoTRT) * 100);
107          videoContainer.vidProgBar.vidProg._x = progPos;
108      }
109  }
110  //-------------</video activate>----------------\\
```

5 Click at the end of the action you wrote in Step 4, press **Enter** (Windows) or **Return** (Mac) to create a line break, and type the following:

`videoContainer.vidProgBar.vidProg._x = progPos;`

This action instructs the movie clip instance **vidProg** located within the **vidProgBar** movie clip, which is located within the **videoContainer** movie clip instance, to set its **x** position (**x** is left and right, **y** is up and down) to be the same as the value of the **progPos** variable. The value of the **progPos** variable is, of course, the percentage of the FLV file played up to that point.

And that's it! This is all you need to move the playback slider to the position representing what percentage of the FLV file has played. Remember, because the two actions you wrote in Steps 4 and 5 are contained within the **onEnterFrame** function, they're continually executed, for as long as the video content is visible, at 21 times per second. So as Flash 8 continually recalculates what percentage of the FLV file has played, it also moves the playback slider to the same percentage value.

---

6 Save your **about_us.fla** file by choosing **File > Save** or pressing **Ctrl+S** (Windows) or **Cmd+S** (Mac).

---

7 Publish an updated SWF file by choosing **File > Publish**.

---

8 Minimize (Windows) or hide (Mac) Flash 8, and navigate to your **Desktop > la_eyeworks > site** folder. Then, double-click **master.swf** to open it in Flash Player 8.

Flash Professional 8 Beyond the Basics : H·O·T

9 When the **About Us** module appears, click the **video** submenu option to display the video content.

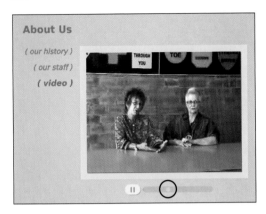

As the FLV file plays, you'll notice the playback progress slider slowly moving across the progress bar underneath it.

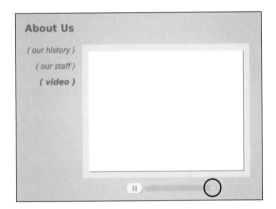

When the slider gets all the way to the right side of the progress bar, you'll notice the video has finished. Awesome!

---

10 When you're finished watching the progress slider do its thing, close the Flash Player 8 window, and return to **about_us.fla** in Flash 8.

The next few steps will be nearly identical to the steps you followed to create the MP3 download progress in the **music_progress.mov** movie in Chapter 10, *"Building an MP3 Player."*

---

11 Make sure you have **Keyframe 1** in layer **a** selected and you have your **Actions** panel open.

---

12 Scroll through the **Actions** panel until you locate the actions you were working on earlier in this exercise—the ones between the **<video activate>** and **</video activate>** comments.

```
 97  //-------------<video activate>----------------\\
 98  function videoActivate() {
 99      scrollDown._visible = false;
100      scrollUp._visible = false;
101      loadedInfo.text = "";
102      videoContainer._visible = true;
103      myNetStream.play("la_eyeworks_video.flv");
104
105      videoContainer.vidProgBar.onEnterFrame = function() {
106          var progPos:Number = Math.round((myNetStream.time/videoTRT) * 100);
107          videoContainer.vidProgBar.vidProg._x = progPos;
108          var vidDlPercent:Number = Math.round((_root.myNetStream.bytesLoaded/_root.myNetStream.bytesTotal) * 100);
109      }
110  }
111  //-------------</video activate>----------------\\
```

13 Click at the end of the **videoContainer.vidProgBar.vidProg._x = progPos;** line, press **Enter** (Windows) or **Return** (Mac) once to create a line break, and type the following all on one with no line breaks:

var vidDlPercent:Number = Math.round((_root.myNetStream.bytesLoaded/_root.myNetStream.bytesTotal) * 100);

As you've seen, this action creates a local variable titled **vidDlPercent** and strict types it to the Number data type. Then, it divides how many bytes of the FLV file (**_root.myNetStream.bytesLoaded**) have downloaded up to this point by the total number of bytes for the FLV file (**_root.myNetStream.bytesTotal**). To translate this number into a percentage, you then multiply the result by 100. Lastly, so you have a nice even number to work with, you use **Math.round** to round the result to the nearest whole number.

Now, just like in **music_progress.mov**, you need to instruct the progress bar mask to set its **_width** property to be the same as the percentage. As the mask width expands, it reveals another bar—carefully positioned on top of the first one—of a different color. This gives the appearance of a progress bar.

```
 97  //-------------<video activate>----------------\\
 98  function videoActivate() {
 99      scrollDown._visible = false;
100      scrollUp._visible = false;
101      loadedInfo.text = "";
102      videoContainer._visible = true;
103      myNetStream.play("la_eyeworks_video.flv");
104
105      videoContainer.vidProgBar.onEnterFrame = function() {
106          var progPos:Number = Math.round((myNetStream.time/videoTRT) * 100);
107          videoContainer.vidProgBar.vidProg._x = progPos;
108          var vidDlPercent:Number = Math.round((_root.myNetStream.bytesLoaded/_root.myNetStream.bytesTotal) * 100);
109          videoContainer.vidProgBar.progMaskContainer.progMask._width = vidDlPercent + 10;
110      }
111  }
112  //-------------</video activate>----------------\\
```

14 Click at the end of the action you wrote in Step 13, press **Enter** (Windows) or **Return** (Mac) to create a line break, and type the following all on one line with no line breaks:

videoContainer.vidProgBar.progMaskContainer.progMask._width = vidDlPercent + 10;

This action simply tells the movie clip with the mask in it, **progMask**, to set its **_width** property to be the same number as the percentage of the FLV file that has downloaded up to this point. Keep in mind, just like the progress slider, these actions within the **onEnterFrame** function will continually execute—while the video content is visible—at 21 fps. So, as the FLV is downloading, Flash 8 is constantly recalculating how much of the FLV file has downloaded and adjusting the download progress mask accordingly.

With those two lines, you just created a progress bar to display the downloading progress of the FLV file. Pretty nifty, if I do say so myself!

Now for the bad news: Because the FLV file is external, you unfortunately can't test the preloader in the Flash authoring environment. This means when you preview your movie in Flash 8—even if you choose the Simulate Download option—the progress bar won't appear to show the downloading progress of the FLV file. Since the FLV file is currently stored locally on your hard drive and will therefore load instantly, the progress bar will just immediately jump to its finished point.

Unless you currently have access to a Web presence provider and can upload your work there and test it using your browser, you'll just have to trust me that it works correctly.

---

15 Save your **about_us.fla** file by choosing **File > Save** or pressing **Ctrl+S** (Windows) or **Cmd+S** (Mac).

In the next exercise, you will utilize the `NetStream` class's `onStatus` event handler to "reset" the FLV file when it has finished playing. Currently, the viewer is unable to replay the FLV file after it has finished playing. In the next exercise, you will write a little script to fix this.

---

7 | Using the onStatus Event Handler

In this exercise, you'll use the **NetStream** class's **onStatus** event handler to detect when the FLV file has finished playing. Once you've detected the FLV file has finished playing, you'll write a few actions to "reset" the FLV file so it can be replayed by the viewer if they choose.

The **onStatus** event handler works somewhat differently than does the other event handlers you've seen thus far. When the **onStatus** event handler detects a change in the status of the FLV file—such as the FLV file starting or stopping—it sends two strings of text to two properties in the **info** object. When you want to find out the status changes of the FLV file, you use an **if** statement to ask the **info** object questions.

The first step is to create the **onStatus** event handler and assign it to a function.

---

1 Scroll through the **Actions** panel until you find the section marked by the **<video>** comments.

```
130 function initializeVideo() {
131     myNetConn = new NetConnection();
132     myNetConn.connect(null);
133     myNetStream = new NetStream(myNetConn);
134     videoContainer.myVideo.attachVideo(myNetStream);
135     myNetStream.setBufferTime(5);
136
137     myNetStream.onStatus = function(info) {
138
139     }
140
141     myNetStream.onMetaData = function(infoObject:Object) {
142         videoTRT = infoObject.duration;
143     }
144     videoActivate();
145 }
```

2 Within the **initializeVideo** function, click at the end of the **myNetStream.setBufferTime(5);** line, press **Enter** (Windows) or **Return** (Mac) twice to create two line breaks, and type the following:

```
myNetStream.onStatus = function(info) {

}
```

Make sure to type a line break between the **myNetStream.onStatus = function(info) {** line and the closed curly brace below it. This gives you a line break where you can start typing some actions.

Like the other event handlers, if you want to do anything with the **onStatus** event handler, you need to assign it to a function. The actions within the function execute when the event handler is invoked. Because the **onStatus** event handler is passing its events to the **info** object, you need to declare the **info** parameter for the **onStatus** function.

Now you need to add branching logic (an **if** statement) to the **onStatus** event to query the **info** object's properties. This enables you to specify what should happen when the **onStatus** event fires.

```
137    myNetStream.onStatus = function(info) {
138        if (info.code == "NetStream.Play.Stop" && info.level == "status") {
139
140        }
141    }
```

3 Click at the end of the **myNetStream.onStatus = function(info) {** line, press **Enter** (Windows) or **Return** (Mac) once to create a line break, and type the following:

```
if (info.code == "NetStream.Play.Stop" && info.level == "status") {

}
```

Make sure to type a line break between the **if (info.code == "NetStream.Play.Stop" && info.level == "status") {** line and the closed curly brace below it. This gives you an empty line break where you can start typing some actions.

This **if** statement essentially says, "If the **code** property in the **info** object is **NetStream.Play.Stop** *and* if the **level** property in the **info** object is **status**...." At this point, you're probably saying to yourself "**code**? **level**? Where the heck did *they* come from?" Well, the table earlier in this chapter lists the various methods, properties, and event handlers of the **NetStream** class. Another table describes the **onStatus** event handlers, listing the event handlers including the **NetStream.Play.Stop** code you just used as well as its **status** level.

Again, the **onStatus** event handler passes strings (bits of text) to the **code** and **level** properties in the **info** object when certain events occur. Because you want to find out whether the FLV file has stopped playing—so you can reset it—in this **if** statement you're asking the **info** object if its **code** property is **NetStream.Play.Stop** *and* (&&) if its **level** property is **status**. If the **if** question results in **true**, the FLV file has stopped. So, every time you have a status change with the FLV file, the **onStatus** event handler is invoked. When it's invoked, it asks this **if** statement question each time. When finally the **if** statement is **true**, it will execute the actions you're about to place within it.

```
137    myNetStream.onStatus = function(info) {
138        if (info.code == "NetStream.Play.Stop" && info.level == "status") {
139            videoContainer.togglePlay.gotoAndStop(2);
140            myNetStream.seek(0);
141            myNetStream.pause(true);
142        }
143    }
```

4 Click the empty line break between the **if** statement and the closed curly brace. Then, type the following three actions:

```
videoContainer.togglePlay.gotoAndStop(2);
myNetStream.seek(0);
myNetStream.pause(true);
```

- The first action, **videoContainer.togglePlay.gotoAndStop(2);**, instructs the Play/Pause toggle button in the **videoContainer** movie clip instance to go to Frame 2. On Frame 2, if you remember, is the Play button. So when the FLV file finishes playing, the Pause button—which is visible when the FLV is playing—returns to displaying the Play button.

- **myNetStream.seek(0);** uses the **seek** method to instruct the FLV file to return to 0 seconds. So, when the FLV file has finished playing, it automatically returns to the beginning. Now, unless you tell it otherwise, it returns to the beginning and start playing again. Because the viewer would probably like to be the one to determine whether it should play again, you should pause the FLV file.

- **myNetStream.pause(true);** uses the **pause()** method to pause the FLV file.

Taken all together, these three actions instruct the Play/Pause toggle button to display the Play button, the FLV file to return to the beginning, and the FLV file to pause. In essence, it resets itself and allows the viewer to play it again by clicking the Play button.

5 Save your **about_us.fla** file by choosing **File > Save** or pressing **Ctrl+S** (Windows) or **Cmd+S** (Mac).

6 Publish an updated SWF file by choosing **File > Publish**.

7 Minimize (Windows) or hide (Mac) Flash 8, and navigate to your **Desktop > la_eyeworks > site** folder. Then, double-click **master.swf** to open it in Flash Player 8.

8 When the **About Us** section appears, click the **video** submenu option to display the video content.

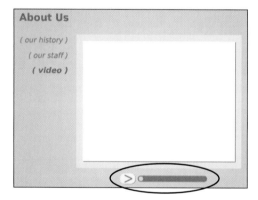

The FLV file immediately loads and starts playing. When the video gets to the end, you'll see the playback progress slider jump to its starting point—because you set the playhead of the FLV file to 0 using **myNetStream.seek(0);**—the Play/Pause toggle switch to the Play button, and the FLV file jump to its beginning and pause there.

Great! When the video finishes, it now resets and waits for the viewer to click the Play button to watch the FLV file again.

9 Close the Flash Player 8 window, and return to **about_us.fla** in Flash 8. Then, make sure you have **Keyframe 1** selected in layer **a** and you have the **Actions** panel open.

8 | Cleaning Up

In this exercise, you'll perform a little janitorial work and tie up some loose ends. You still need to add a few extra items to the video player before it is completely finished.

The first task is to stop the **onEnterFrame** loop you created in Exercise 6. Currently, when you click the **video** option, the FLV file loads and starts playing. Simultaneously, the **onEnterFrame** loop starts looping through its actions, continually making calculations and using up the viewer's computer processing power. However, when the viewer leaves the video section for another section, **onEnterFrame** continues to loop through its actions, even though it's not being used. To help optimize your movie, you should stop the **onEnterFrame** loop when the viewer leaves the video section. Thankfully, you already have a function executing when the viewer leaves the video section, **videoDeactivate**.

---

1 Scroll through the **Actions** panel until you find the actions marked by the comment **<video deactivate>**.

```
114  //--------------<video deactivate>----------------\\
115  function videoDeactivate() {
116      loadedInfo.scroll = 0;
117      scrollDown._visible = true;
118      scrollUp._visible = true;
119      videoContainer._visible = false;
120      myNetStream.pause();
121      delete videoContainer.vidProgBar.onEnterFrame;
122  }
123  //--------------</video deactivate>----------------\\
```

2 Click at the end of the **myNetStream.pause();** line, press **Enter** (Windows) or **Return** (Mac) once to create a line break, and type the following:

```
delete videoContainer.vidProgBar.onEnterFrame;
```

The **delete** operator, as its name implies, deletes a variable or an object. In this case, it deletes the **onEnterFrame** event handler—which, technically, is a part of the movie clip object. When you delete **onEnterFrame**, the loop stops, and the memory and processing power used for this event handler is returned to the system. If you have too many—or have too complex—**onEnterFrame** loops occurring simultaneously, this can slow down the performance of your Flash movie. By deleting **onEnterFrame** loops when you no longer need them, you stop those loops and calculations from occurring and thereby give the processing power and memory back to the viewer's computer system to be used for other tasks. Now, just to waylay any fears of permanently deleting something you can never use again, you can always restart an **onEnterFrame** loop simply by executing the **onEnterFrame** action again.

Next, you need to tell the **myNetStream** object to stop downloading its FLV file—if it is still downloading—when the viewer leaves the video section. If you do not specify this, if the viewer leaves the video section while the FLV file is downloading, the FLV file will *continue* to download even though the viewer has left. The action you're about to write also deletes the FLV file the viewer has downloaded and frees the **NetStream** object to download a different FLV file if necessary.

```
114  //--------------<video deactivate>----------------\\
115  function videoDeactivate() {
116       loadedInfo.scroll = 0;
117       scrollDown._visible = true;
118       scrollUp._visible = true;
119       videoContainer._visible = false;
120       myNetStream.pause();
121       delete videoContainer.vidProgBar.onEnterFrame;
122       myNetStream.close();
123  }
124  //-------------</video deactivate>----------------\\
```

3 Click at the end of the **delete videoContainer.vidProgBar.onEnterFrame;** line, press **Enter** (Windows) or **Return** (Mac) once to create a line break, and type the following:

myNetStream.close();

Imagine this: The viewer comes to the L.A. Eyeworks Web site and clicks the Play button on the MP3 player to listen to some music while cruising around through the site. The viewer visits the About Us section and reads the L.A. Eyeworks history while happily tapping a foot to the music. Then, the viewer clicks the video section. That's when all hell breaks loose. The audio for the video starts playing *while the music is still playing as well.* Obviously, this would *not* be a good thing. But you're a smart, forward-thinking Flash designer/developer, and you'll nip this problem in the bud...so to speak.

You haven't yet integrated the **music.swf** *and* **about_us.swf** sections into **master.swf**. But when you do, **about_us.swf** will load into _level5 where the rest of the content sections also load, and **music.swf** will load one level higher into _level6. So from **about_us.swf**, when you want to instruct the MP3 player to do something—such as stop the music, for instance—you can simply refer to it by typing _**level6**.

```
97   //-------------<video activate>-----------------\\
98   function videoActivate() {
99        scrollDown._visible = false;
100       scrollUp._visible = false;
101       loadedInfo.text = "";
102       videoContainer._visible = true;
103       myNetStream.play("la_eyeworks_video.flv");
104
105       _level6.bgMusak.stop();
106       _level6.musakToggle.gotoAndStop(1);
```

4 Scroll through the **Actions** panel until you locate the actions marked by the comment **<video activate>**. Then, click at the end of the **myNetStream.play("la_eyeworks_video.flv");** line, press **Enter** (Windows) or **Return** (Mac) twice to create two line breaks, and type the following two actions:

_level6.bgMusak.stop();
_level6.musakToggle.gotoAndStop(1);

The top-most action, **_level6.bgMusak.stop();**, instructs the **bgMusak Sound** object to stop playing the music. The second action, **_level6.musakToggle.gotoAndStop(1);**, instructs the music Play/Stop toggle button to display the Play button. Therefore, when the viewer is finished watching the video, they can click the music's Play button to resume listening to the music.

Because you place these two actions within the **videoActivate** function, when the viewer clicks the **video** submenu option and the **videoActivate** function executes, the music will automatically stop playing. Huzzah!

It's subtleties like these that really give an extra edge to a Web site and make it look, sound, and appear professional.

---

5 Save your **about_us.fla** file by choosing **File > Save** or pressing **Ctrl+S** (Windows) or **Cmd+S** (Mac).

---

6 Publish an updated SWF file by choosing **File > Publish**.

---

7 Then, close **about_us.fla**—you won't be needing it in the next chapter.

Congratulations! You finished yet another chapter. In this chapter, you learned how to create a video player to progressively download an external FLV file. You also learned how to allow the viewer to pause and play the FLV file, how to add a playback progress slider, and how to create a progress bar to provide feedback about the downloading progress of the FLV file. If you're understanding—or beginning to understand—the actions and exercises as you work through them, you should really be amazed at what you've accomplished so far in this book. You've already learned a tremendous amount, and you still have more yet to learn. See you in the next chapter!

12

Building the Main Menu

You've now constructed all the sections of the L.A. Eyeworks Web site—minus the Locations module—so you're ready to build the one piece to bring all the separate sections together: the main menu. In this chapter, you will use a few new techniques to construct the main menu, and you will get to see, for the first time, all the modules as they peacefully coexist in **master.swf**.

1 | Previewing What You Are Building

In this exercise, you'll get to preview the main menu *before* you start building it. Therefore, as you're working through the exercises in this chapter, you'll have a better idea of how some of the abstract ActionScript concepts fit together to create a functional piece of the L.A. Eyeworks Web site.

1 Open your preferred browser, and navigate to the following URL:

www.lynda.com/flash8btb/laeyeworks/

2 When the L.A. Eyeworks site finishes loading, move your mouse over the four navigation bar options. As you roll your mouse over each of the options, you'll notice each one turns green. When you roll your mouse off an option, it returns to black.

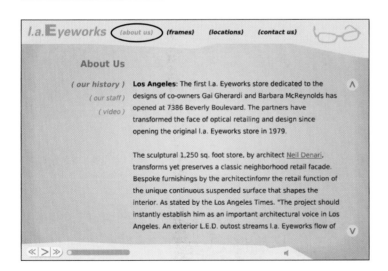

3 Click the **about us** option in the navigation bar. When you do, three events take place. First, the **about us** option turns green and stays green even if you move your mouse over other navigation menu options. Second, the **about us** option becomes disabled, and you aren't able to interact with it. Just like you saw when constructing the submenu for the **About Us** module in Chapter 6, *"Using the TextFormat Class,"* you can use the **enabled** property to disable a menu option for the purposes of usability. Finally, the **About Us** module's content loads.

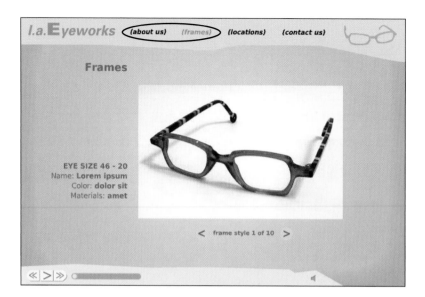

4 Click the **frames** option in the navigation bar. When you do, you'll notice the **about us** option becomes re-enabled, the **frames** option becomes disabled and turns green, and the **Frames** module loads.

As you work through this chapter, you'll likely notice many similarities between the construction of the main menu and the About Us module's content. Because of the similarities, I've included much of the ActionScript to build the main menu in a prebuilt FLA file. However, this chapter isn't all review, and you will be learning some new actions in the upcoming exercises.

---

5 Close your browser when you're finished checking out the main menu.

In the next exercise, you will set up the provided FLA file by adding a font symbol from the shared library and linking the main menu options to the shared font.

---

2 | Setting Up

In this exercise, you'll import and integrate a shared font for use in the main navigation bar options.

---

1 Navigate to your **Desktop > la_eyeworks > site** folder, and double-click the file **main_menu.fla**.

I provided this FLA file for you so you wouldn't need to repeat steps or ActionScript you have already learned.

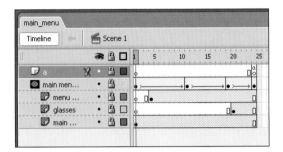

As you can see, this FLA file already has some layers, a mask, a shape tween, and some actions.

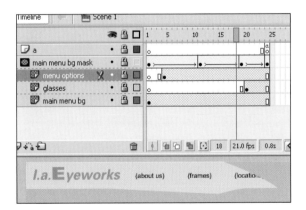

2 So you can see what's going on in this FLA file, drag the playhead down the **Timeline**. Watching the **Stage**, you'll notice the green bar in the background being revealed by an animated mask, which also reveals the L.A. Eyeworks logo, the main menu options, and the glasses image at the top-right corner. At the end of the **Timeline**, you'll also notice some actions have been assigned to a keyframe in layer **a**. Later in this chapter, you will modify these actions to add functionality to the main menu.

Before you can start working with ActionScript, however, you need to import a font symbol from your shared library and assign it to the text making up the main menu options.

3 Make sure you *do not* have **sharedLib.fla** open. If it *is* open, it will interfere with the next few steps, so make sure it is closed before continuing. Then, choose **File > Import > Open External Library**. In the **Open as Library** dialog box, navigate to your **Desktop > la_eyeworks > site** folder, and double-click the file **sharedLib.fla**.

This opens the library *only* for **sharedLib.fla** as you have seen, and done, several times.

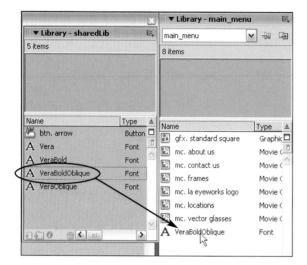

4 Open the library for **main_menu.fla** by pressing **Ctrl+L** (Windows) or **Cmd+L** (Mac), and position it next to the **sharedLib Library** panel. Then, drag the font symbol **VeraBoldOblique** from the **sharedLib Library** panel to the **main_menu Library** panel.

5 Close the **sharedLib Library** panel—you won't be needing it again in this chapter.

Note: You probably noticed by now—in nearly every chapter you're loading the sharedLib Library panel, dragging the shared elements you need into a new FLA file, and then closing the sharedLib Library panel. In a "real-world" workflow, you could easily keep the sharedLib Library panel open and pull elements from it as needed. However, to reduce confusion when working through the exercises in this book, you're closing the sharedLib Library panel each time after using it.

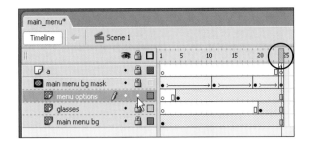

6 In the **Timeline**, move the playhead to the last frame (24), and unlock the **menu options** layer, which is the layer housing the main menu options.

7 On the **Stage**, single-click the **about us** menu option, and open the **Property Inspector** by pressing **Ctrl+F3** (Windows) or **Cmd+F3** (Mac).

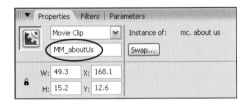

Notice how this option is actually an instance of the **mc. about us** movie clip. It also already has an instance name of **MM_aboutUs**. The other menu options—**frames**, **locations**, and **contact us**— have instance names of **MM_frames**, **MM_locations**, and **MM_contactUs**, respectively. (The *MM* stands for **M**ain **M**enu.)

8 Double-click the **mc. about us** movie clip instance to open it.

9 Single-click the Dynamic text field on the **Stage** with the text **about us** inside it, and open the **Property Inspector**. You'll notice **Font** is currently set to **_sans**. However, to match the look and feel of the rest of the site, you need to change the font face.

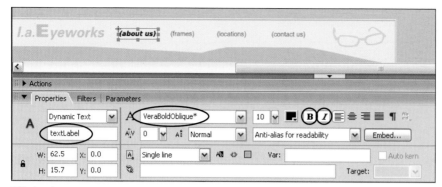

(Windows)

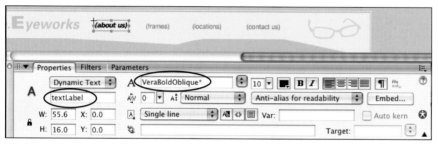

(Mac)

10 From the **Font** pop-up menu in the **Property Inspector**, choose the shared font you imported earlier, **VeraBoldOblique***. If you're working in Windows, also make sure you click the **Bold Style** and **Italic Style** buttons. (If you're on a Mac, you *do not* need to click these buttons.) The remaining options can stay the same; just verify your **Property Inspector** matches what you see in the illustration shown here for your operating system. Also note the Dynamic text field has a preapplied instance name of **textLabel**. As you'll see when you change the font face of the other main menu options, they *all* have the same instance name of **textLabel**. Later in this chapter, when you write the ActionScript to create the `rollOver` and `rollOut` interactivity, it streamlines the process if the text fields all have the same instance name. Because they are all inside movie clips, the identical instance names don't cause any naming conflicts.

11 Return to the **Scene 1 Timeline** by clicking its tab above the top-left corner of the **Timeline**.

12 Repeat Steps 8 through 11 for the remaining three main menu options. All you're really doing is opening the movie clip each option resides in, selecting the Dynamic text field, and changing the font face to the shared font **VeraBoldOblique***. If you're working in Windows, you need to remember to also click the **Bold Style** and **Italic Style** buttons.

13 When you're finished changing the font face for the main menu options, make sure you return to **Scene 1**. You will begin the next exercise there.

And with that, you're all done setting up this FLA file! In the next exercise, you will write the ActionScript to create the `rollOver` and `rollOut` effects for the main menu options.

Scripting onRollOver, onRollOut, and onRelease

In this exercise, you'll write some ActionScript to create the main menu option color rollover effects. Essentially, as the viewer rolls the mouse on and off the main menu options, a function and the `TextField` class's `textColor` property will change the text color of the `textLabel` Dynamic text fields. All in all, it's fairly straightforward to set up.

The first step is to create the variables to hold the color strings to be displayed on `onRollOver` and `onRollOut`.

---

1 Select **Keyframe 24** on layer **a**, and open the **Actions** panel by pressing **F9** (Windows) or **Opt+F9** (Mac).

```
1  stop();
2  MM_logo.enabled = false;
3
4  //---------------<define option colors>---------------\\
5
6  //---------------</define option colors>---------------\\
7
8  //---------------<re-enable menu options>---------------\\
9  function reActivateBtns() {
10     MM_logo.enabled = true;
11     MM_aboutUs.enabled = true;
12     MM_contactUs.enabled = true;
13     MM_frames.enabled = true;
14     MM_locations.enabled = true;
15     changeOptionColor(MM_aboutUs, outColor);
16     changeOptionColor(MM_frames, outColor);
17     changeOptionColor(MM_locations, outColor);
18     changeOptionColor(MM_contactUs, outColor);
19  };
20  //---------------</re-enable menu options>---------------\\
```

2 Toward the top of the **Actions** panel, click after the `MM_logo.enabled = false;` line, press **Enter** (Windows) or **Return** (Mac) twice to create two line breaks, and type the following:

```
//---------------<define option colors>---------------\\

//---------------</define option colors>---------------\\
```

Note: Make sure to include an empty line break between the two comment lines. This gives you a space where you can begin to type some actions.

Next you'll create a couple of variables to hold the colors (stated as a string of numbers and letters) the menu options will change to when the viewer rolls their mouse over and then off those options. Later in this exercise, you will use these variables in the function to change the color of the text in the **textLabel** Dynamic text fields.

```
1  stop();
2  MM_logo.enabled = false;
3
4  //--------------<define option colors>--------------\\
5  var overColor:Number = 0x7DBC6B;
6  var outColor:Number = 0x000000;
7  //--------------</define option colors>--------------\\
```

3 Click the empty line break between the **<define option colors>** and **</define option colors>** comments, and type the following two actions:

```
var overColor:Number = 0x7DBC6B;
var outColor:Number = 0x000000;
```

These two actions create the two variables **overColor** and **outColor** and strict type them to the Number data type. Then, within the variables is a color in its hexadecimal format. The hexadecimal format is simply a color's hex value—which you can get from Macromedia Flash 8's color picker—preceded by **0x** (that's a zero and a lowercase *x*). In this case, the **overColor** color is green, and the **outColor** color is black.

You've now specified the colors the menu options will display on **onRollOver** and **onRollOut**, so you can create the function to actually change the text color. To create a single function to be utilized by both the **onRollOver** and **onRollOut** mouse events, you will incorporate parameters into the function. When calling the function from the **onRollOver** and **onRollOut** events, you can utilize those parameters within the action changing the appearance of the main menu options.

```
1   stop();
2   MM_logo.enabled = false;
3
4   //--------------<define option colors>--------------\\
5   var overColor:Number = 0x7DBC6B;
6   var outColor:Number = 0x000000;
7
8   function changeOptionColor(myOption:MovieClip, myColor:Number) {
9       myOption.textLabel.textColor = myColor;
10  }
11  //--------------</define option colors>--------------\\
```

4 Click at the end of the **var outColor:Number = 0x000000;** line, press **Enter** (Windows) or **Return** (Mac) twice to create two line breaks, and type the following:

```
function changeOptionColor(myOption:MovieClip, myColor:Number) {
  myOption.textLabel.textColor = myColor;
}
```

As you have seen, this creates a function called **changeOptionColor**. In the parentheses after **changeOptionColor** are two parameters: **myOption** and **myColor**. Because the **myOption** and **myColor** parameters are essentially variable placeholders, you can—and should—strict type them just like you would any other variable. Because the **myOption** parameter is going to receive an instance name of a movie clip, it is strict typed with the **MovieClip** data type. **myColor**, being a parameter to receive a hexadecimal color value, is strict typed as a Number data type.

Note: If you need a refresher on how a function's parameters work, refer to Chapter 3, *"Getting Started."*

The action within the function instructs a text field to change its color using the **textColor** text field property. The **myOption** parameter symbolizes the path to the text field. Later, when you call this function, in place of the **myOption** parameter you will specify the name of the movie clip instance holding the main menu option you want to modify. As you remember, within each main menu option movie clip is a Dynamic text field with the instance name of **textLabel**. By keeping the text field instance name the same throughout the individual movie clips, it makes writing this action much easier. Lastly, when you call this function, the **myColor** parameter will be substituted with one of the color variables you created earlier—either **overColor** or **outColor**.

Now it's time to try the function.

```
35  //----------------<about us option>---------------\\
36  MM_aboutUs.onRollOver = function () {
37      changeOptionColor(this, overColor);
38  }
39
40  MM_aboutUs.onRollOut = function () {
41
42  }
43
44  MM_aboutUs.onRelease = function () {
45      reActivateBtns();
46      changeOptionColor(this, overColor);
47      this.enabled = false;
48  }
49  //----------------</about us option>---------------\\
```

5 In the **Actions** panel, scroll down until you reach the actions marked by the comments **<about us option>** and **</about us option>**. Then, click the provided empty line break after the **MM_aboutUs.onRollOver = function () {** line, and type the following:

changeOptionColor(this, overColor);

This action triggers the **changeOptionColor** function and passes two parameters to it when the viewer rolls the mouse over the **MM_aboutUs** movie clip instance. For the **myOption** parameter, you're passing the keyword **this**, which, as you have seen before, is a keyword referring to the object instance the parent function is targeting. In this case, it's the **MM_aboutUs** movie clip instance. For the **myColor** parameter, you're passing the variable name you earlier assigned to the green color: **overColor**. As you are seeing here, when you have a function with more than one parameter, in the action where you call the function and define the parameters, you pass them back in the same order.

Before you test your movie, you should also specify what should happen when the viewer rolls the mouse *off* the **MM_aboutUs** movie clip instance.

```
35 //----------------<about us option>----------------\\
36 MM_aboutUs.onRollOver = function () {
37     changeOptionColor(this, overColor);
38 }
39
40 MM_aboutUs.onRollOut = function () {
41     changeOptionColor(this, outColor);
42 }
43
44 MM_aboutUs.onRelease = function () {
45     reActivateBtns();
46     changeOptionColor(this, overColor);
47     this.enabled = false;
48 }
49 //----------------</about us option>----------------\\
```

6 Select and copy the action you just wrote in Step 5. Then, click the provided empty line break after the `MM_aboutUs.onRollOut = function () {` line, and paste the copied action. All you then have to do is simply change the parameter `overColor` to `outColor`. The rest of the action should remain the same.

This action simply states, "When the viewer rolls the mouse *off* the **about us** main menu option, tell the Dynamic text field **textLabel** within the **MM_aboutUs** movie clip instance to set its color to `outColor` (black)."

And that's all there is to scripting a `rollOver` and `rollOut` color change effect. But some of you might be wondering why you're writing all this ActionScript for something that can be accomplished with a button symbol and requires *no* ActionScript. In essence, it really comes down to being able to easily update your content. If you had manually built all four of the main menu options, including the color change `rollOver`/`rollOut` effects as button symbols, what would happen when the client came to you wanting to change the colors of those options? You would have to spend a good amount of time manually opening each button symbol, selecting the text within the button, and changing its color. Although this may not be too big of a hassle if you have only a few buttons, what would it be like if you had ten buttons? Twenty? By defining the `rollOver` and `rollOut` states using ActionScript—as you have just done here—it takes you all of five seconds to modify the mouse event color effects. All you'd have to do is change the hexadecimal color value in the `overColor` and `outColor` variables and call it a day. Modifying those color values affects *all* the main menu options. For those of you with HTML (**H**yper**T**ext **M**arkup **L**anguage) and CSS (**C**ascading **S**tyle **S**heet) experience, this is analogous to a global CSS file you refer to from all your HTML pages. Making a single change to the CSS file affects *all* the HTML pages linking to it.

Better yet, you could even put those `overColor` and `outColor` variables in a text file and load them into **main_menu.swf** using `LoadVars`. Then even the *client* could easily modify the main menu color `rollOver`/`rollOut` effects if necessary. "Amazing," you say? Yes, I know.

Before continuing, you should test your changes thus far so you can make sure everything is working correctly.

---

7 Save your **main_menu.fla** file by choosing **File > Save** or pressing **Ctrl+S** (Windows) or **Cmd+S** (Mac).

Because the main menu is self-contained and doesn't rely on any ActionScript in **master.swf**, you can preview **main_menu.fla** by itself.

---

8 Test **main_menu.fla** by pressing **Ctrl+Enter** (Windows) or **Cmd+Return** (Mac).

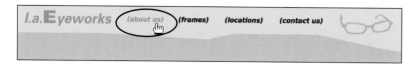

9 When the main menu is revealed, roll your mouse over and then off the **about us** menu option. As you do, you'll see the text change to green and then back to black, respectively. Awesome!

10 Close the preview window. Then, back in **main_menu.fla**, make sure **Keyframe 24** in layer **a** is still selected and you have your **Actions** panel open.

Note: Because creating the **onRollOver** and **onRollOut** actions for the remaining three main menu options are identical to the actions you just wrote in Steps 5 and 6, I've taken the liberty of writing the actions for you. If you're curious, you can scroll down in the **Actions** panel to see what the actions look like. In this case, setting up this functionality really does follow the adage, "Seen one, seen 'em all."

You have the **rollOver** and **rollOut** actions working correctly, but what about **onRelease**?

```
35  //----------------<about us option>----------------\\
36  MM_aboutUs.onRollOver = function () {
37      changeOptionColor(this, overColor);
38  }
39
40  MM_aboutUs.onRollOut = function () {
41      changeOptionColor(this, outColor);
42  }
43
44  MM_aboutUs.onRelease = function () {
45      reActivateBtns();
46      changeOptionColor(this, overColor);
47      this.enabled = false;
48  }
49  //----------------</about us option>----------------\\
```

Within the **<about us option>** and **</about us option>** comments, under the **MM_aboutUs.onRelease** function, you'll notice three prebuilt actions. I provided these actions, like the others, for you because you already know how to construct what they're doing. So you have a good understanding of what's going on, however, here's a quick breakdown of what those three actions are doing and what will happen when the viewer clicks the **about us** main menu option:

- **reActivateBtns();** calls the prebuilt function by the same name. If you scroll your **Actions** panel toward the top, you'll notice a function called **reActivateBtns**. Within that function some actions enable the functionality of the four main menu options and the L.A. Eyeworks logo (which, when clicked, will load the splash graphic), as well as actions to set the four main menu options to display using the **outColor** color (black). Essentially, as its name implies, the **reActivateBtns** function reactivates the main menu options. In terms of functionality, this is *identical* to the **reEnableOptions** function you created in Chapter 6, *"Using the TextFormat Class."*

- `changeOptionColor(this, overColor);`, as you've seen before, simply changes the **about us** main menu option so the text is green.

- `this.enabled = false;` disables the functionality of the **about us** main menu option.

So, when the viewer clicks the **about us** main menu option, the **reActivateBtns** function executes, and *all* the main menu options, if they are disabled, are re-enabled. This way, if the viewer had already clicked another main menu option—thereby disabling it—it would become re-enabled when the viewer clicks a different main menu option. Once *all* the main menu options are re-enabled, the option the viewer clicked turns green (**overColor**) and becomes disabled. Because you know what all these actions do and how they work, I've already completed the other main menu options and assigned similar actions to them to save you some time.

So, you've seen how the main menu options operate when the viewer rolls over them, off them, and clicks them. You should now test the movie again so you can see it all in action.

11 Preview **main_menu.fla** again by choosing **Ctrl+Enter** (Windows) or **Cmd+Return** (Mac).

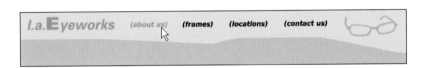

12 When the main menu appears, click **about us**. This immediately disables the **about us** option and changes its color to green.

13 Click a different main menu option. When you do—thanks to the **reActivateBtns** function—the **about us** option becomes re-enabled, and the **frames** option becomes disabled and green. Fabulous! If you'd like, you can click the other options, but you will discover they all behave in the same way. Clicking an option disables its interactivity using the **enabled = false** property, colors it green using the **textColor** property, and re-enables the other menu options using the actions in the **reActivateBtns** function.

14 When you're finished checking everything out, close the preview window, and return to **main_menu.fla**.

Now, all that's missing—of course—is to have those main menu options actually load the appropriate content. That's what you will be constructing in the next exercise.

4 | Bringing It All Together

Your main menu is nearly fully functional, so all you have to do is add the capability for it to load in the appropriate section when the user clicks one of the options. You can build this functionality in multiple ways, but in this exercise you'll have the ubiquitous **myMCL MovieClipLoader** object in **master.swf** to do all the heavy lifting for you. All you'll have to do is write a simple one-line action instructing the **MovieClipLoader** *which* SWF file you want to load and *where* you want it to load.

---

1 In **main_menu.fla**, make sure you have **Keyframe 24** in layer **a** selected and you have the **Actions** panel open.

---

2 Scroll down in the **Actions** panel until you locate the actions within the **<about us option>** and **</about us option>** comments.

```
35  //---------------<about us option>---------------\\
36  MM_aboutUs.onRollOver = function () {
37      changeOptionColor(this, overColor);
38  }
39
40  MM_aboutUs.onRollOut = function () {
41      changeOptionColor(this, outColor);
42  }
43
44  MM_aboutUs.onRelease = function () {
45      reActivateBtns();
46      changeOptionColor(this, overColor);
47      this.enabled = false;
48      _level0.myMCL.loadClip("about_us.swf", 5);
49  }
50  //---------------</about us option>---------------\\
```

3 Within the **onRelease** function, click at the end of the **this.enabled = false;** line, press **Enter** (Windows) or **Return** (Mac) once to create a line break, and type the following:

_level0.myMCL.loadClip("about_us.swf", 5);

As you have seen quite a few times, this simple action instructs the **myMCL MovieClipLoader** object in **master.swf** (**_level0**) to load **about_us.swf** into **_level5**.

And that's it! That's all there is to loading a section's SWF file when the viewer clicks one of the main menu options. Because you've seen this action many times before and because it's a simple action, I've saved you the repetitive task of adding similar actions to the remaining three main menu options. If you scroll down in the **Actions** panel, you'll notice similar actions have already been assigned to the other menu options within their **onRelease** functions. The only change for each menu option is, of course, which SWF file is instructed to load **onRelease**.

As yet, you cannot test the changes you've made thus far. Because you're utilizing the myMCL MovieClipLoader object residing in **master.swf**, you need to preview the main menu only *after* it has been loaded into **master.swf**. So in the next steps, you'll modify **master.swf** to load the main menu.

---

4 Save the changes you've made to **main_menu.fla** by choosing **File > Save** or pressing **Ctrl+S** (Windows) or **Cmd+S** (Mac).

---

5 Publish an updated SWF file by choosing **File > Publish**.

---

6 Minimize (Windows) or hide (Mac) Flash 8, navigate to your **Desktop > la_eyeworks > site** folder, and double-click **master.fla** to open it in Flash 8.

---

7 In **master.fla**, select **Keyframe 10** in layer **a**, and open the **Actions** panel.

```
stop();
// myMCL.loadClip("splash.swf", 5);
myMCL.loadClip("about_us.swf", 5);
// myMCL.loadClip("frames.swf", 5);
```

You'll notice because you've been using Keyframe 10 in **master.swf** to temporarily load SWF files for testing, three other actions are already there to load various SWF files. However, since you have the main menu completed, it will now be the method for which the viewer will access the section SWF files, opposed to manually typing in which files to load.

```
1  stop();
2  myMCL.loadClip("main_menu.swf", 20);
```

8 Delete the three myMCL.loadClip actions in **Keyframe 10**, and under the **stop();** action, type the following:

myMCL.loadClip("main_menu.swf", 20);

As you have seen before, this action simply loads **main_menu.swf** into Level 20. Why all the way up at Level 20? This is simply so the main menu resides in a level above everything else—so it won't get accidentally blocked or obscured by another SWF file—*and* so you have extra room in levels beneath it to load more content if you choose.

Now it's time to see whether your hard work has paid off.

---

9 Save your **master.fla** file by choosing **File > Save** or pressing **Ctrl+S** (Windows) or **Cmd+S** (Mac).

---

10 Then, test **master.fla** by choosing **Control > Test Movie** or pressing **Ctrl+Enter** (Windows) or **Cmd+Return** (Mac).

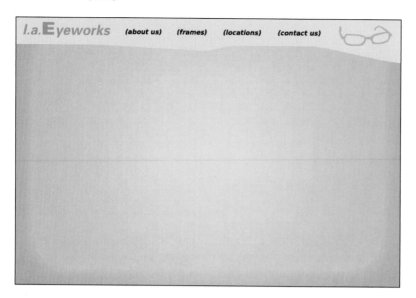

When the preview window opens, you'll see the main menu animate. Ooooh. Aaaah.

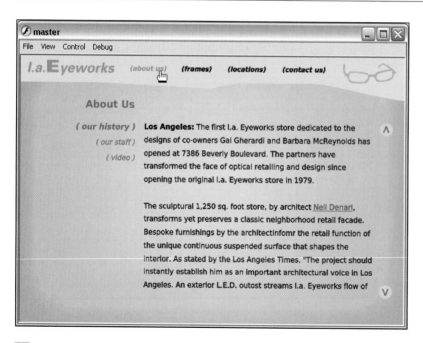

11 Click one of the main menu options. When you do, you'll notice the proper section's SWF file load and display. You now have a working, functional navigation system!

If you click **locations**, it will load and display as well. The **locations** section was not covered in this book because, although it is a necessary addition to the L.A. Eyeworks site as a whole, its construction does not demonstrate any new concepts. However, the **locations.fla** file—and the **locations.swf** file you see when you click its main menu option—are both included in the **la_eyeworks > site** folder so you can refer to them if you'd like.

As you click each of the main menu options, that section's SWF file will load in, replacing the section there previously.

Note: If you click the main menu options but no content loads, chances are you forgot to complete Step 5 in this exercise. Return to Step 5, publish an updated SWF file from **main_menu.fla**, return to **master.fla**, and try testing the movie again.

So, you've gotten the main menu to load and all the sections are now loading, displaying, and functioning to perfection. But what about the animated splash page and the MP3 player? In the next few steps, you will load them as well.

---

12 When you're finished ogling your main menu and congratulating yourself for building such an awesome piece of functionality, close the preview window, and return to **master.fla**.

---

13 In **master.fla**, make sure you have **Keyframe 10** in layer **a** selected and your **Actions** panel is open.

When **main_menu.swf** loads, you also want to load the MP3 player and the splash page. Since they are constructed to all coexist on the Stage simultaneously, you can load them into **master.swf** all at the same time.

```
1  stop();
2  myMCL.loadClip("main_menu.swf", 20);
3  myMCL.loadClip("splash.swf", 5);
4  myMCL.loadClip("music.swf", 6);
```

14 Click at the end of the `myMCL.loadClip("main_menu.swf", 20);` action, press **Enter** (Windows) or **Return** (Mac) once to create a line break, and type the following two actions:

```
myMCL.loadClip("splash.swf", 5);
myMCL.loadClip("music.swf", 6);
```

These two actions load, of course, **splash.swf** into Level 5 and **music.swf** into Level 6. The **splash.swf** file loads into Level 5, which is the same level the section SWF files load into, because you want **splash.swf** to disappear when the viewer clicks one of the main menu options.

---

15 Once again, save your **master.fla** file by choosing **File > Save** or pressing **Ctrl+S** (Windows) or **Cmd+S** (Mac).

---

16 Preview the changes you've made by choosing **Control > Test Movie** or pressing **Ctrl+Enter** (Windows) or **Cmd+Return** (Mac).

When the preview window appears, it should bowl you over. You now have a functional navigation menu, an animated splash graphic swapping out with the content sections, and a functional MP3 player. Essentially, you have a working, complete, Flash 8–built Web site for L.A. Eyeworks. I hope you're proud of what you've accomplished thus far because you certainly deserve it. You've learned a tremendous amount in this book, and you have only yourself to thank for it. Congratulations!

---

17 Close the preview window, return to Flash 8, and close any FLA file you currently have open. If you're prompted by Flash 8 to save your changes, click **Yes** (Windows) or **Save** (Mac).

With that, don't think your work is over quite yet. In the next chapter, I'll show you how to insert your completed L.A. Eyeworks site into an HTML page using Macromedia Dreamweaver 8 and how to build a Flash plug-in detector. I'll see you in the next chapter.

Although there are a gazillion ways of embedding a SWF file into an HTML page, in this exercise you will embed the SWF file so it's centered in the middle—both horizontally and vertically—of the HTML page using tables. Keep in mind, however, that one of the fantastic properties of Flash 8 content is that you can put it anywhere on an HTML page. You can easily use CSS or tables to align and position the SWF file wherever you'd like, just as if you were placing a JPEG or GIF on the page.

First, you need to set the margins of the HTML page so the table can be positioned all the way to the edges.

2 Choose **Modify > Page Properties**, or press **Ctrl+J** (Windows) or **Cmd+J** (Mac).

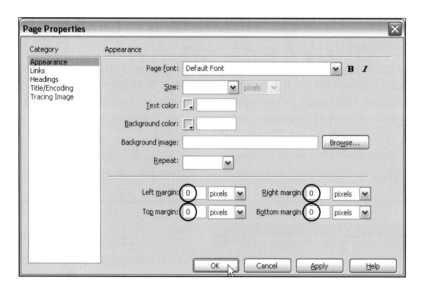

3 In the **Page Properties** window, type **0** in the **Left margin**, **Right margin**, **Top margin**, and **Bottom margin** fields to remove the default margins of the HTML page. This prevents you from pushing content all the way to the edge of the document. Click **OK**.

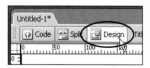

4 Make sure you're looking at the **Design** view by clicking the **Design** button.

Note: If you prefer to watch the HTML code as you construct this page, you can also select the Split view mode. If you choose Split view, just make sure you made your edits and changes in the Design portion of the window so you can follow along correctly with the upcoming steps.

5 Click the HTML page and choose **Insert > Table**.

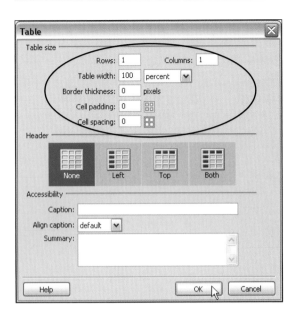

6 In the **Table** window, type **1** in both the **Rows** and **Columns** fields. Set the **Table width** to **100 percent**, the **Border thickness** to **0 pixels**, and the **Cell padding** and **Cell spacing** to **0**. Click **OK**.

This will insert a table with one row, one column, and 100 percent width into the page. But because you want to center the SWF file that will eventually reside within this table, both horizontally *and* vertically (within an average-sized monitor), you need to adjust the height of the table as well.

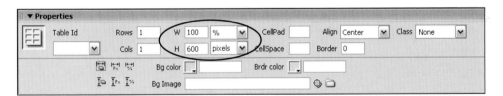

7 Press **Ctrl+F3** (Windows) or **Cmd+F3** (Mac) to open the **Property Inspector**. Change the **H** (height) field to **600 pixels**, which sets the table's height to 600 pixels.

Note: If you don't see options to change the table's width and height, make sure you have the table selected first.

Because the SWF file will be embedded in the sole cell in this table, you'll set the table cell so that any content placed within it will be aligned in the center both horizontally and vertically. By default, the table cell is set to align content placed within it in the center vertically but on the *left* horizontally.

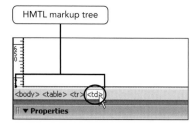

8 Click in the table cell (anywhere on the page, essentially). In the **HTML markup tree**, click the **<td>** tag to select only the cell of the table.

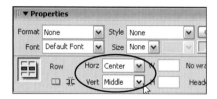

9 In the **Property Inspector**, choose **Center** from the **Horz** (Horizontal) pop-up menu. From the **Vert** (Vertical) pop-up menu, choose **Middle**. This sets the alignment of the table cell so that content placed within it is aligned in the center horizontally and in the middle vertically.

10 Click in the middle of the page.

You'll notice that your blinking cursor is now in the middle. When you place a SWF file into this cell, that's where it will be embedded.

Now, before you can place anything within this HTML page, you should save it first. Dreamweaver 8 needs to know where the content you're placing in the page resides *relative* to where the HTML page itself is saved. To keep your site files organized, you'll save this HTML page in the same folder as the rest of your L.A. Eyeworks site files.

11 Choose **File > Save** or press **Ctrl+S** (Windows) or **Cmd+S** (Mac).

12 In the **Save As** window, navigate to the **Desktop > la_eyeworks > site** folder.

13 In the **File name** field, type **index** and click **Save**. Dreamweaver 8 automatically inserts an **.html** extension on the end of the filename.

Now that you've saved your **index.htm** file into the **site** folder, you can embed the SWF file into the HTML page. All in all, the L.A. Eyeworks Flash 8–built Web site is constructed with approximately 15 SWF files. Out of those, which one should you embed? The SWF file you want to place in the HTML page should be whichever SWF is Level 0, or the root SWF that the other SWFs load into. In the case of the L.A. Eyeworks site, that is **master.swf**. (It's not called "master" for nothing, ya know.)

14 Click in the middle of the table cell so you see the blinking cursor there, then choose **Insert > Media > Flash** or press **Ctrl+Alt+F** (Windows) or **Cmd+Option+F** (Mac).

15 In the **Select File** dialog box, navigate to the **Desktop > la_eyeworks > site** folder, click **master.swf**, and click **OK** (Windows) or **Choose** (Mac).

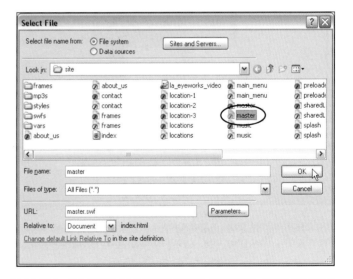

Why Use a Flash Plug-In Detector?

Flash plug-in detectors come in a variety of styles. Some use pure JavaScript to do all the work, and others use a combination of JavaScript and Flash content. The following exercise demonstrates the "recommended method" of creating a Flash plug-in detector.

Keep in mind that Flash plug-in detectors aren't foolproof. Various hardware or software factors could cause the detection script to fail, potentially leaving your visitor staring at a blank page. A *must* when you're creating a plug-in detector is to *always* add text information to the page that contains your Flash content. Then, if a viewer visits your site and either doesn't have the Flash plug-in installed or has an outdated version of it, he or she will still see text explaining why the Flash content didn't appear and how to correct the problem.

2 | Building a Flash 8 Plug-In Detector

Imagine this: A viewer comes to your Web site, and your Flash 8-built Web page loads in his or her browser. Looking for the closest L.A. Eyeworks store, the viewer clicks the **(locations)** option. Nothing happens. No preloader, no loading, no nothing. The viewer clicks again. Nothing. The viewer, with wonder, clicks **(about us)**. Still, nothing happens. Disgusted with this "broken" Web site, the viewer leaves, unaware that it only appears broken because he or she has the Macromedia Flash 6 plug-in, and your site uses the `MovieClipLoader` class to load the appropriate content—a feature that the version 6 plug-in doesn't understand. Thankfully, this hypothetical scenario is preventable. You can install a Flash plug-in detector (sometimes called a plug-in **sniffer**) that catches a viewer attempting to enter your site with an unsupported version of the Flash plug-in. Viewers with the *correct* version, or higher, of the Macromedia Flash plug-in can seamlessly enter your Web site; viewers with an *earlier* version of the plug-in will see alternate information. Unless you're constructing Flash content for projector playback, you should *always* use a Flash plug-in detector so your site doesn't appear broken.

In this exercise, you will build a robust Flash plug-in detector by simply selecting the **Detect Flash Version** option. The first step is to open an FLA. But which one? Because **master.swf** is the root SWF file that all the others load into, you need to open **master.fla** to create the plug-in detector. The detection script that Flash generates for you will reference **master.swf** as the Flash content for viewers with the correct version of the Flash plug-in.

---

1 On your hard drive, navigate to the **Desktop > la_eyeworks > site** folder and double-click **master.fla** to open it in Flash 8.

---

2 Choose **File > Publish Settings** to open the **Publish Settings** dialog box.

---

3 In the **Formats** tab, make sure the **HTML (.html)** option is selected.

---

4 Select the **HTML** tab to display the HTML preferences. Select the **Detect Flash Version** option, and click **Publish**.

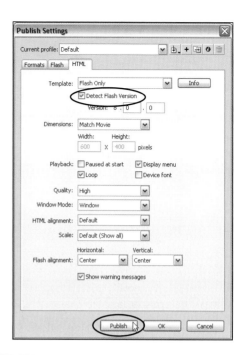

5 Click **OK** to close the **Publish Settings** dialog box.

6 Minimize (Windows) or hide (Mac) Flash 8, and return to Dreamweaver 8.

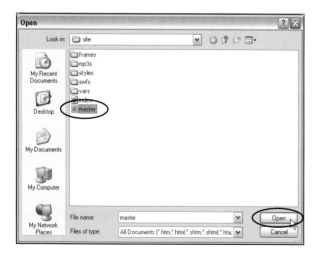

7 In Dreamweaver 8, choose **File > Open**. In the **Open** dialog box, select **master** and click **Open**.

8 Switch to **Code** view.

When Flash 8 created the plug-in detection script, it wrote a few JavaScripts into the **master.html** file. In the next few steps you'll take those two JavaScripts and add them to the page that contains your Flash content: **index.html**.

```
 85   for (i=25;i>0;i--) {
 86      if (isIE && isWin && !isOpera) {
 87         versionStr = VBGetSwfVer(i);
 88      } else {
 89         versionStr = JSGetSwfVer(i);
 90      }
 91      if (versionStr == -1 ) {
 92         return false;
 93      } else if (versionStr != 0) {
 94         if(isIE && isWin && !isOpera) {
 95            tempArray      = versionStr.split(" ");
 96            tempString     = tempArray[1];
 97            versionArray   = tempString .split(",");
 98         } else {
 99            versionArray   = versionStr.split(".");
100         }
101         versionMajor    = versionArray[0];
102         versionMinor    = versionArray[1];
103         versionRevision = versionArray[2];
104
105         versionString   = versionMajor + "." + version
106         versionNum      = parseFloat(versionString);
107         // is the major.revision >= requested major.rev
108         if ( (versionMajor > reqMajorVer) && (versionNum
109            return true;
110         } else {
111            return ((versionNum >= reqVer && versionMino
112         }
113      }
114   }
115   return (reqVer ? false : 0.0);
116 }
117
118 </script>
119 </head>
120 <body bgcolor="#b4cce5">
121 <!--url's used in the movie-->
122 <!--text used in the movie-->
```

Context menu:
- Edit Tag <script>... Shift+F5
- Insert Tag...
- Functions ▶
- Selection ▶
- Create New Snippet
- CSS Styles ▶
- Code Hint Tools ▶
- Open   Ctrl+D
- Find and Replace... Ctrl+F
- Find Selection Shift+F3
- Find Next   F3
- Reference   Shift+F1
- Cut
- Copy
- Paste   Ctrl+V
- Paste Special...
- Print Code...

9 Scroll to the top of the **master.html** code. Several lines down you'll see a line that reads

`<script language="JavaScript" type="text/javascript">`

Select that line and all the lines that follow it down to the one that reads

`</script>`

(In the illustration, it is the **</script>** tag that comes right before the **</head>** tag.)

After you've selected that large block of text, copy it.

10 Switch to **index.html** and make sure you're in **Code** view as well.

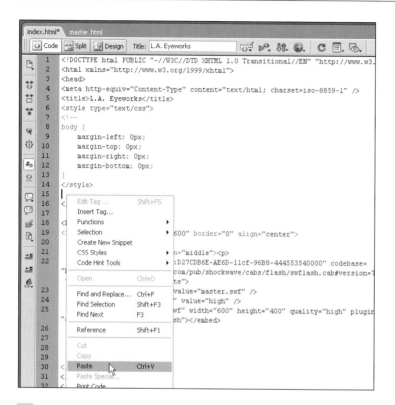

11 Click *before* the **</head>** tag toward the top of the window, create a line break and select it, and paste the text you copied from **master.html**.

12 Switch back to **master.html**.

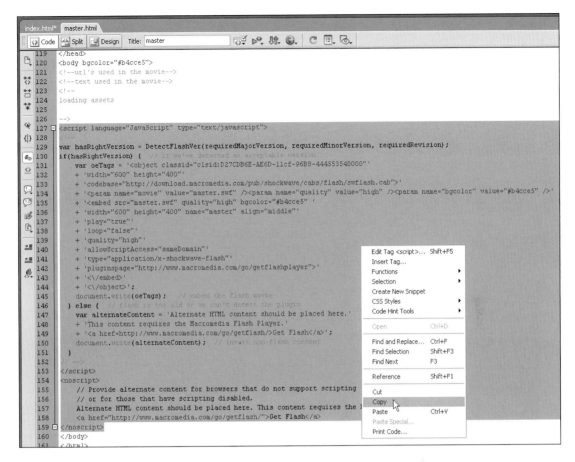

```
119  </head>
120  <body bgcolor="#b4cce5">
121  <!--url's used in the movie-->
122  <!--text used in the movie-->
123  <!--
124  loading assets
125
126  -->
127  <script language="JavaScript" type="text/javascript">
128
129  var hasRightVersion = DetectFlashVer(requiredMajorVersion, requiredMinorVersion, requiredRevision);
130  if(hasRightVersion) {  // if we've detected an acceptable version
131      var oeTags = '<object classid="clsid:D27CDB6E-AE6D-11cf-96B8-444553540000"'
132      + 'width="600" height="400"'
133      + 'codebase="http://download.macromedia.com/pub/shockwave/cabs/flash/swflash.cab">'
134      + '<param name="movie" value="master.swf" /><param name="quality" value="high" /><param name="bgcolor" value="#b4cce5" />'
135      + '<embed src="master.swf" quality="high" bgcolor="#b4cce5" '
136      + 'width="600" height="400" name="master" align="middle"'
137      + 'play="true"'
138      + 'loop="false"'
139      + 'quality="high"'
140      + 'allowScriptAccess="sameDomain"'
141      + 'type="application/x-shockwave-flash"'
142      + 'pluginspage="http://www.macromedia.com/go/getflashplayer">'
143      + '<\/embed>'
144      + '<\/object>';
145      document.write(oeTags);  // embed the flash movie
146  } else {  // flash is too old or we can't detect the plugin
147      var alternateContent = 'Alternate HTML content should be placed here.'
148      + 'This content requires the Macromedia Flash Player.'
149      + '<a href=http://www.macromedia.com/go/getflash>Get Flash</a>';
150      document.write(alternateContent);  // insert non-flash content
151  }
152  // -->
153  </script>
154  <noscript>
155      // Provide alternate content for browsers that do not support scripting
156      // or for those that have scripting disabled.
157      Alternate HTML content should be placed here. This content requires the I
158      <a href="http://www.macromedia.com/go/getflash/">Get Flash</a>
159  </noscript>
160  </body>
161  </html>
```

Context menu options shown:

```
Edit Tag <script>...   Shift+F5
Insert Tag...
Functions            ▶
Selection            ▶
Create New Snippet
CSS Styles           ▶
Code Hint Tools      ▶

Open                 Ctrl+D

Find and Replace...  Ctrl+F
Find Selection       Shift+F3
Find Next            F3

Reference            Shift+F1

Cut
Copy
Paste                Ctrl+V
Paste Special...
Print Code...
```

13 Scroll farther down the code window and you'll see another JavaScript block. As shown in the illustration here, select all the text from **`<script language="JavaScript" type="text/javascript">`** to **`</noscript>`** (right before the **`</body>`** tag). Copy that text.

---

14 Once again, return to **index.html**.

When you copied that last chunk of text from **master.html**, you might have noticed that there are some lines in there that make mention of **master.swf**, as well as its width, height, and so forth. The text you're about to paste into **index.html** is actually the code (mixed in with some other JavaScript that Flash 8 generated) that embeds **master.swf** itself. You'll need to make sure you replace the existing text that embeds **master.swf** in **index.html** with your new and improved text.

```
31  <table width="100%" height="600" border="0" align="center">
32    <tr>
33      <td align="center" valign="middle"><p>
34        <object classid="clsid:D27CDB6E-AE6D-11cf-96B8-444553540000" codebase=
    "http://download.macromedia.com/pub/shockwave/cabs/flash/swflash.cab#version=7,0,19,0" width="600" height="400" accesskey="B" tabindex="1"
    title="L.A. Eyeworks Web site">
35          <param name="movie" value="master.swf" />
36          <param name="quality" value="high" />
37          <embed src="master.swf" width="600" height="400" quality="high" pluginspage="http://www.macromedia.com/go/getflashplayer" type=
    "application/x-shockwave-flash"></embed>
38        </object>
39      </p>
40    </td>
```

15 In **index.html**, scroll down the **Code** view window until you locate the table tags and, contained within them, the **<object>** tags. After you locate the object tags, select all the text from the **<object>** tag to the **</object>** tag, as shown in the illustration.

Note: You can also easily select the text by clicking anywhere between the **<object** and **</object>** tags, and then clicking the **<object>** button in the HTML markup tree.

```
130  <body>
131  <table width="100%" height="600" border="0" align="center">
132    <tr>
133      <td align="center" valign="middle"><p>
134        <script language="JavaScript" type="text/javascript">
135  <!--
136  var hasRightVersion = DetectFlashVer(requiredMajorVersion, requiredMinorVersion, requiredRevision);
137  if(hasRightVersion) {  // if we've detected an acceptable version
138      var oeTags = '<object classid="clsid:D27CDB6E-AE6D-11cf-96B8-444553540000"'
139      + 'width="600" height="400"'
140      + 'codebase="http://download.macromedia.com/pub/shockwave/cabs/flash/swflash.cab">'
141      + '<param name="movie" value="master.swf" /><param name="quality" value="high" /><param name="bgcolor" value="#b4cce5" />'
142      + '<embed src="master.swf" quality="high" bgcolor="#b4cce5" '
143      + 'width="600" height="400" name="master" align="middle"'
144      + 'play="true"'
145      + 'loop="false"'
146      + 'quality="high"'
147      + 'allowScriptAccess="sameDomain"'
148      + 'type="application/x-shockwave-flash"'
149      + 'pluginspage="http://www.macromedia.com/go/getflashplayer">'
150      + '<\/embed>'
151      + '<\/object>';
152      document.write(oeTags);  // embed the flash movie
153  } else {  // flash is too old or we can't detect the plugin
154      var alternateContent = 'Alternate HTML content should be placed here.'
155      + 'This content requires the Macromedia Flash Player.'
156      + '<a href=http://www.macromedia.com/go/getflash/>Get Flash</a>';
157      document.write(alternateContent);  // insert non-flash content
158  }
159  // -->
160  </script>
161  <noscript>
162      // Provide alternate content for browsers that do not support scripting
163      // or for those that have scripting disabled.
164      Alternate HTML content should be placed here. This content requires the Macromedia Flash Player.
165      <a href="http://www.macromedia.com/go/getflash/">Get Flash</a>
166  </noscript>
167      </p>
168    </td>
169  </tr>
```

16 Delete the selected text and paste in the text you copied from **master.html** in its place.

Before calling this plug-in detector finished, you should be aware of a few items in the last text block you pasted. Note the comment tag that reads **//flash is too old or we can't detect the plugin**. After that comment is some placeholder text (highlighted in blue) that starts with "Alternate HTML content should be placed here." Before repeating these steps for your own—or client—site, make sure you replace that text with some text of your own. Additionally, notice the **<noscript>** and **</noscript>** tags with some placeholder text between them. Replace this content with content you want viewers to see if they're using Web browsers with JavaScript disabled.

Congratulations! You've just created—with a few clicks of the mouse button and the waving of a magical Flash wand—a Flash plug-in detector. You should test it just to make sure everything is working as intended.

---

17 Save your changes to **index.html** by choosing **File > Save**.

---

18 Open **index.html** in your preferred Web browser. Normally, you can simply double-click the file to open it in your system's default browser.

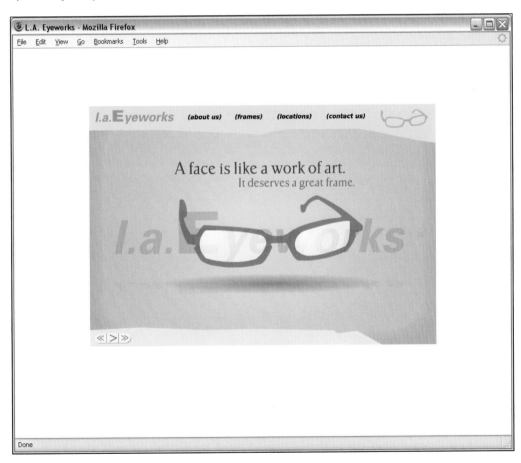

When your browser opens **index.html**, you'll notice—because you have version 8 of the Flash Player installed in your Web browser—your L.A. Eyeworks site successfully appears!

Unfortunately, in the Windows operating system, it's not very easy to disable or deactivate the Macromedia Flash plug-in so you can test whether the rest of the plug-in detector works. If you really, really want to fully test the functionality of the plug-in detector, you can download the Macromedia Flash Player uninstaller from **http://www.macromedia.com/cfusion/knowledgebase/index.cfm?id=tn_14157**, uninstall the Flash Player from your system, test the plug-in detector, and then reinstall the Flash Player when you're finished.

If you really, really want to test the plug-in detector in Mac OS X, you can move the files **NP-PPC-Dir-Shockwave** and **Flash Player.plugin** out of the **/Library/Internet Plug-ins/** folder (and also from your **~/Library/Internet Plug-ins/** folder if it is there as well), test the plug-in detector, and then move **NP-PPC-Dir-Shockwave** and **Flash Player.plugin** back to the **Internet Plug-ins** folder when you're finished. However, rather than go through all those steps, you're just going to have to trust me that the rest of it works as intended.

And that is one of several ways to create a Flash plug-in detector. With the introduction of Flash MX 2004, and now Flash 8, the capability to create a plug-in detector is now *built into* Flash itself. As you've seen, this capability makes it incredibly easy to create a plug-in detector. Now you have no excuse not to add a plug-in detector to everything you build in Flash 8.

Concluding Remarks

In this chapter, you learned how to embed a SWF file into an HTML page using Dreamweaver 8 and how to create a plug-in detector so viewers with an older version of the Flash Player can see alternate content. Your L.A. Eyeworks site is now ready to upload to a Web server so the whole world can see it! Because you've been consistently keeping your L.A. Eyeworks site-related files in the **la_eyeworks > site** folder on your **Desktop**, when you have a Web presence provider and you're ready to upload your work, all you have to do is upload all the files in the **site** folder (minus the FLA files and **master.html**, of course) to your Web server, and you're done!

You're also done with this book as well! A giant, humungous congratulations is in order, too. For those of you who considered yourself "ActionScript challenged" and have made it through to the end of this book, you have earned my sincere respect. This book introduced you to a plethora of ActionScript concepts. From this book, you've learned how to use ActionScript to bring that extremely important element of *dynamics* into your Flash 8 projects. By using ActionScript to build a dynamic site, you (or your client) can now easily manage and update a site by modifying only a few items.

Throughout this book you also learned how to create fun but *useful* and *practical* functionality. For example, you created an MP3 player that doesn't just play MP3s, but also allows the viewer to stop the music, skip to the next or previous track, change the volume, and even observe the playback and downloading progress of the MP3. Many users' general preconception of Macromedia Flash is that it is used to create "intro animations" or other flourishes that serve no functional purpose. As you've seen in this book, nothing could be further from the truth. In these pages, I hope you've learned how to create some really fun things, but more importantly I hope you've learned how to use Macromedia Flash to say or present what you need to in a *functional* and *useful* manner.

Once again, congratulations.

Shane Rebenschied

Technical Support and Troubleshooting FAQ

If you run into problems while following the exercises in this book, you might find the answer in the Troubleshooting FAQ. If you don't find the information you're looking for, use the contact information provided in the Technical Support section.

Technical Support Information

The following is a list of technical support resources you can use if you need help:

lynda.com

If you run into any problems as you work through this book, check the companion Web site for updates:

www.lynda.com/books/HOT/fl8btb

If you don't find with you're looking for on the companion Web site, send Shane Rebenschied an email:

fl8btb@lynda.com

We encourage and welcome your feedback, comments, and error reports.

Peachpit Press

If your book has a defective CD-ROM, please contact the customer service department at Peachpit Press:

customer_service@peachpit.com

Macromedia Technical Support

If you're having problems with Flash Professional 8, please visit the Macromedia Flash Support Center:

www.macromedia.com/support/flash/

To contact Macromedia Technical Support, visit the following link:

www.macromedia.com/support/email/cscontact/

Frequently Asked Questions

Q On the Macintosh, why can't I see any FLA files when I choose File > Open?

A If the FLA file was created on a PC, you might experience a problem seeing those files when you choose **File > Open** from within Macromedia Flash 8 on a Macintosh. You can correct this problem by changing the **Enable** option to **All Files**.

Q On the Macintosh, the FLA file won't open when I double-click it. Why?

A If the FLA file was created on a PC, you might not be able to double-click it to open the file. If this is the case, open Flash 8 and choose **File > Open** to open the FLA file. If you don't see the FLA file listed when you choose **File > Open**, see the previous question. After you save the FLA file (originally created on a PC) on your Mac, you will be able to double-click the FLA to open it.

Q When I select the Text tool, why doesn't my Property Inspector update to show the text options?

A Sometimes the **Property Inspector** will not update when you switch to the **Text** tool. To get the **Property Inspector** to display text options when you select the **Text** tool, click the **Stage**, which updates the **Property Inspector** and displays the text options. However, if clicking the **Stage** also creates a Dynamic or Input text field, press **Esc** and then **Backspace** or **Delete** to delete the text field.

Q I can't get a certain action or script to work correctly. I've gone over what you said and have rebuilt the exercise several times, but it still won't work. Help!

A One of the most common mistakes is often the simplest. Double-check your spelling to make sure everything—ActionScript syntax, variables, and so forth—is spelled correctly. Secondly, Flash 8 is case-sensitive, so make sure you are using capitalization consistently. In other words, if you are creating a variable **var myVar**, but are then later referring to that variable as **myvar**, it won't work. (Notice the difference in capitalization.) Lastly, double-check your semicolons, commas, quotation marks, and so on. ActionScript syntax uses a variety of symbols to represent various things, and the code can get quite complex at times. Make sure you're using those symbols in the same way and in the same order as in the book. If you've performed all these steps, and it still doesn't work, email the support address for this book (**fl8btb@lynda.com**)—with a *detailed* description of the problem and a copy of the FLA (if possible).

Q Can I reuse the elements—graphics, audio, or otherwise—in this book and on the HOT CD-ROM for client work or personal experimentation?

A The assets in the book and on the **HOT CD-ROM** are there as tools to help you learn and understand the exercises and concepts. However, those assets *cannot* be used for client work. If you want to use them in your own experimental or personal work, feel free. But the assets *may not* be used for commercial work.

Flash Professional 8 Resources

There are many great resources for Flash users. You have ample choices among a variety of newsgroups, conferences, and third-party Web sites that can really help you get the most out of the new skills you've developed by reading this book. Here you'll find a list of the best resources for further developing your skills with Flash Professional 8.

lynda.com Training Resources

lynda.com is a leader in software books and video training for Web and graphics professionals. To help further develop your skills in Flash, check out the following training resources from **lynda.com**:

Books

The **Hands-On Training** series was originally developed by **Lynda Weinman**, author of the revolutionary book *Designing Web Graphics*, first released in 1996. Lynda believes people learn best from doing and has developed the **Hands-On Training** series to teach users software programs and technologies through a progressive learning process.

Check out the following books from lynda.com:

Macromedia Flash Professional 8 Hands-On Training
by James Gonzalez
lynda.com/books and Peachpit Press
ISBN: 0321293886

Macromedia Dreamweaver 8 Hands-On Training
by Garo Green and Daniel Short
lynda.com/books and Peachpit Press
ISBN: 0321293894

Adobe Photoshop CS2 for the Web Hands-On Training
by Tanya Staples
lynda.com/books and Peachpit Press
ISBN: 0321331710

Designing Web Graphics 4
by Lynda Weinman
New Riders
ISBN: 0735710791

Video-Based Training

lynda.com offers video training as stand-alone **CD-ROM** and **DVD-ROM** products and through a subscription to the **lynda.com Online Training Library**.

For a free, 24-hour trial pass to the lynda.com Online Training Library, register your copy of *Flash Professional 8 Beyond the Basics* at the following link:

www.lynda.com/register/HOT/flash8btb

Note: This offer is available for new subscribers only and does not apply to current or past subscribers of the lynda.com Online Training Library.

To help you build your skills with Flash 8, check out the following video training titles from lynda.com:

Flash Video-Based Training

Flash Professional 8 Essential Training
with Shane Rebenschied

Flash Professional 8 New Features
with Shane Rebenschied

Flash Professional 8 Beyond the Basics
with Shane Rebenschied

Flash 8 User Experience Best Practices
with Robert Hoekman Jr.

Flash Professional 8 and Photoshop CS2 Integration
with Michael Ninness

ActionScript 2.0 Video-Based Training

Learning ActionScript 2.0
with Joey Lott

Advanced ActionScript 2.0
with Joey Lott

Web Design Video-Based Training

Studio 8 Web Workflow
with Abigail Rudner

Photoshop CS2 for the Web Essential Training
with Tanya Staples

Fireworks 8 Essential Training
with Abigail Rudner

Flashforward Conference

Flashforward is an international educational conference dedicated to Macromedia Flash. Flashforward was first hosted by Lynda Weinman, founder of lynda.com, and Stewart McBride, founder of United Digital Artists. Flashforward is now owned exclusively by lynda.com and strives to provide the best conferences for designers and developers to present their technical and artistic work in an educational setting.

For more information about the Flashforward conference, visit **www.flashforwardconference.com**.

Online Resources

Flash 8 Developer Center

www.macromedia.com/devnet/flash/
Macromedia has created a section of its Web site called the Flash Developer Center. This is a one-stop shop for everything Flash. For example, you can read tutorials and articles about Flash 8, download sample applications, access links to other Flash 8 resources, and read the white papers written on topics related to Flash 8. This is the perfect link to use if you want to get more in-depth information about components, video, or other topics in Flash 8.

Macromedia Online Forums

webforums.macromedia.com/flash/
Macromedia has set up several Web-based online forums for Flash. This is a great place to ask questions and get help from thousands of Flash users. These online forums are used by beginning to advanced Flash users, so you should have no problem finding the type of help you need, regardless of your experience with the program. A list follows describing several of the Macromedia online forums.

Flash General Discussion
Online forum for general issues related to using Flash.

Flash ActionScript

Online forum dedicated, of course, to everything ActionScript. Post your ActionScript-related questions and search for your ActionScript-related answers here.

Flash Site Design

Online forum for design feedback on Flash animations. This forum is dedicated to the discussion of Macromedia Flash design and animation principles and practices. Other issues not specific to the Flash tools, yet important to Flash designers, are also discussed here.

Flash Remoting

Online forum that discusses issues involved with Flash Remoting. Flash Remoting supplies the infrastructure that allows users to connect to remote services exposed by application server developers and Web services. Examples of these are message boards, shopping carts, and even up-to-the-minute stock quote graphs.

Flash Exchange Extensions

Online forum for issues relating to Flash extensions, including how to use them and how to troubleshoot any problems with them. (See also the "Macromedia Flash Exchange" section next.)

Flash Data Integration

Online forum dedicated to the topic of integrating data into your Flash movies. Have questions about integrating database content into your Flash projects? Post your questions or search for your answers here.

Flash Ad Development

Online forum dedicated to discussing "the development of rich media ad units using Flash and the Flash Ad Kit for DoubleClick DART Motif or other advertising-related Flash content."

Macromedia Flash Exchange

www.macromedia.com/exchange/flash/
Here you'll find hundreds of free extensions written by third-party users and developers, which can help you build new features into your Web site. These features are not part of the Flash Professional 8 product, but you can download them when you need them. Many of these extensions have features that normally would require an advanced level of ActionScripting. For example, some of these behaviors enable you to create password-protected areas of your site and to create pop-up menus, scroll bars, complex text effects, and so on.

The Macromedia site is not just for developers but also for any Flash user who wants to take Flash Professional 8 to the next level. If you are a developer, this is a great place to learn how to write your own behaviors to share with the rest of the Flash community.

You can also visit **http://webforums.macromedia.com/flash/** and click the **Flash Exchange Extensions** link to access the online forum for Flash extensions.

Macromedia TechNotes

www.macromedia.com/support/flash/technotes.html
This section of the Macromedia Web site lists all the issues that have been reported and answered by Macromedia Flash staff.

Third-Party Web Sites

www.flashkit.com/

www.ultrashock.com/

http://virtual-fx.net/

www.actionscripts.org/

www.flzone.net/

http://flashmove.com/

http://flazoom.com/

www.were-here.com/

www.popedeflash.com/

www.macromedia.com/support/flash/ts/documents/flash_websites.htm

Books

Macromedia Flash 8 Bible
by Robert Reinhardt and Snow Dowd
John Wiley & Sons, 2006
ISBN: 0471746762

Macromedia Flash MX 2004 Bible
by Robert Reinhardt and Snow Dowd
John Wiley & Sons, 2003
ISBN: 0764543032

Macromedia Flash MX ActionScript Bible
by Robert Reinhardt and Joey Lott
John Wiley & Sons, 2004
ISBN: 0764543547

Macromedia Flash Professional 8 Training from the Source
by Tom Green, Jordan L. Chilcott
Publisher: Macromedia Press, 2005
ISBN: 0321384032

ActionScript: The Definitive Guide
by Colin Moock and Gary Grossman
O'Reilly & Associates, 2001
ISBN: 1565928520

Flash MX 2004 Games Most Wanted
by Kristian Besley
APress L.P., 2003
ISBN: 1590592360

Flash Web Design: The V5 Remix
by Hillman Curtis
New Riders Publishing, 2001
ISBN: 0735708967

MTIV: Process, Inspiration, and Practice for the New Media Designer
by Hillman Curtis
New Riders Publishing, 2002
ISBN: 0735711658

Macromedia Flash MX 2004 Magic
by Michelangelo Capraro
New Riders, 2003
ISBN: 0735713774

Software and Technology

CSS

The following programs let you easily write and edit cascading style sheets (CSS):

- Macromedia Dreamweaver 8 for Windows and Mac (**www.macromedia.com/dreamweaver/**)

- Adobe GoLive CS for Windows and Mac (**www.adobe.com/products/golive/**)

- CSSEdit for Mac (**www.macrabbit.com/cssedit/**)

- Bradsoft Top Style for Windows (**www.bradsoft.com/topstyle/**)

MP3 Playback/Encoding

The following programs let you encode audio files as MP3:

- Apple iTunes for Windows and Mac (**www.apple.com/iTunes/**)

- Nullsoft Winamp for Windows (**www.winamp.com**)

- Panic Audion for Mac (**www.panic.com/audion/**)

ID3 Editing

The following programs let you edit the ID3 tags in MP3 files:

- Apple iTunes for Windows and Mac (**www.apple.com/iTunes/**)

- Nullsoft Winamp for Windows (**www.winamp.com**)

- Panic Audion for Mac (**www.panic.com/audion/**)

- MP3 Book Helper for Windows (**http://mp3bookhelper.sourceforge.net/**)

Flowcharts

The following programs let you create flowcharts:

- Omni Group OmniGraffle for Mac (**www.omnigroup.com/applications/omnigraffle/**)

- Microsoft Visio for Windows (**www.microsoft.com/office**)

- Edge Diagrammer for Windows (**www.pacestar.com/edge/**)

Getting Your Work Online / Using CGIs

In Chapter 9, *"Building a Form,"* you learned how to construct a feed-back form in Flash 8 using the **TextInput** and **TextArea** components. You also learned that when the viewer fills out the form and clicks Submit, the form results are sent—using a **LoadVars** object—to a CGI script to be processed. The CGI script processes the form results, and in the case of a feedback form like the one you built, emails those results to whichever email address you specify. But where can you get these CGI scripts? Moreover, where can you find a Web presence provider to store those CGI scripts, and your Web site, so everyone can see your work? In this appendix, I will share a few places where you can find CGI scripts to use in your Flash 8 projects, as well as Web presence providers where you can store and display your work to the world.

Web Presence Providers

Once you've designed your Web site, you'll need a place to store it—preferably a place that has a very high-speed connection to the Internet, gives you lots of disk space for your content, and offers you lots of options. The companies that provide these services for you are called **Web presence providers**. There are easily thousands and thousands of Web presence providers all around the world. So which one should you choose? Which ones stretch your dollars the furthest? The following sections list a few U.S.-based Web presence providers that I've hosted my work on, as well as some that I've heard great things about.

Web Site Hosting

The following Web presence providers offer services to host your content. They all offer plans that allow access to prebuilt CGI scripts as well as the ability to install your own custom CGI scripts.

- Pair Networks (**www.pair.com**)—I hosted sites with Pair for years. They have a great reputation in the industry; they offer great options at great prices; and their customer service is top-notch. If some of their competitors didn't offer more for less, I'd still be hosting my personal site with them.

- Media Temple (**www.mediatemple.net**)—This is the "hip" place to host your work on the Internet. I've also hosted my work with Media Temple in the past, and I currently have friends that host their content with them as well. The fantastic thing about Media Temple is that they also offer the use—for an additional monthly fee—of a Flash Communication Server. The Flash Communication Server lets you do true streaming (RTMP) of your MP3 and FLV files. Media Temple also offers Macromedia ColdFusion MX services, which let you integrate database content into your Flash 8 movies. If you build Flash 8 content for a living, and you want access to all the bells and whistles, Media Temple is the place to be.

- DreamHost (**www.dreamhost.net**)—This is the presence provider that hosts my personal Web site blot.com. I've been with them for only about a year so far, but they provide great service with lots of disk space at an awesome price.

Flash Communication Server Hosting

Special server software called the **Flash Communication Server** lets you, among other things, truly stream (RTMP) media such as MP3s and FLVs. For more information about the benefits a Flash Communication Server provides, see the "What Is Progressive Downloading, and What Is Streaming?" section in Chapter 10, *"Building an MP3 Player."*

The following presence providers offer Flash Communication Server accounts:

- Media Temple (**www.mediatemple.net**)—See the preceding section for a description of Media Temple.

- Uvault (**www.uvault.com**)—Uvault offers Flash Communication Server options similar to those offered by Media Temple, but Uvault also maintains servers in Europe. If the majority of your client base is in Europe, you should look into the Uvault services.

- NI Solutions Group (**www.nisgroup.com**)—NI Solutions Group offers both Flash Communication Server services as well as ColdFusion hosting.

You can also see an up-to-date list of providers that host Flash Communication Server accounts here: **www.macromedia.com/partners/flashcom/**.

Additionally, if you just want to be able to have your FLVs RTMP streamed (instead of just progressively streamed off of a Web server), Macromedia has partnered with a few services to offer **Flash Video Streaming Service**. You can read more about this service, as well as which providers Macromedia has partnered with, at the following URL: **www.macromedia.com/software/flashmediaserver/fvss/**.

CGI Scripts

If you already have a Web presence provider, or if you're signing up with one of the providers listed here in Appendix C, check with them before searching all over the Internet for CGI scripts to use with your Flash 8 project. Every Web presence provider I've seen offers pre-installed CGI scripts that come with your account. Check in the support section of your Web presence provider's home page to see which CGI scripts are already installed for your use.

When locating a CGI script to use in conjunction with your Flash 8 feedback form, you're essentially looking for one that processes form results. This CGI script is often called **FormMail** or **formmail.pl**. The CGI script doesn't need to be built specifically for Flash 8–based forms; in fact, most of them aren't. Usually, as long as the CGI script accepts form results from an HTML form, you can use it with your Flash 8 form as well. As you learned in Chapter 9, *"Building a Form,"* the FormMail CGI script accepts your Flash 8 form results, processes them, and then emails them to whomever you'd like. Once you've located a CGI script that can process your Flash 8 form results, you simply have to look through the instructions or README file that came with the CGI—or look on the support section of your Web presence provider's home page—to see which variables the CGI script is expecting and which are "required." Then, as you saw in Chapter 9, you simply associate those variables with the fields in your Flash 8 form and you're good to go.

But if your Web presence provider doesn't have a **formmail.pl** script—or something similar—where can you find a free one online? Before you go looking for a form-processing CGI script, first make sure your Web presence providers give you access to your **cgi-bin** (a special folder to store your CGI scripts) and let you install your own CGI scripts. Here are some places where you can get free CGI scripts for your Flash 8 projects:

- Matt's Script Archive (**www.scriptarchive .com**)—The original free script archive on the Internet. You can find his FormMail CGI script here, complete with installation and usage instructions: **www.scriptarchive.com/readme/ formmail.html**.

- The CGI Resource Index (**www.cgi-resources .com**)—Everything CGI-related is here. The CGI Resource Index tracks scripts, books, and resources alike. So much so, that if you do a search for "Form", it returns over 140 form-related CGI script results. You can see CGI scripts that process form results here: **http://cgi.resourceindex.com/Programs_and_ Scripts/Perl/Form_Processing/**.

Remember, if you're having trouble installing or configuring a CGI script on your Web presence provider's servers, don't feel shy about calling their technical support. After all, that's part of what you're paying for!

Index

Q–R

S

Virtual FX Web site, 417

volume_slider.mov (HOT CD-ROM videos folder), 315

W–Z

Web design, video-based training, 416

Web forums, 416–417

Web Navigation: Designing the User Experience, 21

Web presence providers, 421–422

Web ReDesign: Workflow That Works 2.0, 21

Web sites
  ActionScripts, 417
  Adobe, 419
  Apple, xi
  Bradsoft, 419
  CGI Resource Index, 422
  Cloudforge, x
  construction process
    content, 17
    deployment, 20–21
    development, 20
    implementation, 20
    layout and design, 18–20
    target audience, 17–18
    uploading and testing, 20–21
  Dreamhost, 421
  Flashforward Conference and Film Festival, ix
  FLZone, 417
  font installation, 24
  Gnome, 24
  iTunes, 419
  L.A. Eyeworks. *See* L.A. Eyeworks Web site
  lynda.com
    book registration, ix
    Online Training Library, ix
    technical support link, viii, 411
    training resources, ix

Web sites (*continued*)
  Macrabbit, 419
  Macromedia, xiii, 411
  Macromedia Flash Exchange, 417
  Media Temple, 421
  Microsoft, 19, 419
  modular development, 5
  MP3 Book Helper, 419
  NI Solutions Group, 421
  Omni Group, 19, 419
  Pacestar, 419
  Pair Networks, 421
  Panic, 419
  Peachpit Press, 411
  Rebenschied, Shane, 411
  Script Archive, 422
  third-party resources, 417
  Uvault, 421
  Web presence providers, 421
  Winamp, 419

Weinman, Lynda
  Adobe Illustrator CS Hands-On Training, 23
  Adobe Photoshop CS2 for the Web Hands-On Training, 23
  Designing Web Graphics, ix
  Designing Web Graphics 4, 415

Were Here Web site, 417

West, Jeff van
  Adobe Illustrator CS2 Essential Training, 23
  Adobe Illustrator CS Hands-On Training, 23

What You *See* Is What You Get (WYSIWYG) HTML editor, 110

Winamp Web site, 419

Windows
  file extension visibility, xii
  Flash Professional 8 system requirements, xiii
  making exercise files editable, xii
  opening files on Macintosh, xi

WYSIWYG (What You *See* Is What You Get) HTML editor, 110

THIS SOFTWARE LICENSE AGREEMENT CONSTITUTES AN AGREEMENT BETWEEN YOU AND, LYNDA.COM, INC. YOU SHOULD CAREFULLY READ THE FOLLOWING TERMS AND CONDITIONS. COPYING THIS SOFTWARE TO YOUR MACHINE OR OTHERWISE REMOVING OR USING THE SOFTWARE INDICATES YOUR ACCEPTANCE OF THESE TERMS AND CONDITIONS. IF YOU DO NOT AGREE TO BE BOUND BY THE PROVISIONS OF THIS LICENSE AGREEMENT, YOU SHOULD PROMPTLY DELETE THE SOFTWARE FROM YOUR MACHINE.

TERMS AND CONDITIONS:

1. GRANT OF LICENSE. In consideration of payment of the License Fee, which was a part of the price you paid for this product, LICENSOR grants to you (the "Licensee") a non-exclusive right to use the Software (all parts and elements of the data contained on the accompanying CD-ROM are hereinafter referred to as the "Software"), along with any updates or upgrade releases of the Software for which you have paid on a single computer only (i.e., with a single CPU) at a single location, all as more particularly set forth and limited below. LICENSOR reserves all rights not expressly granted to you as Licensee in this License Agreement.

2. OWNERSHIP OF SOFTWARE. The license granted herein is not a sale of the original Software or of any copy of the Software. As Licensee, you own only the rights to use the Software as described herein and the magnetic or other physical media on which the Software is originally or subsequently recorded or fixed. LICENSOR retains title and ownership of the Software recorded on the original disk(s), as well as title and ownership of any subsequent copies of the Software irrespective of the form of media on or in which the Software is recorded or fixed. This license does not grant you any intellectual or other proprietary or other rights of any nature whatsoever in the Software.

3. USE RESTRICTIONS. As Licensee, you may use the Software only as expressly authorized in this License Agreement under the terms of paragraph 4. You may physically transfer the Software from one computer to another provided that the Software is used on only a single computer at any one time. You may not: (i) electronically transfer the Software from one computer to another over a network; (ii) make the Software available through a time-sharing service, network of computers, or other multiple user arrangement; (iii) distribute copies of the Software or related written materials to any third party, whether for sale or otherwise; (iv) modify, adapt, translate, reverse engineer, decompile, disassemble, or prepare any derivative work based on the Software or any element thereof; (v) make or distribute, whether for sale or otherwise, any hard copy or printed version of any of the Software nor any portion thereof nor any work of yours containing the Software or any component thereof; (vi) use any of the Software nor any of its components in any other work.

4. THIS IS WHAT YOU CAN AND CANNOT DO WITH THE SOFTWARE. Even though in the preceding paragraph and elsewhere LICENSOR has restricted your use of the Software, the following is the only thing you can do with the Software and the various elements of the Software: THE ARTWORK CONTAINED ON THIS CD-ROM MAY NOT BE USED IN ANY MANNER WHATSOEVER OTHER THAN TO VIEW THE SAME ON YOUR COMPUTER, OR POST TO YOUR PERSONAL, NON-COMMERCIAL WEB SITE FOR EDUCATIONAL PURPOSES ONLY. THIS MATERIAL IS SUBJECT TO ALL OF THE RESTRICTION PROVISIONS OF THIS SOFTWARE LICENSE. SPECIFICALLY BUT NOT IN LIMITATION OF THESE RESTRICTIONS, YOU MAY NOT DISTRIBUTE, RESELL OR TRANSFER THIS PART OF THE SOFTWARE NOR ANY OF YOUR DESIGN OR OTHER WORK CONTAINING ANY OF THE SOFTWARE on this CD-ROM, ALL AS MORE PARTICULARLY RESTRICTED IN THE WITHIN SOFTWARE LICENSE.

5. COPY RESTRICTIONS. The Software and accompanying written materials are protected under United States copyright laws. Unauthorized copying and/or distribution of the Software and/or the related written materials is expressly forbidden. You may be held legally responsible for any copyright infringement that is caused, directly or indirectly, by your failure to abide by the terms of this License Agreement. Subject to the terms of this License Agreement and if the software is not otherwise copy protected, you may make one copy of the Software for backup purposes only. The copyright notice and any other proprietary notices which were included in the original Software must be reproduced and included on any such backup copy.

6. TRANSFER RESTRICTIONS. The license herein granted is personal to you, the Licensee. You may not transfer the Software nor any of its components or elements to anyone else, nor may you sell, lease, loan, sublicense, assign, or otherwise dispose of the Software nor any of its components or elements without the express written consent of LICENSOR, which consent may be granted or withheld at LICENSOR's sole discretion.

7. TERMINATION. The license herein granted hereby will remain in effect until terminated. This license will terminate automatically without further notice from LICENSOR in the event of the violation of any of the provisions hereof. As Licensee, you agree that upon such termination you will promptly destroy any and all copies of the Software which remain in your possession and, upon request, will certify to such destruction in writing to LICENSOR.

8. LIMITATION AND DISCLAIMER OF WARRANTIES. a) THE SOFTWARE AND RELATED WRITTEN MATERIALS, INCLUDING ANY INSTRUCTIONS FOR USE, ARE PROVIDED ON AN "AS IS" BASIS, WITHOUT WARRANTY OF ANY KIND, EXPRESS OR IMPLIED. THIS DISCLAIMER OF WARRANTY EXPRESSLY INCLUDES, BUT IS NOT LIMITED TO, ANY IMPLIED WARRANTIES OF MERCHANTABILITY AND/OR OF FITNESS FOR A PARTICULAR PURPOSE. NO WARRANTY OF ANY KIND IS MADE AS TO WHETHER OR NOT THIS SOFTWARE INFRINGES UPON ANY RIGHTS OF ANY OTHER THIRD PARTIES. NO ORAL OR WRITTEN INFORMATION GIVEN BY LICENSOR, ITS SUPPLIERS, DISTRIBUTORS, DEALERS, EMPLOYEES, OR AGENTS, SHALL CREATE OR OTHERWISE ENLARGE THE SCOPE OF ANY WARRANTY HEREUNDER. LICENSEE ASSUMES THE ENTIRE RISK AS TO THE QUALITY AND THE PERFORMANCE OF SUCH SOFTWARE.

SHOULD THE SOFTWARE PROVE DEFECTIVE, YOU, AS LICENSEE (AND NOT LICENSOR, ITS SUPPLIERS, DISTRIBUTORS, DEALERS OR AGENTS), ASSUME THE ENTIRE COST OF ALL NECESSARY CORRECTION, SERVICING, OR REPAIR. b) LICENSOR warrants the disk(s) on which this copy of the Software is recorded or fixed to be free from defects in materials and workmanship, under normal use and service, for a period of ninety (90) days from the date of delivery as evidenced by a copy of the applicable receipt. LICENSOR hereby limits the duration of any implied warranties with respect to the disk(s) to the duration of the express warranty. This limited warranty shall not apply if the disk(s) have been damaged by unreasonable use, accident, negligence, or by any other causes unrelated to defective materials or workmanship. c) LICENSOR does not warrant that the functions contained in the Software will be uninterrupted or error free and Licensee is encouraged to test the Software for Licensee's intended use prior to placing any reliance thereon. All risk of the use of the Software will be on you, as Licensee. d) THE LIMITED WARRANTY SET FORTH ABOVE GIVES YOU SPECIFIC LEGAL RIGHTS AND YOU MAY ALSO HAVE OTHER RIGHTS, WHICH VARY FROM STATE TO STATE. SOME STATES DO NOT ALLOW THE LIMITATION OR EXCLUSION OF IMPLIED WARRANTIES OR OF INCIDENTAL OR CONSEQUEN-TIAL DAMAGES, SO THE LIMITATIONS AND EXCLUSIONS CONCERNING THE SOFTWARE AND RELATED WRITTEN MATERIALS SET FORTH ABOVE MAY NOT APPLY TO YOU.

9. LIMITATION OF REMEDIES. LICENSOR's entire liability and Licensee's exclusive remedy shall be the replacement of any disk(s) not meeting the limited warranty set forth in Section 8 above which is returned to LICENSOR with a copy of the applicable receipt within the warranty period. Any replacement disk(s)will be warranted for the remainder of the original warranty period or thirty (30) days, whichever is longer.

10. LIMITATION OF LIABILITY. IN NO EVENT WILL LICENSOR, OR ANYONE ELSE INVOLVED IN THE CREATION, PRODUCTION, AND/OR DELIVERY OF THIS SOFTWARE PRODUCT BE LIABLE TO LICENSEE OR ANY OTHER PERSON OR ENTITY FOR ANY DIRECT, INDIRECT, OR OTHER DAMAGES, INCLUDING, WITHOUT LIMITATION, ANY INTERRUPTION OF SERVICES, LOST PROFITS, LOST SAVINGS, LOSS OF DATA, OR ANY OTHER CONSEQUENTIAL, INCIDENTAL, SPECIAL, OR PUNITIVE DAMAGES, ARISING OUT OF THE PURCHASE, USE, INABILITY TO USE, OR OPERATION OF THE SOFTWARE, EVEN IF LICENSOR OR ANY AUTHORIZED LICENSOR DEALER HAS BEEN ADVISED OF THE POSSIBILITY OF SUCH DAMAGES. BY YOUR USE OF THE SOFTWARE, YOU ACKNOWLEDGE THAT THE LIMITATION OF LIABILITY SET FORTH IN THIS LICENSE WAS THE BASIS UPON WHICH THE SOFTWARE WAS OFFERED BY LICENSOR AND YOU ACKNOWLEDGE THAT THE PRICE OF THE SOFTWARE LICENSE WOULD BE HIGHER IN THE ABSENCE OF SUCH LIMITATION. SOME STATES DO NOT ALLOW THE LIMITATION OR EXCLUSION OF LIABILITY FOR INCIDENTAL OR CONSEQUENTIAL DAMAGES SO THE ABOVE LIMITATIONS AND EXCLUSIONS MAY NOT APPLY TO YOU.

11. UPDATES. LICENSOR, at its sole discretion, may periodically issue updates of the Software which you may receive upon request and payment of the applicable update fee in effect from time to time and in such event, all of the provisions of the within License Agreement shall apply to such updates.

12. EXPORT RESTRICTIONS. Licensee agrees not to export or re-export the Software and accompanying documentation (or any copies thereof) in violation of any applicable U.S. laws or regulations.

13. ENTIRE AGREEMENT. YOU, AS LICENSEE, ACKNOWLEDGE THAT: (i) YOU HAVE READ THIS ENTIRE AGREEMENT AND AGREE TO BE BOUND BY ITS TERMS AND CONDITIONS; (ii) THIS AGREEMENT IS THE COMPLETE AND EXCLUSIVE STATEMENT OF THE UNDERSTANDING BETWEEN THE PARTIES AND SUPERSEDES ANY AND ALL PRIOR ORAL OR WRITTEN COMMUNICA-TIONS RELATING TO THE SUBJECT MATTER HEREOF; AND (iii) THIS AGREE-MENT MAY NOT BE MODIFIED, AMENDED, OR IN ANY WAY ALTERED EXCEPT BY A WRITING SIGNED BY BOTH YOURSELF AND AN OFFICER OR AUTHO-RIZED REPRESENTATIVE OF LICENSOR.

14. SEVERABILITY. In the event that any provision of this License Agreement is held to be illegal or otherwise unenforceable, such provision shall be deemed to have been deleted from this License Agreement while the remaining provisions of this License Agreement shall be unaffected and shall continue in full force and effect.

15. GOVERNING LAW. This License Agreement shall be governed by the laws of the State of California applicable to agreements wholly to be performed therein and of the United States of America, excluding that body of the law related to conflicts of law. This License Agreement shall not be governed by the United Nations Convention on Contracts for the International Sale of Goods, the applica-tion of which is expressly excluded. No waiver of any breach of the provisions of this License Agreement shall be deemed a waiver of any other breach of this License Agreement.

16. RESTRICTED RIGHTS LEGEND. Use, duplication, or disclosure by the Government is subject to restrictions as set forth in subparagraph (c)(1)(ii) of the Rights in Technical Data and Computer Software clause at 48 CFR § 252.227-7013 and DFARS § 252.227-7013 or subparagraphs (c) (1) and (c)(2) of the Commercial Computer Software-Restricted Rights at 48 CFR § 52.227.19, as applicable. Contractor/manufacturer: LICENSOR: LYNDA.COM, INC., c/o PEACHPIT PRESS, 1249 Eighth Street, Berkeley, CA 94710.

4442a

W9-ATO-24

This Large Print Book carries the
Seal of Approval of N.A.V.H.

HOW TO MAKE A SPACESHIP

How to Make a Spaceship

A Band of Renegades, an Epic Race, and the Birth of Private Space Flight

Julian Guthrie

THORNDIKE PRESS

A part of Gale, Cengage Learning

GALE
CENGAGE Learning

Farmington Hills, Mich • San Francisco • New York • Waterville, Maine
Meriden, Conn • Mason, Ohio • Chicago

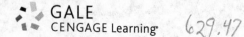629.47

LIBRARY OF CONGRESS CATALOGING-IN-PUBLICATION DATA

Names: Guthrie, Julian, author.
Title: How to make a spaceship : a band of renegades, an epic race, and the birth of private space flight / by Julian Guthrie.
Description: Waterville, Maine : Thorndike Press, a part of Gale, Cengage Learning, [2016]
Identifiers: LCCN 2016039889| ISBN 9781410495204 (hardcover) | ISBN 1410495205 (hardcover)
Subjects: LCSH: Outer space—Civilian use—History. | Astronautics—Research—History. | Entrepreneurship. | Large type books.
Classification: LCC TL794.7 .G88 2016 | DDC 338.4/76294—dc23
LC record available at https://lccn.loc.gov/2016039889

Published in 2016 by arrangement with Penguin Press, an imprint of Penguin Publishing Group, a division of Penguin Random House LLC

Printed in the United States of America
1 2 3 4 5 6 7 20 19 18 17 16

To the memory of my late father,
Wayne Guthrie,
and to my mother, Connie Guthrie.
Thank you for your love and strength.

CONTENTS

7

PART THREE: A RACE TO REMEMBER

FOREWORD

BY RICHARD BRANSON

Prizes have spurred great milestones and launched industries. The British government's Longitude Prize, offered in 1714, ended up saving both sailors' lives and ships. I was already a believer that prizes can make an incredible difference when Peter Diamandis came to see me about funding his $10 million XPRIZE. As Peter shared his idea about a prize to encourage small teams to jump-start space exploration, my instinct was to say yes. My nickname is, after all, Dr. Yes, and in those days I was running ahead of myself, spending money before I had it. But for some unknown reason, "no" came out of my mouth!

By the time we met again in the late 1990s, I had made quite a few trips to various places to see people who claimed they could go to space. Most were father-son types of operations and many had elaborate plans and no hardware to show. There was a rocket in the Mojave Desert in California called the Roton, which promised to "put NASA out of business." But the rocket appeared impossible to control, and looked quite perilous to me. So I kept looking.

Space was something that I had dreamed of for decades. I can still clearly remember sitting with my mum and dad and my two sisters watching Apollo 11 land on the Moon. I was nineteen years old and spellbound by these men who had traveled to another world. It went without saying that in my lifetime ordinary people would get to travel beyond the Earth's atmosphere. Then decades passed and governments were not sending the general public to space. In 1999, I registered the name Virgin Galactic, believing the right opportunity would come along.

Burt Rutan, who was already well known in aviation circles, and I worked on a ballooning project called Earthwinds. We were a small team trying to make the first nonstop circumnavigation of the globe in a balloon. Burt, whose shop was in the Mojave Desert, was helping to build the capsule. A few years later, while collaborating again with Burt and adventurer Steve Fossett on a plane to fly solo nonstop around the world, the Virgin Atlantic *GlobalFlyer,* Burt said he was building something "even cooler." He was secretly building a spaceship. And he was competing for Peter's $10 million prize. At that point, I thought, "This may be my dream come true."

If anyone can pull it off, it is Burt.

The story of Peter Diamandis, Burt Rutan, Paul Allen, and a group of big thinkers and crazy dreamers — I use the word "crazy" here with admiration — is as entertaining as it is inspiring. It tells of a turning point in history, when entrepreneurs were offered the chance to do something only governments had done before. Whether you are nine years old or ninety-nine, this is a tale that will capture your imagination. The drama in these pages played out over many years and is filled with unforgettable people. There were high-adrenaline, high-emotion moments that I witnessed firsthand and will never forget. These moments, and the bravery, brought tears to my eyes. I feel honored to have been a part of this great history that set out to rewrite the rules.

Rules are meant to be broken. I left school at sixteen to start a magazine run by students to make a difference in the world. The Vietnam War was going on and I wanted to be a voice to stop it, to play some little role. It wasn't about making money or becoming an entrepreneur. Virgin began as a mail-order record retailer in 1970, then it was a record shop and a recording studio. Soon the biggest music acts flocked to our label. We signed the Sex Pistols and the Rolling Stones and became the biggest independent label in the world. No one thought any of this was possible. In an effort to beat the record for the fastest boat to cross the Atlantic, we ended up sinking the first time but succeeding the second. When we tried to fly a balloon across the Atlantic, we failed the first time but were successful the second. You learn by doing, by falling forward. There isn't much of a difference between being an adventurer and an entrepreneur. As an entrepreneur, you push the limits and try to protect the downside. As an adventurer, you push the limits, and protect the downside — which can be your life.

As you read Julian Guthrie's book, you will meet people who set huge and seemingly unachievable challenges and then rose above them. Without Peter, who is a pretty unique individual, commercial spaceship travel would simply not have happened. Thanks in part to the XPRIZE, billions of dollars have been invested in commercializing space. My dollars might not have gone to his initial prize but they have built Virgin Galactic, the fulfillment of a dream long held by me and countless others and an endeavor that, as you will read in this book, will forever be linked with Peter and the XPRIZE. If I'd said yes to Peter in those first meetings when he was pitching me on funding the prize, I don't know if I would have actually gotten into the spaceship business. Instead of spending $10 million to fund the XPRIZE, I will now end up spending half a billion dollars to commercialize it!

Our goal with Virgin Galactic is to open space to change the world for good. That includes realizing the dreams of thousands of people around the world of seeing the majestic beauty of our planet from above and the stars in all their glory. We believe there are untold benefits to this human experience and we want every country in the world, not just a privileged few, to have its own astronauts.

The story of the XPRIZE is the dramatic prelude of many more chapters to come, chapters that are being built now with some of the same people — like me and Paul Allen — who were inspired by the XPRIZE. Building our commercial spaceline has taken longer than we thought, and been more painful than we thought. We accept the risks and time line of commercializing flights to space that would otherwise be possible for only a few brave pilots. One of the messages of this book — and my own personal philosophy — can help provoke positive change in the world: Life is best lived looking forward — and up.

Sir Richard Branson
Founder, Virgin Group, bestselling author, entrepreneur, and philanthropist

PROLOGUE:
MOJAVE DESERT

Alone in a spartan black cockpit made from carbon fiber and epoxy glue, sixty-three-year-old test pilot Mike Melvill rocketed toward space. He had eighty seconds to exceed the speed of sound and begin the vertical climb to 100 kilometers, a target no civilian pilot had ever reached. The rocket motor burned liquid nitrous oxide and a form of solid rubber fuel, generating a violent seventeen thousand pounds of thrust that knocked him back into his seat and screeched like metal scraping metal. Wind shear rocked the plane 90 degrees to the left and Melvill, right hand on the stick and feet at the rudders, tried to correct the problem but trimmed the plane 90 degrees to the right, banking a full 180 degrees, a move bordering on aerobatics. He was off course by 30 miles, shooting nearly straight up and closing in on Mach 1,* the

---

* Mach 1 is when the speed of a vehicle exceeds the local speed of sound. Below Mach 1 is subsonic. Above Mach 1 is supersonic. The region in between

chaotic, once-mythical region around 700 miles per hour known to pummel planes and kill their pilots. There was a chance he would not make it back alive. If he did, he would make history as the world's first commercial astronaut.

"Please, Lord, don't let me screw this up," Melvill said under his breath, paraphrasing the test pilot's prayer.

Melvill would lose stick and rudder control as he went faster than the speed of sound, as shock waves dampened control surfaces and the air refused to move out of the way. The self-described daredevil, known to kayak over waterfalls and do headstands on boulders at the edge of cliffs, was hurtling through the atmosphere in an air-launched, podlike rocket the size of a small bus, built by a team of about forty engineers in California's high desert. The idea was to do what only the world's biggest governments — the Soviet Union, the United States, and China — had done before: get people to space. More than twenty thousand people — Buzz Aldrin

---

is transonic. The term *Mach* came from Austrian physicist Ernst Mach, who studied the shock waves of bullets at supersonic speeds. Mach speed decreases with higher altitude and lower air density. At sea level Mach 1 is about 760 miles per hour; at 60,000 feet Mach 1 is about 660 miles per hour.

among them — had made their way by car, bike, plane, and motor home caravan to the Mojave Desert, 100 miles north of Los Angeles, to see the early morning flight of the winged ovoid called *SpaceShipOne*. Peter Diamandis, an entrepreneur who had dreamed up an improbable private race to space, with a $10 million prize for the team that made it there first, was watching from the desert floor. His life's work had brought him to this day, when a manned spaceship, built and flown without the government's help, would attempt to rocket out of Earth's atmosphere and return safely to a runway just a dozen feet away. So much was at stake, not only for would-be space travelers, but for Diamandis himself. Melvill's six-thousand-pound, hand-flown spaceship streaked through the sky nearly straight up, slashing the blue expanse with a jagged white line.

"Very rough ride initially, a lot of pitching," Melvill said, his breathing labored as he talked to flight director Doug Shane in Mission Control overlooking the Mojave flight line. Directly behind Melvill's seat was the hybrid rocket engine with three thousand pounds of nitrous oxide and eight hundred pounds of rubber fuel. Melvill added, "Slowing down on me. The engine shut down. I did not shut it down. It shut down on its own. . . . It didn't run very well." The engine had cut off at around 170,000 feet after a seventy-seven-second burn, but inertia propelled his craft toward apogee, toward his target of 62 miles above Earth, or 328,000 feet. This was the Karman line,[*] named for Hungarian physicist Theodore von Kármán and widely accepted as the altitude above the Earth's sea level representing the start of space.

"Start the feather up" came the call from Doug Shane. The "feather" was the rocket plane's secret weapon, wings that bent in half to add drag — aeronautical concept designer Burt Rutan's promising but still unproven invention for delivering man and machine back to Earth. Rutan was a master of the improbable, creating flying machines out of unconventional composite materials and surfboard technology, moving wings forward and engines back, and delighting in defying symmetry and being a creative battering ram to establishment aerospace. But he had zero experience sending people to space. There were times in the program, especially on days

[*] While the Karman line offers a nice intrinsic definition as the putative boundary between the atmosphere and space, there is no real "boundary" of space, just a thinning of the atmosphere until, above 100 km, the air is so thin that trying to fly an airplane is pointless, requiring flying at rocket speeds to stay aloft.

like today, when Rutan thought to himself: *This is really out there. We are absolutely crazy to be taking this kind of risk.*

"Feather unlocked. Feather coming," Melvill said as the white rocket rotated in the thin air. "Trying to get it upright." Melvill had flown 9,500 hours in more than 150 different types of planes — even piloting one whimsical Rutan design by riding on top of it like a jockey rides a horse. But he had never encountered the violent power of a rocket. He peered out the small, round, double-paned plastic portholes — there were sixteen nine-inch-diameter windows around the nose. The inside window was made of Plexiglas, and the outside was the even stronger polycarbonate. During the building and testing phase, Rutan handed his pilots welding axes and challenged them to break the windows.

It was around eight A.M. in California, and from near the top of his parabolic arc,[*] Melvill could see frothy clouds along the Los Angeles coastline, browns and beiges of the desert, the shimmery coast of Baja California, and the forests and mountains of the Sierra

[*] Parabolic arc is a flight path that ascends until apogee — its highest point from Earth — and descends in a mirrored path, like a rock or ball thrown into the air.

Nevada — enormous peaks that from this height looked as flat as the desert to the south. The clouds were varied, in shades of white, platinum, and gray. Wisps turned thicker like silvery cloth, and waves of ethereal gray rolled in the sky like waves on an open ocean. Lakes and sinewy rivers glistened liquid gold. The Earth's thin blue line looked a million miles away. He now understood why astronauts were forever changed by "Earth gazing," by taking in how fragile and beautiful this little blue marble looked from above.

Melvill was not far from the skies above Edwards Air Force Base, where they had been given permission to fly in the tightly restricted area known as 2515. Edwards was the dry, hot, isolated Valhalla of test pilots and the Mecca of experimental planes, the place where the sonic boom was born, where pilots were tested for skill and mettle and some of the world's fastest, most powerful planes were let out to gallop. Melvill watched the energy height predictor, an instrument that gave a digital readout of the final altitude the plane would reach once the engine was off. His friend and mentor Albert "Scotty" Crossfield, the first pilot to fly twice the speed of sound, and the pilot with the most experience flying the military's X-15 — a matte-black brute of a rocket plane that in 1963 first reached an altitude of 100 kilometers — told him he would feel disoriented after lighting the rocket motor and pulling back on the stick. "You will think the nose is coming up and you're going to go over on your back," Crossfield told him. "Everyone in the X-15 felt that."

"Doing a good job with RCS," Doug Shane said of the cold-gas reaction control system, small thrusters used to maneuver the vehicle's orientation.

"Everything is good here, Doug," Melvill reported.

From Mission Control came the announcement, "Three-twenty-eight," and the sound of clapping, which quickly dimmed. After that moment of euphoria, it was uncertain whether Rutan's *SpaceShipOne,* registration number N328KF, had made it to the start of space. They would have to wait for the data to come in to be sure. Rutan and his team settled back into their chairs. The toughest part of the mission lay ahead. Space shuttle *Columbia* disintegrated during reentry the year before, in 2003, killing all seven astronauts on board. The X-15 — the only other winged vehicle to get to space — had ferocious loads when reentering Earth's atmosphere, traveling at Mach 5 and coming in at a forty-degree, nose-down attitude. X-15 pilot Mike Adams, a friend of Rutan's, was killed in 1967; after reaching a peak altitude of 266,000 feet, the thirty-seven-year-old Adams, a scholar and top test pilot, was at around 230,000 feet when he went into a violent Mach 5 spin and couldn't recover. The rocket plane broke apart, pieces scattered for nearly 60 miles on the desert floor.

Melvill looked at the instrument panel. Pilots were told to trust their instruments more than their bodies, but Melvill needed to *feel* the plane. He flew through the seat of his pants, literally feeling the plane through his rear end, the same way he once rode motorcycles in races. Planes, like people, had their quirks. Melvill flipped the switch on top of the stick to move the horizontal stabilizers, the movable flaps used for pitch and roll control. He reset the trim for reentry to thirty degrees on each side. He waited and watched. The feather had deployed perfectly; with the engine off, he could hear the feather make a thud against the forward tail booms. He looked again at the instruments.

Something was wrong.

"I'd like to see the stab trim here," Shane said quickly. Control of the plane's horizontal, fixed-wing stabilizers and elevons — the hinged flaps on the trailing edge of the stabilizers — was operated by sophisticated electric motors and gear boxes mounted in the tail booms and used at high altitudes and speed when stick and rudder were ineffective. The stabilizers had to be precisely set at plus-ten degrees for reentry.

Rutan studied the telemetry. For a moment,

no one moved. No one said a word. The only sound in Mission Control came from more than 60 miles up, from Melvill repeatedly, quickly, flipping switches.

"Whoa! Pull the breakers!" said Rutan's chief aerodynamicist, Jim Tighe. The breakers initiated the backup motor. Melvill had tried that. Nothing. The stabilizers were unevenly positioned, with the left one at thirty degrees and the right at ten degrees. A twenty-degree difference would result in a high-speed, potentially fatal spin. Melvill knew enough about physics to know that his rocket motor took him out of the Earth's atmosphere at Mach 3 — three times the speed of sound — and that gravity would pull him back at the same speed. There was little if any chance of surviving reentry with asymmetrical stabilizers. The only way out of this rocket was through the nose; unlike in the X-15, there were no ejection seats. In an emergency, Melvill would have to first depressurize the cabin, unlatch the front end of the plane by pulling a lever from the floor up, pop the nose of the plane right off, and somehow jump out the front — all while traveling faster than a speeding bullet. Scotty Crossfield had said that trying to punch out of a rocket plane was "committing suicide to keep from getting killed."

Melvill had the sensation of falling back. There was no panic, only sadness. *Man, all of this effort and this is how it ends,* he thought. A small team in the desert had a shared dream of a new golden era of spaceflight, of doing what most deemed impossible. The engineers and builders could not have worked harder. His wife of more than five decades, the cute blonde he'd run away from home with, was on the flight line below, probably clasping their son's hand. Wiry, watchful, and still very much besotted with him, Sally had pinned their lucky horseshoe on his flight suit — a piece of jewelry he designed for her in 1961, engraved "Mike and Sally." Sally was his first and only love. He tried the switches again.

The left stabilizer would not move.

Jim Tighe said darkly: "This is not good."

Rutan, sitting to Shane's right, grimaced slightly and hunched forward. Mike was his best test pilot and best friend. He was his first employee at Rutan Aircraft Factory. Sally had wanted her husband taken off the flight test program of *SpaceShipOne.* She had a bad feeling about the rocket and tried to make the case that Mike had done enough for the program already. Rutan had seen how Mike was uncharacteristically nervous before the morning's takeoff. Mike wanted to make history — for himself, for the team, for those who were never supposed to amount to much. There was also Peter Diamandis's $10 million cash prize dangled out there, offered

26

to a team like theirs that could fly to the start of space twice within two weeks. Today was a day to make history, but it also got them one step closer to the prize.

Before the 6:47 A.M. takeoff, when the gusting wind and enveloping dust of the night before had calmed and the orange sun rose over the pale landscape, Rutan had reached into the cockpit and clasped his friend's hand.

"Mike, it's just a plane," he said. "Fly it like an airplane."

■ ■ ■ ■

PART ONE:
THE INFINITE
CORRIDOR

■ ■ ■ ■

1
UNRULY

At around ten P.M. on July 20, 1969, eight-year-old Peter Diamandis positioned himself in front of the large television set in the wood-paneled basement of his family's home in Mount Vernon, New York. His mom, dad, younger sister, and grandparents were seated nearby. Peter, in pajamas and cape, aimed his mom's Super 8 camera at the screen, panned the room, paused on his white German shepherd, Prince, and returned to the television.

On the carpet next to Peter were his note cards and newspaper clippings, organized by NASA mission — Mercury, Gemini, and Apollo — and by rockets — Redstone, Atlas, Titan, and Saturn. The third-grader, unable to sit still under normal circumstances — his mother called him *ataktos,* Greek for *unruly* — fidgeted, bounced, and rocked in place. This was the moment Peter had dreamed about, a moment that promised to be better than all the electronics he could buy at Radio

Shack, cooler than every Estes rocket ever made, more exciting even than the M80s lit on his birthday, sending his mom and friends diving for cover.

The Sears Silvertone TV was turned to *CBS Evening News* with Walter Cronkite, the seasoned newsman who was at Cape Kennedy, Florida. Peter, with the camera on, read the words "MAN ON THE MOON: THE EPIC JOURNEY OF APOLLO 11." He listened to a clip from a speech given by President Kennedy in May 1961: "I believe that this nation should commit itself to achieving the goal, before this decade is out, of landing a man on the Moon and returning him safely to the Earth. No single space project in this period will be more impressive to mankind, or more important for the long-range exploration of space; and none will be so difficult or expensive to accomplish." The onscreen countdown began for Apollo 11 astronauts Neil Armstrong and Edwin "Buzz" Aldrin to park their lunar lander on the surface of the Moon, a quest for the ages, a Cold War imperative, and a high-stakes contest between nations that had begun when the Soviet Union launched Sputnik, the world's first artificial satellite, on October 4, 1957. Now, almost twelve years later, America was trying to make history of its own. Astronaut Michael Collins, piloting Apollo 11's command module *Columbia,* had already separated from the lander and was alone in lunar orbit, waiting for his fellow astronauts to walk on the Moon.

If all went according to plan, Collins, Aldrin, and Armstrong would reunite in orbit in less than a day. About seventeen thousand engineers, mechanics, and managers were at the Florida space center for the launch. In all, an estimated four hundred thousand people had worked on some part of the Apollo program, from the women in Dover, Delaware, who did the sewing and gluing of the life-protecting rubberized fabric of the spacesuits, to the engineers at NASA, Northrop, and North American Aviation who worked for years on the clustering, three-chute parachute system for *Columbia.* The cost of the program was put at more than $25 billion.

Peter daydreamed constantly about exploring the glittering and dark expanse in his own spaceship, like the Robinson family in the television series *Lost in Space,* with the precocious nine-year-old son Will Robinson and the humanized and weaponized Robot. But on this night, the TV screen had his undivided attention.

Cronkite, in his deep voice and languid manner, said, "Ten minutes to the touch-down. Oh boy . . . Ten minutes to landing on the Moon." The program flashed between streamed images of the Moon and simulations of the landing done by CBS with NASA's help. The signal from the lunar camera had to be transmitted a quarter of a million miles to the Parkes Radio Astronomy Observatory west of Sydney, Australia, and then across the Pacific Ocean by satellite to the control center in Houston. From there, the images would go to television networks and finally to television sets in the United States and abroad.

In the first few minutes of flight, the Saturn V first stage — which had its design origins as a ballistic missile used by the Germans in World War II — had used four and a half million pounds of propellant, and the craft's velocity relative to Earth had gone from zero to 9,000 feet per second in ascent. [*]

Cronkite announced: "Go for landing, three thousand feet."

[*] This was for the first of three stages. At first-stage cutoff, the Earth-fixed velocity was approximately 7,900 feet per second, and the space-fixed velocity was approximately 9,100 feet per second. Orbital velocity was achieved after the third-stage cutoff, at a space-fixed velocity of approximately 25,500 feet per second. Total oxidizer plus propellant for all three stages was approximately 5.7 million pounds. Earth-fixed velocity is lower because the rockets are always launched in the direction that Earth is rotating, getting a free approximately 1,000 miles per hour of space-fixed velocity.

"*Eagle* looking great," said Mission Control in Houston, as grainy black-and-white images of a barren, rock-strewn landscape appeared on television sets.

"Altitude sixteen hundred feet," Cronkite narrated. "They're going to hover and make a decision. . . . Apparently it's a go. Seven hundred feet, coming down."

"Nineteen seconds, seventeen, counting down," Cronkite said. It was just before dawn on the Moon, and the sun was low over the eastern horizon behind the lunar lander.

Peter focused his camera on the screen. He had used his mom's camera to film NASA television broadcasts before. He had clipped countless newspaper and magazine stories of space missions and written letters to the National Aeronautics and Space Administration. He had a "Short Glossary of Space Terms," issued by NASA, and he memorized terms like "monopropellant" and "artificial gravity." He won first place in a county dental poster contest with his drawing of the launch of Apollo to the Moon and the caption "Going away? Brush three times a day." He and his elementary school friend Wayne Root made their own stop-motion movies, using *Star Trek* models on fishing line as props. Peter learned that he could scratch the film in postproduction to make spaceships fire laser beams. On weekends, Peter loved to sit his family down in the living room upstairs and give lectures on stars, the Moon, and the solar system, explaining terms like "LEO," for low-Earth orbit.

The launch of the Saturn V rocket on July 16, four days before the scheduled Moon landing, had been to Peter every Fourth of July rolled into one. *Three men riding on top of a fiery rocket aimed at space! Five F-1 engines burning liquid oxygen and kerosene and producing 7.5 million pounds of thrust!* It was like sending the Washington Monument rocketing skyward.[*] Peter littered his schoolbooks with sketches and doodles of planets, aliens, and spaceships. He had drawn the Saturn V over and over, with its first stage, second stage, and third stage, its lunar module, service module, and command module.

At 363 feet, it was taller than a football field set on end, both beauty and monster, weighing more than 6.4 million pounds when prepared for launch. Peter had watched Neil Armstrong and Buzz Aldrin climb through the docking tunnel from *Columbia* to *Eagle* to check on the lunar module. The lunar module — the LM, pronounced "LEM" and originally called the Lunar Excursion Module

[*] The Washington Monument is actually 50 percent taller than the Saturn V and weighs fourteen times as much (not including the monument's foundation).

— had never been tested in the microgravity of the Moon. Peter was not alone in wondering whether this spaceship would make it back to Earth. *Columbia* would return at more than 17,000 miles per hour. If its descent was too steep, it would burn up; if too gradual, it wouldn't make it through the atmosphere back to Earth. Even when coming into the atmosphere perfectly — threading the needle at supersonic speeds — *Columbia* would be a fireball, with temperatures on the outside exceeding three thousand degrees Fahrenheit. Peter's father, Harry Diamandis, appreciated this moment in history and welcomed any news that wasn't about the Vietnam War or the emotional civil rights struggles of the day. But he couldn't understand his son's fascination with space, given the challenges of life on Earth. He and his wife, Tula, had come from the small Greek island of Lesbos, where he grew up tending goats and bartering for food — olives for almonds, kale for milk — and working at his father's café. Harry's mother, Athena, was a housekeeper who would bring home surplus bits of dough in her apron pockets to bake for the family. One of Harry's favorite Christmas presents was a red balloon. He was a village boy, the first in his family to graduate from high school and go to college. Harry had wanted to be a doctor, and passed his medical boards in Athens before setting his

37

sights on America. He arrived in the Bronx speaking no English. Their journey from Lesbos to America, and Harry's path to becoming a successful obstetrician, at times felt like its own trip to the Moon, with improbable odds, an element of fear, and a feeling of being a stranger in a foreign land.

On the television screen in the Diamandises' living room, images showed a simulation of the lunar landing. Then Apollo 11 commander Armstrong radioed, "Houston, Tranquility Base here. The *Eagle* has landed." The *Eagle* sat silently on the Sea of Tranquility in the Moon's northern hemisphere. Mission Control radioed back, "Roger, Tranquility. We copy you on the ground. You got a bunch of guys about to turn blue. We're breathing again."

"The lunar module has landed on the Moon," Cronkite marveled. "We're home. Man on the Moon."

More than five hundred million people, from crowds gathered before screens in Disneyland to American soldiers in Vietnam, watched as the white-suited, tank-headed Armstrong, a ghostly, blocky figure, backed out of the module and made his way down the steps. Tula watched Peter, hoping her son remembered to breathe. Armstrong said, "I'm at the foot of the ladder. The surface appears to be very, very fine-grained as you get close to it. It's almost like a powder. I'm going to step off the LM now."

It was just minutes before eleven P.M. in the Diamandis household. From Earth, the Moon was in a waxing crescent phase. Slowly, Armstrong moved his cleated foot onto the talcum surface, becoming the first human to ever touch another celestial body. "That's one small step for man," Armstrong said, "one giant leap for mankind." The view was desolate but mesmerizing, a desert scrubbed clean. The sky looked thick and dark like black velvet.

Peter stopped filming. This was the difference between believing in God and witnessing God. It was both answer and question, new frontier, old Earth. It was NASA doing what it said it would do. The astronauts were modern-day Magellans.

Cronkite rubbed his hands together and dropped his paternal demeanor. "There's a foot on the Moon," he said, removing his black-rimmed glasses and wiping his eyes. "Armstrong is on the Moon. Neil Armstrong — thirty-eight-year-old American — standing on the surface of the Moon! Boy, look at those pictures — 240,000 miles to the Moon. I'm speechless. That is really something. How can anybody turn off from a world like this?"

It was close to midnight when Tula finally got the kids to bed. Marcelle, who was six, was asleep before her head hit the pillow. Peter, still wired with excitement, told his mom once again that he was going to be an astronaut when he grew up. Tula's reply never varied: "That's nice, dear. You're going to be a doctor." Medicine was known; space was experimental. Besides, the first-born son in a Greek family always followed his father's path. Family friends were already calling young Peter the future Dr. Diamandis. Tula had given Peter a child's doctor's kit, and he would sometimes have her recline on the sofa so he could check her pulse and listen to her heartbeat. Being a doctor would be an honorable profession for Peter.

After Tula left the room, Peter turned on his flashlight and ducked under his tented bedspread. He made entries in his secret diary: The Moon was freezing in the shadows but baking in the sun. He would need a suit and the right boots — maybe his ski boots. There was no air to breathe on the Moon, so he'd need oxygen. He'd need food, water, and of course, a rocket. He drew more pictures of Saturn V, and of the astronauts. Late into the night, drawings and notes scattered around him, Peter fell asleep wondering how he could possibly be a doctor when he needed to get to the Moon.

In the years following the lunar landing, Peter began making his own rovers, among other machines. He was predatory in his pursuit of motors to hack. In one case, the lawn mower motor disappeared, turning up later on his go-kart. Then the bedsheets went missing, revealing themselves eventually as parachutes for the go-kart. The Diamandis family lived in the middle of the block on a middle-class street on the north side of Mount Vernon, New York, about thirty minutes from New York City and bordering the Bronx. Their house was a two-story white Dutch colonial with blue shutters, a big front yard, and a narrow gravel driveway where Peter liked to set up jumps for his bike. The house also had a side yard and backyard, with cherry trees and a swing set put together with great effort by his dad and uncle.

Peter drove his lawn mower–powered go-kart down the street from his house, turned onto Primrose Avenue, and pushed the cart to the top of an enormous hill. Wearing no helmet, he blasted down Primrose Avenue like a junior John Stapp,[*] the Air Force colonel who studied g-forces by famously riding rocket-powered sleds to a top speed of 639 miles per hour. Peter deployed his go-kart's "parachute" only when precariously close to the busy intersection.

Peter took particular delight in his sister's

[*] Stapp famously coined an appendix to Murphy's Law called Stapp's Law: "The universal aptitude for ineptitude makes any human accomplishment an incredible miracle."

toys, eyeing them as a raven stares at a meaty carcass. When Marcelle received a new Barbie Dream House, Peter discovered that its motor was perfect for one of his projects, and the Barbie window shades provided the ideal chain to automate the arm of one of his robots. Marcelle and her parents went from amused to exasperated. Peter also hatched various weapon-related plans, including one that used a pipe cleaner fashioned as a projectile for his BB gun. When it didn't work, Peter mistakenly tried to suck it out of the barrel, only to have the discharged pipe cleaner shoot straight down his throat. He was rushed to the hospital and back to his experiments by nightfall. Peter got good grades, but his teachers wrote on his report cards, "Peter talks too much," and he could "work a little harder on settling down."

Every Sunday, Peter and his family drove to the Archangel Michael Greek Orthodox Church near Roslyn, where Peter was an altar boy, tasked with carrying the incense, candles, or the large gold cross and helping with communion. Confession wasn't required, but he talked openly with the kind Reverend Father Alex Karloutsos, telling him that he regularly took his sister's toys and too often made his parents worry. And he told him about his love of space; it was his "guiding star."

Peter shared with Father Alex his belief that

they were all living in a biosphere, a kind of terrarium seeded with life by aliens. The aliens returned, Peter confided, to collect people as specimens or seedlings, but only in rural places like Nebraska where they wouldn't be noticed. Father Alex liked listening to Peter and knew that he was not a boy who could be placated by statements like "God is love." Father Alex told Peter that the greatness of the universe was a reflection of God's presence in our lives.

In early spring, Peter was out riding his gold Schwinn Stingray banana-seat bike when he came across a neighborhood boy selling fireworks. Not long after, when it came time for Peter's birthday, Tula and Peter went over the party plan. Peter wanted to light off his new "fireworks." Tula, concerned about the noise, decided she could mute the sounds by burying the M80 — Peter kept insisting these were everyday fireworks — under a pile of gravel in their narrow driveway. She said she would light the fuse herself. Peter's buddy Wayne Root was there with camera in hand. Tula told the kids to step back, nervously lit the red fuse, and scurried off. There was a long pause. The suburban neighborhood was quiet. Then — the sounds of gunfire. *Pop! Pop!* Tula yelled out, "Duck! Everybody duck!" Gravel flew, glass shattered, and she and the kids dove for cover.

When Tula finally looked up, there were

clouds of lingering smoke and wide-eyed kids. Wayne was still holding his camera. Miraculously, no one was injured, and — at first glance — only a small side window of their house was cracked. Tula, heart racing, feeling as if they'd all just been shot at, gave Peter a you're-in-*big*-trouble look. Peter did his best to appear solemn, all the while thinking excitedly about the power and possibilities of projectiles powered by a fraction of a stick of dynamite.

The Diamandis family moved from Mount Vernon to Kings Point, Long Island, in the summer of 1974, when Peter was entering eighth grade. Harry Diamandis's medical practice was thriving in the Bronx.

They moved to Long Island for the schools, and because Tula fell in love with a century-old house she saw advertised in *The New York Times,* which had been on the market for three years. It was eight thousand square feet, at the bottom of a hill, with access to a community tennis court, swimming pool, and marina. Where others saw a white elephant and a lot of hard work, Tula saw possibility, and quickly set about restoring the house room by room.

Great Neck, a thirty-minute commute to Manhattan, was the fictional setting for F. Scott Fitzgerald's *The Great Gatsby;* it had sprawling verdant lawns, long driveways leading to estate homes, and nine miles of waterfront along Long Island Sound and Manhasset Bay. The Diamandis home was in Kings Point, the village at the northern tip of the Great Neck peninsula in Nassau County.

Peter claimed the third floor of the house for himself, posting a green and white "ADULTS KEEP OUT" sign, printed on his new dot matrix printer, at the top of the stairs. Peter's domain consisted of three rooms, one for sleeping and studying, one for projects — robots, rockets, chemistry, general experimentation — and the third for playing Ping-Pong, rerouting his electric train set, watching TV, and listening to music and studying.

Peter still decorated his bedroom with NASA posters, but now the posters were of the Apollo 17 astronauts Eugene Cernan, Ronald Evans, and Harrison Schmitt, NASA's first scientist-astronaut. Their mission in 1972, two years earlier, had spanned twelve days and included three days of exploration on the surface of the Moon. Cernan, who drove the Lunar Rover more than twenty miles collecting geologic samples, made a wishful statement before departing the Moon: "As we leave, we leave as we came and, God willing, as we shall return, with peace and hope for all mankind." The Apollo missions were over, but the new space shuttle program had begun, announced by President

Nixon in 1972 as a rocket that would land like an airplane and would be "a reusable orbital vehicle that will revolutionize transportation into near space, by routinizing it." In Peter's mind, NASA could do no wrong, though he thought the name "space shuttle" was uninspired when compared with Apollo.

It didn't take long for Peter and a new friend in Great Neck, Billy Greenberg, to realize they were going to need more money for their projects and experiments. Cannibalizing household appliances and siblings' toys would get them only so far. They rounded up like-minded friends Gary Gumowitz, Danny Pelz, and Clifford Stober, pooled their cash, and set off on their bikes to the bank.

The boys explained to the teller that they wanted to open an account to pay for cool stuff for their club.

"Does your club have a name?" the teller asked.

The boys looked at one another quizzically. "Well, what do you do?"

"I don't know," Peter said, "we build stuff."

"Like what?"

Rockets, trains, robots, remote-control planes, remote-control cars, boats.

"It sounds like you do everything," the teller said finally. "Why don't you call it 'The Everything Club'?"

The loosely formed Everything Club was officially launched. The boys met in Peter's tree house, intentionally built with a stepladder too rickety to support adults. And they met in Peter's project room. They ordered Estes rocket kits organized by skill level, beginning with the classic Der Red Max, which had red wood fins, a black nose, and a skull and crossbones. Standing sixteen inches tall, the rocket flew to around 500 feet and had parachute recovery. The boys had a schedule to work their way up the skill levels, from one to five, and then start building their own rockets and making their own propellant.

Peter and Billy and the rest of the boys joined the Great Neck North High School computer club, math club, and future physicians club. They started programming on Hewlett-Packard and Texas Instruments calculators, and then programmed on computers that were offered as vocational training for high school students. They learned electronics by building Heathkits, making small transistor radios with resistors, capacitors, diodes, transistors, a rheostat, and a small loudspeaker. Their classmate Jon Lynn was the first in their group to build a working computer, the Sol-20 by Processor Technology, similar to the early Altair. Their first "computers" relied on punch cards for programming, based on the same mechanical principle as the Jacquard loom, with the punch-card reader converting the perforations into on/off electrical signals, which the computer interpreted as numbers and instruction codes for the calculation. Carrying the punch cards around school was like being a part of a secret fraternity.

After school, the boys hung out at the Gold Coast video arcade, playing *Pong, Tank,* and *Speed Race.* One of their favorite games was *Lunar Lander,* where they used arrow keys to rotate the lander and change the thrust, with the goal of landing safely on an *X* on the Moon. Peter was on the high school diving team, and though he was never very interested in sports, he was muscular like a wrestler and could do a backflip from the standing position. He had thick and dark feathered hair, wore a gold chain with a cross, and got teased for his height — he had topped out at five feet five inches tall.

Peter and his friend Billy's outlook for building and flying powerful rockets improved greatly when they found themselves in the popular Mr. Tuori's chemistry class. Mr. Tuori, who had taught chemistry at Great Neck North for decades, favored experiments that woke kids up and left an impression. Peter and Billy were lab partners and watched attentively. This was learning they would use.

In class, lab coats and goggles on, Peter and Billy followed as Mr. Tuori took metallic-looking gray iodine crystals from a small jar and put them into a beaker. Mr. Tuori then relocated to the fume hood to pour a small amount of concentrated solution of ammonia over the crystals. He shook the mixture gently, explaining that the new compound, nitrogen triiodide, with three iodine atoms stuck around a single nitrogen atom, was pretty safe while wet. Once dry, though, anything could set it off, from a snowflake to a feather. After giving the chemicals time to react, Mr. Tuori filtered the mud-colored mixture to get rid of the excess ammonia. It was critical, Mr. Tuori again cautioned, to set it down before it had time to dry. When it came time for testing, Peter and Billy were front and center. Using a long pole, Mr. Tuori reached toward the charred-looking material. Peter noticed a fly buzzing just above the nitrogen triiodide. He gently elbowed Billy to look in the direction of the six-legged inter-loper. As Mr. Tuori's stick approached the compound, the fly landed on the powder — setting off a loud and sharp *snap*! A poof of purple smoke followed. The unfortunate fly was blown to smithereens.

Soon, shipments of explosives began arriving at Peter's door in boxes marked with a skull and crossbones and the warning "DANGER: EXPLOSIVES" stamped on top. The boys discovered they could find whatever they wanted through chemical supply companies advertised in the back of *Popular Science* magazine. They could have chemicals sent in bulk by UPS directly to their door. Peter secretly turned one of his third-floor closets into a chemical supply room, apprehending the boxes before his mom and dad made it home. Peter and Billy split the supplies in half, so if one of them was found out, they'd lose only half their supply.

The boys ordered equipment for their chemistry labs: beakers, Bunsen burners, flasks, stoppers, droppers, funnels, and thermometers. Peter was drawn to the alkaline earth metals, especially magnesium, which burned a bright white light. He ordered boxes of magnesium ribbons and powder, and he'd add barium to make it burn green and strontium to make it burn red. He did tests with calcium and — of course — loved potassium nitrate, sulfur, and charcoal, the mainstays of gunpowder.

The only thing that Peter didn't like was that potassium nitrate and sulfur needed oxygen to burn. He wanted to find something that wasn't saddled with that requirement. To Peter, chemistry pushed into the unknown, into what felt like the opposite of ordinary schoolwork. It held mystery, order, and logic. Chemistry reminded him of being a little boy again and jumping into rain puddles. Only now, he got to make the puddles *and* cause the ripples.

Peter began studying rocketry, reading books by the Russian teacher and physicist

Konstantin Tsiolkovsky, who was born in 1857, was nearly deaf, largely self-educated, and introduced ideas about space travel and rocket science still in use more than a century later. In the late 1800s, Tsiolkovsky wrote about the effects of zero gravity on the body, predicted the need one day for pressure suits for space travel, developed Russia's first wind tunnel, envisioned rockets fueled by a mixture of liquid hydrogen and liquid oxygen, and developed the mathematical formula for changes in a rocket's momentum and velocity.* Peter also read about Robert Goddard, the American physicist who built and launched the world's first liquid-fueled rocket

* Tsiolkovsky invented the rocket equation, the formula describing how much speed you gain from a rocket engine. It depends on the exhaust speed of the gas and the net change in mass of the rocket as fuel is expended. The rule of thumb is that the change in velocity ΔV = (exhaust gas speed) × (logarithm of the initial mass/ final mass). For example, if the rocket burns enough fuel to decrease the total mass by a factor of 3, then the velocity increase approximately equals the exhaust gas speed. If the mass decreases by a factor of 9, then the velocity increase approximately equals twice the exhaust gas speed. The takeaway is that you want to burn as much as quickly as possible, and expel it as fast as possible. The faster you burn, the lighter the rocket gets, and the easier it is to change the velocity.

in 1926, an event likened in significance to the Wright brothers' flight at Kitty Hawk. Goddard was ridiculed when he stated his belief that a big enough rocket could one day reach the Moon, but he drew support from aviator Charles Lindbergh. Peter appreciated how Goddard's rocket experiments as an undergraduate at the Worcester Polytechnic Institute yielded explosions and smoke that sent professors running for fire extinguishers.

Peter learned about German physicist Hermann Oberth, also a believer in liquid-fueled rockets over solid-fuel rockets, and another German, Wernher von Braun, father of the Saturn V, which came out of his work for Nazi Germany on the V-2 ballistic missile during World War II.* Peter knew that if it weren't for von Braun and his group of German engineers, the United States would not have reached the Moon by the end of the 1960s.

On weekends, Peter and his rocket-making pals packed their creations, along with various remote-controlled planes, into their backpacks and hopped on their bikes. They rode to the nearby Merchant Marine Academy in King's Point. Sometimes they'd pick a football field just outside the gates to launch their Estes rockets. It never took long before

---

* The entire Saturn rocket management team was composed of ex-V-2 engineers from Peenemünde.

the academy guards chased them away.

Other times, the boys persuaded one of their parents to drive them to Roosevelt Field, where Lindbergh took off in the *Spirit of St. Louis* to try to fly to Le Bourget Field in Paris. The field had a parking lot and vast open space. The boys filled their rockets with homemade gunpowder, sometimes getting a poof, other times a firework, and sometimes an unwanted ballistic missile that tore at them like a flying snake, coming close on at least one occasion to taking out an unsuspecting Harry Diamandis.

One of Peter and Billy's best creations was a rocket series they called Mongo, with Mongo 1, 2, and 3 getting progressively taller and driven by the most powerful motors they could get their hands on. They built an autonomous launch system that could fire up to three rockets in sequence using a circuit they designed around the 555 Timer IC. This way, when it was just two of them, one rocketeer could be downfield tracking the launch and the other taking photos. This won them first place in an Estes rocket design competition, awarding them certificates to buy more rockets. While working on their arsenal and making their way down the periodic table, Peter and Billy made an important discovery: potassium chlorate made better explosions than potassium nitrate.

Peter also discovered important properties about potassium perchlorate. Not only was it highly explosive, but it also produced its own oxygen when it decomposed. He bought the colorless crystalline substance — common in fireworks, ammunition, sparklers, and massive rocket motors — in five-pound boxes. He experimented by drilling holes in film canisters and covering the holes with automotive body filler. To make an explosion with potassium perchlorate or chlorate, he would need to combine it with something else that would combust, like sulfur or aluminum powder. The right concoctions shot out of the filled hole; some fizzled or failed altogether.

One winter afternoon, the boys met up at Jon Lynn's house. They filled film canisters with various potions, wrapped them in duct tape, and lit them off in the icy driveway. One flew directly at a boy's head, several worked as planned, and a few fizzled. After more experimentation, a new plan was hatched: They should take one of their potassium perchlorate film canister bombs and put it *underwater* to see what would happen. Potassium perchlorate didn't need oxygen to burn.

The boys ran to the back of the house, where the Lynns had a swimming pool, which was partially frozen over. They put one of the canisters in the water below the ice. The boys stood slightly off to the side, watching and waiting. Nothing happened. Seconds passed. Then they heard a muted *booosh!* The ice rose up an inch — the boys stepped back — and then it appeared to settle. Peter was relieved. But then came an enormous, clear *crack.* Jon Lynn's mom, Suzanne, inside preparing dinner, suddenly felt the house move.

It was becoming more and more evident that this suburban neighborhood was not a big enough canvas for Peter's rocket dreams.

2
EARLY REGRETS

Peter sat alone in his dorm room at Hamilton, a New England–style liberal arts college of 1,800 students in Clinton, New York, almost five hours north of his home in Great Neck. The school had a beautiful campus, but after only a few weeks there, Peter was feeling like he had made a big mistake.

His love of space, chemistry, and rocketry was stronger than ever, yet he was on a premed track at Hamilton, not on a path to becoming an astronaut. Making matters worse, it didn't look like the school would permit him to double major in biology and physics, a compromise he hoped would allow him to continue his dual desires of space and medicine. This was not a place for a science-based double major, let alone a serious student of space.

Peter was at Hamilton because he hadn't felt smart enough to apply to Ivy League schools, though most of his friends had ended up there. The premed track was for his parents. The boy who couldn't be contained was now contained.

Not long after his arrival at college, the eighteen-year-old wrote in his journal: "I must admit I've been having second thoughts about Hamilton. I wanted a larger selection in courses. I'm trying to get a major in biochemistry set up. Don't know if I can do it."

A page later: "I'm extremely bothered by this paradox I've encountered about Hamilton (though I strongly hope it's false). First I hear it to be extremely hard scholastically, harder than many of the larger 'better' well-known schools. Yet I don't know if it will be considered when it counts, on entrance to graduate work."

When Peter returned home to Great Neck for Thanksgiving break, he ran into Michael November, a former high school classmate who was now a college freshman at MIT. They set up a tennis match at the Shelter Bay tennis court adjacent to his home to get some exercise and catch up with each other. As they rallied on the cold but dry late-fall day, Peter admitted to Michael, who had been in his advanced-placement chemistry class, that he was already starved for science and technology. Whenever Hamilton hosted a science-related talk from a visiting professor, Peter was front and center taking notes. "I eat it up," Peter told his friend. "Philosophy is great and literature is fine, but I want more."

Michael, who had played football at Great Neck High and loved math the way Peter loved space, was having the opposite experience. Between tennis shots, Michael told Peter about a program at MIT called UROP, the Undergraduate Research Opportunities Program, giving undergraduate students the chance to work on research in fields as varied as nuclear science, urban planning, and solar-photovoltaic systems for houses.

Michael told Peter that he was working on fusion experiments involving the building of a scaled-down version of a tokamak, a vacuum inside a circular steel tube that used magnetic fields to confine fusion. His project leader was Professor Louis Smullin, who had helped create the school's Department of Electrical Engineering and Computer Science, and was head of the radiation laboratory in the early 1940s when the lab developed airborne radar used during World War II.

Peter stopped playing. He couldn't believe a *freshman* was getting to work on *fusion.* "Ohmygod, that's incredible," he said.

Michael was also taking a class on relativity from Professor Jerome Friedman, director of the school's Laboratory for Nuclear Science. His freshman physics class was taught by Professor Henry Kendall, who was working with Friedman on breakthrough research into subnuclear particles called quarks.[*] By the time the tennis match had ended, Peter couldn't get MIT out of his head. He spent the rest of Thanksgiving break working on his car, a Pontiac Trans Am with a V8 engine and a golden firebird on the hood. He had modified the carburetor intake manifold to take in more oxygen, and he toyed with the idea of putting in a nitrous injection system.

When Peter returned to Hamilton after Thanksgiving, he called MIT to learn about its transfer policies. Buoyed by what he learned, he scheduled a tour and interview in early January; the admissions application for transfer students would be mailed to him. He wondered whether he even had a chance; MIT was one of the most competitive universities in the world, and it was even harder to be accepted when transferring. In the meantime, though, Peter would try to make the most of Hamilton, while also reaching outside

---

[*] The name "quark" was invented by Murray Gell-Mann, a colleague of Richard Feynman's at Caltech, reputedly based on a quote from James Joyce's book *Finnegans Wake:* "Three quarks for Muster Mark!" Gell-Mann wanted it pronounced as "quork." The quark model unified in a single stroke the whole disorganized pile of miscellaneous particles that had been observed up until that time.

the campus for science and space. He started a biology study group to meet two to three times a week. He sought out professors and local authors with connections to space. He wrote letters to NASA, including:

Dear sirs:
   I am writing to you in regards to my education. I'm presently a college student, and eventually I hope to enter the space program. First, however, I wish to enter graduate school to obtain an MD, hopefully in conjunction with a Ph.D. (probably in biochemical engineering). My question is, does NASA offer any educational programs which would be of interest to me? . . . Also if possible, please send me any information you can about entering the space program, astronaut training, etc., and an application if possible?

Sincerely,
Peter H. Diamandis

When January finally arrived, Peter and his mom drove to Boston and headed to the Massachusetts Institute of Technology in Cambridge, across the Charles River. Peter and Tula walked along Massachusetts Avenue, past the Harvard Bridge,[*] continued

[*] The official length of the Harvard Bridge is 364.4 Smoots plus one ear. Distances on the bridge are

up a well-worn staircase, past a row of grand columns, and into the entrance of 77 Mass Ave., the marbled and domed rotunda at the heart of campus. Peter took in every detail, from the inscription in Greek under the dome to the long hallway stretched out ahead.

The winter sun streamed through the tall windows behind them, filling the travertine lobby with a muted buttery light. Students were bundled up in puffy jackets and carried books and backpacks, their chatter echoing in the cavernous space. The lobby led to a hallway running 825 feet in length, connecting to other parts of campus. Tula, who loved architecture, thought the building was as breathtaking as the Pantheon in Rome. Peter had a feeling he couldn't describe. Maybe it was how his mom felt when she spotted their Great Neck house, or how his dad felt when he saw his mom for the first time, wearing

---

indicated with a colored paint mark every Smoot and a number every ten Smoots. Oliver Smoot was a pledge at the Lambda Chi Alpha fraternity, and he got picked as the standard unit for the bridge in the 1958 pledge season. Some of his "brothers" laid him out three hundred times along the bridge until the cops came and chased them off. Smoot's cousin George Smoot became very famous for his work on the COBE satellite, which first measured anisotropy in the cosmic microwave background radiation.

her Friday night dress, and *just knew.*

Peter and Tula walked slowly down the long hall, and Peter studied the posters and flyers on bulletin boards and in display cases. There was a sign for UROP, the undergraduate research opportunities program that Michael November had touted. A student told Peter and Tula about "MIT Henge," where for a few days every year in late January, the setting sun lined up with the string of buildings on the north edge of Killian Court and shined all the way through building 7 and reached building 8, with the best viewing from the third floor.

The hall, known on campus as the Infinite Corridor, ran through parts of buildings 3, 4, 7, 8, and 10. MIT was number-centric — students, classes, and buildings were all assigned numbers. Classroom doors had opaque creamy glass with black, hand-painted department and professor names, reminding Peter of doors he'd seen in old detective shows. Peter wanted to open every door and explore every subject. He was uncharacteristically silent, soaking in all of the details. He and his mom passed buildings 10 and 11 and stopped at building 8, the physics department. Created in the nineteenth century by MIT founder William Barton Rogers, the department had among its faculty and graduates a dazzling array of Nobel Prize winners and some of the field's greatest minds, from

Richard Feynman (quantum electrodynamics), Murray Gell-Mann (elementary particles), Samuel Ting and Burton Richter (subatomic particles), to Robert Noyce (Fairchild Semiconductor, Intel), Bill Shockley (field-effect transistors), George Smoot (cosmic microwave background radiation), and Philip Morrison (Manhattan Project, science educator). Physics classes at MIT had been flooded with students in the years following the launch of Sputnik and the success of Apollo.

Peter and his mom made their way to the biology department. He had an understanding with his parents that if he was accepted at MIT, he would stay on his premed track. The biology department here had much more to offer. Peter and Tula doubled back through the corridor, studying more of the photos, posters, and signs for events and clubs, from salsa dancing to stargazing. Peter had two departments he had to see before leaving. The first was in building 37, devoted to astrophysics. It was a field both ethereal and real, where words and equations tried to interpret vibrant colors, patterns, and formations of the cosmos.

The very last stop on their tour was building 33, AeroAstro, which had produced more astronauts than any other place outside U.S. military academies. Military officers had received aviation training for World Wars I and II here. Breakthroughs in hypersonic flight testing were achieved. Buzz Aldrin got his PhD here in 1963. Other astronauts — Jim Lovell, Apollo 13; Ed Mitchell, Apollo 14 — took MIT's astronautical guidance class.

There was a picture of a half dozen NASA astronauts visiting the Instrumentation Lab: three men were the Apollo 1 astronauts — Virgil Grissom, Roger Chaffee, and Ed White — who died during a prelaunch test. Next to them were MIT students and astronauts Dave Scott, Rusty Schweickart, and Jim Mc-Divitt.

Peter studied the department time line: Charles Stark "Doc" Draper started at MIT in the 1920s and founded the Instrumentation Laboratory in the 1930s. Peter kept reading, stunned by what he was learning. The inertial guidance system for Apollo — the computer that got man to the Moon — was developed here in the Instrumentation Lab. *Right here!* The guidance system came to life at a time when computers took up entire rooms, when typewriters with carbon paper were the norm, and when television was black and white. A small team from MIT had figured out how to use a new technology, the integrated circuit, to send man and machine to the Moon and back. Baseball fans had Wrigley Field. Golfers, St. Andrews. Surfers, Mavericks. Climbers, K2. This was Peter's hallowed ground.

Peter looked at space relics, including parts from the Instrumentation Lab's Mars probe. Built in the early 1960s, the probe never launched, but its technology evolved into the guidance computer for Apollo. MIT was awarded the first NASA Apollo contract for the guidance computer in the months following Kennedy's famous speech. Jim Webb, the administrator of the newly formed NASA, knew Doc Draper, engineer, inventor of inertial systems, and a pilot who tested parts he made by flying the planes himself. According to Draper, Webb had called him and said, "Doc, can you develop the guidance and navigation system for Apollo?"

"Yes, of course," Draper said.

"When will it be ready?" Webb asked.

"When you need it," Draper replied.

"And how do I know it will work?"

"I will go along and operate it for you," Draper said, formally volunteering to be an astronaut at age sixty.

Draper could not have known that he and his team were capable of building a computer to get men to the Moon. It hadn't been done before. But Draper didn't hesitate to put everything on the line by saying yes to one of the most difficult technical challenges in history. He believed in himself, and in his team. Walking through the labs, Peter jotted down another note, this one involving one of his idols, Wernher von Braun, who was asked early in the Apollo program: "Wouldn't we do a lot better if we collaborated with the Russians?" Von Braun replied, "If there were collaboration with the Russians, there wouldn't be a program in either country." Peter wrote, *Competition got America to the Moon.*

As Peter and Tula headed out into the late afternoon cold, Peter's mind went over the array of classes, subjects, and breakthroughs in this one location. This was a place of limitless possibilities.

Back at Hamilton after his tour, Peter was antsy. MIT had been another reminder of the audacity of NASA, of what had been accomplished in less than a decade. He wanted those glory days restored. The 1970s were in many ways the opposite of the 1960s. Money had been redirected to the Vietnam War and to myriad social problems.

During the 1960s, NASA's budget was around 1 percent of the total federal budget, and the agency had more than 400,000 employees and contractors at its peak in 1965.[*] By 1979, NASA's percentage of the federal budget had been cut in half, and the agency

[*] NASA's biggest total employment year was 1965, when the space agency employed 34,300 in-house employees and 376,700 out-of-house contractor employees.

counted around 20,000 employees. NASA canceled its mission to send a spacecraft to do a flyby of the famed Halley's Comet, set to pass close to Earth in 1986 and not return for another seventy-five years. Apollo 18, 19, and 20 were canceled even though most of the hardware had been bought and built. The Moon had been reached, and critics said the government was "shooting money into space." Design and development of the space shuttle were delayed, and plans for a U.S. space station in low-Earth orbit ended. Lovers of space wondered what was next. It was the withering away of a dream.

Desperate to do something space related at Hamilton, Peter created and circulated a pro-space petition to send to every elected leader he could find, from local representatives to President Jimmy Carter's adviser on space affairs. Peter expressed his concerns about the "slow but sure degeneration of the U.S. space program's goals and budget." He collected about two hundred signatures from Hamilton students and faculty — significant for a campus of 1,800. Peter then penned a letter that he hoped would be published in the science magazine *Omni:*

I am directing this letter to college students. Having learned of the death of both the Galileo and Halley's Comet/T II missions and the embarrassing delay of the shuttle program — and having seen the space program pushed aside by our government — it is about time that those of us who support our space program, our future, address the issue.

The method for letting the government know how we feel is simple: begin a petition at your college, collect signatures, and submit them to the proper offices of the president and Congress. There are nearly 1,000 colleges and universities in the United States, with an average of 2,000 students per institution. We represent a powerful force and we can change our future.

Peter H. Diamandis
Great Neck, NY

In early February 1980, Hamilton hosted a lecture by visiting professor Jim Arnold, founder of UC San Diego's chemistry department, consultant to NASA, and one of the first to study rocks and soil returned from the Moon. Arnold talked about the rich and useful resources to be mined from the Moon and near-Earth asteroids. Peter had never heard of mining asteroids for metals like nickel, iron, and platinum. When the talk ended, he met two visiting students representing what they called the "international school of the future," who were intent on establishing a "space micropolis." Walking back to his dorm, Peter looked at the cards they had given him. This had been a good night, but the lectures were few and far between at Hamilton, and he wouldn't hear from MIT for at least another six weeks.

A key course required for premed students at Hamilton was intro to biology by Professor Frank Price. The course was tough and had a reputation for winnowing the number of students who continued on the premed track. The study and dissection of a fetal pig made up 50 percent of the student's grade.

Peter's class had around eighty students, and consisted of three hours of lectures and three hours of lab work per week. On the first day of class, Professor Price, a biology teacher at Hamilton for five years, gave a stern talk about the importance of treating the fetal pigs with respect and care. He cautioned that "under no circumstances are the pigs to leave the lab." There was one pig for every two students; the course instruction focused on physiology, organ functions, and the patterns of blood circulation through the heart, lungs, stomach, and liver.

Two weeks before the all-important dissection exam, Peter came down with the chicken pox and had to spend a week in the school infirmary. He missed crucial lab time and test practices. He knew that if he didn't do well on this test, he wouldn't have a chance at a top medical school, and he wouldn't be considered for MIT. Peter could not do poorly on this exam. The thought kept him awake all night. Finally, he hatched a plan: he would "borrow" a fetal pig to study over the weekend. He enlisted help from his lab partner, Philip, who was also a dorm mate. It was decided after class that Philip would casually *brush* the pig into a book bag, held open by Peter.

The following Monday, Professor Price asked for everyone's attention. He didn't look happy. "It has come to my attention," he said, "that a fetal pig has been stolen. I would like to have whoever has done this to please turn themselves in. And if you know who's done this, it's your duty on the school's honor code to turn him in."

Peter looked over his shoulder at Philip, *terrified.* Hamilton's strict honor code was signed by students at the start of school. Academic dishonesty resulted in expulsion or automatic course failure. The pig, about a foot long, was in a plastic bag with formaldehyde-soaked paper towels hidden at the back of their dorm's refrigerator. After class and back at the dorm, the worst scenario unfolded: Peter was told that a suite mate was going to turn him in.

My life is over, Peter thought. He asked the suite mate for a day to deal with it on his own. In a state of panic, Peter and Philip met in his room and decided to get rid of the evidence. They walked the campus, eyeing Dumpsters and secluded spots. They were searching for somewhere the pig would never be found. That night, Peter and Philip headed to the woods; Hamilton was in a rural area with hundreds of acres of wooded land. The pig was buried, and the burial spot marked. All Peter could think about was that he would be expelled; his family would be disgraced, and he would never get to MIT. He was physically ill.

Peter called his father. Harry and Tula were at a friend's house playing cards. Harry excused himself to talk in private, returning more than an hour later. When Tula asked what was wrong, Harry said it was taken care of. Peter told his dad about the mess he had gotten himself into, and said he intended to turn himself in the next day.

Harry Diamandis had listened closely to his son. After a long pause, he presented another idea. Peter was to call the doctor in the infirmary and explain the situation. Harry had visited Peter while he was sick, and found the campus doctor to be kind and smart. The physician should be enlisted as an ally, Harry said. The doctor would talk to Professor Price, and then Peter would return the pig to the lab and have a candid talk with his teacher.

Peter returned to the woods and exhumed

the pig. Late in the afternoon, he entered Professor Price's lab. His hands shook as he took the pig out of his bag. Professor Price could see that Peter was ashen and appeared on the verge of tears. The professor had experienced the theft of his pigs before. He had seen them hanging from nooses in students' dorms, and pigs had been used for pranks in students' beds and bathrooms. Professor Price, who had talked with the infirmary doctor, asked Peter, "Did you learn your lesson?" Peter nodded, fighting back tears and stammering, "I'm so sorry." Peter looked at his professor. *Is my life over, or will I be shown mercy?* After a pause that seemed to go on forever, Professor Price said, "Good luck on your exam, then."

A few weeks later, Peter got his letter from MIT. His eyes filled with tears. *"Peter, On behalf of the Admissions Committee, it is my pleasure to offer you admission to MIT. . . ."*

Professor Price had given him a second chance, a lesson of grace and generosity Peter would never forget. There would be no more shortcuts, no more bending of rules. Getting to MIT was a gift. Peter would return to the Infinite Corridor, open some doors, join clubs — and maybe even launch something of his own.

3
PETE IN SPACE

It wasn't long after his arrival at MIT in the fall of 1980 that Peter got a new nickname: "Pete in Space." His fraternity brothers at Theta Delta Chi called him "PIS" for short, and had fun with "space cadet" and "spaced out" jokes. Peter took the friendly ribbing in stride and started signing his name as PIS; he was happy to be at MIT.

With each passing day he grew more impressed with the university's diversity of programs in molecular biology, physics, computer science, electrical engineering, astrophysics, aeronautics, and astronautics. His new school was dazzling. But as he walked the halls of the Infinite Corridor, scanning announcements and posters, he discovered one thing missing: MIT did not have a student space group.

How could there not be a student space group at MIT, of all places? Peter went to the campus activities administrators to ask about space-related clubs for students. There were computer clubs and astronomy clubs, but no space club. He was told that if he wanted to start a club, he needed four signatures and a name.

Peter got the signatures from his fraternity brothers and a friend and drew up a list of potential names: Student Space Society; Children of Icarus; Students for the Preservation of the Future; Students for the Exploration and Development of Space; Space Cadets of America; and Space Cadets at MIT. He nixed the space cadet options after hearing how the potheads in his house loved the name. He eventually settled on the name Students for the Exploration and Development of Space (SEDS), because it best explained the group's mission. He made a couple hundred flyers, blanketed the campus, and took special care in finding a prime spot in the Infinite Corridor. He used a transfer letter kit for the block lettering of SEDS, and wrote in thick pen, "If you care about your future in space, join me in the student center."

The nineteen-year-old Peter was already juggling a heavy class load and two undergraduate research projects, one space related, and the other for his premed track. Many nights, his lab work kept him so busy that he wouldn't get back to his fraternity house until three A.M. On the premed side, in the genetics lab of Graham Walker, he worked on plasmid instability of PKM-101 in *E. coli.* To feed his space-related passion, Peter had scored a UROP project in the Man Vehicle Laboratory (MVL) in AeroAstro, building 37. Peter worked in the windowless ground floor, where the design, cabinets, floors, and even some of the equipment felt like it hadn't changed in a half century. It all transported Peter to the days of Apollo.

Peter's work in the MVL was far from glamorous, but he loved it. MVL research focused on the physiological and cognitive limitations of humans in aircraft and spacecraft. Founded in 1962, the lab worked closely with NASA to study space sickness for astronauts in the early Apollo program. It now had another NASA contract to work with a new breed of astronaut, the payload specialist, scientists trained to conduct experiments in space aboard the shuttle. Peter helped design and build an electrogastrograph to record the electrical activity of the stomach during motion sickness. Later in the school year, he would begin to research and construct an experiment tracking involuntary eye movements called nystagmus, a part of motion sickness that astronauts faced. Peter was told he would get to work one-on-one with astronauts. He was also aware of the buzz that NASA needed more astronaut physicians for future shuttle flights and had plans for an eventual space station. Peter was officially premed, but passionately pre-astronaut.

On the scheduled Wednesday night of the first meeting of SEDS, Peter waited nervously in his reserved second-floor room in the Stratton Student Center. Only five people had signed up, and he feared that no one would come. He watched anxiously as students passed by. A few paused, as if they were about to come in, and then continued walking. He bit his nails, a habit he had been trying to give up. Within a few minutes, several people ventured in, then a few more. To his great relief, about thirty people gathered in the room — not a bad turnout.

Peter welcomed the group and talked about his background, saying he "drank all the Tang" — *Star Trek, Star Wars,* Apollo. He talked about why the time was right to start a student space organization: "This is our future we're talking about. We can't have myopic politicians say where it goes. We need to stand up for the future of space."

Peter talked about the momentum of the Apollo program in the sixties carrying through to a lesser degree in the seventies, with Apollo 17; the *Voyager* probes reaching the space between stars; and Skylab, the U.S. space station launched by a modified Saturn V, providing the first glimpse of space station technology. But progress had slowed, the space shuttle was delayed and over budget — it was being called the "$9 billion spaceship that refuses to fly" — and NASA had no new plans to send people to the Moon or beyond. Public interest in space had dropped. Peter enthused about all of the spinoff technologies that came from the space program, including cordless appliances, compact integrated circuits for navigation, implantable pacemakers, and freeze-dried food.

"Our goal," Peter said, surprised by his own fervor, "is to enlighten our government, private industry, and the general populace regarding the benefits of a strong space program."

Peter was asked whether he would consider making SEDS/MIT part of a national space group called L5, formed around the ideas of Princeton University physicist Gerry O'Neill. As author of *The High Frontier* and founder of the Space Studies Institute, O'Neill called for establishing a colony of about ten thousand people at L5, a gravitational sweet spot between the Earth and the Moon where a spacecraft could remain stationary, always more than 350,000 kilometers from Earth.

Peter shook his head. "I want an organization created for students run by students," he said.

A man at the back of the room raised his hand and introduced himself as Eric Drexler. "I think Peter made a case for a student-led organization," Drexler said. "I don't think this group should be part of L5." Drexler had worked for O'Neill at Princeton for two summers making a mass driver, an electromagnetic cannonlike device to shoot payloads of lunar material from the Moon. His master's degree was in aeronautical engineering from MIT, and his thesis was on a high-performance solar sail system for space. He was a PhD candidate studying the groundbreaking field of molecular nanotechnology.

The meeting closed as Peter gathered names and addresses. He stayed late answering questions and brainstorming the future of SEDS. When he finally walked outside, the air was still warm. The sky was clear with stars. The moment felt perfect. He'd had this feeling before, when he walked through the hallway of the Infinite Corridor and was sure he was entering something big, something real. Walking through campus, posters under his arm, Peter felt as though he could reach out and touch the future.

Chapters of SEDS were soon announced at Princeton and Yale. Scott Scharfman, a friend of Peter's from Great Neck High, started the Princeton chapter while another former Great Neck classmate, Richard Sorkin, initiated the Yale chapter. Peter, Scott, and Richard drafted a four-page constitution; started a national petition drive directed at President-elect Ronald Reagan and the U.S. Congress, urging funding for solar power satellite research; created a club logo that included the space shuttle; and sent off a carefully worded letter to *Omni,* known for its mix of hard science and pseudoscience, stating, "The steady deterioration of the U.S. space program's goals and budget endangers our future and demands an organized response from our nation's campuses. . . . We invite you and the other students at your college to begin a chapter and join us in our cause." The international headquarters of SEDS was 372 Memorial Drive — Peter's fraternity.

Omni published the letter in April 1981. That month, space shuttle *Columbia,* STS-1, was finally launched, generating international attention and a resurgence in national pride. The mission was the first of four planned orbital tests of the shuttle, which took off like a rocket, cruised in orbit like a spacecraft, and returned to Earth as a glider. It was the world's first reusable manned spacecraft and marked the first launching of American astronauts in nearly six years.

Thousands of spectators had poured onto the beaches across the Indian River from the Kennedy Space Center. As the countdown reached its final seconds, crowds chanted "Go, go, go!" As *Columbia* was pushed straight up, crowds roared, yelled, and prayed.

Returning to his fraternity after class one day, Peter slowed to a stop inside the front door. There in the foyer of his fraternity house, in the midst of the dozens of wooden slots, was his mailbox. It was overflowing with letters, packed in like a thick deck of cards, with a few jutting out at odd angles. *Was this a prank?* Peter carefully pulled the letters out and examined the envelopes, with all different handwriting, stamps, and postmarks. He sat down in the foyer and began to read. A student in Bombay wanted to form a SEDS chapter. A woman at Arizona State University was interested in meeting like-minded students to form a chapter in Phoenix. A man in Lubbock, Texas, said he was studying "colony ecosystems, mass drivers, etc." to reach space if "Uncle Sam defaults." An engineering student from Toronto wrote, "It is hard to express my reaction to your idea; ecstatic is probably close. An organized student voice in support of the space program is long overdue, and your initiative has sparked a welcome feeling of optimism inside me." He suggested that the goal of SEDS become not just national, but international, and he offered his services as Canadian coordinator.

The letters poured in day after day. Peter's fraternity brothers took notice. Now when they called him "PIS," it was with an air of respect.

Over the next two years, SEDS grew from a three-campus group to a student association with close to one hundred chapters in the United States and abroad. Peter, who was now serving as chairman of SEDS, traveled to visit nearby chapters and juggled putting out newsletters and passing his finals. He worked on his public speaking, trying to improve his cadence and confidence, and got his first lessons in fund-raising when he set out to secure $5,000 to cover the cost of printing and mailing the SEDS newsletter to all of the chapters. Fund-raising meetings were set up through friends and faculty, but Peter had a hard time actually asking for the money. He feared rejection.

When he landed a meeting with administrators at Draper Lab, started by Doc Draper of Apollo guidance system fame, Peter knew he needed to do his best. He made his pitch with all the passion he could summon. Afterward, the Draper Lab folks said they loved what Peter was doing with SEDS, but the lab was nonprofit and unable to give him the money. Peter nodded with understanding, but as he began to walk out of the lab, he had another idea. He turned back and asked, "Those newsletters I'm trying to get printed, any chance you have the ability to print them here at Draper?" The response was yes. Peter continued, "Any chance you can mail them out to our chapters for us as well?" Again, the answer was yes. Peter learned a lesson that would stay with him: there is always a way.

Peter organized conferences at universities in the area — Tufts, Harvard, Boston University — attracting notables from academia, NASA, and other established space groups. The first annual international SEDS conference was held over four days in July 1982, with NASA deputy administrator Hans Mark speaking primarily on the government's military motivations to get to space. In another celestial coup, Peter was invited to attend a United Nations conference on space in Vienna. The meeting would focus on the peaceful, nongovernmental use of space.

Peter searched for the cheapest plane ticket he could find. He would fly to Austria with Bob Richards, chairman of SEDS–Canada, and the engineering student from Toronto who had written to him after reading his letter in *Omni*. Bob had graduated with degrees in industrial engineering and aerospace and had started a SEDS group in Toronto. He studied at Cornell, and was an assistant to space scientist and author Carl Sagan. Peter and Bob had become allies and close friends with another student, Todd Hawley, who started a SEDS chapter at George Washington University, where the 1982 international SEDS conference was held. Todd, who spoke Spanish, French, and Russian, was a double major in economics and Slavic language and literature at GWU. Hawley had introduced them to David Webb, who was chairman of the nongovernmental space conference at the United Nations.

Peter, Bob, and Todd had become so unified in their vision and presence that people often called them by one name, *Peterbobtodd.* They were even the same height: Peter had feathered brown hair, parted down the middle; Todd had dirty blond hair and round, wire-rimmed glasses; and Bob had strawberry blond curls and a cherubic face. Todd believed that space was where differences could be erased. Bob looked at the cosmos as the next step in humanity's evolution. Peter was interested in the hardware of space, and the adventure.

Peter and Bob found their cheap tickets on an Austrian airline, Arista Air, while Todd made his own way to Vienna with his girlfriend, MaryAnn. About nine hours into their flight, Peter and Bob were awakened by a terse announcement that they would be landing in Budapest, Hungary, not Vienna. Upon landing in Hungary — still a part of the Communist Eastern bloc — their plane was boarded by military police with guns and dogs. Bob was convinced they were being hijacked. Peter got out his camera and began taking pictures, until an officer told him to put the camera away. The plane baked on the tarmac, and Peter and Bob waited, worried, and sweltered. This was not how Peter envisioned the first international mission of SEDS would unfold. Eventually they were told that all Viennese citizens on board had to get off the plane and take a bus. There was reportedly an issue with someone's not paying the landing fees in Austria. Peter and Bob remained in their seats, and the plane eventually took off for Vienna. The two wondered whether the rest of their trip would be as strange.

The next day, Peter and Bob rendezvoused with Todd and MaryAnn, and the four made their way to the United Nations conference. At the front of the majestic building — adorned with flags from dozens of countries — horse-drawn carriages were parked next to satellite trucks. Peter took a picture of a satellite truck with the lettering "MOSKVA, USSR." He attended sessions called "Tomorrow's Peacemakers," "Remote Sensing Centers," and "Land Use Information Through Space." He shared a table with a man who told him that he had left his job as a scientist working on Reagan's Star Wars initiative because he believed the program was dangerous. He told Peter that he'd had his passport stolen and had a KGB woman try to befriend him.

On their second morning in Vienna, Peter, Bob, and Todd stood in the lobby and studied the roster of speakers. The three of them were scheduled to speak the following day. Suddenly, Bob whispered excitedly, "That's Arthur C. Clarke!" Todd couldn't believe it. Peter, unaware of Clarke's godlike status, said, "So?" Clarke was the author of *2001: A Space Odyssey,* an originator of the idea of geostationary satellites, and a futurist known as the "prophet of the space age."

As Bob and Todd stared at Clarke, Peter said, "Let's go talk to him." Before the starstruck Bob and Todd could respond, Peter headed straight for Clarke, who was flanked by an entourage. Peter got close enough to Clarke to extend his hand and gesture back toward Bob and Todd.

"We are from SEDS and . . ."

Clarke walked away. Peter shook his head. He couldn't leave it at that. Bob was embarrassed by Peter's brashness. As the crowd slowly made its way into the auditorium to hear Clarke speak, Peter moved quickly and snagged front-row seats. Clarke talked about the future of the telecommunications industry. Decades earlier, Clarke had written a famous paper in *Wireless World* that defined the geostationary orbit and proposed using space satellites for global communications.

Peter was fascinated by Clarke's concept of geostationary satellites and was determined to connect with him. He whispered to Bob, "We're going to have dinner with him." Bob rolled his eyes.

After the talk, Peter intercepted Clarke — again.

"Mr. Clarke, we're from Students for the Exploration and Development of Space, and we'd love to take you to dinner tonight," Peter declared, just as Clarke was being shuffled off to an interview. "Here's the telephone number of our hotel and our room number. We'd love to tell you what we're up to."

Clarke looked at the three young men and said in his deep British accent, "I'll call you."

Back in their shared hotel room, Peter and Bob sat on their beds and stared at the phone. Peter and Bob were now making bets on whether Clarke would ever call. Peter was confident. Bob was skeptical. They watched the clock: 5:30. 5:35. 5:50. *Rriiiinnngg.* Peter grabbed at the phone. Bob held his breath. Peter said, *Uh huh, yes, okay, the InterContinental, sure.* He put the phone back on the receiver.

"Well?" Bob implored.

"That was Arthur," Peter said impassively. "He said he can't allow us to take him to dinner."

Bob sighed.

"He wants to take *us* to dinner!"

Bob didn't know whether to hug Peter or punch him.

That night, Peter, Bob, and Todd met Clarke in the lobby of the InterContinental

Hotel. They went to dinner and listened, rapt, to Clarke's stories of growing up in the 1940s, reading pulp fiction, and his early days with the Planetary Society. He talked about how he came up with his ideas around geostationary communication satellites, and spoke passionately about what he saw as the unifying bond that came with a shared interest in space. He had met all of the major rocket scientists from space programs in the Soviet Union, China, and Japan. "They all have a common sense of space," Clarke said, urging Peter, Bob, and Todd to think of students from all languages, nationalities, governments, and ideologies coming together over a shared love of space. "Focus on young people," he said.

He used a line the group loved: *Any sufficiently advanced technology is indistinguishable from magic.*

Toward the end of dinner, Peter said, "If you don't mind, can we call you 'Uncle Arthur'?"

The answer was yes, and soon Uncle Arthur, the prophet of the space age, had signed on to become an adviser to SEDS.

Back in the Man Vehicle Lab at MIT, working with Professor Chuck Oman, Peter affixed adhesive electrode patches to the face of a man he considered royalty — Byron Lichtenberg, test pilot, Vietnam fighter pilot,

MIT-trained mechanical engineer and bio-medical engineer, and new breed of space traveler.

Selected as a payload specialist in 1978, Lichtenberg was excited by the space shuttle's promise of about forty-eight flights per year, doing science, satellite deployment, and building of the space station along the way. But it had already taken three times as long as planned to launch the shuttle, and the astronauts were expecting to do only a third as many flights. It was the winter of 1983, and Lichtenberg was scheduled to fly the shuttle's first Spacelab mission by the end of the year.

One of the key areas of research for the payload specialists was space sickness, something the tough-guy astronauts of Mercury, Gemini, and Apollo — all former military test pilots — were loath to admit. Russia's Yuri Gagarin, the world's first astronaut, reported no sickness in space. Russia's second cosmonaut, Gherman Titov, who orbited Earth seventeen times, earned the distinction of being the first man to vomit in space. Apollo 9 astronaut Rusty Schweickart suffered space sickness on his first day in orbit. Buzz Aldrin told his friends in the MVL that he had felt extremely queasy returning to Earth.

With electrodes attached to his head and stomach, Lichtenberg was seated in Peter's rotating chair. He was spun in one direction, moving his head in another until the symptoms of nausea began. Data were recorded and responses compared. Peter and his professors also spent a great deal of time in the chair.

There were interesting findings — once you feel the onset of nausea, full recovery takes thirty-five minutes — and new questions. Lichtenberg planned to wear a head-mounted accelerometer made by the folks in the MVL on his shuttle flight and keep detailed notes of how he felt. The work in the MVL was about "bringing space sickness out of the closet." The director of the MVL, MIT professor Larry Young, was selected as principal investigator to perform a series of space experiments on the crew of Spacelab 1 — the first pressurized laboratory to be carried into space on the shuttle.

When Peter and Lichtenberg weren't doing experiments, they talked about the life of an astronaut. Peter wanted to know what was asked during the interview process. He wanted to be ready. Lichtenberg told him that the standard questions focused on the hardware and software of spaceflight, the training, and effects on his family life. But there were some obsure and silly questions, including: "What is the lifetime of an average red blood cell in your bloodstream?," "Don't you think we faked the Moon landings?," and "We hear aliens visit the space shuttle and hop on board with you guys. What do you think?"

Peter peppered Lichtenberg with questions about the odds of becoming an astronaut. Lichtenberg said that NASA received about six thousand applicants for every round of hiring, and usually no more than ten of those applicants became astronauts — 1 out of 600, less than .17 percent. Selections could be "random or political," and the vetting process was brutal, he said.

It suddenly occurred to Peter to mention that he had a small tear in his retina, the result of getting kneed in the eye while playing football.

"Would that get me thrown off?" he asked.

"Yep," Lichtenberg said. "That would get you tossed out of the selection process."

Peter was stunned. He didn't know what to say.

"NASA is risk averse." Lichtenberg shrugged. "Heck, even if you are selected, it doesn't mean you'll actually fly. Most astronauts are called penguins: they have wings but don't fly."

Peter had dreamed of being an astronaut for as long as he could remember. What would he do if he couldn't reach space through NASA? What would he try? What would he risk? Was it even possible to get to space without the government's help?

Nearly three thousand miles away, in California's high desert, an airplane designer disenchanted with government-run programs was asking similar questions. For now, he was working on a low-flying plane that he hoped would do laps around the best that the U.S. military had to offer. But like Peter, this dreamer in the desert had high hopes of one day reaching the stars.

4
MOJAVE MAGIC

Burt Rutan stared down one of the longest runways in the world, the seven-and-a-half-mile partially paved stretch at Edwards Air Force Base in the California desert. He was sitting in a chase plane, and just to his left was one of his most audacious creations yet: the *Voyager*.

Weighing about 2,500 pounds when empty, the aircraft was flat and white like stretched taffy, with the twin booms of a catamaran, and 7,000 pounds of fuel packed into long, spindly wings.[*] Within minutes, the *Voyager* was scheduled to take off for its death-defying mission, a flight around the world without stopping or refueling. Aviation experts gave

---

[*] The *Voyager* design bears some resemblance to that of the famous World War II Lockheed P-38 Lightning. Burt moved the horizontal stabilizers forward, relocated the two engines into the center fuselage, and made one a puller and the other a pusher, thereby allowing him to lighten up and extend the wingspan.

the *Voyager* little chance of success, because of the compromises Burt had made in its design and construction, and because his aim was nothing less than to *double* an aviation record that had stood for almost a quarter century. There was every reason to believe the *Voyager* would land for no other reason than pilot exhaustion. This was a test of flying skill, physical endurance, and breakthrough design.

Just as Charles Lindbergh had done with the *Spirit of St. Louis* in 1927, Burt had pared down the *Voyager* to its lightest possible weight. The in-flight tools, whether wrenches or screwdrivers, were hollowed out. The top of the plane got only a light coat of white paint, to keep the structure cool in the hot desert sun. The plane's skin consisted of only two layers of graphite fiber composite, with a paper honeycomb in between. There were virtually no redundancies: if a part failed, there was no backup.[*]

Burt was off to the *Voyager*'s right on the runway. He wondered if the plane would be controllable with such a heavy fuel load.

But Burt had a habit of finding breakthroughs where others saw nonsense. He'd been dreaming up and engineering planes

---

[*] Fortunately, the *Voyager* had a backup attitude indicator. The primary one failed before they were halfway around the world.

since the time before computers, relying on pencils, slide rules for calculations, and French curves for airfoils. The maverick with the Elvis sideburns and the glint in his blue eyes, who could look at a plane and guess its weight within a pound or two, moved in the contrarian footsteps of the self-taught R. T. Jones, inventor of the theory of the swept-back wing, basic to commercial airliners today.* Like Jones, Burt delighted in silencing his skeptics in the aviation world.

Socially indifferent, mischievous, and anti-establishment, Burt lived in a three-level hexagonal pyramid house among the Joshua trees of the Mojave Desert, not far from Edwards Air Force Base. His pool table, dining table, and conference table in the energy-efficient bermed house — most of it was underground — were custom built to have similar hexagonal angles. His favorite mural in the house was of the Egyptian pyramids, and included Egyptian girls, palm trees, and a pharaoh. He challenged visitors to try to find two tiny and unexpected things in the mural: a wind generator and a flying saucer. He had spent years studying the building of

* There had been numerous experiments and even production aircraft with swept-wing designs, but the theory was missing. Jones experimented with thin delta wing aircraft, which is an extreme case of a swept-wing design.

the pyramids, concluding that the pyramid builders were likely able to cast and machine limestone and even granite; he had also spent eight years studying the Kennedy assassination, and came to his own contrarian conclusions. His mailbox, across the driveway from his sagebrush-dotted helipad, was the tail section of a scaled-down version of an experimental military plane called SMUT (Special Mission Utility Transport).

Born in 1943, Burt grew up in the small town of Dinuba in California's Central Valley. His father George was a dentist, and his mom, Irene, took care of the kids on their small farm. The Rutans were strict Seventh-day Adventists, observing the Sabbath from sundown Friday to sundown Saturday. Burt couldn't play team baseball, basketball, football, or any other sport requiring weekend practices or games. He couldn't see movies, chase girls, or race hot rods. Instead, he flew, chased, and crashed airplanes.

He and his mother would drive to San Francisco, about four hours north of Dinuba, to shop at a small hobby store. Burt wanted parts, but he didn't want planes built from a kit. He had no interest in building something that he already knew would fly. At age eight he designed and built a model of an airplane that had engines under swept wings, looking a lot like the Boeing 707 years before it took flight. He began entering designs in model aircraft shows, and by the time he was sixteen, Burt was off to the nationals with nine different entries. Mom Rutan, as she was known, hitched a trailer to the family wagon, loaded the large models into the back, and drove Burt to competitions as far away as Dallas.

The tall and lanky teenager with the flat-top haircut was also interested in rockets, and closely followed the Soviet Union's launch of Sputnik, cosmonaut Yuri Gagarin's first flight, and the promise of America's space program. At age twelve, his favorite television program was the futuristic "Tomorrow Land" segment on the *Walt Disney's Disneyland* TV series, hosted by Walt Disney himself, which asked questions about life on other planets, weightlessness in space, the origin of stars, and lunar exploration, and featured interviews with scientists including Wernher von Braun. Burt learned to fly at age sixteen, paying Dinuba's radio station DJ Johnny Banks, who moonlighted as a flight instructor, $2.50 an hour. The plane rental cost $4.50 an hour. After logging less than six hours of flight instruction, Burt soloed in an Aeronca 7AC Champ. But Burt's passion was design. He graduated from California Polytechnic State University at San Luis Obispo halfway between Gagarin's flight and the Apollo 11 Moon landing.

After getting his degree in aeronautical engineering from Cal Poly in 1965, Burt took a job as a civilian flight test engineer at Edwards Air Force Base, where he was responsible for figuring out why one of their jets, the McDonnell Douglas F-4 Phantom, a workhorse fighter bomber, was having so many accidents. More than sixty accidents were characterized as "departures from controlled flight," where the plane would enter a stall or spin by itself, without pilot inputs. So in 1968, at Edwards, a test program was run to investigate the problem, and Burt was the project flight test engineer. He flew in the backseat of an F-4 with pilot Jerry Gentry, and the two subjected themselves to life-threatening spins. From these test flights, Burt came up with major revisions to the F-4 pilots' manual to help them avoid departures and spins, and to help them recover from them. He also developed a training film titled *Unload for Control.* He and Gentry then personally briefed every USAF F-4 pilot in the world, going on a whirlwind tour of forty-eight locations as far away as Incirlik, Turkey, and Bangkok, Thailand. Edwards, of course, was where some of the military's fastest and most experimental jets were tested, where Chuck Yeager was the first to fly faster than the speed of sound, and where the X-15 reached suborbital spaceflight.

Burt left Edwards in 1972 for what turned out to be an ill-fitting corporate job with Bede Aircraft in Kansas. He quickly realized he wanted to follow his own calling and, in 1974, he returned to California to open the Rutan Aircraft Factory on the Mojave flight line, designing and developing prototypes for small planes to be put together by amateur builders. The business of kits for homebuilt planes took off, but by the early 1980s, aware of the risks in the business, where he could be sued for a builder's mistakes, Burt folded his company and founded Scaled Composites to build a range of plane types and create prototypes.

Now, in 1986, as Burt scanned the hallowed Edwards runway on a cold December morning, he was concerned whether his new creation could get off the ground, let alone make history. The light plane had never carried this much weight. Burt calculated the mechanical reliability of the craft: His crew had done sixty-eight test flights with a total of 375 flight hours over a period of two years. They had serious mechanical failures on seven of those flights, ranging from a cockpit fire to a failed propeller that ripped the engine from its mounts. Now their flight plan would have the plane up in the air for more than 200 hours nonstop. The first part of the flight, carrying the heaviest fuel load, was westward over water toward Hawaii. The plane didn't do well for long in turbulence. Burt concluded the flight was improbable.

But if there was any pilot who could pull it

off, it was Burt's pilot. His brother.

Dick Rutan handed off his black cowboy hat before climbing into the *Voyager* cockpit, about the size of a phone booth laid on its side. His copilot, Jeana Yeager (no relation to Chuck), petite and known to be fearless, was behind him wearing no seatbelt — another weight-saving measure. The two pilots had once been lovers, but now they were barely on speaking terms as they set out to fly around the world.

Dick, forty-eight, was sure that he was going to die in this terrible flying machine. Two days earlier, he had made a "death tape," saying good-bye to his team. He handed the cassette to his crew chief, Bruce Evans, to be played when he died. The decorated fighter pilot, labeled "aggressive among the aggressive," and his copilot, thirty-four, a skilled mechanical draftsman who had worked for Navy inventor and rocket engineer Bob Truax, were trying to double a record set twenty-four years earlier by U.S. Air Force pilots in a Boeing B-52 Stratofortress. Dick and Jeana had lived this dream for five years. They had put everything they had into the *Voyager,* including so much of their own money that they had none left over to pay their rent. They had pitched dozens of possible backers, including American businessman Ross Perot, who was close to sponsoring their flight, but declined in the end because Dick and Jeana were not married. The owner of Caesars Palace was willing to fund them if the flight started and ended in the casino's parking lot, an impossibility given the need for a long runway. The fragile aircraft, constructed in a hangar donated by the Mojave Airport, was funded through hundred-dollar contributions, and built with donated parts and a mostly volunteer crew.

Dick had fed on the adventure of flight since childhood. His mom took him to an air show, where he got his first ride. The plane was an old two-seater yellow Piper Club, the tires had no tread, someone came out to hand-prop the plane, and takeoff was from a grassy field. As soon as they were aloft, Dick unfastened his safety belt and stood up in the back of the tiny plane. He needed to see what the pilot was seeing. He knew in that moment this was the view he wanted for life. He got his pilot's license the day he turned sixteen. When Dick wasn't flying, he was tearing through narrow rows of vineyards on his motorcycle, delighting in his ability to evade the local police, who were always warning him to slow down. Dick dreaded the Sabbath even more than Burt. He snuck into movies, sat way in the back where no one would see him, and left through the back door instead of the front. He was told throughout his childhood that the end was coming. The only end he lived for was the end of the Sabbath each week. Beginning Saturday afternoon, he'd sit and watch the horizon, waiting for that great moment when the sun had set and purgatory was over.

In 1958, at twenty years old, Dick enlisted in the Air Force Aviation Cadet Program even though Seventh-day Adventists were conscientious objectors. He flew the military's F-100 Super Sabre supersonic jet over North Vietnam, returning from aerial combat in planes riddled with bullet holes. He thrived on the adrenaline. The more he flew, the more he sought out dangerous missions. He saw colleagues and friends killed. Some were burned alive in cockpits. He saw a colleague on the ground being chopped up by a machete. In the middle of a mission, he felt no fear. When it was all over, back on the ground, he would occasionally walk over to the edge of the runway and throw up.

It seemed natural for him to sign on to the *Voyager* flight as soon as Burt had proposed it. By the early 1980s, Dick was working for Burt as a test pilot. He had already set distance records in his personal Long-EZ — one of Burt's kit designs — and was looking for a new adventure. Burt, Dick, and Jeana were having lunch at the Mojave Overpass Café when Dick said he was interested in a new type of plane for aerobatics. Burt said he had a better idea, something he'd been thinking about for years, given the advent and availability of carbon fiber and composite materials for planes. Between bites of teriyaki steak, Burt grabbed a napkin and sketched a plane with a single long wing. Burt, Dick, and Jeana immediately grasped what it would mean to do a nonstop, nonrefueled flight around the world. They saw it as a milestone, the last first in aviation.

Burt calculated that it would take seven pounds of fuel for every pound of airplane structural weight to go around the world. The challenge was how to squeeze in enough fuel to fly nearly 25,000 miles and yet keep the aircraft light enough to take off. Part of the answer came from carbon fiber, which would make the plane half the weight of conventional aluminum construction, but would give it the needed strength. The aerodynamic efficiency, as well as the propulsive efficiency, would have to be better than that of any other light aircraft. The propeller had to be more efficient, and the engines had to do a better job of turning gasoline into energy. The flight would be low altitude because the cockpit would not be pressurized.

Dick and Burt battled over weight versus stability. Dick said he couldn't turn the plane. Burt said he was flying around the world and didn't need to turn at all. Dick said the plane would come apart in a rainstorm. Burt told him not to fly in the rain. Burt questioned the need for radar. Dick said he wasn't about to fly blind. Most people knew to walk away when the Rutan brothers went nose to nose.

But the two siblings eventually found compromises. From childhood, Burt designed planes and Dick flew planes. Their sister Nell was a stewardess. The *Voyager* would have long, slender wings, so frail they would flap like a bird's. The airplane comprised nineteen separate fuel tanks. Seventy-three percent of the total takeoff weight of the plane was fuel — Dick would basically be piloting a flying gas tank.

"Edwards Tower, this is *Voyager* One," Dick Rutan said from the runway of Edwards Air Force Base on the early morning of December 14, 1986. "We are ready for takeoff."

"Cleared for takeoff, and Godspeed" came the reply at eight A.M.

Nearby, in the chase plane, Burt took a deep breath as Mike Melvill, a world-class pilot in his own right, prepared to follow the *Voyager* on the initial stages of its flight.

Jeana called out speed: *forty-five, sixty-one, sixty-five* —

As the *Voyager* gained speed, the fuel-laden wingtips began to droop, like the long leaves of tulips. Then the ends touched down on the runway and began to scrape.

"The wings are *grinding on the ground*," Mike said, following the plane. "There is fuel right at the wing's tip."

"Tell him to pull back on the stick!" Burt yelled. "Tell him he's got wings *on the ground.* Pull back on the stick!"

Jeana, in a monotone, continued to call out the speed: *eighty-four, eighty-seven, ninety.* Mike was afraid there would be a fire. The *Voyager* had to reach one hundred knots to have adequate climb capability after takeoff.

Slowly, as the *Voyager* gained speed, the wings lifted just an inch. Then two. Then three.

"The wings went up!" Mike said. "Wow. They bent up!"

Jeana called out: *ninety-four, ninety-seven, one hundred.* The plane took flight.

"One hundred knots! Hot damn!" shouted Burt. "We got one hundred knots!"

Mike, Burt, and Mike's wife, Sally, sitting in the back of the chase plane, were quiet. It had taken so much just to get to the starting line. Flying in Burt's twin-engine Duchess, they would follow the *Voyager* until they could no longer see California. The wingtips looked bad. Wire dangled from the end, and the winglet — the small vertical fin at the end of the wing — was barely holding on. As Burt had Dick perform stability tests, the right winglet tore off. The other one looked poised to do the same.[*]

[*]The right winglet landed in the backyard of a

Burt was telling Dick, "Don't abort. Don't abort." Dick was listening and shaking his head. He wasn't about to quit. He had "W" in his compass, signaling "west," and he was on his way. As the fuel gauge in the Duchess dipped lower, Burt, Mike, and Sally needed to turn around immediately if they wanted to make it back to Edwards. Mike banked the plane to wave good-bye. Burt was silent, his eyes searching the horizon. There was water for as far as he could see.

The *Voyager* team in Hangar 77 in Mojave, led by Bruce Evans — one of the few people Dick listened to unconditionally — stayed in contact with Dick and Jeana around the clock. Burt and Mike spent their days flight-testing their newest business plane, the Beechcraft Starship. Burt was on call to talk to his brother, or to give him space — whatever he needed. Mike spent nights tracking the *Voyager*'s journey, talking to Dick and Jeana throughout. He also ran interference, keeping Burt away when he knew he would only agitate his brother by giving Dick advice on things Dick didn't need to hear.

When they had first lifted off from the

---

woman in Lancaster, who had been watching the *Voyager* takeoff on television. The left winglet tore off over the Santa Barbara area.

Edwards runway, when the fragile wings were finally taking flight, Dick said excitedly, "I can fly the airplane! I can fly the airplane!" Jeana, who was lying on her back looking up at him, said, "I knew you could." Dick didn't know whether she was being confident or naïve, but the encouragement was important. "The *Voyager* is flyable by the velvet-arm test pilot," he said happily. He had known that if the tip of the wing continued to tear, if the fuel tank ruptured, they were dead. He had put that information in what he called his I-don't-give-a-shit box.

The sense of danger never went away. He and Jeana spoke on an as-needed basis. Jeana managed the fuel log but never flew the plane. She had built sections of the plane by hand and had been key to the mission's success. She had passed certification requirements to fly the *Voyager,* including getting her multiengine rating and instrument rating, but she did not learn other key systems to fly the plane. She hadn't learned how to use the radar or set up autopilot or navigation or talk on the radio. Dick slept for occasional two-hour stretches, weather permitting, by using the autopilot. He flew in a semisupine position, looking at instruments he and his team had built by hand, going over the checklists that Jeana had painted in tiny, perfect, artistic script. The mission could not have happened without her, but he was now the only one capable of keeping them aloft and alive.

Even during short periods of rest, Dick feared the autopilot was going to do something terrible. Every time he tried to close his eyes, the plane pitched up in his mind. They encountered storms, low visibility, and no visibility. On day two, they flew through Typhoon Marge. On day three, the autopilot failed. Day five, crossing central Africa, they ran into fierce thunderstorms and monsoons, the worst storms Dick had ever encountered. The plane pitched and heaved as he flew in and out of clouds, and the airplane rolled into a ninety-degree bank. *Here it is,* he thought. But then came the reprieve, the kind pilot Ernest Gann wrote about in *Fate Is the Hunter:* "The peril was instantly there and then almost as instantly not there. We peeped behind the curtain, saw what some dead men have seen, and survived with it engraved forever on our memories." When the worst of the African storms had passed, they flew in a black haze that was so thick and inky that Dick imagined walking on it. On another day, they almost flew right into a mountain peak. Over Sri Lanka, they had an engine coolant leak. Over the Pacific, they lost oil pressure. Dick was taking a twenty-minute nap when Jeana woke him and pointed to the red oil pressure light indicating the plane was starting to overheat.

He felt like he was playing Russian roulette

every day. Pull the trigger. Click. Survive another day. His body focused his mind on what he needed to do to stay alive. But every day, he looked out and thought, *Out there someplace is disaster. It may be tonight over water or tomorrow during the day, but at some point, this mission is going to end and we are going to die.* If faced with a structural error, they wouldn't be able to get out of the cockpit. The centrifugal forces would wind up the plane and prevent them from moving until impact. They wore small parachutes with nylon harnesses and had a vacuum-sealed raft about the size of a football. Dick put their chances of opening the hatch and jumping out at slim to none. His whole world had collapsed into the cocoon of their cockpit. After a couple of days of flight, he couldn't imagine anything outside.

Nine days after takeoff, news arrived that Dick and Jeana were not far out from Edwards, having flown up the California coast after a night crossing of Costa Rica. Burt and Mike jumped into the Duchess, hoping to join up with the *Voyager* over the ocean west of San Diego. About sixty miles off the coast, in the dark, early morning hours of December 23, Burt and Mike spotted a strobe light. They couldn't be sure it was the *Voyager*. The plane had no running lights; they had been lost with the winglets.

Mike radioed, hoping it was his wingman Dick, and instructed him to cycle the strobe on and off. The strobe went off. When the strobe flashed back on, Mike and Burt did something neither one expected: they began to sob. There they were, bawling like babies. Collecting themselves, they smiled and wiped their eyes. Soon, in the gray light of the rising sun, they could make out the silhouette of the *Voyager.* When they'd last seen the plane, it was bent and damaged. Now it was flying straight and slow, looking more like an ethereal boat floating on currents of air.

In the *Voyager* cockpit, Dick wondered whether he could land back at Edwards. About twenty minutes out, he still had his doubts. *They're flight-testing big bombers and fighter jets and I'm a little homebuilder from frickin' Mojave. Who is going to care about us?* Then he thought, *What if I can't land there?* If they couldn't land at Edwards, their record wouldn't count. The Fédération Aéronautique Internationale, the world sanctioning body for aviation records, required closed-course record seekers to take off and land from the same place.

Dick called the tower at Edwards. "We're twenty minutes out," he said. "I know you're real busy. Could you let me land in the restricted area?" He figured he could land in a remote area of the restricted dry lake — so as not to bother anyone.

The tower came back: "This is Edwards Tower. Sir, we have canceled flying today and we are all here waiting for your return."

Dick was dumbfounded. *They canceled flying for us?* None of it made sense, but then he had just gone nine days on no real sleep, stuffed into a capsule with the noise level of a freight train. Dick had no idea the *Voyager* was on the cover of that week's *Newsweek,* with the headline: "THE INCREDIBLE VOYAGER, HEADING AROUND THE WORLD WITHOUT A STOP."

There was a solid cloud layer as Dick flew over the San Gabriel Mountains. Closing in on the southern end of Edwards, he looked down, expecting to see the beige canvas of the base. Instead, he saw black and silver and beige. He saw thousands of people. There were trucks, satellite dishes, and motor homes framing the runway. The 747 that carried the space shuttle to the Cape was in front of the massive NASA hangar. The sight was unforgettable. Using Mike as their wingman to count wheel height, Dick and Jeana touched down. Nine days, three minutes, forty-four seconds: 26,358 statute miles. The event was televised live worldwide.

Dick had told the *Voyager* crew that he didn't want anyone running up to the plane before the FAI inspector arrived to certify the flight. He had nightmares of doing the flight and not getting the credit for it. Dick opened the cockpit and saw all of the commotion, with cameras and microphones and a crowd closing in.

Now he faced a new challenge: he wasn't sure he could walk. He pulled himself up and out of the cockpit and took a seat on the top of the plane. His legs felt like noodles, atrophied from nine days of no exercise. He pushed himself farther back on the fuselage, moving and stretching his legs. He would not let himself be carried off the plane; his fighter pilot credibility would be shot. He figured he'd sit and wave, and jostle and tense his legs. Postponing the move for as long as he could, Dick — black cowboy hat back on — carefully made his way onto the ground.

Burt was the first in line to give him a hug. It was December 23 — the best Christmas present ever.

That year had started in a very different way. The space shuttle *Challenger* had disintegrated seventy-three seconds after liftoff on January 28, 1986, killing the seven astronauts, including a high school teacher, on board. The accident was found to be part mechanical failure, part management failure. Members of the Rogers Commission, appointed to determine the causes of the disaster, found among other things that NASA managers had not accurately calculated the flight risks. Commissioner Richard Feynman, the Caltech physicist and Nobel laureate, concluded, "The management of NASA exaggerates the reliability of its product, to the point of fantasy."

Burt had followed the commission's findings only from afar. One of the more memorable things to come out of it was something he heard from test pilot Chuck Yeager, who would swing by to visit on occasion. Yeager was appointed to the commission and attended the first meeting, where discussion centered around the shuttle's O-rings, which failed due to the cold temperatures on the morning of the launch. (In one meeting, Feynman took an O-ring and put it in ice water, showing how the material was compromised by the cold.) Yeager, big on courage but short on patience, listened as discussions dragged on for hours. He could predict how NASA was going to limit shuttle flights for years to come. He walked out of the first meeting with no plans to return. Asked in the hallway why he was leaving, he shot back, "Give me a warm day and I'll fly that sonofabitch."

There were plenty of things not to like about Yeager — he was all about Yeager — but Burt admired his spirit. Yeager got into a plane shaped like a .50 caliber bullet with a needle nose and flew into the unknown, pushing the X-1 faster than any pilot had flown. Burt knew that his brother was cut from the same cloth. All Dick ever wanted was to do something significant in a plane. He had made that happen. A scrappy team in the desert had defied reason, ignored skeptics, and made history. Burt was given the moniker "Magician of the Mojave." He had a lot more tricks up his denim sleeve.

5
SPACE MEDICINE

Peter drove his black Trans Am along Mass Ave., slowing as he passed the entrance leading to the Infinite Corridor. He turned onto Memorial Drive, home of the Stratton Student Center, where SEDS was launched on a perfect starry night. Across the way was building 37, the place of real-life astronauts and cutting-edge space technology. Boston's "Don't Look Back" played on the radio. Peter blinked back tears. MIT was in his rearview mirror.

Peter graduated from MIT in June 1983 with a bachelor's degree in molecular biology. He had worked on some dazzling things, ranging from space-bound experiments to genetic engineering. He was now headed to medical school. Peter had been accepted to Stanford on early admission — and moved out to Palo Alto, loving the weather — only to learn over the summer while backpacking in Greece that he was accepted to Harvard Medical School as well. Specifically, he was admitted to Harvard's MD-HST — Health Science and Technology program — something Peter embraced as a "geeky medical degree." The Harvard HST program was Peter's first choice, but the odds had been against him, given that only twenty-five students were admitted to the program each year.

Harvard took some getting used to. He quickly discovered that telling someone he attended Harvard Medical School was "dropping the H-bomb." It felt impossible to say the school name without sounding like a snob. On the positive side, it could prove effective in picking up girls, though a social life in medical school was as hard to come by as sleep. The medical school was about fifteen minutes across the Charles River from the Harvard University campus. Its epicenter was the Quad, a grassy area surrounded in a horseshoe shape by five marble-faced buildings. Peter lived in the student dorm, Vanderbilt Hall, on campus his first year. Surrounding the medical school buildings were hospitals. Peter loved the school's history and its miles of underground corridors. On the rare occasion he landed a date, he would suggest they go to the museum above the medical school administration building. The Warren Anatomical Museum detailed the history of health care and was filled with artifacts — many macabre — including nineteenth-century surgery kits, early microscopes and microscopic imagery, plaster casts of faces for phrenology and of the right hands of great surgeons, and sterilizing devices from the earliest days of surgery. The coolest exhibit was the skull of Phineas Gage, the man who survived a terrible accident that drove a steel bar straight through his skull.

The first real eye-opener of medical school, though, was anatomy class. Peter and his lab partner were given the choice of working on the cadaver of a small elderly lady or the cadaver of a large man. Peter chose the elderly female cadaver, hoping the smaller frame would make the dissection easier. Peter named her "Aunt Molly." The woman had died at age seventy-three of pancreatic cancer. On dissection day one, Peter and his lab partner covered Molly's face and hands with cloth to depersonalize the experience. They cut into her thorax, and then had what Peter considered the brutal experience of sawing her ribs with a handsaw. Not long after, they were tasked with dissecting Aunt Molly's groin area. This was followed by the study and dissection of the arm and hand. Before work began on the arm, the professor carried from table to table a perfectly dissected arm on a tray. Peter and his lab partner placed a nickel in the open outstretched hand, generating some laughs. Dissection under way, Peter was struck by the brilliant biomechanics of the arm, wrist, and hand, with the delicate and dexterous arrangement of muscles in the palm and forearm, the bands of connective tissue, tendons, joints, and nerves. He was reminded of the prosthetic hand Luke Skywalker was given in *The Empire Strikes Back*. And he was reminded of some of the robotic arms he had made in his upstairs room in Great Neck. He had always been enamored with the physics of the hand.

When the day came to uncover Aunt Molly's face, Peter paused. This felt like the most psychologically difficult part of the course. The cloth was set aside and students had to remove the skin of the face. In a later class, Peter had to open up Molly's skull, sawing it with a rotary saw in a line running from about an inch above the ear all the way around her head. Peter worked methodically to extract her brain to examine the cranial nerves, cerebral veins, and various components, from neurons and dendrites to synapses. Her tissue, he found, was like semisoft cheese. The smell was terrible, but seeing the inside of a skull was something he would not soon forget. What struck him was how this small brain, gray and slightly slippery like a rock lifted from a river and weighing only three pounds, held all of Aunt Molly's thoughts, memories, skills, loves, wants, and desires. Molly's entire life was lived in this matter until one day it just blinked off. Those memories, housed in the patterns of synaptic connections between neurons, were locked in this meaty human hard drive, never to be accessed again. Peter had recently bought one of IBM's first desktop personal computers, with two five-inch floppy drives. He could back up his files, but there was no way to back up the human mind. He was awed and saddened by what he held.

Early one morning on his first third-year medical rotation, while on a shift in the Baker Building at Massachusetts General Hospital, Peter had his first life-or-death encounter with a patient. It was around three A.M. and Peter was catching some sleep on a cot. He was jolted awake with "Code Blue Baker five." Someone on the fifth floor was having a cardiac arrest. Peter raced up a flight of stairs and was the first to reach the patient, who'd had open heart surgery the day before. He began chest compressions. The man's sternum cracked with each compression, and all Peter could think was, *Ohmygod this is real.* It was one thing to do this on a dummy, another on a human. This night ended well. There were other times when Peter felt overwhelmed and overloaded. He met an angelic sixteen-year-old girl who had lymphoma and was given very little chance of living. He saw premature babies fighting for life. He developed a friendship with a rheumy-eyed homeless man, an alcoholic with liver failure, and discovered that he was a Harvard graduate. The two had great conversations when the man was sober. Peter worked with a frail and elderly patient with impacted bowels and had to don gloves and disimpact him. He did his first spinal tap and first breast exam. He also began to see previously healthy men come in with debilitating infections, including pneumonia and Kaposi's sarcoma. The men were among the first diagnosed cases of HIV/AIDS. A mix of anxiety and hysteria surrounded the disease — the religious right called it "the wrath of God against homosexuals" — and Peter experienced it all from the front lines. With every patient, whatever the problem, Peter thought the same three things: *If only they knew how little I know, I'm doing my damnedest, I hope I don't fuck up.*

The problem was that Peter didn't love what he was doing. He sometimes fell asleep in class — from exhaustion, but also from finding many of the lectures tedious and uninspired. He thought the school's anatomy lab looked like it dated to the Civil War. He took a pathology class and found the subject matter similar to what he'd covered in seventh grade. One of the few subjects that intrigued him was something they spent too little time on — atrial fibrillation, where the class did an in-depth math analysis that left Peter thinking, *Now that was actually interesting.* He and his lab partner rushed out of anatomy class one day to attend a student-faculty council meeting only to find that no faculty showed up. His fellow HST students — an eclectic group that included a professional surfer, a former Ringling Brothers circus clown, and an eighteen-year-old whiz kid from Columbia — all knew of what Peter called his *space affliction.*

To Peter, one of the best things about the HST program was that Harvard Medical School collaborated academically with MIT, incorporating engineering principles into traditional medical school teachings. They would study the human heart and then work with MIT professors to build an electronic circuit diagram to represent the heart.

But Peter made a beeline whenever he could for MIT's Man Vehicle Lab, volunteering for research and gleaning details on new space projects. He was still running SEDS, which had grown by the mid-1980s to around 110 chapters, including a new chapter he'd started while at Harvard Med. He held big and impressive space fairs at MIT, inviting students, faculty, and executives from NASA, Boeing, and Lockheed. As he rode the bus back to Harvard early one evening, he wrote in his journal, "Oh how I wish I could cut loose of expectations. Have I been doing what I do to impress Dad?"

Though medical school was duty over passion, a family obligation, Peter believed on some level that there was a chance a medical degree might get him closer to space. He had done the research and learned that if he wasn't going to be a fighter pilot, then an MD might be the ticket to getting into the Astronaut Corps. Peter rationalized that at the very least, it might help him learn how to extend the human life span long enough so that technology could catch up with his dream of accessible space travel. The longer he lived, the better his chances were of getting off planet. He also liked the idea of being a polymath, the boy who played three roles in his Cub Scouts play. Peter's newest fictional hero was Buckaroo Banzai of *The Adventures of Buckaroo Banzai Across the 8th Dimension.* Buckaroo was a top neurosurgeon, a particle physicist, a race car driver, and a rock star. Buckaroo had perfected a wide range of skills; why couldn't he?

Sitting in Amphitheater A on the Harvard Medical School campus, Peter listened as the teacher went over the forms being handed out. The paperwork was to be filled out with information on where students wanted to be "matched" for internships and residencies after their fourth year. Peter had passed part one of his medical boards, and would take part two at the end of his fourth year. If he passed, he would begin his internship. At the end of the internship, he would take part three of the medical boards to get his license to practice. Then the residency would begin, ranging from a two-year to a seven-year commitment, depending on the chosen branch of medicine.

Peter looked at the forms. He was supposed to know his top choices of hospitals? He needed to declare a specialty? He thought, *I just want to go build rockets.* Through his first and second year, and even now in his third year, in the midst of clinical rotation, he had managed to get away with medical school as a part-time undertaking. He was running SEDS, doing his MVL research, and hosting national space conferences. And space was becoming more real. Shuttle missions were flying with increasing frequency, from two flights in 1981 to nine now in 1985. Looking at the papers on his lap, Peter felt a rising sense of panic. There was no way he could keep juggling medical school *and* space as an intern or resident. He would make a mistake that would kill someone. At the very least, he would turn into a frustrated doctor not living his dream. Sometime later, lost in his thoughts, he looked around and noticed that everyone had left the cavernous room. The lights were being turned off. Stuffing the papers into his backpack, anxious and worked up, he headed to the administration office. He had a long-shot idea.

He asked the receptionist if he could make

a call to the Man Vehicle Lab at MIT. He needed to talk to *his* Obi-Wan Kenobi, lab director Dr. Larry Young. Peter was lucky to find Dr. Young in the lab. Peter quietly explained his situation at Harvard and asked, "Is there some way I can come back to MIT and do my master's or PhD in sixteen?"[*] He wanted to take a leave from Harvard, enter the aeronautical and astronautical engineering program, and defer this critical decision about medicine. Dr. Young told Peter that he would have to apply for admission, but that he would help fast-track the application. He had seen Peter's dedication in the lab, and wondered when Peter would move from the science of medicine to the science of space.

Larry Young's own love of space began the day the beach-ball-size Sputnik satellite orbited Earth on October 4, 1957. He was traveling by ship to France, where he had a Fulbright scholarship to study applied mathematics at the Sorbonne. On the night he arrived in France, everyone was staring up at the sky and listening to handheld radios. Young decided in that moment to shift his studies to space. When asked why space, he would reply, "It's a little like falling in love. You can't explain it rationally; but you know it." The license plate on his car read 2MARS.

[*] Course sixteen is an introduction to aerospace engineering and design.

His student Byron Lichtenberg had become America's first payload specialist, and many of the experiments developed in the MVL were flying on shuttle missions. Young saw Peter as smart and enthusiastic and filled with one big idea after the other. Peter had more excitement in his eyes than just about anyone he'd ever met.

Where Harvard was interesting, being back at MIT was joyous. Peter was now doing exactly what he wanted to do: aerospace engineering. He reassured his parents that he was simply adding another degree, but would return to medical school. He was surrounded in labs and classrooms by real turbines, flight simulators and models, and photographs of planes and rockets. Even the make-or-break two-semester course, Unified Engineering, taken by sophomores, was a welcome challenge. Peter was four years older than his classmates and sat in the front row, learning the underlying math equations and principles behind solid mechanics and materials, fluid mechanics, thermodynamics, and propulsion. Because of the sheer amount of interdisciplinary material covered in Unified Engineering, students were required to work collaboratively on problem sets. Peter returned to his old stomping grounds, the Theta Delta Chi fraternity, and found a new group of fraternity brothers to study with. There were also break nights, with movies — the latest James Bond film, *A View to a Kill* — and parties that lasted into the early morning hours with dancing to the Go-Go's. There were times when Peter longed for a girlfriend, and other times when he realized love would have to wait.

Shortly after returning to MIT, Peter had met with Dr. Young to talk over his idea for his master's thesis project. Peter was interested in somehow creating artificial gravity to alleviate the muscle deterioration, loss of bone calcium, and other known maladies that came with weightlessness. He told Dr. Young he was thinking about a small-radius rotating bed that could create gravity while the astronaut slept.

Any prolonged stay in space would require humans to figure out how to create artificial gravity or some other countermeasure, such as extensive exercise. The astronauts of Skylab, the NASA space station that orbited Earth between 1973 and 1979, had come home in worse shape than when they'd left. Owen Garriott and William Pogue — who set records at the time for the number of months spent in space — were examined upon their return, and the flight surgeon's official report read, "Capable musculoskeletal function will be threatened during prolonged space flight lasting one and a half years to three years, unless protective measures can be developed." In addition to muscle atrophy and bone density loss, the astronauts had balance disorders that persisted after the other conditions were fixed. Some stumbled in the dark, lacking visual clues as to which way was vertical, and continued to try to float things around them as they had done in the space station.

Both Konstantin Tsiolkovsky and Wernher von Braun had imagined a large, circular space station that would rotate to generate artificial gravity. A NASA Ames research study begun the year after the Skylab program ended also imagined a space station shaped like a wheel that would rotate at one revolution per minute, fast enough so the centrifugal force at its rim — where living accommodations were to be located — would be the equivalent of normal gravity on Earth. In the movie *2001: A Space Odyssey,* the *Discovery One* spaceship included a large spinning centrifuge inside the crew compartment.

Dr. Young liked Peter's topic but needed details and was worried about the effect on an astronaut's inner ear. Fortunately, inspiration came to Peter. Out on a walk with his mom, dad, and sister, who were visiting MIT, Peter found his answer on a playground. Tula, who had a habit of asking Peter the moment she saw him if he'd met any nice Greek girls, liked the idea of Peter's looking wistfully at kids. But Peter was stopped by something other than children. He was looking at the playground roundabout — the flat disk with handrails that spins like a merry-go-round. His mind started spinning: *centrifugal force, the force created by spinning,* is a function of the velocity squared and the radius from the center of rotation. At the center, the acceleration would be zero. And if an astronaut's head, more specifically his vestibular system, was placed at the center, there would be no axial acceleration to mess with the inner ear. Peter grabbed his sister's hand and ran toward the play structure. After persuading the playground kids to take a break, he instructed his sister to lie down with her head at the center. She protested to no avail. Inwardly, she smiled. This was Peter, the boy who often had a distracted, I-am-elsewhere look. First she was spun around, eyes closed. Then it was Peter's turn. He stayed on until a few moms began standing next to the play structure, throwing unhappy looks their way. Back at school later that night, he sketched out his idea. He needed something small enough to fit inside the space shuttle and eventually live at the International Space Station, outlined the year before by President Reagan and under construction with segments reportedly close to launch. Peter wrote in his journal, "What if you can give a dose of gravity, like medicine, while someone sleeps?" The next Thursday, Peter was in the Man Vehicle Lab and talked with Dr. Young about the specifics of his plan. He had done three sketches: of a rotating plank on the floor, a plank on the side of the craft in a storage area, and a positionable beam. He dubbed it the Artificial Gravity Sleeper, or AGS.

"If you put people on a centrifuge, they can't do anything else," Peter said excitedly. "If they centrifuge while they're sleeping, they can work their cardiovascular system and stimulate their immune system."

Dr. Young looked at the drawings and said, "It's not a dumb idea." Still, he remained skeptical that someone could sleep while being rotated. But Peter told him he had spent time at the playground, and had even dozed off while spinning. Peter reasoned that if one could sleep in a gravity field, gravity could be thought of as a medicine and could be given in doses of four hours, six hours, and so on. In space, the bed's centrifugal force would act like gravity, making the body work harder than when it was weightless. The astronaut's head would be at the center, like the center of a record player, with no gravity.

Peter was able to get $50,000 in grants from the Space Foundation, NASA, the National Institutes of Health, the American Heart Association, and the AeroAstro department of MIT. He went to work building his motorized rotating space bed. He did drawings, calculations, and the hands-on building of the device, which was a two-meter-radius centrifuge. The bed, which could run at a rate as high as 40 rpm, providing 3 gs, would be made of a honeycombed aluminum and had counterweights and telemetry signals flowing through gold-plated slip rings to monitor the person being spun. The AGS sat atop concentric six-inch and eight-inch–diameter steel piping connected by sealed ball-bearing fittings. Peter offered MIT students thirty dollars if they would spend the night sleeping while spinning. His friend Todd B. Hawley, a leader at SEDS, was his first and best volunteer, spending nine nights in a row in the device. Peter noted in his observation log: "What amazes me is that it's working! TBH is actually getting a good night's sleep on the device. Todd has been really fantastic about cooperating, and has not really complained @ all." Peter evaluated sleep through observation, and by the data readouts. One day, Dr. Young stopped by and volunteered to get into the contraption. He stayed on for a few minutes before climbing off and saying he thought it was great. The next time Peter powered up the machine, the piping unwound off the flange and the whole thing toppled down. Peter was mortified, realizing he could have killed the Obi-Wan Kenobi of the MVL. Peter corrected the problem and continued with his experimentation. He also built the device for exercise, adding a "cycle ergometer," with pedals for use while the astronaut was supine. Peter loved every second of it: He was the little boy back building Estes rockets and experimenting with chemistry. Only this time, he was building something that might help people live in space.

In April 1987, Peter, Todd Hawley, and Bob Richards hosted a conference to realize a new and even bigger dream: the founding of a space university dedicated to space studies in every discipline. The gang of three, *Peterbobtodd,* had been exploring the formation of a graduate-level university for several years. The goal was to create the world's first nonprofit, nongovernmental university focused on space studies. The three men were counting on their body of work — SEDS and their popular national space fairs — to give them credibility and contacts. It worked: over three days in April, Peter, Bob, and Todd hosted hundreds of people at MIT's Stratton Student Center, the birthplace of SEDS. Peter, who was ten months shy of earning his master's degree and one year shy of an MD, again had the support of MIT president Paul Gray, and the conference drew space delegations and top leaders from the Soviet Union, Canada, Japan, China, the European Space Agency, and NASA.

The opening session drew more than five

hundred people. Peter welcomed attendees to the Founding Conference of the International Space University Project and gave an impassioned talk about the state of the nation's space program. He noted that after the Apollo 11 landing, NASA had appointed a task force to chart three courses — fast, medium, and slow — for continuing beyond the Apollo program.

"The time line set forth in the fast-paced scenario reflects what we might read in today's science fiction stories," Peter said. "The slowest of the three scenarios goes as follows," with dates of completion:

Space Station and Shuttle: 1977
Space Tug: 1981
Lunar Orbiting Station: 1981
Lunar Surface Base: 1983
50 Person Space Base: 1984
Mars Expedition: 1986
100 Person Space Base: 1989

Peter asked the group, "What has happened in the last eighteen years? . . . It is time to revitalize the motor and the vision which will put humanity in space — and that motor is composed of yourselves, of the students around the world. This is where I see ISU playing its greatest role."

Closed sessions were led by notables including Byron Lichtenberg; John McLucas, the former U.S. secretary of the Air Force; and Joe Pelton, a director at Intelsat, the governmental consortium managing a constellation of communications satellites. Subjects of discussion and debate ranged from the university's mission statement to classes to be offered. From the start, it was Todd who insisted the university be truly international.

Peter, Todd, and Bob sat at the end of long tables, surrounded by distinguished-looking executives and professors and attentive groups of students. Their plan was to open their university the following summer, in 1988, with an inaugural eight-week session. They would borrow the bricks and mortar — a campus — and hire faculty from their own universities. Their goal was a permanent campus of their own, and their dream was a campus in space. They had already signed on a notable to be chancellor — their Uncle Arthur — Arthur C. Clarke.

For the second time, Peter walked out of the student center believing he was onto something big. Step by step, all of this effort had to make a difference. He had to excite and inspire a new generation of space dreamers. Since the space shuttle *Challenger* disaster the year before — Peter had watched the launch from a closed-circuit TV in the Man Vehicle Lab — risk seemed to go from something laudable to something lamentable. *Fail-*

ure is not an option solidified as NASA's mantra. At least for now, nothing was flying; the shuttle program was grounded. There was only eulogizing, finger pointing, debating. There were commissions formed, reports written, and town hall meetings held. Fear supplanted courage.

Late that night, the three-day conference over, Peter picked up the book he had just finished, *Atlas Shrugged*. Todd had given him the tome, and it became almost a playbook. Peter was moved by the story of what happens to the world when the most productive members of society — the thinkers, the engine of creation — go on strike. *What happens,* Peter pondered, *when a small group of thinkers and builders create a vision of a future they want when the politics of government let them down?*

Peter looked through his dog-eared, marked-up copy. It was interesting, he realized, how he had said in his opening speech earlier in the week: "It is time to revitalize the motor. . . . *You* are the motor." Flipping through the book, he came across a quote he'd underlined. It was by Hank Rearden, the indefatigable industrialist he most identified with, a man who spends a decade working to invent a new type of metal, and who undergoes a transformation over the course of the journey. Peter read the quote by

Rearden aloud:

"All that lunacy is temporary. It can't last. It's demented, so it has to defeat itself. You and I will just have to work a little harder for a while, that's all."

Peter would also have to work harder to figure out his own path. His dream was always about space. His parents' dream for him was always about medicine. He wanted to honor his family legacy, yet also be true to himself.

A similar struggle for identity was playing out on an icy mountain across the country. There, a man a few years younger than Peter was also searching for his true self, but weighed down by a famous last name.

What Peter couldn't know was how this man — and his legacy — would change his life.

6
BEING A LINDBERGH

Erik Lindbergh woke at two A.M. and peered out of his tent on the icy slopes of Mount Rainier. The black sky was milky with stars — radiant, muted, cloudlike, an ethereal carpet unfolded above, a connect-the-dots of constellations all around. The air was still, the mountain slumbering. The twenty-one-year-old closed his eyes and inhaled the cold air, knowing the day ahead would be anything but calm.

Erik's goal on this early August morning in 1986 was to summit the 14,411-foot mountain, the highest peak in the Cascade Range. Climbing Rainier wouldn't be a history-making event like his grandfather's plane flight, the 1927 journey across the Atlantic to Paris that made Charles Lindbergh a hero and at the time arguably the most famous man on Earth. But — for now — scaling Rainier would be Erik's Paris, his milestone. He was intent on staying clear of anything too predictably "Lindberghian." A friend was trying to persuade him to get his pilot's license, but Erik found it way too obvious. Family members had learned to fly, but no one was a pilot. The only flying Erik planned to do was off the cornices at his favorite ski mountains.

Erik began packing up his gear. He was at Camp Schurman, 9,440 feet above sea level on the eastern side of Mount Rainier, an active, icy volcano about an hour southeast of Seattle in Washington state. He would start before three A.M. in a bid to get off the icy part of the mountain before the sun warmed the snow and increased the avalanche risk.

Mount Rainier was postcard beautiful, with glaciers toward the top, and wildflowers, lakes, and old-growth forests on the valley floor. But the peak was dangerous year round. It was riddled with crevasses. Rocks tumbled, the weather turned, and the glaciers were always shifting. Five years earlier, in the worst recorded climbing accident in American history, eleven hikers were killed on Mount Rainer, their bodies never recovered. A massive piece of the icy mountain had exploded like dynamite and rained down on the climbers.

After a quick breakfast of oatmeal, Erik, his brother, Leif — four years older and a more experienced mountaineer — and cousin Craig Vogel set out in the darkness carrying fifty-pound packs. Leif took the lead, and

Erik carried his old green external-frame nylon pack nicknamed the "meat wagon." Stained and beat up, the backpack had accompanied Erik on family deer hunting trips when he was a teenager. He and his siblings and father would climb the steep trails of the North Cascades high country, returning with the meat wagon filled with deer meat wrapped in cheesecloth.

But on this cold morning, Erik had much higher aspirations: he was trying to reach the summit for the first time. Roped together and wearing battery-powered headlamps, the Lindbergh group made its way up the Emmons Glacier trail one booted step at a time in hopes of arriving at the destination in eight hours. From the top, they would still have to hike back down to Camp Schurman to gather the rest of their gear, and then continue to the trailhead at the White River Campground at 4,400 feet.

Erik had tried the same climb twice before and failed. He had made novice mistakes of packing too much gear — his dad's cast iron crampons, skis, extra boots — and taking the wrong route and overshooting Camp Schurman by 1,000 vertical feet, arriving at camp at two A.M., just as other hikers were waking up to start their climb.

Tall, wiry, and athletic, Erik was unaccustomed to failing at any physical challenge. He had been the Washington state gymnastics champion at age twelve. His strongest discipline was the floor exercise, but he won for all-around performance. Shelves in his bedroom were filled with water-skiing trophies. He could climb a rope in gym class with just his hands, held his high school record for chin-ups, and as a student of tae kwon do, would do a jumping sidekick at head level.

While in high school in a small island town a short ferry ride from Seattle, Erik was a major ski bum — working as a dishwasher and shoveling snow at the Crystal Mountain Resort, not far from Mount Rainier. He also spent a ski season in Sun Valley, Idaho. He now lived in Olympia, Washington, and attended Evergreen State College, where he was studying political ecology. College, like high school, didn't engage him the way it should. He was thinking of opening his own backcountry luxury skiing company. He preferred working his body over his brain, favored action over intellectualizing.

Erik and his siblings had learned from early childhood to keep their heritage to themselves. As a boy, Erik had little understanding of the significance of his family name until a classmate told him he was reading his grandfather's Pulitzer Prize–winning book, *The Spirit of St. Louis*. Erik knew his grandfather not as the world-famous aviator Charles Lindbergh, but simply as "Grandfather." He was the tall and balding man who offered

Erik fifty cents if he could learn to wiggle his ears (as he could), bought him a toy model of a Sikorsky helicopter,[*] and seemed more at ease with children than adults.

Known to his children as a perfectionist, list maker, and lecturer, Charles could also be affectionate when away from the public eye. There was a tacit understanding among the Lindbergh clan that one should not ask Grandfather about his 1927 flight. Erik's uncle Land Lindbergh — the third child of Charles and his wife, Anne — did ask and was directed to "read the book."

In high school, Erik was struck by how people treated him differently when they discovered his lineage. They would clutch his arm, stand too close, and tell him stories about the man they idolized, the man who risked everything for a dream he believed in;

[*] Erik learned much later that his grandfather had worked with Igor Sikorsky, the Russian inventor of the first helicopter, who became a close family friend. The first helicopter was genius. It had a cyclic (essentially a joystick that controls the pitch of the helicopter by controlling the pitch of the main rotor blades), a tail rotor (which prevents the helicopter from spinning around with the main rotor), and landing skids (which effectively distribute the load of a vertical landing). A modern helicopter pilot would easily recognize the craft, and could very probably fly it.

who galvanized commercial air travel; who even inspired America's first astronauts through his dangerous journey into the unknown. There was also a controversial side to his grandfather, a man who was anti-interventionist during World War II, was impressed by the military might of Nazi Germany, and made anti-Semitic statements. Occasionally, the idolatry from strangers would focus on Erik's grandmother, Anne Morrow Lindbergh, herself a pioneering aviator — the first American woman to earn a glider pilot's license — and acclaimed writer. But Grandmother's legacy was gentler — she was gentler. Where Charles was tall, forceful, and peripatetic, Anne was petite, contemplative, and grounded.

Erik's father, Jon Lindbergh, was the second child of Charles and Anne. Their first son, Charles Jr., was the cherubic, curly-haired twenty-month-old toddler who was kidnapped from the Lindbergh home in 1932, held for ransom, and killed. The baby, taken from his second-floor nursery, was found dead in the woods close by, killed by an apparent blow to the head. The fame from the 1927 flight — ticker tape parades, autograph seekers, photographers following the family's every move — had made the Lindberghs a target. The media circus around the crime, and the con artists who emerged to make false claims, sent the Lindberghs into exile in

England, where they lived for a period under assumed names. The message to descendants was clear: you put yourself out, you pay.

On the corridor of the Emmons Glacier, the first hints of dawn had lightened the sky from black to pale blue and rimmed the horizon with vibrant orange. Soon the sun rose above the clouds and dusted the white landscape in pink and mauve. Erik studied the massive mountain underfoot. The immense beauty of where they were was eclipsed by the personal agony of taking thousands of uneven steps. He and his brother were on a softly sloped area, but the sound of falling rocks was as constant as the crunching of snow. Leif, a skilled storyteller with an ironic sense of humor, was quiet today. Breathing grew more difficult as the air thinned. The brothers snaked their way up the glacier. Their goal was two breaths per step.

Pausing to rest, Erik looked back down and saw clusters of hikers at Camp Schurman looking up at them. They were now ten hours into their climb, which should have taken them no more than nine hours. They passed dramatic-looking seracs, giant columns of intersecting glacial ice, which could topple with no warning. They were on a painfully indirect trajectory, and this final pitch was grueling. Erik had been strangely sluggish from the start, and was feeling worse and worse the higher they climbed. His backpack was heavy, and his legs were uncharacteristically weak. He rubbed his forearms and wrists. They were now within sight of Columbia Crest, the mountain's official summit. Erik called up his strength for the final push.

Finally, short of breath, weighed down by their packs, and operating on little sleep, Erik, Leif, and Craig reached the summit of Mount Rainier. Leif wanted to stay and explore the summit, with its 360-degree view, caves, false summits, and calderas. The view was like a moonscape: different from anything Erik had ever seen before, filled with dangerous couloirs and turquoise crevasses hundreds of feet deep. There were places on the mountain that man would never be able to touch.

After about twenty minutes, the three men began their trek back down the mountain, aiming for a far more direct route. Within ten minutes of the descent, Erik, who had felt lousy for much of the climb, started to breathe better. But then he developed an epic nosebleed, and his nostrils felt sunburned. His feet throbbed, and his wrists were swollen and sore. The pain would not go away.

Erik finally arrived back at Camp Schurman, where he and Leif gathered up their gear, adding ten more pounds to their packs. His feet and shoulders ached. His head hurt. He had always pushed his body beyond its comfort zone, but this time felt different. It felt far worse.

At eight thousand feet, they left the ice and were on rocky terrain, no longer roped in. They saw powerful-looking Canada geese flying in arrow formation above, and agile black-tailed deer darting through the trees. The valley floor was laced with purple and yellow flowers, and snow-fed rivers glistened in the dwindling sun. As a student of ecology, Erik worried about losing pristine places like this. Nature was his religion; the place where he found peace, inspiration, and answers. He felt allergic to organized religion. As a boy, he spent hours watching eagles and herons swoop and hunt. He built sandcastles, marveled at the sea life of Puget Sound, and collected oddly shaped driftwood for its beauty. He and his five siblings often slept outside on the upstairs porch, watching for shooting stars.

Erik's grandfather had the same love of nature. Charles Lindbergh, by all accounts a restless spirit, traveled extensively after World War II and became as fixated on the environment as he had been on his history-making flight. He supported and spearheaded conservation efforts, became a director of the World Wildlife Fund, and fought for the protection of parkland and endangered species around the world, from the gray whale in Baja to a small buffalo called the tamaraw in the Philippines. He lived among indigenous tribes in the Philippines, Brazil, and Africa, eating stewed monkey and sleeping in huts with palm-thatched roofs. He was instrumental in working with locals to secure land for the establishment of Haleakala National Park in Hawaii. He had a particular love affair with the Philippines, where he worked to save the endangered monkey-eating eagle, the largest eagle in the world. Erik's grandmother was equally interested in the interplay between humans and the environment, writing a cover story for *Life* in February 1969 about nature in the midst of America's new spaceport. Anne wanted to understand whether the natural beauty and abundant wildlife of Cape Canaveral — where she and Charles had camped with their children decades earlier — could persist next to the brawny and fiery technology of space. The title of her story, published the week of the Apollo 9 mission, was "The Heron and the Astronaut," and concluded, "without the marsh there would be no heron; without the wilderness, forests, trees, fields, there would be no breath, no crops, no sustenance, no life, no brotherhood and no peace on earth. No heron and no astronaut. The heron and the astronaut are linked in an indissoluble chain of life on earth." The story, with photos of the indigenous wildlife — egrets, wood ibis, pelicans, alligators, armadillos, and rattlesnakes — ended with, "Through the eyes of the astronauts, we have seen more clearly than ever before this precious earth-essence that must be preserved. It might be given a new name borrowed from space language: 'Earth shine.' "*

Now close to the trailhead, where their painful adventure up Mount Rainier had begun, Erik took another break. He saw a marmot poke its furry head above the rocks. Sunlight steamed through the fir, pine, and cedar trees. Had he not been a Lindbergh, Erik might have worked in logging. It was outdoors and physical. But he had embraced a statement that his grandfather had made to *Life* in the sixties: "The human future depends on our ability to combine the knowledge of science with the wisdom of wildness." The Lindbergh Foundation, established three years after Charles's death in 1974, was focused on the intersection between technology and conservation.

It was around eight P.M. when Erik made it back to the parking lot near the Mount

* Anne Morrow Lindbergh wrote of a "cheerful" meal she and her husband shared with a group of astronauts, with Charles marveling over the amount of fuel consumed by an Apollo launch. "In the first second, he figures out, the fuel burned is more than ten times as much as he had used flying his *Spirit of St. Louis* from New York to Paris." Charles typed the *Life* story up for Anne, using two index fingers at a time.

Rainer trailhead. He set his pack down on a rock. When he tried to pick it up again, he couldn't use his hands.

Had he sprained his wrists? He tried to make light of it, saying mountaineering wasn't his sport. But something wasn't right.

Months after the Mount Rainier climb, Erik finally went to see his family doctor. He would be fine for weeks, only to have the pain suddenly return. After competing in a water-skiing competition, both of his knees hurt and were swollen. The pain was intense, as it had been in his wrists. His doctor did some tests and said he wasn't sure whether Erik was just overexerting himself or had something more serious.

The doctor told Erik there was a chance that he had a degenerative condition. There was a *chance,* the doctor said slowly, that Erik had something called rheumatoid arthritis. One symptom of the chronic disease was a mirroring of pain in the body: both knees, both wrists, both feet, both ankles. It could be triggered, the doctor said, by something physically excruciating, whether a marathon or — for women — a particularly difficult childbirth. The doctor said the disease could damage and deteriorate joints, but he wouldn't give Erik a worst-case scenario. He wanted to watch Erik over time.

Erik walked out of the office shaken but

telling himself there was no way he had rheumatoid arthritis, or any kind of arthritis. That was something afflicting the elderly, not an accomplished twenty-one-year-old athlete.

Erik's mother, Barbara Robbins, was quiet when she heard the news. She knew nothing about rheumatoid arthritis. Now divorced from Erik's father, Barbara sometimes felt the Lindbergh name had a curse to it: her in-laws lost their beautiful baby Charles Jr. Her sister-in-law, Reeve (Charles and Anne's youngest child), had lost her first son, Jonathan, when he too was just a toddler. Reeve had been staying at her parents' new house in Connecticut when the baby died of a seizure in the night.

For Barbara, living with Erik's father, Jon, had been full of ups and downs. When they married — having met as students at Stanford — everything had to be done in secrecy. The newlyweds were out of town when they began reading concocted stories of their wedding and the gifts they had received. Syndicated gossip columnist Walter Winchell wrote about Charles Lindbergh's gift to his son and new daughter-in-law, saying he had given them a new sports car, when in fact they drove an old blue Ford wagon that turned purple in the sun. *Redbook* ran an interview with them that had never happened.

Jon was a Navy "frogman," an underwater combat and demolition specialist (frogmen were the precursors to the Navy SEALs). After the Navy, he went into business diving on gas lines and off oil rigs, reaching unprecedented depths and experimenting with breathing mixed gases for decompression. He volunteered to fight fires and was one of the world's first "aquanauts," having lived underwater for more than twenty-four hours.

Now Barbara contemplated the prospect that her son Erik might have a degenerative disease. Barbara had met only one person who had rheumatoid arthritis — he was a young man who spent his days in a rocking chair.

Erik had been the easiest of her six babies; as an infant, he would just sit and smile and kick his legs happily. Erik looked just like Barbara's father, Jim Robbins, a Swede with blue eyes and angular features, but Barbara knew that Erik was a Lindbergh, and like his father and grandfather before him, he would define himself by what he could do physically. Her son had his whole life in front of him, but she worried whether Erik would get the adventure he needed, the adventure that was part of the Lindbergh DNA.

7
A CAREER IN ORBIT

It was after midnight when Peter and his friend John Chirban settled into a booth at the Deli Haus in Kenmore Square, across the Charles River from MIT. John loved the chicken livers, matzo ball soup, and cheese blintzes, and Peter liked the huge pastrami sandwiches, burgers, and cheesecake. The two drank coffee, listened to music, and watched the colorful scene that flowed in and out. They marveled that there were still punk rockers in the late 1980s, though the discussion for the night — as it often was for the two men — was not music, fashion, or food. It was the connection between the truth of science and the truth of faith.

John, ten years older than Peter, was friend, mentor, and consigliere. He admired Peter's passion for space but didn't share it. A Harvard-trained psychologist and professor — and fellow Greek American with a second doctorate in theology — John was committed to understanding and advancing spirituality.

He had spent nearly two decades interviewing the famous and influential behaviorist B. F. Skinner, discussing similar topics of free will versus determinism, and whether spirituality could be rational. While John argued that feelings could be independent of behavioral conditioning, Skinner denied the existence of the soul, saying it was "silly" and "prescientific."

Peter had been introduced to John through his parish priest. The space-loving college student was questioning the Greek Orthodox traditions that had suffused his youth, and though Peter still attended church when he was home with his family, he rarely went on his own. He told John that he felt "weird" about not being actively religious and still found the smell of incense comforting. In the same way medical school was more about duty than passion, church was tradition. It was what his family did on Sundays.

Science, though, was Peter's rock. What he questioned was what existed *beyond physics.*

"Do I believe there's something spiritually out there?" Peter asked, sipping black coffee. "Do I believe there's energy beyond the physical matter? Where does energy that drives life come from?" He looked at John and said, "Did life on Earth originate as a result of aliens?"

John smiled, knowing Peter was serious. Peter's view of the energy of life came closer to the Force in *Star Wars* than what he was taught in church. John found in Peter an innocent competing and excelling in the academic big leagues, a young man with a great family and a foundation of love. Peter was his favorite type of person: a truth seeker. Peter had the zeal of a missionary, only his gods were Goddard and von Braun and his bible was a cross between *Atlas Shrugged* and *The High Frontier.* John believed in God's ability to transform lives, something he articulated to Skinner, who had a deep disdain for religion because of his upbringing. Skinner's work as an adult was rooted in the idea that there is neither choice nor freedom, and that all behavior is shaped by environmental conditioning — negating any role of God. John told Peter that Skinner had made *science* his religion. John chuckled remembering the day he invited Skinner to go with him to listen to Mother Teresa of Calcutta, who was visiting Harvard. Skinner declined, saying he thought Mother Teresa was "very narcissistic." Where John and Skinner came together — and where Peter and John came together — was over central questions of truth: *What is the nature of existence? How should one live life, given that so much remains unknown and perhaps unknowable?* With Peter, John made the case — quoting Albert Einstein — that "science without religion is lame, religion without science is blind."

When Peter was in high school and still an altar boy, his priest asked him to give a Sunday sermon. Father Alex often invited parishioners to give prepared talks, and on this day, Peter stood in front of a congregation of about two hundred people. Peter talked for quite a while without mentioning the word "God." Instead, he spoke of "meta intelligence," a generative force beyond words. Peter said that this meta intelligence was "beyond our comprehension, beyond human terms." Understanding, he said, would come through the exploration of space. He also said, "We may not be the only beings in this universe. We may not be the most intelligent species." Father Alex listened with interest, believing Peter was using nontraditional language to describe his relationship with God. He likened Peter's use of "meta intelligence" to Aristotle's cosmological "first cause" principle, where God is the uncaused cause. Father Alex smiled to himself, even as he saw perplexed looks on the faces of parishioners.

Peter was always drawn to the deeper philosophical concerns presented by science. He had once written a paper on why it was okay to clone people. In medical school, he struggled to understand the animating material of life, and what happens when the vital force goes dark. Now, in the early spring of

1988, Peter was at a crossroads. He had received his master's degree in aeronautical engineering from MIT. Dr. Larry Young had signed his thesis. And NASA had committed funding for three years of continued research involving his Artificial Gravity Sleeper.

Sitting in the Deli Haus diner, Peter poked at his cheesecake. It was after two A.M., and he and John were still talking about faith and truth seeking. John pointed out that many great scientists and engineers, including Einstein and Nikola Tesla, recognized "different kinds of truth and shifting levels of consciousness." Famous founders of science held Christian beliefs, including Blaise Pascal (who was a Jansenist), Galileo, and Johannes Kepler. It was Einstein, John noted, who said, "Whether you can observe a thing or not depends on the theory which you use. It is the theory which decides what can be observed." And Tesla, John continued, wrote about the relationship between matter and energy, saying: "If you want to find the secrets of the universe, think in terms of energy, frequency and vibration. What one man calls God, another calls the laws of physics."

Peter told John that he had recently spent six months reading the Bible every day. "I tried to think of the meaning," Peter said. "I was studying it for myself versus reading the gospel chosen for me on Sundays in church." Had he been asked in high school whether he believed in God, he would have said yes. "Now? I'm agnostic. I'm searching." But he acknowledged, "When the shit hits the fan, like when I had stolen this fetal pig at Hamilton and I thought I was going to be expelled, I prayed."

As the two stood to leave, Peter tossed out his own quote by Konstantin Tsiolkovsky: "You know what I believe?" Peter asked. "Tsiolkovsky said, 'Earth is the cradle of humanity, but one cannot remain in the cradle forever.' " Peter was two months shy of his twenty-seventh birthday. He had one big hurdle to go before he could focus full time on moving humanity out of its cradle. He needed to finish up at Harvard Medical School, either by graduating or by gracefully bowing out. And he had a certain ambitious side project — one that was drawing attention from all over the globe.

At the world headquarters of the International Space University — a tiny second-floor office above a bagel shop on Beacon Street — Peter and Todd Hawley marveled at the postmarks on the applications: the Soviet Union, China, Japan, Kenya, Switzerland, Germany, France, Poland, India, Saudi Arabia. In all, there were more than 350 applicants from thirty-seven countries vying for one of 100 spots at ISU's inaugural summer session, just months away.

Hardly a day went by without Peter and Todd scrutinizing letters and résumés for clues to which students had the best chance of helping them get to space. They looked for leadership and engineering skills, creativity, and hints of a willingness to set aside political and nationalistic differences. Peter and Todd lined up big-name sponsors and visiting professors, and worked on endorsements, seeking Senators Edward Kennedy and John Glenn, and Elizabeth Dole, former U.S. secretary of transportation, among others.

Peter and Todd drew support from astronauts and scientists, including Byron Lichtenberg, Rusty Schweickart, rocket pioneer Hermann Oberth, and *The High Frontier* author himself, Gerry O'Neill. The inaugural summer session would be held at MIT, with eight fields of study: space architecture, business and management, space engineering, space life sciences, space sciences, policy and law, resources and manufacturing, and satellite applications. The first lecture would be on June 27 on space resources and manufacturing by Charlie Walker of McDonnell Douglas Astronautics Co. The final discussion would be on August 16 by Roger Bonnet, head of the European Space Agency. In all, there were speaking commitments from more than one hundred visiting lecturers. Peter and Todd winnowed the hundreds of applicants to 104 and worked on getting visas for all of the international students. More than $1 million in funding came in from a mix of foundations, individuals, companies, and governmental agencies. Tuition was set at $10,000.

Peter and Todd started taking flying lessons together in Piper Cherokees. They came up with pages and pages of sketches and ideas for an array of inventions. When they went skiing together, they concluded that the resort's setup was inefficient: too much time wasted riding the ski lift, not enough time spent skiing. They sketched a new lift and slope design, with a 180-degree slanted turnaround tunneled into the mountain, leading to an elevator to pop them back to the top.

Like Peter, Todd kept a daily journal. But instead of writing the month, day, and year above entries, he wrote the number of days he had lived — by now more than nine thousand. Peter soon adopted Todd's "life-timer clock," and the two envisioned a clock they could sell that would "keep track of how many days/hours/minutes you've been alive!" They signed and dated their clock concept, with Peter on his 9,791st day and Todd on his 9,828th day. Another idea came one day while the two were having lunch at the Trident Café on Boston's Newbury Street and a waitress stumbled and dropped a tray of food. Peter proposed a food tray with an internal spinning magnetic disk. Peter jotted ideas: "This device is a gyroscope stabilizing serving tray. What is unique about this device is that it does not carry along with it a motor or battery. When the tray is placed on the counter to load the food, the magnetic disk is spun up to speed." The two devised their own written language called ALFON, derived from the UNIFON alphabet, which matched the most important sounds in the human language with a symbol.

But despite their shared creativity and passion for space, there were days when the two squabbled and disagreed, and Bob Richards had to step in to play peacemaker. Todd was the unrelenting idealist; Peter was the driven pragmatist. There were days when Peter found Todd inexplicably quiet. But there was no time to dwell on personality differences; the two had a university to launch.

A few months later, on the night of Friday, June 24, 1988, 104 graduate students from twenty-one countries gathered for the opening ceremony of the International Space University at MIT. Students from the Soviet Union stood next to American delegates, and students from the People's Republic of China shared dorms with attendees from Saudi Arabia.

After a weekend of socializing and settling into dorms, classes and lectures began early Monday morning. Students formed teams to work on the summer's chosen design project, which was to come up with blueprints for a working lunar base. They would tackle issues including transportation, surface operations, human behavior, environmental impact, and how to control machinery in real time on the Moon. Peter, Bob, and Todd bounced between classes and lectures and checked in on the lunar base teams. They hosted parties, directed faculty, and handled housing mix-ups. For the first week, there were constant questions and little sleep. Their crazy dream had come true. Peter also met people he was sure would become friends for life, including two men: Harry Kloor and Ray Cronise. Harry had earned simultaneous bachelor's degrees in physics and chemistry and intended to do the same with simultaneous PhDs in physics and chemistry. Ray was a scientist at Marshall Space Flight Center and had done countless hours aboard NASA's zero-gravity plane. Almost as impressive to Peter were the attractive women whom both Kloor and Cronise seemed to surround themselves with. The inaugural ISU summer session came to a close eight weeks later. A graduation ceremony for the class of 1988 was held on Saturday, August 20, from ten A.M. to noon at Kresge Auditorium, and featured opening remarks by David C. Webb, the eloquent trustee and early backer of both SEDS and ISU, who said, "This is about much more than a learning experience. It is a creative experience: You are creating your future. In your future lives the future of the human species."

Chancellor Arthur C. Clarke was beamed in via a double satellite bounce — courtesy of Intelsat — from his home in Sri Lanka. Uncle Arthur congratulated the students and gave credit to what he called "the gang of three: Peterbobtodd."

In his sonorous voice, Clarke said he hoped the students would continue to collaborate and create "lasting ties to foster international goodwill." He urged the graduates to go forward to "shape the destiny of many space efforts and lay the groundwork for new evolutionary and perhaps revolutionary fields." It was education and the world's first universities, Clarke noted, that moved humanity out of the Dark Ages and into the Renaissance. Clarke closed with a Chinese proverb: "To plan for a year, plant a seed; to plan for a decade, plant a tree; to plan for a century, educate the people." Peter listened and smiled. It was Uncle Arthur who had planted the seed for ISU. From their first meeting in Vienna, Clarke had talked about how political and cultural differences could be erased when there was a shared dream of space.

Finally, Peter, exhilarated and exhausted, took the stage. He said that the past eight weeks had been the most "intense and challenging" period of his life.

"It has, without a doubt, also been the most rewarding and exciting time," Peter said. "The experience has changed me in fundamental ways. Never again will I look at the many nations represented here as 'foreign.' From now on, these nations are the homes of my friends." He went on, "You attended over 240 hours of classroom lectures, typically equivalent to more than a full semester at MIT. In addition, you put about 280 hours each into the lunar design project. And you spent at least 300 hours in cross-cultural training, better known as partying."

At this, the graduates cheered.

Back at Harvard, Peter juggled the continuing demands of ISU — the next summer session was in the works, to be held in Strasbourg, France — with his return to medical school. He completed his neurology rotation, which had him on call at Mass General every third night, and required him to work seven A.M. to seven P.M. daily. He was miserable, writing in a notebook, "I have before me, in living color, all the reasons I'm not going into clinical medicine — an environment with continuous demands, little room for creativity, little monetary return, low success rate. In any event, it is not the fulltime career for me."

In late September of 1988, he finished up his OB/GYN rotation. He had participated in the delivery of twenty-two baby boys and fourteen baby girls. November and December would see him in surgery rotations, requiring him to set his alarm for 4:30 A.M. daily. He was assured by his sister, Marcelle — who had gotten married earlier in the year and was a second-year surgery resident — that he would get used to the hours. Peter didn't believe that he would get used to 4:30 A.M., and he was incredulous that his little sister was now married. He barely had time to go on a date. Marcelle often gave him a hard time about Harvard, saying he knew so little and was getting away with so much. Peter, for his part, was impressed by the academic rigor of Albany Medical School. He would say, "Thank God I'm at Harvard. It's hard to get into and harder to fail out of."

The difference was, his sister wasn't running a university on the side. And Peter piled on yet another passion-driven challenge: he was cofounding his first for-profit company, called International Microspace. The idea was to do what only the government or huge corporations had done before: launch satellites into orbit. A NASA engineer named Bob Noteboom, who had a unique ultra-low-cost multistage launch vehicle, was hired as the chief engineer, and funding came from a space lover and communications entrepreneur named Walt Anderson, who had risen from college dropout to multimillionaire, and sometimes preferred to pay people in gold bullion over cash. Anderson was a dreamer like Todd Hawley, an Ayn Rand fan, an extreme libertarian, and an early financial backer of ISU. The new company was based in Houston, home of the Johnson Space Center, and testing of their rocket engine was already under way. With each passing day, Peter's to-do list was getting longer and longer.

One of Peter's functions at ISU was chairing the curriculum committee, which met twice per year to update what was taught each summer. Peter reserved a room in the posh Harvard Club in Boston's Back Bay neighborhood to host the upcoming curriculum meeting in preparation for the 1989 Strasbourg summer session. All of the department chairs that he'd hired were confirmed, including Harvard Medical School professor Susanne Churchill, director of ISU's life sciences department; Giovanni Fazio, head of the Harvard-Smithsonian Center for Astrophysics; and Dr. Larry Young from MIT. Peter was free of medical school commitments on that particular Saturday and looked forward to the planning meetings, which often turned into semifriendly battles over which departments could secure the most lecture slots.

Then, just days before the long-planned session, Peter got unwelcome news. He was told he had psychiatry rotations on the day of the curriculum meeting. The medical school controlled his schedule, and rotations were mandatory. He was required to go from hospital to hospital, visiting psychiatric wards and meeting with patients and doctors.

He could not miss the rotations, and he could not cancel the ISU curriculum planning meeting. He considered his dilemma. He sat down and drew up a map, charting distances from the Harvard Club on Commonwealth Avenue to the area hospitals. It was only 1.7 miles from the club to Mass General, but would take about twenty minutes to walk, seventeen minutes on public transit, and under ten minutes by taxi. He did calculations for time and distance between the hospitals on his rotation and from the hospitals back to the club.

On the morning of the meeting, Peter stuffed his doctor's coat, scrubs, medical notes, and gear into his backpack. Arriving at the Harvard Club, he stashed his backpack in the bathroom. He checked in with the professors and outlined the day's agenda. As soon as the planning was up and running, with discussions about how to organize lectures, Peter slipped out of the room. He walked as fast as he could without drawing attention to himself, went into the bathroom, took off his suit, stashed it in a corner, got into his white coat, and ran out of the building. He hailed a cab and headed to the first psych ward of the day. As soon as he made sure that his resident or staff physician noticed him, he skulked out to hit the next hospital. When he couldn't find a taxi, he took off on foot, often arriving at his next destination damp with sweat. This pattern continued until late morning, when he needed to be back at the Harvard Club. After lunch, the clothing change and taxi hailing began again, making Peter feel like Clark Kent changing into Superman, only this Superman was lacking a much-needed ability to fly.

Inside the Harvard Club, Professor Susanne Churchill was unfazed by the frenetic blur of Peter Diamandis. She knew him well enough to know he rarely sat still. She wouldn't forget the night Peter phoned her at home to tell her his idea for an international graduate-level space university. She knew him as an MD student at Harvard and saw he had a burning interest in space. The two had talked about her work developing an instrumented primate model to simulate the effects of microgravity on the cardiovascular system. That night on the phone, Susanne, standing in her kitchen, listened as Peter talked about his and his colleagues' — all in their twenties —

vision for ISU. When Peter asked whether she would be the founding chair of the life sciences department, her reaction was, "Are you out of your mind?" By the end of the conversation, though, she said yes. She had found the first ISU summer session to be the most mind-expanding time of her life, watching as a gaggle of students from the Soviet Union attended with KGB minders in tow. The Berlin Wall had not yet come down, and America's communication with the other space-faring giant was closed off. She was awed, too, when Peter and crew managed to get the first Soviet physician cosmonaut, Oleg Atkov, to attend ISU, also with his KGB minder. At the end of the day — after the rush between space and medicine — after the hospital visits were done and the curriculum meeting was over, Peter sat alone in the Harvard Club. He was exhausted, and uncertain that he'd actually pulled this off. He was aware during his rotations at the psych wards that a few of the doctors were looking at him as if *he* were the one needing treatment.

A few weeks later, a letter from the dean's office showed up in Peter's student mailbox. Peter tore into it, his heart racing. He flashed to a recent surgery rotation where he had darted out of the room to take a call on his brick-sized Motorola cell phone. Bob Noteboom, his chief engineer at International Microspace, had been calling from Houston to brief him on their latest rocket-motor tests. Dan Tosteson, dean of the Harvard Medical School, wanted Peter to stop by his office. Peter held the dean in high regard. He always invited first-year students to his home for a welcoming barbecue, and was a skilled scientist in his own right. But Peter knew this gentle summons could not be good.

When the day came, Peter sat across a desk from Dean Tosteson. Pleasantries were exchanged, before the dean got right to it: "Listen, your interns and residents are telling me you're not paying attention the way you should be. I'm told you're showing up late or not showing up at all, and that you're on your phone all the time."

Peter was sure the color had drained from his face.

The dean told Peter he was concerned and wanted to know what was going on in his life. Were there financial problems? A family crisis? Was he in some sort of trouble?

Peter was suddenly back at Hamilton, feeling like his life was over because of a borrowed fetal pig. He had put in more than three out of four years of medical school. How could he *not finish* when the end was in sight? He would never be able to face his parents.

Peter exhaled. He told the dean everything:

"I'm running an international space university," he began. "I've got this rocket company in Houston, where I'm CEO. I've taken in millions of dollars of investor money and I have to make it work. And there's no way I can't finish medical school. It would devastate my family."

The dean shook his head, offered a bemused half smile, and said, "Only at the HST program." He looked at Peter for confirmation: "You're running a university, a rocket company, *and* trying to finish medical school?"

Peter nodded.

"What do you want to do?" the dean asked.

"I'm interested in medicine, but I'm really interested in putting humans in space," Peter said. "I thought getting my medical degree would make my parents happy, and it might be my avenue to space."

The dean asked, "Do you want to practice?"

"No," Peter answered honestly and sheepishly. "But I do want to finish the degree."

The dean paused. "Okay, I'll make you a deal," Tosteson said. "If you complete your rotations and can pass part two of the medical boards, I'll let you graduate."

As the two stood to leave, Tosteson looked Peter in the eyes and added, "Peter, you have to promise me one thing."

Peter nodded. "Anything."

"You have to promise me you will never practice medicine."

Peter had dedicated nine years to his college and graduate studies. The finish line was in sight, but elusive. He wrote in his journal, "Even as I spend my days at the hospital learning the healing arts, my mind and heart remain in the heavens. I know I will not practice medicine. It seems almost comical after I've come so far, but I truly hope that I have the strength of will to finish this degree." He spent three weeks studying around the clock for the board exam, resenting the time it took away from working on ISU and International Microspace.

In the weeks following the exam, Peter would run to his brass-plated mailbox to see whether the results were in. He was unable to sleep, worrying he hadn't passed. And he had other concerns: Todd Hawley had been acting erratically, often not showing up at the ISU office, other times wandering in late. Peter believed that ISU wouldn't work without Todd. But he couldn't figure out what was wrong, and Todd wasn't talking.

Finally, Peter opened the mailbox. There it was. The letter from the National Board of Medical Examiners, dated September 1989. He carefully opened it. His eyes went to the pass-fail box on the right side of the results page. There was just one word: Pass.

He stared at the piece of paper for a long time, his eyes welling with tears. He would graduate from Harvard Medical School. He was done. The passing score on the exam was 290, and he had gotten 360. His highest scores were in psychiatry — and OB/GYN. He smiled and thought, *That's for you, Dad.*

Peter was awarded his medical degree on November 21, 1989. The expression on his face that day as the dean handed him his diploma on stage was, *Really? Are you sure?*

After all of the celebrations were over, Peter — now well past his ten thousandth day on Earth — climbed into bed. He wrote in his journal: "Today is the beginning of the rest of my life. I am free, finally free, of my intellectual and emotional obligation to medicine and now my spirit and my mind focus with laser-like intensity upon the frontier of space."

8
STRUGGLES IN THE REAL WORLD

On a beautiful fall morning in 1991, Peter went to Hopewell, New Jersey, to build robots with his pal and business partner Gregg Maryniak, a director at International Microspace, on the faculty of ISU, and Peter's adopted "big brother." Peter had met Gregg almost a decade earlier, when Gregg was invited by Todd Hawley to give a talk at the 1982 SEDS meeting at George Washington University. In more recent times, Peter and Gregg got together to design and make things for the fun of it. The creative sessions in Gregg's basement workshop helped get their minds off the troubles of their satellite launch company, International Microspace.

But on this day — Saturday, October 19 — the skies were unusually clear, the weather unseasonably warm, and the rich and fiery fall palette too irresistible for Peter and Gregg to remain indoors. So they headed to the Princeton Airport, about fifteen minutes away, and rented an old Cessna 172, registration number N65827. Peter was copilot and sat in the right seat in the single-engine, four-seat, high-wing plane. It was a pilot's dream day. "CAVU all the way," Gregg said, using the aviation term for "Ceiling and Visibility Unlimited."

Gregg got the Cessna to an altitude of about 2,500 feet, flying northeast from Princeton to the mouth of Raritan Bay, and then east with Staten Island to the north and the Jersey Shore to their right. Gregg turned left to fly over the Verrazano-Narrows Bridge and continued up the Hudson River corridor. Small towns tucked in by blankets of foliage in hues of orange, red, burgundy, and green were behind them. The gray and shimmering Manhattan skyline, a mix of beauty and swagger, with buildings jammed shoulder to shoulder, was ahead. The green-cloaked lady, the Statue of Liberty, was to their left, Manhattan to their right. They flew lower than the top of the Twin Towers of the World Trade Center.

This was the most fun Peter had experienced in months, given his worries about International Microspace, which was $300,000 in debt and had no immediate source of cash. Some employees were "asked to seek alternative employment," and the board raised the possibility of filing for bankruptcy. Just when Peter was sure that his satellite company was at its bleakest hour, he would land an investor willing to put up $50,000 or $100,000, just enough money to keep the firm afloat. But how long could he keep this up?

No longer burdened by medical school, Peter had expected International Microspace to take off quickly, in ways similar to SEDS and ISU. In his mind, the goals of the satellite company were straightforward: reduce the cost of getting something to space, offer an alternative to the government monopoly, and use the low-Earth-orbit launchers as a stepping-stone to reaching the stars. But nothing in this enterprise had been simple; in fact, most everything had been tedious — and contentious. For starters, fundraising for the satellite company was harder than the launch of ISU and SEDS combined. And in stark contrast to the impassioned, idealistic space discussions that he had savored at MIT, Peter now found himself immersed in talk of legalities, contracts, licensing partners, strategic partners, vendors, customers, finance, government regulations, and valuations.

Peter tried to keep his spirits up, likening himself to Batman and Gregg to Robin, saying, "Batman is in an inescapable trap set by his archenemy. . . . Will Batman and Robin ever get out of this sticky mess? Or will it be curtains?" He told Gregg that he was confident financing was just around the corner. "I am on the line," Peter said. "This *has* to succeed."

Flying around La Guardia airspace in the Cessna, Peter and Gregg decided to take a short detour before heading back down the Hudson corridor. They wanted to fly over the Diamandises' home in Great Neck. Peter was nostalgic as he pointed out the house, with its sprawling lawn, long driveway, and nearby tennis courts. The house looked somehow different, the way an elementary school does when you go back inside as an adult.

Peter enjoyed being caught up in youthful memories, but it was tough to escape the realities of his current situation. He was no longer in the protective environment of academia, a cocoon in which he had stayed until he was almost thirty. Though he remained publicly optimistic about International Microspace, he asked himself, "What is it that continually drives me to set goals beyond my reach? Do I have what it takes to pull this off?" The tug of parental expectations remained, but it was different now. He was in the unusual position of having graduated from Harvard and then decided not to pursue what surely would have been a lucrative career in medicine. Until he succeeded in space, Harvard and what-could-have-been would hang over him. He could hear his mother's words: *Medicine is secure, space experimental.* After nearly two hours of flying,

Peter and Gregg returned to the Princeton airport. Peter, animated by the flight, told Gregg that he would get his pilot's license at last. Gregg had gotten his pilot's license at seventeen — he was now thirty-seven — and had a dozen friends who'd become pilots after flying with him. Gregg wanted to do whatever he could to get his space-loving friend aloft.

Gregg had been running the Chicago Society for Space Settlement when Todd Hawley called in 1982 to introduce him to a new student-run space group, SEDS, started at MIT. Gregg had just walked into his house in Oak Park, Illinois, and set his briefcase down when he found himself on the phone with an impassioned stranger. Todd was so fascinating, his enthusiasm so palpable, that the two ended up talking for two hours. At the time, Gregg was working as a trial lawyer, though his passion had always been for space. In Todd, Gregg met a kindred spirit — a fellow space geek who would inspire him to give up pencil pushing and focus on something he really loved.

Gregg agreed to become a senior adviser to SEDS and quickly bonded with Peter, Todd, and Bob. Three years later, in 1985, Gregg, who had been teaching orbital mechanics and dabbling in space science in his free time, officially made the leap from law to space. He went to work with scientist and author Gerry O'Neill, running the Space Studies Institute at Princeton. Gregg's wife, Maureen, joked that O'Neill had promised: "You could earn as much as *some* poets!" Gregg, involved in the founding of ISU, was now a director with Peter, Todd, and Walt Anderson in International Microspace.

Gregg's thinking around space was influenced by three books: *The Limits to Growth, The Population Bomb,* and O'Neill's *The High Frontier.* The first two books made dire predictions about unsustainable growth and an exploding population chasing after finite resources, resulting in mass starvation and societal upheaval. O'Neill agreed in *The High Frontier* that Earth's resources were limited and that a population explosion was inevitable. But his book provided an exit strategy and a path to sustainability. Well known as a physicist before he became an author, O'Neill detailed in his 1977 book the coming age of space settlements and the limitless and valuable energy and materials of space. O'Neill wrote, "The concept of the humanization of space can stand on its own merits, survive detailed numerical checks, and survive logical debate. To support it requires no act of faith, only the willingness to study unfamiliar ideas with an open mind." The book was for many the first to articulate a path for a private-sector push into space, without the government's help. For Gregg, *The High Frontier* was an awakening. It was an antidote to doomsday scenarios — positive, pragmatic, and egalitarian. Working as a trial lawyer had been about who got what piece of a finite pie. As Gregg saw it, O'Neill was trying to expand thinking and expand resources. He wanted to make more pie.

Gregg believed that humanity was capable of addressing its challenges. The nonprofit Space Studies Institute at Princeton was established to realize the vision and concepts of *The High Frontier.* The institute held space manufacturing conferences and inspired students to build equipment for space, including mass drivers to catapult materials off the Moon for colonization of space. The prototype mass drivers, with electromagnetic drive coils and a payload container, were made at Princeton and MIT.[*]

Now, in late 1991, with a recession and high oil prices in the wake of Iraq's invasion of Kuwait the summer before, Gregg and Peter talked almost daily about the financial challenges of International Microspace,

[*]O'Neill invented the storage ring technique for particle colliders, which led to the building of the Stanford Linear Accelerator Center. He also invented a mass driver to move materials mined on the Moon into Earth orbit.

which had been relocated from Houston to Washington, D.C. Houston was where NASA's human launch systems were based; the Washington area was where satellite companies were finding financing.

Gregg knew better than anyone how Peter was struggling with International Microspace. Gregg felt that his role in the business was to be the steady force, the constant source of calm. If International Microspace was the starship *Enterprise,* Peter was the Captain Kirk, and Gregg was his Mr. Spock. More and more, Gregg was becoming concerned about his younger friend, who put a lot of pressure on himself — and who was about to face some very tough decisions.

Peter prepared for a private social meeting at his home in Rockville, Maryland — but in the back of his mind, he knew it was part of a mission to rescue International Microspace. He also realized that this strategy could come back to haunt him on a personal level, but there was no choice: the company's very survival was in question.

Already, Peter had met with potential investors across the globe. He had even approached a group he referred to lovingly as the "Greek Mafia," his parents and twelve of their friends. At this point, his satellite launch company had several failed rocket firing tests and was now building a small launcher of a new design to take one-hundred-pound payloads — experiments, signaling, imaging, whatever the customer wanted — to low-Earth orbit.

Peter likened the company's trajectory to a staging rocket: it had let go of its original unneeded weight and ignited new engines. The company had new designs, new management, and a new board of directors that included the last man to set foot on the Moon — Gene Cernan — and Andy Stofan, former director of launch vehicles at NASA and former associate administrator for the space station. Peter had pulled in $10 million in financing. Even the name of the rocket had changed from the Galt vehicle — after John Galt in *Atlas Shrugged* — to Orbital Express.

But International Microspace couldn't add to its momentum and was struggling to meet payroll. One major reason for this standstill was that investor Walt Anderson was vehemently libertarian and antigovernment, describing himself as a "pretty rampant pacifist." Walt had contributed about $80,000 to finance ISU and put $100,000 into founding International Microspace. As a condition of Walt's early backing, Peter was not to pitch anyone with government ties. This had turned out to be a major impediment: the few private companies that had done small launchers were now a part of governmental agencies or relied on government contracts.

■ ■ ■ ■

The most successful of the companies, the darling of the private launch business, was Orbital Sciences, started by MIT and Harvard business school graduates. Their rocket, the Pegasus, was designed by former MIT professor Antonio Elias, who as a boy growing up in Spain loved nothing more than to search the sky for planes. The Pegasus, built to carry payloads of up to one thousand pounds to low-Earth orbit, was modeled after some of the X-series planes and the McDonnell Douglas F-15 Eagle fighter jet. It was air-launched horizontally from a NASA B-52 aircraft at 40,000 feet before engines ignited and shot it toward space. On April 5, 1990, Pegasus made history as the first privately developed, all-new space launch vehicle. Its first customer was DARPA, the Defense Advanced Research Projects Agency of the U.S. military. The rocket's delta wings, fins, and wing-body fairing were designed by Burt Rutan of *Voyager* fame, in Mojave. Rutan, who decades earlier had spent several months working on the F-15 Eagle, was impressed with the air-launched system. He saw how relatively inexpensive and flexible it could be in delivering payloads to the start of space.

Now, on this day in 1991, Peter was hoping that International Microspace could tap into the government's considerable payload of money. He had scheduled a social meeting with a man he considered a friend, yet someone whom Walt Anderson would consider the devil himself. The friend was Pete Worden, the newly appointed head of technology for SDI, the Strategic Defense Initiative, otherwise known as "Star Wars," the program begun in 1983 under President Reagan to build a new missile defense system.

Worden was an astrophysicist and a straight-talking Air Force colonel who had enough clout to be hired by NASA even after criticizing the agency as a "self-licking ice cream cone" and saying the name meant "Never A Straight Answer." Worden and Peter had met in the late 1980s, when Peter was running ISU and Worden was working as director of new initiatives in the White House's National Space Council. At the time, Worden had no money to offer — only contacts. These days, though, Worden had a multibillion-dollar budget at his discretion. And he was a believer in the need for small, low-cost satellites.

After Worden arrived at Peter's home, they had a long and winding discussion about humanity's expansion into space. Worden was no longer a fan of the space shuttle, saying it had been "an interesting experiment that didn't work." It didn't allow man to go back to the Moon or on to Mars, and it failed in its primary mission of providing routine and affordable access to space.

Soon, Worden and Peter agreed to set up a follow-up meeting about International Microspace. That face-to-face occurred in Worden's office in Washington. The discussion ranged from the space shuttle to Brilliant Pebbles, a program under design that would send a swarm of small and smart satellites into orbit to be used as a missile defense. Peter and Worden both concluded that there needed to be a vibrant private sector, but one that involved the government. "You build the equipment and work from the outside, and I'll work from the inside," Worden told Peter. By the time the meeting ended, Worden made it clear that if International Microspace had a viable vehicle that ideally was "somewhat cheaper than Pegasus," then the "government has a good reason to support a second supplier." Peter walked away confident that he had a deal. It was great news — salvation for the company — but was it selling out?

Predictably, when Walt, then chairman, learned of Peter's likely deal with Worden, he blew up and announced he wanted out. He told Peter and members of the board that he would sell back his shares at fifty cents to the dollar — getting $50,000 on his $100,000 investment — in order not to be involved. He said he never wanted his name associated with the company again, and never wanted anything to do with Peter Diamandis. This was not the starry-eyed Peter he had met and admired. Now Walt labeled him a "liar" and worse. Todd Hawley, another idealist, had an equally strong but more personal reaction.

Todd sent Peter a six-page handwritten letter that began "I am as <u>DISTRESSED</u> now with my own role in [International Microspace] as I am with your drive to succeed at all costs. I fear that you're now set to create another incremental institution that won't ultimately change much. The present company vision and approach is so much like the old guard that it essentially is all but another, small cousin of existing giants. Nowhere is a radical new approach in sight." While Todd acknowledged that Peter was leading the company to a "place of possible profit," the final product would be diluted at best. "The countless hours of unusually driven, visionary and idealistic people will never show up on the bottom line. I believe you've abandoned any and all of our non-economic objectives." The letter was signed, "Sincerely, Todd."

The words — and final signoff — stung. Peter's friends were saying that he had sold his soul. It wasn't lost on him that the founders' original vision, hatched over coffee-and-excitement-fueled all-nighters, had been severely diluted. Their dream was to unleash rapid experimentation in space, sending out hundreds of private Sputniks. But Peter was responsible to the shareholders. Without this deal with Worden, which was moving forward fast, they had nothing. Peter knew this decision was pragmatism over passion. It was Harvard Medical School over MIT. It was the real world over academia.

Peter sat down several times to write Todd a letter, taking more than a month to get his thoughts straight. He finally wrote: "Since January 6th of 1982, some 9 years, 2 months (3,344 days), since we first met, we have shared emotions, triumphs, experiences, adventures and challenges like no one else I know. I feel safe in saying that we have spent the highlight of our lifetimes together, side by side. I love you as a brother and respect you as a colleague — together we have accomplished many great things. From the moment we met, I knew that our energy and vision would enable the development of space. I have been greatly saddened that our friendship has drifted apart. I speak here of friendship — not business or work relationships. Todd, it *is* okay to disagree, to hold differences in opinion, to learn from each other. I want to put the time and energy into something very valuable to me — our friendship. With love, your brother, Peter."

Gregg saw the situation from both sides, but in the end stood by Peter. It was Peter who had thrown everything he had into trying to make the company successful, asking family, friends, former professors, colleagues, fraternity brothers, and astronauts to invest. He traveled the world pitching any investors who would listen. He had nearly moved the company to Alaska after being wooed by the governor to settle the company in Poker Flat, north of Fairbanks. Gregg saw Peter and Todd as the "Damon and Pythias of space," referring to the ancient Greek story of friendship, where two men are each willing to risk their lives to save the other. On other days, when Peter and Todd were feuding or refusing to speak, Gregg would tell them: "Quit this bullshit. You have one of the most amazing friendships I've ever seen."

But for months, even after Peter's letter, Todd was silent.

Finally, happily for Peter, the silence ended. Todd wanted to meet Peter at the Deli Haus near MIT. On the appointed afternoon, the two found a booth and settled in. Peter was relieved to see his friend, but Todd was somber and said he had some news to share. Peter assumed it was about International Microspace. He had thought about what he wanted to say. But as he sat sipping his coffee, Peter could feel something else was going on. Todd looked away, avoiding eye contact. He moved his plate, picked up his silverware and put it back down again. He looked at Peter, frowned slightly, and said it: "I've been diagnosed with AIDS."

Peter was physically jolted back in his seat. He looked at Todd and for a moment said nothing. He closed his eyes. Peter had known that Todd was gay for some time now, though for years Todd was closeted, bringing his "girlfriend" MaryAnn to events and on trips. When Todd first told him he was gay, Peter had reacted negatively. He didn't know how to handle the news, was homophobic — he and Todd were always sleeping at each other's homes — and he shut Todd out. Peter realized months later that he was being an idiot, called Todd, and told him he loved him unconditionally. Now, in the Deli Haus, with loud music playing and dishes and silverware rattling, Peter fought back tears. He had treated AIDS patients at Mass General. AIDS was a death sentence. Since the early 1980s, about a hundred thousand people — mostly young men ages twenty-five to forty-five — had succumbed to AIDS. Magic Johnson had just told the world that he was HIV positive. There were one million confirmed cases of HIV infection in the United States. These men were emaciated, pockmarked, and unfairly ostracized. Todd was brilliant, handsome, and full of life.

Peter collected himself and vowed to find Todd the best treatment possible. His childhood friend and rocket-making buddy Billy

Greenberg, now a doctor, was involved in an experimental AIDS treatment. Peter would contact him. The anti-HIV drug AZT was on the market. Todd listened to Peter and smiled slightly. As the moments passed, the two found a way back to laughter, recalling the meetings where they were in way over their heads but acted so cool and confident. They marveled at how they had talked brilliant professors into working for them, and how they had brought together like-minded people from across the globe at a time when personal computers didn't exist and electronic mail was not yet conceived. Through Todd's insistence, they had gotten America's putative enemy — the Soviets — to attend their university before the Cold War's end. It was Todd who had said, "We're not excluding fifty percent of the space-faring part of Earth because Americans have a phobia about Russians." Todd asked Peter whether he remembered the day they got the call from their bank, and were sure they'd be told they were overdrawn. Todd reluctantly took the call. The banker said, "Mr. Hawley, I want to let you know the international wire transfer you expected has come in." Todd perked up and asked whether it was from Spain or Sweden. The man responded, "It's from the USSR Ministry of Education — for $120,000." Todd nearly fell out of his chair. The Soviets were sending twelve students to the first ISU summer session. Cash from the Cold War villains saved ISU!

After a few hours at the Deli Haus, Peter and Todd hugged good-bye. Peter promised to support him in whatever ways he could. He told Todd that he loved him: "You are strong. You will persevere."

That night, Peter wrote in his journal, "Like a superconducting magnet, this news has brought us back together."

It was a beautiful fall day in 1993 when Gregg was in New Hope, Pennsylvania, on the Delaware River just west of Princeton. He and his family, spending the day there relaxing, wandered into a bookstore. Gregg was soothed by the filtered light and sense of quiet, like sitting in a church pew on a weekday afternoon. He meandered through the shop, and stopped when he accidentally kicked a book left on the floor. He picked it up and dusted it off. It was like an old friend to Gregg: *The Spirit of St. Louis* by Charles Lindbergh. Gregg was fourteen when he read Lindbergh's story of his dangerous, history-changing flight from New York to Paris.

Gregg opened the book to an earmarked page. He smiled as he read the words, "Suppose I really could stay up here flying; suppose gasoline didn't weigh so much and I could put enough in the tanks to last for days. Suppose, like the man on the magic carpet, I could fly anywhere I wanted to — anywhere in the world." A few pages later, Lindbergh wrote of how he considered making the transatlantic feat, something no one had ever done. "Why shouldn't I fly from New York to Paris? I'm almost twenty-five. I have more than four years of aviation behind me, and close to two thousand hours in the air." A few paragraphs down, the aviator wrote, "The important thing is to start; to lay a plan, and then to follow it step by step no matter how small or large each one by itself may seem." Lindbergh knew he didn't have enough money to buy the right plane for the trip. He considered raising money. He wrote of a tantalizing prize that had been offered to the first person who could make the treacherous journey: "Then there's the Orteig prize of $25,000 for the first man to fly from New York to Paris nonstop — that's more than enough to pay for a plane and all the expenses of the flight. New York to Paris nonstop! If airplanes can do that, there's no limit to aviation's future." Lindbergh was right, Gregg thought. He changed the world's mind about air travel, seeing a future that others didn't see. Before Lindbergh flew, Americans were afraid to fly. After he landed in Paris, the world wanted to fly. In 1929, nearly 170,000 paying passengers boarded U.S. airliners, nearly three times the 60,000 that had flown the previous year.

At the bookstore cash register, Gregg's daughter asked why he was buying a book he already had. "It's for your uncle Peter," he said. Gregg hoped the book would inspire Peter to finally get his pilot's license. More than that, he hoped it would remind Peter of the importance of impossible dreams.

9
MEETING THE MAGICIAN

Looking out the window of the plane, Peter saw carless roads and grids of streets for development that had never been developed, all on a flat stretched canvas of beige and sand. His eyes followed an empty railroad line running through the desert, with a sprinkling of arthritic-looking trees on either side. A gaping crater turned out to be the Mountain Pass rare-earth mine. As Peter's plane descended toward runway 30 of the Mojave Airport, he took in the bleached hangars to the left and what looked like a plane boneyard to the right. Mojave was a place where planes were born; Peter hadn't known it was also a place where some old birds came to die.

After the plane taxied to a smooth stop, Peter climbed out to get the lay of the land. The peaks and slopes of the mountains to the west and south gave the lapis-blue sky a jagged border. Heat radiated up from the runway. It was not exactly John F. Kennedy

International. The only signs of life were a handful of crows stationed above the Voyager restaurant, and a tortoise that tucked its head into its shell, camouflaged by rocks and burrow-weed. Peter half expected Gary Cooper to appear as a sheriff facing off against four killers in the Mojave version of *High Noon. We are in the middle of nowhere,* Peter thought.

Desperate to escape the corporate drudgery of International Microspace, Peter had co-founded another new venture in 1993 called Angel Technologies, which sought to jump on the nascent and restless commercialized Internet, opened only a few years earlier to the public domain from the academic and scientific community's ARPANET.[*] Peter

[*] The ARPANET was the first packet-switched network. Packet-switched networks were the work of many hands: Leonard Kleinrock (UCLA) and Paul Baran (RAND), as well as Bob Kahn (DARPA), who is related to futurist and nuclear strategist Herman Kahn, and Vint Cerf, who connected with Kleinrock at UCLA, worked with Kahn at DARPA, and works at Google. ARPANET was all about breaking down messages into little self-contained packets like postcards that have a "from" and "to" address and can shuttle through a hetero-geneous network of cooperating computers. As long as all the computers share enough information about what the "from" and "to" addresses mean,

and his Angel business partner, Marc Arnold, wanted to provide low-cost, high-speed Internet access to the developed and developing world. Instead of laying cables underwater, under roads, or on telephone poles, their plan called for a faster, cheaper alternative. They wanted to deliver broadband from above the stratosphere.

Peter had been introduced to Marc through their mutual friend David Wine, the ISU supporter who had invested in International Microspace. Marc had made his money by selling a hospital services company to Smith Barney in 1991. After the sale, he pursued soaring (also known as gliding) as a sport, buying a Stemme sailplane and becoming the North American dealer for the plane. His love of soaring led to his interest in high-altitude projects.

Peter and Marc's Angel Technologies plan had competition. Cable operators, software companies, and start-ups were looking at a range of broadband delivery methods, from launching hundreds of satellites to using low-voltage electricity grids. A company called

---

they can forward the little packets to their eventual destination. It's a robust and organic process. There is no center, no controller, and no simple point of failure. A truly brilliant technology that completely changed the world.

Sky Station International, a project of former secretary of state Alexander Haig, envisioned beaming Internet service to cities using football field–size balloons hovering in the sky. Marc and Peter's plan was to send solar-powered, high-altitude airplanes to circle above populated areas at 61,000 feet to provide news, entertainment, and information. The vehicle's name, HALO, stood for "high altitude, long operation," but it was also intended to evoke positive feelings as customers looked up and saw their planes flying in circles, leaving halo-shaped contrails of water vapor.

Before they could go further with their venture, Marc and Peter needed a plane that would be able to do routine operations at high altitude. They needed a world-class engineer, an original thinker and a dreamer. There was only one person for the job — Burt Rutan.

Rutan emerged from his office, looking as tall as a cactus, dressed in denim, with sideburns shaped like Idaho, and grinning ear to ear. Burt stood six feet four, making Peter — at five feet five inches tall — feel dwarfed. After exchanging brief hellos on the runway, Peter, Marc, and Burt made small talk around Marc's plane, a twin-engine turboprop Cessna 421 Conquest. Nearby were a few Pipers, Beechcraft, and another Cessna. The plane graveyard across the way was apparently where aircraft were retired, dismantled, and recycled. The planes resembled giant beached whales that had been pushed up and onto a sandy beach from all directions. Locals sometimes heard explosions and artillery fire coming from the boneyard in the early morning hours — the military occasionally used the planes for hostage rescue simulations.

The three men walked into Scaled Composites, which was a collection of buildings and hangars in various states of upgrade, looking out onto the flight line. Inside the main entrance were pictures of Burt's planes and his many awards. Peter marveled at the range, from the homebuilt planes and an AD-1 with its pivoting wing à la Robert Jones, to the Grizzly, built for camping and landing in meadows, and the Solitaire, a self-launching sailplane. Hanging upside down from the rafters was the Catbird, first flown in 1988. Burt's brother Dick had recently broken a world speed record in the light aircraft, flying a 1,243-mile-long course at 246 miles per hour. Some parts of the shop were curtained off so visitors couldn't see what was under development. Not far away were several delta wings for Orbital Sciences' Pegasus rocket. Peter could have spent hours just talking about the development of those wings.

Burt's reputation as an aviation concept designer was well established, but he was also becoming an innovator in the rarefied air high above the clouds. Peter had talked on the phone with Burt once before, about potential launch vehicles for International Microspace. He knew of Burt's remarkable design of the *Voyager.* Peter was also following the progress of the DC-X, the Delta Clipper Experimental, a vertical-takeoff, vertical-landing reusable "rocket for the people," being funded by the Department of Defense and supervised by Pete Worden. Burt and the crew at Scaled Composites had built the DC-X's aero-shell.

After the tour of Burt's planes, Marc, Peter, and Burt headed into a conference room. Before the Angel Technologies presentation began, Peter talked about his lifelong goal of getting launched into orbit. Burt listened and thought, *This guy is a true space geek.*

"Diamandis," Burt said abruptly, "since you're such a space nut, tell me the rockets used for the first four manned space programs."

Burt's tone had shifted — from playful to needling — faster than the sand moved on the dusty Mojave runway. But Peter began ticking off the answer: "Mercury, Gemini, Apollo . . ."

"No, no! Wrong!" Burt said, seeming to delight in Peter's error. "Gagarin was first with Vostok." Peter knew that, of course, but thought Burt had been talking about the U.S. space program.

Burt asked, "What was next?"

"Mercury," Peter replied.

Burt shook his head, almost triumphantly. A heavy silence filled the room.

"Redstone! Redstone 3 was the second one," Burt exclaimed. "I'm not talking about the capsules! I'm talking about the rockets! What was the third?"

Peter hadn't felt this intimidated since transferring from Hamilton to MIT.

"Gemini," Peter said.

"No, the third was Atlas, for John Glenn's flight!"

Peter looked at Marc, who kept quiet. Burt was clearly enjoying this. Peter knew the space program as well as anyone, but Burt was looking for *his* answer.

"I could be in a room with so-called NASA historians and no one could answer this," Burt said. "What was the fourth one?"

Peter wondered whether he should even try to respond.

Burt answered for him: "The fourth one was the X-15. Fifth was the Titan II for Gemini. Sixth was the Russian Soyuz. Seventh was Saturn 1B (Apollo 7). Eighth was Saturn V." When the impromptu exam was over — and none too soon for Peter — it was time for the three men to address the challenge at hand: getting an unmanned solar-powered plane to the mesosphere.

Peter and Marc felt like evangelists for

something potentially great, something that could democratize access to information — and maybe even teach an industry how to do its job better. Marc took the lead, going through a slide presentation on Angel Technologies. Marc itemized what he and Peter were looking for in a high-altitude plane: It would need to carry 1,800 pounds and have an eighteen-foot-diameter antenna pod facing downward. It would need a level payload antenna while the plane was in a seventeen-degree bank, and require liquid payload cooling. Under Marc and Peter's plan, the solar-powered plane would transmit high-speed Internet service — phone, video, information — to customers with cone-shaped antennas on their roofs, creating what they called a "cone of commerce."

Peter listened to Marc and watched Burt, who was either sketching an idea, doodling, or taking notes — Peter could not be sure which. The three then discussed unmanned aerial flight and solar-powered flight. The discussion turned to the engineer Paul Mac-Cready, the father of solar-powered flight who had earlier won several Kremer prizes for innovations in human-powered flight.*

* Named for British industrialist Henry Kremer, who was instrumental in the commercial development of construction materials, including plywood, chipboard, and fiberglass.

MacCready's winning planes included the lightweight *Gossamer Condor,* which became the first human-powered aircraft to do a figure eight over a closed course; the *Gossamer Albatross,* flown human-powered from England to France; and the "bionic bat," which set a human-powered air-speed record. MacCready's early breakthroughs in human-powered flight came in part from studying the low-energy mechanics of birds in flight, measuring time, bank angle, and turning radius for the fun of it. Burt and MacCready were friends, attended many meetings together, but had never formally worked on a project together. MacCready had a concept for a plane to go after the around-the-world record if the *Voyager* failed, and had sent a photo of himself with no hair and the note: "If Rutan Flies Around the World, I'll Shave My Head!"*

After the *Voyager* succeeded, MacCready showed Burt drawings of his plane design. He said there was no value in building it now that the around-the-world milestone had been reached. Instead, MacCready's company, AeroVironment, focused on building the remote-controlled, solar-powered *Pathfinder,* being readied to fly to 50,000 feet,

* The photo showed MacCready, smiling, with no hair. The hair loss, though, was due to chemotherapy treatments.

and the *Helios,* a 247-foot-long solar electric wing under development for NASA. Peter and Marc were banking on the idea that similar solar-powered technology could benefit their project.

In the conference room, Burt was excited by their high-altitude broadband idea, even if he doubted whether a solar-powered vehicle would work for this purpose. But Burt didn't express these misgivings, and he told Peter and Marc that he would begin sketching designs.

Talk turned to Burt's service on the U.S. Air Force Scientific Advisory Board, a short-term position that gave the home builder from Mojave a Pentagon badge and the power to make recommendations on what the Air Force should do following the cancellation of a program called the Orient Express. Announced by President Reagan in his 1986 State of the Union address, the program promised a "new Orient Express" — the X-30 space plane — that could fly into low-Earth orbit at 17,000 miles per hour. But the space plane was shelved as technologically unfeasible. By way of response — and out of his own frustration with government-run space programs — Burt had started a file he called "Logic Gone Amok." It said, in essence, "Okay, you don't have the guts to do the Orient Express. I propose for the next ten to twelve years that NASA should cut its budget in half," and reserve the other half — seven billion dollars — for a single prize to be given to anyone who can design, build, and fly a spaceship that had Orient Express capabilities. Burt explained, "My logic was, if this was really impossible, the government spends nothing. If it is possible, it's a win-win."

Peter loved the story. He told Burt an abbreviated version of his loving-NASA leaving-NASA tale. Peter said that when he started realizing that NASA was not going to be the one to get him to space, he began to think of his medical degree in a different light. He wanted to better understand human longevity. He believed he needed to invent something in the field of life extension to get beyond the 122-year maximum for a human. He had hoped that Harvard Medical School might give him just the advantage to figure out how to live long enough to reach space.

After Peter and Marc left, Burt scratched his head. *This space geek earned two degrees from MIT and graduated from Harvard Medical School, with no intention of practicing medicine?* Burt wondered, *Who would go through all the shit of medical school and not become a doctor?*

On the flight home, Marc and Peter couldn't help but talk about the charismatic and enigmatic Burt Rutan. They wondered whether he'd even been listening. Peter had a sense that Burt was above all an artist, a modern-day da Vinci. Burt was the type who would get involved *if* he found a project challenging and *if* he could do something entirely new. Marc and Peter both wondered what they would see when they returned to Mojave for the concept presentation.

Marc and Peter also discussed the Kremer prize; they hadn't known that MacCready had gone after it for practical reasons: he owed $100,000 to the bank after guaranteeing a loan for a relative's business that failed. Burt said it dawned on MacCready that the Kremer prize, at 50,000 pounds, came out almost exactly to $100,000. While the winning of the prize was important to MacCready — allowing him to pay off his debt — the innovations that followed proved even more significant.

Marc told Peter that he and a friend had put up $250,000 to start the Feynman Prize in Nanotechnology. The prize was run through the Foresight Institute, and was an incentive award to be given to the first person who could design and build two nanotechnology devices, a nanoscale robotic arm and a computing device that could demonstrate the feasibility of building a nanotechnology computer. Marc said the catalyst for the prize came from reading the book *Engines of*

Creation: The Coming Era of Nanotechnology, by Eric Drexler.

Peter's head was swimming with ideas, impressions, and memories. As Marc talked about *Engines of Creation,* Peter remembered how it was Drexler who stood at the back of the student center at MIT in 1980 when he launched Students for the Exploration and Development of Space. Drexler spoke up at that meeting to say SEDS should remain independent from the L5 space organization, despite some urging to the contrary. Peter hoped to one day thank Drexler for his vote of confidence in SEDS.

As they continued the flight back east, Peter talked of Gerry O'Neill's passing. He had died at age sixty-five on April 27, 1992, seven years after being diagnosed with leukemia. Peter attended O'Neill's memorial on May 26, with Gregg Maryniak and the "GKO extended family," as followers of Gerry K. O'Neill were known. Peter viewed O'Neill's life as both inspiration and cautionary tale. Just as there was incredible work accomplished — and so many people inspired — there were revolutionary scientific projects that O'Neill dreamed of that were never realized.

Peter now had two ambitious companies running — International Microspace and Angel Technologies — and a third under development called Zero Gravity Corporation (ZERO-G). He was working with Byron Lichtenberg and ISU alumnus Ray Cronise on a plan to give civilians the experience of weightlessness using a modified Boeing 727–200 airplane. Still, Peter hadn't been sleeping much, feeling increasingly antsy that he wasn't getting enough done. He created a two-page contract with himself, listing his strengths, weaknesses, and goals. He wrote about ways he needed to improve himself: consolidate his entrepreneurial efforts, strengthen his piloting skills, put a stop to being a nail biter, commit himself to a regular workout routine, and find a soul mate. He was thirty-two years old: his life clock was ticking.

10
AN OUT-OF-THIS-WORLD IDEA

Visiting his parents' retirement home in Boca Raton, Florida, for the Christmas holidays, Peter sat down and began reading the dog-eared copy of *The Spirit of St. Louis* that Gregg Maryniak had given him the year before. The book was filled with revelations. Peter had always assumed that Charles Lindbergh crossed the Atlantic in 1927 as a stunt, or maybe a dare. He'd had no idea that Lindbergh had made the first-ever flight from New York to Paris *to win a prize.*

As it turned out, Lindbergh was one of nine pilots who competed for the $25,000 Orteig Prize, named after its benefactor Raymond Orteig. The competition was riddled with drama, casualties, and deaths, as some of the world's top pilots and newest planes were lost to the cold expanse of the North Atlantic. *The New York Times* labeled it "the greatest sporting event of the age," and the public took to calling it "the world's greatest air derby." The barriers were both psychological and technical: The distance of 3,600 miles from Paris to New York was almost twice the distance that had been previously covered by an airplane on a single flight.

The successful flight not only made airmail pilot Charles Lindbergh famous, but it also created a global perception that flight was safe and available to the common man. Lindbergh was, after all, an Everyman-turned-Superman story: he dropped out of college to pursue his dream of aviation and then used his own engineering skills to get off the ground. He embodied the belief that adventure is essential to civilization, and that risk reaps rewards.

In between feasts of Greek food at his parents' house, Peter underlined passages and wrote notes in the margins of the book. Raymond Orteig, who grew up a shepherd in Louvie-Juzon, France, on the slopes of the Pyrenees, had immigrated to America as an adolescent and found work as a busboy in the restaurant of the Hotel Martin in mid-town Manhattan. Within a decade, he was café manager, then hotel manager, and eventually, with money saved, he purchased the hotel and later another. In the years following World War I, French airmen often stayed at Orteig's hotels. He loved to hear the stories of aerial combat and developed a passion for aviation and a deep respect for the airmen. On May 22, 1919, Orteig sent a letter to president Alan Hawley of the Aero Club of America in New York City:

> Gentlemen, as a stimulus to courageous aviators, I desire to offer, through the auspices and regulations of the Aero Club of America, a prize of $25,000 to the first aviator of any Allied country crossing the Atlantic in one flight from Paris to New York or New York to Paris, all other details in your care.

The prize would be offered for a period of five years, which came and went without anyone claiming it. Orteig was unfazed and renewed the offer for another five years. Peter calculated that the nine teams competing for $25,000 had spent around $400,000 — sixteen times the value of the cash prize. "Orteig didn't spend one cent backing the losers," an amazed Peter wrote in the margin of his book. "By using incentives, he automatically backed the winner . . . great return on his money. Sixteen times the purse prize."

When Peter finished the book in December 1993, he saw something that he felt had been staring him in the face for a long time. *A space prize.*

The idea of prizes and competitions was not new to Peter. He had talked with Gregg Maryniak and Pete Worden about the potential of prizes and had studied other incentive prize competitions. He had read about the longitude prize of 1714, when the British Parliament offered 20,000 pounds for the discovery of a way for ships to ascertain longitude. Nearly a century later, Napoleon and his ministers, searching for a way to end scurvy and feed troops, had offered a prize of 12,000 francs for a simple invention that could preserve food. In addition to the Orteig Prize, there were dozens of other early aviation prizes, given for everything from staying aloft for fifteen minutes straight to being the first pilot to cross the English Channel.

While the notion of a space prize seemed like the natural next step, Peter didn't know what such an award would look like or how much the winnings would be. But he was already thinking that the goal of the competition would be suborbital rather than orbital, because orbital was so much more difficult to achieve. It would be a big first step.

Peter girded himself in his seat as the small turboprop plane rattled and jolted its way from Stapleton Airport in Denver to the town of Montrose about an hour away. The wind gusted at 35 miles per hour, and visibility was less than five miles. A thick mixture of fog and snow churned in the darkness on the other side of the plane's cold windows. Peter had organized a three-night, four-day "build a rocket" brainstorming retreat for rocket scientists and space lovers at a friend's private home near Montrose in February 1994. The log "cabin" where they were meeting had 16,000 square feet, eight bedrooms, 7.5 baths, an indoor pool, and meeting rooms with high ceilings, arched wooden beams, chandeliers, and large stone fireplaces. The home was not far from Telluride and — more important — close to Ouray, Colorado, also known as "Galt's Gulch," the mystical and secluded valley of *Atlas Shrugged,* where John Galt and the "men of the mind" went on strike to safeguard rational self-interest.

The goal of the Montrose gathering was to see whether a dozen men and women meeting over a weekend could hatch a new breed of rocket, finding inspiration in the improbable beginnings of many great companies: Harley-Davidson, Walt Disney, Hewlett-Packard, Apple, and Microsoft were conceived in garages or sheds. Likewise, engineers and pilots, not governments, had started the aviation industry. A space lover named Jeff Bezos — who had served as president of the SEDS chapter at Princeton while a student there — was reportedly starting a book company from his house to capitalize on the next big thing — the Internet.

David and Myra Wine, who owned the outsized shack in the woods in Montrose, hoped that whatever prototype was dreamed up could be built in their backyard. David and Myra had met in Daytona Beach in 1969 during the Apollo days, when Myra was working for a NASA program. David was a founder of Geostar, the satellite company based on the invention patented by Gerry O'Neill. David had been weeks away from flying three of his Geostar satellites on the space shuttle when the *Challenger* disaster happened, grounding all flying. David and Myra always told their friends, "We are spacey people."

As the shaky turboprop made its descent into Montrose, Peter tried to ignore the turbulence and focus on the meeting ahead. His goal going into the weekend was nothing less than to come up with a new rocket design that would take paying passengers to space. But he had another idea, too, one he had been studying in stealth mode.

On day one of the meeting, after a big breakfast made by Myra, after travel war stories were exchanged, the group gathered in the conference room. Peter, wearing black pants and a thick black turtleneck, wrote on the whiteboard: "SMALL TEAMS CAN DO BIG THINGS."

It was something he needed to believe in now more than ever. Like a projectile veering off course, Peter had landed in unfamiliar terrain. He had managed to sell his beleaguered International Microspace to CTA of Rockville, Maryland, which designed and manufactured satellites and made software and hardware for ground- and space-based systems. CTA bought International Microspace because of the deal that Peter forged with Pete Worden. Although the Defense Department deal was valued at $100 million for ten launches, relatively little cash was handed over up front. The money would be paid when satellites were ready to launch, something that was appearing less and less likely. Peter had scrambled to keep the company one step ahead of bankruptcy, but he now found himself doing something he never wanted — climbing a corporate ladder as a midlevel executive at CTA. He was going on thirty-three and in a job that wasn't for him. He needed to get back to his scrappy roots — of launching SEDS and ISU, of designing, building, and testing out gravity-defying ideas in the Man Vehicle Lab.

The Montrose attendees began discussing how to build a new rocket for space travel. Peter's friend Byron Lichtenberg, the astronaut, said he thought it was time to "prove that this work can be done by someone other than NASA." The year before, he, Peter, and Ray Cronise had started ZERO-G, with the bold goal of taking paying passengers on parabolic flights using the modified Boeing airplane. They had raised a few hundred thousand dollars from two adventure-investors, Mike McDowell, who had run tourist operations to the North and South poles, and Richard Garriott, better known as "Lord British" in the video game world, and son of Skylab and space shuttle astronaut Owen Garriott. If approved by the Federal Aviation Administration, ZERO-G would be the first private company to offer nonastronauts the chance to experience weightlessness.

Peter, in introducing everyone, noted that Byron had now flown more than three hundred orbits, logging 468 hours — nearly twenty days — in space. Colette Bevis, seated nearby, had headed marketing for Society Expeditions, a company trying to break into commercial space. Across the table was Gary Hudson, a college dropout who had taught launch vehicle design at Stanford, and was an entrepreneur who had been pushing for private spaceflight development since 1969, when he was nineteen. He just wanted to build and ride in a reusable spaceship, preferably one that did both vertical takeoffs and vertical landings. David Wine had known Peter since the early ISU days and was an investor in International Microspace. Wine had been in talks with Burt Rutan about moving Scaled Composites from the Mojave Desert to Montrose. Engineer Dan DeLong worked full time for Boeing and had been a subcontractor for NASA, doing the air and water recycling systems for the space station. De-

Long was still in high school when he built his first submarine, electric bicycle, and a tape recorder out of a first-generation computer. Since then, he had a habit of walking away from perfectly good high-paying jobs to join experimental space start-ups. His problem with NASA was that it spent $17 billion a year and "didn't do much." He was working on a NASA contract in January 1986 when the *Challenger* broke up. Within an hour, he knew what the problem was, because he had designed thousands of O-rings and seals. He learned that on the night before the launch, as well as early the next morning, engineers had urged NASA not to launch in temperatures below 53 degrees, and were overruled. "Ten good engineers are better than one hundred," DeLong had come to believe. He was certain that the private space industry could improve on NASA's record of one catastrophic vehicle destruction for every one hundred flights.[*] Looking around the table, DeLong chuckled to himself. He was surrounded by people, like himself, best

[*] Richard Feynman wrote in the Rogers Commission report: "It appears that there are enormous differences of opinion as to the probability of a failure with loss of vehicle and of human life. The estimates range from roughly 1 in 100 to 1 in 100,000. The higher figures come from the working engineers, and the very low figures from management."

described in incongruent terms: hard-nosed idealists.

The participants presented ideas for vehicles ranging from a modified Learjet to multistage rockets. Gary Hudson did drawings of the holy grail of suborbital spaceflight, the SSTO, the Single Stage to Orbit vehicle. There was talk of propulsion, considered the key to space exploration. Formulas learned long before were now scribbled on the whiteboard. Tsiolkovsky's rocket equation (also called the "ideal rocket equation") calculated how much speed you gain from a rocket engine:

$$\Delta^v = v_e \ln(m_0/m_1)^*$$

* $\Delta^v = v_e \ln(m_0/m_1)$ where: Δv = change in rocket velocity, v_e = exhaust gas speed, m_0 = initial mass of rocket, m_1 = final mass of rocket, after the burn, and $\ln(..)$ is the natural logarithm — roughly speaking $\ln(N)$ = twice number of digits in the number N. The formula describes how much speed you gain from a rocket engine. It depends on the exhaust speed of the gas and the net change in mass of the rocket as fuel is expended. The rule is that the change in velocity ΔV = (exhaust gas speed) × (logarithm of the initial/final mass). For example, if the rocket burns enough fuel to decrease the total mass by a factor of 3, then the velocity increase approximately equals the exhaust gas speed. If the mass decreases by a factor of 9, then the velocity

There was mention of the teachings of Maxwell Hunter — Gary Hudson's mentor — who helped design the Thor, Nike, and other missiles during the Cold War and wrote *Thrust into Space*. There was animated discussion around speed and how to achieve it. The year before, in 1993, American sprinter Michael Johnson set a world record by running the 400-meter race in 43.18 seconds, traveling an astounding *30 feet per second*. An arrow launched from a bow can go about 350 feet per second. The average bullet travels 2,500 feet per second. To get to the inner line of outer space — 62.5 miles — requires a velocity of about 5,800 feet per second, or nearly 4,000 miles per hour. Reaching orbital velocity requires 30,000 feet per second, or more than 20,000 miles per hour.

"Going to orbit is so much harder than suborbital flight, and there's a good market for suborbital missions," Byron said. "There's a lot of scientific work that can be done seven to eight minutes out of the atmosphere."

Discussion turned to liquid engines, hybrid motors, and solid motors. Standing at the whiteboard, Peter wrote under "Propulsion Options":

---

increase approximately equals twice the exhaust gas speed. The faster you burn, the lighter the rocket gets, and the easier it is to change the velocity.

— Liquid air/jet engine
— Hybrid rocket
— LOX/kerosene
— RL-10
— H_2O_2/kerosene

Peter scribbled a dozen formulas on the board, and shared his sketch of a small space plane. It had a bullet-shaped fuselage with passengers up front, wings with slats, ailerons and flaps, and triangular horizontal stabilizers.

Engineer Bevin McKinney, who had built a prototype commercial satellite launcher called Dolphin (which had a hybrid motor and was sea-launched in 1984), believed that everything being discussed was possible. The challenge was money. As Gordon Cooper said to Gus Grissom in *The Right Stuff*: "You boys know what makes this bird go up? FUNDING makes this bird go up." Grissom replied, "He's right. No bucks, no Buck Rogers." In John Clark's 1972 book *Ignition!,* a technician running a rocket engine test, and using an exotic and expensive boron-based propellant, remarked that every time he pushed the "run" button, he felt the price of a Cadillac go down the pipes.

Both of McKinney's private rocket companies had breakthroughs, but were driven out of business by government-backed competitors. McKinney's American Rocket Company had spent years developing its hybrid rocket motor technology, only to have NASA fund a competitor to duplicate its work. Gary Hudson's Pacific American Launch Systems was outmaneuvered by a program funded by the Defense Department.

On Sunday afternoon, with less than a day remaining in Montrose, Peter decided to share with the group his under-the-radar idea: the space prize. Standing at the whiteboard, Peter wrote, "PRIZES WORK."

"Prizes help to focus energy," Peter began, as if thinking aloud. "They provide a spirit of competition which has been one of the most important driving forces during the entire history of humanity." The more he talked, the more animated he became. "Space needs prizes. Space needs a return to small, well-articulated goals. Goals which involve and excite the general public."

Peter handed out a paper he had drafted titled "Spaceflight Prize Strategy." The copies were marked *proprietary and confidential.* The paper read in part:

There is a strong technology available which helps humans in achieving difficult, sometimes seemingly impossible feats, this technology is a forcing function which helps to focus the whole of human ingenuity at the same well articulated goal. . . . This concept, the forcing function, this technology, is the competitive "Prize." Not prizes for spelling bees or prizes for a lifetime achievement, but prizes which lay out impossible goals and tempt man to take great strides forward. Prizes such as those which were set out to the aeronautical world for speed, distance, endurance, etc. Prizes which brought forward adventurers, dreamers, and doers. Prizes such as the $25,000 Orteig Prize. Where no government filled the need and no immediate profit could fill the bill, the Orteig Prize stimulated multiple different attempts. Where $25,000 was offered, nearly $400,000 was spent to win the prize — because it was there to be won.

Peter wanted to do for space what Orteig — through Lindbergh — did for aviation. He now had everyone's attention.

Peter told the cautionary story of Richard Feynman giving a Caltech lecture to the American Physical Society entitled "There's Plenty of Room at the Bottom," where he spoke of building atomic- and molecular-size machinery. To promote the idea, Feynman offered $1,000 to the first person who could build a working electric motor no larger than one sixty-fourth of an inch on each side. He envisioned that novel technologies would have to be developed to permit the manipulation of individual atoms to win such a prize. A month later, one of Feynman's graduate students asked him to step up to the microscope and take a look inside. The student with a steady hand had used a very fine jeweler's forceps, patience, and ample magnification to construct a conventional, microscopic electric motor that met the prize rules. Dismayed, Feynman paid the winner the $1,000. Feynman later told a friend of Peter's that the "enemy" of the incentive prize was the "smart aleck grad student" who met the conditions of the prize without achieving the breakthrough spirit of the prize.

With that in mind, Peter emphasized the importance of clearly articulated and logical rules for the award: The prize must involve a human feat with a level of danger and drama that would capture the interest of the public. The prize must involve a feat in which the public could someday imagine themselves participating. The prize must involve competitors racing against time and each other. The prize must be sufficiently lucrative to entice a number of competitors and must be well advertised.

It was not long before the conferees came up with a flurry of questions. Would a prize for a spaceship require the vehicle to fly more than once? What would be the turnaround time, given that the goal was to introduce to the market a reusable, privately funded spacecraft? How many people would be in each vehicle? Max speed? Air launch versus ground launch? What about hybrids for the mission?

Peter, who had thought out this plan to the nth degree, was quick with his replies: The spaceship must be built privately for a cost and using a method that can be repeated. The spaceship must be reusable. The flight must return the crew and spaceship safely to Earth. The entrant must demonstrate the ability to refurbish the spaceship within seven days for a repeat of the flight. And the spaceship cannot be a surplus vehicle from any government program.

The discussion then moved on to a key criterion: the definition of the start of space. Americans consider 50 miles out from the Earth's surface "space," whereas Europeans draw the line at 62.5 miles (100 kilometers). The U.S. military and NASA had awarded astronaut wings to pilots who had flown above 50 miles.[*]

Dan DeLong said the goal for contenders should be to reach the Karman line — 62.5 miles. "A lot of international organizations and agencies respect this as the definition of the start of space," he said. "This should be an international competition. The other

[*] Russian cosmonaut Yuri Gagarin was the first person to reach space, in April 1961. The first American in space was Alan Shepard aboard Mercury 7 in May 1961.

reason is that's about the peak altitude you can go to and still do a pullout from vertical to horizontal with a reasonable load on the plane and pilot."

Next came literally the million-dollar question: What would be the size of the prize? Peter responded in a way that only a space geek could:

"If we use the Orteig Prize ($25,000) from sixty-seven years ago and adjust it at a compound rate of 6 percent inflation, this would yield a current value of $1,240,000 (1994 dollars)." He went on, "This value is probably at the lowest end of the right ballpark for our suborbital spaceflight prize. A prize somewhere in the neighborhood of $1.5 million to $10 million should attract a large number of entries yielding on the order of $30 million to $60 million of invested effort into getting man off the planet in reusable spaceships."

The funding of the prize would come from two primary sources, Peter said. The first would be individuals who want to create a "living monument" to honor someone. The prize would become a "shining light so strong, so compelling, that it will cause all individuals of dreams to aspire, to think, and to strive toward greatness." The second source of funds might involve "pledges from the space advocate population," through phone-a-thons and direct mail campaigns.

As the group discussed the plan, Peter excused himself and slipped out of the room. He took the stairs to his room two at a time. Sitting down at his desk, with his view looking south to the snow-capped Ouray Mountains, he began to type:

CHARTER

"The John Galt"
The challenge of the spaces between the worlds is a stupendous one; but, if we fail to meet it, the story of our race will be drawing to a close.

— *Arthur C. Clarke*

There are few chances in one's life to aspire to greatness. When such an opportunity comes along, the most difficult job is to recognize it, the second most difficult job is to take the risk of acting upon it. The project described in this Charter is one such opportunity. It cannot be ignored — it must be acted upon. All those who join The John Galt Team and sign the last page of this document recognize the challenge, the sacrifice, the fun, and the need to accomplish this goal.

Throughout all of history, the greatest accomplishments of the human race have been instigated and acted upon by the individual or the small group — never have the masses brought about innovation. We have the accomplishments of Charles Lindbergh and the Rutan/Yeager Voyager team as our guiding stars, and every NASA program since Apollo as our incentive to bring about change.

Peter envisioned both a prize and a rocket. The rocket would be called the John Galt and would be built in Montrose. It would either become a part of the competition or be a separate space taxi. He completed the mission statement, the rationale for the project, and the time line. Above the signature lines, he included a list of required reading to give members of the team a current base of experience and an understanding of similar successful undertakings in the past. Peter's required reading list included *Atlas Shrugged; The Spirit of St. Louis; Voyager,* by Dick Rutan and Jeana Yeager; and *The Man Who Sold the Moon,* by Robert Heinlein.

Hours later, Peter delivered the charter to the group. It was to remain confidential, known for now only to this group. One by one, signatures were gathered.

Dan DeLong was already sketching ideas for a spaceship that he believed could win the prize. Gary Hudson had a vehicle in mind. David Wine said they needed to get Burt Rutan involved. Byron Lichtenberg said it would be crucial to find a group of backers as strong as the ones Charles Lindbergh had. Lindbergh had written: "My greatest asset lies in the character of my partners in St. Louis."

Back in his room, Peter grabbed his leather-bound journal and wrote, "This is the story of men and machines and the dreams that entwine their lives. It is, perhaps, our oldest fable: the attempt to touch the heavens."

Since childhood, Peter had continued to move inexorably toward space, in the same way Cézanne kept painting the same apples; his latest idea for his canvas of space was his most ambitious yet. Peter left Montrose suffused with the feeling of certainty and promise, the way he'd felt as a child when he watched Apollo 11.

■ ■ ■ ■

PART TWO:
THE ART OF
THE IMPOSSIBLE

■ ■ ■ ■

11
EYES ON THE PRIZE

Peter stood between *Friendship 7,* the titanium-skinned capsule that took the first American, John Glenn Jr., into orbit, and a display of a lunar rock sample said to be four billion years old. Not far away were the *Wright Flyer* from 1903 and the *Voyager,* the spindly winged Rutan flying machine that made it around the world in 1986 without stopping or refueling. Next to Peter was the one and only Apollo 11 command module, *Columbia,* and directly above was the international orange Bell X-1, the first plane to exceed the speed of sound. Suspended next to it was Charles Lindbergh's *Spirit of St. Louis,* the single-engine, single-seat monoplane with its skin of treated cotton fabric and dappled aluminum nose cone. Lindbergh was all of twenty-five when he furnished the plane with a stiff wicker chair and charted his route by placing a string on a large globe and dividing the journey into segments.

Peter had been to the Smithsonian National

Air and Space Museum a dozen times before. He came to the Milestones of Flight gallery to sit and think, watch and listen. He was inspired and humbled by the genius, imagination, and perseverance on display. This was his Fenway Park, Ganges River, and Mount Kilimanjaro rolled into one.

But on this evening of May 25, 1994, Peter was looking for connections — not milestones. Dressed in a tuxedo and holding a glass of wine, he was there to do what most business advisers caution against: crash a party, furtively elbow your way to the host, and pitch your idea. The host tonight was Reeve Lindbergh, the second daughter and youngest child of Charles and Anne Morrow Lindbergh. The event was the Lindbergh Award gala. Peter hoped to get the Lindberghs to endorse his concept of a spaceflight prize.

Scanning the gala program, Peter read that Reeve was a director of the Lindbergh Foundation, and that the award was established in 1978 to recognize leaders who preserved the environment while making technological strides. This year's award recipient was Samuel Johnson Jr., who had been called "corporate America's leading environmentalist."

Peter searched the room and spotted Reeve, with her sandy hair, wire-rimmed glasses, and engaging smile. Heading her way, he rehearsed his summary and hoped he wouldn't get tossed out for bluffing his way in. He waited for an opening in the conversation before introducing himself and launching into his spiel. Talking quickly, he explained his vision for a space prize modeled after the Orteig Prize, the award that had galvanized Reeve's father to make his historic flight. Peter painted a picture of teams of rocket hobbyists and established engineers building spaceships in backyards, garages, deserts, and machine shops — daring to do what only a few governments had done before. He wrapped up his pitch by dropping the names of astronauts who had already pledged their support for his prize, and said that the prize would be offered to the first team that could reach the suborbital altitude of 100 kilometers. The winning team would change the world — just as her father had done in 1927.

Reeve was impressed by Peter's enthusiasm but had no idea what he was talking about. What she got was that he wanted to do something very new modeled on something very old that had appealed to her father decades earlier. A children's book author, Reeve was accustomed to people mythologizing her parents. Her mother was a Smith College graduate. Anne Morrow Lindbergh's mother had been a writer and poet who had served as president of Smith College. Anne's father was a partner at J. P. Morgan, a U.S. senator, and a U.S. ambassador to Mexico when Anne and Charles first met, in 1927, during the famous aviator's goodwill tour. When the two married, Anne, who loved books more than anything, adopted Charles's physically demanding life. She learned to fly and use Morse code, and with her husband set records with flying adventures around the globe. She was the first woman in America to earn a glider pilot's license. Of Anne and Charles's children, Reeve was the most comfortable dealing with the adulation and controversy that came with the Lindbergh name. The legacy was more than a story for Reeve and her siblings: their older brother was the Lindbergh baby who was kidnapped and killed. Reeve and her siblings were raised to live quietly and modestly — buy used cars, never give an address or list a phone number — so as not to draw attention to themselves. But in a family of recluses, Reeve, born in 1945, was venturing out. The former second-grade teacher was working on a memoir about her upbringing in Connecticut after the war, about her loving, perfectionist, list-making father and her mother, who needed to write as she needed to breathe. In a similar way, writing felt inevitable to Reeve. Her mother wrote beautifully, and her father won the Pulitzer Prize for his book *The Spirit of St. Louis.* Reeve was at the point in life where she needed to set down her memories and deal in her own way with what some in the family called "Lindberghophobia."

At first, public events had been overwhelming to Reeve, until she learned to listen, nod, and smile and let people say what they desperately wanted to say. She recognized the glow in people's eyes when they learned her parentage. Now, this energetic man before her — who wasn't wearing a name tag — was talking about launching an "Orteig Prize for space." He said it was his "mission and moral imperative" to open the space frontier.

Peter, realizing his time with Reeve was up, said, "Would you consider being on our advisory board?"

Reeve thought for a moment and replied, "You should talk to the pilot in our family, Erik. He's the flying Lindbergh."

It was months later when Peter finally tracked down the flying Lindbergh, and additional months before a meeting was scheduled. Peter and Byron Lichtenberg were in a restaurant near Seattle when they saw a man with long graying hair and a white pallor headed their way. He used a cane to walk. When he introduced himself as Erik Lindbergh, Peter did his best to hide his surprise. Erik was four years younger than Peter, but looked considerably older. Erik was living in a yurt on a ten-acre organic farm on a small island near Seattle. He was not exactly the flier and adventurer that Peter had envisioned. He seemed artistic and bohemian; not the guy who was going to help get Peter's space prize off the ground.

Peter, Byron, and Erik settled into their table at the Yarrow Bay Grill in Kirkland on Lake Washington. Byron had brought his usual trove of signed astronaut photos and memorabilia.

Erik took to Byron right away, but found Peter fidgety. Peter chewed his fingernails when he wasn't talking, and kept looking around, as if expecting someone else. He reminded Erik of an antsy kid. But Peter's résumé was lacking nothing. Erik learned that Peter and Byron had met at MIT, where Peter earned two degrees before graduating from medical school. Peter had started a national student space group, founded an international space university, and built a satellite launch company. Now he wanted to create an international competition to get rocket enthusiasts to build their own vehicles to fly civilians to space. Erik smiled. No wonder his first impression of Peter was *odd.* This was not an everyday undertaking.

Byron talked about his path to the Astronaut Corps. As a kid, he was a member of the science fiction book-of-the-month club, and devoured the works of Isaac Asimov, Robert Heinlein, and A. E. van Vogt. He was thirteen years old when he heard John F. Kennedy describe the nation's space mission as "the most hazardous and dangerous and greatest adventure on which man has ever embarked." Byron's dad was in the Army during World War II, and later worked as a dairy equipment salesman. His mom ran a dress shop in their small hometown of Stroudsburg, Pennsylvania. After Byron learned that America's first astronauts, the Mercury 7 crew, were all military test pilots, he became a fighter pilot. He earned a doctorate in biomedical engineering to enhance his chances of getting to space. The strategy paid off: he had become what NASA billed as a "new breed of space travelers," more scientist than career astronaut. He had experienced the magic of NASA, was close to the missteps, and had lived through the tragedies.

Byron shared with Erik the story of where he was on January 28, 1986, the day the space shuttle *Challenger* exploded seventy-three seconds after liftoff. He had given three talks earlier that morning to six hundred high school kids in eastern Connecticut. It was the first time that a teacher was being sent to space, and Christa McAuliffe planned to give lessons from orbit. On his drive back to the airport, Byron turned the car radio on. That's when he heard the news. Tears filled his eyes, forcing him to pull off Interstate 91 and roll to a stop. There on the side of the road, he began to cry. The astronauts were his friends.

He flashed to the six hundred students who had been captivated by the mission. He imagined the millions of students across the country who were watching the event live. He wondered what would happen to the shuttle program. He was seven months out from his next scheduled mission. But it would be six years before he would fly again, he told Erik.

When the conversation shifted to his experiences in space, Byron became joyful. He said that in the weeks leading up to a launch, he feared every cough, twitch and headache. Before going jogging or working out, he reminded himself to take it easy and watch his every step. Preflight astronauts got into this "Howard Hughes mode," he said, and wanted to go into a bubble. "So when you're finally strapped in, it's 'Wow, I've been training for this for five years. This is the real thing. Let's go!' "

Sadly, there were only a limited number of opportunities for people to fly to space. "Out of thousands of applicants who apply to NASA every few years, only a handful are chosen for the Astronaut Corps," Byron said. "Of those, a few will get to fly." Byron believed that NASA's future should involve buying seats to low-Earth orbit from commercial providers and spending its research money on exploration missions.

Peter nodded. "The government is not going to get us there," he said. "It is not in the business of taking risks." The three talked about the flight of Erik's grandfather, and the risks he took as the chief pilot on the St. Louis–Chicago airmail route. Twice in the latter part of 1926, the year before the transatlantic flight, Charles narrowly escaped death when his plane's motor failed and forced him to jump out and make a parachute descent. Thirty-one out of forty of his fellow airmail pilots perished in crashes.

It was Wernher von Braun, Peter noted, who had talked about the parallels between the *Spirit of St. Louis* flight and the Apollo voyage. Both missions had a shared goal of capturing the public's imagination and proving that outsized dreams were attainable. Von Braun said, "I do not think that anyone believed that his [Lindbergh's] sole purpose was simply to get to Paris. In the Apollo program, the Moon is our Paris." For Peter, Paris was getting to the start of space in a privately built spaceship. He told Erik what he had told Reeve: He was inspired by the *Spirit of St. Louis* and struck by the impact of the Orteig Prize. His new prize was to be called the XPRIZE. The *X* would be replaced with the eventual benefactor's name; *X* was the Roman numeral for ten and also stood for "experimental." The $10 million prize would be awarded to the first nongovernmental team that could build and fly a three-person rocket to the start of space twice within two weeks.

Erik listened to Peter and Byron talk in more detail about the rules of the XPRIZE: contenders were required to give sixty days' notice of their intent to fly; the flight would have one pilot and a ballast of 396 pounds to simulate two passengers; the spaceship would reach 100 kilometers twice under the dictated two-week time line; and the pilot had to stay alive for at least seven days after the winning flight.

Erik shifted in his seat to try to feel less discomfort. All he could think of was, *We've got enough problems here on Earth. Why do we need to spend $10 million to get to space?* He had flown Estes rockets as a kid and dreamed at one point of flying into space. He had heard talk of space at home, and knew his grandfather was a champion of the work of rocket pioneer Robert Goddard and had been convinced that Goddard's work might one day lead to a trip to the Moon. His grandfather even persuaded philanthropist Daniel Guggenheim to give Goddard $100,000 so he could continue his work. When Apollo 8 became the first manned space mission to orbit the Moon in 1968, Charles Lindbergh sent the astronauts a message saying, "You have turned into reality the dream of Robert Goddard."

Until recently, Erik had been a dreamer and

risk taker. Even after his climb to the summit of Mount Rainier, after the mysterious and troubling symptoms of mirrored pain and swelling persisted and abated only to return again, he believed that things would be okay. But as the months passed, his denial gave way to concern. He felt worse for longer periods. He reluctantly returned to his family doctor, where he got the diagnosis: rheumatoid arthritis. The disease was punishing, effectively turning one's immune system against itself, bringing pain, swelling, and deterioration of the joints. If tissue atrophied, the bone structure would change, causing severe deviation in the fingers and wrists until they were gnarled like trees in winter. Erik felt betrayed by his best friend — his body, the body that climbed mountains, laid tracks in fresh powder, did running flips across gymnastic mats. No doctor would tell him how bad it could get. As his condition worsened, Erik tried everything, from prescribed prednisone and methotrexate to homeopathic remedies. Nothing worked. Methotrexate made his mouth painfully dry and left him with a metallic taste. He tried vodka-soaked white raisins and an array of extreme foods and diets. When he learned that beekeepers rarely had rheumatoid arthritis, he subjected himself to bee stings. He eventually found a doctor to give him syringes of bee venom, which he shot under his skin. He swelled from rheumatoid arthritis *and* bee venom. He exercised his limbs and focused on trying to prevent his fingers from curling. The only thing he hadn't tried yet was something considered a last line of defense, the injection of gold salts. The decades-old treatment was known to turn skin mauve and gray. Erik, who had never been depressed for more than a day or two at a time, now struggled with profound sadness. Standing for five minutes was sometimes difficult. Sitting hurt. Talking was no reprieve. But then, with no warning, he would have days where the symptoms blessedly subsided.

At a friend's relentless urging, Erik had earned his pilot's license. It was the obvious choice he had avoided, but it was also an interest that persisted. He immediately loved the physical part of flying — takeoffs, landings, and dealing with crosswinds — but found the memorization of rules and regulations and all of the math calculations difficult. Still, the boy who was bored in high school, maintaining a C-minus average, earned a 4.0 in flight school. He soloed for the first time on October 31, 1989, got his private license to fly the next spring, earned his commercial pilot's license in July 1991, and got his flight instructor rating in September 1991. His first job was at the Bremerton Airport in Bremerton, Washington, before he moved to Port Townsend and worked for a company called

Ludlow Aviation. Erik did his best to keep his family name to himself. When the local newspaper ran a small story about a certain flight instructor with a famous last name, Erik was nervous and his boss was happy. He made $12 an hour as a flight instructor, earning money only when the tachometer was turning.

In his first years of flying, he binged on books by Ernest Gann, from *Twilight of the Gods* and *Fate Is the Hunter* to *Soldier of Fortune.* It was Gann who wrote, "Flying is hypnotic and all pilots are willing victims to the spell." And it was Gann's words that resonated with Erik now: "It's when things are going just right that you'd better be suspicious. There you are, fat as can be. The whole world is yours and you're the answer to the Wright brothers' prayers. You say to yourself, nothing can go wrong . . . all my trespasses are forgiven. Best you not believe it." It was similar to the warning that Charles Lindbergh gave his children: "It's the unforeseen. It's always the unforeseen."

Erik earned money doing woodworking when he could, but it was hard on his hands. He had married in 1988, and his wife, Mara, was a massage therapist. The monthly rent on their yurt — located on a farm owned by a friend — was $50.

Finally Erik looked at Peter and Byron and

said what was on his mind. "I can think of a lot of ways to use ten million dollars right here on Earth."

Byron nodded. He could see that Erik was in pain. He told him that "up in space, a change comes over you." He explained, "In an hour and a half, you orbit Earth. You see everything that holds civilization. You look down and see this beautiful Earth and look into the void of space with its blackness and white dots and you have to admire what we have. You realize that we're all on Earth together. The Earth's atmosphere looks like this one-inch-thick line and you think, 'That is what is keeping us alive.' " He didn't know of an astronaut who wasn't changed by the view, who didn't want to take better care of Earth after looking at it from afar. "When you see it with your own eyes, it's not the same as looking at pictures. I've been very blessed to go twice."

They talked about *Earthrise,* the photo of Earth shared from orbit on Christmas Eve 1968 by Apollo 8 astronauts William Anders, Frank Borman, and Jim Lovell. It was the first time people had seen home from space. The photo, called "the picture that changed the world," showed a perfect blue and white marble surrounded by a black sea. The astronauts read from the book of Genesis, and Lovell said of the image, "The vast loneliness is awe-inspiring and it makes you realize just what you have back there on Earth." The image would play a role in doomsday books by the likes of Paul Ehrlich and bleak scenarios by the *Limits to Growth* researchers. It inspired the modern environmental movement.

What Byron said resonated with Erik. He understood that on one critical level, the XPRIZE was about giving more people that view of Earth. He could see how the goals of the XPRIZE were aligned with the Lindbergh Foundation's mission of using technology to enhance life and preserve the environment. Erik brightened, temporarily forgetting the pain of sitting for too long. After being hit with waves of bad health news, he felt different in this meeting with Peter and Byron. He felt hopeful. Byron came across as part scientist, part philosopher. Peter came across as the mechanism to make this crazy idea work. Before dinner ended, Byron shared one of his favorite quotes, by Calvin Coolidge: "Nothing in the world can take the place of persistence. . . . The world is full of educated derelicts. The slogan 'press on' has solved and will always solve the problems of the human race." It spoke to the vision of the XPRIZE, Byron said. Erik thought it spoke to his life. He needed to press on, to find a way to a better life.

As the three stood to leave, Erik did his best to walk normally. He could still drive, though it was painful to use the manual transmission, and he couldn't afford a new car. He had a handicapped parking sticker, but hated to use it. Outside the restaurant, Peter and Byron asked Erik whether he would take part in an event being planned in St. Louis to formally announce the XPRIZE. Peter said they would return to the Racquet Club where Erik's grandfather and his backers had signed their pledge to pursue the transatlantic flight. There would be city leaders, astronauts, aviation designers, and rocket makers. It would mean a great deal if they had the support of the aviator's family.

Erik looked at the two men and promised he would think about it. He had never been to St. Louis. It was Grandfather's city, with Lindbergh Boulevard, the Lindbergh museum, the Lindbergh school district, and a replica of the *Spirit of St. Louis* hanging in the airport. On his drive home, Erik reflected on the night. Peter and Byron had come to him in hopes of connecting with the "flying Lindbergh." He could barely walk, and only occasionally fly. But the meeting reminded him of the question he was asked all the time by fans of his grandfather: "And what are you going to do with *your* life?"

Peter stood in the slow-moving line to touch the lunar rock in the Smithsonian's Milestones of Flight gallery. He was back a year after meeting Reeve Lindbergh here, and a few months after meeting Erik in Seattle. He exchanged sad smiles with his friends Bob Richards, Gregg Maryniak, and others. One by one, Peter and the group inched forward, pausing to touch a piece of the Moon and to reflect on the meaning of the day. It was supposed to be a celebration of life, but it felt more like one of the sky's brightest stars had blinked out. Their friend, leader, and co-conspirator Todd Hawley had died from AIDS. He was thirty-four.

Many of the men wore suits and ties, while others wore T-shirts from the inaugural ISU summer session held eight years before. Lapels were adorned with laminated buttons with a close-up photo of Todd's smiling face. There were family members, professors, and ISU loyalists. Peter, wearing suit and tie, touched the moonstone and closed his eyes. He had seen Todd twice in the months before his passing: for an ISU founders' reunion in April, where he, Bob, and Todd had their last photo taken together here in the Milestones of Flight gallery, and later in San Francisco, where Todd was living with his partner. The founders' reunion had been held in part to draw up an "ISU Credo," crafted and signed by Bob, Todd, and Peter on April 12 — the day before Todd's thirty-fourth birthday and on the anniversary of Yuri Gagarin's 108-minute orbital flight. More important, the reunion had brought together the Gang of Three, *Peterbobtodd.*

For nearly two years, Todd had isolated himself from Peter and Bob. He had shut himself off from the space community. He broke the silence in early 1995, saying he wanted to see his friends and work together again. Writing the credo in Washington, D.C., reminded them of the adrenalized early days of ISU. They had always joked that they were "triaxially stabilized," strongest as a team of three. Their credo, which had been articulated hundreds of times but never formally written down, set forth the founding principles and goals of the space university. Comprising six paragraphs on one page, it began: "International Space University is an institution founded on the vision of a peaceful, prosperous and boundless future through the study, exploration and development of Space for the benefit of all humanity." It concluded, "This, then, is the credo of ISU. For all who join ISU, we welcome you to a new and growing family. It is hoped that each of you, as leaders of industry, academia and government will work together to fulfill the goals set forth herein. Together, we shall aspire to the Stars with wisdom, vision and effort."

Around the same time, Todd learned that he was being awarded the Tsiolkovsky Medal, given to individuals and organizations that popularize the ideas of Konstantin Tsiolkovsky. Todd was humbled by the award.

Shortly after the reunion, Todd suffered a collapsed lung and was hospitalized. Peter's last visit with the man he called his closest brother was in San Francisco's South of Market neighborhood. Even under heavy sweatpants, Todd looked gaunt. The two went for a walk and Todd had a nasal cannula and pulled a small oxygen tank. The experimental treatments in Russia had failed. Peter and Todd, only a month apart in age, had spent countless hours walking together, talking about everything from space governance structures to the development of new economic systems. On this foggy day in San Francisco, they walked slowly. Todd, a Francophile and a student of history, loved Peter's idea and inspiration for the XPRIZE. They talked about the Frenchman Raymond Orteig, and about great explorers, from Meriwether Lewis and William Clark to Ferdinand Magellan. They laughed at the term they used for their own space endeavors: "benign conspiracy." It was their goal to change the world for the better. But Todd's once-buoyant stride had turned to a shuffle. The man who always seemed to be looking up at the sky with a smile was now focused on making it one more step. When Todd tired after a few short blocks, they turned back. More than once, Peter was forced to look away so Todd wouldn't see his eyes filling with tears. As they walked, Peter remembered the consecutive nights that Todd spent in his antigravity sleeper, smiling through it, never once complaining, sleeping as if he were already in space.

In line at the space museum to touch the lunar rock was Todd's partner, Riq Hospodar, who in the final months of Todd's life changed his name to Yuri Hospodar, to honor Todd's love of space, which began with Yuri Gagarin's flight when Todd was one day away from entering the world. Yuri touched his "commitment ring" to the smooth stone. Bob Richards felt the lunar stone and thought of Todd's eternal optimism. He had talked with his friend the morning he died. Todd called to relay his final wishes. He wanted his celebration of life held in the Smithsonian's National Air and Space Museum. He wanted his ashes placed at the permanent ISU campus. Bob promised he would fulfill his wishes. He was pained as he listened to Todd struggle for breath. Hours later, Yuri called Bob to say Todd was gone.

After everyone had passed by the lunar rock, the group moved to a reserved hall nearby to share memories. Photos were shown of Todd, a blond, blue-eyed kid and with horn-rimmed glasses, next to his dog and siblings. Todd playing cowboys and Indians. An older Todd in a suit and tie, now wearing gold-rimmed glasses, giving a talk at

ISU. Todd with Peter, Bob, and Uncle Arthur in Vienna. From childhood to the end of life, Todd's smile stayed the same. In a video interview, Todd talked about his "life mission." His dream, he said, was "no less than the establishment of an entire world off the Earth, inhabited by individuals including you and me." Before the tribute ended, Todd's sister took to the dais to share stories. She said half jokingly that her brother had dreamed of dying at the Air and Space Museum.

In time, the group moved to the steps of the museum. As pictures were taken, they waved and yelled in unison, "Hi, Todd!"

Born April 13, 1961, Todd died on July 11, 1995. According to his own life clock, he spent 12,507 days on Earth.

12
COWBOY PILOT

In January 1996, Mike Melvill and his wife, Sally, arrived at work at eight A.M., unlocked the door, and let themselves in. They headed through the carpeted reception area to Mike's office, which looked out onto the Mojave flight line. Their boss, Burt Rutan, was standing over his drafting table. Burt looked up, startled, squinted at them as if they were blurry, peered outside the window, and checked his watch. He muttered that his wife was *going to be mad.* He'd worked straight through another night, standing at his drafting table, nursing his umpteenth cup of black coffee, wearing his clothes of the day before.

Mike and Sally exchanged knowing looks. They had worked for Burt for nearly eighteen years, saying goodbye to him at five P.M. and returning many mornings before eight to find him where they had left him. They knew his brilliance and his quirks. He was the boss who took them on exotic vacations, only to announce a day after arriving that they were leaving because he couldn't think on a white sand beach in paradise. He was the boss who did wind tunnel testing on top of his 1966 Dodge Dart station wagon; who always said his best plane was his next plane; and who knew airplanes better than just about anyone alive.

These days, Burt was working on his thirty-first plane, the Proteus, a high-altitude research aircraft named for the Greek god who changed his shape to take on any form. The Proteus was being built for Angel Technologies to deliver broadband services from just above the stratosphere. Mike had recently attended a meeting with Burt to discuss the project, and had met Angel founders Peter Diamandis, Marc Arnold, and David Wine, and Angel chief technology officer Nick Colella.

Several times a day, Burt would wave Mike over, or appear at his drafting table with an idea or a sketch for a plane or a part that more often than not had the whimsy of a Dr. Seuss drawing. Burt was deliberately contrarian, moving engines back and wings far forward and co-opting materials once reserved for boats and surfboards.

As Burt's go-to test pilot, Mike had plenty of experience with Burt's convention-defying aircraft. He would fly anything Burt dreamed up.

■ ■ ■ ■

Mike didn't learn to fly until he was thirty years old in 1969, but the South Africa native was drawn to danger long before his love affair with the skies began. His strong, compact frame made him a star on the local gymnastics squad, and his agile acts on the parallel bars were only the beginning.

Mike inherited a competitive spirit from his father, a world-class target shooter who routinely defeated younger rivals. A motorcycle enthusiast, Mike also got his father's auto mechanic skills. But his ability to build and fix things did not translate into confidence in the classroom. Mike found much of the teaching mind-numbing and was frustrated that the curriculum gave him no opportunity to work with his hands. He failed his senior year math final and didn't graduate from high school.

Mike met his match early when he encountered Sally, a high-energy, petite blonde with a strong will and a thirst for adventure. Sally's parents wanted her to go to finishing school and marry a wealthy sugar farmer. Sally wanted only Mike. She defied her family and left Durban on the back of Mike's motorcycle, with her angry father in hot pursuit. Mike and Sally went to England, where Mike became a carpenter. They were married in

Scotland and immigrated to the United States in 1967 to join Sally's brothers and her now friendly father. They settled in Indiana, where Sally's family had a rotary die-cutting factory called Dovey Manufacturing. Mike ran the machinery while Sally took orders from customers. His aptitude for building was apparent from his first day on the engineering-based job. He started making some of the company's tool products, and when those expensive tools failed, broke, or were incorrectly used, he was dispatched to troubleshoot.

To do that part of his job, he jumped on a plane once a week, spending long days just getting to the companies. Finally, Mike concluded that someone in the company needed to learn to fly. Most of the repair jobs he went to were near small airports. Sally's brothers had no interest in flying, so it was decided that Mike would get his pilot's license on the company dime. But Mike didn't take to flying in small planes the way he took to machining parts. He vomited every time he and his instructor were airborne. Thankfully, his instructor, Dick Darlington, told him that plenty of people were nauseated when they first learned to fly. He assured Mike that the sickness would diminish and then disappear. He was right. Mike earned his private and commercial pilot's licenses, and was soon arriving at work wishing that someone's equipment, somewhere, would break so he would have to fly off to fix it.

Flying became freedom. It was a different way of looking at the world — as Amelia Earhart described it, "You haven't seen a tree until you've seen its shadow from the sky." Instructor Darlington, aware of Mike's intense interest in flying, suggested he consider making his own plane, given that he had the skills and tools of a machinist.

Mike had no idea that people made their own planes. Darlington told him about a place in Wisconsin called Oshkosh, where the Experimental Aircraft Association held an annual gathering of pilots and their homebuilt or modified aircraft. In the summer of 1974, Mike and Sally attended. One of the first things they saw at Oshkosh was a crazy-looking plane with a tail on the front and engine in the back. "What *is* that?" Mike asked, intrigued. Its name was the VariViggen, and it was flown by a man named Burt Rutan. The name VariViggen came from the Viggen, a highly innovative Swedish fighter aircraft built by Saab. The Viggen had "canards," essentially wings moved from the back to the front. As Mike watched Burt give people rides in the plane, doing short take-offs, short landings, and turning on a dime, Mike said, "Now that's a plane." Burt sold kits for the VariViggen out of the back of his plane parked on the Oshkosh flight line. Mike handed over fifty-one dollars in cash — Burt didn't trust banks — returned to Indiana, and began studying the plans. He knew how to build things from blueprints, but these were not engineering plans. They were sketches and photographs and had a comic book–style narrative.

Undeterred, Mike started building. He made progress on one part, only to find himself confounded by the next part. He called the Rutan Aircraft Factory (RAF) in Mojave, and Burt walked him through the problem. At the end of three years, Mike, ever competitive, became Burt's first customer to finish building a VariViggen. Not long after finishing the plane, Mike and Sally flew the VariViggen from Indiana to a business meeting in California.

To confirm that Mike had built the plane right, they flew into Mojave. Burt was so impressed that he invited them to dinner. He told Mike and Sally that he'd left his job as director of development for Bede Aircraft in Newton, Kansas, and opened RAF in 1974. He asked Mike what he did for a living and ended up offering Mike and Sally jobs. Burt said he needed help so he could focus on designing new planes. Sally could do bookkeeping, and Mike would help him with the homebuilt airplane business. He offered the Melvills a starting salary of $22,000 a year — to be split however they wanted. They were each earning double that in Indiana.

In September 1978, Mike and Sally gave up their secure jobs in the family business and moved from central Indiana, with its bone-chilling winters, hot summers, and flat landscape, to the Mojave Desert, with its crisp winters, baking arid summers, and sandy, tumbleweed-strewn landscape. The Melvills' sons, Graham and Keith, were fifteen and twelve. Sally cried for a year, lonely for her extended family, but Mike settled in. He had found his niche. The renegade spirit suited him, and his newfound love affair with planes was the oldest story in this dusty town. Where others saw wind, sand, and Joshua trees, aviators saw a dreamland of unlimited heights and speeds. They saw a sky that was almost never obscured, a place where nearly every day brought a call from the flight tower of "severe clear." A cast of characters flew in and out of Mojave, stopping in at Burt's shop to share stories. Over time, Mike befriended legendary pilots, notably Scotty Crossfield, the first to fly twice the speed of sound, and Fitz Fulton, who set early altitude records for the military and was the first to fly the modified Boeing 747 when it carried the space shuttle out of Edwards Air Force Base.

Mike started at RAF doing whatever was needed, from sweeping shop floors to helping Burt design and flight-test new planes, including the kit-built VariEze and Long-EZ. Mike improved the instructions in the kits. Thousands of the VariEze kits sold quickly, at $54 apiece. The Long-EZ kits were snapped up for $250 apiece. Burt told Mike that the idea for the first kit for the VariViggen came in part from the Simplicity sewing patterns used by Burt's wife, Carolyn. Burt had seen Carolyn make her own dresses by pinning patterns to fabric and cutting along the dotted line, and wondered why he couldn't do the same for aircraft. Burt loved the idea that someone could build a plane in his or her garage and go and fly it.

By the early 1980s, Burt told Mike that they needed to phase out the homebuilt plane business. The money was good, but the builders needed a lot of support, and the liabilities were great. When the U.S. Air Force needed a trainer for a new fighter plane, Burt built a scaled-down replica that would give them the same flight test data. Scaled Composites opened for business in 1982. Burt set a standard for working hard, but he also evangelized the need for fun. He would stop meetings to say, "Are we having fun yet?" Employees would yell, "Yeahhhhh!" Instead of spending money on employee Christmas parties, Burt took 1 percent of the company's net profit for the year and divided it equally among employees. Burt gave himself the same bonus as the shop floor sweep. On

Fridays, when the company was small, Burt announced that everyone had been working too hard. "It's time for clam chowder," he'd say. Employees would jump into planes and off they'd fly to their favorite greasy spoon in nearby California City.

In the same way a surfer studies the sea, waiting for that perfect wave — looking for a glassy surface, an offshore breeze, and the right amount of spray coming off the top of the lip — Burt was captive to the sky. One afternoon, Burt found Mike and said excitedly, "Have you looked outside?"

"Yeah," Mike answered tentatively.

"The clouds!" Burt said.

"Yeah, there are clouds."

"We need to go flying!"

Mike, Burt, and Burt's brother Dick grabbed cameras, piled into a plane, and hit the sky to fly through the rare clouds of Mojave.

Mike took advantage of any opportunity he had to become a better pilot, practicing landings and takeoffs again and again until he got it right. Burt, who had been a flight test engineer — not a test pilot — knew the maneuvers needed to get the desired telemetry, whether on directional stability or stall characteristics. Burt demonstrated a maneuver in his own twin-engine Duchess and then had Mike do the same thing. Mike learned that flight tests proceeded in incremental steps — slowly, steadily. Mike learned to take a plane that had never been flown before and start by taxiing it around the runway to make sure the brakes and steering worked and the plane cooled well. The plane was then returned to the hangar, and the team would debrief with the data and Mike's analysis. This would continue for days or weeks, until they felt the plane was flight ready. The first "flight" would be in the thin cushion of air inches above the runway.

Mike got his long-distance flying and formation training from none other than the velvet-armed Dick Rutan. The Rutan brothers agreed that Mike was one of the most instinctive stick-and-rudder pilots they had ever met. With time, Burt grew confident that Mike could do dangerous flying in a plane that had never been pushed — performing stalls and spins — and bring his baby back safely.

There were times, though, when Mike sat on the runway before a first flight test, looked at whatever unconventional contraption he was belted into, and wondered, *Am I going to be alive for long after I push the throttle?* Mike narrowly averted disaster many times, including the day a mechanic left a wrench inside a wing of the prototype Starship, flown in 1983. The controls jammed midflight. Mike tried everything he could think of before grabbing the stick and putting all of his weight on it. He was lucky; the wrench popped loose.

Sally served as Scaled's director of human resources. It wasn't easy being the wife of a test pilot of experimental planes. When someone asked what it was like, she pointed to her wrinkles. But being a pilot herself, Sally said, "It's for Mike to question whether the plane is safe." Both she and Mike had to believe that Burt would never put Mike in a plane that wasn't safe.

But Burt pushed the limits. In 1992, Mike and another Scaled pilot, Doug Shane, endured a plane that Doug called "a new and unwelcome experience," and that Mike labeled "harrowing." Burt had designed a new radio-controlled unmanned aerial vehicle (UAV), intended for forty-eight-hour flights at 65,000 feet. The drone was called the Raptor and had a wingspan of sixty-six feet. It was designed to carry a 150-pound payload, including underwing antimissiles. The fuselage was too narrow to accommodate a cockpit. The Raptor was part of a ballistic missile defense concept, engineered by Nick Colella while he was at Lawrence Livermore National Laboratory.*

---

* "Raptor" stands for "Responsive Aircraft Program for Theater OpeRations," and the slightly fanciful idea was to have UAVs loitering on the edges of a battlefield where they would detect and respond to

258

Mike arrived at work one morning to find the shop guys having fun with a saddle they'd thrown over the newly built Raptor. The maintenance manager was a horse owner, and the crew had apparently been taking turns in the saddle. When the guys somewhat nervously asked Mike whether they could take his picture up in the saddle, he was game and climbed aboard, just in time for Burt's arrival. For a moment, no one said a word, fearing the boss would not be amused. But Burt studied the situation and exclaimed, "That's it! That's what we needed and I never thought of." Burt had been worried about losing the unmanned prototype on its first flight tests. That morning, again to the surprise of the crew, Burt had the shop build a fiberglass saddle with a back and shoulder support. He would give the pilots the ability to override the remote controls. *They could just ride on top of the plane!* He'd give them parachutes, too, just in case.

When it came time for the Raptor's test flights, Mike climbed warily into the fiberglass saddle on top of the plane, put his helmet on, and got his feet into the stirrups. Sally

---

theater ballistic missile launches and intercept them in the launch phase with a hypervelocity TALON missile. It was to be a direct predecessor of the Predator and Reaper UAVs.

was deep inside Scaled — not about to come out to witness the love of her life riding *on top* of a plane. Project engineer Dave Ganzer controlled takeoff and landing remotely, making Mike — straddling the fuselage — feel like a pawn in someone else's nutty video game. The landings proved particularly terrifying, as the Raptor came in at nearly 100 miles per hour. There was Mike, riding on top of a plane in the open air without even a windshield. It took every bit of his strength not to reach for the controls.

A few days into the testing, Mike got airborne and very quickly realized he had no rudder control. Ganzer and his crew were in a chase van on the runway, and Ganzer reported the same problem. Mike couldn't land if he couldn't line up with the runway. Mike radioed Ganzer to say he was going to fly over to the dry lake bed in Rosamond and try to land there. He didn't have the option of parachuting out, as he couldn't gain even a foot of altitude. Ganzer sped out of Mojave, following the imperiled Raptor's path. Ganzer was in Burt's old white van with the roof cut out to make way for a plastic bubble. Ganzer would stand up in the bubble holding the controls to fly the Raptor.

With the dry lake bed below, Mike considered putting one wing down to drag himself to a stop. The plane would surely break apart. Ganzer had said something to him about the

Raptor's "adverse yaw." This suggested the plane would react in an opposite way to the normal push of the stick. If he pushed the stick to the left, the plane would initially yaw or turn to the right. Mike said his pilot's prayer and plunged the stick all the way to the right. The plane turned to the left initially and then had one beautiful moment of leveling out. Mike immediately put the plane on the ground and taxied to a stop in a cloud of dust. By the time Ganzer and crew came tearing in, Mike had dismounted from the death trap. He was *almost* breathing normally again when Ganzer and the crew came to a stop. Ganzer discovered there on the lake bed that a relay that controlled the rudders had locked up. The relay was replaced, and Mike was asked to fly the drone back to Mojave. His first reaction was "No way! I thought I was dead!" As the hours passed, though, it was clear that the only way to return the Raptor to Mojave was for Mike to fly it. He reluctantly got back in the saddle.

Now, in early January 1996, Mike was getting ready for the first test flight of another new plane, the Boomerang, a five-passenger twin-engine that took defiance of convention to a new level. It was intentionally asymmetrical, and looked all wrong. The wings didn't match, with the right wing coming in fifty-seven inches shorter than the left. One of the engines was mounted on the fuselage, the other on the left boom, and the right engine was more powerful than the left. The horizontal stabilizer, joining the fin on the twin tails, extended past the right fin but not past the left. The "door" for the copilot and pilot was through the windshield. Burt's goal with the forward swept-wing plane — thus the name Boomerang — was to solve the problems and dangers of engine failure and asymmetric thrust — the "P effect"[*] — in conventionally designed twin-engine planes. Burt assured Mike that the asymmetrical design was actually "more symmetric than a symmetric airplane" when flown. He said that

[*] The P effect is caused by asymmetry in the action of a propeller blade that is running into the air at an angle. Picture a spinning propeller as a disc. If the disc is facing straight into the direction of motion, then the action of the blades is completely symmetrical. But if the disc is tilted as it would be when the aircraft is climbing, then the lower edge is ahead of the upper, and the blades on the way "down" the disc are moving faster into the air than on the way up. The effect is to move the center of thrust. In a single-engine plane, this puts the center of thrust along a line parallel to but offset from the centerline of the airplane. It tends to yaw the craft, and you compensate with rudder control. Burt's asymmetric design made this effect go away: the asymmetries cancel out.

the P effect slowed a symmetric plane down, requiring rudder, but that the P effect on an asymmetric plane made it symmetric at low speeds and asymmetric at high speeds, when the pilot wouldn't notice it.

Before leaving the office, Mike checked out the drawings for the Proteus, the Angel Technologies' high-altitude plane still in the drafting phase. The plane shared similarities to a Klingon warship from *Star Trek,* a praying mantis, and a dragonfly. The Proteus needed to be capable of doing small circles in the sky for up to fourteen hours at a time and carrying payloads of different size and weight. "You'll have to wear a Moon suit for this," Burt said. Mike had no doubt Burt was serious and noted happily that at least the plane had a cockpit — and no stirrups. Mike studied the drawings and realized that the temperature cycling would be extreme: the Proteus would have to be capable of taking off in the Mojave summer of 110 degrees, and at 50,000 or 60,000 feet would encounter temperatures of minus 110 degrees, a delta of 220 degrees.

As he was pondering this, another Proteus drawing on Burt's drafting table caught Mike's attention. In this sketch, the Proteus carried a rocket underneath. Mike looked closer; there was a *cockpit in the rocket.* This couldn't be serious, he thought.

Burt smiled at him expectantly. Mike had

seen that dreamy expression before. He had to wonder: What on Earth was Burt going to build next?

13
HISTORY REPEATS ITSELF

It was the morning of Saturday, May 18, 1996, and Peter was pacing in front of his hotel in St. Louis, studying the names of confirmed participants and going through his checklist. Today was the day he would formally announce the $10 million XPRIZE and invite teams around the world to compete, and he needed everything to go perfectly. He had local and national media attending. He had commitments from more than twenty astronauts, including his childhood hero Buzz Aldrin. He had top honchos from NASA and the Federal Aviation Administration, as well as rocket designers and aviation stars like Burt Rutan. And he had Erik Lindbergh and his brother Morgan in St. Louis for the very first time — the city where Charles "Slim" Lindbergh had found the support he needed to fly.

Peter finished his cup of black coffee and watched as the superheroes of his youth, the astronauts, began to appear outside the lobby, looking like Secret Service agents in dark suits and aviator shades. As a line formed to board the van to take them to a spot near the city's Gateway Arch, Peter went over logistics with Byron Lichtenberg, who had corralled many of his fellow astronauts into coming. When he looked up from his notes, Peter saw Burt talking with Dan Goldin, the head of NASA. Something about their body language didn't look right. While the line was moving, the two men had faced off and were not moving. Peter walked closer.

Burt loomed over Goldin like Apollo Creed over Rocky Balboa. He was chiding the space agency for its lack of innovation and declared that NASA should be pronounced "nay say." Peter bit his nails. "There is no growth. No activity. Nothing," Burt said. "Why isn't NASA doing this?" he asked, gesturing around. "Because risks don't register with NASA today."

Goldin, who grew up in the Bronx, ran marathons, and did 100-mile bicycle races for fun, was not about to let anyone attack his agency or employees. He gave it right back to Burt. Burt didn't have to live under the constraints of government rules or expectations. He didn't have to answer to the president, the Congress, or the American people. He could do his thing in the Mojave Desert, with no interference, little oversight, and without the "gotcha" media watching and waiting. Goldin respected Burt, considered him brilliant, and had been at the receiving end of his needling before. NASA was a lot of things, he said, but it was *not* risk averse.

" 'Failure is not an option' was the mantra from *one human being during Apollo 13!*" Goldin said angrily. "[Gene] Kranz wasn't speaking for *all* of NASA. He was saying, 'These three people's lives are at stake. We cannot fail. We gotta bring them back.' It has been misinterpreted." Goldin said that people expected "perfection from NASA, and it's a news story when NASA fails." Goldin was the first to admit he had never wanted to run the space agency, but got what he called the "hug of life" from President George H. W. Bush. When he took the position, he pushed for a "faster, better, cheaper" approach. Four years into his tenure, he was a passionate and irascible defender of NASA and didn't tolerate anyone in any domain calling NASA "mediocre" or "risk averse" — or for that matter, "nay say."

As Peter watched the titans go head to head, he feared that his big event could end before it began. He was angry with Burt for being so antagonistic, but he had seen before how Burt could go from playful to challenging. The men moved forward, but were still sparring like prizefighters heading to the ring. Peter whispered to an aide that he wanted the two separated on the bus. Goldin told Burt that he wanted NASA to experiment with different approaches. Failure was a "way out of mediocrity," Goldin said loudly. Fear of failure "would keep America grounded," and expecting perfection was "unfair to the wonderful people at NASA."

Burt shook his head. "You've got a budget of *fourteen billion dollars*. Why don't you take the money NASA spends on *coffee* at its centers and do what the XPRIZE people are trying to do? Why don't you take one percent of that, or a half a percent — you wouldn't miss it — and just throw it out there for someone to do this stuff? Someone will have a breakthrough, and it would be the best money you would spend while you're running NASA."

Finally, Goldin thawed. He knew Burt was critical of the space agency because his life's work had been inspired by the X-planes of the forties and fifties, and NASA of the sixties. Burt was Burt in large part because of the risks taken by the likes of Chuck Yeager, Wernher von Braun, Alan Shepard, Neil Armstrong, and Buzz Aldrin. What he was saying was that he wanted NASA to keep inspiring.

"I'm here," Goldin said by way of response. "I'm clearly very receptive to wild and crazy things."

■ ■ ■ ■

On the van heading to the Gateway Arch, Erik Lindbergh and his brother Morgan heard the last of the barbs between Goldin and Rutan. Erik was amused, intrigued, and impressed. He had figured that NASA's administrator would be an agreeable civil servant, but Goldin was the opposite. Erik liked the passion coming from both sides and thought, *Alpha dogs in the presence of other alphas will fight.* The trip to St. Louis had been memorable from the moment the Lindbergh brothers arrived, and they'd been here for less than a day.

Starting at the airport, they were treated like celebrities and surrounded by homages to their grandfather. It had been nearly seventy years since their grandfather had set out from St. Louis to win the Orteig Prize, but his presence was everywhere in this city. It was here he found his backers and believers. The city also happened to be steeped in aerospace history, as the headquarters of McDonnell Douglas, builders of the Mercury and Gemini capsules, the Skylab space station, and the new Delta Clipper.

Unfortunately, Erik was in pain just riding in the small bus. His rheumatoid arthritis was worse than when he had first met Peter and Byron in Kirkland a year earlier. He had slowly warmed to the idea of participating in the XPRIZE, though he remained wary of being a public Lindbergh. Morgan, on the other hand, had taken to the XPRIZE dream right away. He was the youngest of Jon and Barbara Lindbergh's six children and had gone through his own challenges in dealing with the complicated Lindbergh legacy. At one point, Morgan disassociated himself from the family altogether. He found his way back only after reading his grandfather's autobiography. Morgan was moved by how his grandfather's time in the air gave him powerful insights into the vastness of the universe and man's place in it. A practitioner of meditation, Morgan was searching for his own epiphanies. When he read that his grandfather had sat on a beach and studied his own hand as a sort of time travel to primitive life, Morgan's mind drifted to Apollo 13 astronaut James Lovell as he famously looked back at Earth from space, put his hand up to the window, and realized he could hide all of Earth with just his thumb. Morgan was certain that the world needed the XPRIZE; that peace and wisdom were attainable through access to space. He intended to talk onstage about the need to inspire a new generation of dreamers. Morgan had another motivation that went beyond giving a speech: he wanted to help his older brother find his passion again.

As dozens of members of the press and about one hundred invited guests filed into the staging area under the Gateway Arch, Peter took a moment to look around. He noticed Erik Lindbergh, moving slowly to his seat, relying on his cane. He saw astronauts representing Apollo missions 7, 10, and 11, Gemini missions 6, 9, and 12, and a dozen Skylab and space shuttle missions. Burt and Dan Goldin had arrived in one piece, to Peter's great relief, and now the two men were exchanging friendly banter like the best of friends.

Peter had garnered endorsements from key organizations, including the U.S. Space Foundation, the National Space Society, the Space Frontier Foundation, the Society of Experimental Test Pilots, and the Explorers Club. Byron Lichtenberg, a founding member in 1985 of the Association of Space Explorers, had gotten many of the international fliers and astronauts to attend. Peter had snagged commitments from Patti Grace Smith, associate administrator for commercial space transportation at the Federal Aviation Administration, and from a group of St. Louis civic leaders.

Two months earlier, on March 4, 1996, committee members had convened at the historic brick-façade Racquet Club in the leafy Central West End of St. Louis. Taking a page from Lindbergh's playbook, Peter and the XPRIZE backers gathered at the very same table that Lindbergh and his supporters had used to sign their intent to enter the race for the Orteig Prize. Lindbergh had found his support slowly. His first backers were insurance executive Earl Thompson; Frank and Bill Robertson of the Robertson Aircraft Corporation; and Major Albert Bond Lambert, the city's first licensed pilot and an avid balloonist. He heard enough noes for a lifetime. The fund-raising challenge surprised him. He wrote in *The Spirit of St. Louis:* "Aside from Mr. Thompson and Majors Robertson and Lambert, I've found no one willing to take part in financing a flight across the ocean. The men I've talked to who are interested don't have enough money. Those who have enough money consider the risk too great." Lindbergh thought about raising money by popular subscription. "Maybe I could get a thousand people in St. Louis to contribute ten dollars each." His luck improved when he met Harry Knight, president of the St. Louis Flying Club, who introduced him to others, including Harold Bixby, head of the St. Louis Chamber of Commerce, and E. Lansing Ray, publisher of the *St. Louis Globe-Democrat.* Lindbergh soon had the financial fuel needed to fly. As Bixby handed the aviator a check for $15,000, he asked him, "What would you think of naming it the *Spirit of St. Louis?*"

Some of St. Louis's biggest names showed up for Peter's March 4 organizing event, invited by Al Kerth, a civic leader, senior partner at the public relations firm Fleishman-Hillard, and Peter's newfound guardian angel; Doug King, chief executive of the St. Louis Science Center; and Dick Fleming, head of the St. Louis Chamber of Commerce. Kerth's idea was to get one hundred people in St. Louis to donate $25,000 each — $25,000 was chosen because it was the amount of the Orteig Prize. Seven people agreed to donate $25,000 each, becoming the first members of the "New Spirit of St. Louis" group. The funding was enough to get the XPRIZE up and running. Ralph Korte, president of Korte Co., a construction company based in Highland, Illinois, was the first to write a check. Support also came from Dr. William Danforth of Washington University; Enterprise Holdings' Andrew Taylor and his father, Jack Taylor; Sam Fox of Harbour Group; Hugh Scott, former mayor of Clayton, Missouri; Steve Schankman of Contemporary Productions; John McDonnell of the McDonnell Douglas Corp.; and lawyer Walter Metcalfe.

Peter had also gotten help from his Angel Technologies partner, Marc Arnold, who had moved Angel to St. Louis and was connected with members of the Young Presidents' Organization. Many locals embraced the

XPRIZE as a chance to revitalize the city and revisit its most glorious chapter. It came at a time of city renaissance efforts; St. Louis had committed to a multibillion-dollar renovation of its historic properties. At the end of the organizing event in March, Peter raised his glass of gin and tonic to toast Al Kerth, who raised his glass of scotch. Kerth was Peter's Harold Bixby and Harry Knight rolled into one. He had not hesitated when Peter pitched him on the XPRIZE idea, nearly jumping from his chair. "I get it! I get it!" Kerth had said. "Let's do it!" He was proving to be an indomitable force. Kerth had come up with the XPRIZE logo, created the bronze medallions for "New Spirit of St. Louis" members, and hatched the idea of unveiling the prize under the Gateway Arch.

Now, as the final guests arrived at the arch for the May 18 ceremony, Peter took one last look at his checklist. He'd set out to make this event impossible to ignore, something he described as launching "above the line of super credibility." Peter wanted this event to be heard around the world.

The show began with the luminaries of old space and new space, reluctant Lindberghs and born-again Lindberghs, St. Louis old-timers and newcomers. Buzz Aldrin paused on his way to the stage to sign autographs. The stressed steel Gateway Arch glistened in the late-morning sun. Every seat was filled.

Peter, in suit and tie, his parents in the front row — supporting him while not yet fully grasping the importance of a prize for suborbital flight — began, "The *Spirit of St. Louis* carried Charles Lindbergh from New York to Paris and into the hearts and minds of the world. Today, all eyes are on St. Louis again."

To rousing applause, he said, "The XPRIZE has been created for one major purpose, to accelerate the development of low-cost, reusable launch vehicles and thereby jump-start the creation of a space tourism industry."

Gregg Maryniak, who had plotted and planned this event with Peter, listened with pride. Peter was the most relentless person he knew. At the dais, Peter talked about the incentive prizes of the 1920s and 1930s, "the hundreds of aviation prizes that pushed the envelope of speed, distance, endurance, and safety in the fledgling aeronautical industry. In 1926 and 1927 alone, more than $100 million worth of prizes (in 1996 dollars) were offered to challenge the flying community. Today, only seventy years later, aviation is a global multibillion-dollar industry. This is the first-ever human spaceflight prize." Peter told the story of Raymond Orteig and his prize — a competition that was not without casualties. In the summer of 1926, Charles W. Clavier and Jacob Islamoff, two members of Captain René Fonck's flight crew, died when their plane, designed by Igor Sikorsky but grossly overloaded, crashed and ripped apart on takeoff from Roosevelt Field on Long Island. In spring of 1927, U.S. naval pilots Noel Davis and Stanton H. Wooster perished during a final test of their aircraft. Weeks later, on May 8, 1927, French aviators Captain Charles Nungesser and Captain François Coli flew westward into the dawning skies over Le Bourget, France, and were never seen again. While Orteig expressed sadness at these losses, he never wavered from his offering. On May 20, 1927, Charles Lindbergh departed from Roosevelt Field, flying nonstop, thirty-three hours and thirty minutes in a single-engine, single-pilot aircraft to Le Bourget Field outside of Paris. There had been others to fly across the Atlantic, but Lindbergh was the first solo pilot to fly nonstop and connect these major cities.[*]

Peter expressed his hope that vehicles born from the global XPRIZE competition would "bring about change in the stagnant aero-

[*] On June 15, 1919, in pursuit of another prize — of 10,000 British pounds offered by the *Daily Mail* — John Alcock and Arthur Brown were the first to fly nonstop across the Atlantic. They flew approximately 1,890 miles across the shortest part of the Atlantic, taking off from St. John's, Newfoundland, and landing in what was described as a "gentle crash" in a bog in Ireland.

space world."

When Peter was done, Erik Lindbergh made his way to the podium. At first, he spoke softly, and then he gained confidence.

"I found some notes taken by my grandfather when he was preparing to get funding for his flight across the Atlantic," Erik said. "There are some notes here about why he wanted to make the flight: 'Make America first in the air. Promote and demonstrate the perfection of modern equipment. Advertise St. Louis as an aviation city.' I think there are some great parallels for what is going on with the XPRIZE today." Erik believed that the XPRIZE had the ability to start an industry and bring humanity together. "That's where the XPRIZE has the most potential."

Erik offered another insight from his grandfather, this one written as the foreword to astronaut Michael Collins's book *Carrying the Fire*. His grandfather acknowledged the "awareness" that came with scientific and technological breakthroughs, whether with his flight or the push into space. He wrote: "Alone in my survey plane, in 1928, flying over the transcontinental air route between New York and Los Angeles, I had hours for contemplation. Aviation's success was certain, with faster, bigger, and more efficient aircraft coming. But what lay beyond our conquest of the air? What did the future hold? There seemed to be nothing but space. Man had used hulls to travel over water, wheels to travel over land, wings to travel through air. Was it remotely possible that he could use rockets to travel through space?"

In closing, Erik said, "The XPRIZE is an event that has the potential to capture the world's imagination. It has the potential to shift people's interest from conflict and war to an adventurous goal."

Morgan Lindbergh also gave an impassioned talk, but with a focus on the potential and imperative of the XPRIZE to inspire young people. Buzz Aldrin, sixty-six years old, took to the microphone and lamented that close to twenty-five years had passed since man had stepped foot on the Moon with Apollo 17. He hated to see America lose its leadership role in space exploration and was pouring his energy into campaigning for new resources for space travel. "America must dream again," he said. "I am still awed by the miracle of having walked on the Moon. That sense of awe in all of us can be the engine of future achievement."

Toward the end of the ceremony, NASA chief Dan Goldin stepped up to give his endorsement of the XPRIZE. "We need to encourage the participation by as many people, by as many organizations, in this noble venture," he said, wearing an XPRIZE pin on his left lapel. "I hope that my grandson, Zachary, who is two years old, will be able to go with his children on a trip to a lunar hotel."

Gregg Maryniak, taking it all in, believed that the XPRIZE would soon find its benefactor, and the *X* would be usurped by the person's name. Attracting teams, on the other hand, might be more difficult, he thought. Gregg watched the Lindberghs and saw Erik trying his best not to show his physical discomfort. Occasionally, a grimace would make its way through. Erik demonstrated a lot of strength by being here.

As the crowd dwindled and the television trucks rolled away, Peter looked back at the 630-foot-high Gateway Arch, a monument to fur traders and explorers, to the spirit of pioneers. It was the shape of a parabola, the very trajectory he imagined a homebuilt spaceship would one day fly to win his $10 million prize.

Hours after the announcement under the arch, Peter and the XPRIZE crew were cleaned up, dressed in black tie, and at the St. Louis Science Center. The evening gala, cochaired by Buzz and Erik, was to include fog machines, an elaborate laser show, and talks by luminaries. Tickets went for $500 per person.

When it was time for the dinner to begin, Hollywood producer Bob Weiss found his seat in the tented dining area. Bob, who had met

Peter the year before, found a certain poetry to the entire day, with the army of astronauts, captains of industry, and the parallels to a sixty-nine-year-old dream. Bob had produced a range of films, including *The Blues Brothers,* and had a new science fiction TV series out called *Sliders.* He was a self-professed space geek who went to space conferences and had grown tired of listening to pessimistic projections of when man would return to space. He had found Peter's XPRIZE idea brilliant: offer the right incentive, use Darwinian forces, and stimulate innovation. It was taking human nature and marshaling it for a specific purpose.

Settling in at the table, Bob soon began to wish that he could direct this event. He was happy to be across the table from Burt Rutan and wanted to hear what he had to say, but with no warning, the fog machine would come on and make half the table disappear. People said Burt's mind was in the clouds; now he was in a cloud. Once the fog dissipated, Al Kerth gave the welcoming remarks and introduced a narrated film that combined clips from Kitty Hawk, Lindbergh arriving in Paris, Neil Armstrong and Buzz Aldrin walking on the Moon, and Burt Rutan at his drafting table creating what would be the *Voyager.* Peter spoke on video, saying, "Sixty-nine years ago, Charles Lindbergh and the *Spirit of St. Louis* changed the way people think about air travel. The XPRIZE is trying to change the way people think about space travel." There were humorous clips of Jimmy Stewart as Lindbergh, talking with Robert Cornthwaite, who played Harry Knight.

Knight, looking serious, said to Lindbergh, "Slim, you understand we have to make sure we're not financing a suicide."

Lindbergh replied, "The idea of suicide never crossed my mind."

"Except you're flying over the ocean," said one of the men at the meeting.

Lindbergh responded, "But the idea is not to set it down on the water. The idea is to set it down on Le Bourget."

"Will this stimulate aviation?" another man asked. "I mean, a man went over Niagara Falls in a barrel. Did that stimulate an industry?"

"That was a stunt," Lindbergh replied. "I'm not a stuntman; I'm a flier."

Next up was a video message from Peter's longtime supporter Arthur C. Clarke:

"I'd like to send my fondest greetings to Buzz and Peter. I recently had the pleasure of having Peter here. He explained the commitment you have made to launching a new era in private space travel. Thirty years ago, Stanley Kubrick and I made this little movie, *2001: A Space Odyssey.* We predicted by that time, space tourism would begin and if you had money, anyone who wanted to could go to orbit. Sooner or later this will happen, and I hope the XPRIZE will contribute to that. I think I may need to revise my predictions to the date 2004 instead of 2001."

Clarke smiled and went on, "It's always been our nature as humans to explore our surroundings and turn frontiers into future homes. Now, space beckons. During the birth of the space age, it was the competition between the former Soviet Union and the U.S. that drove it so far and so fast, from Yuri Gagarin's flight in 1961 to landing on the Moon only eight years later. It is my belief that the XPRIZE will reintroduce in a constructive fashion this element of competition. I invite teams from every nation in the world to lay their plans and begin the competition for the prize. May the best team win. I am Arthur Clarke, signing off in Sri Lanka, to you in St. Louis — to be known one day as the gateway to the stars."

Peter grew anxious when it was time for Burt to speak. Burt had told him he planned to talk about the importance of prizes in aviation history. Peter just hoped that Burt would rouse the crowd, not roil them.

At the podium, Burt, wearing a tuxedo and a New Spirit of St. Louis medallion on a ribbon around his neck, opened by saying he wanted to share "what's in my heart" when it comes to the meaning of the XPRIZE. Peter grew even more nervous.

"Imagine something that didn't happen but could have happened," Burt began. "Back in the golden age of the development of aircraft, back when people had this fantasy to leave the Earth and fly through the atmosphere, we had XPRIZEs — we had a lot of them. Over a tiny amount of time from the Wright brothers to when you could buy a ticket to Chicago or have a private airplane to enjoy the skies. But let me imagine . . . let me ask you to imagine . . . what if in those days, we didn't have XPRIZEs? The prize for the first flight over the Alps. The prize for a flight across America. What if we had, between 1903 and 1920 or 1930, a government-owned, government-developed, government-flown program, where they are the only ones who could go into the air? You would have seen large and extremely expensive craft. You would have seen the government's airplane fly with seven pilots, and only those who had worked for fifteen years got to fly twice. That could've happened.

"I feel not just embarrassed as an American citizen, in a society that is supposed to be free, but frankly I am mad as hell that we have the kind of limitations we do for us to leave the atmosphere.

"I believe seriously that this XPRIZE is what is going to break that open. I have seen myself, personally, all of a sudden, get extremely creative in design. I have dreamed of making a homebuilt spacecraft since I've been doing homebuilt aircraft. That's since 1968, when I started on the VariViggen. But I have never, by myself, been as creative as I have been in the last couple of months, eyeballing this goddamn prize.

"I am not going to tell you what I've come up with because I want to win this thing, but I am going to tell you I'm not the only one that's going to be creative. I'm going to tell you to try to think about something entirely different from what you imagine to be a spacecraft. It's not a throwaway Atlas. It's not a space shuttle. The guys who were barnstorming in the old days, they'd fly a Jenny [an early 1900s biplane] over and land in a field and give people rides for two dollars. Could they have imagined a 747 or a Concorde or TWA's baggage system?" The crowd laughed. "Think about it: Did they have that kind of info? Could they have imagined a Bonanza or a Long-EZ? They had no idea. I'm telling this crowd tonight I have myself just got a touch of this.

"I'm looking out here at some very sharp entrepreneurs who are going to go after me like crazy, and they're going to have phenomenal breakthroughs. What's going to happen is way beyond our imagination, and it's going to happen very soon. It's going to create the best roller coaster in the world. We'll be sending people to orbit. We're going to the planets and the stars — and we're going to do that because of Peter Diamandis."

Burt got a standing ovation. Peter was stunned by Burt's compliment, and by what Burt said about the prize. Was he serious? Had Burt Rutan just announced he was a contender for the XPRIZE?

Later, when most of the dinner attendees had gone home, Peter lingered with a close group of friends and family. It was after midnight, and Peter shared the story of how he had first met Buzz Aldrin eight years earlier. He told them how Aldrin had agreed to talk at the founding summer conference of the International Space University. After his talk, Buzz had dinner with Peter and some of the students and faculty. They ended up at the MIT faculty club, where they spent five hours, captivated by Buzz's stories.

Putting his weary feet up on a table, Peter asked Gregg for his thoughts on the night. Gregg was amazed, he said, that everyone who RSVP'd yes actually showed up. He looked at his hands, with more than their share of nicks and cuts from stuffing envelopes, and said, "We're not far from our SEDS days of getting paper cuts after midnight." On the table were copies of their eight-page, full-color invitation. The cover image was of a family of space travelers standing in front of rockets shooting at different trajectories. The rockets were given names: John Galt, Byron Lichtenberg, Doug King. The biggest of the rockets was reserved for their friend Todd B. Hawley.

As Peter gathered his belongings and his strength — the man with seemingly limitless energy was finally exhausted — his mom and dad appeared with a birthday cake blazing with candles. His name and the XPRIZE were on it. Peter was about to turn thirty-five, and the XPRIZE had just come to life. He made a wish and blew out the candles. No one had to ask what he wished for.

14
THE SPACE DERBY

Thin, pale, and prone to dressing in Zombie Apocalypse T-shirts, John Carmack was still in his "larval stage" of rocketry when he first heard about the $10 million XPRIZE, news of which was quickly making its way around the globe.

The twenty-seven-year-old Carmack had long been fascinated with space and had dabbled with Estes rockets in middle school, but his interest then went dormant for years as he focused on computers, coding, and video games. Once called "a brain with legs," the multimillionaire Carmack had attracted a cult following for creating some of the hottest games of the computer underworld, including *Commander Keen*, *Wolfenstein*, *Quake*, and *Doom*. As a founder of id Software in Mesquite, Texas, he had helped pioneer the first-person shooter genre, giving players the feeling of being inside the game.*

Carmack had started designing video games

* First-person shooter games are made by building

when he was in the third grade, when his favorite pastimes were reading comic books and *The Lord of the Rings* and playing *Dungeons & Dragons.* He liked the logic of computers. Unlike his home life — where his games were dismissed as a waste of time — and unlike the religious "myths" he was taught in parochial school, computers made sense to him. There was no magic, no mystery. He might not understand something at first, but if he put in the time, he could eventually unravel every seemingly weird and quirky behavior. He could look at a computer and understand its operating system, interconnect protocol, compiler, chip set, and peripheral hardware. The beauty of programming was in the knowledge that a computer could be controlled. The specific programming language was less important. Carmack felt less at odds with the world when he learned to command computers.

But by 1997, around the time he released the source code for *Doom 3,* Carmack felt he'd achieved all he could in the realm of

---

a perspective picture, such as of a scary basement. Then as the player moves the controls, the perspective changes, creating the illusion of turning or moving forward or backward. The problem is to store all the textures and images that compose the constantly changing scenes.

video graphics and games. He had built fast games and bought fast cars — a Ferrari Testarossa and Ferrari 328, to which he added a turbo engine — and he was beginning to look around for the next hot rod to hack. So when one of his programmers at id Software, Michael Abrash, started feeding Carmack some old Robert Heinlein books — *Stranger in a Strange Land, The Moon Is a Harsh Mistress, The Man Who Sold the Moon,* and *Rocket Ship Galileo* — it was not long before Carmack's passion for rockets was reignited. Carmack loved the archetypal Heinlein hero, the fierce individualist who uses technology to solve problems. He believed to his core that building things was the best way to shape the world.

In short order, Carmack was shelling out thousands of dollars for seminal rocket textbooks, including *Rocket Propulsion Elements* by George P. Sutton, and *Modern Engineering for Design of Liquid-Propellant Rocket Engines* by Dieter K. Huzel and David H. Huang. The rocket treatises filled bookshelves and consumed his mind. Carmack pored over NASA publications from the early sixties and seventies, impressed by the nuts-and-bolts descriptions of what worked and didn't work for the Mercury, Gemini, and Apollo programs. The early NASA studies were dazzling in their details, right down to diagrams of welding procedures. NASA publications from more recent times proved the opposite: full of meta-analysis of surveys of simulations. During his embryonic phase of rocket study, Carmack also looked online for tutorials and signed up for all the right mailing lists.

When Carmack got to the point where he felt like he could hold an intelligent conversation with industry types, he began attending space conferences. At first, he wandered around asking questions without anyone knowing who he was. He was just another space geek who dreamed of the stars but looked like he never felt the warmth of the sun. Soon, though, whispers circulated that he had the magical designation of an "accredited investor," a high net worth individual who could make risky investments. Suddenly, around every corner came a new pitch.

That's when Carmack discovered the XPRIZE. He also learned about the $250,000 CATS (Cheap Access to Space) Prize, which would be given to the first private team to launch a 4.4-pound payload into space, 124 miles or higher, by November 8, 2000. Carmack wasn't sure whether to finance a team for one or both contests, but he was certain of a few things: He wasn't in this for the money — none of his work had ever been about the money. Truth be told, he relished the idea of entering a new arena where many of the folks would know a lot more than he did. He would always love computers, of course, but it was time to look beyond the screen in front of him.

In Bucharest, Romania, Dumitru Popescu had just sat down in an Internet café to browse a Web site called Astronautix when he saw something about the XPRIZE. The twenty-year-old aerospace engineering student had come to the café to research the liquid fuel used in SCUD missiles when his attention was drawn to the words *ten million dollar prize* and *suborbital flight*. By the time he got a few paragraphs in, he downed his espresso, hurried to find his phone, and called his wife.

"You need to come to the café," he told her, as they didn't have e-mail at home. "I have to show you something." His wife, Simona, arrived within the hour, took a seat, and read the story. Before she could respond, Dumitru said, "Let's try to do something on our own."

She could see he wasn't joking. "We are students," she said by way of protest. "We have no money. We don't have a thousand dollars to even *enter* the competition." Dumitru shook his head. "Let's start building something and maybe we will be able to attract sponsors."

That afternoon, Dumitru went from the

Internet café to the campus of the Faculty of Aerospace Engineering at the University Politehnica of Bucharest, where he was a sophomore. He wanted to discuss the XPRIZE with his peers and professors. The reaction he got was "This is unreachable for us," and "Forget it." But he couldn't forget it. His father was a policeman, his mother an accountant. Life seemed more about drudgery than dreams. He had a degree in theology, which was his parents' idea. Now he was studying aerospace, which was his idea. He wanted to build manned rockets, and feared the Romanian space agency was making no progress in this direction.

Soon, Dumitru had persuaded his wife to help him. Together, they talked her father into letting them build their rocket in his backyard in a small town west of Bucharest.

Thirty-two-year-old Pablo de León was talking with friends in Buenos Aires about the lamentable monopoly on space by the world's largest governments when he heard of the XPRIZE. "This is right out of science fiction," he said excitedly. After researching the prize, he confided his interest to colleagues. He had founded the nonprofit, nongovernmental Argentine Association for Space Technology, and his friends there told him, "Pablo, listen, don't even think about it. This is something that just isn't possible. You'll burn your credibility."

But de León couldn't shake the idea. When he read that Burt Rutan was a possible contender, he said to himself, *Boy, I have to do that. If Rutan is thinking about it, then it's serious.* He already knew of Peter Diamandis as a founder of the International Space University. De León had wanted to attend ISU for many years, but couldn't afford both the flight and tuition. After eight years of applying, he had finally been accepted on full scholarship. He believed the stars were aligning in the direction of the XPRIZE.

De León had been captivated by space for as long as he could remember. When he was five years old in July 1969, his parents woke him up in the early morning hours to watch the lunar landing of Apollo 11. There he sat with his parents and grandparents on their farm in Cañuelas, Argentina, watching man walk on the Moon. He remembered the dim lighting in their small family room and the quiet that fell over the family when images of the astronauts appeared on-screen. They were one of the few families in town that had a TV. By the age of nine, he was launching homemade rockets in the pasture out back, scaring the cows and sheep and getting stern warnings from his parents. He went on to design and build spacesuits used at Kennedy Space Center and wrote two books about the history of the orbital efforts in Argentina, the only country in South America with a space program.[*] At the time he heard of the XPRIZE, he was working from Buenos Aires as a payload manager for seven experiments to be launched on the space shuttle in early 2000.

Pablo would find a way to enter the contest. As the designer of any future craft, he would surely have to fly it, too, he told himself happily. He could picture the rocket, and he already had a name for it: *Gauchito,* for Little Cowboy.

Steve Bennett was working as a laboratory technician for the toothpaste company Colgate in Manchester, England, when a coworker showed him a small newspaper story about a prize being offered from America for

[*] The Argentine space program consists of two main components: scientific satellites and the development of a small launch vehicle, the Tronador. The country also has two communication satellites in geostationary orbit, launched by European Space Agency Ariane rockets. They've done a few scientific satellites, mainly in collaboration with NASA; however, the first Argentine satellite was launched from Russia. The last Argentine scientific satellite was launched from the United States on a Delta 2 from Vandenberg Air Force Base in California. The Argentine government space program is not pursuing human spaceflight as one of its priorities.

anyone who could build and fly a rocket without the government's help to the start of space. Bennett had taught himself the ins and outs of rockets, from types of propulsion to ablative skins. He was thirty-three years old, but he had never forgotten how his parents had refused to wake him up for the Apollo 11 landing in 1969, when he was five. His mother had told him that he had school the next day, a Monday, and assured him there would be "plenty of rocket launches to see later." By the age of thirteen, he was on a first-name basis with workers at the local chemical supply company, buying ingredients to propel his homemade rockets. As a young adult, he watched in dismay as England's auspicious space program regressed. In its aeronautical heyday of the sixties, England had a sophisticated and impressive satellite carrier rocket called Black Arrow. The rocket was retired in 1971 by decision makers who opted to go with less expensive American-made vehicles.

Now, as Bennett toiled in the toothpaste factory, he saw rockets in the shapes of the tubes and propellant in the texture of the paste. He wanted to live and breathe rockets, but he couldn't leave Colgate until he had another source of income, however paltry. His wife wouldn't hear of it.

To Bennett, humanity's destiny was outside Earth and required bravery, exploration, and adventure. He wanted to see space, with its luminosity and darkness, milky patterns, planets, stars, galaxies, and nebulae. On breaks from work, he began sketching his rocket. It would be at least forty feet tall and have a capsule on top. Like the boy with the purple crayon, he drew himself into the cockpit.

There were many others rumored to be gearing up to make a run for the XPRIZE. Brian Feeney, an inventor from Toronto, was living in Hong Kong when he happened upon a story about the prize while browsing his local newsstand. Geoffrey Sheerin in Canada was already said to be designing the ultimate homebuilt hot rod, a fifty-four-foot-long rocket modeled after Germany's V-2 missile. A team in Russia was reportedly interested in using a solid engine to power something resembling a mini space shuttle. A former NASA propulsion specialist in Texas was building a ship in a rice field. The vehicle would launch vertically from water and land horizontally like a seaplane. In California, Peter's friends Gary Hudson and Bevin McKinney — who had been at the John Galt gathering in Montrose, Colorado — were working on a Buck Rogers–style ship, only with helicopter blades on top.

Even the grandfather of rockets, Bob Truax, who had been pushing for space tourism since before Peter Diamandis was born, was eyeing the race. The eighty-five-year-old Truax[*] had a forty-foot-long spaceship, two fuel tanks, and a rocket engine in storage just outside of San Diego. Having designed and built Evel Knievel's Skycycle, Truax had known both success and failure. At an age when most of his peers were relaxing into retirement and a round or two of golf, Truax confessed, "I just like to go out and play with rockets."

In trying to decide which rocket team to finance, John Carmack first reached out to contenders for the CATS Prize. This was a much less ambitious contest than the XPRIZE, but the methodical Carmack had always taken measured steps — and the smaller prize was the perfect place to start.

Carmack found out that the CATS Prize was in response to the XPRIZE: the money

---

[*] Truax was involved with some of the highest-profile U.S. military rocket programs of the twentieth century: Thor, Viking, Polaris (submarine missile), and Sea Dragon. He was interested in space tourism, with his "Volksrocket." And he built Evel Knievel's Skycycle, a steam-powered rocket with wheels that Knievel used to try to launch across the Snake River Canyon in 1974. The parachute deployed early, and the vehicle drifted back to the canyon floor.

was put up by Walt Anderson, who'd had the bitter falling out with Peter during their time together at International Microspace. The smaller prize was being run by Rick Tumlinson, president of the Space Frontier Foundation and a longtime space advocate who had resigned from the XPRIZE board because Peter had announced the award without having the $10 million. Tumlinson told Carmack that he'd said to Walt, "If you want to poke at Peter, endow this little prize."

Carmack didn't know Peter or want to get involved in any intramural fights; he was focused on looking carefully at the CATS competitors. He sent letters out introducing himself and saying he was interested in possibly sponsoring a few teams. Several teams never bothered to respond. After interviewing the others, Carmack came to a conclusion: he found that a great number of people in the space community were out of touch with reality. Several team leaders told him how they would use his money, but didn't offer any plans for testing hardware. When Carmack asked about this, he was told by one team, "We're not going to tell you how to make video games, so don't tell us how to make rockets." He repeatedly heard how easy it was going to be to win the CATS Prize, but few people were building anything. He met people with thirty years of experience in the industry who had never screwed a nut onto a bolt but insisted, "There are no technological challenges. All we need is funding." One company founder told him he needed "a million dollars to turn the lights on." Carmack talked with Patrick Bahn of TGV Rockets and was impressed by his business plan, but worried how the company could go for so long without having a rocket to show for it. Carmack marveled, too, at how space professionals attended conference after conference, presenting the same presentation decks with only minor tweaks. After months of research and interviews, Carmack drew up a list, putting teams into three categories: Loony, Unrealistic, Maybe.

He ended up funding a few groups, including XCOR Aerospace in Mojave, which he found to be the best of the bunch. He gave $10,000 to JP Aerospace, a volunteer-based, do-it-yourself effort that balloon-launched high-powered rockets — or "rockoons." Carmack went to a few launches of hardware by other companies, including one in the Black Rock Desert of Nevada, where he waited hours and hours only to see the vehicle blow up on the pad. He favored that over doing nothing. When he saw hardware built and launched — even if it failed — he was happy. Failure meant learning.

As he continued working full time at id Software and sponsoring the efforts of a handful of rocket makers, Carmack began studying the programming required for rockets. He delved into high-reliability programming, designed not to fail under stress or regular use. NASA specialized in designing systems with three duplicate computers calculating the same thing, such as navigational positioning or main engine burn. For safety, the engineers would compare the three results and use the majority result. Aircraft control systems were subjected to automatic verification of no errors. Error-correcting systems had to tolerate storage and network errors by using redundant data encodings. In a way, game code and rocket code were like the same play cast in two different ways, two apparently different objects with substantially identical underlying structures.

To Carmack, game development was far more complicated than rocket development. Games involved millions of lines of software code. Games contained more program objects. A single game might contain thousands of items that needed to be tracked, updated, and rendered. A rocket, by comparison, had a small set of sensor inputs and control surfaces, such as the angle of the rocket nozzle. Reliability requirements, though, were biased the other way. A game flaw had few repercussions. Nobody got hurt if something went awry. But a bug in a rocket control code could cost millions of dollars and endanger lives. In the end, the rocket code was smaller,

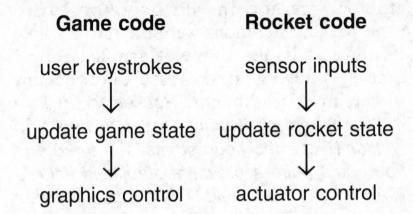

Game code	Rocket code
user keystrokes	sensor inputs
↓	↓
update game state	update rocket state
↓	↓
graphics control	actuator control

but needed more validation.

Carmack wanted to make the programming of rockets more like software development. He didn't want to write software the way the space shuttle team did it, where everything was reviewed to death and changed every few weeks. The method could work, but it was cost ineffective and schedule ineffective. His observations and interviews also taught him what he didn't want to do if he started his own rocket company. He didn't want to work for six months to a year, make a pilgrimage to the desert, push a button, and see something go wrong. He wanted to build and test something new every week, to let problems express themselves. He wanted to be open source with rockets as he had been with video games, posting all he learned, right down to where he'd purchased the parts. The breakthroughs of the Internet, personal computer, and smart phones came from a production-efficient method in which failures were expected and iterations were the norm.

One day in his office, Carmack found himself studying the exposed ductwork on the ceiling. He thought, *Rockets should be made by spiral welding tubes. Then you wouldn't have the hoop stresses in there and you could build a pressure-stabilized vehicle like the Atlas. You could build a Saturn V out of sheet metal.* Returning home that night, he waded through boxes of rocket parts filling his garage and hallway, and through the rocket textbooks stacked on the hood of one of his Ferraris. When Carmack had first started his research, he had assumed that he should finance other rocket builders, but he had slowly realized that many of the so-called experts had no idea what they were talking about. During his computer career, Carmack had turned the video game industry inside out; he wondered if he could show the aerospace industry how to build spaceships in a faster and cheaper way. He knew it was time for him to stop watching and start doing.

Carmack reached out to the president of the Dallas Area Rocket Society to see whether anyone there would be interested in joining him in developing and building experimental rockets. He was given some names, and began to think about the team he needed.

The best times at id Software involved over-loaded circuits that made their basement office go dark, pizza- and Coke-fueled all-nighters, and a belief they were doing something entirely new. Over the years, that passion was replaced by schedules, output, production, and professionalism. With rockets, he would be back to tapping unexploited energy and traveling into the unknown.

15
EPIPHANIES IN THE MOJAVE

Dick Rutan was in the pressurized capsule of a giant hot air and helium balloon, climbing to a cruising altitude of 30,000 feet. The higher he went, the calmer he felt. It had been a year of nonstop planning and building to get to this point, day one of attempting to be the first to circumnavigate the globe in a balloon.

It was early January 1998, twelve years since Dick's historic around-the-world *Voyager* flight, which had gotten him an invitation to the White House and speaking engagements across the globe. But his newfound fame as a pilot hadn't made Dick any less hungry for his next run at the record books.

Ten minutes into the balloon flight, which had begun in New Mexico, everything felt right. Dick monitored the carbon dioxide scrubber he had built to balance the nitrogen and oxygen in their hermetically sealed, eight-foot-diameter carbon fiber sphere. His co-pilot, Dave Melton, controlled the helium release during ascent, creating the right amount of buoyancy.

Dick checked his Inmarsat satellite communications and radio altimeter, and continually fine-tuned the pressurization in the chamber. He removed his gold Rolex watch — a gift from a sponsor — and replaced it with his trusty Casio, which could do things the Rolex couldn't. He set the Rolex on a shelf. As the balloon reached its target altitude, the buoyant force equaled the craft's weight. Melton removed his boots, tucked them away, and put on his slippers. It was time to relax a bit — this balloon would be their home for the next month. Dick had constructed the balloon's capsule, which his brother Burt had designed, and now the craft was in the stratosphere, heading east. "Cruisin' now," Dick said. On their way.

Suddenly — *BOOM!*

The capsule floor jumped up like a trampoline. The bottom of the helium cell ruptured. Parts of the inside of the balloon hung in shreds. They were falling. Not like a freefall, but going down. Dick was on the radio: *MaydayMaydayMayday! It ruptured . . . we're on our way down.* He grabbed his knife to cut the survival gear free, but stopped himself. *I'm going to use this parachute,* he thought. *I better not cut it with a knife.* The sounds were not comforting — ripping, tearing, rushes of air. A rip to the very top and the helium would release. They would zigzag to the ground like a small party balloon with helium let out. The three-story-high silver balloon would be a flag marker for the point of impact.

This is the end of a nice day, Dick thought drily.

"Can you continue to fly it?" Mission Control asked. Dick and Melton depressurized the cabin and started throwing things out to slow the descent. They pulled the emergency helium release valve and used the long rope to tie it off and keep it open. The two men and the mission controllers went back and forth on what to do, until Dick made the call: "We have an airborne structural failure . . . it's deteriorating . . . we're going to bail out." He had bailed out of burning planes in Vietnam and parachuted into hostile Viet Cong territory. He could get out of a balloon above the New Mexico desert. Dick helped Melton into his boots and parachute. Melton peppered him with questions: *When do I pull the rip cord? . . . How much time do I have to wait?* Dick grew mad as hell: Melton had told him earlier that he had done thirty-five parachute jumps. Dick had asked because he wanted to make sure that Melton had the training — in the unlikely case they had to bail out. *His experience ap-*

pears to be slim to none, Dick thought as they stood at the edge of the capsule.[*]

Melton said repeatedly, "Don't hit me, don't hit me, don't hit me."

"What the hell do you mean?" Dick asked. "You think I'm going to coldcock you with my fist?"

"Don't fall on me when you jump," Melton said.

Dick shook his head. *He doesn't know jack shit about this. The guy has no concept of separation in skydiving. This is not good.* The winds were at least 40 miles per hour on the ground, dangerously high for a parachute landing. He looked up: the aluminized Mylar was shredding on the inside, with strips pulling like tentacles. Melton asked more questions. Dick realized he just had to get him out and under a parachute.

Dick told him: "Keep your head down. Arms in. Jump. Wait a handful of seconds. Pull the rip cord down by your crotch. It should open."

Finally, Dick said, "Go!" Melton jumped, pulling the cord almost as his feet left the

[*] In Melton's defense, he was a last-minute replacement for the flight. Dick had worked for over a year with balloonist Richard Abruzzo, who quit the race only weeks before the scheduled departure. Melton was a talented and experienced balloonist, but he and Dick had little time to prepare.

capsule. Dick didn't have time to tell him to land backward in high winds and always protect the arms. *I don't have time for Parachuting 101,* he thought.

Now about six thousand feet above the ground, Dick got himself ready to jump. There was no time to retrieve his $5,000 Rolex. He saw the pilot Clay Lacy and business magnate Barron Hilton in Hilton's Learjet. Hilton was sponsoring Dick and Melton's flight, and a half dozen other teams in various locations were vying to be the first to race around the world in a balloon. A film crew was following along. Dick stood ready to jump. *I'm going to wait until they come close, so as I jump I'll be right in frame for the camera,* he thought. *You gotta make the best of a bad day.*

Dick had taught people how to jump out of balloons and planes. But he was distracted — by the film crew, by the shredding balloon. He kicked off when he jumped, just as he told students not to do, and started falling and rolling. He tried to grab air. As he plummeted, he yelled at himself: *Don't flip over! Don't flip over! Don't do it!* He flipped over. *I'm pissed.* Then he got himself into a freefall position. He turned and maneuvered, and loved the feeling. He was caught up in the reverie of flying, free and unencumbered, until he realized he had flown to terminal velocity of 125 miles per hour and couldn't pull back. *Crap, this is really going to hurt,* he thought, pulling the chute. He had an emergency parachute, designed to open fast. He shouted: *Holy bananas!* He was sure he'd have crotch burns and raspberries for life.

Dick surveyed the terrain of eastern New Mexico: patches of snow, desert, scrub brush, sloping hills, roads, power lines, cows, a few pastures. There were high winds on the ground. He had not had time to tell Melton that if you land forward going forty miles an hour, your feet hit, you break your toes and kneecaps, you slam down hard, you hit your face. If you put your hands down — your natural instinct — you'll injure your arms and fingers and you won't be able to disconnect from the canopy. You need both your hands. If you can't land backward, there's a chance you'll be dragged to death through the desert.

It was quiet as Dick neared landing. He could hear the ripple of air going through his parachute. He looked between his legs and saw the ground going by in a blur. He turned backward — an uncomfortable feeling. *Resist the urge to turn around! Don't turn around! Low enough now. Elbows in. Ground close, no turning now. Grab the four risers! Hold them.* Bam! *Feet hit. Pull the risers across your chest!* His back slammed to the ground. Then his head.

Did my helmet crack?

Dick lay motionless. He looked up and around. *I'm in a goddamn cactus patch,* he muttered. *Cholla cactus. The most hated cacti around. A cactus that grabs you, that has a straight needle that turns and hooks under your skin. Cholla all over my face.*

He'd crashed his motorcycle enough to know that seconds could pass before the pain really kicked in. He waited. The cholla on his face and hands was one thing. *There isn't any horrible pain elsewhere,* he thought. Ops check time: *Neck works, okay. Hands work, okay. Knees work, okay.* He looked to his feet — the big test. *Can I move my feet? Yes! The central nervous system is working.* His right hand was full of needles, which left him in a quandary. *Do I take the hand already full of needles to get needles off my face, or do I use the good hand, and get needles in that, too? Maybe I can find a knife.*

Seconds later, a television news helicopter landed. Soon, a cameraman — with a huge camera on his shoulders — walked around him in a big circle. He didn't say, "Hey, Dick, are you okay?" He filmed everything and said nothing. Dick soon heard the helicopter shut down and told himself the pilot would come to his aid. *Okay, a fellow aviator is going to get out and help me.* The helicopter pilot appeared and looked at Dick, wearing his

310

jumpsuit and helmet, and said, "You okay?" Dick, still supine, responded, "Yeah. How about getting this fucking cactus off my face?"

Wearing gloves, the pilot carefully extracted the cactus. Dick's nose and cheeks looked like they'd been in a fight with a tiger. The pilot took Dick's hands — needles now removed — and carefully, slowly, pulled him to his feet. Dick was able to walk away. Melton wasn't so lucky. When he landed, his femur went through his hip socket, and he went end over end. But Melton was alive. He would be okay.

Their balloon eventually hit a power line in north Texas that cut the envelope loose. The envelope landed in a cow pasture. The capsule, infused with 100 percent oxygen and propane, caught on fire and burned like a cauldron when it crashed down. Dick and his crew chief, Bruce Evans — who had been on the *Voyager* team — went to collect it. There was no sign of the Rolex; nothing at the crash site stood higher than a pair of shoelaces.

Erik Lindbergh sat at a table in a restaurant in Mojave and listened in awe as Dick Rutan told the jaw-dropping story of his attempt to fly the Barron Hilton balloon around the world. It was one of the most incredible adventure stories that Erik had ever heard, one that got better and better as it got worse and worse.

Dick was recounting his balloon misadventure in mesmerizing detail for a small XPRIZE event that had drawn board members, local aviators, and rocket makers to Mojave. Erik was happy to be there; the XPRIZE was a fresh, daring venture. Attending events like this one helped him forget his own misery. Erik repositioned himself in his chair. He was recovering from a fusion of the talonavicular joint in his right foot, a surgery that involved screws and a bone graft. Somehow, Dick's colorful storytelling made Erik's pain more bearable.

Dick told the gathering that if anyone completed the around-the-world balloon journey, a $1 million prize would be offered by Anheuser-Busch, the beer company. But he emphasized that money was never a motivation for him.

"I did this for a milestone," Dick said. "There are a certain amount of milestones in aviation. We looked at the *Voyager* as the 'last first.' People set all sorts of *records* for speed, altitude, and distance. But there are only certain events that happen that are *milestones.*" He ticked off a few: the first Moon landing; John Alcock and Arthur Brown's first nonstop transatlantic flight in 1919, crossing from Newfoundland to Ireland; Leigh Wade's flight around the world (in segments and with four planes) in 1924; Lindbergh's New York–to–Paris flight in 1927; British captain

Charles Kingsford Smith's first flight across the Pacific Ocean in 1928; his *Voyager* flight. "These are events that are landmarks, that mark a change in development, in what is possible. It's more than a record, where, okay, you get your name in a record book."

Other participants in the balloon race had included Steve Fossett in his *Solo Spirit;* Richard Branson, the billionaire head of the Virgin Group, in his *Virgin Global Challenger;* Swiss psychiatrist Bertrand Piccard and crew in the *Breitling Orbiter;* and Kevin Uliassi in the *J. Renee.* So far, no balloonist had ever come close to achieving such a distance — more than 25,000 miles — and several had died trying.

"I didn't know anything about ballooning when I started," Dick told the group. "I started asking questions, and talked to some people and said, 'We oughta fly a balloon around the world. I know something about flying around the world. Why not?' " Dick said the problem with the Barron Hilton balloon was a manufacturer's defect that caused the helium cell to rupture. He was already working on building a second capsule for his next attempt. He had a new constrained volume helium lifting system, and a new name — *World Quest.*[*]

[*] In 1999, the team of Bertrand Piccard and Brian Jones became the first balloonists to circumnavigate

313

Erik stretched his legs. *This guy has courage,* he thought. He spends a year building the capsule by hand in Mojave, planning, getting ready, lifting off. He would fly over hostile areas with uncertain clearance: Russia, China, Afghanistan, Iraq. Then, about twelve minutes after hitting the stratosphere, just as he thinks they're off and cruising — the balloon explodes. And it intensifies from there, right down to landing in a massive cactus patch. But he makes the most of it. *You gotta make the best of a bad day,* Dick had said.

Erik's rheumatoid arthritis brought a lot of bad days. He was still trying to figure out how to operate in a world that he couldn't attack physically, as he was used to. He was figuring out how to make a living when he didn't know whether he would wake up able to move or not. He'd had the one foot operated on, and was going to have to have his left foot fused as well. Dick ended his talk by sharing a story about his brother.

"There are two things I always say about Burt's designs: no way is this going to work, and no way can we get it done that fast. Then Burt comes back and uses his favorite saying,

---

the globe with a nonstop, nonrefueled flight. At that point, once they succeeded, Dick Rutan was no longer interested in making the flight.

'Gray today, white tonight.' The plane is gray now, but you can paint it white tonight." Dick laughed. "We'd be like, 'There's no frickin' way. It's twenty percent done!' But Burt would stay with his 'white tonight' mantra, and more often than not, miracles happened."

The talk of miracles stayed with Erik. Change *was* always possible, always right around the corner. Erik told himself, *Gray today, white tonight.*

A few months later, on July 25, 1998, Mike Melvill walked out onto runway 30 at the Mojave airport to take his first flight in the Proteus, the Angel Technologies high-altitude experimental plane developed to deliver broadband services. The plane's design had evolved from solar-powered to twin-engine early in development. Burt knew that a solar-powered plane wouldn't be strong enough or reliable enough to carry and power the payload. It also had to fly at night, when there is no solar power. If all went according to plan, the completed Proteus would fly higher than Mike had ever gotten close to flying. The all-composite plane with graphite-epoxy construction was designed to fly to above 60,000 feet and carry a large, downward-pointing antenna.

The plane was beauty and beast; big yet delicate. After getting into the aircraft, Mike and flight test engineer Pete Siebold taxied down the runway. The Proteus flexed, twisted, and bent. When Mike tested the brakes, even the wide-stance landing gear seemed to flex back and forth. He took his time, taxiing it around the Mojave runways, becoming familiar with the plane's behavior on the ground. When he was comfortable, he moved on to do the plane's first high-speed run along runway 30. He carefully lifted the nose wheel off the runway, reduced the power, and let it run the length of the runway on the main wheels. He got a sense of how the plane would look when he touched down his main wheels for the first landing. Approaching the end of the runway, he lowered the nose wheel to the runway and applied the brakes. He turned the Proteus around and used more power, rapidly accelerating to Burt's predicted liftoff speed, then reduced power to maintain the speed and pulled back on the side stick control, lifting the Proteus just a couple of feet into the air.

Mike smiled. As he flew toward the end of runway 12, still only a few feet in the air, the plane felt remarkably controllable. He gingerly tried small inputs of all three axes of control, and was happy with the handling qualities in ground effect. In time, he reduced the power to idle and gently landed. Burt, chasing him in a company truck, looked thrilled with the two high-speed runs. They taxied back to Scaled, where the ground crew would go over the plane, like a groom with a prized racehorse. They would prepare the Proteus for its first flight up high the next morning.

Months before, Mike and Siebold had traveled to Beale Air Force Base in northern California to learn about high-altitude flying and get trained in the use of pressure suits. When Mike first stepped into the fitted suit, he wasn't sure he was cut out for the Astronaut Corps. He felt terribly claustrophobic. He spent two days at Beale. Enduring rapid decompression tests on the second day, the chamber crew, including a doctor, monitored him from the other side of windows. The atmosphere was raised to 70,000 feet from sea level in less than two seconds. The experience was terrifying, even with the classroom training he'd had the day before. Instantly, the Gore-Tex pressure suit went from a soft fabric to one of baseball material, making it hard for Mike to move his legs and arms, and nearly impossible to simulate flying. The efforts were exhausting. Mike saw a bowl of water on a windowsill inside the chamber. As he passed 63,000 feet, the water boiled furiously until there was none left. This was what would happen to his blood if he were not wearing a functioning pressure suit.* *This*

* A metaphor describes what was happening with

317

space stuff is scary, he thought to himself.

Early on the morning of July 26, on a beautiful, clear, windless day, Mike and Siebold — a talented young engineer and naturally gifted pilot — suited up, donned their parachutes, and climbed into the Proteus. It was time for the plane's first real flight. Mike taxied out to runway 30 and applied maximum power to the two jet engines mounted on the aft fuselage. The Proteus accelerated rapidly down the runway, rotated, and lifted into the sky for the first time. The rate of

---

the boiling water: The water molecules are trying to jailbreak from the liquid phase (their prison) through the surface (the steel bars) into the open (the vapor phase). Either you give them a more powerful drill (that is, more heat) or you make the bars lighter by reducing the external pressure. At the Armstrong limit (63,000 feet), the bars all but vanish, and the molecules escape en masse, free at last. It's water below the line and water vapor above the line. The molecules bounce around and eject off the surface into the vapor layer above the bowl of water. The atmosphere is bearing down on the surface, making it harder for the molecules to get out. You can either give them more energy by heating the water or make their life easier by reducing the atmospheric pressure. At the Armstrong limit, the pressure is so low that water at human body temperature will boil away.

climb was smooth as could be. Mike reached 12,000 feet, circling the airport to remain within gliding range. He went through the test card, including approaches to the stall, which he found benign. Roll forces were higher than on most planes he had flown, but appropriate for an aircraft of this size. Pitch and yaw forces were light and just about perfect, while control authority in all three axes was outstanding.* Because the plane had a canard — a forward wing — it flew in some ways like the Long-EZ, but had a flexible airframe and an unsettling ride in turbulence. The main wing was long and narrow, and bent more than any aircraft he had flown, almost like a car with soft suspension. As soon as Mike got used to the flexing, though, the Proteus proved a comfortable ride.

With the first flight tests behind them, Burt and the Scaled crew began thinking about late September as a time for the first public flight of the Proteus, which would also be the flight attended by their clients, Marc Arnold, David Wine, and Peter Diamandis. Burt and

---

* During yaw the nose of the aircraft moves from side to side. During pitch the nose moves up or down. During roll the nose rotates around the direction of flight like a spinning football. The rudder creates yaw force around the aircraft center of gravity, the elevators create pitch force, and the ailerons on the wings create rolling motion.

Mike also talked excitedly about the possibility of setting national and international world altitude records in the Proteus in its weight class. The plane was impressive, and attracting some major attention.

Burt was in his office on the Mojave flight line when he looked out the window and saw a Boeing 757 Business Jet taxiing to a stop. It wasn't every day that a 757 — measuring 155 feet long with a wingspan of 124 feet — arrived in off-the-grid Mojave, but Burt was expecting a visit from Microsoft cofounder Paul Allen and Vern Raburn, who handled Allen's technology investments.

Burt gazed at the 757, sitting way up high, as it came to a stop in front of Scaled. He frowned. Mojave had no commercial infrastructure, and was not the kind of airport with a mobile stairway to use for the next billionaire who rolled up. Burt grabbed a couple of his guys and headed outside. The 757 was the same plane used by the vice president for Air Force Two. Suddenly, the door to the 757 opened. Out flipped, in a sort of seamless triple flip, an elegant air stair. Burt looked up at Paul Allen and thought, *God is here.*

Allen and Raburn were in Mojave because Allen was investing heavily in broadband, buying cable systems, Web portals, wireless modems, and fiber builders. He was staging an initial public offering to raise billions for his cable firm, Charter Communications. He was looking at all areas of infrastructure of the Internet, and flew from Seattle to Mojave to find out what the Proteus could do. He was intrigued by the high-altitude plane, which was designed to stay at altitude for twelve hours, spit out broadband, and be replaced with the next plane for another twelve-hour shift.

Burt told Raburn and Allen that he had done the Proteus's preliminary design work between November 1994 and May 1996. The second phase, involving a more detailed design and the building of the prototype — the idea was to have a fleet of these planes — began in December 1996. The plane's general mission capabilities included commercial telecommunications, communication and data relay, atmospheric sciences, reconnaissance, and microsatellite launch. The midfuselage area was the dedicated payload component, and Burt had made the wing and canard tips extendable to adapt to the aerodynamics of a wide range of payloads. As a mechanism for broadband delivery, the Proteus was less expensive than broadband delivered by satellite, could go for twelve hours with 12,500 pounds at takeoff, and circle at altitudes of between 52,000 and 64,000 feet.

Burt went over the other figures for atmospheric science, reconnaissance, and microsatellite missions. Then he got to a final possible use for the Proteus, one he hadn't discussed publicly: space tourism. Burt broached the possibility that the Proteus, or some version of it, could be employed to launch a spaceship from the air. The spaceship would then rocket out of the atmosphere, giving the crew about four minutes of zero gravity and about the same view of Earth that you would see from orbit, and then fall back for landing.

As soon as he uttered this idea, Burt knew he had the quiet billionaire's full attention.

Allen, born in 1953, was ten years younger than Burt. He was a classic space geek: he loved science fiction, grew up knowing the names of the Mercury 7 astronauts, and followed every NASA launch. Like Burt, he built balsa wood model planes and made and launched model rockets. In 1969, the tenth grader who loved music and machinery in equal parts had a banner year. In May he went to his first rock concert — Jimi Hendrix — and in July, watched Apollo 11 land on the Moon. In more recent times, he had commissioned architect Frank Gehry to build a rock-and-roll and science fiction museum in Seattle. Allen was the world's third richest man (after Bill Gates and Warren Buffett) with a net worth of $22 billion. He owned the Portland Trail Blazers basketball team and the Seattle Seahawks football franchise.

He had a yacht the size of the White House, and the Boeing 757 was but one of the planes in his stable.

Burt told Allen that he wasn't entirely convinced that the Proteus was the right vehicle for suborbital spaceflight, but that the Proteus was inspiring sketches for another space plane, possibly an air-launched craft modeled after the X-15, which had been carried aloft by a modified B-52. His idea was to design something "safer and cheaper, something you could sell tickets for." Burt made it clear he wasn't looking for money, and told Allen and Raburn, "I don't know if I can do this, it's just something I've been thinking about. It's something that might happen." Allen made it clear that he was interested. If Burt got to a point where he believed his design would fly to space, Allen wanted to be the first to hear about it.

A short time later, Allen and Raburn boarded the 757. The elegant air stair retracted with the ease of a red carpet being rolled up. Off they flew into the cloudless Mojave sky.

After Allen and Raburn had left, Burt stood in his office thinking about the XPRIZE. He had been approached early on by Peter to help develop and refine the rules and requirements. Burt told him, "I will not help you. I may want to compete and win this, and it wouldn't be a good idea if I was involved in writing the rules." Looking at some of the sketches he'd done for the Proteus, he felt it would be tough to launch something into space with three seats — as was required by the XPRIZE. He had all sorts of ideas, including launching a capsule with parachute recovery, like Mercury and Gemini. He considered helicopter recovery, knowing he could use his neighbor's Huey helicopter to attempt in-flight pickup of a capsule, where the helicopter grabbed the top of the capsule's parachute and set it carefully on the ground right in front of Scaled.

But there were tough obstacles. Even the world's largest governments hadn't succeeded in building a fully reusable manned space vehicle.[*] And Peter didn't have the $10 million prize money; Orteig had put up the $25,000 right away, just like Kremer for human-powered flight.

As Burt worked throughout the day, he thought of his meeting with Paul Allen and brainstormed about the most vexing part of human space-flight, the holy grail of manned missions: the return to Earth. He sat down and began to draw. When he looked up again, everyone had gone home.

---

[*] The space shuttle came the closest. The fifteen-story external tank of the space shuttle was the only component not reused.

16
PETER'S PITCHES

The XPRIZE gala dinner at the St. Louis Planetarium was sold out. Once again, Peter had astronauts. He had renowned space scientists. He had military brass. He had captains of industry and a who's who of endorsing organizations. He had members of competing XPRIZE teams. He had artwork and models of the teams' designs. He had attention from the media. He even had an elaborate trophy for the eventual winner. It was what he didn't have that weighed on him.

After issuing a clarion call to rocket makers, investors, and entrepreneurs, Peter had contenders with ideas for vehicles in all shapes and sizes, from the familiar to the flying saucer. He had assurances from teams that funding was secure or imminent. But at the end of the day, no one appeared to be building anything. In Peter's mind, the competition would be real only when the hardware was real.

In the same way Peter was jonesing for

hardware, he was hustling for dollars. He was pitching his heart out, and here he was, in the middle of a dot-com bonanza, when wildly speculative companies including Pets.com and Webvan were taking in hundreds of millions of dollars in investment capital, and he was coming up empty handed, for something that could make history and launch an industry.

To make matters worse, his keynote speaker for the XPRIZE gala had canceled at the last minute. Buzz Aldrin had phoned a few days before the event to say he couldn't make it. Adding even more to Peter's headache was the reality that the one possible contender with actual hardware was Burt Rutan. Burt still hadn't officially registered for the XPRIZE competition, but he was making moves in that direction with the Proteus aircraft. Aware of the major conflict of interest, Peter sent out a letter to the teams disclosing how funding for the Proteus had come in part from his company Angel. He really didn't want the Proteus to be Burt's solution to win the XPRIZE competition.

Al Kerth, emcee of the St. Louis gala dinner, opened the evening by noting, "Attendance tonight has grown by more than thirty percent over last year. This is a sellout crowd. Only the stock market has shown more growth recently. I was thinking the only other difference between the stock market and the XPRIZE is we know the stock market is going to crash." He paused for the laughter. "Okay, bad joke."

After welcoming representatives of the XPRIZE teams, Kerth talked about exciting developments in the realm of space, including a half dozen shuttle missions; the Clementine unmanned mission, which revealed water ice at the lunar south pole; the Hale-Bopp comet paying Earth a visit; the Pathfinder landing on Mars; and the Global Surveyor entering the orbit around Mars. He noted that aviator, balloonist, and adventurer Steve Fossett was in attendance, as was Pete Worden, DC-X engineer Bill Gaubatz, and Clementine deputy program manager Stu Nozette. Peter's parents, Harry and Tula, were there, and had donated $25,000 for a New Spirit of St. Louis membership.

At the dais, Kerth was handed a note. Reading it, he looked up and scanned the crowd. He said he had an announcement to make. The surprise news was that someone in the audience had just bought not one, not two, not three, but *four* New Spirit memberships, valued at $100,000. Kerth said, "The donation comes from a man of surprises. You know him already as a great author — of books including *The Hunt for Red October, Red Storm Rising, Patriot Games, Clear and Present Danger, Without Remorse.* But how many of you knew he started as a humble insurance agent? He's also an investor in one of the XPRIZE competitors, Rotary Rocket. He's part owner of the Baltimore Orioles. His personal military contacts rival those of most nations. His job tonight is to lay to rest the rumor that the XPRIZE is really a secret conspiracy propagated by aliens stranded here." He paused for effect. "His name? Tom Clancy."

Clancy, drink in hand, made his way to the stage. At the podium, he said, "Let me tell you a story. July 20, 1969. Apollo 11. It was the night of the watermelons. I was driving home. There were all of these watermelons everywhere. I finally catch this tractor. I see watermelons falling out the back. July 20 was a great day to be an American. That was when NASA really meant something. The people at NASA are good people and smart people, but they are working in a system that doesn't reward achievement. The government doesn't really work.

"When the government wants to do something intelligent, they need us. Who invented the personal computer? The government? No. IBM? No. Two college dropouts named Jobs and Woz in a garage! Okay, it takes a big garage to build a rocket, but that's the American way. The difference between private industry and the government is we have to be efficient. If we don't make money, we go out of business. We need to create a private industry around space."

He continued, "America has brought democracy to the world. Freedom. Liberty. It happened here. Now, our job as Americans is to get the hell back out there in space. Progress depends on the unreasonable man."

He concluded, "Let's have some fun. I just pledged $100,000 for this — because it's fun! How often do you get a chance to make history? How often do you get a chance to see something cool happen and say, 'I had a piece of that'? To tell your grandchildren, 'I kind of helped.' Our next legacy will be to start human expansion into the next dimension.

"We do impossible things. That's why we're here. Look at things that never happen and say, 'Impossible?' Impossible means we don't know how to do it today. We'll figure it out. The future is something we will build." The evening ended with enthusiasm, encomiums, and more Tom Clancy dazzle. Funds were raised, and the night was a success. What still eluded Peter, though, was a big-name sponsor.

Peter's very first pitch, after the XPRIZE announcement under the arch, had been to St. Louis civic leader Bill Maritz, who ran a billion-dollar business, Maritz Inc., structuring in-house sales incentive programs for companies including General Motors. Peter and Gregg Maryniak believed that Maritz would be a perfect title sponsor, given his awareness of the XPRIZE and the company's focus on incentive-based competitions.

Gregg had flown in from New Jersey. He and Colette Bevis — now doing marketing for the XPRIZE — met Peter at a Kinko's in downtown St. Louis at around nine P.M. the night before the meeting. They had copying, printing, and binding to do. They wanted to make high-resolution, full-color prints from nearly sixty slides. Hours into the project, copies done, they used a 3M adhesive spray for the backing of the eleven-by-seventeen-inch color images. They managed to get as much glue on themselves as on the heavy cardboard stock. They didn't leave Kinko's until three A.M., returned to their hotel at four A.M., and were at the meeting with Maritz at nine A.M.

There were about ten people on the Maritz side. Peter did most of the pitching, starting out with an overview of the XPRIZE goals. "We had no money and no teams when we kicked off the XPRIZE," Peter said. "Our goal is to incentivize a twenty-first-century Charles Lindbergh." He went on for several minutes.

Al Kerth, who was present at the meeting, discussed the impact that the prize would have on St. Louis. A local sponsorship would change people's view of St. Louis from a "has been" to a "futuristic" city; create a new industry in St. Louis; excite youth about St. Louis's image — "space is sexy"; and offer "huge revenue potential for the city and its surroundings." Kerth had dreams of the prize being waged and won in St. Louis and recreating the romance and pride of the 1904 St. Louis World's Fair, which attracted visitors from near and far.

Maritz and his team wanted to know why NASA wasn't doing what the XPRIZE was attempting. Maritz asked about the risks to the sponsor if something went wrong. He wanted to know the likelihood of anyone pulling this off. While there was a flurry of questions, there was also considerable warmth and encouragement. When the meeting ended and Peter and crew walked out, Gregg surmised they had a "fifty-fifty chance."

"They seemed to really get it," Gregg enthused. Peter thought the odds were even better. That night, Peter and Gregg let themselves imagine what it would be like to land their title sponsor on their very first try.

A few days later, Peter got a call from Maritz's office. The idea was great, Peter was told, but it didn't "align with who we are."

That was the beginning of passionate pitches and succinct noes. Peter pitched to the founders of Enterprise Rent-A-Car, selling it as EnterPRIZE. He and Gregg and crew did the same with just about every major company in St. Louis. Then they moved on to Boeing, Cadillac, Champ Car, Charter Cable, Cisco, DHL, DuPont, Echo-Star, Emerson, E*TRADE, Gateway Computers, JetBlue, Hilton, Lexus, Mars Inc., Miramax, Orbitz, Red Bull, Sprint, Wendy's, and more. Every time, there were the same concerns: "Why isn't NASA doing this? Can any small team really do it? Isn't it too dangerous? What if someone dies?"

A few months of failed pitches later, in late 1998, Peter, who was living part time in St. Louis and part time in Rockville, Maryland, had a meeting in London with the man he was sure held his winning lottery ticket. This was their guy. Peter could feel it. He was scheduled to meet with none other than Richard Branson of the Virgin Group. Branson, the rebel billionaire. Branson, the adventurer. Branson, the space lover.

The Virgin Group, started in the sixties with a magazine called *Student* and a record shop that evolved into a label called Virgin Records, was now made up of hundreds of companies, including Virgin Atlantic Airways. Branson lived on his privately owned Necker Island, which was, naturally, located in the Virgin Islands. He exuded gusto, with his mane of blond hair, year-round tan, and open-collar shirts. He had an international best-selling book out, *Losing My Virginity.* He was a humanitarian, and he was on a quest to break records — in balloons, boats, and amphibious vehicles. Peter wanted to convince Branson that it was time to trade in his dangerous balloon adventures for something more sedate, like spaceships.

Peter met up with his friend and business partner Eric Anderson at the airport in Newark, New Jersey, to fly on Virgin Atlantic to Heathrow Airport in London. Eric was twenty-three, fresh out of college, and working for a software company in Philadelphia. Eric and Peter had met several years earlier, in the mid-1990s, when Anderson was an aerospace student at the University of Virginia. Eric, a member of UVA's SEDS chapter, interned for Peter and spent the summer living in his basement, helping him in the early days of both the XPRIZE and ZERO-G Corp. He and Peter had just started a new company called Space Adventures with Mike McDowell, who had founded a polar expedition company called Quark Expeditions. Space Adventures was an umbrella organization for all things space, from private tours of rocket facilities with astronauts to classes on propulsion systems to zero gravity experiences. They wanted to broker deals between viable rocket providers — including in Russia — and wealthy citizens interested in the ultimate joyride.

Peter and Eric arrived at Heathrow before seven A.M. London time. Peter told Eric they would be met at passenger pickup by a Virgin Limobikes, courtesy of Branson. Eric had never heard of a motorcycle limo, but was too tired to give it much thought. It was freezing outside: drizzly, gray, snow seemingly imminent. They met their motorcyclists, were given leathers and helmets with microphones, and watched as their wardrobe bags were strapped to the back of the bikes. They took off in a blur, and held on as the red Virgin motorcycles darted in and out of morning rush-hour traffic. Eric's mind was on strong hot coffee. Peter was having a great time. They arrived at Branson's three-story town house in Holland Park, and were directed to a den off the living room. The first thing the two noticed was a model of Vela Technology's Space Cruiser displayed on the mantel. Peter and Eric fretted that the Vela folks had gotten to Branson before they had. Eric wondered if Branson would milk them for information on Vela, which was doing its own thing and wasn't involved in the XPRIZE. The company, based in Virginia, was trying to develop a fully reusable, two-stage rocket to carry at least six passengers for $80,000 each on suborbital flights. Eric knew the company was trying to raise more than $100 million.

Fifteen minutes later, Branson walked down the stairs, smiling warmly as he greeted them. Branson was in his trademark khakis and white shirt. He appeared relaxed, and asked about the motorcycle limo service. Peter, who had been anxious about the meeting — Branson was someone he deeply admired — began his pitch, talking up the power of the "Virgin XPRIZE," and detailing some of the contenders and likely entrants.

Branson said he had been to Mojave years before to meet Burt Rutan to get a sense of his thinking on pressurized balloon capsules. Peter, who had brought mockups of Virgin XPRIZE logos, told Branson about Charles Lindbergh and the history of the Orteig Prize. Branson was intrigued, and said he loved the idea. He had been drawn to space as a teenager and was nineteen when Apollo 11 landed on the Moon. Branson had a number of favorite space quotes, including one by Carl Sagan about the richness of the cosmos: "The total number of stars in the universe is larger than all of the grains of sand on all of the beaches on planet Earth."

As Eric talked about Space Adventures' mission of broadening access to space by offering zero-gravity experiences, suborbital expeditions, and orbital flights on Russian hardware, Branson asked a question that took Eric by surprise. The billionaire wanted to know whether there was really a market for space tourism. No private citizens had ever flown on a commercial rocket to space. Private space as an industry did not exist.

"Is there really a market for people going up and floating around?" Branson asked. "I mean, I would do it, but I'm kind of crazy."

Peter listened, sure Branson already knew the answer and was playing devil's advocate. Eric thought Branson seriously doubted that a market existed. Peter and Eric talked about different events that showed the public appetite for private access to space. In 1958, Bantam Books published an "extraterrestrial travel reservation form" in the back of selected science fiction paperbacks. It asked readers to "Reserve a future trip to the planets. Your name and destination request will be kept on record until the technology is available to take you there." More than 250,000 responses poured in. Ten years later, during the height of the Apollo program, Pan Am Airlines offered reservations for a trip to the Moon. Ninety-three thousand people signed up. In 1985, hundreds of people put down $5,000 deposits for a private flight to orbit, this one offered by adventure travel agency Society Expeditions. Major checks from wealthy individuals soon followed. When NASA refused to sell shuttle seats to Society Expeditions, Gary Hudson was hired to design and build a private spaceship. That pursuit ended when the *Challenger* exploded.

Branson listened and nodded. He was a dreamer; these guys were dreamers. His motivation, though, was not necessarily to create another company because he saw a market for it. He started companies because of simple urges: to listen to better music, to have a better experience flying, to get a better drink at a juice bar, to get to London from Heathrow faster. If *he* had the desire to do something, he figured a lot of other people would, too. He definitely had an urge to go to space. He looked at Peter and thought, *Everything tells me I should say yes.*

Days later, when Peter was back in the States, he got word from Branson's people. Dr. Yes, as he was known, had said no. Peter sat in shock. He wondered: "If Richard Branson says no, who will say yes?"

In early 1999, Peter landed another major meeting, with another major billionaire, who also seemed *the perfect fit* for the XPRIZE. This time, he was heading to Seattle to meet with Jeff Bezos, head of the impossibly fast-growing Amazon.com. The e-commerce company, not yet five years old, had a stock market value of more than $30 billion. The stock had risen 1,000 percent in a year, making the Seattle-based company more valuable than blue-chip giants like Texaco. Bezos, thirty-five years old, was worth at least $9 billion — and he was a space lover. Peter and Bezos had an e-mail exchange in which Bezos agreed to the meeting but cautioned, "I'm so busy I'm trying to optimize my tooth brushing time."

Peter couldn't help but get his hopes up again. As a kid, Bezos watched *Star Trek* religiously and spent recess playing Spock or Captain Kirk. When he graduated as valedictorian of his high school class, he spoke of building colonies for millions of people in orbit to "preserve the Earth." Before graduating summa cum laude from Princeton in 1986 with degrees in electrical engineering and computer science, Bezos served as the chapter head of the campus SEDS group. Peter and Bezos had been in the same circles but had never met.

The two got together for breakfast at a diner in downtown Seattle. Bezos, *Time* magazine's person of the year, was dressed in jeans and wore a watch that updated itself thirty-six times a day from the atomic clock. His laugh was quirky and unabashed. They talked about their shared interest in space, and about the SEDS days at Princeton. The SEDS chapter hosted movie nights, showing 16 mm films ordered from NASA about the history of the Apollo program. They had Friday night showings of James Bond films. They would charge $2 or $3 for tickets and sometimes make a few hundred dollars. The money paid for field trips to air shows, the Smithsonian Air and Space Museum, or nearby Air Force bases. They sent students to symposiums on Robert Goddard and conducted campuswide polls asking students how they felt about the U.S. space program.

Like SEDS chapters elsewhere, SEDS at Princeton was all about networking with like-minded students, learning more, and plotting a more active future in space. Up to two dozen students showed up for regular meetings, held in hallways or open rooms of the Princeton student union. Their biggest meeting followed President Reagan's speech about diverting nuclear weapons by building a peace shield. An advocacy group formed, and soon a meeting was held on the subject, drawing hundreds of people and high-ranking military leaders.

Peter and Bezos were seated in a booth in the dark-wood diner. Peter, three years older than Bezos, explained the XPRIZE idea. He talked about the teams and showed him vehicle drawings. He went over specifications and propulsion systems. Bezos listened closely and asked highly technical questions. The two talked about Gerry O'Neill, who was at Princeton while Bezos was a student, and about their shared long-term vision of going to the Moon and mining space for resources. By the end of the meeting, Peter was clear on one thing: Bezos wasn't going to fund the XPRIZE. As an engineer, Bezos didn't want to just sponsor spaceflight; he wanted to be involved in making this dream come true himself. He wanted to get a smart group of people together to design and create his own star chaser. Bezos told Peter that Amazon was his means to make money to get to space. The more money Amazon made, the better his chances were of opening space. Amazon was his focus at present. As the two stood to leave, Bezos picked up the check. Peter noticed that Bezos ripped up the receipt and left it there. He was well beyond the point of expensing a meal.

The two parted ways but agreed to stay in touch. Another space-loving billionaire had turned Peter down. Peter was disappointed again, but also felt that if the XPRIZE didn't succeed, Bezos had the wealth and vision to one day pull it off himself. As Peter trudged up the hilly streets of Seattle, the drizzle soon turned to a downpour. He didn't have an umbrella.

Filmmaker Bob Weiss watched Peter talk to anyone and everyone about the XPRIZE. He was the evangelist going door to door to win converts. When the two first met in New York years earlier, Peter had excitedly told Bob about a screenplay he'd written that he expected to sell in Hollywood to fund the XPRIZE. Peter believed the script would garner millions up front and millions more once the movie was made. Bob listened, moved his glasses lower on the bridge of his nose, and began telling Peter the reality of

Hollywood. He was sorry to have to disabuse him of his "fantasy notions of the economics of movies."

Bob told Peter that even if he did manage to sell the movie rights, the chances were remote that he would get any real money. Bob found Peter exceedingly bright, and Peter had in his soul what Bob called "the extraterrestrial imperative." He was driven to get off the planet. Bob had the same imperative and wanted to help Peter make his dream come true. It was science fiction come to life. Bob came from Hollywood, where his job was to create alternate realities. This story of Peter Diamandis and the XPRIZE had a similar mission. Since their first meeting, Bob had worked as much as he could on XPRIZE matters, until his wife reminded him they had children in private school. Then he'd go back to moviemaking to make some money before returning to the XPRIZE.

It was now nearly three years after the 1996 announcement under the arch, and the XPRIZE was pulling in just enough money to stay afloat. Peter had done at least fifty pitches for sponsorships, meeting with executives at Sony, Chrysler, Anheuser-Busch, Rolex, Breitling, Ford, FedEx, Airbus, Northrop Grumman, AOL, Discovery, Enterprise, Nissan, and Xerox, to name a few. All turned him down. The New Spirit of St. Louis memberships had kept the XPRIZE alive, and Tom Clancy's support had come at just the right time. But the memberships were increasingly scarce. The XPRIZE was getting $25,000 here, $25,000 there. Peter was like a gambler hooked on intermittent rewards. He was either going to win the jackpot or go broke trying. There was nothing in between.

Peter passed by the XPRIZE office in St. Louis near the St. Charles Airport on his way home from another trip and checked messages left by his assistant. Flipping through the notes, he saw one reading, "First USA called about donation." Peter laughed and thought, *Someone is asking* us *for a donation?* He started to crumple up the note to throw it away, but decided at the last minute to have his assistant call the following day to get more information.

The next day, his assistant came back with promising news. First USA Bank was not *seeking* a donation, but wanted to *make* a donation to the XPRIZE. The bank executives based in Boston had apparently read a story in *The Christian Science Monitor* about the XPRIZE gala event where Tom Clancy donated $100,000, and they were interested in meeting with Peter for a possible deal.

Within a week, a meeting was scheduled at the St. Louis Science Center. Peter met Gregg, Al Kerth, and Doug King there. The four were standing curbside when four First USA executives clad in black suits stepped out of black limos, prompting Peter to quietly refer to them as the Men in Black. Once inside, the executives told Peter, Gregg, Al, and Doug that they were interested in creating an XPRIZE credit card. They explained how they made specialty credit cards for colleges, alumni associations, airlines, and the like. They believed the space community was sizable enough to attract new cardholders. They would want access to the XPRIZE mailing lists, to pilot and general aviation lists, as well as mailing lists for a number of space clubs and organizations. First USA XPRIZE cardholders would get a chance to win various space-related flights, including eventual ZERO-G flights, and flights on Russian MiG jet fighters. Cardholders would also be able to donate directly to the XPRIZE.

A deal came together quickly — and it was big. First USA Bank, anticipating significant revenues through the XPRIZE cards, agreed to fund half of the purse prize. But the offer came with a caveat: the $5 million would be awarded only if the prize could be won by a certain date — December 17, 2003, the one hundredth anniversary of the Wright brothers' historic flight. And there would be no prize unless Peter could come up with the other $5 million.

Back from his trip to St. Louis, Peter got on his running shoes to head to the gym. He was filled with mixed emotions. On the one hand, he could announce to the teams that he had secured half of the $10 million. On the other, his title sponsor remained elusive. Still, in the face of a torrent of noes, the reality was that someone had actually said yes.

Peter Diamandis displaying the model of an atom he made for his first grade science fair. He was upset he took only second place.

Peter Diamandis

Peter with his dad, Harry, mom, Tula, and sister, Marcelle.

Peter Diamandis

Six-year-old Peter Diamandis playing doctor with a kit his parents gave him. He checks his mother's vital signs.
Peter Diamandis

Peter when he first met Arthur C. Clarke at the United Nations' 1982 Unispace conference in Vienna, Austria.
Peter Diamandis

Peter (right) and his rocket-making friend, Billy Greenberg, with their homemade Mongo rocket.
Peter Diamandis

Peter (right) and Todd Hawley clasping hands when Peter turned over
the SEDS chairmanship to Todd at George Washington University.

Peter Diamandis

Peter and his father upon Peter's graduation from Harvard Medical School in 1989.

Peter Diamandis

At a gathering (the "John Galt meeting") of rocket makers and space enthusiasts in Montrose, Colorado, Peter and others shared ideas for getting to space without NASA's help. This was where the idea for the XPRIZE began to take shape. *Peter Diamandis*

The "build a rocket" brainstorming session in Montrose drew a half dozen commercial space enthusiasts to the home of David and Myra Wine. *Peter Diamandis*

(Left to right) Peter, Todd Hawley, and Bob Richards in the Smithsonian Air and Space Museum in 1995. This was the last picture taken of the three of them. *Peter Diamandis*

The $10 million XPRIZE is announced in St. Louis in 1996. St. Louis was chosen as the city for the announcement because that was where the young aviator Charles Lindbergh found his backers to make his transatlantic flight.   *Peter Diamandis*

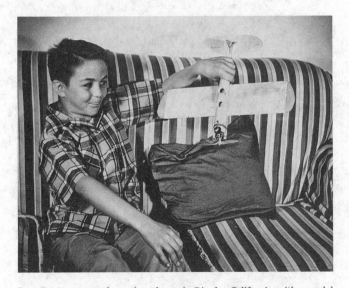

Burt Rutan at around age six at home in Dinuba, California, with a model plane he built. Burt never built models through kits, preferring to make his own designs using mixed pieces of balsa wood.   *Burt Rutan*

Burt Rutan, sixteen, with model planes of his own making assembled for entry in the 1960 Academy of Model Aeronautics national competition. *Burt Rutan*

The *Voyager*'s historic flight by Dick Rutan and Jeana Yeager in 1986, trailed here on the final leg home by brother Burt Rutan and friends Mike and Sally Melvill in their Duchess chase plane. *Mark Greenberg*

Scaled Composites engineer Steve Losey works on the cockpit of what will become *SpaceShipOne*. *Dave Moore*

The construction of Burt Rutan and Paul Allen's secret spaceship program, *SpaceShipOne*—the rocket "mated" with the *White Knight*—at Scaled Composites in a hangar in the Mojave Desert, California. *Dave Moore*

Scaled Composites unveiled its spaceship program to the world in April 2003. Here, Burt (left) with Mercury and shuttle spacecraft designer Max Faget (center) and astronaut Buzz Aldrin. *Bradley Waits*

LEFT: Also at the April 2003 rollout of the *White Knight* and *SpaceShipOne*, Scaled's pilots (left to right) Doug Shane, Mike Melvill, Pete Siebold, and Brian Binnie. *Bradley Waits*

RIGHT: Steve Bennett, a Brit, left a secure job in a Colgate factory in England to start his own company and build rockets. He was the first XPRIZE contender to launch a vehicle. Here he is with his rocket in Morecambe Bay, England, in 2001. *Starchaser Industries Ltd.*

Argentinian space scientist Pablo de León and his XPRIZE capsule in Argentina. His colleagues warned him he would lose his credibility if he tried to win the XPRIZE.

Pablo de León

Romanian Dumitru Popescu dropped out of aerospace engineering school in Bucharest to build a rocket that could win the XPRIZE. Here he is with his XPRIZE contender in September 2004.

Dumitru Popescu

Erik Lindbergh, the grandson of Charles and Anne Morrow Lindbergh, after double total knee replacement surgery. He fought to get his life back after being diagnosed with rheumatoid arthritis. *Barbara Robbins*

A triumphant Erik Lindbergh lands his Lancair at Le Bourget Field in Paris in 2002, seventy-five years after his grandfather made his historic flight. *The Lancair Company*

Burt Rutan (seated left) hosted Microsoft cofounder Paul Allen (seated center) and Virgin Group founder Richard Branson (seated right) at his Mojave home on June 20, 2004—the night before Scaled Composites' attempt to make history with the world's frist private manned space program. The "vision summit," as Burt called it, focused on goals for exploring and inhabiting space.
Tonya Rutan

ABOVE: Cars pour into the Mojave Desert in California in the early morning of June 21, 2004, in hope of witnessing history.
Mark Greenberg

LEFT: Burt Rutan's *White Knight* carries *SpaceShipOne* to altitude. After being released from the *White Knight* at 48,000 feet, spaceship pilot Mike Melvill lights the rocket motor and tries to make it to the Karman line—sixty-two miles up.
Mark Greenberg

Experimental test pilot Mike Melvill is surprised by his celebrity status following his June 21, 2004, suborbital flight, where he took off and landed on a Mojave runway, just a few dozen feet from cheering spectators. Here, Melvill signs a woman's back as others ask for his autograph.
Mark Greenberg

Burt Rutan turns and smiles as pilot Mike Melvill (center) and *SpaceShipOne* backer Paul Allen greet photographers and others in Mojave following the historic June 21, 2004, suborbital flight.
Mark Greenberg

Following the flight, a triumphant Mike Melvill holds a sign plucked from the crowds by his boss and friend Burt Rutan. Burt and Paul Allen (in cap) ride on the back of a truck as the rocket is towed back to its hangar in Mojave.
Mark Greenberg

Mike and Sally Melvill fell in love as teenagers in South Africa and ran away together to get married. Here they are in Scotland the day before their wedding on October 6, 1961. *Mike and Sally Melvill*

Mike and Sally Melvill share a private moment before the first XPRIZE flight on September 29, 2004. Sally was acutely aware of the danger of flying the spaceship and feared losing the love of her life. *Mark Greenberg*

On October 4, 2004, the morning of the "money flight," Mike Melvill (left) tells Brian Binnie that he'll do great. Binnie is out to win the $10 million XPRIZE and to restore his reputation as an ace pilot. *Mark Greenberg*

A special anguish is shared by the wives of experimental test pilots. Here, Brian's wife (left), "Bub" Binnie, and Sally Melvill on the runway right before the start of the October 4, 2004, flight. *Dave Moore*

After a lifetime of dreaming, Peter Diamandis (right) and his father, Harry, watch the winner-takes-all flight of *SpaceShipOne* on October 4, 2004. October 4 was chosen by Burt Rutan to commemorate the anniversary of the launch of Sputnik (1957), the world's first artificial satellite to orbit Earth. *Peter Diamandis*

The *White Knight*, carrying *SpaceShipOne*, takes off for its XPRIZE flight.
Mark Greenberg

As thousands of spectators cheer, *SpaceShipOne* pilot Brian Binnie comes in for a landing to try to win the $10 million XPRIZE.
Mark Greenberg

Richard Branson (in white shirt) hugs Burt Rutan after *SpaceShipOne* wins the XPRIZE. For both men, the day heralded a new era for commercial spaceflight.
Mark Greenberg

An exultant Peter addresses the crowd after the XPRIZE is won, October 4, 2004.

Peiwei Wei

The XPRIZE is won. (Right to left) Richard Branson, Brian Binnie, Burt Rutan, Paul Allen, Peter Diamandis, Amir Ansari, and Anousheh Ansari, October 4, 2004.

Dave Moore

17
A Lindbergh
Sculpts a Dream

Erik Lindbergh sat with a doctor considered brilliant in the field of rheumatology. He was at the Mayo Clinic in Rochester, Minnesota, and had endured day two of being processed like meat, moved from test to test he didn't know he needed, being shuffled along in lines wearing flimsy paper gowns ignominiously open at the back. Erik had tried anything to get better, meeting with alternative healers and osteopaths, adopting the latest in experimental treatments. Nothing worked. Finally, his dad told him, "You have to talk to somebody good," and offered to pay for him to go to the Mayo Clinic. So here Erik sat, across from an esteemed rheumatologist. The doctor studied his X-rays and records, swiveled in his chair and said matter-of-factly, "It's obvious. You need knee replacements. Both knees."

Erik didn't hear much after that. He knew his knees were shot, but no doctor had been this blunt. The doctors he had seen before didn't put expectations on him; they treated him where he was rather than looking too far ahead. Erik left the hospital in a stupor. He was by himself, relying on his cane to navigate the icy walkways and make it down the steps. Instead of staying at a hotel connected to the Mayo Clinic campus by heated and covered walkways, he had tried to save money by booking a room in a motel across town. He kept hearing the words: *total bilateral knee replacement.*

Arriving back in his room, he sat down on the bed and didn't bother to take off his coat. There was a jagged line of brown liquid creeping down one wall. The light was dim and flickering and the radiator sputtered. The thick shag rug was the color of mustard. Someone outside yelled to the manager that there was a rat in the pool. He moved his hands along his long legs. Strong, agile, ready for adventure. Fly down a trail on a mountain bike. Carve glassy water with a slalom ski, huge spray, controlled, aggressive cuts through the wake. Aerial cartwheels, boxes of trophies. That was then. Now his legs were thin, brittle. Stuck like rusted metal. The room, the sounds, the doctor's words, the feeling of his legs. It hit him. He curled up on the bed and cried. Hours passed. The light in the room was tobacco brown. He slowly got up and forced himself to look in the mirror. Really look. For most of a decade, he looked past his reflection. He shied away from having his picture taken. He even avoided his shadow. He was young and fit. Erik the gifted athlete. Not frail and hobbled. His smile would conceal his pain; no one would notice the cane. He was still the same Erik. This is what he told himself. The disease, with its pattern of attack and retreat, pain and easing off, was complicit in his denial. It enabled him to put off acknowledging that he had a serious and chronic disease. He studied himself in the mirror. He felt his beard. He was not yet thirty-five, but he was an old man.

The good thing, Erik told himself later, was that there was nowhere to go but up from the motel in Rochester. Six months later, he had new knees. He kept his old knees — chunks of bone — in a jar in the refrigerator until his wife, Mara, said the knees had to go. He had wanted to hold on to them for as long as he could, maybe even have a burial. He reluctantly moved them out of the fridge and put them in a wooden box outside, where they were eventually eaten by mice. The recovery was slow and painful. He had eight-inch vertical scars over both knees. But the pain of surgery and recovery was better than the pain of rheumatoid arthritis. He spent his recovery at the small beach home of his mother, Barbara, on Bainbridge Island. He needed constant care. His friends came to visit, and physical therapists were in and out. Not long after surgery, with his knees still huge from swelling, Erik was up and walking around. Barbara returned home one day to find Erik had somehow made it down the stairs and was out wading into the salt water. She just watched him — her happy-go-lucky boy who rarely complained about anything. It wasn't long before he could walk steadily and without a cane. Barbara worried, though, about what was ahead. She feared that the new knees were like new tires for an old car. His wrists were shot from using the cane so hard. He still needed his right foot fused like the left. And the surgeon who replaced his knees cautioned that he would need to go through the same surgery again in a decade or two.

In his drive to get better and have a normal life again, Erik learned of a new medicine called Enbrel. The drug was a "biologic," made in living cell cultures rather than through a manufactured chemical process. The cultures were made from genetically modified Chinese hamster ovary cells. The hamster's ovary cells were said to produce the proteins needed to combat rheumatoid arthritis by stopping joint damage and inflammation. Erik's rheumatologist was cautiously optimistic about Enbrel, but told him that his health insurance wouldn't cover the cost of the drug. Fortuitously, his doctor was involved in a double-blind efficacy study on Enbrel. He got Erik into the trial and told him that if he showed improvement while on the drug, his insurer would then probably cover the costs of the medication. His doctor warned him that the treatment required suppressing his immune system, which in turn could make the body vulnerable to everyday infections or more serious problems. He also said the long-term side effects were unknown, and that it "may cause cancer."

Erik listened to all the warnings, but didn't hesitate. Parts of his body were worn out, bone on bone. Even with his new knees, his quality of life was so low that he was willing to take the chance. He was given a kit with a sterile powder and solvent to mix at home. He would inject the drug once a week just below the skin of his thigh. After about three weeks, he began to feel something, like coming back from a debilitating and prolonged flu. The active inflammation, caused by his immune system turning against itself, was stopped. Gradually, everything began to hurt less. He felt more stable and could sleep through most of the night again. As the months went by, Erik put on needed weight, even adding muscle mass. He felt less brittle. Bumping into things no longer brought searing pain. New damage was being halted. He was told that if improvements continued, he wouldn't need the right foot fused like the left.

With his improved mobility, Erik began taking long walks on the beaches around Bainbridge Island, a ferry ride from Seattle. As he walked, he picked up pieces of driftwood. He had made furniture for years, but only intermittently because of the flare-ups. The first piece of furniture he made was a bench inspired by a gorgeous piece of maple driftwood. The wood looked like a wishbone, which he split into two to form the legs. He used a large chunk of redwood for the seat, and had another perfect piece for the back of the bench.

He knew of cancer patients who planted rows of baby trees, determined to be a part of something living and growing. Erik needed to carve and build, to take something unwanted, strangely formed or riddled with knots, burls, and twisted grain, and make it beautiful, strong, and useful. He pulled wood destined for the furnace or fireplace and gave it permanence. He needed to carve and build almost as he needed to move. He found two pieces of beautiful wood that formed oddly complementary lines of an X and brought the sculpture to an XPRIZE event. He made a lamp of twisted juniper and madrone wood, carved a butterfly from juniper and dogwood, and made a "Felix the Chair" out of holly and cherry wood. He brought his furniture to the local farmers' market, and talked about the shapes and types of wood. He got to know some of the regulars, including a man who asked him whether he would consider making a sculpture of the *Spirit of St. Louis*. Erik demurred, telling him he could buy a model from an aviation magazine. But the would-be client persisted, saying he had become a pilot after reading *The Spirit of St. Louis* and loved Erik's bohemian style. Erik returned to the woodshop, thinking about the request. He sifted through pieces of driftwood, studying the shapes, colors, and grain. He went out in search of wood, looking in neighbors' wood piles, walking through forested areas, and finding old and worn branches. He hauled pieces into the shop. Then he went back to the shoreline, to spots he knew were laden with sea-scrubbed driftwood in all shapes and sizes. The pieces were knotted or satin smooth, weathered by sand, sun, rain, and sea.

At the same time he searched for wood for his grandfather's plane sculpture, these walks on the beach connected him to his grandmother, Anne Morrow Lindbergh. As he collected driftwood, he thought of Grandmother out collecting seashells. Her book *Gift from the Sea* was about lessons learned from the shells she collected on Captiva Island, on Florida's Gulf Coast. First published in 1955, the book had by now sold millions of copies.

His grandmother was easier to think about than his grandfather. She was a softer presence. She was a candle, he was a spotlight. Grandmother was forty-nine years old when *Gift from the Sea* was released. She organized the book as a collection of meditative essays on how to find inner peace, outer harmony, and meaning, particularly as a woman. Each chapter focused on the shape, purpose, and meaning of one kind of shell, whether an oyster or a channeled whelk. The shells spoke to simplicity and paring back, to the beauty of solitude, to different needs at different times of life.

Erik's grandmother was now ninety-two and living with his aunt Reeve. On the surface, Grandmother was a delicate flower. Inside, she had the strength of a redwood. She raised five children after having her first son kidnapped and killed. She married Charles when he was the most famous man on Earth and became a decorated pilot herself. She lived through her husband's adulation and endured his castigation. His isolationist views during World War II and his praise of Nazi Germany's military and aviation programs turned him from hero to villain. Grandfather had died in 1974 at the age of seventy-two, when Erik was nine. Grandmother was soft-spoken and eloquent and called Erik "nature's nobleman" because of his love of the outdoors and his easygoing mien. He marveled that she could see through his growing-up-in-a-pack-of-boys energy.

Erik often returned to his favorite passages from *Gift from the Sea.* He loved what his grandmother wrote about serendipitous finds: "One never knows what chance treasures these easy unconscious rollers may toss up, on the smooth white sand of the conscious mind; what perfectly rounded stone, what rare shell from the ocean floor. Perhaps a channeled whelk, a Moon shell, or even an argonaut." She wrote: "The sea does not reward those who are too anxious, too greedy, or too impatient. To dig for treasures shows not only impatience and greed, but lack of faith. Patience, patience, patience, is what the sea teaches. Patience and faith. One should lie empty, open, choiceless as a beach — waiting for a gift from the sea."

That was the perfect way to walk along the beach — though in the Pacific Northwest, driftwood was more abundant than shells. While embracing his grandmother's call to accept what came his way, Erik felt happy to be in a greedy phase. He had a fever to create. Building was more than a meditative act. There was the commerce of it — he needed to make a living — and there was the catharsis.

Back in the shop, he was surrounded by the smell of wood and the tools of the trade, the grinders, sanders, and drills. He arranged a dozen pieces of wood on the table and hoisted a heavy piece of lumber. He'd spotted the beauty in his neighbor's woodpile — destined for the fireplace — and asked whether he could have it to make art. He loved wood weathered by salt; it was like seeing smile lines on a beautiful face.

He looked at the pieces of wood laid before him. He was reminded of the stories of the astronauts he'd met through the XPRIZE. They talked about the unparalleled force of the rocket engine, the black sky, the g-forces, the weightlessness, and leaving the bonds of Earth. The rockets that launched them were ballistic capsules and missiles, flying like supersonic bottles to space, skyscrapers launched to the heavens. Erik hadn't known what to do with these oddly shaped pieces. Now he saw it: *That is a smoke trail for a rocket ship!* He picked up a branch he'd found in eastern Washington. *That's a parabolic arc!* Another piece was Jupiter with its ring. The wood from his neighbor's pile would make amazing rocket ships. Images of traditional Buck Rogers–style rockets, abstract rockets, and even a few of the Estes models he'd built as a youth played like a slideshow. He didn't need to search for pictures; he had it all in his mind. If he could do spaceships, he could certainly do the *Spirit of St. Louis.*

He needed the right wood. The *Spirit of St.*

Louis was not the most stable plane. Grandfather had designed it to bump and rattle and keep him awake. And it was not the best-looking plane. Astronaut Neil Armstrong once called it a bird only its mother could love. Erik couldn't sculpt a replica; the plane was too iconic. It was entirely Grandfather's.

He could make his version of *Spirit* aerodynamically improbable, if he wanted. He could make it abstract beyond obvious recognition. He could make it as *he* saw it. It was like walking in his grandfather's footsteps without feeling obligated to fill his shoes.

He remembered a story about his grandfather's friend Jilin ole "John" Konchellah, a Masai warrior. Konchellah had to slay a lion with a spear to become a man. Erik's grandfather had to cross the unforgiving sea. Erik's father had to dive to the ocean's uncharted depths. His grandmother removed herself from everything familiar, finding lessons in collected shells. Erik was reduced to nothing by a foreboding room in Rochester, Minnesota. Maybe he had to break before the fixing could begin. He studied a piece of wood and saw what he had been searching for: swells of the Atlantic in the waves of the grain. He held it up and started flying the piece around the shop. For the first time, he imagined himself in the cockpit. He thought of what it must have been like for his grandfather to fly the plane for more than thirty-three hours nonstop. *What was it like to take off in relative anonymity and land in global fame?* The flight changed his grandfather's life — and it changed the world.

Erik held the wood up to the light. He flew the piece through a ray of sun flecked with sawdust and imagined his grandfather flying through the night to get to a golden dawn. It no longer made sense for Erik to keep running away from being a Lindbergh. He had done that all of his life, and it had gotten him nowhere. Like old lumber rescued from the fire pit, he had been given a second chance.

18
PETER BLASTS OFF

The first thing Peter noticed when he pulled up to Idealab in southern California was the show of cars: limos and Porsches were double-parked out front. Inside the office — all open space, exposed ductwork, doors used for desks — employees didn't walk, they ran. This was not Pacific Standard Time; it was Internet time.

Peter had sold his Rockville, Maryland, home in one day, put his furniture and all of his belongings into storage, and moved west to run a new Idealab company called Blastoff. The mission of Blastoff was to be the first private company to land a rover on the Moon and transmit images back to Earth. Peter had made a deal that once the Blastoff lunar mission was fully funded, the XPRIZE would get funded next. It was his riskiest venture yet, but all Peter could think was: *I was offered the Moon, the fucking Moon, a funded mission to the Moon.*

It was early 2000, and the tech-heavy

NASDAQ had doubled in little over a year, though it had started to drop. The beleaguered "old economy" Dow was in retreat. Equity trumped cash and e-commerce elbowed out brick and mortar. Netscape had gone public five years earlier, Google had begun operating in a garage in Menlo Park two years earlier, and eToys had a value of $7.8 billion on its first day public in 1999.

Idealab, founded by a small, wiry, constantly-in-motion engineer turned entrepreneur named Bill Gross, was worth $9 billion and comprised more than forty dot-com companies, including eToys, Pets.com, Friendster, NetZero, and CarsDirect. An inventor from an early age, Bill Gross had found inspiration for Blastoff from a new company called eBay. Bill had gone to the online auction site to try to buy a Moon rock, which he had dreamed about owning since he was eleven years old and transfixed by the Apollo 11 lunar landing. Bill told his brother Larry, "Someone must have it at some price." But their eBay search of lunar souvenirs left them empty-handed. They learned that all Moon rocks were exclusively owned by the government, locked up in hurricane-proof vaults in Houston or loaned to teaching institutions like the Smithsonian. Even lunar dust was supposed to be the property of the U.S. government. At that point, Bill decided to form a private company that would send a human to the Moon to collect and return lunar samples to sell on eBay. The second iteration of Blastoff replaced the astronaut with a machine — an unmanned robotic rover, equipped with a camera, would land on the Moon and collect the samples. The mission would be covered on television, beamed through the Internet, and financed by sponsors. Bill disliked the idea of plastering ads on a rocket and a rover, but he had even more disdain for the government's hold on space.

Jim Cameron, a pioneer of special effects and director of some of the world's top-grossing films, including *Titanic* and *Terminator,* was interested in filming the lunar spectacle for Blastoff, and filmmaker Steven Spielberg was an investor. The technical head of Blastoff's space missions was the white-haired, Einstein-like Tony Spear, project manager for the NASA Pathfinder mission, which landed a rover on Mars on July 4, 1997. Bill and his brother Larry had taken notice when the Pathfinder landing drew more than eighty million Internet hits a day in the first few days, including nearly fifty million hits to the Jet Propulsion Laboratory Web site, where cameras were trained on Spear and his team as they watched, waited, and celebrated.

A few of Bill's aerospace friends told him that he could probably land something simple and efficient on the Moon for less than $10 million. But as the project grew, so did expenses. No matter. Bill was starting companies the way the Treasury printed money. An IPO for Idealab was planned for later in 2000, an event that would make the forty-one-year-old a decabillionaire. Besides, if the online grocer Webvan — another of his companies — could raise more than $800 million just so people could have groceries delivered to their door, the cost of his little Moon project would be pocket change. The fact that there hadn't been any private space missions didn't matter, either; in the halcyon days of the Internet, when things like profit were irrelevant, anything was possible. Bill could lure the best rocket scientists, the best filmmakers, and the best space entrepreneurs, including Peter Diamandis.

When Bill, who had recently raised more than $1 billion in private equity, recruited Peter as the CEO of Blastoff, he told him that he had set aside up to $60 million for the Moon exploration company, but wanted Peter to bring in outside funds where possible. Funding for the XPRIZE would kick in once Peter was able to raise outside financing for Blastoff.

Peter, who had grown tired of friends' telling him they were making a mint on Internet companies, was the eighteenth employee at Blastoff, based in Pasadena in Los Angeles

County, and down the street from Caltech and the Jet Propulsion Lab. Opting for a lower salary and more stock, Peter had a base pay of $145,000 and 1.3 million options. Peter believed that Blastoff would be the rising tide to carry the XPRIZE and his other space ventures. He still had Gregg Maryniak and the team in St. Louis working on the XPRIZE, and he planned to continue managing it from the West Coast.

Working at Internet hyperspeed, Blastoff had a mission date of summer 2001 to get to the Moon, just in time for a fall 2001 IPO. As Bill saw it, the private lunar landing would be an Internet phenomenon and another billion-dollar business. As Peter saw it, Blastoff was a way to make all of his space dreams come true.

Peter and Larry Gross, who was on Blastoff's board of directors and involved in day-to-day oversight, met with Jim Cameron at his Santa Monica office, where the Terminator T2000 robot stood just outside the door. In a corner of Cameron's office was the ship's wheel from the *Titanic* film. Cameron, known for his love of the oceans, had an equally strong fascination with space, and grew up on a steady diet of science fiction. For many years, faced with a long bus ride to school, he read a book a day, devouring works by Arthur C. Clarke, A. E. van Vogt, Harlan Ellison, and

Larry Niven. He was fascinated by aliens and interstellar travel and liked the blurring of lines between reality and fantasy, science and art.

During the two-hour meeting, Larry and Peter offered the director 300,000 shares in Blastoff, discussed his level of involvement, and tossed out ideas for the title of the lunar film. Peter suggested that Cameron serve as Blastoff's "mission producer," but Cameron had a similar title with Fox. The three decided on "imaging supervisor."

The biggest thing to come out of the meeting was Cameron's insistence that they needed not one camera-equipped rover, but two. "You need one that is going this way and another that sees it, so you have this point of view," Cameron said, mapping out the camera angles on a whiteboard. The two cameras playing off each other would promote stronger audience involvement.

Meetings like this prompted Peter to start an audio journal that he hoped would document history in the making. In his tape-recorded observations about the Cameron confab, Peter said that he found the director extremely smart, friendly, and generous with his time — but Cameron's handlers were a different story.

"The big issue now," Peter said in his audio journal, "is dealing with his lawyer, Bert Fields. Cameron and Spielberg play super nice on their side, but then you have to deal with their accountants and lawyers who are basically recalcitrant. I was impressed today by how Jim gave us all the time we needed. His organization, on the other hand, is frenetic trying to take care of him."

Peter also noted in his audio journal — which he often recorded in his car — that although it was exciting to have Cameron on board, the move to two rovers instead of one would double the cost and workload of the program and send the engineers into over-drive. Peter wondered how these strange bedfellows — hardwired aerospace, frenetic Internet, and fantastical Hollywood — would work together. On the passenger seat next to Peter was Heinlein's *The Man Who Sold the Moon,* written in 1949 about a businessman obsessed with the idea of being the first to reach, control, and monetize the Moon, sell-ing naming rights to craters, offering public-ity stunts, and returning diamonds from the lunar surface.

It was a novella that Peter assigned to the entire Blastoff team to read.

One of Peter's first staff meetings at Blastoff lasted for seven hours. Peter and the team went over all of the systems requirements. Peter wanted the company to have the "cul-ture and spirit of the early days of Apple Computer," when a pirate flag flew over the building.* The team went over particulars, from the landing site and new hires to the rovers and the delivery rocket that would get both lander and rover to the Moon. Buzz Aldrin had ruled out Bill Gross's original idea of landing near the Apollo 11 site, where the flag planted in 1969 was no longer standing. Bill's vision was to move the rovers slowly toward the iconic site — cameras rolling — and have a rover pick up the flag and replant it. Aldrin nixed the idea, saying they couldn't "traipse all over the historic site," make tracks and "go over our footprints." The footprints should remain for millennia.

The Blastoff team consulted with Harrison Schmitt, a geologist and Apollo 17 astronaut who was the twelfth man to set foot on the Moon and the second to last to leave (right before Gene Cernan). The team considered the Taurus-Littrow valley and highlands, the landing area for Apollo 17, but settled on the Apollo 15 site at the foot of the Apennine mountain range. Schmitt told team members that the photographs of the Moon released to the public decades earlier were not entirely accurate. The original photos, taken with Hasselblad cameras, were put into a vault

---

* The team behind the early Macintosh hoisted the pirate flag over their office as a testament to Steve Jobs's statement that it's more fun to be a pirate than to join the navy.

and copies were made into prints. Schmitt said the Moon was not white and colorless as portrayed, but had a range of colors, mostly in shades of brown and brick-red.

Discussion turned to landing times that coincided with spaceflight milestones, lunar cycles, and IPO targets. Bill wanted the craft to land on the Moon, American flag in tow, on July 4, 2001. The engineers were looking at the end of 2001. The new Moon for December 2001 would fall on December 17, with the full Moon on or around December 28. Students across the globe could begin studying the mission and its physics and technology in the fall. One of the engineers pointed out that December 25 was Isaac Newton's birthday.

Rex Ridenoure, Blastoff's chief mission architect and number-two hire (after a Czech-born engineer named Tomas Svitek), went over some of the systems challenges, including transmitting video, images, and data from both lunar rovers back to Earth. The plan, he explained, was to transmit video and data from the rovers independently to the lander — the mother ship — via the same sort of radio links (a 2.4 GHz microwave radio band) used by remote-controlled cars and toy drones. The data streams would be merged on board the mother ship. All of this could be done live or in record/playback mode. To ensure transmission to Earth,[*] the mother ship would have to be parked in a certain orientation on the lunar surface. The command link on the lander could be active at any time, even when the mother ship was on the move. Commands from Mission Control to the rovers would be routed through the link with the mother ship.

Ridenoure, who like the Gross brothers was a graduate of the California Institute of Technology, had been recruited to Blastoff from SpaceDev, one of the first commercial space exploration companies. He had met Peter around 1992, when he was working at the Jet Propulsion Laboratory, managed for NASA by Caltech. Peter had come to JPL to talk about the potential launch services of International Microspace. Ridenoure believed in the Blastoff mission and thought they had a good shot at becoming the first to launch a private venture to the Moon.

[*] The Moon-to-Earth link would be established through a higher-frequency X-band radio link from a fan-shaped medium-gain radio antenna on the rover to a global network of space-mission tracking antennas and dishes operated by the U.S. company Universal Space Networks (USN). The USN antennas would also be used to send commands to the rovers from Blastoff's Mission Control. The USN dishes were capable of transmitting commands to the mother ship at relatively high power levels.

The group discussed the types of rockets that could be used to carry the mother ship to the Moon, including Orbital Sciences' Taurus XL rocket, a Boeing-designed Delta II rocket, and the Russian Dnepr launch vehicle, a converted SS-18 Satan ICBM. As they brainstormed design ideas, tension began to emerge between the engineering side and the marketing side. The engineers wanted function; the marketers wanted form. They wanted a cute "family" of rovers, where the mother ship would dispatch two childlike rovers to "play and explore." The rovers would need to be anthropomorphized, with squat white bodies, thin necks, big eyes, and maybe even some sort of cap or eyebrow features.

The engineers debated the best approach to reach the Moon. They could go by "direct injection," à la Apollo 11, where the rocket would take three to four days to reach the Moon. The challenge with this approach was to time the launch at just the right period when the Earth-Moon geometry was lined up. Direct injection gave engineers at most one try a month. By contrast, a "phased orbit" would put the hardware in a low- or medium-Earth orbit, require trips around the Earth (of varying times based on low or medium Earth orbit), and allow for multiple slots per month to inject to the Moon.* The Blastoff team went with the phased orbit strategy.

Peter left the office late, and exhausted. Walking to his car, he looked at the Moon in the midnight sky and said, "That's where we're going."

For Peter, months after arriving in sunny Pasadena, the euphoria of Moon missions and Internet time began to dim. Peter was feeling unsettled by the seemingly infinite iterations of Blastoff. The mission statement changed faster than cars pulling in and out of Idealab. During pitches to potential investors, Bill Gross touted Blastoff as an education company. Then it was an entertainment company. Next, it was a sports venture, with rovers racing on the Moon. The latest pitch by Bill to venture capitalists had Blastoff as the "broadband Napster." Peter listened and thought, *This has zero validity.* As much as he tried to accept the new way of doing things, Peter felt whiplashed by the pop-up business ideas. Larry Gross said they needed to create a "level of pizzazz," a vision that would excite

* With the Moon's twenty-eight-day trip time around the Earth and a Moon-bound spacecraft orbiting the Earth once every two days, say, you may get up to fourteen times per month to inject to the Moon.

people. Peter was dispatched to Brazil twice to work on the "Olympics on the Moon" concept, with corporate sponsorships of national flags. The idea was to have the mother ship carry six rovers — now six! — representing six nations. Children from different countries would man the joysticks and control the rovers as they planted their national flags and raced on the lunar surface.

The engineering team remained more rooted in reality. They believed they were eighteen months from launch. They had invited a serious top-to-bottom technical peer review of the entire project, with sixteen experienced space project managers. The reviewers included a former JPL director, JPL deputy space mission project managers, former senior Department of Defense space managers, expert rocket engineers, and more. The consensus was that their designs were solid and the goal was attainable, if the money kept coming in.

That was the problem. So far, Bill had allocated only $12 million for Blastoff, and Peter was told he needed to personally raise another $10 million before Idealab would kick in what would be a final $10 million. The budget would be capped at about $30 million, even though $60 million was supposed to have been set aside in the first place. "I didn't sign up to raise money," Peter said in one of his late-night audio recordings. "I signed up to make this company work. The capital promised — $60 million — is not committed. Is this the Internet way, to lure someone in and then yank the rug out from under them?"

Peter scheduled a meeting with Bill and Bill's wife, Marcia Goodstein, Idealab's chief operating officer. He loved meeting with Bill, who was the consummate optimist and brainstormer. He dreaded meeting with Marcia, who was steely, by-the-numbers, and made every meeting personal and unnerving. At the meeting with the two, Peter was told he needed to "make it work" with what he had. He was told they wanted to support him, but the softness in the market was delaying the Idealab IPO and making things generally "squeamish." Some pundits and economists believed that a market correction was under way, while others, including Bill, said the fundamentals remained solid and the boom would continue. Still, as summer turned to fall and the markets continued to drop, money was becoming impossible to raise.

Unwelcome surprises presented themselves at every corner. One engineer resigned, fed up with what he saw as unsubstantiated promises made to potential investors. Blastoff management was trying to hawk a product that engineers found illegitimate. Dot-com companies, meanwhile, were running out of cash or liquidating. Idealab's Pets.com, with its popular sock puppet, had closed its doors and filed for bankruptcy.

During a meeting in early November, Peter asked his team for support, as part of his feverish bid to save Blastoff from the same fate. But Peter got no sympathy. Blastoff's avionics systems head, Doug Caldwell, told Peter in the meeting that he didn't have the backing of engineers. Caldwell said point-blank that engineers wouldn't support him because they didn't respect him. What was being told to investors was not reality. Peter listened and felt a mix of anger and betrayal. He felt that many of the engineers — while brilliant — were naïve or ignorant when it came to marketing and raising the capital needed to save their jobs. They were upset that the mockups he was showing to venture capitalists didn't reflect actual hardware. As Peter let the engineers vent, he thought to himself, *How the hell did I get stuck in this situation?* He had sold his house for far less than he could have made had he taken his time, and he'd gotten pennies to the dollar when he'd brought his things out of storage and held a one-day estate sale. Now he was trying to inspire engineers while fighting for the company's survival. He was selling what he still believed in his heart was possible, but it was hard when no one seemed to believe in *him*.

Peter felt even worse because he had personally recruited a number of people away from JPL, including a brilliant young engineer named Chris Lewicki, who grew up in the dairy country in northern Wisconsin and was a leader of the SEDS chapter at the University of Arizona. Lewicki and many others had left stable, high-paying jobs to join this mission to the Moon. Peter had moved into a house in the hills of Pasadena, and two of his talented recruits — inventor Dezso Molnar and space entrepreneur George Whitesides — were his roommates. Peter had also brought in Bob Weiss as his number-two man and the head of marketing. It took Peter months to persuade Weiss to take the job. Weiss thought that Blastoff sounded like a project, not a business. But Peter was unrelenting, and would track Weiss down on vacation to woo him with some new angle. Weiss would retreat with phone in hand to a quiet room or even a closet so his wife wouldn't hear his latest idea about leaving moviemaking — to go to the Moon. Eventually, Peter sold him on the idea.

The public relations team at Blastoff, led by Diane Murphy, who had boundless energy and great contacts, had a massive media rollout in the works, including a multifaceted Web site and a polished video that began, "What if we told you that for the past year, an amazing team of scientists has been working on a mission to the Moon? . . . What if we told you this was not a part of a secret government program?"

But with each passing day, the dreams were turning to desperation.

Peter was in save-the-ship mode, working around the clock, sleeping a few hours here and there. He and Larry Gross were in talks to buy an Athena II rocket built for the Navy by Lockheed Martin. The government had canceled the project after spending $40 million, leaving Lockheed with a brand-new rocket. Lockheed said Blastoff could have it for $20 million.

Dezso Molnar, who had been involved in private space for more than fifteen years — he started working with rocket maker Bob Truax in 1984 — knew that a bloodbath was coming. He had been hired at Blastoff after running the land-speed racing team for Craig Breedlove in the Black Hawk Desert, where the goal was to build a car to break the sound barrier. At Blastoff, Molnar told everyone to go to the doctor or dentist while they still had health coverage. "George, have you been to the dentist?" he asked George Whitesides. "I'm calling to make you an appointment. You're about to lose your job. I've seen this movie before."

By the end of 2000, Blastoff was splashing down. A decision was made to keep people on through the holidays. In early January, Peter and Bill called a meeting. The mood was grim, like standing on the deck of the *Titanic*. "Guys, I hate to say it," Peter began, "but this mission is being put on hold." Bill apologized that Idealab wasn't able to support the mission in the way it had intended. There were talks of resurrecting Blastoff when the economy improved, of Hail Mary passes, of investor meetings still scheduled.

Bob Weiss watched as employees packed up their things. An engineer carrying a box with belongings stopped at his desk on the way out the door. The engineer offered a joke.

"Hey, Bob, what did one aerospace engineer say to the other?"

"I give up," Bob said.

"You want fries with that burger?"

It took Bob a few moments to get it.

The pace had slowed to a stop at Blastoff. The parking lot was now mostly empty. Peter stayed at the company after the last employee left. He needed to circle back on contracts, including the deal with Lockheed, which tied Blastoff to monthly payments of $1 million. He needed to figure out what to do with the impressive hardware and software developed by Blastoff.

Bob Weiss had been in talks with a Japanese company that wanted to invest in Blastoff and deploy some sort of inflatable house on the Moon. Peter had a meeting with Jeff

Berg, head of the talent agency ICM, who had leads on potential investors. Filmmakers Ron Howard and Brian Grazer had been about to come on board when the market tanked.

Early in 2001, Peter was forced to do some more personal downsizing, moving out of the gorgeous house in the hills above Pasadena and into a small two-bedroom apartment in Santa Monica. The address was 2408 Third Street, an address Peter remembered as: 2 (to the first power); 2 (squared); and 2 (cubed). Before leaving the Pasadena house, he sat by the pool and remembered how he, George, and Dezso had envisioned great pool parties. He had gone swimming maybe once.

Now it was time to refocus on the XPRIZE. He couldn't let the failure of Blastoff end his most important dream. Peter used the second bedroom of the Santa Monica apartment as his office. It had been nearly five years since the XPRIZE was announced under the arch in St. Louis. Gregg Maryniak and his team had kept things going — but barely. Peter had spent some time almost every day on the XPRIZE — connecting with teams, talking with board members and benefactors — but his focus had been on Blastoff, on this crazy moonshot, on the promise that Blastoff would generate millions for his real baby, the XPRIZE. He knew that teams were building actual hardware. Insiders told him Burt Rutan was working on something predictably counterintuitive and super cool. The XPRIZE had all of the ingredients it needed, except the prize money. He had $5 million promised and needed $5 million more. This was becoming a familiar refrain for Peter. In joining Blastoff, Peter had taken the biggest gamble of his life. And he had lost.

19
ELON'S INSPIRATION

Peter's part-time assistant, Angel Panlasigui, opened the door to Peter's Santa Monica apartment late in the morning and saw what was becoming an increasingly familiar sight in early 2001: Peter still in his bathrobe, hair disheveled. The place was dark, the shades down. Peter had yet to emerge from the rubble of Blastoff.

Things hit a new low in early March, when Peter sat with a copy of *Fortune* magazine featuring Bill Gross on the cover. The title of the story by Joe Nocera was "Why Is He Still Smiling? Bill Gross Blew Through $800 Million in 8 Months (and he's got nothing to show for it)." It was painful to read the piece, which made no mention of Blastoff. Peter also had nothing to show for his last ten months. Unlike Gross, Peter had put everything on the line.

Then, in May 2001, when Peter was whiling away another afternoon in his apartment, Angel said there was a call from Larry Gross.

"Peter," Larry said, "I've got a fortieth birthday present for you."

Peter arrived at the Skybar, a rooftop watering hole on Sunset Boulevard, a week after Larry Gross told him he knew who was going to fund the continuation of Blastoff. It was two men who had made a fortune on the Internet and who were interested in space. Peter had never heard of the men, so he wrote down their names: Adeo Ressi and Elon Musk.

Peter usually approached pitch meetings with great enthusiasm, but tonight he felt subdued. He spotted Adeo by the Skybar pool, smoking a cigarette and looking out at the gold and glimmering Los Angeles sunset. He was tall and thin, a Giacometti walking man figure, and immediately affable. Adeo said Elon was running late but on his way. Elon was working on getting his pilot's license and was flying down from San Jose with his instructor. He had a new plane being built.

It was Sunday, June 3, 2001, and Adeo, Elon, and Peter were scheduled to have dinner at Asia de Cuba, adjacent to the Skybar in the Mondrian Hotel. Peter took in the beautiful women in filmy tops and short skirts, and felt overdressed in his suit and mock turtleneck. Adeo was in casual slacks and a shirt open at the collar. The music was pulsating, the lychee up martinis flowing, and the entire hotel was bathed in white, with minimalist accents of Hermès orange. Even the matches were stylish, with lime-green tips. Peter had taken notice of the white-clad valet team when he pulled up to the white-façade hotel. The valet attendants all clasped their hands in exactly the same way.

Peter joined Adeo for a drink near the pool. Adeo, who knew Larry Gross from a two-month stint as CEO of Idealab in New York, had just sold his Web development firm Methodfive and was working on turnarounds of lagging public companies. He said he and Elon had been housemates at the University of Pennsylvania. Elon was South African and had founded Zip2, a mapping and business services company, and cofounded PayPal, the online payment service being bought by eBay.

Their shared interest in space came to light during a late-night car ride the weekend before Memorial Day. As they drove back to New York City from Long Island on a cloudy night, talk turned to what they wanted to do next. As a joke, one of them said, "Why don't we do something in space?" When the laughter died down, Elon said, "Well, why *can't* we do something in space?" The debate went back and forth: Space was too expensive. *Why was it so expensive?* Space takes a lot of infrastructure. *Why does it take so much infra-*

structure? Space is controlled by governments and strict regulation. *What happens if it is taken out of the government's hands?* Finally, they asked each other, *Why do we even think space is interesting?* This led to a discussion of where they would go if they could go to space. By the end of the car ride, they had their answer about what to do next. They knew exactly where they wanted to go.

Before Adeo could continue, Elon arrived and apologized for being late. The three men moved with drinks in hand from the Skybar to the restaurant and ordered a feast: pan-seared ahi tuna, miso grilled salmon, the Asian noodle box, and more. Tracks from the Buddha Bar collection played in the background. Peter found Elon immediately likable: good chemistry from the start, soft-spoken, polite, his words well chosen. Adeo was also great, but more of an extrovert who seemed to enjoy playing devil's advocate. Peter knew very little about the two coming into the night's dinner. He'd had a quick conference call the week before with Elon and Adeo, thought they said all the right things, and took Elon's accent to be British.

Adeo made Peter laugh knowingly when he said, "I think every geek is a bit of a space buff." Peter talked about Blastoff, the XPRIZE, ZERO-G, and Space Adventures, his company with Eric Anderson, which had brokered the final part of the deal to send the world's first space tourist, Dennis Tito, to the International Space Station aboard a Russian Soyuz spacecraft for $20 million. Peter talked briefly about how NASA had tried to stop Tito from flying, but Tito had launched on April 28 and landed safely in Kazakhstan on May 6. It was big news in space circles that Tito, an American, had to fly with Russian cosmonauts and was not allowed on the U.S. side of the space station. Peter had met Tito when he came to California to interview with Bill and Larry Gross for the Blastoff position. Peter pitched Tito on an XPRIZE sponsorship, but Tito said he didn't want to sponsor a prize; he may want to fund a team and compete himself.

As Peter talked about what the "ultimate space company" would look like, putting on Moon missions and suborbital and ZERO-G flights, Elon and Adeo said they had set their sights on something different, something even more difficult. They wanted to reach the Red Planet. Their mission, decided that night on Long Island, was to put humanity on Mars. They wanted to spend money to "shame, embarrass, or prod" the government into doing a human mission to Mars.

Peter cautioned that he had seen a lot of great missions fail because one wealthy backer or another expected other wealthy individuals to support his vision. "But every wealthy person has his own vision," Peter said. To make such a mission work, Peter now believed, one very wealthy and determined person would need to be willing to pay for everything, something he had yet to encounter. As Elon listened to Peter talk about Blastoff and his other companies, he thought Peter's heart was in the right place, and it was obvious that he cared deeply about the future of space travel. But the Blastoff plan didn't make sense to him. He didn't think sending a rover back to the Moon was going to reignite space travel.

Returning to the subject of Mars, Elon said, "We want to do something that's significant enough but does something for a reasonable budget — for a couple million." Adeo added that they had $10 million to $15 million to spend, but wanted to start with a $1 million or $2 million project.

Peter was stunned to hear such a low figure of "a couple million," but knew that in aerospace, a couple million often led to many more millions. He listened to them with interest, but made sure not to get his hopes up. Still, at the very least, even if Elon and Adeo did nothing, Peter had met some smart guys who would be friends. Elon was a major Trekkie. He had watched all of the episodes as a kid in South Africa, dreamed of spaceships, and read Heinlein, Asimov, and Douglas Adams. He said his successes in Silicon Valley had paved the way for his future in space — not unlike what Jeff Bezos had told him.

Adeo, Elon, and Peter shared an interest in using small teams to accomplish what only the government had done before, though Elon remarked that he saw the government as "a corporation — the biggest corporation." And like Peter, Adeo and Elon didn't see NASA as the bad guy, but instead saw the public's expectation of perfection as an unnecessary speed limit on innovation. The expectation that everything needed to go right caused NASA to be overly cautious.

Elon talked about how he had been trying to understand why the world had not made more progress in sending people to the Moon or Mars. "There was a lot of excitement with the Apollo program and the dream of space travel," Elon said. "It was ignited, and somehow that dream died or was put into stasis." He said he was "trying to figure out if there is anything we can do to bring back the dream of Apollo. Maybe even a philanthropic mission."

Peter could see that Elon — a logician and engineer above all else — needed to understand the physical and psychological limitations of why rockets hadn't improved since the sixties. Peter knew that Elon and Adeo were in research mode, talking to a mix of major players and fringe players in the world of aerospace. Peter told them he thought

Mars was a great place to set up a future colony, but "the Moon was economical. The Moon is a place where you can go to gain access to resources and you are close enough to Earth that you can build on it."

But Elon was not interested in the Moon. "Maybe we do a mini greenhouse to Mars," he said. "Maybe mice to Mars. Maybe we grow samples of food crops." He said it had been obvious to him since childhood, when the Moon was already reached, that "Mars is next." Also, Mars was even more mythical, more unattainable. The Moon was 240,000 miles away from Earth. Mars was about 34 million miles away when their orbits were together on the same side of the sun, but as much as 250 million miles apart when the two planets were on the opposite sides of the sun. The Moon was the talcum face in the night sky. Mars was the out-of-reach gem. Mars would take at least half a year to reach, using optimal energy cost. It would take a year and a half for the planets to realign,* and then it would take another six months to return. Elon said he thought such a mission

* A craft departing Earth naturally has all of Earth's orbital velocity plus the rocket velocity toward Mars. You time the journey to intercept Mars, taking into account that it is also orbiting. Going back to Earth, the craft has Mars's orbital velocity plus the rocket velocity toward Earth.

sounded entirely doable. Earlier, in May, Elon had attended a Mars Society event with Jim Cameron, who was working on a six-episode TV miniseries on the Red Planet. Over breakfast the next morning with Mars Society cofounder Robert Zubrin, Elon had pledged $100,000 to the cause.

Peter, who had been in constant pitching mode for what felt like an eternity, tried to sit back and listen, but he kept finding himself back in the mode of selling. Elon and Adeo asked whether a manned mission to Mars was possible for less than $10 billion. *Now the budget is edging closer to reality,* Peter thought. Peter said enticingly, "I've got a way for you to do it for a tenth of the cost, for one billion." Everyone leaned in. "You could build a one-way mission with existing Russian hardware. You send a few people with the goal of their living on Mars for five years until a resupply or rescue mission gets there. They will be the world's first Martians." Adeo and Elon loved the idea and spent the next hour in a fast-paced discussion, going over details and obstacles. Peter then told them that whatever they did in space, they needed to first prove themselves, "step by step."

Even though Peter had figured out quickly that Elon and Adeo had no interest in Blast-off, he admired how these guys were willing to gamble on space. And the evening offered a pleasant surprise: Elon loved the XPRIZE idea. "I could be a supporter of that," he said. Elon thought that unlike Blastoff, the XPRIZE could jump-start an industry and rekindle public interest in space. Elon and Adeo appeared keenly interested as Peter talked about the *Spirit of St. Louis*, Charles Lindbergh, and the teams that had signed up.

"I'd love to meet some of the teams," Elon said. Adeo offered to join the XPRIZE board.

Well after midnight, the men finally walked out of the restaurant and were greeted by the white-clad valet. They had plans to meet the next morning to continue the discussion at the Idealab office.

As Peter drove back to his apartment in Santa Monica, he turned on his recorder and began to reflect. It was strange, he said, how until tonight, he had felt like the kid in the room. Now, at forty, he felt more like the elder statesman. Both Adeo and Elon were weeks shy of turning thirty.

They were just starting on space; he had never been anywhere else. "They only have ten million to fifteen million to spend," he said as he drove. "It's not going to be on Blastoff. They could be backers of the XPRIZE. Regardless, I get the feeling we'll be friends. I really liked this guy Elon. He was quieter, but sounded serious about space. I think I planted some ideas, some seeds, maybe some direction, tonight."

He continued, "It amazes me when I hear there is apathy about going to the Moon. Not from these guys tonight so much as from people who are not drawn to space at all. They have this kind of been-there-done-that mentality. People are fickle. What gets them excited?

"I think about sports teams and to me — BFD, so what? Why would people spend so much on sports? I guess they want to relate to that person. They want to be out on the court. Here I am, talking about sending robots to the Moon, and it's an apathy-inducing agent? Space has to be developed for more than science. It's about daring to do great things. That alone is valuable."

Peter paused as he pulled into his garage, the sound of his car blinker magnified by the silence, a kind of metronome to his thoughts. "Blastoff is dead," he said. "But my heartfelt passion of space is not."

Another few moments passed. "Dammit, I can't let this go," he said. "My mission in life is to make all of this happen. I've learned a ton of lessons. Whatever I do from here on out is going to be my show."

20
Burt and Paul's
Big Adventure

"Let's go fly some models," said an excited Burt Rutan, rounding up a handful of engineers at lunch hour on a cool spring day in Mojave. The crew at Scaled Composites grabbed small foam airplanes and headed outside, walking down the flight line to the Mojave Tower. There, on the seventh-floor deck, eighty-seven feet up, Burt and the others began chucking model space planes into the air. The models, with variable shapes, were designed to have extreme drag and stability. They had models with fishing line, and models with streamers to measure the angle of attack. Some dropped straight down; others rode the air like gentle waves.

Burt watched, smiled, frowned, and studied. The foam models had different drag mechanisms, or ways to slow the plane: crude sorts of elevators on the trailing edge of the wing or tail for nose-up, high-drag descent; rudimentary ailerons on the ends of the model plane's wings to roll to the left or the right. One model had a large top flap intended to provide high drag and to raise the nose to an extreme angle. The strings helped to visualize the angle of the airflow during descent. Burt, who was right-handed in everything except controlling flight line models, suggested different angles for the planes to be thrown from. He and the crew were assessing whether the models were stable, tumbled, or descended at bizarre angles. If a plane looped, did it recover or flip over backward? Today's field trip was the latest exercise in Burt's quest to design a first-of-a-kind, affordable, and reusable spaceship. Burt knew that these crude models did not give an accurate answer, because a real atmospheric spaceship entry would be done at supersonic speeds, where the aerodynamics are very different. Burt loved the idea of the XPRIZE — and even more the idea of winning it — though he still found it disconcerting that Peter had announced the race without funding for the prize. Peter now had $5 million — for a $10 million prize. Burt was aware there were a number of teams in contention, with ideas ranging from rocket and balloon combinations to vertical-takeoff, vertical-landing missiles. Peter, who called Burt regularly to fish for information on what he was doing, kept assuring him that full funding of the prize was close at hand. And no one else had launched anything — yet.

At this point, Burt no longer considered one of his latest creations, the Proteus, to be a viable launch platform for the space competition, though its design was still very much influencing his thinking. Burt had toyed with the notion that the craft could be used to launch a single-seat rocket from high altitude to the edge of space, in the same way the B-52 had shot the winged X-15 skyward from 45,000 feet. But Burt had concluded that the Proteus would not work carrying a three-passenger cabin, an XPRIZE requirement. Since then, he had talked with a few engineers about other ideas he had for suborbital spaceships. From time to time, he shared sketches: some looked derivative, others futuristic, others uniquely Burt Rutan. He sketched on paper and by computer, and drew in pen and pencil on restaurant napkins. There was a delta wing (isosceles triangle) space plane with a bubble-shaped cabin up front to hold a half dozen space tourists, including the pilot. There was a Redstone-inspired rocket with a *Friendship 7*–like capsule on top. Burt's version of the rocket and capsule would detach after boost, return to Earth by parachute, and then be set down in front of Scaled by helicopter. He'd also drawn an oblong capsule tapered on one end, with two small feathered wings jutting out from the sides like arms.

The visit to the tower with the foam models

would allow Burt to do basic hand calculations to determine the efficacy of his latest, more advanced designs. The calculations on lift and drag were not unlike those he'd done on planes as a kid, when he would build whatever he imagined using balsa wood pieces bought for sixteen cents apiece. Now, of course, he could turn to the computer and work with his aerodynamicist to look at hundreds of different calculations involving how air flowed around a design.[*]

The foam models were concepts, but they gave clues. Burt would see how they would do subsonically first. Like his doodles on napkins, the models were a part of Burt's process. With every new type of plane, Burt plotted and planned and worked out hundreds of details in his mind before testing

[*] By 2000, computational fluid dynamics had advanced pretty far. The first computer programs for numerical simulation of Navier-Stokes–derived equations appeared in the sixties. By the 1980s there were a number of them running quite effectively. Every aerospace company had its own. By 2000 these computer programs had become quite sophisticated and were approaching the hard problems: dealing with viscosity, and dealing with vortices. If you include both, you have the Navier-Stokes equation. If you include only vortices, you have the Euler equation. If you exclude both, you have the so-called full potential equation.

anything in a computer. There was never an epiphany, a single "aha" moment; only iteration after iteration, layer after layer. Aesthetics were a part of performance. If a wing reached its performance goal, it was beautiful. If he put a sweep on a wingtip that looked like a shark fin, it was to improve performance. The fact that it looked cool was an unexpected benefit. He worked on every project until he reached the point where something in his gut told him he was right. Once he had that gut feeling, he was in a hurry.

Already, the spaceship project had Burt tapping into his likes and dislikes. In his mind, the most impressive manned launch system ever was the Northrop Grumman Lunar Module, designed less than four years after the world's first manned spaceflight and flight-tested three years later. It descended from orbit, landed on the Moon, took off, and then ascended to lunar orbit. The most impressive plane was Lockheed's SR-71 Blackbird, a Mach 3-plus reconnaissance craft, designed just a decade and a half after the world moved away from slow piston-powered aircraft. Burt's philosophy was that small improvements to designs were not interesting. What mattered to him was "reaching way out."

Burt didn't like parachutes for recovery and couldn't imagine space tourists wanting to be inside a capsule that parachuted back to Earth and landed in the ocean. And despite his early drawing of a rocket and a capsule like the one that lobbed Alan Shepard to suborbital spaceflight forty years earlier on a fifteen-minute ride, Burt wanted his pilots to fly and land the craft. Amazingly, there had been only four manned suborbital spaceflights in U.S. history where the astronaut or pilot reached higher than sixty-two miles: Mercury-Redstone with Alan Shepard and Gus Grissom, both in 1961; and Joe Walker in the X-15, who in 1963 reached 354,200 feet, or sixty-seven miles. The gunmetal black X-15, built to test manned suborbital spaceflight, had smashed world speed and altitude records. Carried aloft under the wing of a modified B-52, the X-15 rocket plane was drop-launched for a rocket ascent followed by an unpowered glide back to Earth. Burt was at Edwards in the 1960s when the X-15 was flown, and was now consulting on his space plane with former X-15 test engineer Bob Hoey.

The most challenging part of the space plane equation was figuring out how to slow the descent after the craft coasted through apogee. Everything changed in space. There was no air, and therefore no aerodynamic forces. Burt needed to come up with a configuration that would give the ship maximum drag and natural stability as it returned through the upper atmosphere, and could be built quickly and cheaply and be safer than anything done before. He had begun looking at ways to have the craft returned in the thin atmosphere belly first. That would put the vehicle at close to the theoretical maximum drag: zero lift from the wings, maximum cross section in the direction of motion. If he didn't reorient the craft, it would plunge nose first at dangerously high speeds. This situation resulted in high aerodynamic loads (high stresses on the structure) and heating of the airframe. He wanted something that could approach the atmosphere at any attitude or flight path, then naturally reorient itself to the right angle without relying on the pilot or computer to do it. The X-15 had relied on a special nickel alloy with a space-age name, Inconel-X, for heat protection up to 1,200 degrees Fahrenheit and speeds up to Mach 6.7. The space shuttle used thousands of individually made tiles filled with high-grade sand. Anything Burt made would be built of composite materials, and have far lower heat tolerance than metals or custom-made tiles.[*]

[*]The space shuttle tiles were six by six inches. There were about twenty thousand unique tiles. The shuttle was thus sometimes referred to as the "flying brickyard." The tiles, including the borosilicate coating, weigh less than a comparable piece of Styrofoam. They were 90 percent air. The heating of the

Additionally, his lightweight, high-drag ship would decelerate much higher up in the atmosphere than the X-15, where the loads and heating are considerably less.

Now, after years of thinking about what a homebuilt spaceship would involve, Burt was convinced that he was closing in on designing a craft that would work. To cut fuel costs and add safety, his rocket would be carried aloft like the X-15 by a mother ship similar to the Proteus. The rocket-powered plane would drop-launch from the mother ship's belly like the X-15. This would mean Burt would have to build his own B-52 equivalent *and* his own rocket. And here's where things got interesting. His idea for reentry — after sketches, models, debates, dreams, and analysis — was to bend the tail booms of the spacecraft upward while in space, where there is no aerodynamic load on the structure. The design was tricky. The feathering configuration would be used only for the flight phase where the ship is decelerating as it enters the

---

tiles was due to convection, not friction. At Mach 15-plus the shock wave prevented air from slamming the shuttle underbelly. Heat was transmitted from the shock front to the surface via convection of a superhot layer of plasma. The tiles insulate so well that you can hold one by the bottom corners, even when the rest is red hot.

atmosphere. After deceleration, it could descend to any altitude desired because it is flying slowly. However, it must defeather to be able to make a proper gliding approach to land on the runway. The only design remotely like it was something that Burt had made as a teenager and brought to the Academy of Model Aeronautics national competition in Dallas. He was seventeen years old in 1960 when he built and flew a Nordic towline glider that used a mechanism called a dethermalizer to flip the horizontal stabilizer of his model glider upward midflight. He had soaked cotton in saltpeter and lit it before takeoff. The ignited cotton burned through a rubber band slowly, flipping the tail up.

Burt asked X-15 engineer Bob Hoey, who lived nearby, to help by looking at the hazards of the program. Hoey took one look at his friend's design for bending the tails and booms and thought it was as strange as anything he'd seen before. But he said the idea just might work. Hoey had also been a modeler as a youth, and had used dethermalizers. The concept was practical, but the application in space was entirely unknown. It had never been done before. Having lived through the high-risk, high-reward X-15 program, where every week brought agitation and exhilaration, Hoey told Burt that he and his team at Scaled were about to fly into the unknown. He said they should prepare to live with the likelihood of catastrophe. But Burt knew he could do this; he now had that feeling in his gut.

After a few more launches of the foam models from the Mojave Tower, twenty-six-year-old engineer Matt Stinemetze looked around. Burt was long gone. Matt chuckled. Burt made you feel like anything was possible, that the out-of-the-ordinary was ordinary. This was Scaled, where it wasn't unusual for someone to show up in the lobby with a suitcase of cash and insist he had the next great idea for aviation. Pilots flew in to show off their tricked-out, homebuilt planes, including one number that resembled a walrus. The running joke about living here was "How many people live in Mojave? . . . About half of them."

Matt had moved to Mojave shortly after graduating and a week after his honeymoon. He understood why Burt settled here: cheap rents, space to build and fly, and little oversight. The area was classified as "unpopulated" by the Federal Aviation Administration, perfect for testing and flying experimental and homebuilt aircraft. As Matt saw it, it was also a place that brilliantly weeded out those who were not serious about the job. Mojave's main drag was nothing more than truck stops, motels, gas stations, and fast food. Trash blew in and got caught on cyclone fences. The desert was not for the meek. One of the longest-living plants on Earth — the creosote bush — prospered in Mojave, along with the lethally venomous Mojave green pit viper. But this was also home to the *Voyager,* and to dozens of original planes made from unexpected materials. Twenty-three miles down Highway 58 was Edwards Air Force Base. Mojave was made by the frontier spirit. It remained a place where outsized ideas were not to be tamed.

Stinemetze, in T-shirt, jeans, and with hair halfway down his back, had been at Scaled Composites for more than two years, and was still intimidated by the man he'd dreamed of working for since he was a kid in Kansas. This was the reason Matt had come to Scaled. As he put it, wonderfully weird shit happened here all the time. He'd known about Burt as the face on the cover of aviation magazines his dad read. He thought Burt's backward-looking planes were the coolest things he'd ever seen outside the Kansas Cosmonaut Space Center.

Matt was having a great time flying the models off the tower; it was a hobby that had filled his childhood. He'd never had the money to spend much time in or around real planes, but he always made and flew models, the stranger the better. He was seven years old when the space shuttle flew for the first time in 1981, and he watched as his dad, a city sanitation worker, snapped pictures of it on TV. His parents let him use sharp tools with big blades when he was just a kid, and he nearly cut off a finger or two. He got stitched up and never made the same mistake again. He worked on old cars and even built his own all-composite sailboat modeled after the Koch brothers' America's Cup catamaran.[*] In college at Wichita State, where he earned his aerospace degree, he led a team that built a small jet. When Matt interviewed at Scaled, Burt seemed most interested in what he was building for fun. Scaled was filled with guys like him who were not Ivy League, but who were aerospace graduates or had simply been born with a need to make stuff, including their own planes.

When Matt arrived at Scaled, business was slow and the company took on projects to keep everyone employed. Matt was given the job of building a twenty-one-foot-long carbon fiber spine of a cow for a prominent artist in Washington, D.C. He then worked in the bids and proposals department with his mentor Cory Bird, an artist, perfectionist, and self-taught aerodynamicist who arrived for work

[*] Burt and the team at Scaled designed the first hard sail ever used in an America's Cup race. The wing sail was for Dennis Conner's catamaran *Stars & Stripes,* raced in 1988.

on his first day at Scaled with his own toolbox. Matt was then involved in a cruise missile project, followed by the building of a prototype plane for the carmaker Toyota. It was in a meeting in 2000 when Matt began hearing Burt talk in detail about doing a spaceship. Burt spent an entire lengthy meeting one day talking about how he'd make the cabin door of the ship. Matt had never sought out projects directly run by Burt, finding him unnerving. Matt was wiry and watchful; Burt was big and had blue eyes that cut right through you. Matt had intentionally kept his head down while learning the ropes.

Now, flying a foam model straight off the tower deck, Matt thought about the idea of sending a privately built ship to space from Mojave. He felt he was ready for something new, maybe even working with the man himself.

In a matter of weeks, in fall 2000, Burt was seated across the table from Microsoft cofounder Paul Allen in Allen's office in Seattle. Soup and salad were served, but Burt didn't touch the food. He knew his time was limited. Burt got to the point. Since their last discussions about using the Proteus not just for broadband communications but possibly for single-person spaceflight, Burt had looked at the problem of reentry with the goal of finding a generic solution to get people to and from space. When he told Allen in earlier meetings that he didn't have the solution yet, Allen said to come and find him when he did. Now, Burt told him that he'd figured out the technology. He was confident that he had come up with a breakthrough design that would provide a "carefree" reentry.

Allen listened and said little, occasionally looking out the window. The view to the west was of the city's waterfront and the Olympic Mountains. To the southwest was the Seattle Seahawks' new football stadium, under construction. Allen had bought the NFL team in 1996. To the south was Mount Rainier and the Cascade Mountains. Allen had followed Burt's career from afar, thought he had a brilliant body of work, and had studied his safety record, noting that none of his designs ever crashed during testing. He and Burt had talked several times about a shared desire to get America back to space. They also shared a passion for coming up with new and unconventional solutions to old problems. Allen wanted to bring back the sense of daring, imagination, and technological skill that gave NASA its successes, but get there with private industry. Both men believed that the "little guy" needed to restart manned spaceflight, or it wouldn't be done at all. Allen was intrigued by the XPRIZE, but had been told that the financing for the award was shaky — they were four years in and $5 million short.

During the lunch in Allen's office, Burt talked about the fatal crash of the X-15 involving his friend Mike Adams, and about his plans for slowing his vehicle. He used the term "feather" to describe how the wings would bend up to create drag and turn the ship belly first for its trip back to Earth. Allen, who loved playing badminton as a youth, likened the feather concept to a badminton birdie, which, launched from a racket, oriented itself nose first in the direction of flight. *This is a genius approach,* Allen thought. *It can go subsonic, supersonic, go to space, and come home as a benign glider.* Allen had great respect for NASA, but believed its systems had become too expensive and that innovation had gotten lost. It was time for the torch to be passed to entrepreneurs.

Burt said that based on his decades of experience building airplanes quickly, using composite materials and techniques similar to the building of boats or surfboards, he could do a space project "real quick." He would keep costs down by building it basically with cable and pushrod flight controls. He didn't want a computer as the pilot. He loved the idea that the last time anyone went supersonic in a mechanically controlled plane was Chuck Yeager in 1947.

"Have you done a rocket before?" Allen asked.

"No," Burt replied. "But I believe in this so strongly, that I would fund it myself if I had the money."

At that, Allen stood up from his chair, reached his hand out, and said, "Let's do it."

It took almost a year from the handshake for Burt and Paul Allen to sign an operating agreement. There were provisions in the contract that Burt was not about to accept. The biggest point of contention was the stipulation that if Allen for some reason ended the program at his discretion, Burt would not be allowed to use any of the ideas he had developed. Allen would own the intellectual property — ideas, concepts, drawings, and models developed even before the two started working together. When Burt protested, Allen's lawyers told him that they'd had people before who would "bail and go compete with Mr. Allen with someone else." The lawyers reassured him that they were protecting Mr. Allen's liabilities. "This is normal, don't worry," they said. Burt wasn't worried; he was *haunted* by the idea that he could be the only guy in America who could not do a space plane. Burt told his employees at Scaled, "I'm going to stick with it until we get something that doesn't look so bad."

Slowly, the two sides found compromises

and set up a company called Mojave Aerospace Ventures. Allen's point person on the venture was Dave Moore, who handled a number of Allen's investments and had been an early Microsoft employee. Moore thought the deal should be simple: At the very beginning, Burt and his company would own the majority share in the joint venture. As Allen funded it, that share — and their ownership — would be diluted.

The tricky part for Moore, a self-described "hard-ass" when it came to negotiations, was how to put a valuation on an idea that was still unproven but came from someone who was a "preeminent star," and was considerably smarter than just about everyone in the field. Moore always had the advantage of negotiating from a position of strength; his boss had the billions.

Moore had started at Microsoft as a software designer in 1981, when the company had fewer than seventy employees and personal computers were just getting started. When Moore went for his interview at Microsoft, he was asked math-related questions and given a technical test. When he passed the test, he was moved up to talk to Paul Allen. Allen asked him what he'd been working on in his previous job, and Moore said he was creating an electronic exchange to design parts on a computer and then send the parts to manufacturing to run the machines. When he mentioned he was using "spline," a mathematical method to determine shapes, Allen said excitedly, "You know about *splines*?" Allen got up and went next door to Bill Gates's office, came back and said, "Bill would like to talk to you." Moore then gave Bill Gates a ninety-minute tutorial on splines.[*] Moore was hired to work on Microsoft's first business graphics. He left Microsoft in 1997, when the company had 25,000 employees, and began doing technical due diligence for venture capital firms. He was soon pulled back into the Microsoft fold

[*] Splines are complex curves formed by gluing together simple curves. Simple equations can represent only simple forms. They are "simple" precisely because they are easy to describe; you need only a few numbers — or parameters. But a simple curve described by few parameters will be "rigid" — you can't force it to pass through very many points in given directions. A spline, though, can pass through as many points as you like in whatever direction you like, because it's stitched together from little pieces, each of which is simple and passes through a few of the points. The next piece passes through the next set of points, et cetera. The trick is how you stitch the curves together. Naturally you want the ends to meet up. That's a given. But you want more. You want the ends to meet up nicely, for some definition of "nicely." The most common splines are "cubic splines," polynomials of degree 3.

when Allen asked him to look into some of his potential investments. Moore had worked closely over the years with a number of innovative and "unique" thinkers, so he welcomed the chance to work with Burt Rutan.

Before the handshake between Burt and his boss, Moore had met with a number of people who wanted Allen to fund their space companies, even talking at one point with Buzz Aldrin. Aldrin was on the board of directors of a green technology company, and when the subject turned to spaceflight and advanced avionics, Burt's name came up. Moore asked Aldrin whether he thought Burt could build a manned suborbital spaceship, and Aldrin said no; he thought Burt "wouldn't be successful." Moore had also met with Peter Diamandis, who pitched him on Blastoff and made an argument for Allen to come in as the title sponsor of the XPRIZE. Moore listened to Peter's pitch, but never let on that his boss was in talks with Burt. Moore met with Gary Hudson, who'd been at the Montrose, Colorado, weekend event when the XPRIZE idea was hatched. Hudson had a company called Rotary Rocket, funded in large part by none other than Walt Anderson. Moore had flown to Mojave in his own plane, a Socata TBM 700, and sat in the Rotary's simulator. Even though Moore was an experienced pilot, and was in the process of getting his helicopter rating, he couldn't come close to landing the simulator. Moore thought the propulsion system on the craft, called Roton — with a spinning wheel of engines on its base to lift the rocket and another set of spinning rockets on rotor blades to recover the vehicle like a helicopter — sounded "crazy." He returned to Seattle and told Allen, "You shouldn't invest." Allen didn't. In 2000, Rotary Rocket closed, after having burned through about $30 million. The Roton, standing 63 feet high — the same height as the tail of a 747 — was now on display at the entrance to the Mojave Airport.

When contract talks started, Burt gave Moore a bid based on twenty-one tasks to be completed during the spaceship program, from building a flight simulator and performing glide tests to flying "three people twice above 100 km in less than 2 weeks with same spaceship . . . achieve the goal defined by the XPRIZE organization." The twenty-first task was to fly the spaceship every Tuesday for five months to show its reliability and direct operating costs. Burt thought it was a neat task, but got cold feet as he couldn't put a price on the costs before development was under way. Task twenty-one was nixed. The jointly owned Mojave Aerospace Ventures would hold the intellectual property developed during the program. Moore would be CEO of the new venture. During the drawn-out negotiations, Burt didn't get a nickel from Allen and wondered whether he ever would. But he still charged ahead with the design of the rocket and mother ship and began studying types of propulsion.

After months of back-and-forth, Burt finally got a contract he could accept. Allen would be the majority owner of Mojave Aerospace Ventures, and Burt would have a strong minority interest. In March 2001, the two sides signed a deal. They agreed on the need to do the program covertly. They didn't want anyone — including NASA — to find out what they were doing.

In April, Burt and Moore met to go over insurance, launch licenses, the timing of permits, patents on new technology, and when powered tests might begin. When the meeting ended, the two walked down the hall, pausing before heading outside. The price tag of the whole program was put at about $18 million. Turning to Burt, Moore said, "Well, how much do you need to get started?" Burt went over figures in his head: *Thirty thousand? Eighty thousand? One hundred thousand?* He was calculating what would come first when Moore said, "Why don't I just put $3 million in a bank account now and let me know when you need more."

Burt tried not to smile too big. Three million to start. That would work.

■ ■ ■

By early June 2001, Burt had completed his preliminary design of the launch aircraft, the rocket motor, and the basic spaceship. Burt had given the rocket the in-house name of *SpaceShipOne,* which wasn't popular. Dave Moore came up with names close to his boss's heart, including "Faye" — for Paul's mother — as well as some Native American names for various birds. Burt defended his name, saying that kids fantasized about flying to space and always used the term "spaceship." He wanted to emphasize the informal, fantasy nature of the first nongovernmental manned space program. Fabrication of the mother ship was set to begin. He sent employees armed with wrenches to the local junkyard to pry handles off cars to be used temporarily for the simulator and spaceship. He sent one of his builders, who happened to look like a biker, to another junkyard to buy J-85 engines on the cheap. He found his hybrid rocket propulsion expert in Huntsville, Alabama. The guy hadn't flown any rockets to space, but he had built a rocket-fueled bike that he rode at impressive speeds along the back roads of Alabama.

In a cordoned-off area of Scaled's hangar, the mother ship — which would carry *Space-ShipOne* to altitude for a drop launch — was given a name: the *White Knight.* It was named by Cory Bird, who referred to the windows as slits in a knight's helmet and the sharp slender boom fronts as jousting spears. In another curtained-off area, the rocket-powered *SpaceShipOne* program appeared stalled. A few things were being built, but it didn't have the momentum of the *White Knight.* To get the rocket part of the equation moving, a new project engineer was named: Matt Stinemetze.

Stinemetze, thinking about the pressure of running the spaceship program, realized the goal of a manned space program was so preposterous that it fit with Scaled. Burt didn't give a shit about doing stuff that was impossible or nuts. Why should anyone else give it a second thought?

21
A LIFELINE FOR THE XPRIZE

When the invitation came in to join a group of friends on a ski trip in early January 2001, Erik Lindbergh hesitated. He was doing better, thanks to the breakthrough arthritis drug Enbrel, but he hadn't skied in more than seven years. After returning from the Mayo Clinic, Erik had taken stock of his past and future. He looked over his treasured Atomic telemarks, Dynamic VR27s, and Völkl Snow Rangers, and said, "Who am I kidding? I'm walking with a cane." He sold nine pairs of skis, each representing a different kind of joy: skis for powder, skis for downhill, skis for slalom racing.

But now here he stood, on his oldest and sturdiest pair of cross-country skis, at the top of a gentle sloping hill, situated about twenty miles east of Stevens Pass in Washington. He was wearing the one pair he hadn't sold, his Black Diamond Vector cross-country skis, and his leather telemark boots. He figured that if he could walk, he could still cross-country ski. His wife, Mara, was with him, and they had a new addition to the Lindbergh clan: their six-month-old son, Gus, bundled up in a carrier on Erik's back. The skies were blue, the sun shined, and four inches of fresh powder beckoned.

Starting out that morning from their friends' cabin in Scottish Lakes High Camp, Erik had planned to just tool around and do the best he could. He had two relatively new knees, one fused foot, and the wear and tear from years of living with rheumatoid arthritis. He didn't know how he would hold up. But after he and Mara had cross-country skied about a quarter of a mile, Erik felt great. The only thing feeling old and stiff was his gear. Still, there was a difference between walking and running — between cross-country and downhill.

"I have to try it," he told Mara after they reached the top of the hill. It was a gentle rolling slope, a far cry from the slalom courses and cornices of his youth. But the gentle slope looked like a blast. He took nothing for granted anymore, not walking, sitting comfortably, or sleeping through the night. This was all a gift: like the gnarled lumber of his sculptures, he had been handed a second chance. And now he was a dad who could carry his son on his back.

He pushed off with his skis and had that familiar feeling of gravity's tug and momen-

412

tum's pull, and of air — cold, fresh air. It was effortless.

"I can ski again!" Erik yelled out.

A moment later, he added with a laugh, "And I need better gear again!"

Erik was back home working in his wood-shop and putting the finishing touches on one of his sculptures when he stopped what he was doing to call Gregg Maryniak. He had been toying with an idea that was both rebellious and reverential. It was something friends and strangers had asked him about for years, something he would dismiss before the person could finish the sentence. The idea had been hatched months earlier when he was holding wood pieces up to the sunlight, and the plan had taken shape in his mind as he finished the *Spirit of St. Louis* sculpture. The idea was affirmed by his days on the ski slopes and by the mornings when he woke up feeling great.

Erik caught Gregg at work. Gregg was the only salaried employee left at the XPRIZE, and he was working part time and hustling for outside sources of income. He kept the office open in the St. Louis Science Center in case someone called about a possible sponsorship. Everyone else, Peter included, was off salary. Erik was on the XPRIZE board and attended meeting after meeting where desperation had set in around fund-raising. Peter, back to the XPRIZE after the letdown of Blastoff, was calling on friends and family to keep operations afloat. He was putting in his own money to sustain his dream.

Erik told Gregg that he had landed on an idea that could save the XPRIZE, get a ton of attention, and be a huge personal challenge. "I want to recreate grandfather's flight," Erik said.

There was silence. Finally, Gregg said he thought it was a very bad idea. "It's way too risky," Gregg said. "Erik, you have a nice wife, a young child. *Why?* It's thirty-six hundred miles over wet stuff. A helicopter can rescue you the first fifty miles or the last fifty miles."

Even in a modern plane, nonstop solo transatlantic flying was risky, Gregg noted. Erik was still living with the residual damage from rheumatoid arthritis, and the flight would have him seated, alone, in a cockpit, for close to twenty hours straight. Modern technology could help to a degree. Gregg likened it to the difference between climbing Mount Everest when Edmund Hillary did it in 1953 and climbing Everest today; the modern climber had better equipment, communications technology, and training, but the potential perils remained: unpredictable weather, equipment failure, human error, and exhaustion.

Erik was undeterred. He explained he'd come up with the idea while making the *Spirit of St. Louis* wood sculpture, and it became more plausible when he found himself gaining strength after finding the new treatment for his rheumatoid arthritis. He told Gregg he had even started skiing again. His reasons for wanting to do the flight were threefold: to better understand what his grandfather had experienced; to show people — especially kids — that if they were suffering, they could get their lives back; and to spotlight how far aviation had come and, with the XPRIZE, how far it could go.

"I think we can raise a lot of money and attention for the XPRIZE," Erik said, noting that the flight would be done in spring 2002, on the seventy-fifth anniversary of his grandfather's flight.

As Gregg listened to the reasons, he started warming to the idea, with certain caveats. They needed to do a feasibility study of what would be required to make the flight. He suggested they meet with Peter, Byron Lichtenberg, Marc Arnold, and a fellow named Joe Dobronski, a well-regarded chief test pilot and engineer for McDonnell Douglas who could advise them on the type of plane. Gregg was emphatic that even though transatlantic flights by small craft were common, Erik would have to undergo ditch and survival training. If he crashed at sea, Erik would need to know how to survive until a rescue operation could arrive.

The other part of the feasibility study was possibly the riskiest: Erik needed to broach the subject with his reticent and reclusive Lindbergh family. The idea of Erik's flight was taboo, like adding a new layer of paint to the *Mona Lisa*.

One of the first people Erik talked to was his aunt Reeve, Charles and Anne Morrow Lindbergh's youngest daughter. Her response was supportive, but she was the only family member who was publicly a Lindbergh. And this assertiveness had taken time. When she married her first husband, Richard Brown, she was happy to be Mrs. Brown. There were no expectations. But over time, she became Reeve Lindbergh Brown and then Reeve Lindbergh. Her way of dealing with the Lindbergh legacy was to write about it; her newest book was a memoir detailing her mother's final seventeen months living with her on her farm in Vermont.

Reeve told Erik that the flight sounded daring. It seemed to her only yesterday that Erik could barely walk because of his rheumatoid arthritis. But she cautioned him that others in the family would be less gracious in their responses. They would probably say he was doing a "big commercial publicity stunt." For decades, a family lawyer named James W.

Lloyd had been charged with enforcing Charles and Anne Lindbergh's instructions of "no use of name, likeness or signature [of Charles or Anne] for commercial purposes." This left the nonprofit Lindbergh Foundation dancing around the delicate issue of fund-raising while trading on the legacy. And in the end, it prevented the foundation from securing a sustainable endowment. Family members referred to Lloyd somewhat lovingly as "Dr. No." Although, when Erik brought fake "official Charles Lindbergh merchandise" to his attention, nothing was done. Reeve advised Erik that if he was to do the flight, he should emphasize *his* name, and reference who his grandparents were.

Erik's mother, Barbara, was troubled by the idea of the flight. She feared for her son's physical safety during and after. While long divorced from Erik's father, Jon Lindbergh, she still felt constricted by the tacit rule that you don't publicize who you are. If you do, bad things happen. When Erik and his siblings were growing up, she told them they could use her maiden name, Robbins, as their last name if they wanted. A few did, but most — like Reeve — eventually returned to Lindbergh.

News of Erik's plans spread fast among family members, and Barbara was soon getting calls from her other children. The men in the family were opposed to the idea, some more vociferously than others. The women in the family were concerned about Erik's safety. Erik's brother Morgan was a supporter of the XPRIZE and could see how the seventy-fifth anniversary flight would generate money and attention. But what if Erik's flight failed? How would that affect Grandfather's legacy? And why did Erik have the right to take this piece of family history and make it his own?

After weeks of back-and-forth with family members, Erik had another conversation with Reeve. She concluded that the women in the family feared he wouldn't make it, and the men feared he would.

But Erik had made up his mind. He was going to do this. Erik was done being crippled by this disease and hobbled by his legacy. As his grandfather once said in response to critics and skeptics, "Why shouldn't I fly from New York to Paris?"

Erik met Gregg and Peter in St. Louis to go over plans and budgets for the flight. Dobronski, Arnold, and Lichtenberg joined them. Peter had first heard of Erik's idea through Gregg. Peter didn't share Gregg's initial worries. He thought the flight would be life changing for Erik — affirming both his legacy and his restored health — and told Gregg, "That's awesome. I'm all in." He found it profound that Erik just might save a competition inspired by his grandfather.

A pilot for four decades, Gregg agreed that the XPRIZE financing effort had reached a point where it had run out of "altitude, ideas, and airspeed." They were scraping by and needed a cash infusion to keep operations going long enough so they could find a sponsor. Doug King, director of the St. Louis Science Center, had already rescued them several times.

Erik began sketching out a budget and goals, and talk turned to the type of plane that Erik would use for the transatlantic journey. Someone suggested they buy a Beechcraft Bonanza, a single-engine, six-seat general aviation plane, and then sell it after the flight. Dobronski said, "No, why don't you talk to Lancair, in Oregon? They make the best state-of-the-art airplane" for this type of flight. Erik and Gregg — now project manager for Erik's mission — agreed to go and take a look at what Lancair had to offer. They set a fund-raising goal of $1 million for the XPRIZE, and additional sums for the Lindbergh Foundation and the Arthritis Foundation.

Erik left the meeting thinking: *I'm going to recreate Grandfather's landmark journey in my own single-engine light monoplane and fly the same path over the Atlantic without stopping.*

Peter left the meeting thinking, *This is oxygen for the XPRIZE.*

22
A DISPLAY OF HARDWARE

Steve Bennett stood on the wet thick sand of Morecambe Bay on the northwest coast of England, preparing for the launch of his four-story-high rocket, Nova 1. The sand flats were beautiful and brutal, a place where pink-footed geese and delicate hairstreak butterflies coexisted with shifting channels, deadly quicksand, and a tide that came in fast and quiet like an advancing army.

It was early morning on November 22, 2001, and Bennett was here for the test flight of Nova 1, a two-stage rocket that he'd been developing in the five years since hearing of the XPRIZE. When he first started telling people he wanted to build rockets to go to space, he got looks like there was something seriously wrong with him. But when he began telling people he wanted to win an international competition involving *ten million dollars,* it suddenly became about beating the Yanks at their own game. Ordinary people were taking interest. Though the prize was only half funded, that had done little to dampen the enthusiasm of Bennett and other space entrepreneurs around the world: they had forged ahead full steam and now had hardware to show for their efforts, even if some were more viable than others.

Nova 1, one of the most serious entries in the field, would be the first rocket actually flown as a part of the XPRIZE. Soon after hearing about the XPRIZE, Bennett had left his job at the toothpaste maker Colgate — which at first supported his rocket pursuits by offering six months of paid leave — and founded Starchaser Industries. He spent the next three years living off his credit cards. A part-time teaching job at the University of Salford, just outside of Manchester, had kept what he described as "the wolf from the door." The job gave him access to a small laboratory, an office and telephone, and students who were interested in space technology and wanted to help him. He landed a huge break when one of his rockets featured on a Discovery Channel segment attracted support from a deep-pocketed, space-minded benefactor.

If this morning's launch went according to plan, Nova 1 would be the largest privately built rocket ever flown from British soil. The gleaming white rocket with the tapered throat — all Bennett's design — had the XPRIZE logo splashed across its fins. Nova 1 was big enough to carry one person, but Bennett would need a capsule fit for three to win the XPRIZE. Although no one was inside the Nova capsule, Bennett had every intention of one day flying to space in his own ship, and this flight would be an important stepping-stone toward that goal.

Today's flight would test the hardware, including the mobile launch tower, the Nova airframe, booster system, capsule parachute descent, and avionics. Bennett's rocket, the stuff he'd dreamed about both as child and adult, was big: more than 37 feet high, 4 feet in diameter, and weighing 1,643 pounds on liftoff. The estimated speed would be 500 miles per hour.

Bennett surveyed the scene, with its earthly beauty and untested machine. The shellfish grounds and shrimping channels of Morecambe Bay had been plied for generations, first by using horse and cart and later with tractor and nets. When Bennett first started coming here to test out smaller rockets, he met with the local cocklers, fishermen who eked out a hard living collecting the small, heart-shaped mollusks called cockles. The cocklers knew the lay of the land in Morecambe Bay: the fast-moving tides, unpredictable channels, and invisible areas of quicksand. Today, launch day, the cocklers were being paid to shuttle media and VIPs on the back of their tractor beds from the main road to the rocket staging area.

The biggest question on Bennett's mind was whether the solid rocket motor propulsion system would work. He had nineteen solid motors that needed to ignite at precisely the same time. If they didn't ignite at once, the rocket would probably cartwheel over. The igniters had been tested three times in the shop, and there were four igniters in each of the nineteen motors — they had quadruple redundancy to make sure everything worked. Another concern was the nuclear power station five miles away. It would not be a good day if the rocket crashed into a nuclear power plant.

Bennett had arrived that morning before sunrise, when ground and air were blurred by heavy moisture, reminding him of a J.M.W. Turner landscape. The team relied on floodlights to set up. The cockle fishermen were happy to earn a little extra money and to have a break from the tedium of their days. Bennett had limited time before the tide returned. At around nine A.M., carrying duct tape and wearing a white construction helmet and a jacket with the Starchaser logo, Bennett was up in a cherry picker at the top of Nova 1. Three helicopters flew nearby. After years of dreaming, scrimping, building, and testing, the moment of truth was here. This was what he'd worked for — the answer to his fears that he would go through life as a "conventional person," that he'd be lying on his deathbed, bills paid, but unfulfilled.

Back down on the ground, Bennett positioned himself with a vantage point to take in the guests, media, and Mission Control, which in this case was a cabin resembling a carnival ticket booth set down on the back of a tractor bed. He had a full-time team of twenty, a legion of volunteers, reporters, and television crews, his benefactor, Paul Young, who had made his money in cell phone technology, and a group of cocklers, who had never seen anything like this. The Civil Aviation Authority, England's version of the Federal Aviation Administration, said Bennett needed to keep Nova 1 from flying above 10,000 feet. He was fine with that; just under two miles high was sufficient to test all of the systems.

At 10:30 A.M., a hush fell over the crowd. The countdown began: 10, 9, 8, 7 — Bennett took a deep breath — 5, 4, 3, 2, 1 . . . ignition!

The rocket lifted off with an earsplitting screech. A fiery plume became a thick white line, straight at first, then jagged, then billowing. The nineteen motors lit perfectly. At around 10,000 feet, the capsule separated from the rocket, and both began to float back to Earth by parachute. The cocklers cheered; Paul Young had a tear in his eye. Bennett tracked the trajectory of the parts against the cool blue sky. The wind was blowing at around 15 miles per hour, enough to cause concern. Both sections landed on target, but the capsule was picked up by the wind and dragged for some distance before it could be stopped.

The boy whose mom wouldn't let him stay up late to watch the Apollo 11 landing on TV had staged his own show. It wasn't the Moon, but he had succeeded without any help from the government. He'd built and flown the largest nongovernmental rocket ever launched from the United Kingdom mainland. His next challenge would be even bigger, even better: Nova 2, with room for three.

Bennett remained at Cape Morecambe Bay, as he'd taken to calling it, after everyone but the fishermen had gone home. The tide would soon wash in, erasing any hint of what had happened that day.

For their new rocket company, video game legend John Carmack and his wife, Katherine Anna Kang, came up with the name Armadillo Aerospace — a nod to the nocturnal animals that were well represented across Texas, and that often scurried around the Carmacks' property. A small armadillo in a flight suit was their team logo.

After his "larval stage" of research into rocketing, and after giving small amounts of cash to a few aerospace companies going after the CATS Prize, which no one won, Carmack had called the Dallas Area Rocket Society and asked whether anyone wanted to help him build experimental, high-powered rockets. Carmack hinted over the phone that he wanted to work on "a little bit of a special project, something extreme."

Neil Milburn, a member of the Dallas rocket group, was one of a handful of guys who responded to Carmack's invitation, drawn in by the promise of "something extreme." He and the other rocket enthusiasts went to meet with Carmack after hours at the id Software office. Milburn watched a guy with long hair, John Lennon glasses, T-shirt, and shorts amble down the stairs. Realizing it was Carmack, he thought, *What the heck am I getting myself involved with here?* But after an hour of talking, it was obvious that Carmack was exceedingly sharp and had done his homework; soon, a core group of nine people was in place, including Carmack and his wife.

Beyond the XPRIZE competition, Carmack's long-term goal was to create private suborbital manned spaceflight. He wanted to be credible in what he was doing and told the volunteer group, "I want this to be a rich man's hobby, not a poor man's aerospace company." That meant he would fund the company out of his own pocket, and the team would focus on building, testing, and flying.

They would not have to create simulations of what they would do if only they had the money. Their goal, Carmack said, was to operate more like a software company, to be open source, post their successes and failures, and "celebrate the positive but don't get torn up about the negative."

And so the development process began on their rocket, Black Armadillo. Carmack bought one hundred acres of land east of Dallas to use for high-energy tests and helicopter drop tests of the capsule. Four months after team members had a space to work in, they managed to get a small craft to hover. Then the building of Black Armadillo proceeded. The rocket would be cylindrical, the nose cone providing the space for the occupant, similar in design and flight mission to the DC-X Delta Clipper with vertical takeoff, vertical landing. Russ Blink, an entrepreneur considered the electronics whiz of the group, was also the daredevil, doing freefall parachuting for fun. He would be Black Armadillo's pilot. Carmack had found a used Russian spacesuit on eBay for Blink to wear.

The all-volunteer group met twice a week, for four hours on Tuesday nights and eight to ten hours on Saturdays. Carmack had committed $500,000 a year to cover overhead, buy parts, and pay for launch costs. Everyone volunteered out of a shared goal of getting to space quickly and cheaply. The key members of the team were Blink, Milburn, and Phil Eaton.

There were many successes, and even more failures. Carmack was surprised that rocket building was more difficult than he'd expected. And while team members faced an array of technical challenges, they also found the bureaucratic side equally painstaking, reminding them of Wernher von Braun's quote: "We can lick gravity, but sometimes the paperwork is overwhelming." There were times when there were more people at the FAA's Office of Commercial Space Transportation working on their launch license than Armadillo had building the rocket.

Their propellant of choice was rocket-grade hydrogen peroxide, over 90 percent concentration compared with the household 3 percent variety. But team members soon found they would have a hard time buying large quantities of rocket-grade peroxide in the United States because the company they'd first purchased it from was concerned about lawsuits if Armadillo had a fatality or a major accident. As an alternative, Carmack had been enticed by the idea of concocting a mixed monopropellant of their own, that is, mixing a fuel with an oxidizer, in this case 50 percent strength hydrogen peroxide. This still had the simplicity of just hydrogen peroxide, and the purchasing requirements were straightforward. So they ended up using a mixture of 50 percent peroxide and alcohol, a relatively safe combination, but one that was harder to get working.

Black Armadillo would stand thirty feet tall and be up to six feet in diameter. It would do a DC-X-style landing, freefalling back through the atmosphere until it reached 15,000 feet above ground, when the engines — two banks of four engines — were relit. It would then continue falling tail-first before the engines would slow it to a safe landing, Buck Rogers style. The crew cabin was beneath the fuel tank, directly above the engines. Each engine would have about five thousand pounds of thrust. By far the most dangerous part of the mission was the return to Earth: if the engines didn't relight the way they were supposed to, there would be little chance of survival.

By early 2002, team members were getting ready to do more drop tests of their rocket. They hoped the rocket would fly in 2003. As Carmack and the team raced ahead, Carmack's wife, Katherine Kang, served a different role: she became the adult in the room.

Since their marriage in 2000, Katherine, a self-described "type A personality," managed the business side of things. She supported the idea of her husband's starting a rocket company, but she wanted it run as a business, in an orderly way, with the goal of one day making money. She expected results beyond flawless engine firings and a rocket that shot up and returned safely.

When she and John first started dating, she learned that he had a significant amount of money parked in a zero-interest checking account. He didn't know what to do with his millions, and didn't have time to think about investing. She told him that he needed to at least think about moving his money from a zero-interest account to a money market. She laughed years later remembering it. When he saw he was making money on his money, he thought it was "neat."

They shared a similar background of growing up without much parental support and having to pay their own way at a relatively young age. At around the time she and John began talking about a rocket company — he was still working at id Software — they separated funds into His, Hers, and Family. Katherine had begun looking into costs of insurance, launch licenses, lawyers, and environmental impact studies, and told John, "We need some reasonable ceiling. Any other hobby is manageable by comparison." The $500,000 a year was an underestimate. She could see that rockets burned through money faster than fuel.

As time passed, Katherine knew that some on the Armadillo team thought of her as the bad guy. She was monitoring the money. Still, the cash kept flowing out at Mach speed. She realized she needed something to illustrate to her husband just how much they were spending. She needed something tangible, something that would get his attention. After pondering different ideas, she sat him down one night and told him that for every dollar he spent on rockets, she was going to spend, too. On diamonds.

At the time, she wasn't particularly interested in jewelry, though that changed as she started collecting. If John wrote a check for $50,000 for insurance for a launch license, she would have $50,000 to spend shopping for diamonds. As her diamonds got bigger and bigger, her plan worked. John took notice. One day, seeing Katherine's haul, he said, "Whoa! *How much am I spending?*"

But she could see that John was happier than he'd been in years, working with a small team on a hugely challenging project. He told her he felt like he was back in his apartment in Wisconsin, bringing 3-D *Wolfenstein* to life. But instead of a virtual game where a World War II spy goes after Nazis, John was now writing software and building hardware to fly to space. They had engines to fire and launches to realize. And she had more diamonds to buy.

Across the globe, teams were at work on a range of rocket concepts. A group called TGV

Rockets (Two Guys in a Vehicle) in Bethesda, Maryland, had a design for a rocket called Michelle B., described as a "suborbital bus service" that would take people sixty-two miles up and back. The group was heavy with aerospace veterans and military test pilots, but light on cash. Nonetheless, they were determined, fixed on the goal of offering no-frills suborbital flight priced by the pound.

One of two Canadian XPRIZE teams, Canadian Arrow, run by Geoff Sheerin, had constructed a full-scale engineering mockup based on the World War II–era V-2 rocket. Sheerin shopped the model around on the back of a flatbed truck in hopes of getting funding, hauling it to New York to display it in Rockefeller Center — quite a sight in the months following 9/11 — and going on the *Today* show to talk about the rocket, the XPRIZE, and his space dreams. The team also built a V-2-style engine, which was made of steel, had brass propellant injectors, and would use liquid oxygen and alcohol as propellants to burn for fifty-five seconds.

The other Canadian team, da Vinci Project, was led by Brian Feeney. Feeney had been living in Hong Kong when he first read about the XPRIZE. His vision was of a rocket-powered spacecraft called Wild Fire, which would be air-launched from the world's largest reusable helium balloon at about 65,000 feet. Feeney was also building hardware as he searched for backers of his manned "rock-oon."

In Hitchcock, Texas, Jim Akkerman, who spent his youth making and racing turbo-charged go-karts and spent thirty-six years working as a NASA engineer, was toiling away in semiretirement (though he preferred to say he "graduated" from NASA) on his XPRIZE rocket, the Mayflower II. His plan was unlike any of the others, at least in terms of where it would start. He planned to launch the massive vehicle, weighing fifteen thousand pounds, from about thirty miles offshore in the Gulf of Mexico. According to his plan, the titanium rocket would bob upright like a buoy, and would have two ten-thousand-gallon fuel tanks: one for liquid natural gas, one for liquid oxygen. A cockpit would be on top of the rocket, and passengers would ride below. It would be powered by eight TRW engines, producing forty thousand pounds of thrust.

Akkerman had a pilot signed up. He named his company Advent Launch Services to represent the start of a new and private era of space. For now, its base of operations was a rice field near his house. He estimated that the Mayflower II would cost $10 million, which he was trying to raise. In the meantime, he was funding what he couldn't get donated out of his retirement savings. A devout Baptist, he wanted to win the XPRIZE, but

434

he was really out to make the world a better place by giving more people access to God's great universe.

And down in a town south of Buenos Aires, Argentina, Pablo de León was making progress on his Gauchito "Little Cowboy" rocket. He had recently performed the first drop tests of a fully instrumented, reduced-scale model of the capsule out of a C-130 Hercules aircraft at 54,000 feet. Another drop test of the tomato-red Gauchito capsule was done from 90,000 feet, which set an altitude record for XPRIZE tests at the time. With both tests, de León was able to track the capsule and record GPS data and video from the descent, parachute opening, and recovery. At the same time, de León also did stratospheric glider testing and thermal testing of the spacesuit he had designed and constructed to use for eventual Gauchito launches.

De León had an impressive résumé, having managed the project that sent the first Argentine-made payloads to space on space shuttle *Endeavor* in 2001. His house was filled with rocket parts, including a small satellite that came to rest on his kitchen counter. He had made pressure suits for underwater use and spacesuits for NASA. But despite public enthusiasm for his project in Argentina, he was pulling in only around $50,000 a year in sponsorships, nowhere near what was needed. He and five engineers worked full time on the project, and he had more than thirty volunteers, most from local universities. Through scrounging and relying largely on donated time and goods, they built Gauchito's full-scale capsule out of wood and fiberglass, and also built a full simulator. The capsule was a concept demonstrator with running simulation software. The next goal was to build a 50-percent-scale rocket.

De León, who had recently met Peter Diamandis at the ISU summer session he attended on scholarship, felt a sense of camaraderie with the other rocket makers in the XPRIZE competition. Like everyone else, he searched for any news he could find on Burt Rutan. The last thing he'd heard was that Rutan was building a rocket to be drop-launched.

De León was the only competitor from Latin America. All he needed to do next — he told his team with a laugh — was come up with six unmanned flights before he could certify Gauchito for occupancy. But even without the funding he needed, De León was happy. He was certain he was taking part in something important; it felt like access to space was about to crack wide open.

Dumitru Popescu was in Bucharest, Romania, at the same Internet café where he'd first come across a story about the XPRIZE when he heard the news that Steve Bennett had successfully launched Nova 1 in England. Popescu got on the phone and called his wife. "We need to move faster," he told her.

Popescu had by now dropped out of the university where he was studying aerospace and worked around the clock in his father-in-law's backyard in Dragasane, a town about 100 miles west of Bucharest. When Popescu wasn't building the rocket, he was reading about building rockets. His parents told him he was wasting his time, and friends weighed in to say he was nuts. But his father-in-law, Constantin Turta, a skillful mechanical technician who prepared molds at the largest shoe factory in the area, was happy to share all he knew. Popescu's wife, Elena Simona Popescu, a French major, supported him by learning about rocketry, and was soon casting composites herself. The building of their rocket and engine had begun. Like Nova 1, their two-stage vehicle would separate in the sky and return to sea by parachute.

Earlier in 2001, Popescu had landed a meeting with Romania's first and only cosmonaut, Dumitru Prunariu, in the hope that Prunariu would support his team. Prunariu had flown aboard the Soyuz 40 in 1981 and been given a hero's welcome by both Soviet leader Leonid Brezhnev and Romanian president Nicolae Ceauşescu. The cosmonaut had coauthored several books on space and space technology and was now president of the

Romanian Space Agency, ROSA. Popescu arrived at the Ministry of Research building in Bucharest and was welcomed into Prunariu's office.

Popescu found the cosmonaut predictably impressive and outgoing. Prunariu talked about his 1981 spaceflight, telling stories about the difficulty of sleeping in space and the challenge of walking when he first set foot back on Earth. Popescu told the cosmonaut about his rocket and engine designs, propellant ideas, and hopes of winning an international competition started in America called the XPRIZE. He shared photos of his work as well as drawings and simulations. Prunariu listened and smiled, but said the space agency would not be able to help. Before the meeting ended, though, Prunariu told him that the agency was holding a competition to generate new ideas for aerospace projects. He would be happy to include Popescu's ideas as a possible way to get him funding.

When the winners of the state-sponsored competition were announced, Popescu and his team had not been considered. When Popescu asked Prunariu why his team, ARCA — Aeronautics and Cosmonautics Romanian Association — was not included in the competition, the cosmonaut became considerably less friendly. Not long after, when Popescu's team began attracting attention from the local media, Prunariu was quoted as saying that

ARCA was a group of "amateurs" with no idea what they were doing and no chance of winning the XPRIZE. Relations worsened from there. In an e-mail exchange between Popescu and Prunariu, the cosmonaut said that in light of the terrorist attacks of September 11, 2001, Popescu and the work of his team "could be used for terrorist activities." Prunariu said that Popescu did not have the "clearance to manufacture missile guidance systems," and such work could only be done under government control. Popescu was worried by the implication that his work would be of potential interest to terrorists. It felt like the head of his country's space agency was linking him with terrorism. He learned that some in Parliament had begun asking Prunariu how it was that a group of students with no obvious funding source was managing to build a rocket when the government-funded ROSA appeared to be doing nothing.

Popescu and his volunteer team did their best to ignore Prunariu's increasingly public criticism and forge ahead with their work. Popescu wanted to build something that flew *and* looked great. He set out to create rockets the same way Apple created its products — the company had just released its first iPod — with attention to shape, color, and symmetry. Working outside year-round presented challenges, though. The weather was beautiful in the fall and spring, but freezing in the winter and stifling in the summer. One summer day, when Popescu and three others were building their orange launchpad, the temperature was 104 degrees Fahrenheit. They tried to protect their welder from the sun by having two people hold a blanket over him and another fan him with paper.

Popescu kept thinking about the launch of Nova 1 and figured other teams were soon to follow. Despite being labeled amateurs in public and linked to terrorists in private, ARCA picked up momentum, even finding a sponsor who donated hydrogen peroxide and other combustibles. The building of the fuel tank, the feed lines, and the launchpads was under way. A few neighbors who knew of the project occasionally wandered over, donating cash, tools, or old machine parts. A few stayed on to volunteer, and others set up chairs to watch.

After months of work on a rocket motor and the completion of the test stand, operations were moved to an open field at the far end of Popescu's father-in-law's property. Popescu had dug a deep trench one shovel of dirt at a time, until a bunker was made about 100 yards from the test stand. Construction helmets and ski goggles were donned as Popescu, his wife, father-in-law, and two volunteers readied for the test. The propellant was hydrogen peroxide and ethyl alcohol. They were confident. It was their first big test of whether the engine would be a success.

The moment of ignition came — and went. Nothing. They looked at one another. Seconds later came the loudest explosion anyone had heard in peacetime Romania. The Popescu team peered out from the bunker. Everything was lost: test stand, fuel tank, rocket engine. Blown to smithereens. A perfect bomb; a very bad rocket engine.

Within minutes, police had swarmed the property. Windows were apparently shattered for a two-mile radius.

Popescu, still rattled, did his best to appear calm and play the whole thing down, saying they were just university students testing a rocket for a school project. He hoped the police had not read stories about them. He didn't want the explosion to end up in the press and be connected to the XPRIZE. He feared he could be disqualified.

"Come with us," the police said, taking him to the station. That afternoon, waiting to be questioned, Popescu considered what had gone wrong. He was pretty sure they had mixed the ingredients prematurely *and* had a delay in the ignition, allowing too much fuel to accumulate in the chamber. After some time, Popescu was released with the promise that he would be more careful next time.

He arrived back at his father-in-law's house and found the team quiet and sullen. He told them they'd lost expensive parts but learned invaluable lessons. He said he'd had an idea while riding to the station in the back of the police car. They needed to have a build-a-rocket party and invite the town.

23
ANOTHER LINDBERGH
TAKES FLIGHT

Erik Lindbergh had been home on the morning of September 11, 2001, when he heard over the radio that a jetliner had smashed into the South Tower of the World Trade Center in New York and that another plane had hit the North Tower. He heard that a third plane crashed into the Pentagon in Virginia, and a fourth plane, originally headed for San Francisco and identified as United Airlines Flight 93, crashed into a Pennsylvania field. Erik and his wife, Mara, held their son, Gus, who was one, especially close. Erik felt shock, anger, sadness, and a changed reality.

In the days that followed the attacks, the entire airspace of the United States and Canada was closed to civilians. Under a little known and never before used national security plan, only military and medical planes were allowed to fly. Most small private planes wouldn't fly for weeks.

Erik was scheduled to make his transatlantic

flight in six months. In committing to this flight, he had overcome not only debilitating health issues, but also the considerable doubts of his family and friends. But in the wake of the attacks, he had wondered whether his flight was irrelevant. Erik had posed the question to Peter. As it turned out, Peter was being urged by some XPRIZE board members to give up on the space travel competition; because of 9/11, it simply wasn't going to happen. Peter was told, "No one will fund you now."

Peter refused to give in and told Erik he believed that the terrorist attacks made it even more imperative that Erik embark on his flight. The country needed something positive now more than ever. It needed everyday heroes. Others urged Erik to fly as a reminder of one of the most inspiring chapters in American history. Gregg also pushed his friend to go ahead with the flight. He wanted it for Erik, and for the XPRIZE.

Erik didn't know about being anybody's hero, but he did know that he wanted to help the XPRIZE raise much-needed operating income. The XPRIZE had lit him up when everything else in his life was dark. It made him think about how to solve problems in a different way, whether it was something grand like getting out of Earth's gravity well into space, or running when he should probably be walking. Once reduced to a life of sitting, of barely walking, he now wanted to soar.

But first, he had to live through his survival training.

The fuselage of the airplane began to fill with water, first to Erik's feet, then to his thighs, next to his waist. He would soon be submerged, strapped into his seat in the cockpit. As the water rose to his chin, he told himself: deep breaths, prepare to close your eyes. He raced through his mental checklist. The water will be saltwater. Maybe filled with oil, debris, gasoline. Don't unfasten early. Water pressing against the window and door makes it impossible to get out. Wait for the pressure to equalize, inside and out. Final deep breaths. He was under.

Eyes closed, Erik fumbled to free himself from his four-point harness. Feeling for the exit handle, he pushed open the door, kept a hand on it, and established his path out. He pushed himself up to the surface and opened his eyes. His heart was racing. He did it. There was his friend Gregg, also in a soaked flight suit and helmet, having made it out the other side of the cockpit. Their trainer, close by in the deep pool in Groton, Connecticut, gave them a thumbs-up. It was time to do it again.

Erik's transatlantic mission was now three months away, in May 2002. Within minutes, Erik and Gregg were back in the simulator, which resembled the body of a Huey helicopter. It was raised eight feet above the pool. Their trainer gave a hand signal from behind his back to the simulator operator to dunk them. Erik's mind hurried to review what they'd gone over in their morning classes: Lean forward before impact to lock in the shoulder harness. Move thumbs to the front of the yoke. The impact of a crash landing could break your thumbs. Know the primary and secondary exits. Know the location of the emergency equipment.

The fuselage hit the water; they were going under. Faster this time. And they were being inverted, turned upside down. Erik told himself to breathe sooner this time. The water scrambled him, swirled bubbles all around. He was strapped into his seat, upside down. He closed his eyes. Same steps as right side up. Find egress, unfasten harness, feel for the path out.

He did this eleven more times that afternoon, in every crash landing simulation imaginable: fuselage right side up, upside down, jutted sideways, spinning, lights on in the facility, all lights off, dark as night. Hours later, waterlogged yet adrenalized, Erik and Gregg climbed out of the pool. Erik did additional training that day: using underwater emergency breathing devices after his sinuses had already filled with water, practicing how to brace for impact, and escaping from a cockpit filled with smoke. He even did a simulated, plucked-from-the-water helicopter rescue.

Survival Systems, the company providing their training, was just across a parking lot from the Long Island Sound. The company had been one of the first to sign on as sponsors of Erik's flight and was providing training at no cost. For Erik and Gregg, their second day of lessons would be even tougher: they were going to be tossed into the frigid waters of the Atlantic Ocean.

The next day started early. Gregg and Erik boarded a small boat with their trainers and headed out onto Long Island Sound. The wind whipped at around thirty knots, turning the gray sea into menacing swells. The air temperature hovered at around zero degrees Celsius (32°F), and the water temperature was around thirty-five degrees. Erik and Gregg stepped into their orange immersion suits, which left only their faces exposed. The suits were recommended for pilots flying over water below fifty-five degrees, and provided a thermal barrier and up to fifty pounds of buoyancy.

Erik and Gregg had practiced climbing into life rafts in the pool, but not in roiling water like this. The two took Dramamine in hopes of staving off seasickness.

Erik pulled the operating cord — the painter's line — to activate the CO_2 and inflate the raft. The raft was in the water, and Erik and Gregg took the plunge. In the water, Erik was breathing fast in shallow interrupted breaths as three-foot waves slapped his face. Without an immersion suit, he would be incapacitated in no more than twenty minutes, as blood moved away from his extremities toward his core. Fatal hypothermia would set in quickly. Heavier people would survive longer, given that they had more of an insulating layer. Erik was tall and lean like his grandfather, who was six feet two and weighed 170 pounds when he made his 1927 flight.

The raft separated from the Survival Systems boat, which needed to head toward shore to get out of the waves splashing over the sides and avoid hitting the raft. Erik and Gregg were on their own. They had already learned that climbing into a raft wasn't as easy as it looked, even in a pool. And now they had to do it at sea. Erik imagined how hard this would be if he were injured. Using a boarding ladder, they got themselves up and into the raft. Erik had turned green. Seasickness was stronger than Dramamine. From inside the raft, only waves and ocean were visible. They knew the critical steps they would need to take from here — get the canopy up if it didn't pop up on its own, rid the raft of any water, ensure all sharp objects were secured, and find first aid, flares, flags, and signal lights. Erik was having a hard time just sitting up.

When the Survival Systems crew returned, Erik and Gregg made their way slowly, unsteadily, from raft to boat. Still in their immersion suits, they slumped down on the deck, backs against the side of the boat. They had been in the raft for a little over an hour, and neither one felt like moving or uttering a word.

Finally, after a year of planning, training, and drama, the morning of the flight arrived — May 1, 2002. Erik walked toward his Lancair 300, ready to begin the trip to Paris. Like his grandfather, Erik had actually begun his journey at the San Diego International Airport — now known as Lindbergh Field. Erik flew from San Diego to St. Louis and days later flew to New York, where the most famous and difficult part of the flight was set to begin.

Charles Lindbergh's plane, the *Spirit of St. Louis,* was built for $10,580 by the scrappy Ryan Airlines company in San Diego. Its engine was a 220-horsepower (at sea level) Wright Whirlwind J-5C. It weighed 5,250 pounds fully loaded, including 450 gallons of fuel. It had a maximum airspeed at the start of the flight of 120 miles per hour, and 124 at the end, when the plane was lighter. Its range was put at 4,110 miles with zero wind and ideal economical airspeeds of 97 miles per hour at the start. Made of wood, metal, and treated fabric, it was painted silver and given the registration number N-X-211 (X was for "experimental"), which — along with *Spirit of St. Louis* — was painted in black. Charles was twenty-five when he set out on his journey. His pilot's chair was wicker, intentionally uncomfortable to keep him awake. He brought water and five ham sandwiches with him. For navigation, he had a compass, the stars, a wristwatch, and paper maps — with edges trimmed off to save on weight.

Erik's plane was a modified Lancair Columbia 300, sleek, single engine, and built for just under $300,000 by the Lancair Company in Redmond, Oregon. Christened the *New Spirit of St. Louis,* the plane had a 310-horsepower Continental engine driving a three-bladed prop. Erik's expected cruising speed was more than 180 miles per hour, and he would fly at an altitude of between 7,000 and 17,000 feet, depending on the weather. The airframe was all composite, painted white, and had the registration number N142LC. It weighed 4,260 pounds loaded. Erik was thirty-seven years old and would spend the flight in a leather seat, one of four in the plane. Erik had five ham sandwiches, his smeared with mustard. It was Erik's first trip to Europe, as it had been for his grand-father.

At this point, Erik had already flown three hundred hours in the Lancair 300 and knew its quirks and handling qualities. It was a fast, fixed-gear aircraft with controls that were nimble at lower speeds and stiffer at higher speeds. He had flown cross-country, dodging storms, icing, and turbulence. A high-tech, state-of-the-art Mission Control was set up in the St. Louis Science Center with Gregg at the helm. He would be there from takeoff to landing. Erik's plane was equipped with a global positioning system — which told him where he was, his speed, and the expected duration of his flight — and an Iridium phone. The Lancair's position would be updated every five minutes.

Erik would be taking off from Republic Field in Farmingdale, New York. Roosevelt Field, where his grandfather flew from — and where Peter once launched rockets — was now a shopping center.

On the tarmac of Republic Field, Erik stopped to hug Peter, who was going to hop on a commercial plane with Erik's luggage and beat him to Paris. Peter could not have imagined when he first read *The Spirit of St. Louis* that Erik Lindbergh would become so important to realizing his dreams. Erik was rescuing the XPRIZE during otherwise bleak times. Peter was also struck by the picture of

Erik now versus when they'd first met in the restaurant in Kirkland. Erik looked healthy and strong — something miraculous to behold — and ready to repeat his grandfather's historic and physically demanding feat. Peter hugged Erik one more time and told him, "See you in Paris."

With his orange immersion suit unzipped at the waist, Erik climbed into the Lancair cockpit. Unlike his grandfather, who had barely slept the night before his flight — awakened at 2:15 A.M. by the very man he had stationed at his door so as not to be bothered — Erik slept perfectly, a solid seven hours. And unlike his grandfather, who took off on a cold and misty morning — the tires of the *Spirit of St. Louis* were rubbed with grease to keep the mud of the runway from sticking — Erik would begin his flight on a picture-perfect day.

In a matter of minutes, Erik taxied off. Soon, the *New Spirit of St. Louis* was in the air. Just as his grandfather had done, Erik tilted the wings to the left and the right to wave good-bye, delighting the hundreds of spectators below.

Erik's communication with Mission Control began immediately. Gregg was running the show, pacing, talking, and checking data. Meteorologists studied weather patterns. A team from Lancair monitored the plane. Byron Lichtenberg, Marc Arnold, and Joe

Dobronski were the three "Capcoms," capsule communicators, authorized to talk with Erik during the flight. Gregg had search and rescue groups at the ready. Erik would do a systems check every thirty minutes, going over oil pressure, fuel flows, cylinder head temperatures, and more.

About an hour into the flight, Erik was finally able to settle in. His grandfather's words, recounted in his book, were with him: "My cockpit is small, and its walls are thin; but inside this cocoon I feel secure, despite the speculations in my mind. . . . Here, I am conscious of all elements of weather, immersed in them, dependent on them. Here, the earth spreads out beyond my window, its expanse and beauty offered at the cost of a glance. Here are no unnecessary extras, only the barest essentials of life and flight. A cabin that flies through the air, that's what I live in. Through months of planning, I've equipped it with utmost care. Now, I can relax in its solitary vantage point, and let the sun shine, and the west wind blow, and the blizzard come with the night."

In between the talking and the checklists, the satellite communications and Iridium phone, Erik came to relish something unexpected — solitude. It wasn't quiet, as the sound of the engine was constant. But just being in the air on his own was a relief. Like the exhausted but exultant feeling at a marathon's end.

Erik was flying roughly the same course that his grandfather flew. To figure out the shortest path from New York to Paris, Charles had placed a string on a globe. He found that in the higher latitudes, the shortest route from New York to Liverpool was not an east-to-west parallel, but — because of the Earth's curvature — an arc across New England and Canada, west of Nova Scotia, and through Newfoundland.*

Erik was happy to leave the coast of North America behind and begin his journey across the ocean. In the hours that followed, he saw storm clouds and clear skies. He saw Mother Nature's finest monochrome paintings in changing palettes of blue and gray. When night came, there was tedium, but also moments of unexpected humor. He got himself on the same air-to-air frequency of commercial pilots who were flying 20,000 feet or so above him and listened to their chatter. Soon they were asking Erik about his plane and flight. They were enthralled to hear he was the grandson of Charles Lindbergh. At one point, Erik asked, "Hey, can you check

* The great circle path between two points on a globe is determined by stretching a rubber band between the two points. The rubber band will naturally find the configuration with the least tension, and this will be the shortest path.

to see if you have a guy named Peter Diamandis on board?" He was flying from New York, JFK, to Charles de Gaulle in Paris. Erik heard the Delta pilots say they would check. Then Air France chimed in to say they would check. Finally, someone from American Airlines came back and said, "We've got him. What do you want me to do?" Erik shot back, "Wake him up!" A few minutes later, the pilot said, "We went to wake him up but it was someone else." Erik laughed. Peter had apparently been bumped to business class. Not long after, they found him, woke him up, and told him they'd been sharing the sky with his friend Erik Lindbergh, who would see him in Paris.

As Erik flew over the open ocean at night, spotting icebergs below, he was again reminded of his grandfather's observations of "white pyramids below — an iceberg, lustrous white against the water." Grandfather wrote: "I've never seen anything so white before. Like an apparition, it draws my eyes from the instruments and makes me conscious of a strange new sea." Erik saw clouds as textured and dramatic as the Grand Canyon, and — like his grandfather — found in the Moon a "forgotten ally."

Erik knew that sleep haunted his grandfather, whose eyes were dry from the air. Charles didn't have communication satellites. He didn't have anyone to talk to. He had himself, and the reminder of his good partners in St. Louis to keep him awake. Grandfather wrote, "How could I ever face my partners and say that I failed to reach Paris because I was sleepy?" He continued, "[I've] lost command of my eyelids. When they start to close, I can't restrain them. They shut, and I shake myself, and lift them with my fingers." His grandfather had resorted to diving down and pulling the plane up sharply to try to jolt himself awake. He got to the point where he wanted sleep more than anything in the world. During the seemingly endless stretch between dusk and sunrise, his grandfather expressed relief that they didn't make his plane more stable.* Erik grew weary, too — the early morning, predawn hours were the toughest — but he had constant chatter, systems checks, and questions from his friends at Mission Control.

The communications went down just once during Erik's flight. Erik hit a stormy patch, and contact was lost. While Mission Control feared something terrible had happened, Erik found himself relishing the seclusion. In those fleeting moments of quiet, he felt cradled in

---

* Charles Lindbergh had designed the plane without dihedral, which is less stable. He did this because if he started to fall asleep, the plane would bank and the noise created from this would wake him up. Erik joked that this was a primitive form of autopilot.

the same sky as his grandfather. He marveled at the quality of the air — invisible but with weight and substance during flight — and the power of wings. He imagined going far higher and getting to see the splendor of Earth from space. He was in a modern plane, safe, dry, and warm and with technology that surely would not be mute for long. He realized that his grandfather, barely insulated from the elements, experienced a poetry that he could only glimpse.

"The *Spirit of St. Louis* is a wonderful plane," his grandfather wrote. "It's like a living creature, gliding along smoothly, happily. . . . *We* have made this flight across the ocean, not I or it."

When Erik saw the coast of France, the joy was a shared joy. His grandfather had been amazed to find he was on course. Erik was on course. "Ireland, England, France, Paris!" Grandfather wrote. "The night at Paris! This night at Paris! Yesterday I walked on Roosevelt Field, today I'll walk on Le Bourget. What limitless possibilities aviation holds when planes can fly nonstop between New York and Paris!"

Erik was now in his sixteenth straight hour of flight, and he was over the coast of France. Grandfather said it came to him "like an outstretched hand to meet me." Erik had maybe an hour to go. He was sleep-deprived and rummy. AIIRRRIK. That's what his childhood friends called him because he was always flying — skiing, jumping, climbing high. That was before, when all that mattered to him was physical. When he won competitions and tournaments, when he was the only kid in his high school who could climb the rope to the gym ceiling, using only his hands and not his legs. Then came Mount Rainier. There was life before the summit and after the summit. His body became foreign. All he knew went away, like a beloved house shredded by a tornado. Hope was lost in that squalid hotel room in Minnesota. Knees replaced, titanium in his foot. An old man afraid of his shadow. His blue eyes welled with tears. Life — this plane, this day, this body, this moment — was a gift. He was AI-IRRRIK again. But so much better.

Erik would land at Le Bourget in the morning. His grandfather came in at night. Charles had never landed the *Spirit of St. Louis* at night. The final lines of Grandfather's book were with Erik now. Brilliant. Emotional. Pure. The sod came up to meet him. Grandfather faced nothing but night. No lights on the plane, or the field. He questioned whether he should climb back up for another try at landing, then — the wheels touched gently, the nicest greeting he'd ever had. He kept contact with the ground. There was still only blackness. The plane swung around and soon stopped rolling, resting on "the solidness of earth, in the center of Le Bourget." As Grandfather started to taxi back toward where there were now floodlights, he suddenly noticed it: "The entire field ahead is covered with running figures!" More than 100,000 people were there to greet him.

Erik prepared for the final descent, going through his own checklist. In the clouds, flying on instruments, he was vectored around Paris's Charles de Gaulle airport.

I have to grease this landing, Erik told himself. *I can't come down and bounce it.* He made some small turns and limbered himself up. He was stiff, and the plane felt stiff. He came out of the clouds and there was Le Bourget. He was ready. *Grease this.* Seconds later, he was down. *Smooth as butter!*

"Are you down?" Gregg asked anxiously from St. Louis.

"I AM DOWN!" Erik replied to whoops and hollers in Mission Control. Grandfather had made the flight in thirty-three hours, thirty minutes. Erik's flight took seventeen hours and seven minutes.

Erik climbed out of the plane, taking a moment to look at the sky. The golden light on the horizon had been even better than he'd imagined. To applause and cheers, Erik walked a few feet on the tarmac — amazed he wasn't terribly stiff — got down on his knees, and kissed the ground. Nearby were Peter and Erik's mother, Barbara, both reveling in this unlikely moment of history. Soon he would get a call from President George W. Bush, thanking him for "inspiring the country" after the attacks of September 11. Erik had raised more than $1 million — keeping the XPRIZE alive at a critical time, and supporting the Arthritis Foundation and the Lindbergh Foundation. Stories about his flight had reached half a billion people. The History Channel filmed the flight and planned to air the documentary later in May. Erik took it all in. The flying had felt easy compared with the obstacles he'd faced on land. Having rheumatoid arthritis had leveled him, and being a Lindbergh had limited him. He was leaving all of that behind.

The XPRIZE had thrown Erik a lifeline when he needed it most. Now Erik had returned the favor.

24
A Hole in One

Since Erik's dramatic transatlantic flight, the XPRIZE had gotten a new lease on life, receiving more public attention than ever. The renewed spotlight brought in significant cash infusions, keeping the operation afloat and motivating the teams to race ahead building rockets and engines. But the XPRIZE still needed a title sponsor to seal the deal, something that Peter had chased for six long years. Peter was still $5 million short of what he needed, and the First USA funds would disappear after December 17, 2003 — now less than a year and a half away.

Bob Weiss was sitting with Peter and Gregg in his office at Paramount Pictures in Los Angeles when he presented an "out-there" concept to get the XPRIZE fully funded. The idea, which indeed sounded crazy — at least at first — was to get a group of professional gamblers to wage a $10 million bet *against* anyone winning the XPRIZE.

Peter and Gregg laughed. But Weiss was

461

serious. He told them how an insurance company had agreed to pay out $1 million if a randomly chosen fan at a professional basketball game could make a three-quarters-court shot on his first try. The insurance company was of course betting that the fan would miss the extremely difficult shot. In the case of the XPRIZE, the insurance company would have to analyze the probability that one of the contenders — Burt Rutan, Dumitru Popescu, Jim Akkerman, Brian Feeney, or someone else barely on the radar — could make a lob shot to space, not once but twice within two weeks.

Peter welcomed any and all ideas. He'd recently pitched the XPRIZE concept to film-maker George Lucas, and to the heads of Intel, Sony, Discovery, Fox, Rolex, Emerson, and Ford. Plans A, B, and C had failed, as had D, E, and F. Now he was moving on to G, H, I, and J.

Weiss said that when he was going to school in Illinois, the archdiocese of Chicago had offered a $1 million prize to someone who could catch a fish tagged with a religious medallion in Lake Michigan. Weiss remembered asking himself how the Catholic Church could afford to host a $1 million charity fishing contest. Was the archdiocese going to write to the Holy Father and request the money? Was the church going to cut the check? What he learned, he told Peter and

Gregg, was that the archdiocese had secured something called hole-in-one insurance. Local church officials paid a premium to purchase a policy that the insurers believed would never be paid out. In this case, the insurance company bet right. No one caught the fish. But in the case of the random fan winning $1 million by making a shot from the foul line on the other end of the court, American Hole 'n One insurance bet wrong. The fan nailed the long shot on one try, winning a promotional gimmick in front of more than seventeen thousand cheering fans at Chicago Stadium in April 1993.[*]

"Here's the deal," Weiss said. "We're going to get someone to bet against us and then we're going to pull the rug out from under them because we are going to pull it off. Then we'll have our prize money."

Peter considered Weiss's proposal; he'd had people betting against him from the start. He found something poetic in the idea that he might actually raise money from those who were sure he would fail. Peter reached out to two friends, Bruce Kraselsky and Jean-Michel Eid, of Aon, a risk management company, to

[*] The insurance company ended up refusing to pay the fan, saying he lied about not having any pro or college basketball experience. His $1 million still got paid, but by the Bulls, Coca-Cola, and the Lettuce Entertain You restaurant.

see if they could take brokerage experience for insuring satellite launches and spin it into hole-in-one space insurance.

The man tasked by Aon to take on the important first step in weighing the probability of anyone winning the XPRIZE was aerospace engineer Jim French, who had worked for NASA for years and was now an independent consultant viewed as both extremely competent and unbiased. He had helped test and develop rocket engines for the Apollo and Saturn launch vehicles, and worked at the Jet Propulsion Laboratory on the Mariner, Viking, and *Voyager* missions. Peter asked him whether he would be interested in interviewing as many of the teams as possible, assessing credibility, and writing a report that could be given to Aon, which was trying to broker the hole-in-one deal for the XPRIZE with XL Specialty Insurance Company.

French was open about his longtime interest in seeing commercial space become a reality, an affliction he attributed to reading way too much Heinlein as a kid. He felt that humanity's long-term survival depended on an expansion into space, though he didn't think private industry was going to get there anytime soon. He was happy to do the analysis for the XPRIZE and began contacting the contenders, meeting with some in person and interviewing others in far-flung places by phone. He didn't have time to interview everyone, but he was willing to look at any team whose idea "didn't violate the laws of physics." He asked detailed questions about hardware, funding, and credentials of team members.

French started with Burt Rutan. The two had worked together years before on the DC-X Delta Clipper, where French was in the program office that funded it. They had talked at the time about Burt's interest in space and the different designs he had in mind for a spaceship. French also remembered in the eighties when Burt and his brother Dick first talked about a plane that could fly around the world nonstop without refueling. French felt at the time that it couldn't be done. He'd come to see that Burt was exceptionally good at setting his sights on a specific goal and building a plane to meet that goal.

French visited Burt at Scaled Composites in Mojave, listened to his plan for a spaceship, and asked: "Can you do this?" Burt knew French as an experienced space guy. He pondered the question. It wouldn't be honest to say his chance was 1 percent, and it wouldn't be honest to say with certainty he could do it. He told him the truth: he was taking big risks, including "building a Mach 3.5 plane with no wind tunnel testing."

French asked whether he could do it by December 17, 2003, the target set by the insurance company and the date established by First USA. Burt said he didn't think so. Then French asked about his funding. Burt again replied honestly. "We are adequately funded," he said. No one knew just how adequately funded he was, or who was backing him.

French went through the list of contenders. A few teams were composed of a handful of smart guys with bright ideas and no money. Several were not credible. But others had a chance of doing something *if* funding came in. He really liked what Pablo de León was doing in Argentina and felt if funding came in he had a serious shot. He talked to Dumitru Popescu and thought the Romanian team could surprise everyone, but needed money like a rocket needs fuel. He thought the V-2 rocket and engine of Canadian Arrow was a reasonable approach — though expensive — and he was impressed that the self-taught Steve Bennett had successfully flown a serious rocket from the United Kingdom. He looked at Kelly Space & Technology in San Bernardino, California — a company formerly focused on satellite launches that was now building a rocket-powered delta-wing aircraft intended for suborbital flights. The technical smarts were there, but the funding was not.

In the end, French wrote a report saying he thought Burt had the best chance of winning. But French believed that Burt wouldn't be able to accomplish the feat by the Wright brothers' anniversary and possibly even by the end of 2004 — if at all. For as long as French could remember, private space travel was always just a few years away. He was skeptical that someone could pull off what was needed to win the XPRIZE. But at the same time, he saw how teams were intoxicated by it. Inventiveness had been sparked. Pablo de León told him he'd grabbed the leg off a chair to use as a last-minute lever in the testing of a small rocket engine. Armadillo Aerospace in Texas used a trunk latch mechanism for a variety of things, including parachute release. Brian Feeney of the da Vinci Project in Canada worked out of the back of a scuba shop and bought parts at Home Depot. Jim Akkerman had recruited retirees to work with him out in a field in Texas on a rocket that he dreamed of water launching. Scaled Composites was trying out used paintball gun tanks to hold air for the spaceship's reentry control thrusters. Many of the teams regularly went shopping for odd parts in a McMaster-Carr catalog.

Once French had completed his report, the insurance company had the job of taking French's findings and doing its own analysis of probabilities. The challenge of the XPRIZE was that it was a "unique event" — something where no prior data existed. A nonunique event, by comparison, like the roll of a die, could be repeated ad nauseam, results tabulated and outcomes predicted with high precision based on the main assumption that things would continue to work the same way in the future as in the past. Making a wager on a unique event was more textured. How would you determine the probability of someone flying to space without the government's help when it hadn't been done before? Probability, in this case, had to rely on a *belief* about the outcome. It had to rely on something called Bayesian inference, the idea of taking any a priori belief and then systematically accumulating evidence that conditioned the belief. Any and all evidence under Bayes's law would be considered.

A unique event usually fell into a set of categories that the insurance company would assess, collect evidence on, and then come to a conclusion largely based on the disparate evidence. The conditions for the XPRIZE would be historical data regarding Rutan's success rate, tech prizes in general, failure rates of all launch vehicles, failure rates of known private launch vehicles, related historical evidence, and the informed opinions of people like Jim French.

The actuaries at XL Specialty Insurance began calculating the odds. Their hard work could yield surprisingly good results, but in the end, it still came down to systematic guesswork. It came down to beliefs.

Peter, Gregg, and Bob Weiss had the uncomfortable feeling of talking out of both sides of their mouth. When they talked to potential sponsors, the XPRIZE was possible and near term. When they were dealing with the insurance company, the prize was daunting and somewhere in the unknowable future. In the end, both sentiments rang true.

On August 18, 2002, Peter received a call from Bruce Kraselsky, who delivered the news: he had his deal with a group of doubters. XL Specialty Insurance wanted to move ahead with a policy for the XPRIZE, inferring that it was the easiest money they would ever make. The policy had two target dates. First, XL agreed to insure a $5 million payout if a team could win the contest on or before the one hundredth anniversary of the Wright brothers' famous flights at Kitty Hawk in their first powered aircraft. First USA would kick in the other $5 million. The second part of the XL contract dealt with what would happen if no one won by the 2003 date. Peter got XL to extend the contract by a year and double it to a $10 million payout.

But the insurance company wasn't the only one making a multimillion-dollar wager. In exchange for the promised prize money, Peter would have to come up with $50,000-a-month premium payments for more than sixteen months, as well as make a one-time balloon payment of $1.3 million. The XPRIZE was operating with a handful of people — Peter, Gregg, Bob, and Diane Murphy — who all relied on outside jobs or other sources of income. If at any point the XPRIZE missed a payment, XL would keep all the payments made to date and the hole-in-one policy would be null and void. Peter was at a loss for how he would cover the monthly premiums or the $1.3 million balloon payment, until, that is, he got the phone call that he'd been dreaming of for six years.

The good news came from Anousheh Ansari; her husband, Hamid Ansari; and her brother-in-law, Amir Ansari, who had recently sold their telecommunications software company, Telecom Technologies, to Sonus Networks in a deal worth $1.2 billion.* Peter wouldn't be getting the title sponsor he had sought, but the family pledged $1.75 million up front — an amount that would cover the insurance balloon payment and some of the related

---

* The value of the sale of the Ansaris' company was between $400 million and $1.2 billion based on the stock price and whether certain targets were met. All targets were met, so the payout was $1.2 billion.

expenses. The Ansaris also said they would help Peter fund-raise. If they raised an additional $4.5 million or greater, they would get their $1.75 million back.

Months earlier, in the spring of 2002, Peter and Byron Lichtenberg had flown to Dallas to meet the Ansaris for the first time. Peter had come across the Ansari name as he flipped through *Fortune* magazine's list of the forty wealthiest self-made people under forty in the United States. Anousheh, who was thirty-five years old, was number thirty-three on the list. But it wasn't her money that caught his eye. It was a single word she used in the interview: *suborbital.* He read the paragraph three times:

> Anousheh Ansari wants to see stars. But not the Hollywood kind. Sitting in the lobby of Manhattan's Peninsula Hotel, the 35-year-old Sonus Networks VP — one of two women on this year's rich list — is talking about her desire to board a civilian-carrying, suborbital shuttle. "It would be nice," she said, "to get outside the planet and see the universe for what it really is."

Both Anousheh and her brother-in-law, Amir, had listened intently to Peter's pitch during the meeting in their Dallas office. Amir felt guilty for having given up on his space dream so easily compared with Peter.

He and Anousheh both grew up watching *Star Trek* in Iran and dreaming of interplanetary travel. But no one from Iran had ever flown in space. NASA was not taking paying customers up there. There had been only two tourists — Dennis Tito and South African entrepreneur Mark Shuttleworth — and they'd forked over tens of millions of dollars for rides into orbit aboard Russian launchers.

Anousheh listened to Peter in that first meeting and tried not to smile. She had never met anyone with Peter's passion and commitment. *With this guy, if you close one door, he's going to open another,* she thought. Amir thought a space prize was an odd approach, but just cool enough that it may work. Peter also talked about his efforts with Byron to get the Federal Aviation Administration to issue permits so they could offer civilians zero-gravity flights in their modified Boeing 727, something they'd been pursuing for eight years. Peter said their ZERO-G Corporation would offer the world's first parabolic flights to the public and could be used to train NASA astronauts, scientists, and engineers. After a labyrinthine legal battle, they believed they were close to winning the necessary permits.

Anousheh's husband, Hamid, watched Peter make his pitch at what seemed like 100 miles per hour. "If someone wins the XPRIZE, we can all go to space," Peter said.

Hamid didn't have the "space DNA" of his brother and wife. Their interest in space was not a wish or a game; it was who they were, like the color of their eyes. Hamid was drawn to the idea of the international competition, and the daredevilry required to win it. He wasn't at all afraid of the obvious risk of something going wrong along the way. Risk had been good to the Ansaris. His family had fled Tehran at the start of the revolution under Ayatollah Khomeini, arriving in America with little money and speaking no English. Anousheh and her family had left Mashad a few years later, when conditions in Iran had worsened. Hamid and Anousheh had met in the United States in the mid-eighties, when Anousheh, a computer and electrical engineering major at George Mason University, applied for a summer internship at MCI, where Hamid worked. Anousheh, Hamid, and Amir all worked together at MCI and eventually took $50,000 in savings from their jobs to start Telecom Technologies.

As Peter showed pictures of XPRIZE events and talked about the contenders and what was being built, Anousheh, Hamid, and Amir exchanged looks. Anousheh did her best to keep a poker face while listening to Peter. She had dreamed of space for as long as she could remember. Her favorite book as a child was *The Little Prince,* which she'd read in Farsi. As a child, she loved sleeping outside on her grandmother's balcony. She would stare up at the stars and fall asleep to the same fervent prayer: that aliens would come and take her away. She was incapable of being outside without looking up to see the stars. Anousheh asked Peter a few questions, including how these private teams could afford to build a rocket. Then she asked why commercial space hadn't happened yet. "Who is the enemy?" she wanted to know. "NASA?"

Peter had been living with this question for decades. "The opponents are multiple," he said. "The opponent is the government by being the regulatory body that makes it difficult. The opponent is NASA for establishing the mind-set in the sixties, seventies, and eighties that only governments do this. The opponent is our risk-averse society that is resistant to any of this. The opponent is the laws of physics. The opponent is the capital markets that don't value these risks and want the cheap and fast return of an Internet play. Those are the opponents."

When the meeting concluded, the Ansaris said they needed some time to think about it. Peter then heard the familiar refrain: *We'll get back to you.*

As the group headed to the door, Peter walked with Anousheh. He turned to look her in the eyes and said, "I promise you I will do everything in my power to get you to space."

She believed him. And now, Peter had a fully funded hole-in-one policy, and a $10 million XPRIZE, *there to be won.*

At home in his Santa Monica apartment, Peter sifted through paperwork and found the John Galt charter written eight years earlier in Montrose, Colorado, when the XPRIZE came to life. He reread his impassioned words and realized how naïve he was when it came to funding. But he still believed every word in the charter. He cut out a paragraph and posted it above his desk:

There is a strong technology available which helps humans in achieving difficult, sometimes seemingly impossible feats, this technology is a forcing function which helps to focus the whole of human ingenuity at the same well articulated goal. . . . This concept, the forcing function, this technology, is the competitive "Prize." Not prizes for spelling bees or prizes for a lifetime achievement, but prizes which lay out impossible goals and tempt man to take great strides forward. Prizes such as those which were set out to the aeronautical world for speed, distance, endurance. Prizes which brought forward adventurers, dreamers, and doers. Prizes such as the $25,000

Orteig Prize. Where no government filled the need and no immediate profit could fill the bill, the Orteig Prize stimulated multiple different attempts. Where $25,000 was offered, nearly $400,000 was spent to win the prize — because it was there to be won.

Six years after the announcement of the prize under the arch in St. Louis, Peter had his promise of $10 million. He wondered whether this was how Charles Lindbergh felt after securing his financial backing in St. Louis. Lindbergh had the money, but he still needed to build the right plane, get to the starting line, and make it to the finish alive. Peter still had to come up with $50,000 a month in premium payments, something he'd taken to calling his "fifty-thousand-dollar Fridays." He and others would start dialing for dollars on Monday, needing the fifty grand by week's end. Peter had moved one big step closer, but he still had his ocean to cross. And now the clock was ticking: If no one succeeded by 12:01 A.M. on January 1, 2005, the $10 million would vanish.

■ ■ ■ ■

PART THREE:
A RACE TO
REMEMBER

■ ■ ■ ■

25
A Fire to Be Ignited

On November 21, 2002, after delays, false starts, and missed deadlines, Burt Rutan's Scaled Composites was ready to do a first hot fire test of its hybrid rocket motor. At this point, the still-secret *SpaceShipOne* — Burt's hope of getting beyond the atmosphere — remained a work in progress, and time had become an issue. But a successful motor test would be a turning point in what Burt considered the most important project in his company's history.

Getting to this day had been difficult. Scaled Composites had wanted to build everything related to the outside of the motor, including the propellant tank, case, and nozzle. But Scaled was an airplane company, with no experience making rocket engines. Fabrication problems quickly surfaced with the case, throat, and nozzle. There was uncertainty that Scaled's nitrous tank design could handle the required pressures. Alabaman Tim Pickens, hired early on by Burt for his work in propulsion, design, and fabrication — and because his side projects included rocket-powered bicycles, rocket-powered backpacks, and rocket-powered pickup trucks — agreed with Scaled's call to outsource the nitrous oxide tank, which would transport the nitrous. Pickens found a guy in Texas who owned a scrap yard and said he could help build a nitrous trailer. The Texan already had a tank with a generator for refrigeration that could hold ten thousand pounds of nitrous. A deal was made, and not long after, the Texan pulled up to Scaled with nitrous trailer in tow. An old beat-up truck was thrown into the deal to haul the tank and generator around.

Burt was confident he could build the solid motor case, but didn't feel he had the expertise to build the parts that see the highest temperatures — the ablative throat and nozzle. Scaled engaged a specialty company, AAE, to supply these components, knowing they had supplied ablative nozzles for all the big companies that made rocket motors. But Scaled also needed to find some source for many other components it did not have expertise building: injectors, igniters, valves, controllers — the critical metal components on both sides of the big tank.

In order to maintain secrecy, Scaled sent out RFPs (requests for proposals) to all the big rocket companies, using a cover story about building a hybrid rocket motor for an unmanned sounding rocket whose mission was to measure the top of the atmosphere for NASA's earth-sciences programs. But they got only two types of responses: no bid at all — apparently revealing an attitude that the project was hopeless — or bids to build custom-designed components at a cost that exceeded the entire *SpaceShipOne* budget. Quickly switching to another plan, Scaled set up visits to the community of small operators, including Gary Hudson, eAc (Environmental Aeroscience Corporation), and SpaceDev. Two of them immediately self-unselected by staging failed tests during their visits.

Burt decided to fund the two most impressive small shops with the promise that the best components identified during the tests would be used on a historic new space program. Scaled set up a fixed-price competition between SpaceDev, based on the West Coast, and eAc from Florida to see whose components would fly on a manned ship out of the atmosphere.

The hybrid motor had been sketched on a napkin in Huntsville, Alabama, by Burt and Pickens. Instead of using the common rocket fuel of liquid oxygen and liquid hydrogen, their motor would use laughing gas and rubber (nitrous oxide and hydroxyl-terminated polybutadiene, or HTPB). The rubbery part was pliable and could be touched without gloves. Some Scaled employees had coffee coasters made from the stuff.

The promise of the first hot fire test energized the crew. A quote by Plutarch was scribbled on a whiteboard: "The mind is not a vessel to be filled but a fire to be ignited." Ignition was the word of the day. This motor test would be by SpaceDev, and eAc would get its chance six weeks later in early January. Burt went over safety procedures and talked about how far the company had come in its design of all the components. He talked about the safety of hybrids and said there wasn't much that could go wrong with the day's main event.

On a bright and cool Mojave day, with light winds out of the east, the SpaceDev motor, about the size of a van, was mounted on a stand in the desert. The transfer of the nitrous began. A small control room, about the size of a horse trailer and called the SCUM truck — for Scaled Composites Utility Mobile — was situated two hundred feet away, protected by steel shipping containers. Among those inside the truck was Scaled pilot and engineer Brian Binnie, who watched as both a hopeful future pilot of the spaceship and as the person managing propulsion development.

Standing about three hundred feet from the test site were Burt and Tim Pickens. Burt could feel the excitement in the air. And Pickens was more than ready. He had, after all, grown up in Huntsville, aka "Rocket City," where the booms of Saturn V motor tests were a part of life, like the honking of taxis in New York.

Joining Burt and Pickens at their vantage point were Dave Moore, who was running the spaceship project for Paul Allen, and Jeff Johnson, whom Moore had brought in to try to get Scaled on a better production schedule. Paul Allen had not been pleased by the delays, saying in one meeting: "I know you had a slow start, but you mean to tell me that after three months of work you're three months behind?" At the next meeting, Allen said, "You mean you've slipped another three months on top of the other three months you told me about last time?"

Just before test time, Moore said to Pickens half jokingly that he was going to stick with him just in case something went wrong. But Pickens was thinking about nitrous — nitrogen and oxygen combined — as an energetic substance on its own, even without the rubber. Nitrous usually had to be hauled around at close to zero degrees, but when team members filled the rocket tank, they'd need it at around sixty-three degrees. This nitrous would perform two thirds as well on its own as opposed to when it was combined with rubber fuel. As soon as the command was sent from the control room, a valve in the tank of nitrous would open, and nitrous would flow in a controlled way. That was the idea at least.

The countdown began. When it reached "zero," there was white smoke, a small flame, and then — a violent explosion. Binnie jumped inside the SCUM truck, thinking, *This is what we're going to fly on top of?* The motor was supposed to fire for fifteen seconds and then shut off. Fifteen seconds came and went. Hands were raised for high-fives. The hot fire was successful! The program had reached a milestone. A few seconds later, though, congratulations turned to watchful silence. All eyes were focused on a small potential problem: a flame continued to flicker out the nozzle, like a snake's quick tongue. Jeff Johnson was the first to say, "It shouldn't be doing that."

Dave Moore turned to ask Pickens what he thought, only to find that Pickens was gone. He looked around again and spotted their propulsion expert — 50 feet back, crouched behind a truck. Moore darted toward him to get more information, and Pickens said, "This could be bad. Real bad." Pickens said the valves had shut, but the seal was blown. The system was full of nitrous oxide, and the plumbing could only support a short test. He feared what would happen next, as extreme heat soaked back into the nitrous tank. He told Moore that the whole motor could blow up, sending huge metal chunks flying. There were still people on both sides of the tank; the one fire engine on the scene was not moving.

Moore, crouched behind the truck with Pickens, watched the persistent flame. This was not the start they were looking for. What if the thing exploded? It didn't help that Pickens was wondering aloud whether the nitrous inside the tank was turning to gas. An American flag flapped in the wind, looking vulnerable next to the semidormant giant. A full five minutes later — watching and waiting for Armageddon — the fire truck finally moved close to the motor and began spraying foam.

Burt, exasperated, pointed out that the fire truck was spraying *the wrong end* of the motor. It needed to spray the *nozzle end,* where the fire was coming out. About fifteen minutes later — an eternity when an explosion feels imminent — the flickering flames were extinguished. They were lucky; the tank hadn't blown up. One of the problems, Pickens believed, was that Burt had asked for three igniters instead of two, the way SpaceDev had originally designed the motor. Burt wanted the additional ignition energy. Before the test, Pickens had told Burt and a few others that he didn't have a good feeling about how the day would be run. SpaceDev engineers had said they would start flowing the nitrous *before* they hit ignition. Pickens had said, "This is a really bad idea." Burt responded, "Well, this is a competition. We have to let them learn."

Dave Moore and Jeff Johnson headed back to Scaled for a debriefing to review the video and telemetry from the test. One of their biggest concerns was that the tank and the test stand were damaged, which would create more setbacks and delays. Moore was already thinking about the report he would need to send to Paul Allen detailing the day's events.

Moore had brought Johnson in to get a better sense of what was going on inside Scaled. Johnson had a knack for ingratiating himself with the right employees, the ones who dealt in reality over fiction. Moore had learned that although Scaled had talented and resourceful builders and engineers, the company lacked some basic project management. The topdown structure — Burt ruled — was not working for this project. Moore needed real schedules, not a guessing game or wishful thinking. Moore had twenty years' experience at Microsoft, and Johnson had ten. The program management that Moore was trying to bring to Scaled was something he'd worked on with Bill Gates to ensure that software projects remained on track.

At one point, Moore told Burt, "You need to walk around and ask people when they think a certain part is going to be done. They really have to believe it." Burt took this to mean he had to *convince* people. Moore said, "No, it's the other way around. They have to believe intrinsically that this date is the real date." Moore also said he'd rather see them pick conservative dates and stick to them than string them along with "guesses." They also needed people assigned to specific jobs. At one point, Burt had said he wasn't going to assign engineers to the program. He was going to give them different tasks at different times. Burt had said, "The engineers are like mothers-in-law. Once you assign an engineer, they move in, take over, and never leave."

As Moore and Johnson saw it, Burt was the solution — he was the genius. None of this would be happening without him. But he could be elusive when it came to scheduling. There were points in the program when Moore looked at the Scaled crew and thought, "They're a bunch of motorcycle mechanics in the desert building a spaceship!" He said this with admiration or exasperation, depending on the day.

Before the less-than-ideal rocket motor test, the Scaled team had already succeeded in flying the *White Knight* — the mother ship. Resembling the Proteus, but bigger and more beautiful, the *White Knight* would take *SpaceShipOne* to around fifty thousand feet up before releasing the rocket for its final ascent to space. The *White Knight*'s first flight had been memorable: it lasted two and a half minutes. Pilot Doug Shane reported after the flight that "everything was good" — except for the minor issue of the J-85 engines producing "a small fire." There was also the matter of the spoilers flapping and banging, prompting Burt to order them bolted down. The first flight had earned the *White Knight* a new nickname, "White Knuckle Knight." Fortunately, the flying had been fire-free ever since.

Things were not going so smoothly with the production of the spaceship — it was, after all, a spaceship. Scaled was put on what came to be known as the "blood schedule." Johnson and Moore showed up regularly to play good cop, bad cop. The Scaled team worked nights and weekends. The main area of concern was the fabrication of the spaceship. Matt Stinemetze, who spent his first two years at Scaled avoiding Burt out of intimidation, was now the one who had to needle Burt to stay on schedule. They had set a target of spring 2003 for the public unveiling of the whole program. The XPRIZE was now fully funded, and there was a chance someone could beat them to the starting line.

By early 2003, the spaceship was in the build phase; everything was started but nothing was finished. The craft was in a walled-off hangar next to the *White Knight* and looked more like a picked-over carcass than a supersonic rocket. Its dark gray shell had unfinished portholes and wires dangling out. The Scaled team was in the midst of what felt like a million "cure cycles," where the uncured fiber resin was shaped and "cooked" into desired parts. The team needed fairings — smooth composite panels — for everything from landing gear to wingtips. The plumbing and fittings weren't done. The gear was being assembled. The reaction control system and the feather — both pneumatic, driven by high-pressure air fired through thrusters — all had to be built, from bottle to tubing. They had a chemist mixing up different recipes of thermal protection for the rocket. The difficulty of getting to space wasn't so much distance as it was the required speed, which in turn generated heat. The team had looked into what NASA used for thermal protection and learned it was too expensive and sold only in large quantities. So Scaled had its own scientist cooking up mixtures for the day its ship would go supersonic. One of the more recent mixtures, tested at high temperatures, had begun to sizzle, like the sparklers Stinemetze had lit as a kid. The chemist was returned to his recipe cards.

On the positive side, the *White Knight* was now flying beautifully, and was photographed by locals every time it was taken out of the shed. Stinemetze and others started bringing in clips of the latest blogs speculating on their space program. They tacked them up to the inside wall of the hangar.

The Scaled team began to gain momentum on the rocket, employing the disciplined style of Moore and Johnson while preserving the best of Scaled's creative culture. The myriad components — from landing gear to nose cone — were finally coming together in this one-of-a-kind puzzle. Two new hot fire tests of the hybrid motor — by SpaceDev and eAc — went off without a problem. No unwanted flames. No explosions. And the gray carcass was starting to look like the spaceship of Burt Rutan's dreams.

On Saturday morning, February 1, 2003, Stinemetze was at home with his wife, Kathlene "Kit" Bowman, who had joined Scaled as a process engineer. She came into the bedroom with a worried expression. "*Columbia* came apart," she said slowly. He didn't understand at first, as he hadn't been watching the news. But then he learned: space shuttle *Columbia*, STS-107, was returning to Earth after sixteen days of research in space when it broke apart. It had been traveling at eighteen times the speed of sound at 200,000 feet above Earth when communication was lost. The seven astronauts were twelve minutes away from making their landing. Instead, their one-hundred-ton spaceship disintegrated in the blue sky.

Later that day, a stony-faced President George W. Bush appeared on television to make a statement: "The *Columbia* is lost. At nine A.M. in Mission Control in Houston, we lost contact with space shuttle *Columbia*. Debris fell from the skies over Texas. There are no survivors." He went on to reference "the difficulties of navigating the outer atmospheres of the Earth." Stinemetze could not pull himself away from the news, thinking of the astronauts, and thinking, inevitably, of Scaled's own space program. What was required to reach orbit and stay there was very different from what was required to get to the start of space. The space shuttle flew at Mach 25. The Scaled pilots would need to fly at Mach 3-plus. Still, they were trying to reach space with a team of only a few dozen people. NASA had been at this for decades and was spending more than a billion dollars for every shuttle flight. Stinemetze asked his wife: "What are we doing?"

On Monday morning, Stinemetze pulled into the Scaled lot, turned off the engine, and sat in his car for a few minutes. It was raining and gloomy, and the wind was whipping the flags on the tops of buildings. He was still thinking about *Columbia*. The space program he grew up believing in felt bereft. Early reports on the cause pointed to damage to the left wing by foam insulation that had come loose from the orange external tank on liftoff.[*] As Stinemetze got out of his car, he realized his job was more like a mission. There could be no motor misfirings, no loose or faulty pieces. They had to get everything right.

The rollout of *SpaceShipOne* was now scheduled for the morning of April 18, 2003 — Good Friday. Burt was working around the clock, drinking copious amounts of coffee. In earlier days, he liked to rib Mike Melvill for wasting time cycling and staying fit. Burt would say his best exercise was at home on his couch, raising his spoon from tub of ice cream to mouth. Nowadays, he didn't even have time for the ice cream.[†]

Finally, the morning of the unveiling arrived. Guests were driving and flying in from near and far. Hundreds of people were

[*] Bits of foam insulation from the external tank came loose and hit the shuttle several times previously. When the program restarted after *Columbia,* NASA instituted mandatory external inspections of the shuttles once in orbit. Also, they launched only when a backup vehicle was ready to go in case a rescue was needed. For *Columbia,* the *Atlantis* shuttle was queued up for STS114, but it was not ready to fly.

[†] Burt had been on a healthier program in recent years, after suffering serious heart problems in the late 1980s.

expected, with a few notable no-shows. Paul Allen wasn't going to make it. He didn't think it was a good idea to announce his sponsorship so soon after the *Columbia* tragedy. While rumors had swirled that Allen was Burt's backer — Burt's customer, really — Burt dispelled such questions with comments including, "I hadn't heard that one." Allen was also being hit with more than his share of bad press. A harsh biography, *The Accidental Zillionaire,* had just been released, portraying Allen as a great party thrower, a lucky Microsoft stockholder, and a bad investor. A *Newsweek* story in February had described Allen as having a "reverse Midas touch."

Burt scanned the crowd as guests began seating themselves in the Scaled hangar. He was thrilled when he spotted Maxime "Max" Faget. Faget had designed the shape of the Mercury capsule, been involved in the designs of Gemini and Apollo, and was a lead designer of the space shuttle. Burt had worked with him in 1992, when he, Faget, Antonio Elias, and Caldwell Johnson met in Houston to discuss the preliminary design of a carrier aircraft that would have a range of capabilities, including air launch to orbit.[*] Burt had called Faget a few weeks earlier to invite him

---

[*] This preliminary design would eventually become Stratolaunch, a mobile launch aircraft designed by

to the *SpaceShipOne* event. "Max, come and tell me if my 'feather' reentry idea will work," he said. Faget declined, saying, "I'm in my eighties and I don't travel much anymore." After a pause, Burt said, "Max, what do you plan to do with the rest of your life?" The conversation ended with Burt assuming he wouldn't come. A day later, Faget's daughter called and said, "I am bringing him to your rollout."

Burt had never invited the public to see any of his planes before they flew, but he was making an exception for his rocket. Peter was there, having driven over at four that morning from his apartment in Santa Monica. Erik Lindbergh was nearby, along with the Ansari family, and Pete Worden, now brigadier general in charge of the U.S. Air Force's center for space transformation. A few seats away in the crowd was millionaire adventurer Steve Fossett, whose *GlobalFlyer* was being built by Burt to try to set a speed record for an around-the-world solo flight. Also present was space tourist Dennis Tito, and Kevin Petersen, head of NASA's Dryden Flight Research Center. Buzz Aldrin was in the front row. Burt was introduced by Academy Award–winning actor and good friend Cliff

---

Burt and funded by Paul Allen that will be the largest plane ever built, with a wingspan of 385 feet.

Robertson.

Suffering from a terrible cold and a hoarse voice, Burt began, "This is not just the development of another research aircraft. This is a complete manned space program." Flashing his inimitable isn't-this-cool smile, he added, "We are not seeking funding and are not selling anything. We are in the middle of an important research program to see if manned space access can be done by other than the expensive government programs. Nothing you will see today is a mockup. I didn't want to start the program until we knew this could happen."

The star of the show, cordoned off behind a blue curtain dotted with yellow stars, was about to take center stage. At Burt's command, the curtain was pulled away and the spaceship was revealed. Guests in the back stood up to get a better look. Cameras were pointed at the small, strange-looking rocket — white, pristine, blue stars painted on its belly, a nozzle out the back. The name *Space-ShipOne* was on the side, with the FAA registration number N328KF — for 328 kilofeet (about 100 kilometers), the designated start of space and chosen finish line of the XPRIZE.[*] Its body reminded people of a bullet, a bird, even a squid. Aldrin sat forward in his chair studying the design. Burt, two

---

[*] The registry number N100KM was already taken.

months shy of his sixtieth birthday, was smiling ear to ear. He was a kid again, back at his model airplane shows, wowing the pros and confounding the traditionalists.

After the commotion died down, Burt talked about Scaled's history, saying proudly that they'd never had a significant accident or pilot injury during flight test activity. Looking toward the spaceship and trying again to speak up despite his nonexistent voice, he said, "This program, if successful, will result in the first nongovernment manned spaceflight above one hundred kilometers altitude. If I'm able to do this with this little company here, there'll be a lot of other people who will say, 'Yeah, I can do it, too.' "

He noted that suborbital manned spaceflight had been achieved before by Mercury-Redstone in 1961 and by the B-52/X-15 in 1963. Burt marveled, "Even though the experience — as described by Alan Shepard, Gus Grissom, and Joe Walker — was *awe-inspiring,* suborbital spaceflights were ignored for the next forty years. Our goal is to demonstrate that nongovernment manned spaceflight operations are not only feasible, but can be done at very low costs."

At this, Burt asked his crew chief Steve Losey, who had grown up in Mojave and was now seated in the cockpit of the spaceship, to activate and extend the "feather" — his solution to giving the craft drag and slowing it for reentry. It took thirteen seconds to raise the wing to full extension of sixty-five degrees. Burt then asked Losey to fire up the thrusters for the pneumatic jets. The crowd cheered.

The plan, Burt said, was to attach the three-person spaceship to the turbojet *White Knight,* which would climb for an hour to reach 50,000 feet. The spaceship would then drop from the *White Knight,* the pilot would light the motor, and the rocket would "turn the corner" and make a vertical climb at speeds of 2,500 miles per hour. After the engine shut off, the ship would coast to its target altitude of 100 kilometers (62 miles) before falling back into the atmosphere. During that time, the pilot would have weightlessness for three to four minutes, and the ship would come back into the atmosphere "carefree," thanks to the feather — which had only two positions, up or down. Then, the ship — feather back down — would become a conventional glider, allowing a "leisurely" seventeen-minute glide down to the runway in front of Scaled. Max Faget couldn't take his eyes off the spaceship. He thought the feather was clever and unique, and had a hunch it would work.

"The program is a lot like the X-15," Burt quipped, "but we had this minor annoyance: we had to build our own B-52." The crowd laughed. Burt was referring, of course, to the

White Knight, which was not only a launch platform, but also an in-flight systems test bed. The cockpits of *SpaceShipOne* and the *White Knight* were functionally identical, so the *White Knight* could be used as a training simulator for the rocket.

Burt also took a moment to single out Peter, saying that the "rules of the XPRIZE had stood the test of time" and were as valid today as when they were announced under the arch in St. Louis seven years earlier.

After the unveiling, the crowd made its way outside to see the *White Knight,* which by now had flown fifteen times, including more than twenty hours at altitudes of about 50,000 feet. On the tarmac, Mike Melvill and Doug Shane climbed into the cockpit of the *White Knight* and taxied out. Minutes later, the *White Knight* came roaring back, dove down in front of the crowd, pitched its nose up, and tore eighty degrees skyward. At around 10,000 feet, it rolled over and then did a few more high-octane air show–style maneuvers. The crowd loved it.

Burt smiled and exclaimed, "Dammit! Those guys are having too much fun. I'm gonna have to stop paying them." Then he said, "You ain't seen nothing yet!"

That night, Peter and a small group of friends met up at an Asian fusion restaurant called Typhoon, which overlooked the runway of the Santa Monica Airport. He was joined on the second-floor terrace by some XPRIZE board members, including Adeo Ressi, technologist Barry Thompson, Anousheh Ansari, and Erik Lindbergh. The sake flowed and wine was poured, but the fuel at this table was optimism. Both Ressi and Thompson had saved the XPRIZE on different fifty-thousand-dollar Fridays, stepping in with last-minute cash infusions to cover the hole-in-one insurance premiums. Peter had also paid the premiums, as had his parents.

Ressi, who had joined the board in 2001 and had been at the morning's unveiling in Mojave, congratulated Peter for driving innovation. After the dot-com crash, Ressi feared that innovation had died, but the XPRIZE was bucking that trend and finding a way to resurrect inspiration. What he had seen in Mojave — and as he traveled to meet some of the XPRIZE contenders — was creativity unleashed. And he saw real determination, a willingness to get down in the dirt and dig a ditch for a homemade rocket bunker; sacrifice a steady job for a crazy dream; or spend retirement savings to make a giant spaceship.

Peter relished the excitement that the *SpaceShipOne* unveiling had brought. As he watched planes take off and land on Santa Monica's 4,973-foot runway 21, he was reminded that *SpaceShipOne* was as small as a private plane. He pictured it being pulled out of a hangar, rolled out onto the runway, and flying off to space. That was his dream — spaceships for personal use.

As if on cue, in walked Elon Musk. Since meeting Peter shortly after the demise of Blastoff, Musk had set out on his own quest for space, motivated by the question: if one was to make a rocket, what would be the best choices to make it cost effective? Ressi and Musk had gone to Russia in 2001 to try to buy rockets, only to find a sort of criminal-filled Wild West, where missiles of any sort could be had for the right amount of cash. The Russians got them drunk on vodka, and by their next visit, the price of the rockets had tripled. Ressi had kept one of the vodka bottles that their Russian hosts had made for them, complete with a logo featuring Ressi, Musk, and a palm tree on Mars.

Ressi and others had tried to talk Musk out of starting a rocket company. Ressi reminded him that there had been "a long line of rich guys who had lost fortunes on space." He and Peter and a handful of others had shown him clip after clip of rockets blowing up. For Peter, the reason was simple. He told him, "Building rockets is hard. Most people fail. A better mechanism is to fund the XPRIZE." Ressi told Musk, "Dude, don't do it. Don't do it. Don't do it." Musk responded, "I'm going to do it."

In June 2002, around his thirty-first birthday, Musk started his own company called SpaceX. His dealings with the Russians had convinced him that he should build his own engines, rocket structures, and capsules. His first launch vehicle would be the Falcon, a two-stage, liquid oxygen and kerosene–powered rocket, named after the *Star Wars Millennium Falcon.* He was hoping to launch by the end of the year.

Musk was impressed by what the XPRIZE was trying to do and saw how it was getting the general public excited about space again. He liked Burt's idea for the feather, saying he thought it was a good solution for suborbital flight. "It's something that only works for suborbital," he said. "It won't work for orbital."

Ressi, looking at Musk, playfully raised the possibility of certain well-funded "secret teams" entering the XPRIZE race at the last minute. Talk turned to Amazon founder Jeff Bezos, who was also getting into the space field and had a new, under-the-radar company called Blue Origin, headquartered in Seattle in a one-story warehouse — its windows covered in blue paper.

Soon, the discussion at the dinner table turned to the *Columbia* shuttle disaster and the national outpouring of grief. Elon remarked that it had shown him just how much people still cared about space and admired their astronauts. There was a feeling among the group that night that they had arrived at an unexpected moment in history. NASA had grounded manned flights, but because of the XPRIZE — and because of entrepreneurs including Elon — the prospects for getting humans off planet had never looked better.

Peter listened to the animated chatter. He looked at the daring group around him and thought of the morning in Mojave with Burt. There were teams building rockets in backyards, rice fields, and deserts. They were willing to risk everything, from ridicule and debt to their personal safety. They were modern-day explorers who shunned federal sponsors. Peter knew there would be errors of illusion and assumption. There would be imperfect starts and certain failure. But this moment felt as real to him as anything before. A changing of the guard. A new beginning. Hypergolic — that's how it felt. Parts coming together and igniting.

26
THE TEST OF A LIFETIME

Inside the shop of Scaled Composites, Matt Stinemetze frowned as he studied the nose of *SpaceShipOne*. Instead of looking sleek, forceful, and aerodynamic like the tip of an arrow, the front of the rocket had the look of a dry lake bed. There were cracks and superficial pieces missing, apparently lost during the morning's latest glide test.

The Scaled crew was searching for the perfect homebrew of thermal protection. Types and ratios of fillers and resins had been changed, quantities added and subtracted, in pursuit of the formula that could protect *SpaceShipOne* as it cut through the atmosphere on its return to Earth. But so far, nothing was working.

The rocket plane had already gone on seven successful glide tests and was fast approaching its first powered flight, set for December 17, 2003, the one hundredth anniversary of the Wright brothers' milestone in Kitty Hawk. Even if all went well today, Scaled was still months away from a trip to space. Burt's deadline now was the end of 2004, when the XPRIZE's hole-in-one insurance was set to expire.

Before *SpaceShipOne* could fly to the start of space, it needed to prove that it could safely go supersonic. The December 17 powered flight would be telling, revealing the integrity of the motor, the craft's sturdiness, and the pilot's ability to handle the spaceship. But the concoctions for thermal protection were failing time and time again.

Burt kept saying they needed something light and easy. Stinemetze examined the cracking coat on *SpaceShipOne* and stated the obvious: "This is not going to work when we go to high altitude." Burt took one look and said, "Take this stuff off. Clean up the lumps and bumps. Put some body putty on it." At one point, his in-house chemist had tried to talk Burt into putting forty-two pounds of thermal protection on the ship. Burt said "bullshit" and talked him down to fourteen pounds, which eventually became four pounds. In the end, though, Burt felt the mixture was overdeveloped. *Body putty should do the trick.*

"Body putty . . ." Stinemetze said, raising his eyebrows.

"Body putty," Burt said, walking away.

Stinemetze exchanged looks with a couple of the guys in the shop. "Okay," he said.

"Body putty it is."

Before he could paint the putty on the parts of the ship that would be exposed to the greatest heat, Stinemetze would need to test the substance to around eight hundred degrees, as he'd done with the other pixie dust concoctions that ended up sizzling, sparkling, cracking, or falling off. As he worked, he kept thinking, *body putty*? It was standard stuff in aviation. Like Bondo, only epoxy based, highly versatile, and used to smooth over dents and nicks. It was basically glue and filler. A smooth layer of the stuff would dry like hard candy.

Stinemetze tested a layer of putty. The results astounded him. *It worked.* The space shuttle had used fancy, high-grade synthetic sand for its thermal protection. Could Scaled really go to space with body putty? Stinemetze tested it again. And again. Finally, he headed off to find Burt.

"This stuff is awesome!" Stinemetze said. "Body putty. It works!"

Burt got the same excited look in his eyes as when those rare clouds over Mojave beckoned to be flown through, or the guys in the shop gave him the idea to put a saddle on one of his planes. "You need herbs and spices!" Burt said. "You can't just use *body putty* for thermal protection *on a spaceship*. Thermal protection has to be high tech! It has to be a proprietary recipe. Get some herbs and spices."

Stinemetze smiled. He understood. He had heard Burt tell stories about his days at Bede Aircraft. People would ask about a certain high-tech goo that was apparently uniquely effective. Burt loved to tell people that he couldn't reveal the top secret proprietary mixture. He would cite ITAR — international regulations limiting the disclosure of certain information — before confiding conspiratorially, "Okay, I'll tell you. It's made from the eyelashes of Nicaraguan racing spiders." In reality, Bede's secret "goo" was a new fiber invented by DuPont. It was Kevlar. In those days, Bede was testing it for possible use in aviation.

Stinemetze and one of the shop guys, Leon Warner, headed to the grocery store for herbs and spices. They bought red dye, oregano, and cinnamon. Back at Scaled, Stinemetze mixed the herbs and spices with the putty, turning their homebrew potion a lovely pinkish-red. The color would complete the patriotic triumvirate — with the white paint and scattered blue stars. The top-secret thermal protection was painted under the nose, belly, and wings. If someone looked closely enough, they might even see a sprinkling of oregano.

Scaled Composites had three pilots doing the flight testing of *SpaceShipOne:* Mike Melvill, sixty-three, Burt's longtime go-to guy to bring the plane home; Pete Siebold, thirty-two, a whiz kid pilot and a Cal Poly engineer who irritated people because he was so skilled; and Brian Binnie, fifty, a straitlaced, Ivy League–educated engineer and U.S. Navy–trained pilot. All three were talented and smart and could handle different planes the way a professional jockey can ride any horse. But their courage — that ineffable quality that couldn't be taught — was about to be tested like never before.

Binnie was first up, chosen to pilot the spaceship's maiden rocket-powered flight test. Scaled had never built a plane that broke the sound barrier; in fact no private company had ever independently built a piloted craft to fly faster than the speed of sound. But that's what would be required before Burt's spaceship could reach space: it would need to show that it could push from subsonic to transonic — which started at about .7 Mach — and then to supersonic.

Binnie knew the *SpaceShipOne* motor better than most. He was managing the development of all of its parts, from nozzle to propellant. Plus he was the only pilot at Scaled who had experience flying supersonic jets, courtesy of twenty years in the U.S. Navy, where he flew dozens of combat missions over Iraq. Binnie had also survived the harrowing test flights of Rotary Rocket's Roton, which was

Gary Hudson and Bevin McKinney's answer to a reusable rocket. Binnie had been sure that if the test flights had continued on the Roton, the day would come when he climbed into the cockpit of the cone-shaped contraption and didn't climb back out. It was just a matter of time.

Burt had seen past the short-sleeve, button-down Navy guy with the perfectly combed hair, creased pants, and polished shoes. He saw a man who turned down a job pushing paper in a comfortable office in the Pentagon to fly experimental rockets in the Mojave Desert. There was nothing buttoned down about that.

Born in 1953 in West Lafayette, Indiana, Brian was that kid who loved anything that flew or otherwise left the ground. His father was a physics professor at Purdue University, and the family lived in university housing behind a golf course. Brian spent hours running around the golf course with his two sisters, flying a rubber-band-powered airplane that launched like a rocket and slowed with wings that popped out for a glide back to the ground. When the family lived in Scotland — his mother and father were Scottish born — Brian's school was close enough that he would walk home for lunch. At around age seven, in 1960, his mother asked what he wanted to be when he grew up. Brian contemplated the question, thinking "football players are famous, so that would be nice. Or maybe a policeman or a fireman." His mother shook her head. "No, if I was a wee laddie, I'd want to be an astronaut," she said, talking in a dreamy way about rockets, stars, and planets. She was the one in the family with the adventuresome spirit. When the Binnies moved from Scotland back to the United States, Brian had an experience he wouldn't soon forget. It was a hot summer day when Brian walked off the plane at Logan Airport in Boston. The smell of asphalt and plane fumes overwhelmed him; he loved it. It became both inspiration and anodyne. He went on to graduate from Brown University with a bachelor's degree in aerospace engineering and a master's degree in thermodynamics and earned a second master's degree in aeronautical engineering from Princeton.

While at Princeton, Brian ran into some Navy pilots who urged him to consider flying with them. He'd been dreaming of planes, studying planes, and working on planes, but never had the money to actually fly planes. As it turned out, his lack of flying experience proved to be a good thing, as he was open to the Navy's way of teaching. Brian took to it readily, passing one test after another. He spent three years training in Florida and eventually earned his Navy wings — as cherished as his wedding band. The training continued with flight refueling, simulated air-to-air combat, close flight formation, night flying, and low-level night flying. Every day presented an opportunity to fail. The scrutiny was intense. But Brian loved what he was doing and thrived in the single-seat aircraft, where he was alone in the cockpit with his instructor flying in his own plane alongside. It was one man, one machine, make-or-break flying. Before he got into a plane, Brian flew every formation in his mind. He drew flight patterns out on the carpet in his room. He dreamed about airspeed and maneuvers.

His next challenge combined the precision of a high-wire act with the power of a drag race: landing an F/A-18 Hornet on an aircraft carrier at sea. It was a moving target where any mistake could be his last. The runways were no more than 500 feet long, and landing was done at speeds of up to 150 miles per hour. He had to come in and catch with his tail hook one of the four "arresting" cables strung in parallel lines across the deck of the ship. Catching the third wire was the goal. A counterintuitive challenge was to touch down with engines full throttle. If the plane didn't catch a wire, Brian needed enough speed to take off for another pass. All of this was to be done on a heaving and swaying ship.

Brian would spend twelve to thirteen hours flying the same pattern, all under the unforgiving watch of the meanest guy on deck, the air boss. The air boss was impossible to please, barking orders and running the show. Brian spent much of his training on the USS *Lexington,* which had only three trip wires. Every pass was graded A through F. If a pilot got an F on a flight, he'd be talking to the admiral and his career was in danger. Brian also trained on the USS *Enterprise,* which had four wires. One day while training off the USS *Independence,* a typhoon was sweeping in through the North Philippine Sea, and all the pilots were called back to the aircraft carrier. Brian was on his landing approach and gave his call signal — with his type of plane and amount of fuel — so the cables could be set at the right tension. As he neared the back of the ship, the bow of the *Independence* dipped down and the stern came way up. Brian stared at the propellers whirring out of the water. The landing signal officer — charged with keeping his pilots alive — said calmly, "Deck's up. Looking good. Keep it comin.' " The bond that developed between pilot and landing officer was intense. *I gotta trust in something,* Brian thought. "Okay, I'm comin' in." Sure enough, the deck reversed pitch and he saddled into the wire, pulling off a respectable landing in roiling seas.

Night training was even more demanding. "Okay" was the language of the Navy. Not "great" or even "good." "Okay" was what every pilot wanted to hear, making him feel like King Kong for the next fifteen minutes — or at least until he had to do the run all over again. Brian flew in Operations Desert Shield, Desert Storm, and Southern Watch. He flew thirty-three combat missions over Iraq, primarily in the F/A-18. He was a Navy commander when he retired in 1998 at the age of forty-five.

Not interested in being relegated to a cubicle in the Pentagon, he started looking around for other jobs that would keep him in the air. When he saw a job posting to flight-test an experimental rocket in the Mojave Desert, he was intrigued, applied, and got the job at Rotary Rocket. He, his wife, and three kids had been living at Point Mugu in southern California, finding it paradise compared with many of the bases they'd called home. It had mountains, the Pacific Ocean, golf courses, and strawberry fields. They left that for the dry and flat town of Rosamond, thirteen miles south of Mojave and just west of Edwards Air Force Base. Brian had long considered his wife, Valerie, who went by "Bub," an angel — now he had proof.

Just as his family wasn't prepared for desert dwelling, Brian struggled with civilian life. Going from the military to Mojave was like entering the Twilight Zone. At Rotary, it felt like there were no rules. Everything was "fluid." Schedules were amorphous. Some of the employees looked and sounded more like agitators than engineers. Brian took one look at a guy with green hair and nose rings and asked, "Who is this guy? What does he do?" He was told, "You better get over it, pal. This guy is designing your flight controls." When he overheard some employees talking about recreational drug use, he made it an issue, saying he wasn't going to fly a rocket built by guys on drugs. Again he was scoffed at. He didn't believe a word of Rotary's "schedule" for approvals, licenses, and flight tests. He had seen how slow the government moved. Still, there was money coming in to Rotary, and the promise of more.

Brian started at Rotary in 1998 as one of two pilots — the other was Marti Sarigul-Klijn, another Navy-trained engineer and pilot. Brian also served as program manager. He knew of Burt Rutan by reputation and had seen him around, but the two had never met. Scaled had been hired by Gary Hudson to build the shell for the Roton. When it came time for a design review of the project, Burt and a handful of others were invited over. Brian had the last presentation of the day, from 1:30 to 2:30 P.M. At the end of his presentation, Brian asked whether anyone had any questions. Brian saw Burt's hand shoot up. His heart sank. He felt like he was in the crosshairs of the lion. "Yes, Mr. Rutan."

"If we quit right now," Burt said cheerfully, "we can still get in nine holes. What do you think?"

Brian thought it was a great idea. The two became golfing buddies, and when Rotary closed its doors in 2000, Burt brought Brian to Scaled.

On Wednesday, December 17, 2003, one hundred years to the day after two bicycle mechanics named Wright managed a powered and sustained flight in a flimsy aircraft that no one thought would fly, a bunch of "motor-cycle mechanics in the desert" were ready for the first powered flight of *SpaceShipOne*. The *White Knight* and *SpaceShipOne* were rolled from the hangar of Scaled into the early morning light. The plan for the flight was straightforward: achieve a fifteen-second burn of the rocket motor and supersonic flight. Brian would assess how the motor lit and performed, how it felt going through tran-sonics, and how the feather did at a relatively high altitude. Of these things, the sound bar-rier posed the greatest challenge. The little craft with the pointed nose sprinkled with oregano had never flown so fast or so high.

Brian was in the cockpit of *SpaceShipOne,* to be carried aloft by the *White Knight.* He focused on the instruments before him. The rocket controls were simple. Two switches: one to arm, one to fire. The avionics suite had a dedicated propulsion display that showed important motor parameters that could be monitored by the pilot and Mission Control. The pilot couldn't throttle the rocket. At around 48,000 feet — Burt liked to say the first 50,000 feet were free — *SpaceShipOne* would be dropped like a bomb from the hooks of the *White Knight.*

With relatively little fanfare — a few invited guests and media — the *White Knight* took off into the hazy blue sky. The ground below was a palette of beige and sand. Six miles north of Mojave, Brian did a systems check. They were close to their desired altitude. Brian got the green light; he and *Space-ShipOne* were ready to be dropped from the *White Knight.* The countdown began: 5-4-3-2-1-mark!

"Good release," came the call from Cory Bird, piloting the *White Knight.*

"Nose wants to drop," Brian reported. Then, "Control checks are good."

"Status — go for light."

"Armed," Brian said. "Green light."

Brian, in the rocket and free from the mother ship, stared at the FIRE switch. He had seen, heard, and felt the rocket motor hot fires. It was the Brahman bull angered, and today was the day the bull left the chute. With his head back into the seat and his finger on the FIRE switch, Brian girded himself. He flipped it. Both his hands

515

clutched the stick like the horn of a saddle. He was jolted up and back until he could barely keep hold of the stick.

He had landed on carriers and flown in combat, but this was something else. Chuck Yeager had brought his own leather football helmet, knowing the X-1 would knock him around. Brian was jostled. "A lot of oscillation," he told Mission Control euphemistically. He tried to focus on the velocity vector, which told him where he'd be in the next few seconds. His trajectory was nearly perpendicular to the ground. He feared he would go over backward, but the flight path maker told him otherwise. Brian was now in the transonic corridor, where he was hit by even more buffeting. A sad-sack cowboy being flung around like a rag doll.

Just then, a giant boom was heard across the desert floor, signaling that *SpaceShipOne* had flown faster than the speed of sound. Brian was at Mach 1.2, wondering how much longer he could hold on. Then, as fast and as violently as it all began, the rocket motor shut down — marking the end of the longest fifteen seconds of his life.

Brian still had to get back to Mojave. He activated the feather that bent the wings in half, locking them in place at sixty-five degrees. After his fifteen-second foray into the supersonic, he was returning through the unfriendly transonic region with more pitching and swerving. He almost laughed when he got the call from Mike Melvill, in a chase plane: "Brian, you look great!"

Then, at around 60,000 feet, there was a gift, better than the blue expanse or a pillow of clouds. It was calm and quiet. No bucking, jostling, jerking. No noise. One man, one machine.

Brian exhaled. "That was quite a wild ride from Mr. Rutan," he said, prompting laughter from Mission Control. At 50,000 feet, he got the nod to "defeather" and move the wings back into glide position.

As he made the final descent into Mojave, everything finally felt familiar. Mike was off to his left in a chase plane, monitoring and encouraging him and ready to call out wheel height. This was good. Brian could sense impending triumph. He had fired the motor, gone supersonic, and operated the feather. It all worked. The runway was just ahead. The years of hard work on *SpaceShipOne* were paying off. If the Scaled crew could go supersonic, they could go to the start of space. The celebrating would begin with touchdown. On the ground, to mark this important next step on the way to space, were the few invited guests and media, and their benefactor, Paul Allen.

Brian lined up with the runway and dropped the landing gear. He was almost home. Then suddenly, the nose started to slip to the right. He tried trimming it, but that made things worse. The wings wobbled, refusing to stay level. Mike called wheel height as Brian wondered whether he would land upright. He relaxed pressure on the stick, but this just dropped him closer to the runway. *Was the airspeed indicator off?* He could *not* crashland, not after all this effort. Brian pulled the nose up and flared the plane before touchdown, but that didn't help, either.

He was going down.

SpaceShipOne hit the runway hard, its left landing gear crunching and collapsing. Brian skidded down the runway and veered off it into the sand. He was enveloped in a cloud of dust.

Brian threw off his helmet and used every expletive in the book. Burt was among the first to reach him and dust him off. Paul Allen, who was using the day to officially announce that he was backing Burt's space program, was conspicuously absent from the crash site. His handlers didn't think it was such a good idea for him to be pictured with his newly crashed spaceship.

Burt told Brian that he'd done a great job: he'd gone supersonic and he'd feathered. The hard landing was caused by last-minute modifications they'd made to make the plane more stable, Burt said. He told him they'd have the plane flying again in weeks.

But Brian was inconsolable. He believed that he had been working up to this flight all his life. He was a war veteran, a skilled Navy fighter pilot, and a family man. He had done everything right, but in this moment, all of those accomplishments seemed for naught. He felt like an Olympic athlete who had won every heat, jumped every hurdle, and then stumbled right before the finish line, when everything mattered most. That's how he would be remembered — he was sure of that. It even seemed irrelevant to him that he had made history that day, piloting the first private plane to reach supersonic speeds.

Brian's colleagues at Scaled only reinforced his doubts about whether he had the right stuff as a pilot. In the wake of the test flight, some were saying the Navy aviator had landed the spaceship as if he were landing an F/A-18 on a flight deck — hard and fast. Even Mike, who'd watched from the chase plane, said Brian had flown the craft into the ground. The name *Brian Binnie* was suddenly synonymous with *crash landing.* But all the negative talk couldn't make Brian feel worse than he already did. As repairs were made to the spaceship, Brian feared he'd be relegated to writing up the test cards for missions he'd never fly.

That Friday afternoon, only two days later,

Burt, Brian, and Scaled colleague Kevin Mickey took off early for a round of golf in Bakersfield. Mickey had grown up in Mojave and spent most of his youth peering through the chain-link fence to see what this guy named Burt Rutan was building. He had started as a floor sweep at $6 an hour and was now a vice president.

Out on the course, Burt took out his laminated spreadsheets detailing different clubs and holes and projections for how far the ball would carry and roll on the fairway, greens, and in the rough. Brian had worked his way down to a five handicap, and Burt was a solid ten. Mickey could hold his own. Brian's strength was off the tee, while Burt had a strong short game. Once Burt got inside a hundred yards, he could be formidable. He had built his own putter, which was similar to a belly putter, with a "T" as the head. He called it the Titanic because he trusted it to sink any putt. While relaxing on the links was the primary goal, it wasn't unusual for Burt and company to get into discussions around the aerodynamic properties and ballistic coefficient of different clubs, club heads, and even golf balls — talking dimple depth and shape, including hexagons. Would a bigger driver head create more drag, or give the golfer more confidence in hitting the ball, thus a better chance at striking the ball with more power? How did the grooves in a golf ball reduce drag?

Burt could see that Brian was still depressed about the crash landing of *SpaceShipOne*. As they were finishing up their round in Bakersfield, Burt asked Brian whether he knew the story of Doug Sanders, the American golfer who had been one shot away on the eighteenth hole from winning the British Open at St. Andrews in 1970. Brian said no.

"He missed a three-foot putt against Jack Nicklaus to win the Open," Burt said. He won twenty PGA tour events, but that one thing changed the course of his life. Burt had heard Sanders asked years later how often he still thought about that missed putt. Sanders said that "maybe nine or ten minutes" went by when he didn't think about it.

The story stayed with Brian, distracting him as he drove home. Brian thought, *I didn't come this far to have* that landing *define me. I'll be damned if that's the way it's going to be for me.*

27
FLIRTING WITH CALAMITY

It was the middle of the night on June 21, 2004, and a warm Mojave wind whipped up the sand and tipped over chairs, tents, and anything else not tied down. Even the Porta Potties had to be pushed back up. Not far from Scaled Composites, a makeshift RV park was now full. A long line of cars snaked from California Highway 58 into the newly renamed Mojave Air and Spaceport. Big crowds were amassing here to witness the test flight of all test flights — *SpaceShipOne*'s first journey to space — and, if successful, a preview of its first XPRIZE attempt.

Burt Rutan arrived at Scaled before three A.M. The sky was dotted with stars, and the Moon was a waxing silvery crescent. Pilot Mike Melvill had spent the night in an RV in the hangar because gridlook was predicted. A preflight meeting was scheduled for 4:45 A.M. Inside the hangar, *SpaceShipOne* and the *White Knight* were gleaming and ready. The rocket plane had flown two powered flights since Brian Binnie's supersonic milestone in December. The craft's broken landing gear was replaced and other fixes made. A wider nozzle for the rocket was installed, along with a new fairing that ran from the back of the fuselage over the nozzle to reduce drag. Each test flight had taken the craft incrementally higher and faster — to 211,400 feet and Mach 2.3 the month before. That put Scaled team members at about 64 percent of where they needed to get to today, which was 328,000 feet, the internationally recognized boundary of space.[*]

[*] The 211,400 feet achieved on the May flight just reached the mesosphere, the third layer in the four layers of our atmosphere. The 328,000 feet sought on June 21, 2004, needed to reach the fourth layer, the thermosphere. The atmosphere consists of four thin onion skin–like layers around the Earth. The troposphere starts at the Earth's surface and extends 8 to 14.5 kilometers high. This part of the atmosphere is the densest. Almost all weather is in this region. The stratosphere starts just above the troposphere and extends to 50 kilometers high. The ozone layer, which absorbs and scatters the solar ultraviolet radiation, is in this layer. The mesosphere starts just above the stratosphere and extends to 85 kilometers high. Meteors burn up in this layer. The thermosphere starts just above the mesosphere and extends to 600 kilometers high. Aurora occurs and satellites orbit in this layer. The mesosphere still

Today's flight was the biggest gamble yet. Each test flight — whether glide or rocket-powered — had anomalies. On one occasion, a dangerous tail stall during a glide test had turned into a harrowing loss of control. During a powered flight, the avionics display suddenly blinked off, forcing Mike Melvill to decide in an instant whether to fly blind or abort. As X-15 engineer Bob Hoey had warned, the *SpaceShipOne* team was living with the constant threat of calamity. But team members also got to experience the wonder and validation of what they were getting right. In the weeks leading up to this day, Burt had found it hard to work and hard to sleep. He hadn't even been to space, but he was already drawing up plans for what would come next: orbital vehicles. Only hours earlier, he'd spent the evening hosting Paul Allen and Virgin billionaire Richard Branson for dinner at his pyramid home. Before dinner, he sat them down on his sofa — one billionaire on each side — and showed them a forty-four-slide PowerPoint presentation titled "Manned Space Vision Summit." He talked excitedly about private space stations,

---

contains clouds — although very thin ones — the famous noctilucent clouds. But the atmosphere is still thick enough that meteorites burn up as they cross from the thermosphere into the mesosphere.

zero-gravity hotels, and orbital ships. He shared his renderings for an "upgraded *SpaceShipOne* with room for seven passengers." Between the slides and musings, Burt said to both men, "You're probably asking what we should do this year and next year, right? The only way you can make an intelligent decision on what to do this year and next is to know the answer to one very important question." He paused. The room went quiet. "The question is, what do you want to see happen before you die?" Allen smiled. He could see that Burt had been bitten by the space bug. Allen was too, but he was satisfied with what they were attempting with manned suborbital flight. Branson was interested in how Burt's ideas and creations could open space to the masses.[*]

Bouncing around the Scaled offices at 3:45 A.M., Burt realized he was the only one present who wasn't immediately mission critical. He looked at the clock: he had forty-five minutes to do whatever he wanted. So he headed straight down the flight line to find Stuart Witt, a no-nonsense former top gun Navy pilot who was now the airport director. Witt had recently pushed the Federal Avia-

---

[*] Paul Allen and Richard Branson had begun discussions about Branson's buying the rights to *SpaceShipOne* in March, three months before this dinner in the desert. But no deal had been made.

tion Administration to authorize the transformation of the airport into a spaceport. The plan had been Burt's idea, presented with his typical urgency. Burt had marched into Witt's office — he always came through the side door by the flight line — and said, as if in midconversation: "I need a fourteen-thousand-foot runway and you've only got a ten [thousand]."

"Why do you need it?" Witt asked.

"Oh, I need it as soon as you can build it. Need a throat [a turn in the runway] this big," Burt said, gesturing hugely.

"Who is going to pay for it?"

"Hell, I don't know."

Witt lobbied Congress and got the funds for the longer runway and new turnaround. In the weeks leading up to today's big test flight, Witt had been working around the clock, determined to run the show with military precision. This morning, his busy schedule included orchestrating the uprighting of the Porta Potties, handling security, and fielding last-minute calls, including one from the general over at Edwards Air Force Base, who was asking to land but wasn't on the day's fly-in list.

Now, here stood Burt in the middle of the night, with another idea, this one more mischievous than ambitious. "I've got about forty-five minutes — now less — and I can't think of anything I'd rather do," Burt said.

Witt couldn't resist. The two hopped in Witt's truck, parked outside the door. It was still dark as the two drove down the runway and past the flight tower. Before Witt came to a full stop, Burt was out of the truck. When he'd first met Burt years before, Burt had told him that the reason he settled in Mojave was simple: he started driving at Brown Field just north of the U.S.-Mexico border and hit every airport heading north until he found one that he could afford and that would give him permission to start his business.

Witt parked and got out of his truck. Burt was heading for an RV parked in a prime viewing spot, suggesting that the vehicle had arrived days before. The Magician of the Mojave wanted to mingle with the rocket fans.

A light was on in the camper, and Burt went ahead and knocked. The door creaked opened. A couple peered out to see a tall man with silvery hair and Elvis sideburns.

"Yes?"

"I'm Burt Rutan, and I want to thank you for coming," Burt said, extending his hand as the two reluctantly opened the screen door. The couple, from St. George, Utah, had two kids sleeping in the back. It slowly dawned on them that the Burt Rutan standing before them was *the* Burt Rutan. The Utah man laughed, and opened the door wide. He explained that he'd come home from work a few days before, listened to his wife talk excitedly about a news story she'd heard promoting the launch of a private spaceship, and he said, "Load up the car, we're going to Mojave!"

Burt continued his meet-and-greet, knocking on a few more campers' doors. He shook hands and thanked people for making the trip to Mojave. He looked around for what to do next. Paul Allen's people hadn't budgeted for public parking. Allen wanted the press and VIPs to attend, but Burt wanted the public to be a part of the day, too. To make it happen, he and his wife, Tonya, decided to foot the hefty parking and police security costs, which were close to $100,000 after all the licenses and red tape. Burt and Tonya paid for about $80,000, and Witt picked up the rest. Burt and Tonya wanted kids to be there so they could later tell their own children that they had attended the world's first nongovernmental manned spaceflight.

In the RV area, Witt could now see that Burt was fixated on some drivers a short distance away who appeared to be struggling to make a ninety-degree turn to park. Burt walked up to a parking attendant, startled him by relieving him of his lighted baton, and said, "Let me help you." He moved into position and began directing traffic, even opening car doors with a "Welcome to Mojave!" Some people recognized him — including a group wearing "GO BURT GO!" T-shirts

— and grabbed for their cameras. Others were just happy to have a parking spot.

As a hint of orange light on the horizon announced the dawn, visitors inured to the wind staked out their places in fold-out chairs, ready for showtime. Witt and Burt both needed to be back for preflight meetings. They left the parking area and headed up the flight line. A steady stream of private jets had been arriving. The sunrise would be a gorgeous orange, turning the mountains dark brown. Witt and Burt were silent as they took in the sea of cars, campers, and people. Witt looked at his seatmate. Burt had tears in his eyes.

Inside Scaled, Mike, now in his flight suit, joined the engineers and flight team managers at the conference table, mission notebooks in front of them. As others talked, he was lost in thought. If everything went right, he would become the world's first civilian pilot — not working for the military, not working for NASA — to fly out of the Earth's atmosphere. But Mike knew better than anyone that this was a big "if." A lot could go wrong.

At sixty-three, he was past the mandatory retirement age for an airline pilot. He was also too much of a "cowboy" and didn't take instruction, according to an e-mail from fellow pilot Pete Siebold that got passed on to Burt in the weeks leading up to today's flight.

Burt read the e-mail, headed across the hall and dropped the paper on Mike's desk, saying, "See what you're up against?" Mike was the first to admit he wasn't as good in the simulator as Siebold — who built the simulator and wrote much of the software. Siebold was a Cal Poly graduate like Burt; Mike didn't graduate from high school and was a self-taught engineer. Mike had never played video games; Siebold was a master. Mike flew by how the plane *felt.*

Despite Siebold's criticisms, Mike had done the majority — eight out of thirteen — of the manned test flights of *SpaceShipOne.* He was the pilot of *SpaceShipOne* when the avionics went out and he continued to fly blind, something Burt applauded and Siebold criticized. Brian Binnie had done a great job with his flight, until he crash-landed. Siebold pulled off a strong powered flight, but hesitated too long before firing the motor. Once dropped from the *White Knight,* Siebold hadn't trusted the handling qualities of the rocket. He dropped more than a mile as he assessed the problems, until Mission Control told him he had to light the motor. Landing with a full load of fuel would be far too dangerous. Siebold's analytical engineering brain had overridden his test pilot moxie. Still, he had pushed hard to pilot today's historic flight to space and had mission director Doug Shane in his corner. But Burt hadn't been pleased with Siebold's May 13 flight. The cowboy was up.

Burt had never invited the public to watch a critical experimental flight test. There were too many things that could scrub a launch or derail a takeoff. The *Voyager*'s around-the-world trip had drawn global attention, but the ubiquity of the cameras and multimedia was something entirely new. With this flight, there were cameras everywhere, from inside the pilots' locker room to the cockpit of the *White Knight* and the spaceship. If something went wrong, the world would know. The risk was palpable. Burt trusted Mike to get the job done.

During the early morning briefing, the schedule was reviewed and Shane noted, "We're still trying to taxi out at six-thirty." Crew chief Steve Losey went over the system checks of the vehicle. Looking at his friend Mike, he said, "We're good to go." Mike nodded slightly, but his mind was rehearsing the day's flight. More details were discussed: the weight of the fully loaded spaceship, pilot included, was 6,380 pounds; the target altitude for the *White Knight* to release *Space-ShipOne* was 46,000 feet; and wind limits to takeoff were fifteen knots crosswind.

Shane, who had perfected the art of impassivity, noted with his usual poker face that the "unique nature of the day" presented new challenges, including "lots of people," and

531

the "ears of the world tapped into Mission frequency." They also had what they called a "higher tortoise jeopardy." Under their licensing agreement with the Federal Aviation Administration's Office of Commercial Space Transportation, Scaled was required by the Environmental Protection Agency to do a runway sweep to ensure that runways were free of the endangered tortoise. At an earlier point in the rocket program, an idea was hatched to take one of Mojave's finest turtles to space. But under the licensing agreement, Scaled personnel were not allowed to touch, nudge, or move these reptilian interlopers. Scaled was required to call in a specialist trained in tortoise relocation. Witt, who almost didn't take the Mojave job so that he could catch lots of fish in British Columbia instead, noted drily that they had been doing about three hundred movements across the runway every day — planes, equipment, trucks, aircraft, and helicopters — and had never once been asked to do a runway check for tortoises. "But by God, we're told to do it for *SpaceShipOne*," Witt said, "so we're going to do it."

The meeting ended, and Mike and Brian Binnie headed to the pilots' room to grab their parachute packs. Neither said a word. Brian felt like something of a "bus driver" in the *White Knight*; he was determined to work his way back from the mother ship and into the cockpit of the spaceship again someday. In the hangar, employees signed the nozzle of *SpaceShipOne*. Paul Allen, using a gold Sharpie, signed the nozzle and autographed the inside of the cockpit. Pete Siebold wished Mike a good flight and said with a hint of wistfulness, "This is the flight that says, 'Hey, NASA, we're here.' " Burt and Paul Allen walked out onto the tarmac together and looked in the direction of the wind cones, which hours before were whipping and full of air, but were now quiet. Burt told Paul that the Mojave wind always calmed when it was time to fly, like a child who knows when it's time to behave.

Peter Diamandis was in Mojave with Erik Lindbergh and a group from the XPRIZE, including William Shatner. Virgin's Richard Branson had arrived there, too, as had Buzz Aldrin and aviator Bob Hoover, whom Chuck Yeager had called "the greatest pilot I ever saw." Peter had been hosting parties leading up to the flight and made his way to the tarmac as the sun was coming up. If Scaled succeeded today, the next trip to space would be the first flight for the XPRIZE. Teams were required to give Peter a sixty-day notice of intent to fly. Several teams had told him they were close to launching hardware, and one team hinted that manned flight was not far off. As Peter waited for the test flight to begin, he dreamed of even bigger parties in

Mojave — of back-to-back flights to space. He had the $10 million prize money, but under the arrangement of his hole-in-one insurance policy, time was fast running out.

Off to a quiet side of the hangar, away from the clutch of employees and photographers, Mike and Sally stole a minute to themselves. They held each other close and kissed. Mike brushed Sally's hair off her face and said, "I wouldn't trade anything I've done for anybody else's love." Sally looked at Mike and told him, "Come home to me." She pinned their lucky horseshoe on the sleeve of his flight suit. He kissed her again before heading to his plane. Test pilots, like astronauts, had training, simulators, flight plans, flight suits, helmets, talismans, and people praying for them. The wives of test pilots had that last kiss.

It was time. The manning up of the vehicles was under way.

Mike walked to *SpaceShipOne,* helmet under his arm, mind on the mission. Burt had never put him in a plane that wouldn't come home. Mike trusted this man with his life — he had to. Burt had never let him down, and he hadn't let Burt down. He wasn't about to let that change today. Still, Mike was afraid.

Before the cockpit door was closed, Burt leaned in. "This is the big one, Burt," Mike said, his voice full of emotion.

"We got the right guy," Burt said, his voice breaking. He clutched Mike's hand. "Forget about space," Burt said. "It's just an air-plane."

The door was soon closed, and Mike was alone in the cockpit. Burt's last message resonated with him: *Just fly it like a plane.*

Standing on the runway, Burt told Paul Allen that Mike's fear would vanish like the winds of Mojave as soon as he was in the air and had a job to do. "Test pilots are like that," he said. Paul was anxious. When he made the deal to sponsor Burt in his quest to build a spaceship, he hadn't been thinking about the pilots, and the pilots' families. Now he was friends with the pilots and their wives and aware of all that was at stake.

Inside the *White Knight,* Brian Binnie was at the controls, with Matt Stinemetze in one of the plane's two passenger seats. Stine-metze's job would be to pull the handle and release the spaceship. Two chase planes were ready on the runway: a high-altitude Alpha jet owned by Paul Allen, and a Beechcraft Starship, one of Burt's early designs. The *White Knight* began its roll down the runway. As the craft taxied, Stinemetze peered out the side windows. He was disappointed to see only a hundred or so spectators. Flood-lights were pointed their way, making it dif-ficult to see to the sides. "These are the only people who showed up?" he asked.

But as the *White Knight* passed the tower, the view from the windows changed. It was row after row of people, as far as Stinemetze could see. "Holy crap!" he said. "Will you look at that!" He took in the satellite dishes, cars, and campers. He said it again: "Holy crap!" Brian marveled at the thousands of people who lined the runway fences. "Oh boy," Brian said, "let this be a good day."

From out in the crowds, cheers rang out as the twin-engine *White Knight,* carrying *SpaceShipOne,* approached. A young girl yelled out excitedly, "The *White Knight* is coming! The *White Knight* is coming!" Minutes later, the applause and cheers erupted again: the *White Knight* was taking off toward the southern Sierra Nevada.

It took sixty-three minutes for the mother ship to reach 47,000 feet and the targeted drop point. The countdown began for the release. The spaceship was dropped and the motor armed.

Mike said, "Armed and . . . fire!" The acceleration knocked his head back into his seat. He was flying almost straight up, quickly closing in on the transonic region. The strong wind shear was making it difficult to control the ship, and sending him off course in a way that might sabotage his goal of getting high enough to reach space. Then Mike heard three ominous bangs — one big bang and two smaller bangs. He couldn't see outside the rocket to know what had happened and worried that the ship was damaged or that something had fallen off. The flight had not gotten off to the best of starts.

Seventy-seven seconds into the flight, the motor of *SpaceShipOne* shut down, as it was supposed to do. Mike felt the motor hadn't run well and was still concerned about the earlier banging noises.[*] He was anxious that the craft might not have the inertia to make it to the Karman line.

In Mission Control, there was clapping when it appeared that the spaceship had made it to 328,000 feet. But the applause quickly stopped. The crew would need to wait on the final altitude report. Burt sat to Doug Shane's right, and Paul Allen and two officials from the FAA's Commercial Space Transportation division stood toward the back.

Down the flight line, thousands of people looked through powerful camera lenses or binoculars. Others held hands to the sky like a universal salute, trying to catch a glimpse of the spaceship, now a white dot with a long white contrail. The spaceship was flying in

---

[*] It was later determined that the bangs were a normal noise the motor made as it used up the last of its fuel load in the rocket's motor case.

the direction of the sun. Someone yelled, "Go, Mike, go!" Nearby, a man with a tinfoil hat sold T-shirts reading "SAY HELLO TO MY ALIEN MOTHER" and "TAKE ME TO SATURN." A woman wielded a sign: "WE ARE GOING TO SPACE AND THE GOVERNMENT IS NOT INVITED." Another sign read "I'VE BEEN WAITING 40 YEARS FOR THIS." Sally was on the flight line with her son, looking anguished as she searched the sky.

Mike configured the feather to prepare it for the reentry, which would happen four minutes later. He unlocked and feathered it, and felt the thud as it was forced into its sixty-five-degree angled reentry position. *No problem there,* Mike thought. Studying the display in front of him, Mike noticed that the stabilizers on the feather, used for high-altitude control, were unevenly set. One was at ten degrees and the other at thirty degrees. *This has to be a mistake,* he thought. But it wasn't. *This is bad.* Mike knew it was potentially fatal: a twenty-degree delta in the settings would force the spaceship into a spin from which he couldn't recover. If he didn't find a solution, he wouldn't make it back alive. The only way out was through the nose — an impossibility in the midst of a supersonic spin.

In Mission Control, Shane called for "more stab trim." Aerodynamicist Jim Tighe, sitting one row back from Shane, told Mike to pull the breakers to start the backup motor. Mike had tried that, but the backup motor had failed. Mike audibly exhaled. He took in the beauty with sadness. He was more wistful than panicked. Thousands of people were watching and waiting; he was alone in this experimental space capsule.

Suddenly, Mission Control lost its connection to *SpaceShipOne.* Paul Allen could see a change in the team's body language. Burt and Doug leaned forward in their chairs.

"Ground to *SpaceShipOne,*" Doug said.

Nothing.

"Ground to *SpaceShipOne.*"

No response.

Doug's lips trembled slightly.

"Ground to *White Knight.* Contact *Space-ShipOne.*"

Still nothing.

"WhiteKnight to *SpaceShipOne."*

A few moments later, Mike, now desperate for a solution, decided to try the trim system again. This time, for a reason he couldn't understand, the left stabilizer moved.[*] *Oh my God — it worked,* Mike thought.

"*SpaceShipOne* to ground," Mike said, as a

---

[*] Unbeknownst to Mike and the folks in Mission Control during this flight, the sophisticated motor controlling the stabilizers was programmed to shut itself down to prevent overheating. The motor would work again after a two-minute cooldown period.

collective sigh of relief was heard in Mission Control.

Jim Tighe said quickly, "Back up stab trim, got it. Leave the trim alone."

Shane added, "The trim is adequate for landing."

Mike took in the majestic view outside his windows. He just might live another day. "Wow," Mike said slowly, his heart rate coming down as his eyes followed the curvature of Earth. "You would not believe the view. Holy mackerel."

He was now in his three to four minutes of weightlessness. He unzipped the left pocket of his flight suit to take out an item that he'd purchased at a convenience store en route from home to work: M&Ms. He unfurled a handful of the multicolored candies, which went into the air like a cool spray of water on a hot summer afternoon. The treats floated in the sunlit cockpit, clicking as they bounced off surfaces. Small pieces of a rainbow surrounded him.

"He is twenty miles south of the bull's-eye," Shane said.

"We need to head northwest," Tighe said.

Gravity took hold too soon, and the ethereal M&Ms clattered to the cockpit floor.

"Here come the gs," said Mike, his breathing labored as he came back through the atmosphere at more than five times the normal force of gravity. Parts of the outside of the plane were heated to one thousand degrees — body putty, cinnamon, and oregano as his shield.

"Coming down, gs past," Shane said when Mike was through the supersonic region. Then, as he looked up at the television monitor, he said, "Spaceship in sight."

"Mike, you doing okay?" Shane asked.

"Doing great," Mike said, though he was still anxious to have one of the chase plane pilots do a visual inspection of the spaceship. In a matter of minutes, the look-over was complete. Mike was told there was only a small buckling around the nozzle, but nothing compromising.

On the desert floor, the crowd caught sight of *SpaceShipOne* and erupted into the biggest cheers of the day. The spaceship looked tiny in the blue expanse, like a kite drifting way up high. Sally clasped her hands to her face and said, "Come home, Michael." People chanted, "Go, baby, go!" A man yelled: "This is what America is all about." No one knew just how difficult the flight had been.

The landing gear was extended. *SpaceShipOne* was coming home, flanked by its mother ship and the chase planes. The birdlike craft cast a dark shadow on the tarmac. Seconds later, it touched down to more cheers. A man drew more applause when he said of Mike: "That guy is a badass!"

In the cockpit, Mike let out a "Yeehaw!"

The space cowboy had lived for another day.

In Mission Control, Shane — the man who specialized in showing no emotion — wiped tears from his eyes. Paul Allen patted Burt on the back, and the two headed out to greet Mike. They had seen the data: 326, 327, and some thought it reached 328 — the 62-mile point. No one knew for sure, though, whether they'd officially made it to space. They needed to wait for the tracking data from a privately run group and a team out of NASA Dryden at Edwards Air Force Base.

Mike pulled himself out of the cockpit and stood unsteady for a brief moment on the runway. When Burt and Paul reached *SpaceShipOne,* Mike and Burt hugged like best friends kept apart for years.

"If we can do this, we can do anything." Mike beamed.

"How do you feel?" Burt asked.

"I've never felt this good."

"You did a super job," Burt said.

Sally ran to her husband's arms.

Then something happened that had never been seen after any manned spaceflight. With Burt and Paul sitting on the tailgate of a pickup, *SpaceShipOne* was towed right to the crowd line so everyone could see the rocket up close. Burt scanned the crowd. Suddenly, he was gone, running off into the rows of spectators. He returned with a sign he'd plucked from the crowd and handed to Mike. Before long, Burt and Paul were back on the tailgate as *SpaceShipOne* was towed back to the hangar. Mike stood on the top of the spaceship, holding the borrowed sign reading: "SPACESHIPONE GOVERNMENTZERO."*

Scaled soon got confirmation: Mike had made it to space — by a nose: 328,491 feet. He had passed the Karman line by less than 500 feet — one tenth of 1 percent of 62 miles.

In a ceremony that day, sixty-three-year-old Michael Winston Melvill, who didn't become a pilot until he was thirty and was a career machinist before meeting Burt Rutan, was awarded the first ever commercial astronaut wings from Federal Aviation Administration director Marion Blakey and Patti Grace Smith, associate administrator for commercial space transportation. That day, and for the days and weeks that followed, Mike was stopped by strangers and asked to sign T-shirts, coffee mugs, and anything people could find. He was deeply touched, and would say, "I think of myself as an ordinary guy who flies around the Mojave Airport."

For Burt, it was the culmination of a dream

---

* Mike said only half jokingly later that standing on top of the spaceship as it was towed was the most dangerous part of the day. The top of *SpaceShipOne* was slick, and he feared he would survive the flight to space only to fall on the Mojave tarmac.

that had begun in 1955 when he was twelve years old. He had been transfixed watching Wernher von Braun talk with Walt Disney on the television segment "Tomorrow Land" about his pragmatic vision of space. Von Braun went over the development of pressurized suits for space, John Stapp and his rocket sled, and man's ability to take great acceleration forces. Von Braun said, "I believe a passenger rocket could be built and tested within ten years if we follow a step-by-step research and development program." Later, the German scientist said something else that had always appealed to Burt: "I have learned to use the word 'impossible' with the greatest caution."

By late afternoon, campers were packed up and it looked like the wagons were rolling out of the Wild West. Scaled had opened its hangar to hundreds of invited guests to come by and celebrate the world's first privately manned spaceship. The rocket wasn't cordoned off; the point was to make space accessible. Guests checked out the cockpit and leaned against the ship for photos. They couldn't climb in, but many paused to imagine themselves in the backseat heading to space.

Behind the scenes, there was already talk of the XPRIZE and what had to happen to improve performance. The rocket had been pared down to its minimum weight for the flight and had barely reached the Karman line. To qualify for the XPRIZE flight, Burt's team would need to add four hundred pounds — the equivalent of two backseat passengers — to the spaceship. They would need to do what they'd done today — only better — and twice within two weeks. And they would have to do it soon. The first XPRIZE flight would be on September 29. For Burt, there wasn't a lot of time to bask in the excitement of the day. He needed a rocket with more power, and he had just the idea.

28
POWER STRUGGLES

After the June 21 flight, Burt started questioning for the first time whether his homemade craft could pull off the XPRIZE feat. *SpaceShipOne* had barely reached its goal of space, and pilot Mike Melvill had endured the flight of his life.

To the public, it appeared Scaled Composites had hit a home run, hosting an estimated 25,000 people for the first private spaceflight and certifying the world's first commercial astronaut. But privately, Burt was worried that the flight had exposed weaknesses in his spacecraft. During the ascent, Mike had ended up in airspace over the populated city of Palmdale — way off the two-mile-by-two-mile flight path approved by the Federal Aviation Administration.

Burt told his propulsion guys to pull out all the stops and do whatever they could to get more energy out of their hybrid motor in time for the first XPRIZE flight, called X1. Under the XPRIZE rules, the spaceship would have to carry the full six-hundred-pound ballast — the equivalent of a pilot and two passengers. Burt instructed Stinemetze and crew chief Steve Losey to put the spaceship on a diet by finding any way possible to reduce its load. The same was being done for the *White Knight,* in hopes the mother ship could fly higher before dropping *SpaceShipOne.*

But Burt had more on his mind than simply cutting pounds from *SpaceShipOne* and the *White Knight.* He had some shopping to do. For missiles.

If Burt couldn't get the oomph he needed from his hybrid motor, his idea was to strap Sidewinders onto *SpaceShipOne.* The small but mighty air-to-air missile, developed at the Naval Air Weapons Station at China Lake in the Indian Wells Valley, would get them where they needed to go. Burt had an old friend who was confident he could secure the Sidewinders. At the same time, Burt dispatched Brian Binnie to use his military contacts to find alternative suppliers as a backup. Brian, who had been overseeing propulsion development, concluded they would need *nine* Sidewinder missiles. Brian looked at the situation and thought, *This is getting scary.* Flying the spaceship already felt like a ride on a Sidewinder.

Brian then talked with folks at Raytheon, which made a large air-to-air missile called

AMRAAM (Advanced Medium Range Air to Air Missile). If Scaled went with those missiles, it would need only two of them. The problem was that Raytheon wasn't sure whether it was such a good idea to pull production away from the armed forces at a time of heavy demand to make missiles for an experimental spaceship program in the desert. Raytheon also feared that it would be sued if something went wrong.

Brian then went to Alliant Techsystems (ATK), which had produced a solid motor used for the Titan IVB rocket. ATK was happy to work with Scaled and sent them blank motor casings so the team could start figuring out the placement of missiles. Paul Allen's guys, Dave Moore and Jeff Johnson, got into discussions with the Scaled team about the logistics, testing, and pricing of missiles.

Burt's idea was to install the solid missiles inside the aft fuselage, alongside the hybrid rocket motor. In the past, missiles had been used to boost gliders, airplanes, and jets, and solid motors had been employed to propel rockets to space. But combining a hybrid motor system with solid missiles for a private space venture had never been done. The basic premise was to use the hybrid motor to get *SpaceShipOne* "around the corner" and pointed up. Then, when past the unpredictable transonic region, the pilot would ignite the solid motors to launch the ship like an arrow to its target. The risks were considerable. If one solid motor lit and another didn't, the asymmetric thrust would mark the end of *SpaceShipOne.* Solids, which carried their own oxidizer, also had a greater chance of exploding.

For Burt's plan to work, the solid missiles would have to be installed at the proper angle, and the exhaust vented so as not to melt parts of the vehicle. All of this required a major reconfiguration of the spaceship less than two months before the big flight. There was the all-important feathering system to think about, the landing gear, and other key parts tucked into the back of the craft. The addition of missiles would require a rewiring from the cockpit to the motors, so the pilot could arm and fire at the right time. Once solid motors were lit, they couldn't be turned off. A pilot could only hang on for the ride. There was also the question of how to test the new system. Would the first "test" be with a human on board for the XPRIZE flight, watched in real time around the globe?

Burt was brilliant much of the time, and right most of the time. But this was a rare instance in which his employees were universally opposed to his idea. For more than a year, the group had been preached to by propulsion experts that solids were dangerous and hybrids were safe. Now, practically overnight, they were talking about bringing the devil to the party.

While Burt and Brian were out shopping for surplus armed forces hardware, the propulsion team was working feverishly to figure out how to get more energy from what they had. Their reputations were on the line. *SpaceShipOne*'s rocket motor, developed almost entirely in-house by Scaled, was the largest nitrous oxide hybrid rocket motor ever flown and the only one to fly a human outside the atmosphere.[*]

In the meantime, Stinemetze and Losey scoured the spaceship for what could be removed. They looked at the vehicle piece by piece, even sanding for better aerodynamics. They switched out all of the steel fasteners for lighter titanium fasteners. They removed any extra material from the access doors, literally cutting out fabric between bolts. They removed all extra testing instrumentation typically carried by a prototype and looked for unnecessary wires. Anything overbuilt was cut back. Similar scavenging was done on the *White Knight* in the hangar next door. The mother ship was being wet

[*] eAc of Miami built the components on the front of the big nitrous tank — valves for fill, dump, and vent system. SpaceDev of Poway, California, built components on the tank's back, the valve, injector, igniters, controller, and the casting of the solid fuel.

sanded and fairings were added to reduce drag.

Elsewhere, the hybrid motor component vendor was studying its two options: add more propellant, or make the existing propellant more efficient. They were looking at increasing the motor's performance from its original requirement, set by Burt at 630,000 pounds-seconds — a measure of pounds of force and seconds of duration — to at least 700,000 pounds-seconds and possibly higher. Frank Macklin, the chief propulsion engineer for SpaceDev, had been working closely with Scaled's in-house propulsion expert John Campbell.* The pressure to come up with a solution was intense.

At the same time a solution was sought for the motor, Brian was in pursuit of a second chance. After a long day at work, Brian arrived at his home in Rosamond after six P.M., changed from his work clothes into his running attire, and headed out. It was still close to 100 degrees outside, and the desert town offered little shade. He'd had four knee operations, all stemming from a single judo injury in high school. Running was painful, but it was now his nightly routine. It was

---

* Tim Pickens had left early in the program to return to Alabama and at one point formed a team to compete for the XPRIZE.

about relieving stress and pressing on despite the pain. Ultimately, it was about getting back inside the cockpit of *SpaceShipOne*.

After his crash landing seven months earlier, on December 17, 2003, Brian had spent Christmas trying to find meaning in what had happened. He would wander back into the hangar on his days off and see the broken spaceship looking like an injured bird.

Though Mike's historic trip to space on June 21 was now in the record books, it remained unclear to Brian and everyone else who would pilot the X1 flight: Mike, Pete Siebold, or Brian. Making the call would be Scaled flight director Doug Shane. Brian thought of him as the oracle of Greek mythology who delivers prophecies where nothing is clear yet nothing is questioned. For clarity on the X1 flight, Brian took to hanging out by the office coffeepot. There was a constant shifting of alliances between the Oracle, the Master (Mike), and the Protégé (Siebold). Brian told his wife half jokingly that the shifting of loyalties made him feel like the reality show *Survivor* had set up inside Scaled Composites. Even Mike wondered about the way Scaled went about its pilot lineup. Shane generally kept the decision to himself until the day before a flight. Mike figured it was Shane's way of getting them all to train hard to be ready, but Mike worried that the approach divided the three pilots instead of bringing them together. Whatever the case, Brian was determined to be ready if the call came his way.

After a quick sequence of stretches in front of his house, Brian headed out on his regular loop from home to a small park with trees offering dollops of shade. He didn't listen to music, as he had his own track to play over and over. It was more of a movie, really. As he set out, the reel began: the four phases of piloting *SpaceShipOne.* The first phase began with him in the cockpit — at 48,000 feet, ready for separation from the *White Knight.* He pictured it: His thumb on the FIRE switch. Ready-set-FIRE! Five seconds of being in combat. Life as you know it erupting, shaking. Control or abort? Picture it. Stay calm, clear.

The next phase — transonics. More shaking, pitching, buffeting. Thunderous sounds. The third phase — the longest segment, maybe forty-five seconds. Nose up to eighty-five degrees. Stabilize. Start burning the oxidizer.

The final phase — endgame. Nitrous at end of liquid phase. Transition. Liquid moves through combustion chamber, followed by gas, followed by slugs of more liquid. Thrust difference is tenfold. Motor bounces between vibration and thrust. Hands shake, head shakes. Wakeup call for final part of flight. Thrust coming out of engine no longer aligns with axis of the vehicle. Body beaten up, shaken. Add fleeting aerodynamic control. Air is thin. Get it right the first time. An error at Mach 3 takes you to Palmdale — or somewhere you won't recover from. Slowing down, coasting to apogee, unlock the feather. Make it to space. Make it home. Not like last time. Nail this landing. Find redemption. Stop on the centerline. Spectators cheer.

Pounding the hot pavement on his nightly run, Brian almost forgot his discomfort — until he came to a stop in front of his house. Every jog was the same: he went through the four phases of the flight four times from start to finish. He never missed a run.

Then the mornings started early. Brian tried to get to Scaled before anyone else so he could grab time in the *SpaceShipOne* flight simulator. At first, he had found the sim "piss poor" — to use a Navy term — but liked the bells and whistles added of late. The sim had the same display as the spaceship, but not the stick force. The views in the sim were not representative of what you would see in the spaceship. Imagination was required, as there was no motion or sound. But a clever feature was added by Jim Tighe to reset each "flight" for different motor characteristics and external forces, such as wind shear. On the rare days Brian couldn't practice in the sim in the morning, he was in it during his lunch break. Sometimes he practiced with Siebold — who also badly wanted to pilot the X1 flight — and the two spent hours trading techniques and strategies to deal with problems that lurked around every corner. Brian and Siebold both worried that they were never going to fly the spaceship again, saying, "The only guy who's going to fly it is the guy who has flown it." That was Mike.

Brian now believed that the hit to his reputation in the wake of the crash landing wasn't justified. Since his December flight, he had discovered that the spaceship's controls had stiffened up in the approach to landing because of the dampers installed to prevent the elevons from fluttering. The dampers — similar in concept to dampers used on a car to smooth a driver's path over potholes — got cold on the December flight and stiffened, making it difficult to control the landing flare. From this flight forward, heaters were installed on the dampers to keep them from binding. Still, Brian knew the shop talk: he was the Navy guy who hit the runway the same way he landed on a carrier — full throttle to catch an arresting cable that didn't exist. That portrayal wasn't accurate, but Brian saw no point in protesting or defending. The only thing he could do was to prove the doubters wrong.

At work in early August, Brian ran into Mike,

who had been away from Scaled a great deal since his June flight, doing public talks and media appearances, including the Jay Leno show. Mike's new celebrity status drew old-time celebrities to Scaled. Everyone wanted to take a look at *SpaceShipOne.* One day Harrison Ford popped in, unannounced. Another day, it was Gene Hackman.

These days, Mike was basking in unofficial semiretirement, saying he was never going to top the accomplishment of becoming the world's first commercial astronaut. He didn't announce that he was out of the space travel lineup, and he was still doing flight tests. Yet in his mind — and certainly in the mind of his wife, Sally — the space cowboy had set aside his wings to spend some quality time at the ranch.

On this morning at Scaled, Mike sidled up to Brian, put his arm around his shoulder, and said he had an idea for him. He'd seen how Brian was living in the sim. He knew that Brian wanted back in the spaceship. Mike told him he was going to take him under his wing — in every sense of the word. The high school dropout would mentor the Ivy League–educated Navy pilot.

The two began training in Mike's Long-EZ, the two-seat plane that he and Sally had built by hand and he had flown around the world in formation with Dick Rutan. Mike and Sally considered the craft their own personal taxi, taking it to Alaska, to Death Valley for lunch, to see their kids when the mood struck.

Stinemetze went to work doing the math to produce a cardboard cutout mask for the Long-EZ that mirrored the inside of *SpaceShipOne*, with the small windows on the side and no visibility straight ahead. The idea was to make the cockpit of the Long-EZ feel like the cockpit of *SpaceShipOne*, with a similar window pattern. Burt offered to pay for gas. Mike, who thought Brian was a good pilot who lacked experience in small planes, said he would kick in new tires as needed, since they would be doing plenty of landings.

Mike told Brian that in many of his early test flights, he had to rely on the chase plane pilots to call out wheel height, to tell him how close he was to the runway when visibility was limited. He also said he would go out and make a dozen landings in any plane he could get his hands on. During training flights in the Long-EZ, Mike would station himself in the backseat, simulating wheel height calls on landing.

The Long-EZ was the perfect trainer. It flew toward the runway at the same speed as the spaceship. Mike instructed Brian to come in with an approach speed of 155 knots, then round it out, pull the stick back, and touch down at 115 to 120 knots. After Brian got the approach and speed right, they started honing the landing. After doing a minimum of ten landings in a row every flight, they would work on perfecting the landing. Master and apprentice went around and around, flying over Mojave some days, California City and Tehachapi the other days. At one point, after another round of landings and takeoffs, after the two put the plane away, Brian said, "I really appreciate what you're doing, but it may be all for nothing. I don't think they're going to let me fly."

Mike told Brian that he wouldn't be chosen if he wasn't ready. They kept at it, working every Saturday and Sunday. The Long-EZ went through two new sets of tires. Brian did eighty-four landings. The final ones were perfect.

In August 2004, just a month before the XPRIZE flight, Burt arrived at a meeting of about twenty people at Scaled. Unbeknownst to him, everyone in the room had been anxiously rehearsing how to tell their genius boss that they didn't think his missile idea was going to fly. Burt had always carried the team. It was his vision and his absolute daring that had pulled everyone through; if Burt believed, everyone believed. But now, for the first time, it was Burt who had been having doubts about his homemade spacecraft — and in his team's view, their inventive leader had been overcompensating for his rocket's propulsion problems.

Instead of merely lodging complaints, however, Burt's team members did something remarkable: Taking a page out of Burt's playbook, they'd come up with an ingenious solution of their own. Everyone — from the floor sweep to the crew chief — worked harder and sacrificed more. They made the spaceship and mother ship lighter, smoother, more aerodynamic. Pilots trained pilots. And the propulsion guys came up with what they believed was a missile-free solution.

As the meeting began, Burt's most loyal lieutenants, one by one, voiced their opinion that the missile option wasn't feasible, necessary, or safe. It was unanimous. Burt took the news with a mix of good nature and slight exasperation. After all, Scaled's mantra around safety was "Always Question, Never Defend." This meant to ask questions up front, don't defend when something goes wrong. After considerable back-and-forth, Burt said, "You are questioning me so much it makes me want to defend!"

Burt was still convinced that his missile idea was workable, and he had made a career of defying skeptics with his revolutionary, and very successful, plane designs. To him, the missile solution would take "simple calculations" to work. Yet he knew that time was running out — the missiles were still not procured — and his team had landed on a different type of a solution. Burt had always promoted moxie and ingenuity, and he welcomed ideas from any corner of the shop.

Talk turned to the non-Sidewinder solution. The answer, according to the propellant guys, could be found in one odd word: ullage. This is the space in a bottle, cask, barrel, or tank not filled with liquid, or there because of loss through evaporation. What *SpaceShipOne* needed, John Campbell explained, was more nitrous, less ullage. The empty space in the tank wasn't needed, because the oxidizer didn't heat up and expand as much as originally thought. The pilot always took off in the cool early morning and climbed to colder altitudes. The nitrous was spent by the time they were heading home, when things heated up. The team would just add more propellant, the same way a hiker adds more water to his pack when he needs to climb higher. While this solution meant adding weight, it was the right kind of weight.

"If we pull out all of the ullage and we fly a perfect trajectory," Frank Macklin said, "we're going to make it."

The trick, the team acknowledged, was that nitrous oxide's liquid density was highly dependent on temperature. It was critical when warming nitrous to allow for sufficient ullage for the liquid nitrous oxide to expand into. Campbell and Macklin dealt with this through pressure-relieving devices. Macklin said, "We'll have no ullage. We'll fill this to the brim and then we'll monitor the heck out of the temperature to ensure we don't over-pressurize the tank." Also, the density of nitrous oxide goes up significantly when the temperature is lowered. They would do what they could to load it a little cooler.

Macklin and Campbell were confident that their hybrid motor was up to the task. They knew the temperature profile on the ascent and devised a new process by which to load the nitrous into the vehicle with very little ullage. Campbell figured out how to insulate the tank more efficiently. He then built a small air-conditioning unit to blow cool air on the ends of the oxidizer tank. He and Macklin also devised a memorable — and admittedly primitive — way of mixing the nitrous. They tested their systems out on the Mojave runway at two A.M., the time they would load nitrous before an actual flight. Campbell would climb into the driver's seat of an old tractor and begin pulling the trailer with the nitrous tank. Nitrous stratifies in unwanted ways if left to sit, becoming warm at the top and cold at the bottom, making the pressure higher at the top. Under the new zero-ullage plan, getting the right pressure was more important than ever. The nitrous needed to be mixed before loading. So out on the runway, floodlights trained on them,

Campbell said to Macklin, "How about if I just get it going a bit and mash on the brakes?" Campbell's idea was to cruise along in the old tractor as fast as it could go and then suddenly stomp on the brakes to slosh and mix the nitrous around. Macklin would run alongside the trailer checking pressure gauges. Without millions of dollars to spend like NASA, or years to launch a study, the two men had tractor, trailer, and an open Mojave runway. They would stay out until the first signs of dawn. Their shaken and stirred system was working.

Tests showed that zero ullage made all the difference. The propulsion experts had no doubt that if flown correctly, the spaceship would shoot right past the Karman line. They had been able to work fast, thanks to an approach pushed by Burt from the beginning. Normally, motor development begins with subscale testing and moves on to larger testing, and finally there is testing of the real and heavy hardware. Burt, however, had wanted them to do flight hardware testing from the start. He wanted to test what would be flown as fast as possible. The reconfigured zero-ullage hybrid motor was now cranking out between 750,000 pounds-seconds and *1 million* pounds-seconds.

As the Scaled team readied the hardware, Peter Diamandis and the XPRIZE team began transforming Mojave into something that was a cross between a giant fairgrounds and a sporting event. They had three months until their pieced-together $10 million prize vanished, and they needed to see history made not once but twice. Peter now had a dedicated team and an army of space-loving volunteers.

Meanwhile, also in the weeks before the first XPRIZE flight, mission director Doug Shane announced that he was putting in a new system for the pilots: There would be a primary pilot for X1 and a backup pilot. The backup would step in if the primary pilot wasn't ready or got sick or injured. The lineup was announced: Pete Siebold was the pilot for X1, and Brian was the backup. No one was named for X2. Brian was okay with this; he was just happy to be included.

But not long after the lineup was announced, in mid-September, Siebold had a closed-door meeting with Burt. He had serious news. He told Burt that he was taking himself off the *SpaceShipOne* flight program. His wife had just had a baby. He was having lingering stomach pains. And he felt the zero-ullage plan was unsafe and insufficiently tested.

Although the news came at a critical time — just eight days before the X1 flight — Burt wasn't entirely surprised. He had watched Siebold struggle to light the motor after being dropped from the mother ship on his first powered flight in May. Siebold also wasn't comfortable with the handling qualities of the spaceship.

Burt believed that had Siebold been in the cockpit on an earlier flight when the navigation display went black, he would have aborted the mission. Mike had continued to fly by looking out the window, saying afterward that it was a "blessing" because he had gotten to see the sky go from blue to purple to black. He never considered shutting down the motor. Siebold was talented, but he was more careful than Mike. He was an engineer *and* a pilot, and sometimes those things conflicted. He was not as much of a cowboy. In Burt's mind, test pilots had to be cowboys. They had to climb into a cockpit with a leather football helmet on, ignore the fact that they had broken ribs from an accident the night before — as Yeager had done — and fly right through the sound barrier like a bat out of hell.

Mike was in Texas doing a demonstration of the Proteus when he got a call from Doug Shane saying he needed him to hustle back to Mojave.

Arriving at Scaled, Mike dropped his things in his office. He found Burt, Doug, Pete, and Brian in Burt's office. Sally was standing in the hallway. She hadn't been told what was going on, but had figured it out. Doug delivered the news matter-of-factly. Pete was out for X1. Mike was in. Brian sat stunned, thinking, *When did the backup pilot become not the backup pilot?* To avoid having the press get wind of the fact that Pete was out because he wasn't comfortable with the safety level of the program, Scaled would stick to the story that Pete was sick. There was no time to re-assure Pete and no time for more tests; they had an appointment in space the very next week.

Little else was said, and the meeting ended. When Mike emerged, Sally looked at him imploringly. Mike nodded. Sally knew he was back in the flight program, despite assurances she'd received from Burt that Mike had done enough already. She and Mike had believed that the dangers of *SpaceShipOne* were in their rearview mirror. Now they were a week out from the XPRIZE flight, and Mike hadn't been seriously training. He'd let down his guard — as had Sally — and wasn't mentally prepared. Mike knew how important this flight was to Burt and the whole team. He also knew that Sally believed he had pushed his luck in the spaceship as far as it would go.

Brian left the office early, afraid of what he might say if he stayed. Arriving home, he stared at his running shoes. For an hour, he did nothing except walk around in a defeated daze. He picked up a book by one of his favorite authors, Dean Koontz. Koontz wrote: "Sometimes life is not about how fast you run the race or with what degree of grace. It's about perseverance. Finding your feet and slogging forward no matter what." As the light in his home dimmed, he made a decision. He went and found his running clothes. Brian was heading back out.

29
In Pursuit of a Masterpiece

Dumitru Popescu and his small team were ready for their big event, the first high-altitude launch of a major civilian rocket from Romania. They arrived at the Air Force base at Cape Midia next to the Black Sea on Wednesday, September 1, 2004, and planned to launch within nine days. Their rocket, the Demonstrator 2B, was fifteen feet long and made entirely of composite materials. The rocket fins were emblazoned with the XPRIZE logo. Almost one hundred journalists from four countries would be on hand to cover the flight.

Popescu had launch clearance for two days only, September 8 and 9. Adopting an Apollo 13 imperative, he told his wife, Simona, "Failure is not an option." The launch would be televised live. Popescu and his team had poured all of the money they had into this launch. They were now flat broke and would be unable to try again anytime soon. Popescu had always believed that the XPRIZE was going to make history. He wanted to be part of it, but in his mind, that would happen only if he launched hardware he'd built — and only if he launched it before XPRIZE front-runner Burt Rutan made his first flight, now just weeks away.

After assembling the launch complex, rehearsing procedures and emergency response, testing firing control systems, and giving members of the media an up-close look at the rocket, Popescu and his team were ready for liftoff on September 8. The Demonstrator, gleaming with Popescu's attention to aesthetic detail, had a reusable, all-composite engine. It stood on its platform, smooth white rocket and tall white gantry set against the deep blue waters of the Black Sea. Popescu would watch from closed-circuit television inside an old bunker built during the First World War. Simona Popescu was two miles away, playing host to ninety-six journalists.

Everyone was in position, with the countdown set to begin. Systems checks were done and hopes were high. Suddenly — there was a problem. A hose was leaking propellant. The 70 percent hydrogen peroxide fuel was leaking into the motor and valves. The launch was aborted. Popescu and his wife hustled to reassure the media and VIPs that the launch was being postponed for only a day.

Behind the scenes, though, things unraveled fast. In addition to the hose malfunction, Popescu and his team learned of a problem with the fuel pressure. Next, Popescu was told by Romanian air force officials that a storm was approaching, with winds expected at more than 40 miles per hour and pummeling rain. The military officers were not comfortable with a launch, fearing for the safety of spectators. The nearest major town of Constanta, the oldest continuously inhabited city in Romania, was just thirteen miles away. There was also the matter of all the journalists near the site. Things could go bad quickly.

Popescu and Simona were staying in a small house on the air force base. Neither could sleep that night. "The Romanian Space Agency is going to smell blood," Popescu said, thinking about the unrelenting criticism, innuendo, and undermining he had faced from cosmonaut Dumitru Prunariu. If he didn't launch, Prunariu would win — at least that's how it felt. Late in the night, Popescu ventured outside to study the sky. Trees were being bent by the wind. Then came thunder and lightning. Standing under the dark and hostile sky, he thought, *This is the worst night of my life.* At the first sign of dawn, after about an hour inside tossing and turning and in his futile attempts at sleep, Popescu headed back out for a walk. He needed to think. He reflected on the work of one of his heroes, Hermann Oberth, who took a teaching job in

Romania in 1930 and received his patent for a liquid-propellant rocket from the Romanian Patent Agency. Oberth left Romania for Germany, where he became a mentor to a young Wernher von Braun, who would call Oberth "the guiding light of my life." Oberth had to leave Romania to make his mark. Popescu wondered if he would make a mark in the country he had always called home.

As Popescu watched an enormous sun rise behind his rocket, he was approached by the commanding officer of the base. Popescu braced for more bad news — and he got it. He was told that one of his engineers, Andrei Comanceanu, had left the base in the night to go into the small town of Novadari. He had been caught earlier that morning trying to jump back over the wall. Fortunately, Popescu was told, the armed guard who spotted him, recognizing that he was an engineer with team ARCA, didn't fire a warning shot. Popescu apologized and went to find his friend, who had been a year behind him in aerospace engineering school.

When Popescu saw him, Comanceanu fell to his knees and began to cry. He said he was sorry, but he was not able to handle the stress. Popescu, skinny, unshaven, and with dark shadows under his own eyes, propped his friend up and told him they were going to launch and he needed to stand proud. "Two people built the first flying machine," he reminded him of the Wright brothers. "We were brave enough to get this far. We are not giving up." Privately, Popescu berated himself as "probably stupid or something" for refusing to give up.

With little time to spare, he told the now calm Comanceanu that he had come up with an idea for how they could launch without endangering anyone. In the night, when he wasn't out eyeing the angry skies, he had run simulations on what would happen if they used less fuel, given the strong winds that threatened to turn the rocket into a missile. "We reduce the fuel level from one hundred percent all the way to nineteen percent," Popescu said. "The rocket will have a higher velocity off the launchpad, and it will be less affected by the wind." They would not achieve the 28,400 feet they had projected, but they would launch. He told his friend, "When you're in this business of building rockets, you can be a hero or a loser in a matter of seconds. We are going to be heroes today."

Their launch window would close after four P.M. Journalists were reassembled and ready for a noon launch. There were delays. One P.M. passed. Then two P.M. Then three P.M. Whitecaps tumbled on the Black Sea. Just minutes before four P.M., Popescu, back in the bunker, ordered the launch to commence. Everything moved fast from there — go! go! go! were the commands.

Finally, it happened. The Demonstrator shot off the pad. In that moment, time slowed for Popescu. He ran outside. His rocket flew above him, soaring like an arrow shot straight up. Strangely, it felt like it was right over his head. The rocket looked black, not white, and the plume was the color of the storm clouds. This was Popescu's first-ever rocket launch, and it was perfection. It was his. All of the work, struggle, ridicule, and doubts suddenly felt worth it. Flying with its limited fuel, the rocket made it to 4,000 feet before it began to fall back. It crash-landed in the Black Sea. There were cheers all around. The normally reserved military brass hugged Popescu like a brother. It was the purest moment of Popescu's life.

A day later, Popescu learned that Turkish fishermen, fishing illegally in the waters off Romania, had found parts of the Demonstrator rocket. They wanted money in exchange for what was found. The fishermen had watched the news, learned Popescu was involved in a $10 million competition in America, and figured he was rich. Popescu's next source of laughter came when he read several stories in which cosmonaut Prunariu was quoted as saying that the flight was a big deal only to Popescu and his team and "had no real significance." It didn't escape Popescu that these words were coming from a man who had all the government's resources at his disposal — yet had launched nothing.

Popescu was broke, but he had created a company and a brand. He had flown a rocket as a part of the XPRIZE. "We have the energy, the inertia," he told his team. "We will not give up. What we are doing is revolutionary."

John Carmack and his team from Armadillo Aerospace headed out to their one-hundred-acre parcel in Mesquite, Texas, optimistic that it was the perfect day for flying. The skies were blue and the wind was calm. The team planned to fire its forty-eight-inch-diameter rocket, which just days before had hovered in the air for sixteen seconds with no hint of a problem. After arriving at the site and setting up, the Armadillo team loaded the propellant and pressurized the vehicle. Carmack, Russ Blink, Neil Milburn, and a half dozen others holed up a safe distance from the unmanned, cone-shaped rocket, which was ready for a full-throttle test. John's wife, Katherine, was nine months pregnant and had to miss the launch.

Yet there was a hitch: the engine wasn't warming up. Carmack used about 20 percent throttle, and nothing happened. He gave the engine more slugs of propellant until the temperature began to increase the way it should. Until now, the engine had been operated only at hover thrusts. There had been some apprehension about what would happen at full throttle, but with Burt Rutan's first XPRIZE flight on the horizon, it was time to proceed if they had any chance of competing with him.

Finally, happily, they had ignition and liftoff. The rocket shot straight up and was on an impressive trajectory toward 600 feet. The only sound came from grasshoppers in the hot Texas sun. A second or two later, before the rocket reached its targeted height, the ship began to rotate at around fifty degrees per second. This was a problem.

Russ Blink watched, aware that the team — in their crisp white Armadillo team T-shirts — had never crashed anything big before. There'd been a crash of a lander from around forty feet high. But this was very different. The vehicle was falling tail-first. Just before impact, it turned on its side and hit the ground sideways, though with a little tail first. The 450-pound fiberglass tank, pressure still in it, was punted from its impact point about two hundred yards away. Dirt and debris were sprayed across the field of grass and sunflowers.

This was not what team Armadillo had hoped for in the weeks leading up to Rutan's XPRIZE flight. They had hoped to fast-track their test flights.

When the dust settled and the stunned silence ended, Carmack and the team proceeded to the crash site. There was a sizable crater flagged by mangled parts. A few pipe fittings were intact. The fiberglass tank was ruptured. The onboard camera was destroyed, but it appeared the tape had survived surprisingly unscathed. The team spent hours searching and digging for remnants, taking photos of what was recovered. Some parts were splayed open, wires severed and protruding, while other pieces were mangled together from the high-speed, head-on crash. They hauled whatever they could find back to the shop for a thorough postmortem, and used a plasma cutter to open up the engine to figure out what went wrong. They studied the telemetry. They learned that they had blown about two thirds of their propellant out onto the ground during the engine warmup, when Carmack was urging it along with slugs of fuel. Their vehicle had run out of gas. They were using a type of engine that had a prolonged start-up sequence involving the slow heating of the catalyst material. Clearly, this was too difficult to control. They needed a different type of engine for future launches.

Not long after the crash, Carmack wrote in an online post: "We gave up our last glimmer of hope to have a vehicle ready" for the XPRIZE. He added, "The only stacked-miracles path that could have worked was to have perfect test flights with the 48″ diameter vehicle, then build out the 63″ diameter carbon fiber vehicle and have perfect flight tests with it, then get some combination of influential senators and popular support to lean on the AST [office of Commercial Space Transportation] to fast-track our launch license and launch site work. Not a very likely scenario." Despite the loss of the $40,000 vehicle, the team remained in good spirits, calling the collected rocket parts "Armadillo droppings." And Carmack noted of his latest video game, "It's a good thing *Doom 3* is selling very well."

But when Carmack thought about it, he realized that Armadillo had fallen out of the XPRIZE running the day they were forced to give up on using the 90 percent hydrogen peroxide formula that was central to their rocket design. The vendor had refused to sell the propellant to them for fear of liabilities and because Armadillo wanted relatively small quantities. The Armadillo team then had to spend a year developing a mixed monopropellant. Carmack believed that if they'd had an uninterrupted supply of 90 percent hydrogen peroxide, Armadillo would've had a shot at the XPRIZE.

By mid-September, the building of a new and improved engine and vehicle was under way. Carmack was taking what he had already learned about structuring, reliability, and simplicity in his coding for rockets and applying it to his work in software. Yet he loved the hands-on aspect of rocketry, of taking a bar of solid metal and working on it until he had a gleaming and useful part. He would follow the XPRIZE flights in Mojave, but he was undeterred in his own goal of accessing space. He told his team, "We'll see if we have a one-hundred-kilometer vehicle ready for testing this time next year."

Carmack was also staying true to his hacker roots, and to the hacker creed. He was intent on sharing all that he learned. He would continue to build everything from scratch, from the bottom up. He believed in the beauty that could be attained through working with one's hands, whether on a keyboard or with a soldering iron. Results mattered more than rules, and everything should be free — not free of charge, but free to change. He was determined to play a part in the hacking of aerospace, in taking it away from the government and putting it into the hands of the people.

In the United Kingdom, XPRIZE contender Steve Bennett was in the process of building Nova 2, following his successful launch in 2001 of Nova 1 from Morecambe Bay. The Nova 2 would be bigger and fly higher than Nova 1, standing 57 feet high and reaching a target of 120,000 feet. Bennett saw his new rocket as the key to his future manned space program.

He did ground systems tests on the Nova 2 capsule with a pilot and two passengers sealed into the cabin for two hours at a time. Bennett took the capsule to Florida to have it fitted with parachutes, and then to Arizona for piloted drop tests from 13,000 feet. Everything was working. Around this time, though, he found his work sidelined by the unexpected.

Without warning, a story appeared on the BBC Web site alleging that the self-taught rocket maker was designing a death trap, and that his spaceship was nothing more than "a converted cement mixer." Bennett believed that the author of the BBC piece had a vendetta against him. He spent twenty months and 250,000 pounds on a lawsuit against the BBC. Eventually, the BBC issued an apology to Bennett and paid his legal fees. But that wouldn't bring back the two years lost to litigation. He did find solace in an education program he'd started that was aimed at introducing the Nova 1 to schools across England. He would bring rocket models and rocket scientists into classrooms and talk to the kids about the importance of following their dreams. "It's kind of an American thing," Bennett would tell students. "Americans are brought up to dream big things. It's the land of opportunity. We don't do that enough in this country, and we should. You should."

Even though Bennett had resumed building Nova 2, it was clear to him by late summer of 2004 that Burt Rutan was within arm's reach of the XPRIZE. Rutan was smart, had a great team and a billionaire backer. Bennett had heard that Paul Allen put $25 million into Rutan's space program. No one else came close to having that kind of funding. But everything was still relative, Bennett thought. NASA would have spent that kind of money on blueprints alone.

Bennett had met Rutan in 2003, when the XPRIZE invited teams to Los Angeles to show their models and share some of what they were doing. The visit included a field trip to El Segundo, California, where Elon Musk had started SpaceX in an empty 75,000-square-foot hangar. One of Bennett's favorite moments was on the bus ride to SpaceX, when he overheard Rutan talking on his phone in a low tone about who was attending the event. Bennett smiled when he heard Rutan say, "Bennett's here."

To be sure, the XPRIZE was a competition, but there was also a shared mission and friendships forged. Brian Feeney of the da Vinci Project was there, and had the nickname "Flying Brian," because he was always "just days away from flying." Bennett saw the full-size model that Feeney had built. He talked with Carmack's team of volunteers and thought they had cool hardware. He was also impressed with Pablo de León of Argentina and his plans for suborbital flight. Bennett remembered Dumitru Popescu telling him how they were so short on cash that at one point one of his workers resorted to closing his eyes while welding because he didn't have proper eye protection. Bennett met fellow Brit Graham Dorrington, an aeronautical engineer who was one of the first people to register for the XPRIZE but hadn't gotten far beyond paper studies for a vehicle called the Green Arrow.

All in all, Bennett was proud that he had followed his dream, despite the years of challenges. He could have kept his secure job at the toothpaste plant, avoiding financial troubles, tensions with his family, and media hits. But like an artist in pursuit of a masterpiece, he had no choice but to go on. He was a rocket maker, and that was that.

In September 2004, Peter Diamandis invited Bennett to attend Rutan's first XPRIZE flight. Bennett wished that his own rocket was the one ready to soar, but that didn't change the fact that he had been the first XPRIZE contender to fly hardware, even making history in his country. And the specter of someone else's winning the XPRIZE wasn't going to stop him from completing his own suborbital ship. In the not too distant future, he would shuttle passengers to the start of space, just for the fun of it. For Bennett, and for fellow competitors like Popescu and Carmack, this was just the beginning.

The XPRIZE was already shaping a legacy — even before its first official flight.

30
ONE FOR THE MONEY

It was late September 2004, more than ten years after Peter hatched the XPRIZE idea in Montrose, Colorado, and eight years after the private race to space was announced to great fanfare in St. Louis. That memorable night, in the city that Charles Lindbergh put on the aviation map, legendary airplane designer Burt Rutan had stood at the dais and revealed his dream of making a home-built spacecraft. Burt was now ready to display that dream — and so was Peter. All eyes were on Mojave, where the XPRIZE competition was finally set to begin.

Peter's army of volunteers descended on the small desert town. The troops were culled from space organizations and university engineering departments and managed by Loretta Hidalgo, who had attended International Space University and also ran Peter's "special ops" team, a smaller group that did everything from pick up dignitaries at the airport to help mainstream journalists understand the technicalities of this space story. Another ISU graduate from years before, Harry Kloor, had reentered Peter's life and was pitching the XPRIZE story to dozens of media and television outlets. It was critical to Peter that the event represent more than a competition and a prize. He wanted to see a global shift in the way people thought about space travel. For help with this, Peter called on his longtime friend Dan Pallotta, a California entrepreneur who pioneered multiday charitable events, including the AIDS Rides. Pallotta knew how to create pop-up tent cities for a massive audience. Pallotta, like Peter, was born in 1961 and reared on the magic of Apollo.

Peter, Bob Weiss, Pallotta, and Stuart Witt, director of the Mojave Air and Space Port, spent long hours going over the message of the XPRIZE that they wanted conveyed to the world and the minute-by-minute schedule of events. They had grids of the airport, VIP and hospitality tents, souvenir booths, food vendors, Jumbotrons, emergency personnel, and contingency plans, including those based on the number of medical emergencies expected given the anticipated crowd size. (Two heart attacks were expected for a crowd of thirty thousand.) Weiss was applying all he'd learned directing Hollywood movies to the scene in the Mojave Desert. Everyone, from the organizers to the onlookers, understood that this reality show could end in victory, defeat, or despair.

Everything was coming together for Peter — and at the same time. After a decade of battling the Federal Aviation Administration — a bureaucratic quagmire — Peter, Byron Lichtenberg, and Ray Cronise had gotten approval for their company, ZERO-G, to offer the first parabolic gravity-free flights to the public. Cola company Diet Rite was sponsoring a twelve-city tour of the ZERO-G plane, with media stops along the way. Peter's life had been divided between introducing the world to the thrills of zero-gravity flights and planning for the XPRIZE.

The race for the XPRIZE was shaping up to be one of the biggest news stories of 2004. Peter, who had gambled before and lost, now had all his chips on Burt Rutan and *SpaceShipOne*. The hole-in-one contract with XL Specialty Insurance would expire in three months. At that point, the $10 million prize money would dry up, and he had no Plan X, Y, or Z. After Scaled's successful June 21 flight, Peter was called to Santa Barbara for a meeting with the insurance executives. The executives, apparently figuring out a tad late that it had been unwise to bet against Burt Rutan, wanted to offer a new deal: they would lower the altitude requirement, from 100 kilometers to 50 kilometers, and proposed that the insurance payout be reduced by half, to $5 million. Peter would have none of it. "You guys are ridiculous," he said on his way out the door. "You are writing a check for $10 million."

Peter arrived in Mojave on the Monday before the Wednesday X1 flight. He was joined by his parents, Tula and Harry, his sister Marcelle, and someone else near and dear — the woman he was falling for, Kristen Hladecek, an artist and a vice president of creative advertising at 20th Century Fox. It was as if Peter had needed to get the XPRIZE to a secure place before he could find a secure relationship. He was joined by his close friends and allies Erik Lindbergh and Gregg Maryniak, Adeo and Elon, Bob Richards and Jim Cameron, Diane Murphy, who was running marketing and publicity for the XPRIZE, and Harry Kloor, his friend from early ISU days, and the Ansaris. With no one else stepping forward as a title sponsor, the XPRIZE had been renamed the Ansari XPRIZE.

Mike Melvill drove from his home in Tehachapi to Mojave. In the months leading up to this big day, he had been doing more media interviews than rigorous training. He thought he was done with *SpaceShipOne* flights. There had been only eight days to prepare after being summoned back into the cockpit. He had spent time in the simulator, an apparatus that the instinctive pilot had never taken seriously. Mike also did strenuous workouts on his bicycle. Luckily, Mike was already in great shape, and this was not exactly his first rodeo. Getting ready now was more mental than physical. He needed to put his test pilot's Teflon suit back on.

As he drove to Mojave, he looked out toward Edwards Air Force Base and wondered, *What will this day bring?* This was the land of coyotes and Joshua trees, dry lake beds and long runways, where B-24s had thundered in the sky and pilots in P-38s had strafed their practice targets in training before heading off to battle in World War II. The skies were layered with the memories of pilots and planes that had gone before. It was where the turbojet revolution began with the Bell XP-59A and the Lockheed XP-80 Shooting Star, where high-testosterone test pilots competed to see who could fly higher and faster. It was where supersonic flight became almost commonplace and some of the coolest-looking planes shredded the sky. It was also where some machines broke apart, where brave pilots lost their lives in deadly spins. This was the reality of the skies here. Mike wanted Scaled's little rocket program to be a part of that grand history. He was not ready to join the bravely departed.

Just as Mike arrived at Scaled in the early morning hours before his September 29 flight, he saw how dusty Mojave was turned into a tent city. Music pulsated down the flight line. Parties were being held, with dancing and DJs spinning tracks. Mike took it all in and then headed inside. Security crews were already out on the runway, and the sky was dusky pink. The early arrivals delighted in watching private planes come in and land, like birders thrilled to spot exotic feathered species. Among those early arrivals was Peter. The first thing he saw was a bird of a different feather on the runway. It was an airplane splashed with Virgin logos, perfectly positioned in front of all the TV cameras. *Impressive ambush marketing,* Peter thought. He had pitched Virgin chief Richard Branson not once but twice to fund the XPRIZE. Now that they were at the starting line, Branson was all in. Branson had paid Paul Allen $2 million the day before this flight to have the Virgin logo painted on the tail end of *Space-ShipOne.* Then Branson's people had called airport director Stuart Witt late in the night before this first XPRIZE flight with a last-minute request: make sure the Virgin logo was visible from the runway when the sun came up and the television cameras were on. There was only one airplane in Mojave — besides *SpaceShipOne* — with the Virgin logo. That was the *GlobalFlyer,* sponsored by Virgin, designed by Burt, and soon to be flown around the world by Steve Fossett. While Peter was still at his hotel, Witt had called some of the Scaled crew, and together they pushed the *GlobalFlyer* out of the hangar and onto the runway, in prime viewing position for the crowds and media. Witt had anticipated Peter would be startled to see Virgin front and center. Peter was also trying to get the best visibility for his XPRIZE sponsors — something he'd been working on for years.

Out on the runway, Peter looked at the logo-decorated plane with a mix of respect and disbelief. The XPRIZE was spending a small fortune hosting this event — not knowing whether there would even be a second flight — and now it felt like a Virgin commercial. Peter also found it ironic that he had met with Paul Allen's lieutenant, Dave Moore, several times in a bid to get XPRIZE funding, but no one had let Peter in on the little fact that Allen was actually financing *SpaceShipOne*.

But Peter refused to let anything dampen his spirits. He considered Branson brilliant and was cheered by the news that the Virgin chief was investing in commercial space. A few days before the X1 flight, Branson and Burt had held a press conference in London for the British press announcing that Virgin was forging a deal to buy the technology behind *SpaceShipOne* with the goal of sending ticketed passengers to space. Peter wished Branson had come in earlier, before everything was done, but he appreciated that he was in now. Space needed talented and deep-pocketed believers.

Inside Scaled, the preflight briefing was under way and lasted for close to an hour. The hybrid motor was ready. The nitrous oxide had been stirred and was now loaded into the spaceship, with temperatures carefully monitored. Crew chief Steve Losey had gone over the spaceship inside and out. He had made a promise to Sally long before that he would never put Mike in a plane unless it was safe to fly. Losey stayed with the plane through the night, like a groom with a prized racehorse. Even the paint job had been perfected for the big day. Dan Kreigh, an engineer who had structural responsibility for the spaceship — taking Burt's designs, making any fine-tune adjustments, and then instructing the shop on building — was also Scaled's in-house artist. For *SpaceShipOne,* he and Brian Binnie had worked out a patriotic theme. Because the plane was going to space, Kreigh became obsessed with finding a subliminal graphic design idea. He wanted *SpaceShipOne* to look like it had flown through a magical cloud of stars — and brought some back. The *White Knight* would carry the red stripes to complete the image. Kreigh and his wife, Rojana, would touch up the plane in the middle of the night, cutting all the vinyl decals and stripes and painstakingly applying them. Recent nights had brought them to the hangar to apply the Virgin logos. They had also affixed the smaller decals of the various XPRIZE sponsors that had kept the dream alive along the way: the St. Louis Science Center, Champ Car World-series, M&Ms, and 7UP.

After the preflight briefing, Mike headed into the locker room to finish getting ready. Sally was there, and soon Burt appeared holding a small vial that looked like a sand dial. He asked Mike to put it in one of his pockets for his flight. Burt said it was a bit of his mother's ashes. Irene Rutan, diminutive but forceful, had always been Burt's biggest supporter, driving him to his model plane competitions when he was a child and tallying how many of his plane designs flew in each year to Oshkosh. Burt wanted his mom to take another journey with him, this time to space. Mike looked up and down the front and sides of his green flight suit. Sally pointed out that the new suits had no pockets, so Mike tucked the vial into his helmet bag. He and Sally then made their way out to the tarmac. Photographers snapped pictures, and well-wishers appeared from out of nowhere to shake Mike's hand and offer salutations. Dick Rutan was there as a commentator for CNN.

It was showtime. Peter took to the stage and looked out at the crowd. His parents were front and center.

"Ladies and gentlemen," he began, "we are at the start of the personal spaceflight revolution, right here, right now. It begins in Mojave, today. What happens here in Mojave is not about technology. It is about a willingness to take risk, to dream, and possibly, to fail." Peter said he believed that *SpaceShipOne* would reach space today, and again within two weeks.

Anousheh Ansari followed Peter onstage. "This is an exciting day for all of us," she said, "a day our dreams will come true. I'm grateful to Burt, and to all of the teams that competed. Without their courage and willingness to achieve the impossible, this dream would never happen."

"I believe we are changing the future of space exploration," she added. "By being here, we are supporting the XPRIZE teams and foundation. We are no longer just dreaming about going to space. We are making it a reality. Each of us has a responsibility." Anousheh knew a thing or two about dreams coming true. Early that morning, she had run into her childhood hero, William Shatner, Captain James T. Kirk. She was speechless when she saw he was wearing an ANSARI XPRIZE baseball cap.

Not far away, out on the runway, Mike and

Sally embraced. Sally was shaken by the belief that luck eventually ran out. The two held each other close, and Sally again pinned their lucky horseshoe on Mike's sleeve. After a few more moments, Burt pulled Mike aside for a final pep talk. Like a coach reviewing the game plan with his quarterback, Burt reminded Mike that the rocket had never carried such a heavy load. Mike needed to get the rocket turned vertical as quickly as possible. Mike nodded, and the men hugged.

Mike climbed into the spaceship. He felt the horseshoe pin on his sleeve and closed his eyes for a brief calming moment. Behind his seat was a container holding all sorts of mementos thrown in by Scaled employees. There were dozens of wedding rings, bundles of coins, photos, and personal talismans.

Soon, the *White Knight,* coupled with *Space-ShipOne,* began rolling down the runway. In the *White Knight,* Brian Binnie was again the "bus driver," and Stinemetze was in the passenger seat. A consummate team player, Brian still had mixed emotions about today's flight. He should be in the cockpit of *Space-ShipOne,* he thought; his piloting abilities had been unfairly maligned. Yet he had deep respect for Mike, not only as a pilot but also as a person. Over the past few months, Brian had relentlessly trained in case his name was called, but he couldn't escape from a nagging feeling that his hard work would be for naught — and that Mike would end up piloting both XPRIZE flights.

The crowd went wild when the *White Knight* took to the air. An hour later, as commentators, including Peter and Witt, addressed the crowd from various stages, and onlookers aimed powerful lenses at the sky, *SpaceShipOne* was released from the *White Knight.* X1 was under way, watched by a global Webcast and live television. Even the hotshots at Edwards Air Force Base were tuning in; they were testing a high-resolution missile-tracking camera that would observe the flight from takeoff to landing.

Seconds after the release of *SpaceShipOne,* Mike, in helmet and aviator shades, said, "Armed-fire."

"Good light," he said, thrust back into his seat. The rocket was on its ascent.

In the crowd on the desert floor, a man pointed to *SpaceShipOne*'s contrail and said, "Look at that sucker move! Man!"

Cameras from outside the spaceship beamed images to the Jumbotrons. Witt, onstage, said, "Cross your fingers and say a prayer. Here we go, guys."

In the cockpit, Mike's breathing was heavy.

In Mission Control, Burt sat next to Doug Shane, and Jim Tighe was a row back. Paul Allen and FAA heads Patti Grace Smith and Marion Blakey were also in the room.

"Twenty seconds, Mike," Shane said when the motor was twenty seconds into the burn. "Thirty seconds coming."

"Doing good," Mike offered, sounding upbeat.

"Coming forty seconds," Shane said. "Forty-five seconds."

Mike, wanting to get as close to vertical as he could, pulled hard on the stick, briefly exceeding 90 degrees. He stopped the rapid pitch up at 91.6 degrees by gently pushing the stick forward, which got him back to 90 degrees. Now the wing was generating no lift at all, and the plane began to oscillate slightly in yaw, then it pitched up 8 degrees and simultaneously yawed 15 degrees.

Mike now had a new and serious problem. He was spinning — slowly at first, then faster like a figure skater in a parallel spin. He was going up — fast. But it was roll after intense roll.[*] Mike told himself that the spinning would eventually stop. If he cut the engine, the bid to win the XPRIZE would be over.

[*] Detailed analysis by Scaled determined that the rolls resulted from a mild thrust asymmetry, which could not be offset by pilot inputs at a flight condition of low directional stability. This flight condition had not been tested on previous flights. The low directional stability occurs only at high Mach numbers and at very low (zero or negative) angles of attack.

He would have to ride it out.

Witt, seeing the rolls in the sky and on the screens, said, "Uh oh, uh oh. He's in a roll." His fellow commentator said, "It does not appear to be a scripted maneuver."

Silence fell over the crowd. Richard Branson looked over at Sally Melvill. Her anguished expression said it all. Branson dreamed of private spaceflight, but knew this was pushing the limits. Paul Allen watched, feeling himself age twenty years in a few stressful moments.

Dick Rutan was talking with Miles O'Brien live on CNN when the rolls began. Dick said to O'Brien, "This is probably not how Mike planned it." Dick looked up at the sky and thought that there was a real chance that Mike would not recover.

From the stage, Peter had the same feeling he'd always had watching manned rockets fly: rapture, awe, and uncertainty. He stood up and said, "Mike is going to be out of the atmosphere soon, and he has a reaction control system he will be able to use to nullify the roll. He'll be okay." Then he said it again, "He'll be okay." Peter's mom, Tula, wasn't so confident. She said a prayer, asking for everything to be okay. A bad outcome for the pilot would also be a bad outcome for her son. Witt could be heard saying, "Come on, Mike. Come on, Mike." He told the crowd, "Communications with air show center are shut off. These are tense moments, folks. We are waiting to hear Mike is okay." A downlink camera showed the view of Earth from *SpaceShipOne*.

In the cockpit — the crowd couldn't see this, only Mission Control — Mike held the stick and kept his focus on the instruments before him. He was going straight up at more than 2,000 miles an hour. The cockpit was a strobe, spinning dark-light dark-light, with the brightness of the sun and the blackness of space flashing through the cockpit windows. If he looked outside, he got disoriented fast. He had a roll rate of 283 degrees per second. He found that if he concentrated on one thing on the instrument panel, his disorientation abated. Mike stared at the rate of roll indication, a small display of digital numbers showing degrees per second of rotation. The numbers were the size of typewriter keys, and Mike had to look closely to read the display. He held the stick against the left stop, and the left rudder pressed forward as far as it could go, opposing the roll motion to the right.

Reprieve came in the slowing of the strobe, like a figure skater opening her arms after a tucked spin. Now he had longer periods of sun and space, dark and light. Mike had gone out of the atmosphere and was spinning at 160 degrees per second. During his years of flight testing, Mike had deliberately spun planes. He didn't know until now that you could spin while going straight up. Now that *SpaceShipOne* was out of the atmosphere, the aerodynamic controls no longer had any effect. The control stick and rudder pedals became "loose" and were completely ineffective with no air to press against.

But in short order, the spinning began to ease even more, and communication with the air show center was returned. "He held on," Dick Rutan said to O'Brien. "That's courage — and skill."

With the telemetry returning to normal, Shane asked Mike how he was doing. This time, Mike answered tentatively, "Okay."

Jim Tighe said Mike would need a lot of the reaction control system to orient the ship. "Start the feather up," he said.

Seventy-seven seconds after the release of *SpaceShipOne,* the motor shut down at 328,000 feet — the targeted edge of space — and Mike was still shooting up. There was clapping in Mission Control, and cheering on the Mojave floor. Sally clutched her hands together. It wasn't over until Mike was beside her.

Mike put the feather up and activated the reaction control system, which consisted of four pairs of small jetlike nozzles mounted near the nose, with four more pairs on top and under the wingtips. He used up almost all of the compressed air in both the A and B bottles to finally bring the roll rate to near zero.

When he was sure that *SpaceShipOne* had achieved a sufficient altitude, Mike reached under the instrument panel for a small camera and took pictures out the oval-shaped windows. The next three to four minutes, marked by weightlessness, would be the calmest stretch of the trip. As he had done on his first flight to space, Mike admired the blurry blue sapphire below. But this second trip made him marvel, more than ever, at the beauty down on Earth: his wife, his son, everything he held dear.

The feather was up, roll rates down, and the reaction control system was working. *SpaceShipOne* was at 330,000 feet, and finally 337,000 feet. Now it was time to make it back down. He got ready, knowing he was about to fly three times the speed of sound and five times the force of gravity.

On the desert floor, Witt said, "Coming back down. Okay. Here it comes. The gs build. There's a rapid rate of acceleration. He's coming in now at Mach 2.2, higher. Some rumbling and buffeting. G rise. He's ballistic right now."

Moments later, Witt couldn't help but break into a smile, now that *SpaceShipOne* was no longer spinning and Mike appeared back in control. He believed there always came a moment in life when you were asked to pull it all together — all you had learned, trained for, all you had deep inside. When he'd come to Mojave to interview for the job, the offices reminded him of a 1940s Marine Corps operations center with louvered doors and dust flying in. But he saw a place where people could be given permission to take extraordinary risks outside the reach and arm of the federal government.

Looking at Mike flying some 60 miles up, Witt said, "Can you imagine the technology required to bring a spaceship from 328,000 feet back to landing? It's a goose-bumps day. Mike now has tail feathered to reduce the rate of descent."

He continued, "Now they will need to re-configure it back to a plane. Looking for feather. Feather down. Okay. Now the crowd can pick up sight of *SpaceShipOne*. This space plane, this rocket plane, is now a glider. We now have a glider back inbound for the money run."

After a pause, Witt added, "This is flight test at its purest form. It's risky business. There's the boom — the sonic boom! Folks, Mike Melvill's comin' home."

But Mike wasn't done with his air show. Feeling joyful as hell to still be alive, the sixty-four-year-old wanted to squeeze one last bit of dare-devilry out of *SpaceShipOne*. He had already done twenty-nine spins — why not make it an even thirty? Mike pitched the nose of *SpaceShipOne* down and picked up speed. The pilot of the Alpha jet, on his wing, knew exactly what the cowboy pilot was doing. The pilot exclaimed, "Mike's going to do a roll!" Jeff Johnson, sitting in the back of the jet, began to laugh. Mike got to around 190 knots, pulled the nose up, and began the roll.

In Mission Control, Shane could see what Mike was setting up for. This was *not* on the flight card, and he had the head of the Federal Aviation Administration standing behind him.

At the end of the roll, Mike let out a "YEE-HAWWW!"

Shane realized that he needed to make Mike's audacious maneuver appear planned, so as not to arouse the suspicions of the FAA folks. He said coolly, "Roll evaluation complete."

The flight above the start of space was confirmed. X1 was achieved. As soon as the red-white-and-blue space plane was on the runway, Burt was there to greet his wingman. After dashing off to shake hands with spectators pressed against a rope line, Burt returned and jumped in the back of the truck to begin the towing of *SpaceShipOne.* Seated between Richard Branson and Paul Allen, Burt made jokes about what would happen if a billionaire was accidentally bounced off. Mike was back on the top of slippery *Space-ShipOne* — happy to have good balance from his earlier days as a gymnast. He waved to the crowds, and singled out his sweetheart.

When he was back down on the ground, Sally looked at Mike and said, "Now we can grow old together."

Peter and his girlfriend Kristen watched as *SpaceShipOne* was cheered on like the best float in a ticker-tape parade. Kristen didn't have a background in engineering or even an interest in space. When she met Peter, he was living in a small and dimly lit two-bedroom apartment — one bedroom doubled as his office — and driving an old BMW. He told her stories about the XPRIZE and suborbital flight and tried to explain something called hole-in-one insurance. He told her of the CEOs he'd pitched and the endless noes he'd heard. Kristen was drawn to Peter because he refused to give up on a dream that most people said was not going to happen. What she fell for was the purity of his intentions and his almost naïve soul. As the cheers continued for the improbable *SpaceShipOne,* its brave pilot, and ingenious designer, talk on one of the stages turned to the one remaining flight needed to win the $10 million prize. But in Kristen's mind, the star of the day, the one who had won, was Peter.

Burt and his Scaled team did not have much time to celebrate. They worked through the night of the first XPRIZE flight to figure out what had caused the twenty-nine rolls and how to prevent the dangerous situation from happening again. But there was also a new glitch, this one on the ground.

"I'm out," Mike said.

Hours after his X1 triumph, Mike revealed to Burt and Doug — Paul Allen was also present — that he would not be flying X2. He was firm about his decision. He had done enough, and he believed that Brian deserved a chance. "I've been working with Brian," Mike said. "I've trained Brian. He is ready."

Mike noticed that Paul looked incredulous. Brian was the guy who had crashed his spaceship in December, only ten months before. Shane also couldn't believe that their go-to guy would not be available for this critical flight. Burt, to his credit, kept quiet. He had flown in dangerous planes and understood there comes a time when you say enough is enough. Mike felt he had already done it: he had the world's first private astronaut wings. He'd been the first person to fly to space alone since Alan Shepard in 1961. And he'd been the only guy to fly to space stick and rudder. Now he'd done it twice.

The next afternoon, on September 30, the Scaled folks met again to talk about the X2 flight. Burt, fond of staging important flights on anniversaries of big aviation events, had chosen October 4 as the date for the second flight. This was the forty-seventh anniversary of the day the Soviet Union launched Sputnik and started the government-sponsored space race.* Now the goal of the Scaled team was to create a new anniversary, for private space-flight.

The meeting was winding down at around six P.M. when Steve Losey said he'd like to finish going over the spaceship and then turn it over to the propulsion crew. He needed one more piece of information to complete his logbooks. This required an important bit of data: the weight of the pilot who was going to fly. He asked Burt, "Who is going to fly?"

Brian was at the table, having worked with Jim Tighe and Pete Siebold, reviewing the telemetry and flying the sim. He was unaware of Mike's bombshell the day before. Shane was across the table from Brian, and Burt was at one end, opposite Losey. Burt deferred to Shane.

Brian waited for the answer, feeling his life was in the balance. Would he be given this

* The beach-ball-size Sputnik 1, the world's first artificial satellite, was launched by the Soviet Union on October 4, 1957, and jumpstarted the space race with its ninety-eight-minute orbit of Earth. One month later, on November 3, the Soviets launched Sputnik 2 with a dog named Laika inside. The press used terms like "Muttnik" to describe the canine cosmonaut, who died in space.

chance, or would he be remembered for his missed putt? He was fifty-one years old. This opportunity wasn't going to come around again. Yet for all his training and dedication, Brian felt in his gut that the nod would go to Mike: the pilot who has flown gets to fly. This notion was reinforced when Shane wouldn't even look at Brian.

Then Shane said flatly, "Brian's the pilot."

Brian did his best to take a page from the Oracle and show no emotion, to make it appear that he had known all along. But inside, he was sprinting with perfect knees. He had made the perfect landing on the carrier in the dark of night. He had chipped in for a birdie on the eighteenth green of Pebble Beach. He saw his wife's smile, as beguiling now as when they'd met so many years before.

He had three days to make sure he was ready for the most important day of his life.

31
ROCKETING TO REDEMPTION

In his living room, Brian Binnie watched on television as the irrepressible Burt Rutan talked to CNN about the XPRIZE flight scheduled for the next morning, Monday, October 4. The Scaled team was not just going to hit a "home run," Burt told the CNN interviewer. They were going to hit a "grand slam." Brian couldn't help but think, *Ohmygod, isn't the bar high enough already?*

Brian paced the room, his emotions bouncing between fear and optimism. When the interview ended, Brian turned off the TV. He settled into the couch, where he was spending the night so his in-laws could have the master bedroom upstairs. His wife, Bub, had thought the arrangement would be best for him, allowing him to wake at 2:15 A.M., make his coffee, and be out the door early as needed.

But just as he started to doze off, he was jolted awake with some new worry. The family dog, an oversized golden retriever named

Tanner, trying to claim his usual territory on the couch, wasn't helping either. Instead of counting sheep, Brian tried going over the numbers of his flight. He'd been in the simulator almost nonstop since finding out at six P.M. Thursday, three days before, that he was the pilot for X2. There on the couch, he visualized the course. He was inside the cockpit. Dropped from the *White Knight,* he positioned *SpaceShipOne*'s nose at about sixty degrees. To avoid the spins that Mike had endured, Brian would fly at between eighty-one and eighty-seven degrees.

He dozed off again, numbers and images swirling in his head. Then he'd wake up, panicked he'd slept through his alarm, only to find his dog's paw across his face. At some point, he got up and wrote down the goals of the flight:

1. Get to 100km = $10M
2. Don't leave the atmosphere out-of-control = (Richard) Branson's future interest
3. Beat the existing X-15 altitude record = Burt's personal desire
4. Land with grace = My personal salvation

Then he wrote, "1 & 2 are mandatory. 3 is more in the nice to have territory & 4 is all about me."

Even in his half sleep, he was lucid enough to know he was in limbo, caught between reality and dreams, past and future. With the ticking of the clock, he was moving closer to clarity. The gift of this flight was in the possibility it presented. The cloud of sand that had enveloped him after his crash landing had dissipated quickly. The cloud of doubt remained.

His wife had been praying for him more than usual. A devout Catholic, Bub had jumped into action when she learned he was getting a second chance. She started a prayer chain that by now had stretched across the globe. She made sure the prayers being offered were the same, and that they were specific. "God likes specifics," she said to her fellow Catholics. "Be specific in your prayer." The prayer she sought for Brian was this: "Safe flight up. Safe flight down. Safe landing."

Brian put his faith more in American ideals than in biblical commands, but he welcomed help from any corner. At some point in his fitful night, he even said his own prayer, promising God that he would be "forever grateful" for a successful flight start to finish.

When the alarm beeped at 2:15 A.M., it was almost a relief. Brian was already up. He wanted to be at Scaled by 3:00 A.M. Once outside his house, he inhaled the cool fresh air. The night was clear and silent. He gazed at the stars and spotted the Milky Way. The sky seemed to be beckoning.

On his fifteen-minute drive to Mojave, he turned on the AM radio and landed on a show called *Midnight in the Desert: Late Night Paranormal.* The show's host, Art Bell, was talking about the "other dimension" that exists beyond the reach of most people. As Brian listened to this odd early morning show, his mind revisited an encounter he'd had a few days after his December 17 flight of *SpaceShipOne.* It was one of the strangest things that had ever happened to him. He had been awake in bed, waiting for his 5:45 A.M. alarm to sound, when suddenly the bedroom lit up like a television had blinked on. Only it wasn't the TV. He got out of bed and went to the window, where slivers of bright light peeked through the curtains. His backyard was lit up like daylight, while the rest of the neighborhood was dark. There were bubblelike shapes — the size of beach balls and volleyballs — roaming, airborne, playful looking. After only a minute, this magical performance of translucent shapes faded back into darkness. He stood still for several minutes, not wanting to move or speak. He didn't believe in the paranormal or in extraterrestrial beings, but he knew what he had seen. It was beyond understanding. For whatever reason, the moment gave him hope at the time and buoyed his spirits now.

Turning in to the Mojave Air and Space Port, Brian looked again at the sparkly sky. What did the heavens know that he would soon find out?

Before five A.M. in nearby Palmdale, about 1,500 schoolchildren boarded buses from three different pickup sites to be driven to Mojave to watch *SpaceShipOne,* a junket that had been dreamed up by Stuart Witt, Peter, and the XPRIZE planning team. The once-in-a-lifetime field trip was funded and organized — permission slips, insurance, chaperones, and buses — by a local real estate developer, R. Gregg Anderson, who saw an opportunity to place kids in a moment of history that would inspire them for the rest of their lives. Anderson also wanted to see local youth introduced to the aerospace industry and to glimpse how the team at Scaled Composites had achieved a global audience. Witt had said to Peter in one of their early planning meetings, "You see pictures of Kitty Hawk and there are no children." Peter thought the idea would create a "Lindbergh moment" for a new generation. Instead of Le Bourget, they would have Mojave.

Upon arrival at the spaceport, the kids were escorted to the flight line, where they watched, waited, and cheered at the sight of the *White Knight.* The mother ship approached and then did a hairpin turn in the direction of the mountains.

Near the runway, Peter took a moment to appreciate every detail: the crowds, reporters, celebrities, billionaires, kids, astronauts, NASA and FAA administrators, his family, the cloudless blue sky, and the strangely beautiful *White Knight* mated with the spaceship. He didn't know what today's flight would bring, but he was struck by how far they'd come. As his childhood friend Scott Scharfman had reminded him: he had launched a space prize without the prize money; he had wanted to do something privately that only governments had done; he had believed it was possible to make a spaceship that wasn't thrown away after one use; and he believed that if he offered a prize, teams would come. One more flight was all that was needed. The other teams founded to capture the XPRIZE were continuing to build; the dream of space was not going away if the prize was won. The passion would persist. Rockets and hardware were being built in Romania, England, Argentina, Texas, and elsewhere. Richard Branson had secured a deal to develop SpaceShipTwo, using Rutan's technology and feather design. Peter's friend Elon Musk was taking on the aerospace establishment with his private rocket company, and former SEDS chapter head Jeff Bezos was beginning to apply his massive wealth to space. This was the inflection point, Peter believed, in which the downward spiral of manned spaceflight turned around.

Peter watched *SpaceShipOne.* He had three treasured books in the ballast box behind Brian's seat: *The Man Who Sold the Moon; The Spirit of St. Louis,* given to him by Gregg Maryniak; and *Atlas Shrugged,* a gift from Todd Hawley. He and Todd had that favorite line: "All that lunacy is temporary. It can't last. It's demented, so it has to defeat itself. You and I will just have to work a little harder for a while, that's all."

After the preflight briefing, Burt reminded the crew, "This is the money flight." *He keeps adding on the pressure,* Brian thought. *A grand slam! The money flight!* Brian got into his flight suit and headed to the hangar. He stepped on the scales holding a small bag that he planned to bring on board. He was five feet eleven and weighed 165 pounds, having lost weight through all of his running and stress. He had two American flags that he wanted to fly to space — one a heavy-duty cloth flag and the other polyester — and an assortment of things handed to him at the last minute by colleagues. The official ballast boxes were already full and included ten thousand pennies added by Dave Moore to make weight and have as space souvenirs. Brian's weight allocation was 200 pounds, and he was slightly over. He reluctantly opted to bring the lighter polyester flag and, taking a cue from Charles Lindbergh, tore unnecessary pages out of a hefty flight checklist. He was in trouble if he didn't know the flight checklist by now. He wore multiple pairs of socks to protect his feet from the minus-seventy-degree air on the other side of the rocket. Only three layers of carbon fiber separated his toes from the outside world. He wasn't going to pare back on his socks. Finally, when he'd made weight, Brian began the walk to the plane.

On the way, he was intercepted every few feet by a procession of well-wishers. Brian finally gave up trying to stay in his game-day zone, and now understood one reason for sequestering astronauts before a flight. Test pilot Chuck Coleman, who had survived more crashes than anyone could remember, and who would pilot the chase plane today that would guide Brian toward his landing, said, "Meet you at fifteen thousand feet." Robert Scherer, who owned the Starship chase plane, said solemnly to Brian, "The world is with you. The heavens are with you." Jeff Johnson, who knew of Brian's determination and efforts to get back into the cockpit, embraced him. Brian saw Erik Lindbergh and Peter Diamandis, who told him that he was "the day's Charles Lindbergh," the one who was going to make history.

Heading his way next was his mother-in-law, Maria Anderson, looking well rested and holding a cup of McDonald's coffee. The woman had never been shy, and was not easily thwarted. Brian eyed the coffee and his mother-in-law with equal wariness. Before he could say anything, she threw her arms around him in an expression of good-luck and do-right-by-my-daughter. What came next happened in a rush: the tight mother-in-law hug, the hot liquid flowing on his neck and down his back. *Hot,* he thought, *just as advertised.* The contents of the sixteen-ounce cup soaked his white T-shirt under his flight suit. After the shock and awe, as he called it, he somehow found humor in the moment, pointing out that she had generously saved about four ounces of the sweet-smelling vanilla-flavored stuff for herself. Aerodynamicist Jim Tighe assessed the situation in terms of weight added by the coffee and its possible impact on the altitude reached. He informed Brian that he was "wearing about four hundred feet of apogee," close to the margin that Mike had made it to space on his June 21 flight.

Brian continued his march toward the plane. Bub was now at his side, wearing a shirt that she had made with the pattern of the American flag. She kissed him, removed her wedding ring, and tucked it into his pocket, saying, "Think of me being with you up there." She had her crystal blue rosary with her and would feel the beads as Brian flew. Her prayer group was similarly armed and ready.

Soon, Sally Melvill approached. She offered Brian their lucky horseshoe, which he gladly accepted. Then there was Mike, mentor and friend. Brian knew Mike had gone to bat for him to get this flight, but he didn't know that Shane had told Mike this morning, "We'll soon know whether this was a good decision or not." But Mike was confident and told Brian, "You can do this. I know you can do this." That was exactly what he had said when they were out in the Long-EZ. Mike added, "We're going to have a great day." For this flight, Mike was the bus driver, piloting the *White Knight.*

Finally, there appeared Burt — boss, friend, golfing buddy. He looked excited rather than nervous, leaned into the cockpit, and delivered his advice — in golfing terms — for how Brian should fly: "Take out the driver, swing smooth, and go long." Seconds later, the door closed and Brian was alone, back in the cockpit that held his dreams and fears. Instead of experiencing some profound moment of illumination, Brian was overcome by something else — the smell of French vanilla coffee.

At 6:49 A.M. local time, the *White Knight*

reached 130 miles per hour and lifted off runway 30. Brian had an hour-long ride underneath the *White Knight* as it flew its approved pattern and climbed to altitude. Brian hadn't known how he'd feel being back in the hot seat, waiting for his moment to fly. But he was ready. And he was calm.

Exactly one hour later, at 7:49 A.M., the *White Knight* was at 47,100 feet. Brian pushed the control stick forward to prepare for the release.

Mike called the release: "Three-two-one — release," and Stinemetze pulled the lever to drop *SpaceShipOne.*

"Released, armed, fire," Brian said.

"Holy crap, that was close!" Stinemetze said of the spaceship's quick turn upward. Brian had charged out of the gate.

A handful of seconds later, Shane in Mission Control said, "Rates look good and low. Doing okay?"

"Doing all right," Brian said. This time, he knew the bull he was riding. He expected to be shaken, tugged, and beat up. He waited for the noises that sounded like the start of World War III. His breathing was steady. He had this.

"Little lateral oscillations," Brian said.

Shane said, "Copy. Thirty seconds. A little nose-up trim. Forty. Trajectory perfect."

Mike added, "Brian looks great."

On the Mojave floor, crowds held cameras

to the sky. They had seen the separation, where the *White Knight* veered to the left and the rocket shot straight up, leaving a thick white vertical contrail. The wind was calm, the visibility perfect. Stuart Witt was back providing commentary, as was Gregg Maryniak. Today, the cheers were, "Go Brian!"

It was time for the motor's transition from liquid to gas, when the nitrous oxide begins to run low in the oxidizer tank. Brian focused on exiting the atmosphere without any rolls.[*]

"Three-fifty, recommend shutdown," Shane said. The altitude predictor showed that Brian would end up at 350,000 feet if the motor was shut down now. This already put him safely past the Karman line.

Brian wanted more. He was going to squeeze every molecule of energy from the motor. He started a slow-motion response, hoping to see 370,000 feet on the predictor.

At eighty-four seconds, the engine finally shut down. Mike had flown the engine to seventy-seven seconds on X1 and seventy-six seconds on June 21.

---

[*] The initial thrust of the motor, the "kick," ranged between sixteen thousand and eighteen thousand pounds before tapering off to about eight thousand pounds before entering the liquid to gas transition phase, when the shaking and vibrating commenced at about one minute into the burn.

Shane formalized it: "Engine shut down."

"Feather up," Brian said. "Feather green." Then, looking out at the black sky, he said, "Wow. I'm upside down." He was in space. And he'd gotten there without a hint of a roll.

During his journey past the Karman line, Brian had felt strangely *guided,* and not by Mission Control. The feeling was as clear as this morning's sky. Now, away from the pull of gravity, he gazed at the pale blue curvature of Earth against a black dome.

"Feel good?" Shane asked.

"I'm feeling great," Brian said. "Wow, it's quiet up here."

"Copy that."

"Better get the camera out."

"Roger that."

Brian took pictures and then released a paper model of *SpaceShipOne* that someone had given him before the flight. The paper spaceship effortlessly took its own gravity-free flight around the cockpit.

Then Brian heard Burt's voice: "X-15 record."

In Mission Control, Burt pumped both fists in the air. Paul Allen patted Burt on the back. Brian was more than 10,000 feet above the highest altitude ever reached by the X-15, which was 354,200 feet in 1963. This was the boss's grand slam.

Burt was studying the numbers. The engine

had shut down at 213,000 feet, going Mach 3.09, and *SpaceShipOne* had continued like a ball tossed in the air on its own momentum. But the amount of that momentum was a surprise. The spaceship kept going upward until it reached 367,550 feet.

"Outstanding," Brian said.

Having reached its top altitude, *Space-ShipOne* began its quick descent. Brian could still smell the vanilla-flavored coffee.

"Here come the gs," Shane said.

"Five gs," Brian called.

Burt took notes on a legal pad and alternated between looking at Shane and studying the screen.

"Peak gs are done, coming through seventy-five thousand feet," Shane said to applause in Mission Control.

"Feels a little loosey-goosey now," Brian said of the spaceship.

"Copy," Shane said. "Get the roll trim back to neutral as you defeather."

At around 63,000 feet, Brian retracted the feather. Mission Control watched anxiously as the tail booms went from their upward bend of sixty-three degrees slowly back down to locked position.*

---

* Burt reduced the feather angle from sixty-five degrees to sixty-three when they installed a bumper insert to reduce the hammering when the actuator came to a stop.

"Feather lock," Brian said to more cheers in Mission Control. Burt's ingenious design, taking inspiration from the dethermalizing model planes of his youth, had performed flawlessly. The moment was not lost on Burt, who wiped tears from the corner of his eyes. After all, Burt knew that his entire space travel program would succeed or fail based on how the feather worked. Many experts had told him that the feather was unworkable, that it was sheer lunacy. But once again, as he had done all his life, Burt found breakthroughs where others saw nonsense.

With only the landing remaining, Burt and Paul Allen headed out onto the tarmac to join Richard Branson, Peter, Erik Lindbergh, and the pilots' families. At one point, Burt, Paul, and Richard could all be seen pointing up at the sky with their left hands.

Nearby, Bub was working her prayer beads, believing all of the prayers were guiding Brian home. Their kids held up signs: "GO DAD!"

The wind socks on the runway were hanging calm. Mojave was green for landing.

Brian extended the landing gear for the moment of truth. Would he stumble again at the finish line? In his heart and soul, and after his breathtaking experience in space, Brian knew the answer: He was going to make that perfect stop. He was going to let his confidence take over — and vanquish his doubts once and for all.

Brian focused, not like a quarterback who needs to throw a Hail Mary pass, but like a painter poised to make the perfect last stroke. He heard the call: "Looking good, right down the middle."

SpaceShipOne was gliding in, the motor now spent. There was no wind, no buffeting. Brian didn't see the cheering crowds or satellite trucks or emergency response vehicles. He saw only a centerline. The little spaceship, its nose clouded with stars, was close to touching down.

From the chase plane, Coleman made the calls: "Two hundred mph, one hundred, looking good."

Brian thought about all those practice landings in the Long-EZ, about all the training runs, about all the work in the sim. Brian kept it coming, leveled off, the small shadow of his ship sweeping the runway below. There was no aircraft carrier, no arresting wire. This was his canvas.

Three-two-one-down. Softly, on the centerline. It was perfect.

"Congratulations, Brian!" Shane said. The Oracle was showing some emotion.

In the mother ship, Mike couldn't help himself, offering another "Yee-haw!" — this one for Brian. Then, with his voice choking, Mike added, "Proud of you, man."

Brian responded to his mentor, "Thank you, Mike."

■ ■ ■ ■

Out on the runway, Burt reached Brian and congratulated him. "How 'bout them apples! You got the X-15! This is so cool."

Sally and Bub jumped into a truck on the flight line — the wife of a test pilot knows to have keys to a response car — and headed straight for Brian. When their truck got close, Bub jumped out and ran the rest of the way. She climbed into the cockpit and said, "You did it!" over and over. Brian held her close and blinked back tears. He didn't trust himself to speak yet. Elton John's song "Rocket Man" blasted across the spaceport: *I'm a rocket man/Rocket man; Burnin' out his fuse up here alone.* He'd nailed it. He'd earned his astronaut wings.

As the crowd continued to cheer, the schoolchildren were shepherded to their buses. They still had a day of classes ahead. When a reporter for the local *Antelope Valley Press* stopped and asked a group of middle schoolers whether they wanted to be astronauts, all hands shot up — no hesitation.

There was singing, dancing, and the spraying of champagne. Several of the XPRIZE contenders were there, including Pablo de León, standing next to Loretta Hidalgo and

George Whitesides.[*] "This is the beginning of a new era," de León said, tears in his eyes. "There is a before day and an after day. Things will never be the same after today. This is the end of the government's monopoly over manned launch." The celebration moved to an area in front of Scaled. Peter stood on a makeshift platform with Burt, Paul Allen, and Richard Branson. Erik Lindbergh and the Ansaris were close by. Peter's voice carried to the end of the long runway and back:

"For forty years, we have watched as spaceships have flown," Peter said. "Crowds of people had to be moved five miles away while those few astronauts got on board and ignited those engines. Today, *SpaceShipOne* has landed, and stands not five miles away but five feet away."

Peter continued, "We are at the birth of a new era — the personal spaceflight revolution. It is our pleasure to announce today in Mojave, California, that *SpaceShipOne* has made two flights to one hundred kilometers and has won the Ansari XPRIZE."

When Peter returned to the crowd, he stood with his family and Kristen. His parents might not understand orbital versus suborbital, and they couldn't begin to know all of

* George Whitesides, Peter's roommate during the Blastoff days, would go on to become Virgin Galactic's CEO.

the planning, heartache, and passion that went into making the XPRIZE happen. But in their own way, Tula and Harry were the ones who could understand best just what this meant to him, to the boy who had raced around with the energy of a rocket and could not be contained. The boy who sat them down for lectures on space and kept note cards on every episode of *Star Trek*. The teenager who stashed explosives in the house and made experimental rockets that often turned into missiles. The college student who started student space clubs and a space university. The grad student who finished medical school to please them, but always had his own dreams, including one that came true today.

Tula allowed, jokingly, that she should probably stop asking Peter when he was going to practice medicine. Harry told Peter that he had brought great pride to the family name. To Peter, this day was a beginning. As he listened to Burt, he kept thinking one thing: *We lit the fuse of a new Space Age.*

Burt addressed the crowd and said, "If you look at the twelve months after Yuri Gagarin was flown to space by the Russians in 1961, that first year, there were five manned spaceflights. Now, this year — *forty-three years later* — how many spaceflights are there? There are five. We did three of them with our little program, and the Russians did two. Our little team was able to show American exception-alism."[*]

Brian, standing next to Burt, was up next. He spoke forcefully: "I wake up every morning and thank God I live in a country where all of this is possible. Where you have the Yankee ingenuity to roll up your sleeves, get a band of people who believe in something, and go for it and make it happen." Just hours earlier, Brian's fate was uncertain. Now he was the 434th human to go to space.

Later that day, after most of the crowd had pulled out of Mojave, Peter, Paul Allen, Burt, Mike, and Brian and the Scaled team gathered in a conference room. They had a call coming in, from President George W. Bush.

[*] Burt believed that the *SpaceShipOne* program would be historic and wanted every Scaled employee to be able to tell his or her grandkids that they played some part in helping design, build, or test it. There were eight people involved in the initial design and planning; twenty-five people involved in building *White Knight* and designing and testing the rocket; and about sixty people working on both *White Knight* and *SpaceShipOne,* the avionics and simulator. During the year leading up to the flights to space, there were thirty people directly involved in the space program. In all, Burt estimates that about eighty people had a role in the success of the world's first private manned space program.

The president, aboard Air Force One, noted that his plane was not nearly as cool as *SpaceShipOne,* and not nearly "as exciting as Mike's and Brian's flights."

Mike and Brian were side by side — Mike the world's 433rd astronaut — across from Burt and Peter. The rest of the crew huddled close. After some pleasantries about the program, President Bush said, "The sky of Mojave is very big. And you've got very big dreams there." He added, "Thank you for dreaming the big dream."

That night, Stinemetze, Losey, and the others lingered over beers. There was a quiet and calm they hadn't felt in years.

"People talk about the magic of the early days of the Apollo program," Stinemetze said. "That's what it feels like happened here. All the right people just showed up to play a part. Every person was key to the success. We had magic."

Not far away, as *SpaceShipOne* was being put away for the night, Burt had told the team, "You put your hearts and your talents into this. This is not an end. It's just a *very good* beginning."

In a month, Burt, Paul Allen, and the team at Scaled would head to St. Louis for the awarding of the $10 million check. Then *SpaceShipOne* would take to the skies one more time, under the mother ship's wings, toward its final destination.

32
HALLOWED COMPANY

It was an hour before closing time in the Milestones of Flight Hall in the Smithsonian National Air and Space Museum. Peter was there by himself, having stolen some time while in Washington, D.C.

He had come here over the years seeking inspiration, often following frustrating meetings with officials at NASA or the Federal Aviation Administration to discuss International Microspace, Angel Technologies, or ZERO-G. He would arrive at the Air and Space Museum numb from battles with bureaucracy, in need of a reminder of the rewards that came with risk.

While the Infinite Corridor at his alma mater remained Peter's place of limitless possibilities, this hall of flight was a validation of dreams achieved.

As soon as he walked into the sunlit hall, he lost himself in the stories behind the machines. There was much he knew, much more he wanted to learn. So many untold stories of late sleepless nights, fights over funding, arguments over design. Standing under the orange Bell X-1, he thought of what it must have taken to build this bullet-shaped craft and then find the right Air Force pilot to fly it faster than the speed of sound when it had never been done before. There was the rocket-powered North American X-15, built to explore man's role in space. It wasn't known at the time that pilot and plane could leave the atmosphere and safely return.

Peter made his way over to the Mercury spacecraft, imagining the courage of John Glenn in becoming the first American to orbit Earth. Looking at the Apollo 11 command module *Columbia* always made Peter euphoric. The craft had changed his life, mesmerizing him when he was eight years old with the grainy black-and-white images of man's first steps on the Moon.

Peter looked up and saw the world's fastest jet-propelled aircraft, the titanium-alloy SR-71 Blackbird, built in Lockheed's clandestine "Skunk Works" division. He wandered toward Burt's *Voyager* aircraft, which answered the question of whether a pilot could make it around the world nonstop without refueling. Each milestone probed deeper into the unknown, each built on what had been learned before.

Peter watched how people paused for a moment, if at all, in front of these heroic achievements. He wondered whether they thought of the designer, engineers, funders, pilots, materials, setbacks, heartaches, and break-throughs. With everything he looked at, he imagined the decade before its debut. He thought of the improbable odds of these vehicles coming into existence at all. He wondered who had to be pitched, who had to be convinced, how the funding came in, how many doors were closed, and who was there to keep opening the next one.

In a more personal way, the hall held memories representing gifts and losses. This was where he and Bob Richards came with Todd Hawley in the spring of 1995 after formalizing their International Space University charter. He kept a picture of the three of them — *Peterbobtodd* — standing in front of the *Spirit of St. Louis* and the Bell X-1, a space in between the planes. Three months later, Todd had died. His best friend — the man he called his brother — was memorialized here. Everyone had stood in line to touch the Moon rock, as if seeking a final connection with Todd. It was also in this hall where he'd met Reeve Lindbergh, who would introduce him to the "flying Lindbergh." Erik's life had been transformed by the XPRIZE, and Erik in turn had helped rescue Peter's dream when things looked bleak.

Peter made his way back to the front entrance, continuing to stop along the way and pose his silent questions: How many people lost their lives for this? How many marriages were ruined? What suffering was endured to build these crazy vehicles? Now for the first time, he had all of the answers to one icon of flight: *SpaceShipOne.* The little rocket's final destination was here. It was installed a few months earlier, in October 2005, on the one-year anniversary of the winning XPRIZE flight. This was one story Peter knew well — crazy, traumatic, glorious, exhausting, thrilling, and almost-didn't-happen.

Where there had been the unoccupied space between the *Spirit of St. Louis* and Chuck Yeager's X-1, there was now the world's first privately made, financed, and flown spaceship. The *Spirit of St. Louis* was wing to wing with the wonder from Mojave. The two vehicles came to life seventy-seven years apart, but shared contrarian ideas, confident creators, and a race for a prize. And just as Charles Lindbergh had asked, "Why shouldn't I fly to Paris?" Burt Rutan had said, "Why shouldn't I fly to space?"

As the museum was preparing to shut down for the night, Peter took one last look at *SpaceShipOne,* the rocket with the star-spangled nose that now shared rarefied air with the greatest achievements in aeronautical history. It was Peter's 16,157th day on

Earth — and he had proof that the impossible was possible.

Epilogue:
Where Are They Now?

Peter H. Diamandis continues to run the XPRIZE Foundation as founder and executive chairman. The XPRIZE has expanded into a global organization creating incentive prizes to solve some of the world's biggest problems in fields ranging from energy, environment, space, and oceans to education, health, and global development. To date, the foundation has awarded more than $34 million in purses, is currently offering $82 million in active prize purses, and has more than $100 million in prizes under development. The Foundation's largest prize, the $30 million Google Lunar XPRIZE, will be awarded to the first team to land a robot on the Moon, travel 500 meters on the surface, and transmit video back to Earth. The Google Lunar XPRIZE "is Blastoff reincarnated," Peter says of the ill-fated dot-com company he ran in Pasadena. Today both SEDS and International Space University (ISU) continue to thrive. Peter has also taken what he learned from his days running ISU and cofounded Singularity University (SU), an educational think tank and incubator headquartered in Silicon Valley for entrepreneurs and executives to launch or refocus companies. SU focuses on the application of exponential technologies and operates globally. Most recently Peter has cofounded two new companies that continue his duality between space and medicine. The first, Planetary Resources, Inc., is building deep-space drones for the prospecting of asteroid resources (as well monitoring terrestrial agricultural and energy resources). The second, Human Longevity, Inc. (HLI), is a genomics-, stem-cell-, and machine-learning-driven company focused on "extending the healthy human lifespan." HLI is Peter's mechanism for achieving longevity — his Harvard Medical School redux — so he can one day be assured his trip to space. In addition, the ZERO-G Corporation has flown more than fifteen thousand people, ages nine to ninety-three, into weightlessness. In 2007, Peter and Byron Lichtenberg flew Professor Stephen Hawking, the world's expert on gravity, into zero gravity. ZERO-G is now the sole provider of parabolic flight services to NASA. Peter lives in Santa Monica, is the best-selling coauthor of *Abundance* and *Bold,* and travels the globe talking to Fortune 500 CEOs and advising entrepreneurs. He and his wife, Kristen, have twin boys, Jet and Dax.

— Erik Lindbergh's lifelong quest to escape from the gravity of life inspired him to start a new venture called Escape from Gravity. His new company is about helping people claim strength and grace in the face of aging. Lindbergh explained, "I'm delighted to have gotten a second chance at life, survived to the ripe old age of fifty-one, and I'm still rockin' it — this is the best time of my life. Escape from Gravity is about sharing stories of people rockin' their spirit in life and using that passion for social good. *My* Escape from Gravity is through aerospace, art, and adventure. How do *you* escape?"

— After retiring from Scaled Composites in April 2011, Burt Rutan and his wife, Tonya, moved to Coeur d'Alene, Idaho. Burt came out of his short-lived retirement to build his forty-seventh new type of aircraft — in his garage. The amphibious plane, called the SkiGull — with retractable skis for landing — was designed to be able to fly from California to Hawaii without refueling and be capable of landing on water, snow, grass, or hard surfaces. Burt and Tonya, who received her private pilot's license in a seaplane, plan to use the SkiGull to explore the world in their own Walter Mitty-like adventure. Burt insists the SkiGull, which is saltwater resistant, is the last plane he will ever design and build himself. Six of his planes, including

SpaceShipOne, hang in the Smithsonian National Air and Space Museum.

— Mike Melvill retired from Scaled Composites in October 2007. He still flies his Long-EZ and Pitts biplane, logging at least 120 flight hours a year. He is also privileged to fly a friend's collection of World War I fighter aircraft. Sally retired at the same time as Mike, and has since found her calling — volunteering in a kindergarten classroom two days a week. Mike recently said, "We are happy we left when we did. Burt was the best boss either of us ever had. He was the most generous and the most exciting guy to work for. Never a dull moment, always something neat or cool going on. When we started working for Burt in September 1978, the whole company consisted of Burt and Sally and me!"

— After the success of *SpaceShipOne,* Scaled Composites began work on Space-ShipTwo for Richard Branson and his spaceship company. Brian Binnie spent the decade after Scaled won the XPRIZE working through the many issues related to scaling *SpaceShipOne* into the considerably larger SpaceShipTwo, which will have two pilots and six passengers. Brian left Scaled in 2014 to work on a completely different suborbital spaceship called the *Lynx,* being built by XCOR Aerospace. As the senior test pilot and engineer, he has worked to ready the vehicle to take off from the runway under its own rocket power, fly to space, and return (like many of its predecessors) as a glider. The *Lynx* is about the same size as *SpaceShipOne* and has room for carrying one space participant who will sit side by side in the cockpit with the pilot/astronaut. Brian considers his days at Scaled as the most creative and rewarding years of his professional life. He said, "I've never been in an organization that was so flooded with incredible talent and genuinely nice people. It is an environment that reflects the genius and humanity of Burt Rutan." Brian and his wife, Bub, eventually hope to retire somewhere along the western coastline, where the more rustic weather and temperatures remind him of his Scottish roots.

— Paul Allen, who spent around $26 million on *SpaceShipOne,* said that seeing *SpaceShipOne* hang in the Smithsonian was a day he'll never forget. "I haven't had any days prouder than that one," Allen said. "The whole experience was something I'd dreamed about. It was a very singular, peak experience to be a part of that amazing team." Allen remains involved in space but was happy to hand the manned spaceflight aspect over to Richard Branson. "I was not so enamored of being in the commercial spaceflight business," Allen said, noting that sooner or later, errors — or "deviations from a plan" — are inevitable. Allen's company Vulcan Aerospace contracts with Scaled to build Stratolaunch, the largest aircraft (by wingspan at about 117 meters) ever made, designed to launch payloads and vehicles to orbit. Burt Rutan, responsible for the initial concept of Stratolaunch, remains on the board but has little interface with the Scaled team working on the craft.

— The $10 million XPRIZE purse was shared 50–50 between Burt Rutan's company and Paul Allen. Burt took the money and handed bonuses out to every employee who had some role in making *SpaceShipOne,* from the guys who cleaned the shop to the engineers and pilots. The bonuses were the equivalent of the employee's salary for a year. Scaled Composites is now fully owned by Northrop Grumman Corp. A number of people have left Scaled to work at Virgin Galactic, including Doug Shane and Steve Losey, the former crew chief of *SpaceShipOne.* Virgin Galactic is just down the flight line from Scaled Composites. Stratolaunch is being built in an enormous hangar in a far corner of the Mojave Air and Space Port.

— Richard Branson's Virgin Galactic was established to build on the work of *SpaceShipOne* and open access to space for more people and payloads, starting with commercial suborbital flights. The company faced a setback and tragedy during a test flight in October 2014. SpaceShipTwo (named VSS *Enterprise* after the *Star Trek* craft) violently broke apart when the feather was unlocked at the wrong time. The test pilots were Pete Siebold and Mike Alsbury. The cause, according to the National Transportation Safety Board, was an error by Alsbury, who inexplicably unlocked the feather *before* reaching Mach 1 instead of after, as Burt had intended and the pilots had been trained. The breaking apart of the craft killed Alsbury instantly. Siebold, who found himself hurtling through the air still strapped into his pilot seat after the plane broke apart, lost and then regained consciousness in time to unclip from his seat and pull his parachute. He landed with only a shoulder injury. Alsbury was Mike Melvill's protégé; he trained him, and he was planning to leave him his Long-EZ. In February 2016, Richard Branson held an event in Mojave to unveil the second SpaceShipTwo, named VSS *Unity,* based on the same Rutan feathering design — though now with a feather lock safety mechanism. Theoretical physicist Stephen Hawking said at the unveiling, "I would be very proud to fly on this spaceship." Branson noted, "I thought we would be where we are today a lot quicker than we have been, and I was hoping we'd get there with a lot less pain. But once again we are not far off.

If it hadn't been for the XPRIZE, we wouldn't be here today. Yes, it's taking people to space, but I believe that so many fascinating things will emerge from what we are doing — and what Jeff Bezos is doing and Elon Musk is doing. People want to do extraordinary things and push the limits."

— In September 2006, Anousheh Ansari became the world's first female space tourist, the first Iranian woman in space, and the fourth space tourist to fly to the International Space Station. Her dream of flying to space became a reality thanks to her association with Peter Diamandis. The company he cofounded with Eric Anderson, Space Adventures, brokered the deal.

— John Carmack and his team at Armadillo Aerospace went on to build piloted rocket-powered airplanes for the Rocket Racing League and launch computer-controlled rockets close to 100 kilometers. They even had a year when they showed an operating profit. After the team went from all-volunteer to full-time salaried employees in 2006, Carmack began to notice what he calls "creeping professionalism." He explained, "Once it became people's jobs, they had other hobbies — go-karts and model airplanes and other distractions. When it was two days a week, everyone was much more focused on really getting things done. We started doing work with NASA and there were blueprints and diagrams and technical reviews. It slowed the team down." Carmack, who is now the CTO of Oculus Rift, says, "There are still aerospace ideas that interest me, so there is a decent chance that I will return to try again after virtual reality is all sorted out. I don't regret any of the work. We didn't achieve all the goals we wanted, but we took a good shot at it."

— When the XPRIZE was won and entrepreneurs including Branson, Musk, and Bezos were starting private space companies, Argentinian Pablo de León looked around and realized there would be a need for spacesuits for the private sector. Building on his previous work, he became a recognized spacesuit expert, founding a company to develop commercial spacesuits. In 2004, he began working at the Department of Space Studies at the University of North Dakota, first as a researcher in human spaceflight and, since 2013, as a professor. De León secured several NASA grants to develop new-generation spacesuits for the Moon and Mars and secured more than $2 million of external funding for the university. He currently has a NASA grant to develop an inflatable Mars base prototype.

— Dumitru Popescu left Romania in 2014 to establish the headquarters of ARCA Space Corporation in New Mexico. The company now makes large drones, including electric-powered ones that can fly higher than commercial aircraft, high-altitude balloons, and suborbital vehicles. Popescu recently unveiled the ArcaBoard, an all-composite mattresslike board that "surfs" a foot above the ground, giving the rider the feeling of flying. Popescu said his participation in the XPRIZE changed his life. "I knew it would make the history books from the moment I first read about it. It never crossed my mind to give up. We created a company, a brand. We had inertia on our side."

— Steve Bennett of Starchaser Industries in England said, "For me, the XPRIZE legitimized what I was trying to do. Before the XPRIZE, people humored me. After the XPRIZE, the same people began knocking on my door, asking when I will be able to send them into space." In the years following the XPRIZE, Bennett's company focused on the development of its liquid oxygen/kerosene rocket engines. In 2007 Starchaser won a competition to land a European Space Agency (ESA) contract entitled "Study of European Privately Funded Vehicles for Commercial Human Space Flight." Between 2008 and 2009 Starchaser won UK Development Agency funding to carry out the research and development on an eco-friendly rocket engine suitable for space tourism vehicles. As part of this project, the Starchaser team successfully designed, built, and test-fired a series of hybrid rocket engines. Starchaser's educational outreach program continues to grow, providing rocket- and space-related workshops, shows, and presentations for around two hundred schools every year. Bennett is working his way toward launching the company's Nova 2 man-rated rocket in 2017. "2017 will be a special year for us," Bennett predicted. "It will mark the twenty-fifth anniversary of the founding of Starchaser and the sixtieth anniversary of Sputnik and the dawn of the space age. The launch of Nova 2 will set the stage for flying our first Starchaser astronauts into outer space."

— Other XPRIZE contenders, including Jim Akkerman in Texas, continue to work on manned spaceflight programs and applaud the pervasiveness of private enterprise in the field of space. Jeff Bezos's company Blue Origin has had consistent success with its New Shepard suborbital rocket, which has a propulsive vertical landing system. The New Shepard is achieving reusable and relatively low-cost spaceflight. Bezos is starting with suborbital on his way to orbit. Elon Musk's SpaceX, founded in an old hangar in El Segundo, California, and given little chance of succeeding, has repeatedly made history. Starting with a team of thirty, SpaceX now has more than four thousand employees and some of the most advanced rockets and engines in the world. After three highly publicized rocket failures early on — a fourth would have put Musk into bankruptcy — SpaceX succeeded and went on to become the first private company to send a rocket to orbit, the first private company to deliver cargo to the International Space Station, and the first private company to land an orbital booster back on the launchpad. SpaceX has a $1.6 billion contract with NASA to fly cargo resupply missions to the ISS and to carry crew. NASA has contracted with SpaceX and Boeing to fly astronauts to the International Space Station. Both companies say they are on track for manned launches in 2017.

AFTERWORD:
SPACE, HERE I COME!

BY STEPHEN HAWKING

I have no fear of adventure. I have taken daredevil opportunities when they presented themselves. Years ago I barreled down the steepest hills of San Francisco in my motorized wheelchair. I travel widely and have been to Antarctica and Easter Island and down in a submarine.

On April 26, 2007, three months after my sixty-fifth birthday, I did something special: I experienced zero gravity. It temporarily stripped me of my disability and gave me a feeling of true freedom. After forty years in a wheelchair, I was floating. I had four wonderful minutes of weightlessness, thanks to Peter Diamandis and the team at the Zero Gravity Corporation. I rode in a modified Boeing 727 jet, which traveled over the ocean off Florida and did a series of maneuvers that took me into this state of welcome weightlessness.

It has always been my dream to travel into space, and Peter Diamandis told me, "For now, I can take you into weightlessness." The experience was amazing. I could have gone on and on.

Now I have a chance to travel to the start of space aboard Richard Branson's Virgin Galactic SpaceShipTwo vehicle, VSS *Unity*. SpaceShipTwo would not exist without the XPRIZE or without Burt Rutan, who shared a vision that space should be open to all, not just astronauts and the lucky few. Richard Branson is close to opening spaceflight for ordinary citizens, and if I am lucky, I will be among the early passengers.

I immediately said yes to Richard when he offered me a seat on SpaceShipTwo. I have lived with ALS, amyotrophic lateral sclerosis, for fifty years. When I was diagnosed at age twenty-one, I was given two years to live. I was starting my PhD at Cambridge and embarking on the scientific challenge of determining whether the universe had always existed and would always exist or had begun with a big explosion. As my body grew weaker, my mind grew stronger. I lost the use of my hands and could no longer write equations, but I developed ways of traveling through the universe in my mind and visualizing how it all worked.

Keeping an active mind has been vital to my survival. Living two thirds of my life with the threat of death hanging over me has taught me to make the most of every minute. As a child, I spent a lot of time looking at the sky and stars and wondering where eternity came to an end. As an adult, I have asked questions, including Why are we here? Where did we come from? Did God create the universe? What is the meaning of life? Why does the universe exist? Some questions I have answered; others I am still asking.

Like Peter Diamandis and those who fill the pages of this book, I believe that we need a new generation of explorers to venture out into our solar system and beyond. These first private astronauts will be pioneers, and I hope to be among them. We are entering a new space age, one in which we will help to change the world for good.

I believe in the possibility of commercial space travel — for exploration and for the preservation of humanity. I believe that life on Earth is at an ever-increasing risk of being wiped out by a disaster, such as a sudden nuclear war, a genetically engineered virus, or other dangers. I think the human race has no future if it doesn't go to space. We need to inspire the next generation to become engaged in space and in science in general, to ask questions: What will we find when we go to space? Is there alien life, or are we alone? What will a sunset on Mars look like?

My wheels are here on Earth, but I will keep dreaming. It is my belief, and it is the message of this book, that there is no boundary of human endeavor. Raise your sights. Be courageous and kind. Remember to look up at the stars and not at your feet. Space, here I come!

Stephen Hawking
Theoretical physicist, cosmologist, and bestselling author of six science books and five children's books coauthored with his daughter, Lucy

AUTHOR'S NOTE

I met Peter Diamandis in the spring of 2014, when I interviewed him for a story in the *San Francisco Chronicle.* I remember asking Peter at the time a seemingly simple question, "How did the XPRIZE begin?" Peter laughed and asked how much time I had. I was immediately drawn into Peter's story — of the space geek kid who can't let go of an out-of-this-world dream — and the even bigger tale of how the private race to space was launched. I love underdog stories, and this embodies a great David versus Goliath struggle.

I had just finished doing publicity for my last book, on Larry Ellison and his quest for the America's Cup — and his unlikely partnership with a radiator repairman who was the commodore of a blue-collar boating club. I realized Peter's story, and the story of the men and women who went after the Ansari XPRIZE, would make for a compelling book. Peter said he had been waiting to find the right writer to tell this story of how history was made. I began researching this subject in October 2014, on the tenth anniversary of the winning of the XPRIZE. But I didn't commit full time to it until early spring of 2015.

I traveled to Florida to meet with Peter's mom, dad, and sister, and to sift through boxes of photos, albums, and newspaper clippings. I made several reporting trips to the Mojave Desert, including a memorable visit with my son, Roman, then nine, who marveled at the intricacies of a rocket engine. He said he had never seen anything that looked so complicated. I spent countless hours with the engineers at Scaled Composites and had long and wonderful talks with Brian Binnie and his wife, Bub. Brian's story of getting knocked down and of his determination to get back into the proverbial ring wowed me. I pored over flight logs of *SpaceShipOne,* watched hours of video, listened to audio recordings, and read notes taken during the test flights and XPRIZE flights. I interviewed spectators and competitors as well as aviation and space historians.

I spent a great deal of time with Mike and Sally Melvill and got to fly with Mike in his Long-EZ. The experience was enlivened when Mike casually relayed — as we were high above the mountains of Tehachapi — that he was going to do some rolls and other high-adrenaline maneuvers to give me a feel for the plane. It was an amazing experience to fly with the world's first commercial astronaut, who also is a world-class guy: humble, brave, self-taught, and kind.

I had the privilege of long talks with Dick Rutan and Burt Rutan. These brothers were born to build, test, and fly planes. They're pioneers and mavericks. Burt, especially, is still this kid whose eyes light up with the joy of a new idea and tear up with memories of milestone moments. He is revered in the world of aviation, but my hope is that his story and his genius will also become known to those who are not aviators. Burt is truly one of America's great innovators. It all started for him as a kid making model planes.

There are many others I interviewed for this book, from Elon Musk, Richard Branson, and Paul Allen to NASA's Dan Goldin and the FAA's Marion Blakey. I did well over one hundred interviews and many of these people put up with my returning again and again with seemingly infinite questions. I traveled to Dallas to meet with Oculus Rift CTO John Carmack, who was both considerate and exceedingly smart. I met with Russell Blink and the team from Armadillo Aerospace, driving to remote corners of the Lone Star State to find these persistent rocket makers and to see the remnants of their XPRIZE vehicle. I visited Seattle to meet Erik Lindbergh. What a story he has! I found Erik to be smart and soulful, and was struck by how his fate was inextricably tied to the XPRIZE. I even went to St. Louis to visit the Racquet Club where Erik's grandfather Charles Lindbergh met with his supporters and where, decades later, the XPRIZE found its backers.

And, of course, there is Peter Diamandis, a true force of nature and probably the most tenacious person I've ever met. Beyond sharing his time over the last year and a half, Peter shared his contacts, photos, and video and audio archives. I listened to hours of his recorded thoughts and was even a fly on the wall in certain meetings that he recorded. I was entrusted with scrapbooks from his earliest SEDS and ISU days. I interviewed his childhood friends and a handful of his influential teachers and professors. Peter exhumed long-sealed boxes containing his personal, handwritten journals, spanning from 1979, his senior year in high school, to 2006, two years after the XPRIZE was won. These journals were as private and revelatory as any diary. They were raw in their expression of dreams, desires, frustrations, failures, and successes as the boy grew into the man. Collectively, they revealed someone with a sincere and unrelenting belief in the beauty and bounty of space. And they helped bring to life his herculean effort to open space to private industry — a dream that is a reality today.

ACKNOWLEDGMENTS

First, I want to thank David Lewis, my friend and editor who has guided me through all of my books and got me through this one — which brought with it a complex cast of characters spread across the globe, a lengthy passage of time, and sophisticated science, technology, and aerospace history, all written under a tight deadline. Next, I want to thank my technical adviser, Paul Pedersen, who is as smart as he is inquisitive, and helped me understand a range of intellectual challenges, was never daunted by my odd or arcane questions, and happily forged ahead with formulating many of the book's footnotes.

I'm grateful and humbled to have the foreword of my book written by the irrepressible Virgin founder Richard Branson and the afterword by Professor Stephen Hawking. I am awed by the life stories of these two men. Fitting with the theme of this book, they believe that rules are meant to be broken and limits transcended.

Special thanks go to my longtime agent, Joe Veltre of the Gersh Agency, who believed in me before my first book was sold. Thank you; what a fun ride we're on! A special note of gratitude goes to Scott Moyers at Penguin Press, for embracing this story from the moment he read my proposal. It was Scott who came up with the book title, *How to Make a Spaceship.* We had gone back and forth with dozens of titles over many weeks, and even crowdsourced a half dozen different titles. Nothing felt just right. *How to Make a Spaceship* fit for a number of reasons: As I see it, people *make* things while governments *build* things. There is a great renaissance under way with the maker movement and do-it-yourself culture. This book is about rolling up your sleeves and making things yourself. It is about making your own spaceship-like dreams come true. I'm grateful for the opportunity to work with such a savvy and inspired editor as well as with the talented team at Penguin, notably: Christopher Richards, Yamil Anglada, Chris Holmes, Matt Boyd, and Sabila Kahn.

I have been lucky to have worked with the XPRIZE team and owe a thank-you to Marcus Shingles, Esther Count, Eric Desatnik, Greg O'Brien, Cody Rapp, Maxx Bricklin, Joe Polish, and Diane Murphy. Thank you to others who spent a great deal of time talking with me, including Gary Hudson, Gregg

Maryniak, Dezso Molnar, and Byron Lichtenberg.

Last but not least, thank you to my family — my amazing mom, Connie Guthrie; my smart and creative brother, David Guthrie, and his kids, Wayne, Lauren, and Garrett; and my special and forever friend Martin Muller. I now have a tradition of ending my books with a note to my son, Roman, who watched this process of reporting and writing up close and personal, who put up with my late nights, long days, and vacations spent working. Roman, this is a story you and your peers should love: full of rockets and rebels, mind-blowing innovations, a major dare followed by a huge prize, and high-adrenaline moments that came together in California's high desert. Roman, take inspiration from these pages: follow your dreams, ignore the naysayers, and make really cool stuff. And listen to Stephen Hawking, who says that the best way to transcend limits is "with our minds and our machines."

The employees of Thorndike Press hope you have enjoyed this Large Print book. All our Thorndike, Wheeler, and Kennebec Large Print titles are designed for easy reading, and all our books are made to last. Other Thorndike Press Large Print books are available at your library, through selected bookstores, or directly from us.

For information about titles, please call:
(800) 223-1244

or visit our Web site at:
http://gale.cengage.com/thorndike

To share your comments, please write:
Publisher
Thorndike Press
10 Water St., Suite 310
Waterville, ME 04901

HARLEM MOON ✴

BROADWAY

HARLEM MOON

BROADWAY BOOKS

NEW YORK

GUMBO

A Celebration of
African American
Writing

EDITED BY

Marita Golden
and E. Lynn Harris

DESIGNED BY DEBORAH KERNER/DANCING BEARS DESIGN

PRINTED IN THE UNITED STATES OF AMERICA

ISBN 0-7394-2979-5

Acknowledgments

From Marita Golden:

Clyde McElevene, my friend and fellow cultural worker, without whom the Hurston/Wright Foundation would not exist.

E. Lynn Harris for the zeal, dedication, and generosity with which he has supported the Hurston/Wright Foundation and for suggesting this anthology.

Janet Hill, for her energy, intelligence, and vision; and for making this big project more fun than I suspected it could be.

From E. Lynn Harris:

Thanks to Marita Golden and Clyde McElevene for their friendship and leadership of the Hurston/Wright Foundation and for allowing me to be a part of their mission.

Janet Hill, for her leadership—and for proving to me time and time again that she is among the best editors and people in the business.

All of the writers who didn't think twice when we asked them to contribute a story for free. This couldn't have happened without you.

Contents

THIS I KNOW IS TRUE • •   277

x ..

About the Hurston/Wright Foundation

Since 1990, the Hurston/Wright Foundation has been in the forefront of developing programs that support the national community of Black writers. The Hurston/Wright Award, the country's only national award for college writers of African descent has recognized over thirty emerging writers, six of whose books have been published by leading national imprints.

Hurston/Wright Writers' Week is the country's only multi-genre summer writers' workshop for Black writers, held on the campus of Howard University. Over five hundred writers have attended Hurston/Wright Writers' Week, and three alumni of the workshop have had books published. The Hurston/Wright Foundation also offers classes in creative writing for high school students in Washington, D.C.

The Hurston/Wright Legacy Award is a new national award for published Black writers, presented by the Hurston/Wright Foundation in partnership with Borders Books and Music. Three winners in the categories of Fiction, Debut Fiction, and Nonfiction will receive, respectively, $10,000 for the winner and $5,000 each for two finalists.

The Hurston/Wright Legacy Award is the only award to published Black writers presented by a panel of their peers, and honors the works of Black writers who represent the tradition of excellence and innovation established by Zora Neale Hurston and Richard Wright.

For more information on the Hurston/Wright Foundation you may visit our Web site at www.hurston-wright.org Or email us at hurstonwrightlit@ aol.com. Our address is P.O. Box 77287 Washington, D.C. 20013; our phone is 301-422-0152.

Note from E. Lynn Harris

Early in my career I started supporting the Hurston Wright Foundation because I believed in their mission. The Foundation was addressing a need that was missing by providing workshops and programs for writers of color. Judging from the outstanding collection we've been able to gather in the form of *Gumbo,* I'm happy that other writers feel the same way and want to show the same support. Black authors are at a very critical point right now in proving to mainstream publishers that African American literature is viable not only in the sense of temporary renaissance, but now and forever.

Imprints such as Harlem Moon will give voice to those writers perfecting their craft and will allow them to share their words with many hungry readers.

Gumbo includes a broad spectrum of current writers—from those who have established popular followings, to those writing with a literary or social slant, as well as some unpublished authors who may become the stars of tomorrow. Some of you will reacquaint yourself with old friends in the form of stories you've loved that were previously published but you'll also be able to meet some new friends and be introduced to authors who have been waiting for the chance to meet you.

By buying and supporting this collection, you'll ensure that there will always be entertaining, heartfelt and poignant stories by a wide range of writers who will always tell the stories of people of color.

Thank you so much for your support.

Warmest regards,
E. Lynn Harris

Note from Marita Golden

Our mission is to tell the truth at whatever cost.

RICHARD WRIGHT

I am not tragically colored. There is no great sorrow damned up in my soul, nor lurking behind my eyes. I do not mind at all.

ZORA NEALE HURSTON

The Zora Neale Hurston/Richard Wright Foundation was started with $750 and a dream. The money was mine. The dream belonged to every writer, everywhere, and it was the desire for recognition, support, and community. The African American writer has, of necessity, been visionary and witness, a channel for an individual sense of story even while recognizing that for Black people in America, writing is fighting. The most important and crucial lesson I have learned from other writers about the lonely, difficult, rewarding-beyond-measure, dangerous, amazing, misunderstood endeavor we undertake is the lesson of courage. Courage not only in the face of a society and a world that often seeks to silence the complexity and beauty of the experience of African people, but courage in the face of the fear and narrow-mindedness and orthodoxy that bedevils our own community. Writing *is* fighting. But it is also building and loving and confirming and creating. It's a job. A lifestyle. An honorable and even sacred way of living in the world.

Zora Neale Hurston and Richard Wright exemplify all the contradictions, all the peaks and valleys of the writer's life. They made their lives their epitaph, and their spirits remain vivid, combustible, energizing, and inspiring, continually altering the world. The more I learn about the life of Richard Wright, every time I read or teach his autobiography, *Black Boy*, I am rendered nearly mute with admiration for his guts, his bravery, and the powerful things that words became when he used them. Every time I read *Their Eyes Were Watching God*, or just think about how Zora Neale Hurston strode through her life as though it was a gift not only for her but one she was bound to share, I know that I can face today and tomorrow. The world doesn't create many writers like Zora Neale Hurston and Richard Wright. The African American community in America did, and I wanted to show that to the world.

It was 1990, and I was a faculty member in the MFA Graduate Creative Writing Program at George Mason University. Like many MFA programs, ours received few applications from Black students. Nevertheless, when I founded the Hurston/Wright Foundation, naturally I hoped that some of the winners of the Hurston/Wright Award for Black college fiction writers would apply to and enroll in the program at George Mason, where the foundation was housed (in my office) for the first four years.

I was watching with enormous pride and excitement what can only be called the third major wave of literary activity after the Harlem Renaissance and the Black Arts Movement, and wanted to encourage emerging Black writers. I'd had a little success with a novel, *Long Distance Life*, and I wanted to "give back." So with $750 I underwrote the first Hurston/Wright Award. With a cadre of several other "true believers" the foundation was incorporated, and we set about changing the American literary landscape.

Because we wanted to give as much encouragement as possible, after the first year, we decided to choose three winners, not one. The support of HarperCollins, publishers of Wright and Hurston, made this possible. In addition, from the very first award, the winners were invited to receive their prize at a ceremony at which they were recognized and honored by established writers. I wanted to create a ritual, a ceremony in which young Black writers were acknowledged and embraced by their peers, their elders, their fellow writers, on behalf of the Black community and the larger society. And so Nikki Giovanni, Maxine Clair, David Bradley, Colson Whitehead, Jewell Parker Rhodes, Gloria Naylor and others have spoken words of praise and encouragement to the winners. I wanted to model encouragement of activities that still gets short shrift in many pockets of our community—reading and writing. I wanted people to believe that it is as exciting for a young person to grow up to be a writer as it is for them to grow up to be Michael Jordan, or Mary J. Blige. I wanted to say to young Black writers that there was a group of people who believed in them, who would always "have their back." The prize winners check went into their bank account, but I hope the meaning and significance, the import of the awards ceremony, went straight to their hearts.

I will never forget how my father raised me on stories of Hannibal, Frederick Douglass, Sojourner Truth, and Cleopatra. These stories introduced me to larger-than-life heroes and heroines and, listening to my father, I subconsciously learned the tenets of good storytelling. My mother simply told me when I was fourteen that one day I was going to write books. And because I was an obedient child, I did. My parents were my first literary mentors. When I moved to New York City in the early seventies, Sidney Offit, who taught the first fiction class I ever took; poets Audre Lorde and June Jordan; novelist Paule Marshall, all gave me the charge to continue writing and to believe in myself. To this day I remember how much their words meant to me. The belief and support of this unofficial coalition shaped my sense of what was expected of me. I was to write, to fulfill my gifts. I was also expected to pass on the sense of possibility that I had received to others.

I named the award and foundation for Hurston and Wright to bring together the spirits of two major American writers who simply couldn't stand each other's work. Wright thought that Hurston's stories of rural Black life, drenched in folklore, humor, and emotional resilience, offered up characters who were buffoonish and played into the worst White stereotypes of Black life. Hurston felt that Wright, in his blistering condemnation of American racism, created Black characters devoid of humanity, dignity, and pride.

Of course the tragedy of this particular literary spat is that only through a close and complete reading of both of these geniuses of the American South do we get a clear picture of the African American experience and how it speaks to universal humanity.

When I started the foundation, the bitter gender-based cultural battles over feminism and *The Color Purple*, movie and book, while past, still cast a pall over the Black writing community and echoed the ego/cultural battles of Hurston and Wright. Somehow we had survived this cultural/literary Battle of the Bulge, the kind that plagues intellectual/artistic communities.

Because of the significance of the foundation and the new award, I felt its name had to symbolize the best writing we'd created and invite Black male and female writers to "sit down together." As an inheritor of the literary legacy of Hurston and Wright, I felt myself "called" to unite them, to join their legacies and their artistic boldness. As an inheritor and protector of their legacy it was my job, to perhaps be even bolder that they had been able to be. So I linked them. A legacy is a contract that obligates the recipient to rise to meet the best that the legacy symbolizes. Hurston and Wright were not saints. But they *were* major literary voices of the twentieth century. They were both rebels, opinionated individualists who gloried in re-creating themselves, and who at various times during their long careers were castigated, marginalized, and rejected as often by Blacks as by Whites. Maybe they had not been able to see that they were bound inextricably by all this, but I could.

I have been a literary and cultural activist for more than thirty years. Nonetheless, the growth of the Hurston/Wright Foundation into a major literary institution, I have to admit, caught me by surprise. This development was, of course, planned, hoped for, even prayed for; yet I still don't think anyone is ever really prepared for their dreams to come true. I also was not prepared for how much the hard work and long hours of working with others to build this foundation would enrich and positively transform my life. It has been enormously gratifying to see the foundation receive the kind of wide-ranging and diverse support that has kept us not just afloat but growing. Virginia Commonwealth University provided an office, and administrative *and* financial support for seven years. Publishers HarperCollins, Ballantine, and Doubleday recognized the significance of our mission. The National Endowment for the Arts, visionary and major support from Borders Books and Music and many corporations have made our work possible.

The national writing community bought into the idea of the foundation and supported it from day one. One of the most satisfying aspects of the work that I do is to work with other writers and to see how many of us are dedicated to cultural work. Terry McMillan, John Grisham, Connie Briscoe, John Edgar Wideman, Gloria Naylor, and many others have made the foundation possible. And it was E. Lynn Harris, the hardest-working man in the book world and one of the most generous, who suggested this anthology and who has been extraordinarily generous with time, spirit, and treasure.

The most daunting challenge I faced in the twelve years of the foundation's growth was how to balance my need and my call to write with my need and my call to build this institution. Fortunately there were so many role models for me to follow—the philanthropy of Gwendolyn Brooks; the fierce, nation-building/nation-time work of Amiri Baraka and Toni Cade Bambara; my friends Susan Shreve and Alan Cheuse, who worked with the PEN/Faulkner Foundation, and who provided helpful advice about how the build the Hurston/Wright Foundation. I looked to these writers and others and saw that it could be done. In fact, the twelve years of the Hurston/ Wright Foundation have been years of consistent and satisfying creativity for me. I have been charged, energized, renewed, and inspired by this work.

Gumbo arrives at an auspicious moment. Never before have more Black writers been read by more people, not just in America but around the world. And don't believe the old frequently flaunted notion that "nobody but Blacks" read books by Black authors. Black writers are raising Cain, moving mountains, rewriting the script, redefining notions of character, story, place, literature.

Who can forget the summer of 1998, when Terry McMillan, Toni Morrison, and Alice Walker were on the national bestseller lists *simultaneously?* Black *and* White folks put them there. The works of scores of *living* Black writers are being taught in universities and colleges across the country, despite the assault on Affirmative Action and multiculturalism. Black writers are in the canon and ain't going *nowhere.* Several years ago, as part of a United States Information Agency tour of Turkey, I lectured at several universities there about contemporary African American writers. The interest among students and faculty was passionate. One faculty member had shared photocopies of *Their Eyes Were Watching God* with her students because the book was unavailable in the country. The Turkish people loved Hurston because in her wise, enduring rural folk they saw themselves. Paule Marshall told me of a Richard Wright Society in Japan, made up of scholars devoted to a study of Wright's work. We are a community that has traditionally created stories that speak to and nourish the world, and we still are.

Never before have Black writers mastered as many genres—literary fiction, (winning major awards from Pulitzer to Nobel), commercial fiction (making major money and racking up major sales figures), extending and enlarging science fiction, mystery, detective writing, wiping out the borders that separate genre and literary fiction altogether (à la Walter Mosley). In some quarters there is much hand-wringing about the "commercialization" of Black literature. And some have even charged that popular, clearly commercial fiction by Black writers is a threat to the future of Black writing. I think the only threat to the future of Black writing is a Black community that fails to understand and rejoice in the fact that it has a story that the world cannot get enough of, a Black community that fails to honor and *read* its literary writers as well as its commercial writers, a Black community content to let others define its story and establish the prevailing standards by which it will be judged. A Black writer getting a six-figure contract puts more money into our community. At least that's how I do the math.

Gumbo presents an enticing overview of where we are now. Gumbo is an African-inspired dish, and an African-inspired way of speaking. The stories in this anthology will nourish you and introduce you to a hearty stew of Black writers speaking a New World African language that mixes it all up and that calls on all of our traditions and creates some new ones.

Hurston/Wright Award winners David Anthony Durham, Tayari Jones, Nelly Rosario, Ravi Howard, Erica Doyle, Faith Adiele, Genaro Ky Ly Smith, Amy DuBois Barnet, and William Henry Lewis, whose stories you will read on these pages, are all carrying on and extending the tradition established by Zora Neale Hurston and Richard Wright. *Gumbo* is also filled with many other writers, some of whom you may meet for the first time in these pages, who are working in that same tradition. But for me the significance of *Gumbo* is that it brings together a tasty, spicy sampling of *all* the stories we are writing now. It resonates with the sound of our longing from whatever vantage point we live out the African American and African diasporic experience. *Gumbo* is a literary rent party. And like the rent parties of old, everybody here had to *pay* to get in. This time, however, the currency was a story. And so the narratives in *Gumbo* are boogying in the middle of the living room floor with an audience circling them, egging them on; they are locked in the upstairs bathroom doing the nasty; sitting on the porch plotting the future of race; in the kitchen, eating jerk chicken and black-eyed peas; on the porch falling in love. And who's here? Danzy Senna, Eric Jerome Dickey, Van Whitfield, Tananarive Due, Edward P. Jones, and a whole lot more, including some surprise guests who brought *totally new jams* with them. *What kinda party is this?* The kind we've needed to have for a long time.

If you are reading this book you are attending the party. If you bought this book you are an investor in the future of Black writing, and the stories are your immediate dividend. The strong, assured future of the Hurston/Wright Foundation, down the line, will be, in the words of the godfather of soul, "The Big Payback." But for now, come on in. Let me have your coat. If you've got to smoke you have to do it outside. The bar is over there. Food's in the den.

Richard and Zora?

They're around here somewhere. I just saw them . . .

GUMBO

Family Tree

The Dew Breaker

Anne was talking about miracles right before they reached the cemetery. She was telling her husband and daughter about a case she'd recently heard reported on a religious cable access program about a twelve-year-old Lebanese girl who cried crystal tears.

From the front passenger seat, the daughter had just blurted out "Ouch!," one of those non sequiturs Anne would rather not hear come out of her grown child's mouth, but that her daughter sometimes used as a short cut for more precise reactions to anything that was not easily comprehensible. It was either "Ouch!," "Cool," "Okay," or "Whatever," a meaningless chorus her daughter had been drawing from since she was fourteen years old.

Anne was thinking of scolding her daughter, of telling her now that she was grown up she should talk more like a woman, weigh her words carefully so that, even though she was an "artiste," others might take her seriously— but she held back, imagining her daughter's reaction to her lecture might be, "Okay, whatever, Manman, go on with your story."

Her husband, who was always useful in helping her elaborate on her miraculous tales, and who also disapproved of their daughter's sometimes limited use of language, said in Creole, "If crystal was coming out of her eyes, I would think she would be crying blood."

"That's what's extraordinary," Anne replied. "The crystal pieces were as sharp as knives, but they did not hurt her."

"How big were these pieces?" the husband asked, keeping his eyes on the road. He slowed the car down a bit as they entered the ramp leading to the Jackie Robinson Parkway.

Anne took one last look at the surrounding buildings before the car plunged into the parkway. They were lit more brightly than usual with Christmas trees, and Chanukah and Kwanzaa candles in some of the windows. Anne tried to keep these visions of illuminated pines, electric candles, and giant cardboard Santas in her mind, as they entered the parkway.

She hated driving through the parkway's curvy narrow lanes, even as a passenger, and would have never put herself through the ride, on Christmas Eve of all times, had it not been so important to her to go to her daughter's apartment in New Rochelle and convince her to attend Christmas Eve Mass with them, something the daughter was probably doing out of guilt because her mother and father had shown up at her front door. While in college, her daughter had declared herself an atheist. Between her daughter, who chose not to believe in God, and her husband, who went to the Brooklyn Museum every week to worship, it seemed, at the foot of Ancient Egyptian statues, she felt outnumbered by pagans.

Anne was just about to tell her husband and daughter that the crystal pieces that had fallen out of the Lebanese girl's eyes were as big as ten-carat diamonds—she had imagined her daughter retorting, "I bet her family *wished* she cried ten-carat diamonds"—and that as crystal slid out of her eyes, the girl had visions of a man on a white horse telling her he was a messenger of God, when they reached the cemetery.

Every time she passed a cemetery, Anne always held her breath. When she was a girl, Anne had gone swimming with her two-year-old brother on a beach in Jacmel and he had disappeared beneath the waves. Ever since then she'd convinced herself that her brother was walking the Earth looking for his grave, and whenever she went by a cemetery, any cemetery, she imagined him there, his tiny wet body bent over the tombstones, his ash-colored eyes surveying the letters, trying to find his name.

The cemetery was on both sides of them now, the headstones glistening in the limited light, each of them swaying, it seemed—perhaps because the car was moving so fast—like white sheets left out overnight to dry.

She held her breath the way she imagined her brother did before the weight of the sea collapsed his small lungs and he was forced to surrender to the water, sinking into a world of starfish, sea turtles, weeds, and sharks. She had gone nowhere near the sea since her brother had disappeared, her heart racing even when she happened upon images of waves on television.

Who would put a busy thoroughfare in the middle of a cemetery, she wondered, *forcing the living and their noisy cars to always be trespassing on the dead?* It didn't make sense, but perhaps the parkway's architects had been thinking beyond the daily needs of the living to the fact that now and then the dead might enjoy hearing sounds of life going on at high speed around them. *If this were so,* she thought, *then why should the living be spared the dead's own signs of existence? Of shadows swaying in the breeze, of the laughter and cries of lost children, of the whispers of lovers, muffled as though in dreams.*

"We're way past the cemetery now," she heard her daughter say.

Anne had closed her eyes without realizing it. Her daughter knew she reacted strangely to cemeteries but Anne had never told her why, since her daughter had concluded early in life that this, like many incomprehensible things her parents did, was connected to "some bizarre event that happened in Haiti, right?," mysterious customs the daughter had never shown the least interest in.

"I'm glad Papa doesn't have your issues with cemeteries," the daughter was saying, "otherwise we'd be in the cemetery ourselves by now."

The daughter pulled out a cigarette, which the father objected to with the wave of a hand. "When you get out of the car," he said.

"Whatever," the daughter replied, putting the loose cigarette back in its pack. She turned her face to the bare trees lining her side of the parkway and said, "Okay, Manman, tell us about another miracle."

Anne had lost her two brothers, her only siblings, one to the sea, and the other, a grown man, to her husband, who had killed him in prison. That's the miracle she wanted to tell her daughter about on this Christmas Eve night, the miracle of her daughter being alive, but once again she could think of no reason to make herself do it. What was the use of disturbing her child's peace, of inciting her husband's constant sense of guilt?

She was not an adherent to the all-revealing culture here. What harm could it do her daughter not to know any of this? About the young brother who had drowned? About the older brother, a Protestant preacher, who had been tortured to death, but not before leaving three circular bite marks on the face of the man who would soon after become her husband? So rather than entertain thoughts of sharing, or clarifying these events, for she was worried that if the daughter ever found out about them she might think her an accomplice in both deaths, she told them about another miracle.

This one concerned a twenty-one-year-old Filipino man who had seen an image of the Madonna in a white rose petal.

She thought her daughter would say "Cool" or something equally meaningless, but the daughter actually asked, "How come these people are all foreigners?"

"Because Americans don't have much faith," the father replied.

"Faith is the evidence of things unseen," Anne concurred. "Here you see everything."

"Hello?" the daughter said as if calling them from some great distance on the telephone. "Maybe people here are more practical, so if I see a woman's face in a rose, I'd think somebody drew it there. But there where people see everything, even things they're not supposed to see—or if you see it, Manman—you think it's a miracle. Here we can make miracles happen. There, in Haiti, the Philippines, or wherever, people are always looking for miracles. I don't believe in those things. Maybe if they happened in a different place, I'd believe anyway, even if they happened here, I wouldn't believe them."

"Why not?" Anne's husband asked.

"Because it's like I told you, here we could make them happen, but there, in the Philippines, or wherever, they might not have the means."

"You could use vegetable dye to paint a face on a rose petal," Anne's husband said. "You don't need technology for that. So how do you know they don't have the means?"

"Because Manman is saying it is a miracle."

Anne hated it when her daughter dissected the miracles, coming up with critiques to explain them away.

"Let me add that I don't think Americans are faithless," the daughter said. "It reads 'In God We Trust' on the money, doesn't it? Besides here we are going to this Mass thing and I know we're not the only ones doing that."

They were coming out of the Jackie Robinson Parkway and turning onto Jamaica Avenue. Anne tried to bring her thoughts back to the Mass.

When her daughter was a girl, before going to the Christmas Eve Mass, they would walk around their Brooklyn neighborhood to look at the holiday lights. Their community associations were engaged in fierce competition, awarding a prize to the block with the most nativity scenes, lawn sculptures, wreaths, and banners.

Anne, her husband, and daughter would walk or drive around to see these holiday decorations because their house had none. Each year, Anne suspected that their neighbors detested her family because their house had been the only nonornamented home on the block, had perhaps been the cause of their section only receiving an honorable mention yet again.

She and her husband had put up no decorations, fearing, irrationally perhaps, that lit ornaments and trimmings would bring too much attention to them. Instead, as they would later discover, their lack of participation made them stand out. But by then they had settled into their routine and could not bring themselves to change it.

When her daughter was still living at home the only things Anne ever did to acknowledge the season—aside from attending the Christmas Eve Mass—were to put a handful of shredded brown paper under her daughter's bed and hang a sprig of mistletoe over her bedroom doorway. The frayed paper—put there without her daughter's knowledge—was a substitute for the hay that had been part of the Baby Jesus' first bed. The mistletoe was acquired from the Christmas tree vendor who parked himself across the street from her beauty shop each year, because she'd once heard someone on a Christmas television special say that mistletoe was considered a sacred plant, one with all sorts of reconciliatory qualities. So much so that if two enemy warriors found themselves beneath it they would lay down their weapons and embrace one another.

By not offering each other or their daughter any presents at Christmas, Anne and her husband had tried to encourage her to be thankful for what she already had—family, a roof over her head—rather than count on what she would, or could, receive on Christmas morning. Their daughter had learned this lesson so well that aside from the drive from block to block to criticize the brightest houses, Christmas disinterested her.

"Look at that one!" the husband would shout, pointing to the arches of icicle lights draped over one house from top to bottom. "Can you imagine how high their electricity bill is going to be?"

"I wouldn't be able to sleep in a place like that," the daughter would say, singling out a neon holiday greeting in a living room window. "It must be as bright as daylight in there all the time."

Even now, they were doing the same thing, her husband talking about enormous light bills, and her daughter saying that an extravagantly embellished house across the street looked like "an inferno."

Even though the Mass would not begin for another fifteen minutes, the church was packed. Anne and her husband found three seats in a back row, near a young couple who were holding hands and staring ahead at the altar. Anne sat next to the woman, who acknowledged her with a nod as Anne squeezed into the pew. Their daughter was outside in the cold, smoking.

The daughter soon joined them, plopping herself down on the aisle next to her father. Anne had tried to convince her to wear a dress, or at least a skirt and a blouse, but she had insisted on wearing her paint-stained blue jeans and a lint-covered sweater.

Anne thought the church most beautiful at Christmas. The nativity scene in front of the altar had a black Mary, Joseph, and Baby Jesus, the altar candles casting a golden light on their mahogany faces. The sight of people greeting each other around her made her wish that she and her husband had real friends, not just acquaintances from their respective businesses, the beauty salon and barbershop. She wanted to rethink the decision she and her husband had made when they came here, not to get close to anyone who might ask too many questions about his past. The only reason they'd set up shop on Nostrand Avenue, at the center of the Haitian community, was because it was the best chance they had of finding clients. But soon after the barbershop's opening, the husband had discovered that losing eighty pounds, changing his name, and giving Jacmel, a village deep in the mountains, as his place of birth, meant no one asked any more about him. He hadn't been a famous "dew breaker," or torturer anyway, just one of hundreds who had done their job so well that their victims were never able to speak of them again.

The church grew silent as the priest walked in and bowed before the altar. It was exactly midnight. Midnight on Christmas Eve was Anne's favorite sixty seconds of the year. It was a charmed minute not just for her, she imagined, but for the entire world. It was the time when birds began chirping their all-night songs to greet the holy birth, when other animals genuflected and trees bowed in reverence. She could picture all this as though it were being projected on a giant screen in a movie theater: water in secret wells and far off rivers and streams turning into wine, bells chiming with help only from the breeze, candles, lanterns, and lamps blinking like the Star of Bethlehem, the gates of Paradise opened, so anyone who died this minute could enter without passing through Purgatory, the Virgin Mary choosing among the sleeping children of the world for some to invite to Heaven to serenade her son.

Once again she hoped the Virgin would choose her younger brother to go up to Heaven and sing with the choir of angels. Technically, as he had never been properly buried, he was not sleeping, so his spirit was somewhere out there, wandering, searching. But perhaps if he were chosen to go up to Heaven, the Holy Mother would keep him there. She hoped too that her older brother would be allowed to slip into Paradise, even if it wasn't her idea of Paradise, but his—his Protestant one—which he had always told her included spending eternity in the same crystal palace as "His Savior."

The priest was incensing the altar, the smoke rising in a perfumed cloud toward the thorn-crowned head on the golden crucifix. Her daughter chose that exact moment to mumble something to her father while pointing to someone sitting diagonally on the aisle three rows down from them.

Anne wanted to tell her daughter to be quiet, but her scolding would mean more conversation, and her daughter's murmurs were already drawing stares from those sitting nearby.

When her daughter's garbled whispers grew louder, however, Anne moved her mouth close to her husband's ear to ask, "What is the problem?"

"She thinks she sees Emmanuel Constant over there," her husband calmly replied.

Now he pointed at the man her daughter had been aiming her finger at for a while now. From her limited view of the man's profile Anne could tell he was relatively tall—even from his seated position his head stood above those around him—had dark brown skin, a short afro, a beard, and a mustache. All this was consistent with the picture a community group had printed on the WANTED FOR CRIMES AGAINST THE HAITIAN PEOPLE flyers that had been stapled to lampposts all along Nostrand Avenue a month before. Beneath the photograph of Constant had been a shorthand list of the crimes of which he had been accused—"torture, rape, murder of 3,000 people"— all apparently committed between 1993, when Constant had founded a militia called FRAPH, to Christmas Eve 1994, when he had arrived in the United States.

For a month now, each morning while opening up and again at night while lowering their shutters, both Anne and her husband had been casting purposefully casual glances at the flyer on the lamppost in front of their stores. But they'd never spoken about it, even when—bleached by the sun and wrinkled by the cold—it had slowly begun to fade; the letters and numbers disappearing so that the word "rape" became "ape" and the "3" vanished from "3,000," leaving a trio of zeros as the number of Constant's reported casualties.

Even before the flyer had found its way to her doorstep Anne had followed the story of Emmanuel Constant through Haitian newspapers, Creole radio, and cable access programs. Constant had created his death squad after a military coup had sent the democratically elected president of Haiti into exile. FRAPH members had sought to silence the deposed president's followers by circling neighborhoods with gasoline, setting houses on fire, and shooting fleeing residents. Anne had read about incidents of facial scalping, where FRAPH members were said to have peeled back the skin from their victims' faces so no one would be able to identify them. Constant had been tried in absentia in a Haitian court and sentenced to life in prison, a sentence he would probably never serve.

And every morning and evening as her eyes wandered to the paling flyer on the lamppost, she had had to fight a strong desire to pull it down, not out of sympathy for Constant, but out of a fear that even though her husband and Constant's reported offenses were separated by more than twenty-five years, she might arrive at her store one morning and find her husband's likeness on the lamppost rather than Constant's.

Now that her husband had whispered that name so long unspoken between them, she found herself turning to her husband's face, not the supposed Constant; the circular bite marks reminding her of the three zeros on what was left of the WANTED flyer in front of their shops.

"Could that really be him?" she whispered back to her husband.

He shrugged as someone behind them leaned over and hissed "Shush" into her ear.

The man her daughter believed to be Constant was looking straight ahead, watching the choir sing a Christmas carol. It could not be Constant, Anne decided. Why would he come to a church filled with Haitians when so many despised him? Wouldn't he be afraid for his life? Why would he want to taunt his survivors, or the friends and relatives of his victims who might recognize him?

The daughter was fuming, shifting in her seat and mumbling under her breath, all the while keeping her eyes fixed on the man's profile.

Anne was proud of her daughter, proud of her righteous anger. But what would her daughter say if she ever found out about her own father? About how he had tortured dozens, hundreds of people; how he had taunted his prisoners before they'd taken their last breaths, bullying them into card games with the false hope that they could earn back their lives from him; how he had collapsed into Anne's arms outside the prison gates, after he'd murdered, among others, her own brother; how he'd tried at first to make her think he was an escaped prisoner even when she had seen him enter the church and remove her brother from his pulpit.

Because of the political sermons he was preaching at his church, her brother knew his arrest was inevitable, so he'd prepared for it by practicing biting "6s" on the back of his hands.

"My murderer will carry the mark of the beast until the end of his days," her brother had said. "I will brand him with three sixes, even more if I can."

When her husband, then a stranger, had collapsed into her arms with those marks on his right cheek, she'd known then that her brother had succeeded. As he raced out of the prison gates, his face bleeding, she'd run toward him to make sure the marks were there. But she and he had both whispered the word "Help" to each other at the same time. And believing, as she had often been told, that people who simultaneously utter the same word are meant to die together, she quickly grabbed his hand and held it tightly, as though it were her brother's fingers between hers. Since her brother was now surely gone, she wanted to become the guardian of his killer, and of the mark her brother had left on him. It was the last thread connecting her to her brother, and she was not willing to separate from it.

At some point while she was holding his hand, he asked her to see him home.

Soon after they arrived at his apartment, on the lower floor of a two-story house nearby, he crawled onto a bare mattress on the floor and fell asleep. She watched him sleep until dawn, sitting in a corner of his bedroom, trying to think of ways to take his life.

In the morning she stumbled to an open market to buy a knife to plunge into his chest, but next to the knife vendor was a seller of the fernlike fèy wònt, the shame plant, a *Mimosa pudica* in a small plastic bag with soil and roots still attached.

She bought the plant and carried it back to his apartment. By then he was awake, darkened blood caked over the bite marks, which she was suddenly desperate to see again. So she got some water and scrubbed his face as he closed his eyes and grimaced. The marks were still there, three large "Os" that looked more like circles than numbers.

He noticed her mimosa and assumed she had gotten it for the tiny leaflets, which could be used to heal cuts. He looked ashamed when he reached over and touched the prickly spines and the leaves bent, then collapsed onto themselves, as though to shut him out, but the plant's miniature leaves soon opened up like a baby's fist. His face lit up; he smiled, even while groaning from the pain. He spent most of the morning tapping the leaves to watch them close, then open and close again. She noticed that whenever he smiled the bite marks shrank and disappeared into the folds of fat on his cheek, and she wished she had never bought the mimosa.

Maybe this was when she lost her mind, watching him enjoy the shame plant. Seeing her brother's teeth imprints carved into his cheek, she felt as though she could hear her brother's voice speaking to her from the wound.

"Stay with him," her brother was saying, "and hopefully you will live to see shame and regret tear at him until he takes *his* last breath."

So she became a different person, a woman with no past, no present, and no future. She would do whatever was necessary to realize her brother's dream.

That afternoon when he went to the national archives to get the birth certificate of one of his victims, she followed him there. She went along when he got them passports and paid for someone to immediately get them visas for New York.

A week later, when an old army friend of his met them at the airport in New York and he introduced her as his wife, she did not disagree. During sex that first night, and other nights after that, she insisted he keep the light on so she could stare at the marks which grew smaller and less defined as they healed and slowly shrank in size as he lost more and more weight. But the marks were still like a grave she could visit every day. Each time she looked at them, she felt her brother near her, his entire life reduced to his final rebellious act. When she touched or kissed them, it was as though she were holding a part of her brother that he'd left behind, just for her.

The day their daughter was born, she realized some good could come out of their union. He had insisted on naming their daughter Ka, after something having to do with Egyptian statues, which he was becoming more and more interested in.

She agreed to the name Ka as long as her daughter's middle names could be Erica and Justine, after her brothers. She regretted that even if her daughter wanted to, she'd never be able to trace her paternal lineage, because he'd taken on someone else's name and has used it ever since. Though Anne knew his real name, she preferred to call him by the assumed one and did so until it became so natural that she sometimes forgot the old one.

As her daughter grew up, she had a recurring dream of her daughter returning to Haiti after her father's death to look for his family and confronting the dead man's relatives. But she never let on she was aware he was the one who had arrested her brother, even when he told about the people he had "worked on" at the prison, describing his interrogation methods in detail.

At first, she couldn't get enough of his stories, asking him question after question. Then she led him to the narrative of his last killing, to his wrapping his bare hands around the neck of the man who had leaped at him and in quick succession gnawed the three bite marks into his face. After that story, they never spoke of prisons or torture again.

Perhaps if her daughter knew all this, she would hate both her and her husband in equal measure, like Anne did at times. Perhaps they would repulse her for months, years. But maybe she would also pity them, even deny to herself that they had ever been anything but a barber and a beautician, a husband and wife, mother and father. Maybe their daughter would teach herself to forgive them over and over again, convincing herself that loving them was giving her life more purpose than she had ever dreamed it would have.

The congregation was now getting up to walk to the front of the church to take Holy Communion.

"How lucky we are," said the priest, "that Jesus has given of his flesh for us to take into ourselves."

When her turn came, Anne got up with a handful of people from her pew, including the young couple sitting next to her, and proceeded to the altar. Uninterested and unconfessed, her husband and daughter remained behind.

Standing before the priest, Anne opened her mouth as wide as she could to accept the wafer. She then took a mouthful of wine, more than the portion she usually allowed herself. Crossing herself, she followed a line of people walking back in the other direction to their seats.

As she neared the pew where her daughter believed Constant was sitting, she stopped for a second to have a good look at him. Though he looked enough like Constant to be a relative, he was not Constant. Constant was older, fatter, almost twice the size of this man. He also had a wider forehead, bushier eyebrows, larger, more bulging eyes, a longer nose, and fuller lips.

Anne lingered at the edge of the pew, glaring down at the man until he looked up at her and smiled, appearing uncomfortable.

Someone tapped her shoulder from behind and she continued walking, her knees shaking, until she got back to her seat.

"It is not him," she whispered to her husband, who relayed the message to their daughter.

"It is not him," Anne repeated under her breath, to herself. "I knew he would have never come here."

She felt strangely relieved, as though she, her husband, and daughter had just been spared bodily arm. Her daughter, however, was still staring at the man, looking doubtful.

Anne knew at that moment that she would never attend Mass at this church, or any other Mass again. What if someone were to sit there, staring at them the same way her daughter stared at that man?

She couldn't wait for the Mass to end. They would leave the church as soon as it was over, avoiding the meetings and greetings at the end.

As they stepped out of the church, ahead of everybody else, the first thing Anne noticed was the extravagantly embellished house across the street, the one her daughter had referred to as "an inferno."

Looking over the icicle lights covering every available inch of the property and the life-size Santa, sleigh, and reindeers on the rooftop, Anne had to agree. The place did look like an inferno. But at least it was a temporary inferno, unlike their own.

FROM **Erasure**

BY PERCIVAL EVERETT

My journal is a private affair, but as I cannot know the time of my coming death, and since I am not disposed, however unfortunately, to the serious consideration of self-termination, I am afraid that others will see these pages. Since however I will be dead, it should not much matter to me who sees what or when. My name is Thelonious Ellison. And I am a writer of fiction. This admission pains me only at the thought of my story being found and read, as I have always been severely put off by any story which had as its main character a writer. So, I will claim to be something else, if not instead, then in addition, and that shall be a son, a brother, a fisherman, an art lover, a woodworker. If for no other reason, I choose this last callus-building occupation because of the shame it caused my mother, who for years called my pickup truck a station wagon. I am Thelonious Ellison. Call me Monk.

I have dark brown skin, curly hair, a broad nose, some of my ancestor were slaves and I have been detained by pasty white policemen in New Hampshire, Arizona, and Georgia and so the society in which I live tells me I am black; that is my race. Though I am fairly athletic, I am no good at basketball. I listen to Mahler, Aretha Franklin, Charlie Parker, and Ry Cooder on vinyl records and compact discs. I graduated summa cum laude from Harvard, hating every minute of it. I am good at math. I cannot dance. I did not grow up in any inner city or the rural south. My family owned a bungalow near Annapolis. My grandfather was a doctor. My father was a doctor. My brother and sister were doctors.

While in college I was a member of the Black Panther Party, defunct as it was, mainly because I felt I had to prove I was *black* enough. Some people in the society in which I live, described as being black, tell me I am not *black* enough. Some people whom the society calls white tell me the same thing. I have heard this mainly about my novels, from editors who have rejected me and reviewers whom I have apparently confused and, on a couple of occasions, on a basketball court when upon missing a shot I muttered *Egads*. From a reviewer:

> *The novel is finely crafted, with fully developed characters, rich language and subtle play with the plot, but one is lost to understand what this re-working of Aeschylus'* The Persians *has to do with the African American experience.*

One night at a party in New York, one of the tedious affairs where people who write mingle with people who want to write and with people who can help either group begin or continue to write, a tall, thin, rather ugly book agent told me that I could sell many books if I'd forget about writing retellings of Euripides and parodies of French poststructuralists and settle down to write the true, gritty, real stories of black life. I told him that I was living a *black* life, far blacker than he could ever know, that I had lived one, that I would be living one. He left me to chat with an on-the-rise performance artist/novelist who had recently posed for seventeen straight hours in front of the governor's mansion as a lawn jockey. He familiarly flipped one of her braided extensions and tossed a thumb back in my direction.

The hard, *gritty* truth of the matter is that I hardly ever think about race. Those times when I did think about it a lot I did so because of my guilt for not thinking about it. I don't believe in race. I believe there are people who will shoot me or hang me or cheat me and try to stop me because they do believe in race, because of my brown skin, curly hair, wide nose, and slave ancestors. But that's just the way it is.

Saws cut wood. They either rip with the grain or cut across it. A ripsaw will slice smoothly along the grain, but chew up the wood if it goes against the grain. It is all in the geometry of the teeth, the shape, size, and set of them, how they lean away from the blade. Crosscut teeth are typically smaller than rip teeth. The large teeth of ripsaws shave material away quickly and there are deep gaps between them which allow shavings to fall away, keeping the saw from binding. Crosscut teeth make a wider path, are raked back and beveled to points. The points allow the crosscut saw to score and cleave the grain cleanly.

. . .

I arrived in Washington to give a paper, for which I had only moderate affection, at a conference, a meeting of the Nouveau Roman Society. I decided to attend out of no great affinity for the organization or its members or its mission, but because my mother and sister still lived in D.C. and it had been three years since my last visit.

My mother had wanted to meet me at the airport, but I refused to give her my flight information. For that matter, I also did not tell her at which hotel I'd be staying. My sister did not offer to pick me up. Lisa probably didn't hate me, her younger brother, but it became fairly clear rather early in our lives, and still, that she had little use for me. I was too flighty for her, lived in a swirl of abstracts, removed from the *real world*. While she had struggled through medical school, I had somehow, apparently, breezed through college "without cracking a book." A falsehood, but a belief to which she held fast. While she was risking her life daily by crossing picket lines to offer poor women health care which included abortions if they wanted, I was fishing, sawing wood, or writing dense, obscure novels, or teaching a bunch of green California intellects about Russian formalism. But if she was cool to me, she was frozen to my brother, the high-rolling plastic surgeon in Scottsdale, Arizona. Bill had a wife and two kids, but we all knew he was gay. Lisa didn't dislike Bill because of his sexuality, but because he practiced medicine for no reason other than the accumulation of great wealth.

I fancied occasionally that my brother and sister were proud of me, for my books, even if they found them unreadable, boring, mere curiosities. As my brother pointed out once while my parents were extolling my greatness to some friends, "You could rub your shit on a shingle and they'd act like that." I knew this before he'd said it, but still it was rather deflating. He then added, "Not that they don't have a right to be proud." What went unsaid, but clearly implied, was that they had a right but not a reason to be proud of me. I must have cared some then, because I was angered by his words. By now however, I appreciated Bill and what he had said, though I hadn't seen him in four years.

The conference was at the Mayflower Hotel, but as I disliked meetings and had little interest in the participants of such affairs, I took a room at a little B&B off Dupont Circle called the Tabbard Inn. The most attractive feature of the place to me was the absence of a phone in the room. I checked in, unpacked and showered. I then called my sister at her clinic from the phone in the lobby.

"So, you're here," Lisa said.

I didn't point out to her how much better *So, you made it* might have sounded, but said, "Yep."

"Have you called Mother yet?"

"No. I figured she'd be taking her afternoon siesta about now."

Lisa grunted what sounded like an agreement. "So, shall I pick you up and we can swing by and get the old lady for dinner?"

"Okay. I'm at the Tabbard Inn."

"I know it. Be there in an hour." She hung up before I could say "Goodbye" or "I'll be ready" or "Don't bother, just go to hell." But I wouldn't have said that to Lisa. I admired her far too much and in many ways I wished I were more like her. She'd dedicated her life to helping people, but it was never clear to me that she liked them all that much. That idea of service, she got from my father, who, however wealthy his practice made him, never collected fees from half his patients.

My father's funeral had been a simple, yet huge, somewhat organic event in Northwest Washington. The street outside the Episcopal church my parents never attended was filled with people, nearly all of them teary-eyed and claiming to have been delivered into this world by the great Dr. Ellison, this in spite of most of them being clearly too young to have been born while he was still practicing. I as yet have been unable to come to an understanding or create some meaning for the spectacle.

Lisa arrived exactly one hour later. We hugged stiffly, as was our wont, and walked to the street. I got into her luxury coupe, sank into the leather and said, "Nice car."

"What's that supposed to mean?" she asked.

"Comfortable car," I said. "Plush, well appointed, not shitty, nicer than my car. What do you think it means?"

She turned the key. "I hope you're ready."

I looked at her, watched as she slipped the automatic transmission into drive.

"Mother's a little weird these days," she said.

"She sounds okay on the phone," I said, knowing full well it was a stupid thing to say, but still my bit in all this was to allow segue from minor complaint to reports of coming doom.

"You think you'd be able to tell anything during those five minute check-ins you call conversations?"

I had in fact called them just that, but I would no longer.

"She forgets things, forgets that you've told her things just minutes later."

"She an old woman."

"That's exactly what I'm telling you." Lisa slammed the heel of her palm against the horn, then lowered her window. She yelled at the driver in front of us who had stopped in a manner to her disliking, "Eat shit and die, you colon polyp!"

"You should be careful," I said. "That guy could be a nut or something."

"Fuck him," she said. "Four months ago Mother paid all her bills twice. All of them. Guess who writes the checks now." She turned her head to look at me, awaiting a response.

"You do."

"Damn right, I do. You're out in California and Pretty Boy Floyd is butchering people in Fartsdale and I'm the only one here."

"What about Lorraine?"

"Lorraine is still around. Where else is she going to be? She's still stealing little things here and there. Do you think she complained when she got paid twice? I'm being run ragged."

"I'm sorry, Lisa. It really isn't a fair setup." I didn't know what to say short of offering to move back to D.C. and in with my mother.

"She can't even remember that I'm divorced. She can recall every nauseating detail about Barry, but she can't remember that he ran off with his secretary. You'll see. First thing out of her mouth will be 'Are you and Barry pregnant yet?' Christ."

"Is there anything you want me to take care of in the house?" I asked.

"Yeah, right. You come home, fix a radiator and she'll remember that for six years. 'Monksie fixed that squeaky door. Why can't you fix anything? You'd think with all that education you could fix something.' Don't touch anything in that house." Lisa didn't reach for a pack of cigarettes, didn't make motions like she was reaching for one or lighting one, but that's exactly what she was doing. In her mind, she was holding a Bic lighter to a Marlboro and blowing out a cloud of smoke. She looked at me again. "So, how are you doing, little brother?"

"Okay, I guess."

"What are you doing in town?"

"I'm giving a paper at the Nouveau Roman Society meeting." Her silence seemed to request elaboration. "I'm working on a novel, I guess you'd call it a novel, which treats this critical text by Roland Barthes, *SI/Z*, exactly as it treats its so-called subject text which is Balzac's *Sarrasine*."

Lisa grunted something friendly enough sounding. "You know, I just can't read that stuff you write."

"Sorry."

"It's my fault, I'm sure."

"How is your practice?"

Lisa shook her head. "I hate this country. These antiabortionist creeps are out front every day, with their signs and their big potato heads. They're scary. I suppose you heard about that mess in Maryland."

I had in fact read about the sniper who shot the nurse through the clinic window. I nodded.

Lisa was tapping the steering wheel rapid fire with her index fingers. As always, my sister and her problems seemed so much larger than me and mine. And I could offer her nothing in the way of solutions, advice, or even commiseration. Even in her car, in spite of her small size and soft features, she towered over me.

"You know why I like you, Monk?" she said after a long break. "I like you because you're smart. You understand stuff I could never get and you don't even think about it. I mean, you're just one of those people." There was a note of resentment in her compliment. "I mean, Bill is a jerk, probably a good butcher, but a butcher nonetheless. He doesn't care about anything but being a good butcher and making butcher money. But you, you don't have to think about this crap, but you do." She put out her imaginary cigarette. "I just wish you'd write something I could read."

"I'll see what I can do."

I've always fished small water, brooks and streams, and little rivers. I've never been able to make it back to my car before dark. No matter how early I start, it's night when I get back. I fish this hole, then that riffle under that undercut bank, that outside bend, each spot looking sweeter and more promising than the last, until I'm miles away from where I started. When it's clear that the hour is late, then I fish my way back, each possible trout hiding place looking even more exciting than it did before, the new angle changing it, the thought that dusk will make the fish hungry nudging at me.

My mother had just awakened from her nap when we arrived at her house on Underwood, but as always she was dressed as if to go out. She wore blush in the old way, showing clearly on her light cheeks, but her age let her pull it off. She seemed shorter than ever and she hugged me somewhat less stiffly than my sister had and said, "My little Monksie is home."

I lifted her briefly from the floor, she always liked that, and kissed her cheek. I observed the expectant expression on my sister's face as the old woman turned to her.

"So, Lisa, are you and Barry pregnant yet?"

"Barry is," Lisa said. She then spoke into our mother's puzzled face. "Barry and I are divorced, Mother. The idiot ran off with another woman."

"I'm so sorry, dear." She patted Lisa's arm. "That's just life, honey. Don't worry. You'll get through it. As your father used to say, 'One way or another.' "

"Thank you, Mother."

"We're taking you out to dinner, madam," I said. "What do you think of that?"

"I think it's lovely, just lovely. Let me freshen up and grab my bag."

Lisa and I wandered around the living room while she was gone. I went to the mantel and looked at the photographs that had remained the same for fifteen years, my father posed gallantly in his uniform from the war in Korea, my mother looking more like Dorothy Dandridge than my mother, and the children, looking sweeter and cleaner than we ever were. I looked down into the fireplace. "Hey, Lisa, there are ashes in the fireplace."

"What?"

"Look. Ashes." I pointed.

The fireplace in the house had never been used. Our mother was so afraid of fire that she'd insisted on electric stoves and electric baseboard heat throughout the house. Mother came back with her bag and her face powdered.

"How did these ashes get here?" Lisa asked, sidling up to the subject in her way.

"When you burn things, you make ashes," Mother said. "You should know that, with your education."

"What was burned?"

"I promised your father I'd burn some of his papers when he died. Well, he died."

"Father died seven years ago," Lisa said.

"I know that, dear. I just finally got around to it. You know how I hate fire." Her point was a reasonable one.

"What kind of papers?" Lisa asked.

"That's none of your business," Mother said. "Why do you think your father asked me to burn them? Now, let's go to dinner."

At the door, Mother fumbled with her key in the lock, complained that the mechanism had become sticky lately. I offered to help. "Here," I said. "If you turn the key this way and then back, it turns easily."

"Monksie fixed my lock," she said.

Lisa groaned and stepped down ahead of us to her car.

Mother spoke softly to me. "I think there's a problem with Lisa and Barry."

"Yes, Mother."

"Are you married yet?" she asked. I held her arm as she walked down the porch steps.

"Not yet."

"You'd better get started. You don't want to be fifty with little kids. They'll run your tail into the ground."

My father had been considerably older than my mother. In June, when school ended, we would drive to the house in Highland Beach, Maryland, and open it for the summer. We'd open all the windows, sweep, clear cobwebs, and chase away stray cats. Then for the rest of the summer we would all remain at the beach and Father would join us on weekends. But I remember how the first cleaning always wore him out and when it came time to take a break before dinner and play softball or croquet, he would resign to a seat on the porch and watch. He would cheer Mother on when she took the bat, giving her pointers, then sitting back as if worn out by thinking about it. He had more energy in the mornings and for some reason he and I took early strolls together. We walked to the beach, out onto the pier, then back, past the Douglass house and over to the tidal creek where we'd sit and watch the crabs scurrying with the tide. Sometimes we'd take a bucket and a net and he'd coach me while I snagged a couple dozen crabs for lunch.

Once he fell to his butt in the sand and said, "Thelonious, you're a good boy."

I looked back at him from the ankle-deep water.

"You're not like your brother and sister. Of course, they're not like each other, either. But they're more alike than they're willing to admit. Anyway, you're different."

"Is that good, Father?" I asked.

"Yes," he said, as if figuring out the answer right then. He pointed to the water. "There's a nice fat one. Come at him from farther away."

I followed his instructions and scooped up the crab.

"Good boy. You have a special mind. The way you see things. If I had the patience to figure out what you were saying sometimes, I know you'd make me a smarter man."

I didn't know what he was telling me, but I understood the flattering tone and appreciated it.

"And you're so relaxed. Hang on to that trait, son. That might serve you better than anything else in life."

"Yes, Father."

"It will also prove handy for upsetting your siblings." Then he leaned back and proceeded to have a heart attack.

I ran to him. He grabbed my arm and said, "Now, stay relaxed and go get help."

That turned out to be the first of four heart attacks he would suffer before just out and shooting himself one unseasonably warm February evening while Mother was off meeting with her bridge club. His suicide apparently came as no surprise to my mother, as she called each of us, in order of age, and said the same thing: "You must come home for your father's funeral."

Dinner was typical, nothing more or less. My mother said things that made my sister roll her eyes while she smoked an entire pack of imaginary cigarettes. Mother told me about telling all her bridge buddies about my books, asking as she always did if there wasn't a better word for "fuck" than "fuck."

Then my sister dropped me at my hotel and perfunctorily committed herself to lunch with me the next day.

I was scheduled to present my paper at nine the next morning, so my intention was to get to bed early and maybe sleep through it. However, when I entered my room I found a note that had been slipped under the door that told me to return a call to Linda Mallory at the Mayflower. I went to the lobby for the telephone.

"I was hoping you would come to the conference," Linda said. "The secretary in your department told me where you'd be staying."

"How are you, Linda?"

"I've been better. You know, Lars and I broke up."

"I didn't know you were together. I suppose asking who Lars is at this juncture is pointless."

"Are you tired? I mean, it's early yet and we are still on California clock, right?"

"Is that Bay area talk? *California clock?*" I looked at my watch. 8:20. "My paper's at nine in the morning."

"But it's only eight o'clock," she said. "That's five for us. You can't expect me to believe you're going to bed at five. I can be over in fifteen."

"No, I'll come there," I said, fearing that if I declined completely, she would show up anyway. "I'll meet you in the bar."

"There's one of those little bars in my room."

"In the bar at eight-forty-five." I hung up.

Linda Mallory and I had slept together three times; two of those time we had sex. Twice in Berkeley when I was doing some readings and once in Los Angeles when she was down doing the same. She was a tall, knock-kneed, rather shapeless-however-thin woman with a weak chin and a sharp wit, a sharp wit when men and sex weren't involved at any rate. She zeroed in on male attention like a Rottweiler on a porkchop and it became all she could see. In fact, before her ears perked to male attention she could be called attractive, dark eyes and thick hair, lean and with an easy smile. She liked to fuck, she said, but I believed she liked saying it more than doing it. She could be pushy. And she was completely without literary talent, which was both irritating and, in a weird way, refreshing. Linda had published one volume of predictably strange and stereotypically "innovative" short fictions (as she liked to call them). She'd fallen into a circle of "innovative" writers who had survived the sixties by publishing each others' stories in their periodicals and each others' books collectively, thus amassing publications, so achieving tenure at their various universities, and establishing a semblance of credibility in the so-called real world. Sadly, these people made up a good portion of the membership of the Nouveau Roman Society. They all hated me. For a couple of reasons: One was that I had published and had moderate success with a realistic novel some years earlier, and two, I made no secret, in print or radio interviews, what I thought of their work. Finally, however, I was hated because the French, whom they so adored, seemed to hold my work in high regard. To me, a mere strange footnote to my obscure and very quiet literary career. To them, a slap in the face perhaps.

Linda was already in the bar when I arrived. She wrapped me up in a hug and I remembered how much like a bicycle she had felt in bed.

"So," she said, in that way people use the word to introduce beating around the bush. "We had to come three thousand miles to see each other when we live in the same state."

"Funny how things work out."

We sat and I ordered a scotch. Linda asked for another Gibson. She played with the onion in her glass, stabbing it with the red plastic sword.

"Are you on the program?" I asked. I hadn't seen her name, but then I hadn't looked.

"I'm on a panel with Davis Gimbel, Willis Lloyd, and Lewis Rosenthal."

"What's the panel?" I asked.

" 'The Place of Burroughs in American Fiction.' "

I groaned. "Sounds pleasant enough."

"I saw the title of your paper. I don't get it." She ate the onion off her sword just as our drinks arrived. "What's it about?"

"You'll hear it. I'm sick of the damn thing. It's not going to make me any friends, I'll tell you that." I looked around the bar and saw no familiar faces. "I can just feel the creepiness here."

"Why did you come then?" she complained.

"Because this way my trip is paid for." I swallowed some scotch and was sorry I hadn't requested a water back. "I'd rather admit to that than say I came here because I care about the proceedings of the NRS."

"You have a point." Linda ate her second onion. "Would you like to go up to my room?"

"Smooth," I said. "What if we don't have sex and say we did?" After an awkward spell, I said, "So, how's Berkeley?"

"It's fine. I'm up for tenure this year."

"How does it look?" I asked, knowing full well it couldn't look good for her.

"Your family's here," she said.

"My mother and sister." I finished my scotch and became painfully aware that I had nothing to say to Linda. I didn't know enough about her personal life to ask questions and I didn't want to bring up her recent breakup, so I stared into my glass.

The waitress came over and asked if I wanted another drink. I said no and gave her enough for the two Gibsons and my scotch. Linda watched my hands.

"I'd better get some rest," I said. "I'll see you tomorrow."

"Probably."

FROM **RL's Dream**

BY WALTER MOSLEY

Inez used to kiss him at night when she thought he was asleep.

She'd come to his corner of the big room after he'd been in bed for a while. First she'd strike a match on a piece of sandpaper that was tacked up on the wall. Then she'd puff on the pipe in little gasps until Atwater could smell the sweet smoke of her cured tobacco.

Inez came very close but he kept his eyes shut, not even making a peep, because "li'l boys s'posed t'be 'sleep when it gets dark outside—an' thas all they is to it." But he wasn't asleep. He was wide awake in his cot, fooling Inez; and that made him want to laugh and dance. But he couldn't make a sound while she was still there.

Inez hovered over him. He could feel it like you could feel the harvest moon when it was over the frail sharecroppers' huts in the Delta. And like that moon she brought sweet smells and slight breezes that tickled his skin the way Kiki did over sixty years later up on the fourth floor.

The child had ants in his hands and feet. He wanted to laugh out loud and caper to let Inez know that he was fooling her. He couldn't keep it in, but if he moved, Inez would get mad. Inez got mad when children couldn't control themselves. She wasn't like Ruby. Ruby was rounder and darker and she smiled almost all the time. Inez was sweet-smelling but Ruby smelled like bread.

Ruby didn't get mad even when Atwater kicked over the bucket of cleaned and peeled turnips, or when he threw that rock and broke Ruby's grandmother's colored window (which Ruby's mother had given her from the deathbed). Ruby never got mad. She'd just let her eyes get real big and say, "Atwater! How did we let that happen?" and then they'd get together and work hard to clean up the mess before Inez could find out.

But it was Inez who came out to check on Atwater at night after the alcohol lanterns were turned down. It was always Inez. And Atwater was always scared that he wouldn't be able to control himself and would make a peep and then Inez would be mad and he'd have bad dreams.

But, just when he knew he had to let go, Inez would take a deep draw on her pipe and blow a sweet wave of smoke over him. The ants became long dewy blades of cool grass between his fingers and toes. The moon gave way to blue sky and Atwater was rising and falling like one of the great box kites that Fitzhew made for the windy days of fall.

Atwater Wise came out of the sky and hit the ground running. Faster than the dive-bombing bumblebees and with nobody to tell him when to come in. There was chest-high yellow grass to run through and a hundred different odors of earth. There was the blood from his ankle, once, from a sharp rock hidden in the moss of Millwater Pond. There were the hilly nests of fire ants that would swarm over grasshoppers and tired dragonflies.

Cold water was good. Blood, scabbing over and sluggish, was good. Even the fire-orange specks on the shiny green eye of the dragonfly were good.

The wind through the stiff yellow grass wheezed like an old woman. Hidden in there were all kinds of birds that were named for their colors and sizes and personalities. They sang and warbled and croaked.

Crows came from the devil but they couldn't catch him. They called his name in crow words but the little boy just laughed.

His dreams were full of colors and smells and music. There, under the blanket of Inez's sweet smoke, he ran and played while she sat back—too old to have fun anymore.

And then the kiss. Warm and moist. It was only when she thought that he was asleep that Inez kissed Atwater. The loud groan of a timber and the snick of the door told the boy that Inez had gone back to the big bed with Ruby. He could open his eyes, but now he was too tired to move.

The young boy fell asleep but the old man came awake. Tears saved up from over half a century came for the death of that poor dragonfly. The red bird, the gray fat warbler—lost. Soupspoon had tears over the great herons and the train that ran right through town carrying the big bales of cotton down to the Mississippi River.

He remembered the one-eyed cat that came to the window to look into the house; looking for Inez's praying mantis like Death searching for that one soul who slipped away behind some trees and was overlooked, half forgotten.

Soupspoon remembered days and days down by the river with his little boyfriends—fishing, rafting, swimming among the catfish and carp.

He remembered the cotton fields and all the men and women lumbering off to work from the plantation barracks. Hollers and calls came from the fields even before the sun was up. But it was silence he heard at the end of the day.

"I'm way past tired to almost dead," Job Hockfoot would say. But by midnight on Saturday he was dancing full out.

A Negro didn't own too much back then, but he had the ears to hear music and the hands and mouth to make it. Washboards, washtubs, and homemade guitars. Mouth harps from the dime store and songs from deep down in the well . . .

"No, daddy," Kiki cried. Her voice was small and helpless. Soupspoon wondered if it was her nightmare that woke him. He sat up to look. The blankets were all kicked off her bed. Her naked behind was thrust up in the air because she was hunched over the pillow and some sheet.

"No."

A white woman; skinny butt stuck out at me like a ripe peach on a low branch. There was nobody left to tell. Nobody left to understand how strange it was, how scary it was. Nobody to laugh and ask, "An' then what you did?"

An' then I died, Soupspoon said to himself. There was nobody there to hear him. And even if there was—so what?

That was the blues.

He was eleven years old the first time he heard the blues. The year was 1932. It was on a Saturday and Atwater had been hanging around at a barn party. He got to stay late because Inez forgot to send him home.

It was Phil Wortham playing on a homemade four-string guitar with Tiny Hill working a squeeze-box. It wasn't like anything that Atwater had ever heard. The music made him want to move, and the words, the words were like the talk people talked every day, but he listened closer and he heard things that he never heard before.

Your heart breaking or your well running dry. Things like cake batter at the bottom of the bowl and the mist clinging to the road on summer mornings.

The music made Atwater want to dance, so he knew that it had to be good.

A good friend of the boy's—an older man named Bannon—had been killed only a week earlier. Atwater hadn't shed a tear.

People died in the Delta; they died all the time. Atwater hadn't cried, but a dark feeling came over him. He didn't know what it was until he heard Phil and Tiny play at the barn party. He didn't know that he had the blues.

That music had changed him. From then on at night, after Ruby and Inez had gone to bed, he'd go out the window and make it down to the Milky Way.

The Milky Way was a beat-up old chicken barn that had been coated with tar and dotted with yellow splotches of paint that were supposed to be stars. It was a lopsided ugly building in the daylight. But at night, when you came through Captaw Creek and around the old elm, it looked like something magic; like, Atwater thought, a hill house of God.

He was too young to go into a juke joint, but he made up his mind to try on his birthday.

And so on a summer's evening, when the sun was still out, Atwater told Ruby that he and Petey Simms were going to set nets for crayfish down at the creek. But really they meant to take the quarter that Fitzhew had given Atwater for his birthday and get two glasses of whiskey from Oja, the midget owner of the Milky Way.

Petey made it as far as the old elm—where he stopped and gawked as Atwater walked on ahead.

"Wha' wrong wichyou, Petey Simms?" Atwater asked when he turned to see that he was alone.

Petey just shook his head. He was a long-necked heavy-eyed youngster who everybody but Atwater called Turtle.

Atwater followed Petey's gaze to two women who were standing out in front of the juke. They were big women wearing loose dresses that flowed in the breezes, flaring up now and then to expose their legs. They had very big legs. Petey was looking at those women (especially, Atwater knew, at those legs) and shaking his head.

Atwater was scared too but he thought that they'd be safe as long as they stuck together.

"Come on," he said. "They ain't gonna bite you."

He said it loudly to shame his friend, but he didn't expect the women to hear.

"Hey you," one of them shouted.

Petey took off like a scared hare. Shoop! He was gone.

"Hey, boy!" the voice called out again. "You!"

One of them was coming toward him. She had a kind of rolling motion in her thighs as she walked. She waved for him to come to her while her friend stayed back near the juke, shading her eyes to see.

"Me?"

"Come here!" the woman shouted—none too kindly. She was tall and heavy-chested with hair that was combed straight back from her head.

"Come here!"

Atwater's bare feet obeyed, but he didn't want to walk down there.

"Hurry up, boy! I ain't got all night!" The big woman was smiling, one meaty fist on her hip.

"Yes, ma'am?" Atwater said when he stood before the woman.

"Elma," she said. Her smile revealed that one of her upper front teeth was gone. Another one had been broken in half. "Elma Ponce is my name. What's yours?"

"A-A-Atty . . ."

"A-A-Atty," Elma mocked the poor boy. "What you doin' out here, A-A-Atty? Yo' momma know you here?"

"Elma, what you messin' wit' this baby for?" The other woman had come up to them.

They seemed like women then, but now, on Kiki's couch, Soupspoon remembered them as teenagers—maybe eighteen. But they were women to Atty Wise. They wore the same cut of loose dress. Elma's dress was blue while her friend's was a washed-out orange.

"Jus' playin' wit'im, Theresa." Elma took Atwater by the arm. "What you doin' here, Atty?" The sweetness in her voice was not lost on him.

"My birfday," he whispered.

"What? Talk up."

"My birfday today."

Elma showed her snaggle teeth again. "Yo' birfday? An' you come down to Milky Way to get a kiss?"

"N-no . . ." Atwater said. He could feel himself shaking but couldn't stop.

"You scarin' the poor boy, Elma," Theresa laughed. "Let him be."

"I come to get a drink on my birfday day," Atwater said. He said it fast to keep Elma from getting mad. He didn't want to see her mad. "I come t'get a drink wit' my birfday quatah."

"You got a quatah?" Theresa asked. She was black-skinned and good-looking the way a handsome man looks good.

"Uh-huh. Yes, ma'am."

Elma, still holding the boy by his arm, pulled Atwater toward the door of the Milky Way. "Come on," was all she said.

The dark blue front door had a big drippy yellow circle painted in the middle. That circle was supposed to be the moon.

Elma pushed the door open, dragging Atty in behind her. Theresa followed up the rear, holding on to his pants.

Elma went up to the bar and shouted, "Oja! Bring a pint bottle ovah here!" She pointed across the dark room to a row of makeshift booths hammered together against the far wall.

"The hell I will," small fat Oja replied. He climbed up on his stool to face her. "Where you gonna come up wit' money for a pint an' not ten minutes ago you couldn't even buy no beer?"

Theresa pinched Atty's butt and giggled in his ear.

He was thankful for her closeness, because the Milky Way on the inside scared him to death. The floor was black and sticky, covered with crushed peanut shells. It smelt of sweat and sour beer. The ceiling was uneven and low; at some points a full-grown man wouldn't have been able to stand up straight.

And it was hot.

"I can't pay for it," Elma hooted. "But my boyfriend here could."

Elma yanked Atty's arm, pulling him away from Theresa and up next to her.

"Well? Pay the man, Atty," she said. "You want yo' birfday toast, don't ya?"

Atwater took the quarter from the pocket of his cutoff trousers and handed it to Elma.

"Not to me. Give it to the barman an' tell'im what you want. That's what you do when you a man."

Oja had a mashed-in black face with a long cigar stuck out between his battered lips. He was too small to work in the cotton fields, so he had to go into business for himself.

"Well?" the bartender asked.

Atty pressed his quarter into the pudgy little hand.

"Yo' a'ntees know you down here, boy?" Oja asked once the coin was in his pocket.

"Yes sir."

"You sure?" Oja had this thing he did with his eyes. He'd open one very wide and close the other until it was just a glistening slit.

"Put that eye back in yo' head, nigger," Elma warned. "He done told you that they know an' he done give you his money, too. So pull down that pint. The *deep* brown stuff, too."

After they collected their whiskey and tin cup, Elma pushed Atty until she had him dammed up between her and the wall in the booth. Theresa sat on the other side. She held his hand from across the table. After tasting the first drink, Elma leaned up against him, rubbing his chest and holding the cup to his lips.

"Drink, Atty. Thas it. Take some more, baby. This here will make you into a man."

His tongue and throat burned. The fumes from that homemade brew made his eyes tear and his breath come short. But what Atty felt most was Elma rubbing and pinching his chest.

"We gonna grow some hair right ovah here tonight," she whispered.

Theresa's smile was bright against black skin.

They all drank. Atwater held his breath as he watched the cup go from Theresa's lips to Elma's mouth and then to him. Their hands were all over him and they laughed more and more with the liquor.

Elma was almost on top of him. She let her arm rest in his lap.

"I think A-A-Atty like me, Theresa," she said.

Theresa reached over and grabbed Atwater by the back of his neck. She pulled on him until they were kissing across the table.

"You better let up from him, bitch," Elma said in a serious tone. "I'm the one found'im. He mine tonight."

When they weren't fighting or feeling on Atty the women talked trash. Atty learned that they lived on Peale's Slope: a little shantytown where most Negroes slept under propped-up shelters with no walls or right outside on the ground if the weather was good. Elma stayed with her old uncle up there in a small cabin. Theresa had lived with them since her boyfriend had left her.

Atwater wanted to know everything about these women. He could repeat every word of what they said, but he didn't understand it all. For years after that night he'd remember things they said and suddenly, because of something that would happen, he'd realize what they meant.

As evening came on, people began to fill up the bar. It got noisier and smokier but Atwater hardly noticed. Theresa and Elma were enough for him. When Elma would lean close he looked down between her breasts and she'd give him her shattered smile and say, "Atty? What you lookin' at?"

"How you girls doin'?" A slender man slid in on the bench next to Theresa, but he was looking Elma in the eye.

"Who you askin'?" Elma replied. She took Atty's hand and held it tight.

"You, baby. Who else I'ma be talkin' to?"

"All I know, nigger, is that you was s'posed t'be here nine days ago."

"Nigger?" The man had a baby face, but when he smiled he looked evil. Elma's hand tightened under that smile, and Atwater's heart began to race.

"I don't know what you smilin' at. Atty here took me out for a drink, so he my boyfriend tonight." Elma's voice had lost all of its play.

The fine young face turned toward Atty. He smiled again without showing his teeth.

"Cody," Theresa asked, "what you doin' here?"

"I said I was comin'," he said.

"That was more'n a week ago."

"I had sumpin' to do, woman. I got here as soon as I could."

"What you had to do?" Elma asked.

"I don't see what's it to you. You done already got another boyfriend."
Cody smiled and reached down beside him. He brought out of his overalls a
full quart bottle of store-bought Old Crow whiskey. "I planned to say I was
sorry wit' this here, but I guess I got to find me another girlfriend.

"You still wit' John, Theresa?"

The handsome black woman's mouth came open and she shook her head
to say that she was not.

"Theresa!" Elma shouted.

"I ain't did nuthin'," Theresa screamed. She licked her lips and avoided
Cody's smiling eyes. "He jus' axed an' I told'im."

"You ain't gonna go messin' 'round right under my nose," Elma said. She
was crushing Atwater's hand.

"Come on, girls," Cody said. "Don't let's fight. They's whiskey for all of
us. Right, Atty?"

"I-I think I had enough," the boy answered. The room was hot but his
forehead felt like ice. "I got . . . I gots to go home."

Cody reached down into his pants again and came out with a long homemade knife. The blade was from a five-inch metal saw that had been shaped
and sharpened by a grinding stone. It was black and jagged but Atwater
could see that it was still sharp. The haft was wadded cork wound tightly
around with fly-green fishing twine.

Cody put the knife down next to the bottle and said, "You not refusin'
my hospitality now is ya, man?"

"Cody . . ."

"Shet yo' mouf, Theresa. Ain't nobody axed you. If this man here is man
enough take my woman then he man enough t'drink wit' me."

Elma sat stock-still. She let go of Atty's hand. That was the scariest moment for Atwater, because he knew that if Elma was scared then he didn't
have a chance.

"I drink it," Atty said.

While he was still smiling, Cody poured the tin cup full to the brim and
then pushed it in front of Atwater.

"Cody, he cain't drink all that," Theresa said. "He ain't no man."

Cody raised his hand and Theresa flinched back so hard that she banged
her head on the wall.

Atwater picked up the cup and started sipping. Fifty and more years gone
by and he was still amazed that he had the strength to drink as much as he
did.

Cody put a finger to the boy's throat to make sure that he was swallowing.

When Atty finally put the cup down, Cody smiled and said, "That's only
half."

The room changed after Atwater drank. Most of what he heard was just noise but he could hear some talk, even from across the room, very clearly. Colors became stronger and the yellow paint on the walls really did look to be stars.

Elma was saying something but he couldn't make it out.

"I gotta go," Atwater said.

"See?" Elma pointed at him. "You done made the boy sick."

She moved quickly to get up off the bench and let Atwater out. He slid over with no problem, but standing up was a whole new experience. One leg gave way and then the other. He struck the table with his chin, but the feeling was more sweet than it was painful. He was afraid of falling to the sticky floor, but Cody caught him before he tumbled all the way.

The evil baby face came up close to his and said, "You go out an' do yo' business an' then come on back, ya hear?"

The boy thought about nodding—maybe he did.

" 'Cause if you ain't back in two minutes I'ma come out there an' cut you bad."

Then Cody pushed Atwater toward the door. It was a crooked path to get there; bouncing off one body and then into somebody else. It was like a playful child's dance with everyone laughing and pushing. He didn't mind the horseplay though, because, even in that small room, he was too drunk to find the door by himself.

There was the moon again. About three-quarters floating in a thick black eye. The night clouds were golden shoulders for that cyclops. The air was chill and for deep breathing, not like the hell smoke of the Milky Way.

While Atwater relieved himself he laughed because it felt so good. Then he started walking. The leaves crackled and the stream sounded like baby bells. Every footfall was a bass drum going off.

He was lost but that didn't matter. He had a long talk with his murdered friend and said good-bye.

He scraped and scuffed himself and finally fell face forward in the cold stream. The water sobered him for a moment and he sat on a big rock and wondered where he was.

Once he heard somebody call his name. At first he thought that it was Inez out looking for him. He almost called out but then he worried that it might be Cody. So he kept quiet and played dead.

The next morning he awoke in Alyce Griggs's barn, just about a quarter mile from his house. A white hen was clucking and dancing around his feet.

"What you doin' in here, boy?"

When Atwater lifted his eyes to see the woman he felt sharp pain throughout his head and jaw.

"Sorry, Miss Griggs," he said to the elderly white woman. "I got drunk at Milky Way an' I landed here in yo' barn."

"That's the devil in you, Atty," the scrawny white woman warned. "You know that, don't ya?"

"Yes, ma'am," he said, and meant it.

"Go on now. I hope Inez hides you good."

He never did get a beating for that night. When Atwater came through the door he was staggering from fever. The chill and the whiskey had made him sick. For three weeks Ruby and Inez took turns sitting over him, covering his forehead with damp towels and feeding him foul home remedies one after the other.

His lungs filled up and his dreams walked around the house with a life of their own. He choked and coughed and finally accepted that he was going to die. He made his goodbyes to Ruby and Inez so bravely that even stone-faced Inez cried.

When Atwater got out of bed again he knew that he was a man.

"Daddy?" Kiki was sitting up in the bed.

"You okay?" Soupspoon asked.

Fully naked, she got up from the bed and came over to the couch. She sat spread-legged before him and held out her hands for him to hold.

It wasn't sex on her part. It was a frightened girl, no older than Atty at the Milky Way, holding out her hands to be saved.

"What's wrong?"

"I don't know. I'm scared," she said all at once. "I'm scared of . . . of . . ."

"What?"

Kiki told him about her dreams of a stone boy stalking her with his knife.

"It's okay, honey," Soupspoon said when she was through. "He ain't gonna get in here."

"That's not all," she said, avoiding his eyes.

"What else is it?"

"I can't tell you yet. I . . . I have to wait."

"Okay," he said, trying to catch her eye without ogling her orange-brown crotch. "I'll be here when you ready."

"What's wrong?" Kiki asked. "Why you look away from me?"

"I don't know. It's just that you're a nice girl. You should cover up in front of a old man like me."

"You shy?" She smirked while trying to get him to meet her gaze.

"Naw, I ain't shy. I seen it all. But I like you an' I feel like I don't wanna get the wrong idea."

Kiki's face went smooth when he said that. Her eyes became perfect circles with tears beaded up on the lashes. She leaned forward as if she meant to hug Soupspoon but then she got up and went to the bed and rummaged around on the floor. She came up with a ratty brown robe and wrapped herself in it.

She held out her arms as she came back to the couch.

"Can I hug you, Mr. Wise?"

"Sure."

"I won't let anything happen to you," she whispered into the embrace.

Soupspoon was thinking about little Atty wandering through the wilderness over stones white as skulls.

FROM **The Harris Men**

BY R. M. JOHNSON

Caleb sat on a slab of rock and watched two old men play chess. One had a beard, and one was wearing an old fishing hat. They were both filthy. It was an interesting game, so Caleb couldn't just get up and leave in the middle of it, he had to see who won. He looked down at his watch and it read 11:52 A.M. He had gotten out of the house at eight o'clock, telling Sonya that today would be the day that he would find a job. He had even put on his only pair of real pants, a pair of cotton Levi's Dockers. They were a little big and a little long because he had bought them at a discount store, but they still looked kind of professional. Stuffed in his pants pocket was a clip-on tie that he had taken off during the intense chess game.

When the game was over Caleb moved to a park bench and opened the paper to the job section. He started to glance over the tiny blocks of advertisements. "Computer Analyst," one announced, and the ten blocks under it marked positions. Sales Manager, Nurses, Engineers wanted, Electricians, Marketing Executives. These were the ads that caught his attention and all they did was discourage him. There was no way in the world he could qualify for one of those positions with his limited education. He hadn't even graduated from high school, for God's sake.

He sank his face in his hands and wondered why he was even going through the trouble. It didn't make sense to look, get all dressed up and walk around like a fool panhandling for a damn job. Something would come along eventually, it always did. Somebody who knew somebody else would offer him a job, didn't really matter what it was, but he'd take it and everything would be cool. And if that didn't happen, he'd hit Sonya up again. She worked at the unemployment office, and she'd get him a couple of inside tracks just like she had last time, even though he screwed those up.

Happy with himself, his actions all planned for finding a job, he tossed the job section in the trash can near where he was sitting, and folded the rest under his arm. It was too beautiful a day to be out begging for a job. He looked at his watch again and it was only 12:15. Sonya wouldn't expect him back till at least three, so he would find something to do.

He hopped on the bus, showing the driver the crinkled little piece of paper he used to transfer from one bus to the next. He had to squeeze his way through the people because the bus was crowded with the lunchtime rush. A woman was getting up and he took the seat, even though another woman seemed to have been waiting patiently for the vacancy.

The bus was heading in the direction of the inner city housing projects, the many tall identical buildings that lined one of the major highways of Chicago. They stood there, hundreds of feet tall, as a constant reminder of how poor black folks were in this city. They were like building-size billboards, Caleb thought, screaming "Blacks folks be po'! Hey, just look where we live!"

The crowd on the bus started to thin because of the direction the bus was traveling. No one wanted to end up among the project buildings if they didn't belong there.

Across the aisle from Caleb was a man wearing one of those fancy business suits like Austin always wore, the kind Caleb hated so much. But he had to admit, of all the ones he had seen, this was one of the nicest. He was a man of about forty-five or fifty, Caleb figured, and on his lap rested, of course, a briefcase. The man was black, neat-looking, clean-shaven, with shiny shoes and those thin little black socks that you can see through. He wore a diamond ring on his right hand, a wedding band on his left, and on his wrist was a very nice watch. He sat facing Caleb, looking out the window behind him. Caleb looked him up and down; the attention didn't seem to bother the man. He reminded Caleb of Austin, so damn caught up with his suits and ties, watches and rings. He would have bet anything that this guy was just as much a joke as Austin was.

He looked him over again, and wondered what the man was still doing on the bus—they were closing in on the outskirts of the danger zone, and looking the way he was, Caleb figured he should've gotten off the bus long ago. But the man just continued looking out the window as if the surroundings were nothing new to him. Caleb wondered how much money he made, what he did, and what the hell he was doing so damn far away from the suburbs where all the other un-black black folks lived. The man must have felt Caleb's stare. He smiled slightly and nodded. Caleb nodded back, feeling the man was as phony as a three-dollar bill.

"Hey, what's your name?" Caleb asked, not feeling at all out of place.

The man looked up, raising his eyebrows as if to ask, "Me?"

"Joseph Benning," he said, seeming comfortable speaking to a stranger. "And what's your name, young man?"

Caleb thought about not answering, not liking the "young man" remark, but he figured compared to his old ass, he was a young man.

"Caleb. My name is Caleb Harris."

"Nice to meet you, Caleb Harris. Nice day, isn't it?" He smiled, looking out the window. Caleb looked out the window behind him, the same one Benning was looking out, as if it was the only one with the view of the nice day.

"Yeah, I guess so." Caleb looked over the man again, paying close attention to the watch, the big diamond that was where the twelve should have been, the shiny gold of the rings, and the expensive look of the briefcase. He wondered what the street value would be for all that stuff. That is, if he were still into robbing, which he wasn't. But he was sure it would've been reason enough to risk taking it off the old guy. Besides, he probably had it insured, and if he didn't, Caleb was sure he made enough to run out and buy replacements.

"How, how much you make?"

"Excuse me?" The man smiled, seeming embarrassed by the question.

"You know what I mean. How much money you bringing in? I know it has to be a lot if you're walking around with all that on," Caleb pointed a finger in the general direction of the man's hands and wrist.

"That's not the sort of question you ask someone you've just met. That's really not the sort of question you even ask a friend."

"Yeah, I know all that, but I wanted to know, so I asked. All you can do is say no, right? I'd just be right back where I started. So how much?"

The man laughed. He looked at Caleb, appearing to consider the question.

"I make enough," he finally replied.

"All right then, you don't have to tell me. All the people making the big money don't want the little folks to know how much it is, like they're ashamed of their big salaries 'cause they know we aren't making nothing."

"Well, how much do you make, Caleb? If you don't mind me asking."

"No. I don't mind you asking." Caleb paused for a moment, feeling a bit ashamed of himself. "I don't make anything. I don't have a job. I'm out here looking, that's why I got the schoolboy getup on." He reached in his pants pocket and pulled the tie out a bit so Benning could see.

"And how is it going?"

"It ain't. It's tight, man. I been all through this paper, and ain't nothing in here for me to do." He tossed the paper to the seat next to his.

"And what is it you do?"

"Damn, you ask a lot of questions."

"If I'm prying, just ask me to stop." He placed his briefcase to his side and crossed his legs.

"Yeah, well, I do the basic stuff, you know, hands work. Lifting boxes, washing dishes. Stuff like that." Caleb looked away.

"So do you think—"

"What do you do?" Caleb interrupted, taking the spotlight off himself.

"I'm a manager and partial owner of a large computer software supplier downtown. Main Frame Software, you heard of it?"

"Yeah, I think so." Never hearing the name before in his life. "So what you doing on this side of town? You a bit far from the Gold Coast, don't you think?"

"I'm visiting a friend, she's sick."

"Don't you have a car, making all the money you do?"

"Yes, I do, making all the money I do." He smiled. "It's in the shop getting the window replaced. Someone broke into it."

"Mercedes, Lexus, BMW, something like that, right?" Caleb asked.

"Something like that."

"Well, if you keep coming around places like this, it's going to stay in the shop. You don't belong out here, you think?" Caleb asked.

Benning looked out the window at what was passing outside.

"Why don't I?"

"Cause you . . . you know. You rich. You got all that. These people out here, we don't have nothing. You never know, man. They might try and knock you over the head. If I were you, I'd be scared."

"Why, are you scared?"

"Naw, hell no," Caleb said. "I ain't scared. Besides, I don't have nothing. I'm referring to you." He pointed a finger.

"Well, I'm sorry to say, but I disagree. I don't think that a man should fear places that his own people live in just because he has nice things. Besides you make it appear as though everyone here, or individuals without money, are bad people and can't be trusted."

"Well, I almost want to say that's right," Caleb said.

"I don't think you're a bad person, Caleb Harris. Are you?" He looked intently in Caleb's eyes.

Caleb looked back, then smiled and laughed a little. "Very funny, I see your point, but I'm just telling you, you should watch your back, that's all. I'm just looking out for an old guy," Caleb said, joking. "You know, you're out of your element. It's rough around here."

"I'm not as old as you think, but thanks for the gesture." Benning stood, grabbed his briefcase, then looked out the window. "Well, this is my stop. Interesting conversation. I wish we had more time to continue it."

"Yeah, me too," Caleb said, nodding his head.

"I tell you what." Benning reached into his jacket pocket, took out a tiny leather folder, and pulled out a little white card. "This is my business card. If you would really like to continue this conversation, give me a call and we can meet somewhere for lunch or something."

Caleb took the card, looked it over. " 'Main Frame Software, Joseph Benning, Dept. Manager.' Yeah, okay, I'll do that."

"Good." Benning extended his hand and Caleb shook it vigorously.

"Good-bye, Mr. Harris." Benning walked toward the front of the bus, but stopped. "Oh, yeah, and the remark you made about me being out of my element—I'm not. This is where I grew up." He smiled at the look on Caleb's face and stepped off the bus.

He grew up here? Caleb thought. He's lying. He's making too much money to come from this. It couldn't be. He looked down at the card again. He held it with both hands, almost caressing it. Department manager grew up in the projects, that's something. Caleb felt good that he had met someone that had actually made it out of the wretched place, that is if the old guy was telling the truth. He was a cool old guy, and he had a lot to say. Caleb was genuinely sorry that they couldn't keep talking. He could have learned a lot from the man, or at least found out how much money he made. But he had already decided that he would call him. He would call him and they would do lunch. He really didn't have much else to do during the day. Caleb Harris and this important, rich, money-making old dude that grew up in the projects would talk.

Caleb felt good about himself, felt proud, as though he had accomplished a great deal. He wanted to tell someone, but he didn't feel like going back home. He wanted to celebrate, get a forty-ounce bottle of beer or something. He got off the bus, stepped into the liquor store, and grabbed a bottle of beer. Miller High Life, his favorite. He paid for it with loose change, then set off to find a couple of his friends. He knew they'd be hanging out on a nice day like this, because they had no jobs, either.

He took off down the street, carrying the bottle of beer, small paper bag covering it halfway, exposing the neck. It was almost two o'clock and the sun was getting warmer. It was pretty bright and it seemed to improve the looks of everything. Even the streets of the projects didn't look that bad. The abandoned cars, the bits of trash that grew along the curbs as if they were flowers that belonged there, the areas of hard-packed gray dirt where grass used to grow. Nothing looked as bad as it did on glum, dull days when the sun wasn't out. When Caleb saw his friend Blue sitting on a park bench with a couple of other guys, he said loudly, "Hey, man, what's up with your black ass?" They called him Blue because he was so black—so black that he was blue.

Blue looked at him weirdly, as if he had never seen Caleb happy. "What's up with you? Finally win the Lotto or something?" He had a bottle of beer himself. He was sitting on the backrest of the bench, his feet planted on the seat. He reached down and grabbed the forty-ounce bottle from between his legs.

Caleb had known Blue since they were kids, the better part of his life, and like Caleb's, Blue's life seemed to be moving in every direction but the correct one. Blue's father hadn't cut out on him, but he was gunned down on his way home from work one day. Wrong place wrong time. So Blue knew what it was like to grow up without a father, and that was one reason the two of them were so tight. Whatever it was they were missing by not having fathers around, they found in each other, and Caleb could no longer count how many times they had saved each other's asses from sticky situations. Blue had always been there for him, just like a brother, even when Caleb's real brothers weren't.

"What you doing all spiffed up, looking like you coming from church?" Blue said, taking a swig from the bottle of beer. The remark provoked a chuckle from the two other guys, one standing and one sitting.

"Been looking for a job, man. Had to," Caleb said, slapping Blue's hand.

"Sonya been riding that ass again, huh?" He did his Sonya impression, raising the sound of his voice. "You better get your ass out there and find you a nine to five, or don't think about bringing your butt back in this house!" He took another swig from his bottle, this time a longer one. Caleb could see the tight little ball in his neck go up and down as the beer slid down his throat. Blue pulled the bottle away and smiled, the gold tooth in the front of his mouth reflecting sunlight.

"Naw, it ain't nothing like that. I got responsibilities, that's all," Caleb said.

"Well, did you get one? You find a job?"

"Naw, but I met this dude. Real cool dude. Grew up in the projects, got this software company, and make big cash. We talked on the bus. He got a lot to say, and I'm going to listen. I'm going to get a job from him, just listen to what I'm saying."

"Yeah, all right, that's cool," Blue said, with little enthusiasm.

"I'm for real. Look at this." Caleb reached in his pocket and pulled out the card. He held it in front of Blue's face, not allowing him to grab it.

"Let me hold it," Blue said.

"Naw, you going to get it dirty, bend it all up, just look."

Blue took a quick glance, then dismissed it. "All right, man, that's great. Happy birthday. Now why don't you put your toy away and crack that brew, 'cause if you ain't, you can pass it this way."

Caleb did what he was asked, and decided that his friend would never make more of himself than what he was at that moment: one more brother sitting on a bench, swigging on a forty. Sure Caleb was doing the same thing at that moment, but he wouldn't be there for the rest of his life.

They sat and talked, the four of them. They talked about life and women and the white man keeping them down, lack of job opportunities, the destruction of the world, and whatever else floated into their heads. One of the other guys that Caleb didn't know—his name was Pete—took out a small, crumpled piece of aluminum foil. He opened it up, then pulled out of his pocket a small booklet of thin papers. He proceeded to roll the contents of the foil into the paper, licked it a couple of times, then lit it.

"Now you talking," Ray Ray said. That was the other guy, big afro on his head. He was a huge lethargic guy. Pete passed Ray Ray the joint, and he took a long drag from it.

"See, the white man want us to work a nine to five. That's where he want us, see," Ray Ray said, already high. "Because if we work a nine to five, he'd have control over us. He'd be monitoring us, you see. Have us piss in a bottle to see if we be enhancing. They don't want us enhancing our minds with the herb, because they know that it gives us knowledge, it clarifies shit." He took another puff, pulled the joint from his mouth, and held it before him, staring at it, marveling as if it was the cure for cancer. "I'll fuck a motherfucker up, he try and take this from me."

"Just pass the shit and stop tripping!" Blue said. "I ain't working that shit, 'cause it's just like slavery. They want you to sweat, break your back for them, and what do they give you? Some money so you can run out and buy some insignificant shit on credit. Then they have you paying them, not just one time but for two years, or three years, or five years." He took a hit of the blunt and held the smoke in as he finished talking, his voice sounding strangled. "And then don't just have you paying them for years and years, but have you paying for more than the shit actually cost—interest and shit." He blew the smoke out through his nose and mouth. "Black folks think they arrived when they get a credit card and a car note, but they don't realize, they just jumped into a funnel, and it goes nowhere but down." He passed the joint to Pete.

"But what do you have?" Pete asked. "You ain't got shit but them gym shoes on your feet, and you need to be buying a new pair real soon, 'cause those starting to talk."

Everyone laughed a little, except Blue.

"That's cool, too. I ain't got no car, and I don't have no credit card either, but you know what else I ain't got? Debt. I don't owe no one shit. You hear me. Shit! Big fat zero. So yeah, I ain't making no money, but I sure as hell ain't spending none, either. Am I right, or what, Caleb?"

Caleb looked over at Blue and considered what he had said. "You right, man, for the most part. I don't like it either. I don't like no one telling me what to do, sizing me up, condemning me 'cause I put the square peg in the circle hole. And you right about folks being so far in debt that they never going to see they way out. They going to die still paying off that TV that they renting to own. But if you got responsibilities, if you going to live, you got to make money. That's just the way life is. White folks made it that way so we got to work, and that brings us back to them controlling us."

"I don't care what you say, I'm living, and I ain't working. I'm living, smoking this here joint, and it's what I'm going to continue to do until I find out what it is I really want to do," Blue said.

"And when is that going to be, when you fifty?" Ray Ray said.

"That's going to be when that's going to be. I ain't rushing for nobody."

"I'm glad you got it like that, but some of us can't be taking our time," Caleb said. He wanted to continue, letting them know that some of them, speaking of himself, had a girlfriend that practically was his wife, and a child to raise, plus rent to pay and food to buy, but they wouldn't have understood. All they thought about was sitting out, talking shit, and getting high.

There was a time when that was all that interested him as well, but lately he had been getting ridiculed from all sides. Sonya had done everything but come out and call him a complete loser. She'd leave the day's paper on the table with the job section open, things circled, things that she thought he should check out. She'd always ask him how things were going, had he found a job yet? It all seemed like gentle nudging, something that she referred to as "support," but he found it painfully annoying. Like she had to remind him every day that he had no job, that he brought no money into the household. He needed no one for that. He could simply dig in his pockets, and the lint there spoke loud and clear.

Caleb downed the last of his beer and looked at his watch. It was a little after four o'clock and he figured it was time he got home. He said good-bye to his friends. "Yeah, better get that ass home before you get in trouble," was Blue's farewell.

Caleb only had to wait about five minutes before he saw the bus slowly roll down the street.

He didn't like the pressure, not just from his girlfriend but also from his brothers. Marcus kept telling him that he should do this and do that. Maybe enroll in school, take the GED, and maybe he'd find out that he had a new liking for school. That shit would never happen. First of all, he wasn't the slightest bit interested. Secondly, he was scared as hell of all the book stuff. He could never get it. The math, the science, it was too far above his head, and he just felt like a fool even attempting to make an effort. It was just easier if he didn't have to bother with it at all, so he dropped out, and he would not return, no matter what Marcus said.

Then there was Austin. Caleb realized that Austin really didn't give a damn anyway, but he still felt pressure. Not pressure directly from Austin, but pressure from himself to do something, if for no other reason than to prove his brother wrong. It seemed from as far back as he could remember, Austin had written him off as a loser. He didn't know why, and it was something that had bothered him even as a child. He could remember his father would give him the same loser treatment, as if he wasn't as deserving as his older brothers, or as if he always got in the way of their time together. Caleb just figured that Austin's treatment of him stemmed from his father's treatment, considering how much Austin looked up to the man.

Caleb would do something. He would have to. He couldn't just continue to live the way he was living, freeloading off his girlfriend, not being able to contribute a single dime toward their expenses. He pulled out the card again and held it before him. "Mr. Joseph Benning," he said softly to himself. He smiled, then put the card safely back in his pocket.

The Boy-Fish

BY DAVID ANTHONY DURHAM

When Eldon spoke, his voice was slow and muffled. "Sutekh, go up and wash."

Sutekh looked up from the book in his lap. He stared, not at his father's face, but at his T-shirt. He pursed his lips, shaping them into a momentary, silent protest, and then he stood up and walked across the small room. In the hallway, he passed the pictures of old people captured in straight-backed postures, in shades of black and white, with eyes that seemed to follow him. He sought out the image of the woman who had been his mother. He knew her picture well: the creamy tones and fine lines of her features, her thin eyebrows and gentle eyes, the long black hair, so straight, cast over her shoulder as solid and thick as a rope woven of seaweed. And he knew her name,

Anita, so often on his father's lips. But his memory of her was fading as each day of the last nine months pushed between them.

The bathroom was a cramped space, with an old bathtub and a slowly dripping sink. It smelled of mildew and of moisture trapped in towels. Faint city sounds entered through the tiny window above the tub. Sutekh closed the door, turned on the water, and undressed. His body was small, skinny, light brown, and smooth as an eggshell, gentle as a marble statue, marked only by a paisley-shaped slash of pink across his forehead, a birthmark. He had a face of delicate features, with a narrow, aquiline nose, and eyes so gray they seemed almost translucent.

Looking through the window, Sutekh caught sight of a gull swooping through a cloud-laden sky. He watched its erratic flight until he heard footsteps coming up the stairs. He stepped into the tub, scowled at the heat, and stood there, listening. The noise had stopped. He held one hand to his heart; the other rested on the cool yellow tiles. Finally, he reached for the cold-water knob. Just as he touched it the door opened. Sutekh looked up and there was his father. He shifted his eyes to his father's chest and sat down, wincing at the heat of the water.

The man swayed as he walked in. "Stand up," he said.

Sutekh rose.

Eldon touched Sutekh's head. He slid his hand from the boy's forehead, up over his hair, and traced his fingertips down the boy's spine. He cleared his throat, closed his eyes, and swallowed. "Let's clean you up," he said. "Okay? We'll just wash."

Eldon had a light chestnut complexion, with freckles under the eyes that jiggled as he talked. His features were well formed and evenly spaced, with the slightly pudgy quality of a young boy. He leaned on the wall beside the refrigerator, the phone to his ear. With one finger, he pushed plastic magnets around on the metal door: pears and apples and bananas; several alphabetical letters.

Sutekh sat at the kitchen table, a book in his lap. He ran his fingers over its smooth cover and along its edges. His gaze drifted around the wall near his father and settled on a dim stain on the flowered wallpaper, the splash of some liquid.

"Yeah, Gen," Eldon said into the phone. "Yeah. It's all right. I mean, I still have the same job. I don't know for how long, but it's all right . . . You know what I do. The furniture reupholstering . . . Right . . . Of course." Eldon glanced over at his son. "Yeah, Sutekh is fine." His finger knocked off an apple-shaped magnet. It fell to the floor, bounced off his foot, and twirled under the refrigerator. He kneeled down and slid his hand underneath the appliance. The metal grating at the bottom of the refrigerator dis-

lodged and fell onto his fingers. He pulled his hand, and the grating clanged
to the floor. "Damn it!" he said. "No, I dropped something and now the
damn grating fell off the fridge."

He stood up, kicked it, backed away a few steps, and put his palm up to
his forehead. "Forget it. So, Gen, why is everyone always after us to come
visit? Jesus. It's either you or Momma, but somebody's always nagging. Told
her we'd come out next week. Might just leave Sutekh with them for a couple days, let the old man play his granddad games."

Sutekh looked down at his book. It was a large, thin children's book. On
the cover there was an illustration of a boy in a bulky yellow raincoat and
hat. The boy held a duck out before him, grasped by the leg. The duck was
captured in mid-squawk, and the boy appeared to be pulling back, surprised. Sutekh traced a line around the boy with his finger.

"Yeah, yeah. Okay. We'll come by soon. But first Momma wants to have
Sutekh stay over there for the weekend or something." Eldon had been rubbing his injured palm with the fingers of his other hand. He stopped and his
gaze shot over to Sutekh. "Okay, hold on. Sutekh? Come talk to your Aunt
Genevieve." Eldon extended the phone toward him.

Sutekh rose and, holding the book under one arm, took the phone from
his father. The receiver was warm and greasy with moisture. "Hello?"

"Hey, Sutekh!" said Genevieve, her voice exhilarated, almost breathless.
"How are you?"

Eldon walked away and stood next to the table.

"Okay," Sutekh said.

"Okay? Well, all right. Great. I haven't seen you since the Fourth of July.
Remember the Fourth of July? When we took that boat ride to Saint
Michaels and had all those crabs?"

"Yeah."

"You were scared of them at first, remember?"

Sutekh tucked his head and smiled. " 'Cause they had pinchers," he said.

"I know. They are pretty ugly. But they're good on the inside."

"Yeah." Sutekh nodded. He raised his book up as if just remembering it.
"Gen, I have a book."

"Really? What book?"

"Um . . ." Wrinkles stood out on the boy's forehead. He looked down at
the cover. "About a boy and a duck."

"Yeah? Hey, that reminds me—How's school? You just started school,
right?"

Sutekh glanced over at his father. "No."

"No what? You didn't start school?"

"No."

"What?" Genevieve's voice grew serious. "Why not? Didn't your father take you to school? I can't believe this. You should be starting school. You're going to be behind already. Let me speak to your father."

Sutekh shook his head. He looked over at his father, who was watching him. "No. It's okay, Aunt Gen. Right? I don't want to go so much."

"Well, of course you don't, but that's just because it's something new. Once you try it you'll like it fine. And anyway, you have to go. It's not a choice. Let me speak to your father."

Sutekh turned toward the wall. "I have a book—"

"Sutekh, honey," Genevieve said, her voice both gentle and commanding, "put Eldon on."

The boy turned back to his father and held the phone out toward him. The corners of Eldon's lips dipped, but he grasped the phone. "Yeah?"

Sutekh walked back to the kitchen table and sat down, book balanced on his knees.

"Gen . . . I'm taking him. You just don't know how things are. It's not easy . . . He's been coming to work with me . . ." He listened for some time. He nodded, and when he spoke his voice had softened. "I don't know. It's just been these last nine months. I'll take him, but sometimes I'm afraid to have him out of my sight. Other times . . ." He ran a hand up over his hair. "Other times I just don't know. Anyway, fuck it, Gen," he said, not angrily, but with an exasperated sigh. "I'm hanging up now. You should watch what you ask for. Some day I might drop him on your doorstep for good." He hung up the phone and stood leaning against the wall for a few moments, one hand in a fist that slowly rapped against the wall.

He turned around.

Sutekh didn't look up at him, but said softly, "I just said I had a book."

Sutekh's bedroom was a small space, cluttered by articles of clothing, toys, and books. A single bed ran the length of the wall, its crumpled bedspread trailing across the floor. The walls were painted a thick, innocuous yellow, and were bare except for a poster of the Earth viewed from space and a calendar featuring football players frozen in motion. The room's one window opened onto the wall of the next row house, just below an opposing window.

Sutekh walked in, clothed in light blue pajamas, his bare feet padding lightly across the hardwood tiles. He tossed his book down on the floor and stood still in the center of the room. His eyes drifted up to the window across the alley. The light was on, and a person's vague shadow moved across the scarlet and gold curtains.

He took a few steps toward his bed, then jumped as he approached it, landing with a bounce on the mattress. The jostling of the mattress and sheets tossed several objects into the air: two *Star Trek* action figures, a miniature automobile, a small brass elephant figurine. The boy picked up the Star Trek figures and stood them face-to-face with each other, control-ling their arms with his fingers. One figure gently touched the other on the forehead. Suddenly they began to wrestle, their bodies pushed clumsily to-gether. Then Sutekh picked up the elephant and tilted it upward. A faint sound escaped his lips, a high-pitched, somewhat horse-like whine.

"You call that an elephant roar?" Eldon asked. He stood leaning against the doorframe.

Sutekh stopped moving. The brass figurine fell from his fingers.

"That's no elephant roar. That sounded like a mouse roar or something." He entered the room and sat down on the corner of the bed. He placed a hand on Sutekh's back.

The boy didn't move, his eyes fixed on a wrinkle in the blanket.

"If I was an elephant, I'd roar like this . . ." He let out a roar, a guttural cry that went from low pitched to higher pitched, ending with an expulsion of air somewhere between a laugh and a cough. "Well, something like that." He swiped in the air with a hand. "Something like that . . ."

The humor with which he had just spoken faded quickly, his expression changing to one of exhaustion. The bags below his eyes were more pro-nounced than usual, with a bluish tint to them. His gaze drifted around the room, over his son's back and shoulders. He moved his hand from Sutekh's back to his head and stroked his hair. When he spoke again, his voice was limp, each word falling heavily from his lips. "Have you ever seen an ele-phant? You never have, have you?" He stretched out on the bed beside his son.

Sutekh squirmed away a few inches and rolled over on his side, facing his father. The man's breath carried the stale scent of alcohol and onions.

"I went to see the elephants with your mom, at the circus," he said. "She didn't like the circus, but she liked the elephants. She talked about Hannibal and how he rode elephants across the mountains and fought the Romans. That must've been something . . . Anita could tell such good stories. I'll tell you about Hannibal sometime. But I can't tell it as good as her. I can't do anything as good as her." Eldon exhaled a long breath and looked past Sutekh at the wall. He closed his eyes and inhaled. "Sutekh, your dad's go-ing crazy," he said, his voice barely a whisper. "He's going crazy, and he doesn't know what to do." With his eyes still closed, he reached out and felt for his son.

Sutekh moved back a little, but let his father grasp him around the arm. The man's fingers were firm in their grip, but still gentle. The boy watched his father's face, the lines around his mouth, the flutter of his eyelids, the movement of his lips.

"She shouldn't have gone. You didn't have to, Anita. You didn't . . ." He pulled Sutekh close to him. "I would have fought the snakes with you. I

wouldn't have let them get you, never. We could have fought anything together. That's all I ever wanted. To fight back the world with you. To make a
place for us."

Eldon opened his eyes and liquid burst forth from both of them, lingering momentarily on the rim of his eyelids, then sliding over the bridge of his
nose, down his cheek, and falling onto Sutekh's head, which the man held
under his chin. He closed his eyes again and rubbed Sutekh with comforting gestures, his hand making gentle circles on the small of his back. He
said, "Shhh," softly, as if it were the boy who was crying. "Shhh." It was
only very gradually that his own body began to move, that his comforting
gestures became caresses, and he began to rub the boy's body against his
own.

Eldon drove the car slowly down Frederick Avenue, a quiet street of lumpy
asphalt, shaded by tall gum trees and an occasional pine. Sitting among the
trees were houses of varying sizes and designs. Some had the aged look of
antebellum estates, with large porches and fold-out windows. Others were
modern structures, small houses of simple geometry, in pastel shades of light
blue and mint green, with plaster shingles and fake shutters. They sat quietly among the trees, with the silence of a ghost town. Behind the houses on
the right, the surface of a small harbor sparkled with the auburn shades of
the setting sun.

"Hey, little man, remember you stayed down here last summer?" Eldon
asked. "You do a lot of fishing then?"

Sutekh slipped his seat belt underneath his arm and pressed his face close
to the car window. His eyes floated slowly over each object they passed, lingering on the wake left by a slow moving boat in the harbor, following the
flight of a flock of ducks. The houses to the west momentarily thinned out,
and the glow of the sun lit Sutekh's face. He watched his image reflected in
the glass and saw his lips move. "Some," he said.

"Yeah, that's your granddad," Eldon said. "I guess he's got to do something with himself. I don't know why it's fishing, though. I never really liked
fishing that much. Maybe it was the getting up early." He reached up and
turned the rearview mirror toward his face. He looked at himself, drew his
lips back from his teeth. "Your granddad will probably complain that I'm
depriving you by not taking you fishing and stuff. I don't know if I would
know how anymore." He moved the mirror back to its original place. "Like
fishing really matters."

Eldon slowed the car down and pulled over in front of a small, single-
level house. "Here we are." He turned off the car and reached into the backseat for a duffel bag. "Go on, get out."

Sutekh untangled himself from his seat belt and climbed out of the car.

He stood on the concrete walkway and looked at the house. It looked back silently, a white, flat-faced facade, with two front windows set on either side of the door. The three steps leading up to the door stuck out like a protruding tongue. There was a light on near one of the windows, it cast a corrugated glow through the blinds. The only noticeable decorations were the three plaster kittens that clung to the roof's green shingles.

"Come on." Eldon nudged Sutekh forward.

Just as he began walking, the front door opened and his grandmother, Rosella, appeared silhouetted within the door frame. "Sutekh! Come here to your grandmother," she said. She pushed open the screen door and extended her arms toward him.

Sutekh walked steadily up the pathway, the stairs, and, when he reached her, was engulfed by her arms, pressed into her torso. She took his face within her two hands and looked at him for a long moment. Her face was pale and covered with delicate wrinkles. Her cheeks had the soft quality of half-baked dough, and her eyes were a deep brown, flecked with bits of yellow. She kissed him on the forehead.

"It's so good to see you. Every time I see you you've grown a few inches." She backed up and motioned for them to enter. "Hi, Eldon. Come on in. I've just about got dinner ready."

The interior of the house was cluttered with furniture: a couch, numerous chairs and endtables, and lamps. The walls were littered with plaques and awards from various clubs and organizations, framed photographs, and several aged needlework pieces. Each flat surface was occupied by something, an ashtray or magazines, wooden figurines and other items, the various knickknacks collected over a lifetime. The television was on, tuned to the news, and the scent of fried chicken was thick in the air.

"No dinner for me, thanks," Eldon said. "I'll just drop Sutekh off and get going."

"You sure?" Rosella asked. She leaned forward when she spoke, and furrowed her brow with a look of concern. "Your father isn't home yet, but he should be any minute. He just went to the store."

"Yeah." Eldon plopped the duffel bag down in a chair. "I have to meet someone in a little bit."

He looked from his mother to Sutekh, puffed up his cheeks and exhaled. "Hey, Sutekh, what do you say I just take off? Your grandmother will take care of you. All right?"

Sutekh sat down on a chair in the living room. He looked back at his father and shrugged. "All right."

Eldon's eyes flicked up to Rosella. She was watching the boy, her head tilted slightly to the side, her face fixed in a smile. "Okay," he said. "Um . . . So what, I'll be back Sunday night?"

"Sure," Rosella said. "Whenever. We'll be here."

"Okay. See ya, Sutekh. Have fun, right? Remember what I told you." He walked back to the front door and paused there a moment, looked back. Rosella watched him. "Okay," he said. "Bye."

"Bye, Eldon. We'll look for you on Sunday."

He stepped outside and shut the door behind him.

Rosella turned back to Sutekh. "I'm making your favorite—fried chicken for dinner. I should go check it. I'll just be a minute." She shuffled from the room toward the kitchen.

Sutekh turned and looked through the blinds, out the window. His father stood next to the car, saying something to Norman, Sutekh's grandfather, who had just pulled into the driveway. Norman held a grocery bag to his chest with one arm. He walked around the front of his car, as Eldon walked to the driver's side of his. They got no closer than this, and after exchanging a few words that Sutekh couldn't hear, Eldon waved and Norman turned toward the house.

Sutekh released the blinds when he heard Norman open the door. They snapped back into place.

Norman's skin had a smooth texture, a hue like raw sienna, marked by deep lines that etched his features. The edges of his forehead extended far up into his thinning hairline. He held up a spoonful of buttered corn and paused, leaning his elbow on the table. "So, you're ready to get up early, right?" he asked. His tone was serious, as if conducting official business. "You know that's when the fish are hungry. Early in the morning. If you go out much past sun up you're not gonna get much. It's the early worm that catches the fish." He smiled, slipped the fork into his mouth, and chewed rapidly, his thin, gray-flecked mustache jiggling up and down like a living creature.

Sutekh sat across from him at the dinner table, next to Rosella. He held a chicken leg in his fingers. He nodded and took a bite.

"Is that all you can talk about?" Rosella asked. "You'd think you fished for a living."

Norman wiped his mouth with a napkin, which he held crumpled in his hand. "That's why I retired, isn't it? A man's got to do something with his time. Can't just sit around doing nothing. Right Sutekh?"

Sutekh nodded. He wiped his hands on the napkin in his lap.

"That's why you work your whole life," Norman said. He pointed at Sutekh with his knife. "You work your whole life so that one day you can stop working and retire. Buy yourself a house by the water and do some fishing with your grandson. That's what it comes down to in the end. That's got to be what it comes down to, because thirty years spent working behind a desk, handling other people's money, ain't much of a life. But you've got to put in the time. Lord knows I've done mine and now—"

"Norman, don't lecture the boy."

Norman scowled. "I'm not lecturing. I'm talking to my grandson. Somebody has got to educate the boy. I'm just telling him what work is about. Figure Eldon don't tell him nothing."

"Norman—"

"Don't say you think Eldon knows anything about work. You know he doesn't. Never did. That boy never had an ounce of backbone in his body, not from day one. He's got a spine like one of them salamanders." He raised a forkful of corn to his mouth, but pulled it away, spilling a few kernels back onto his plate. "But Sutekh, you're gonna do better, aren't you? You know what you are, son?"

Sutekh looked up at him. He shook his head.

Norman leaned forward. "You're the hope of this family. You know that? You're the only one left to carry on for me. You're my only grandson, my right-hand man. The only one I'm ever gonna have." He lowered his voice. "You know why? Because your Aunt Genevieve only likes women. She's what they call a 'female fag.' "

Rosella's knife and fork clanked down against her plate. She watched Norman with her lips puckered, her cheeks drawn in.

"What do you think of that?" Norman asked. "My own daughter. Your own aunt. A woman's woman." He began to put the fork in his mouth, but, seeing it was almost empty, he put it down and picked at his chicken breast. "The hope of the family."

"Norman, give it a rest and let Sutekh eat."

Norman spoke while still chewing. "I'm not saying anything but the truth. Did everything I could in this world and I still ended up with two messed-up kids. If I had my way I would send them back and start over again. Just start from scratch."

"Thank the Lord you don't have that option," Rosella said. She turned toward Sutekh. "How's everything, Sutekh? Save room for dessert. Norman got some ice cream for you. See, when he's not in a grumpy mood he's really pretty nice."

"I'm not grumpy," Norman said. He wrung his hands on his crumpled napkin. "Not really. You hear, Sutekh? How could I be grumpy when I'm going fishing with my grandson in the morning? To tell you the truth, I'm feeling downright pleasant. Grumpy is another thing entirely."

Sutekh and Norman sat together on the pier, with fishing rods and hooks and worms. A steady flow of waves passed beneath them. Moisture from the chill air clung to their clothes, tickled their skin. The garbled hum of a clam boat crept across the surface of the water; the blanket of morning mist soft-ened the sharp-edged cries of gulls. A pelican flew out of the void and glided low across the water. Its head was stretched intently forward and its wings were held still in motionless speed. "Well, look at that," Norman said. "That's a pelican. He's a fisherman, too." As quietly as it appeared it was gone into the distance.

Sutekh held his fishing rod between his legs, one thumb pressed against the fishing line. His feet dangled off the pier. On the surface of the water, the gray sky seemed to heave and undulate. Minnows swam beside seagulls through the clouds.

"Look," Sutekh said. "There's fish in the clouds."

Norman watched the water for a moment. He stroked his mustache with the tips of his fingers. "Well, yeah, I guess you could say that. You've got a funny way of saying things though."

Sutekh looked up at his grandfather. Norman looked down and slowly the crevices of his face stretched into a smile. He adjusted his hat and was about to speak when he suddenly jerked backward. "Hot damn! I got ya!" he yelled. He struggled to rise as his fishing pole bent and jerked. Sutekh put on the rubber glove from the tackle box and felt the metal spikes of its palm. He stood, holding his fishing rod in one hand and the glove in the other, watching the old man struggle.

Norman turned to him. "Come here. Stick that away and take this here."

Sutekh jumped, secured his fishing pole in a crack between the boards, threw off the glove, and took the man's fishing pole carefully into his hands. Instantly, he felt the vigorous tug of the fish shooting through the line. He wound the reel, bending forward and back. His heart pumped furiously, aroused both by the tugging and the fear of being pulled from the pier.

"It must be a big one," Norman said. He stood protectively close, slap-ping his hands frequently on his legs.

The boy's hands began to falter, barely able to turn the reel. Norman pointed over his shoulder and there it was, the fish surging against the string in a wide arch, a streak of silver in the water. "Keep her steady," the grandfa-ther said. "Bring her in slow." Eventually, the boy slowed so much that Nor-man reached over and helped him bring the fish up.

The fight ended, but now began the futile flapping. The fish sparkled with tiny scales. It still tried to breathe. The mouth opened and closed rhythmically, showing rows of small teeth, sharp like bits of glass.

"Careful of her mouth. If she gets a grip on your finger, she'll take it," Norman said. He grabbed the fish with the glove. There was a crunch as the spikes dug in. The fish tried to wiggle free, but Norman yanked at the wire going into its mouth. The hook wouldn't come out. "It's a bluefish. Proba-bly a foot long." He reached down into the tackle box and pulled out a tool the size of a screwdriver, a short pole with a corrugated bulge at the end, for extracting hooks. He shoved it down the fish's mouth and twisted. "Yeah, this'll be good eating," he said. Then he yanked out the tool, bringing with it the hook and pieces of gill and blood. The fish stopped fighting, only tried to breathe a little longer, then went limp.

"That'll do it," Norman said. He tossed the fish into an empty bucket. Its tail peeked over the rim. "What do ya say? You caught a real blue, boy. Catch another one like that and we got dinner."

Sutekh nodded. He looked at the pier, toward the bucket, at his grandfather. "We're gonna make you a fisherman yet," Norman said. "Check your line."

Sutekh turned slowly, as if he didn't understand, and pulled his fishing rod from the crack. As he reeled it in he looked back at the bucket, at the fishtail.

The kitchen's fluorescent light sputtered on. Sutekh and his grandfather walked in and set their things down; the fish by the sink, tackle box and rod on the floor.

"Your grandmother must be at Helen's," Norman said. He leaned back against the counter. "Okay, now comes the dirty part. I ever teach you how to clean fish?"

Sutekh said, "No."

"I haven't? Seven years old and you never cleaned a fish? It's your daddy's fault, you know. He's been in the city too long is what it is. He hasn't been out here in years, has he? He just comes and drops you off and is gone like a flash." Absently, he added, "Ain't been no good since your mother passed. That's got him messed up in the head."

Sutekh looked as if he was about to say something, but the words evaporated before they escaped his lips. Instead, he just looked up, his eyes searching his grandfather's features.

Norman motioned for Sutekh to pull a stool up to the counter, and dumped the bucket of four fish into the sink. "Now, you have to be careful with the knife or you'll take off a finger. Hear?" He turned the water on and let it wash over the fish, pulled a long, thin knife out of a drawer and dipped it under the stream. He put a fish on the counter and grabbed it by the tail. "Now, first you got to scale it." He scraped the blade up and down fish's side. Scales flaked off on the knife or popped onto the counter. He flipped the fish over and did the other side. "See, you gotta get these off. You wouldn't want to eat them." He put the blade of the knife behind the fish's gills and leaned down. The creature's head dropped into the sink with a dull thud. A rich maroon substance oozed from the hole where the head had been. He slit the fish's belly open and pulled out its insides with his fingers.

He flicked them into the sink with a quick snap of his wrist. "You see what I been doing? Just slit it down here and pull out the mush." He turned the fish around and sliced the tail off with a quick thrust. "And there you go. Clean and ready for the pan." Norman held the fish up and smiled at Sutekh. "You ready to try?"

Sutekh stepped down from the stool and backed away a few steps.

"Whatsa matter, son?" Norman asked.

Sutekh looked him in the face for a moment, but then leaned back against the counter, with his head down.

"Son? Don't you want to scale your fish?"

Looking down, Sutekh saw the man's shoes, dock shoes, dirty from salt and fish and use, against the swirling pattern of the linoleum floor. "Granddad," he said. Sutekh closed his eyes and spoke without lifting his head. His voice was pained like bending wood. "Sometimes I think that's not supposed to happen."

"You think what's not supposed to happen? What are you talking about?"

"Daddy."

Norman stood up straight and cleared his throat. "What's wrong with your father?"

"He rubs on me," Sutekh said.

"What? You're not making sense."

"He rubs on me."

"Son, I don't know . . ." Norman began, but before he could complete the sentence some thought muffled his words. The questioning wrinkles around his eyes faded. His jaw went slack, and he seemed to pause in the middle of a breath. His gaze drifted away from Sutekh.

When Sutekh saw his grandfather's shoes step away a few paces, he looked up, his face tight, his lips quivering. "Granddad?"

The man was still, with his back turned toward the boy. His spine was crooked, one hand touching the wall, one shoulder higher than the other. His body looked broken and limp. He shook his head, said something under his breath, and placed a hand over his forehead. "Stop. Stop talking this foolishness."

Sutekh's forehead furrowed. He reached up and tugged at his lower lip, his eyes never leaving his grandfather. "He rubs on me. Sometimes in the bath—"

Norman moved. He turned and stepped forward and his hand rose, stiff as a board, and smacked Sutekh across the cheek. The force threw the boy's head sideways and knocked him from the chair.

"You dirty . . ." Norman stood above him, one hand raised as if to strike again, the other reaching down in a gesture almost comforting. He hesitated. Both hands trembled, and, when he spoke, his voice wavered. "I said stop talking that. You need to listen when I tell you a thing. You think I want to listen to—" He cut himself off and turned away. "That's enough. Your grandmother will finish cleaning the fish." Without another word, he left the room. The patio door banged shut behind him.

Sutekh lay still, with his arms wrapped tightly around his torso. There were scales on his face, but he didn't seem to notice. He had bitten the tip of his tongue, and a trickle of blood escaped the edge of his lips. He didn't seem to notice this either. When he finally moved, he did so carefully, silently. He placed his hands up to his throat, and gently probed the skin with his fingers, as if searching for some object lodged beneath the flesh.

The Way I See It

BY TERRY MCMILLAN
FROM *A Day Late and a Dollar Short*

Can't nobody tell me nothing I don't already know. At least not when it comes to my kids. They all grown, but in a whole lotta ways they still act like children. I *know* I get on their nerves—but they get on mine, too—and they always accusing me of meddling in their business, but, hell, I'm their mother. It's my job to meddle. What I really do is worry. About all four of 'em. Out loud. If I didn't love 'em, I wouldn't care two cents about what they did or be the least bit concerned about what happens to 'em. But I do. Most of the time they can't see what they doing, so I just tell 'em what *I* see. They don't listen to me half the time no way, but as their mother, I've always felt that if *I* don't point out the things they doing that seem to be causing 'em problems and pain, who will?

Which is exactly how I ended up in this damn hospital: worrying about kids. I don't even want to think about Cecil right now, because it might just bring on another attack. He's a bad habit I've had for thirty-eight years, which would make him my husband. Between him and these kids, I'm worn out. It's a miracle I can breathe at all.

I had 'em so fast they felt more like a litter, except each one turned out to be a different animal. Paris is a female lion who don't roar loud enough. Lewis is a horse who don't pull his own weight. Charlotte is definitely a bull, and Janelle would have to be a sheep—a lamb is closer to it—'cause she always being led out to some pasture and don't know how she got there.

As a mother, you have high hopes for your kids. Big dreams. You want the best for them. Want 'em to get the rewards from life that you didn't get for one reason or another. You want them to be smarter than you. Make better choices. Wiser moves. You don't want them to be foolish or act like fools.

Which is why I could strangle Lewis my damnself. He is one big ball of confusion. Always has had an excuse for everything, and in thirty-six years, he ain't changed a lick. In 1974, he did not steal them air conditioners from the Lucky Lady Motel that the police just happened to find stacked up in the back seat of our LeSabre way out there in East L.A. Lewis said his buddy told him they belonged to his uncle. And why shouldn't he believe him? All of a sudden he got allergies. Was always sneezing and sniffling. He said it was the smog. But I wasn't born yesterday. He just kept at it. Said he couldn't help it if folks was always giving him stuff to fix or things he didn't even ask for. Like that stereo that didn't work. Or them old tools that turned out to be from Miss Beulah's garage. Was I accusing him of stealing from Miss Beulah? Yes I was. Lewis was always at the wrong place at the wrong time, like in 1978 while he waited for Dukey and Lucky to come out of a dry cleaner's with no dry cleaning and they asked him to "Floor it!" and like a fool he did and the police chased their black asses all the way to the county jail.

For the next three years, Lewis made quite a few trips back and forth to that same gray building, and then spent eighteen months in a much bigger place. But he wasn't a good criminal, because, number one, he always got caught; and, number two, he only stole shit nobody needed: rusty lawnmowers, shovels and rakes, dead batteries, bald tires, saddles, and so on and so forth. Every time he got caught, all I did was try to figure out how could somebody with an IQ of 146 be so stupid? His teachers said he was a genius. Especially when it came to math. His brain was like a calculator. But what good did it do? I'm still waiting for the day to come when all them numbers add up to something.

Something musta happened to him behind them bars, 'cause ever since then—and we talking twelve, thirteen years ago—Lewis ain't been right. In the head. He can't finish nothing he start. Sometime he don't even start. Fortunately, he ain't been back to jail except for a couple of DUIs, and he did have sense enough to stop fooling around with that dope after so many of his friends OD'd. Now all he do is smoke reefa, sit in that dreary one-bedroom apartment drinking a million ounces of Old English, and play chess with the Mexicans. When ain't nobody there but him (which ain't often 'cause he can't stand being by hisself more than a few hours), he do crossword puzzles. Hard ones. And he good at it. These he *do* finish. And from what I gather, he done let hundreds of women walk through his revolving door for a day or two but then all he do is complain about Donnetta, his ex-wife, who he ain't been married to now going on six years, so most of 'em don't come back.

And don't let him get a buzz going. Every other word outta his mouth is Donnetta. He talk about her like they just got divorced yesterday. "She wanted a perfect man," he claimed, or, "I almost killed myself trying to please that woman." But even though Donnetta was a little slow, she was nice, decent. After I'd left Cecil for the third time, I stayed with 'em for close to a month. By the second week, I was almost ready for the loony bin. First off, Donnetta couldn't cook nothing worth eating; she wasn't exactly Oprah when it came to having a two-way conversation; cleaning house was at the bottom of her things-to-do list; and that boy needed his ass beat at least twice a day but she only believed in that white folks' "time-out" mess. She didn't have as much sense as a Christmas turkey, and how you supposed to lead a child down a path when you lost your damnself? I understood completely when that chile turned to God, got saved, and finally stopped giving Lewis dessert at night. A few months ago she sent me a pink postcard from some motel in San Diego saying she got married, is seven months pregnant and they already know it's a girl, and her new husband's name is Todd and he wants to adopt Jamil, and what do I think about all this? And then: P.S. Not that it should matter, but Todd is white. First of all, who she marry is her business, even though Lewis'll probably have a stroke when he find out. But one thing I do know: Kids love whoever take care of 'em.

Lewis been lost since she left. And he blames everybody except Lewis for his personal misery. Can't find no job: "I'm a threat to the white man," he says. "How?" I ask. "You more of a threat to yourself, Lewis." He huffs and puffs. "I'm a victim." And I say, "I agree. Of poor-assed planning!" And then he goes off and explains the history of the human race, and then black people, and then finally we get to the twentieth century and the castration of the black man that's still going on in society today because just look at how successful the black woman is compared to us! This is when I'd usually hand him another beer, which finally either shut his ass up, or he'd nod off into a coma.

Tragedy is his middle name.

For years I fell for his mess. Would lend him my Mary Kay money. My insurance-bill money. Even pawned my wedding ring once so he could pay his child support. But then it started to dawn on me that the only time he call is when he want something, so I stopped accepting the charges. Last week he come calling me to say another one of his little raggedy cars broke down on the side of the freeway, way out in redneck country, where Rodney King got beat up, and I guess I was supposed to feel sorry for him, which I did for a hot minute, but then I remembered he ain't had no driver's license for close to a year, and then he asked could I wire him $350 till his disability check came, and this time, this was my answer: "Hell, no!"

He got mad. "You don't care what happens to me, do you, Ma?"

"Don't start that mess with me, Lewis."

"You don't understand what I'm going through. Not one bit. Do you?"

"It don't matter whether I understand or not. I'm your mother. Not your wife. Not your woman. And I ain't no psychiatrist neither. What happened to Conchita?"

"It's Carlita."

"Comosita, Consuela, Conleche . . . whatever."

"We broke up."

"I'm shocked."

"I need your help, Ma. For real."

"So what else is new? You ain't even supposed to be driving, Lewis."

"Then how am I supposed to look for work or get to work?"

I decided to just pretend like I didn't hear him say the word "work." "I don't know. Call one of your friends, Lewis."

"I ain't got no friends with that kind of money. It's tough out here for black men, Ma, and especially if you handicapped. Don't you know that?"

"I didn't know you was handicapped."

"I got arthritis."

"Uh-huh. And I'm three months pregnant with triplets."

"How come don't nobody ever believe me when I tell the truth? I can't hardly ball up my fist, my knuckles is so swollen. And on my right wrist, the bone is sticking out. . . . Oh, never mind. Ma, please?"

"I have to go now, Lewis. I ain't got no three hundred and fifty dollars."

"Yes you do."

"You calling me a lie?"

"No."

"I'm telling you. All my money is spent."

"Where's Daddy?"

"Barbecuing. Where you think?" I say, lying my butt off.

"Could you ask him? And tell him it's for you?"

I just started laughing. First of all, I ain't seen Cecil in over a month, but I didn't feel like getting into it right then.

He groaned. "How about two hundred dollars, then?"

That's when I slammed the receiver down, because I couldn't stand hearing him beg. My hands was shaking so bad and my heart was beating a mile a minute, so I reached in the kitchen drawer, grabbed my spray, and took two or three quick puffs. Seem like he ain't gon' be satisfied till he use me up. That thought alone made me start crying, and I don't like to cry, 'cause it always do me right in. I couldn't get no air to come through my nose or mouth, and I clenched my fist and said in my head, "God give me strength," as I made my way to my room and sat on the edge of the bed, turned on my machine, grabbed that plastic tube, and sucked and sucked until my palms got slippery and my forehead was so full of sweat that I snatched my wig off and threw it on the floor.

I love Lewis. Would give him my last breath. Lord knows I don't want nothing bad to happen to him, but Lewis got problems I can't solve. It's some things love *can* do. And it's some things it can't do. I can't save him. Hell, I'm trying to figure out how to save myself.

Now, Charlotte. She a bull, all right. And I wish I didn't feel like this but I do: Half the time I can't stand her. I don't know how her husband can tolerate her ass either. I feel sorry for Al, really. He's one of them pussy-whipped, henpecked kinda husbands but try to pretend like he Superman in front of company. *Everybody* know Charlotte is a bossy wench from the word go. We ain't spoke this time going on four months. I think the record is five or six. I can't remember. But, hell, all I did was tell her she need to spend more time at home with them kids and she went off.

"When was the last time you worked full-time, took care of three kids and a husband, ran a household *and* three Laundromats, Mama, huh?"

"Never," I said.

"So how can you sit there on your high horse telling me what you think I *should* be doing?"

"Get some help and stop trying to do it all yourself."

"Do you know how expensive housekeepers is these days?"

"Oh, stop being so damn cheap, Charlotte. You don't have no trouble spending it."

"Cheap? Let me . . ."

"I heard Tiffany got expelled and Monique is running her mouth so much in class that she might be next."

"Who told you this—Janelle? With *her* big mouth? I know it, I just know it. Well, first of all, it ain't true."

"It is true, and it's your fault for not being there to keep their behinds in line."

"I'ma pretend like I didn't hear that. But let me tell you something, *Mother*. Tiffany did *not* get expelled. She got sent home for wearing too much perfume, 'cause half the class—including the teacher—started getting nauseous. And for your information, Monique just told a joke that made everybody laugh."

I knew she was lying through her teeth, but I didn't dare say it, so I just said, "Un-huh."

"And since Janelle's running her mouth so much, did she bother to tell

you that Monique is also having a tough time 'cause we regulating her medication?"

"I got her medicine, all right."

"Mama, you know what? I'm so tired of your sarcastic remarks I don't
know what to do. Sick of 'em! You never have nothing nice to say about my
kids!"

"That's bullshit, and you know it!"

"It ain't bullshit!"

"When they do something good, then I'll have a reason to say something
nice."

"See, that's what I mean! Has Dingus thrown a touchdown pass lately?
And what about your darling Shanice: Did she get straight A's again? Go
ahead and throw it in my face. I could use some more good goddamn news
today!"

"You better watch your mouth. I'm still your mother."

"Then don't call me until you start acting like a mother and a grandmother to *my* kids!" And—bam!—she hung up.

The truth always hurts. This ain't the first time she done slammed the
phone down in my face or talked to me in that nasty tone: Like I'm somebody in the street. I ain't gon' lie; It hurts and cuts into me deep, but I refuse
to give her the satisfaction of knowing how bad she makes me feel. To be
honest, Charlotte just likes people to kiss her ass, but I kissed their daddy's
behind for thirty-eight years, I ain't here to pacify my kids. No, Lordy.
Them days is over, especially since they're all damn near middle age.

Charlotte came too quick. Ten months after Paris. I did not need another
baby so soon, and I think she knew it. She wanted all my attention then.
And still do. She ain't never forgiven me for having Lewis and Janelle, and
she made sure I knew it. I had to snatch a knot in her behind once for putting furniture polish in their milk. Made 'em take a nap in the doghouse
with the dog and fed 'em Alpo while I went downtown to pay some bills.
Had 'em practice drowning in a bathtub full of cold water. How many steps
could they jump down with their eyes closed without falling. The list goes
on.

Now, all my kids is taller than average, as good-looking as they come and
as dark as you can get, and I spent what I felt was a whole lotta unnecessary
time and energy teaching 'em to appreciate the color of their skin. To not be
ashamed of it. I used to tell 'em that the blacker the berry the sweeter the
juice, 'cause everybody know that back then being yellow with long wavy
hair meant you was automatically fine, which was bullshit, but here it is
1994 and there's millions of homely yellow women with long straggly hair
running around still believing that lie. Anyway, no matter what I did or said
to make my kids feel proud, Charlotte was the only one who despised her

color. Never mind that she was the prettiest of the bunch. Never mind that she had the longest, thickest, shiniest hair of all the black girls in the whole school. And nothing upset that chile more than when Paris started getting breasts and learned how to do the splits and Charlotte couldn't. She was the type of child you couldn't praise enough. Always wanted more. But, hell, I had three other kids and I had to work overtime to divide up my energy and time. What was left, I gave to Cecil.

Where's my lunch? I know this ain't no hotel, but a person could starve to death in this hospital. Would you look at that: It's raining like cats and dogs and here it is March. This weather in Vegas done sure changed over the years. It sound like bullets hitting these windows. I wish they would turn that damn air conditioning down. My nose is froze and I can't even feel my toes no more. I hope I ain't dead and just don't know it.

Anyway, it ain't my fault that right after we left Chicago and moved to California, Charlotte didn't like it and put up such a fuss that we sent her ass back there to live with my dinghy sister, Suzie Mae. She forgot to tell me and Suzie Mae she was damn near four months pregnant when I put her on the train. Young girls know how to hide a baby when they want to, and I'm a hard person to fool. I pay attention. Don't miss too much of nothing. But Charlotte is good at hiding a whole lot of stuff. She snuck and got married, and wasn't until another two months had passed when Suzie Mae come calling me saying, "You could send your daughter a wedding present or at least a package of diapers for the baby." What baby? Did I miss something? But I was not about to ask. I sent her a his-and-her set of beige towels from JC Penney, even though I didn't know nothing about the boy except his name was Al and he was a truck driver whose people was from Baton Rouge, so I couldn't get no initials put on 'em. I bought a mint-green booty set for the baby, 'cause they say it's bad luck to plan so far ahead, and right after her honeymoon (they didn't go nowhere except to spend the night at the Holiday Inn two exits off the freeway from where they live), Charlotte woke up in the middle of the night in a puddle of blood. She was having terrible cramps and thought she was in labor, except later on she tells us that the baby hadn't moved in two or three days. The doctors had to induce labor, and the baby was stillborn—a boy. I asked if she wanted me to come there to be with her, and she told me no. Her husband would take care of her. And *that* he did.

With so much going on, college slipped her mind altogether. She got that job at the post office and worked so much overtime I don't know when they found time to make anything except money, but somehow they managed to generate three more kids.

Now, Tiffany—that's her oldest daughter—got those big gray eyes and that high-yellow skin and that wavy plantation hair from her daddy's side of the family—they Louisiana Creoles—which is why she walk around with her ass on her shoulders thinking she the finest thing this side of heaven. She is. Ain't big as a minute, and prettier than a chile is supposed to be. But folks been telling her for so long that sometimes I can't hardly stand her behind, either. She thirteen going on twenty. Can have a nasty attitude. Just like her mama. Ask her to do something she don't wanna do and she'll roll them eyes at you like a grown woman. I threw a shoe at her the last time I was there and accidentally hit her in the eye, which is probably one more reason why me and her mama ain't speaking. The child stays in the mirror. Change her hairstyle at least two or three times before she leave for school, which is apparently the reason she don't have no time left to do her homework. Every time I see her she washing and rolling a ponytail or cascade and putting it in the microwave to dry, which is why the whole upstairs smell like burnt hair. I told her, Being pretty and dumb won't get you nowhere in this day and age. There's *millions* of pretty girls in the world. You just one. Put something else with it.

Now, Monique is on the verge of being sweet, but something stops her. She supposed to have some kind of learning disorder they giving out to every other child who don't pay attention, but let one of those music videos come on BET and she'll drop whatever she doing and go into a trance. Know the words to every rap record and hippity-hop song that come on the radio. And can move her behind so smooth she look like a pint-size woman practicing what she gon' do to her man the next chance she get. But I give her this much credit. She can play the flute so sweet it make you close your eyes and see blue. She know how to read all the notes, too. She taught herself how to play the piano. But once she get up off that bench, she too grown. I bought some videos for both of 'em when I was visiting last year and just slap me for buying PG-13s. "Granny, don't you know that all the best movies are rated R?" she asked me. Monique had her hands on what one day might be hips. "If ain't no sex, blood, or don't nobody get killed, it's boring, huh, Tiff?" And Miss Thang put the glue down and started blowing on her $1.99 Fancy Nails and said, "Yep." I couldn't say shit. At the rate they going, if these two make it outta high school without a baby, it'll be a miracle. This ain't wishful thinking on my part, it's what I see coming.

Now, Trevor is the only one in the house with a ounce of sense, but it's hard to tell what he's gon' do with it. He smart as hell—get straight A's and everything—but he don't seem to be interested in too much of nothing except his sewing machine and other boys, and not necessarily in that order. His mama refuse to believe that he's like that, but I saw it in him when he was little. He was always a little soft. Did everything lightly. But he can't help it. And even though I don't like it, Oprah has helped me understand it. He has a right to be who he is, and I'll love him no matter where he put his business. I just hope he don't grow up and catch no AIDS. He dance better than both of the girls, like ain't a bone in his body, and he been blessed with more than one talent. Besides clothes designing, the boy can also cook his ass off. It wouldn't kill his mama to take a long hard look in his room to get a few decorating ideas either, 'cause her mix-and-match taste ain't saying nothing. One minute she Chinese and the next she Southern Gothic or French Provincial. Some rules ain't supposed to be broken. Class is one more thing Charlotte think she can buy.

Trevor call me collect from time to time. "I can't wait to get out of here, Granny," he say each and every time we talk. "But it's okay. Two more years, Granny. And I'll be free."

Is that a real-live nurse coming in here carrying a tray? Yum yum yum. More babyfood? Who can swallow when you got a tube going down your throat and through your nose? I done already had two breathing treatments since this morning, what she want now? Nothing. All she do is look up at the numbers on those machines and then smile at me. "Comfortable?" she ask, and I shake my head no, since she know good and damn well I can't hardly mumble, but she just kinda curtsy and say, "Good," then turn around and walk out! If I was able to open my mouth I'd say, "Huzzy! I'm hungry as hell, cold as hell, and I could sure use a stiff drink." But I can't talk. And Lord knows I'm scared, 'cause I'm still here in ICU and I'm bored and I wanna go home, even though I know ain't nobody there waiting for me. Cecil been gone since the first of the year, but I don't feel like thinking about his old ass right now. That's another reason why I'm glad I got kids.

Now, Paris is the oldest. And just the opposite of Charlotte. Probably too much. Never gave me no trouble to speak of. And even though you love the ones that come afterwards, that first one'll always be something special. It's when you learn to think about somebody besides yourself. At the time, I was sixteen and watched too many movies, which is how I got it in my mind that one day I was going to Paris and become a movie star like Dorothy Dandridge or Lena Horne and I'd wear long flowing evening gowns and sleep in satin pajamas. I wanted to speak French, because Paris, France, seemed like the most romantic place in the world, and back then I craved romance something fierce. But I didn't expect it to come in the form it came in: Cecil. I used to close my eyes, laying right between my sisters: Suzie Mae on one side and Priscilla on the other. I'd smell bread baking and see red wine being poured in my glass and pale-yellow cheese being sliced and I could see the mist through those lace curtains and feel the cobblestone beneath my spiked heels. I heard accordions. Saw small wooden boats in dark-green water. But by the time I married Cecil and got pregnant—or, I should say, by the time I got pregnant and married Cecil—I knew the chances of me ever getting on a airplane going anywhere was slim to zero, so I named my daughter after the place I'd probably never see.

I made two mistakes: Married the first man who was nice to me, who showed me some unfiltered attention and gave me endless pleasure in bed. But because of my particular kind of ignorance, my second major mistake was dropping outta high school at sixteen to have a baby. It wasn't until five or six years down the road, when I was watching *Casablanca* on TV one night—alone—that I had to ask myself if I really loved Cecil. Would I go this far for him? Long before Humphrey and Ingmar even made it to the airport I knew the answer to that question was no. What I felt back then was comfortable—not comfort—just comfortable. There was no guesswork to our lives. But over the years all of it melted and turned into some kind of love, that much I do know.

Speaking of heat. All my kids are too hot in the ass—which they got from their daddy's side of the family—and Paris ain't no exception. It's probably the reason they all been divorced at least once (except for Charlotte, of course, but that's only 'cause she just too stubborn to admit defeat). All four of 'em married the wrong person for the wrong reasons. They married people who only lit up their bodies and hearts and forgot all about their minds and souls. To this day I still don't think they know that orgasms and love ain't hardly the same thing.

Paris sure don't know how to pick no man. Every one she ever loved had something wrong with him. Nathan—that's my grandson's daddy—scores very high on this test. I don't know why, but she seem to pick the ones that's got major wiring problems. They should've been wearing giant signs that said: "Defective" or "Lazy" or "Retarded" or "Not Father Material" or "Yeah, I'm Good-looking but I Ain't Worth Shit." I guess she think her love can fill in their blank spots, 'cause for some strange reason she gravitate to these types. The kind of men that drain you, drag you down, take more from you than they give, and by the time they done used you up, got what they want, they bored, you on empty, and they ready to move on to greener pastures.

She love too hard. Her heart is way too big and she's too generous. To put it another way: She's a fool. Ain't nothing worse than a smart fool. And she's smart all right. Got her own catering company. Well, it's more to it than just cooking and dropping the stuff off in those silver trays with little flames underneath. No sirree. This ain't no rinky-dink kind of operation. First of all, you need some real money if you want to eat Paris's food, 'cause she's expensive as hell. Say you having a big party—not just your regular weekend type of bash, I mean the kind you see in movies: like *The Godfather Part I*, for example, when the food don't look real, or too good to eat, and you too scared to touch it. Give her a theme: She'll cook around it. Give her a country:

She'll transform your house. Make it look like you in Africa or Brazil or Spain or, hell, Compton. All you gotta do is tell her. She make all the arrangements: from the forks and tablecloths, to the palm trees, hedges, and flowers, to the jazz band or DJ. One of her assistants, and she's got a few of 'em, will even make hotel arrangements for the guests and have folks picked up in limousines at the airport.

Anyway, she got class, and she got it from my side of the family. She been in the San Francisco newspaper, and I think the *L.A. Times*, too. Been on a few of them morning talk shows, where she pretended to cook something in a minute that she really made the night before. One of the local TV stations asked her about doing her own cooking show, but like a fool she said no, because she said she had enough on her plate. Like what?

Food must run in our family. Me and her daddy opened our first barbecue joint, which we named the Shack, fifteen years ago. But Vegas ain't the same no more. With all the violence and gangs and drugs and kids not caring one way or the other that you the same color as them while they robbing you at gunpoint and can't look you in the eye 'cause you probably favor somebody they know, we had to close two down and ain't got but one left. It's been a struggle trying to make ends meet. Paris stopped cooking like us years ago. She think our kinda food kill folks. She right, but it's hard for black people to live without barbecue and potato salad and collard greens with a touch of salt pork, a slice of cornbread soaked in the juice, a spoonful of candied yams, and every now and then a plateful of chitterlings. Her food is so pretty that half the time you don't never know what you eating until you put it in your mouth, and even then you gotta ask.

In spite of all the money she make and that big house her and my favorite grandson, Dingus, live in—yes, I said favorite—she ain't happy. What Paris need ain't in no cookbook, no house, or no garage. She need a man quick and in a hurry, and Dingus need a daddy he can touch. Another baby wouldn't be a bad idea. She ain't but thirty-eight but swears up and down she's too old to be thinking about a baby. I said bullshit. "As long as you still bleed, you able." She rolled her eyes up inside her head. "And just where am I supposed to find a father?" Sometimes she make things harder than they really are. "Pick one!" I said.

I don't know how she's survived over there all by herself. Hell, it's been six years since her divorce. To my knowledge, Paris don't love nobody and don't nobody love her. She put up a good front, like everything just so damn hunky-dory. Only she ain't fooling me. I know when something wrong with any of my kids. They don't have to open their mouth. I can sense it. Paris spend so much energy trying to be perfect, trying too hard to be Superwoman, that I don't think she know how lonely she really is. I guess she think if she stay busy she won't have to think about it. But I can hear what's missing. She too damn peppy all the time.

I'm here to testify: Ain't no time limit on heartache. Cecil done broke mine so many times I'm surprised it still know how to tick. But forget about me. Paris been grieving so long now for Nathan that she done pretty much turned to stone. I think she so scared of getting her heart broke again that now she's like the Ice Queen. Can't nobody get close to her. They say time heals all wounds. But I ain't so sure. I think they run around inside you till they find the old ones, jump on top until they form a little stack, and they don't go nowhere until something come along that make you so happy you forget about past pain. Sorta like labor.

What time is it? I know my stories is off. I watch *Restless* and *Lives* and occasionally *World*, but some days they piss me off so bad that I can't hardly stand to watch none of their simple-asses. Ha ha ha. I'm "trippin'" as Dingus would say, laying in a hospital bed in intensive care thinking about some damn soap operas when what I should be doing is thanking the Lord for giving me another shot: Thank you, Jesus.

To be honest, I didn't trust Nathan from the get-go. Paris hadn't known him but two months when they got married. He was in law school for seven of the eight years they was married. Even I know it only take three. I just bit my tongue and gritted my teeth when she told me she wasn't taking him to court for no child support. "I don't want the hassle," she said. That was what, 1987? Here it is 1994 and I can count on one hand how many times he done seen his son since he went back to Atlanta. He don't hardly call. I guess he forgot how to write, and ain't sent nary a birthday card and not a single solitary Christmas present in the last three years that I know of. I ain't heard her mention nothing about no surprise checks either—not that she need 'em—but that ain't the point. She handled this all wrong. If a man ain't gon' be there for his kids then he should at least help pay for 'em. It's the reason we got so many juvenile delinquents and criminals and gangs running through our neighborhoods. Where was they damn daddies when they needed one? Mamas can't do everything.

The one good thing that came out of that marriage was my grandson Dingus. He's turning out to be one fine specimen. Just made the varsity football team. The first black quarterback in the history of his high school. He in the eleventh grade and I ain't never seen a C on his report card. He ain't never come home drunk and he told me drugs scare him. He say he gets his high from exercising and eating vegetables and drinking that protein stuff everyday. I got my money on him. That he gon' grow up and be something one day. Putting the boy in that Christian school all them years was the smartest thing Paris could've done. Going to church at least one Sunday a month wouldn't kill her though. I just hope I live long enough to see him in college. And mark my words: if he wins a scholarship or goes on any kind of TV, watch and see if his daddy don't come rushing out of nowhere to claim him then.

The day before I got here, Paris had called the house and after leaving three messages on my answering machine and she didn't hear from me, she called emergency and they told her I'd been admitted, that I was in ICU, and of course she was all set to hop on a airplane but I grabbed that doctor's arm and shook my head back and forth so many times I got the spins. He told her I'd probably be home in three to four days. That I was almost out of the danger zone. That if I kept improving they would move me to a regular room on Thursday, which is tomorrow, and if my breathing test is at least 70 percent I can probably go home Saturday morning. It don't make no sense for Paris to spend unnecessary money to come see me when I'm still breathing and she can take that very same money and slide it inside my birthday card in three weeks.

Sometimes I feel like they made a mistake in the hospital when they handed Janelle to me. She a case study in and of herself. Been going to college off and on for the past fifteen years and still don't have no degree in nothing. Hell, she should *be* the professor by now. Every time I turn around she taking another class. One minute it's stained glass. The next it's drapes and valances. But I think she was tired of being creative and now she wanna be a professional. Did she tell me she switched over to real estate? Who knows? Maybe all them years of comparing one child to another messed her up. Treating her like a baby is probably why she still act like one. Me or her daddy didn't have such high expectations of her like we did with the first ones, and maybe this is what made her not have too many for herself. I don't know. But I have to blame Cecil for the chile being so wishy-washy. He lived and breathed for that girl. Spoiled her. Janelle couldn't do no wrong. But back then neither one of us knew we was doing it.

Even still, Janelle is as sweet as she wants to be, a little dense, but the most affectionate child of the whole bunch. She even go to psychics and palm readers and the people that read them big cards. I don't know what lies they telling her, but she believe in that mess. And she say some of the dumbest shit sometime that you can't even twist your mouth to say nothing. The chile live from one holiday to the next. If you don't know which one is coming up, just drive by her house. For Groundhog Day, you can bet a groundhog'll be peeking up from somewhere in her front yard. On St. Patrick's Day: four-leaf clovers everywhere. On Valentine's Day: red and pink hearts plastered on everything. She had seven Christmas trees one Christmas, in every room in the damn house, and a giant one in the front yard! And now here come Easter.

Ever since Jimmy got killed back in '85, Janelle been a little off. He was her second husband. She wasn't married but twenty-two days the first time. He beat her up once and that was enough. But Jimmy is Shanice's daddy. Once Janelle finally got back into the dating game—the last few men she dealt with was all married. I told her it was wrong, but she said this way she didn't have to worry about getting too serious.

Well, guess what? She married this last one. He left his wife of a million years for her. His name is George. He's ugly and old enough to be her daddy. But his money is long and green and he don't mind spending it on Janelle. That's her whole problem: she always want somebody to take care of her. Ain't this the nineties? Even I know this kind of attitude is ridiculous in this day and age and I'm almost a senior citizen. This is the reason so many of us became slaves to our husbands in the first place, and why so many women don't have no marketable skills to speak of now. Can't no man take better care of you than you can take of yourself. Janelle is thirty-five years old and still ain't figured this out yet.

I have tried my damnedest to like George, be nice, act civilized toward him, but I can't pretend no more. He's head of security at LAX, but work for the LAPD. Janelle brag that he got over six hundred people working under him. I ain't impressed in the least. Now, Shanice, she's my granddaughter who's all of twelve, came to spend last Christmas with me and Cecil. That was three months ago. I knew something was different about her but I couldn't put my finger on it. First of all, she wouldn't take off that stupid baseball cap, but I know it's the style these days, so I didn't say nothing. She wasn't here but two days before I noticed how strange she was acting. Not her usual talkative self. She seemed nervous. Downright fidgety. Like her mind was somewhere else. Almost burnt up my kitchen frying a hamburger. Forgot all about it. Dropped three eggs on the floor and sliced off a chunk of her finger helping me chop up the celery for the dressing. When she wasn't the least bit excited after she opened her presents—some ugly clothes she asked for—I said, "Hold it a minute, sugar. Take that hat off and look at me." She shook her head no. "I know you're not saying no to me—your granny—are you?" She shook her head no again. I walked over and snatched that cap off her head, and when I looked down I could not believe my eyes. All I saw was big beige circles of scalp and strands of hair here and there. "Cecil, get my spray for me, would you?" But I forgot he went down to Harrah's right after the game, and I looked around till I saw one on the table next to the couch and I grabbed it and took two deep puffs. Shanice didn't move and I didn't take my eyes off her. "Why is your hair falling out?" She didn't answer. Just had this blank look on her face. "Is it from a bad perm?" She shook her head no. Shit. Then what? I looked at her hand moving up toward a strand and she started twirling it tight. "You pulling it out?" She nodded yes. "Why?" I'm waiting and trying not to cry, 'cause I want to know what the hell is going on here, but that's when the chile crumpled over all that wrapping paper like somebody had stuck her with a knife. "Tell Granny what's wrong, baby." She just kept crying. "You scared?" She shook her head yes. "Scared of what? Who?" She wouldn't say nothing. "Is it somebody we know?" She shook her head no, then yes. "Talk to me, Shanice. Sit your butt up and talk to me." She sat up but looked over at the Christmas tree. "Is it George?" She nodded her head yes. "Has he been putting his hands on you?" When she shook her head no, I wasn't sure if she understood what I meant. I put my arms around her and rocked her. When she finally stopped, she said that George is mean and sometimes he hits her and she's scared of him. "You got any marks on you?" She shook her head no. "You sure that's all he's done is hit you?" She nodded yes, but for some reason I didn't believe her. "Have you told your mama?" She shook her head yes. "And?" She started crying again, but by now I grabbed my spray and snatched that phone out the cradle and got Janelle on the phone. "Shanice just told me George been hitting her and she tried to tell you and you don't believe her. Tell me this ain't true."

"Mama, George has never hit Shanice. She's been lying about a lot of things lately. She's just being dramatic."

"Oh, really. What about her hair? How dramatic is that?"

"The doctor said some kids do this."

"Have you at least confronted George?"

"Of course I have. Mama, look. George is a good man. He loves Shanice like she was his own daughter. He's done everything to get in her good graces, but she has never really cared for him, so this is just another desperation move on her part to get him out of the house once and for all."

"What makes you so sure?"

"Look. Why don't you send her on home?"

I took a few more puffs off my inhaler, then slammed it down on the counter. I changed ears. "I'll tell you something. A home is where a child is supposed to feel safe, protected."

"I know this, Mama, and she should . . ."

"Apparently, your daughter don't feel this way."

"Are you about finished?"

"No. I'm just getting started. I'll say this. You better watch that motherfucker like a hawk, 'cause he doing more than hitting her. You may be blind, but I ain't. And I'll send her home when I'm good and damn ready!" And I hung up.

My granddaughter ain't no actress, and them tears was real. Since she run track and had a big meet coming up, I sent her home, but promised her I would look into this. I told her to dial 911 the next time he so much as bump into her. I just been patting my feet, trying to figure out what to do about this mess. Cecil told me to mind my own business. I told Cecil to kiss my black ass. This chile got my blood in her veins.

The more I think about it, I'm beginning to wonder if we ain't one of them dysfunctional families I've seen on TV. A whole lotta weird shit been going on in the Price family for years. But, then again, I know some folks got some stuff that can top ours. Hell, look at the Kennedys. Maybe *everybody* is dysfunctional and God put us all in this mess so we can learn how to function. To test us. See what we can tolerate. I don't know, but we don't seem to be doing such a hot job of it. I guess we need to work harder at getting rid of that d-y-s part. I just wish I had a clue where to start.

I won't lie: None of my kids turned out the way I hoped they would, but I'm still proud to be their mother. I did the best I could with what I had. Cecil worked two jobs back in those days, which meant I had to do everything: like raise 'em. I tried to teach 'em the difference between right and wrong, good and bad, being honest, having good manners, and what I knew about dignity, pride, and respect. What I left out they shoulda learned in Sunday school. Common sense is something you can't teach, which is why there's some things kids should blame their parents for and some shit they just have to take responsibility for on their own.

I still can't believe they all came out of my body. Grew up in the same house. I tried my best to spread my love around so none of 'em would feel left out. Even lied to 'em so each one would feel special. I've tried to steer 'em in the right direction, but sometimes they just didn't wanna go that way. They had their own destiny in mind, which was okay, except when ain't no clear path in front of 'em you kinda wonder where they headed.

I've watched 'em make all kinda mistakes over the years. Been scared for 'em. Worried myself gray. Prayed like a beggar. But I done finally learned that you can't carry the weight for everything that happen to your kids. For the longest time I have. But not no more. I'm letting go of the coulda-woulda-shouldas and admit that I was not the perfect mother, but I broke my neck trying to be a good one. I'm tired of mothering 'em. It's time for them to mother themselves. I can't do no more than I already have. And from now on I'm standing on the sidelines. I've made too many trips to this hospital from worrying about husbands and kids, which is why from now on the only person I'm worrying about is Viola Price.

That's me.

I'm pushing fifty-five. Twenty-three more days and I'll finally qualify as a senior citizen. I can't wait! April 15. A day don't nobody want to remember but can't nobody forget. Hard to believe that me and Charlotte was born on the same day. Them astrologers don't know *what* they talking about. We different as night and day. All I know is when I get outta here this time, things gon' be different. I'm about to start living. I can't wait to start doing some of the things I've been meaning to do but never have for one reason or another. The day after my birthday, I'm going straight to Jenny Craig so I can lose these thirty or forty pounds once and for all. When I look good, maybe I'll feel good. By then, maybe I can figure out what I'm gon' do with the rest of my life. Selling Mary Kay ain't exactly been getting it. I just did it to get away from barbecue and smoke—to stop myself from going completely crazy being home. As hard as I tried, I couldn't take the smell of all that perfume they put in their products, and at the rate I was going it woulda took me about twenty years before I ever sold enough to get me one of them pink cars.

That phone could ring. Paris shoulda told Charlotte's evil ass by now, and I know she called Janelle first, and somebody shoulda put out a SOS to Lewis, and Cecil of all people should know I'm in here. I just heard it through the grapevine that he over there living with some welfare huzzy who got three kids. He must really think he John Travolta or somebody. But his midlife crisis done lasted about twenty years now. Hell, he pushing fifty-seven years old. I can't lie. Cecil was driving me nuts after he took early retirement from bus driving for the school district, and on top of that, he had to quit putting in time at the Shack altogether, 'cause his sinuses took a turn for the worse. We had to hire strangers to run it, and we didn't need no bookkeeper to see that they'd been robbing us blind. Cecil didn't know what to do with so much free time on his hands. Vegas being a desert, and where our little stucco house is, ain't no grass to cut, no hedges to trim, no weeds to pull, no pool to clean, so this is when he started hanging around the crap tables and at the same time discovered he could still drive his truck: ram it into some little dumb cunt who probably thought she'd found herself a genuine sugardaddy. Unfortunately, Cecil's truck ain't had no pickup in years so what this chile is getting I don't know.

In all honesty, I really ain't missed him *personally*, but what I do miss is his presence. That raggedy house feel even smaller without him in it. Like all the moisture been sucked out. I can't even smell him no more. Ain't nothing to pick up. Or hang. Ain't washed but once this past week, but even that was only a half a load. And plenty of leftovers. Never learned how to cook for just two people, let alone one. If I thought about him long enough, I guess I *could* miss him.

He stopped by last month to pick up his little pension check, looking all embarrassed, and, boy, was he surprised when he saw all his stuff stuffed in old pillowcases and balled up in old sheets and stacked on top of each other in the storage closet right off the carport. The spiderwebs was already starting to do their business. I only did it to impress him. I wanted him to think I can live without him. I'm sure I can, I just ain't figured out if I want to or not yet. He didn't mention nothing about coming home, and I didn't bring up the subject either. I can't lie: right after he left, I was relieved, like I was getting a much-needed vacation. It was like the part of me that used to love him had been shot up with novocaine. I didn't shed a single tear. I been numb too long. Even still, another part of me is scared, 'cause I ain't never lived by myself. Always had him or the kids here: somebody.

"How you feeling, Vy?"

Well, look who's here: Cecil! At first I pretend like I'm already dead. I want the guilt to eat his ass up. But he can see the oxygen coming through this mask, hear me breathing through these tubes, see that monitor zigzagging with my life in green. He take my hand and I snatch it back. When I open my eyes, he look like a bear. He smell like curl activator. Cecil will not cut off his Jheri Curl to save his life. I told him a thousand times to look around: this "do" ain't been in style for years. But he don't care. He think, 'cause he dye it black, it makes him look younger, which ain't hardly true. He think he still "got it going on," as Dingus would say. To set the record straight, Cecil look like he about four months pregnant. He wearing his exciting uniform: them black polyester pants that don't need no belt, his Sammy Davis, Jr.–pink shirt without the ruffles (thank the Lord), and those lizard shoes he bought at the turn of the century, when we still lived in Chicago. He look like a lounge singer who just got off work. But other than this, I'd say he still might be handsome, all things considered.

"I was worried about you," he say like he mean it. "You doing all right?" If I ain't mistaken, them look like tears in his eyes. I know how to do this, too, which is why I ain't the least bit moved by this little show of—what should I call it, emotion? I open my eyes wide—like a woman who done had too many face lifts—grab the little notepad from my tray, write, "Take a wild guess," and hand it to him. He look somewhat hurt and sit down at the foot of my bed. The heat from his body is warming my right foot. I feel like sliding both feet under his big butt but I don't. He might get the wrong impression.

"Is everythang all right at the house?"

I nod.

"You want me to bring you anythang?"

I want to point to my mouth but I don't. I shake my head no. My friend Loretta promised to bring me my teeth, which I know is somewhere on the dining-room floor, 'cause I heard 'em slide across the wood when the paramedics picked me up and slung me onto that stretcher. But her car's been in the shop. Loretta is my next-door neighbor. She's white and nice and a brand-new widow. She even trying to teach me how to play bridge. I just hope she watering my plants and got the rest of that stuff out the refrigerator, 'cause I was cleaning it when I first felt my chest go tight.

"You looking good," he say. If I had the strength, I'd slap him. I look like hell froze over and he know it. My hair is still in these cellophaned burgundy cornrows, 'cause they won't let me put my wig on. Cecil just sit there for a few minutes, looking like a complete fool, like he trying to remember something only he can't. I guess the silence was starting to get to him, 'cause he take a deep breath and finally say, "So—when you get to come home?"

I hold up three, then four fingers.

He stand up. "You need a ride?"

I shake my head no.

"I can come back and see you tomorrow."

I shake my head no. He shake his head yes. "After I get off work."

My eyes say: "Work?"

"Just a little security job. Part-time. It's something."

I'm wondering if it's at Harrah's or Circus Circus or Mirage: his second homes. I write the word "SHACK" down.

"Shaquan got robbed again, so we boarded the place up. I can't take the stress no more."

No more barbecue.

"I'll stop by the house to check on things," he say and bend over and give me a kiss on my forehead. Either he still love me and don't know it or he feel sorry for me. I don't much care right now, but all I know is that his lips is the warmest thing I've felt touch my body since I was greasing Shanice's scalp and she fell asleep in my lap. I hate to admit it, but Cecil's lips sure felt good.

I turn my face toward the window and close my eyes. I'm hoping these tears can hold off a few more minutes. I hear the soles of his shoes squish against the tile floor. The door opens. A shot of cold air comes in, and then the click of that door. I look at the clock. Cecil was here for all of eight minutes. When that door pops back open, I turn, thinking he done come to his senses, done had a change of heart, wanna say something mushy to me like they do on *All My Children*: Something that gon' make me feel like I got wings and can fly outta this hospital bed straight into his arms, where I can sink against his soft chest and he'll hold me, rock me like he used to, and I'll be able to take one deep breath after another.

But it ain't Cecil. It's a nurse. Finally bringing me my lunch. Some thick green soup and mashed potatoes and it hurts when I swallow, but I don't care: I'm starving. I eat every drop of my tapioca, even though I can't usually stomach smooth-and-creamy nothing. I drink my apple juice, wishing all the time it was a beer. When I push the call button so they can take my tray, something metal hits the floor. They're Cecil's keys. Ha ha ha.

. . .

I musta dozed off for a few minutes after they picked up my tray and the doctors checked my numbers. I know I'm in bad shape. I hate having asthma. I wasn't even born with this shit. I was forty-two when Suzie Mae called me at four-thirty in the morning to tell me that Daddy's sixteen-year-old grandson by his first wife, who he had took in, had stabbed him thirty-six times and killed him 'cause Daddy wouldn't let his girlfriend spend the night. I had a anxiety attack and couldn't catch my breath. The doctors treated me for asthma, and I been on this medication ever since. Each time I try to stop taking it, I have a attack, so my feeling is the doctors gave me this damn disease. I can't win.

And I can't lie. This attack scared me. In the back of my mind, I'm thinking: Is *this* gon' be the one? In a split second you remember everybody you love, and in the next one you ask yourself: Did I do this thing right? Did I do everything I wanted to? What would I change if I could do it all over? Did I hurt anybody so much that they won't be able to forgive me? Will they forgive me for not being perfect? I forgive myself. And I forgive God. But then you feel your eyes open and you realize you ain't dead. You got tubes coming outta you. Lights is bright. Your heart is thumping. You say a long thank-you prayer. And you lay here thinking about everything and everybody, 'cause you got another chance to live. You ask yourself what you gon' do now. My answer is plain and simple: I'ma start doing things differently, 'cause, like they say, if you keep doing what you've always done, you'll keep getting what you've always gotten. Ain't that the truth, and who don't know it?

So this is the deal, Viola. First of all, if I don't do nothing else, I'ma get this asthma under control, 'cause I'm tired of it running my life. Tired of grown kids and husbands running my life. Tired of being smart but ain't got no evidence to prove it. I wanna get my GED. I don't see why not. It ain't never too late to learn. I just hope what they say about the brain being a muscle is true. The way I see it, I figure I owe myself a cruise to *somewhere* before I hit sixty, especially since I took Paris, France, outta my dreams a million years ago. Hell, I ain't been *nowhere*. How I'ma get the money is a mystery to me, but I'll get it. If it's meant to be, it'll be. I should try to get some decent dentures: the kind that fit and don't look false. But if me or my kids ever hit the lottery, I'ma get the kind that don't come out. Paris and Janelle think playing is a waste of time and money. Paris say only emigrants and legitimate senior citizens ever seem to win. But Charlotte play Little Lotto three times a week, and Lewis, whenever he get a extra dollar, which ain't all that often. Both of 'em promised that if they ever hit, they would split the winnings with me. I told 'em I'd divide mine three ways if I didn't win but twenty dollars, and I would.

The first thing I would do is buy myself a house that don't need no repairs, and walk around barefoot, 'cause the carpet would be just that thick. Hell, a condo would do the trick, as long as I had a patch of dirt big enough to plant some collards, a few ears of corn, some cherry tomatoes, and hot peppers to pickle for the winter. And I'd like to know what it feel like to drive a brand-new anything. I know I'm dreaming, but deep down inside, when you know your life is at least 80 percent over, you ain't got nothing left to live for but dreams.

More than anything, if something *was* to happen to me, I pray that each one of my kids find happiness. I want 'em to feel good. Live good. Do what's right. I just hope I live long enough to see Lewis get hisself together and start acting like the man I know he is. Lord knows I'd love to see Paris marry somebody worthy of her and I'd pay cash money to be there when my grandson throw a touchdown pass on nationwide TV. And Charlotte. I hope she stop getting so mad with me for every little thing and realize that she ain't no stepchild of mine, that I love her just as much as the other kids. I want the day to come when Janelle stand on her own two feet and get rid of that rapist she married. And if I don't get my old husband back, hell, I'll settle for a new one. One thing I do know about men and kids is that they always come back. They may be a day late and a dollar short, but they always come back.

FROM **Pride**

BY LORENE CARY

At this point in my life I don't think there's anybody I would have done a wedding for except Bryant. Maybe my son. My daughter we won't even discuss.

But once I took it on, though, you'd better believe that this wedding was going to be a very special affair, and classy too—even if the bride was pregnant and barely eighteen years old, and the wedding party put together couldn't have financed a used Chevrolet. I wanted to dignify and elevate their union, and show them what was possible. Hiram and I practically raised Bryant, and I refused to see him and his girlfriend stand up in some JP's office in their sneakers as if they didn't have anybody who was willing and able to do better. That's a terrible way to start out.

Plus, since they were getting married at our country house in Chester

County, and since Hiram was looking toward Congress in a couple of years, this was my opportunity to invite a few of our neighbors and supporters out there. What that meant was that I had to keep a very firm hand on the proceedings. I told the kids they could bring their hip-hop music to the reception and all, but for the ceremony, at least, we were going to do this thing right.

Despite everything. Despite the fact that the bridesmaid arrived with her hair stuck out all over her head talking about her cousin was supposed to do it, but the cousin's boyfriend's house caught on fire, and the kids were staying over with him, so the cousin had to go get them, and now what was she supposed to do, and did we have a beauty shop out here she could go to?

Not hardly.

So I gave Audrey my car so she could drive back to the city to get my daughter Nicki's dryer. Audrey is my old, old girlfriend and Bryant's mother. We took him after she divorced her husband and went back to finish nursing school. When her drinking got bad we kept him. Bryant is like a son to both of us.

Audrey never did like Bryant's girlfriends and couldn't abide this one. She was not totally on board with the wedding, and she did not approach the hair dryer emergency like a team player.

"I got sober so I could watch my one son throw his life away for some big-face, big-titty, big-ass gold digger with a lisp? And then run my ass ragged because the maid of honor shows up to the train station with hair look like she had first-period gym? I don't think so, Roz. She'll have to march down the aisle with them nappy spikes lookin' just like that."

I would have sent my daughter, Nicki, but she was already upstairs trying to help take in the girl's dress where the bodice hung off her chest like it was pouting. I mean everybody had to pitch in on this one.

I wanted to light into Audrey point-blank, like: "Well, what the heck *did* you get sober for?" But at this point, better, I figured, just to stay positive, *period*, with everybody.

"You know what Hiram said, Audrey. With a girl like that, the boy's sort of livin' large." I had to laugh. It just made her madder.

" 'That tho thweet. Y'all tho funny. . . .' "

"She does have *some* ambition," I said. "I've talked to her. I can tell these things."

"What ambition? To marry my son, that's her damn ambition."

Audrey was right, but I wasn't going to give in. "She tells me she wants to open a manicure shop," I said.

"Oh, piss."

"Now, I'ma tell you again, since you seem a little slow on the uptake, Audrey: The dryer is in Nicki's closet, up on the shelf. And take this money."

"What do I need money for?"

"You always need money, Audrey; even if you don't need it, it's good to have. And take the cell phone."

Audrey calls me "bourgie"; she calls me all kind of names, but I don't care. You see who was throwing the wedding, don't you?

In fact, quiet as it's kept, if this had happened any sooner, Audrey would've been out of the picture altogether. It hadn't even been a year since she'd called us at three in the morning to come get her from behind some bucket-o'-blood bar where two men supposed to be giving her a ride took her in the alley and raped her. Hiram went and took her to emergency, where they examined her and brought in a rape counselor, advised her to get therapy and get sober, and released her. Didn't Hiram drive her straight to the city's detox and rehab center—which is right behind Betsy Ross's house, if you can believe that.

Then Hiram being Hiram, he strikes up a friendship with the young black guys who admitted her. He bought them breakfast and listened to their dream of creating a community-based rehab afterwork program. Hiram's put them in touch with Neesie's church and some funders, so it may actually happen. And Audrey's sober; that's the main thing. She's part of our lives again.

I walked Audrey to the car and repeated my instructions about the burglar alarm system to make sure she understood how to work it. She wasn't hardly listening to me.

"Here," I said, reaching into the car for my traveling pad and pencil, "I'll write it down."

"You know that yellow heifer tricked him," Audrey said.

Written directions or not, it was even money she'd set off the alarm when she got there.

"God knows I am trying to get this pulled off with some semblance of dignity and style. Will you help me, Audrey?"

"You know she got herself pregnant just so she wouldn't lose 'im."

What could I say? Bryant is like a throwback—steady and responsible to a fault—and I'd be willing to bet money that Crystal had to maneuver to get him to slip up. I'm sure Audrey was right again.

"My grandmother used to say, 'Who knows what goes on when two people close the door to their bedroom?' "

"They didn't have a bedroom. Probably didn't have a damn door."

Forty-five minutes later she called from the house to say "No dryer." So I ask Nicki, and she tells me that after she and the new Boyfriend-Who-Could-Do-No-Wrong went native with the dreads, she lent her dryer I bought her to some girl at her school who's on scholarship from Camden. Which means I can kiss that hair dryer good-bye.

"You should've asked me."

Asked her? Who bought the doggone dryer? "I know you're not talkin' to me," I said.

She shrugged and kept working on the dress. That boyfriend was a real pain in the neck. A know-it-all. Got her acting like she was a woman grown, and the fact of my presence was stunting her growth.

The maid of honor is sitting there looking me in the face talking about "That's all 'ight. She don't have to bother. With the little veil, ain't nobody gonna see. Plus I got gel."

I used every trick in the book to get Audrey to zoom out to the beauty supply place. I didn't care: guilt, shame, bribery. She called me names. I told her to take that money I gave her and buy a Gold-N-Hot hard hat and extra-strength perm, too. The bridesmaid's roots were pure steel wool—I swear to God—and steady whining.

"I told you just some gel take care of that."

Now, you don't want to be rude, because children these days take such offense, but I had to let her know very politely that there was no gel in the whole wide world could fix what she had crawling down the back of her neck.

"I have a plan for this evening, honey," I said. "And one part of that plan is for you to be as beautiful as we both know you can be. Will you work with me on this?"

My daughter, Nicki, rolled her eyes, but people respond to that sort of appeal. Besides, my other girlfriend Tamara kept popping her head in every half an hour saying, "Cut it. Just let me cut it down to the roots. I'm telling you, with eyeliner and Fulani hoops, you'd be *stunning*. Aesthetically, this could be a real turning point for you."

When we were kids Tam would tease you until you almost wanted to hit her, except she'd hit you back. All this poor girl could do was look at me with those big eyes like: please don't let that five-foot-ten woman with the dreads get near me with no scissors.

I told her to put on a sweatshirt and come trail around and give me a hand putting out the flowers.

The place looked gorgeous, if I do say so myself. It's an old farmhouse, built by a black caretaker on land given to him in the eighteen hundreds by the family he worked for. He built the front section, I understand, from local stone that he dug out of his own fields. In later years, his children and grandchildren added rooms, but then, I guess, the gene pool ran shallow, because they messed over the building and then messed up their finances so bad that we got the property for next to nothing. The one thing I'd expect that living out here would have taught them is the advantage of inheritance. White people out here hold on to their land, and they hold on to their money, which is why they have no debt and why everybody else in America is fighting over what's left.

I told her that this land has been under black ownership for more than a hundred and fifty years. And I explained to her about the original owner and showed her the gravestone that he carved every day for fifteen years before he died out of a piece of quartz shaped like a cross he found in the creek. Fifteen years, a little at a time. He finished the carving and died a month later. It's a wonderful story. If the family didn't have the sense to keep the place up, well, too bad. I have no qualms about making use of the history they threw away. Whether it made any effect on the bridesmaid, I couldn't say.

Since everybody knew the kids didn't have any money, and the bride's family didn't have a pot to piss in, I tried to keep the presentation humble. Tamara hooked up this "whole village" theme. Tam being Tam, she did it tongue-in-cheek. But, ironic or not, Tamara understands the spirit of a thing like this, or what the spirit ought to be, and then she can translate that into something tangible. Tamara must have made fifty phone calls to get everybody in the bride's and groom's families to donate Bryant's and Crystal's favorite dishes. Then she made up cards with *kinte* cloth around the edges and that person's name, like Aunt Clara's Uncanny Corn Pudding or Uncle Sonny's Hot Sauce, with a big circle with a diagonal line through it like the NO SMOKING signs, except for where they put the picture of a cigarette were the words CANDY ASS, which is what Sonny always says: "If you're a candy ass, don't eat this stuff."

Now, she did all of this, mind you, even though she personally thought that half the food was "uninspired" (her word) and that only two dishes were "truly extraordinary"—the yellow mustard hot sauce and the black-eyed peas and rice with smoked turkey butts. So she filled in with her own creations, which are fantastic. I tried to get her to make this thing I read about where you bake a ham on a bed of fresh-cut grass, but she launched into a diatribe against Martha Stewart and the taste police and Ralph Lauren ads, so I let well enough alone.

She baked a gorgeous wedding cake with lemon custard in the middle and butter-cream icing and tiny broomsticks and candied pansies and mint leaves cascading down one side, which was about as far into haute cuisine, she said, as she was willing to go. It was plenty. That thing was exquisite. Tamara brought it down from New York in three cardboard boxes in the back of her little red Karmann Ghia and assembled it at the house. I mean, she outdid herself for this wedding.

I ordered twenty flats of purple and yellow pansies for the inside and outside of the house and, because it was Valentine's Day, red and white roses for the formal arrangements. The house is mostly muted beige and cream and yellow, so the color just popped.

Then there was the wedding party. I wanted little Empire-waistline dresses in red velvet with puffy taffeta sleeves for the bridesmaids. A classic look, young, but with style. But, no. Girlfriend had to have one of those black-and-white weddings. She thought it was *da bomb*, as the kids say. Well, you have to have a very good eye to pull those things off. And money.

And I'm sorry, but it was too late for white.

She wore it, though. Blue-white to hurt your eyes and shiny and tight. I always say: A place for everything and everything in its place—and that cheesy white satin dress was not the place for that big old pregnant belly and butt. God knows baby got back *and* front to begin with, which is why Audrey started calling her T&A.

By the time the deal went down, her three attendants dropped to one. To make a long story short, they were trifling. There's no excuse. The one attendant left was the pitiful girl who had brought us the original bad hair day—although she looked fine once we finished with her, thank the Lord—in a black off-the-shoulder dress. Despite Nicki's work, the pointed tips of the bodice stuck off her chest like some kind of crazy plumes. The shoes were so big, she wobbled. Somebody gave her the idea to wear some off-white stockings that went way beyond bad to comical. Child was so busy trying to do sultry, she ended up making herself look like a crow.

I tried to tell them that an evening wedding is not the same thing as a nightclub act. But the bride was marrying the most promising young black man she'd ever met, so, hey, she knew everything there was to know about everything. Put the *B* in bad taste, but how could she tell? I gave them like a Currier and Ives backdrop and they come on stage doing Heckle and Jeckle. Hurt your feelings if you think about it like that for too long.

So I didn't. I just sat up in the front in a red peplum jacket and—just to go along with the program—a black full-length straight skirt with a side slash, not to mention a long-line bra for control under the jacket, a long-line girdle for the skirt, and control-top panty hose underneath everything to try to control whatever was left. Dear God. My midsection was so bound up I could feel the gas pockets forming down in my gut before the service even began.

But they were happy. And I refused to be anything but. Bride's gown too white and too tight? The maid's dress too black and too big? Music out of a boom box while the groom's own mother could play piano like an angel? Hey, no problem. Therapist used to say I didn't have any boundaries with my kids, so guess what? I let them plan this whole mess by themselves. Don't come back to me ten years from now saying I made them do this or that, and they got the wrong start in their married life, and it's all my fault. I let them tack it up—some of it—to their hearts' content.

And they loved it. Or, as we used to say, they *loveded* it. All the kids, mine, too—my son, Hiram Junior, standing next to Bryant as his best man, and my daughter and her boyfriend, the so-called Afrocentric intellectual—I swear they acted like we were at the Penn relays instead of a solemn event. They put their hands up in the air and did those doggie hoots like the audience on the old Arsenio Hall show.

"They gonna make this thing into a fuckin' farce," Audrey said through her teeth. "It'th da bomb!"

I just put my head down and said a prayer.

When I looked up Arneatha was standing in front of the fireplace completely unperturbed. Arneatha can fall over her own shadow, she's so clumsy, but let her stand still somewhere and she exudes calm. I've seen her do it in a classroom: The peacefulness spreads right through the children. Bryant and Junior were so handsome in the tuxes Hiram got them, and Bryant looked so much like Audrey's father, I couldn't help remarking on it.

"Don't even say it."

Arneatha indicated with a finger that the bridesmaid should step back and give the bride room to squeeze in next to Bryant. The ring bearer started to have a fit because he couldn't see, so Junior scooped him up and held him in one arm for the rest of the service. When the wedding party was still and the guests were finally silent, Arneatha let out that beautiful voice. It is a voice that is rich and smooth, not overpowering, but intense. It's a gift and, when she wants to, Arneatha knows how to use it.

"Dearly beloved," she began, "we are gathered together here in the sight of God and the ancestors and in the presence of these witnesses to join this man and this woman in holy matrimony."

At the point in the ceremony where you can read something, the bridesmaid and Junior stepped forward. The ring bearer, who was spoiled rotten, wouldn't get down, so Junior shifted him to his left arm and read holding his papers in the right:

" 'There is no sweeter name than that of my friend, my love, my soul's companion.' "

Then the girl read: "For the Bible says: 'Rise up, my love, my fair one, and come away. For lo, the winter is past, the rain is over and gone; the flowers appear on the earth; the time of the singing birds is come, and the voice of the turtle is heard over the land.' "

Tamara leaned forward and whispered into my ear, " 'The voice of the turtle?' "

"And the Bible also says," he continued, " 'A faithful friend is the medicine of life.' "

Then the bridesmaid started to sing "You Are So Beautiful to Me." Her voice was husky and smallish, but right on pitch and from her throat, not all up in her nose like most of the children sing today. Audrey nodded her head. It was just right.

When she finished Arneatha went into her signature wedding prayer: "Father God, we ask your blessings on these two people. They are so very young. We ask that you teach them how to care for and care about each other, knowing that in a marriage nobody gets his or her way all the time, knowing that in many cases, Lord God, you will ask that they rise to the occasion when they swear they cannot, and share when they feel they do not have enough, and give what they never got themselves."

I commenced to crying right on cue. Like a big baby. I'd been keeping up a good front, but I was exhausted, and Lord knows that like Audrey, I wished he'd held off a few years. And sitting there I had another thought: That of all the people in the room, Arneatha herself was the one who should've had the babies. It wasn't too late yet, but it almost was. We were becoming grandmas already.

Why else was I crying? I don't know.

"Dear God, help them build a life for themselves and their children. We don't fall in love, we receive love from God and we use it in our lives. We know what's in everyone's mind at this wedding, Lord. You've already blessed them with fertility. Teach them how to make love work in the home they will now build together."

I probably wouldn't have boo-hooed like that had it not been for the cancer. And, as these things go, I had it easy—I contracted one of the *good* cancers. The girls teased me that I had the rich white women's cancer with the 96 percent cure rate. But something like that rocks your world. It just does. And then there's the other 4 percent.

What I did, the minute I was diagnosed, was I decided to fight this monkey. To my mind, that means not giving in. I like life rich. Like the kids say: phat, large. I made up my mind to that a long time ago. I am going to eat my beef and my pork. Sorry. Pigs' feet is what kept our people *alive*. I mean it. That's why God gave Adam dominion over the animals. And I am going to put cream in my coffee. I will not let this cancer dictate my every move. I will not live in constant fear. I swear, I think that makes it grow more.

I didn't go to the cancer support groups the hospital sponsored because of the same reasons. I do not want to sit up in a room with a bunch of bald-headed white women talking about how scared we are that the cancer's going to come back. Arneatha told me I was missing an opportunity for spiritual growth, and I told her that I loved her dearly, but that I was growing just about as fast as I could take. I told her, I said: "I got *you*; what I need the group for?"

So, as Arneatha was saying that marriage is an honorable estate, she looked at me and it felt like the look she gave me in the hospital when I asked if she believed in heaven. "All I know," she said, "is that life is short, and that this is no dress rehearsal."

Jesus have mercy.

This is the real thing, I kept thinking, and it's already half over. Half a lifetime ago, I was standing up there myself. I wasn't but nineteen when I got married to a grown man—Hiram was thirty-one—and I knew precisely what I was doing. I'd worked at his bar for eight months. He'd been watching me, but kept his distance. So one day I pulled him aside and told him that I knew his political ambitions. I told him that I knew exactly the kind of wife he needed, and that I could be that wife. I told him that not many women could think as big as I knew he was thinking, and very few could live up to the vision. But I had imagination—and I knew how to stick. Then I stood there waiting for an answer. Thinking that I couldn't possibly be serious, I guess, he told me that he had a thing for blondes. What about that? Could I be a blonde for him? He said it kind of offhand. I *was* awfully young.

Now, I was not some poor, pathetic child slinking around the world dying to be a wife. I was on a mission—we all were, our set, our little pride, as one of our teachers at Girls' High called us, us four lionesses lying out on our rock in the sun, watching the water hole, just seeing what was going to turn up for us. That makes it sound like we were going to gobble up whoever came along, but too bad how it sounds. If you're a black woman with ambition—or man, for that matter—you better be aggressive and expect that somebody's not going to like you. Because we are supposed to be *sub*. Subservient. Subsistent. Substandard. Subliterate. Subordinate. Subdued. America doesn't want us off welfare. They want us *on* welfare, right where they can keep an eye on us.

Far as women are concerned, a lotta men want you to be sub, too. Not Hiram. Hiram expects you to be on equal footing, which is hard sometimes because he is larger than life. It's why people vote for him. Hiram walks into the room and people turn to see who it is. He disturbs the air.

So, there are women, inevitably. I didn't quite figure that in at nineteen, but then, you don't at that age. It hasn't been so bad, really. Nothing I could ever really point to specifically. No disrespect.

He has very strong principles across the board, and where it counts. It wasn't enough for him to own a bar; he wanted to move the drug dealers off his corner so neighborhood people could come in for a beer without being afraid. We had a couple of little light-bright old schoolteachers on the block, lived together in a perfect little house with green shutters—I swear they were lesbians—and he made us make a pitcher of iced tea for them so they could stop in after school on Fridays and have a glass with us. That sort of thing. He brought in a local DJ so people could dance outside the bar on Saturday nights and sold soda and water ice and roast beef sandwiches from a sidewalk table. You have never seen a bar like Hiram created. It was like the family barbecue that most of us wished we had.

So when he said the blonde thing, I decided not to take offense. I didn't go off about how here's another brother wants white women and all that. What I did, I took it as a challenge. Everything with him is a challenge, a competition. I said—to myself, that is—OK, Negro, you want blond? I'll see you your blond, and I'll raise you.

I went home and bought some Dusky Sahara-something-or-other and dyed my hair. Then I had my girlfriend, Audrey's cousin, give me a new cut and curl. I told her I wanted it bone straight, with just a bang at the bottom for movement so the highlights could catch the light, but short, sophisticated. And I'll tell you a funny thing—see, people think fashion and hair and all is frivolous, but how are we introduced to one another if not through our eyes?—when I picked up the mirror that night, it was as if the woman looking back was exactly who I was meant to be all along, as if that little girl with that rhiney red hair and freckles was the ugly duckling, and, now, I had become the swan. Blond swan. I swear. I decided who I was going to be for Hiram Prettyman, and I can look anybody in the face and tell them: I have lived up to it, too.

When Arneatha got to the part in the service about married people present renewing their commitment, I reached over and squeezed Hiram's hand. Twenty-one years. I remember thinking at that moment maybe that's when marriages, like people, came of age.

Arneatha told Bryant to kiss his bride, and, honest to God, he just went for it. Tamara leaned forward over my shoulder and said to me, "Remember you asked what he saw in her?"

And I have to say, until that moment I never could picture it. You don't, with your own children. Or at least I don't see them as, you know, sexual persons. Tam would. But then, she's the one went down on some little Negro at a house party—and we were only sixteen—so I figured, consider the source.

Audrey saw it, too, which is why she always called the child T&A. Audrey does have a nasty mouth on her sometimes, and that's no more than the truth. In fact, when we had our big falling out fifteen years ago over Bryant—that time she said she was coming to get him to take him to the zoo, but she didn't, and he fell asleep right there by the front door, in his own chair, dressed up in the little blue blazer Hiram bought him—we got into the fight of our lives, and Audrey said some things to me that to this day I will not repeat. But God knows she has paid for it. For every drink she poured down her throat, she has paid a terrible price.

I can't forget, but I surely can forgive, and it's as if I had saved a place for her in my heart all along. Bryant will take longer, though. He gives her her due respect, but he is very, very cool. I can understand that.

Tamara slipped out to get the food and the toast going. I swear, she should've been a caterer. Caterers make good money. College professors do, too, but I have always thought that she was trying to prove something. She said as much herself—that the only thing her Jamaican parents wanted was money and middle-class respectability, even though they couldn't stand respectable, middle-class Americans. So, her compromise was to teach college, drive a thirty-year-old sports car, and stay single.

But if you watched her constructing that wedding cake, putting in straws between the layers to hold the thing together, and then piping the butter cream like they blow insulation into a crawl space under the shed kitchen, you would have seen her whole body come alive. I mean, she twisted and turned and maneuvered. Then she'd put a dab on her finger and come over to me and put her finger to my mouth. The butter and lemon and some drops of raspberry liqueur blended on my tongue like I never could have imagined.

"Tastes like spring, doesn't it?" she asked. "You said you wished we could've had a spring wedding. So, here's the taste of May. And look—"

She opened a mail-order box from out of the fridge and showed me purple and yellow pansies crusted all over with sugar.

"They're crystallized," she said. "They'll match the ones you put out front."

They were so beautiful I didn't know what to say. So she tore one, popped half in her mouth, half in mine, and then went back to cementing the top tier of the cake with butter cream.

Tamara may dog Martha Stewart, but I say, if you don't like what she's doing, go out and do it better. I told Tamara that I think, in the nineties, America's ready for a tall, gorgeous, dark-skinned woman with her own TV show on cooking. Oprah has prepared them. Audrey went for the idea so much that she called cable companies and got information about every public access channel in the Delaware Valley.

Tamara wouldn't take us seriously.

"Oh, I get it," she said. "I'd be like a cross between Martha Stewart and Grace Jones. That'll make 'em take notice."

OK, I told her. We only have but so many schemes to make one another rich and famous, and she already threw away Audrey's idea to do a line of divorce cards back when she was in art school and nobody else was doing them. Now even Hallmark publishes divorce cards. But why listen to us? I'm just the high school graduate who does charity balls and Audrey's the temp nurse. Like what do we know?

FROM **What Looks Like Crazy on an Ordinary Day**

BY PEARL CLEAGE

• 1

I'm sitting at the bar in the airport, minding my own business, trying to get psyched up for my flight, and I made the mistake of listening to one of those TV talk shows. They were interviewing some women with what the host kept calling "full-blown AIDS." As opposed to half-blown AIDS, I guess. There they were, weeping and wailing and wringing their hands, wearing their prissy little Laura Ashley dresses and telling their edited-for-TV life stories.

The audience was eating it up, but it got on my last nerve. The thing is, half these bitches are lying. *More* than half. They get diagnosed and all of a sudden they're Mother Teresa. "I can't be positive! It's impossible! I'm practically a virgin!" Bullshit. They got it just like I got it: fucking men.

That's not male bashing, either. That's the truth. Most of us got it from the boys. Which is, when you think about it, a pretty good argument for cutting men loose, but if I could work up a strong physical reaction to women, I would already be having sex with them. I'm not knocking it. I'm just saying I can't be a witness. Too many titties in one place to suit me.

I try to tune out the "almost-a-virgins," but they're going on and on and now one is really sobbing and all of a sudden *I get it.* They're just going through the purification ritual. This is how it goes: First, you have to confess that you did nasty, disgusting sex stuff with multiple partners who may even have been of your same gender. *Or* you have to confess that you like to shoot illegal drugs into your veins and sometimes you use other people's works when you want to get high and you came unprepared. Then you have to describe the sin you have confessed in as much detail as you can remember. Names, dates, places, faces. Specific sexual acts. Quantity and quality of orgasms. What kind of dope you shot. What park you bought it in. All the down and dirty. Then, once your listeners have been totally freaked out by what you've told them, they get to decide how much sympathy, attention, help, money, and understanding you're entitled to based on how disgusted they are.

I'm not buying into that shit. I don't think anything I did was bad enough for me to earn this as the payback, but it gets rough out here sometimes. If you're not a little kid, or a heterosexual movie star's doomed but devoted wife, or a hemophiliac who got it from a tainted transfusion, or a straight white woman who can prove she's a virgin with a dirty dentist, you're not eligible for any no-strings sympathy.

The truth is, people are usually relieved. It always makes them feel better when they know the specifics of your story. You can see their faces brighten up when your path is one they haven't traveled. That's why people keep asking me if I know who I got it from. Like all they'd have to do to ensure their safety is cross this specific guy's name off their list of acceptable sexual partners the same way you do when somebody starts smoking crack: "No future here." But I always tell them the truth: "I have no idea." That's when they frown and give me one last chance to redeem myself. If I don't know *who*, do I at least know *how many*?

By that time I can't decide if I'm supposed to be sorry about having had a lot of sex or sorry I got sick from it. And what difference does it make at this point, anyway? It's like lying about how much you loved the rush of the nicotine just because now you have lung cancer.

I'm babbling. I must be higher than I thought. *Good.* I hate to fly. I used to dread it so much I'd have to be falling-down drunk to get on a plane. For years I started every vacation with a hangover. That's actually how I started drinking vodka, trying to get up the nerve to go to Jamaica for a reggae festival. Worked like a charm, too, and worth a little headache the first day out and the first day back.

I know I drink too much, but I'm trying to cut back. When I first got diagnosed, I stayed drunk for about three months until I realized it was going to be a lot harder to drink myself to death then it might be to wait it out and see what happens. Some people live a long time with HIV. Maybe I'll be one of those, grinning like a maniac on the front of *Parade* magazine, talking about how I did it.

I never used to read those survivor testimonials, but now I do, for obvious reasons. The first thing they all say they had to do was learn how to calm the fuck down, which is exactly why I was drinking so much, trying to cool out. The problem was, after a while I couldn't tell if it was the vodka or the HIV making me sick, and I wanted to know the difference.

But I figure a little lightweight backsliding at thirty thousand feet doesn't really count, so by the time we boarded, I had polished off two doubles and was waiting for the flight attendant to smile that first-class-only smile and bring me two more. That's why I pay all that extra money to sit up here, so they'll bring me what I want before I have to ring the bell and ask for it.

The man sitting next to me is wearing a beautiful suit that cost him a couple of grand easy and he's spread out calculators, calendars, and legal pads across his tray table like the plane is now his personal office in the air. I think all that shit is for show. I don't believe anybody can really concentrate on business when they're hurtling through the air at six hundred miles an hour. Besides, ain't nobody that damn busy.

He was surprised as hell when I sat down next to him. White men in expensive suits are always a little pissed to find themselves seated next to me in first class, especially since I started wearing my hair so short. They seem to take it as some kind of personal affront that of all the seats on the airplane, the bald-headed black woman showed up next to them. It used to make me uncomfortable. Now I think of it as helping them take a small step toward higher consciousness. Discomfort is always a necessary part of the process of enlightenment.

For the first time in a long time, I didn't grip and pray during takeoff. It wasn't that I was drunk. I've been a lot drunker on a lot of other airplanes. It's just that at this point, a plane crash might be just what the doctor ordered.

• 2

I always forget how small the terminal is in Grand Rapids. Two or three shops, a newsstand, and a lounge with a big-screen TV, but barely enough vodka to make me another double while I wait for Joyce, who is, of course, a little late. I truly love my big sister, but I swear if she was ever on time for anything, I'd probably have a heart attack at the shock of it.

The bartender seemed surprised when the drink he poured for me emptied his only bottle of Absolut. He set the glass down in front of me on a cocktail napkin printed with a full-color map of Michigan.

"Sorry I don't have lime," he said. "Most people come through here just drink a beer or something."

"It's fine," I said, taking a long swallow to prove it. I knew that if he could think of something else to say, he would, but our brief exchange seemed to have exhausted his conversational skills. He headed back to the TV.

It feels strange to be sitting here writing all this down. The last time I kept a diary was when I first got to Atlanta in 1984. Things were happening so fast I started writing it all down to try and keep up. Just like now. I was nineteen. I had a brand-new cosmetology license, two years salon experience, and an absolute understanding of the fact that it was time for me to get the hell out of Detroit.

When I was growing up in Idlewild, my tiny hometown four hours north of the big city, the motor city had always seemed as close to paradise as I could probably stand. Two years of really being there showed me how truly wrong I could be.

I had heard that if you were young and black and had any sense, Atlanta was the place to be, and that was the damn truth. Those Negroes were living so good, they could hardly stand themselves. They had big dreams and big cars and good jobs and money in the bank. They had just elected another one of their own to the mayor's office, they were selling plenty of wolf tickets downtown, and they partied hard and continuously.

My first week in town, I hooked up with a sister who was going to work for the new mayor, and she invited me to a cocktail reception at one of the big downtown hotels. When we got there, I felt like I had walked into one of those ads in *Ebony* where the fine brother in the designer tux says to the beautiful sister in the gorgeous gown: "I assume you drink Martel." Folks were standing around laughing and talking and pretending they had been doing this shit for years.

My friend was steadily working the crowd, and by the end of the evening, I had been introduced to everybody who was anybody among the new power people. My first impression was that they were the best-dressed, best-coifed, horniest crowd I had ever seen. I knew my salon was going to make a fortune, and it did. I'd still be making good money if I hadn't tried to do the right thing.

When I got the bad news, I sat down and wrote to all the men I'd had sex with in the last ten years. It's kind of depressing to make a list like that. Makes you remember how many times you had sex when you should have just said good night and gone home. Sometimes, at first, when I was really pissed off at the *injustice* of it all and some self-righteous anger seemed more appealing than another round of whining, I used to try and figure out who gave it to me in the first place, but I knew that line of thinking was bullshit. The question wasn't who gave it to me. The question was what was I going to do about it. Still, when I think about all the men I slept with that I didn't even really care about, it drives me crazy to think I could be paying with my life for some damn sex that didn't even make the Earth move.

When I called Joyce and told her what I was going to do, she told me I was crazy and to let sleeping dogs lie, but I felt like it was only fair. I didn't even know how long I had been carrying it and I sure didn't know who I got it from. Atlanta is always full of men with money to spend on you if you know how to have a good time, and I used to be a good-time somebody when I put my mind to it.

So I sat down and tried to figure out how to tell these guys what was up without freaking them out. "Hey, Bobby, long time no see! Have you been tested for HIV yet?" "Hey, Jerome, what's up, baby? Listen, it might be a good time for you to get tested for HIV." I don't remember what all I finally said, except to tell them I was really sorry and that if they wanted to talk, to call me anytime.

To tell the truth, I was a little nervous. I'd heard a few stories about people going off on their ex-lovers when they found out, but nobody contacted me for a couple of weeks, so I figured they were all going to deal with it in their own way. Then one Saturday, the salon was full of people, and in walks this woman I've never seen before. She walked right past the receptionist and up to me like we were old friends, except her face didn't look too friendly.

"Are you Ava Johnson?" she said.

"Yes," I said. "What can I do for you?"

"You can tell me what you think you're doing sending my husband some shit like this through the mail." She reached into her purse, took out one of my letters, and waved it in my face, her voice suddenly rising to just short of a shriek.

As noisy as the salon always was on Saturday afternoon, it got so quiet so fast, all I could hear was the Anita Baker CD we'd been playing all morning. I tried to stay calm and ask her if she wanted to go into my office so we could talk. She didn't even let me finish.

"I don't want to go anywhere with you, you nasty heifer!"

I knew she was upset, but she was pushing it. I wondered if he'd given her the letter to read or if she'd discovered it on what was probably a routine wifely search through his pockets.

"All right then," I said. "What do you want?"

"I want you to take it back," she said.

"Take it back?" I was really confused now. What good was that going to do?

"You heard me, bitch!" She shouted over Anita's soothing admonitions about the importance of finding your own rhythms. "Take it back!"

I held up my hand to let her know she had gone too far, and she drew back and slapped me across the mouth. Two of my operators grabbed her and pushed her out the door, but all the time she's hollering at the top of her lungs, "This bitch got AIDS! This bitch got AIDS!"

I tried to play if off, but it really shook me up. I finally had to cancel the rest of my appointments and go home for the day. I was distracted, and that's when you run the risk of leaving the perm on too long, or cutting the bangs too short, or putting the crimp in sideways and your life isn't worth two cents. Sisters will forgive you a lot, but do not fuck up their hair.

The slap didn't do me any serious damage, but the rumors that scene started didn't help business any. I sent out a letter to our clients explaining the difference between HIV and AIDS, but they were scared. They started calling to cancel appointments or just not showing up at all. That's when I really started to understand how afraid people can be when they don't have any information.

All those folks who had been giving me those African American Businesswoman of the Year awards and Mentor of the Month citations and invitations to speak from the pulpit on Women's Day stopped calling me. When people I'd known for ten years saw me out, they'd wave and smile and head off in the other direction. Everybody knew, but nobody mentioned it. They acted like it was too embarrassing to bring it up in polite company. I guess we were all still supposed to be virgins instead of just stupid.

When I got a good offer from a hotshot young developer for the downtown land the salon building was sitting on, I figured this was a good time to take the money and run. It was time for a change. I wanted to open another business that didn't require doing heads or frying chicken, and I was truly tired of living in a place where so many people still thought getting AIDS was proof that you were a child of Satan.

I know as well as anybody that being diagnosed HIV-positive changes everything about your life, but it's still *your life*, the only one you know for sure you got, so you better figure out how to live it as best you can, which is exactly what I intended to do. I wanted to move someplace where I didn't have to apologize for not disappearing because my presence made people nervous. I wanted a more enlightened pool of folks from which to draw potential lovers. I wanted to be someplace where I could be my black, female, sexual, HIV-positive self.

The salon sale gave me enough money to finance a big move without stress. Add to that the money I made when my house sold immediately and I was set for a couple of years without working at anything but living right. From where I was sitting, San Francisco looked like heaven, earthquakes notwithstanding. Natural disasters were no longer my main concern. That's one of the things about being positive. It focuses your fear. You don't have to worry about auto accidents, breast cancer, nerve gas on the subway. None of that shit. You already know your death by name.

When I called Joyce to tell her I had decided to move to the West Coast in the fall and ask her if she wanted some company for the summer, she did the big-sister thing, got all excited and started talking a mile a minute. She started some kind of youth group at her church, and now that Mitch's insurance settled out, she's quit her job as a caseworker with the Department of Family and Children's Services so she can work this thing full-time. She said all the young people in Idlewild are going to hell in a handbasket and if *we* don't do something pretty quick, the town is going to be just as violent and crazy as the cities are.

I tried to say "What you mean we?," like that old joke about the Lone Ranger and Tonto, but she sounded so much like her old self again, all happy and optimistic, I didn't want to discourage her. After Mitch, her husband, died, I never thought I'd hear her sound like that again. She hardly talked at all for months after, but I should have known that was only temporary. Joyce always finds a way to make it better.

She's had some bad luck, too. In fact, until recently, I thought Joyce had been given our family's entire allotment. Two kids and a husband, all dead before she hit forty. One baby died in her sleep two weeks after they brought her home from the hospital. The other kid was walking home from the school bus and got hit by a drunk twelve-year-old who stole his mother's keys and then passed out behind the wheel of the family station wagon.

Mitch drowned two years ago this February, and in the dictionary under the words "freak accident," there would be a picture of that shit. A couple of years ago the lake in front of their house got real popular with ice fishermen. These guys would come out early in the morning, drill a big hole in the ice, and sit there all day drinking beer, peeing in the hole, and wondering why the "spose to be that stupid" fish didn't swim on up and commit suicide for a chance at a plastic cricket.

By evening, the fishermen were too drunk and disappointed to clearly mark the area with safety flags like they're supposed to do, so the lake was dotted with all these open holes. Once it got dark, they froze over with a thin sheet of ice, not enough to support your weight, but just enough to camouflage the hole.

Mitch and Joyce went walking beside the lake on this particular night and he started sliding around on the ice, doing tricks, showing off for Joyce. They had been married twenty-three years and he still acted like she had just accepted his invitation to the senior prom. So he got up some speed, slid way out, opened his arms into the wind, hollered, "I love my wife!" and disappeared. By the time they pulled him out, he was gone. Mitch was the sweetest man I ever knew, and for a long time after he died, I kept thinking how unfair it was for him to die that way. I was still naive back then. I thought *fairness* had something to do with who gets to stay and who *gots to go*.

In the bad-luck department, there's also the fact that my mother chose Joyce's wedding night to mourn my father's death five years earlier by taking all the sleeping pills she'd been hoarding for this occasion and drinking herself to death with a fifth of Johnny Walker Red. She left a note for Joyce, who was almost eighteen, saying she was sorry and that maybe Joyce would understand if anything ever happened to Mitch. I was still a kid and didn't even have a boyfriend yet, so she didn't leave anything for me.

I don't know whether or not Joyce finally understood when Mitch fell through that ice, but my mother's choice made a lot of sense to me when my doctor gave me the bad news. It occurred to me for the first time that there might be circumstances where what you don't know is infinitely preferable to those things of which you are already certain.

I was glad me and Joyce were going to get a big dose of each other before I moved three thousand miles away. I waited for her to take a breath and then told her I'd be on the four-o'clock flight to Grand Rapids on Tuesday and for her to *swear* she wouldn't be late to pick me up. She swore, like she always does, but I knew she was still going to be late.

Before we hung up, Joyce asked me if I ever prayed. I told her I had tried to start up again when I got sick, but I quit because I knew I was just hedging my bets. I figured if I was smart enough to know that, God must know it, too, and would probably not only refuse to grant my selfish prayers, but might figure I needed to be taught a lesson for trying to bullshit him in the first place. I know once you repent, Jesus himself isn't big on punishment, but according to all the Old Testament stories I ever heard, his father was not above it.

• 3

Joyce sent wild Eddie Jefferson to pick me up. I couldn't believe it. I'd been sitting there for an hour and a half, which is a long time to be waiting, even for Joyce, when I see this brother with a head full of beautiful dreadlocks, some kind of weird-looking Chinese jacket, and some Jesus sandals walk up to the gate and look around. Now, there is no reason for the look since everybody else on the plane has been picked up by their grandparents or caught a cab to meet their boyfriend and ain't a soul in sight but me. The way he's looking, you'd have thought it was rush hour at Grand Central Station and he was trying not to miss somebody in the crowd. He takes his time like he's got no place to be but here and nothing to be doing but looking.

At first I thought I recognized him, but I didn't want to stare, so I looked away. The last thing I needed was some wanna-be Rastafarian thinking I wanted company for the evening. When he didn't move on, I took another look at him, just to be sure. He had one of those smooth, brown-skinned faces that could be any age from twenty-five to fifty. He had great big dark eyes and he was looking right at me in a way that you don't see much in the city anymore. Like he had nothing to prove.

When he caught me looking at him, he walked right up, stuck out his hand, and called my name like we were old friends.

"Ava?" he said. "You probably don't remember me. I'm Eddie Jefferson. Mitch's friend."

As soon as he smiled, I knew exactly who he was. Remember him? *Was he kidding?* The exploits of Wild Eddie Jefferson were *beyond* legendary. He had done everything from getting into a fistfight with the basketball coach to threatening his father with a shotgun for beating his mother. He drank, smoked reefer before I even understood that there was such a thing, and had two babies by two different women before he got out of high school. One of them graduated and moved away. The other one, a thirty-year-old divorcée, went back to her ex-husband, convinced him the baby was his, remarried immediately, and lived happily ever after.

Mitch was always so straight-arrow, nobody could believe they were friends, but they were so close, they might as well have been brothers. The last time I saw Eddie was at Joyce's wedding. He was Mitch's best man and he brought a date from Detroit who had on a red strapless dress and silver shoes at eleven o'clock in the morning. After that, he got sent to Vietnam, and by the time he came back, I had finished high school and headed up the road to Detroit.

I'm sure he was at Mitch's funeral, but I don't really remember. That whole thing is still a blur to me. Besides, he looked so different, I probably wouldn't have recognized him, although I'd sure have remembered that hair. I wanted to touch it to see if it was as soft as it looked.

"How ya doin', Wild Eddie?" I said before I thought about it.

He cringed a little like he'd just as soon I forgot the history that produced the nickname. "Just Eddie."

Joyce had sent him to pick me up because some woman had shown up on her doorstep in labor and had to be driven to the hospital in Big Rapids, more than an hour away. They left so quickly, Joyce didn't even have a chance to call Eddie until she got there, which is why he was so late.

That was typical. Anybody with trouble knew if they could get to Joyce, she'd take care of it. Her feeling was that all crises could be handled if some-one would take responsibility and start *moving*. Joyce could get going faster in an emergency than anybody I ever saw. When I first called and told her I was sick, she was on a plane and at my door by nine-thirty the next morn-ing. Once I explained everything the doctor had said, I think the hardest part for her was realizing that there was nothing she could start *doing* that would fix it.

Eddie's truck was so clean, I could see my reflection in the passenger door. The truck was old, but its bright red exterior was polished to a high gloss and the inside was spotless. The old fabric on the seat was soft and smooth when I accepted Eddie's hand, hopped in, and slid over to pop the lock for him.

I'm sorry automatic door locks eliminated the necessity to lean over and open the door for your date after he helped you get seated. In my younger days, I liked that lean because you could arch your back a little and push your breasts up and out just enough to make sure your boyfriend noticed. I didn't do it this time, though. It's a little late for all that now.

"Do you always keep your truck this nice, or were you expecting company?"

He smiled to acknowledge the compliment. "Don't you recognize it? This is Mitch's truck."

I was amazed. That meant this was the truck I learned to drive a stick shift on the summer I graduated from high school. I was on my way to Detroit as fast as I could get there and I was honing my survival skills. I didn't want to ever find myself needing to make a quick exit from someplace I probably had no business being in the first place and find I couldn't because the getaway car wasn't an automatic. Mitch agreed to teach me and we spent a day lurching up and down the road until I finally got the hang of it.

"Joyce gave it to me after he died. She knew I wanted it and I think she likes the way I restored it."

I guess she does. To say he *restored* the truck implies that it once looked this good and had now been returned to its former glory. *No way.* Mitch ran this truck so hard it would rattle your teeth. Now it rode soundlessly over the bumpy road.

I was wondering what Eddie had been doing for the last couple of decades, but I couldn't figure out a polite way to ask without opening myself up for a lot of questions in return, so I just looked out the window as we rode. Things didn't seem to have changed much around here, despite Joyce's conviction that her church group was all that stood between Idlewild and the Apocalypse. I was always amazed that Joyce had chosen to make her life here. You can't help where you get born, but as soon as I was old enough to know there was a world outside the confines of Lake County, I started making plans to get there.

"How long since you been home?" Eddie said.

"Almost two years," I said. "How about you?"

"This is home," he said. "I moved back for good."

"That sounds pretty final," I said, but he just shrugged.

"It was time."

He didn't offer to tell me *why* it was time and I didn't ask him. Timing is truly a personal thing. It's not such a bad place, I guess. Some people really love it. Look at Joyce and Mitch, but they're probably not a good example since when you're in love like that it doesn't matter as much where else you are.

The two-lane highway into town still offered cheap motels for vacationers on a tight budget, fast-food joints, and bait shops with vending machines out front where you could put in a dollar's worth of quarters and pull out a small box of live crickets or a ventilated container full of fat night crawlers. The smell of sweet grass was blowing in the window and I was remembering what I wrote on page one of the diary I bought when I first moved away: "Good-bye, Idlewild! Hello, world!"

• 4

When you first come to Idlewild, there are two stories the old-timers will tell you. It's strange, too, since it's an all-black town and both the stories are about Indians, but the place has never been known for making much sense. The first story is about The Founder.

The Michigan history books were always full of stories about courageous Indians and wily fur traders and white guys who wore stiff uniforms and built forts and thought there could really be such a thing as Manifest Destiny. We still said *Indians* back then. Not out of any disrespect. We thought they were cool. It was the word we *knew*.

Pontiac was one of the most famous of the Indian chiefs, according to the books we read anyway. He was also one of the baddest, but he still got tricked. When it came down to the final moment, he negotiated with the stiff white guys from a position of as much strength as he could muster and did the best he could, but it was all downhill from there.

Once Pontiac signed the papers and got his picture painted for the history books, nobody seemed to need him anymore and gradually his people died off, or moved away and left the guys in the stiff uniforms to their own devices. Except for one. This one Indian stayed around because he had decided to try and figure out what happened. He wanted to understand how his people had been defeated so rapidly and displaced so completely. And he wanted to structure his life in such a way as to avoid as much future contact with his enemies as humanly possible.

A noble quest, and one that still engages great minds from Atlanta to Capetown, but this one remaining Indian was not concerned about all that. He was looking to understand some things a little closer to home as he settled in for a long period of intense contemplation in the section of the Great North Woods that is bounded by towns with names like White Cloud and Wolf Lake and Big Rapids. Places where the lakes freeze solid and the first big snow is already old news by the middle of November.

One early fall morning, he was walking along through the woods and the day was perfectly clear and absolutely quiet and every once in a while he would see deer melting off into the trees of either side of him, and suddenly *he understood.* He went back to his house and took out all the money he had saved doing all the things he had been doing and bought up as much land as he could and wrote into his covenant that no white folks would be allowed to live in this small but identifiable sector he was bringing under his control. He welcomed his own blood brothers and sisters and any black people who would promise not to act a fool. And then he went back and sat down on his porch and sighed a deep sigh because he was finally at peace. He had not only figured out *who* and *what* the problem was. He had figured out a solution.

By this time, most of the remaining Indians had been moved farther west or had walked on over into Canada, but there were a lot of black folks with new money in their pockets crowded up in Detroit and Chicago and Cleveland who didn't know anything about The Founder's vision of an all-colored paradise, but who were soothed by the beauty of the lakes and moved by the mystery of the pine trees. First came one-room cabins for men-only fishing trips. Then, maybe a little reluctantly, summer cottages for the whole family. Enterprising Negro entrepreneurs opened businesses and stayed on year-round to keep things ready for the summer folks who always came flocking the first of June with lungs full of city grit and fists full of factory dollars, ready to enjoy the all-black paradise in the middle of the Great North Woods.

No one is sure how The Rajah came to Idlewild, but people always talked about his arrival as if The Founder had passed things on like Carl Lewis leaning into the last leg of the relay even though he and The Founder weren't even the same kind of Indian. The Rajah was supposed to be a *Bombay* Indian, as opposed to an Iroquois, or a Lumbee, or a Sioux, so he didn't come from generations of people who had lived and hunted and wandered in these woods. One day he was just there, his big square head wrapped in a snow white turban, and shoes on his feet that seemed to turn up at the toes even if they really didn't. He bowed low when he talked and he was traveling with a not-so-young white lady who seemed to be his wife or his business partner or both, but ultimately it didn't matter. She was *white.* That was the critical thing about her.

Everybody knew right off The Rajah was a regular Negro and not an Indian. *Bombay by way of Hastings Street,* they used to say. Why would a *real* Bombay Indian bring a white woman all the way to Idlewild, Michigan, to open a restaurant? He wouldn't. But this brother was laying it on thick, with an accent and everything, and *what the hell?* He wasn't the first Negro to opt for exotica as the most viable protective coloration and he sure wouldn't be the last one.

Back then, the place more than lived up to its name with *idle men, wild women*, and unlimited night life featuring stars like Dinah Washington and Jackie Wilson and Sammy Davis, Jr., before he went solo. For his part, The Rajah was convinced that Idlewild could support his establishment in much the same way that the community sustained The Paradise Lounge, The Flamingo Club, The Purple Palace, and a boardinghouse called The Eagle's Nest, renting exclusively to young Negro women, looked after by a large, handsome matron who never knew that after she rolled her hair at ten o'clock and went to bed, the ones who were working as shake dancers in the big nightclubs sometimes went skinny-dipping in the moonlight.

The Rajah's place was too small for shake dancers and too intimate for live musicians. There was only room enough for eight couples at a time, a modest number, but one that allowed The Rajah to treat each customer like the royalty he seemed to believe they were. Obsessed with service, The Rajah was the kind of host who *hovered.*

The place did good business right from the very beginning. The lighting flattered sun-kissed faces. The food was delicious, and the service, exquisite. Even when the place was full, The Rajah made each patron feel pampered. The water glass was never empty. The napkin was always freshly laundered. The butter rested in individual pats on beds of crushed ice in fluted silver dishes. The Rajah had *class* and a clientele who recognized and appreciated it. From the carefully made-up doctors' wives who no longer had to do their own manicures, to the misplaced romantics who spent all their time and hard-earned vacation money trying to impress the unimpressible showgirls, The Rajah's place was *the* place to see and be seen.

Now, the white woman was pretty much out of sight during this time, so everybody just assumed she was the cook because somebody was back there cooking up a storm and it wasn't The Rajah, who was forever out front being *smooth.* But nobody can say for sure whether that had anything to do with what happened. Everybody said it was a shame, too, because the place was doing so well.

The story is that one night, long after closing time and cleanup, a big party of folks came strolling over, drunk and happy and wanting something good to eat. Although he was locking up for the night and the white woman was already standing at the foot of the porch steps, he couldn't say no. He graciously unlocked the door, turned on the lights, and ushered them inside to a table.

The woman didn't move. The Rajah went to the door and spoke to her firmly. The woman still didn't move. The Rajah spoke to her again, more sharply this time, and it is at this point that the two versions of the story diverge. In one version, she hisses *"nigger"* at him from outside so loudly that the patrons can hear the insult from where they sit. In another version, she comes back in and shouts it at him from across the room.

In any case, wherever she was when she said it, *she said it*, and The Rajah narrowed his eyes and turned away from the chair he was holding for a bronzed beauty in a calico sundress and leaped at the white woman like a *for-real* Bombay tiger. They fought all the way out the door and down the steps and disappeared into the Great North Woods with her hollering and him hollering and that turban and that accent and that shouted charge of secret negritude flying *every which-a-way*, and nobody ever saw either one of them again.

Which just goes to show you, the oldsters would say, leaving you alone to consider all this while they eased off to pour themselves another drink, *wherever you go, there you are*.

Mourning Glo

BY LORI BRYANT-WOOLRIDGE

What's happened? Clinton again?" Esme inquired following my lack-luster hello.

"He just called to un-invite me to his client dinner tonight. He claims none of the other wives and girlfriends are going, so I shouldn't either. This is the second time this month," I explained, trying to wave off the niggling thought that Clinton was becoming a practiced liar. "Es, what's going on here?"

"I don't know, but I'll be over in a hour to help you figure it out."

"Okay, but it's going to be one of those nights. You bring the ice cream. I'll take care of the rest." I hung up the phone, grateful that Esme Bass, my best friend since the sixth grade, was coming over to rescue me from stewing in my own suspicions. With her uncanny knack for comprehending all the little nuances of people and situations that seemed to slip past the rest of us, hopefully I'd gain some insight into why it felt like my boyfriend of fifteen months was starting to give me the big ig.

Sixty minutes gave me plenty of time to whip up a pan of Esme's favorite double-chocolate chip brownies. More fat calories were the last thing my 5′ 4″, 171-pound frame needed, but I was depressed so my desire for chocolate was truly medicinal. Plus, serious fuel was required for the exhaustive and torturous evening of conclusion-jumping that lay ahead.

Half hour later, the glorious scent of cocoa saturated the air as I sat in front of the television taste testing the brownies and wondering about Clinton. I was enjoying my chocolate buzz when the ever perky voice of Mary Hart announced that world-renowned photographer, Glodelle, a.k.a. Glo Girard, was in the Royal Marsden Hospital in London, dying from an undisclosed illness.

At first I didn't really pay much attention when the nut-brown, dreadlocked-framed face of this art world icon filled the screen. She looked familiar, but I was sure it was because the woman was a celebrity. And of course I knew of her work. Anybody acquainted with black art knew that Glo Girard was famous (or infamous, depending on which conservative city official or museum curator you spoke to) for her outrageous takes on cultural and religious symbols that the world held sacred. Her lengthy career was filled with as much controversy as genius, and her reputation for being quirky and bold was legendary. Glo Girard was the black, female Andy Warhol, whose fifteen minutes of outrageous fame had audaciously spanned over two decades.

I watched disinterestedly as they flashed examples of her work across the screen, that is, until they displayed a photograph that I'd never seen before but shared an immediate connection with. Through a magical mix of light and technique, Glo had captured on film a winged archangel, adorned like an African warrior, holding an infant. The body was ethereal and otherworldly, but the angelic face was definitely human and instantly recognizable. It belonged to Michael Henry Taylor—my father.

My fork clanged on the floor as I hurdled over the coffee table to get a closer look, but by the time I got my nose to the screen, the image was gone. What was going on here? Why was my father the subject of a Glo Girard photograph and why had he never mentioned that he knew her? Another topic to add to tonight's agenda.

"So you held out on me, old man? What other secrets did you take to the grave with you?" I asked, my words floating toward the ceiling. God how I missed that man. Ms. Girard had certainly captured my father's true essence. He had been such a special person and certainly my angelic hero.

I was the only child of two only children. My mother died when I was three years old. I grew up with my father, a rock-steady tax accountant whose single mission in life was to keep his little girl safe and happy. He never remarried, but instead learned to expertly blend the roles of mother and father, and perform both with loving grace. He was the one who dried my tears when bullies teased me about growing up motherless and he held my hand through measles and menstrual cramps. It was Daddy who helped pick out my prom dress, guided me through the minefields of teenage love, and warned me about the delights and dangers of sex. There wasn't a day I regretted not having a mother to love, but my father tried so hard I never complained.

When he passed suddenly from a massive heart attack two years ago, I was devastated. Between his insurance and social security, I was financially set for life, but without a family. Six months after his death, I met Clinton. I was convinced that he was a parting gift sent from Daddy to keep me from being alone, which was all the more reason I had to figure out how to hold on to his love.

E.T. moved on to a story about Will Smith and I sat back to enjoy the man's charm and wit but was interrupted by a loud thumping. I jumped up and threw open the door to find Esme hugging a quart of vanilla Haagen-Dazs. For such a sprite of a girl, she had the knock of a lumberjack.

"No need to bang the thing down. Get in here. You won't believe who and what I just saw on *Entertainment Tonight*," I said and proceeded to tell her about the photo of my father.

"You're kidding me. When did Michael meet Glo Girard?" Esme asked, stepping inside and throwing her wrap on the nearest chair.

"I have no idea. He never mentioned he knew her."

"Do you think they were lovers?"

I could already see the wheels turning beneath Esme's mop of tight curls. Inside that pharmaceutical saleswoman was a mystery writer dying to be born.

"Who knows?"

"This is too good not to investigate further," Esme declared.

"Let's look her up on the Internet," I suggested. "If she took one picture of him, maybe there are others." Thanks to my status as a professional student (other than a one year break between graduate school and going back for my Ph.D. in history last year, I'd never *not* been in school), I was confident in my ability to locate anything on the Web.

I went to my makeshift office in the corner of my dining room and turned on my laptop. By the time Esme had fixed us both a plate of brownie a la mode, I'd logged on to Google.com and a long list of articles about the woman and her work appeared.

"These are incredible," Esme said, commandeering the mouse and clicking through the virtual gallery. Filling the screen in a dozen two-inch squares were several evocative portrayals of the female nudes that Glo Girard was famous for. We moved on to another site and pulled up further examples of the woman's contentious talent. It was a series of black angels, posed as winged guardians in a variety of positions—most compromising, a few divine. As with all the others, the light and shadows combined with her compositional inventiveness begat visual poetry.

"Wait a minute. I've seen these photos," I said, inspecting each image as it came through the printer. "They were on exhibit at the Whitney about five years ago. I thought they showed the entire series, but the one with my dad wasn't displayed. I wonder why?"

"Well, I wonder what she was thinking when she staged some of this stuff," Esme remarked, pointing to a set of winged pimps hovering over two prostitutes. Next to that was the curvaceous backside view of woman standing over a chalice and wearing a red lace corset and feathered wings.

"Maybe that even hos go to heaven," I suggested with a laugh.

"Actually she's really pretty deep," Esme commented as she quickly read through the accompanying interview. "These photos are her first body of professional work. She says she got the idea after the birth of her first child. She says she was tired of angels always being depicted as white and watching over blond, blue-eyed children. Apparently this anger pushed her to do a series of images depicting angels of color standing guard over black people in a variety of historical and cultural situations."

"Here he is. My dad," I said, suddenly spotting him. "Can you make it bigger?"

Esme clicked on the image, and in seconds it expanded on the screen. Together we studied the photograph, both noting details I was unable to garner during the television report, like how young and handsome he looked and the visible love he exuded as he gazed upon the infant in his arms. The baby was naked but for tiny shackles on its arms and legs and an ornate rosary around its neck.

"Oh shit." The words escaped my mouth on the tail of a sigh. "Can you zoom in more?" I asked Esme. She double-clicked once again on the image, bringing it closer. "Oh shit," I repeated, then jumped up from the table and ran straight to my bedroom.

I hurried over to the dresser and emptied the meager contents of my jewelry box, sifting through the costume earrings, bracelets, and necklaces before finally locating it. Clutching the black velvet pouch tightly in my hand, I hurried back to the computer.

"Look," I demanded, thrusting at her a soapstone cross bejeweled with cowrie shells hanging from a rosary of amber beads.

"Oh my God, it's the same cross. Where did you get this?"

"My mother gave it to me when I was baptized." A startling thought suddenly occurred to me. *If the warrior was my father, could I be the baby he was holding?*

"You know, I'm thinking that maybe your dad isn't the only one in your family in this photo," Esme remarked, reading my thoughts. "But here's what I don't get. According to this article, Glo didn't start her career until 1973, but this photo was taken in 1970, three years earlier."

"I guess that's why it's never been displayed with the rest of the series."

"It also means that they knew each other before she became professional," Esme said. "So, how did you and your father end up in a photo taken by Glo Girard before she was famous?"

"Unless she was a friend of my mom and dad's."

"Or unless she's your mother. Listen to this." Esme continued reading. " 'I've always been attracted to the concept of angel power,' the outspoken artist proclaimed. 'Those who ride on the wings of angels ride in the arms of God. That's why both of my children are named after angels. I wanted them to be reminded of the strength and power they possess in this heaven on Earth.' "

"So?"

"Seraphim, work with me here. You're named after an angel. You're in a photo with your dad wearing a rosary your mother gave you, taken the same year you were born. You don't think this is more than a mere coinkidink?"

"The woman can not be my mother," I emphatically informed my friend.

"Why not?"

"First of all, my mother was a second-grade teacher named Etta Taylor, not a photographer named Glo Girard."

"Ever heard of professional names? Writers, actors, artists—they use them all the time."

"Second," I continued, totally ignoring her argument, "she died in a car accident twenty-eight years ago. Third, and most important, my father would never lie to me about something that significant."

"You're probably right," Esme conceded, though I could tell by her expression that she wasn't convinced. "So you've seen her death certificate?"

"No, but . . ."

"It wasn't in the safety deposit box with your dad's things?"

"No."

"No obituary? No funeral program?"

"Not that I know of. They were probably destroyed in the fire."

"Oh yeah, the same fire that burned up every picture that existed of her. A fire you can't remember."

"So? I was young, and anyway, it happened before we moved from California to Atlanta."

"You always said you didn't know much about your mother because your dad didn't like to talk about her. And you don't find it questionable that other than this rosary there doesn't seem to be a shred of evidence that the woman lived or died? You gotta wonder."

I sat there in silence, trying to find the words to defend myself against the onslaught of Esme's questions.

"I can wonder, but there's no way to ever know, so why bother?" I countered.

"You should call her in London and ask."

"Ask what? Are you my mother? This isn't some children's story. Esme, my mom is dead. Why are you trying to create all this drama around a stupid photograph?"

"Well, if you're a hundred percent sure there's no possibility, then forget it," she began before reaching into her pocket to retrieve her vibrating cell phone. "Okay, see you there." Moments later Esme was at the door on her way to meet Derek for an impromptu nightcap. I think it was more like a booty call, but who was I to judge?

"I have to go. You going to be okay?"

"I'll be fine," I assured her.

"Okay, but . . ."

"But what? Go on. Say it."

"Sera, the woman is dying. If there is even an inkling in your gut that I might be right, what's the harm in making that call before it's too late to ever know?"

"Thanks for coming over," I said, refusing to acknowledge her comment.

"Okay. I get the message. Case closed. Look, if I got a bit overenthusiastic about the Glo thing, I apologize. But you must admit, we might be onto something and even if we aren't, it did keep your mind off Clinton."

I closed the door, acknowledging the truth in Esme's words. The discussion had temporarily cleared my worries about Clinton, but Esme's line of questioning had left me feeling uneasy and off balance. And despite my insistence otherwise, a little voice in my heart was telling me that I needed to further investigate the connection between my father, Glodelle Girard, and myself.

Tidying up after Esme's departure allowed me to strategize how to go about looking deeper into this mother lode of a mystery. She had brought up several salient points that, if eliminated immediately, could quickly clear up this entire matter. Like a record of Etta's death. I looked at my watch. It was after eleven. It was Friday. The Office of Vital Statistics wouldn't be opened until Monday morning and I needed answers now. I'd have to begin elsewhere.

Start with the box, my mind suggested despite the fact that for two years I'd kept the lid on those memories closed as tight as a mummy's tomb.

"Back to the Web," I decided, ignoring my thoughts. I packed up my laptop, the prints of Glodelle, and with the remaining brownies retired to my room. I set up shop in my double bed, arranging pillows and bedcovers to make myself comfortable for a long night of Web surfing. Forget sleep. Forget class in the morning. And for now, forget Clinton. I had some serious questions and unless my Toshiba blew up before I got some answers, I was settling in for the duration.

Immediately I went to my favorite search engine, typed in the words "death certificates," and waited a miraculous 0.8 seconds for a list of starting places to appear. I began with the California Death Menu (how sick is that?) and after a click here and a click there, I came across several databases that looked to be helpful. I skipped the Social Security index, knowing that I had no clue as to Etta's digits. In fact, come to think of it, there was a lot I didn't know about my mother. The only two pieces of information I knew for certain were her birthday, October 19, 1942, and the date she died, January 3, 1973. Both occurred in Oakland, California. Every detail in between was an unknown.

I started with the obituary registry, which revealed nothing about Etta but led me to the California newspaper database, which also provided zip, but took me to the grave search, which directed me to search for burials on the cemetery database. By 2:30 A.M. I had found nothing to confirm that my mother, Etta Taylor, had left this Earth.

Suppressing a yawn with a corner of brownie, I unwound my stiff legs from underneath me and stood up to stretch. The Web was leading me nowhere. I felt like a mouse, seduced by the fragrance of some exotic cheese, running around a cybermaze where every corridor led to another dead end. It was time to move on to the one thing I'd been putting off since my father's death.

I took a deep breath and dropped to the floor. Slowly I wedged my thick frame in between the carpet and bed until I could reach the two long boxes I'd found in the attic of my father's house and brought to my apartment. The seals were still intact, proof that I hadn't been ready to review my happy life with him when I wasn't yet accustomed to living without him.

I sat on the floor with the box labeled "Seraphim" between my legs and carefully ripped away the packing tape. The box flaps bounced open, revealing a trove of memorabilia from my childhood: report cards, programs from school plays, artwork. They were simply thrown inside the box, but I knew that haphazard pile held the same love inherent in the neatly arranged scrapbooks owned by the kids with mothers. My dad had kept every scrap of my adolescence and this show of love brought me to tears.

Along with the souvenirs of my youth were photos of me costumed for various life events: ballet recitals, my First Communion, and the high school prom. There were also many snapshots of family vacations through the years: camping in Yosemite, shell hunting in Jamaica, and mugging with

Mickey in Disney World. And, as usual, most of the prints had been sabotaged by my self-deprecating expressions.

I instinctively cringed as I inspected myself making a face in a Parisian café on my sixteenth birthday. Even now, as an adult, I hated having my picture taken. Clinton always got upset when we had film developed and the shots came back looking like publicity stills for Ringling Brothers, but I could understand why cultures in Northern Africa and elsewhere considered photographs to be a personal invasion—a stolen piece of one's soul—although I don't think I was that deep about it. I simply hated the way I looked in person, so why capture it forever on film?

After an hour tripping down the trails of my past, I pushed the contents aside and pulled the second box close. It was much lighter than the first and examining the exterior gave me absolutely no hint of the enlightenment within.

Inside a large manila envelope, I found a candid photo of my mother and father on their wedding day. The two of them were standing in front of the open doors of a church with another man and woman, obviously their witnesses. My parents made a striking couple. Michael looked tall and handsome in his dark suit and crisp white shirt. Positioned full face to the camera, his mouth was open in cheerful joy, his arm wrapped lovingly around his bride's waist. Etta's short white dress and veil were appropriately hip for the late sixties and she was holding a small bouquet of what looked to be white roses. Her face was unfortunately revealed only in profile, but I was still mesmerized by the features I could make out. She wore a wide and toothy grin of glee as she gazed upon my father. They looked genuinely happy together and truly in love. If this was the only photo saved from the fire, why had my father never shared it with me? Eager to see more images of my mother, I reached into the large envelope and pulled out a smaller business-size one.

Inside were divorce papers terminating the marriage of Michael Henry Taylor and Etta Glodelle Taylor. Also listed was their last address shared as husband and wife—265 Girard Place, Oakland, California.

"Glodelle Girard," I muttered with disbelief. My breath ceased to flow when I noted the date, January 3, 1973, the same date I had been told my mother had died, the same year Glo Girard, professional photographer, was born.

The scream of despair started in my toes and ascended through my body, playing pinball with each vital organ. By the time it reached my vocal cords it had evaporated into dead air that escaped my mouth not as a wail but a despondent whine.

Etta Taylor hadn't died. Only her marriage had. The realization caused a flurry of questions to invade my head. Why did she leave without me? Why had she chosen to divorce both my father and me? What had we done to make her stop loving us? And what had she done to make my father cut her out of our lives like she never existed?

I continued to sit, stunned into paralysis, not knowing what to think and having no one to call for comfort or further edification. Just hours ago I was parentless and pathetic. Now I was still pathetic but the daughter of a famous mother. What seemed like hours drifted by before I picked my emotionally weary body up from the floor and dropped it back onto the bed. I rummaged through the printouts until I found a head shot of Glo. Carrying it over to the vanity, I taped it to the left side of the mirror and studied her face next to my own.

Even though the image was grainy, I could see my mother was a stunning woman. Not in a glamorous movie star kind of way, but in the way that confidence and personal style could pick you up from the average heap, and deposit you among the femme fatales. There was a twist to her lips and a defiance in her eyes that was translated into her work. It was a look that told the world that Glo Girard had arrived to divide the observer from his comfort zone and conquer any preconceived biases.

Already I could see that my mother and I were vastly different. While she'd spent the last twenty years taking on the world with her camera, I'd spent them hiding in a classroom. My life had been one long preparation to *do* something, but I hadn't been brave enough to actually *try* anything. During my brief stint as a working girl I had realized that being in the real world didn't exactly live up to all the hype. After Daddy died I had gone back to school because I never felt better or safer than when I was in an environment of higher learning. But now I had to wonder. If I had grown up under the adventurous influence of Glodelle Girard, would I, too, be courageous enough to define and capture my dream?

I peered into the trifold mirror, into the betrayed eyes of the woman in the looking glass, trying to find something in my face to connect me with this larger-than-life woman. Aside from the color of my skin and the seductive slope of our cushiony lips, there was little resemblance. Glo's face was an exercise in aesthetic exposition—interesting bits and pieces mixed together to create a work of art. Mine, on the other hand, was an example of the universal principle: you've-got-to-give-some-to-get-some. The get: A smooth, supple light-brown complexion that actually looked better without makeup; perfectly arched eyebrows, and long thick eyelashes to fringe my wide, almond-shaped eyes. The give: Not a cheekbone in sight, a forehead big enough to advertise on, and a two-layer chin. My face, like my body, was a series of soft, round lumps and curves, nary a taut straight line to be found. Nothing like my mom's, but just like my dad's.

I pulled my father's photo from its frame and taped it to the right side of the mirror, then squeezed my own face in between, creating the family portrait I'd always dreamed about. My eyes traveled back and forth between the two, trying to register who was to blame for the drastically unfair way I had been treated. At that moment I had mixed emotions about her—a cocktail of admiration and anger. But the disappointment and rage toward my father was so intense I physically ached.

"How could you have done this to me?" The words slid from my clenched teeth as I cleared the vanity with one angry sweep. Watching my toiletries crash to the floor, I wondered how the one person I had trusted most in this world could have deprived me of knowing my own mother.

I had to talk to someone. Esme was with Derek, and I wasn't quite ready to share all of this with her anyway. Her flair for the dramatic would only complicate my already complicated emotions. That left Clinton. Hope and habit caused me to pick up the phone and dial his home number. It was nearly four A.M., but I wanted to hear his voice. I needed comfort and advice from the man I loved. It rang thirteen times before I hung up. I dialed his cell phone number. Another dozen jingles and still no hello. The echo of unanswered rings mingled with the sound of my sobs, plunging me farther into despair. I wished that I'd never met Clinton . . . never turned on the television . . . never seen that photograph . . . never learned that my mother was alive and my father was a liar.

A small voice whispering in my ear woke me. *Call her*, it suggested. I turned over to look at the alarm clock. Seven-thirty. I'd managed to escape this familial nightmare for less than three hours. Lifting my head from the pillow, I was greeted by a throbbing head, the apparent hangover of a long night of intense emotion.

Call her, the voice implored again. The phone rang, hurting my head but silencing the commentator inside.

"Sorry to call so early. I'm on my way to an all-day conference," Esme said, staying true to her habit of just diving into a conversation without even a hello, "but I couldn't leave without finding out what you're going to do."

"About who? Clinton?"

"We'll deal with that asshole later. I was talking about Glo Girard."

I considered pleading pain and hanging up, but decided I could use a sounding board. First, though, I needed relief. "Hold on a minute. I'll be right back." I crawled out of bed and into the bathroom in search of an Advil and some time to consolidate my scattered thoughts before Esme imposed hers on me. When I returned, I shared with her all the information I'd found last night. Esme listened with concern, stopping only to interject a few excited gasps here and there. "Anyway, I plan to apply directly to the Office of

Vital Statistics for a death certificate, but it looks like she and Etta are one and the same."

"So, Glo Girard is your mother," Esme whooped, the I-told-you-so unspoken but strongly implied. "You know, it's a little after noon in London. A perfect time to make that call."

"For what reason? Esme, the woman wanted nothing to do with me my entire life. Why start now?"

"When people are dying they always want to get stuff off their chests. You know, clear their conscience before they do the heavenly meet-and-greet."

"My father certainly didn't," I angrily interjected. "Look, it's pretty obvious that I was the property settlement in their divorce. He got me and she got the chance to live her dream. Out of sight, out of mind. Everybody's happy."

"Maybe, maybe not. There could be a million different reasons why your mom never contacted you. Maybe she thought *you* were dead . . ."

"Maybe she just didn't want me and my father was trying to protect me," I interrupted, the sudden thought mellowing my fury.

"Maybe. But the only person who knows the truth can't tell you unless you contact her."

"I don't know," I replied, picking up the amber rosary from the nightstand and sliding the beads between my fingers.

"Well, then think about this. That article said that Glo named *both* her children after angels. Sera, you have family out there. If for no other reason, let her hook you up before it's too late."

We talked a few minutes more, but after Esme's comment about siblings nothing really penetrated my brain. My mind was consumed with the notion that with Clinton's apparent defection, I was teetering on the edge of total abandonment. It took another twenty minutes for the Advil to kick in, but once I could hold my head upright I booted up my computer and found the Web site for the hospital mentioned on television. Along with the phone number, I learned that the Royal Marsden Hospital had a worldwide reputation for cancer care and research. Another mystery revealed.

Even though she was a stranger, the thought of Glodelle dying of cancer in a foreign hospital depressed me. Was she in pain? Was she alone or surrounded by family and friends? Was my brother or sister with her? Was she thinking of me as she slowly slipped away? That thought caused my tears to flow, both from anger and concern. Defiantly I picked up the phone, deciding that if I wasn't on her mind, I would be.

I swear I could hear my heart beating as I dialed the number. When the operator answered I asked to be connected with Glo's room. In a clipped British accent she informed me that Ms. Girard was in a private room accessible only to family. I bit my lip and took a deep breath before giving my name and demanding that I be connected to my mother's room. I'm not sure where that audacity came from, but it worked, because within seconds she was transferring my call.

I considered hanging up at least a thousand times in the short span it took for my call to be connected. But my mind was too consumed with anxious queries to command my hands to act. Who would pick up the phone and would they believe my claim of relativity when I barely believed it myself?

"Hello." A female voice with no discernible accent answered.

"Uh . . . this is . . . um . . . Seraphim Taylor," I began, wondering if I could be related to the voice on the phone. "I'd like to speak to . . ."

"Who did you say you are?" My ears registered a mix of caution and disbelief.

"Seraphim Taylor. I live in America and I have reason to believe . . ."

"Oh my God. Phimie is it really you? How did you know? Where are you?" The woman's questions flew like bullets from an AK-47.

Phimie. The sound of that particular diminutive made me sit up straight. My father hated that nickname. He preferred the use of my full name, barely tolerated the use of Sera by my friends and teachers, and had always refused to allow anyone to call me was Phimie. Was it because my mother had used this name? My skin pimpled by the realization that the person on the phone knew of my existence. "Who is this?"

"This is Mame Anderson. I'm your mother's lawyer, and if you're Seraphim Nicole Taylor, daughter of Michael Taylor, born April 27, 1970, then you're her daughter."

"Then it's true. I am her daughter. How do you know me?"

"I've been helping Glo put her affairs in order."

"Then she's mentioned me?" My words were barely audible, even to me.

"Yes. We've actually been trying to contact you, but the last known address we have for you is Atlanta, Georgia."

"I live in New Jersey now." As I explained to Mame how and when I'd learned of Glo's existence, my mind raced ahead. My mother wanted to see me. She had tried to contact me. This realization, while doing little to erase my feelings of betrayal, seemed to take the hard edge off her lifelong denial. "Why did she wait so long to find me?"

"Glo alluded to the fact that she was estranged from both you and your brother, but I really don't have any further details."

I had a brother. Damn. Forget pouring rain. I was standing in the midst of a monsoon. Still, the confirmation of this fact delighted me. Suddenly alone didn't feel quite so lonely. "Is he there with you?"

"No, unfortunately we've been unable to locate him as well. Perhaps we'll get lucky and he'll see the news before it's too . . ."

"How bad is she?" I interrupted, hoping for a miraculous denial of the truth.

"It won't be long now. I'm afraid your mother has lymphatic cancer. She hasn't been conscious in days but the doctors are doing everything to keep her comfortable."

"I'd like to see her." My mouth released the words without contacting my mind for permission. But once airborne, retrieval was impossible.

"I'm sure she'd like that. But come immediately. There isn't much time."

I hung up the phone, my head a whirling blend of varying sentiments—curiosity and confusion reigned. What was I going to do? In less than twenty-four hours I'd located my mother, but unfortunately on the lost side of found. What was the point of flying thousands of miles to say good-bye to an unconscious woman whom I wouldn't recognize if she sat down next to me? Why, when she wasn't capable of answering the questions that I most wanted to know, like why had she and my father conspired against me and why had it been so easy to give up her only daughter?

The answers to those questions would die with her and there was nothing I could do about it. And just as potent was my regret over the lost opportunity to know if the adage "like mother like daughter" applied to Glodelle and me. Certainly, Glo Girard exceeded all of my childhood fantasies of what my mother had been like. She was dynamic, talented, fascinating, and famous—all the things I wished I could be. But perhaps if I went to her, held her hand, and looked into her face, some Glo would rub off. Maybe in London I'd find the piece of my mother that was me.

Those maybes convinced me to phone my travel agent and book a flight to London that evening. I hung up and immediately called Clinton to fill him in and let him know of my plans, but of course, he was unavailable. All the better, I decided. I'd simply leave town and let him wonder about *me* and *my* intentions for a change. I left a message for Esme on her cell phone, knowing she'd applaud my decision and zealously pump me for every detail when I returned.

I was busy packing when the phone rang. The connection had that long-distance crackle to it. I knew immediately it was Mame Anderson from London with bad news.

"Phimie, I'm sorry, but your mother died about an hour ago."

My eyes filled with tears as I realized what I had gained and lost in the span of a day. I was once again officially an orphan, but now I had a brother and a solid link to my past. I took a minute to allow my grief and disappointment to make room for gratitude, then told Mame I would be arriving in the morning to help with the funeral arrangements.

I walked over to the mirror and once again placed my head between the suspended photos of my parents. "Take care of her, Daddy," I requested, wiping away my tears. I smiled at my reflection, intuitively knowing the search for my mother had just begun.

FROM **These Same Long Bones**

BY GWENDOLYN M. PARKER

As if he'd been shaken, Sirus McDougald abruptly opened his eyes. There was a merciful moment of forgetfulness. The sheet was tangled about his long legs. He lay for a second at the center of a haze, moist and open from sleep, his limbs relaxed and peaceful, the recollection of a smile still puddled at the corner of his full lips. It was near dawn, and Sirus had been dreaming. He had dreamed that nothing would ever awaken him again. He had dreamed that he could stop life at his bedroom door. He had dreamed that he could force time to retrace its steps. But even as he turned to avoid it, the sun stole into his room, creeping into his sleep.

Sirus rubbed a broad hand across his face and looked drowsily around him. The dust in a beam of light that streamed through the blinds sparkled like fireflies near his slippers. Next to his head, on the small folding table he used as his nightstand, the light caressed the items he had laid out the night before: a small tortoiseshell comb, his pocket watch, his mother-of-pearl studs edged in gold, the loose pieces of paper on which he'd absently scribbled as he spoke to the reporter from the local paper. The light seemed to halt on the words on the top sheet of paper—"Brown, brown, 5'3", reading." What could the reporter he'd spoken to yesterday possibly print that would be news?

At once, Sirus's lingering ease was gone. His eyes widened, his chest swelled with air, and his mouth opened, gaping. He seized the piece of paper from the table, crumpled it, and stuffed it into his mouth.

A moan escaped. His daughter, his precious girl, his only child, was dead. Of what importance was the color of her hair and eyes, her height or favorite hobby, when even the paper boy knew more than that: Knew that she liked to sit in the narrow tunnel made by the honeysuckles between their house and the Senates', knew how she banged out of the house with her skates already on, how she stopped on the grass at the edge of the walk to tighten them, knew the way she posed to wave good-bye, one hand on her hip, the other straight in the air, an elongated little teapot.

No, there was no news to convey, talking to the reporter was just a formality, one among dozens that were expected of him. So he rented all ten of Jason's cars for the funeral and he called people personally with the news, and he readied his house as if for a party. These were the things that were done, and he did each of them, when it was time, in turn. He knew that his neighbors and friends were similarly busy: the women baking pies and hams and fretting over who might not know and still need to be told; the men collecting money, arranging for their own transportation and clean black suits; even the children, bent over basement tables, cutting construction paper to serve as backings for paper flowers and poems.

Sirus forced his legs stiffly to the edge of the bed. Get up, he said to himself, spitting the paper onto the floor.

Outside, cars slowly traveled past his house. Some carried strangers: a Northerner in search of a relative's home, vacationers from farther inland heading for the coast, a delivery truck with vats of sweet cola syrup. But most carried Sirus's friends and acquaintances, unable to resist taking an extra turn past his house in an attempt to catch a glimpse of him or to see the large black and purple wreath hung on the door.

How was he holding up? Why was his wife, Aileen, sleeping over at her mother's house? Had they, following the country way, covered the mirrors with black paper? Like Sirus, the people who had settled this part of town—the colored section, which butted up against the white part of town and then turned back on itself—were primarily the descendants and relatives of farmers. As they'd spread throughout the city, one brother and then one cousin following the next, they'd left the country but brought their country ways: an unflagging belief in cause and effect—after all, hadn't they always reaped what they sowed—leavened by a large measure of fatalism bred by bugs, fire, and a too hot sun, and bound together by clannishness based on proximity, shared cheekbones, and common values. For these farmers and their progeny, holding the line against the sorrow of history, there was absolute virtue in hard work, an education was a lifeline, and life was an inevitable mystery. These things were givens, like the choice of good land, from which everything else that was good would proceed. And to these descendants of farmers, death itself was both sower and reaper, an unreasoning though sometimes benevolent messenger from God.

Sirus himself was born on a farm that produced three hundred baskets of tobacco a season, in a town called Carr, in the upper coastal plain of North Carolina. It was a typical pocket of life in the South, crammed with contradictions and ellipses of time. There were the Cherokee and the Tuscarora, who had lived on the land for always; the slave and the free Africans who'd settled beside them; and the Scottish farmers, who had worked beside the others. Sirus's parents, like those of his neighbors, were descended from these Africans, Cherokee, Tuscarora, and Scots, and these people, when they were not farmers, were blacksmiths, barbers, cabinetmakers, grocers, and traders. They built everything they would have one day from these skills. And Sirus absorbed in his greens and hog crackling and corn bread the peculiar mixture of building and dreaming that was the heritage of these people. Now, in the wake of death, he was as much a part of this town of some five thousand colored people as the red dirt that ringed the manicured lawns, or the North Carolina light that was at once bright and hazy, or the ash, willow, cedar, and pecan that were native to the land.

Sirus stood now, some thirty-five years past his birth, in the late summer of 1947, in this town of Durham, North Carolina, which bustled with progress, in a house on Fayetville Street that was one of dozens he'd built, wishing he were the one who was dead. From his bathroom, the sun streaming in the window, Sirus could still hear the cars as they slowed to pass his house. He stood his shaving brush on its base, bristles up, to dry, and carefully shook the last drops of water from his razor. He looked at his face, now clean-shaven, in the mirror.

There was still the familiar broad chin, the wide cheekbones, the long thick nose, the thick black hair that formed a sharp contrast to his unbearably light, almost pearl-toned skin. The cold water had restored some color to his face; his gray eyes were smooth and clear. He marveled at his own composure. How could his features reveal so little while he felt as if every aspect of him, every thought and desire, every feeling and habit, was hurtling inside him at such speed and with such force that he could be an atom exploding, shattering into oblivion?

From the moment he had learned of Mattie's death, from each second that moved forward, he was dragged backward, caught in a great rush of time away from the present, away from the husband he'd been, the prosperous businessman the town had grown to rely on, the solid friend that so many came to for advice. And in his place loomed the specter of another Sirus, a youth, a boy he believed was long gone, a boy who was all quiet and softness. This boy, his eyes permanently wide, followed after him in his own house, relentlessly padded after him in his own shoes.

There had been nothing authoritative about Sirus as a child. He had been thin and too pale, his elbows always at the wrong angles, his energy too volatile, kinetic, as likely to lead him in one direction as another. But as the years went by his skin had gained a translucence and his energy had cohered, coalesced, so that it no longer erupted jerkily in his limbs but rode high in his chest, girded by his thickening muscles. As a man, he was loosegaited, solid but warm. If he wanted to command attention, he had only to stand, releasing heat into the air like fire.

He dropped his gaze from the mirror to the basin and watched the spot where the water continued to run. A small green stain glinted at the bottom of the bowl. On any other day it was just green, a color, but today it summoned half a dozen memories: the color of new tobacco in the fields, the color of his mother's eyes when she stood in the light on their porch, the transparent color of an old penny, or the color, in spring, of all the land of his youth. The color, this green, came rushing up at him with its freshness and longing, setting off an embedded charge. Sirus doubled over, an intense wave of pain and nausea gripping his gut. He grabbed the sink, shaking.

Tears welled up and just as quickly receded. With careful steps he returned to the bedroom, took a clean shirt from his wardrobe, and slid his arms into the cool, crisp cotton. Then, slowly, he walked to the window. The starch in his collar was exactly as he'd requested, but now it felt like a gag. He watched the cars continue in an endless procession out on the street, until a black limousine appeared. It was Etta Baldridge's car, turning onto Fayetville from Dupree, already bearing down the road with that ominous cadence reminiscent of halting steps stumbling toward death. If its headlights had been on, it would have looked as if it were already part of the funeral procession.

As the car crept down the street, Sirus could easily imagine Etta's voice and her short, sharp fingers tapping on the back of the front seat right below her driver's neck. "Albert, Albert, slower," she'd be saying. From where Sirus stood at the window he could imagine Etta's head, peeping forward from the relative darkness of the back of the car, her mouth moving animatedly, her face nearly pressed against the window. "Albert." Etta had been the first person to call on him when he had moved into this house. "I'm Etta Baldridge. Welcome to Fayetville," she'd said, pressing her face against the inside screen at the front door, an unofficial welcoming committee. Etta was always one to be pressing.

He thought he heard his housekeeper's key in the lock downstairs. Thank God, he thought. Mrs. Johnson could talk with Etta if she insisted on stopping. He reached for his pants from his wardrobe and his suspenders from the back of the cane-bottomed chair by the window. He knew that if he went out to the porch, Etta would ask Albert to stop altogether, would wave her arms and hands frenetically until he came out to the car. Once he was there, she would clasp him with those same grasping hands, her eyes sweeping greedily over him, hunting for a stain on his shirt, a cut from shaving, some food left on his lips, some sign of his grief—anything she could carry away with her to the bank or the insurance office or the beauty parlor where she would find an ear in which to deposit her find. If Etta saw him at this moment she might also be able to spy the child who was hiding in his face. He reached for his suit jacket, feeling a wave of relief as the car passed.

Downstairs, Mrs. Johnson was at the back door, pushing it open with her hip as she always did. She held her key in one hand and, in the other, the bag with her change of clothes, her morning paper, and a pair of flat shoes. She was a sturdy, compact woman, with blunt fingers and short, thick legs, and when she hung up the light raincoat she wore, regardless of the weather, her roundly muscled forearms showed. Her face was diamond-shaped, a dark brown flecked through with magenta, crowned by a wide forehead and dominated by closely placed, expressive eyes. She had worked for Mr. Mac, as she called him, for over fifteen years, beginning when he first came to Durham from Washington after college, continuing through his marriage to Aileen Bryant twelve years ago, through Mattie's birth, and on up to the present day.

She tugged at the chain to the overhead light and lit the oven and the burner under the kettle in rapid succession. On any other morning, she would also have turned on the radio standing on the counter next to the sink, softly tuning in to *The Sunny Days of Glory Hour,* which was broadcast from eight till ten. This morning, however, as she had yesterday and the day before, she went about her work as quietly as she could. She gently closed the catch on the cabinet where the coffee was stored, took her flat shoes from the bag without rustling the paper, and turned off the heat under the kettle as soon as it began to whistle. She thought of Mr. Mac upstairs, still asleep, she hoped.

If asked, she always described Mr. Mac as a firm but fair man to work for, though in the privacy of her home or among close friends she usually elaborated on his kindness with great passion. To her, this tragedy, which was the precise word she used to describe Mattie's death, was not only God's will but also the work of the devil, the latter having cruelly shut out the light in Mattie's eyes, the former having blissfully caused them to reopen in the temple of His everlasting love. As she construed it, Mattie's death was also a test of a special and particular nature.

Mrs. Johnson had been the one to find Mattie lying on the ground in the backyard (a fall from her slide, the doctor later confirmed), her neck at an impossible angle. As soon as the housekeeper recovered her senses, her first thought had been, oh, my Lord, how will Mr. Mac survive? Mattie was his treasure, his precious girl. They blurred together in each other's company, he and Mattie, an edging of the hardness that was him into the softness that was her, until the exact point at which one finished and the other began was obscured, as if they actually shared one body and one heart. Mrs. Johnson could not begin to imagine how he would survive this loss. Certainly Mr.

Mac would need help—everyone did in such circumstances, and Mr. Mac would be no exception—but she was hard pressed to say where it would come from. He seemed to value her opinion, but that was not the kind of holding up he would need. There was his friend Jason, but she had never known Mr. Mac to rely on him in that way. The logical place to look would be to his wife, of course, but Mrs. McDougald's own collapse had been immediate and complete. Yes, Mrs. Johnson concluded, this was going to be a trial, a difficult one, and she would do what she could to support him. After all, hadn't Mr. Mac helped her with her Cora's tuition? And with extra money for shoes and pants for the two boys those three years in a row when they both kept growing?

"Good morning, Mrs. Johnson," Sirus said, appearing suddenly in the kitchen. He was completely dressed; he looked severe in his black suit, his light skin made all the paler by the contrast.

"Good morning, Mr. Mac," she answered. "You're up early. I'd hoped you'd be sleeping at least another hour." She ran her gaze over him methodically, as if weeding a garden, looking first at his eyes, then at the lines around them, then at the slope of his shoulders inside his suit.

"I didn't sleep well," he began. "Why don't you bring the coffee to the front room so we can talk for a minute." He waited for her nod before he left the room. Mrs. Johnson shortly followed with his coffee, careful to use his favorite cup and saucer. He definitely hadn't slept well, she decided, looking again at the shadows under his eyes and the pinched set of his shoulders.

"I think we have enough food now," he said as soon as she sat down. He sipped some of his coffee, holding it in his mouth until it cooled, and let her know it was how he liked it. "Every lady from the church will bring something," he continued, "and I don't want it to appear as if we're not grateful." He fastened his eyes on an old photograph of his father, which sat on the table beside her.

Mrs. Johnson continued to watch him carefully, encouraging him to go on.

"It's okay if you go ahead and fry up those last two chickens in the freezer, but after that I think we have more than enough."

Mrs. Johnson still said nothing. Of course there was too much food. There were three hams and two turkeys and pots and pots of collards and turnips and cabbage, not to mention rolls and pies and cold salads. On occasions like this there was always too much food. But no matter how much there was, it always got eaten. They both knew this.

"It's not as though any of these people will make their only meal here," he added.

"No, Mr. Mac, I don't expect they will," Mrs. Johnson said. "But it's always been the way to have more than enough, as long as a body can see their way clear to that."

Sirus pointed at her with his cup. "Just because I can afford it is no reason to waste both food and money," he said sharply. The coffee in his cup splashed up on one side.

"No, I didn't say there was," Mrs. Johnson said evenly. She sought his eyes, but they remained resolutely fixed on the point to the left of her. "I merely said it's usually the way, that's all. The food will keep, at any rate, and not go to waste; you can rely on me for that."

"Then you'll just cook what I said," Sirus said quietly, and drained the last of his coffee. He reached into his pocket for his watch, and Mrs. Johnson took his pointed hint, picked up his coffee cup along with hers, and left the room.

As soon as she was gone Sirus realized that he'd sounded foolish. He never talked to Mrs. Johnson this way. Yet the thought of all that food amassing in the kitchen nauseated him. It also made him think of another wake, at another time, at the home of a carpenter he'd known a long time ago in Wilson County, a man who had lost his wife and two of his three children in a fire.

The fire that killed them had erupted suddenly, its origin a mystery. The flames were already extinguished by the time the carpenter returned from a night of hunting with his youngest boy. He and the boy sat in his shed as smoke hung in the air, the same shed in which, in happier times, the man had often boasted he could make or repair anything made from wood: a wagon wheel, a table, a sideboard—anything that a use was known for. Now, ringed by the neighbors who had battled the blaze, he sat quietly. A thick layer of soot was everywhere: on the tools and chips and wood shavings that lay all around, on his clothing, on those of his neighbors. He sat precisely on the edge of the chair someone had dragged to the center of the shed. His arm was loosely draped around the shoulders of his son. Later, at the wake, with the food spread from one end of a table to the other, he'd held his son in the same slack manner, his eyes fixed on the three coffins that crowded the front of his house, taking up the space where a worn sofa and two chairs normally stood.

It was only later that it happened, what people referred to as "the change." First he kept his son home from school; then, when he allowed him to go out, he tightly buttoned the boy's shirtcuffs and layered both a vest and a sweater underneath his overalls, even in the summer. And later, or so Sirus heard his parents whispering, he rubbed the boy every night with a mixture of tar and pitch. It was so strange, so secretive, these private protections, but no one intervened. Nor did anyone step forward when it ended, finally, with the slaughter and ritualized eating of his animals. It was a story that even the busiest seemed loath to tell: how he had begun with his goat, gone on to the spindly-legged mule that drew the cart in which he delivered his work, and then to their dog, a mutt, with one brown ear and one yellow. It was rumored to have taken him weeks to finish this grisly task, and no one said a word to him about what he had done. Later, when the spring came, the carpenter and his boy simply moved away.

It was the carpenter and his son Sirus had been picturing when he spoke to Mrs. Johnson about the food. He thought about the boy chafing and sweating under the vests and the sweaters, about his mumbled excuses when he tried to explain his absence from school, and about what the boy's skin must have looked like after being covered with that stinging tar and pitch. Most of all, though, he thought about those beasts, their large, surprised eyes blinking shut against the spurting blood, their flesh cracking and smoking. Sirus never saw the flames that licked the animals clean; he only heard of their agony. But now he saw the animals multiplied, walking into the flames, two by two. And those images became mixed with others—of food piled high, stacked like a funeral pyre; of people eating so much that their bellies became distended; of a ladder made of food on which Mattie disappeared into heaven. Sirus was sure that he had to draw the line somewhere, anywhere, as a cordon of order and reason. Death and even his young self might stalk him, but he was resolved that he would not go the way of the carpenter, would not find himself, in the middle of the night, clinging to another body, his hands raw and stained, rubbing and covering and praying, and killing and consuming, doing anything at all that was necessary to keep from facing the truth, that he had lost the thing on earth he loved best.

A few blocks away, Etta Baldridge was back at her home, leaning against a pillow she'd bought on her last trip to New York. "I've got a stomach like a cast-iron skillet," she said to her best friend, Ophelia Macon. The remark concluded the conversation about food and digestion and bowels that Mrs. Macon had begun some five minutes earlier. The women left a respectful pause before launching into the subject they had gathered to discuss.

"I've never felt such a sorrow," Mrs. Baldridge began, interrupting the sound of her own breathing. "Never," she added dramatically.

Mrs. Macon nodded.

"Now I can't say how I would feel if it were my own Lily, but you know what I mean. Nobody outside 435 Fayetville loved that child more than me."

Ophelia Macon added a high sound of her own breathing, whistling up her nose.

"Wasn't I her godmother? Didn't I go to every birthday, every church play, every little thing they had at school?"

Mrs. Macon again showed agreement, lifting her chest so that her whole upper body shuddered. The two women sat at opposite ends of the beige and blue couch Mrs. Baldridge had had recovered only a month before. They sat in almost identical poses: their hands folded in their laps, large upper torsos perched precariously atop narrowly proportioned waists, hips, and legs, lips momentarily pursed against the torrent of words each always carried in her mouth. Mrs. Baldridge sat to the right, near the entrance to her dining room, her feet flat and even on the floor. Mrs. Macon sat to the left, near the archway to the front hall, her legs crossed at the ankles. On the low mahogany table in front of them sat two glasses of iced tea, with a sprig of fresh mint in each. The two women had had their hair dyed the day before, Mrs. Macon's a dark red, Mrs. Baldridge's a paler red, like new mahogany finished with clear resin.

"Have you seen them? Do you know how they're holding up?" Mrs. Macon asked, leaning in Mrs. Baldridge's direction.

"I've given them privacy, of course," Etta answered, thinking of her calls to Sirus, how he had ignored her hints for an invitation to come over. "I called, but there'll be time enough for them to lean on their friends. In the meantime I've been praying to the Lord to fill my bosom with comfort."

Mrs. Macon looked as if she too had been filling her bosom.

Mrs. Baldridge continued, "There're the days right through now, of course. Holding up Aileen. Being a post for Sirus so he can carry out his duties. But what grieves me to think about is later."

Mrs. Macon bowed her head.

"Remember Fran Farmer, her poor daughter, lost to TB?"

Mrs. Macon looked up, her eyes wide. "Oh, yes. Poor Fran Farmer."

"And remember how we took turns sitting with her? I mean her with no family, and only here in Durham five years."

"Oh, yes, she had no one."

"And we all kept coming, till a week after the funeral I think it was, and then someone said, 'Maybe we shouldn't intrude.' Why, I think it was Evelyn Knight who said it first."

"Was it Evelyn? Oh, mercy."

"I believe it was. I can't think who else would say something like that, can you?"

"No, I'm sure you're right. I'm sure it was Evelyn."

"Yes, I know it was. But we have to share the blame, too. Didn't we take what she was saying to heart? I mean, she put it so well. 'Who really knows her?' she said. And she had a point. She kept to herself pretty much all those years."

"But all and still," Mrs. Macon interjected.

"Yes, that's just what I was saying," continued Etta Baldridge, "but all and still. We should have kept going but we didn't, and who's to say if we had, why, that poor Fran might not have gone and followed her baby."

The women gasped simultaneously, as if the horror of Fran Farmer, found lying with her head resting—"like on a pillow," the preacher said— on the door of her stove, had suddenly pressed itself, for an instant, against them, and then, as quickly, had retreated, leaving them just that one image and a story to tell.

"You don't think?" Mrs. Macon began after a respectful silence.

"No, no, don't even mention such a thing."

But for a few long minutes both women imagined the worst. For Mrs. Macon it was one sorrowful scene after another: the wailing sound of the ambulance from Lincoln Hospital, ladies at the church wailing and fainting, the large, beautiful house on Fayetville once again draped in black and empty. For Mrs. Baldridge the images were much more far-ranging. She saw herself and her daughter Lily not exactly ostracized, but no longer occupying a place of importance. No more parties for Lily with the daughters of the other leading colored families of Durham: the McDougalds, the Gants, the Wilsons, the Gerards. She imagined a pall settling over the families, over all their hard work and their dreams of "progress for the race," until the whole fragile structure wilted and lay dead. She imagined an edgy despair spreading through the town, so that when someone fell on hard times people turned away instead of coming by with a pot of greens or a pile of carefully folded clothes. No one lending money to anyone anymore. No eligible young men, with the right education and the right family connections, coming by for Lily when the time was right. In Mrs. Baldridge's mind, Sirus was the knotted thread that bound them together. As you ringed salt around a stain or stitched a wound with pig gut, you relied on Sirus to be the stanch, to keep the tear from spreading. Driving past his house today, Etta had asked Albert to slow down so that she could concentrate on this. She had seen it clearly, how he had to hold together, not just avoiding the way of Fran Farmer, but going beyond, going from bad to good. Sirus had to re-deem this tragedy; that was how she saw it. He had to swallow it whole like a bitter root, not alone, but with the assistance of his friends and neighbors. And after the sweating from the poison was over and the shaking stilled, he had to rise up and be new. Mrs. Baldridge was as sure of this as she had been that her husband would die before fifty, and he'd died abruptly, as she had predicted, just two years before.

"Sirus will be strong," she said. "And with his strength Aileen will find her own. We just have to help him know his own resilience."

Mrs. Macon showed her agreement, staring at Mrs. Baldridge.

"I think we should arrive early. Not at the same time, of course, but within the half hour."

Mrs. Macon took a large swallow of her iced tea. "Are you going to read a prayer?" she asked.

"Well, nothing planned." Mrs. Baldridge let her shoulders fall against the back of the couch. "Of course I'll bring my Bible, and some subject may present itself."

"There are so many passages that bring comfort," Mrs. Macon observed.

In response, Mrs. Baldridge suddenly bellowed, " 'And though after my skin worms destroy this body, yet in my flesh shall I see God.' "

"Oh, my goodness, yes. Amen," Mrs. Macon replied.

" 'I will lay me down and take my rest,' " continued Mrs. Baldridge.

"Blessed be the Lord," echoed Mrs. Macon.

" 'The Lord is my light and my salvation; whom shall I fear? The Lord is the strength of my life; of whom shall I be afraid?' "

"Praise the Lord."

" 'Weeping may endure for a night,' " Mrs. Baldridge nearly yelled, lifting her hands from her lap, palms lifted. " 'But joy cometh in the morning.' " She dropped her hands back into her lap with a loud clap.

"Joy, oh, joy, oh, joy," Mrs. Macon said softly, clasping her hands.

"Yes, joy," Mrs. Baldridge concluded, staring ahead as if the word were printed in the air.

Upstairs, in her room, Lily heard the word *joy* erupt like a dissonant chord. Oh, God, what was her mother bellowing about now? She sat at her desk and looked at the words she had written so far:

Mattie was my friend so dear
Her face so full of grace
And now that she has left us here
No one can take her place.

It was a poem she was writing to read at Mattie's funeral—her mother's idea, of course. She would have preferred to sit quietly in the back and do nothing, but her mother had insisted. "You were her best friend," she said, "and I was her godmother. How would it look if you didn't say or do anything while someone like Cottie Moore sings a song, or Jane Henson does a dramatic reading?" Lily didn't care what Jane or Cottie was going to do; she didn't like them anyway. And even though she was Mattie's best friend, she still didn't want to read a poem in front of everyone.

She stared at the blank space under the four lines. She wanted to say something about Mattie's hair, which was a thick bushy brown, or her eyes, which were dark dark brown and always alert, but she couldn't think of any rhymes for hair or eyes, or any adjectives to go with them. Why couldn't she just sit at the back of the church like she wanted to? She hated the idea of everyone staring at her while she read her poem. Lily knew she was what was called a funny-looking child. She looked like both her mother and her father, but all mixed up in a jumble. She had her father's nice full lips, broad nose, and thick kinky hair. But she'd also gotten her mother's fair skin and light hair, and together she knew she looked a little like a duckling, awkward and ungainly. The only feature that was truly hers were her eyes, which were wide and round and sparkling brown, and drew people to her. Lily knew, however, that up on the podium, raised above the pews, she would only look yellow and strange.

She shifted her gaze out the window, hoping to find an adjective to describe Mattie's hair. Why couldn't she just show one of the pictures she had sketched of Mattie? There was the one of Mattie sitting on the steps of her front porch, with acorns in her mouth. Or the one of the baptism, where she had drawn Mattie, Edie Senate, and Floyd Turner all sitting in a row at the back of the church altar, waiting for the preacher to call them down into the pool of water, where he would rest his hand over their noses and mouths and dunk them, fully dressed, in the water. Or even the one she had drawn of Mattie today, of the two of them, sitting on Mattie's front porch the night before she died. They put up flowers at funerals, so why couldn't they put up one of her pictures, like a little flower? And that could be that. It would mean telling about the drawings, of course, and if she did that, her mother would want to see them all. Maybe it would be easier to read the poem; at least it would be over quickly. If she told about the drawings, there'd be no end to it.

There was a quick rap on the door, and as soon as she slid a piece of paper over what she was writing, her mother was in the room.

"Oh, Lily, I'm so disgusted," her mother said, huffing from the flight of stairs. She dropped onto the edge of Lily's bed and immediately began picking at a loose thread on the bedspread.

Lily watched her mother's eyes frenetically sweep around the room.

"Really, I can't even begin to tell you," Mrs. Baldridge continued. "No one seems to have the vaguest notion of how to behave tonight." She stared at a pile of books on top of Lily's dresser and read the title of each one. She focused on Lily's shoes and then at the hem of Lily's dress. "And do you know what I saw today as I drove past the McDougalds'? No, of course you don't know. You couldn't even begin to guess." Her gaze at last rested on Lily's face. "Guess," she said sharply.

"I don't know, Mother. What?" Lily answered.

"A skate," she announced. "Do you hear what I'm saying? A skate."

Lily was puzzled. She was sure her mother could read her expression.

"You don't understand what I'm saying, do you?"

Lily shook her head slowly.

"It was her skate," her mother elaborated. "Right under the front bush."

Lily's eyes widened.

"Right," replied her mother; "that's just what I'm saying. It was as plain as day. I'm surprised Sirus hasn't seen it. But he hasn't. His mind has been too busy, I expect. But there it was and, I imagine, still is. Do you understand what I'm saying?"

"Yes, Mother," Lily said quietly.

"I mean, anyone could see it tonight. Sirus. Oh, God, poor Aileen. What a shock that would be."

Lily tried to imagine how the skate had gotten there. Had Mattie fallen, flung it there in anger, and then clumped into the house on only one skate? Or had she put it there on purpose; was there something wrong with the skate that she wanted to hide?

"I'm at a loss," continued her mother. "Completely. I can't very well go over there and pick it up myself. What if someone saw me in the bushes, for goodness' sake? And it can't be left there. What a cruel thing that would be."

Lily suddenly imagined running over to Mattie's house right now to pick it up, not so that it would be gone, but to make it hers.

"Well," Mrs. Baldridge said, leaning toward Lily. "Do you think I'm just talking to hear myself speak? What do you think we should do?"

Lily wished she had seen the skate first and had it now, under her bed, safely wrapped in a blanket.

"Can you really see it from the road?" she asked.

"Like buckshot in a deer's eye."

Lily winced. "Then I guess someone should pick it up." Her voice trailed off at the end of her sentence.

"Do what?" her mother fairly yelled. "Speak up."

"Pick it up," Lily said louder.

"Well, what do you think I've been saying? I mean, have you been listening to a word I've said?"

"Yes, ma'am, I'm listening." Lily made an effort to sit straighter in her chair and bring her eyes to her mother's.

"What have you been doing up here all this time, anyway?"

Lily wished they could return to the skate, but she knew her mother would not be satisfied with that.

"I cleaned my room," she answered, "and ironed my dress for tonight."

"Oh, really? Let me see it."

Lily took her dress from the closet and held it up to herself, holding it out at the hem so that the skirt flared.

"There's a wrinkle there, on the left side," her mother said, taking the material in her hand and balling it lightly. Lily knew that this would not only mark the spot that needed ironing, but make a new wrinkle as well.

"And your ears? Let me see them," she continued as Lily hung the dress back in her closet.

"Yes, ma'am." Lily returned and leaned forward so that her head hung just within reach of her mother's hands. Her mother took her chin in one hand and turned it first to one side, where she inspected one ear, and then to the other. "There's wax at the back of both of your ears," she concluded.

Lily backed her head away, willing herself to move it slowly. What was it her mother was moving toward?

"You might as well know, I'm worried about this whole thing."

"You mean about the skate?" Lily asked.

"That, and the whole thing." Her mother waved her hand listlessly in the air.

Lily wasn't at all sure what her mother meant. "You mean about the funeral tomorrow? What you're going to say?"

"No, not that . . . You think I'm worried about something so minor when this house, our car, all those fine things you wear, your whole future and mine is what's at stake?"

"No, I guess not," Lily ventured.

"No, of course not. Do I look like somebody's fool?"

"No, Momma, of course you don't."

"Oh, if your father were alive, it would be different. He'd still have his job, his position, and we'd have our place from his, but since he died, it's all dependent on everyone else. Did you know we get an allowance from the bank every month, something the bank board voted on after he died? Well, what do you think would happen if Sirus McDougald were not heading up that board? Do you think those others would be so generous? No, I don't think so. They'd just as soon forget we even exist; that's what I think. I wouldn't trust a one of them. And what about this house? Who do you think owns it? Do you think there's a deed with my name on it? Of course there isn't. And do you think it's anyone else down at the bank that argues for us to stay? Not for a minute. The rest of them don't think of anyone but themselves."

Lily had had no idea of any of this. It was the first she knew that everything they had wasn't really theirs.

"I don't understand, Mother," she began. "Why would anything change now? Is Mr. McDougald going somewhere?"

Her mother groaned loudly. "Don't you know anything? Must I spell everything out for you? Things change. Death changes things."

Lily still didn't understand. Of course death changes things. It meant she and Mattie would never go to the beach together again, or ride in the Mc-

Dougalds' car. It meant there'd be no one sitting on the porch or standing in the yard that she could yell hey to when she rode past on her bike. Oh, a hundred and one things would change. But nowhere was there the kind of change her mother was talking about, and she couldn't see, even for a moment, why it should be so.

"Why am I talking to a child?" Her mother looked around the room as if there were someone else to talk to. "I mean, here is a child who doesn't have the sense the good Lord gave her at birth, and I'm expecting her to understand something as vital as her own future? The good Lord must think I've lost my mind."

Lily lowered her head. She knew her mother would be through soon— she always was when the good Lord began to have an opinion.

"Be downstairs and dressed in an hour," her mother added as she left the room.

"Yes, ma'am," she said quickly. But her mother was already down the stairs by the time she got the words out.

Just down the street from Sirus, Jason Morgan, Sirus's friend and the leading colored undertaker, climbed behind the wheel of his hearse. His two young assistants, Lucas and Earl, were in the seat behind him, and the small coffin that held Mattie lay in the cabin beyond them. Jason pulled the car smoothly out of the driveway and into the right lane. It would not take long to drive Mattie's body the five short blocks from the funeral parlor to Sirus's house. When he and Sirus were boys, back in Carr, the distance between their farms had been nearly two miles along a pounded dirt road. But back then, even that distance had flowed like water. Back and forth, back and forth, one or the other of them made the journey. Those two miles seemed no more than these five blocks did now.

Throughout their childhood, they had been best friends. Jason was more uniformly muscled than Sirus, with knobby wrists that sprouted from the cuffs of his cotton shirts, large, knuckled hands, small flat ears, and a long skull that curved back and away, giving his head an elfin look that matched the sinewy shape of his body. Sirus, by contrast, was made of pieces that seemed not quite whole; his feet were too large, his legs thin and muscled only in the thighs, his chest narrow and sloping inward, his light skin delicate and easily bruised.

Jason was the one who played softball well, who won when they raced each other, who vaulted over any chairs and logs in his way. Sirus was uneven and distracted at sports, lost his train of thought when something upset him. At school Jason was considered the regular fellow, jovial and good-humored, emotional but unaffected, so quick to recover from easy tears that by the time anyone might have begun a jeer he was all smiles and jokes again. Sirus was more likely to be confused, to cry and fall silent, or to feign indifference and then brood over an event long after it was finished for everybody else. Sirus enjoyed Jason's easy fit with others, his sincerity, his uncomplicated response to things; Jason enjoyed Sirus's curiosity, quiet intensity, and his energy, which easily matched Jason's own.

Whenever they were together as boys, it was as if there were no space between them, until that time when it changed. One late July day, the air thick with wet heat, he and Sirus had lain in the tall grass behind Sirus's house, beyond the four stripping barns, next to the woods that ran the length of the road. Their heads were cushioned by the matted grass; their sneakered feet rested in the red dirt path. Sirus had brought with him his collection of dried skins: a copperhead, a flat mouth, an Indian moccasin, and a tiny field mouse, treasures he had found in the fields or woods and carefully placed on a broken stripping shelf in a barn to dry. Jason had brought his new Sears, Roebuck softball, a present for his birthday; his hand-stitched glove, made by the tanner in town, was propped under his knees like the bump in an old sofa. They had had a game of catch and searched fruitlessly for more skins, and then lay nearly stuporous in the shade.

It was Sirus who decided it was too hot for clothes. He jumped to his feet and peeled away his socks and overalls and tightly buttoned cotton shirt with one unexpectedly graceful motion, as if he were shedding his skin. It was just the kind of surprising thing, back then, that Sirus would do. He stood in the path next to Jason's feet, the sun bouncing off the right side of his body, casting a shadow on the ground between them. As he stood there, naked, the skin under his clothes paper white, he looked not so much like a boy of ten as like a newly hatched creature that had been deposited on the narrow path. Jason was too lazy to stand, but he kicked off first one sneaker and then the other as he randomly unsnapped and unbuttoned his clothes. While Jason undressed, Sirus seemed suddenly set free. Pretending to be a Cherokee warrior, he pranced in the path and the grass, waving his arms, hooting, cawing like a crow, kicking his legs and flapping his arms.

He carried on for five minutes, a mist of sweat covering his body. "You going to catch the grass on fire, you keep rubbing those stick legs of yours together like that," Jason said, laughing, still not undressed. Then he heard a crackling in the pine underbrush. He sat up and hooked his arms around his knees, squinting into the dappled woods. He searched the path that wound between a stand of cedars, but he didn't see the two men until the moment they emerged from the woods, their rifles nosed toward the ground. Startled at first, he was quickly relieved to see they were men he and Sirus both knew.

Ezra Carter, short and the color of cocoa, owned a small dry-goods store and was a fanatical hunter. Hank Prinde worked in Ezra's store. Ezra wore a brown felt hat with the brim rolled up on one side, pushed back on his head. His mouth worked furiously on a large piece of chew. "Fool boy" was all he said as he gaped at Sirus, who stood frozen, his chest neither rising nor falling, his hands at his sides as if they were plumbed. Ezra spat on the path and shifted the heft of his gun.

"Looks like a bird; think I'll shoot it," Hank Prinde said, coming up behind him and laughing in three short bursts that sounded like a small dog barking. He raised his rifle from the ground, leveled it directly at the center of Sirus's thin chest, and cocked the trigger. He moved the barrel up toward Sirus's eyes, then down to his Adam's apple, which seemed to be shriveling in the boy's throat, and next to his private parts, which were indeed no bigger than a small bird. They stood like that for a full minute.

"Boy, put your clothes on," Ezra said finally. "You look like some goddamn savage." He motioned to Hank, who barked his laugh again, and they both turned, making their way back across the field, swaying with the weight of the rows of rabbits slung across their backs.

"Damn, nearly scared me," Jason said, turning to Sirus. Sirus stood without moving; the quiver in his lips had spread to his arms and legs, like a giant chill coursing from one end of his body to the other.

"That Hank's the one who's a savage," Jason said, "pointing his gun like that." He wiped his hands on his coveralls. "You'd think a grown man would have more sense than that."

Sirus continued to stare after the two men.

"C'mon, Sirus, let's start back." Jason stood and reached forward to swipe at Sirus's leg with his hand. Sirus jerked away.

"Don't," he said quietly.

"Well, okay." Jason let his hands fall beside him. He wished that he could just tell Sirus again that it was Hank who was the fool, but Sirus's stillness inspired his own. He felt uncomfortable in his own skin. A second ago, Sirus's dancing had made him glad, and now the men had taken that away. It was as if some rule had been broken, but neither of them could say what it was. He fumbled with his own clothes, buttoning and snapping what he had undone. A chasm had suddenly opened between them, and he felt himself on one side, with Sirus on the other. Ah, just forget them, he tried to say with his hands, willing the gesture to be nonchalant, but Sirus wasn't listening. He harshly forced his legs and arms back into his clothes, as if he might tear off his skin with the rough corduroy and cotton. Those men, Jason thought as he watched Sirus dress, have snatched something away from us.

He and Sirus didn't talk about what happened, but the two boys were never again so free with each other. A stiffness, a small measure of furtiveness insinuated itself into their physical selves. Jason sometimes looked back and wondered how it was that that had happened. And whether there was anything he could have done to make it different. And what about now? What special part of his friend would death chase away? Would he fail Sirus now as, he felt, he had failed him then?

He thought about the work he had just completed on Mattie's body, which lay nestled inside the molded pink couch of her coffin, underneath a spray of yellow roses, at the back of the hearse. The hands that gripped the wheel—a little more tensely than he would have liked—were the same large and knuckled hands he had had as a boy. He had a mustache now, thin but nicely curved, and sideburns, which came to the middle of his sloping ears. Though he did not cry quite as frequently as he had as a child, he still cried easily.

Despite the smell of formaldehyde that clung to him like burdock, and the sometimes quizzical looks he got from someone new when he identified his profession, Jason enjoyed his work as an undertaker. He liked working with his hands, liked to be as respectful and gentle to the bodies as his work allowed, liked particularly to let his own deep capacity for tenderness and empathy find a rightful and appropriate home. Unlike some undertakers, who needed to conjure up a display of sorrow, Jason had sympathy that flowed as naturally as his love for his wife and three children. He loved them and his work freely, simply, without reserve or conflict. And because he loved so freely, there was nothing to hold back his grief.

When he first heard the news about Mattie, he was at the drugstore, talking to the pharmacist, Dr. Gerard, about the smelling salts he thought he might need for an upcoming funeral. In the middle of their conversation, Dr. Gerard got the call. Jason left everything just where it lay on the counter: the box of salts, aspirin for his wife, Edith, and two comics for the girls. He rushed from the store and drove without stopping. When he pulled into the driveway at Sirus's house, the sight of Sirus's own car in the garage seemed suddenly to make the tragedy real. He jumped out of his car, ran up the steps of the porch, and rushed into the house. Dr. Gant sat in the foyer, his large leather bag at his feet, filling out the death certificate. Sirus sat opposite him in a high-backed leather chair, his head frozen to one side, his shoulders hunched forward. Jason had never seen Sirus look so small or so pale.

In one swift motion, Jason grabbed Sirus's hands, pulled him up out of his chair, and folded his arms around him. Without even knowing that he did, he rocked his friend in his arms, and for a moment Sirus's full weight collapsed against him.

Jason now knocked at the front-door screen of Sirus's house as Lucas and Earl waited with the hearse at the curb. Jason strained to see into the darkened front parlor, but Sirus got to the door before Jason's eyes adjusted so that all he could make out was Sirus's broad frame.

"Hello, Sirus," Jason said, stepping back as Sirus swung open the door.

"Morning, Jason," Sirus said, nodding also toward Jason's two assistants, who now stood in the middle of the sidewalk.

Jason turned slightly to include Earl and Lucas in his statement. "We've brought her home," he said. "Do you want to go upstairs while we bring her in?"

Sirus didn't move. "No, I'll wait here," he answered, sliding the metal hinge that held the door open along its rod.

"Are you sure, Sirus?"

"I'm all right, Jason," Sirus said. "Please, just go ahead."

"Okay," Jason answered. "It'll take us about five minutes to get things all set up."

He turned and walked down the porch and sidewalk, motioning to Lucas and Earl to precede him back to the hearse. They swung open the heavy black door, one of them on either side, and pulled out a folded metal cart. Watching them, Sirus remembered that until a few days ago he had been able to carry Mattie easily, sweeping her up in a second, her arms around his neck, supporting her whole weight with one arm. Now it would take three men and five minutes to bring her inside.

"Sirus, why don't you roll back the edge of the rug?" Jason called from the steps of the porch.

The coffin rose up in front of Sirus like a whale breaking from the sea. For a second, if he closed his eyes, he thought it could be a month ago, at Highland Beach: Mattie's face breaking the water, her mouth spouting salt water, laughing, her thick brown hair holding the water and salt like a sponge so that it caught the sunlight bouncing on the surface of the ocean.

"Catch me, Daddy, catch me."

She had flopped toward him, her arms stretched out over her head, her legs and feet beating the top of the water like butter. And he had caught her up, just under the ribs, swinging her around in the water so fast that there was, for a moment, only spray and motion, making a small circle in the middle of the ocean around them.

"Again, Daddy, again," she had called out in her high, breaking voice, pushing off with her feet against his thighs. She had flopped and smacked and dived and he had caught and swung and lifted until his arms felt there was nothing else they had ever done before but catch her and carry her and whirl her around deliriously in the midst of her zest and joy. When he asked Aileen that night to put salve on his shoulder, she had said, "Sirus, you spoil that child. Why didn't you just tell her your arms were getting tired?" "She's a lovely child, Aileen; we couldn't have asked for one better," was all he said in reply.

Jason cleared his throat.

"Of course," Sirus said, flipping back the edge of the carpet with his foot. Jason and the boys pushed the cart up the last step and through the doorway, steadying it carefully as the wheels ran over the threshold. So she was coming home, Sirus thought, stiller than she had ever been, with a stillness that felt more still than death.

"We'll put her here," Jason called, as they traveled across the living room like a small caravan, "by the window." By the time Sirus turned, the coffin was off its cart and resting on a pedestal the same color as the coffin.

"We'll be able to bank the flowers here nicely," Jason continued, spreading his arms out on either side like long sails. "And if we move these two chairs"—he pointed at the two wing chairs that flanked the coffin—"we'll have a walkway for people to spend their time with her to say their goodbyes."

Jason moved about the room, touching various pieces of furniture. There was something hypnotic in the way he spoke, as if the scene he was describing were not real. Behind his words, Sirus thought, another scene seemed to unfold. In that scene Jason's arms, raised and lowered, were a shepherd's arms; the square, slightly formal living room was a wide meadow; and Mattie's coffin contained not a dead child, but something magical, something created for a moment of worshipful celebration.

Sirus interrupted Jason, took him by the arm, and led him, Lucas, and Earl into the kitchen. There, Sirus pressed biscuits and coffee and eggs on them, encouraged by Mrs. Johnson. He left them there, Jason in the wide-bottomed oak chair he usually sat in, the boys scooted up to the table, their brown caps resting on their knees, as Mrs. Johnson turned to the stove and tended her biscuits, which were browning. Sirus, in the armchair next to the head of the coffin in the living room, could hear their voices.

"He's quite a man, that one," Mrs. Johnson said somberly as she lifted the tray of biscuits from the oven. "Not a better man to work for in this world." She dropped the tray on the counter, where the water beneath it made a hissing sound.

"He's a good man, all right," Jason agreed.

"You better believe it," Mrs. Johnson continued. "Don't let a person come anywhere near me saying anything different."

"Yes, indeed."

"Did I ever tell you about how my Cora used to do her homework, right here at this table?" Mrs. Johnson continued. "Mr. Mac would come in, take a look at it for her—I mean, sometimes reading a whole report, cover to cover, like it was an important paper from the bank—and when he'd be done he'd say, 'Well, Cora, that's really fine,' or 'You ought to try and change how you end it. I got a little confused along the way.' Whatever he thought."

"Umm-hmm," Jason murmured, taking a bite of the hot biscuit.

"And those Genene girls, didn't he have one, then the next, then the next, till all three of them lived here at one time or another, every one of those girls coming up from the country to go to school. And they went, too, every one of them, and their parents decent hardworking people. But you know what I'm saying, about the expense and all. And the whole time, Mr. Mac not saying a word to anybody, except something about how he needs help down at the real estate office. I guess there might have been something they could have done, but who could for the life of them say what a country girl would know about all that work Mr. Mac is always doing. You know what it is I'm saying."

Jason nodded, swallowing and chewing almost simultaneously.

"And don't tell me anything about loving that child," she went on. "Oh, mercy, think I'd like to die myself than have to live to see the day something happen to that child, then die again to keep from living long enough to see Mr. Mac have to go through it." She turned on the water in the sink full force. "He's been like something right out of the grave himself, walking and breathing, but not much more. Oh, Lord, I thought I'd never see this day."

Jason looked at her, soap rising from beneath her hand swirling under the stream from the faucet. His large eyes clouded over. "It's a terrible thing," he agreed.

"Terrible ain't even the beginning of it." Mrs. Johnson turned to face him and the boys. "If I weren't afraid of blasphemy, I'd talk about pestilence and flood; that's how bad this thing strikes me. Must be near on to hell and damnation."

Earl's and Lucas's eyes met across the table, their mouths motionless as they contemplated Mrs. Johnson.

"But I ain't saying nothing about that subject in this house." The boys resumed their contented chewing. "Got to remember the good times, especially now you've done gone and brought her soul's house on home." She stared at Lucas and Earl. "You boys brought her in here okay, yes? You been gentle and careful like with a lamb?"

They bobbed their heads.

"Good. I wouldn't want nothing more to disturb that child on her way to glory, and praise the Lord, I know that's where she's bound."

"Praise the Lord," Jason responded, bowing his head briefly as if in prayer.

Mrs. Johnson's words seemed to have caught up to her, and her eyes filled with tears. "Oh, Lord, that was one sweet child," she said mournfully.

"That she was," said Jason.

Sirus now heard silence in the kitchen. He had been aware of Jason's being there and of what his presence represented: the things they needed to discuss. But as long as he heard the voices, that moment seemed distant. Now, in the silence, it was a presence standing beside him. This was the moment he had been dreading, what he wished he could avoid, to face yet again this stillness that was supposed to be his Mattie.

When Aileen left the house yesterday, fled, really, she had insisted that she would never be able to sleep, knowing that her baby would be coming home in a box. She could not bear to see it, she told him. And she warned him, pleaded with him, not to let them make Mattie look like someone else. "They're always doing that," she said tearfully. "Remember my father's mouth, how they filled it with cotton and his cheeks were all puffed out so that he looked like he was pouting and angry? Or they get the color all wrong. She's our child, a bright chestnut, a happy child," she kept saying. And Sirus had promised that he would be careful, that he would handle this detail, make sure it was done right. But how on Earth could he do it, he wondered. Where would he find the strength to look in the coffin, much less talk with Jason about anything else that might need to be done?

He looked around the room. The sun was streaming through the window behind him; he felt it hot on his shoulders, spreading a warmth that his muscles yielded to in spite of himself. If he closed his eyes, with the feel of that sun, he could escape this room, he could once again be a small boy on his parents' tobacco farm, the sun reflecting on the tall grass that ringed the house. In that imaginary field, lit by this sun, he could keep his eyes closed, and what he sensed was not this coffin but something else, something more closely resembling a mysterious presence. He felt that if he were to turn and approach this inexplicable something, it would be with anticipation, a feeling tinged with yearning.

Drifting with the sun's warmth, he felt himself sink deeper into this scene. He became aware of an altered sense of time, a feeling of long hours, long days, no, long years, bringing him to this point. He kept imagining himself as the boy in that grass, looking to this future, and if he were to open his eyes, then or now, what he'd see would hold all of the years that had gone by. He could feel all of the tension held in his body over the past two days flow out of him. Gone were all the times he had held himself in check, all the movements toward or away from someone. All that was left was this thing, this something. As he drew nearer in his imagination, his heart swelled so that it nearly burst with anticipation.

Yes, that was what he was feeling, he thought giddily, a kind of rejoicing. Things were not as they seemed, he wanted to shout. Look, look, something wonderful has occurred, and he was the only one who knew or was allowed to see it. Privately, secretly, he alone was going to be given a glimpse, permitted only once in a lifetime, of something he couldn't name. And almost joyously, he opened his eyes and turned his head, and as he did, the living room slid into view. What was visible was not this magnificent presence, but the coffin, suspended. The vision faded, not all at once, but as a dream fades. His giddiness slipped away, and then his trembling hope, and the overwhelming joy he had expected to taste. One by one his senses returned him to himself, and what he saw and heard and felt was exactly what was here in this room—and no more.

He was alone. There were no sounds around him. He rose from his chair and lay his hand atop the coffin. She was gone. He ran his hand along the curved top of the molded lid. It was both smooth and cool. If he were to lift the cover, she would lie before him, lifeless. Her smile, her laughter, her smell of leaves and tart apples, her plumply muscled arms folded over her painfully angular legs would be shrouded, still. They would never move again, never explode from the center of the room. The cool, quiet body lying in this box would never again hurtle toward him, take his breath away. Now they were at an end. Now they were removed to a region of memory and shadow. Now he would never experience her again.

He heard Jason come into the room and felt his warm presence beside him as distinctly as a bell pealing in his ear.

"We have a few more things to discuss," Jason said quietly, resting his arm across his friend's shoulder.

"Yes, of course." Sirus's voice was close to breaking. He reached into his pocket for something, anything, and his hand came out empty. "I need my glasses, my pen," he mumbled. He backed away from Jason and the coffin, then turned, stumbling over his feet. He regained his balance, hurried across the front parlor, and disappeared up the stairs.

Your Child Can Be a Model!

BY DAVID HAYNES

Football pools. Rumor mongering. Daylong seminars on the changing face of the twenty-first-century consumer. Apparently this is what Americans did at work. Sheila had no idea. Eighteen months ago she'd been a housewife. Who knew the glass on top of a copy machine could support a grown man's behind?

When Whispering Pines Junior High School rings her cellular to tell her that her son Briggs has been sent home from school for misbehavior, Sheila is arrayed across the entrance from her boss's, Marketa Winthrop, office in the sort of pose a really bad exotic dancer might mistake for sexy. She is trying to keep the production manager from stabbing Marketa Winthrop with an Exacto knife. The knife is right there in his hands, its edges bristling with bits of rubber cement and trimmed copy. Marketa Winthrop wants the blushing beauties on the bridal announcement page arrayed in alphabetical order. Ralph Johansen has his own scheme. He waves the paste up in Sheila's face.

"Ugly, bootiful, ugly, bootiful." He fingers the alternating faces and assumes the bizarre and unrecognizable accent he adopts when he is angling after a date with her. Gypsy or marginally Latino, she thinks, but who could imagine? Ralph is from Eau Claire, Wisconsin.

"It's ten o'clock in the morning," Sheila says to the assistant principal. "What do you mean sent home?"

"Dismissed. Until you bring him back for a conference."

"You can't just send children home," she says. She keeps Ralph at bay with her foot.

"I weel now keel her with my ber hends," he seethes. Olive-skinned and vaguely ethnic like the villains on daytime television, Ralph has steely black eyes and a goatee, the same look sported by pictures of the devil on low-budget religious tracts.

"Important call," Sheila mouths, but Ralph ignores her.

"Che ees evil, no?" He grabs her free hand and kisses the darker side, licking it with his tongue. Why did cute men have to be so nasty? Or maybe it was the other way around.

"I've got a district policy manual right here on my desk that says that I *can* send Briggs home. And my file says you agreed to this plan, two weeks ago."

She did? Sheila doesn't remember, but she might have agreed to anything John Antonio said. Twenty-five years later she could still be intimidated by junior high assistant principals.

"Jou are bootiful when jou are engry." The slobber on her hand tickles. She stifles a giggle.

"I'm sorry you find this amusing."

"I don't." Sheila clears her throat to indicate just how serious she is and also to stifle her laugh. These people didn't need more ammunition against her. She bares her teeth at Ralph. Ralph growls in response.

"Where is my child?" she demands.

"He should be landing on your front porch any minute now."

"Briggs doesn't have a key."

"That's for the two of you to work out. Can I expect you for a conference in the morning?"

"You can expect me in twenty minutes." She tumbles into Marketa Winthrop's office, mashing Ralph's fingers in the jamb, and locks the door behind her.

Sheila is Marketa Winthrop's personal assistant. Sheila gets her dry cleaning, her oil changed, picks up her snack cakes at the 7-Eleven. Marketa Winthrop is a victim of magazines like *New Black Woman* and *Essence* and *Self*. She reads in these magazines how successful entrepreneurs of the kind she imagines herself to be all have personal assistants: Camille Cosby, Linda Johnson, Jada Pinkett-Smith. Those gals snap their fingers and mountains of annoyance disappear. Marketa Winthrop believes this can happen to her. She believes that by modeling herself on rich and glamorous women, she, too, will become lithe and loved the world over. The Fresh Prince of Bel Air will move into her bed. Who is Sheila to disabuse her of this notion?

"I need to run up to school," Sheila tells her boss.

Marketa Winthrop flips the page of another magazine. "Did Ralph redo the wedding announcements?" she asks. Her boss subscribes to dozens of magazines. Sheila delivers them each morning with a jumbo coffee and a bear claw from the convenience store. Marketa Winthrop spends much of her day paging through the glossies, dreaming of the big move she promises Sheila they will be making soon to the national publications scene.

"ABC brides," Sheila lies. As if the order of suburban princesses mattered.

"Good girl. Because one thing Marketa Winthrop won't be having is a bunch of pissy mothers-of-the-bride." Marketa Winthrop always uses both her names, always introduces herself as if the person she were speaking with had been hearing about her for years. "Hello, Marketa Winthrop," she'll say, extending her hand. This despite the fact that, as the owner of a chain of suburban weeklies, the only place they might have encountered her name was on the masthead of one of her throwaway shoppers, just above the announcement for the garden club meeting and a full page ad for Cooper's Super Value.

"Pick up some Twinkies on the way back." Marketa Winthrop shoos her on her way with a trill of fingers.

Sheila makes a left by the trusty 7-Eleven, onto the road to Maple Villas, where she and Briggs reside. Washington County scares her. What were farm roads three crops ago are now lined with strip malls and condos and industrial parks, each cluster of buildings shamelessly jury-rigged—cheap

Tudor veneer on Ye Olde Shoppes. Months old and the whole shebang already looked worn out. There are no landmarks here. Down in the city, where they had lived with the ex, you navigated using the brewery, the steeple of St. Cecilia's, the smokestacks at the auto plant. In Washington County not even the old-timers knew their way around. "I think you turn down by the old Jamison place. Go another mile or so to where they tore down the silo." Pale faces eyed her with mild contempt, as if a black woman didn't deserve a home on the grange. Or perhaps they blamed her personally for the distant city landing on their former cornfields in all its four-lane glory. Sheila turns past the crumbling sandstone cairns that mark the entrance to her apartment complex. There are no maples and the villas are peach-bricked, generic boxes, with opera balconies and too many yucca plants.

One thing for Briggs: He has the good sense to know when not to push his luck. He is waiting on the porch, just as he knew she'd expect him to be, one less thing to go off about. Fourteen years: She'd depleted her repertoire of responses to the boy. Hysterical mom. Frustrated mom. Blasé. Rageful. Shaming. She could mount a full season of one-woman shows—Hey, there was an idea: The Psychotic Divorced Mother's Repertory Company. Rent out a church basement. Sell gin and tonics and Prozac at the concession stand. Begin each season with *Medea*.

She rolls down her window. "Get in this car and start talking," she orders. She'd save the small talk for the suits at school. Climbing in, Briggs slouched down next to her.

"Well, you see, the thing is, it was just that me and Cedric . . . Oh, by the way: You're looking fine today, Ma. That's a really nice dress."

"Don't even, Briggs." Sheila rolls her eyes. Instead of a theater company, how about an anticharm school? She could make piles of money training philandering politicians and your garden-variety teenage-male alternatives to being unctuous when caught with their pants down.

"Out with it," she orders.

"Like I said. Me and Cedric . . ."

"Cedric and I." What did they teach in these damn schools anyway?

"Yeah, that. We were sitting in class, and we were just sitting there and this one kid said that Cedric had ashy legs and then Miss Stephes said turn around and then Cedric said your mama's breath smells like socks and cheese and then I laughed and then Ms. Stephes said go to the office."

Sheila monitors Briggs' face while she negotiates a turn. Sincerity to contrition, dissolving too quickly to oily self-pity.

"You don't even believe that story yourself," she chides.

"Yeah, I do. That's just how it happened. Except . . ."

And there it was: there was always an "except." Sometimes Sheila thinks she should carry in her lap posterboards with large numbers written on them that she could raise and vote on the most promising rendition. Version two of the story is parallel to version one "except" for the fact that Briggs had been the one making the comment about socks and cheese, and said comment had occurred after numerous attempts on the part of Miss Stephes to quell the squawk fest. Briggs looks gravely off into the distance as he delivers this tale, the same way the elderly grandfathers do on *Masterpiece Theater*. A gullible person would be moved to tears. Version three of the story, also fairly parallel, went into great detail about the baneful Miss Stephes, who evidently had installed a torture chamber directly beneath her classroom specifically for the purpose of making Brigg's life a living hell.

"She's evil, Ma. You don't know." Briggs quakes a little, remembering, no doubt, the grip of thumbscrews, the pull of the rack.

Sheila sighs. Another Briggs three-pack. Somewhere in the middle of all these words is the truth. Or *a* truth. The frustrating thing is that Sheila knows her son isn't really a liar. His father? Now *that* was a liar. There was a man who could drag himself in at three in the morning, reeking of knock-off Chanel, with a pair of panties slung around his neck, look you right in the eye and tell you he'd spent the evening at the bowling alley. Briggs on the other hand is basically an honest boy. It's the basically part that troubles her. Like filling out your income taxes, with Briggs it was a game of approximations. Round up a little here, round down a little there. This was America: You develop a poker face, tell your best story, and stick with whichever version doesn't get you audited. What Briggs and his father had in common is that they both believed every word that came out of their mouths. Sheila spent sleepless nights worrying about quarters she'd neglected to return to petty cash. Briggs slept the sleep of angels, as serene and innocent as his first nights on Earth.

Sheila makes a left onto a short and nameless freeway that had been constructed for the sole purpose of carrying people like her from one side of the county to the other. What was she doing in a place like this? People like the kind of person Sheila had intended to become lived in the city, in red-brick and ivy-festooned neighborhoods, with coffee bars and cute restaurants that served things like couscous and tiramisu. These days it was the ex and his various sluts who got to sit under the ailanthus trees, read the *New York Times* and sip espresso. Sheila got to go to the 7-Eleven and to junior highs and drive on nameless roads past buildings too slick for growing things.

"Honestly, Briggs," she says. "What am I supposed to say to these people?" That smug and priggish AP, who fired statements at you about your child and then dared you to come up with an appropriate response. Last time it was "We discovered your son and his buddies beneath the bleachers during a pep rally with a pair of binoculars and a flashlight," and then he sat waiting with his fingers folded on his desk.

"Boy, I'm sure you'd hate to do something like that" is what Sheila had wanted to answer, though this was not the sort of response that won you the prize money. "He'll be dead by sunset" was the sort of thing they had in mind.

"We were collecting the money that dropped from kids' pockets." That had been Brigg's excuse for the bleachers, though he really needed to work on his delivery. A truly unfit mother would have given some pointers. Smile and nod, son. Show some confidence. Try not to make each statement sound like a question.

Briggs, Briggs, Briggs. Just look at the darling boy. Wasn't it only yesterday he was burbling in his crib, taking his first baby steps? Now he was arguing with lunch ladies, cruising the hallways like a shark, firing off Vegas-style one-liners. Sunrise, sunset. A veritable storehouse of smarmy remarks, her son: "Hey girl, bring them twins over here." "Stop by my locker so you can meet my friend." "Baby, you know I could rock your world." Briggs could give Ralph pointers on gross. She considered sewing his lips together, but that still left the hands.

"Your son had better learn where those mitts of his belong," Antonio had warned.

Sheila remembers the sweet and endearing olden days at her own junior high, when squeaky-voiced boys would put an arm around you and maybe try to grab a feel. Silly things: They'd pretend to walk into walls. They'd bang their heads into lockers because you were such a knockout. But when you woke up one day and it was your son with the smart mouth and the fast hands and the too-smooth demeanor, the word "endearing" went the way of Quiana blouses and the Jackson Five.

"Understand our position, Miss Braxton. We're responsible for these young women." That's what the John Antonio had said, a leaky hiss on the "ss" in Miss. Well, Sheila thought, fine: but slap a dickey over the cleavage of Miss C cup over there, and tell the rest of these hussies to stop calling my house at all hours of the day and night.

Didn't any of these people have children of their own? Wasn't there one person at Whispering Pines who had ever been fourteen? Maybe everyone here had been like those AV club boys who at sixteen already wore white shirts and looked like they were about to knock on your door and sell you a subscription to the Watchtower. Maybe they were all like Miss Stephes, right out of teacher college and fresh off the farm. An ordinary brownskin boy like Briggs set her atremble. Imagine! Briggs! Harmless as a calf! What on earth would she do if she ever came across a truly tough customer?

No wonder they wouldn't help you. Sheila had pleaded with Antonio for advice.

"I'll do anything," she'd begged.

He'd inhaled sharply through the nose in that way that all former coaches had of letting you know that they were about to tell you something that anyone other than an idiot such as yourself would already know.

"Bottom line, Miss. Boys need a strong hand. You either find a way of getting him in line, or he'll have to find another place to go school."

What was it they were always saying about how it takes a village to raise a child. Sure sounded good, but try being a mother with a son. Then it became "You squeezed the bastard out, now you do something about him, or else."

Traffic on the nameless expressway is backed up at the last of its two exits. Traffic is always backed up here, as unfortunately there are no other non-dirt roads connecting the two halves of the barbell-shaped region. In the seat beside her Brigg's long legs have begun bouncing the way they always do when he worries.

"It's a beautiful day today," he cheers, brimming with false enthusiasm.

"I'm not doing nice," Sheila responds. "Does the word 'mortification' mean anything to you?"

"Ain't she the mom on *The Addams Family?*"

"Don't try and make me laugh." She gives him the evil eye and then laughs with him anyway. Damn cute boys. What could you do but shake your head, throw up your hands, and join the fun? She'd even gone to her boss for help.

"I'm having some problems with Briggs," she'd proffered.

Marketa Winthrop had riffled a page in her *Black Enterprise.* "This Briggs is your boyfriend, right?"

"My son." Which Sheila had told the woman a thousand times.

"And he would be how old?"

"Fourteen. The school called again and . . ."

Marketa Winthrop had cut her off by waving her hand. "Look, honey," she'd said. "Fourteen. Hair on the balls. I can sum this up in two words: military school."

Ralph, who that day had been compositing personal ads on the computer, shared Sheila's outrage at this comment.

"It would be my hunnor to keel for a bootiful wummun lak jou," he'd said, flashing and flexing his eyes at her. She'd recently had the misfortune of observing her own son practicing the same faces in the bathroom mirror.

"Oh, but you mustn't," she'd demurred. She wondered if the mothers of fourteen-year-old boys were allowed to be ingenues.

"Lat me tek jou avay to peredize," he'd cooed, and she remembers thinking, this is what Eve must have felt like when her big snake came along: scared and excited at the same time.

Sheila had declined. As a consolation prize, Ralph offered her a list of reputable, male-only boarding schools, the efficacy of which he could personally vouch for.

"Jes look vat thev dun for me."

Indeed, she thought. She received similar advice from her parents and even from Brigg's father. Everyone so anxious to dump adolescent males. What was up with that? Maybe there was something she wasn't being told.

"But he's such a sweet boy," she'd told Marketa Winthrop.

Marketa Winthrop had snapped her gum and taken a drag on her Kool and said, "Hun, that's about ninety-eight percent of your problem right there." Then she'd sent Sheila off to the 7-Eleven for more donuts.

Ahead, just off the unnamed freeway, Whispering Pines Junior High looks to Sheila like the sort of building where secret plans are hatched to assassinate third world leaders. Beige trapezoids of white-stuccoed concrete, no windows, sit in the middle of parking lots, which sit in the middle of bulldozed fields, which back up against farms, which still have cattle grazing in the field. No pines can be seen, and nothing and no one here whispers about anything. When they'd come to register, Sheila and Briggs had been escorted on a tour by a helmet-haired woman who was advancing her career in public education by spouting phrases such as "child-centered" and "high tech, high touch, and high teach." The woman was well put together for a school person, but around her eyes she had applied her makeup in a way that indicated to Sheila that at some point she had lived at least a marginally wild life. Did she ever imagine, back on those nights, haunting the bar at the TGI Fridays, that she'd be spending the rest of her life escorting herds of mothers and their sullen offspring on tours of a public school? Her junior tour guide had been one of those student council treasurer types, with a little too much enthusiasm for Sheila's taste.

"This is where we eat lunch. It's really neat. That's the library. It's really neat." Everything had been "neat," not just all the classes and teachers but also the girl's fingernails and hair and brand-name sweatshirt. She was the sort of girl that Sheila and her friends would have backed into a stall in the girls' bathroom and glowered at until she broke down in tears.

The former wild liver had described Whispering Pines as the Triple A+ Magnet School of the Future.

"Your children can take Aikido, Mountaineering, Reader's Theater, Cooking with Math. It's a rich and dynamic environment."

Did they have any regular classes here, anything resembling literature or history? These were the sorts of questions that Sheila had wanted to ask, but the whole business of finding a place to live after the divorce and a school for her son had numbed her into silence. She had discovered that in the years she had been out of circulation, the leasing offices and schools had replaced all the people who used to answer questions—simple questions such as where's the laundry room and does this school have bus service—with well-groomed robots who only knew the words memorized from scripts. If you interrupted them, they had to go back to the beginning of the tape.

"Your child will absolutely love it here," Helmet Hair had said, and for the most part Briggs did love it, but then Briggs could make friends anywhere. He'd probably win the congeniality award on death row, which is the place these people would like her to believe he was headed.

She should have known this was the wrong school. Too much perkiness in the hallways. Too many straight white teeth in too many expensive outfits. Too many Jennifers and Heathers and Jacobs and Sams. She'd had to resign from the Whispering Pines PTA after one too many conversations with parents who'd already put down deposits on their childrens' Ivy League educations. What do you have planned for Briggs? they'd asked. "I was kind of hoping he'd impregnate your daughter Brittany and move into your house," she'd thought. Sometimes Sheila wants the bumper sticker on her Neon to read "My C Student Kicked Your Honor Roll Student's Wimpy Ass."

Thank God Briggs was resilient. These Whispering Pines people could stamp their damn cookie cutters on him all they wanted and Briggs would still be Briggs, at least that's what she hoped. But didn't resilience wear down? Wasn't it like the rustproofing on your car? A year of rain, fine, but five years and all warranties were off.

She eyes him there in the seat beside her. Head nodding gently to some tune in his head, oblivious, whistling—against fear perhaps, but it was hard to say with Briggs. He had never been the whistle in the dark type. All Briggs knew of the hard streets he'd learned from the make-believe videos on MTV. Damn cute, silly, silly boy. He really believed he was the life of the party, everybody's best friend. He didn't even have a clue as to how much trouble he was in.

The point of all of this, of course, was to raise them up and send them off into the world, into their own happy families and into fabulous careers of their choosing, but thinking of this only causes Sheila shudders. Frankly, she was barely employable herself. Twelve years of diapers, volunteering at school, cooking nutritious meals, and then, just like that, she'd been out on the street. And while child support looked good on paper, she wasn't about to rely on regular checks from a man who couldn't figure out to at least take a cat bath before leaving some whore's motel room.

Publisher's personal assistant: that seemed like a glamorous enough position. On the days Sheila feels great she even believes that she is the glue that holds her office together. Most days, however, she knows this is hubris—a good former English major word. For the most part Sheila gets paid for returning clogged nail polish and to shop around for humane poodle groomers.

Even so, despite spending her days with a woman who believed it was a good idea to wear cruise wear to the office everyday, Sheila knew that there were many worse jobs. Winthrop and Rolle left plenty of time to make another plan and for her, as of late, weekly visits to Whispering Pines Junior High. The only really bad part were the hourly trips to the 7-Eleven. It had occurred to her only last week that the Pakistani man behind the counter believed that she herself consumed the mountains of junk food she hauled out of there each day.

"Not for me," she'd shouted last week, waving her hand over an assortment of Ding Dongs and packaged nuts.

"Very good, very good," he'd said. At the time she'd thought it polite, now she believes it's the Pakistani version of "Whatever."

That could be Briggs, she thinks. My son, spending his life trapped behind the counter of the convenience store, bagging up junk food for lying binge eaters.

She pulls into the visitor's parking space by the front entrance.

"Sorry I'm so bad," Briggs says.

Something in Sheila's chest does a somersault. She feels herself filling up with that sensation she remembers so well from when Briggs was an infant. She would get this way when someone, usually an older woman, would lean over the carriage and cluck over her adorable child.

"Yes, he is precious," she'd concur, despite his being covered at the time with chunky yellow bits of gummed Zwieback. She'd always found this emotion unnamable. What would you call it? It wasn't pride and it was something other than love. It was a kind of ecstasy, and mixed in with that the absolute conviction that if anyone so much as plucked a hair from her angel's head, she'd hunt the barbarian to the ends of the Earth and peel him alive with a dull vegetable knife.

The parking lot bustles with her fellow happy strivers, picking up their children for the orthodontist or delivering them from the pediatrician. Shiny, bright faces of the kind that Ralph pasted into ads suggesting "Your Child Can Be a Model!" Antiseptic and crisply pink, the children in those ads, you'd order them out of the catalog, you really would. Call in your Visa number and receive in the mail one perfect blank slate, ready to mold to order. Operators are standing by.

No, honey, she thinks, *you're not bad.*

Tomorrow Sheila will take some personal time and drive all over this

God forsaken wilderness and find some sort of school that makes sense for her child. She will take the whole day, the rest of her life if she has to. Later today she will make sure the little stud in the seat beside her understands that he has gotten on her last good nerve, that he's not anywhere near as funny and cute as they both know that he is, and—on the off chance he thinks she's playing—that she has a list of junior service academies that will permanently erase that smirk right off his handsome brown face.

For now though she leans over to her son and hooks a fingernail beneath his chin. "Listen up, Al Capone," she says. "We're going in there and we're going with version two. Tell it so even I believe it's true."

FROM **Song of the Water Saints**

BY NELLY ROSARIO

INVASIONS • 1916
SANTO DOMINGO, REPÚBLICA DOMINICANA

Graciela and Silvio stood hand in hand on El Malecón, sea breeze polishing their faces. Silvio hurled stones out to the waves and Graciela bunched up her skirt to search for more pebbles. Her knees were ashy and she wore her spongy hair in four knots. A rusty lard can filled with pigeon peas, label long worn from trips to the market, was by her feet. Silvio's straw hat was in Graciela's hands, and quickly, she turned to toss it to the water. The hat fluttered like a hungry seagull, then was lapped up by foam. Silvio's kiss pinned Graciela against the railing.

It was a hazy day. The hot kissing made Graciela squint against the silver light. Beyond her lashes, Silvio was a sepia prince.

—That yanqui over there's lookin' at us, he murmured into Graciela's mouth. He pulled out his hand from the rip in her skirt. Graciela turned to see a pink man standing a few yards away from them. She noticed that the yanqui wore a hat and a vest—he surely did not seem to be a Marine. When she was with Silvio, Graciela forgot to worry about anyone telling on her to Mai and Pai, much less panic over yanquis and their Marine boots scraping the cobble-stones of the Colonial Quarter.

Passion burned stronger than fear. Graciela turned back to Silvio.

—Forget him. Her pelvis dug into his until she felt iron.

. . .

Graciela and Silvio were too lost in their tangle of tongues to care that a few
yards away, the yanqui was glad for a brief break from the brutal sun that
tormented his skin. With her tongue tracing Silvio's neck, Graciela couldn't
care less that Theodore Roosevelt's "soft voice and big stick" on Latin America had dipped the yanqui the furthest south he had ever been from New
York City. Silvio's hands crawled back into the rip in Graciela's skirt; she
would not blush if she learned that the yanqui spying on them had already
photographed the Marines stationed on her side of the island, who were
there to "order and pacify," in all their debauchery; that dozens of her fellow
Dominicans somberly populated the yanqui's photo negatives; and that the
lush Dominican landscape had left marks on the legs of his tripod. Of no
interest to a moaning Graciela were the picaresque postcard views that the
yanqui planned on selling in New York and, he hoped, in France and Germany. And having always been poor and anonymous herself, Graciela would
certainly not pity the yanqui because his still lifes, nature shots, images of
battleships for the newspapers had not won him big money or recognition.

—Forget the goddamned yanqui, I said. Graciela squeezed Silvio's arm
when his lips broke suction with hers.

—He's comin' over here, Silvio said. He turned away from Graciela to
hide his erection against the seawall. Graciela watched the man approach
them. He had a slight limp. Up close, she could see that his skin was indeed
pink and his hair was a deep shade of orange. Graciela had never seen a real
yanqui up close. She smiled and folded her skirt so that the rip disappeared.

The man pulled a handkerchief from his vest pocket and wiped his neck.
He cleared his throat and held out his right hand, first to Silvio, then to
Graciela. His handshake swallowed up Graciela's wrist, but she shook just as
hard. In cornhashed Spanish the man introduced himself: Peter West, he
was.

Peter. Silvio. Graciela. They were all happy to meet each other. The man
leaned against the seawall and pulled out a wad of pesos from a pocket in his
outer jacket. His eyes never left Graciela and Silvio.

—¿So, are you with the Marines? Silvio asked in an octave lower than
usual, and Graciela had to smile secretly because her sepia prince was not yet
old enough to wear long pants.

The yanqui shook his head.

—No, no, he said with an air of importance. His thumb and index finger
formed a circle around his right eye. Graciela looked over at Silvio. They
wrinkled their noses. Then more cornhashed Spanish.

With the help of a Galician vendor, Peter West explained, he had accumulated an especially piquant series of photographs: brothel quadroons
bathed in feathers, a Negro chambermaid naked to the waist, and, of course,

he remembered with the silliest grin Graciela had ever seen, the drunken sailors with the sow. In fact, the sun was not so mean to him when he wore his hat and jacket. And fruit was sweet, whores were cheap.

Graciela reached for the pesos before Silvio did; after all, Peter West had thrust them in her direction when he finished his convoluted explanations. But he quickly pulled the pesos away, leaving Graciela's fingers splayed open.

With the promise of pesos, Graciela and Silvio found themselves in the Galician vendor's warehouse, where Peter West had staged many ribald acts among its sacks of rice. How happy they had been to help this yanqui-man push together the papier-mâché trees, to roll out the starched canvas of cracked land and sky. Silvio straddled the tiger with its frozen growl while Graciela pried open the legs of a broken tripod to look in its middle. When West lit the lamps Graciela and Silvio squealed.

—¡Look, look how he brought the sun in here!

Silvio shaded his eyes.

—This yanqui-man, he is a crazy.

Graciela's whisper rippled through the warehouse when the fantasy soured. The pink hand tugged at her skirt and pointed briskly to Silvio's pants. They turned to each other as the same hand dangled pesos before them.

—¿You still want to go away with me, Mami, or no?

Silvio's whisper was hoarse.

Graciela's shoulders dropped. She unlaced her hair and folded her blouse and skirt. In turn, Silvio unbuttoned his mandarin shirt and untied the rope at his waist. Graciela folded her clothes along with his over a pile of corn-husks. In the dampness, they shivered while West kneaded their bodies as if molding stubborn clay.

They struggled to mimic his pouts and sleepy eyes. Instead of wrestling under heavy trees by Rio Ozama, or chewing cane in the fields near bateyes, or scratching each other's bellies in abandoned mills, or pressing up against the foot of a bridge, they were twisted about on a hard couch that stunk of old rags. Bewildered, they cocked their necks for minutes at a time in a sun more barbarous than the one outside. Their bodies shone like waxed fruit, so West wiped them with white powder. Too light. So he used, instead, mud from the previous day's rain.

"Like this, you idiots."

Where his Spanish failed, West made monkey faces, which finally made Graciela titter—only to reveal gaps where her teeth had been knocked out in a fall from a cashew tree. She found it difficult to sweetly gaze up at the beams of the warehouse as he had instructed. Her eyes remained fixed on the camera.

Then Graciela and Silvio watched in complicit silence as West approached the couch and knelt in front of them. Graciela's leg prickled with the heat of his ragged breathing. One by one, West's fingers wrapped around Silvio's growing penis. He wedged the thumb of his other hand into the humid mound between Graciela's thighs. Neither moved while they watched his forehead glitter. And just as they could hear each other's own sucks of breath, they felt piercing slaps on their chins. West ran to the camera to capture the fire in their faces.

As promised, the yanqui-man tossed Silvio a flurry of pesos. Graciela rubbed caked mud from her arms while Silvio, still naked, wet his fingers to count the bills. Graciela wondered if he would hog up the money, then go off to porches and storefronts to resoak her name in mud. As she wiggled her toes into her sandals, cigar smoke made her bite the inside of her cheek.

—Me amur, ¿qué pase?

This time the knotted Spanish was in Graciela's hair, the grip on her shoulder moist. Before she could demand her own flurry of colored bills, a crash echoed throughout the warehouse. Glass and metal scattered across the floor. The photographer ran toward the crash and in his frenetic efforts to salvage the film plate did not bother to strangle Silvio.

Graciela and Silvio ran from the warehouse and hid behind barrels along the dock, suppressing adrenaline giggles.

—You liked it, she said.

Silvio made a fist, then pointed to the pockets of his shorts.

—¡Gimme my earn, you! Graciela hissed. She clutched at his pocket. A puff of hair flopped over her eye.

—You liked it too, he said.

They wrestled, the strange arousal they had felt in the warehouse pumping through them again.

—I'll hold it for when I come for you, Silvio said in between breaths.

Graciela had to trust Silvio. She tied up her hair into four knots and ran to the market, where she should have been, before Mai sent her brother for her. Silvio kept his head down to try to hide the recently-paid-man brightness in his eyes. He should have been home helping his father with the coal. Graciela and Silvio did not know they had just been immortalized.

Absentmindedly, Graciela plucked four pieces of yucca for barter from the vendor's selection. Silvio's narrow back had disappeared into the market crowd in a swagger that thickened the dread in Graciela's throat. She was about to hand the vendor a lard can's worth of pigeon peas, only to realize that she had left it at the warehouse.

—Devil's toying with my peas.

Graciela bit the inside of her cheek. She turned away and fled.

—¡Ladrona! the ever-suspicious vendor yelled into the crowd, but today, as usual, no one listened.

Away from the mass of vendors, fowl, and vegetables, Graciela's chest heaved under the stolen yucca and her hair unraveled again.

Once her stride slowed down, she banged her forehead three times with the heel of her hand. ¡Sugar! She was supposed to buy sugar, not yucca, which already grew in her father's plot. Graciela sucked her teeth, almost tasting the molasses hanging heavy in the air from the smokestacks eclipsing the hills.

—Graciela, your mai looks for you.

A woman with the carriage of a swan and a bundle balanced on her head walked from the nearby stream. Her even teeth flashed a warning as she stepped onto the road.

—Mai's got eyes all over me.

—You be careful with those yanqui-men ahead, the swan woman responded with a finger in midair. Then she walked toward the whistling ahead, bare feet sure and steady.

Graciela shaded her eyes. Tall uniformed men in hats shaped like gumdrops sat on the roadside. They drank from canteens and spat as far onto the road as they could. Graciela squatted in the dense grass to see how the fearless swan woman would move safely past them. The yanqui-men's rifles and giant bodies confirmed stories that had already filtered into the city from the eastern mountains: suspected gavillero rebels gutted like Christmas piglets; women left spread-eagled right before their fathers and husbands; children with eardrums drilled by bullets. Graciela had folded these stories into the back of her memory when she snuck about the city outskirts with Silvio. The yanqui-man in the warehouse seemed frail now, his black box and clammy hands no match for the long rifles aimed at the swan woman.

"Run, you Negro wench!" The soldier's shout was high-pitched and was followed by a chorus of whistles.

A pop resounded. Through the blades of grass, Graciela could see the white bundle continue down the road in a steady path. The woman held her head high as if the bundle could stretch her above the hats. Another pop and Graciela saw the woman drop to the ground. The soldiers milled around the screaming and thrashing in the grass. Some already had their shirts pulled out of their pants.

Behind the soldiers, Graciela scrabbled away in the blades of grass. By the time the pack of men dispersed, they had become olive dots behind her. The yucca grated inside her blouse. Twigs and soil lodged in her nails. Half an hour later, with all four hair knots completely undone, Graciela was relieved to catch a glimpse of donkeys and their cargo, vendors with their vegetable carts, a rare Model T making crisscross patterns on the road.

The air was tight as she pulled herself up and ran past neighbors' homes. No children played outside. Graciela did see horses—many horses—tied to fenceposts along the way. She could not shake the urge to yawn and swell her lungs with air.

The main road dropped into a dustier, brushier path, leading to the circle of familiar thatched cabins. Two horses were tied to the tree by the fence. Graciela could not hear her mother yelling to her younger brother, Fausto, for coal, or the chickens clucking in the kitchen. Fausto was not sitting on the rickety chair making graters from the sides of cans, saying,—Mai was gonna send for you, stupid harlot.

Instead, from the kitchen came the clatter of tin. As Graciela moved closer, the stench of old rags flared her nostrils again. Inside, Mai knelt by a soldier whose fists entangled her hair and had undone the cloth rollers. Fausto, a statue in the corner. A man wearing his mustache in the handlebar style of the yanquis calmly asked Mai where her husband hid the pistols and why he was away in the hills. Mai's face was marble as she explained that her husband had no weapons, he was a God-fearing farmer, and there was her daughter at the door with yucca from his plot, see how dirty she was from working so hard with her beloved father, come Graciela, come bring the fruits of his sweat so these gentlemen can see how hard we work.

Graciela stepped forward with thin, yellow-meat yucca she was too ashamed to say her father had harvested. The interpreter shoved Graciela against the cold hearth and jammed his face against hers.

Must be cane rum coloring his bloodshot eyes, she thought, Devil toying with her peas again, trying to stick pins in her eyes to make her blink.

—Pai don't got pistols, he only got cane rum, Graciela said.

Her eyes still on the man, Graciela pointed to a shed outside. The man twisted the ends of his mustache. With the same fingers he clamped Graciela's nose and held it until there was blood, which he wiped against her blouse.

—Now you've got my aquiline nose, he said, then sucked the rest of her blood from his fingers. This overeager display of barbarism fueled in Graciela more anger than fear. Mai, Graciela, and Fausto watched as he helped the yanqui-men load their horses with bottles of cane rum. Before taking off, they rinsed their hands in the family's barrel of fresh rainwater.

The mandatory disarmament of the city and its outskirts left a trail of new stories that would find their way back to the eastern mountains. By 1917, the country fell prey to young American men relieved that their incompetence had landed them in the tropics instead of Europe, where fellow soldiers had been dropped into a bubbling World War. For the next eight years these men sparked a war, equipped with sturdy boots, uniforms, and rifles, against machetes, rusty revolvers, and sometimes bare feet. It was a battle between lion and ant. And when an ant pinched a paw, the lion's roar echoed: in Mexico, Panama, Cuba, Haiti, Dominican Republic.

A passionate creditor, Woodrow Wilson, demanded that the country's debt dollars be paid back in full while World War I shook across the ocean. At roughly 23°30´ north longitude, 30°30´ west latitude, Graciela and Silvio could not distinguish the taste of gunpowder from salt in the air of El Malecón.

Graciela's swollen nose stung as she peeled away the yucca's husk. Yellow and gray veins tunneled through the tuber's white flesh.

—¡Sugar! I send you for sugar, and you take the morning with you, Mai said, panic still twisting her voice.

For a moment Graciela wished that the soldiers had worked harder on Mai, had left her eyes swollen shut so she could not notice Graciela's unraveled hair.

Of course Graciela could never reveal that in the two hours she had been gone the seasalt was good against her skin, and so was Silvio, and that she was even able to earn some extra money . . .

Mai blared about hard-earned peas, and money for coal, money for shoes, money for sugar, about what green yanqui soldiers do to girls with skirts aflame, how lucky they all were to have been spared. Mai whacked her daughter on the back with a cooking spoon, squeezed the tender cartilage of her ears, wove her claws into Graciela's knotted hair. And Mai sobbed at only having her own flesh and blood with which to avenge humiliation. Excuses for the lack of peas, or money, or sugar on the table were postponed until the following day, when Pai returned from the bush with better crop and a heavier whipping hand.

Pai did emerge from the bush with better crop, but with hands too blistered by a week of harvesting to draw out confessions. He unearthed the pistols from under the water barrels and, with a furrowed brow, oiled them in the privacy of the outhouse. Graciela was perversely relieved by his preoccupation with who had snitched him out to the yanquis, and she carried on with her household chores, rag-doll dramas, fights with Fausto. Whenever she thought of Silvio buying tamarind balls with their money, Graciela bit the roughened inside of her cheek.

—Get yourself a whipping branch, Pai said days later to Graciela after he had devoured an avocado. He sat in front of the house repairing his only pair of shoes while she reluctantly climbed the cashew tree. As she handed over a thin branch, Graciela saw where mercury still stained the cuts on his hands.

—I told you to get a thicker branch, girl, he said.

After she had chosen the branch and wet it as he had instructed, Graciela followed Pai to the back of the house; Mai had already laid out the rice and stood a few feet away with her arms crossed. Without being told, Graciela removed her dress and knelt on the grains.

—You beat her good so she learns, Mai said to Pai. Then she disappeared into the kitchen, where Graciela could see her spying between the wood planks.

The first strike of the branch burned across the back of her thighs.

—Cry hard, girl, and satisfy your mai.

Pai thrashed the dirt around them. Graciela kept the smirk that she knew could make Mai's voice turn to pieces of breaking china. Finally, Pai cut the branch across the soles of her feet and hurled it to the bushes. Exasperated, he set a brand-new lard can full of peas on her head.

—Girl, you stay there till you lose that insolence.

Rice grains cut into her knees and the can of peas ignited a migraine. Still, Graciela would not confess; nothing she could have said would put her in a favorable light. Better to withstand the bursts of pain in her knees than to tell of her travesties with Silvio and multiply the existing worries in the household.

To numb herself Graciela sang songs, counted to ten twenty times, made popping sounds and saliva bubbles, concentrated on the caterpillar by the outhouse. Her thighs pressed tighter to hold back urine. After the breeze had chilled her raw skin, she began to itch where Pai's forgiving whip had left inevitable welts. A bug tickled her ankle. A sneeze crippled her side.

—¡Move and I shoot! Fausto said. He wore a gourd on his head, pointed a long piece of sugarcane at her, and revealed his own gaps for front teeth.

Two lizards copulated behind the barrel of rainwater. And suddenly Silvio waved pesos across Graciela's mind. He had not snuck around to their grove of cashews with his telltale whistle since the day of the yanqui. The clouds above Graciela did not move. In her agony, her anger and longing for Silvio became interchangeable.

Had Pai known of what she did with Silvio, he would have let the whip open her skin. He might have had Silvio hunted like a guinea hen. Might have scared him with a fresh-oiled pistol. Or turned him over to the yanquis.

With the frozen clouds and the sun baking circles in her head and the can of peas tumbling to the ground and the rice grains up against her flushed cheek, Graciela decided she would hunt for Silvio herself and make him put a zinc roof over her head.

SILVIO • 1917

Silvio never gave Graciela her share of the earnings. He spent the pesos on spicy sausages, on the winning cock, Saca Ojo, and on his favorite patient whore. Nor did Silvio dare muddy Graciela's name on porches or storefronts. (—You liked it too, he remembered her knowing words.)

Silvio withstood a year of Graciela's demands for a house of their own. He joined the yanquis' new Guardia Nacional Dominicana, where he was outfitted in starched slacks and sturdy shoes. It was an accomplishment, Silvio insisted to naysayers, for a man as dark and illiterate as he to be entrusted with yanqui guns. He was not a traitor, he explained, but a quality man with goals, who had already started wearing long pants. At fifteen, his penis swelled when the same elders who had tattled on him took off their hats in his presence. And when, at the sound of his voice, porch girls fanned themselves faster.

A quality man of goals must also head a household. Silvio agreed to elope with Graciela. One night at last, he blew his telltale whistle among the cashews. Like sudden thunder, Silvio invaded her home in his fresh yanqui haircut and pushed aside Pai's machete while Graciela ran past her shrunken mother to gather her few belongings.

Silvio had cleared a plot of land for them. He knew Graciela was disappointed to find that, instead of the turquoise palmwood and zinc house behind her lids, their new place was not much different from the thatched cabins she had left behind.

—This will have to do for now, Silvio said and brushed off dust from the knees of his slacks.

Inhumane military training demoted many an eager cadet back to civilian status. Silvio's own starched slacks, real shoes, and arrogance disappeared after a Marine ordered him to string his own friend Euclides from a mango tree. Euclides, in his zeal for trouble, had stolen the Marine's shoes. Euclides had taken them in jest, Silvio explained to the shrimp-skinned Marine, who, in near-perfect Spanish, had called him in for "a little talk." By the time Silvio tracked down Euclides to warn him, he knew that despite three meals a day and an enviable uniform, belonging to the yanqui police force came with too many problems. As did life with Graciela.

Within a year of their eloping, the fever of Silvio and Graciela's clandestine meetings had dwindled to predictable lukewarm pleasure during siesta and after sundown. Graciela was no longer Silvio's, despite his having her under a roof and being able to hitch up her skirt at will. Just a year ago, she had been completely his when she let him pick off every baby tick that had stuck fast to her ankles from running through a field of grass. And Silvio certainly believed Graciela his shortly before the yanqui-man incident, when she confided about a deadly disease afflicting the women in her family, which causes them to bleed between their legs every month. But the patient whore he frequented recently told him that all women had the disease, and now, more than ever, Silvio felt he had lost Graciela to a world bigger than himself.

But those were crazy moonshine thoughts, because daily life itself seeped into Silvio and Graciela's bodies like cement. As when, throughout their meals, Graciela would chew her food slowly and stare at him with what Silvio increasingly saw as the wide eyes of a cow. ¿What? ¿What? he would yell, hoping she would not bring up again the goddamned turquoise palmwood and zinc house.

Graciela's cow eyes and Euclides' murder convinced Silvio that he preferred the unpredictable ways of the waters to the whims of shrimp-skinned generals and to Graciela's irritating company. Silvio planned to join a fishing fleet that circled the Caribbean. He let his hair sprout out from its yanqui haircut. One night he sat by the fire he had made of his uniform and shoes, and the next morning he kissed Graciela goodbye after a hearty breakfast of cocoa, breadfruit, eggs, and boiled bananas.

On the morning of his first voyage, Silvio had dragged Graciela to her parents' house. Even with his grip, Graciela stirred the dust around them.

—¡Don't need to swallow my own spit 'cause you wanna fish!

—Just for peace of mind, mi cielo, he said.

—Don't worry yourself, Silvio. Not one of your kids will look like you. Graciela punctuated her words with a fisted index finger.

Mai received Graciela and Silvio with crossed arms.

—You're a man of few words, Silvio, but you need to be firm with this one, she said and jutted her bottom lip toward Graciela.

Once Silvio left for the docks, however, Graciela walked back to her own house in another haze of dust, followed by a grumbling Fausto, whom she forced to help file down the series of padlocks. In turn, Fausto ran home to tell Mai of Graciela's hammock-rocking, and the idleness of his sister's broom, the cold in her kitchen.

In the evenings, neighboring women brought Graciela some food. Then they undid the kindness as if slowly unraveling a swatch of silk by a single thread.

—¿That you want to ride on a ship? ¿With feet in lace-ups and those raisins of hair under a hat?

Celeste, Graciela's childhood friend, always spoke the loudest and made

the others cackle. She wondered aloud when the trail of daily chores left undone would catch up with Graciela and freeze over her dreams.

—Ah, but you'd wear lace-up shoes too if El Gordo had them for you,
Celeste my love. Because Graciela knew how much Celeste would give to
bed down El Gordo, who had more ranch cattle than Celeste's impotent
husband.

There was also the not-so-pious woman they all called Santa, who
brought Graciela lavish goat meat and vegetable dishes. After Graciela consumed her portions, Santa would sweetly say to the women gathered in the
kitchen,

—Our dear Graciela's hearth is colder than a witch's breath.

One day, to everyone's surprise, Graciela invited Santa over for a midday
meal of mashed plantains, ham, and cheese. Afterward, Graciela offered
Santa a rock-candy sucker. Only after Santa' had sucked the candy down to
a nub, did Graciela say,

—¿Was it all good, Santa?

—¡Oh by far the best I've had!

—Well, that sucker is what my armpit tastes like after a long hot morning at this hearth.

And though Santa did not speak to her for weeks, the rest of the women
could not stop asking Graciela how she had managed to cook with the
sucker lodged in her armpit the entire time. News of the prank spread, with
camps dividing between those who liked Santa and those who didn't, between those who liked Graciela and those who were beginning to distrust
her.

Still, the women liked to forget their work as Graciela wrung the rain out
of their clouds. When there was no major news to chew on, they could always set their tongues on Graciela and her ways:

—That poor girl's lazier than an upper jaw.

—Show me her pots and I'll show you her bed.

—That fool's wasting her life waiting on that other fool.

For months after Silvio's departure, Graciela rocked in a hammock when
visitors were not coming around. Out of loneliness, she would sometimes
visit her parents, where she found herself having cordial, yet strained morning teas with Mai and clipped exchanges with Pai, when he descended from
the hillside. He would occasionally slip a coin into the pocket of Graciela's
apron; from the way Graciela quickly slurped her tea and darted her starved
eyes when Mai clattered the dishes, Pai suspected that Silvio had not been
sending any fishing money home after all. Pai's concern grew when he realized that Silvio would not be returning any time soon. He then forced a reluctant Fausto to go protect his sister from the "roaming men of low virtue"

that had assaulted the city and its outskirts. Just two years younger than Graciela, Fausto had already mushroomed into an animal of a boy who, according to Pai, was built like a yanqui on an ox. Though Pai was giving up a much-needed workhand, he armed his bumbling twelve-year-old son with a pistol and sent him off to live with Graciela until Silvio's return.

—Learn now how to really defend a household, he told Fausto. Always careful, Pai had already sent word to neighbors to keep watch over Graciela.

Outside on her hammock, Graciela could ignore the disarray inside her home and stare at the wispy cirrus ships in the sky. In the clouds, she wore lace and carried a parasol in the park of a place where the talk was garbled but pretty. Rocking in her hammock, Graciela imagined Silvio on the high seas, sprawled on the deck, maybe looking for her in the clouds. Fool with ideas, she scolded herself. Her eyes closed against the humid breeze.

Forget dirty tongues, she told herself further. They were all over the place: in the town, in the soup, even in her own head. Always trying to stop her from doing what she wanted. She would sit and let her home shrivel if she wanted. It was hers. And if she wanted to wait for Silvio for months, she would. He was hers as well.

Graciela stood up and stretched until she heard a snap somewhere inside her body. Now that Fausto was here, maybe he could help her finish the little plot she and Silvio had started behind the main cabin a few months back.

—Fausto, she called out. He emerged from the kitchen shed, chewing on a piece of lard bread.

—¿Can't you do anything but eat 'round here? Graciela said. Fausto looked down at her, then brushed some crumbs from his lips.

—I got the pistol, so I do whatever I want. Pai says I run this house, Fausto said. From his shorts pocket he pulled out a piece of cheese and brushed the lint from it.

—And if a yanqui were to come here this minute, ¿what the Devil would you do to save us?

Fausto reached into his other pocket, then dropped the piece of cheese.

—¡My pistol! ¿Where the hell is my pistol?

Fausto turned in circles, patting himself on the hips. When he looked up at Graciela, he found himself face-to-face with the pistol's barrel.

—Donkey-face. I dare you to go and tell Pai. You tell him to send Graciela herself to defend me next time. She's a better son than you are.

In one deft move the pistol disappeared behind the neckline of her blouse.

. . .

Graciela had always been a fool with ideas, everyone said, long before she
had waited for Silvio to whistle for her in the cashew grove and take her
away.

—Mai, God willing, I'm gonna ride ships. Big ones with tiny waists, she
had sung at nine years old.

Mai had not looked up from her ironing. A pair of Pai's underwear lay
smoothed out on the table. Graciela stretched the underwear to show the
width of the metal whale that could take her to where sky and water met.

Mai looked up from her ironing. A momentary glimmer. Then she saw
Graciela's idle hands.

—Ideas, ideas. That head in the clouds won't do your chores or fill your
gut.

Mai spat and let the iron sizzle.

And then there were the three Spanish nuns with bunioned feet who had
paid everyone in town a missionary visit when Graciela was four. Graciela
had snuck behind the kitchen to hear the added *s*'s in Mai's speech, the lisp
reserved for rare visitors.

—I have always tried to instill God into this little girl, her mother had
said, hands clasped at her chest.

The following week, Graciela found herself in the colonial church, hairline pulled taut with bits of cloth from old dresses. The church's dilapida-
tion testified only to outward neglect; mission work was still going strong.
Church beams spread out like protective arms above Graciela. Blocks of
sunlight cut into the darkness to illuminate pews, statues, bits of floor. Graciela had the urge to stand inside the blocks of sunlight.

—¿That where Jesus is? Graciela had asked, pointing to the blocks of
light.

—Jesus is everywhere, said the nun who called herself Sol Luz and led her
toward a small room behind the altar. There were children already there,
milling around an object in the middle of the room. They took turns spinning a colorful ball fixed to a metal arc. Graciela pushed and pinched her
way through, until her fingers reached the ball, which she learned was called
a "globe."

Only after she had sung all the holy songs and gulped down a hunk of
stale bread with near-sour milk, was she allowed to return to the globe and
turn it on its axis as if it were a rotisserie.

—You are here.

Sol Luz bent close to put Graciela's finger over a speck rising from the
globe's surface.

—¿Me? ¿On the head of an iguana? Graciela narrowed her eyes. The
iguana head was but a nick on her fingertip. She saw other animals: the

haunch of a sheep, a goat, a dog. They encompassed as many as four of her fingers.

—I am from here—España—and came here.

Sol Luz dragged her finger to the left of the dog's leg, across an expanse of blue.

—I rode a ship all the way here, where you are, she said.

—¿Why did you come to this iguana and not go to the dog's ears over there?

Graciela moved Sol Luz's finger in the opposite direction.

—I came to bring Jesus, she said, leaving some spittle on the globe.

¿Why bring Jesus to such a small iguana when there were bigger animals? New questions prickled Graciela's throat before she could finish asking the last; the answers mattered less.

—Ah, the dilemma of mission work, the nun said, as if trying to sort out for herself why she was there on that speck of land with so much misery.

—¿And does anyone live here? Graciela pointed to blue bulls and horses.

—Not always good for a little girl to ask so many questions, Sol Luz said.
—No one lives in the ocean. Sure, the Lord created fishes and sea animals, but not the sinful women with fish-tails, or pirate ghosts, or the water saints that you people talk about.

Sol Luz's eyes became fixed stones and Graciela thought for a moment that she looked like a fish.

Each Sunday thereafter, Mai would drag Graciela home by her pigtails.

—¿Can't I bring the globe home with me?

—Ask as many questions about Christ as you do about that pitiful ball, Mai said.

¿But how much bigger could the world be when the head of a tiny animal was her whole world? Graciela's fingers traced mountain ridges and the dips of rivers. ¿Would the people there be engulfed in a shadow and look up to the sky to see the swirls of her fingerprints hovering over their lands?

Graciela begged Sol Luz to run outside and watch the sun as she ran her finger over their speck on the globe.

—¿See my finger? Graciela's voice echoed throughout the church.

—No harm in humoring the poor child, Sol Luz thought to herself as she walked to the church doors. Indeed, it was unusually dark outside, and with her heart in her throat Sol Luz lifted her eyes. She was ashamed of herself when, expecting colossal fingertips, she found a heavy cloud hovering over the church. A cool breeze signaled rain, and with a grunt at her own foolishness, she ran back inside.

. . .

When Graciela thought she would pack her rags to break the monotony of her days, Silvio returned for the New Year celebrations. Sea breezes rushed ahead of him to their cactus fence. Fausto returned to Mai and Pai's home when he saw Graciela stuff her knotted mass of hair under a scarf and bury Pai's pistol near the rainwater barrel. Quickly, she stoked the fire for a meal, swept the yard, tried to erase the look of pining she was sure Silvio expected.

Silvio returned with kingfish and squid strung on his back. There was licorice for Graciela in his pockets and Madame C.J. Walker grease to replace coconut oil for her hair. A yellow-ochre tinge lit up his crown from the sun and salt of his travels, making his hair look like the macaroni he told her he had tasted in St. Lucia. Kisses and long stories made her forgive his absence—only to discover later the rash on his groin.

During his first stay at home, he complained to Graciela how the stillness of land, the permanence of the ground underneath his feet made him feel as if his joints were welded together.

—Devil's still dancin' in my head, he said when Graciela's chamomile tea failed to stop the hammer tearing apart his temples. In their bed, Silvio flopped over, long after Graciela had fallen asleep, then his ragged breaths would wake her before dawn. And twice a day Graciela had to send for Fausto to refill the water jug that would cure Silvio's insatiable thirst.

Despite Silvio's uncharacteristic neediness, Graciela was glad to have him back home. She was impressed by the skill with which he prepared barbecued fish, and conch soup, and vinegary ceviches. Unlike hers, his hands stayed uncut when digging out the meat from a crab, which he fed to her in slimy bits. —Try it, you squid, he said, when she refused the seaweed and onions entangled in his fork. A strange man of the sea he had become to the land-anchored Graciela, and it made her proud. No, Silvio was not like all the other dull men in town, with his narrow back, his yellowed naps, his sea speech. But their three weeks of reacquaintance were over—just when Graciela had begun to get used to the extra salt in their food, just as she was feeling proud of herself for not harrowing him about the turquoise palm-wood house.

So Silvio came and went with the tides. Twice a month, his weekend stays heated the kitchen with frying fish and boiling plantains. Folks arrived to hear tales of ghost ships abandoned at sea. Silvio told of real and invented ports where the crew stopped to sell their catch. He described his searches for pirate loot at the bottom of the ocean. And when Graciela was out of earshot, he confirmed that white women had the fragrance of the sea and its treasures. When the fish was sold, given away, and eaten; when the travel stories were told, and had worn thin; when people no longer exclaimed "¡Llegó Silvio!"; and when he was ready for brine again, Silvio would tie up his bags.

—Take me, Silvio.

He would put his finger to Graciela's lips, but later she followed him to the docks with her own bags. Each time, sea mates teased Silvio for his inability to wrest himself from his hound.

One afternoon in early February, Silvio departed for the sixth time, according to Graciela's tally. On this occasion, he hopped on the boat and turned to face the horizon even as Graciela waved. Long after the boatful of those leather-faced men sailed around the turn of shore, Graciela lingered by the water sucking salt from her lips.

—¡Thief!

She spat her bitterness into the water, whose currents drew Silvio away and lapped at the seawall; whose depths contained jewelry unhooked from the wrists of the wealthy, whole bodies of metal sea animals with fractured waists, and hundreds of ball-and-chained bones trapped in white coral.

Nausea came to Graciela. That February the goat had not been slaughtered; her rags remained bloodless for the first time since she was ten. No more waiting.

Graciela collected some belongings, and tied them up in the hammock. She wanted to leave the capital, perhaps head north to Santiago, the Heart of the Country. The new life inside her pulled her daydreams down from the clouds. Up north in the pulse of the country, they could build a bright turquoise palmwood house with a zinc roof for their new family. She would wait for Silvio's return, and then convince him, and if he did not join her, she would leave without him, and take up washing or cleaning until the child was born. Then she would make her palmwood house, and call on Silvio to show him that she was not a woman to be kept sitting and waiting idly for her life to happen . . .

Graciela's dreaming also set in motion Fausto's plan. He invited a friend over to help him till the small plot of beans he had been helping Graciela tend. As the boys rolled up tobacco joints, Graciela could hear Fausto's put-on baritone through the bread-fruit trees.

—Once Sis leaves, I'll bring that little number down from Villa Consuelo to live here with me, you'll see.

But the moon went through its faces and still no Silvio. Common talk brought greetings from him, which Graciela knew were fabricated by pitying friends.

It was already August—half a year since anyone had last seen Silvio. In six months, the speculations surrounding his extended absence bubbled up like a foul gas. Out of consideration, someone suggested to Graciela that his boat had floated far out to the Mona Canal. There was talk of sharks and trouble with Marines. A lynching. Celeste, as always, offered the possibility of a distant woman, one who perhaps did not squabble as much.

The real story people feared.

—Those butchers left the fishermen hanging in a bunch like a hand of bananas, said Desiderio to whoever would listen at Yunco's.

The local bar was packed with Prohibition-free Marines, and Yunco, always out to profit from fortune and misfortune alike, covertly turned his home into the "locals' local" bar after curfew. Desiderio, a regular "yunquero," had heard the lynching story from his cousin, who had heard it from Flavia the johnnycake woman, who lived with El Gordo, who worked in the sugar mill of the Turks. And El Gordo, who was eating out of Celeste's kitchen unbeknownst to Flavia and Celeste's husband, heard the tale from the Turks themselves.

And the Turks, who seemed neutral enough in matters between Dominicans and yanquis, ran an information exchange out of their sugar mill. They bribed Dominicans for details on the gavillero rebels and any other anti-yanqui activities, then sold it to the yanquis. But to assuage their guilt in aiding the yanquis, they also bought information from yanqui-friendly Dominican spies to distribute freely among the people. It was in this web of information that Silvio's fate became enmeshed:

That one of the fishermen in Silvio's fleet deserted them because of a dispute over money. That he went to the Turks. That the Turks then gave the yanquis detailed information on a fleet of so-called fishermen who made trips to the Caribbean. That these fishermen would swing around the nose of the island to the east instead, where they unloaded weapons for the gavilleros hiding out in the hills.

—This is what I heard myself.

El Gordo pounded his chest in competition with Desiderio.

—And those yanquis then chopped them down from the tree. They say that in El Ceibo pigs were shitting buttons and bits of nails, Desiderio said, proud of his contribution to the grains of information.

—Now no one eats pork in El Ceibo, he added with a wink.

—Things are really bad in the east. Bad like purple gas. El Gordo sighed and took a swig of rum.

By September, Graciela had stopped rocking in her hammock. Her seven-month belly popped one of the cords, prompting her to fold up the hammock and tightly wrap up most of her belongings in it; she prayed she would not have to later unwrap it to wear her black skirt and mourning veil. If Silvio did not return before her labor, Graciela was determined to push out her child, pack up the rest of her things, and head north, wailing baby strapped to her back and all. ¿So what if it was a foolish thought not to wait out the forty postpartum days? Tired she was of waiting for her life to truly begin. A departure would be progress, she was sure. Living in this cluster of ramshackle shacks had not been part of her vision of life with Silvio, and now there were more than two futures to think about. Asking the clouds for mercy and ignoring the vivid memory of a straw hat being lapped up by sea foam, Graciela waited one more month for her own signs of Silvio.

It was an easy pregnancy, with Graciela sending Fausto all over town on errands. Water bread and not lard bread, she insisted, and Fausto had better make sure to sift any maggots from the sugar if he purchased it from Joselito. When Fausto was out of the house, Graciela would curl up in bed to work on a rag doll for the future baby. Then she cried herself to sleep when its uneven button eyes gawked back at her, one red and tiny, the other black and large.

Everyone who used to laugh at Graciela's ship-and-lace dreams knew that her baby must have been crying in the womb. They also knew that Silvio's body had been found so riddled by bullets, there was more kindness in saying sharks had devoured him.

The day her daughter was born, Graciela had rocked under anvils of cumulonimbus ships. Gray clouds tumbled after each other, herded by winds to where they could relieve their weight. Must be difficult labor, rain, she thought, rubbing her belly. Crows squawked over the waving trees, dipping over her as if flaunting their gift of flight. A blanket of smoke, of burnt ashes in the ominous sky—the death of her Silvio, she speculated. Thunder changed her mind. No, no, their fruit is life, a good sign. In the silver underbelly of one of the ships, Graciela was certain she saw Silvio. Alive. He was sure to return to her that night, she understood.

The air had cooled, causing land crabs to scurry out of their holes. Cashew leaves turned their waxy sides up and field mice ran up the trunks of trees. Fausto stabbed a spot in the yard with an ax, while Graciela shooed the chickens inside the house and closed all doors. The rest of the day she spent adorning her home and combing her hair tangled from the coming rains. Fausto's whistling and the sharp jabs in Graciela's womb kept her awake before Silvio's arrival.

In the October night, Graciela woke to rain dripping into the pot at the foot of her bed. Fausto was curled in a cot, sleeping soundly, despite heavy ozone in the air. Graciela waited for the sea breeze to enter through the creaking door. The tiny voice had echoed again, languishing at the bottom of her spine, then crawling to her forearms, where cold had already tightened the tiniest of hairs.

—¡Silvio! ¿That you?

For the first time she was afraid of what jumped inside her. She wanted

Silvio to arrive before the child; for the pain of childbirth to be only in her womb and not in her heart.

—¡Fausto!

He snored louder than the thunder outside.

—¡Fausto! ¡Go get Ñá Nurca!

He snored louder than the thunder outside.

—¡Fausto!

Cold and whirring in her womb ate at her. The night howled when Graciela pried open the door. Rain cloaked her.

—¡Silvio!

Spongy ground sucked at her feet. The sky growled as she broke into a jog. A flash of blue lightning found the ax in the yard, and the nerves of the heavens seemed to converge at its handle. Graciela stopped; her feet were buried in unusually warm mud. The rain was saltier than her own tears. She whiffed a sharp sulfuric odor, then the undeniable smell of excrement. Graciela crossed a flooded ditch, wading to her shins in sewage.

The small cement house was a refuge at the end of the road.

—¡Ñá Nurca! She beat on the door until the elderly midwife opened and, without a word, led Graciela into the house by lantern light.

—Like the Devil himself you smell, Ñá Nurca said.

—And I'm about to have Juan the Baptist himself, Graciela yelled with the jolt in her womb. Used to the hysteria of life-givers, Ñá Nurca cupped Graciela's face and complained that Graciela should have sent word with Fausto to the yawning servant girl.

—Go boil water and prepare the birth bed, for the love of God, Ñá Nurca snapped at the girl.

Graciela's moans were muffled by the crackling of the skies. Ñá Nurca's teas and tinctures opened her womb, sending Graciela to the tenuous membrane between life and death. In the velvet behind her lids, she saw Silvio's muted face, then that of a child's.

—Come back, woman, come back, Ñá Nurca said to Graciela.

The servant girl, accustomed to the trials of childbirth, gathered the soiled cloths as fast as she could. Ñá Nurca's gnarled hands massaged Graciela's body relentlessly in an attempt to coax out new life with her own.

By morning, as the storm subsided, the bleating of Graciela's labor had alerted the neighbors. The elaborate word-of-mouth network eventually drew Mai away from her duties. With soup and clean linens she appeared at Ñá Nurca's—not before boxing Fausto's ears for having slept through the night.

That afternoon, Graciela's baby was born, healthy, kicking furiously out of the muting pillows of her mother's warmth. Ñá Nurca wrapped the after-birth in a cloth for burying and saved the umbilical cord for Graciela's safekeeping. She joked about the child's big fists as she wiped her with warm water.

—Mercedes, Ñá Nurca, call the chichí Mercedes, Graciela mumbled.

—¿This little hurricane with the name of mercy? Ñá Nurca said, noting again the unusually large fists and discovering a mole on her toe.

Ñá Nurca swaddled Mercedes in a fresh blanket before putting her to Graciela's breast. The child latched on tightly to her mother, not letting go even after Graciela's breasts were drained of their milk.

Miss Prissy and the Penitentiary

BY YOLANDA JOE

MISS PRISSY,
PRISCILLA EDGEWATER

It's mine!" I yelled at my best friend Penelope.

"Get for-real," she yelled back. "It's mine!"

How'd we get in this mess? Here we are in the hair salon, all by ourselves, straddling chairs, fighting over this big beautiful gold box with lilac and pink bows nestled on top. And I guess we got into this mess because this isn't just any present, but a present from SANDER.

I'm torn between my curiosity about what's inside and my anger at Penelope for trying to claim it. And I'm not giving up. I'm holding on for dear life, glaring across at Pen. She'd had the unmitigated gall to leave her computer analyst job early to come here and pick a fight with me. Her suit jacket and skirt are bunched up around her little body (clothes too tight as usual), and she's staring me down with those big, black, killer eyes, acting like a monster out of one of those sci-fi books she's always reading.

Why won't she let go?

I'm four times her size and can whip her little butt if I've a mind to.

Why won't she let go?

She's my business partner in this shop and supposedly my best friend, best friend since childhood, when everyone started calling me Miss Prissy and Penelope, Miss Penitentiary. That's when she promised, and now twenty-five years later, Pen is breaking that very promise.

PENELOPE PARKINS, MISS PENITENTIARY

Lies, lies, all lies! I am not breaking our promise, she is! Priss is. I'm not letting go of this box. What for? It's mine, period dot com. Sure it arrived with
no name, addressed only to "The P&P Salon," but why would Sander send
it to her? He loves me. Not her. I wonder if it's something sexy? Expensive?
Oh, there she goes pulling at the box again.

"Priss!" I hissed at her.

"Pen!" she whipped back.

I don't want to be vain, but I can see through people like they're cellophane. Priss latches on to men like handcuffs because she's a big mama.
Once a deliveryman came into the beauty shop to bring in a new dryer and
he saw Priss and joked, "Damn baby, you big and fine, how much you
weigh?"

Priss gave her trademark curtsey and cooed, "Good and plenty, and sweet
just like the candy, thank you for asking." She practically rode the man's
back out of the store trying to get his phone number just because he gave
her a little flirt-flirt.

Priss gave that snappy answer because it was a Saturday and the place was
packed and she didn't want to get her face cracked. But I know how self-
conscious Priss is about being big. So when a man shows her the least bit of
attention she turns into a heroine out of one of those romance novels she's
always reading. Priss doesn't know fact from fiction. Just look at her, holding
onto my present with that press-on set of claws! I grinned my sneakiest of
smiles and jerked the box—and two of those press-ons popped off like
smart bombs, flying damn near up to the ceiling.

"You did that on purpose," Priss said, giving me her standard dainty, in-
dignant look.

"Damn skippy," I said right back with attitude. "C'mon Priss, give it up.
Sander wants me, not you."

Priss growled, "Wake up. You always did throw yourself at men—even in
second grade."

"Lies, lies, all lies!" I told Miss Prissy. "Tell me when?"

MISS PRISSY

It was Good Friday. I had only been enrolled at Garvey Academy for a
month, because my family had just moved into a new house. Mama and
Daddy worked double shifts and overtime at their jobs for two years so they,
their daughter, and three sons could live in a three bedroom, two bathroom

house instead of a two bedroom, one bathroom, leaky faucet, warped floor, broken screen door, loose-latched, third-floor walk-up apartment.

It was tough for me to leave our old place. Grandma lived upstairs and my second cousin Willa lived downstairs. It was comforting having that much girl family around because my brothers were, well, brothers. Men are men.

But grown up or not, women are girls. And Grandma and Cousin Willa were fun loving girls. We played jacks and card games like pitty-pat and made stick figures out of Play-Doh. I didn't have a best friend then, they were my best friends even though my mother explained that this wasn't natural; that a child should have friends their own age. Well I was bigger than the other kids on the block, even those who were two to three years older, and it is a tragic situation to be *too* different as a child. If ever a person wants and needs to mesh in with a crowd, it's as a child. I didn't mesh so I stayed in the house, not wanting to be teased for being too big and too tall.

At my new school, it was a triple whammy. They teased me for being too big, too tall, and too new. Particularly this one little girl, Penelope, who resembled a nappy-headed kewpie doll.

Even our teacher, Mrs. Melton, and Penelope did not sit horses because Pen was a pint-sized terror. She wasn't big as a minute, but could wreak havoc twenty-four hours a day. She'd toss the games in the fun room if she lost, gargle with her milk, chew crayon, and spit chips like scud missiles out of that powerful mouth of hers. One kid's face looked like it was peppered with glitter when she got through. And Pen really hated me because I liked Noah and Noah liked me.

Noah was the funniest looking boy in class. He had a round head, sleepy eyes, a little gap between his front teeth, and an odd way of standing: one leg straight as a pencil with the other silly putty cocked inward to the right. He was so funny looking he was cute. But Penelope liked Noah too, so she was static on me all the time. And while Noah in the Bible was a one-woman man, Noah in the second grade was a playah.

When she wasn't dealing with Pen, Mrs. Melton was kindhearted. As Easter approached she decided to put me in the Good Friday play in an effort to boost my confidence. My part was this: after the crowd dropped palms in Jesus' path I was to scoop them up and run off the stage saying, "And the masses praised his arrival to Jerusalem and the palms he touched were blessed." And everyone was to leave the stage following behind me shouting, "Hallelujah! Hallelujah!"

Mrs. Melton put Pen's skinny butt on the floor with the other bad buggas, not trusting her to be in the crowd with the other children. Noah got the part of Jesus because he had a big head and the fake beard fit his face without falling off.

The day of the play we're all in our places and the play was going great. I was nervous but my grandma and cousin were in the second row so I wasn't shaking too badly. Standing in the wings, I was getting ready for my part. Penelope, sitting Indian style—though no self-respecting tribe would have her—was throwing static at me. "Hurry up and get off the stage, too. Don't nobody wanna see you!"

Here it was my big day and she was giving me the business. I had on my pink satin dress, pink ankle socks with lace, and white patent leather shoes with pink bows. There must have been one hundred plaits in my head, each with a barrette. I had had enough. When I got out onstage I looked out in the crowd at my relatives and instead of scooping up the palms, I started picking them up one at a time and giving a curtsey after each one. The more Penelope talked the deeper my curtsey got and the better I bopped my step. I looked good and the crowd cheered like crazy. I wasn't used to this so I spun around a bit. Mrs. Melton began jumping up and down shouting, "C'mon, c'mon!"

I did not care. I was a star. I did a split and picked up the last palm. The crowd was on its feet cheering and laughing. Grandma yelled, "That's my baby!"

Finally I said my line and started to run back across the stage leading everyone off for the curtain to close. I was skipping along, just thinking, I'm a star. I could be on the Cosby Show with Theo and Rudi. That's when some low-down somebody stuck out her foot and tripped me.

Insert domino theory here.

MISS PENITENTIARY

I had a *comic view* of the entire thing.

Bah-boom, bah-boom, and boom: One right after the other, they rolled across the stage. Waxed for the occasion, the floor was slick as a giant slide and all of the kids went *whoosh*. The girls with those two big flat pointy braids sticking outta the sides of their heads? They sailed further 'cause those braids gave them a little Flying Nun action. But in the words of Chaka Kahn, AIN'T NOBODY, and I mean nobody, rolled like Priscilla. She looked like a pink beach ball. There was only one unfunny part about the whole thing. Priss, round as a beach ball, rolled right over me; knocked my one barrette off my bangs and the wind right out of my body. When she sat up and saw it was me, she commenced to bounce! It was a miracle, but Noah was the only one left standing. I wasn't too surprised though; after all, he was playing Jesus. Noah laughed at Priss bouncing on me, "Pen, she tearing you up!"

I started struggling then. I wasn't about to be shown up by HER. I pinched her leg, she jumped up, and the fight was on. Now Mrs. Melton was onstage trying to get the kids up, but kids kept sliding on the floor on purpose, pretending to be slipping, refusing to stand up. Priscilla and me had locked barrettes and were pushing each other back and forth. Poor Mrs. Melton was near tears, her play ruined. Finally the principal ran up on stage and closed the curtain. Over? Not yet. Priss and me, we had tussled forward and were the only ones left front and center. Mrs. Melton separated us and shook me out like a wrinkled sheet, "Miss Penitentiary!" Then she tried to shake Priscilla, "Miss Prissy!"

Trah-ble. We had no recess for the next month but had to stay inside, straighten up the cloakroom and clean the black boards. None of the other kids were talking to us either, mad now that we made them mess up the Good Friday play. Even Noah ignored us except for sticking out his tongue through the window in between getting hit in the head playing dodge ball.

Isolated like that, we got to be friends. One day while squatting on the floor of the cloakroom (who ever wore a cloak to school anyway?), cleaning away chewed up gum that some nut had stepped on and spread across the floor, Priss said, "Pen, let's make a promise. Never to fight over a stupid old boy ever."

"Yeah, they just trah-ble—always digging in their noses and wrestling on the floor. Forget them."

And we shook on it. Sure did. That was the promise. Now Sander was coming between us.

MISS PRISSY

Now most of the girls in the beauty shop are wondering what the hell is so special about Sander?

Sander is a man's man. He went into the navy right after high school, did a double stint. I saw a picture Sander had in his wallet. The photo was of Sander and a friend after they'd won some kind of a competition. They were wearing their frog suits holding a trophy.

Heard that saying, Feel froggish jump?

Well I saw that sexy picture and my heart started to jump, not to mention the fact that I wanted to jump the man's bones. But che-che no-no; I am too sophisticated for that.

Pen knew that I was digging on the brother, but I saw him first. Sander was coming out of Independence Bank, across the street on the corner. Every business in the community used Independence. Sander was coming out of the bank carrying a sack of nickels.

But that body of his ain't no chump change.

Sander had come home to take over his father's hardware store business, and Miss Pen started running in their every other day—I mean damn, how obvious can you get? I mean Pen doesn't even own a hammer but she was throwing herself at the man like some *Home Depot Harlot looking for a screw, excuse my French.*

Anyway, I saw Sander outside the shop yesterday, that's why I know the gift is for me. He said, "Where are you off to looking so fine and cheery?"

The boy has an eye, don't he?

I said, "To get something special for Aunt Tilly."

"Oh," Sander said, those gorgeous eyes sparkling, "that's the nice old lady who checks your clients in, right?"

"Right, she's been working in the shop for ten years now. We're going to have a little anniversary party for her. Wanna come?"

"Depends," he smiled, the sexy gap in his front teeth exposing itself to me.

"Depends on what?"

"If you're doing the cooking for the party. Heard you can burn up some pots."

"Well," I giggled, "I wasn't planning on cooking. I'm trying to cut back, lose a few pounds."

Then I sucked in my gut.

"Aww woman, don't change. Big is beautiful."

Then he smiled and began walking away.

That was joy to my ears; I skipped behind Sander, shouting, "Come Saturday. I'm fixin' short ribs with red beans and rice."

Now tell me that gift isn't for me?

MISS PENITENTIARY

It's not.

Just because the man likes to eat, and isn't hating on Priss because she does too, doesn't mean Sander wants to start a relationship with her.

I'm the one he eyeballs when I walk past his business on the way to the shop after work. I'm the one Sander grins all over himself at when I go into the hardware store to buy some nails.

So here we are both latched onto this beautiful box. And I'm about to tell my best friend to get a grip when I remember: I remember our promise back in second grade. I remember that slope-footed, melon-headed Noah. And I laugh, laugh right out loud.

"What you laughing at Pen? Steve Harvey ain't in here cracking jokes."

I let go of the gift box and slide down off the stool. Priss's big butt almost flips over backwards, into the sink, but I grab and hold her, thanking God that I'd been working out, digging in so hard that my spike heels leave Dracula marks in the vinyl floor.

"Wheez! Thanks Pen. But I still don't know what's so funny."

"I thought about our second grade promise is all, that's why I let go. How are we going to let a man come between us, after all the drama we've been through?"

Priss thought hard for a moment, drawing her lips into a prissy pout, then said in a baby voice, "You right."

We hugged and both looked at the beautiful gift box.

"What are we going to do with that?" Priss asked.

"Go upside Sanders head," I answered, "for trying to come between us. He was playing games with us, had to know we both were digging on him."

"We can't beat the brother down for not knowing which one of the gorgeous ones to pick, can we?"

I laugh when she does this in a Mae West voice with a boom-shockahlockah hip shake.

Then we decide on a plan. It's a quickie; had to be because the guests for the anniversary party would be at the shop within the hour—all the guests—including Sander.

MISS PRISSY

The party at the shop was rocking. All the clients came bearing gifts for Miss Tilly. She's a sock-it-to-me senior with go-go boots on and close-cropped silver gray hair. She even has a tiny tattoo on her shoulder—"SOB"—stands for Sweet Old Broad.

Everyone was listening to the juke box—Ella Fitzgerald, Bobby Blue Bland, and Aretha—when Sander walked in.

Pen and I exchanged glances and I put our plan into motion. I looped my arm around Sander, dragged him over to the coat rack and took his leather jacket, feeling on his muscles as I peeled it down those hefty arms of his.

"I made a plate especially for you, baby."

Then I nodded toward a little table off to the side with a single chair and a place setting.

"Thank you," Sander said, "I can't wait."

You'll wish you hadda, I thought.

I sat him down and Pen came sashaying with the plate. The girl ain't got no hips as it is, but the half a pack she had for Pen shook it to the West and shook it to the East.

"What did I do to deserve so much attention?" Sander asked with a smile.

"Don'tcha know?" I purred and ran my hands along my bountiful hips. "I made this plate of food just for you, baby. Eat up!"

And brother man did.

Sander commenced to making a face.

Wonder if it was the cayenne pepper I added.

His throat started clenching.

Wonder if it was the castor oil I glazed his ribs with?

He jumped up and mouthed the word "water."

My girl Miss Pen said, "We fresh out. Next time you better bring your own and don't ever try to play us off one another again."

Then we stood beside one another, blocking Sander's exit like two super heroes. He looked confused, but it was kindah hard to tell, because his face was also looking kindah blue.

Finally Sander burst through the two of us and scurried out the door. All the women in the shop turned and looked in our direction. We two? We just laughed.

Miss Tilly, she came stepping over to us in her go-go boots. She said, "Where'd that nice boy go? I didn't get a chance to thank him for my beautiful gift."

Then she held up the box me and Pen had been fighting over. We could have died.

"For you?" Pen spit the words out as if they were laced with castor oil like the short ribs we'd fed poor Sander.

"Yeah," Miss Tilly explained, "didn't realize till the other day that I knew his grandmamma way back. So he dropped off this anniversary gift for me and like the old-timer I am, I left it here on accident. What run him off so?"

Then Pen and I had to tell the truth, what else could we do? All the girls gave us what for, especially my mother and my aunts. They marched us down to his hardware store to apologize. Poor Sander, he had barricaded himself in—wouldn't unlock the door.

"Go way! Y'all tried to poison me!"

Then he drew the blinds.

Our little party crew glared at us: "Always Miss Prissy and always Miss Penitentiary."

And ya know what, ain't it the truth?

"What are we gonna do with the two of y'all?" our family members asked.

"Make us start off the soul train line when we get back to the party?" Pen said sheepishly.

And we did.

Pen and I did the bump down the line.
Always Miss Prissy. And always Miss Penitentiary.
Always.

Luminous Days

BY MITCHELL JACKSON

Friday. Payday, and Rhonda quickly found a place in line at the check-cashing store. A faded blue Taco Fever uniform hung loosely around her thinning frame. Fresh stains covered older stains that persisted despite several washings. She fidgeted, trying to eliminate any negative thoughts. But the more she tried to escape them, the stronger they became. Rhonda knew there wasn't any money to spare. There never was any money to spare. Three hundred and twelve dollars, two weeks pay, just enough to pay rent, the light bill, and buy a few groceries for her empty cabinets and refrigerator.

She scanned the office trying to suppress the steady whirl of anxiety twisting the pit of her stomach and hoping the few people in the store wouldn't notice the increasingly harsh trembling of her hands, or the persistent twitching of her left eye. Her feet throbbed, swollen from a full day standing. The smell of ground beef seemed to be ground into her clothing. She considered her options or, in reality, her one option—Champ.

Maybe she needed him. He could help with the money. But calling him now, even though it seemed the best alternative, would mean admitting she was weak again. What would she tell him? She needed an escort to cash her check and pay the bills, because without one the bills wouldn't get paid? She couldn't tell him. She couldn't bear to see the disappointment in his eyes. Better to risk a secret relapse than to endure his disappointment.

A stumpy Hispanic man stood in front of her, irritating the counter woman with his poor English. Two more people entered the small store. Rhonda caught their faces in the security mirror. They were dark, a man and a woman, and judging from their rumpled clothes and wild hair were in the midst of an extended binge. She kept her back to them and hoped they wouldn't recognize her. Luckily they were engrossed in conversation.

"We're gonna cash this and go see Hype," the man said, his familiar voice coming from a few feet behind Rhonda. Ricky. She shuddered.

"Whatever," Ricky's female partner said, "just remember we splittin' this.

You not gonna smoke it all yourself—I'm the one who hit the lick for us in the first place."

Rhonda wished she couldn't hear them, couldn't feel their eyes on her back. She kept her gaze forward and waited impatiently for her turn at the window. More people entered the office. Rhonda watched them all in the mirror terrified at the prospect of recognition.

The Hispanic man was futilely explaining something to the counter woman. Her coworker apparently had no intention of helping anyone else in line. Reading a multicolored paperback book, she removed her eyes only to sip from her Coke.

Finally, the man snatched his check from the small slit beneath the glass and stormed out of the office ranting what sounded like a flurry of Spanish obscenities.

Rhonda moved toward the counter pulling the check from her pocket.

"You'd think if they're gonna stay in our country the least they could do is learn our damn language."

Rhonda signed the back of the check and slid it under the glass. The woman grabbed it and asked her for some identification. She fumbled through her pockets, pulled out her I-D, then pushed it beneath the slit and watched the counter woman scribble some numbers on it.

"How you want your money?" the woman asked, sliding the check between some kind of stamping device.

"Big."

Big bills were safer. Less risky than the small bills that lulled Rhonda into a false sense of security. The ones that made her think she could take a few dollars and get high. As if stopping was a realistic option once she started.

"Fifty, one hundred, fifty, two hundred, fifty, seventy, ninety, one two three dollars and twelve cents," the counter woman said, carefully separating each bill.

Rhonda snapped up the money, stuffed it in her pants pocket, and moved toward the exit. Glancing up, her eyes met Ricky's briefly, but she hurried out the door before he had a chance to speak. Outside, she took the bills from her pocket and stuffed them inside her bra.

Darkness ushered out dusk hanging over the city with the promise of nightfall. The air smelled of rain. Rhonda walked down the sidewalk swiftly, hoping to reach the apartment before any drops fell. She had forgotten her umbrella at home. Her coat didn't have a hood. She turned off the main street and down a small alley that was a shortcut to her apartment. She wanted to rest before grocery shopping.

Her entire body was listless. Even her heart seemed to beat a little slower than normal. The bill paying would have to wait until Saturday. She kicked a glass bottle into an unfenced yard just as two headlights shone against her back.

"Rhonda," a male voice yelled from the car over the grumbling engine noise. She picked up her pace pretending not to hear.

"Rhonda," the voice called louder. The car sped up until it trailed her by only a few feet. "Yo, Rhonda it's me—Ricky. I just saw you come out the check cashin' store. You need a ride?"

Rhonda paused just long enough to respond, "No, I'm fine Ricky. I'm goin' home. I don't need no ride."

"Don't be silly, girl. You look tired. What—you just gettin' off work? Let me give you a ride."

The inside of the car was completely dark except for the two pairs of eyes that glowed like full moons. A painfully familiar glow to Rhonda.

"Ricky, I said no thank you. I don't want no ride. Why you so interested in givin' me a ride anyway? I'm not gettin' high. You're just wastin' your time!"

Ricky stopped the car as Rhonda turned and walked away.

"Rhonda," he called, trailing a few feet behind her now. "Why the hell you always got to bad mouth somebody. You don't wanna smoke. I ain't said a goddam thing 'bout smokin'. Hey! Quit walkin' away from me when I'm talkin'."

Rhonda turned, now thoroughly irritated. She recalled her last few encounters with Ricky. The bus ride home from DePaul when he tempted her unsuccessfully. She blamed him for her first relapse. And here he was blatantly trying again.

"Ricky, just please let me be."

Rain began to fall, gently at first, more harshly moments later. She thought about her walk home, a walk she now dreaded.

"Look it's pourin' now. I know you don't wanna walk home in this shit. Quit trippin'. Come on and get in the car. You ain't got no umbrella." Ricky's voice softened.

Rhonda's canvas tennis shoes were soaking up the wetness like a towel.

"Take me straight home and drop me off in the parking lot."

A triumphant smirk flashed across Ricky's face as Rhonda walked toward the idling car. They sputtered down the alley.

"We just got to make one stop." Ricky said, studying her face in the rear-view mirror.

Saturday night. Champ pulled into the parking lot, circling twice in search of a safe spot for the Lexus.

"It's packed," Bump said, straightening the bandanna around his freshly braided cornrows.

Champ maneuvered between two cars and killed the engine.

"Stash the heater under the seat."

Bump pulled the gun from his belt buckle and slid it beneath the passenger seat.

Walking toward the club they straightened, brushed, and looked themselves over. Bump wore baggy cargo pants and Timberland boots. A long sleeved T-shirt served as backdrop for a navel-length gold medallion. Champ wore leather boots squared at the toe, soft jeans, and a fitted silk shirt. Diamond studded earrings pulled at his lobes; a diamond ring and watch dazzled in the overhead light.

Music pulsated. People glanced at them as they waded through the crowd toward the bar. Champ ordered a double Hennessy, Coke-chaser; Bump ordered the same.

Heavy fog filled the room. Everywhere the clang of glasses, the buzz of conversations, the thud of base. Champ drifted through the crowd dispersing mandatory handshakes, hugs, and nods. Colors filtered through the room like light bending through crystals.

He greeted everyone as friends, all with a smile of familiarity. He saw everything unfold in the third person, like he imagined a well-seasoned director would notice every detail of a scene. He cut through the dance floor, found an empty table against a mirrored wall, and sat sipping his drink.

Champ's mind wandered, captured only faintly by the woman staring at him from across the room. He stirred the ice in his drink with a long straw watching it swirl in choreographed circles inside the glass. She sauntered across the room impervious to gawking eyes that followed her like radar. He stood, then leaned over and whispered, "How you doin', beautiful?"

She smiled. "Fine"

"What's your name?"

"Raven."

"Very nice to meet you, Raven," he said, extending his hand. "I'm Champ." Lights reflecting at precise angles made his ring glitter. "You from around here?"

"Moved here a few months ago."

"Figured that," he said, almost stepping on her reply. "I don't forget pretty faces and I haven't seen yours."

"You talk a nice game . . . Champ."

Champ smiled. He liked the way she said his name. He loved the way she looked. Beautiful. Flawless mahogany skin, almond shaped eyes, mesmerizing long, toned legs.

"I like your style . . . Champ." She paused, overtly sizing him up. "Different. Not like the rest of the brothers I've met."

"Thank you."

He took another sip, more from habit than necessity. "You empty-handed or just not drinking?"

"Just finished one. So I guess that makes me empty-handed."

"Well, drinks on me the rest of the night. A pretty lady like you shouldn't be empty-handed if you don't wanna be. Here, have my seat. What you drinkin'?"

"Sex on the Beach." She smiled, revealing a set of perfect gleaming teeth.

Guilt crept up on Champ on his way toward the bar, his mind overwhelmed with thoughts of Kymm. He needed to hear her voice. He ordered the drink and took it back to Raven.

"Here you are," he said, his voice flat. "It was cool meetin' you, but I got to make a call."

Raven's face twisted in a puzzled expression. Champ walked toward the far end of the club and told Bump he was going outside. He needed quiet to make his calls.

His watch read 2:15. He dialed his home number; the phone rang three times before she picked up.

"Hello," Kymm's voice answered groggily.

"Hey baby."

"Champ, why're you calling this late? I thought you were at the club?"

"I am at the club—well I'm outside the club. I was just thinking about you."

Kymm didn't respond.

"I was just thinking about how much I love you, that's all, and I wanted to tell you."

"What did you do? You must have done something wrong."

"No. I haven't. I just wanted to tell you that. Now go get some sleep. I'll be home in about an hour. I've got to drop Bump off."

Champ called his mother's number next, counting seven rings before hanging up. On the second call the phone rang ten times. His next call went to Bump's pager. He punched in his cell phone number with a 9-1-1 behind it.

"Hey man, I'm ready to go."

"What for? I thought you were just going to the car for a minute," Bump screamed over the blaring background noise.

"I was, but I'm ready now."

"What's the deal?"

"I just called my mom's apartment and she wasn't there. I'm gonna run by and check on her. You can stay if you want, but you gotta find your own way home."

"All right, bro. I'ma hold tight. Moved a little piece of work. We gonna lay up 'til the mornin'."

"Cool. I'll holla tomorrow."

"Eh, bro—don't forget about the heat. Let me know what's up with moms."

Rhonda stumbled along the back streets toward her apartment, the pant legs of her Taco Fever uniform dragging beneath a pair of men's tennis shoes, almost double the size of her feet. With her purse missing and the money gone, only one thing remained: home. A place for recuperation. She hated Ricky, hated him for exploiting her weakness. If it weren't for him she'd be home, not walking. Asleep instead of tearfully awake. Most important, she wouldn't be trying to shake another high. She blamed Ricky, even though she knew sole blame was completely hers. She despised her weakness, her vulnerability. But despising it wouldn't change the last day and a half. Nothing could return the wasted dollars. Her money and pride were smoke blown in the atmosphere.

The shoes felt like blocks of cement. Sharp pains pierced her empty stomach. Nothing compared with the smell. An awful reminder that clung to her clothes and sank into her skin.

Eight more blocks and she'd be home, she thought, walking with her arms folded feebly against the chilly air. Eight more blocks and she could forget this happened. Again.

A car approaching from the rear highlighted Rhonda's stumble over a sidewalk crack. The car slowed, but she kept her head straight and moved as briskly as her weak legs would allow.

The car pulled slowly to a cruise beside her. Still, Rhonda avoided acknowledgment.

"Mama, mama," the voice called.

Rhonda's pace increased.

"Mama, stop! What the hell are you doin'?"

Rhonda froze mid-stride, then turned her head slowly; a reply was trapped somewhere between her throat and lips.

"Get in."

They rode in silence. Painful silence infiltrated only by the steady hum of the engine and the faint sound of breathing.

"Please just take me home, Champ," she said, eyes fixed outside of the window. "Please just take me home. I don't wanna talk right now."

Quiet.

Champ pulled into the parking lot, studying his mother in the faint overhead light. No words were spoken. He watched her exit the car and disappear behind the fence into the darkness.

She trudged in the house and headed straight for her bathroom, where she inspected herself in the gray light. It was self-imposed punishment. Her hair was wild; her lips red, dry, and cracked. The sight of her chipped finger-nails and blackened fingertips caused her eyes to tear. Eyes that were glazed, and frightened. Could he see all this in the darkness? A sharp pain stabbed her gut reminding Rhonda of her hunger. She walked into the kitchen and opened the refrigerator. Empty. The stomach pain returned—fiercer.

FROM **Only Twice I've Wished for Heaven**

BY DAWN TURNER TRICE

The Chicago Sentinel *Tuesday, November 8, 1994*

Inmate Alfred Mayes dies of heart attack

CHICAGO—Alfred Mayes, one of Illinois's most notorious inmates, died of a heart attack Monday in the Friersville Correctional Facility.

Mayes, 82, was the street preacher sentenced to life imprisonment in 1976 for the brutal murder of 12-year-old Valerie Nicholae, a resident of the affluent Lakeland community.

Warden James Delaney said Mayes's body was found by a prison guard at 8:04 Monday morning. According to the prison coroner, Mayes died in his sleep.

CHAPTER 1

Miss Jonetta Goode (that's Goode with an e):
"And the truth about Valerie's passing and Alfred Mayes and that whole mess?
Oh, the truth was buried nearly twenty years ago."

You see, I growed up in a place called Annington County, Mississippi.

In my day, colored folk up and died whenever white folk got a notion for us to. Mostly our men, but sometimes women and children. You look up one day and they gone, like a speck of dirt just blowing on the breeze. Sometimes with grown-ups, you almost had to remember if they was ever there in the first place, because you couldn't tell who was who by the graves. But with the children, there was never no wondering. People always left rocks behind, sticks, X 's, half-pushed into the ground. It was parents' way of burying parts of themselves with their babies. What remained, they numbed, just to get by.

So we all learned to stand together; we learned to help one another. It was something nobody even thought about. A child needed you, you was there. You helped a little boy lean against a hoe handle until hard dirt crumbled. Then you stayed with that child to drop a seed or two inside. When a little girl was sick, you mopped her mouth and served her stew in your Sunday pot, with the biggest chunks of sausage and carrots and potatoes you could find. Wasn't no skimping, mind you. No skimping for a child. Or you hid a so-called wayward boy in your crawl space, telling him to hush up—hold his breath if he had to—until the sheriff's boots stomped off the front porch, back down that dirt road. . . . Many nights after Valerie died, I asked myself what could I've done to help her. How could I've saved that baby from so much sickness?

Down south, we worried about white folks with their shotguns and lynch ropes, which made them God. Gave them the key to a heaven my papa wasn't rushing to get his girls to that fast. So in 1932, when we came up to Chicago, to Thirty-fifth Street, I thought I was a lifetime away from all that mess. Hell, the last thing I thought I'd have to worry about up north was black folks and their guns and lynch ropes and drugs, shooting all kinds of blues in their veins. And the nasty men, the Alfred Mayeses of the world, who liked to prey on little girls.

One thing is sure, you don't get used to death. Oh no, honey. Even old, old folks want to live forever—even if before long all they can do is hang like antique pictures on the wall. Relatives come by and stroke their chin and nod and smile while looking at their old kin. Take a rag every now and then and knock dust off them when it's due. But when they leave this earth, it ain't easy to take. So you know it's near impossible to make sense of having to pat dirt onto a child's face.

I saw Valerie only once, but after Child told me the hell her little friend was traveling through, I felt like I knowed her all her days. Could say I knowed her as good as I knowed Child. Just ain't fair for one person to have so much pain. Seems like God shoulda had better sense in piecing it out like that. Seems like since Creation, God had done gave Thirty-fifth Street's children more than their share of pain. Oh, Thirty-fifth Street was a horrible mess. For the longest, even the city had wanted to forget it was there. The mayor started by taking every city map and drawing a row of X's on the grid line between Thirty-fourth and Thirty-sixth streets. Stores hadn't been inspected in years. Mail wasn't delivered right, just left in one big pile. People never even had the dignity of a address. Thirty-fifth Street was all. Just Thirty-fifth Street. Only ten blocks made up the colored side of that street, and at every intersection, young souls was always dropping off. Like pecans from a tree. And not all of them dying in ways that call for burying, either. Sometimes that's the worst way.

So when Valerie died and the city finally got a notion to close down all the stores—to do what the street preachers had been trying to do for nearly half a century—I must admit, I was happy to get my notice. But it left a great big old hole in my heart that that damned street couldn't go up in flames without taking them two little girls with it: Valerie lifted on up to glory, and Child, who was left behind. Left to roam this here wilderness.

Every now and then, I think about the funeral, all them flowers surrounding Valerie's tiny white coffin, and a funny feeling still pass over me. Flowers are fine and good. But how come people forget to give children, especially little girls, flowers when they can enjoy them? Oh, the flower don't have to be a rose or a daisy. A flower is a "How do?" A kind word. A bouquet is no worries or cares or disappointments. It's giving a little girl a chance to enjoy a good breeze—to fix herself on a dream. And a child can't dream if she afraid to death to close her eyes at night.

I remember the day Child come running into my store, telling me a new girl come to the class. "Miss Jonetta, Miss Jonetta!" She was running so fast, her uniform had turned sideways and she was bouncing like she had jumping beans in her britches. Well, back then that wasn't nothing all that unusual for Child. She was born under a busy moon. I told her often: "Honey, us girls ain't suppose to look like something the cat drug in, like we throwed our clothes up and plopped in 'em. And stop all that hopping up and down, too. That ain't right, neither. You take a chance on mixing stuff up and having them moving to places they ain't suppose to be."

But that day, I couldn't worry about her clothes or her carrying-on. "Miss Jonetta, Miss Jonetta!" she kept yelling.

"Sit down and settle yourself first, honey," I told her. She breathed in and out, swelling her chest up, like you do at the doctor's office when he say take a deep breath. "Now," I said, nearly cracking my sides, "tell me what bug done got a piece of you."

"Today . . . in school? A new girl came to class," she said. "And she sit right in front of me. She even seem pretty nice, not like the other Lakeland girls."

"I thought I told you not to worry none about them other girls," I said. "They ain't got no color is all."

"I ain't worried about them," she said. She took a peek down at those old brogans of hers like they was making more sense than me. But that day? Believe me when I tell you, nothing and nobody, not even those prissy Lakeland heifers, coulda made Child feel low.

That year, Child was eleven years old, going on ninety. She thought nobody understood her. She thought nobody understood what it felt like to want to fly somewhere and be free. That's why she wandered over to Thirty-fifth Street. She was looking for a place to run to. Her hair was too red, so she thought. Her father didn't love her anymore, so she thought. And her family had just moved to this new hankty place where she felt she didn't fit in. With Valerie over there, and me on the other side of that fence, the two of us made her feel like she belonged.

And the truth about Valerie's passing and Alfred Mayes and that whole mess? Oh, the truth was buried nearly twenty years ago. Only today it can finally be resurrected. All them years ago, I told Child that if she didn't want to tell the truth right then, she wouldn't have to. She had my hand to God that I wouldn't utter a word. But I warned her from my own experiences that secrets don't always stay down. They rise like hot bread; spread like melting butter. I told her one day she'd have to tell this thing. And it wouldn't matter if the miles stretched like canyons between us, because I would help her. One day she'd have to gather the events the way you would loose petals on a flower and piece them together again. Slowly. Into the whole story. From the day she and her family moved to Lakeland to the day that no-good Thirty-fifth Street finally went up in flames. And she and Valerie helped set all them souls free. I told her she'd have to tell it, when it was time.

It's time. So listen.

CHAPTER 2

Tempestt Rosa Saville ("Child"):
"When you learn the truth."

When I was a little girl growing up on the far South Side of Chicago, my father and I would sit on our back porch—sometimes it would seem like all day. The sun would be sitting straight up in the sky and my father would be watching me chase butterflies, running from rock to rock, jumping up on the limbs of our near-dead apple tree with my hands poised, ready to pinch at their shiny wings. To this day, I can sometimes feel what was left of the morning dew squishing up between my toes, and the rose thorns and weeds scratching against my little legs. My father would laugh at me when I'd finally get tired of chasing the butterflies and I'd plop right down next to him.

Then when twilight would come and the butterflies had flown away, he'd see me smacking mosquitoes. "I hate them old ugly mosquitoes," I'd tell Daddy. "I just hate them."

One evening, he looked at me and laughed.

"You know, Temmy," he said, "you'll learn as you get older that there really isn't that much difference between your so-called pretty butterflies and your so-called ugly mosquitoes."

I looked at my father and I wondered if the sun hadn't beaten down too hot on his head. Didn't he see how light and free those butterflies were? Didn't he see how the sun fanned rainbow colors into their wings?

Well, twenty years have passed since my father and I last sat on that porch. And after Valerie died, with each year's passing, I finally began to understand what he meant.

That mosquito bites you now and it dies. It leaves a little mark, but nothing to really talk about, nothing that doesn't go away after a day or two. But the butterfly, that pretty, pretty little butterfly, bites you in another way: It makes you think life is full of color and light and easy. When you pinch its wings, it even sprinkles some of its magic onto your fingertips, like gold nuggets, making you think all you have to do is reach out for it. And you can buy yourself a forever. That's when it bites you. Unlike the mosquito, it doesn't die. But slowly you do. When you learn the truth.

CHAPTER 3

Tempestt:
"Good morning and welcome to Lakeland."

I was only eleven years old but deeply rooted in our South Side bungalow when my father moved my mother and me across town to Lakeland. Our move took place in early September 1975. I remember sitting in the backseat of our well-aged Volvo, which Daddy had spit-shined himself the night before, picking at the tear in the vinyl between my legs. The more I picked and pulled at the wadding, the easier it was to forget about the itchy ankle socks and the pleated skirt my father had forced me to wear.

"Daughter of mine," he said, glaring at me over his shoulder. "Daughter of mine" was his new way of referring to me. The words fell clankety on my ears and felt completely inappropriate for two people who had swapped bobbers and minnows and baseball cards, including a 1968 Ernie Banks number that only I could have made him part with. That particular one I kept by itself, wrapped in wax paper in one of Daddy's old tackle boxes under my bed. Though my mother never understood why a little girl would need such things—including several pairs of All Stars that Mama made me

lace in pink, explaining only, "Because I said so!"—when cleaning my bedroom, she always, always cleaned around them. She also demanded that my
father, from time to time, bring me roses in addition to model airplanes and
finely crafted fishing rods with walnut stock handles.

"Daughter of mine," Daddy continued. This time, he squinted into the
rearview mirror. "I won't ask you again to stop picking at that seat. Sit up
straight, dear."

"But—"

"No buts, Temmy, and close your legs. You're a young lady. Didn't our
talk last night mean anything? Weren't you listening? We're almost there
now. Sit up straight, I said."

I suppose my father's metamorphosis didn't happen all at once. But it
seemed that way to me. In truth, it was probably a gradual thing, like an apple left sitting on a counter. One day it's all red and softly curved and the
next you find yourself slicing off sections, trying to find places the mold and
sunken-in dark spots haven't yet reached. As we drove closer to Lakeland, I
wanted just to shake my father, make him wake up and come back to himself. I wanted him to shave off that silly mustache he'd recently scratched
out of his face and toss off that too-tight striped necktie. The house, though
sold, was still empty. We could move back in, patch it up, make it pretty
again, I thought. But of course my thinking was simplistic. My father would
never again see the house at 13500 South Morrison Street as our home.

For me, our bungalow, our neighborhood, was the only home I'd ever
wanted to know. From the day I'd learned our address and our telephone
number by heart, it had become as much a part of me as my name. My parents had created a life that was sturdy and robust, existing as so much color:
yellow-and-blue-trimmed bungalows that lined perfectly square city blocks;
Miss Jane's red compact—the size of Daddy's hand—which Mama said
Miss Jane held like a shield while sitting where the sunlight was best on her
front porch, warding off the years; and Mr. Jenkins's broad purple boxers
that were always line-drying on his back fence across the alley. How the
prospect of ivory towers and debutante balls could ever compare to this
world was completely beyond my understanding. I also wondered how my
father could not only choose Lakeland but yearn for it. It was a lifestyle he'd
once believed to be too "one size fits all," and as loosely woven and thin as
tissue paper.

At stoplights, Daddy busied himself by flicking lint off my mother's sky
blue cardigan and attempting to blot her perfectly smudged lipstick. Mama
batted his hand away, warning with side glances that he was acting a fool.

"Thomas, you'll draw back a stub," she said calmly, refusing a full head
turn to her left. So, after Daddy pulled the radio's knob and Mama pushed
it back in (saying the static, all that popping and cracking, was trying her

nerves), he folded several sheets of Kleenex and wiped his loafers. These, I must say, were the same loafers that just one year before he swore pinched his toes and were fit for nothing more than pulling weeds in our garden.

It used to be, before night school transformed my father from a cabdriver into a teacher, that Daddy watched me with a sense of ceremony as I played in our backyard. He would watch as I skipped around our partially painted picnic table and climbed the bottom branches of our apple tree. He clapped when I completed a somersault; he cheered when I shattered the Coke bottle with the slingshot he'd seen me eye in the Woolworth two blocks from our house. And with him and often my mother as my audience, that tiny backyard—with its thick rows of collards and cramped tomato vines—grew under endless possibilities. Back then, Daddy admired my socks that rarely matched, and my prickly hair, his shade of red, which he once chuckled with Saville pride was so wild, a comb would break its neck getting through.

But on that morning, when my father reached a heavy hand back toward me, it was only to brush wayward strands, forcing them, too, into submission.

The night before our move, Daddy rummaged through the house, deciding what was fitting and proper to take to the kingdom of the drab and what was best left behind. We had packed most of our things and sent them ahead. What remained, the movers would take the following morning. There wasn't much need for furniture because Lakeland's apartments, Daddy said, were "impeccably" furnished. The only redeeming quality about that final night was that Mama allowed my friend Gerald Wayne to sleep over with me. We spent the early-evening hours in the backyard in my tent before going inside. It was one last opportunity to listen to all the crickets and grasshoppers and the pitter-patter of alley rats, whose size often put some cats to shame.

Gerald Wayne and I had been friends since the second grade. Though I had seen him often in school, we met one Saturday while he was sitting on the curb in front of Wilson's Fix-It shop, playing by himself, as he often had. (I inherited both my parents' penchant for the down-and-out.) I just happened to be walking by, when he looked up at me, smiled, exposing two vacant spaces where front teeth should have been, and said in a most sincere voice, "You dare me eat this worm?" Had he given me ample time, I suppose I would indeed have considered the question. Only he didn't. Before I could utter a word, he dangled the worm over his mouth, let the squirmy little thing stare into his tonsils, then scarfed it down. Oh, he was nasty. He didn't even flinch.

Children always teased Gerald because of his dietary habits. But he had yet another unbearable affliction: He reeked—smelled just like a goat. None

of us truly understood why, especially with his family living on the west side
of the el train tracks, near the old soap factory. I suppose we thought proximity alone would have an impact on his condition. Even back then, Gerald
was the cutest little boy in the second grade. He had smooth brown skin,
dark brown eyes that twinkled, and a smile that sometimes made even me
feel faint. But he had this black cloud that formed a capsule around his entire body. It was as if no other part of the atmosphere would allow it to enter, so it clung to Gerald for dear life. It even shimmied in the moonlight.
Mama said all the child needed was a bath. Daddy later obliged him with
one and threatened that if he didn't make "dipping" himself part of his daily
routine, he would be banned from our house. Gerald liked having a friend,
so he washed, religiously.

The night before we moved, Gerald and I sat in my tent with our legs
crossed and the flashlight dimming between us as we sighed, grasping for
topics that didn't smack of corny recollections or mushy farewells.

"My dad said you guys are lucky to be moving to Lakeland," Gerald said,
interrupting several seconds of silence. "The construction company he
works for helped build it. 'Yep,' he said, 'the Savilles are some lucky black
people.'"

"Oh, shut up, Gerald," I said, choking back tears. "Nobody's lucky to be
going nowhere—I mean, anywhere." Daddy had begun to drill me on my
double negatives.

Outside the tent, a soft breeze nudged the wind chimes on the back
porch, which alone held many of my childhood memories. It was there
where Gerald helped me dig a hole to bury the horrendous Cinderella dress
our neighbor Miss Jane had bought one Christmas, expecting me to wear it
to church with her. Mama knew I had buried it back there. She pretended
not to see one of the bells jutting up from the ground. But she never said
anything, because she hated it, too. In the knotholes in the pine of the ban-
ister I had stuffed so many wads of purple and green bubble gum that after
several years, they seemed to hold the old rickety thing together. And once I
had even caught Mama and Daddy under that porch, moaning and touching one another in places that made me giggle.

Feeling sick, I opened the flap of the tent. I told Gerald I had to use the
bathroom, then went into the house to find my father. I didn't want Gerald
to see one teardrop. I don't know when it happened, but Gerald considered
himself my protector, my shadow and shield. No, I'm not sure when it happened, because I was the one who often protected him. Like the day I had
rubbed his head when Sandy Roberts shoved him to the ground. Daddy had
told him that it was never acceptable for a boy to fight a girl, so Gerald
couldn't hit her back. But I could.

In the house, I saw my father scurrying about and I wondered what was lifting him, when my mother and I felt to leave was one of the most wrenching things that could happen to us. One final box marked Garvey, Du Bois, Merton, and Robeson sat in the hallway. My father had so many books that the movers had to make two trips for them alone. He was about to prop the box against the front door when he noticed me staring at him.

"Hey, princess," he said.

"Hey," I said, picking at the newly painted lime green wall. I unpigeoned my feet, remembering my mother's warnings about them one day turning completely inward.

"You, okay? Seems like you got something on your mind. At least I hope you aren't so rude that you'd leave my boy out there by himself for nothing. Come here." He reached out to me with those huge arms of his and made me sit on his lap.

"I don't want to leave," I muttered.

"Daughter of mine," he said. "I thought we talked about this. It's a once-in-a-lifetime opportunity, dear. There's a waiting list a mile long to get into Lakeland. And our name"—he thumped my chest, then his—"our name was pulled in the lottery. Where we're going is a much better place than this."

He brushed his hair back in frustration, revealing a row of reddish gray strands. Then he looked up at the top of the stairs, where Mama was standing, folding towels. She, too, was listening; she, too, needed another dose of convincing. At first, my father looked everywhere except directly at me. I followed his gaze to the empty living room. Without furniture, it was all too apparent the floor sloped too much toward the fake fireplace, and oddly, the room seemed smaller than it had before.

"Lakeland is a wonderful place," he said finally. "That apartment will be three times the size of this old place. You'll have your own huge bedroom with your own balcony. . . ." He paused. "Temmy, you're too young to understand this, but soon this neighborhood will have gone to pot. Already young boys are hanging out on the corners. It won't be long before this place won't be worth half of what we paid for it."

"I don't care," I moaned.

"You haven't heard one word, have you, honey?" Daddy took a long, deep breath. "There was a time, when I first met your mama, that I would never have even considered living among the 'bourgeoisie.' But there comes a time when you have to mix some ideas. You get older and understand that nothing is all good; nothing is all bad. You know why I decided to go back to school? I wanted to give you somebody who does more than drive a cab, and write letters to newspapers and hand out pamphlets in his spare time. I had to ask myself, What more could I offer my wife, my daughter? In a few months, you'll be twelve years old. Soon, you'll be going off to college. I want you to be proud of where you come from and I want you to be proud of me. I'll be a teacher, honey. Your old man a teacher at a fine, fine school."

As I walked back to the tent, I wondered what I had done. I had always been proud of my father, and I wondered when he thought I'd begun to feel otherwise.

Down the hall from the stairs was a small, pantry-sized room that my father had used as his office. There were no windows, just his cold marble-topped desk and his favorite leather chair, cracked and worn, tired-looking from years and years of our weight. Daddy had found the set in an alley in the downtown legal district one afternoon while picking up a fare. He brought it home and dusted it off, and many nights I would stop in just before bed. Though I rarely understood the depth of Emerson or Tolstoy, I knew it was nearly impossible for me to find slumber without the melody of his baritone rocking me to sleep. Those nights, I believed with all my heart that as the years passed and my legs would begin to dangle far below my father's lap, below the final bar of missing gold tacks, we would always fit into the perfectly molded cushion that we'd created. That was until my father decided to leave the set behind.

Gerald had fallen asleep. I knew this as soon as I reached the kitchen, which led to the back porch. For such a small child, he had a tremendous snore, thunderous snatches of gasping and wheezing. Mama and I stood on the porch for a second, listening to him, watching his figure, silhouetted by the light, heave up and down.

"You know everything's going to be okay, don't you, Temmy?" she asked. For years I told myself—I suppose because everybody seemed to agree—I looked just like my father. But that was because of the hair. The red hair tended to blind people to the rest of my features. The truth was that I had a lot of my mother's face, her broad eyes, olive-brown complexion, and heavy, good-for-whistling lips. That night, Mama didn't wait for an answer. I suppose she knew I didn't have one.

"Stay out fifteen more minutes, Tem," she said. "Then I'll come get you both ready for bed." She smiled at me, then kissed me on the lips.

The next morning, I awoke to the scent of my mother's country bacon. I jumped out of bed and ran to wake Gerald in the guest room. By the time I got there, he was already watching the sun rise over the Jenkinses' tree house across the alley, and the garbagemen, sweaty, their pants sliding down their butts, hurl huge barrels of our un-Lakeland-like belongings into their truck. Too soon afterward, it was time to leave. I gave him my new address and he promised to write and visit as soon as he could. From my backseat in the car, I watched my friend, hands crammed into the pockets of his baggy jeans, turn and head for his side of the tracks. I waved, but he didn't see me. Still, I continued until we turned the corner at Alexander Street, and soon the house, Gerald, the Woolworth, everything, leaned in the distance and eventually was completely out of sight.

The clock on the gate showed 10:00 A.M. when our car pulled up. My father made certain it was ten exactly. The guard said, "Good morning and welcome to Lakeland." He checked Daddy's driver's license against a clipboard of notes, then handed him a map and showed us how to maneuver Lakeland's labyrinth of twists and turns to the Five forty-five building, our new home. Finally, he opened a massive iron gate that groaned as it parted, and we were allowed in.

As I looked out the car window, my fingers began to tingle and turn cold. Let my father tell it: This place was straight out of a fairy tale. One square mile of rich black soil carved out of the ghetto. One square mile of ivory towers, emerald green grass, and pruned oaks and willows so stately, they rivaled those in the suburbs and made the newly planted frail trees in the projects beyond the fence blend into the shade. The four high-rise apartment buildings were the tallest structures I'd ever seen, and already janitors were hanging from scaffolds, washing beveled-glass windows, making sure everything shined in tandem.

Men, women, and children were out in droves, reading under the trees, sitting on hand-carved wooden benches, or walking dogs along winding cobblestone streets—appropriately named Martin Luther King, Jr., Drive, Langston Hughes Parkway, Ida B. Wells Lane. When we passed a field of children taking turns riding a pony, I got on my knees to look out the back window. Then, remembering my father's warnings, I slid back down the vinyl. I was surprised to see him smiling at me in the rearview mirror. We turned onto a path that followed the lake, and a flock of white gulls flew over the car. I scooted from one side of the seat to the other to watch their pearl gray wings stretching across the sky as they squawked like restless, hungry babies, back and forth between the rocks and a lighthouse in the middle of the water.

In Lakeland, Daddy said, was the world's wealth of top black professionals: surgeons, engineers, politicians. Lakeland had begun in the early 1960s as part of Chicago's Life Incentive Project. As an apology to the rat-infested and blighted tenement houses blacks had to endure during the migration, the mayor garnered support from the state capital to the White House to build this urban utopia. It was an idyllic community, stripped of limitations and bounds. According to the *Sentinel's* annual obligatory article, Lakeland had every amenity: a twenty-seven-hole golf course, an Olympic-size swimming pool, coffeehouses with the classics lining oak shelves, and an academy whose students were groomed and pointed, some said from the womb, in the direction of either Morehouse, Spelman, Harvard, or Yale. Even Lakeland's section of Lake Michigan was different from that of every other community that bordered the shore. In Lakeland, the water was heavily filtered and chlorinated—sometimes even helped along by food coloring—to look the aqua blue of dreams.

This generation of residents, once removed from salt pork, fatback, and biscuits, now dined on caviar and escargot. Neatly draped Battenberg lace scarves on marcelled heads replaced dingy do-rags and stocking caps. And plump, curved saffron to dark brown behinds that once jiggled like jelly and made little boys long to be men were now girdled and clamped down, as stiff and rigid as paddleboards.

Despite what lay outside the fence on Thirty-fifth Street, whatever the world had told black people they couldn't do or be or wish for, it didn't apply to the residents of Lakeland. Within the confines of that ivy-lined wrought-iron fence lived this elite group of people who had been allowed to purge their minds of all those things that reminded them of what it meant to be poor and downtrodden. Once here, Lakelandites didn't look back. They surely didn't want to go back. All they had to do was sign a two-part contract in which they agreed to pay a monthly rent that was lower than the average mortgage. And they vowed to put their bodies and their beliefs into this great blender and leave it there until the whitewashed folk who came out no longer resembled the pageant of folk who had entered. The women made the Stepford Wives look like members of the Rainbow Coalition. The men, with their expensive pipes, plaid pants, and stiff white collars, were about as individual as the curds in white milk.

"This is Lakeland," Daddy said, pulling up in front of our building. He beamed almost as if he had built the place, or, worse yet, birthed it.

He patted the steering wheel and told the Volvo to be nice. For his sake, even I was hoping it wouldn't sputter and spit the way it usually did when he turned it off. I was happy it didn't embarrass him. A doorman rushed the car, opening the door for my mother, then for me. Solemnly, Mama and I walked up a slight incline to the oak double doors, which led to a lobby of glittering marble and crystal. Daddy, however, floated in on air.

Sonny-Boy

BY AGYMAH KAMAU
FROM *Pictures of a Dying Man*

[NOON]

Midday. The sun directly overhead and so scorching hot it bleaches the blue from the sky.

And the *palang! palang!* of the school bell disgorges a rush of children from the schoolhouse. Playful voices yelling, screaming, laughing in the schoolyard and here and there a boy in khaki short pants and shirt, a girl in navy blue tunic, white blouse, and panama hat walking or running home for lunch.

And Sonny-Boy, strolling across the village in the hot sun to his son's bungalow, rapping at the front door and waiting, knocking again and waiting before finally hearing footsteps inside the house.

And when Isamina opens the door her eyes are swollen and puffy, the face of a woman who has been crying.

"You never meet me," Sonny-Boy says. He stretches out his arm for a handshake. "I's Gladstone father."

Isamina is staring at him as though she just woke up from a deep sleep. "Yes. Yes," she says at last. "We have a photo of you." She shakes his hand. "Come in," she says. "Come in."

She walks ahead of him toward the dining room where a pile of notebooks are scattered on the table. She clears away a spot in front of one of the chairs. "Excuse the mess," she says. "But I was just looking through Gladstone's diaries. Have a seat. Have a seat."

She flips through one of the notebooks, still standing up.

"Funny," he hears her say. "You think you know somebody, live with them for years, then you discover you never really knew them at all."

As Sonny-Boy tells me later, he is impressed with the proper way she talks.

"Here," she says. "Look at this."

Sonny-Boy takes the book she hands to him. It is open. And he reads:

Dear diary,

New York April. Horns honking; pedestrians bumping, freight trucks fart fumes, stirring gritty, eye-stinging dust amidst noises, harsh voices, while the Menthol fresh breeze caresses, raises dresses as funk rises from my parka, sweatshirt, layered clothes of odd sizes, feet aching, sweating while I need a shave, feel a cigarette crave. And on a bench on the corner, a face behind a newspaper, no emotion behind it, looks up as I ask, "Do you have a minute? . . . To talk a little bit?" He folds his newspaper, gives no answer, stands, moves farther away. No answer.

And Sonny-Boy says, "This belong to Gladstone?" And there's surprise in his voice.

"Yes," Isamina tells him. "All of these," flinging her hand out indicating the notebooks scattered on the table. "His whole life, it looks like. He left them for his daughter. Did you know he has a daughter? Yvette?"

Sonny-Boy is silent. Yes he knows but he doesn't want to say the wrong thing, so he keeps his mouth shut. Gladstone always was secretive but he didn't think he would be so secretive as not to tell his wife about his daughter.

Looking at the diaries strewn on the table in front of him he recalls times in New York when he would come home tired and hungry to see Gabby chewing a pencil and staring into space or scribbling in a notebook. And when he would fuss about coming home and nothing en there to eat, wanting to know if it was too much to ask for Gladstone to at least start the pot till he got home, Gabby would say is homework he doing. Perhaps some of those times he was writing things like this. Is true what Gladstone wife just say: Funny how little you can know about people, even your own flesh and blood.

And as he's thinking this Isamina asks him, "Can I get you something to drink?"

"Got any rum in the house?"

She nods. "How do you want it?"

"A little bit of Coke. Not much. With some ice."

After emptying his glass for the second time he says, "Just leave the bottle on the table. Save yourself the trouble, heh heh heh."

He pours his third drink and begins to talk, wanting to know why Gladstone didn't call him if he was having trouble. If he want somebody to talk to (and he looked at Isamina saying, "I don't mean no disrespect to you"), why he didn't call him? He was his father, after all. They coulda talk man-to-man. Perhaps if he'd done that and got whatever it was off his chest, perhaps he woulda been alive today. Because problems ain't nothing but obstacles and ain't no obstacle so high you can't get over it. And nothing certainly ain't so bad that you got to take your own life.

But from when he was small Gladstone always was the kind of child that would keep everything to himself. And instead of growing out of it, look like he get worse. Look what happen in New York.

He, Sonny-Boy was living in Florida, true, and Gladstone was up in New York. But what is distance when your son in trouble? If he knew Gladstone was catching hell he woulda jump on the first plane and go and see what happening. Gladstone didn't have to suffer through no hard times. He woulda even take him back to Florida till he catch himself.

"Don't blame yourself, Mr. Belle," Isamina says. "Things happen."

Easy for *her* to say. How could he help blaming himself when is he who send for the boy? He thought he was helping him. But what Esther say to him not long ago is true. America not for everybody. It is a place where good people, just to survive, can put a shell around them so tough that you stop seeing the person you used to know. He, Sonny-Boy, see it happen all the time. But Gladstone never develop that shell and look how it almost kill him. And is his fault for bringing his own son to a city where human decency is as rare as a virgin in a whorehouse, and even when it is there it seem to be buried deep beneath the filth and garbage that surround everybody.

He didn't even recognize Gladstone when he walked out from the airport with a traveling bag over his shoulder, a carton with four bottles of rum in his hand, and a mustache above his lip.

But Gladstone recognized him. "Pa?" he said.

And he stared at this man that was almost as tall as him, so thick-skinned that he know Esther was feeding him like he was the man in the house.

He say, "Gladstone?"

And Gladstone say, "Yes, Pa. It is me. And this for you." And he holding out the carton of rum like he want to hand it over quick before he forget.

Those early days was good days. Good days. Showing Gladstone around, going to places he never went to in all the years he was in New York.

"This is the Empire State Building," he remember saying. And Gladstone staring up at the building, making Sonny-Boy chest swell out because he can bring wonder to his son face just by showing him things that he pass by every day without even noticing.

He remember Gladstone saying, "When you going show me where you work, Pa? I want to see where you work."

But he was embarrassed. Didn't want the boy to know he was only a janitor. Told him he was an office services engineer. That is what they was calling themselves: office services engineer. Because nobody en what they is anymore in America. Everybody is some kind of engineer or technician. Hell. Nobody en even plain stupid no more—they mentally challenged. You know that? That is the new-fashion word: challenged. What a stupidness, eh?

Anyway, he was always giving excuses like "One day when things not so busy," or "They don't like you bringing people on the job." Excuses like that.

He couldn't understand why he was embarrassed. After all, it wasn't like he had a big job back home before he left. If he had, he wouldn't have had to leave so he could get the money to send Gladstone to high school.

After a while Gladstone stopped asking and it seemed around that time that distance begin to widen between them, probably because he began to hint to Gladstone that he could do with some help. He knew Gladstone was in college and had to study but perhaps he could get a little part-time job to help out. *He* was working two jobs trying to make ends meet and still save a little something—doing janitor work at night cleaning offices in the city, knocking off at seven o'clock in the morning and going straight to his next job at a gas station in Queens till four in the afternoon, then going home and sleeping till nine, when he had to get up and get ready for his eleven-to-seven night job.

It was hard.

Meanwhile all Gladstone doing, as far as he could see, is reading books. So he told him one day, "In America you have to get up and get. Nobody don't give you nothing free. They always take something in return, even if it is only your dignity."

And all Gladstone saying is "okay, okay." Till one day Gladstone look at him and say, "Look, it is you who send for me to come here and study. And it was you who come over here as soon as I pass for secondary school and left me and my mother there to scramble. Least you can do is help me out now."

What a blow, eh? What a blow. That is one Sonny-Boy didn't expect. It knock the wind out of him so hard he had to sit down. When he catch himself he say real soft, "That is what you think? After all the money I send for school fees, for books, the barrel of clothes and school supplies and food I send every year, you saying I left you and your mother to scramble for yourself? That is the thanks I get? That is what education does do to people? Turn them stiff-necked and ungrateful?"

But it seem that Gladstone had it in his head that Sonny-Boy owe him something so he living in the apartment like he is Lord Byron while Sonny-Boy working his tail off and coming home and cooking food for he and Gladstone like he is Gladstone mother or woman, one of the two—Gladstone say his mother never learn him how to cook.

One day Sonny-Boy couldn't take it no more. "Look, Mr. Big Shot," he say. "Money don't grow on trees over here, you know. You see them people you see going back home spending money and showing off? Well they just like me, working like a mule from the minute they land here. Like now, I working these two jobs just to support the two of we. Time for you to get up off your backside and help out, too."

That wasn't too much to ask, eh? But Gladstone bust out with, "Why you send for me, then?"

So now the blood really flying to his head. "Wait a minute!" he bawling. "Wait a gad daim minute! I send for you. Yes. But not for you to live like a king while I slaving to support you! This is America. Every tub got to sit on its own bottom over here. You think it easy? Eh? You see gold on the streets here? Eh?" He steups his teeth. "You just like these black Americans over here. Lazy. Living off welfare and food stamps and expecting somebody to help them. . . ."

And Gladstone butting in saying, "You know how you sound? Eh? You know how you sound?" And asking him if Francine that live across the hall is a black American. Because if he not mistaken, the last he know she was from back home just like them and ent she living on welfare? Eh? What about that? And he going on to give this lecture about how all kinds of people get welfare and that more whitepeople living on welfare than blackpeople, as if Sonny-Boy concerned about what other people do. Is he own color he care about. But this young generation? You can't tell them nothing. You can't reason with them.

So all Sonny-Boy can do is stare at his own son to see how the boy turn just like these Yankee children—contradicting their elders; talking, talking, talking and not stopping to listen and learn. And all he can say to the boy is, "This is what all this book learning doing for you? Turning you stupid and disrespectful? If that is the case, you better off back home."

That is when he feel his heart pounding so hard he think it going bust in his chest. He inhale, take a deep breath and sit down, and he thinking, look his crosses, this boy only here a few months and already with his American rudeness he giving him heart attack. But he also realizing that this isn't the only time here of late that his heart racing like that.

When he get home from his gas station job, even though he tired as a dog, sometimes it taking him a long time before his heart can settle down enough for him to drop off to sleep.

Not only that, he don't have time for enjoyment anymore. He used to be able to go to a dance every now and then on Saturday nights, even when Gladstone first come over. Now his days off at the gas station job is Tuesday and Wednesday, so he working there Saturdays and Sundays and when he get home he too tired to do anything but sit down in front the TV and doze off.

Couple mornings after that argument is when he collapse in the bathroom and when he wake up he find himself in a hospital breathing out of an oxygen mask and with a tube in his arm and Gladstone standing up next to the bed looking down at him.

First thing Gladstone say after he ask Sonny-Boy how he feel is, "Pa, I have a job."

All Sonny-Boy was able to say was, "Uh huh?" And he thinking, Look at this, eh? He had to nearly dead with a heart attack and end up in a hospital bed for the boy to get off his backside and find work. But he got a good feeling inside him anyway and he resting his hand on Gladstone arm.

When he come out the hospital things was better, with Gladstone holding down a little job at the college library and helping out with the bills. But Sonny-Boy decide that even though the heart attack wasn't serious (the doctor tell him he could live a long healthy life but he had to slow down), he would hold on a little bit till he figure his son could handle himself, then he would move to Florida where his cousin write and tell him things not so fast down there and the cost of living lower.

When he left for Florida, Gladstone had two part-time jobs: the one at the college library plus another one at a bank.

Next time he see his son, the boy sitting on a park bench like he sit down there waiting for his father from the moment he hang up the phone from calling him in Florida.

And Sonny-Boy can scarcely recognize his own son, this young man with bushy hair and fidgety hands but with his clothes clean somehow.

At first he feel himself standing there like he stick to the spot; then he have to control himself from rushing over, shouting out his son name and hugging him. Instead he walk over calm and cool and say, "Gladstone?" real easy.

Gladstone look up, see him, and start crying, tears running down his face and dripping off his chin.

. . .

Dear diary,

Here I am, weeks away from my forty-eighth birthday yet in my memory the day my parents got married feels like yesterday when I, a child of no more than about two or three, am being tossed up among the rafters by my father who is looking up at me with his mouth wide open in laughter, his hands open and waiting to catch me while I laugh with the thrill and fear of suspension in midair.

Forty-six years later I still see through the eyes of that two-year-old infant a tarpaulin stretched from poles at each corner of the yard, turning the entire yard into a tent filled with grown-ups eating, drinking, talking, merrymaking.

And my father's gold tooth glistens as he catches me and asks, Enjoying yourself, Brute?

His hands grip me under my armpits while I look down at the floor far below, screaming, kicking, and laughing the same way I yelled and laughed years later on my first roller coaster ride with him, years older and gray-haired, sitting beside me tense and clenching the bar in front of him. And walking home later after the bus ride back I glanced at him breathing heavily from too many years of cigarettes and I say, You know, I had a real good time today.

And without looking at me he says, Me too.

That evening we sat in the apartment watching TV together and I was content in a way I never felt before.

But happiness is as evanescent as a raindrop on a hot stone at midday. Because it wasn't long after this that I stood in a room watching my father lying in his hospital bed with a tube in his nostrils and clear liquid dripping from another tube into his arm.

Not long after that he moved to Florida leaving me alone in a city surrounded by strangers, searching my memory for childhood recollections of him, which was like peering into a darkened room and glimpsing the outline of a man with a golden-toothed smile coming in at night while the lamplight cast flickering shadows on the walls and danced in the corners of the house as I lay on my bedding on the floor; hearing him wake up early on mornings and the sound of his bicycle ticking along the side of the house as he pedaled off for an early-morning sea bath, and seeing him later flinging one leg over the bicycle saddle and riding off to work; watching him walk out through the front door one night while I am doing my homework at the dining table and hearing him say, I am going to have a kick out of life, and hearing Mamuh mutter, Well, I hope life don't give you a stiff, hard kick in your ass.

That was the year I passed the eleven-plus exam for secondary school with a scholarship to go to Wilberforce.

The day the letter came my old man went straight down by the rumshop after work. He got to brag with he friends, Mamuh said. But she could not hide the faint smile on her face. Earlier in the day she couldn't keep the news to herself either, telling Miss Clarke next door, The government paying for everything—school fees, books, uniform, everything.

Pa didn't come in till late that night, drunk and happy, singing and waking up me and my mother. But that night she didn't quarrel, just said, Keep quiet and go to sleep.

Two weeks later another letter came from the Ministry of Education.

To this day I've never seen the letter but I remember my mother opening it with the sound of the postman's bicycle *tickticking* away in the stillness of noonday, and my mother standing next to the morris chair by the front window staring at the letter with her mouth slightly open, then saying after a while, Error? What they mean error? and sitting down in the chair clutching the letter in her lap and staring through the window.

What happen? I asked her.

She stared at me, and it was a long moment before she said, You pass, but not with a scholarship.

Which didn't make sense. The letter from the Ministry of Education saying that I had a scholarship for Wilberforce was right there in the shoe box under the bed with all the other important papers like birth certificates and so forth.

But her eyes were still locked on and mine as she waved this new letter and said, They say they make a mistake.

And right then, at the age of eleven, I learned that folks like us who didn't have connections to influential people would suffer disappointments and face obstacles in life, or as Ma said as she sat staring through the window with the letter in her lap, Boy, if you don't have a godfather in this country, you suck salt. Or as Pa said later that night to Ma, If you stand up under a coconut tree a coconut bound to drop down and bust open your head.

Ma gave him a long, hard stare and then burst out, Harold, what stupidness you talking, eh? This is the boy future we talking about. Why you always got to be talking gibberish? What wrong with you?

But nothing was wrong with Pa. He couldn't help himself. He was a man thrust by circumstance into a role he wasn't prepared to maintain.

I still remember the night, one of many nights when rum made his head light and his tongue heavy, when Pa made a statement so heavy, so profound, that his rum friends opened their eyes wide and their mouths fell open in astonishment. At least that's the way the story was told when it started to spread the next day.

To this day everybody has a different version of what Pa said that night, which means that no one really remembers. But Miss Clarke, our next-door neighbor, came to the house bright and early the next day and told my mother, Sonny-Boy is a prophet.

And Ma stared at her. A prophet? she said.

Yes, Miss Clarke said. Like in the Bible.

In the Bible?

Which caused Miss Clarke to ask Ma, "What happen to you? You's a echo?" Then she began to tell the story of what happened at the rumshop the night before.

That evening before Pa could get in the door Ma asked him, "What this about people saying you's a prophet?"

So now it is Pa's turn to look puzzled and say, "Prophet? What you mean 'prophet'?"

It wasn't long before people began to come knocking at the front door, sometimes as soon as he got home from work, before he even had a chance to eat, asking for all kinds of advice. It is like all of a sudden Pa had turned into an obeah man with people saying things like:

—"Yvonne acting funny, like she got another man. What I should do?" and;

—"I like this fella that does work for the waterworks company, but all I try to catch his attention, he en paying me no mind. What you think?"

People coming from far and near, and Ma grumbling and asking Pa why he don't charge them. He's the only body she know does give away free advice. And Pa saying how God give him a gift to help people and how she expect him to charge them? If people want to give donations that is one thing, but he can't charge. And Ma saying low so that only I can hear, "Is one thing to be kind, is another thing to be stupid." But that comment doesn't reach Pa's ears, otherwise wise man or no wise man her ass would've been in trouble.

And the whole thing reaching national proportions when Dear Suzy who used to give advice to people every day in the newspaper began ending her columns with a warning to her "Dear readers" not to seek the advice of barefoot charlatans who only want to take their money. And the woman who does housework for her, who happen to live in the Village, coming to Pa and saying how Dear Suzy going to obeah man for him because Pa taking away her business. And Pa's only response is to shake his head and say, "Poor woman," which really impressed the woman who brought the news and she's telling people that Pa really is a holy man who, in her words, "have no fear of man nor beast." Which is a big joke to Ma who knows better.

It is around that time that I came to learn another lesson: when people say they want advice, what they really mean is they want you to confirm whatever it is that they already decided. Or at the very least they want you to tilt them in the direction they already were intending to go.

And it seems that Pa learned the same lesson after Gladys came to him with this question: Sammy en doing so good in school. You think you can help him?

To which Pa replied, I can't work miracles, adding that he knew Sammy since the boy was a baby in diapers and to the best of his knowledge her son always had a hard head and in his opinion she should try to get the boy apprenticed to somebody to learn some kind of trade because Sammy never going to be a scholar. The boy just not academically inclined, Pa saying.

You see, Pa had got into the habit of telling people whatever was on his mind, like he thought that whatever gave him the gift of wisdom would also shield him from the wrath of people when he told them what they didn't want to hear.

Gladys started raising her voice. "Wanting to know what kind of prophet you is, eh? Telling me to send my boy to learn a trade? Why you don't send that little, bony boy of yours to learn a trade, eh? Why you don't do that?" And she's looking me up and down with scorn while she's saying this.

That hurt my feelings.

But Pa was calm, replying how he never tell nobody he is no prophet. That is something they put on him. And if she not satisfied with his advice, then she should do like Dear Suzy and go see Papa Sam the obeah man who going tell her some mumbo jumbo and take her money.

Gladys flounced out of the house. Next thing you know, she is spreading a rumor that every night when Pa got drunk he would always come knocking at the side of her house whispering and begging her to let him in. But she is a Christian-minded woman, so she always tell him to go home to Miss Esther and stop bothering her. He should be ashamed of himself. Prophet? He en no prophet. If people stupid enough to believe that, well that is their business but she know better.

As soon as Ma heard this, she stopped speaking to Pa, sulking around the house and talking to him through me, saying things like "Tell your father his food ready," or "Tell your father to pick up some fish when he coming in from work this evening."

And Gladys's next-door neighbor, Mildred, is telling people what a lying hypocrite Gladys is, calling herself a Christian, when some nights she can stay over in her house and hear Gladys moaning and carrying on. And it en Sammy's father that causing her to carry on so, because everybody know Sammy father left her and living with another woman. Mildred figuring she doing Pa a favor by calling Gladys a hypocrite, but she's only making things worse.

After that, Pa stopped giving blunt advice and instead began answering people in baffling, head-scratching parables. So, grown people would come up to me after they talked to my father, asking me questions like, "What your father mean by *so-and-so*," or "What he mean by *this-and-that*?"

But if they couldn't understand my father, how could they expect me to? I was only a boy; they were grown. But of course I couldn't say any of this because in those days children couldn't talk back to adults (not like nowadays), so I would just stare at them or shrug, which would only get them vexed and cause them to suck their teeth and fling off their arms and walk away muttering about how I just as stupidy as my jackass father.

Well, needless to say, the flow of people coming for advice began to trickle, although it never really stopped. Once in a while somebody would come to see him as a last resort.

But the parables never stopped. Sometimes he would be sitting quietly and all of a sudden, out of nowhere, he would let loose a parable.

So the night when Ma told him about the letter that said I didn't have a scholarship, his proverb about a coconut busting your head was the last straw.

That was the first time I could remember Ma raising her voice in the house. But I suppose the frustration that had been building up from having to listen to Pa's stupid parables, plus the shock of shattered expectations were too much to bear, so she let loose.

"These stupid sayings of yours got people looking at me funny! You know that?! People laughing behind my back when they see me, or else they feeling sorry for me and Gladstone—you can see it in their face. You en know you is a big joke?!" she asked him. "You en care you making your whole family a laughing stock?!"

All the while I'm sitting at the dining table expecting Pa to defend his sayings either with another of his parables (as he had a habit of doing) or by telling Ma shut up, woman, what you know. But instead he stared at the tablecloth as if there was something there that only he could see.

Finally a long sigh *whooshed* out of him and his shoulders slumped even more. "What they expect we to do, uh?" he said.

A beetle pinging against the lampshade gave the silence in the house the heaviness of molasses. Crickets chirped in the bushes outside. Frogs croaked.

Pa gazed at the letter in his hand. "First they tell we the boy got a scholarship. Now look at this. Eh? Look at this. What they expect we to do?"

And that night for the first time I saw what defeat looks like on the face of an adult.

Ma gazed at Pa for a long time then sighed. "God will find a way," she said.

To which my father replied, "Well he better hurry up. The school term soon begin."

"Hush," Ma said right away. "Don't talk like that." And she's glancing over her shoulder like she expects God to strike Pa dead.

But the slump of her shoulders says she doesn't really have much more faith than Pa does.

I never found out where Pa got the money to pay my school fees and buy textbooks, nor where he got the money to take me into town and buy a cricket bat for me after I came second in class that school year.

Even now the smell of linseed oil always triggers the memory of Pa and me walking out of the store with the midday hot sun beating down, me holding the cricket bat, and Pa looking down at me and saying, You got to cure it with linseed oil.

If my life can be told in chapters, that day marked the beginning of the end of one chapter, the one that ended with Pa shaking my hand man-to-man in the airport building and walking toward a plane that took him to Away, a place I couldn't even imagine and only later got an idea about through reading books I borrowed from the public library.

For weeks after Pa left I would find myself listening for him to come home from work, and several times I heard his bicycle bang against the side of the house. But those are the kinds of illusions that loneliness can create.

Many nights I would lie in bed listening for him to come singing and stumbling home, waking up Ma when he came in the back door saying, "Esther! I home! The Boss has arrived!" and then coming over to where I was sleeping on the floor and saying, "Sleeping, Brute?" and Ma stirring in bed and mumbling, "How many times I tell you don't call the boy no Brute. And keep quiet, for God's sake. People trying to sleep."

And sometimes Pa would take his food from the larder and warm it up (Rum drinking made him ravenous. I know. The same thing happens to me), and we would eat at the table with the kerosene lamp flickering before us.

Once when our cricket team was playing down in Australia Pa and I sat every single night next to the radio up to three, four o'clock in the dead of night listening to cricket commentary and eating salt herring and biscuits.

But all of that stopped the day Mr. Gaskins's old Morris Minor came bumping down the road to take the three of us to the airport.

When we reached the airport, Pa and Mr. Gaskins each carried a suitcase into the terminal building, with the weight of each suitcase behding their bodies sideways.

Ma and I watched from afar as Pa showed the woman at the counter his papers. It was as if Ma was already putting distance between herself and Pa so that when he really left the shock wouldn't be so great.

After Pa checked in we stood in the middle of the terminal—Ma in her good beige dress with white lace trim around the neck, broad-brim straw hat and shining black pocketbook, Pa in his only dark-gray suit with the two-button jacket and dark-brown felt hat cocked at an angle. It looked to me like he was outgrowing his suit, which didn't make sense because grown-ups don't grow. Mr. Gaskins wore a long-sleeved white shirt with the sleeves rolled up to his elbow.

With all the talking that was going on and the aroma of food, the only difference between the airport and the market was the voice coming over a loudspeaker every now and then.

". . . flight number 461 now boarding . . ."

That is my plane, Pa said.

And the noise in the airport almost drowned out Ma's voice reminding Pa of the two dozen flying fish she fried that morning and wrapped in plastic and newspaper and packed in the suitcase. "Those will hold you for a little while," she said. "What you don't want right away you can freeze."

Pa said, "All right, all right." He didn't say it, but you could tell he was thinking he was a big man who didn't need nobody telling him how to take care of two dozen fish.

Then Ma said, Write as soon as you get there.

"Soon's I get pay I going send something," Pa said.

"Get yourself settle first," Ma said. Don't worry about we.

Pa pulled on his cigarette and at that moment he looked like a movie star with his hat cocked at an angle and his shirt opened at the neck under his jacket.

He stamped the cigarette butt under his foot and hugged Ma. She stared over his shoulder with water brimming in her eyes.

Then he stuck out his hand and looked me full in my eyes. "You in charge now, Brute," he said.

We shook hands, man to man, with me looking him full in his face and with my lips pressed together knowing that if I opened my mouth to speak I would cry, which I couldn't do because men don't cry.

We watched Pa walk toward the door with his travel agency bag over one shoulder and a carton of rum like a valise in one hand.

"Come," Ma said.

So I didn't learn until years later that he stopped at the top of the airplane steps and searched for us among the crowd behind the guard rail on the roof of the airport building, and even though he didn't see us he waved, not knowing that we were already in Mr. Gaskins's car headed back home with Mr. Gaskins making conversation to lighten up Ma's spirits.

"He soon come back," Mr. Gaskins said. "Soon as he make enough money he going come right back to you and Gabby here. Look at me," he said. "I work like a slave in the London Transport. But you think I was going stay over there? No sir. That en no place for human beings to live, far more die. But if I didn't do that, if I didn't go away, you think I woulda had this little motorcar to help me make a few little extra cents? Things going work out," he said.

That night I lay on the floor and heard Ma crying softly. And it brought to mind another night when Ma and I were sleeping and Pa came in, drunk as usual. For some reason he and Ma started shouting and next thing I know, *PAKS!* He delivered a slap to Ma's face. Ma held her face. The house was silent. Then she uncoiled and began windmilling her hands, hitting him every which way and yelling, "You come in here with your drunk self and hit me? Eh? In front your son? That the kind of example you setting?" And Pa hitting her back, but not with any force. After a while he walked back out of the house and Ma lay in bed sniffling into her pillow the same way she was crying that night after we came back from the airport.

It was the first of many such nights.

FROM **Water Marked**

BY HELEN ELAINE LEE

Delta moved aside as Sunday came through the doorway, and in an instant, they felt their manifold heritage of silence and remorse, and the pull of common history and blood.

Sunday called her sister's name, and Delta's hands began to reach for her, before pausing and returning to her sides. She offered a determined smile, and then, seeing Sunday seeing her, she smoothed down her hair, oiled and halved by a careful part.

As Sunday looked at her, Delta nodded, reminded of her sister's aptitude for sight, and wondered if she could sense the toll of misbegotten love. She felt a sudden kinship with a tree she had once known, lightning-struck and fired from the inside out, a few singed spots the only clues, but changed, unmistakably changed. Her roomy, flowered shirtwaist offered no cover at all as she seemed to thicken, further, under Sunday's gaze, and she crossed her arms over the fullness of her waist and breasts and fumbled toward speech.

"Well . . ." she said, damning herself as she spoke for her ineptitude in launching their reunion with that word that was all-purpose and meant nothing, asking herself why she could never find the right way to begin, the right thing to say, even to her own sister, and there she was groping, idiotically groping as she heard her own voice trail off, her alarm at the impending silence and her own impotence spreading, and again, "Well," this time as if it were a statement, the completion of what she had started.

Each one took a step forward, and then Sunday reached for Delta, smelling Ivory soap and Kool Milds, and Delta felt herself enfolded in the soft, loose weave of her baby sister's clothes. She tightened her balled-up hands and inhaled the woody musk, the train, the oil paint in her neck, identifying them all in a tumbled rush of memory as the thin, gold music of

Sunday's earrings quieted against her face and hair. She hadn't been held for so long, and here were Sunday's wiry arms around her and her fingers spread wide across her back.

"Wing stumps," Sunday whispered as she touched her sister's shoulder blades, giving her own childhood explanation for the protrusions of bone. Delta laughed as she remembered how Sunday had once drawn herself holding a set of folded wings, prepared for flight.

Delta freed her hands from her pockets and patted her sister stiffly as she eased herself away, noticing as Sunday moved to the center of the living room how tall she seemed beneath the layers of overlapping aubergine cloth. Her hair was unstraightened and unconfined, and she was so tall, so purple, so much, she seemed to fill the room.

"I know I was supposed to call, but I forgot, and it seemed easier just to come. That way I got to walk through the neighborhood."

Delta stepped back from her and focused on the different textures of cloth, some nubby and fibrous and some watery smooth, and what was that she had on, anyhow, she wondered silently, unable to tell if it was pants or a skirt, and where the top ended and the bottom began, and standing out from those waves of purple, from the corkscrews of bark-red hennaed hair and strings of beads that rang together as she moved, were her eyes, unquiet and night-black, taking in the details of sister and house.

Sunday saw the green and rust that had appeared again and again on her own canvases, and the familiar symmetry of the room, where crystal candlesticks stood like sentries on the ends of the mantel and lamps of bulbous, tarnished brass sat beside the easy chairs that flanked the window. Little was changed, aside from the new afghan of alternating brown and white crocheted squares that Delta had recently made, folded neatly at the end of the couch.

Following Sunday's gaze, Delta looked around and saw threads escaping the bound edges of the sculptured pea green carpet, the dark, beetle-shaped cigarette burns climbing up the threadbare arms of her chair, the fingermarks around the switchplates on the walls. She saw that the brown oak leaf pattern on the drapes had faded, the curtain rod sagged in the center, and she would have to get the side cords unknotted. Everything was in its place at least, but she hadn't realized how shabby some aspects of the house had grown. She need not feel embarrassed, she told herself as she looked at the room crowded with furniture and knickknacks, for they had both grown up there.

Sunday's beads sounded against each other as she turned in a circle and then stopped, caught by the ribboned light coming through the half-opened venetian blinds. Feeling for the edge of something she couldn't place, just a feeling, maybe, a color or a shape that might be, for her, like a first word, like the start of speech, she stepped into the banded light.

Delta watched her. Nate had walked right into that light, too, she thought, recalling that his arms, bare and muscular, had been briefly tattooed with stripes as he extended them, offering plenty. She found that he visited her in sudden alarming flashes: She would see a customer at the post office who waited tensely, flexing his jaw as Nate had done, and it would freeze her fast until she could recover and return to the present moment. Why, she asked herself, did mistakes have to stalk you, no matter how hard you tried to right them and forget? She didn't seem to be able to lose Nate Hunter, and here he was now, walking, uninvited, into her living room light. She shook the memory off and went to the kitchen to restart the kettle, watching the blue fire of the burner leap into a mesmerizing ring.

Absorbed in her study of the room, Sunday didn't realize Delta had left. She felt a pang of guilt at her scrutiny, hearing the voices of those who had told her it wasn't gracious to look so hard at things. Countless times she had tried to defend herself, to say that looking was her job. She approached each object hungrily, seeking something without even knowing what: some clue that would bring understanding, some key thing that she might find in the landscape if she read it closely enough.

She recalled the cloudy rings on the coffee table and its veneer rising up along the edges, exposing warped and naked wood. The mosaic tabletops and trays that Dolora had made were still displayed around the room, overlapping spirals of color and glyphs of private and ancient languages. She could see the few survivor plates and ceramic figurines behind the glass doors of the china closet, and tiny pieces of glazed tile and stones were scattered on the shelves like bits of excavated treasure.

The missing leg of the phone caddy had been replaced with three of the secondhand encyclopedias Dolora had purchased over a five-year indenture: Q through S. Sunday stared at it and thought about the bound, compiled world of facts in the hall bookcase, the gold letters on the spines harder and harder to make out, missing an entire chunk of information two-thirds of the way through, missing quartz . . . rhinoceros . . . scarab . . . She reached out to straighten one of her first paintings, hanging where it had been placed fifteen years ago, recalling that as Nana was putting it up, Delta had said that she liked the texture, but wanted to know what, exactly, it was supposed to be. The plaster had crumbled above in places, leaving a fine grainy film on the picture glass.

The walls and furniture were still marked with horizontal lines from years of flooding, when rain burst the river and filled their home. She remembered sitting on the stair landing, watching wastebaskets, colored pencils, and even chairs float, and recalled the dank smell that remained when the water receded and left its dark, wavy line across their lives.

She could still detect it, she thought, sniffing, just a trace. Either that wetness or a recollection, surfacing.

Their lives had always seemed open to water. Loose, rattling windows and their ill-fitting frames accepted heavy rain into the house, into the ceiling that every now and then grew distended like a swollen belly. There was always a saucepan or that blue bread bowl of Nana's sitting in the middle of a floor upstairs to catch some drip from the roof that failed them again and again. The border of the oak floor was scarred with dark blots around the arching ribs of radiators that hissed and knocked and leaked.

She looked around the cramped, moist house she had been desperate to leave. Although she had never managed to lose it in her work, she had returned annually after leaving for school, and not once in the past five years. After Dolora and then Nana died, she had wondered if the present could exist for her in that house.

There was Nana's photo across the room. That last time, when they were supposed to be comforting each other, she thought, they had given in to a kind of smallness that had made Sunday feel disgraced before Nana's memory. It all came back to her as she passed through the hallway: the airborne tumbler of bourbon, the arsenals of words and tears, the resentments, grown thick and malignant, fed by absence and discontent. But the thing she had never been able to forget or forgive, the thing that came to her at night, just before sleep, was how she had heard Delta come softly to her bedroom door.

Sunday had heard her in the hallway, and had chosen to stand on the other side, separated from her sister by a piece of hinged and hollow wood, so close that she could almost hear her inhale and exhale. Not knocking, Delta had stood there for a full minute and then left, and Sunday had neither spoken, nor opened the door.

Blinking away the image of that door, she saw the piano resting in the corner, its closed keyboard piled high with library detective novels, magazines or horoscopes, mail order catalogs. So many things in the house made her want to either flee or weep. The try at cheerful domesticity of Delta's ruffle-edged apron brought tears to her eyes, and the crowded dining room with its crocheted doilies and centerpiece of plastic lilies reawakened the cornered sense of longing she had felt as a girl.

But there had been touches of beauty, she thought, while her mother was alive. Her mosaics had always given the house a distinctive quality, as had jelly glasses and coffee cans filled with fresh flowers. Mason jars of vibrant canned fruit and preserves had stood on open shelves in the kitchen. And in the daytime, the venetian blinds Sunday had always hated were raised; there had been light.

Overwhelmed with remembering, she went into the bathroom and sat on the chenille-covered toilet seat, collecting herself. I have never left this house behind, she thought, touching the dusty crocheted doll, no doubt bought from one of Delta's post office coworkers, whose skirt concealed an extra roll of toilet paper. Standing, she looked at her face between the abstract shapes where the mirror's silver backing of paint had cracked and flaked off, and pulled the mass of unruly ringlets from her face to force it into one of the elastics she had around her wrist.

She followed the ridged path of the yellowed plastic runner across the carpet, listening for the *rrrrrrh* her shoes made. When she entered the kitchen she remembered the women who had regularly inhabited that room, Nana's voice leading the others, and she could almost hear their wooden spoons and smell the flour and sharp yeast. Standing in the doorway behind her, Sunday watched Delta straighten the quilted rooster-shaped toaster cover and raise her fingers to the half-moon stainless steel handles of the white metal cabinets and drawers. With her sturdy, flat-heeled shoes and her broadened hips rising under the pastel cabbage roses of her dress, she looked upholstered from the back.

Glancing away, Sunday could see the dent above the baseboard and a dark trace of splashed whiskey. How would she meet this woman who was her sister across the chasm, not only of their past but of their adult lives? She sat at the round oak table and took out the gift she had brought as Delta turned around, retied the bow on her apron, and flattened her palms along its fading green and yellow fruit. She took her cigarettes and plastic lighter from the counter and placed them on the table as she sat down.

"A peace offering," Sunday said as she pushed the foil-wrapped box a few inches toward Delta with her fingertips. She hoped the gift wasn't too extravagant, recalling how Nana had told her you had to be careful what you gave middle-class black folks, for if you brought jams or wine to dinner, they might be insulted, construing the gesture as a declaration that they couldn't afford, or didn't know enough, to get such things for themselves.

Delta opened the box slowly, anxious that she wouldn't know how to respond or might not understand its importance or its use. It might be some artsy thing she had never heard of, or some cosmopolitan gadget that was all the rage. And she was embarrassed that she had not thought to get Sunday a gift.

When she saw the dangling, pewter fish earrings, crafted into hinged and moving pieces, she smiled carefully. Sunday knew immediately that again she had chosen something discordant with her sister's quiet taste; she had chosen the gift she herself would like to receive. And she also knew that Delta would try to like them, and would wear them, at least once, before she left.

"They're . . . dramatic," Delta said, pulling one out of the box. She went to the hall mirror to put them on, and returning to the kitchen, unable to think of what to say, she began to apologize for not having a gift.

Sunday interrupted the repentance with a wave of her hand, and they both focused on the tabletop.

"It was definitely him, then?" Sunday asked, raising her head. "You're sure it was him?"

Delta nodded as she reached into her apron pocket to pull out an engraved gold locket the size of a half dollar. She placed it on the table between them.

"What I'd like to know," said Sunday, staring at the dented face of the locket, the letters of their mother's monogram looped together in a continuous line, "is how. How, I ask you, did he manage to die twice?"

The locket lay between them on the table as they looked at each other. "It came in the mail, along with what you might call a note," Delta explained. "He had kept it all these years."

Sunday's mouth went dry. She wanted to ask for every detail and then devour Delta's answers, but she couldn't seem to pose even the first questions: Where was the locket mailed from and what did the note say? She didn't understand why Delta was silent, why she didn't say everything then, right then. She looked up and saw herself in her sister's face. She had her skin, her oval face, her hairline. And unlike their mother's mouth, lean and carefully governed, theirs were liable to transform suddenly into reckless smiles.

Although Delta's hair was pressed straight and divided into the two dark curtains that Sunday remembered, its smooth surface had been invaded by recalcitrant white hairs that stood up at the temples and along the part. They had both sat on the edges of their beds while growing up and rolled the ends of their hair with pink foam-rubber curlers, but she had long ago abandoned that ritual. Delta's was turned under, as it had been for twenty years, in an even pageboy. Her deep-set eyes were sheltered by heavy brows, which she had plucked back to narrow pointed arches as a teenager, until Nana had convinced her to let them be. She still had the habit of smoothing them down with her fingertips, first the right one and then the left.

She seemed different to Sunday, but it wasn't her roundness, or her graying hair. As Delta raised her gaze from the table, Sunday sensed a change within the restive eyes. She searched the striated browns of her sister's irises, seeing behind the folded shutter of russet and seal brown and weathered grass something scorched and too quiet. The aftermath of fire.

She watched as Delta moved from taming her eyebrows, to turning her spoon over and over and over, to circling the gilt edge of the saucer with her fingertips. Delta took out a cigarette and tapped the filtered end against the table, and Sunday remembered how her fidgeting had unsettled Dolora, who had impatiently told her, "Be still . . . be *still*." Only Nana had been able to quiet her. "Be *here*," Nana had urged in her hoarse and gentle voice.

Delta jumped up to escape the discomfort of her sister's eye and emptied the coffee grounds from the pleated filter. As she rinsed the pot she also searched for a way to start the talking, glancing sideways at the locket in Sunday's rough, discolored hands, the nails cut close and straight across, the cuticles bearing traces of brown and yellow paint. Sunday examined the gold wafer intently, as if her touch and concentration could make it surrender its story, and Delta noticed the lines, like Nana's, that appeared in her forehead as she focused.

Reaching into the bag she had dropped next to her chair, Sunday rummaged through pens and sketchbook, lipsticks and barrettes, and the collection of found stones she carried with her. She unearthed her eyeglasses and put them on to inspect the details of the gold engraving that she had been taking in with her hands, and pried open the gold disk with her blunt fingernail.

Inside she found a faded picture of Dolora at fifteen or sixteen, her hair free of the French roll they had always seen her wear, her face plump and unworried, lovely in its innocent excitement at the just-opening world. Although Delta had looked at it when it arrived, she wiped her hands on her apron and came closer, bending over Sunday's shoulder to peer at the photograph that was cracked and water-warped. Together, they thought how different the young girl was from the mother they had known.

They had opened the locket, but they would have to work their way toward what it meant. They sat at the table chatting about local news. Then Sunday pulled the beaded brass chain that hung between them, flooding the room with soft, warm light.

"Remember Mama's jewelry box?" Sunday said as she eased her glasses up onto her forehead, where they stayed, like a second pair of eyes. "How when you slid the little brass button on the front the flat catch popped up, and each of us wanted to be the one to open it. Remember the embossed pink leather . . ."

"I think it was brown . . ."

"Pink. And it was darker, with the gold embossing fainter along the middle edge from all of our fingers touching it and pulling it open. And we would beg to go through it, getting her to tell us the lineage of each little thing in its velvet-lined division, always asking for more information. Unsatisfied, no matter what she told."

"You would want to try it all on and we'd pretend it was rediscovered treasure and make up our own tales about those things. Then we'd sneak into her closet when she was gone and play make-believe with her purses and shoes. I remember the little necklace with the dangling purple stones. 'Those are tourmalines,' Mama used to say whenever I touched it, as if it were important to her that the stones were authentic, and she could call their name."

"She never said where it came from," Sunday remembered. "She had costume stuff, too, the bracelet of shiny birthstones that must have been fake, and matching pin. But it was all super-real . . . magical, to us. And when you held it or put it on, you were transformed. It was the way into a fantasy."

"And there were the colored plastic bangles that probably came from the five-and-ten, and the one that boy had made her in his ninth-grade shop class from twisted metal." A symbol of love that had never had a chance to fail.

Delta also remembered the everyday, unremarkable things that were in there with the jewelry, and had thereby acquired a magic of their own: tiny safety pins and keys to forgotten or changed locks; buttons, lone ones Dolora must have been meaning to sew back on, and special, cherished ones made of rhinestones or cast brass that she had cut from clothes before giving them away, threaded into clusters with tangled wire.

"Grandpa's watch was in there, too," Delta added. "It's upstairs now. And a ring that was missing its stones. I used to imagine it complete, faceted sapphires intact. And there was a silver belt buckle, I vaguely recall."

Sunday stirred and cleared her throat, but decided to say nothing yet about the buckle she had brought in her coat pocket.

Delta lifted the chain and let the locket swing back and forth before she put it down. "Well, it seems like I've seen this locket, but clearly, it was never there after he left. Maybe she showed it to me beforehand, but maybe not. Probably she created it for us in the telling, 'cause when it came, I knew immediately what it was. What I hadn't known was that he took it with him when he left."

They had heard about the locket again and again, as Dolora made and remade her tale. Always it began in the same way, with her pointing to the empty velvet depression where it had been housed. She recounted her sitting for the photograph, and its presentation as a gift from her father, when she turned "sweet sixteen." As she described its intricate monogram and delicate chain, she looked into the distance and they could tell she was seeing it, repeating chosen pieces of the chronicle with embellishments, until it was a myth with a life of its own. As explanation of its absence, she had said only that it was "lost."

"Tell me . . . tell me the whole story," Sunday said, reaching across the table to take Delta's wrist and to feel the pulse beneath her fingertips, helpless at how little she understood, wondering what it would mean to have the whole story about anything, anything at all.

"Tell me," she said, "about the suicide that wasn't death."

Daunted by the hunger in her sister's voice and the rough hand that encircled her wrist, Delta looked away.

As Sunday watched her, she relived her recent impasse with paint. She wanted to be able to tell how she had gone each morning to her kitchen studio to stare at the blank and half-done canvases that filled the room, reminded of tombstones, and then turned their faces to the wall. Riding the El to the end of the line and back, she had walked the city streets, searching for something, a face, a storefront, a window that would move her from silence. She had even found herself standing at church doorways, attracted, yet hesitant to enter for the first time since she had left home, except in requiem. She had walked the lakeshore, trying to think of the water that stretched before her as ocean, but unable to lose the feeling that she was landlocked.

She had tried charcoal and pencil drawing, collage and modeling clay, never getting past concept to give her beginnings life. She had collected paper scraps and photographs and fabrics, but had been unable to turn them into anything. Her relentless, vague anxiety seeded and took root as she stretched canvases and mixed colors, and then flourished into panic when she tried to begin. She couldn't even focus on the rote drafting projects that were her steady source of income.

And then, after retrieving Delta's note from the box, she had drawn and painted furiously for close to a week. What came to her were shadowy figures bent into fetal question marks and disembodied limbs and hands, floating, buried, rising, layered. Again and again she painted the world from above, patchworks of city and field joined by branching rivers that fractured into overlapping pieces, like shattered trees. But she would come to a stop while painting, as if full sight just closed up, and then her palette began to narrow down.

Reed had walked in one day to find her stuck, trying to make a mark, a stroke, in any kind of blue, but lost. She couldn't seem to choose it, just as she couldn't seem to fully choose him. She knew she was trying his patience, but how could she explain something she didn't even understand?

She wanted to tell Delta how it had been. Fingers still around her wrist, she could only say, "I need it. I need all of what I am."

Except for the moth wings that homed in and trembled on the lightbulb's yellow curve, the room was still. And then Delta pulled away and tightened her pocketed hands into fists. "You see," she answered, "there isn't much I know." Tears filled her eyes and she felt as if she had failed her sister, once again. "We weren't a family that talked about what was gone." She looked at Sunday, apologizing silently for every time she had come up short.

"You know a hell of a lot more than I do," Sunday answered. "You had him for five years, so you've got your memory, for one thing. And by the time I came along, everyone had decided to just keep quiet about his leaving and everything else that had to do with him. I don't even know the smallest things about him, like whether he wore cologne . . . what he liked to eat . . . how he moved his hands. You and I scarcely even talked about him. Maybe everyone was protecting me, but in the end, I was left with my imagination, and a gaping hole."

She leaned into the circle of light. "Delta, this didn't only happen to you; it's both of ours. I know you can't give me what you haven't got, but let's remember together. Tell me, anyway, what little bit you know."

Delta paused. At least she was sure what the beginning was, for it came to her all the time, despite her resistance, as if occupying its own tier of the recessed past. She placed her palms flat on the table.

"Shoes," she said. "What I remember most is that pair of shoes."

Delta could see them. From the witnessing or the telling, or both, they were there, worn through brown to gray and dirty at the squared-off tips from work and daily travel. Laces tucked inside. Heels run-down and placed neatly side by side.

"Yes," Sunday responded. "I heard about the shoes. It's practically the only concrete thing about his disappearance that I do remember hearing. Describe them for me, so that I can see them, too."

She did describe their run-down heels, one eroded to a sharper slant than the other, and they both savored that clue to his walk, imagining him moving along, favoring one leg. She told about the places where the dark brown, dusty leather was strained and bunion-cracked on the sides. The twisted laces and elongated tongues. The mud-encrusted toes. And then they wondered what had happened to them, and Delta said, "Maybe Mama threw them out."

As Delta stared out the back window, seeming to fade farther and farther away, it occurred to Sunday that they might not be able to begin with Mercury's disappearance, which had never, in all their years of growing up, been discussed. Would they have to start to remember him as a person, to make him real, first? "You know," she said, "I wonder what Mama did with the rest of his stuff. There must be something, up in the attic, maybe. Something of him she kept."

"Well, I never heard anyone talk about his belongings, and I can't even recollect what all he had."

"But . . . but you must have kept something of him, then, if not a possession then a memory, some little thing he liked or used to do?"

Delta thought for a while, her hands in motion, turning and tipping the edge of her coffee cup and lighter. What came to her suddenly, despite attempts at forgetting, were his restless and uneven footsteps as he paced the upstairs hallway late at night, reaching one loose and groaning floorboard again and again. She willed away the sound and recounted other things.

"I know. He had a beautiful gray fedora that he always wore when he left the house. Sometimes he would take it off and let me feel the soft, pressed felt and the raised lines in its wide, grosgrain ribbon band, where a couple of feathers were tucked before the hat broke out in a cold-blooded brim. I think he felt really fly in that hat, even if he was just going to the plant. I'm sure Grandpa thought that was ridiculous, but he loved that hat, was proud of it, and when he came home he brushed it and placed it just so on the closet shelf . . . I can see him come through the door and do just that . . . but the clearest thing is me looking up at it, from my little-girl height, as it rested, tilted on his head, surrounding his frowning face with a dark oval that blocked out everything else."

After a pause, she went on. "I remember him playing cards at the dining room table, by himself. He liked to listen to the news while he played, and I can see those cards being turned over, building and shrinking and building in overlapping columns, and then his sudden curse and a hand scooping the mass of them together and cracking the edge on the table, evening them up, before starting again. I was entranced by the ceremony of it, and the mirrored, noble pictures on the cards, the bright red and black and the faces turned, secretively, to the side, as if they knew things they would never tell. But I was afraid of the curse and the sound of them hitting the table, and even more afraid to ask if I could play."

She spoke faster and faster. "And you know what else, Sunday? He used to bring a whole bagful of Mary Jane candies when he got home late. We both loved the thick, chewy molasses taste, and he would take one out and hide it in one hand, and ask me to guess which one. Whichever one I chose, he gave it to me, and we both laughed as we ate them together.

"I hadn't thought of that in a long time. It's small, but it's a good thing, isn't it?

"Mostly . . . he seemed ill at ease with me, like he didn't quite know how to relate to a child or a girl child, anyway. Those Mary Janes were something we shared."

Sunday looked at her expectantly, pushing for more. "So what else?"

Delta continued, "He liked fine things. Champagne taste and beer money, Grandpa used to say. And Nana told me how he bought that belt buckle, which he had engraved, along with a pair of inlaid silver cuff links, and a shirt to go with it, and Grandpa chided him with the uselessness of that. 'French cuffs,' he would say, and suck his teeth. It had turned into a big fight, because Nana had defended him, unable to bear the way he got on Mercury at the slightest provocation, telling Grandpa 'a body's got to have a little something nice, just for himself.'

"Grandpa didn't budge, I guess, even though he had his own weaknesses. He sure loved getting all decked out for Mason meetings, and his ring was so important to him that he made Nana promise to bury him in it. Being a Thirty-second-Degree Mason, the secret rites, the ring, all of that was major, along with the gold pocket watch that he cherished so. But in Mercury, he just couldn't tolerate it. Nana said Grandpa thought a person had to work their way up, to pay their dues before they got nice possessions and respect, and that attitude seemed to make Mercury even more withdrawn. Nana said he had one pair of really good shoes that he changed into after he got home and showered, and they were impractical for the life he led. Thin soles and fine leather . . . and she thought he would change into them to try and mark off the separate parts of his life. It was as if he was saying: This isn't all I am. I am also a man who appreciates the distinctions between things."

Sunday wondered at Delta keeping such details to herself for all those years, and at the slight smile in her eyes as she told them, as if they made her proud. She knew plenty of people like that, who found certain indulgences necessary, whatever their means. As she had studied the belt buckle over the past weeks, she had been struck by its extravagance, and she knew she had that taste for special things in her, too. Reed was forever reminding her of the time she had decided to have a pair of antique fountain pens repaired, when they'd scarcely been able to put together rent money.

Delta went on, "He would shower as soon as he got home and put on that shirt and those shoes and take a walk around town before dinner. The ones he left by the river weren't those; they were his other pair."

"You mean that when he left, he went wherever it was he went barefoot?"

"Well . . . I guess he did."

"I wonder what he did about that?" Sunday pressed. "I mean, how long could he have crossed fields and roads without shoes? I wonder if he stole some or what. Are you sure he didn't take those good shoes, too?"

"Nana said he left the good ones home, of that I'm sure. But the hat, the hat went with him. It was never found."

"The fedora?"

"That's right." She frowned in concentration and then went on, "You know, Nana would sometimes talk to me about him, as if she was trying to give me something of him to hold, and I often wondered if it was her own imagination talking, like she was forming an outlook that she could pass on to me. I remember those times by her gentle voice and her clove smell.

"She told me he had worked delivering papers and groceries and whatever else he could manage, from the time he was nine or ten, and then he had landed that job at the paper mill his junior year, most likely with Grandpa's help. At first he worked part-time, and then, after graduating, he had a regular shift. They still had segregated bathrooms, by unstated policy, though, and the black men used to have to warm their lunches on the radiators outside the makeshift 'colored' washroom, which wasn't much more than a closet with one toilet for the dozens of men, and that had filled Mercury with rage. She said he was a prideful man, who liked words. He read the dictionary sometimes and he liked to work crosswords during his breaks at the plant . . . and, what else . . . I know, he used to say all the time that his white supervisor didn't even know the word 'quandary.' It used to burn him, Nana said, and he would repeat it over and over again, 'Quandary,' and shake his head, as if it summed up everything about the unfairness of the world.

"Nana said he used to walk the river early in the morning, a big branch of oak like a staff in his hand. Looked like he was pretending to be someone in an adventure story, striking out for new ground."

Sunday asked, "But what was he thinking about while he walked? And on his last day here, did he pass the corner store and the little triangular park? Did he nod hello, and good-bye, as it turned out, to those he knew, and stop to chat at the barbershop, with its rippled iron grate and Mr. Odell out front, closing up?"

"I wonder. Maybe he saw that lilac tree downtown as you round that corner near the river, and scent floated up over the curb to greet him."

Sunday thought about that. "Somehow I don't think so. Even if he passed it, he likely didn't really see it. At least for me, that tree, with its tender perfume and cones of star-shaped blooms, might just make me able to deal with things. Really seeing that tree might just make me want to live."

"Well, everyone's different, Sunday," Delta said with irritation as she lit a cigarette. "Seeing . . . seeing a tree might not make some folks want to live. Some folks who might feel unlovely could have a *harder* time going on, with lovely things like lilacs around. People . . . individuals, I mean, see different things in things. Some people might even look up and see a tree as a potential place to hang."

Sunday stared at Delta and then picked up her glasses and began to clean them again. She was taken aback by the despair and resistance in her sister's words, and at the fury with which they had rushed out. Damn, Sunday thought, focusing on getting one lens completely free of lint, you can count on family to be there for you, in the same awful way they always were. And all you have to do to inspire their antipathy is be yourself. I wonder how soon I can get a train.

"I'm sorry," Delta said to the table.

"No," Sunday responded, putting the glasses on, "I wouldn't want to deny you a chance to express a grievance. It's quite okay."

Delta sighed. "Anyhow, I overheard someone say that he left for the paper bag plant that morning, showing no more than his usual dislike for his job. He had been talking in the weeks before, though, about his new assignment of pulling the bags out of the folding machines, where they had been turned from flat sheets into rectangular sleeves, one after another, on, on, and on."

They were silent for a long time, both pondering the embalming force of mechanical routine, from which Sunday had always been escaping and about which Delta knew so much.

Sunday pointed at the locket and finally asked, "How did it get here? When did it come?"

Delta went to the hallway and returned with the shoe box Sunday recognized as the family photo archive. Placing it on the table, she explained how she had been at the post office on sorting detail when it arrived in a small padded envelope, made out to "The Owens Girls" at Nana and Grandpa's obsolete address. She had turned it over and shaken it as she tried to think of whom she knew in Clare County, all the way across the state, and after prying open the stapled end, she had reached in and pulled the contents out: the locket, a long piece of lined, yellow paper folded into a tiny square, and a store-bought sympathy card. As she read the card she heard herself shout, "He was alive," and then she looked around and realized, from the uninterrupted flow of events around her, that no sound had emerged from her mouth.

Delta lifted the gray cardboard top of the shoe box, its edges worn soft, its corners split, and removed the brown padded envelope that held the note and card.

"Well," she said, and then cursed herself silently: There you go again, with that pathetic floundering. Unable to find the words to go on, she placed her fingertips on the envelope and slid it across the table.

Sunday began to sweat as she opened the card from the stranger. The words seemed to wave across the page until she placed it on the table and anchored it with both of her hands, recalling the sight of her thumbprints on Delta's note. She finished reading, put it back in the envelope, and got up for more coffee, her cup rattling against the saucer in her unsteady hold. She would have to do this in two stages, she realized, and she was not yet ready to confront her one and only message from a man who had been dead her entire life. Reaching out to touch the kettle without a pot holder, she felt nothing at first, and then a sharp white heat pierced her numbness and she jerked her hand away. Instead of running cold water on her fingers, she took solace in waking to the throbbing burn.

The card, whose printed message read "With the Deepest Sympathy" in embossed silver script, had a handwritten message inside. It said,

> *Your father he asked me to send this along. He was brother to me these last years. And he was sorry.*
>
> *Sincerely, Clement Woods*

She came back to the table and picked up the folded yellow paper, smelling the chemicals in it and detecting the minuscule fibers within its smooth surface. Aware, suddenly, of the fingers that held the paper, she noticed the dryness of their skin, the paint deep in the cuticles, and the scars the fingers bore. She could hear her heart beating, the air moving through her lungs, and the thunder of the paper unfolding as it grew from a two-inch square to full size.

When she got the creased paper open she found the same leaning, elongated scrawl she had studied on the back of the snapshot she had found. Five words: "I remembered and I paid."

Questions erupted in Sunday's chest, and with them a lightning flash of outrage.

Remembered, remembered and paid? she said to herself. *And that's your offering to me who never even knew you never even saw you and I hope you did pay in fact I'm counting on it and what does that mean anyway that you paid and what does it mean that you were brother and never forgot and were sorry yes sorry you surely were and does it mean you married again and had another family you did not feel the need to leave?*

It was too little, and far too much.

She wanted to know if he had recalled the 704 of Nana's address, and whether he had ever phoned their number and hung up when someone answered, or let his imagination run wild as he let it ring. Whether he had taken anything besides the locket that he had kept all those years, and wondered, wondered, what his fatherless children had grown up into, how they had turned out, if she looked anything like him? Delta, he had a chance at remembering, but what about her? The baby who was not yet born? What about her?

She heard tearing paper and before she understood what she had done, she had ripped the note in half and Delta was crying, "No!" and snatching it from her, running to the hall closet for Scotch tape. There she was again, Delta thought in panic and rage: Sunday, taking everything for her own.

"I'm . . . I'm sorry . . . I didn't realize . . ." Sunday stammered as she stood holding the envelope, aware that once again, she had just made Delta the victim, and had given her something else to hold against her.

Delta leaned over the table, carefully matching up and rejoining the halves of paper, while Sunday tried to find different, more meaningful words than "sorry" to express her regret.

"Do you want me to fix it?" she ventured, reaching out to touch her sister's hand.

"I think I'm capable of doing it," Delta replied as she pulled away.

"I didn't mean . . ."

"Oh damn, I almost had it lined up. Why don't you make some coffee or do something useful?"

Okay, I feel really shitty, Sunday thought as she looked at the paper, bisected with a shiny, Scotch-tape scar, and while I'm at it I'd like to apologize for every wrong I've ever done to you. She knew she had acted impulsively, "before thinking," as Dolora had always told her was her biggest flaw. And selfishly.

Delta smoothed the paper and added tape to the back to reinforce the mend, while Sunday, returning to the padded envelope's postmark in the heavy silence, considered whether she might be able to cope with finding Clement Woods.

They both jumped at the teakettle's shriek. "I figure," Sunday said, after rushing to turn it off, "Mama must have been puzzled by him taking that one thing. Lord knows she had a whole story about that locket that was very important to her."

What had his selection of that one possession meant? they pondered. Had it crushed her and comforted her both, that he had left behind the ring, which had stood for a promise that bound, keeping instead the smooth, gold disk that held a timeless memory of the girl she had been, before the demands of life began. Was it a talisman he had selected for his afterlife, rejecting commitment and choosing love?

While they considered Dolora's feelings about the locket, Sunday reached into the shoe box and started spreading the contents out on the kitchen table. When she came to a photo of her own art school graduation, she stopped. There they all were: she in her cap and gown, waving her diploma in the air; Delta, matronly at twenty-seven, hands folded and pageboy intact; Nana dressed in a navy suit and hat and gloves, head held high; and five of the bread-making ladies from church surrounding them, dignified and proud. The Bread Ladies had arrived on commencement morning by train and returned that same night, trusting neither the cleanliness nor the hospitality of white, city hotels.

There was a picture of Dolora's younger brother, Wilborn, who had gone to the East Coast after college and married Anna, from a prominent black family, who loved to say their people were never slaves. At each family death, she and Wilborn had flown in the morning of the funeral and left that night, only visiting once that Sunday could remember for longer than that. "I know he's embarrassed by me," Delta had overheard Dolora declare tearfully to Nana one night.

Sunday and Delta remembered enduring holiday phone calls placed by Wilborn and his family to Nana and Grandpa, following the arrival of extravagant checks. Everyone was forced to take a turn on the line, composing pleasant summaries of school and health and prosperity. "We're having a really good quarter," Wilborn would always begin, and then he would tell about the earnings of his latest sales line and the gifts he had given that year. Dolora was always reduced to icy withdrawal by what she called Wilborn's "all-out bragging" and Anna's "digs." "Isn't family great?" Sunday and Delta used to say, after hanging up.

Wilborn and Anna sent a yearly form letter detailing family accomplishments, and an annual Christmas photo taken in front of their hearth, in which they wore matching holiday outfits, and even the dog had on a red and green sweater. Sunday found many of these in the box and arranged them chronologically on the counter to observe the changes the years had wrought. She found that although the children grew taller and their parents' faces and bodies aged, the photos were amazingly uniform. They showed the same poses and expressions, the same dark hair, and only slight variations on the outfit theme. And then for three years in a row, they presented forced smiles and hints of discord. Wilborn and Anna had moved apart, to the sides of the fireplace instead of its middle. Her arms were folded tightly in a posture of defense, and she looked tired, unamused with her part. Aha, Sunday thought, there was trouble in paradise. What was it, Wilborn, an affair, unbearably average children, declining revenue? Yet after those three pictures, they resumed their presentation of triumphant harmony. The pictures stopped the year before Nana's death.

Beneath those holiday photos, in the shoe box, was a collection of picture postcards that Nana's cousin, Boykin, had sent from all over the country. They remembered how he had come through town as a traveling salesman, bringing the jokes and tall tales he had picked up on the road, jigsaw puzzles and hand mirrors and folding fans with silky red tassels. They had loved it when he showed up, unannounced, spreading mischief and laughter.

They put Boykin's cards aside and took a brown and white photograph of their grandfather from the box. He had died of a heart attack when she was only four, so that most of what Sunday knew was what she had heard. Delta picked up the photo and noticed right away how it had captured his unyielding, unforgiving gaze, and the resolution and pride in the set of his jaw.

"He was a reserved kind of man," Delta said, "and he took everything he did seriously, never missing a Masons' event and revealing nothing, even to Nana, about those sacrosanct meetings or the lodge. He wore a stiff collar and a coat and tie to work at the store, and kept it on even at home while he sat in his easy chair and read the paper as Nana cooked their evening meal. I always wanted to be in the kitchen with her, and I think he scared me. He seemed to need adulthood from me, when I was just a little girl."

She went on to say that his most unforgettable habit was directing an inventory of questions to Nana or Dolora, about the way some chore had been performed. And after the inquisition, during which his respondent had grown more and more vexed, he would demand with quiet force, "Since we now understand each other, tell me. Tell me that you love me now."

That feeling behind "Tell me that you love me" was what Sunday remembered about him. She felt uncomfortable just thinking about it, and she still responded to compelled affection with flight.

"He wanted things to be done in a certain manner," Delta said, "the way he had seen those he called 'important white folks' do them at various points in his life." She told how Grandpa had also been religious about "upholding the race." Although he was a man of few words, one topic he went on at great length about was "the betterment of the Negro." He had worked since he was seven, first farming soybeans and wheat with his family and then, anywhere he could earn something extra. For many years he had had two or three jobs, and he had always taken on something extra, like picking up people's clothes for the white cleaners downtown or delivering groceries. His experience working for a fancy country club, during the one year of college for which he had managed to pay, left him bitter at white folks and determined to emulate them, too.

He took pride in knowing that he was one of the most hardworking and prosperous men in Salt County, and he had a corner drugstore and several pieces of property to show for it. He always wore a suit to work behind the counter at his store, and he felt his people had to show both white folks, and themselves, that Negroes knew how to do right, that they were capable and responsible. And what disturbed him about Mercury Owens were his inklings that he had neither tenacity nor rectitude.

Delta remembered him checking with her to see that she had done her homework. "Always follow through, child," he had told her, stabbing at the air with his forefinger. "Always follow through."

Delta remembered being perplexed by the difference between Nana and him. In contrast to his distant formality, she was warm and fluid, but one piece of common ground Delta had been able to discern was the church, where he was an alderman and Nana was forever organizing some activity, baking for benefits, and singing in the choir. The other quality they shared was a kind of dignity, expressed in different ways.

"Did you ever hear anything about how he and Nana got together?" Delta asked. "Because I don't believe I did. I don't even know what year they married, or exactly how old they were at the time. Well, I have to think about who else would know, about their getting together, I mean. Opus Green knows, if anyone does."

There were no pictures of Mercury's family in the shoe box, but Delta knew that according to Nana, after his father had been killed in a sawmill accident, when he was three, his mother had tried for a year to feed and clothe them. She told Sunday what she knew about how they had often gone hungry, and how his mother was sick with consumption. She had been forced to leave him with her sister, Edna, who thought it best to try to raise him as her own and to speak of his mother as little as possible. He had been a handful growing up, restless and inattentive in school, a loner who had trouble making friends, and his mother died soon after his aunt Edna took him in.

Delta had seen Edna regularly at church. She had brought them birthday and Christmas gifts, but had never stayed long at the house and had never been there for a holiday meal. Delta recalled Nana commenting that Edna and Mercury seemed to make each other so defensive and ill at ease that her visits were dreaded by everyone, and then, after his disappearance, she rarely came. She had brought food for Dolora and sat with the children several times right afterward, and then she had faded from their lives, moving, a year or so later, to another town.

Sunday made a mental note to see what she could do about contacting Edna, or any of her family who might still be alive.

They put aside the photo of Grandpa and uncovered the last things in the box: two pictures of Mercury, one a yearbook photo and one a riverside snapshot with Dolora, that they had both memorized. They had retrieved the meager bequest from Dolora's closet often when they were growing up, determined to read his expression and posture, to know him through his dimpled chin and folded hands. "Who are you?" they had both puzzled, inspecting the figure in the yearbook pose and the youth at the riverside. "Who are you and how are you mine?" Sunday remembered looking at the second snapshot and imagining what everyday essentials and treasured possessions he had carried in his bulging pockets.

Studying the snapshot with a magnifying glass, Delta had speculated on what things had been withheld and professed. She noticed how their shoulders barely touched and the attention her mother's titled head revealed, and imagined the charged aftermath or prospect of touch on their impatient, adolescent skin. Surely they were dreaming, she thought, of the life they would make together, of the home and family they would one day have. Or had he just told her about some aspect of her beauty, "You have the longest lashes I have ever seen," or "Your waist is perfect for my hand"? Maybe they had laughed a private laugh.

They both imagined the people their parents had, at that moment, been. And then, as there was nothing else for the shoe box to yield up to them, Sunday went to her coat and took out the mosaic coaster, its tiles set within a brass frame. "Oh, that one I remember," Delta said. "In fact, I can picture her making it, for the church sale, and then deciding she didn't want to part with it, because she had gotten the colors just right, and almost hidden in the pattern was a scarab she just couldn't bear to let go."

As she handed Mercury's monogrammed belt buckle to her sister, Sunday thought she saw Delta's face stiffen with resentment while she smoothed her eyebrows, right then left. "So you had the buckle," she whispered. "He wore it only on special occasions, not to work, and he always placed it in a dish on his dresser, where I was told never to go. It was off-limits, you see, to my touch. He used to polish it with a piece of flannel, I remember that."

Sunday explained hurriedly that she had forgotten packing the coaster and the buckle when she left for college, only to find them before she came home.

She didn't tell how, halfway through that night when she hadn't been able to sleep or work, she had opened her taped-up box, cutting the packing tape with her matte knife to retrieve the note. Before she got to it, she read every other piece of correspondence she had saved, arranging Nana's letters and Delta's greeting cards by date, combing through her other boxes for the things she had brought with her from Salt County. Unsure of what she was seeking, but driven, she had unearthed her high school yearbook; her drawing contest awards from elementary school; her first set of markers, now shrunken and dried; and the ticket stub from the first train she had taken to Chicago. Amid the other contents of the box, she had found the coaster and the buckle, which as a child, she had liked to use for bouncing moonlight at the window, pretending it was a signal to contact airplanes and helicopters as they passed high above Salt County.

"Well," Delta said, before she could stop herself, "I'm surprised you found anything from here worth keeping." She placed the photo on the table and stood up to clear the plates. It was quieter than ever, and Sunday's bitterness at her sister's long-standing martyrdom flared. Two small mementos seemed little enough to take, when Delta had every other possession that had been left them right there with her. But nothing between them was free of the past, and Sunday guessed that the paucity of things selected, as well as the taking, itself, had provoked her sister.

She looked at the things on the table, stung silent by Delta's comment, and disappointed, too, that she hadn't been more excited about the items she had found. It made her even more reticent to reveal the bigger yearnings she had in mind, for Delta would surely think her maniacal for deciding to track down the man Mercury Owens had become.

For her part, Delta couldn't believe how sharp her own tongue sometimes got. This was no way to begin a reunion, she thought, and yet Sunday just seemed to get under her skin like no one else. She didn't understand where it came from, when she hadn't even been aware that all that ugly history was still so alive. She suggested that they put the pictures and the shoe box aside and they made lunch, relieved to have a concrete task.

To the background of the clock's steady meter, they made and ate their sandwiches, saying little except to comment on the train ride and the condition of the neighborhood. And then, settling back at the table and taking out a cigarette, Delta told the detail, overheard and never shared, which had caused her untold pain: In the laces of one shoe, Mercury Owens had tied his wedding band.

Once she had added that piece of information, the surviving image of his departure became, for both of them, those side-by-side work shoes. Rundown unevenly at the heels and holding a slim ring of gold.

FROM **October Suite**

BY MAXINE CLAIR

The doctor had already told them that it would be days before he could say one way or the other. To October this meant that he didn't want to tell them. And so she said that they should keep a vigil. Twenty-four hours every day, one of them should be right at Aunt Frances's side. Panic took hold of October every time she pictured Auntie wandering in the Valley of the Shadow. She looked at her—pale against the white sheets, slack and doughy—and prayed. Here it was now, Bible wisdom rolling off her own tongue and none of it went anywhere. "God is love." If this was true, how could God let things like this happen? "Thy will be done." Surely suffering wasn't it. "For everything there is a season, a time for every purpose under heaven." Didn't October already have her season of grief, or was this just a continuation? But she prayed anyway.

Vigil it was. For three days they all took turns watching Aunt Frances breathe, talking to her absent eyes when they were open, catnapping when she slept. Visitors couldn't stop coming—from the church, the paper mill, the hospital, the neighborhood. Some of Aunt Frances's bywords being proven. Reaping the kindnesses she had sown. And there were all the women from the Negro Ladies' League, too—a loosely gathered group that collected food and clothing for the poor. October recognized some of their faces.

The League had always left a sour taste in October's mouth, because her aunties had pushed it so hard. When she and Vergie were girls, the biggest notable event of the year had been the weeklong annual celebration for the Children's Home, and the Negro Ladies' League was always front and center. A season didn't end that hadn't seen those ladies—led by Frances, with Maude Cooper and their nieces—tramping around the Hopewell burial mounds or a Tecumseh site with a ragtag flock of orphans.

Although Aunt Frances had never understood why, October had hated the orphans, and she suspected that Vergie had hated them, too. It made sense, when she thought about it. Vergie and October were orphans, too. But strange ones. Different. They knew it and the orphans knew it. Aunt Frances and Aunt Maude alone had had it in their heads that doing things with the orphans could somehow be good for their two girls. Auntie never let them forget that the two of them were better off because somebody wanted them. And as October sat watching Auntie breathe, she conceded that Auntie had been right.

Toward the end of October's shift on the third day, Aunt Frances opened her eyes again and made a humming noise. Nothing in particular. October took her hand and told her, "Try to rest, Auntie. The doctor says you need to have rest and quiet."

Again Auntie hummed, but this time with an edge to it. Gently, as if she were lifting a wilting flower, October lifted Auntie's head and held a glass of water to her lips. Not so good. Auntie moaned, "Um-umm," meaning no, tried to work her mouth, tried to form some impossible word. Her eyes fixed on the bowl of crushed ice on the nightstand.

"Oh," October said. She took a tiny chip of ice from the bowl and spooned it into Auntie's mouth. Then dabbed her lips with a tissue.

She sat in her chair, and Aunt Frances lay silent but with eyes trying to say it all.

"Remember the chickenpox?" October said. "How you rubbed my blisters with ice?"

With the slightest pressure, Aunt Frances pressed her fingers into October's hand. Yes, she did remember.

"You don't have to stay awake," October said. "It's all right to go back to sleep. I'm not going anywhere."

She heard herself say it. Aunt Frances might not want to close her eyes for fear *she* was going somewhere.

But her eyes soon drooped close again, her grip fell, and October found herself breathing with her aunt's shallow rhythm.

Tallies. Wins. Losses. Aunt Frances had been good to her, period. And she owed her. The bad things always come up at the worst times. October was bound to remember the worst storm that raged between them, when she was seventeen and hell-bent on changing her name. Those years before, and even right then in the hospital room, she believed it was one of the most important things she had ever done. But at seventeen she had been righteous with a capital R. Left no room for Auntie to bless or curse.

Auntie had challenged her, October had prevailed. But the arguments had left her with one regret. There at the bedside, looking down on the fading beacon of her early life, October remembered standing at their front doorway once, with her shortie coat over her arm, big as day. And Aunt Frances saying something final, like "Girl, if you go out that door, I'll make you sorry you were ever born." And October had spewed a perfect cruelty about spinsters—an easy target: Something along the lines of Aunt Frances and Aunt Maude having no life until she and Vergie had come to live with them, and how they had not wanted *them* to have a life either.

What really bothered October that afternoon at the hospital was her remembrance of Aunt Frances's face when—with purest venom—October had proceeded to take away any hold Aunt Frances might have thought she had.

"You're not our mother," she had told her aunt. "You could never be *my* mother. You didn't sign anything legal to keep us, and I don't have to mind somebody who's just a relative."

And she had fairly pranced out the door.

And since that first incident of regret, she had done much worse—brought untold worries and hurts to her auntie's door.

That day at the hospital she thought back and saw her life as if it were a play that had started with one single event and then gotten blown every which way by the whims of God and men. That day at the hospital, she fully realized that life as she knew it had started with the death of Carrie. And wasn't that the way grief worked—throwing you back to what caused what, and who was to blame, and how much you had lost?

Over all the years that she had let the event begin to flood her mind and quickly evaporate, October had come up with a hundred ways to describe it. The word "murder" had never fit. The drama of "tragic death" took away the impact. "Father's crime"—too detached. "Family's shame"—too vague. "A man's insanity"—yes. "A woman's nightmare"—even closer. But nothing ever fit the way "The Killing" fit. It brought her down to the nitty-gritty, brought home just what their father had brought down on their heads.

October had been five years old—just five—a little girl with no idea that there were layers to what was happening. Over the years she had scribbled things, words on bits of paper, trying to get it right: a wall of water crashing against two new sapling trees. A gyre of wind sucking air into its spin and dipping down to touch the great and small thing that had been their lives. A natural disaster. How terrible it must have been for children—this was how she had always felt any emotion around it: as a secondhand sympathy for the children she and Vergie had been. Whenever she called herself grieving, it had been for them as they had been then, two young girls.

It didn't seem logical, but for October the public *fact* of the killing seemed to affect her life more than the private pain of losing her two parents did. Having to be *his* daughter—the daughter of a man who killed some-body. Having to carry that name and that label meant shame on you. Are you an evil person, too? And she and Vergie had grown up without so much as a second cousin to show them what a man was. Fascination comes from that. Leads to all kinds of craziness.

Franklin Brown had been the source of everything that had been wrong in their lives. But October couldn't say that she actually *hated* him. "Hate" didn't touch all the things she felt about him. Maybe disgust began to de-scribe her feelings. And sadness, too, over the terror that Carrie must have gone through. Sadness over Carrie's heart that must have been broken at the thought of dying. October's sympathy, though, always gave way to the wish that Franklin Brown had somehow come to realize to the nth degree what he had done, and then that he had been forced to live with it until his last breath.

Some of her vengeful wishes came from being tainted by someone else's crime. At nine, and still named Lillian, she was a gangly little girl with thick ropes of plaited hair. The white freckle that was supposed to have turned into a mole had become a dime-spot blemish on her cheek.

Vergie, on the other hand, had become a thirteen-year-old whose rounded heft refused to be disguised as ordinary ripening. For Vergie, the burden of child-witness to The Killing had worked itself out in pounds, or so they had all thought—she was older, she had suffered more deeply than her little sister, who had been too young to understand.

They *were* sisters, though. Where there are sisters, the flame of contention smolders, and difference is the very air it craves. They were way past the need for being baby-sat, way past the desire to nose around the landscape of their aunties' rooms. With the way she kept her closet and the files of papers in the cedar chest under that high bed of hers, Aunt Frances had already become the General, law and order.

They knew every piece of paper in the chest by heart. Early school drawings, birth certificates, baptism certificates, attendance certificates, bank papers—all that. And whenever they wanted, they could touch the small white Bible with the crumbly clipping, the *Herald* obituary that announced Carrie's death. Inside the back cover of the Bible, the black ink and back-slanted scrawl of "Carrie Cooper" had faded to brown.

The closet, too, they knew: Starched white uniforms hung like guards over the few other dresses Aunt Frances owned; paired white duty shoes toed a straight line. The bureau drawers gave up old-style white cotton stockings on one side and brown cotton stockings—hideous, October always thought—on the other. And, like a monument to an old dream, a solitary bottle of toilet water—precious in cut glass—on her bureau.

Aunt Maude's space had nothing like order. Lounging, rummaging seemed fine in her room. October remembered how Aunt Maude's clothes—drab to plain—had always been draped in layers over the chair in the corner and piled on her bedpost. She and Vergie always found a coffee cup sitting with the lotion and toilet water and combs and brushes on top of her bureau. Snips of newspaper and scribbled lists made a raggedy fringe around her mirror. And candy. Always a tin full of peppermint, butterscotch, lemon drops on her closet shelf, under her one black hat.

At nine and thirteen, October and Vergie had not outgrown their habit of after-school sweets. School-weary and famished, they had just finished helping Mrs. Hopp make rag rugs for the Children's Home one day and raced through the front door straight up to Aunt Maude's closet. They sat on Aunt Maude's bed, Vergie with the nice candy tin on her lap, and they raked through hard candy for best and next best.

October liked butterscotch, and there was one, but Vergie was faster. She popped it into her mouth before October could say *mine*. That gave them a way to spend the next hour. They could just bicker until October decided that nothing at all was better than settling for the sour lemon drops, which were all that was left.

Later, while they piddled with homework, Vergie went down to the kitchen and came back with a crisp green apple, cut supposedly in half, and a little pile of salt on a piece of waxed paper to sprinkle on the apple. She placed the smaller half—a peace offering nonetheless—on October's bed. "That's yours," she said.

October ignored it. Vergie was hungry, but she dipped-and-bit, dipped-and-bit slowly, until hers was all gone. She kept eyeing the half on October's bed, piddled and glared for a while.

"You know, apples start rotting as soon as the air hits them," Vergie said. "You'd better eat yours before it turns brown." To which October answered, "Let it rot—I don't want it." She didn't want apple, she wanted butterscotch.

Vergie wanted apple. "Okay, then," she said. "Starve if you want to." And she snatched up the other half and chomped off a huge bite.

What happened next had to do with the fact that each year, the Negro Ladies' League had sponsored an annual Children's Home trip, which *The Call*—the only national Negro newspaper—dubbed a "Noteworthy Excursion," to the zoo in Columbus. And each year until October and Vergie were too far into their teens, they were forced to "set an example" by sitting like bumps on a log with the orphans on the rented bus, eating shelled and salted peanuts.

There had been this boy, Clyde, a pipsqueak, but Vergie liked him, orphan or not. She had written his name on page 100 of all her books. And there had been this girl, Lila, fearless and feared. Lila was Vergie's age and had run away several times. "Seen the world"—undoubtedly all of downtown Chillicothe and the river. Wore makeup and smoked cigarettes, mostly butts.

During the zoo outing the year she was thirteen, Vergie had made eyes enough at the Clyde boy to convince him that she would walk over a hundred miles of broken glass barefooted if he would smile her way. With the rest of the orphans, Vergie and October had spent the day swatting flies, licking their shaved ice, looking at the same old animals, all of whom had silly names like Tiny the Elephant, and Gertie, the Hippopotamus. On the bus back to the Home that afternoon, Clyde stuck a wad of gum to the back of Vergie's seat. On a piece of paper he scribbled "Gertie" and stuck the paper to the gum. Hearing all the giggles, Vergie turned around to see what else but Clyde, smiling at her. As the moment hung and trembled, Vergie smiled back. And then the moment hit and shattered. Vergie saw the paper. The orphan runaway Lila smacked Clyde with her fist. Too late.

"Devastated" didn't come close. For three days Aunt Frances and Aunt Maude had cooked and spread banquets for breakfast, lunch, and dinner, and Vergie had gagged and cried through them all. Aunt Frances had cursed the ground stupid Clyde walked on, telling Vergie that the boy was a heathen, an orphan with no home training. And Vergie cried into another day. They shook their heads, wrung their hands. Vergie cried into a second night. Over the third day, October had had the good idea that Vergie might be calmer if she had a new skirt to wear, a skirt like the ones Lila wore. October had just the right length of material, too; Aunt Frances had been saving it for a dress. That very day, Aunt Maude and Aunt Frances and October had pieced it together, and finally Vergie's tears dried up.

And so when Vergie gobbled up October's half of the apple that day a few months later, it was the strategic windfall that can bless all warring children. It would be years before October was able to understand how anger works. Why, in her meanest, cold-blooded fury, she had spat out "Gertie!" in Vergie's face.

Right away, though, October could see that she had hit her mark. Vergie's face began to break. But this time Vergie pulled herself together fast.

She arranged her face, lifted her chin ever so slightly, leveled her eyes at October, and said, "I'd rather be Gertie than a spotted *Lillian* any day."

The words weren't infected with any fatal poison. Some people had extra fingers, some had crossed eyes, some had had polio and would be crippled forever. October's white spot would turn brown again someday. She was fine—her feelings weren't hurt.

Oh, but Vergie had her. With lips all curled, now, Vergie had repeated, "I wouldn't be caught dead with that name." And when she saw that October still did not catch on, Vergie blurted, "Stupid. You're so stupid you don't even know where your sorry name came from."

October's face must have remained blank. She had never thought about it, really. Didn't get the point.

Hand-on-her-hip, Vergie had rained it down. "I'm named after Grandma Vergie Cooper," she said. And then the damning question: "Who do you think you're named after?"

Again, what did October know?

"Your *father's* people," Vergie said, quivering with the pleasure of having it out. "Poppa's sister who raised him. Her name was *Lillian.*"

Dumbfounded, October called up reason to her defense. "You're a lie," she said. She threatened to tell Auntie. Any loose reference to Franklin Brown—his person or possible kin, his crime or punishment—any little remember-that-time about their early lives in Cleveland, their suspicions, old wishes, or nightmares had always brought a swift and unmitigated bawling-out from Auntie and Aunt Maude, too. October was sure that Vergie had made it up.

And then Vergie had spilled out unbelievable details. "His mother died and his big sister raised him and her name was Lillian. Ask Auntie. They used to live in Tennessee."

"Liar," October said, folding fast.

Vergie got louder. "Ask Auntie. She knows. Everybody knows. That's where your spot came from. No-good crooks and slutty women—that's who you are."

Hands now covering her ears, October couldn't listen. How many times had her aunts told her that they were decent girls, that they had come from good people? How many times had they warned "their girls" away from "low-life" people who hung around the barbershop on Keane Street because "our girls" are better than that?

October threw back at Vergie, "We never even *knew* those people," trying to sound sure instead of whipped.

But Vergie was on. "Yes, we did," but there must have been some doubt because she went on with, "Even if we didn't, you still got their . . ." and she drawled, "*Lil-yan.*"

"Shut up!"

"Lil-yan," Vergie slurred. "Lil- . . . Lil-yan . . ."

October swung at her, blindly, and her fist caught the corner of Vergie's mouth. Vergie's teeth cut the inside of her lip. She bled red blood.

Shocked them both for a split second. Then Vergie ran to the bathroom and, when she saw the blood, wailed like a trapped puppy dog. October went after her, but by then Vergie would have no apologizing.

"Get out!" she screamed and locked herself in the bathroom. October stood at the bathroom door, saying "I'm sorry" to the frame, but her words were way past lost.

Things might have gone better if Aunt Frances had been the first to arrive home to straighten out sister-squabbling quickly. But Frances had had the late shift at the hospital and wouldn't be in until midnight. And so as hours passed, the incident ballooned into a crime, like night swelling from a single shadow across the bedroom floor.

Aunt Maude got off from the mill at five, and Vergie burst out of the bathroom and stumbled down the stairs, greeting her with a garbled story, plenty of tears, and a swollen lip. Aunt Maude had calmed and soothed and whimpered with her and dressed her mouth with Mercurochrome. October had sat alone in their bedroom, waiting for whatever was to come next.

Aunt Maude, her face flat, opened the door and stood looking at October for a long time, and then her eyes welled up.

"What are we going to do?" she said, as if they were all lost. She looked into the air for an answer, then closed the door.

No one ate dinner.

Somewhere in what seemed the middle of the night, October was shaken awake, to Aunt Frances' cast-iron "Get up, Lillian, and get dressed."

She had been expecting anything. Vergie had not slept in her bed. Aunt

Maude's voice was an all-night murmur behind her door. Starkly awake, October had gotten herself up and dressed, shoes and all.

"Get your coat!" Aunt Frances yelled from downstairs and October did as she was told.

Frances Cooper—fully prepared in nurse whites and her navy-blue cape with the red lining—waited at the front door. Aunt Maude stood at the top of the stairs in her nightgown and watched as October and Aunt Frances went out into the night. October followed Auntie across the yard to the Hopps', where Mr. Hopp waited on his front porch. Cold night. Cold enough to see his breath huff.

"Okay, Miss Cooper," he said to Auntie. "If you're sure this is what you want to do, come on."

Mr. Hopp worked for the city, although his exact job was a question October could not have answered at the time. Whenever he left for work she had heard keys jangling at the hip of his coveralls. This night the keys jangled, too. Silence like the cemetery rode with her in Mr. Hopp's long, low Hudson to the downtown Chillicothe she had seldom seen at night. Corner lamps, cold and glaring, made sharp shadows against the still buildings, empty streets.

Mr. Hopp pulled up in front of city hall and sat still, looked at the building a while, then went around the block, into the alley, and stopped behind the building. Fumbled with his keys. Where were they going? October couldn't imagine what punishment lay waiting—she knew only that Aunt Frances had thought it up, and it would be pretty bad.

"Okay, let's see what might be waitin in there for this one," Mr. Hopp said. Aunt Frances got out of the car and held the back door for October.

"Come on," she said.

Long hallways waited. And echoes. Two white policemen took Mr. Hopp aside to talk, then left. Aunt Frances followed close on Mr. Hopp's heels and October followed close on hers, down another long hallway that led to an iron door. Mr. Hopp unlocked the door and they entered.

When Aunt Frances pushed her forward, October saw the cells, eight or ten, side by side. In the half-dark she could make out lumps of bodies sleeping in some of the cells. And one cell door standing open. Mr. Hopp walked over to it, motioning for her to follow. Aunt Frances nudged her.

"You want to sleep in here?" Mr. Hopp said.

October shook her head no. Up close, she could see the measly cot with no sheet, the stinky slop jar, the dirty stone floor. She wondered about the police—what would they care about a fight between her and Vergie? But she couldn't guess how far Mr. Hopp could go at the jail, and there was no way to know how far Aunt Frances's wrath would go.

A cold, stone floor at night, being locked away, having to lie on that cot and use that slop jar—would Auntie do that to her? Was she finally just an orphan?

Aunt Frances had then opened the cell door farther and nudged her inside.

"This must be where you want to end up," she said. Then she said, "This is where your poppa ended up. He died in a place just like this. He started out just like you, fighting all the time."

She stepped out of the cell and clanged the door, leaving October inside the bars.

"Franklin may have given you his sister's name," Aunt Frances said, "—that's something you can't help. But you'll not have their ways and live with us, I promise you."

Dazzling. So her name really *did* come from those people—people she knew only as too lowdown and dirty to be mentioned. And what else? Her father had been a character in a storybook, banished to never-never land. She had always thought of him as put away forever. The end. It had never occurred to her that he could die.

An aunt, someone named Lillian, the woman who had raised him? No one had ever bothered to mention this. The whole day had turned into a new life. Her blackberry skin was a given, but until that day the only other family resemblance October had ever taken into account had been the way she favored Carrie or Aunt Frances or Aunt Maude or Vergie. With one word, she had a life times two. She had hurt Vergie more than she had had intended. Just happened. And then Vergie had opened a sewer with all kinds of gullies and gutters feeding it. Such a secret. All this time everybody had known.

October, even at the age of nine, had understood then that she was someone other than herself. That she was different from Aunt Frances and Aunt Maude. Different, too, from Vergie. Unwittingly, Aunt Frances had held a mirror in front of her, and even if she couldn't yet make out what she saw, she knew this: in more ways than one, the reflection coming into focus looked like a leper.

After that night, slowly at first, then whenever it wanted to happen, then with a vengeance, the name *Lillian* had become an accusation. Vergie's way of drawling out "Lil-yan" could be an excruciating jab or a pin-stick, depending on how raw October felt at the time.

Aunt Frances and Aunt Maude would step in a little with "All right, Vergie, that's enough."

But they, too, had got in the spirit of the curse. "Lillian" was the epithet when October's attitude became the stubborn cliff their reason couldn't climb. They tiptoed, never used the name unless they were put out with her. Otherwise they started calling her "Lily" or "Lily Ann."

But she called herself October to herself. October, for the month their mother had died. October, for the lack of any other name that she could put on to say how it felt to become another, stranger person.

Over time, though, she hardened. Turned her secret into a plan. When she got to seventeen, that was it. Old enough. She learned not to flinch so, and Vergie got tired of trying to use a dull weapon. Aunt Frances and Aunt Maude got tired, too, or guilty. However it happened, at some point they all dropped "Lillian" from the list of words they could use when they were mad, and replaced it with a permanent "Lily" for all occasions. Which sure enough proved that the name had kept some evil thing alive for too long. For a time anyway, October was Lillian to the world, Lily at home, and October to anyone who would go along.

It was always with a good feeling that she remembered the long swoon of puberty. A for-real-new person, starting with her body and going on to the music of her own voice, every single nerve ending exposed in every single moment. Without telling anyone, she had fallen in love, first with the deciduous drama of autumn, the pungency of blade and leaf giving up the ghost. Fallen in love with poems, any poem, and with the sound of the flute, or a bird, or train whistle.

She had fallen in love with the boy who worked in Ford's grocery store, and because she never caught that boy's name, she had switched her love to the Reverend's son, home from Wilberforce College. Because he had never been around for long and had never noticed her, she ventured to speak to a boy in the twelfth grade who said hi to her once. He didn't need a name. They didn't need to talk.

Each night before bed, like the leper in *The Good Earth*, October had inspected every inch of her new body for white freckles. She was convinced that the brown would return, and since no other spots had appeared, she got it in her head that the sun had protected her, and spent more time outdoors.

When she had turned seventeen, old enough to give herself a new name, with two aunts who were only relatives, not parents, October found an accomplice. The Reverend's daughter, Dainty Bonner.

Dainty wore her hair twisted around a hair-rat, the way women did, in a crown hoop that she set off with jeweled combs. She smoked and had a boyfriend twenty years old. October had fed Dainty bits of the whole orphan story and the evil family she didn't want to be related to. Tortured friend. And Dainty had agreed that "Lillian" had never been a name that suited her, and that "October" stood out. And Dainty had known exactly where, in the courthouse, they had to go to do the thing right.

October had never done this before. She went to the courthouse unprepared. How could she have known about things like the proof of her birth or birth name, and how much money she would have to pay, and a failproof reason for a name change, and the six-week wait for it to be official. And so, on another not-so-brave day, she and her Dainty friend went back to the courthouse. This time she had rifled through Aunt Frances's cedar chest for papers and emptied her own secret stash for the notary's fifty cents. This time she had announced her intention to Aunt Frances, who had dared her to leave. This time, with her shortie slung across her shoulders, and her hand on the doorknob, she had disowned the only mother she had ever really known.

Under "Justification" on the form, October wrote a version of the truth. Instead of pointing to the bloodline, she wrote that Lillian was the name of the mother of the man who had killed October's own mother: No one would dare refuse her then.

Her mother had died on October 26, 1931. As she sat with Dainty on the bench outside the notary's office, a feeling came over her. She had finished something important, and something else had begun. Finally, she could hold on to autumn no matter what the season was, and have the perfect memorial to Carrie. She could have the perfect way to separate herself from her namesake forever—the perfectly unique name for a girl with a dramatic blight on the brown of her cheek, *October*.

On the fifth day after Aunt Frances had suffered the stroke, Gene brought Vergie to relieve October at the hospital. Reverend Carter had prayed his ardent prayer, and as they all stood around the bed, a nurse came in with a needle and syringe.

"We need to check her catheter," the nurse said. "You-all won't mind stepping out into the hall for a minute, would you?"

Out in the hall, October tried to sound like she knew what she was talking about and at the same time not scare Vergie.

"Vergie, I know that miracles can happen," she told her, "but remember, we have to be realistic, too."

It seemed to October that until she had entered Aunt Frances's hospital room that day, her own life had not been pinned down. As if at any moment she might be able to put her life in reverse and move into the life she wanted. Redeemable, she thought. But now she was beginning to see that Aunt Frances's death would nail things down. Up until then she had seemed to have a "real life" waiting somewhere, and one day she would wake up and be in her real life. One where Franklin Brown had not killed Carrie. Carrie was not in the cold ground. Franklin had not died in jail. She and Vergie had not been orphans. In a sense, up until then, Aunt Frances and Aunt Maude had been aunts, not parents. And in some part of her, October had always held out for the possibility of "real" parents. All of it, even the David chapter, could have been a dream, and there was time for it all to be corrected.

But now Aunt Frances would be the real mother who would be dead and buried, gone forever. Nothing could be changed. October's messed-up life would be the only one she would ever have.

Vergie said, "The doctor said that it may take a long time for her to pull through." October knew Vergie dared not think she might die.

October thought she ought to make it clear to Vergie. "And, Vergie," she told her, "it's possible that she might not be able to pull through—I mean, she might not make it. We don't know."

Fear blazed in Vergie's eyes. "How can you say that?" She stepped closer to Gene and grabbed his hand.

"I'm just saying *might*, Vergie. We have to be prepared for the worst. If there's anything you want to say to her, you shouldn't wait. That's all I'm saying."

"Darn it, October, you never look on the bright side. The doctor never said that, and he ought to know." She wiped a tear with her thumb. Gene put his arm around her, and they went back inside the room.

On October's watch the next morning, she had the sense to take her own advice. Say what needs to be said.

Auntie's eyes were closed, and October took her time forming the right words. Auntie's eyes opened and October gave her a chip of ice from a spoon. Auntie stared, and after a few minutes, October could see recognition in her eyes.

October went into how well she remembered the years, the sacrifices, the fevers soothed, the battles Auntie had mounted against the world for her and Vergie, whether they were wrong or right. As well as she could, she said how bad she felt about bringing a child into the world without a father, and giving him away, and fighting with Vergie. And still she couldn't find the words to say what needed to be said.

Auntie never relaxed her gaze.

October tried again. "There is one thing I want to tell you . . ."

Auntie's eyes burned.

". . . something I said to you once, a long time ago. And I never apologized, I never took it back. I know you know I didn't mean it, but I want to take it back now, anyway."

Auntie pressed her fingers lightly into October's palm. She could hear.

Looking into her mute face, October said, "I just want to thank you."

Auntie then made her little humming sound, but kept her eyes fixed on October's face.

"Thank you for being my mother." The tears came then, but October refused to lose the one chance to have it said. "You were a better mother than I ever gave you credit for—better than you ever knew," she said.

Auntie pressed her palm, and October knew a smile was in there.

October wasn't at the hospital that evening to see Vergie reading the Bible to Auntie, or to see the pain in her sister's eyes when Auntie had another stroke. She stood next to Vergie, though, all through the next day, as Auntie's heart marched weakly on.

It was then that I stood by and held for Frances, my sister. She never opened her eyes or pressed their palms again.

Like Trees, Walking

BY RAVI HOWARD

Those of us already gathered along the beach check the wind. With matches cupped in our hands, we watch the smoke rise into the breeze that comes off the water. The conditions have to be right. The wind has to be blowing east. Rising tide and an overcast sky. Nights like this, when conditions are right along the eastern shore of Mobile Bay, the salt water from the Gulf mixes with the fresh water from the rivers. The fish and blue crabs stop swimming then. Why it happens, I'm not exactly certain—something about the oxygen and the water temperature and the currents no longer running true—but the fish and blue crabs are stunned, traumatized. At the place where the waters meet, they just float on the surface as if they're dead.

When the tide rises in the early morning hours, the silver sides of the flounder shine as they wash up on the shore. The crabs collect in the soft sand just below the surface of the water. We wait for them here. Some gather them with scoop nets and stakes. Others just pick them up in their bare hands and carry them home in washtubs and baskets. Nights like these are called "Jubilee."

I unfold our blankets at the place we like to claim while my son wades ankle-deep in the surf. He shines his flashlight on the wet sand, looking. But it's too early. We have time. My daughter holds my hand and taps my thigh with her plastic shovel.

"Daddy, may I go to the water with Reggie?"

"For a little while. Then I want you to come back so you can take a nap before the Jubilee."

"First graders don't take naps."

"You're not a first grader until September. You know what that means? You're still a Daddy grader. Daddy graders take naps so they're awake when the tide comes in. Is that a deal?"

"Deal," she says, shaking off her flip-flops. She points to the glowing hands on her watch. "When the big hand and the little hand are on the twelve, it's your birthday. I'm gonna sing 'Happy Birthday.' *Happy Birthday to you—*"

"Make sure you stay with your brother."

"Okay. *Happy birthday to you—*" She beats time with the shovel against my leg before she runs down to the water to where her brother stands.

It's 11:45 P.M. In fifteen minutes I'll be forty. Forty is supposed to be a milestone, a "big one" as they say. A party has been planned in my honor. My wife, my kids, and my parents have been up to something. They have that obvious silence about them of people trying too hard to keep a secret. So I'm sure they've gone to a lot of trouble to get everyone together. I'll act surprised.

I'll have a good time as I always do. July means family reunions, the Fourth, fireworks and picnics. July for me means celebrating one more year, and sharing some time with my brother, Paul. I don't see him like I used to.

He was born 362 days before me. We were, as my father would sometime call us, "the damn-near twins." For three days every July, I catch up with him.

Jubilee nights only happen in the summer months, twice, maybe three times a season. Every few years one would fall somewhere between our birthdays and we would celebrate here. There was a Jubilee the night after I turned eighteen, in July 1981. Eighteen was a milestone for me, not so much because of the age, but because of all that happened. That spring I finished high school. That summer I started working full-time with my father at our funeral home before I started college that fall. That July was four months after my brother found Michael Donald's body hanging from a tree on Carlisle Street. Michael Donald was a friend of ours.

My mother saves the newspapers from our birthdays. Tomorrow's early edition will come off the press soon. In the morning she'll add it to the stacks of the *Mobile Press Register*, neatly arranged in blue wooden RC Cola crates that she keeps in the closet under the staircase, stored away from the sunlight. Next to the crates she has a small filing cabinet where she stores her important papers. There she kept the news clippings about Michael Donald, neatly trimmed and filed in order. On the manila folder, in her impeccable schoolteacher handwriting, a simple label: "Michael."

The first clip in the stack was from the evening edition of the March 8, 1981:

Local man found slain on Carlisle

Police follow leads as investigation moves forward

MOBILE—Michael Donald, 19, of Mobile was found dead shortly after 6:00 a.m. on the 1400 block of West Carlisle Street. The body of the deceased had been hanged from a tree. Police officials report that the victim had been severely beaten prior to the hanging.

Paul Deacon, 19, of Mobile, a pulp processor at International Paper, discovered the body and notified police.

The lights are on tonight at the paper mill. At the north end of the bay, the smoke stacks made their own white clouds. The mill operates three shifts a day, every day of the year, Christmas and Easter included.

Some nights the smell of the mill carries across the bay. The stench is awful. It's the sulfur. The sulfur breaks down the fibers in the wood, so the pulp is soft enough to make paper. We learned this from Mr. Lewis, our Cub Scout leader, who was a supervisor there.

In our younger days the members of the Cub Scouts Pack 211 from First A.M.E. Church, Paul and I included, followed Mr. Lewis on a tour of the mill. With goggles and hard hats, we toed a broad yellow line painted on the concrete floor. We felt through our feet the rhythm of the vibrating concrete as the large steel combines ripped the timber to shreds.

Paul was historian for Pack 211. His job was to collect pictures for our scrapbook. In the picture Paul took that day, Michael stood in the back row with the taller boys, next to Mr. Lewis. My mother held on to that photo. She keeps it with the others.

Our uniforms reeked when we left the mill. My mother made us take them off before we walked in the kitchen. While our clothes soaked in a bucket of water and ammonia, Paul stood in the middle of the kitchen, in Scout socks and drawers, recounting in dramatic fashion the motions of the combine.

"Mama, do you know why it stanks so bad?"

"*Stinks*, Paul," she said, grading a stack of composition papers on the kitchen table. "*Stanks* is not a word."

"Sulfur," he said. "It smells like the whole world farted at once."

"Paul, do you want a spanking?" she said. She wanted to laugh, though. I could tell.

"You mean a spinking?"

"Oh, so you *do* want a spanking?"

"No, ma'am," he said. "But, Mama, do you know what else?"

"What else, Paul?"

"I'm gonna work at the mill."

"*Going to*," she said. "*Going to* work at the mill. You aren't going to do anything until you go upstairs and take a bath like your brother."

"Yeah. You smell funky," I said.

"Roy you know I don't like that kind of talk. I have told both of you about being so mannish. When your father gets home . . ."

When our father got home that evening, Paul told his story again during dinner. He reenacted the motions of the combines and the men who tended them. When he got to the part about the sulfur, he said, "It stinks tremendously," and waited for our parents to laugh, and they did. He had a way of making them laugh with the things he said. He had talked himself out of a few spankings, but he had talked himself into some, too.

Before our evening dinner conversation, we carried out the nightly tradition of blessing the food and reciting Bible verses. I would say, "Jesus wept," the shortest verse in the Bible, and be done with it. Paul would go on forever. With one eye open, I would watch the steam rise off the food while Paul recited. Sometimes his eyes were open, too. We'd make faces at one another across the vegetables when no one else was looking. I never remember Paul saying the same verse twice. He was good at remembering.

Paul asked Mr. Lewis when he could have a job at the mill. Mr. Lewis told Paul to ask when he turned fifteen. Shortly after his fifteenth birthday, he started working in the office, filing time sheets, moving boxes, running errands. Paul worked in the office for the rest of that summer and after school during the year. The summer he turned eighteen, he applied for a processing job on the floor, working with the same machines that as children we watched turn trees to pulp.

Once he graduated from high school and started college, Paul worked the night shift, ten-to-six three days a week, and went to class in the afternoons. My father wasn't sure what to make of it at first, but he had always believed in good money and hard work, which is what the mill offered. Paul was serious about it. He worked his shifts on time and when he got home, he soaked his work clothes before washing, drying, and ironing them. My parents were impressed, but they considered the job a temporary pursuit until he was old enough to fulfill his calling.

Paul, champion of Sunday school memory competitions, oratorical contests, and composition prizes, was going to go to be a preacher. He had decided that he would go to the seminary once he finished college. My father accepted the fact that Paul had never been interested in working in the funeral home. But on occasion my father would ask him to eulogize those who had no close family or no minister to bury them properly. We would be their family, and sit in the pews of the mortuary chapel, listening to Paul's words.

From the few comments he gathered from the one or two people who knew the departed, or from the unclaimed things that they left behind, Paul would piece together a message, warm words that seemed so familiar it was hard to imagine that the two people—the one in the pulpit and the departed—were strangers.

People in Mobile knew my father. They knew us all. They had seen our family photo on the church fans parishioners waved on hot days, trying to cool down the humidity or the Holy Ghost. Among the black funeral homes in Mobile, ours was one of the oldest and considered the best. In the picture, my grandfather, my parents, Paul, and I stood on the front steps of the funeral home. In black script beneath our feet, "*Deacon Benevolent: Three Generations in the Service.*"

My mother held on to that family photo in an album she keeps. She also saved our team sports pictures. Flanked by backboards and bleachers, we wore sponsored uniforms and the mean-mug faces of adolescent boys trying to be men. Michael Donald was in some of these, one of the tall boys who stood along back rows, or the kneeling captain who held team trophies. Other pictures she kept as well. Color versions of the school day portraits that appeared on the black-and-white pages of our collected yearbooks. Portraits of Michael Donald and Paul Deacon often shared pages or faced across the fold.

In their senior yearbook, they were five classmates removed from one another. That same photo of Michael appeared in the newspaper and in the pages of the glossy magazines that mentioned his name. These magazines my mother saved in a small twine-bound pile on her bookcase, below our trophies and the diplomas on the wall.

Mobile is bright at night, the lights from the bay bridge, the spotlights on the old battleship, the shipyard beacons. Here it's dark. But the eastern shore darkness is familiar. It took a few minutes for my eyes to get accustomed, but now I can see the shades of dark, the outlines that separate the water, the tree line, and the overcast sky.

The only lights that connect the east and west shores are those suspended above the bay bridge. When Paul and I were young, riding in the back of my father's truck, we lay on our backs and counted them, 240 each way. Beyond the main roads, only a few dim lampposts light the Baldwin County woods.

When my father brought us over to the eastern shore on Jubilee nights, it took a while to reach the place we like to claim. People would stop us and speak. My father would stand for a while and talk to those who greeted him. He stopped and listened as long as they had something to say. He remembered everyone. He said it was his business to remember.

I didn't remember the faces of the people who spoke to us then, but some of the voices were familiar. When I answered the phone during my cartoons some early Saturday mornings, when no one else was awake, the sad, polite voices would ask me how I was doing before they asked me to put my father on the phone. I was old enough to know by the soothing tone of my father's voice—the tone I emulate now—that someone had died and there would be work to do. As he talked to them, my father ran his fingers along the carvings on the edge of his desk and looked out the window to where the ginkgoes grew.

After his night shift, Paul would stop by the Krispy Kreme on the corner of Chastain and Carlisle streets and pick up a dozen glazed doughnuts. When he got home, Paul would sit on the edge of my bed, and we'd eat them while I told him what happened on the late episode of *Sanford & Son* on Channel 44. The day before he found Michael, I told Paul about the episode where Fred and Lamonte went to the junkmen's convention in Hawaii.

"Shit. I've seen that one."

"You've seen them all. They're reruns."

"I just hate it how on the reruns how they show part one of the 'To Be Continued' and never show the part two in the right order. I bet you a dollar they show something entirely different tonight. Watch and see."

"You know what happens anyway."

"It's the principle, brother," he said, mouth full of a Krispy Kreme and digging in the box for another one.

"You wash your hands before you handled my food?"

"I washed my hands at your lady's house."

"I'm just saying you smell like the mill. Before you sit on my bed, you need to wash your stankin' ass."

"Speaking of stankin' ass, your lady told me to tell you hello."

If I was asleep when he came in, he would leave my half of the box on my dresser. He'd bring in the paper from the front steps and leave it on the kitchen table for my parents. On March 8, there were no doughnuts waiting. The morning edition of the *Press Register* was not on the table when I ran downstairs to answer the phone. It was Sgt. Kincaid, his voice familiar from our church choir. The strong, smooth tenor that would lead songs, the rock-steady voice expected of police officers. His voice was shaking somewhat when he asked for my father.

My father didn't say much in the car on the way over. He said as much as he had to: Michael Donald had been killed. My brother had found the body, and we had to go see about Paul.

A crowd had already gathered on Carlisle Street when we arrived. Before we could get over there, an elderly woman who was crying stopped my father. He put his arm around her and told me to go find Paul. I saw Sgt. Kincaid moving a barricade trying to clear the people standing in the street.

"Sergeant Kincaid, where is he?"

"He's still hanging. They won't let us cut him down until the coroner gets here."

"My brother, Mr. Kincaid. Where is he?"

"Oh, I'm sorry. He's in my cruiser." He pointed to the police car parked at the far end of the block.

"Is he alright?"

"He's shaken up. He was holding the Donald boy when I got to the scene. Trying to put some slack in the rope. It was already too late. You look out for your brother—he'll be alright."

"Thank you, Mr. Kincaid."

I had to walk past that tree to get to my brother. I didn't look. I didn't want to see Michael there. I looked instead for the blue lights of the squad car and I saw my brother sitting on the passenger side.

When I opened the door, he was sitting with his hands folded in his lap. Mud was all over his work shirt.

"I'm sorry, Roy. The doughnuts," he said, looking over my shoulder to where the crowd stood. "Roy, I left your doughnuts under that tree. I'm sorry."

"Don't worry about it, Paul."

"I'll go get you some more. I can get you some fresh ones."

"Paul, it's alright."

"No. No it's not."

I didn't walk him past the tree and the crowd. We took the long way around the block to where my father had parked.

Our father was standing there with Sgt. Kincaid. Mr. Kincaid had asked my father to ride with him over to Mrs. Donald's house. She didn't know yet. Daddy put his arm on Paul's shoulder and asked him if he was all right.

"No sir," he said, picking the dirt off the name patch on his shirt. "Not yet." That was the last thing he said before I put him in his truck and drove him home.

The next day, the Donald family asked us to prepare Michael's body. My father told me I didn't have to be there when they worked on him.

"I'll understand," he told me. "He was your friend."

He didn't mean that. He wanted me there. Before I started working full-time with my father, we talked about times like these. He reminded me of the people I might see on the table. Friends and family. If this were to be my profession, he would tell me, I would have to be ready for them.

"No one dies before their time," he would say. "The call comes when it's meant to. It's not for us to question."

So I stayed and helped him prepare Michael Donald. There on the table, his face was so swollen that he looked like a stranger. My father addressed the swelling and bruises. I washed his hands and cleared his fingernails of the blood, gravel, and mud. My father stood over me as I cleared the scrapes and cuts on his knuckles.

"He put up a fight," he said.

Seeing Michael, his hands and his face, I thought of my schoolyard fights and neighborhood brawls. I thought of the fights I'd won, remembering how the rush of victory dulls the pain of taken blows. I thought of the fights I had lost, when I felt the full force of heavy fists on my face. Hard blows, knuckle on bone, followed by the hot rush of blood to the surface. These blows would take the fight out of me.

Turning Michael's hands, there were more cuts and bruises. "Defensive wounds," they call these.

My grandfather was in the room. Long retired, he had come to help prepare the body. He knew how to dress rope-burned skin. He knew how to wire the broken bones of a neck and make it straight again. He knew how to arrange the high, starched collar and necktie so they hid the marks that makeup could not conceal. I watched him as he worked, cradling Michael's head in his hands.

He held it like he held mine in the waters here along the bay, on the summer afternoon he tried to teach me to float. I floated for a while, but when I opened my eyes and realized his hands were gone, and what I felt along my neck and back was just a memory of his fingers, I sank like a rock.

On the morning of the funeral Paul came downstairs in reeking work clothes that he must have slept in. Mr. Lewis told him to take some leave time, but he went to work anyway.

"Do you want some breakfast, Paul?" Mama asked. We had started talking to Paul in questions. Sometimes he would answer.

"No, ma'am."

"You don't have much time, sweetheart. Don't you think you should be getting dressed?"

"I'm already dressed. I got some overtime this morning."

"Aren't you going to go pay your respects to your friend?"

"I already did. I talked to him when he was in that tree. We talked for a good while." That was the last thing he said before he went out the door. As we pulled out of our driveway, my mother tried to dab away the redness in her eyes.

"Talk to your brother, Roy," she said.

"I'll talk to him, Mama. He's going to be alright." This was the assurance I made to my mother as we drove to the funeral.

The sanctuary of New Canaan Baptist Church was filled that day. Hundreds more waited outside for the funeral procession. The pulpit overflowed with the reverend doctors of the world, known and unknown.

After the service, I stood in the vestibule with my father as the pallbearers carried Michael's casket down the aisle. On the wall behind them, in stained glass, Jesus stumbled on the road to Calvary. Next to him stood Simon of Cyrene, the man who helped him carry his load. As Simon reaches down over Jesus, his mouth is near the ear of Christ. Whenever I am in New Canaan, whenever I am burying one of their own, I look at that wall and wonder about the Cyrenean. I wonder what he said.

The pallbearers reached the door and met the sunlight of the March afternoon. The man at the front right looked down as he walked over the threshold. He looked back to the others and whispered. They nodded and lowered their heads as they crossed over. They looked down as they left the church, careful of the spot he warned them of—where the carpet had rolled away from the tacks—careful not to stumble.

Paul had been a heavy sleeper before Michael Donald died. In the weeks after Michael's death, his sleep was uneasy. I could hear him through the walls, saying the same words over and over, words I tried in vain to understand. Then he stopped sleeping altogether.

He stopped eating with us, and I would miss him for days at a time. Some mornings I'd wake up hoping to see him on the edge of the bed, hoping to smell the stench of sulfur that filled the room when he entered and lingered, refusing to let me get back to sleep. I started to miss that. But the only sign of him was the piles of work clothes that built up in the washroom until my mother soaked them, cleaned them, and hung them neatly in his closet.

He worked when he should have been sleeping and when he should have been at school. With only a few weeks left in the semester, he stopped going to his classes altogether. He worked double shifts and overtime whenever he could get it. He had that tiredness about him that eight hours of sleep couldn't shake. My mother believed the tiredness caused what happened. It was the tiredness, she said, that caused him to fall asleep at his machine.

"Hello? Deacon residence."

"Mr. Deacon, I'm so sorry to—"

"Mr. Lewis? It's me, Roy."

"You sound more and more—Is he home? I need to speak to him."

"He's out of town. What's wrong?"

He said nothing, but there was no silence. I heard commotion over the hum of the combines at the mill.

"Can I speak to your mother?"

"I'm the only one here, Mr. Lewis. Tell me what's wrong."

"It's Paul. He had an accident—"

The combine had sliced through the bone and tendons just below his right wrist. It could have been much worse, Mr. Lewis said. Paul's hand could have been caught between the teeth of the blades, and his entire arm could have been pulled through on the intake. I've heard the stories of men whose arms were pulled from the socket. They die sometimes from blood clots or trauma. They said Paul was calm. They said he kept his head about him. I slept at the hospital with him for those first few days. Paul got out of the hospital a few days before Memorial Day.

The investigators said the same thing my mother and Mr. Lewis believed, that it was an accident caused by fatigue. When he came home, he slept more than he was awake, and the medication kept him drowsy. Outside of doctor's appointments, he rarely left the house. I would take his dinner to him in his room, and try to talk to him while he ate, but would only speak when you asked him a question. And then in one word answers most times. Yes. No. Fine.

My mother wanted him to talk to someone, a doctor or maybe someone from the church. But he never did. Mama asked me to talk to him. I tried. When he did start to talk more, it was always about the pain in his arm.

"You know it still hurts, my hand. Nothing even there and I can still feel it hurting. The nerves don't know the difference."

"Do you want me to get your medicine?"

"Pills don't work on something that's not there. It's in my head."

He lifted his bandaged arm, turning his forearm and staring where his hand should have been. He never looked at me when he talked like this.

"I'm sitting right here, looking at it, knowing damn well that it's gone, but I can feel it just the same. If I close my eyes I can wiggle the fingers. See? I'm doing it right now."

He'd say these things then he would go silent again, and the only noise would be was the scrape of utensils against my mother's good plates. I told myself, and my parents, what we all wanted to believe. That he was going to work it out in his own time.

The seat my parents saved for him at my graduation was empty when my name was called. But when I walked across the stage, I saw him standing in the back of the auditorium. He waved. When we got to the parking lot, he stood by my father's car waiting for us.

"Sorry I was late, but tying this necktie was a motherfucker." He laughed for the first time in a long while. We all laughed then. That's when we all believed that things would be alright.

Before we could leave, the man in the car next to us, the father of a classmate I barely knew, congratulated us, patting me on the shoulder and hastily shaking hands with my father before extending his hand to Paul.

My father had taught us the proper way to clasp a hand, a firm, single squeeze without too much shaking. Calibrated just so, for the hands of peers or elders or the children of the deceased. My mother taught me the protocol for taking a widow's or grieving mother's hand in both of my own.

In the days after the accident, I had watched Paul reach for things. Bottles, doorknobs, books. He would forget for a second that it was gone. Paul had that same expression now—standing in the auditorium parking lot, tie loosely knotted—as his left hand was clenched awkwardly in the embarrassed man's right.

I skipped the graduation parties and talked to my brother for most of the night. There was small talk, of *Sanford & Son,* and of many things unspoken during the weeks after Michael and the mill, and reassuring words he said to me before I went to bed.

"You need to stop worrying about me, Roy. It just took me some time to get right. I've made sense of all of this now."

Instead of a big party when I turned eighteen, we had dinner at the house, eating the gumbo my mother made. My daddy played his records. Paul danced with my mother until she got tired and went to bed. When she was gone, my father went to his liquor cabinet, pulled out the big bottle of Crown Royal he saved, and poured thin layers into three of his good glasses.

"To my sons. The damn-near twins."

When I swirled it around, it was just thick enough to stick to the sides of the glass before it rolled back down. That was the same way it felt in my mouth before I swallowed.

This was the first time I'd had good liquor outright. We'd stolen tastes, of course, every once in a while slipping shots into Styrofoam cups and obscuring the taste with too much ice and store-brand ginger ale, but this was the first time I had tasted whiskey full on.

"You can pour yourself another one, Roy," my father said. "You won't be able to drink with the Right Reverend Paul Deacon."

Paul stared out the window like my father would sometimes. He hadn't taken a drink yet.

Then, "To Michael," he said, raising his glass.

That next day, I found on my chest of drawers a note: "Jubilee."

I folded the note in my pocket. Around the wastebasket, I saw the discarded scraps of paper. Imperfect letters that Paul had tried again and again with his left hand, incomplete early versions of the single word he had finally gotten right.

He always got to the eastern shore before me. I saw the truck parked on the side of the beach road. He left the park lights on so I could find him.

"Old man Roy Deacon."

After looking out at the lights, it takes my eyes a minute to adjust so I can see my brother. At first I can only hear his voice. But slowly he comes into focus. Whenever I see him, I am reminded how the years have treated me. I am much rounder at the middle, even when I suck in my gut. My hairline has gone its own way. He's still the same. If other people could see us together, it might be hard to imagine that we were born so close together.

"How's forty treating you?"

"I have five minutes left. Let me enjoy it."

"How does it feel to be on the verge of a grand transcendental moment? On the cusp of something greater than yourself?"

"I'll tell you in five minutes."

It's warm on the beach, and Paul has his shoes off. He has those high-arched feet that look like they're always ready to run. He used to stand in the water and wait for the fish and the crab without looking for them. He'd just feel them as they started to brush against his ankles.

"Transcendental moments need to be marked. Did you bring some punctuation?"

I show him the purple Crown Royal sack.

"You always come through, Roy. Always did."

I give him a sip, and pour a bit more on the ground.

"For the brothers who ain't here," I say.

"For the brothers who ain't here."

I look down at the ground. The bit of Crown I poured is soaking into the sand between me and my brother.

"I can't stay. I just wanted to wish you a good one," he says. *"I wanted to see the kids, too. Where are they?"*

"I let them play in the water for a while. They'll be back in a minute."

The scars on his arm have healed as well as can be expected. The ones along his wrist, from the accident. And the other scars that he put there. When I'd gotten to the eastern shore that night, I'd seen the park lights of

Paul's truck along the beach road. When I'd found him, I thought he was sleeping.

"It's good to see you again, Roy."

On that Jubilee night in 1981, I had planned to meet my brother here on the beach. Instead I found him in the back of his truck. Since it had been hard for him to sleep soundly those months before—with Michael Donald and the pain in his arm—I'd decided to let him sleep until the tide came in. It wasn't until I came back and tried to wake him that I realized.

"You know Roy, when we were kids I wished I could stay here forever."

When I'd turned my flashlight on him, I'd seen the places where the blood had run down the rivets of the payload, soaking the dirt and leaves that had collected there. Some had leaked through the rusted places and pooled on the red clay of the road.

"Forever's a long time."

He didn't leave a note. My doctor said they don't always leave notes. And even if he had, the doctor says it might have caused more questions than it answered. He didn't leave a note, but he left a message, spelled out carefully in neat razor-drawn letters along his forearm. MARK 8 24. Some time later I would find it in his Bible. The verse he had underlined and crossed out again and again until the pen ripped through the parchment.

Tonight, Paul put his good arm on my shoulder. The scars along the arm that hangs at his side have healed as well as could be expected. The red open wounds have closed. In their place, swollen keloids have risen like braille against him.

This is the peace I have made for myself. Here in the place we like to claim. This I need to hold the rest together. While I wait for a harvest I don't understand, while I watch my children play in the water, while I watch how sand adheres to the good liquor I pour for brothers and friends.

I see my brother but I cannot feel his hand along my shoulder. I only feel my daughter's shovel as she taps me on my thigh. The alarm on her watch is beeping. She's singing "Happy Birthday" along with the electronic melody.

"Happy birthday to you, Happy birthday to Daddy . . ."

Give them a hug from their uncle.

"Happy birthday, Pop," my son yells to me from the soft sand at the water's edge.

Take it easy, Roy.

I light a match to check the wind. The wind is blowing easterly, like it's supposed to for a Jubilee. It won't be long now. Tomorrow we'll celebrate my forty years. Family and friends will gather and we'll eat gumbo made from the crab and fish that I'll bring home in the morning. Many of us have gathered along the shore at the water now, looking for the silver sides of the floating fish and the sand-colored shells of beached crab. Some of us have lights on while others look down with eyes adjusted to the eastern shore darkness. We watch and wait for them.

Weight

BY JOHN EDGAR WIDEMAN

My mother is a weightlifter. You know what I mean. She understands that the best laid plans, the sweetest beginnings, have a way of turning to shit. Bad enough when life fattens you up just so it can turn around and gobble you down. Worse for the ones like my mother life keeps skinny, munching on her daily, one cruel, little, needle-toothed bite at a time so the meal lasts and lasts. Mom understands life don't play so spends beaucoup time and energy getting ready for the worst. She lifts weights to stay strong. Not barbells or dumbbells, though most of the folks she deals with, especially her sons, act just that way, like dumbbells. No. The weights she lifts are burdens, her children's, her neighbors', yours. Whatever awful calamities arrive on her doorstep or howl in the news, my mom squeezes her frail body beneath them. Grips, hoists, holds the weight. I swear sometimes I can hear her sinews squeaking and singing under a load of invisible tons.

I ought to know since I'm one of the burdens bowing her shoulders. She loves heavy, hopeless me unconditionally. Before I was born, Mom loved me, forever and ever till death do us part. I'll never be anyone else's darling, darling boy, so it's her fault, her doing, isn't it, that neither of us can face the thought of losing the other. How could I resist reciprocating her love. Needing her. Draining her. Feeling her straining underneath me, the pop and crackle of her arthritic joints, her gray hair sizzling with static electricity, the hissing friction, tension, and pressure as she lifts more than she can bear. Bears more than she can possibly lift. You have to see it to believe it. Like the Flying Wallendas or Houdini's spine-chilling escapes. One of the greatest shows on Earth.

My mother believes in a god whose goodness would not permit him to inflict more troubles than a person can handle. A god of mercy and salvation. A sweaty, bleeding god presiding over a fitness class in which his chosen few punish their muscles. She should wear a T-shirt: "God's Gym."

In spite of a son in prison for life, twin girls born dead, a mind-blown son who roams the streets with everything he owns in a shopping cart, a strung-out daughter with a crack baby, a good daughter who'd miscarried the only child her dry womb ever produced, in spite of me and the rest of my limp-along, near to normal siblings and their children—my nephews doping and gangbanging, nieces unwed, underage, dropping babies as regularly as the seasons—in spite of breast cancer, sugar diabetes, hypertension, failing kidneys, emphysema, gout, all resident in her body and epidemic in the community, knocking off one by one her girlhood friends, in spite of corrosive poverty and a neighborhood whose streets are no longer safe even for gray, crippled-up folks like her, my mom loves her god, thanks him for the blessings he bestows, keeps her faith he would not pile on more troubles than she could bear. Praises his name and prays for strength, prays for more weight so it won't fall on those around her less able to bear up.

You've seen those iron pumping, musclebound brothers fresh out the slam who show up at the playground to hoop and don't get picked on a team cause they can't play a lick, not before they did their bit, and sure not now, back on the set, stiff and stone-handed as Frankenstein, but finally some old head goes on and chooses one on his squad because the brother's so huge and scary looking sitting there with his jaws tight, lip poked out you don't want him freaking out and kicking everybody's ass just because the poor baby's feelings is hurt, you know what I mean, the kind so buff looks like his coiled-up insides about to bust through his skin or his skin's stripped clean off his body so he's a walking anatomy lesson. Well, that's how my mom looks to me sometimes, her skin peeled away, no secrets, every taut nerve string on display.

I can identify the precise moment during a trip with her one afternoon to the supermarket on Walnut Street in Shadyside, a Pittsburgh, Pennsylvania, white community with just a few families of us colored sprinkled at the bottom ends of a couple of streets, when I began to marvel at my mother's prodigious strength. I was very young, young enough not to believe I'd grow old, just bigger. A cashier lady who seemed to be acquainted with my mother asked very loudly, Is this your son, and Mom smiled in reply to the cashier's astonishment saying calmly, Yes, he is, and the doughy white lady in her yellow Krogers' smock with her name on the breast tried to match my mother's smile but only managed a fake grin like she'd just discovered shit stinks but didn't want anybody else to know she knew. Then she blurted, He's a tall one, isn't he.

Not a particularly unusual moment as we unloaded our shopping cart and waited for the bad news to ring up on the register. The three of us understood, in spite of the cashier's quick shuffle, what had seized her attention. In public situations the sight of my pale, caucasian-featured mother and her variously colored kids disconcerted strangers. They gulped. Stared.

Muttered insults. We were visible proof somebody was sneaking around after dark, breaking the apartheid rule, messy mulatto exceptions to the rule, trailing behind a woman who could be white.

Nothing special about the scene in Krogers. Just an ugly moment temporarily reprieved from turning uglier by the cashier's remark that attributed her surprise to a discrepancy in height not color. But the exchange alerted me to a startling fact—I was taller than my mother. The brown boy, me, could look down at the crown of his light-skinned mother's head. Obsessed by size, like most adolescent boys, size in general and the size of each and every particular part of my body and how mine compared to others, I was always busily measuring and keeping score, but somehow I'd lost track of my mother's size, and mine relative to hers. Maybe because she was beyond size. If someone had asked me my mother's height or weight I probably would have replied, *Huh*. Ubiquitous I might say now. A tiny, skin-and-bone woman way too huge for size to pin down.

The moment in Krogers is also when I began to marvel at my mother's strength. Unaccountably, unbeknownst to me, my body had grown larger than hers, yes, and the news was great in a way, but more striking and not so comforting was the fact, never mind my advantage in size, I felt hopelessly weak standing there beside my mom in Krogers. A wimpy shadow next to her solid flesh and bones. I couldn't support for one hot minute a fraction of the weight she bore on her shoulders twenty-four hours a day. The weight of the cashier's big-mouthed disbelief. The weight of hating the pudgy white woman forever because she tried to steal my mother from me. The weight of cooking and cleaning and making do with no money, the weight of fighting and loving us iron-headed, ungrateful brats. Would I always feel puny and inadequate when I looked up at the giant fist hovering over our family, the fist of God or the Devil, ready to squash us like bugs if my mother wasn't always on duty, spreading herself thin as an umbrella over our heads, her bones its steel ribs keeping the sky from falling.

Reaching down for the brass handle of this box I must lift to my shoulder, I need the gripping strength of my mother's knobby-knuckled fingers, her superhero power to bear impossible weight.

Since I was reading her this story over the phone (I called it a story but Mom knew better), I stopped at the end of the paragraph above you just completed, if you read that far, stopped because the call was long distance, daytime rates, and also because the rest had yet to be written. I could tell by her silence she was not pleased. Her negative reaction didn't surprise me. Plenty in the piece I didn't like either. Raw, stuttering stuff I intended to improve in subsequent drafts, but before revising and trying to complete it, I needed her blessing.

Mom's always been my best critic. I depend on her honesty. She tells the truth yet never affects the holier-than-thou superiority of some people who believe they occupy the high ground and let you know in no uncertain terms that you nor nobody else like you ain't hardly coming close. Huh-uh. My mother smiles as often as she groans or scolds when she hears gossip about somebody behaving badly. *My, my, my* she'll say and nod and smile and gently broom you, the sinner, and herself into the same crowded heap, no one any better than they should be, could be, absolute equals in a mellow sputter of laughter she sometimes can't suppress, hiding it, muffling it with her fist over her mouth, nodding, remembering, how people's badness can be too good to be true, *my, my, my*.

Well, my story didn't tease out a hint of laugh, and forget the 550 miles separating us, I could tell she wasn't smiling either. Why was she holding back the sunshine that could forgive the worst foolishness. Absolve my sins. Retrieve me from the dead-end corners into which I paint myself. Mama, please. Please, please, please, don't you weep. And tell ole Martha not to moan. Don't leave me drowning like Willie Boy in the deep blue sea. Smile, Mom. Laugh. Send that healing warmth through the wire and save poor me.

Was it the weightlifting joke, Mom. Maybe you didn't think it was funny.

Sorry. Tell the truth, I didn't see nothing humorous about any of it. God's T-shirt. You know better. Ought to be ashamed of yourself. Taking the Lord's name in vain.

Where do you get such ideas, boy. I think I know my children. God knows I should by now, shouldn't I. How am I not supposed to know youall after all you've put me through beating my brains out to get through to you. *Yes, yes, yes.* Then one you all goes and does something terrible I never would have guessed was in you. Won't say you break my heart. Heart's been broke too many times. In too many little itty-bitty pieces can't break down no more, but youall sure ain't finished with me, are you. Still got some new trick in you to lay on your weary mother before she leaves here.

Guess I ought to be grateful to God an old fool like me's still around to be tricked, Weightlifter. Well, it's different. Nobody ain't called me nothing like weightlifter before. It's different, sure enough.

Now here's where she should have laughed. She'd picked up the stone I'd bull's-eyed right into the middle of her wrinkled brow, between her tender, brown, all-seeing eyes, lifted it and turned it over in her hands like a jeweler with a tiny telescope strapped around his skull inspecting a jewel, testing its heft and brilliance, the marks of god's hands, god's will, the hidden truths sparkling in its depths, multiplied, splintered through mirroring facets. After such a brow-scrunching examination, isn't it time to smile. Kiss and make up. Wasn't that Mom's way. Wasn't that how she handled the things that hurt us and hurt her. Didn't she ease the pain of our worst injuries with the balm of her everything's-going-to-be-alright-in-the-morning smile. The smile that takes the weight, every hurtful ounce and forgives, the smile licking our wounds so they scab over, and she can pick them off our skin, stuff their lead weight into the bulging sack of all sorrows slung across her back.

The possibility my wannabe story had actually hurt her dawned on me. Or should I say bopped me upside my head like the Br'er Bear club my middle brother loads in his cart to discourage bandits. I wished I was sitting at the kitchen table across from her so I could check for damage, her first, then check myself in the mirror of those soft, brown, incredibly loving mother's eyes. If I'd hurt her even a teeny-tiny bit, I'd be broken forever unless those eyes repaired me. Yet even as I regretted reading her the clumsy passage and prepared myself to surrender wholly, happily to the hounds of hell if I'd harmed one hair on her tender, gray head, I couldn't deny a sneaky, smarting tingle of satisfaction at the thought that maybe, maybe words I'd written had touched another human being, mama mia or not.

Smile, Mom. It's just a story. Just a start. I know it needs more work. You were supposed to smile at the weightlifting part.

God not something to joke about.

C'mon, mom. How many times have I heard Reverend Fitch cracking you up with his corny God jokes.

Time and a place.

Maybe stories are my time and place, Mom. You know. My time and place to say things I need to say.

No matter how bad it comes out sounding, right. No matter you make a joke of your poor mother . . .

Poor mother's suffering. You were going to say, "Poor mother's suffering," weren't you?

You heard what I said.

And heard what you didn't say. I hear those words, too. The unsaid ones, Mom. Louder sometimes. Drowning out what gets said, Mom.

Whoa. We gon let it all hang out this morning, ain't we. Son. First that story. Now you accusing me of *your* favorite trick, that muttering under your breath. Testing me this morning, aren't you. What makes you think a sane person would ever pray for more weight. Ain't those the words you put in my mouth. More weight.

And the building shook. The Earth rumbled. More weight descended like god's fist on his Hebrew children. Like in Lamentations. The Book in the Bible. The movie based on the Book based on what else, the legend of my mother's long-suffering back.

Because she had a point.

"People with no children can be cruel." Had I heard it first from Oprah, the diva of suffering my mother could have become if she'd pursued showbiz instead of weightlifting. Or was the damning phrase a line from one of Gwen Brooks's abortion blues. Whatever their source, the words fit and I was ashamed. I do know better. A bachelor and nobody's daddy, but still my words have weight. Like sticks and stones, words can break bones. Metaphors can pull you apart and put you back together all wrong. I know what you mean, Mom. My entire life I've had to listen to people trying to tell me I'm just a white man in a dark skin.

Give me a metaphor long enough and I'll move the Earth. Somebody famous said it. Or said something like that. And everybody, famous or not, knows words sting. Words change things. Step on a crack, break your mother's back.

On the other hand, Mom, metaphor's just my way of trying to say two things, be in two places at once. Saying good-bye and hello and good-bye. Many things, many places at once. You know, like James Cleveland singing our favorite gospel tune, "Stood on the Bank of Jordan." Metaphors are very short songs. Mini-mini stories. Rivers between like the Jordan where ships sail on, sail on and you stand and wave good-bye-hello, hello-good-bye.

Weightlifter just a word, just play. I was only teasing, Mom. I didn't mean to upset you. I certainly intended no harm. I'd swallow every stick of dynamite it takes to pay for a Nobel prize before I'd accept one if it cost just one of your soft, curly hairs.

Smile. Let's begin again.

It's snowing in Massachusetts / The ground's white in O-Hi-O. Yes, it's snowing in Massachusetts / And ground's white in O-Hi-O. Shut my eyes, Mr. Weatherman / Can't stand to see my baby go.

When I called you last Thursday evening and didn't get an answer I started worrying. I didn't know why. We'd talked Tuesday and you sounded fine. Better than fine. A lift and lilt in your voice. After I hung up the phone Tuesday said to myself, Mom's in good shape. Frail but her spirit's strong. Said those very words to myself more than once Tuesday. *Frail but her spirit's strong*. The perkiness I sensed in you helped make my Wednesday super. Early rise. Straight to my desk. Two pages before noon and you know me, Mom. Two pages can take a week, a month. I've had two page years. I've had decades dreaming the one perfect page I never got around to writing. Thursday morning reams of routine and no pages but not to worry I told myself. After Wednesday's productivity, wasn't I entitled to some down time. Just sat at my desk, pleased as punch with myself till I got bored feeling so good and started a nice novel, *Call It Sleep*. Dinner at KFC buffet. Must have balled up fifty napkins trying to keep my chin decent. Then home to call you before I snuggled up again with the little Jewish boy, his mama, and their troubles in old NYC.

Let your phone ring and ring. Too late for you to be out unless you had a special occasion. And you always let me know well ahead of time when something special coming up. I tried calling a half hour later and again twenty minutes after that. By then nearly nine, close to your bedtime. I was getting really worried now. Couldn't figure where you might be. Nine-fifteen and still no answer, no clue what was going on.

Called Sis. Called Aunt Chloe. Nobody knew where you were. Chloe said she'd talked with you earlier just like every other morning. Sis said you called her at work after she got back from lunch. Both of them said you sounded fine. Chloe said you'd probably fallen asleep in your recliner and left the phone in the bedroom or bathroom and your hearing's to the point you can be wide-awake but if the TV's on and the phone's not beside you or the ringer's not turned to high she said sometimes she has to ring and hang up, ring and hang up, two, three times before she catches you.

Chloe promised to keep calling every few minutes till she reached you. Said they have a prayer meeting Thursdays in your mother's building and she's been saying she wants to go and I bet she's there, honey. She's alright, honey. Don't worry yourself, OK. We're old and fuddleheaded now, but we're tough old birds. Your mother's fine. I'll tell her to call you soon's I get through to her. Your mom's okay, baby. God keeps an eye on us.

You know Aunt Chloe. She's your sister. Five hundred miles away and I could hear her squeezing her large self through the telephone line, see her pillow arms reaching for the weight before it comes down on me.

Why would you want to hear any of this. You know what happened. Where you were. You know how it all turned out.

You don't need to listen to my conversation with Sis. Dialing her back after we'd been disconnected. The first time in life I think my sister ever phoned me later than ten o'clock at night. First time a lightning bolt ever disconnected us. Ever disconnected me from anybody ever.

Did you see Eva Wallace first, Mom, coming through your door, or was it the busybody super you've never liked since you moved in. Something about the way she speaks to her granddaughter you said. Little girl's around the building all day because her mother's either in the street or the slam and the father takes the child so rarely he might as well live in Timbuktu so you know the super doesn't have it easy and on a couple of occasions you've offered to keep the granddaughter when the super needs both hands and her mind free for an hour. You don't hold the way she busies up in everybody's business or the fact the child has to look out for herself too many hours in the day against the super, and you're sure she loves her granddaughter you said but the short way she talks sometimes to a child that young just not right.

Who'd you see first pushing open your door. Eva said you didn't show up after you said you'd stop by for her. She waited awhile she said then phoned you and got no answer and then a friend called her and they got to running their mouths and Eva said she didn't think again about you not showing up when you were supposed to until she hung up the phone. And not right away then. Said as soon as she missed you, soon as she remembered youall had planned on attending the Thursday prayer meeting together she got scared. She knows how dependable you are. Even though it was late, close to your bedtime, she called you anyway and let the phone ring and ring. Way after nine by then. Pulled her coat on over her housedress, scooted down the hall and knocked on your door cause where else you going to be. No answer so she hustled back to her place and phoned downstairs for the super and they both pounded on your door till the super said we better have a look just in case and unlocked your apartment. Stood there staring after she turned the key, trying to see through the door, then slid it open a little and both of them Eva said tiptoeing in like a couple of fools after all that pounding and hollering in the hall. Said she never thought about it at the time but later, after everything over and she drops down on her couch to have that cigarette she knew she shouldn't have with her lungs rotten as they are and hadn't smoked one for more than a year but sneaks the Camel she'd been saving out its hiding place in a Baggie in the freezer and sinks back in the cushions and lights up, real tired, real shook up and teary she said but couldn't help smiling at herself when she remembered all that hollering and pounding and then tipping in like a thief.

It might have happened that way. Being right or wrong about what happened is less important sometimes than finding a good way to tell it. What's anybody want to hear anyway. Not the truth people want. No-no-no. People want the best told story, the lie that entertains and turns them on. No question about it, is there. What people want. What gets people's attention. What sells soap. Why else do the biggest, most barefaced liars rule the world.

Hard to be a mother, isn't it Mom. I can't pretend to be yours, not even a couple minutes' worth before I go to pieces. I try to imagine a cradle with you lying inside, cute, miniature bedding tucked around the tiny doll of you. I can almost picture you asleep in it, snuggled up, your eyes shut, maybe your thumb in your mouth but then you cry out in the night, you need me to stop whatever I'm doing and rush in and scoop you up and press you to my bosom, lullabye you back to sleep. I couldn't manage it. Not the easy duty I'm imagining, let alone you bucking and wheezing and snot, piss, vomit, shit, blood, you hot and throbbing with fever, steaming in my hands like the heart ripped fresh from some poor soul's chest.

Too much weight. Too much discrepancy in size. As big a boy as I've grown to be, I can't lift you.

Will you forgive me if I cheat, Mom. Dark suited, strong men in somber ties and white shirts will lug you out of the church, down the stone steps, launch your gleaming barge into the black river of the Cadillac's bay. My brothers won't miss me not handling my share of the weight. How much weight could there be. Tiny, scooped out you. The tinny, fake wood shell. The entire affair's symbolic. Heavy with meaning not weight. You know. Like metaphors. Like words interchanged as if they have no weight or too much weight, as if words are never required to bear more than they can stand. As if words, when we're finished mucking with them, go back to just being words.

The word *trouble*. The word *sorrow*. The word *bye-and-bye*.

I was wrong and you were right, as usual, Mom. So smile. Certain situations, yours for instance, being a mother, suffering what mothers suffer, why would anyone want to laugh at that. Who could stand in your shoes a heartbeat—*shoes, shoes, everybody got to have shoes*—bear your burdens one instant and think it's funny. Who ever said it's okay to lie and kill as long as it makes a good story.

Smile. Admit you knew from the start it would come to this. Me trembling, needing your strength. It has, Mom, so please, please, a little, bitty grin of satisfaction. They say curiosity kills the cat and satisfaction brings it back. Smiling. Smile Mom. Come back. You know I've always hated spinach but please spoonfeed me a canful so those Popeye muscles pop in my arms. I meant shapeshifter not weightlifter. I meant the point of this round, spinning-top Earth must rest somewhere, on something or someone. I meant you are my sunshine. My only sunshine.

The problem never was the word "weightlifter," was it. If you'd been insulted by my choice of metaphor you would have let me know, not by silence, but nailing me with a quick, funny signifying dig, and then you would have smiled or laughed and we'd have gone on to the next thing. What must have bothered you, stunned you was what I said into the phone before I began reading. Said this is about a man scared he won't survive his mother's passing.

That's what upset you, wasn't it. Saying good-bye to you. Practicing for your death in a story. Trying on for size a world without you. Ignoring like I did when I was a boy, your size. Saying aloud terrible words with no power over us as long as we don't speak them.

So when you heard me let the cat out the bag, you were shocked, weren't you. Speechless. Smileless. What could you say. The damage had been done.

I heard it in your first words after you got back your voice. And me knowing your lifelong, deathly fear of cats. Like the big, furry orange Tom you told me about, how it curled up on the porch just outside your door, trapping you a whole August afternoon inside the hotbox shanty in Washington, D.C., when I lived in your belly.

Why would I write a story that risks your life. Puts our business in the street. I'm the oldest child, supposed to be the man of the family now. No wonder you cried, Oh father. Oh son. Oh holy ghost. Why hath thou forsaken me. I know you didn't cry that. You aren't Miss Oprah. But I sure did mess up, didn't I. Didn't I, Mom. Up to my old tricks. Crawling up inside you. My weight twisting you all out of shape.

I asked you once about the red sailor cap hanging on the wall inside your front door. Knew it was my brother's cap on the nail, but why that particular hat I asked and not another of his countless, fly sombreros on display. Rob, Rob, man of many lids. For twenty years in the old house, now in your apartment, the hat a shrine no one allowed to touch. You never said it but everybody understood the red hat your good luck charm, your mojo for making sure Rob would get out the slam one day and come bopping through the door, pluck the hat from the wall and pull it down over his bean head. Do you remember me asking why the sailor cap. You probably guessed I was fishing. Really didn't matter which cap, did it. Point was you chose the red one and *why* must always be your secret. You could have made up a nice story to explain why the red sailor cap wound up on the nail and I would have listened as I always listened all ears but you knew part of me would be trying to peek through the words at your secret. Always a chance you might slip up and reveal too much. So the hat story and plenty others never told. The old folks had taught you that telling another person your secret wish strips it of its power, a wish's small, small chance, as long as it isn't spoken, to influence what might happen next in the world. You'd never tell anyone the words sheltered in the shadow of your heart. Still, I asked about the red sailor cap because I needed to understand your faith, your weightlifting power, how you can believe a hat, any fucking kind of hat, could bring my baby brother home safe and sound from prison. I needed to spy and pry. Wiretap the telephone in your bosom. Hear the words you would never say to another soul, not even on pain of death.

How would such unsaid words sound, what would they look like on a page. And if you had uttered them, surrendered your stake in them, forfeited their meager, silent claim to work miracles, would it have been worth the risk, even worth the loss, to finally hear the world around you cracking, collapsing, changing as you spoke your little secret tale.

Would you have risen an inch or two from this cold ground. Would you have breathed easier after releasing the heaviness of silent words hoarded so unbearably, unspeakably long. Let go, Mom. Shed the weight just once.

Not possible for you, I know. It would be cheating, I know. The man of unbending faith did not say to the hooded inquisitors piling a crushing load of stones on his chest, "More light. More light." No. I'm getting my quotes mixed up again. Just at the point the monks thought they'd broken his will, just as spiraling fractures started splintering his bones, he cried, "More bricks. More bricks."

I was scared, Mom. Scared every cotton-picking day of my life I'd lose you. The fear a singsong taunt like tinnitus ringing in my ear. No wonder I'm a little crazy. But don't get me wrong. Not your fault. I don't blame you for my morbid fears, my unhappiness. It's just that I should have confessed sooner, long, long ago, the size of my fear of losing you. I wish you'd heard me say the words. How fear made me keep my distance, hide how much I depended on your smile. The sunshine of your smiling laughter that could also send me silently screaming out the room in stories I never told you because you'd taught me as you'd been taught, not to say anything aloud I didn't want to come true. Nor say out loud the things I wished to come true. Doesn't leave a hell of a lot to say, does it. No wonder I'm tongue-tied, scared shitless.

But would it be worth the risk, worth failing, if I could find words to tell our story and also keep us covered inside it, work us invisibly into the fret, the warp and woof of the story's design, safe there, connected there as words in perfect poems, the silver apples of the moon, golden apples of the sun, blue guitars. The two of us like those rhyming pairs "never" and "forever," "heart" and "part," in the doo-wop songs I harmonized with the fellas in the alley around the corner from Henderson's barber shop up on Frankstown Avenue, first me then lost brother Sonny and his crew then baby brother Rob and his cut buddy hoodlums rapping and now somebody else black and young and wild and pretty so the song lasts forever and never ever ends even though the voices change back there in the alley where you can hear bones rattling in the men's fists, "fever in the funkhouse looking for a five," and hear wine bottles exploding and hear the rusty shopping cart squeak over the cobblestones of some boy ferrying an old lady's penny-ante groceries home for a nickel once, then a dime, a quarter, four quarters now.

Would it be worth the risk, worth failing.

Shouldn't I try even if I know the strength's not in me. No, you say. Yes. Hold on, let go. Do I hear you saying, Everything's gonna be alright. Saying, Do what you got to do, baby, smiling as I twist my fingers into the brass handle. As I lift.

FROM **Thieves' Paradise**

BY ERIC JEROME DICKEY

PROLOGUE

Momma shrieked.

The walls echoed her cries for Daddy to get his hands off her, brought her pleas up the stairs to my room. I jumped and my algebra book dropped from my chestnut desk onto the floor.

My father cursed.

By the time I made it to the railing and looked down into the living room, Momma was in front of my father, begging for forgiveness. Her petite frame was balled up on our Aztec-patterned sofa. She was holding her lip to keep the blood from flowing onto the fabric. I watched her rub away the pain on her cinnamon skin, then run her fingers through her wavy coalblack hair.

My old man looked up at me and grimaced. "Go back to your room, boy."

I was fifteen and a half. Less than half of my old man's age.

He stomped toward Momma.

She screamed and moved away from him like she was trying to run away from the madness that lived here every day.

My chest heaved as I stumbled past the grandfather clock and rushed down the stairs. My heart was pounding. I tightened my hands and hurried to my momma's side.

"Momma," I moaned as I kneeled next to her. "You okay?"

"I'm alright, baby. It's nothing. Nothing."

I looked back at my liquored-up old man. He bobbed his head and pointed back at the kitchen. "I work hard all day and come home to no dinner?"

He was slurring and sneering down on us.

I said, "Nobody knew you were coming home tonight."

Momma tried to get up. "I overslept. My pills made me—"

"*Carmen*," he shouted. "Get up off that sofa and cook. *Now. Planet of the Apes* comes on in an hour and I want my food on the table by the time Charlton Heston—"

"Don't ever touch Momma again."

"What you say?"

"He didn't say anything." Momma touched my arm. "I'm okay, baby. Go back and finish studying for your test."

Daddy's back straightened, his bushy mustache crooked as his lips curved down, his eyes widened. "What you say to me, nigger?"

"I'm not a nigger. My name is Dante."

"So, the nigger speaking up for himself."

"You heard me the first time. And I ain't a nigger."

"You challenging me? What, you think because you got a little hair over your dick you're a grown man now? Ain't but one man in this house."

Momma spoke carefully to Daddy. "Don't get upset."

I frowned at the shiny badge on the chest of his tan uniform, then at the gun in his leather holster.

He sucked his teeth, nodded, and jerked the badge off. He threw the gun holster on the love seat. He stepped away from the glass coffee table, opened his arms, and snapped out, "You want to be a man? Come on. I'll give you the first shot. Nigger, I'll knock your black ass into the middle of next week."

Momma gripped my arm tight enough for her nails to break my skin. I glanced at the golden cross she had on her chest, the one she had got from her mother just a few weeks before Grandmamma died. I looked into my momma's light brown eyes, eyes that looked like mine. "Let me go, Momma."

"No." She put her nose against mine and whispered, "Momma's okay. It's just a little scratch."

My knees shook when I stood and faced my old man. When his eyes met mine, his anger held so much power that I forgot how to breathe. Heart went into overdrive. He balled up his right fist, slammed it into the palm of his left hand; it echoed like thunder. "What are you gonna do, nigger?"

I trembled, backed away, and said, "Nothing."

"Nothing, what?"

"Nothing, sir."

I kicked my bare feet into the rust carpet, then slumped my shoulders, wiped my sweaty hands on my jean shorts, and turned around to go back to my room.

Then that motherfucker chuckled.

A simple laugh that stoked up the rage inside of me.

I charged at him as fast and as hard as I could.

Momma screamed.

Daddy's eyes widened with surprise.

Pain. Anger. Fear.

Three screams from three people.

. . .

From the backseat of the police car, I stared through the wire cage at the colorful rotating lights that were brightening Scottsdale's earth-tone stucco houses. I was hostage under a calm sky. The spinning glow from twelve squad cars looked like rainbows chasing rainbows. Colors raced over all the sweet gum trees and windmill palms, moved like a strobe light over the vanhoutte spirea in the front of the three-car garage. The reek of cordite was on my flesh. Couldn't really smell it over the stench of my stress sweating. I concentrated on the colors to make the pain from the tight handcuffs go away. Watched the rainbows come and go.

The door opened. A dry May breeze mixed with the sweltering car air. A police officer stuck his sweaty head inside. His face was hard, his voice angry and anxious. "Your mother wants to say something to you before we lock your ass up. We shouldn't let her say a damn word to you after what you did. Do you mind?

I stared straight ahead. "No."

He raised his voice. "No what?"

"No," I repeated in a way that let him know I thought that all of them were assholes for making me out to be the bad guy. "I don't mind."

He gripped the back of my neck. "You're pretty belligerent."

I was a knob-kneed reed of a boy. Hadn't lifted anything heavier than an algebra book and could barely run a mile in P.E. without passing out. That was before I started pumping weights, before squats, before doing two hundred push-ups in the morning to start my day, doing sprints, before the hooks and jabs and side kicks and roundhouse kicks and spinning back kicks became my trademark.

I said, "Fuck you."

With his other hand he grabbed the front of my throat and squeezed, made me gag and look into his blue eyes. He growled, "Say, 'No, sir. I don't mind, sir.' You insolent bastard."

He let me go when another officer passed by. I gagged and caught my breath while perspiration tingled down my forehead into my eyes. I tilted my head and looked at him.

He smirked. "Now, what you have to say?"

I spat in his face.

His cheeks turned crimson. He stared at me while my saliva rolled down his scarred face into his ill-trimmed wheat-colored mustache.

"That's your ass, boy."

Veins popped up in his neck while he stood there, handkerchief in hand, clenching his teeth and wiping my juices from his eye. He kept watching me, wanted me to break down and show my fear. It was there, but I refused to let it be seen. Another officer passed by and scarface told him what I'd done. It looked like they were about to double team me, but the second officer said they had to report the assault and they both stormed away.

A second later the door opened again and my mother eased her bruised face inside.

She said, "Don't hate me."

"Love you, Momma." I smiled. "Get away from here."

She fondled her wedding ring. Tears formed in her eyes. She dropped the police blanket from her shoulders, took her cross off, and put it around my neck.

She used her soft fingers to wipe the sweat from my eyes.

"Somebody'll come get you out. Maybe Uncle Ray. You might be able to go back to Philly and stay with him for a while."

"Uncle Ray don't like us. We're Catholic; Jehovah's Witnesses don't like nobody but Jehovah's Witnesses."

"Stop saying that."

"It's true."

"I'll call him anyway. I'll tell him you made the honor roll, so he'll know you're still doing good in school. Let him know you might get a scholarship. You could help him around his grocery store in the evenings."

I shook my head. "Don't worry about me. Get away before he hurts you. All he's gonna do is beat you up, then go out to Fort McDowell and spend the night with that Indian woman. He ain't been home in two days, then walks in complaining about some stupid dinner. Tomorrow he'll be mad about his shirts. The next day his shoes."

My old man was standing in a crowd of badges, guns, and whispers. The ambulance crew had bandaged his head and he was back on his feet. I'd beat him with everything I could get my hands on.

He made a single finger gesture for Momma to come.

My beautiful momma looked tired of the life she was living, and that made me sad. She wiped her eyes and kissed the side of my face. "You understand, don't you? You're a big boy now. Almost a man. You can take care of yourself. You understand."

I kissed the side of her face as my answer.

"Don't be angry." She twisted her lips. "Don't be like him."

"I won't." I smiled for her. "Go back inside before you get in trouble. Stop taking so much of that medication."

She rubbed her eyes, then dragged her fingers down across her lips. "It calms my nerves."

"Why you wanna sleep so much?"

"Sometimes," she patted my legs with her thin fingers, "sometimes I have nice dreams."

She was distant, reciting and not living the words.

I said, "Dreams ain't real, Momma."

"Sometimes—" she started, then stopped and kissed my forehead. Her voice became as melodic as the poetry she always read. "Sometimes they're better than what's real."

I fought the dryness in my throat that always came before my tears. I was scared. Fifteen and a half and living in fear.

She wandered away, wringing her hands and looking back at me every other step. We blew each other dysfunctional kisses.

I'd be in juvenile hall, then a boys' home until I was old enough to register for the draft and vote.

Living with criminals would be like going to a different kinda school. Nigerians, Mexicans, whites, no matter what nationality, they were all caught up in the same game. And didn't hesitate to lend to the schooling on everything from Three Card Monte to Rocks in a Box to Pigeon Drops, even broke down how to pass bad checks. A few were bold enough to run telephone scams from the inside.

That was different from the education I was after.

I had dreams of getting into Howard, to a frat life and a world filled with sorority girls. Always wanted to stomp in a Greek Show. Make enough money to get a small place, get Momma to move in with me. I was working on our escape.

But that night, guess I had had all I could stand and couldn't stand no more. I wanted to be like a superhero and rescue my momma. That was my mission in life. What motivated me.

Hard to save anybody when you're locked up, when you're too busy trying to fight to save yourself. When you've made yourself a prisoner.

I did want to save her. That gave my life a lot of purpose.

But there would be no Howard. No sorority girl at my side. And the closest thing to a frat I would see would be a bunch of young hardheads lining up for roll call, all wearing prison blues, most with tattoos. Our Greek Show was marching in sync to go get our meals.

Momma would find her own way to freedom.

My momma would take too many pills and become an angel.

My daddy would be found dead behind the wheel of his Thunderbird at Fort McDowell. Ambushed and shot outside of a married Indian woman's place.

On that night of changes, I sat in the back of that squad car staring at the colorful lights that were dancing in the night to make my pain go away. Watched the rainbows chasing the rainbows.

• 1

The phone rang.

Jarred me from my sleep and severed me from my past.

Time to time, I had nightmares, I felt the pain from the fights and heard the screams from the midnight rapes in juvenile hall. But I learned to kick ass before I got my ass kicked.

The phone rang again.

I opened my eyes. Focused on the red digits across the room.

3:32 A.M.

Not quite yesterday; not quite today.

Traffic in NoHo—that stands for North Hollywood—was breezing by outside my window on Chandler. Somewhere down by North Hollywood High a car alarm was singing a song of distress.

I snatched the phone up and answered, "Yeah?"

"Where've you been Dante?"

I knew who it was. Hearing his voice jarred me all over again. I sat up in my queen-size bed. The room had a chill and I kept the covers wrapped around me.

He chuckled, then said, "I was beginning to think you were dead or something."

"A'ight, how you get my number, Scamz?"

"There isn't a number I can't get."

"Just got it changed last week."

He laughed his irksome, sneaky laugh. "Happy birthday. You made it to the big two-five."

"On a hot wing and a prayer."

"A black man's not supposed to live past twenty-five."

"Then that makes me a senior citizen. I should be eligible for Social Security and a ten percent discount at Denny's."

"You crack me up." He laughed. "That's why I like talking to you."

I yawned, then checked my caller ID. No number was on the box. Last time he jingled, the ID box told me he was in New York, lounging at Fifth and Fifty-sixth at the Trump Tower. That was two weeks back. He didn't leave a message, he never did, but I knew that was my homey. Doubt if Donald Trump would be ringing me up to talk shop about the market. Nobody but Scamz. Time before that he told me he was down in South Beach. Time before that Montreal. Before then it was the W down in New Orleans during the Essence Festival. Before that Playa del Carmen.

I set another yawn free before I asked, "You back out in La La Land?"

"For a hot sec. Wrapping up some business before I go on vacation. You should've accepted my offer and left with me last time. Aspen had great skiing."

"Whatcha been onto?"

He boasted that over the last few weeks he'd been running scam after scam after scam. All nonviolent. Most of his dealings were in credit and green cards. Since he had women who worked everywhere from the DMV to the IRS, I already knew there wasn't any information he couldn't get, so his criminally-gifted butt getting my number didn't cause me to raise a brow. Not right then.

"Up until a few days ago, nobody around the pool hall had seen you for months," Scamz said.

"My job was keeping me busy."

"Thought One Time might've shackled you down and had you on the gray goose heading out to Chino."

"I don't do prisons." One Time was a nickname for the police. I yawned. "Like I said, I was working."

"Was?"

"Got laid off. Everything came to a screeching halt when the commercial side of the company stopped producing and the aerospace side picked up. Been out looking for another j-o-b."

Sounded like he took a draw from his cigarette, then blew the smoke out before he spoke again. "Why do you keep wasting your talents on a nine-to-five?"

Makes me content, that's all that matters. Don't need to be rich to be happy."

"What's the word, any luck?"

I told him I had called my old gig to check my status. Over twenty technicians with more time than I had were waiting to get called back. No one had gotten called back in six months and a few thousand more were getting kicked to the curb. The unemployment office told me to check back in a week or two, which was the same robotic line they ran on the twenty people in front of me.

I'd been hitting a lot of career fairs. Hit one down at the Bonaventure and put in apps with everybody from Aerospace Corporation to Sears. Never seen that many borderline-bankrupt people coming in from all over California and Nevada and Seattle looking for a job. After that I'd flown up to Oakland, hit the Alameda County Conference and Training Center, but five thousand out-of-work people beat me there. Most were in a line that circled the block by sunrise.

I told Scamz, "North or south, ain't nobody hiring."

"There's a synchronous world recession, especially in the high-tech world."

"Translate."

"No jobs out there. Jobs were already scarce, and those terrorists exacerbated the situation."

I said, "I got an interview next week."

"Another widget factory?"

"Labor gig. Slinging boxes on a truck from dusk to dawn."

"You're overqualified for that kind of work."

"A man with no job ain't overqualified for any kinda work."

"Spoken like a true member of the unemployed."

"You got jokes."

"Seems like a lot of people have been humbled."

I cleared my throat. "They're offering twelve an hour, but I know they have a stack of apps thicker than your little black book."

He laughed at that. "What're your ends looking like until that comes through?"

"They ain't looking. Almost as blind as Helen Keller."

"Your economic recession is in full effect."

"Yep. Seems like the world is fucked up."

We said a few words about the war that was going on, on how it had done a number on people both emotionally and financially.

Scamz said, " 'Ours is essentially a tragic age, so we refuse to take it tragically.' "

"Shakespeare?"

"D. H. Lawrence. The opening lines of *Lady Chatterley's Lover*."

I yawned. "A regular Nostradamus."

"Come see me today. I got a few things lined up."

"Can't. I'm a legit man."

Scamz asked, "You heard from Jackson?"

I met Jackson a few years back through Scamz. They were the best of friends when I came along. But Jackson had been off the grift for almost two years. A good woman and a steady job had him on the straight and narrow.

I said, "Yeah. I've been hanging with him almost every day."

"What you two got going on?"

"We've been teaming up and looking for jobs together."

"So, he's getting back on the hustle?"

I debated telling Jackson's business but Scamz wasn't the type to spread the word about someone else's misfortunes. And nine times out of ten, he already knew what was going on.

I said, "His ex is suing him for back child support."

"Sabrina slapped Jackson with a lawsuit?"

"Yep. She filed papers and claimed Jackson never gave her a dime."

"I don't believe that. He cared about his kids if nothing else."

"He showed me the papers from the district attorney."

We said a few more things about that.

In the end Scamz told me, "Be careful where you stick your dick."

I laughed at those sage words. He laughed too. They were laughs of disbelief.

We chitchatted about a few other people from our little clandestine world. A few were on lockdown, a few more were about to get out. A couple had died along the way.

"Big Slim told me you were down at Eight Ball gambling with Nazario," Scamz said.

Eight Ball was a place people went when they were desperate for cash. Trouble and money was always down there. You just had to outrun the trouble to get the money.

"Yeah," I said. "That psycho was so mad he lost his mind."

"Then he didn't lose much."

"He wanted to pay me on the spot."

"People say he made a scene."

"Big time. He made his wife give me her wedding ring to cover his debt."

Scamz said, "He hates to lose, especially in front of a crowd."

"I pawned the ring. Got five hundred."

"You know he's looking for you. He wants a rematch so he can get that ring back. Heard he's been down at the pool hall at least three times a day trying to find you."

"Kinda figured that. That's why I ain't been back down to the pool hall."

"If you're sweating over chump change, you must need some economic relief."

My eyes went to my pine dresser. My bills were over there, piled up next to a stack of job rejection postcards. Frustration was bringing out the wolf in me.

I told Scamz, "Just need something to hold me over until one of these jobs come through."

He said, "Come see me. You're a good worker. I could use your help."

I paused. The jury in my mind went out to make a decision. "I'll pass. I have a few job interviews around the corner."

"Then come make some ends so you can take your woman out and have a good time."

"Me no got no woman. Got my eye on this waitress at Ed Debevic's."

"You ever stopped her yet?"

"Not yet. She has an L.A. face and an Oakland boot that won't quit. Pretty much out of my league."

"How can a waitress be out of anybody's league?"

"True."

"Be a man at all times. Never let a woman scare you. Never."

Scamz was working my disposition in his direction word by word, phrase by phrase.

"Either way," he said, "it's hard to get a woman being broke."

Scamz wasn't lying. L.A. had its own mentality and it cost to be the boss out here. Whenever I hit Atlas Bar and Grill it was five bucks to park, twenty to get in, and close to ten bucks for one drink. If I met a honey, triple that drinking budget. Breakfast at Roscoe's would add another twenty. If I got lucky, a box of condoms would cost another five. Trojans were the cheapest thing on the list. Not using one was the most expensive thing on the list.

Scamz said, "Pussy and money, Dante. Got money, you can get pussy. Got pussy—"

"You can get money."

We chuckled at his phrase.

My eyes closed when I thought about that waitress, saw her dimples, heard her mature voice, even could see her hips when she did her sensual stroll, and wondered what she was doing right now.

A second later I exhaled. "Is this hot or cold?"

Hot meant difficult. Cold meant smooth, minimal problems.

I could hear Scamz smile when I asked that. His easy words had worked me toward his team.

He replied, "Easy rent money."

"Let's be up front. I'm not down for nothing long term."

"What do I have to do to get you to reconsider?"

"You can't."

He didn't say anything for a few seconds. He did that when his mind was in overdrive. Sometimes I thought he had so many thoughts he had to shut down to keep from overloading.

Scamz said, "You know how to find me."

We left it at that. He wasn't going to give me the specifics, not over the wire.

I hung up.

3:41 A.M.

I dialed another number. Jackson answered on the first ring.

I said, "You're up?"

"Yeah. What's up Cool Hand?"

"Scamz called. He's back and it sounds like he has a few things going on."

Jackson hesitated. "Yeah, Dante. We can check on those interviews after I leave court."

I understood why he was talking in code. I said, "Robin must be over."

"Right."

"See you in a few hours."

We hung up. No matter what time of night I called, he was awake. I didn't think much about that because I wasn't sleeping on a regular schedule my-damn-self. Not having a job stole away the importance of an alarm clock. It also made it easy to lose track of my days. When a man didn't have a job, didn't have a Monday, a hump day, and a payday, all days started to blend and lose value. All were just today. All he wanted was a better tomorrow.

I was on edge, a little hungry. I walked over my two-shades-of-brown carpet, went to the kitchen sink, washed my face, dried it with a paper towel, then opened the fridge. Not much in there except leftover salmon and rice and a frozen Healthy Choice meal.

Restless. Scamz had left me agitated.

I did two hundred sit-ups, crunches, worked on my obliques. Did half as many push-ups. Stretched my legs into a split on the left side, did the same on the right, then went down into a Chinese-style split. Shadowboxed against my old memories until a layer of sweat glistened on my skin.

I looked at that stack of job rejection postcards.

Anxiety was all over me, clinging to my skin like a thousand ticks.

More push-ups until my arm burned. More sit-ups until my abs were on fire.

Dealing with Scamz meant I needed to be in shape. Ready to rumble, ready to run.

I rested in my sweat. Put on my Levi Chen *Liquid Gardens* CD. Meditated a few minutes.

Then with that music calming me, I stood in my window and looked out at the palm trees.

I was lonely. Broke and lonely.

L.A. was an expensive bitch. A whore who sucked your dick and swallowed all of your money, then left you sleeping on the concrete.

A man stayed broke and hungry long enough, his value system was bound to change. And when it did, Scamz was waiting.

FROM **P. G. County**

BY CONNIE BRISCOE

arbara stepped back and smiled at her daughter. Rebecca looked regal in her beaded ivory satin gown, and for a moment Barbara forgot the utter chaos on the lawn. She forgot about the tent being decorated with flowers, the tables and chairs being arranged, the band, the buffet, the bar.

Rebecca stood in front of the mirror above her dresser and picked at her upswept do. "Does it need more hair spray, Mama?"

Barbara glanced at Pearl.

"No indeed," Pearl replied as she reached up and fussed with a tiny stray hair on Rebecca's forehead.

From all that Barbara could see, Rebecca's hair looked absolutely smashing. Pearl had done a fantastic job, as always.

"Another drop of spray and it will be sitting up there looking like a rock, child," Pearl continued. "Your hair looks beautiful just the way it is."

"I've never seen you look prettier, sweetheart." Barbara kissed her daughter gently on the forehead, being careful not to muss her makeup, then she turned to Pearl. "Let's get the veil on her now. It's already twelve-fifteen, and the photographers are due at twelve-thirty."

Pearl reached for the floor-length veil sprawled across the bed as Barbara took a quick glimpse out the bedroom window onto the lawn. The wedding planner, a petite black woman named Darlene Dunn, was leading the florist around the grounds as they placed brightly colored centerpieces and other doodads on the tables inside and outside of a large white tent. The caterer and his staff were running back and forth between the four-car garage, where they had set up a temporary kitchen with food warmers, and the buffet being set up under the tent.

Despite the busy atmosphere, everything seemed to be falling into place, Barbara thought thankfully. Well, almost everything. The only exception was that husband of hers. She checked her watch. The photographers would arrive soon to take pictures and video before the family left for the church, and the father of the bride was still out banging his mistress. Unbelievable.

She needed a cigarette badly. But she had promised Rebecca that she wouldn't smoke on this day. She sighed and turned to help Pearl lift the veil just as something outdoors caught her eye. She looked out the window to see a black car turning onto their driveway. Now who on earth could that be? Rebecca's godmother had offered to come by and ride to the church with them so she would be there to supervise the procession of the wedding party and Barbara could take her place in the front pew and relax. But Marilyn drove a tan Lexus.

Barbara frowned with disapproval as the car approached the house. Anyone arriving at this early hour was either extremely rude or just plain ignorant. Her frown deepened as the sporty little car ran right up over the edge of the asphalt on the freshly mowed lawn.

What the devil? Barbara blincked hard. Her eyes must be playing a horrible trick on her. She had been awfully busy planning this wedding lately and sometimes she didn't know if she was coming or going. It was entirely possible that her eyes were giving out.

Barbara blinked again as the little black sports car kept coming across the lawn. This was no illusion. Some idiot had lost control and now the car was plowing straight toward the reception tent.

"Oh my God!" she screamed just as the car smashed headlong into the tent frame. Pearl dropped the veil on the bed and followed Rebecca to the window. Barbara could have sworn the whole tent would come crashing down, but mercifully it didn't. The car, which by now Barbara realized was a small late-model BMW being driven by a woman, backed up. Thank goodness. What an idiot.

But before Barbara could catch her breath, the engine revved and the car jerked forward. Barbara gasped as it picked up speed and rammed into the tent frame. This time the tent sagged on one end.

This woman wasn't drunk. She was doing this deliberately. Barbara covered her open mouth with her hand as Darlene, the florist, the caterer, and the waiters all ran to and fro. It looked like a fire had broken out under a circus tent.

"Lord have mercy," Pearl whispered, clutching her breasts.

Rebecca shrieked. "Who is that?"

"I have no idea," Barbara said, turning toward the bedroom door. "But I'd better get down there."

"That woman is crazy," Pearl said.

"Mama!" Rebecca cried. "Daddy just pulled up."

Barbara turned back to the window to see Bradford's silver Jaguar convertible come to a screeching halt. He jumped out, ran toward the BMW and yanked the driver's-side door open.

Slowly it dawned on Barbara that she recognized the little black car. It belonged to Sabrina, that hussy mistress of Bradford's. Barbara twisted her lips with disgust. This was utterly ridiculous. She snatched her cell phone off Rebecca's dresser.

"I'll be right back," Barbara said hurriedly. "Pearl, can you stay here and help Rebecca finish getting dressed? I know I'm only paying you to do her hair, but—"

Pearl put her forefinger to her lips. "Shh. Don't worry about a thing. Of course I will."

"Thank you so much," Barbara said as she raced to the door.

"Mama, wait!" Rebecca shouted. "Oh my God. She's getting out of the car and yelling and screaming and waving her fists at Daddy." Rebecca lifted her gown and followed Barbara to the door. "I'm going down there with you."

Barbara held her hand out. "Oh no you aren't," she said firmly. "Your father and I will handle this. I don't want you getting involved."

"But Mama, she's—"

"No buts."

Rebecca sighed and ran back to the window and stood next to Pearl. Barbara walked out the bedroom door so fast she nearly bumped into Robin, Rebecca's older sister.

"What's going on? Who is that crazy woman outside?" Robin asked. She was wearing her lavender maid-of-honor dress and fastening pearl earrings.

"I'm going down there now," Barbara replied.

"Do you want me to come with you?" Robin asked.

"Absolutely not. Go help your sister get ready."

Robin blinked, clearly puzzled by her mother's harsh reaction. Barbara didn't like the tone of her own voice. Certainly none of this was Robin's fault. But she couldn't help it, not when Bradford had allowed his whore to pull such hysterical antics on their daughter's wedding day.

She took the back stairs in her satin Ferragamo pumps two at a time, threw the back door open and marched out onto the lawn. Sabrina was still in the driveway screaming at the top of her lungs as Bradford, dressed in a navy running suit, held his hands out and tried to calm her down.

Darlene Dunn and the others stood around in a small cluster nearby, listening and watching like it was the latest installment of their favorite soap opera. Barbara was so embarrassed but determined to stay calm. She had to get this mess straightened out before Marilyn arrived, not to mention the photographer and the three hundred guests expected later that afternoon.

"You bastard," Sabrina screamed. "I can't believe you didn't invite me to the wedding. How could you do this to me, Bradford?"

Barbara couldn't help but notice how young and thin Sabrina was—and how beautiful. The woman couldn't be more than thirty and had one of those size 4 figures with forty-inch boobs. Barbara also noticed how the spaghetti straps to her black negligee kept slipping off her honey-colored shoulders. The skinny little whore hadn't even taken the time to get dressed after her little tryst with Bradford.

"You're going to have to calm down, Sabrina," Bradford said in a firm tone of voice. "Look at the mess you're making here. You're going to ruin Rebecca's wedding, and I won't have that."

"Like I give a fucking shit," Sabrina retorted, oblivious to the black mascara streaming down her cheeks. She ran toward a cluster of tables on the lawn outside the tent and grabbed a chair by the back. She flipped it over, then ran inside the tent and knocked another chair down.

Barbara was appalled. She ought to grab that whore and throw her off their property. But she was wearing a two-thousand-dollar silk suit, and Sabrina looked downright dangerous. Barbara was not about to get into a public fight over a man, even her husband. Better to let Bradford handle it. She wished he'd hurry up and get rid of her. Marilyn would be arriving any minute, and it would be horrible for Rebecca's godmother to see this.

She followed Bradford as he rushed inside the tent.

"After all I've done for you the past year, Bradford Bentley," Sabrina wailed as she stopped in front of the buffet table. "And this is the thanks I get. A whole fucking year I wasted on you. I do everything for you. I cook for you. I listen to you talk about your problems with your wife. I give you every fucking thing you want in bed."

Bradford stole a glance at Barbara. She glared back at him, eyes smoldering. It was about time he noticed her. And yes, she had heard it. Every word.

"Sabrina, don't make me have to force you to leave. It'll be better for everybody concerned if you just go and get in the car quietly."

"Fuck you, Bradford Bentley," Sabrina yelled. She grabbed a carving knife off the buffet table and held it out in front of her.

Bradford clenched his fists and circled Sabrina silently and cautiously just as Marilyn's Lexus pulled into the driveway.

Damn, Barbara thought, as if all this wasn't enough. Marilyn turned off the engine but stayed inside her car. She looked over the scene with a puzzled expression on her face and rolled down the window.

"What's going on here, Barbara?" she called out.

Barbara waved toward the house. "Go on inside and wait for me there."

Marilyn got out slowly, then ran to the front door and disappeared inside the house.

"Bradford, do I need to call the police?" Barbara was damned if she was going to let this woman ruin Rebecca's wedding day. She lifted her cell phone to dial.

"No," Bradford responded without taking his eyes off Sabrina. "Just stay back."

"Bradford, you'd better tell that bitch to put that phone away," Sabrina shouted. Then she swung the knife in Barbara's direction and lunged.

Barbara screamed as Bradford grabbed Sabrina from behind just in time and they both fell to the ground. They tussled for a moment until Bradford wrestled the knife away. He stood up quickly and stared down at Sabrina with such fury that she began to crawl away in fear.

Barbara put her hand to her breast. She was huffing and puffing like she'd just run a marathon. She couldn't believe that woman had come after her with a knife. On her own property. The woman was clearly out of her mind and needed to be locked up. She punched the buttons on her cell phone and marched toward the house.

Bradford took his eyes off Sabrina, who by now was sprawled out on the grass and crying like a baby, and looked at Barbara. "Who are you calling?" he asked gruffly.

"The police. Who else?"

"You don't need to call the cops," he said tersely. I'll take care of this."

Barbara turned and glared at him. Take care of it? You call this taking care of it? Letting her put all your dirty business out in the street? She'd had enough embarrassment as a child to last a lifetime. *Barbara the bag lady.* She didn't need this, especially on her daughter's wedding day.

That was what she wanted to say, but she didn't care to argue with Bradford now. Rebecca was standing at her bedroom window watching her wedding day go down the drain. Not to mention Pearl and Marilyn.

Barbara hung up the phone. "Well, you'd better get her out of here now. We leave for the church in less than an hour and the photographers are coming. You're not even dressed yet."

"I said I'll handle it," he snapped. "The best thing you can do is go on back in the house. You're obviously just making her angrier."

Barbara squeezed the phone until her fingers ached. How dare he make it sound as if this were *her* fault. The bastard. But this was not the time to get into an argument with him, not in front of all these people. She took a deep breath and signaled for Darlene to follow her as Bradford reached down and pulled a still-sobbing Sabrina up from the ground.

"Are you all right?" Darlene asked as they stepped outside the tent.

Barbara nodded. She had to remain calm and somehow get through this. First, she had to deal with the tent. "How much damage did she do?"

Darlene shook her head anxiously. "It doesn't look good. It's going to need some reparis. Give me a minute and I'll make a few calls to try to get it fixed in time."

While Darlene made her calls, Barbara picked up the chairs that Sabrina had knocked over. Bradford was now talking to Sabrina as she sat in the car, and she looked much calmer. Sabrina finally backed out of the driveway and screeched off down the street.

Darlene covered the mouthpiece. "I'm trying to get the rental company back out here to repair it. But they're giving me some crap about being booked all afternoon."

Barbara threw her hands in the air as Bradford walked across the driveway and back toward the lawn. This was all his fault, but she had to stay calm in front of the help. "Bradford, they can't get out here to fix the tent in time for the reception. What are we going to do?"

He walked up to the tent and examined the damaged area. It was all Barbara could do to keep from yelling at him in front of everyone.

Bradford turned to Darlene. "Tell them we'll double their normal fee to get out here and fix it before the reception," he ordered. "Whatever it takes, just get them out here now."

Darlene's eyes lit up. "Whatever you say, sir." Within a minute she was snapping the phone antenna back into place and smiling in victory. "They're sending someone right away. The reception doesn't start until three, so that gives us two and a half hours. In the meantime, we can finish setting things up. I don't think it will topple over."

"Nah," Bradford said. It should hold up fine until they get out here to fix it."

Barbara sighed with relief. She had to hand it to her husband. He was always so good in a crisis, even one of his own making. "So you think everything will be ready on time, Darlene?"

Darlene nodded. "Yes. I think we'll make it."

Barbara smiled. "Thank goodness. Do your best."

Darlene nodded and walked off with the phone at her ear as she directed the other workers to get back to their jobs. Just when Barbara thought she could relax a bit, she noticed a young man walking around on the patio near the house, snapping away with a 35-millimeter camera. "Oh my God," she exclaimed in horror. "Bradford, it's Peter, the photographer."

Bradford followed her gaze. He let out a deep breath. "I'll handle this."

Barbara didn't say a word. She was too stunned to speak. When did he get here? How much had he caught on film? God forbid she should wake up tomorrow morning to photos in the style section of the *Washington Post* or on the Internet of Bradford's mistress wrecking Rebecca's wedding reception tent.

Bradford walked briskly across the lawn to the patio and spoke to Peter for a minute. Barbara let out a sigh of relief as the photographer fiddled with his camera, then handed something over to Bradford. The photographer disappeared into the house, and Bradford turned toward Barbara. "It's OK. I got the film from him."

"This is your fault, Bradford," Barbara snapped. "What the devil was that all about?"

Bradford shook his head with regret, but he didn't say anything. There was no apology and Barbara didn't expect one. The women came and went so often that Bradford seemed to realize that apologizing when he got caught was getting stale.

"Never mind," Barbara said. "We don't have time to get into it now, anyway."

"Where is Rebecca?" Bradford asked. "Did she see any of this?"

"Of course she saw it," Barbara snapped. How could she miss it? Not to mention Marilyn and Pearl and God knows who else. I'm sure we're the laughingstock of Silver Lake now."

"Barbara, please," Bradford said tiredly. "Don't be so melodramatic. I'm going to go get into my tux."

"Fine," Barbara said crisply. "We'll discuss it tomorrow."

"There's nothing to discuss."

"Nothing to discuss? Your mistress just drove up onto our property and . . . and practically ruined our daughter's wedding. Or didn't you notice?"

"You mean ex-mistress. The reason she was so upset was because I called it off."

Barbara scoffed. "You told me last month that you called it off."

"Well, it's true. But she's having problems accepting it."

This was why she tried to avoid these arguments with Bradford. It was impossible to win any of them. He had an excuse for everything. "So that's why you ran over there first thing this morning, I suppose?" she said sarcastically.

"She called last night crying, so I—"

"Bradford, please," Barbara said. "Spare me."

"Look, I didn't want to get into this, but you—"

"Daddy?"

They both turned to see Rebecca and Robin standing in the doorway leading to the patio with frustrated expressions on their faces.

"Yes?" Bradford smiled and moved toward them.

"Who was that woman?" Rebecca asked, her eyes narrowed with suspicion.

Bradford shoved his hands in his jacket pocket. "Nobody for you to worry about."

Rebecca looked from Bradford to Barbara with doubt. "She looked like plenty to worry about to me. Look at what she did to the tent."

"Your father is right. And the tent will be repaired in plenty of time," Barbara said. No doubt Rebecca and Robin had long ago come to realize their parents' marriage was a rocky one, but she never discussed Bradford's philandering with them, or anyone else for that matter. The dirt between her and Bradford would stay between her and Bradford.

"What on earth was she so upset about?" Robin asked.

Bradford shrugged. "She works for a friend of mine, and, uh, she was mad because we didn't invite her to the wedding."

"You've got to be kidding," Robin said.

"What if she comes back?" Rebecca asked, a look of horror on her face.

Bradford smiled and put his arm around Rebecca's shoulder. "She won't. I promise you that. And did I tell you you look stunning? Ralph is one lucky guy."

Rebecca tried to smile. "Thanks, Daddy. But you're not even dressed yet."

"I will be, in fifteen minutes sharp. I've already shaved and showered."

No doubt after you screwed your whore, Barbara thought. Because he certainly didn't shower here this morning. And all that talk about Sabrina losing control because he broke up with her was bull. Bradford could keep a hundred employees in check. He could manage millions of dollars. But he couldn't keep his mistress in her place? Mister Big Shot? Please.

"By the way," Bradford said. "The lieutenant governor called at the last minute and said she was accepting her invitation to the reception."

Rebecca's eyes widened. "You mean Kathleen Kennedy Townsend? Oh my gosh."

"And you waited all this time to tell us, Bradford?" Barbara said. "Honestly."

Bradford shrugged. "She called just this morning."

"She probably sees the reception as an opportunity to line up votes in her campaign for governor," Robin said.

Barbara sighed with impatience.

"What's the big deal?" Bradford asked. "She and the governor have both been here before."

"That was for political receptions, Bradford, not our daughter's wedding. She'll need special seating."

"I'm sure you'll carry it off without a hitch," Bradford said. He kissed Rebecca's forehead and walked into the house.

"I can't believe all this is happening," Rebecca said.

"How could Daddy let that woman in here today of all days," Robin said with annoyance.

"You can't blame him," Barbara said. "He tried to stop her."

Robin shook her head with frustration. "You always defend him."

Barbara grimaced and touched her forehead. So much to do, so little time. She was going to have to get herself together. And fast. She put her arms around both her daughters and forced a smile. "Come on, girls. Let's forget about this. We have a big day ahead of us. The lieutenant governor is coming, not to mention half of Silver Lake and our family and friends. We have to look and behave our best."

Barbara held her head high and led her daughters back into the house.

This I Know Is True

My Heavenly Father

BY DANA CRUM

It's the evening after I sinned against God, and the heat so bad it seem like somebody done wrapped a coat round my shoulders even though I don't need one. I start thinking about Hell. If I go there when I die, the Devil he gon' be waiting for me and he gon' poke me with that big pitchfork he got.

I'm sitting on the steps of the porch, looking over at the houses across the street. Old people is out on their porches, too, rocking in rocking chairs, fanning theyselves to keep cool. Every now and then one of 'em call across the street to somebody and ask how they doing. Them crickets done just started up their racket, and I'm thinking about what I did at church earlier today. That's when my grandma call me.

"An-DRE!" she say, her voice getting high at the end.

I put them quarters back in my pocket real fast like and look over my shoulder. "Ma'am?"

"You get in here before dark, you hear?"

"Yes, ma'am."

She standing behind me on the porch. Hands on her hips, she looking down at me like she trying to read my mind. I can feel my heart pounding like it's about to jump outa my chest. Around me in them bushes, them crickets is getting louder and louder like they trying to tell on me. Then they quiet down and start up all over again. After a while my grandma leave and go back inside. She must not of seen me with them quarters.

Me and her went to church this morning like we always do, but my mama ain't gone with us. She was sick so we had to go without her. Grandma was wearing a dark blue dress and this lil white and blue hat with a blue feather sticking up in the back. You could see her real hair poking out from underneath her wig 'cause her real hair gray and her wig black. She was wearing these high-heel shoes that make her look even taller than she already is. We was late and about to leave, but something was wrong with her hearing aid. It kept making all this noise and you could hear it all through the house. She couldn't get it to act right for nothing.

Pretty soon she got mad and hit it against the table in the living room. It was all right after that. I smiled. She smiled, too. Until she saw I ain't have my tie on.

"Boy, get in there and put yo' tie on," she said, pointing to my room.

"But we late, Grandma."

She frowned and started fidgeting with her pocketbook. "Lord, Lord," she said, shaking her head. "Well, come on then, boy." She put her pocket-book over her shoulder and we left.

I was glad. That ugly brown corduroy suit she made me wear was bad enough. I wasn't going to put that tie on, too. Why I gotta wear a tie any-way? And how come I can't wear my tennis shoes to church? Them dress shoes be hurting my toes. The bell bottoms on my corduroy pants so wide you can barely tell what kind of shoes I got on, anyway.

Anyway, me and Grandma left and I got away with not wearing that tie. She fussed at me all the way to church though. She always fussing at me about something. She say I'm getting too grown for my britches and I got too much mouth. My daddy used to fuss at me, too. But not like her.

I was burning up in that hot suit. It was summertime and I woulda been wearing the other suit I got, except last Sunday I had this pen in my pocket that bust 'cause I forgot to put the top on. Ink spread all over my suit, so my mama had to take it to the cleaners. My grandma started fussing at me about that, too.

"You hot, ain't you? Un-huh. I told you not to put that pen in yo' pocket. One way or the other, you gon' learn. You gon' learn that when you don't do as you told, the Lord will make you pay for it. He see everything you do."

She said I was gon' be lucky if the ink even come out.

By the time me and her got to First Baptist Church, wasn't nobody out-side. I could hear the choir and everybody else singing they hearts out as me and her went up the steps. After they got through with the song, the usher let us in. He a tall man with big heavy hands. He gave my grandma a pro-gram, but ain't give me one. I looked up at him and frowned. He ain't see me, though. So I looked away.

That's when I saw Paul look over at me all mean like. He like to hang with this skinny boy name Hi-C. Everybody call him Hi-C 'cause every time you see him that's what he drinking. Him and Paul live in the projects, them red buildings down the hill from me. My street and the one the school on—they not like the projects. They nicer. My mama and grandma don't like for me to go down to the projects 'cause they say it's dangerous. But all the kids I'm in second grade with live there. Don't no kids live on my street. It's all old people.

Paul the biggest kid in our grade, but we say he the ugliest, too. He got big lips and his hair always nappy. He still mad 'cause I ain't let him scare me the way he be scaring everybody else. I hit him right in his teeth, just like how my daddy taught me, even though I had to jump to do it. He hurt my arm real bad and pushed me down, but I still got him in the belly. Then I hit him in his mouth again. Real hard. So hard my hand hurt. Here in church my grandma kept walking, but I stopped and stuck my tongue out at him. That made him real mad and he balled up his fist and held it up for me to see. I made a face at him 'cause he couldn't do nothing to me in church. But I was gon' have to see him outside of church sooner or later, so I ain't make that face for too long.

I caught up with my grandma. She looked over her shoulder and reached out for my hand. I let her hold it. My grandma ain't sit down till she got all the way up to the front of the church. Her and my mama always sitting in the front. And I always gotta be right up there with 'em. Most kids get to sit in the back. But not me. So I sat down between my grandma and this lady wearing a wide green hat. She had some perfume on. It smelled sweet. Like one of them flowers in my grandma's garden.

It was hot in the church like it was outside, so I took off my jacket. My grandma looked at me like I was up to something. But she ain't say nothing. After a while this old bald-headed man came up to the front of the church talking about Men's day. His head was real shiny. It was round too, round like a bowling ball. He had on a tight, funny-looking suit and kept asking for all the men in the church to help out "so this Men's Day can be the best Men's Day ever."

If my daddy was here with us, maybe he could help them out. A year and a half ago my mama left him and took me with her. We came here, to Alabama, and started living with my grandma. This where my mama from. Back when me and her was up in Michigan, my daddy used to come to church with us sometimes. But only when my mama woke him up and made him. They used to fuss about that and a whole lotta other things. Last month me and him was supposed to go to a preseason Falcons game for my birthday, like how we did last year. He said he was gon' fly down from Michigan and be in Birmingham that Saturday so we could drive to Atlanta for the game the next day. He said he was gon' buy me some of them fat pretzels and some of them hotdogs with ketchup and mustard all over 'em. He said he was gon' get me one of them footballs, too, the ones with Steve Bartkowski's autograph on it. But then he ain't never come. I waited and waited, but still he ain't never come.

I tried not to think about my daddy no more, but the man at the front of the church kept talking about Men's Day and how he needed the men to help out like they did last year. Then he got through, and everybody in the church had to stand up and sing a song from the hymn book. I was sad but I was mad too, and I wanted to hold my own hymn book 'cause they got pretty gold pages on the side. But my grandma wouldn't let me. She made me read on with her, and she held the hymn book down low to make sure I was singing.

When the song finished and everybody had sat back down, the preacher walked up to that wooden thing my mama call "the podium." He fat and got a big belly that make him look like a big ole grizzly bear. He started talking about Revival Services for the summer. I got bored. I looked at my grandma to see if she was watching me. She wasn't. So I pulled out my Matchbox car real careful like. It's a Trans Am. It's red and got doors and a trunk that open up. It's fast, too. Fast like that car on *Starsky and Hutch.* I started rolling it around on my leg, making it turn around and chase the bad guys. *Vroom. Vroom. Errrrrrr!* I kept looking up at my grandma to make sure she wasn't looking. But after a while I musta forgot to keep looking 'cause she popped me on my hand and snatched my car from me and put it in that big black pocketbook she got.

"I'm sorry, Grandma," I said, trying to see if she was gon' give it back.

Wasn't no use.

She just shook her head. "Boy, I don't know what yo' mama gon' do with you," she said in a mean way even though she was whispering. "You just as mannish as you can be."

I folded my arms across my chest. That was my favorite car and she had took some of my other toys and hadn't never gave 'em back.

"Look at you," she said. "You got your mouth all poked out. I told you if you wanna keep them toys, keep 'em at home."

I turned away and wouldn't look at her no more. The preacher started preaching. He talked and talked and seemed like he wasn't gon' never stop talking. He was sweating, moving all around, talking like it was hurting him to talk. But he still kept on going. He wiped his face with a handkerchief and started holding on to the podium. I fell asleep. I guess my head was bouncing around like people's heads be bouncing around when they sleep 'cause I felt somebody shaking me. I looked up and saw my grandma's face, them lights shining in her glasses like fires burning. She was real mad now, like she was getting ready to whoop me right there in church, right there with all them people watching. I really woke up then. I wasn't trying to get no whooping.

The preacher was still up there. He was swaying around, looking up at the ceiling, sweat coming down his face. His voice got louder and it was almost like he was singing.

"I'm here to tell you this morning, huh!, that when you need a friend, huh!, go to your Father, huh! Your neighbors, huh!, may not be there for you, huh! Your spouse, huh!, may not be there for you, huh! My God, your pastor, huh!, may not be there for you, huh! But no matter what, huh!, no matter the hour, huh!, your Father, huh!, He'll be there for you. Can I get an 'Amen'?"

"Amen!" somebody shouted.

"Can anybody out there, huh!, understand what I'm saying? Huh! If you know your Father, huh!, the way that I know mine, huh!, why don't ya say 'Amen'?"

"Amen!"

"Amen!"

"Yes, Lord!"

"Preach it! Preach it!"

I felt sad. I missed my daddy. I wished he was still my friend like the preacher said he was supposed to be. I wished he ain't stop coming to see me. I remembered how back in Michigan he used to wear a gray tweed cap and after work his face would be dark and the hair would always tickle and then hurt my face whenever he picked me up and hugged me. On the weekends me and him would go down to the park and wrestle in the grass and we would be laughing and every time he would let me win. Then we would be laying on our backs, staring up at the sky, watching the lil birds fly by, their wings just a-flapping. At night we used to sit in front of the TV and watch *Monday Night Football,* then I would fall asleep and he would carry me to bed and I could tell he was carrying me even though I was sleep. My mama and grandma don't know, but I heard them talking the other night about how my daddy got him a new girlfriend even though my mama and him not divorced yet. I heard them say my daddy's new girlfriend "pregnant." That was before my birthday, and then when my birthday came, he ain't never show up.

Last week I wanted to ask my mama what it meant that my daddy's new girlfriend was "pregnant." But I knew I wasn't supposed to have heard nothing about that. So I ain't ask. I asked her if my daddy don't like me no more, if that's why he stopped coming to see me.

She started looking sad. "It's not you," she said, hugging me. "It's him. He's not the man he used to be. There's something wrong with him. Not you."

I felt like she was just saying that to make me feel better. Like the time Frisky died and she said dogs go to Heaven and then I asked the preacher if it say anywhere in the Bible about dogs going to Heaven and he put his hand on my shoulder and said, "Heaven is the land of the blessed. It's for us, young man. People like you and me who love God and accept Christ as our Lord and Savior. Pets can't know God the way we do. They can't go with us to Heaven."

So I felt like my mama was just trying to make me feel better. My daddy didn't like me no more. And I knew why. Last year when me and him came home from the Falcons game, my mama told him about my grades. She told him I wasn't studying and I was watching too much football on TV. He got mad and took off his big, long belt and whooped me with it. And he kept on whooping me. Then he pointed his finger at me and said, "Don't you never let me hear 'bout you getting bad grades again. You too smart for that, boy. I want you to make something outa yourself. You hear me?"

I ain't say nothing.

"Look at me when I'm talking to you! Do you hear me?"

I made myself look. "Yes, sir." I tried not to, but I started crying. "I'm sorry, Daddy. I'ma do better."

"Yeah, well, you just make sure you do."

Then he left and went back to Michigan and I ain't never see him again. For a while he ain't even call.

I think he still mad at me. That's why he don't like me no more. Thinking about all that while the preacher was up there preaching, my eyes started hurting. But I wasn't gon' let myself cry. I tried to stop thinking about my daddy. But I couldn't. That's when people started shouting, catching the Holy Ghost. It's always the ladies catching the Holy Ghost. I don't never see none of the men catching it. Maybe the Ghost don't like them as much. That lady next to me, the one with the green hat and the sweet perfume, she threw her hands up and started bouncing around. The whole pew shook. She was a big ole fat lady. She had on a green dress with flowers all over it. All of a sudden, she hopped up, started jumping up and down, moving all around. I was scared she was gon' fall on me and squish me to death so I started doing what she was doing. She throw her hands up, I throw my hands up. She wiggle around, I wiggle around. She jump up and down, I jump up and down.

The lady sitting in front of me saw me and bent over laughing. I stopped then. I just knew I was about to get it. But my grandma—she ain't see me! I was lucky 'cause I had forgot all about her. She ain't see me 'cause she was too busy helping them ushers calm this other lady down a few pews back. They was fanning her and she was laid back against the pew with her eyes closed like she was sleep. Her arms was spread out and they was fanning her. Wasn't nobody around to help that fat lady next to me. She had to keep getting happy till she tired herself out.

The preacher was finished preaching by then. He was sitting down. He had a Bible in his hands and kept tapping his foot to the music. He was smiling. Seem like he was looking right at me! The skinny man sitting next to him stood up. I guess he a preacher, too. He asked everybody to "come forward with the tithes and offerings." I used to couldn't say "tithe" right, but my mama taught me how. Me and Grandma stood up and waited like everybody else. Two men was standing up at the front, below where the preacher was sitting. They had straw baskets in their hands. They looked real serious in them dark suits with them dark ties. They always looking serious. My mama told me they called "deacons." While we was standing, my grandma gave me two quarters to put in the offering. I rubbed 'em. They was smooth and after a while they felt warm in my hand.

When it come time for the offering, they always gotta start with the peo-

ple in the back. Me and Grandma was up front so we had to wait seem like forever to get a chance to walk around the church and put our money in. It was hot in there. My hand started sweating, so I put them quarters in my pocket. Paul walked past along the side aisle and looked over at me. But he ain't ball up his fist this time 'cause my grandma mighta seen him.

When me and Grandma's turn to go up came around, she ain't go. She sat back down and told me to take her five dollars up there for her. She was leaning back against the pew and her eyes was half closed. She looked tired. So I went without her and followed all them big, tall people around the church. When I saw Paul again, he was back in his seat. He ain't see me this time though. He was too busy digging up his nose and wiping boogas on his pants. I said to myself, *If he try to mess with me again, I'ma tell people what he was doing. I'ma tell how he was up in church, wiping boogas on his pants.*

Before I knew it, I was up there at them baskets. I put the five dollars in and came back and sat down. My grandma patted me on the hand and smiled at me. She still looked tired, but she was smiling. My hands was still sweaty, so I started rubbing 'em up and down my pants. They was shiny corduroy pants, and I watched how they turned from dark brown to light brown every time I rubbed 'em.

It was then I felt something in my pocket. It was them two quarters! They was still there! I had forgot to put them in the basket! I had put my grandma's money in but had forgot to put my own in! I stuck my hand in my pocket to make sure it was them quarters I was feeling. It was them all right. I was about to run up there and put 'em in one of them baskets before the deacons took the baskets away. But I ain't want people laughing at me and looking all at me. I ain't want my grandma to get mad and say I was shaming her. I felt bad. Like I had did something wrong, something God was gon' be mad at me for, something He was gon' punish me for. But I ain't even mean to do it!

I know some kids who be doing this all the time. They keep the money their mama or grandma give 'em and go and buy candy after church over. One time this fat boy name Kevin did that, and after church he ate them apple Now-and-Laters till his stomach hurt. I ain't never kept the money I was supposed to put in the basket. Never. Not till today.

I feel so bad I wanna go tell my grandma right now. But she gon' probably think I meant to do it. She always thinking I'm up to something. My mama say Grandma just old and used to the way things used to be when she was young. Mama say I got too much energy for Grandma. Man, I'm glad I wasn't born back when she was. That was way back in 1907! My mama say back then kids was to be seen and not heard. They do anything, they get a backslap.

I don't know what I'ma do . . .

I guess I could keep these two quarters and put 'em in with the two my grandma gon' give me next Sunday. Yeah, maybe I will do that. I guess God don't be caring when He get His money. Long as He get it.

And if God can forgive me, then maybe my daddy can too. My grandma say, "If you have faith the size of a mustard seed, you can move mountains." I have faith and I been praying to God. So that must mean my daddy he gon' forgive me and start coming to see me again.

But to make sure, I wrote him a letter after church. I used a red pen 'cause red his favorite color. I told my daddy how good I did in school last year. I got all As and one B! So he can see for himself, I sent my report card too. The front of it got four shiny gold stars. Next year I'ma get five stars 'cause I'ma make sure I get straight As. That'll make my daddy happy. But I know he gon' be happy when he see how much I done already improved. After I wrote the letter, I got a stamp and a envelope from my mama. I wrote his address on the front and got her to make sure she could read it. For some reason she looked sad when she handed the envelope back to me. I guess she still feeling sick. She been sick all week. I put the letter and my report card inside, and I ran down to the foot of the hill and dropped the envelope inside the mailbox.

I can't wait to see my daddy again. I know he coming back. I know he is. And when he do come back, he can tell me how to beat Paul once and for all. I was lucky last time. If Paul come after me again, I don't know what I'ma do. And he probably is gon' come after me too. Now that I told Hi-C about him digging up his nose in church. Hi-C was walking through the projects, drinking some Hi-C when I mailed my letter. That's when I told him. I lied though and said Paul had ate his boogas. God ain't gon' be the only one mad about that lie. But God gon' forgive me before Paul will.

Maybe my daddy will call soon as he get my letter. Then I can ask him how to beat Paul. I need to know soon. Real soon.

It's nighttime now, so I betta go inside. I don't want my grandma to start fussing at me again. It's cool out here, and the old people that ain't gone in yet don't need to fan theyselves no more. It's getting real dark, dark like that ink that spilt on my suit, and I can hear a lil bird chirping in my grandma's tree. Now he flying away. Planes is like birds, like big metal falcons, and my daddy he gon' get on one and fly down to see me and it's gon' be like it was when he came to see me last time. Like it was when me and him lived in the same house.

And he gon' like me again.

Lion's Blood

BY STEVEN BARNES

Cetshwayo's old hunting injury prevented him from riding, but his twin sons Keefah and Darbul wouldn't have missed a hunt for a fistful of Alexanders. So as the sun dipped low above the *kraal*, Kai and seven highborn men, Zulus and Abyssinian alike, gathered their restless mounts in a mesquite flat abutting a conifer woodland. A dozen lean, alert Zulus accompanied them afoot.

The lead hunter was Shaka Zulu himself, a giant of a man who rode like a centaur. He raised his brawny arms—an ornate spear in one hand, hunting bow in the other, with a quiver on his back—and screamed to the moonless sky. "Let the hunt begin!"

Like Darbul and Keefah, the unmounted warriors were lean, muscular agile men, trained from infancy to be athletes on a par with any in the world. They gripped short stabbing *umkhonto* with elongated steel blades Kai recalled Malik's sober evaluation of Zulu skill: *"Avoid close-quarter combat if there is any chance at all."*

"And if I cannot?"

"Then consign your soul to Allah and prepare to enter Paradise. Just do your best to ensure you reach those gates together."

Abu Ali, Ali, and Kai carried rifles as well as spears. Despite her pleas Elenya remained behind at Cetshwayo's mansion. On a normal hunt the Wakil might have considered allowing her to accompany them. "Why can Nandi go?" Elenya had pouted.

Cetshwayo himself had overheard that last and had laughed heartily after Elenya stalked out of the room. "In the old country, Nandi would not ride to the hunt." He sighed. "But this New World gives girls airs. What can I say? I can't control her any longer." He dug his elbow into Kai's ribs hard enough to make the boy chuff air. "I wish you better luck!"

Shaka's white teeth shone in the torchlight. "Only here and on the battlefield do I feel so alive."

Abu Ali pulled up next to him. Kai's family rode Cetshwayo's mounts specially bred hunting stallions of imposing strength and size. Kai's seemed responsive to a feather touch of his knees, and Abu Ali already rode his as if he had raised the monster from a colt.

Abu Ali glanced doubtfully at Shaka's spear. "Can you really make the kill with such a weapon?"

Shaka's broad, scarred face glowed with amusement. "You had best hope so, my friend."

Distantly, there came the mournful wail of the hunting horn.

Shaka grew ruminative. "We bring the calves five thousand miles and raise them here, that we might honor the ways of our ancestors. He dies today. Perhaps he will claim one of us as well. Haiii!"

With the suddenness of a lightning stroke he wheeled his horse about as if sensing something that the others had missed completely. Abruptly out of the brush not three dozen cubits away charged two hundred *sep* of the most fearsome creature Kai had ever seen in his life. Its black horns looked as if they could punch holes in steel, its breath snorted from its broad wet nostrils in clouds of condensation, its hooves furrowed the earth.

Savannah buffalo. Magnificent, and the most dangerous game animal on the African continent. Crafty, powerful, and fast, the buffalo had killed more hunters than lions and leopards combined, and had no natural predators—save men like Shaka Zulu.

Abu Ali's face went grim and he reined his horse closer to Ali. "They are insane," he whispered. "Hold back a bit. Give Shaka and his men the honor of first contact."

"Gladly." Even gallant Ali looked unnerved.

Kai was still formulating his answer when Nandi rode past them. Her tan riding pants were unadorned, as simply functional as any of the men's. Somehow, the garb merely enhanced her sensuality.

As she passed Kai she spurred her steed and grinned back at him.

As the very wind of her passage ruffled his face, Kai felt her call: primal and wild and stronger than he had anticipated. He felt dizzied. "You would have me marry into this family, Father?" Kai called to Abu Ali. "They are all mad." *And perhaps I am as well,* he thought. "Hai!"

Kai spurred his own horse forward into the fray.

Ali laughed. "Allah, preserve us! I think the boy is in love." And raced after his younger brother.

The footmen's shielded, gas-burning lanterns probed the darkness, but deep patches of shadow remained in the forest. Death lurked within them.

Shaka, his nephews and footmen worked forward in a practiced arc, clearing one segment of grass after another. The buffalo seemed to have disappeared.

Kai's heart was in his throat. How could so large a beast vanish so completely? Twice he had seen the buffalo erupt out of shadows, and the mounted Zulus had scattered, hooting, as its horns came within digits of their horses. Insanity! Worse yet, they treated it almost like a game. Almost. These men were in the finest, highest physical condition he had ever witnessed. Clearly, they were competing with each other not only physically, but in display of courage. And Nandi was right in the thick of it. What manner of man could ever control such a woman?

There! Their prey had raised up again, and snorted as it charged. One of Shaka's footmen thrust at the beast with a spear, and it wheeled, hitting the man from the side. This time, the hunter was unable to spin out of the way, and the horn pierced his ribs. With a despairing wail, the footman collapsed bleeding into the tall grass.

Two more men veered in, jabbing, and the buffalo turned. Shaka galloped back in. "Hold!" he cried. "He is mine!"

Deferentially, the footmen backed away. Almost as if it understood that some ultimate moment had arrived, the beast pawed the earth and faced Shaka. Had the Zulus trained it for such an encounter? Did they somehow prepare the calves to provide such moments of drama? Certainly no wild beast would behave in such a manner. Kai glimpsed, and in a shadowy manner understood, something new about the culture whose daughter he was to marry.

Kai and Nandi were eighty cubits to the side, and Kai was ready to wheel and run for it if the monster broke in his direction. But he was also transfixed by its power, by its lethal sweep of horns and breadth of shoulder. In the darkness, partially lit by torches, it seemed more a creature of myth than reality, and Shaka some conquering hero of legend, not a man of flesh and bone.

Shaka and Keefah drew their bows, pulling steadily . . .

Suddenly, as if finally comprehending its danger, the animal flickered its tail and turned, vanishing into the high grass. As it turned, Shaka loosed his first arrow and it struck behind the buffalo's shoulder. Keefah's shaft, only a moment later, missed the flank and drove into the ground. Roaring with pain and anger, the buffalo made a *chuffing* sound as it disappeared.

Bearing lanterns and spears, the footmen beat the long grass, pushing ahead in a horseshoe configuration. They were supported by horsemen, all holding to the rigid pattern.

Shaka rode along the outside, striving for position. When their prey tried to break away, it was herded back with shouts and spears. The buffalo seemed confused, but far from fatigued.

Shaka raced for a shooting position ahead of his prey, but without warning the animal changed course, racing back straight for the footmen. With insane courage they thrust their spears, shone their lights in its eyes and shouted. Again it wheeled, running for the open, where Shaka waited, bow drawn.

Then the beast doubled back again, suddenly ignoring the shouts and spear thrusts. Several of the men cast their *umkhontos*. Two struck the beast, the hafts flagging out from its back and side like dreadful bamboo stalks, blood running black in the darkness.

The center man was little more than a boy, perhaps seventeen summers. He lost his nerve, cast poorly as the buffalo came straight at him, and missed his mark completely. The men scattered as it charged their line. The beast caught the boy who had missed his cast, gouging his back and sending him flying.

The boy landed hard in the grass, screaming and thrashing, reaching back spastically for the bleeding wound.

"Fool!" Shaka yelled as he rode by. There was a sheen of madness on his face now. His eyes were too wide, lips pulled tight against his white teeth. The footmen had been left behind now—it was up to the horsemen.

Shaka was racing beside the wounded prey now. He gripped his bow and aimed, horse and buffalo seeming to match each other stride for stride.

He released his bolt, and it entered just behind the left shoulder. The buffalo stumbled, rose again, and thundered on. Shaka released a second arrow. As it struck, the buffalo's knees crumpled, and it dove nose-first into the ground with an earth-shaking impact that would have shattered a lesser creature's spine.

Kai held his breath, unable to fully grasp what he had just witnessed, beyond any doubt the most intense experience of his young life. Allah preserve him! He did not even know that men such as these existed!

Shaka raised his hands to the stars. "Haii!"

"Who is the greatest hunter in all creation?" Darbul roared.

And his footmen, gasping now as they caught up with him, cheered in expected response. Shaka trotted his horse over to his trophy—

And it lurched up, catching Shaka's horse in the belly with its left horn. Mortally wounded and neighing in agony, his mount tumbled over backward, and Shaka spilled. Despite his awesome athleticism he crashed awkwardly to earth.

Shaka seemed momentarily dazed, disoriented, and for a moment the entire party was frozen, as if they shared his confusion. As Shaka's mount whined pitiably, the buffalo lurched to its feet. In that instant it could have slain Shaka, but instead it seemed to stare at him, blood drooling from its nose.

The Zulu's face was gaunt and strained. Kai knew that in that moment Shaka Zulu, great hunter, great warrior, was gazing into the face of his own death, and that his soul had recoiled from the awful sight.

Then, twin shots rang out. The buffalo staggered to its knees, then collapsed onto its side.

Kai turned, startled. His father and brother both had their rifles to their shoulders. Smoke drifted from both barrels.

Composing himself as best he could, Shaka rose. His limbs trembled a bit. Perhaps it was the chill of night, but Kai thought otherwise. Shake gave a perfunctory nod of thanks to Abu Ali and his son, and walked off unsteady legs to the buffalo.

Kai found himself looking deep into the beast's eyes. The mighty but falo's breath huffed in painful bursts. Its black eyes were filmed with dust, Kai's next reaction startled him. This poor thing had been stolen in child childhood from its native land, raised only to die for the entertainment of its captors. It had struggled for freedom and life, that Kai could understand Pointless and absurd as it seemed, he wanted to tell the felled creature *we done.*

Shaka snatched a spear from one of his men and drove it into the wounded beast's side. It heaved in pain. Shaka bore down with all his weight, working the spear back and forth until the heart was pierced and the buffalo lay still.

Shaka raised his arms in victory, yelling in musical, staccato Zulu. The men replied in kind.

"*Ngikhuluma isiZulu kancane,*" Kai said haltingly to Nandi. *I speak only a bit of Zulu.* "What did he say?"

"He said that this was no ordinary creature, it was a demon, and in slaying it he has become more than a man." Her eyes shone with admiration. She had apparently seen nothing that was not glorious, nothing in the least disturbing in her uncle's behavior. Was that pragmatism? An understanding that even the bravest men know fear? Or delusion, an inability to acknowledge what she had seen? He wasn't sure which, and that uncertainty troubled him.

To Kai's gaze, Shaka had not yet fully recovered, and his trembling was not from the cold. His men apparently noticed nothing of their leader's momentary weakness. They cheered, beating their spears against the ground. Kai and his family smiled politely, but shared searing sidelong glances.

Shaka wrenched his spear from the dead animal's side. Its tip glistened black with blood. He rubbed his finger slowly along the edge. Ignoring his dying horse, Shaka then ran to the spot where his second man had been injured. Kai broke his mount into a trot to keep up.

The wounded youth was curled onto his side like an injured lizard his right arm still groping back for the bleeding wound.

"You are hurt," Shaka said coldly.

The wounded man looked up at Shaka, his teeth chattering.

"Your stupidity could have killed me," Shaka continued, in a conversational tone.

The wounded man said something in Zulu. Kai had the very clear impression that he was begging for his life.

Shaka spoke to him in the same language, his face calm and comforting. Then with shocking suddenness he raised the spear and thrust it deeply into the hunter's stomach. Kai's stomach fisted as the boy's body serched, as if trying to take the spear more deeply into his belly. Then with deadful finality, he went limp.

Kai felt dizzy and sick with rage.

"Allah preserve us!" Abu Ali said in disbelief. "What have you done?"

Shaka withdrew the spear and wiped it on the dead boy's chest. "What my right." He shrugged as if it was of little consequence. "He would have died in some days. To die on your king's spear is an honor."

The Wakil's face was as stone. "There are no kings in Bilalistan."

Shaka grinned and pointed to his men, who had moved to encircle the party. "Tell *them*," he said.

Kai scaned them. Fourteen now, standing proud and silent, chests high, gripping their spears, ready to kill or die for the man they followed. Kai felt a deep and pervasive cold seeping into his bones.

"There were kings in the days of my fathers," Shaka said. "Mark well—there may be again."

His mood had shifted completely, as if killing the hunter had purged him of all stress. He turned to his men. "Bring me the head! Put my steed from its misery. Bear your brother on a stretcher, he burns tomorrow."

Shaka ordered one of his men off his horse and mounted without a trace of hesitation. If he had been injured in the fall, the injury was already forgotten. His men scrambled to fulfill his orders.

Abu Ali and his sons rode together quietly, watching. Nandi pulled her horse up next to Shaka, clearly worshipful. "Uncle," she said. "You were wonderful. But weren't you afraid?"

Shaka Zulu rode proudly. "Nandi, fear is neither ally nor enemy. I never see fear, my child."

Ali whispered in Kai's ear: "You cannot see what lives behind your own eyes."

"Father," Kai said. "What do we do?"

Abu Ali shook his head. "The Zulus are allies of the Empress—and Shaka is as much royalty as Lamiya. On their land, it is their world. We can do nothing."

They watched the dead man rolled onto a stretcher. His eyes were open and turned up. Blood leaked from his side.

"It is not right," Kai said quietly.

"No, it is not," agreed Abu Ali. "But it is done."

The Knowing

BY TANANARIVE DUE

Our teacher said one day that knowledge is power, and I had to raise my hand even though I don't like to; I like to sit and be quiet and watch people and wait for lunchtime. But I had to ask him if he was sure about that, or if maybe knowledge wasn't just a curse. He asked me what I meant by that, and I said, "Hey, that's what my mama always says." "Knowing is her curse," she whispers, touching my forehead at night, softly, her long fingers like spiders' legs. Sometimes I wake up in the middle of the night and she's there whispering and rocking me. But I didn't tell my teacher that part. I could tell from the way my teacher looked at me sideways and went on with his lesson that he thought I was trying to be a smart-ass. People always think you're something you don't want to be. Mama says that, too.

I like this school in Chicago all right because my math teacher is real pretty, with long legs and a smile that means what it says. But me and Mama won't be here long. I know that already. I was in six different schools last year. It's always the same; one day I walk into wherever we're staying and she looks up at me through her cigarette smoke and says, "Throw your things in a bag." That must mean the rent hasn't been paid, or somebody got on her nerves, or maybe she's just plain sick of being wherever we are. I don't say anything, because I know if she stays unhappy too long, she'll start throwing things and screaming at the walls and the police might come and put me in foster care like that time in Atlanta. I was gone six months, staying with these white people who were taking care of six other boys. Mama almost lost me that time. When the judge said she could take me back, I smiled in the courtroom so he wouldn't see how mad I was at Mama. I hate it when she acts like she's the kid instead of me. I didn't speak to her for a whole week, and when I did, I said to her, "Damn, Mama, you gotta' do better than that." I meant it, too.

And she promised she would. She really tries. Things will be really cool for a while, better than cool, and then I'll walk through the door and see that look on her face and those Marlboro Lights, or whatever she smokes when she's in a smoking mood, and I know we're moving again. I guess she feels like she'll be all right if she just runs away from it, as if you could run away from your own head.

I wish Mama wouldn't smoke dope. It freaks her out. She goes up and down the stairs and walks through the halls wailing and sobbing, pounding on people's doors and shouting out dates. March 12, 2003. September 6, 2006. December 13, 2020. I have to find her and bring her back to the apartment to listen to Bob Marley or Bunny Wailer, something that calms her down. I hug her tight, and when she sobs, I can feel her shaking against me. "It's all right, Mama," I say.

"Nicky," she says to me in a little girl's voice, "I ain't only telling. I make it happen. When they ask me, I say, okay, you're October fifteenth, you're February eighth. I'm doin' the deciding, Nicky. It's me. Ain't it? Ain't it?"

She gets like that on dope, thinking she's God or something. I have to keep telling her, "Mama, it ain't you. Knowing ain't the same as deciding. *TV Guide* don't decide what's on TV."

Then, if I'm lucky, she'll get a smile on her face and go to sleep. If I'm unlucky, she'll keep crying and go back running through the halls and one of the neighbors will call the police. That's what happened in Atlanta. They thought she was crazy, so they locked her up and took me away. Lucky for her, the doctor said nothing was wrong with her.

But he doesn't know what she knows.

In Miami Beach, the last place we lived, our apartment was upstairs from a *botánica*, which is where the Cubans go to find statues of saints and stuff like that, trying to make magic. Mama took one look at that place and almost burst out laughing. She doesn't believe in statues, she says. But she was real nice to the owner, Rosa, who mostly spoke Spanish. Mama told Rosa what she does, what she knows. It took the lady three or four times to understand Mama, and then she didn't want to believe her. "*El día que la gente van a morir?*" Rosa asked, frowning. You could tell she thought Mama was trying to scam her.

Mama sucked on her teeth, getting impatient. She looked back toward an old lady in the back of the shop who was checking out some oils in small glass bottles on a shelf. The lady was breathing hard, walking real slow. Mama can smell sick people, no lie. Mama leaned close to Rosa's ear. "You know that lady?" Mama asked her.

Rosa nodded. "*Sí.* My aunt," she said. "*Está enferma.*"

"She's gonna' die soon. Real soon."

Rosa looked offended, her face glowing red like a dark cherry. She turned away from Mama, straightening up some of the things on her shelves. You should have seen all that stuff; she had clay pots and plates and cauldrons and beads and tall candles inside glasses with holy people painted on them, even a candle that's supposed to burn fourteen hours. And there were teas labeled *Té de Corazón* and *Té de Castilla*. I always pay attention when I'm in a new place. I like to see everything.

"Listen," Mama said to Rosa, trying to get her attention. "You know your days of the week in English? Remember Friday. That lady back there gonna' die on Friday." Mama held up two fingers. "Friday in two weeks. *Viernes.* Nicky, how you say two weeks in Spanish?"

"*Dos*"—I had to think a few seconds—"*semanas.*"

Rosa stared at me, then at Mama's two fingers, then dead into Mama's eyes. From her face, it was like Rosa couldn't tell if she wanted to be mad, scared, or sad. People always look at Mama that way.

"Then you come upstairs and get me," Mama said. "I want to work here."

I had forgotten all about Rosa and her *botánica* when someone knocked on our door on a Sunday morning. Mama was out getting groceries and I was watching cartoons on the black-and-white TV Mama had bought from a thrift shop for twenty dollars. It only got two channels, but one of the channels showed the Road Runner on Sundays, and that's my favorite. Rosa was standing there in our doorway, dressed up in black lace. I almost didn't recognize her because she was wearing lipstick and had her face made up to look nice even though her eyes were sad. It took me a second to remember she must be on her way to her aunt's funeral.

"Mama's not here," I said.

"When she come, you tell her for me, no?" Rosa said. "Tell her she say truth. She say truth."

I wanted to close the door. I was missing the best part, where Wile E. Coyote straps the rocket to his back so he can fly. He always crashes in the end, but at least he flies for a little while. "So, does she have a job or what?" I asked her.

Rosa nodded.

Cool, I thought. Whenever Mama has a job, there's always a little extra money for candy bars and T-shirts and movies and stuff. Mama only works because of me, because she likes to buy me things like other kids. I always felt a little guilty, though. In Miami Beach, I knew I'd better enjoy Mama's new job while it lasted. She could never work long before she had to run away.

At the *botánica*, Rosa put a sign in the window saying she had a psychic inside, and she told people they could go back into the storeroom, past the colorful curtain, to talk to Mama. The thing is, Rosa got it all wrong. She was saying Mama could tell people if their husbands were cheating or if they would get a raise at work, the kind of lame stuff they see on TV commercials. Mama just shakes her head and tells people she knows one thing, one thing only—and when she says what it is, some of them really do turn pale, like *ghost*-pale. Then they stand up as if she smells bad and they're afraid to stand too close to her.

At Rosa's *botánica*, Mama didn't get too many customers at first. But it was still kind of nice because she and Rosa started becoming friends, even though they could barely talk to each other. I like Mama to have friends. When Mama wasn't helping at the cash register, most of the day she'd sit back there watching TV or playing cards with me. Sometimes, when there weren't any customers, Rosa would come back with us and watch Spanish-language soap operas. I liked to watch them, too, because you don't need to know Spanish to understand those. Someone's cheating on somebody. Somebody's pissed about something. Mama and Rosa would laugh together, and Rosa would explain some parts to Mama: "He very bad man," she would say in her sandpapery voice, or "That woman no married to him." But Rosa didn't need to do that, because most things don't need words. Most things you can see for yourself.

So one day there was a thunderstorm, and Rosa was shaking her head as she stood in front of her store window staring out at the dark clouds. Lightning turned on the whole sky with a flash, then it was black again, and the thunder sounded like a giant boulder being rolled across the clouds. Miami Beach has the best storms I've ever seen, but Rosa was only letting herself see the scary parts. "I get killed to drive in that," Rosa said.

Mama grinned. "No you won't. Not today." Mama's grin was so big, Rosa looked at her real close. I could see Rosa's face change, the corners of her lips lying flat.

"Ain't nothin' to worry about. You got a long ways. You want to know?" Mama said.

"*No*," Rosa said through tight lips. All of a sudden, she didn't sound like Mama's friend anymore; she sounded like her boss-lady. She waved her hand in Mama's face. "No. No."

Mama shrugged, trying to pretend she wasn't hurt. She was just trying to be nice. But that's how it is, because nobody wants the only thing Mama knows how to give away.

It took a week at the *botánica* before even one customer decided to hear what Mama had to say. I liked that lady. She was brown-skinned and young, and she touched me on my shoulder when she passed me in the doorway instead of looking right past me like most people do. Maybe if I'd been older, I would have wanted to ask her out on a date. Or she could have been my sister, maybe.

"Are you the psychic?" she asked Mama. She had some kind of island accent, who knows what. Everyone in Miami was like us, from somewhere else.

Mama wasn't in a how-can-I-help-you-today kind of mood. "You want a psychic? Then you need to call one of them stupid-ass telephone services and waste your money to hear what you want. I only got one thing to tell." Then Mama told her what her specialty was.

But the woman didn't run away, and she didn't look scared. She just made her eyes narrow and stared at my mother like she couldn't quite see her. "Are you telling the truth?"

"I ain't got time for lies," Mama said.

"Then I want to know. How much?"

The price is usually twenty dollars for people Mama likes, a hundred for people she doesn't. She asked this woman for twenty, exact change. You always have to pay first. That's the rule. Then Mama makes you sit across from her at the card table, she takes an index card from her pile, and she scribbles a date in pencil, just like that. She doesn't have to close her eyes or hold your hand or whisper to Jesus. It's nothing like that at all.

"Now," Mama said, holding the card up so the woman couldn't see what she'd written, "I'ma tell you from experience, this ain't the best time to look at this, not right now. Some folks like to go where there's lots of light, or nice music, or where you got somebody you love. This ain't nothin' to share with strangers. That means me, too. Save it for when you're ready."

But when Mama gave her the card, the woman held it in her palms like a shiny seashell and stared down, not even blinking. I saw her shoulders rise up, and she let out a breath that sounded like a whimper. I wished she'd listened to Mama, because it makes me feel bad when people cry.

But this woman, when she stood up to leave, she was smiling. A smile as long as a mile. And this time, when she walked past me, she pressed her palm against my cheek. She made me smile, too.

When she was gone, Mama clapped her hands twice and laughed. "Look at that! That girl is something else." Mama is always so happy when she doesn't make people afraid.

"She's gonna' be an old-timer, huh?" I said.

Mama shook her head. "No, child. Ten years almost to the day. May fourth," she said, her face bright like it hadn't been in a long time.

I didn't get it at first. The woman was so young, like in her twenties. How could she be happy to have ten years left? But then I thought, maybe she was sick with something really bad, and she thought she was a goner already. To her, maybe ten years was like a whole new life.

It's weird. I've seen grown men with gray hair and deep lines in their faces drop to their knees and cry after Mama told them they had twenty-five years. No lie. Maybe they thought they had forever, and Mama's telling them the day, month, and year just made it real. And then there are people like this lady, so young and pretty, with no time left at all, and they walk out smiling like it's Christmas. Those people are my favorite kind.

Mama says she wasn't born knowing. She says she just woke up one morning when she was sixteen, looked at her family at the breakfast table, and *knew*. She knew her father was going to drop dead of a heart attack in January, in three years, after giving a Sunday sermon. She knew her mother was going to live to be ninety just like her great-aunt. She knew her brother Joe was going to get killed in an Army accident in 1987, and her sister was going to get shot to death by her boyfriend in 1999. She says she just ran to her room and cried, because all that knowing hurt her heart.

Then it started coming true. Mama says her father dropped dead of a heart attack after giving the sermon the first Sunday after New Year's, in January, and her mother treated Mama like it was her fault. Same when the phone call came about Mama's brother, my dead Uncle Joe.

Mama wanted to hide her knowing, but right after her father died like she said he would, people started coming to the house to see her. Because some people—maybe they're just weird, or they're less scared than other people—think knowing is power. Just like my teacher said. But Mama doesn't feel that way, not at all. A curse, she calls it. She has all this knowing, and there's nothing she can do to stop it once she knows. Even if she prays and fasts, it doesn't change anything. My dead Uncle Joe never even joined the Army because Mama begged him not to, but he got run over by a car on the exact day she said in 1987 anyway, the same year I was born.

Nobody can cheat it, except maybe the other way. Mama knew a boy in high school who got her to tell him how old he would be on the day it would happen, and she said he would be seventy-two. Then, he decided to act stupid and jump off the top bleacher at the football stadium like he was Superman, and he broke his neck. Mama saw it happen, and he was dead on the spot when he was only eighteen. That was the only time Mama was wrong.

Mama told me she had to think about that a long, long time. That was when she left home for good, and she spent more than a year thinking about how she got the date wrong for that one boy. Then, she decided on an answer: Maybe it'll happen faster if *you* make it happen on purpose, but it never happens later. The day is the day, and that's all there is to it. That's what Mama says.

Mama never had a boyfriend or anything, not the kind of boyfriend who gives you flowers on your birthday or takes you to the movies. She never even knew my daddy's name. Some people might not tell their children something like that, but Mama will say all kinds of things. She tells me she was an ugly child coming up, always sassing back and running around where she wasn't supposed to be, sticking her nose in grown folks' business, and the knowing came as her punishment. "God don't like ugly," she always tells me. She says that to scare me into acting right so I won't get punished the way she did, but that doesn't scare me. I wouldn't mind knowing the way she knows. I'd find a way to get rich from it instead of letting it drive me crazy like Mama does.

Grandmama is sixty-eight now. She still lives in the same house in Macon, all alone, and most of the time she won't return Mama's calls, not since Auntie Ree got shot by her boyfriend. Everyone tried to warn Auntie Ree because her boyfriend used to beat her up, but then again, it wouldn't have made a difference anyway, just like with my dead Uncle Joe. Mama saw how it would all happen.

I always call Grandmama collect once a month, no matter where we are. She picks up the phone if she hears my voice on her answering machine, but she won't talk to Mama except by accident. The way I see it, Grandmama's husband is dead and two of her children are gone, too, and I think she's mad because Mama told her she still has so long to wait.

The day we had to move from Miami Beach, I'd just aced a math test, no lie. I had the second-highest score in the class—answers come to me easy if I think hard enough—and on the way home from school I was looking at the palm trees through the school bus window, thinking it would be snowing if we were still living in Detroit like we did last winter. Then when I walked through the door, Mama was sitting there on the sofa with a Marlboro Light. Damn.

"We're moving on," she said. "Pack a bag."

Her face was damp, and there were little wads of toilet paper all over the floor, like there had been a parade. She'd been crying all day while I was in school. "You ain't working today?" I asked her, hoping it wasn't what I thought. I like new places, but I didn't want to leave. Not already.

"I been fired. So we're moving."

"Rosa fired you, Mama? How come?"

Mama's face turned hard, and she dragged on her cigarette, sucking it like reefer smoke. "We had a fight," Mama said. She blew the smoke out while she talked. "She didn't have no right to say what she said. 'Bout how I need help to take care of you right, I need to call Big Brothers or some mess, how I can't give you things like you need. You ain't none of her goddamn business."

The funny thing is, I always wondered what it would be like to be in Big Brothers, to have some dude who wears a suit to his job every day come play ball with me on weekends. It's not the same as a daddy, but it's better than nothing. But it's too bad for Rosa that she said that, because Mama gets pissed when people say she can't take care of me, especially after Atlanta. And she always has the last word in a fight. Once she gets mad, there's no keeping her quiet.

"So you told her?"

"Just go throw your things in a bag, Nicky."

"I don't want to leave here, Mama. Dang," I whined. I sounded like a baby, but I didn't care. "Tell her you lied. Tell her you just made it up."

I could see her hand holding the cigarette was shaking. New tears were running down her face. "I don't know why I said that to Rosa. That wasn't right. Maybe she didn't mean nothin' by it, but she made me so mad, talking about you."

I sat next to her on the couch and reached for her hand. She wouldn't squeeze back. "Tell her it don't mean nothing. We don't have to move just because of that. That ain't nothing."

"No, Nicky . . ." Mama whispered. "Telling to hurt somebody is the worst thing a person can do. Even the devil couldn't do nothing worse."

I'd seen Mama acting crazy for sure, running around in her underclothes, screaming at anybody who could hear, but I'd never seen her quiet. That scared me more than it would have if she'd been throwing pots and pans on the floor. She sounded different.

I got mad all of a sudden. "Shoot, Mama, forget Rosa. Who does she think she is, trying to say you can't take care of me? Nobody asked her."

Mama laughed a little and stared at the floor.

"You are taking care of me, Mama. Better than anybody."

"Sure am . . ." Mama said, still not looking up at me. "I got to . . . until May twelfth."

"Two thousand five," I said, squeezing her hand again, and Mama just closed her eyes.

Until right then, when I heard myself say it, the date had seemed so far away. I'd always known I would be fifteen that year, but I'd never stopped to think it was only three years away. It wasn't so far off anymore.

We left Miami Beach, which is too bad because it's so alive there. There are so many people who sing and dance and laugh and act like every day is the only one left. I wish we could have stayed there. Even in November, it's already freezing in Chicago, and people are dressing warm, walking fast, waiting for spring to come. In a cold place, it's like there's no such thing as today, just tomorrow. *Will it snow tomorrow? Will it be sunny tomorrow?* But Mama said she couldn't face Rosa, so we jumped on a bus and stopped riding when we got bored. This time, we stopped in Chicago. But there's never really anywhere to go.

I guess Mama felt so bad about what she said to Rosa because it reminded her of all the times before when she's lost her temper and said what she doesn't mean to say. I don't think she can help it. I was only six when she did it to me, even though I don't remember what I did that made her so mad in the first place. I was little, but I never forgot what she said: "I'll be through with your foolishness on May 12, 2005, because that's your day, Nicky. You hear?"

I told a friend once, a kid named Kalil I had just started hanging out with at my school in Atlanta, after he told me about something bad that had happened to his family in the country where they came from. We were just standing on the playground, and we told our worst stories. There were soldiers in his story; mine was only about Mama and May 12, 2005.

That was the only time anyone ever looked at me the way people always look at Mama. But the thing I like most about kids is that even though they get scared like anybody else, they can forget they're scared pretty fast. Especially kids like Kalil, who know there's more to the world than video games and homework. I guess that made us alike. He hardly waited any time at all before he said, "Does that bother you?" Just like that.

I'd never thought about that before. We were both ten then, so fifteen was five years off, half my whole life, and by that time I'd be in high school, nearly a man. A whole different person. I told him I didn't think it bothered me. When you grow up around someone like Mama and you hear about it all the time, you know everybody has a turn, and you just try to find something interesting every day to make you glad it hasn't happened yet.

That's why I didn't mind it in Miami Beach when the TV only got two channels—see, I don't need more than two channels, as long as there's at least one thing I can watch. I'll watch the evening news and soap operas in English or Spanish and even golf, if Tiger Woods is playing. Hell, I don't even mind when we don't have a TV, which we usually don't. I read comic books and books from the library and take walks and watch people. Kalil said he wouldn't go to school if he were me, but I don't mind. There's always something interesting somewhere, even at school. Like the way my math teacher smiles, when you can see her whole heart in it. I don't think anyone in my class has noticed that except me.

"You're really brave, Nicky," Kalil told me in Atlanta. I don't feel brave but I do think about it sometimes. I wonder how it'll go down, if it will hurt when it happens, or if I'll be crossing the street and a car will come around a corner all of a sudden like with my dead Uncle Joe. Or maybe I'll see someone getting robbed and I'll get shot like Auntie Ree when I try to stop the bad guy, and everyone will say I was a hero. That would be best. I wonder if it'll happen even if I stay in bed that day and never leave my room, or if I'll just get struck by lightning while I'm staring out of my window at the greatest storm I've ever seen. I never get sick, so I don't think it'll be that. I think it'll be something else, but I'm not sure what.

Even Mama says she doesn't know.

Luscious

BY BERNICE L. MCFADDEN

FROM *Loving Donovan*

efore she was Luscious, she was Rita.

Little wide-eyed Rita, daughter of Erasmus and Bertha Smith, hardworking people who knew God, but not every Sunday. They drank some and sometimes too much. Played their Billie Holiday records for the neighborhood, whether their neighbors wanted to hear them or not. Loved more than they fought, but fought just the same, had the scars and broken knickknacks to prove the latter, Rita to prove the first.

Before she was Luscious with a number and a cell mate she was Rita of Detroit. Rita of Cadillac Avenue. Tall, red-boned Rita who swayed down the street on long lovely legs so well oiled they gleamed. Rita with the green eyes and good hair that touched the middle of her back. Rita so fine, the white people forgave and forgot her thick lips and broad nose.

Before she was Luscious of Brooklyn, Luscious of Stanley Avenue, she was just Rita minding her own business who one day looked up into the eyes of her father's best friend and saw something there that she'd only seen in the eyes of school boys and lately strange men that beckoned her and sometimes brushed their fingers against her arm when she ignored their calls.

Manny Evans, raven colored, bald-headed, broad smiling, pockets heavy with nickels Manny.

Manny Evans who had bounced Rita on his knee, patted the top of her head, dropped nickels into her saving jar, the old mayonnaise jar Bertha had cleaned and put aside for just that purpose.

Manny Evans who had women on corners and a twenty-two in his sock. He wore taps on the heels of his shoes and the *nickel-jingle-clickety-click* sounds he made when he walked down the streets told everybody he was coming, but no one messed with him because they were sure about the twenty-two in his sock, and suspicious about the breast pocket of his jacket and the nickel-free pocket of his pants.

Rita had always liked the way his head shone and as she got older she began to appreciate his color, so black and smooth. She found herself thinking about his shoulders and the gold pinky ring he wore, the one with the black onyx stone. "Black like me," he said, "strong like me."

Rita filling out in places, eyes greener now, hair loose instead of pulled back, stockings replacing knee socks, ears pierced and Rita all of the time licking her lips keeping them moist, keeping them shiny.

Manny Evans dropping paper money in her saving jar instead of nickels, wanting to pat her ass instead of the top of her head, wanting to bounce her on his knee again and maybe on something else.

He visits on Saturday nights. Comes by with a bottle of whiskey after checking on his women, collecting money, and laying his hands on people who've allowed their eyes to slide over and past him when he called out to them, "You got my money Nigga?"

Erasmus and Manny drink, smoke Pall Malls, and play dominoes while Bertha talks to Adele from next door. Adele, tall like a man with hands that wrinkled early and callused two years ago on the palms.

Before she was Luscious on parole and scrubbing floors for white folk in Indian Village, she was Rita and that's what was written on her bedroom door in big black letters so Manny couldn't have mistaken it for the bathroom. But he did.

His fly is down and his dick is already in his hands when he stumbles in stinking of liquor and bleary-eyed. He apologizes when he walks in on her in the middle of drying her just-bathed body, but he don't jump back and close the door or drop his eyes in shame. He just stares at her and his hand, the one not holding on to his dick, reaches behind him and pushes the door shut.

His eyes enjoy her face and then her naked breasts and finally the thin line of black hair that begins two inches below her navel.

Before she was Luscious, she was Rita, confused and held down in her own bed by strong hands. Those same hands covering her mouth, roughly touching and rubbing. Those hands are rough like the steel wool Bertha scrubs the pots with and Rita believes her skin will shred beneath them. She can't imagine a more painful feeling and then she doesn't have to because he's inside of her, pushing into the place where only her index finger had ever been.

Rita, before she was Luscious, her mind bending and her body coming apart on the inside and Manny not allowing her to scream or breathe and when he's done he don't even look at her he just looks down at the bloodstains on his pants and tucks back in the paper money sticking out of his pockets, but he leaves the nickels that have fallen out and onto the bed.

Manny Evans finds the bathroom just fine now and returns to Erasmus, his Pall Malls and liquor and proceeds to win three more domino games.

Rita buds in the spring along with the gnarly limbs of elms and oaks. Her belly pushes out in mid-April, coinciding with the tulip and daffodil blooms and all of the beauty of the season rests in the glow of her skin, but her eyes are as cold as the long-gone winter.

"Who?" her parents ask even though their minds have wandered over the young men that have spent time with Rita on the porch, the ones that have called out to her from open car windows, music blasting, Rita's name lost in the lyrics and strain. Jake's son, Marshall, they assume, or the Tompkins boy, Pierce.

"Coca-Cola man," Rita says rubbing her stomach and looking off at nothing.

Erasmus doesn't stop smoking and Bertha keeps moving her hands up and down her arms.

"The Coca-Cola man?" they say together and exchange glances before looking back at Rita.

"Hmmm," Rita sounds and looks down at her swollen bare feet. "Mama, where the pail at?" she asks as if the conversation is over.

Bertha remembers her own pregnancy and her feet, swelled up and burning at the bottoms, but she can't go for the pail because Erasmus is reaching for another cigarette even though the one he lit a moment ago is still burning in the ashtray.

"White man, then?" Erasmus asks and then holds his breath.

Rita's eyes roam around the kitchen and then look up at her father. "No. Colored man," she says and her eyes move to the ceiling and then down to the floor and then to the window that looks out into the yard.

"Girl, have you taken leave of your senses?" Erasmus laughs before lighting his cigarette and inhaling. His laughter makes the hair on Bertha's neck stand up.

"Why you say that, Erasmus?" Bertha asks, moving closer to Rita.

Erasmus' laughter rocks him and his cigarette falls from his mouth.

"What's so funny? Why you laughing so?" Bertha's head swings between her husband and her child. "Man, you crazy or something?" She asks rubbing at the hairs on her neck and taking another step that puts her right next to Rita.

Erasmus composes himself and bends down to retrieve his cigarette from the floor. Both women see the thin sheath of hair on the top of his head and Rita thinks that in a few years he will be bald like Manny. She shivers.

"This here is 1942," Erasmus says, wiping the tears from the corners of his eyes and sticking the cigarette back between his lips. "And I ain't never seen no colored man driving no goddamn Coca-Cola truck!" Laughter consumes him again and the house seems to shake with it.

They send her down to Fenton, down to Mamie Ray's house.

Mamie Ray is an old woman Bertha had heard about months earlier when Valerie Hope, one of the women she worked with at the hotel got herself "messed up" by some married man who had showered her with "I love yous" until she was so slick from his sweet words that she found it hard to keep her legs together.

Having had her, his affirmations became few and far between and stopped all together when she announced that she was pregnant.

He didn't love her anymore and maybe when the love left so did his vision because he would pass her on the street like a blind man walking past a box full of money.

Aurora had pulled her aside and told her to stop her whining and crying. Told her it was her own fault she was in the situation she was in but it wasn't no use crying over spilled milk and shoved a piece of paper in Valerie's hand.

"You call Mamie Ray and she'll take care of it." Bertha heard her whisper. Gladys, who wasn't even involved in the conversation, sounded, "*Umph!*" and nodded her head in agreement before swinging her mop from one side of the hall to the other.

Bertha, who was only on nodding basis with Valerie and Aurora, approached Gladys about it later. They whispered about Valerie's situation over their bologna sandwiches and thermoses filled with warm coffee and, in the end, Gladys scrawled Mamie Ray's name and number on the crumpled paper bag that still held Bertha's apple.

"Always good to have," Gladys offered. "Like a pistol or a straight razor," she added and popped the last bit of sandwich into her mouth.

Mamie Ray, black, short, and stout with a tangled mass of orange hair that spread out around her head like a feathered hat imparting her with a buffoon-type peculiarity. She had a dead right foot that was larger than her left and hands too small for her body or even a five-year-old.

When Rita stepped off the bus Mamie Ray, body lopsided from years of dragging around her dead foot, was standing on the curb waiting.

"You Rita?" Mamie asked as she grabbed Rita's elbow with her tiny hands.

She hadn't really had to ask that question, Bertha had described her child to a tee, all Mamie needed to look for were the eyes. "Ain't seen another pair like 'em, ever," Bertha had said to Mamie on the phone.

"Yessum," Rita said, her eyes struggling with the woman's orange hair and twisted body.

"How far along you think you is?" Mamie asked, looking down at Rita's stomach.

"Don't know," Rita replied and took a step backward.

"Well, you know when you 'lowed him on top of you. What month it was?"

"I ain't allowed nothing," Rita mumbled. "Cold month, I suppose," she added and chanced a glance at the oversized foot.

Mamie bit her lip and scratched at her head. "After Thanksgiving but before Christmas and New Year's?"

"I dunno," Rita said and her eyes moved to the tiny hands.

"Uh-huh," Mamie sounded and then, "You look strong, you can carry that suitcase," she said and wobbled away.

Bertha is already preparing. She eats late and heavy, drowning her biscuits in butter and then dabbing them in honey. She bakes pies and cakes and consumes them like air. She excuses herself from the conversations that takes place around the bus stop in the mornings and evenings, when she's traveling to and from work. She excuses herself to spit or to move herself beneath the shade of a nearby tree and dab at the imaginary sweat forming on her brow and below her nose.

She calls in sick, falls out in front of the church after service is over and the congregation and choir are gathered there.

She does all of this so they can assume before she has to tell them.

Her hips have already spread and people remember that she carried Rita the same way. "That baby is all in your behind girl!" they say, just as she had planned.

"When you due?"

The questions come like rain.

"Lawd, you want another one after Rita practically grown!"

"My friend Ann had a baby late, too. Change-of-life baby. You probably won't even get your menstrual after this one come."

Erasmus didn't like what Bertha was doing, didn't like it one little bit.

"Bertha, why we gotta hide the fact that Rita done gone and got herself knocked up?"

" 'Cause."

" 'Cause what?"

"Just 'cause." Bertha was done talking about it and went to check on the cornbread and chicken and dumplings she was preparing.

By the time Manny shows up to the house again, Bertha is a good twenty pounds heavier.

"We expectin' you know. Erasmus ain't tell you?" Bertha spouts when Manny's eyes go wide with surprise.

"Really?" Manny says and his eyes stretch wider. "Go 'head man!" He laughs and slaps Erasmus hard on his back. "You still gotta a little left in you!"

Erasmus just grimaces.

"So when you due?"

Bertha drops her eyes and mumbles something Manny can't quite catch.
"What's that?" he asks and leans in closer to Bertha.
"Summer. July. Maybe August." Bertha speaks in a low, unsure voice.
"Is that right? Is that right?" he says again.
"Uh-huh," Bertha mumbles and then looks over at Erasmus.
There's a space of silence. A deep ebbing quiet that makes both Erasmus
and Bertha twist their necks and examine their hands.
Manny considers them for a while and then asks, "Where Rita at?"
"Oh she down in Gainesville, visiting with my mama. She's ailing you
know, so I sent Rita on down there to help out." The lies fall from Bertha's
mouth like stones and Erasmus' body jerks with each syllable.
"She'll be back by the time the baby come. She'll be back by then."
Bertha's voice falters and the smile that had been holding fast to her lips
slips.
"That's good," Manny says and twists his ring around his pinky. "She a
good girl that Rita."

Rita, before she was Luscious, was not called upon to change a diaper or
heat a bottle, was assured that she would never be referred to as Mama or
have to attend a PTA meeting. Bertha is Mama and Rita, before she was
Luscious, is just older sister, eldest sibling, first child of Erasmus and Bertha,
mother of none.
Friends visit; family, too. They bring pink receiving blankets, matching
booties, and bonnets that smell of talcum powder and everything precious
and new.
They stroke the baby's tiny hand and coo at her pursed lips and Bertha
grins and smiles and serves cookies and tea while Erasmus grunts and excuses himself from the sounds of women and the baby smells that swirl
around him and snatch away his air.
Rita, fuller in the hips and heavy-breasted, stays put in her room and listens as the lies her mother tells about pregnancy and childbirth slip through
the crack beneath the door.

They notice her breasts before anything else. Their eyes light on them like
flies on sugar shit and they lick their tobacco-black lips and drag their hands
through their woolen hair and some touch themselves, running their fingers
across their chins or pinching the skin of their necks.
The women turn cold eyes on her and one even spits in her path, another
fixes her mouth to sling an insult but catches the cold glint in her eyes and
the sun fastening onto something long, sharp, and silver sticking out from
her coat pocket and she thinks better of her comment, bites her tongue and
turns her head away instead.

It's just before dusk and the sun is looming and orange in the sky, people are huddled in bunches on the corners, and someone is already cussing up a storm in one of the apartments overhead.

Music is streaming out of Lou's place, and Jake's Spot has set the first batch of porgies in the pan to fry.

Friday night in the Black Bottom, Paradise Valley.

Rita reaches the corner and turns left on Hastings Street. Broken glass litters the sidewalk; there are bloodstains close by and further away a chalk outline of where the body fell dead.

But that was last night and not one person is talking about it because someone else was shot dead outside of Sonnie Wilson's place and another stabbed behind The Flame.

Too many dead people to talk about, living people got other things on their minds; they move up and down the walkways and don't even seem to notice the silhouette on the ground. They trample across its hands, legs and face while they talk about fifths, fucking, no-good men, and bad-ass kids.

Rita turns into the O Bar.

The door sits open but the orange sun can't even work its way past the threshold; it's already midnight inside those walls, just the flicker of cigarettes and the dim light coming off the jukebox exist there.

Rita peers in before stepping into the gloom. The two men seated at the bar turn their heads to consider her but decide after a moment that the drinks sitting in front of them are more interesting.

A woman, satin-colored, long and leggy, moves from the shadows and positions herself near the jukebox. Rita sees that the skin around her eyes is puffy and the lipstick she wears is the color of purple-black grapes.

The woman drapes herself over the jukebox, pressing the side of her face against the curved metal. Slowly, gently, she places loving kisses onto the glass, leaving plum-colored lip marks smeared across its clear face.

Rita watches her for a while before moving to the bar and taking a seat.

"Yeah," the bartender calls from a dark space at the end of the bar.

Rita squints her eyes. "Manny here?" she asks.

"Maybe," the voice calls back.

The two men turn their attention to Rita once more.

"He here or not?"

"Depending on who's asking."

"Tell 'em Rita here."

"Rita who?"

"Erasmus' girl."

There is the sound of wood scraping against wood and Rita catches sight of a worn white T-shirt and muscular brown arms as the bartender moves from his chair to a room behind the bar.

The woman is done with loving the jukebox and pulls up a stool next to Rita.

The men exchange glances and then drop their eyes back down to their drinks.

"What you want Manny for?" The voice is coarse and brittle and Rita's eyes turn to face the puffed skin and scraggly gray strands sticking out from the black blond hair.

"I got something for him," she says.

"Yeah, what you got that no other woman in here got? We all got something for Manny," the woman says and a bitter laugh escapes her. "Gimme a smoke, Lester." She orders without her eyes leaving Rita's.

Lester almost tips his drink over in his hurry to toss a cigarette down the bar, then drops a dollar down next to his glass and rushes out the door.

The woman reaches into her bosom and pulls out a lighter. Her eyes still holding Rita's, she lights the cigarette and inhales deeply.

"They ain't nobody too young for Manny," she mumbles to herself, then blows a stream of smoke into Rita's face. "Shit, I was young once, too, ya know." She spits and slams her hand down on the counter. "Must be them eyes. You got eyes like a cat. Probably sneaky like 'em too."

The man that was left at the bar, digs deep into his pocket, pulls out a dollar and drops it down next to his glass. "Later, Lonnie." He yells over his shoulder before shooting Rita a cautious look and skip-walking out of the bar.

"Hey, Lonnie, he here or not?" Rita asks.

"He said he don't know no Rita or Erasmus," Lonnie says as he lazily flips through the newspaper.

"He don't know nobody he owe, had, or hates!" the woman laughs. "Ain't that right, Lonnie?" she screams and slaps the bar again.

"If you say so, Ursula."

"So which category you fall under, honey?" Ursula leans in and whispers to Rita's cheek.

The rancid stench of scotch and cigarettes accosts Rita's nostrils and she stands up suddenly, sending the stool toppling down to the floor.

"Oooh! This one's a little spitfire," Ursula says. "Yeah, he like 'em like that."

"That's enough, Ursula," Lonnie warns and finally moves down from the dark end of the bar. He's large, over three hundred pounds, and his stomach jiggles beneath his T-shirt with every step he takes toward Rita.

"He ain't here. So either buy a drink or vacate the premises," he says and lays his meaty hands down on the bar.

"He ain't here?" Rita questions sarcastically.

"He always here," Ursula whispers and then breaks down with laughter.

Lonnie shoots her another warning look before turning his gaze back to Rita.

"That's what I said." His tone is angry now.

Rita chews on her bottom lip for a moment. "Okay," she says and then, "Where's the ladies room?"

"For customers only!" Ursula screams and pounds a scrawny fist on the bar.

Lonnie rolls his eyes and says, "At the back and to the left." He turns on Ursula. "I'ma throw your ass out of here, ya here me, Ursula?"

Rita moves slowly toward the dewy blackness of the back. Cigarette smoke hangs heavy in the air and the soles of her shoes makes sucking sounds against the sticky filth of the floor.

She walks slowly then turns her head slightly to see Manny seated in a large leather chair in the room at the back. He's leaned back, sleeping legs stretched out before him, arms folded across his stomach, onyx stone gleaming.

Lonnie is still fussing at Ursula, his sausage-length index finger swaying ominously in her face.

Rita moves right, slips behind the bar and into the room.

She stands there for some time, staring at his gleaming bald head, thick neck, and hands that held her down. Her eyes roll over legs that forced hers apart and shoes that left black polish streaks across her bedspread.

He sneezes and his eyelids fly open, his brown eyes hold the green of hers, the young face soft, plump, and glowing of motherhood. He smiles a sleepy smile and his eyes drop down to firm, full breasts and the small circles of wetness seeping through the pale pink blouse she wears.

Rita steps closer to him and he smells the talcum powder she's dusted her stomach with, the sour milk the baby spewed across her skirt that Bertha dragged a wet cloth across before Rita walked blank-eyed and calm out the door.

"What you doing here?" he finally asks when his eyes grow tired of holding her and the wet spots begin to make him uncomfortable.

Rita is still seeing the shoe polish marks on the bedspread and feeling the gold band of his ring pressed between her fingers. She can hear her insides screaming, screaming and pulling apart and him breathing heavy in her neck, her hair, his skin slapping against hers, the tearing part complete and the silence that swelled inside of her and him so deep within her she feels as if her body will swallow him whole.

"What you want?" he asks, his voice filling with annoyance, his eyes looking behind her for Lonnie.

Rita wonders why she's so calm, so cool. She looks down at her hands that aren't even shaking and thinks about her heart that barely beats enough for her to breathe right anymore. Then she reaches into her pocket and pulls out the knife that Bertha uses to gut fish and before Manny can understand what's happening, before he can reach his big hands up to stop her, she brings the knife down into the center of his head.

A screaming Ursula backs away from the doorway, her purple lips a large circle, her chicken-thin hands cradling her cheeks as Rita, bloody hands and blouse soaked through with mother's milk, moves pass her.

Days later, when the police knock on Bertha's door to come and take Rita away, the O Bar was burned down to the ground when white rioters tossed fire bombs through the glass panes of businesses along Hastings, St. Antoine, and Brush.

By the time Rita was assigned her number and asked to turn front and then sideways for the camera, Manny Evans' chalky silhouette was burned away to nothing and Rita was on her way to becoming Luscious #132541289.

FROM **Crawfish Dreams**

BY NANCY RAWLES

Camille Broussard sat high on the torn vinyl cushion waiting to shake hands with her Maker. Her wrinkled brown fingers worked the rosewood beads that had been her mother's last gift to her. She hadn't expected to die on a Thursday, an undistinguished day in her opinion, and she was disappointed to find she'd be riding to heaven in a heavily-dented Ford pickup truck. Good Catholic that she was, she had hoped for something fancier, a sky blue Cadillac with pleated wings boasting a choir of angels in the back seat. But her life had been one of diminishing returns, so she wasn't altogether surprised to find herself rushing headlong toward a concrete barrier in a vehicle composed entirely of scrap.

She had been looking forward to retiring from her job. For forty years, Camille had been housekeeper and cook for the priests at St. Martin de Porres Catholic Church. Two dozen priests had come and gone, but she was still there. The church had been both sanctuary and snare, located six blocks from her home in a conspicuously unprosperous part of Los Angeles called

Watts. In a place where jobs were scarce, she had depended on St. Martin's for her daily bread. Her seven children had attended the parish school; it had given her great comfort to look up from the stove and see them at play. Now they were grown. Most of them had taken leave of both Watts and the Catholic faith. But whoever wished to see her a final time would have to come to church.

Being matriarch of the Broussard clan, a family of Louisiana Creoles who relied heavily upon ritual, Camille had laid elaborate plans concerning every detail of her death: who to burden with her last secrets, who to allow at her bedside, who to trust with her final rosary. She'd peopled dying moments with a cast of penitent thousands—the scoundrels who had wronged her, the children who had vexed her, the tax collectors who had cheated her out of her hard-earned dimes. Her funeral had been scripted down to the necklace and earrings, the correct shade of velvet for the coffin lining, the number, type, and tenor of hymns, the precise expression to be frozen for eternity. Pallbearers had been preselected along with their understudies. Her plot was purchased and waiting, the stone carved with everything but the final date. She'd envisioned a priest miraculously materializing at the exact moment of death bearing one final body of Christ, one last sweet taste of Jesus which Camille, as a Eucharistic minister, was perfectly capable of feeding herself. However, she wanted the priest to grant her absolution, which she did not wish to grant herself.

In her current condition, she would have no choice but to pardon her own sins. Her plans were literally out the window. In all her planning, she had never dreamed herself foolish enough to hasten her own demise by asking Lester Pep to carry her to San Bernardino and back in his godawful deathtrap of a truck.

Pep struggled to gain control of the lunging demon, jerking the wheel from side to side—an angler with a big one. "Say your prayers!" he shouted. A sixty-two-year-old black man from Watts, he was already five years past his life expectancy.

Camille held fast to the nape of her seat. They were jiggling down the freeway at a mean tilt, seventy miles an hour in the carpool lane, not a seat belt in sight. The curving highway stretched into oblivion, a vast sea of lanes rising and falling over pillars of rock. Box houses, brown skies, beige hills, dry bushes—all were being swept away on time's noisy current. The speed with which the end was approaching confused Camille, who was sure God still had work for her to do. As fragments of her sixty-seven years flashed before her eyes, a strange vision of hope revealed itself to her. Beyond the smog and the steamy desert sun, she thought she saw Watts rising in the distance.

Camille felt a pounding on the glass behind her. Her grandson Nicholas was crouched in the truck bed pitching curses to the wind, his shaved head thumping the glass like a gigantic ball of hail. As cars swerved and dipped all around him, he gripped the metal bars that normally served as guard rails for Pep's lawn mowing equipment. The equipment had been removed to make room for the passenger, but the chains that held it in place were left to rattle and bang against the sides of the truck. Nicholas, who had just been released from three years in prison, rattled and banged along with them. Camille wondered if any beating he might have suffered at the Men's Correctional Institute was as cruel and unusual as this one.

"Mother of Jesus!" Pep delivered a swift uppercut to the steering column and forced the truck off the meridian. The pickup bucked to a stop on the exit ramp, and Nicholas landed with a thud against the window. "Whew! That was a close one!" Pep massaged the dash. "God in heaven, I never pray except when I'm in this truck!" Camille turned around to see if Nicholas was all right.

"Oh, don't worry about him," Pep advised. "Somebody needs to knock some sense into that big head of his. So he knows better than to beat up old ladies."

Camille found herself staring directly into her grandson's eyes and nineteen years of hurt. She had raised seven children but none had tried her the way Nicholas had. Such a beautiful child he had been, but now fury scarred his countenance. She clasped the rosary in her palm. Everyday for the last three years, she had prayed a rosary for the return of his soul. As far as she could tell, a thousand rosaries later, he was not any closer to God. She was face to face with her failure.

She wanted to ask Pep to stop the truck and let the boy off right there on the blacktop in the middle of those chalky white lines. The way he was going, he would end up as a chalk outline sooner or later and she feared the yellow tape more than anything but the toe tag. When people in Watts drove past crime or accident scenes, they craned their necks to see if the yellow tape was mapping their tragedy, if the chalk outline matched the dimensions of someone they loved. Keening could still be heard in their part of town; the daughters of Jerusalem had nothing on the daughters of Watts. Camille could not bear the thought of burying her grandson, but the thought of him playing the angel of death was even more disturbing to her. He had not killed anyone yet, but he had come close enough to warrant a thousand rosaries.

Here was a child who only twelve years earlier had held the promise of a stellar future. He was so handsome that one of the Crenshaw cousins, upon spotting him at the annual beach trip, convinced Raymond and Isabel to sign their son with a modeling agency. He quickly became the family celebrity. By the age of nine, he had money in the bank and college plans, an enthusiastic agent, and two store catalogs under his belt. The limit was the sky, or in his case, the airwaves. The Broussards celebrated with gumbo the night their golden boy's first and only television commercial premiered. There was Nicholas, dressed as George Washington Carver, inventing peanut butter right before their eyes. It should have been his big break, but eminent historians and loudmouthed politicians suggested using Dr. Carver to sell peanut butter was like using George Washington to sell cherries, only worse because the distinguished scientist and inventor never would have uttered the words, "It don't get no betta than my crunchy nut butta." The ad was yanked off the air three short weeks, and like that of so many other budding stars in the city of the angels, the lad's golden age had come to an untimely end.

"Yo, Peanut! What happened to your head?" Some rough-looking young men were standing on the corner in front of the liquor store. Nicholas pounded the glass, in farewell or anger Camille wasn't sure, then climbed out. A lanky boy on a small copper bicycle circled the crowd. Nicholas reached out his hand and cuffed him on the ear.

Camille rolled down her window and shouted after her grandson, "Don't you dare leave without saying anything. You get back over here and thank Pep for the ride." The young men fell out laughing. Nicholas obeyed.

"Hey, man, thanks for bustin' me out the joint. I hope I can return the favor one day." He assumed a cocky swagger for the benefit of his friends.

Camille yanked him back with one lash of her tongue. "You may have paid your debt to society," she snapped, "but you haven't paid your debt to me."

"Get off my back, Grandma. I ain't done nothin' to you." The crowd bellowed its appreciation.

"You done plenty."

"Well, I ain't goin' to confession. You ain't my judge."

"I'm worse than the judge. You fooled the judge. I would have given you life."

"You can't give me life! You ain't God."

"I'm worse than God. God didn't come to pick you up. God didn't sit at your trial everyday hoping for some sign of humanity. I don't know what God has planned for you, but I've got work for you to do. You may have served your time with the California justice system, but you haven't served your time with me."

Howls from the street corner chorus. Eyes wet with tears of laughter.

"Damn, Grandma. Why you gots to be so hard on me?"

"I'm the easy one. What do you want me to tell your father?"

"Tell him I survived the pokey. Tell him the bird man is back."

For three years, Camille had dreaded this day and now it was upon her. His day of freedom was her day of reckoning. From the moment he was dragged from this same corner in handcuffs, she had racked her mind for an explanation. Boy children don't belong to their mothers, her best friend had tried to comfort her, they belong to the world. But it was under Camille's watch that Nicholas had gone from bad to worse, and she couldn't accept that she was blameless. She had turned her eyes away from him and he had wandered into the desert. It was up to her to bring him home.

Broussards did not go to prison. So as long as Nicholas had been locked up, they had pretended he had gone off to school or war or the priesthood. Now he was out, however & they were forced to deal with an ex-con, which was harder than dealing with a dropout, a veteran, or an ex-priest. Already his two younger brothers were following his lead. They had been suspended from school so often that the office had a stack of pink slips pretyped with the Broussard name. For Broussard men, it seemed prison was the equivalent of pregnancy: how to ruin your life, take years off your youth, and shame your family at the same time. And a prison record was more difficult to disown than an offspring.

Nobody else would go get him from prison. His parents were still too angry. His big brother had disowned him. He no longer had any girlfriends, or his girlfriends no longer had any cars. His little sister was too pregnant to fit behind a wheel. Even his Auntie Grace, who often felt kinship with outlaws, could not be persuaded to make the journey to San Bernardino. The prison was located not far from where Marc lived, but Uncle Marc couldn't have picked his nephew out of a lineup.

So Camille wasn't surprised when the phone rang and it was Nicholas wanting to know if she would come get him. She might could, she told him, but she wasn't going to let him stay in her house. He had tried to drive her from her house once but he hadn't succeeded, and she wasn't going to let him have another go at it. Nobody was going to part her from her home. She had been driven from her home in Louisiana by some lowlife white criminals, but she wasn't going to let any lowlife black criminals drive her from her home in Los Angeles, especially not one related to her.

"Ain't you forgive me, Grandma?" he wanted to know.

"No," she said and hung up the phone.

Now, as she watched him stroll away, taking no shame with him, she tried to remind herself that he had once been her joy.

"When I was his age, I wanted to do everything and couldn't do nothin'." Pep turned his head to follow the ambling figure of youth. "Here he is, free to do whatever he wants, and he don't wanna do nothin'." He whipped around and stepped on the gas.

Exhaust from the truck caused the young men to hack and wheeze. They fanned themselves, clutched their necks, pretended they were choking to death. Through the mirror, Camille watched Nicholas disappear into a cloud of smoke and laughter. She pictured his slender youthful fingers plunging a knife into delicate elderly flesh. The crime was his, but she was having the flashbacks.

"I can't just let him run the streets!" Her voice was thick with despair.

"Well, you can't keep him under lock and key," Pep reminded her. "It's up to the government to do that for you." He swung a left onto Hooper.

It was then that they noticed the boy with the small copper bicycle racing alongside the truck.

Pep slammed on the brakes. "Dammit! That kid needs to be in school!"

Camille clutched the dash with one hand and her stomach with the other. The truck started to convulse. The bicycle boy raced on ahead. Pep pumped the gas in a futile attempt to engage the engine. Some children chased each other into the street. Pep blew his horn. They scattered laughing. Eventually, the truck stopped shaking and Pep could not rouse it at all.

She should have driven herself in the Studebaker, but a few weeks before she had gotten into a little scrape. For a hair's length of road, she had lost sight of what she was doing and plowed into the car in front of her. In her forty years of driving, she had never hit a soul. No one was hurt, but a child was crying in the back seat of the stricken car. Camille cried, too. "It's my fault," she kept apologizing, thankfully. By the time Camille drove herself home, it was twilight and difficult to see so the damage to her car one of her headlights was smashed and her right front bumper dented wasn't that noticeable When she got to the house, she parked the car in backyard with all the dead cars her children had left there, and didn't tell them what had happened. When they did notice the damage, she downplayed the incident. Her insurance would surely be raised, that's what they said. But she could hear them whispering amongst themselves. She was no longer the unshakable power.

Age was beginning to take its toll. The ache in her feet was constant. Her eyes strained more to see, her ears strained more to hear. Her blood pressure was high, and so was her blood sugar. She looked at her next door neighbor. Grey had invaded his beard. His hands were veined like cabbage. Neither one of them was capable of picking up a nineteen-year-old and setting him on his feet.

"Where did we go wrong, Lester?"

"Oh, we didn't go wrong, Pretty Miss Camille. All the wells done dried up, that's all. The young people think they got to do bad just to survive. Take your boy . . ."

"He never wanted for anything!"

"You sure? How long his daddy work them shipyards?"

"He hired on just before the Riots . . ."

"Laid off after twenty years! Now, what kind of a upside down thing is that? It's an unforgiving world out there. All the niceties is gone! Where this boy gonna work? They done up and left with all the paychecks. An idle man is a hankering thing."

Pep spoke from experience. When he bought his house from the Broussards in 1959, he was a gardener tending the flowerbeds of Beverly Hills. After the 1965 Riots, his clients discovered they no longer needed him. So he moved his business to Baldwin Hills and Leimert Park, places where black people had enough money and grass to keep him busy. But Pep was a flower man. He didn't care for lawns and he wasn't very good at them. He couldn't compete with the teams of Japanese, then Mexican gardeners. He was used to operating solo. For Camille, this was the problem in a nutshell. What was known to successful gardeners had been known to her for generations. Collective effort brought collective achievement.

"Do you think he's redeemable?" She looked to Pep for encouragement. He had always been a positive fellow, far more optmistic than the Broussards, despite the comparatively poorer hand life had dealt him.

"I don't know, Pretty Miss," he shook his head. "Can't save nobody don't wanna be saved—not if he's too big to carry. You can pull a child out of a burning house, but not a grown man. And he's a child of the Riots, ain't that right? Whole city burning down and he come blazing outta his mama! Ain't smart enough to run the other way."

Camille hated when Pep talked crazy.

"What he needs is a job," she said.

"You gonna give him one? There's kids out here with good records can't find no work."

"Maybe I could pay him a little something to do odd jobs around the house."

The minute the words left her mouth Camille knew she had stumbled upon a truly bad idea. For the eight years since her husband died, she had been saving fifty dollars a month, stuffing it in an envelope taped to the underside of her bedroom bureau. Her job at the rectory paid two hundred dollars a week. Social Security would pay only half of that. She would have to subsidize her retirement with money from the envelope. She didn't have any money to pay Nicholas.

"You know," Pep was saying, "the two of us should put our assets together. We should start a little business."

"What assets?" Camille retorted. She had no more interest in going into business with Pep than she had in getting into his truck again.

"You with your beauty and brains. Me with my green thumb." He was smiling.

"You had a little business. What happened to it?" She wasn't in the mood.

"Minority-owned and everything. Just couldn't get those big contracts!" Pep shook his head. He climbed out of the truck and came around and opened her door.

"Where's a criminal when you need him?" he sighed. "Gotta get that grandson of yours to steal me a new vehicle!"

He threw back his head and laughed. Camille stared at him long and hard. He was not particularly handsome. His teeth were yellow; a couple of them were missing. His beard was badly in need of a trim. His eyes were bloodshot, even though he had stopped drinking a couple of years ago. But unlike Nicholas, with his movie star looks, Pep had never been to jail. He was entitled to his laughter. His only crimes were entrepreneurial.

She wrapped her sweater around her, took his hand, and stepped down into the street. The boy with the copper bicycle was suddenly at her feet.

"Hey, Miz Broussard, 'member me? I used to carry yo' bags."

"Where'd you get that bicycle from?" Pep growled.

"I found it in the L.A. River." The boy looked proud of himself.

"That's the bicycle of one of them boys that drowned after that big rain. You best to take that bicycle back." Pep snatched the bicycle away from him.

The boy protested loudly and held on. "I didn't steal it," he hollered, "I found it. I ain't no thief!"

Camille stared at him hard. "Is that you, Quentin? You getting big. How's your grandma?"

"She awright."

"Ain't seen you round the store lately."

"Ain't workin' there no more."

"You ain't working nowhere," Pep brushed him aside. "You need to be going to school. How old are you? Ten?"

"I'm thirteen! My gramma say I ain't need to go to school no mo'. Gimme twenty dollars, I fix that truck."

"I'll sell it to you for twenty-five." Quentin shook his head. Pep threw down the bicycle. He picked it up and rode off. The copper frame gleamed in the twilight sun.

Camille and Pep set off. Three blocks and they would be home. Before they had gone a good ten yards, children were jumping up and down in the back of Pep's truck chanting rhymes and yelling obscenities. The elders did not look back nor wag their fingers in reprimand, nor add their own voices to the din of posterity. They were tired from a long day spent with the future. Together they walked, his arm supporting her elbow, her hand clutching his wrist, two stalwart spirits teetering on the edge of endurance. If not for their surroundings and not again for their circumstances and not again for their misfortunes, they might have caused a head or two to bow. As it was, theirs were the only heads straining to stay aloft. Burdened with obligations and the apprehension of old people walking a gauntlet of unemployed youth, they struggled to make it home before night descended.

Press and Curl

BY TAYARI JONES

It didn't take them all that long to find Rodney's body. Three weeks after he disappeared, they came across him facedown in an Atlanta creek. And by then I was used to the idea of him being dead. I had watched the children's faces on the news, one by one, since August of last year. Last time I checked, three of the pictures had "missing" up under them and the other ten said, "murdered." None of the "missing" ones ever got found and took off the list. All that ever changed was the word below. Once somebody's picture made it to the news, it was a done deal.

Rodney's family asked if the school chorus could sing at the services. We practiced for three days straight to be ready for Tuesday. Our rehearsals weren't as rowdy as usual, but somebody just passing by also wouldn't think we was getting ready to put a boy in the ground. Truth was, most people was a little excited because the funerals always got shown on TV. I didn't like to watch them, but Mama would sit on the couch with one dry Kleenex balled tight in her hand saying "God spare."

Mrs. Scott, the music teacher, was taking us through "God Is Amazing" for the fifty-millionth time with Cinque Freeman on solo. He had his eyes closed, singing like he Foster Silvers or somebody. Mrs. Scott banged on the music stand with her conductor wand. "Let us not forget why we are here."

I don't think that anyone *forgot* Rodney. It was just that they didn't know him good enough to have nothing much to remember. He was my friend, true, but I was the only one who got to talk to him. Rodney was so shy, like in that song by the Pointer Sisters. Talking to him was sometimes like talking to my grandfather after he had his stroke. I could tell by looking at Papa that he could hear me but his mouth couldn't work for him to answer me. So when I spoke to him, I would say my part and his, too. But most people not going to go through all that with a eleven-year-old, so they never got to know Rodney Green. That's too bad, because he was good people. So it's not that the chorus *forgot* Rodney. It just that they didn't miss him enough to forget that come next Tuesday, we'd all be on television.

Mama must have thought about me being on TV, too, because she made an appointment for me to get my hair fixed the day before the funeral. I had been begging her every Christmas and every Easter since second grade to let me wear curls and every time she said, "What you need to have your hair pressed for? You ain't grown."

What did I need a press and curl for? Sometimes Mama act like she don't have two good eyes to see with. My hair so nappy that it pulls the comb right out Mama hand when she try to fix it for me. By the time she get it into plaits, my head be tender and the comb so full of hair that it look like a little animal. And all that wrestling for what? Nobody ever said to me, "You hair looks real nice, Octavia." If they do notice it at all, it's to say how short it is. Grown people try to be nice and tell me things I can eat or put in it to make it grow. Kids just poke fun and say, "Octavia hair so short she can use rice for a curler."

But my hair not as short as people think. I can pull my braids down till they reach the bottom of my ear, but when I let it go, then pop back up by my eyes. But see, if I could get it straightened it could hang to its full length. Then I could wear it smooth down in the back with a little row of curls. Forsythia Chambers, this girl in my class, wears hers tucked under all the way around so she look like a sweet little mushroom. That's how I want mine. I get tired of stupid boys slapping on my neck because I ain't got no hair to cover it up with.

And as for me being grown, you don't have to be grown to get a press and curl. On Easter I see five-year-olds with they hair twisted into shiny Shirley-Temples. I think they look cute as pie but Mama just talk about them under her breath, "Last thing a little girl need is for people to have a reason to look at her."

Sometimes my Mama act like she don't live in the same world with the rest of us. Listening to her, you would think that you have to be *cute* for people to look at you.

"I want you to get your hair fixed after school on Monday," Mama said. She was in the kitchen boiling neck bones.

"Monday?" I asked. Real beauty parlors are closed on Monday. "Where at?"

"Over Mrs. Washington, where you think?" Mama chopped celery into big chunks.

"Mama, you know I don't eat celery."

"Don't eat it, then," she said.

I couldn't figure out if she was sending me to Mrs. Washington because she didn't have the money to send me to the Pink Fox Salon or if it was because Mrs. Washington is the only one doing heads on a Monday.

"What we having with the neck bones?"

"Rice and gravy. Green beans."

"To drink?" I asked.

"Kool Aid."

So it was a money thing. When she got cash we have Coke with dinner, or juice. Water or Kool Aid meant money was funny. But it could be worse. In the summer when the electric bill gets really high, Mama do her own hair in the kitchen. It looked okay when she get through but the tops of her ears get burnt where she bring the hot comb in too close.

"Mrs. Washington do people hair pretty," I said to show I wasn't tripping. Mama is good for taking something away if I turn my nose up at it.

"Go over there right after school." She didn't look up from the pot she was stirring. "And get rid of that gum. You look like a cow chewing cud."

"Yes ma'am," I said spitting into a napkin. The gum was still sweet but I wasn't about to complain.

Mama gave the pot one more stir before she went in her pocketbook and dug out some money. She gathered the bills in a stack and tried to smooth them out. "Here eight," she said. "You just give her seven. Use the extra one to get you a snack after school."

"Yes ma'am." I was trying to be cool, but a grin came to my face by itself.

"You sure smiling hard for somebody going to a funeral." Mama's soft sad face sucked the happy out of me like a vacuum cleaner. I didn't reach for the money.

"What? Ain't you the same child been worrying me half to death about a press and curl?"

"But you said I wasn't—" I was about to say *grown*, but she cut me off.

"Now I'm saying yes." She shook the money at me. I never noticed that dollar bills had a smell before then. They had a odor like people's sweaty hands and rooms that need to be aired out.

I took it from her without saying anything else. The stack of money was fat and kind of messy. Money on TV always lay flat in thin stacks held together with a little piece of paper. On the *Rockford Files*, Jim could slip a hundred dollars in his coat without it making a bump. But these eight real-life dollars made a stack so big, I couldn't put it in my back pocket without it looking like one side of my booty was lopsided.

Before I went to school on Monday, I folded two dollars at a time and put them in each one of my jeans pockets. That way, at least, people couldn't look at me and see how much I was carrying. But even for all my carefulness, I felt heavy like each dollar bill was a cartoon anchor that could pull the whole ship over. Mama had never trusted me with so much money at one time. She had never sent me for a press and curl. And I had never been to a funeral before. There were just too many had-nevers gettin' away like a handful of water.

Mrs. Washington stay in the for-real projects down the street. All the buildings are colored soft like ice cream but the paint peeled off like scabs. As soon as I got over there, I walked real fast and kept pulling my eyes off the sidewalk. I wanted to look like I came round here all the time, just that this time I was in a hurry. When you look like you not on your home side of the street is when kids try and jump you.

As soon as I knocked on the door, I could hear Mrs. Washington shuffling up to the front. She peeked through the peephole and waited a second like she was trying to see if she should let me in or not. She needed to hurry up. The wind was whipping around corners and I didn't have nothing on my head.

"Who is it?" It wasn't a friendly-sounding question.

"Octavia Griffith," I said. "I'm supposed to get a press and curl this afternoon."

There was all this clicking while she took loose the fifty million locks on her door. The last thing she let go was the chain; it swung to the side with a little click.

To be someone that fix hair so pretty, Mrs. Washington go around looking a mess. Her hair was long down to her shoulders but it was so thin that I could see her brown head between white strings of hair. It was pressed but she didn't put no curl in it so it was like looking at a bowling ball with spider webs all over it.

"Thought you was supposed to be here at two," she said once I was inside.

"No ma'am," I said. "School don't let out till 2:25. I came straight over." I looked down at the bag of chips in my hand. "I stopped quick at the store but that's all." I added that so she couldn't accuse me of lying.

It was dark in there. The only light that came in the living room was what managed to squeeze around the corners of the shades.

"The light bothers my eyes," she said. "Glaucoma."

"Yessum," I said. How could she do my hair in the dark? If I wanted to get a big burn cross my forehead, I could have stayed home and let my mama press my hair for free.

I had half a mind to ask her if heat bothered her, too, because it was freezing. The was furnace turned up just enough to keep your breath from smoking but that was it.

"Let me take your coat," she said.

Even in the half-dark she must have seen me looking at her like she was crazy.

"It's warmer in the kitchen where we going to be. Nobody got money to heat rooms where ain't nobody at."

I was shamed as I pulled off my coat. Like I was being high and mighty, worrying about being cold, trying to run up this old lady electric bill. But I would have gave her the dollar I spent for my snack if she would turn up the heat just for the time I was in there.

The kitchen was green. Green fridge, green counter, green cabinets, green everything. The high white stool in front of the stove was the only thing that didn't match.

"That's where I'm going to sit?"

"Unless you want to sit on the floor."

I climbed up and waited.

"You ate yet?" she asked. The smell of a chicken potpie rushed out when she opened the over door. I turned to get some of that warm air on my cold cheeks.

"Yessum. I had lunch at school and I got a snack off in my bag."

"Well I'm going to have myself a little bite." She bent over and took the potpie out with a blue oven mitt. She set it on the counter and added, "If that's all right with you."

It wasn't okay with me. Why she didn't eat before I got here? But what could I do but wait while she had her dinner standing over the sink? She ate slow and slurpy, but I guess people who have false teeth have to take their time.

She finished finally, and cut on the stove. It took her a few seconds to strike a match with her shaky hands. When she touched it to the gas it caught with a big *whoosh*. One of these days, she going to blow herself up. She set the heavy pressing comb on the blue flame.

Pressing combs are like cast-iron skillets. The first time I saw a brand new one, I couldn't hardly tell that it was the same thing as one that had been put to use; it was shiny as a good idea. Mrs. Washington's pressing comb look like it been in a thousand heads, black as Granny's skillets.

"What we doing with this hair?" She talked slow like people from the country.

"Press and curl."

"You got seven dollars?" She scooped a hunk of Ultra Sheen out of a wide-mouth jar. Her fingers were bent up with old age and lumpy from years of burning and healing.

"Yessum."

She nodded and started unloosing my plaits. "You wash your hair last night?"

"Yessum."

She put her nose to it for a second, which I really didn't appreciate. She the one live in the projects and now she sniffing me like I don't know nothing about personal hygiene. Mama had even put the shampoo through my hair twice and on top of that, used a strawberry creme conditioner. I never seen the ladies in the Pink Fox sniffing on nobody. But I guess that's why it cost twelve dollars.

Mrs. Washington took the comb off the fire and pressed it down on a wet dishrag. It sizzled like chicken frying but it smelled like hot water. Then she put the comb in a little section of my hair and pulled it through; at first my hair was hard to get through like regular but then the naps just let go and the comb went through smooth and easy like baby-doll hair.

I wanted so bad to have a little hand mirror so I could watch what was happening on my head. How long was my hair stretching to? A lot of times, girls who had just regular hair ended up with long hair once they got it pressed. I forgot about the mushroom style and started seeing myself with pretty little curls around the side of my face stretching past my chin, and the rest hanging straight back past my collar.

"You getting your hair fixed for that little boy funeral?" Mrs. Washington said.

For the second time since I got over here, I felt shamed. It was like how the Sunday school teacher let us sit around half Easter morning excited about new shoes and chocolate rabbits and then she reminded us that Pontius Pilate put nails in Jesus' hands and jooked him in the side with a knife. *Twice.*

"Yessum," I said. "I'm singing in the chorus."

"Hush now," she said. "It's hard enough for me to hold my hand steady without you moving your head around talking."

Why she ask me then? Seven dollars ain't as much as twelve but she don't have to be *nasty.* Next time, she put the comb so close that I felt like a piece of toast under the broiler. Grease melted and ran hot down my scalp.

"Ouch!" I jerked forward and the comb touched my scalp.

Mrs. Washington stepped back while I felt my head. Nothing was bleeding.

"Let me know when you ready to be still. That's why I don't like to do children's hair. They can't hold still."

"But you burned me." I was trying not to whine.

"That was just some grease melting," she said. "Pretty don't come easy."

After that, I was too scared to talk or even to move my legs when my butt started falling asleep on that hard stool. Next time, I was going to save the extra five dollars for the Pink Fox. The ladies in there wear nice little coats with their name on the pocket, call you "baby," and show you books with pictures of hair styles. You point at one and say, "I want to look like her," and they get to work. If your hair not long enough, they might let you wear a hairpiece. But this old lady didn't have none of that. And to top it off, she got a bad attitude. Hairdressers supposed to be friendly. And pretty.

By the time that old bat finished with me, I was stiff like it was me with the arthritis. I gave her the money and she counted it before she unlocked the door to let me out of that cold apartment onto the even colder street. She did ask me if I wanted to go to the restroom and look at my hair, but I wanted to get out there. We got a mirror at home.

"Who coming to get you?" she said.

"Nobody," I told her. "It's not that far."

She shook her head and said she don't know what go through young mamas' heads these days. "Run fast," she said while she was undoing her locks. "We don't need no more lost childrens around here."

"Yessum," I answered. She waited til I got to the street before closing the door and starting on her locks.

I had to pass by a liquor store to get to my house. There wasn't no way around it. Even if I took the back way, I would have to go by J&B's. Taking the front way, I had to walk in front of West End Package. Lights in front spelled out LIQUOR and WINE in blue and red. It wasn't night yet, but it was getting there. The last thing I needed was to be caught out in the projects after dark with liquor store lights pointing me out like I'm on a stage. But if I put too much pep in my step, I would seem scared and scaredness draw ugly people to you. And ugly get uglier at night. I made a point to take two steps for every block of sidewalk.

"Psst," said this one man leaning up on a pole smoking a cigarette. If he had been a boy my own age, I would have said, "I don't talk to snakes," and kept walking. But he was a full grown man with a mustache and everything.

"Say," he said.

I had passed by this store before and nobody ever had actually *said* anything to me. As a matter of fact, I had passed right by here on my way to Mrs. Washington house. Did I see this same man earlier? I couldn't remember. There'd been some men standing out here, there always were no matter what time of the day, but none of them had noticed me.

"Psst," he said again.

I crossed my arms in front of me so he couldn't see the outline of my training bra and notice what was sprouting underneath. What did Mama say about little girls with pressed hair? "The last thing a little girl need is to give somebody a reason to look at her."

"Say," he said again and I just took off running. He might could smell fear like a dog but he couldn't run as fast as one.

When I got home, my face was slick with sweat.

Mama was in the kitchen again, washing dishes. "What you doing running like that? I didn't spend seven dollars for a press and curl for you to sweat it out in the same day!" She shook her finger at me; drops of water and soap made little splatters on the floor. "You got to make up your mind what you want."

I was breathing hard, but I was able to say, "It ain't pressed no more?" If it wasn't I wouldn't have been hurt. I only wished that I could have seen it before it went back nappy.

"No," Mama said inspecting my head. "It's still straight. But you can't do all that playing if you want to wear curls."

"Yes ma'am."

She smiled. "You like it?"

"I don't know. I ain't seen it yet." I put my hand to my neck, where my nappiest hair grows. Everything back there was smooth as the green strands inside the corn husk. "It feel good, though."

I closed my eyes when I walked into the bathroom. I wanted to see myself all at once, like a picture when somebody snatches a red cloth from over it. When my hips knocked up against the sink, I knew I was right in front of the mirror. I opened my eyes.

My hair was not hanging down my back. It didn't even make it to my ears. Mrs. Washington had turned it into tight curls about as big around as a magic marker. Each curl sat close to my head in five or six rows like I was recharging fifty batteries on the top of my head.

"It's going to be pretty tomorrow," Mama said.

I didn't answer. Mama didn't spend seven dollars to see me cry.

"We'll comb it out in the morning."

"But it's so short." My voice was shaky.

"She cut it?"

"No. But I thought pressing your hair was supposed to make it long." I couldn't help it now. I let the tears run loose. I stood up against Mama but she didn't hug me.

"What's your problem?" She held me by my shoulders.

"A dog chased me on the way home."

"Well, ain't no dog in here now and ain't nothing wrong with your hair. Seven dollars can't buy a miracle. What? You think Mrs. Washington supposed to put hair on your head?"

I moved away since I could see she wasn't going to give me any sympathy. Even worse, she was getting mad.

"On the one hand, you want to be so grown, then you run in the street like a little kid, turn around, and want to cry like a baby." She put her hands on her hips, shaking her head.

What was she talking about? She was the one who said that pressing hair made you grown. I just wanted to have curls. But not these magic marker rolls. All I wanted was to be pretty. Make it where somebody could look at me and actually *like* what they see.

"Now, get on out of here. I need to get my bath so I can get ready to go to the wake." She stood in front of the mirror. "That poor little boy."

Mama's hair around the edges and in the back didn't lay down like the straightening comb told it to. It curled up in tight, hard knots that kids call "BB shots." Especially behind her scabbed ears.

"Look at me," Mama said. "My hair is all over my head." She looked at me with that Sunday school teacher look. I tucked my head and left the room.

I went in to my bedroom and cried facedown in the pillow, careful not to mash my hair.

I Don't Know Nothin' 'Bout Birthin' No Babies

BY SANDRA JACKSON-OPOKU
FROM *The River Where Blood Is Born*

October 20, 1973

Dear Allie Mae:

How is college treating my baby way up there in Providence?

Don't a day pass when I don't think about you, and miss you, and wonder how you're getting on. I'm counting the days until you home with us for Christmas. Wish we could afford to bring you home Thanksgiving, too. But you know how tight money is. This twenty dollars ain't much, but I hope it helps you some.

We all been doing fine. Benny fell off the toilet up at Waukegan and had to go in the hospital. He's doing better now, praise the Lord. Otis lost his little bit of disability money last month. Those peoples had the nerve to tell him he well enough to go to work, bad as his back is.

You remember Miss Nibbs out to Lombard, where I mind her mother Friday nights? She so happy to hear you in college. She give me these books and magazines she was fixing to throw away, thought you might could use them.

I see one here where they pay peoples to write about *My Most Unforgettable Character*. You know I don't have much education. I don't know much about story writing and what-all. But Lord knows I could use the money. And I have known me some Unforgettable Characters in my time. Maybe you could write it up for me.

I know I ain't never told you much about my childhood. I been spending my life trying to forget. It wasn't an easy thing coming up in Cairo. But if I learned one thing at the age of forty-five, it's the truth of that old church song. "I can't get above what made me." I been thinking a lot about peoples I ain't seen in years.

Let me tell you about Lula Mae Jaspars. You know Cousin Lola, on my daddy's side? Her mama, my Aunt Truly, was my daddy's half sister. I guess you could call us distant first cousins. They were the kinfolk you never saw much of, come from living too close to the white folks' part of town.

Old Sheriff Jaspars was one of the ugliest mens you would want to see. Red face, red hair, big old red nose. Now you got to know he had a red neck. That didn't stop him from keeping his two houses. A big rambling one for his white wife and kids. A little white cottage for Aunt Truly and the kids they had.

I don't know how he done it. Maybe he would switch up days. Say, Mondays, Wednesdays, and Fridays with Aunt Truly. Tuesdays, Thursdays, and Saturdays for Mrs. Jaspars, his white wife. Sunday to rest—you know he needed it. Between his two families, Sheriff Jaspars had twenty-something kids. Lula Mae was one of them.

They say Lula Mae was her daddy's favorite of the bunch. She didn't favor him, except for being kind of on the red side. How ugly Sheriff Jaspars made such a fine gal, I'll never know. Those light, funny-colored eyes of Lula Mae's. I swear they changed with the weather. Rainy days they was gray, sunny days they was green. She got that good hair too, used to wear it all down her back. Never did have the need of no straightening comb.

Lula Mae Jaspars grew up to be a traveling woman. Her daddy sent her all over. New York City. New Orleans. Texas. I wanted to be a traveling woman, too, but I was too chicken-shit to go off on my own. She was in San Francisco when I got it in my mind to go out and see her. I wasn't but about fourteen years old, but I went up there on the train all by myself. First time I ever set foot out of Cairo, I went halfway across country. Took me the better part of a week.

Lula Mae, who had been about the sharpest dresser in Alexander County, had took to wearing sandals, long skirts, headrags, and gold hoops in her ears. She had herself a Mexican boyfriend, and was passing herself off as a Gypsy fortune-teller, but she ain't used no crystal ball. She had a little black spider tatooed in the cup of her right hand, with all the lines in her palm stretched out around it like a web. For a price, she would tell them filthy-rich white womens up on Telegraph Hill what the spider saw in their future.

At first Lola, which is what Lula Mae had started calling herself, wasn't that happy to see her country cousin. But when it came to her that I could be of some help, Lola changed her mind and welcomed me with open arms. She got me on with the MacAvie family doing cleaning. It turned out I was doing her work and mines, too.

You know, thinking back on it, Dennis MacAvie might make a good story. That child was something else. I called him Dennis the Menace. I'd put him in his high chair while I cleaned up the house. He liked to be up high. And he'd be steady watching me with those big old blue eyes. He would wait for me all morning, just as quiet and patient. By lunchtime I would have that whole house spotless and the rest of the day left to play with Dennis.

The older he got, the more he swore I was his mama. But I wasn't soft like Mrs. Hightone MacAvie. I wasn't but fifteen years old, but Callie Mae Bullocks did not take no mess. I remember one day they give me some money to take Dennis to a picture show. Dennis wanted a cowboy picture. I wanted to see *Gone With the Wind.* Guess who won?

"Lordy, Miz Scarlet. I don't know nothin' 'bout birthin' no babies!"

Me and old buck-eyed Butterfly McQueen about the only black faces in the movie house. Dennis just would have to point at the screen and holler out: "Look! There you go, Callie Mae."

Child, I took him out of there and tanned his natural hide. If he had the nerve to show his behind, I had the nerve to whip it for him. Showing me out like that. I might be somebody's housemaid, but I wasn't hardly no-body's slave. If Dennis ain't learned nothing else, I made sure he learned that well.

"Are you my real mother?" he come asking me another time.

"Now, Dennis. How I'm going to be your mother? Look at you. I'm col-ored. You're white."

"No." Dennis shakes his blond head. "I'm colored, too."

I went and got his crayon box and a big sheet of white paper.

"Look at here." I drew a stick figure with the brown crayon. "This is me. What color is that?"

Dennis squinched up his eyes. He was just learning to name his colors. "Brown."

"Alright." I picked out the white crayon. "Now, this is you."

I rubbed and rubbed it on the paper.

"But Callie Mae. Nothing's coming out."

"That's right, child. You see, they call people, like me, "colored," because we're colored brown or black. They call people like you "white," because you don't have no color to you."

He frowned up his face and snatched the crayon away from me. He commenced to scratching it against the paper, trying to get a picture out of it. Finally it broke.

"Ain't nothing you can do to make white colored, Dennis MacAvie."

When it hit him that he couldn't make a colored picture with that white crayon, he bust out crying and wailed the whole afternoon.

Well, I've met colored people who wanted to be white so bad they would take a shotgun to their own shadow. And I've met many a colored person who don't have a thing in the world to hold on to but their color. I was one of them. But I ain't never met a white person who wanted to be colored so bad they would cry about it. Not until that day.

Lola said I was being cruel to the child. But you know as good as I do that Dennis would grow up and learn to love his whiteness. You know he did. But you better believe that he also grew up knowing that darkness can make a mighty mark. And Dennis MacAvie also ain't out there making a mammy out of every colored woman he comes across, or my name ain't Callie Mae Clemmons.

Of course, I didn't have a way in the world of knowing how he grew up until near on thirty years later. Lola got in trouble with the family about bringing a man in the house to sleep in their bed when they was out of town. Dennis got an eyeful and couldn't wait to run and tell. And we were both sent packing back to Cairo.

But Lola wasn't a woman who would stay put for too long. Being run out of San Francisco on a rail ain't put a crook in her step. She hadn't sat down in Cairo good before she was off again to be with a man up in Phoenix. A black man this time. He had a little piece of change in his pocket, too. You know Lola had to have a man with some money.

Back then Clyde Brown owned the only barbershop and funeral parlor in town, right next door to each other. "Clyde's cuts will do you proud," was one of his slogans. "Browns, for the Funeral of Distinction," was the other.

Passing for Creole now (which I guess Creole is just about anything you want to make it), Lola went ahead on and married him. When she had the baby she come back down to Cairo and got me. I guess then she remembered how good I did her all those years in San Francisco when she was supposed to be baby-sitting Dennis. Lola never been too good with kids, anyway. Her temper ain't as long as my toenail.

Anyway, I went on up to Phoenix to be Clyde and Lola's live-in. And here's where I met another one of My Most Unforgettable Characters. He was so unforgettable, I up and married him. But that's getting ahead of the story.

I thank Clyde Brown to this day. If it hadn't been for him wanting to stay home and play with his baby girl, I might not have never met your daddy. His name was Benjamin Peeples, but everybody who knew him called him "King."

Clyde had set Lola up in a little business. She was queen of Lola's Place, a little juke joint that served watered-down drinks and live music. That night Clyde had come home from the barbershop or funeral parlor, one. He woke up Pat and started playing with her. She opened those big eyes and grinned all up in his face, nothing but curls and dimples. A little Daddy's Girl. If I had woke the hussy out of sleep she would have been screaming to beat the band.

"Go on out and have a good time, Callie Mae. I'm baby-sitting tonight."

"Where I'm going? I don't know nobody around here."

"Go on down to Lola's. If you want to meet you somebody, that's where they all at."

So down to Lola's I went. And I met me somebody. A big, black, burly somebody. Six and a half feet tall. King was there taking pictures of the colored folks dancing and drinking and flirting with each other's wives. He'd snap awhile, then duck back in that room behind the bar awhile. It was crowded that Saturday night, seemed like everybody wanted their picture took. King stuck his head out the door and hollered over where I was sitting drinking my soda pop, trying to make like it was something else.

"Come on in here and help me, girl."

Turned out to be, King had a darkroom set up in there where he was printing up the pictures as quick as he could shoot them. I got a quick lesson and was left to develop film and print pictures for the rest of the evening. We were a good team from day one. Just like a key and lock when they're well greased and not rusty. One works the other.

King, he was a natural-born salesman. Loud and friendly, could tell a Shine joke to a church mother and have her laughing at the filthiest lines. People just took a liking to him. He'd jolly them into having their pictures took; sweet-talk the womens, buddy up the mens. We'd sometimes pull in two hundred dollars on a good night. We'd work Chicago, Gary, Milwaukee, Peoria, and every place in between. Lord, wasn't that the good life?

See, me—I was the quiet type. I was happy to be in the back in the dark, with the noise and the music and the laughter floating back to me. I never missed a thing. Anything I ain't overheard, the pictures told the story the minute they start coming to life in the fix.

And if they didn't have nothing to say, King sure would. When the night was over we'd go on back home, count up our money, and King would tell me which woman got drunk and danced the hootchie-kootchie on the bar, who beat whose butt in what fight, what songs the band was singing that night.

King had him a good singing voice. He could croon just as good as that other man they called King who used to work the same juke joints we did before he went and got famous singing:

"Unforgettable, that's what you are."

What went wrong with your daddy and me? The lock ran out of grease. The key wore down. Children started being born.

Maybe I should never have had kids. Lord knows I love you both. But when I had taken care of other people's babies it was so easy. When I had my own, it was hard as day-old biscuits. Hard as a pimp's heart. Hard as the sun-baked row you know you got to hoe. That's why I look after old folks now. Seems I'm better helping ease folks out of life than I am raising them up in it.

Your brother, Benny, wasn't right from the beginning. He wanted to go out of this life the minute he came in it. Maybe they should have let him. They worked on him a good twenty minutes to bring him back. But part of him stayed over on the other side. He always hung back. Slow to crawl, slow to walk, slow to talk. Took him ten years to get up to where most boys would be at two. And he ain't never went no further.

Big, lively King and his slow son, Benny. It broke his heart every time he looked at the boy. And it broke my heart when I saw him looking. He never laid blame, but I always felt to blame. Like I must have done something wrong to make a child that wasn't right. Maybe it was the smoke in the air of all them juke joints. Maybe it was the chemicals I always had my hands in.

When I got pregnant again King made me come off the road.

"You a mother now. Soon to be mother of two. These late nights and smoky taverns ain't the right life for a mother."

You was a normal child, even though you came six weeks early. Black as a raisin and smart as a whip. But Lord, I ain't never seen such a colicky baby. Always wanted somebody to be holding you. If not, you cried. Girl, you could lay up there for an hour, flailing those little legs and wailing those little lungs. Once you got started good, Benny would join in. Sometimes I'd have to go out on the porch just to get away from the noise and have a minute to myself.

King was away working nights, sometimes overnight. And my mind would be working overtime. I'd be seeing him with some woman in the corner of a tavern somewhere. I'd hear his deep laugh mixed in with her soft one, while I sat up and listened to babies screaming.

Motherhood turned me into somebody I didn't like. A prying, jealous, hateful somebody. The kind of woman who goes through wallets and listens in on phone calls. A woman who boils water and sharpens knives. King was a traveling man. I knew that when I met him. One day he went out on the road and didn't come back.

Well, they say what goes around, comes around. And I lived to have a man who would do me like I did King. You know who I'm talking about. A man so jealous-hearted he couldn't stand to hear another man's name on my lips. A man who burned up my clothes on the barbecue grill because he said they showed too much of me. A man who wants to own every step I take, every thought I think, every breath I draw. I know you two never got along, but Otis ain't a bad man in his way. Sometimes I wish I had let him straight alone. It's too late to fret on that now.

And I don't hold hard feelings for King no more. He was a man who couldn't live with chains dragging at him. If I saw him today I would tell him that I lived to understand why he had to go.

Lola, Dennis, or King? Who do you think would make the best story? Or what would you say if I told you this? My most Unforgettable Character is me. Callie Mae Clemmons, forty-five years old. Born in Battle Creek, Michigan, raised up in Cairo, Illinois.

My daddy was a traveling man, too. He was an evangelist who went all up and down the country preaching revivals. He used to say that God got him up one morning and told him to spread the word far and wide. And he never stopped moving until a lightning bolt caught him while driving to a revival one night.

I never knew my mother. They say she used to go out on the road with him, singing gospel and passing the plate. I was born on the road, halfway between a church anniversary in Chicago and a revival in Detroit. My mother died giving birth to me.

Maybe that's why I come up wanting to be a traveling woman. Like that train named the *City of New Orleans* that would come whistling through Cairo in the night. I wanted to cock my hat to the side, jam my hands in my pockets, and jump aboard. Just move any which way the railroad would take me. I wanted to ride that train. I wanted to be that train.

But it took a while for the blood to take. Daddy stayed on the road, I stayed on the truck farm with Big Momma. Working the land, pulling at the roots of sweet potatoes, and feeling like I was growing roots that didn't belong in that place.

I just wanted to be out somewhere. Don't you remember being so little you couldn't even wipe your nose right, but always dreaming? Wanting to be out in the world with people who ain't known you since birth. People with things left to find out about them.

I ain't done too bad. I haven't traveled far, but I've been a lot of places.
From Battle Creek to Cairo. Cairo to San Francisco and back again.
Phoenix, Illinois. The night side of at least a dozen little cities in Illinois and
Indiana. And Chicago, that's where it all ended up.

But don't a day pass when I don't wonder what I would have done and
where I would have gone if I'd lived my whole life as a free woman. With no
babies to keep me home, would I be laughing on King's arm right now in
some other city? Ain't no telling.

Y'all kids are gone now. I'm as free as I'm ever going to be. I could go off
tomorrow if I wanted to. But seems like once I got shed of one anchor, here
come another one to weight me down. A piece of job to go to, a piece of
house to pay on. A piece of man to keep me company as the years go by.
Well, I guess my life wouldn't make no kind of story. I lived it long, but
maybe not so well. But I tell you what.

I got me a daughter who is one Unforgettable Character. That's you,
baby. Allie Mae Peeples. Still as black as a raisin and smart as a whip. I guess
I give you a name something like mine because I thought you would be another one of me. But, honey, ain't no such thing as making yourself over in
somebody else. You don't belong to nobody but yourself. Allie Mae ain't
hardly Callie Mae. I guess you calling yourself Alma now.

It tickled me to death when you went and done like Cousin Lola did.
Changed your name to suit yourself. What you say Alma Peeples means?
"Soul of a people"? It takes a writer to think up with something like that.

When I was coming up it wasn't no such thing as a colored girl making a
living as no writer. But the only difference between *ain't yet* and *could be* is
trying. You sure tried. Through no help of mine, Lord forgive me.

I tried to pass my ignorance on down to you. Tried as hard as I could to
write *can't* on your soul. But I was writing with a white crayon that couldn't
make a mark. So *can't* wasn't never a part of your makeup.

Remember when you started busing? You must have been about twelve
years old. Livia was so happy when we got you and Clarisse in the white
children's school. I wasn't sure about it at first, but Livia talked me into it.
You girls was so smart, but that school you'd been going to wasn't for shit.
To me and Livia, this was a chance to get our daughters a little piece of the
future.

It wasn't nothing special we were dreaming of. You'd get to finish high
school without having a baby. Go to college maybe. Get a job as a schoolteacher or nurse. Just the stingy little dreams of poor colored womens.

I knew it was going to be rough on you girls. But Livia said it like this.
"At least there'd be two of you." White folks was going to make it hard, but
at least you would have each other to lean on. And be getting that good education, couldn't nobody take it away. Y'all got an education alright.

I seen what you went through every night on TV. It was just as bad as Little Rock ten years before. Bunch of grown-ass white womens, carrying signs and hollering at a busload of helpless children. Nothing I had ever taught could have got you ready to be called *nigger* by womens old enough to know better.

Livia didn't get nothing but grief for her dreaming. "What did Clarisse die from?" you used to always ask me. I didn't think that knowing would help, young as you was then. I guess I might as well tell you now. You remember that last time they carried her to the hospital? Clarisse had the sickle cell, she died in the County after having the fit that day in school.

What did I get for my dreaming? It's hard to say. You met the lynch mob at the age of twelve, lost your best friend to it. You know, I wanted to pull you out but Livia wouldn't hear of it. Said her baby's death wasn't going for nothing. Maybe you can tell me now. Was it worth it?

You stayed. Got that good education. And gone on to do much more in life than the raggedy little dreams I dreamed for you. You grew up strong, learning early on that to keep from being a beggar you had to be a fighter. But was it because of, or in spite of, me? I guess I'll never know.

All I know is that I would come home from work so late most evenings, you was already done cooking dinner and putting Benny to bed. You'd be sitting up at the kitchen table, just writing. Sometimes so mad you couldn't even speak. But writing like the lessons on that paper would save your soul. And to tell you the truth, I don't begrudge you your anger. It helped you make a way for yourself in a world where most colored womens scared to walk.

I told you that I ran into Dennis the Menace again? I was on the ward one day, collecting my sheets for the laundry. And here comes this white man loping down the hall after me, hospital gown hanging all open in the back. Thirty years later and Dennis MacAvie still showing his behind.

The money his parents had and the gumption I gave him had made him a big shot in the business world. But he was still little snotty-nosed Dennis the Menace to me, just living high in filthy-rich Lake Forest instead of San Francisco. He couldn't believe that life hadn't taken me no further than the hospital laundry.

"If you'd just apply yourself, Callie Mae, you could conquer the world. Hell, you've got twice the balls of the average corporate CEO out there."

"Nigger," I said. Since the boy had been so interested in being colored, I felt free to call him by some of the worser names we're known by. "Don't be telling me to apply myself. I taught you the ropes when you didn't know your ass from a hole in the ground. You better be out there telling your corporate boys to apply themselves and get they feet off my peoples' necks."

I ain't asked Dennis for but one thing. I figure he owed it to me for raising him. It wasn't nothing for him to get you that college scholarship. And you acted like it was nothing for you to get it, too.

"Payback," I remember you saying when you was packing for the trip out east. "Just paying back a few pennies of the millions they've made off us for the past four hundred years."

I should have knowed that being a schoolteacher or nurse would never be my girl's speed. You been writing things up so long, I bet you still got ink stains on your fingers. I kept everything you wrote, too. Shoot, I still got shoeboxes in the closet, full of the lists and letters and stories you been writing since you was old enough to pick up a pen.

See, you're like your mama and your daddy and grandfolks before you; a traveling woman. You're going places in this life. You know how to go out, yet you know how to come home. You ain't a train, you a ship. Can pull those anchors up, and put them back down again.

Or being a woman of today, maybe I should say my Alma is a plane with wings spread wide. With the Lord beside you and the wind behind you, ain't no telling how far this life will take you.

Now I know what you going to say. "Mama, you lived the life. So you write the story." But I just don't have the experience. So you take it and fix it up, make it so it reads right. I guess since you turned out to be My Most Unforgettable Character, it's only right that I split the money with you. So finish it up just as fast as you can, do we get that little piece of pocket change.

Be a good girl up there, now. Remember what Big Momma used to say. "Boys and books don't mix." Keep your mind stayed on your lessons, don't fool around and get pregnant, and everything will come out alright.

Your mother,
Callie Mae Clemmons

Draggin' the Dog

BY ANIKA NAILAH

I eat. A lot. Some people dance. Some people drink. I eat. So does everyone in my family. I could say we're big-boned, but hell, I'm from New York, okay? We're fat.

We've all got our reasons, you know? Most of it comes from growing up in a house of folk who loved to argue. Everything was a debate, from what channel we should be watching to whose turn it was to do the dishes. Only time we were quiet was when we were sitting around that table eating. That's when folks quit jawin' and got busy. We had some of our happiest times around that table. But that's not my excuse. I eat because I'd rather be fat than on trial for murder.

You see, I'm a principal of a high school where black children are killed every day. And last winter, there was this teacher and a dog . . . She's a big reason why I eat myself into Fat Land. But wait a minute. You're thinking the kids are dangerous, right? You're seeing them walking around with Uzis in their backpacks? You got it all wrong. Thugs don't do well in my building. Would *you* want to mess with a five-foot-eleven, 262-pound black woman with a bad attitude in the middle of a hot flash? The kids know better than to bring Miss Carter nonsense on her own turf. I don't play that. No, it's not the kids. It's the adults who are the problem.

Adults. That's what I'm talking about. Stay with me now. Take the music kids listen to, for example. Okay, we all know it's not Aretha or The Stylistics. Definitely not about no romance no kind of way. "Straight up I'ma do it to ya." As Grandma Lucas says, "It ain't nothin' but nasty," but who you think is responsible for getting this music into our kids' ears and hands? Adults. Honey, let me tell you. Those label people, they'd put their mama in half a skirt above her navel for that Judas purse. So I ask you, who will stand for the children?

When I started here, I was just a teacher. The principal at that time was a wrinkled-up, dry, white man who looked like a dandelion on the way out; thin as he could be, with one or two puffs of white hair on his head. On my first day, he offered me his ghostly hand, then stood there like someone who had walked into a room and forgotten what he came for. Then I realized he was trying to squeeze a smile out of the left side of his face.

We shook hands and he gave me the same speech he gave all the new teachers: "You're gonna love it here. Don't wear jewelry and don't ever take the stairs."

That was my introduction to this school. The teachers' cafeteria was a trip, too. The black teachers sat at their tables. The white teachers sat at theirs. The latinos divided themselves between the two. Every now and then, you'd see a brave soul sitting at a table looking like Sidney Poitier in *Guess Who's Coming To Dinner?*

The conversations were about sports, travel, shopping, and what "the animals" had done that day. Yes, that's what they called the children. Animals. Teachers who'd been there since dirt gave tips to rookies like me about how to survive the day, like it was a recovery room in a trauma ward.

No one listened to what I had to say back then. "You're new here, aren't you?" they'd say, not really asking. Now they have to listen to me whether they like it or not. Most times they don't like it, 'cause teachers are creatures of habit. They don't like change.

First year I made principal, all I did was change. The color of the walls. My hair. Rules. Staffing. Damn near everything but, well, my dress size. I'd been here nineteen years by then. I'd had enough and seen it all. A teacher crocheting and calling it a Reading Class. A teacher coming in high so she wouldn't have to feel low. Another teacher reading the newspaper in front of the class all day, every day, and calling it Social Studies. One teacher exploring himself behind his desk. You guessed it. He taught Biology. I even caught a teacher with a student in the supply room. Let me put it to you like this. She was getting more than paper clips. Educating the children? Well, that's somewhere on the list, but it's like that thing you keep forgetting to pick up at the supermarket, it just ain't there on the kitchen table when you're putting those groceries away.

Don't get me wrong. I know there are some righteous adults out there. There are some good teachers in my building, too. I treat them like kings and queens. Sunup to sundown I'm here for those good ones. They know it.

But back to those other folks—the dead weight—and why I eat. I'd have to say it's because it's better than wringing folks' necks on a continuous basis. Let me tell you a story. You already know it has a dog in it. I'm getting to that part. I need to tell you about the boy first. We'll call him "Ray," alright?

I became aware of Ray when he was just a sophomore. Beautiful boy. Reminded me of my son when he was a little guy and I'd take him places and white folks would say how cute he was. Always bothered me because I knew these same ones who were oohing and aahing him now, as soon as he grew up, they'd be clutching their pocketbooks like he was going to cut their heads off.

Well, Ray was beautiful like that, too, except he was black, blue black, so he didn't know how beautiful he really was. Kids made fun of him so much, he just looked evil all the time. Just had a permanent scowl, you know? But I knew that the beautiful Ray was still in there. I don't just mean how he looked. I mean what he was giving off. The boy was pure. He had something gentle and patient and innocent inside him, like an angel being tested for the first time.

And that was the thing about Ray. Street-smart kids could see he needed protection. They X-rayed him from a distance and knew there wasn't a tough bone in his body. Boys who'd been through the system had seen tough. They knew Ray wasn't it. So he was useful. An easy mark. He could be talked into things. Things he knew deep down weren't right. But these were the guys who were treating him like a brother. To his face. Giving him money. Clothes. Jewelry.

He was a kid. Fifteen. What do you know at fifteen? So, I was sure he could be turned around, you know? Hey, I've been in this game long enough to recognize when a kid turns a corner or crosses a line. The map is in his eyes.

Ray's map had lots of no-name streets, dead ends without signs to let him know where he was headed, stop signs where there shouldn't have been any, and no traffic lights at his most dangerous intersections. Somehow, though, he managed each year, studying just enough to pass.

I noticed him again when he was a junior. I'd see him sometimes, his hands probably sweating inside his pockets, just standing by the staircase near the front door. Standing there like he couldn't decide whether to go up or down, stay in or out.

Now, I have to tell you, I am not a principal who hides in her office behind a pile of papers. I got a secretary who does that real well. I like to move around, see what's going on. You know that bubble-wrap stuff people use to pack things in? Well, I will roll my triple-plus self down the halls in a heartbeat, breaking up those little bubbles of kids standing around. They whisper, "Here come Big Mama," thinking I'm deaf. But even though I don't tell them, I don't mind them calling me that. Least they know this is *my* house and I *am* their mama 'til they get back home.

So, on those standing-by-the-staircase days, I'd call Ray into my office using my principal voice, which is not the one I use when I'm explaining to my pastor why he hasn't seen me in church or the one you can barely hear when my doctor asks me if I'm trying to kill myself or do I just have a thing for refrigerators? So Ray, he'd hear me and suddenly he was no bigger than a minute. He'd egg-step over, walking on his toes like he was scared to break something or wake up babies no one else could see. He'd look up at me when he got closer, trying to give me that what's-this-broad-want-now? face. But you could see he was happy someone had noticed him splashing in the water. 'Cause he was the kind of kid who'd drown before he asked for help.

He'd come into my office, look around, stare at how big all the furniture was. Finally, he'd surrender to the same chair he always sat in. The leather would hold him like some giant suction cup in a science fiction novel, and we would talk.

"Aren't you late for your sixth period class, Mr. Taylor?" I'd ask him.

"Mr. Jacobs don't care I come or not," he'd say.

And we'd be off to the races about how it wasn't about Mr. Jacobs or Miss Lewis or anyone else but him, and didn't he know they were the ones who had already graduated from high school and he hadn't?

One time he told me about his daddy, who drove in and out of his life whenever he got the notion, with one fancy car after another and a different woman every time, and his brothers and sisters all over town he'd never met but heard about, as well as the five he shared a mother with. He was the last of the litter, the baby of three older brothers and two sisters, all but one had grown up and moved away.

"I give my mom big respect. She takes care of me," he said. "Even when she's tired."

Yes, he sure did love his mama, but he was *in love* with Ms. Jamieson, the science teacher he met in his senior year. At least until the trouble happened.

Ms. Jamieson was probably the first white woman who Ray felt had treated him right. He had no behavior problems when he was in her class. He even did all his homework and the extra credit. When she needed someone to stay after class to help her with a classroom project, Ray's hand was the first to go up. All because she'd told him he was smart. No one had ever told him that before. It wasn't like someone had said to him, "You're dumb," but it was the way too many teachers, for too many years had looked at him through their do-right pity, like surgeons whose eyes peek out between their caps and masks, and say without a word there's no sense in trying. The patient is too far gone. You see, Ray had gotten so used to everyone thinking he was stupid, he'd forgotten he wasn't. He'd given up trying to prove that the color of his skin did nothing to diminish the power of his mind.

Quiet as it's kept, when you study this child's records (and this is what I told them at the hearing) you'll find his scores are high, always were, all the way up through the third grade. Then something happened. His grades dropped like a downhill skier who had to pee.

My guess is he stopped feeling that joy of learning and love for himself as a special black boy. He came into the system with a gift, but we didn't have space for it on our paperwork. I always tell my teachers, every child has something, a delicate, little flame, whether it's a pretty smile or his ability to memorize all the words to a song. It's up to us to work that flame. Honey, we got to work it, you hear me, into a bonfire.

Somebody shoved Ray's flame down his throat. It wasn't shining anymore. Just burning him up. Same intelligence, but locked down in a pit of fire. 'Cause somewhere down there, he knew (even if he didn't know how to say it) that it wasn't supposed to be like this or feel like this as he went through life. Dr. Kunjufu says it's a "conspiracy to destroy Black boys." (It gets done to the girls too, but in a different way.)

From fourth grade on, Ray's records showed that there were problems. "Attitude" was what most of the comments were about. But what does that mean? Black folks got to have attitude just to get by in this world. We are characters by necessity. How you think we made it through our first Holocaust? But suddenly Jamieson was a key. Yes, Lord. In his senior year, the flame in Ray began trying to break free. I think he even began to believe he might be halfway smart. I loved visiting his science classroom just to see the process take shape.

And the other good thing about his excitement about Ms. Jamieson's class was having a domino effect on his other subjects. He had lost interest in being with the kids who meant him no good. Or maybe they'd lost interest in him. Either way, he seemed to finally be swimming with a gang of new ideas in a pond of his own. Graduation was on the horizon and maybe even a small community college.

It all fell apart at the Science Fair.

Ray had never thought about entering it before, but his progress in Jamieson's class gave him courage. He outdid himself. Do you hear what I'm saying? Created a project in quantum physics. The child was asking questions like "What is now?" and "How can we prove that time exists?" He did all kinds of research. Even interviewed scientists at the local university. It was brilliant. Okay, granted we all knew he did what he did to please Ms. Jamieson, but so what? Isn't that part of the game? Let them think they're making a big ole boat for you, and when it's all done and pretty and they're standing back and can't wait to see that look on your face, you show them that the boat was really theirs all along and you help them sail away.

Now what do you think happened? There was a tie between him and Wayne, an Asian boy who was used to winning every year. So I came to work one Tuesday morning and hell had not only broken loose, but it had splattered itself into a pool of folk in front of my office door. There was Wayne, his mother, father, and grandmother, Ms. Jamieson and Mr. Wycoff, the self-declared, most important Negro in the school, and head of the Science Department, all talking at the same time and trying to calm each other down. They were all waiting for me. The breakfast I'd bought was also waiting for me inside my pocketbook.

After I stepped inside my office to hang my coat up and gulped down a few quick bites of heaven, I called Jamieson in, because I knew all this commotion had something to do with Ray. Wycoff tried to push his long head through the door, too, but I told him I only wanted to speak with Ms. Jamieson at the moment, thank you very much. I closed the door on him mid-sentence and asked her what was going on. She paced and hemmed and hawed and finally said Wycoff thought Ray had cheated on his science project. That's when I felt a vision of a double cheeseburger and super-size fries coming on. Lord help me, I knew I was going to have to wring some necks that day.

Seems that Wycoff had looked Ray's classwork over and decided that he couldn't possibly have done it. I asked her if Wycoff had any proof Ray had cheated. He didn't. She said he was sort of hoping she would back him up on this. I asked her point blank what she was going to do. I'll never forget the terrified look on her face, her eyes bugging out of her head, but at the same time looking straight ahead, but no voice, no response.

Course Wayne's people wanted to know what their son had done wrong that he wasn't exclusively in first place. After all, everyone knew how smart *he* was.

They all expected me to open my door to their twenty-ring circus. I was not having it. No one, and I mean no one, was going to completely ruin my breakfast. I kept that door closed after Jamieson left. I was eating and thinking, thinking and eating. I decided to speak to each party alone, in a soft voice, with my belly full.

Of course, I had to call Ray in, too. He was nervous. Real nervous. He couldn't sit down. I told him how proud I was of how hard he'd worked this year. I told him not to worry. His graduation was not in jeopardy. Then I told him what he'd been accused of.

Slowly, he sat down.

"Ray," I said, "if you have anything to tell me, now is the time."

"You think I cheated, too?" he asked.

"No, Ray. I don't. Now that we've spoken, face-to-face, I know you're telling me the truth. But I want you to be man enough to face your accuser and tell him that same truth. I'll be right here with you."

"Thanks, Big . . . uh . . . Miss Carter."

That seemed to make him feel better. Now it was time for the meeting between him, Jamieson, Wycoff, and myself.

Ray thought he knew what to expect. He figured Jamieson had to be there because she was his teacher. He was sure she would defend him against Wycoff. He sat through Wycoff's accusations, and all through the speech about why plagiarism is unacceptable and how we have a higher standard at this institution of learning. He kept looking at Jamieson, waiting for her to say something. When he couldn't stand it anymore, fighting tears, he said, "Miss Jamieson? Miss Jamieson? Tell him. Tell him it was my work. You know me. Tell him, Miss Jamieson."

She hung her head and never said a word.

That's when I saw the final embers die in Ray's eyes. This is how they do it, I thought. They kill the children's spirits then sit back and watch them kill themselves.

Ray ran out. I knew exactly where he was headed. Y'all know I couldn't beat him to it. When I finally did get to the cafeteria, I was dripping sweat in places I didn't know I had, and out of breath. The science projects were still there on exhibit but Ray had knocked his over. By the time I saw him, he was stomping it into nothing but a mess of paper and mud. Then he started destroying everyone else's.

I tried to stop him before things got too out of hand, but Ray wasn't even there. He had gone to a place where he couldn't hear me anymore. Plates, glasses, windows, he began smashing everything he saw.

Security called the police, of course. They took him away in handcuffs. His mother showed up in time to see them pushing him into the police car. I held her back so they wouldn't lock her up, too. Should I have called her sooner? Maybe. Would it have made a difference? I don't know.

It was a sad, sad day.

Ray never did graduate. He was in and out of jail after that. Last I heard, about two years ago, he was doing big time somewhere upstate, learning quantum physics from a whole new perspective.

Now, I told you I never forgot that look on Jamieson's face when I asked her what she was going to do that day in my office. Well, I saw that same look one winter day after Ray was taken away, but on someone else.

The snow was thick underfoot and in the sky. It had been coming down pretty heavy for three days. I guess it was about five o'clock or so, because I remember praising myself for getting out of the building, for once, before the sun went down. I was trying to cross the street so I could get into my car when something made me look up. There was a car coming in my direction and it was making a weird kind of sound, like something scraping. As it got closer, I saw that a young white woman was driving. She had that look on her face that I told you about already. Pure terror, but straight ahead. Her hands were gripping the wheel tight, tight. And When I looked down at her front bumper, I saw that a big, black dog was caught underneath it. As she passed by, dragging the dog against the ground, she left a bright red trail on the snow behind her.

I stood there for a minute, the snow striking my face, not believing what I had seen. You can't tell me she didn't know she had a dog stuck underneath her fender. How could she not know? And then a thought came to me just as clear. She was like so many who worked in my school, pretending they were doing what was right by moving forward, getting from Point A to Point B, talking to themselves, plowing through year after year, no longer looking for any signs of life, just moving forward, not even caring that they were dragging the dog.

But you know, as Pastor Richards says, "God puts on his pajamas, but he doesn't go to sleep." Life has a funny way of bringing us back full circle 'til we get it right. Ms. Jamieson was forced to resign last year. Rumor was, someone discovered she didn't really have a degree in Science. In fact, when I did some digging, come to find out she never even graduated from college.

Then Wycoff's wife caught him cheating on her one night with some young chippy. She left him the next day and never looked back.

As for me, I'm still here at Morrison High, searching for a few good pieces of wood, trying to build those bonfires. But all this storytelling's made me hungry. Would you care to join me for a couple of giant burgers with very special sauce?

Museum Guide

BY SHAY YOUNGBLOOD
FROM *Black Girl in Paris*

*P*ARIS. SEPTEMBER 1986. *Early morning. She is lying on her back in a hard little bed with her eyes closed, dreaming in French.* Langston was here. *There is a black girl in Paris lying in a bed on the fifth floor of a hotel in the Latin Quarter. Her eyes are closed against the soft pink dawn. Delicate maps of light line her face, tattoo the palms of her hands, the insides of her thighs, the soles of her feet like lace.* Jimmy was here. *She sleeps while small, feminine hands plant a bomb under the seat of a train headed toward the city of Lyon.*

James Baldwin, Langston Hughes, Richard Wright, Gabriel García Márquez, and Milan Kundera all had lived in Paris as if it had been part of their training for greatness. When artists and writers spoke of Paris in their memoirs and letters home it was with reverence. Those who have been and those who still dream mention the quality of the light, the taste of the wine, the *joie de vivre*, the pleasures of the senses, a kind of freedom to be anonymous and also new. I wanted that kind of life even though I was a woman and did not yet think of myself as a writer. *I was a mapmaker.*

I remember the long, narrow room, the low slanted ceiling, the bare whitewashed walls, the spotted, musty brown carpet. To my left a cracked porcelain sink with a spigot that ran only cold water. On its ledge a new bar of soap, a blue ragged-edged washcloth shaped like a pocket, and a green hand towel. A round window at the foot of the bed looked out onto the quai St-Michel, a street that runs along the Seine, a river flowing like strong coffee through the body of Paris. The *quai* was lined with book stalls and painters with their easels and wooden plates of wet fall colors.

I am there again. It's as if I have somebody else's eyes. The Paris at the foot of my bed looks as if it were painted leaf by leaf and stone by stone with tiny brushstrokes. People dressed in dark coats hurrying along the narrow sidewalks look like small black birds. Time is still when I look out at the pale, gray sky, down to the silvery river below, which by midmorning will be crowded with double-decker boats filled with tourists. In the river, on an island, I can see the somber face of Notre-Dame cathedral and farther down, an enormous, block-long, turreted, pale stone building that looks like a castle, but which I am told is part of the Palais de Justice, which houses in its basement the Conciergerie, the prison where Queen Marie Antoinette waited to have her head chopped off and the writer James Baldwin spent one night after being accused of stealing a hotel bedsheet. Even the prisons here are beautiful, and everything is so old. Back home you can see the bars on the windows of buildings and houses, so you know that they are prisons. Sometimes bondage is invisible.

The first time I woke up in Paris I thought I'd been wounded. My body ached that first morning. My eyes, nose, and lips were puffy, as if my face had been soaked in water. My skin was dry and ashy. My joints were tight. When I stretched the full length of my body, bones popped and crunched like loose pebbles in a jar. The dream I woke up with was like a first memory, the most vivid of all the old movies that projected themselves onto the me that was. I woke up with a piece of broken glass clutched in my left hand. There was a small spot of blood on the sheets underneath me.

Before I left home I cut my hair close to my scalp so I could be a free woman with free thoughts, open to all possibilities. I was making a map of the world. In ancient times maps were made to help people find food, water, and the way back home. I needed a map to help me find love and language, and since one didn't exist, I'd have to invent one, following the trails and signs left by other travelers. I didn't know what I wanted to be, but I knew I wanted to be the kind of woman who was bold, took chances, and had adventures. I wanted to travel around the world. It was my little-girl dream.

I woke up suddenly one morning, at dawn. As the light began to bleed between the blinds into my room, the blank wall in front of me dissolved into a colorful collage by Romare Bearden of a naked black woman eating a watermelon. Against the iridescent blue background lay the outline of the city of Paris. The woman was me. This was my first sign of the unusual shape of things to come. By the time I came back to myself I was booked on an Air France flight to Paris. Paris would kill me or make me strong.

In 1924 at the age of twenty-two, Langston Hughes, *the Negro Poet Laureate of Harlem*, author of *The Big Sea*, arrived in Paris with seven dollars in his pocket. He worked as a doorman, second cook, and dishwasher at a jazz club on rue Pigalle. He wrote blues poems and stories and lived a poet's life. He wrote about the joys of living as well as the heartache.

. . .

My name is Eden, and I'm not afraid of anything anymore. Like my literary godfathers who came to Paris before me, I intend to live a life in which being black won't hold me back.

Baldwin's prophetic essays . . . *The Fire Next Time* . . . *No Name in the Street* . . . *Nobody Knows My Name* . . . were like the sound of trumpets in my ears. Baldwin knew things that I hoped someday he would tell me. The issues in my mind were still black versus white, right versus wrong, good versus evil, and me against the world.

The spring before I arrived in Paris, the city was on alert. I cut out an article from a news magazine that listed the horrible facts: April 2, a bomb aboard a TWA plane exploded over Athens, killing four Americans; April 5, an explosion in a West Berlin disco killed an American soldier and a Turkish woman, 230 people were wounded; April 15, in retaliation, President Ronald Reagan bombed Muammar Qadaffi's headquarters in Tripoli, killing fifteen civilians. Three American hostages were killed in Lebanon in response. April 17, a British woman was arrested in London's Heathrow airport, carrying explosives planted in her luggage by her Jordanian fiancé, who had intended to blow up a Tel Aviv–bound El Al flight. Terrorism was so popular that there were full-page ads in the *International Herald Tribune* offering hijacking insurance to frequent flyers.

I was no stranger to terrorism . . .

I was born in Birmingham, Alabama, where my parents witnessed the terror of eighteen bombs in six years. During that time the city was nicknamed Bombingham. When the four little girls were killed by a segregationist's bomb at church one Sunday morning in 1963, I had just started to write my name. I still remember writing theirs . . . *Cynthia* . . . *Addie Mae* . . . *Carole* . . . *Denise* . . . Our church sent letters of condolence to their families. We moved to Georgia, but I did not stop being afraid of being blown to pieces on an ordinary day if God wasn't looking. I slept at the foot of my parents' bed until I was eleven years old, when my mother convinced me that the four little girls were by now colored angels and would watch over me as I slept. But I didn't sleep much, and for most of my childhood I woke up each morning tired from so much running in my dreams—from faceless men in starched white sheets, from policemen with dogs, from firemen with water hoses. I was living in two places, night and day. In the night place I ran but they never caught me, and in the morning brown angels kissed my face. I woke up with tears on my pillow.

I was no stranger to terror . . .

When I was thirteen years old and living in Georgia I was in love with a girl in my class named Rosaleen and with her older brother, Anthony. Rosaleen and I played touching games in her bedroom, games she'd learned from her brother. We never spoke when we were naked and lying still on the carpet waiting for a hand to move an arm, bend a knee, for lips to kiss, for fingers to caress like feathers. We created still-life compositions with each other's pliant limbs, we were corpses, and for a few moments, a few hours, death seemed like something beautiful I wanted for the rest of my life. The fear of being caught heightened the sensations she awakened in me. Once when Anthony was home from college he sent Rosaleen downstairs to watch television, and he and I played the touching games. In Anthony's eyes I was a pretty brown-skinned girl. He whispered a continuous stream of compliments about my strange narrow eyes, my soft, still tender new breasts that filled his hands. He called me "Sugar Mama." His hands were rough, his smell musky and rank. I didn't struggle against the thick fingers that pushed between my legs, but let the hardness search the stillness inside of me. My feelings about Rosaleen and Anthony created a confusion in me, a terror of choosing. Anthony touched my body, but Rosaleen was the one I wanted to touch me inside. I was afraid to lose Rosaleen, but eventually I did. She got pregnant by a boy she met at the county fair. The baby was sickly and soon died. Rosaleen was sent away to live with relatives in Philadelphia. I never saw her again, but I had been touched by her in a way that would make all other touches fade quickly. After Rosaleen and Anthony I was terrified that no one would ever love me again, that desire was a bubble that would burst when I touched it. Years later I met Leo, who loved my body for a while, then left me when I felt I needed him most.

A bomb can kill you instantly, love can make you wish you were dead.

Within days of my arrival in Paris four separate explosions killed three people and wounded 170. There was an atmosphere of paranoia. The tension was visible in people's eyes. Everyone was suspicious. Every abandoned bag standing alone for more than a few minutes could be filled with explosives set to kill. Anyone could be a terrorist. Bombs were exploding all over the city the fall I arrived, and that made tickets to Paris cheap and suicide unnecessary. I would become a witness. I left my body and another me took over, someone who had no fear of bombs or dying.

It is 1986. I am twenty-six years old. I have 140 dollars folded flat and pressed into my shoes between sock and sole. It is what's left of the 200 dollars I arrived with two days ago. I have no friends here and barely remember my two years of college French. I think that my ticket to Paris will be the beginning or the end of me.

In 1948 James Baldwin, author of *Another Country*, then twenty-five years old, arrived in Paris with forty dollars. During the Sixties civil rights movement he led marches, protests, and voter registration drives. His angry, articulate essays on race shocked France and compelled witnesses to action.

He was awarded the medal of Legion of Honor by the French government. *I was a witness.*

Josephine Baker arrived in 1925, at age eighteen. She danced naked except for a string of bananas around her waist, sang the "Marseillaise" in beaded gowns, and was decorated by the French government for her efforts during World War II. She created a new tribe in her château with children from every ethnic group. Like the character she played in the film *Princess Tam Tam*, she represented to the French the exotic black, sexually independent woman who could learn to speak French and pick up enough manners to dine with royalty.

I was transformed.

Bricktop arrived penniless and taught Paris how to dance the Charleston. Richard Wright was already a celebrity; he joined the French intellectuals and gave voice to the Negro problem in America. There were others and there will be more. My heroes. They dared to make a way where there was none, and I want to be just like them.

I was born again.

This is the place where it happened, where it will happen again.

For once I slept without dreaming. I woke up when the plane touched down on the runway and heard the entire cabin clap and cheer the pilot and crew for our safe landing. As we taxied along the runway I pulled my small French-English dictionary out of my bag to look up in the phrase section how to take a cab. Across the aisle from me was a young woman who had slept through most of the flight. She was blonde with olive skin and had a long face and pretty features. She wore jeans and a black sweater and held a Museum of Modern Art gift bag in one hand and a large Louis Vuitton satchel on her lap. The satchel looked real, not like the imitations everyone at home wanted. I assumed she was American.

"It's my first time in Paris. What's the best way to get to the city? Is there a bus?"

"We can share a taxi if you like. Where are you going?" Her French accent was a surprise.

"I don't know. I was going to ask the driver for a hotel. I don't have much money."

She looked at me as if I was crazy.

"You don't know anyone?"

I shook my head.

"It will be very difficult to find something not expensive." She pursed her lips and blew into the air, a French gesture I would come to recognize and imitate. She said that the students would be arriving for classes that week.

"Many of the hotels not too dear will be . . . *complet.* You understand?"

I quickly flipped through my dictionary and learned that the hotels would be full, no vacancies.

"My name is . . . *Je m'appelle Eden.*"

"Delphine. Come," she commanded. We got up and joined the line of passengers exiting the plane. Charles de Gaulle airport was a maze of lines, people talking fast, signs I couldn't understand, and everywhere, guards carrying machine guns and holding fierce-looking dogs on short leashes. Then I began to be a little afraid of what I had done. I didn't know anyone, my French was practically nonexistent, and I had only enough money to last a few weeks until I found a job. But there was no going back. I took a deep breath and followed Delphine to baggage claim. I was relieved to see my duffel bag circle round in front of me. We stood in long, crooked lines in customs. One for citizens of France and several for everyone else. I gave Delphine twenty dollars to change into francs for me. She said she would meet me outside. When she was out of sight I had the fleeting thought that at home I would never be stupid enough to give a stranger money and watch her walk away, but I was in Paris and I was giving myself up to new angels.

When I offered up my passport, the customs officer, who had had a dry, grim expression for all the passengers before me, looked at me, then back at my passport. He scanned my short natural hair, high forehead, slow, sleepy eyes, broad nose, and full lips, as if to make sure the brown-skinned girl in his hands was me. He pushed my passport toward me and startled me by speaking in English. "Welcome to France, mademoiselle. Enjoy your visit."

During the ride to the city Delphine told me that she was a student at the "Science Po," the Ecole des Sciences Politiques, which I later learned was comparable to Harvard. She wanted to be a lawyer and in the current term she was studying English. When I told her I was a writer her eyes grew large and she could not hide her admiration, as if seeing in me something special she had not noticed before.

"I admire the dedication of the artist, but nothing is certain for you. I am not so brave." She looked out the window.

I did not feel brave, there was nothing else I thought I could do or that held my interest in the same way. The taxi was an old white Mercedes with a gray leather interior. The driver looked African and spoke French. We had loaded our bags in the trunk and got inside. Delphine had given the driver an address and instructions in rapid French. We sat in silence looking out at early morning Paris. The cars on the highway seemed to go faster than in the States. I was so tired I kept nodding off. When the taxi stopped on busy rue de l'Université, in front of a photography shop, I opened my wallet and Delphine took out some of the bills she had exchanged for me and added some of her own.

She pointed out the Sorbonne from the foot of the hill before we turned into the lobby of her apartment building. I followed her up four flights of stairs. She opened the door onto a small studio with high ceilings and cream-colored walls that made the room seem much bigger than it really was. Books and a small compact-disc collection lined the longest wall in the small but neat room, a high-tech stereo system and a small TV found space there as well. A bare desk sat in front of the windows, overlooking the street. Two double futons were stacked on top of each other in a corner. The most beautiful feature of the room was the set of tall French windows covered by metal shutters. Delphine opened the windows, letting in the light and noise of the street below. I went to the windows and looked down into the street. I saw a shop displaying cartons of brightly colored fruit, a florist's shop with spring in huge vivid bouquets that brightened the gray morning. She pointed me in the direction of the toilet. The bathroom fixtures were odd and ancient-looking. I did not recognize my face in the smoky gilt-framed mirror above the wide porcelain sink. There were dark circles under my eyes and my hair was so short. It was still me, a new me in a new place ready to begin again. I felt lost. After my father's funeral I felt as if I were drifting in-side, as if anyone could disappear. Few things were certain. *My father was dead.*

Delphine made us strong cups of coffee in the tiny red-and-white kitchen area—miniature appliances lined up under tall cabinets. Stale bread crumbs were scattered over the counter, a knife left sticking out of a pot of butter. We added sugar to the coffee and drank it black from heavy yellow bowls.

"What will you do?" she asked, sitting crosslegged on the futons next to me.

"I thought I could look for a job as a secretary or an au pair." I sipped the coffee and felt the caffeine spreading through my chest.

"I have heard the American Church has a place to look for jobs. I can check the newspaper for you. There is a black American writer who is every day at a bookstore close to here. He might help you. I think he is a poet."

Delphine made two phone calls, then we left the apartment to look for a room. Her apartment was in the heart of the Latin Quarter, near the boule-vard St-Michel. The streets were filled with people even though it was still early in the morning. Delphine was right, the less expensive hotels in the guidebook were *complet*, and I could not afford the more expensive ones. I could see that she felt pity for me and that she was determined to help me. Perhaps she thought an artist who was destined for a life of poverty needed all the help she could get. It started to rain, and as we were walking along the Seine back to her apartment I saw a hotel with a tiny sign in the win-dow. By some miracle they had one room left, for about thirty-five dollars a night. We were told that it did not have a toilet, I'd have to share one on the floor below, and if I wanted to take a shower it would cost me about three dollars. The shower was in a stone cubicle in the basement. The clerk was a young man who, when he realized I was American, began speaking to me in English. This was a small relief to me, knowing I'd soon be on my own. I agreed without even seeing the room. I only hoped it had a view. It was not far from Delphine's apartment. She helped me carry my bags back to the hotel.

Delphine gave me her phone number and told me to call her when I was settled. She was going away to visit her sister in Lyon for a week until school started. Her cousin Jean-Michel would be in her apartment until she returned and he spoke a little English, so if I needed help I was to call him. I reached out to hug her but she leaned only her face toward me. She kissed me on each cheek and wished me *bonne chance*. She was the one who would need the luck. The very next day a bomb was found on a train headed toward Lyon. It was defused and no one was hurt, but it was only the first sign of more danger to come.

Suddenly it was night, and I was far from home and completely alone. The little room at the top of the stairs was not decorated with a chandelier, gold-leafed antiques, and a canopy bed covered in delicate lace as I'd imagined, but I was thankful to have a place indoors to sleep. On the floor at the foot of the bed were my green duffel bag and a black canvas backpack, which contained everything I owned. A tiny book of Bible verses the size of a matchbook, a *1968 Frommer's Guide to Paris* I'd stolen from the public library. I knew all the major attractions by heart. I used the guide as a dream journal, writing between the lines. Between the pages I filed found poems and movie stubs and photographs. There was the gold pen from Dr. Bernard, three sharp number two pencils, a red Swiss army knife, seven pairs of white cotton panties, two pairs of white socks and one pair of black tights, a navy blue sweater and a pair of black jeans, a fat, palm-sized French-English dictionary, and a new address book with three addresses written in it. On the chair next to the sink, a pair of black stretch pants, a pair of gold hoop earrings, a watch with a thick brown leather band, a green trench coat from a military surplus store, and underneath the chair, a pair of black leather sneakers.

"*Je m'appelle Eden. Je suis une . . .* writer." The new me tried to impress the scratched mirror. I couldn't remember the French word for writer. *Ecrivain.* I said other things in French and practiced forgetting my old life.

My mother told me that she found me lying there, like a lost book or a forgotten hat. Found me crying, hungry, wet, and cold, wrapped in newspaper

at the bottom of a brown paper bag in the bathroom of a Greyhound bus
station. My father confirmed her story.

"*Who am I?*"

"Mama's little girl."

"*Who am I?*"

"Daddy's African princess."

"*How do you know for sure?*"

I discover that nothing is ever certain. A name, a birthday, an entire life
can be invented, and that being so, can be changed. I intended to change all
the ordinary things about myself. When I began to write I kept secret diaries, writing between the lines of books my father found in the trash at
work. Books on law and economics, typewriter manuals. I wrote about the
life I lived in the night place, where I traveled as far as the stars. Before I
could speak my father read to me from his found books, sounding out each
word as if it were an island, as if either of us understood. Having learned to
read so late in life he valued books as treasures of knowledge waiting to be
unlocked.

When I was four years old my parents told me that I was an orphan. My
parents were orphans too. They found each other in church one Sunday.
Hermine was a big-boned, sturdy, pecan-colored woman, with green eyes
and gray hair she kept braided and wrapped around her head. She taught
Prior Walker how to read the Bible, and in return he worshiped her. He was
small for a man, with thick, callused hands, and balding by the time he was
twenty-three. She was a seamstress in a blue-jean factory, and he was the
custodian at a bank. They were old, like grandparents. Kind and patient,
hardworking Christians. They were alone in the world until they found me.
Their family, and therefore mine, was the church. We were happy together.
They called me Eden. I made dresses for my dolls, but I was more interested
in reading books and writing poems than in sewing. One summer Hermine
and I pieced together a quilt made from scraps of clothes Prior and Hermine
had worn out or I had outgrown. She called it the family circle quilt. The
center image was three interlocking circles. She cried when it was done and
sewed a lock of hair from each of us into three corners of the quilt, and in
the fourth corner she sewed a secret. She folded the quilt into quarters and
packed it into the cedar chest at the foot of her bed. In winter when it was
time for me to go to sleep, she pulled the covers up around my chin.

"When you have a family you can put your baby to sleep under your
family circle."

"My baby will have pretty dreams," I said stroking the lines of thread so
lovingly handstitched.

"As long as Singer makes sewing machines, we'll get by," Hermine always
said. The old machine she had must have been one of the first Singers, made

in the late 1800s. She had a new electric model my father had bought her for her birthday, but for the quilt we used the one her mother left her before she died. Hermine told the same story about how her life began over and over again. At the age of two she had been left on the doorstep of a colored orphanage along with a note and the old Singer sewing machine in its case next to where she lay asleep. This was all she knew, but her life was full of stories she made up as she went along.

The only other family we had was Aunt Victorine, my mother's best friend and mine. On the first Saturday morning of each month she used to take me for blessings to the Church of Modern Miracles, where we both pretended she was my mother. When we were together she called me Daughter and I called her Mother, and that was only one of our secrets. Aunt Vic had never married and was childless, and in her way adopted me so that I had two mothers. She had something to do with my wanting to go to Paris. From the time she showed me on a map she drew with a broken pencil on her kitchen wall and told me that black people were free in Paris. Free to live where you wanted, work where you were qualified, and love whom you pleased. At least that was the rumor she had heard. One of her friends in Chicago, where she had grown up, had a sister, an opera singer who went to Paris and married a white man. The opera singer became famous in Europe. According to Aunt Vic the white folks in America didn't want us to know about that kind of living, where a colored person could socialize and marry whom they wanted whether they were white or black, Chinese or Hindu. If she could have chosen, Aunt Vic surely would not have chosen to be a maid for most of her life. She worked two days a week for a rich white doctor in Green Island Hills. That was freedom to her, to choose the life you wanted to live.

"And who would not choose to live well?" Aunt Vic said.

Aunt Vic's stories about Paris had sounded like fantasies. She talked about it as if it were a made-up place. If Paris was a real place, I wanted to go.

"Every day you ought to learn something new, Daughter," Aunt Vic said. I tried to learn new things, and I wrote them down like recipes between the lines of my found books.

I would go to stay with Aunt Vic, who returned me home Sunday morning ready for Sunday school with Hermine and Prior. I slept through most of Sunday morning sermons at the First African Baptist Missionary Church, where the service was orderly, the hymns hushed, and the service short, and nobody cried too loud or shouted that the Holy Ghost had them by the collar. There was no dancing in the aisles. At the Church of Modern Miracles there was a three-piece band—drums, electric organ, and electric guitar—and several ladies in the front row who shook tambourines and their ample hips and tremulous breasts all through the service. People shouted, praised God so their prayers could be heard above the sins of the city, were possessed by the Holy Spirit, who took over their bodies, shaking them with emotion and filling their eyes with tears and their throats with hallelujahs. I could use my voice strong and was put in the young people's choir. Soon I was singing a solo almost every Saturday morning. And Aunt Victorine had me performing at the age of six in juke joints on dirt roads for miles around almost every Saturday night. After midnight, when a juke joint was most crowded, some cigar-smelling man would lift me up onto a table in the middle of the room and somebody else would unplug the jukebox. Sometimes there would be a pianist or a guitar player to accompany me. I would sing songs I'd heard on Aunt Vic's record player. Aunt Vic taught me how to lift the hem of my dress and dance at the end of the song like Josephine Baker and the French can-can dancers who looked so glamorous in the photographs she showed me. The audience would throw handfuls of change and crumpled dollar bills at my dancing feet. I loved the attention. I dreamed about doing the can-can in Paris. If Mama hadn't found out when I was thirteen, I might've become a star on the dirt-floor circuit. Instead I started taking classical voice lessons from a mean old Creole woman who used to be an entertainer. Her long black curls left greasy spots on the collars of her old-fashioned quilted pastel dressing gowns. Miss Candy shouted at me in Creole when I forgot the words to a song. I didn't like her and the lessons didn't last long. Aunt Vic didn't speak to Mama for a long time. She was mad at losing all that income from my singing. And she missed me as much as I missed her. Low lights, Aunt Vic's copper-colored lipstick, and the sparkling dresses she let me borrow to perform in made me dream of a kind of life different from the one I was living. I made maps in my mind that would lead to other worlds.

Aunt Vic loved to be read to. She had grown up in Chicago and still had a subscription to the *Chicago Defender* so she could keep up with the community even though she had left under duress. The circumstances of her leaving the North many years before remained a mystery to me even though I asked her every time she started talking about the old days. Once I got her to admit her leaving had something to do with a man she didn't care to dance with, a gangster who owned the club she worked in. Aunt Vic loved Langston Hughes's Simple stories, which were published in the *Chicago Defender* from 1943 to 1966, Aunt Vic said. His main character, Jesse B. Simple, was everyman, every black man, and she loved him.

"Jesse B. Simple is real, I think that's a real person. I knew somebody just like that back in Chicago. Munro Fish, a sweet-talking jailbird who truly believed that someday he would run for a government office. He had it all figured out just like Simple. Always talking about race."

She had collected all the stories. She cut them out of the newspaper, and every once in a while she would pull them out and I'd read to her. The language was a little salty, but Mama wasn't around to get holy. Simple would talk about having Indian blood, and Aunt Vic would add her commentary. "Like what Southern Negro don't claim that?" she would laugh. We would start packing our bags when he talked about all the colored people in Harlem. She would start singing about speakeasies and going up to Harlem like we were hearing the story for the first time.

The stories made us laugh and feel like we knew what was going on in the world, and we had a lot of our own opinions about that.

Aunt Vic showed me pictures of her old life as a dancer, the girls who went to France, and Josephine Baker, who was to her a symbol of complete freedom. I made up stories and acted out little dramas for my parents, playing all the parts myself. I wrote sad poems about orphans, and I moved through my life taking pictures with a toy camera, recording things in my mind, writing them down between the lines of other books. One day I made up my mind that I would go to Paris to be free.

When I was thirteen my parents gave me a typewriter, for which they had made many sacrifices. I typed my first novel in fourteen days. I wrote all the stories I knew and made up new ones. I typed them and put them in my library, a small bookshelf next to my bed that my father had made and my mother had painted yellow. By then I was reading in the adult section of the library and was certain after reading Langston Hughes's autobiography, *The Big Sea*, that I wanted to be a writer and feast at the banquet of life. Going to Paris would be an hors d'oeuvre. I kept my thoughts pressed between the lines of biology texts and biographies of dead presidents that no one else ever checked out anyway.

The color rust tastes like dirt, and my bones ache. The first blood on my fingers tastes like new nickels. Help me. I stumble on new legs into rooms so full of static sparks fly from my fingertips. As I reach for a vowel with my lips, an "O" softly escapes into the dry air. I need someone to introduce me to the woman who woke up in my skin. Mother, may I? Maman, puis-je?

"My body is breaking," says the me who is not my mother's child.

"It will bend," the mother whispers.

When I got my first blood, my mother told me I was a woman. There was something false about her happiness. Her joy came with conditions that must be followed.

"Don't let boys touch you." Anthony was a man.

"Be a sweet girl." I was hard candy.

My father pushed me off his lap and my mother seemed blind to me. Aunt Vic was my salvation.

"Being a woman is a cross we women must bear," she said.

"When I go to Paris I will leave behind the little orphan girl and all I will take with me is her body and some of her clothes. I'll make maps so other people can get there too, adventurers like me."

This was my little-girl dream.

Before Paris, at university, I studied English literature, and all it was good for in the end was a job as a librarian.

I wanted to hold on to old things, but I wanted new things to make me forget. When I was twenty-five I found a job in the house of dead things. Villa Luisa, known locally as the Dimple Mansion, built by the richest black man born into slavery. The house recalled an Italian villa and had become a museum and a memorial to a family of successful African American entre-preneurs. I was hired by the museum's director to assist him in giving tours and cataloging the collection. The director, Dr. Edgar Bernard, was a seri-ous, scholarly gentleman and looked the part. He was tall, gray-haired, and elegant. His old-fashioned wire-rimmed glasses accented wide eyes that popped from his head like lightbulbs. He wore the same dark gray suit and a crisp white shirt every day. His silk ties looked like pieces of stained-glass windows. The director was a lonely man. He spoke quietly and quickly as if afraid I would lose interest or he would forget to tell me something impor-tant as he veered into heated dissertations on obscure areas of Greek and African civilization. I was fascinated and listened to him with my whole body as if to memorize his knowledge.

When Dr. Bernard spoke there were secrets in his voice. I knew because I had secrets of my own. Dead things locked in a box I kept out of sight. I lis-tened to his lonely, his hurt, and his misunderstood. He had dedicated his life to preserving a dignified memory of his mentor.

Dr. Bernard was a young man when he met Mason Dimple and became his secretary. Dimple sent him to Yale. They traveled the world together.

"Mr. Dimple gave me my first job. I worked in his garden every summer from the time I was fourteen years old. He sent me to school. I studied an-thropology, receiving my doctorate just a few months before Mr. Dimple died.

" 'Edgar,' he said, 'You have worked very hard and I've had to work hardly at all. I hope that you will make of your life something beautiful.' Mason was very good to me." Dr. Bernard's eyes got misty and his voice softened even more when he talked about Mr. Dimple, whom he some-times, slipping, called Mason.

Now Dr. Bernard was married to a large woman who wore too much makeup and laughed too loudly. They were childless. The few times I saw her at holiday parties Mrs. Bernard's sadness and disappointment were clear as the champagne glasses she kept filled to the top.

Everything in the Villa was dead or old except me. The offices were in the basement of Mason Dimple's yellow brick mansion. The house was surrounded by a meticulously manicured landscape of pink and white dogwoods, red and orange azalea bushes, and wine-colored Japanese maples. Inside, the furnishings were opulent, each of the twenty-six rooms decorated in a different period. On the ceiling of each room were painted re-creations of religious scenes by Michelangelo from the Sistine Chapel. Angels floated above our heads all day. The Dimples were not religious, but they had wanted to impress their guests with their culture acquired from trips abroad. The house had marble bathrooms with gold fixtures and bronze-and-crystal chandeliers. The floors were inlaid with rare wood or covered in rare Oriental carpets. English antiques in the living room, French baroque velvet sofas in the sitting room.

A white marble statue of a naked muscled Greek god stood in the foyer, a replica of a famous sculpture in the Louvre. The director had placed a discreet bronze ivy leaf over its private parts after several church groups complained that the statue disturbed the children on tours.

Mason Dimple's bedroom was not included on the tour. Dr. Bernard said that Mason Dimple was so consumed with grief when his parents died in a train wreck when he was almost twenty-one that he stayed in his room for seven days staring into the flame of a candle, trying to pray them back to life. Then he painted his bedroom walls black. When I opened the door to his bedroom I could feel his suffering like cold fingers on the back of my neck. It was like standing in an opulent prison cell.

The Villa held a large collection of European art, English silver, and Greek sculpture. Most museum patrons expected to see a collection of African art because of Mason Dimple's race. But there was nothing African here except a wooden mask from Nigeria half eaten by termites and a few Moroccan tapestries. Mason Dimple hated anything too black or too African. At one time he had wanted to be a part of local white society. He thought his money and barely brown skin would allow him access, but he soon realized that he was not welcome. He made do with occasional contact with the black bourgeoisie that mirrored white society with its balls and charity events.

Dr. Bernard took me on a tour of the house and gave me facts I memorized. The questions from our guests were always the same.

When was the house built? Who was the architect?

How did the family make its fortune?

How did they die?

Why did Mason Dimple never marry or have children?

What are the naked wrestlers on the Greek vase in the study doing?

These were the things Dr. Bernard instructed me to say to the busloads of curious foreign tourists and rowdy school children and locals who had always wondered what went on inside the yellow brick mansion on Dimple Court.

In 1933 Mason's father, Simon Dimple, was the richest black man in the state of Georgia. He had spent his youth as a house slave on a plantation owned by his white father. He had been taught to cook by his mother, who was the plantation cook. He ran away from home when he was thirteen years old and earned his way in the world as a cook for rich white Northern college students. He met his future wife, Daisy, an octoroon girl from Louisiana, on a train in New York. They both were passing for white. He fell in love with her, and they returned to Georgia. He used Daisy and her brothers, who also passed for white, to purchase land and hire labor to build a restaurant on the outskirts of a growing town. They quietly ran the business behind the scenes and joined the local elite black community. Neither Daisy nor Simon could eat in the dining room of their own restaurant because it was for whites only. It was very popular and enabled Simon to invest in other businesses and real estate and make a fortune. The Dimples' firstborn child, Mason, they sent away to boarding school in Switzerland from the time he was a small boy to shelter him from the pain of racism. He spent summers with his family and eventually went to Yale, graduating with a degree in business.

At Simon Dimples' Plantation Restaurant, black women, dressed like Aunt Jemima in red-and-white checkered head kerchiefs, voluminous skirts, and white aprons, served the white patrons with a grin and a shuffle. The entire kitchen staff was made up of black men in white uniforms. The food was old-fashioned Southern cooking. Fried chicken, collard greens, sweet potatoes, macaroni and cheese, chicken and dumplings, lemon cheesecakes, blackberry cobblers, rice puddings, barbecued ribs, biscuits and cornbread. As good as the food was, that was not why the restaurant was so popular. It was the novelty of whites being served in the manner of their ancestors by a wait staff that reminded them of the good old days. The Dimples were members of the NAACP even though many members protested that the Dimples' restaurant perpetuated the stereotype of a slave plantation, where the white masters were still being served by happy blacks.

The Dimples considered themselves good and patriotic Americans. They raised the flag on holidays, bought war bonds, and wanted the world to see them as they saw themselves—successful, sophisticated citizens who contributed to their community. The Dimples were generous philanthropists, donating large sums of money to their church and black colleges and medical facilities all over the South. They were good businessmen and, after his parents died, Mason Dimple sold the offensive restaurant and most of the other properties. He set up a foundation to ensure the preservation of his home as a memorial to his parents after his own death.

A year after Mason Dimple himself died, the board of directors he had set up was ready to hire someone to organize the home's collection. My first job was to catalog everything in the house and develop a system for marking. First I looked through the photographs. Mason seemed to have been a happy child, in short velvet pants, white ruffled shirts, and high buttoned boots. As he grew older his smiles faded to a hard line and he wore pressed tailored suits and posed stiffly for the camera's eye. He still looked like a boy even after his hair had thinned and his small rimless glasses sat on his nose like little windows.

Under the stairs in the basement of the dead man's house there were several boxes of books Dr. Bernard didn't seem to know existed. One rainy afternoon when tours were slow and Dr. Bernard was attending a conference at a downtown hotel, I opened one of the boxes and flipped through the pages of historical novels and murder mysteries that Mason was so fond of. Behind the boxes was a small trunk half hidden by a large, brightly patterned rug. I dragged the trunk into my office and opened it. Inside were a packet of letters and several photographs. In the photographs Mason Dimple's eyes seemed happy only once. In one photograph he was walking through a flock of birds in a square in Venice. He was smiling at a young man who faintly resembled Dr. Bernard and who seemed to be flapping his arms to make the birds fly. There was a well-dressed young woman in the picture. She was wearing a tall hat and stood nearby watching both men with a weary, tight little smile.

The tiny black leather notebook fit in the palm of my hand. I found it sewn inside a linen bag in a secret compartment in Mason Dimple's traveling office trunk designed by Louis Vuitton in the mid 1800s. It was slender, the leather was smooth to touch, and inside, each page overflowed with tiny black lines like marching ants. The words were crowded together carefully as if they had been written in a small, dark place by someone with plenty of time, lots to say, and no one to listen. My hands were trembling as I cut open the neat stitches with my pocket knife. As archivist for the house museum where Mason Dimple was born and died I had access to every silver spoon and faded photograph that made up his life. Mason Dimple was a complicated man, there was no doubt about that. He had wanted to be a poet and so he went where poets went, tried to live as they did, but his money got in the way. He died a bachelor with no heirs and left a substantial fortune in a trust that would preserve the family home and the Dimple name forever.

I wanted to be a poet and I knew early on, but it was not practical for a girl born into a poor family to be a poet. At first I studied biology in preparation for life as a nurse. This was to ease my parents' minds that I would be able to take care of myself, but I became fascinated with history and poetry and the lives of artists. I was never a practical girl. Five years out of college I found myself working in the basement of a dead man's house, sorting through intimate details of his life, discovering common ground.

The letters were faded, but I could read the words, which told a story different from the one I recited to visitors to the house. It was in his handwriting. I knew it from the dull entries in the diaries I had cataloged. Places visited, foods eaten, and the prices in local currency of gifts purchased.

There were love letters:

My tongue is wasted on words when you would be of better use in my mouth.

There were rooms full of secrets:
The Great Hall, where the family received guests and gave lovely parties.

Mother made me scrub the floors on my hands and knees this morning as she recited prayers for my sinful soul.

The music room, where the family entertained their guests.

Mother tied me to the piano bench until I could play perfectly. Finally my fingers behaved. What a bad boy to make Mother unhappy. She speaks French when she is unhappy.

The master bedroom, where the father slept.

It is curious how Father never sleeps alone at night, nor does he sleep with Mother.

The pink bedroom, where the mother slept.

She cries at night. Her weeping is my lullaby.

Mason Dimple's bedroom, closed to visitors.

He is my first love and will be my last. I would be lost without him.

Mason Dimple had many secrets. Secrets I did not tell visitors to the house. Sometimes when it was quiet in the house I could hear a young woman singing and a grown man weeping. I could feel the cold, sad suffering of a mother's love. Some nights I dreamed, some nights I didn't sleep at all. My dreams shift my thinking:

I am in Paris. I climb a spiral staircase seven flights up. I enter a room made entirely of books, the walls, the fireplace, and the ceiling. The floor is a soft carpet of words. Leatherbound books with SECRETS etched in gold leaf along their spines are displayed in elaborate boxes set in the walls behind glass. The smell is haunting, dried ink and musty memories. I lie on the floor and words beneath me whisper in my ear, water words, the names of trees and flowers, parts of the body, parts of the eye. I leave the room and enter a dark hallway heading toward the light. I see my father in the distance, he waves me back toward the living. I whisper good-bye and turn my back on him.

My father died of a heart attack the summer before I went to Paris. All of us who knew him almost died from shock. A pious deacon of the church. A kind neighbor. A loving husband and father. Simply put: a good man gone to glory. "Prior Walker, dearly beloved" was carved in stone. Daddy was stitched onto the tender parts of my heart. My body folded and water fell from my eyes like rain.

The weight of all those dead things pulled me down.

One afternoon shortly after my father died, I had a revelation and a sign. The streets outside were steaming as if little teapots were brewing beneath the city, but I was cool underground. I was working at my desk in the windowless basement office. That morning the principal from a local boy's school called to cancel their one o'clock tour, and I was afraid I would cry all afternoon. A man I'd been dating had called me at noon to tell me he was returning to Detroit. He'd been looking for a job as a radio news journalist the whole year I knew him, but he had been unlucky and he felt that it was time for us both to face facts. For me the reality was more jarring, that he hadn't even asked me to go with him, let alone marry him. I couldn't say I was in love with him. I was just sad to be by myself again. I wanted to run away from so much loss all at once.

I was not allowed to be with my sadness for long. At one-fifteen the front doorbell rang. I went up the stairs, crossed the foyer, and opened the front door. Standing there were a regal-looking, well-dressed older black woman wearing heavy gold jewelry and too much powder on her face and a younger man in a conservative dark suit who I guessed by their resemblance was her son. I invited them in and noticed that they spoke with soft West Indian accents. The son seemed more interested in the house than the mother. Sometimes he would whisper to her in what sounded like French. I gave them the standard tour and the son asked the standard questions. At the end of the tour the son looked around with a puzzled expression.

"I presume that Mr. Dimple was an educated man."

"Yes, he graduated from Yale."

"That is not what I mean. His collection seems incomplete. He traveled to Africa in the Fifties?"

"Yes, but he wasn't much interested in African art. He brought back several tapestries from Morocco, and you saw the Ibo mask?"

The man made a noise in his throat and pitched his eyes around the room once more. "You can tell so much about a man by what he keeps in his house."

"Thank you very much for the tour. It was lovely," the mother said, signing the guest book. I noticed she wrote down Paris as her address.

"How did you hear about the museum?" I asked, curious.

"The concierge at the hotel recommended it."

"Are you West Indian?"

"We are *French*," the mother said, as if I'd insulted her.

The son looked at me as if seeing me for the first time. His eyes assessed me quickly, lingering on my breasts before returning to my face. He seemed to want to continue talking with me.

"There are many black Americans living in Paris, many artists," the son said. "I believe the black American writer James Baldwin makes his home in France. Do you know him?" he asked, as if it were possible for me to know someone famous.

"I know his work. I've been listening to my aunt go on about France since I was a little girl. I'd love to go there someday."

The son warmed to me when I said I wanted to be a writer. He said there were many bohemian artists living in Paris.

"There are certainly enough entertainers," the mother said, dabbing at her perspiring nose with a delicate lace handkerchief.

For the next half hour the son, Maxime Bazille, and his mother, Madame Marie-Lise Bazille, convinced me that Paris was the last red apple on the highest branches of a tree well worth climbing. I thanked them, and for the first time Paris became a real destination, with real places to eat, museums to see, and wide boulevards to stroll. A list of inexpensive hotels, bakeries and cafés, clothing shops and museums neatly printed in Maxime Bazille's elegant hand was folded in my pocket.

By six o'clock that evening the security guard hadn't shown up. I called Dr. Bernard and offered to lock up the house and set the alarm. He agreed, and I began clearing up my desk. I called a local copy shop to find out how much they charged for passport photos. Before setting the alarm I went into the library, and my eyes fell on several books by James Baldwin. I'd seen them every day, but that evening it was as if a laser beam pointed them out to me and I was drawn to them. Each of the books was a signed first edition. *Giovanni's Room, Another Country, Go Tell It on the Mountain, Nobody Knows My Name, The Fire Next Time.* Each book was signed, "Affectionately, Jimmy." I sat in Mason Dimple's reading chair and read into the night, from one book to the next. The most brilliantly illuminating passages were underlined with blue ink. By the time the sun came up, my eyes were red and tired and an overwhelming sadness had clouded the room. When Dr. Bernard arrived he thought I was sleeping. He touched my shoulder and called my name.

His eyes fell on the bundle of love letters on the table next to me.

"I found them behind the stairs."

Dr. Bernard sat facing me in a leather wing chair, wearily, as if it were the end of a long day and not the beginning.

"After Mason read a book he liked or hated or was moved by, he would buy another and underline words and sometimes whole passages. Then he gave them to me. We went to Paris after he read *Giovanni's Room.* It was the happiest time of my life. I love him still." Dr. Bernard began to weep. I reached out and touched his hand.

"Don't take only what life gives you, reach out and take what you want," he said.

We sat quietly in the room thick with memories and desire. Reading my own copy of *Giovanni's Room* a few days later lit a fire in me. The main character, David, a white American living in Paris, begins a passionate affair with an Italian bartender, Giovanni, but because David is ashamed and scared of his desire, his love for Giovanni destroys them both. I was determined to have no such regrets, no such fears. I was still young and thought anything was possible.

I was awake, but I was dreaming about Paris, reading Baldwin, planning a new life. I made a reservation on a flight to Paris. I gave Dr. Bernard one month's notice, he gave me his blessings and a gold pen. When I told Aunt Vic I wanted to go to Paris, she didn't laugh or ask me if I was crazy; she sat down on her sofa, leaned over, and peeled back the carpet. She counted eighteen twenty-dollar bills into my hand and promised to send me more if I needed money to come home.

"I wish *I* had the balls to do it." She hugged me hard.

"Aunt Vic, that's some salty talk."

My mother was still deep in her grief over losing my father. She let her sadness at my leaving roll over her like a fog.

"Child, I wish I could see you married, but I know that's a long ways off. You still restless." She stroked my hair and kissed my third eye.

"Aren't you glad I didn't marry Leo just to ease your mind?"

"He was too handsome to be a husband anyway," she said, trying to comfort me. I had already put him in a box and shoveled dirt on top.

I had saved three hundred dollars, and I figured after selling everything I couldn't carry to France I'd have about five hundred more. I watched ten French videos in fourteen days to prepare my ear for my new language. Four weeks later I had a ticket to Paris.

The day after I arrived in Paris a bomb was found on a train headed toward Lyon. I wondered if my new friend Delphine had noticed a plain package underneath a seat near her. Had she panicked? Did she call the conductor and save the lives of dozens of passengers and her own life as well?

> *In another country, reading the words "two men kissed" makes it possible for me to kiss any lips my heart desires. In another country, the sound of music breathes.*
>
> *In another country, love means this moment, now.*
> *It means remembering your mother's face*
> *when you told her you were leaving,*
> *your lover's smell on that last day.*
> *Good-bye is so final,*
> *say: til then.*

I carry words around in my pocket, put them behind my eyelids, in my mind. I let words float in my mouth. I roll them around on my tongue, taste them until sounds slowly push out of my mouth. Each word is a poem.

parler . . . la verité . . . à minuit . . . regarde . . . une étoile . . . le nuage . . . fumée

This new language I am dreaming, I'm beginning to understand, is soft in my mouth like small satin pillows. These words are not hard to swallow.

Once upon a time, not so long ago and not far from now, there was a black girl in Paris . . . She is lying on her back on a hard little bed with her eyes closed dreaming in French . . . The long narrow room . . . a round window at the foot of the bed . . . All the familiar things are not. A door is not a door. *La porte.* Love is *l'amour*, not an open wound. When I wake up I'll leave this place and I'll find my way back again. I'll find a word and sing it like it's the last song I'll ever sing. Josephine and jazz were here. It is a brand-new world.

My name is Eden and I'm not afraid of anything anymore.

School

BY VERONICA CHAMBERS
FROM *Miss Black America*

The first time somebody called me a liar, I was nine years old. It was in a classroom decorated with faded pictures of rosy-cheeked white kids with blond hair, and that did not escape my notice. Every conceivable surface—the bulletin boards, the wall above the chalkboard, the wood closet doors—were covered with the illustrated adventures of Dick and Jane. There was only one white girl in our class: Brenda. She had red hair just like the comic book character Brenda Starr. She swore up and down that she wasn't named after a stupid comic strip, but that's what we all called her. Brenda Starr.

Our teacher was a middle-aged white woman from Long Island. She told us that the very first day of school. "My name is Mrs. Newhouse and I'm from Long Island." She pronounced "Long Island" in a really funny way, as if each word was chopped up into five or six squeaky syllables. I thought it was strange that she mentioned where she was from. It wasn't as if it was any place interesting like France or India. My third grade teacher, Mrs. Chong, was Cuban Chinese. We only found out about the Cuban part when some of the Puerto Rican kids in class were making fun of her eyes and she went off on them in Spanish. We always thought her clipped, staccato tone was the way all Chinese people talked. But when she started speaking Spanish, she was like Nidia Velásquez' grandmother cursing people out her window. Mrs. Chong put one hand on her hip and one finger in the air and let loose a string of Spanish words that swiveled in her mouth as fast as her hips. It was extraordinary, like watching a normal person turn into a superhero. That's when Mrs. Chong explained that her parents were Chinese, but she'd grown up in Cuba. We knew then that she was the coolest teacher we'd ever have.

"You better watch out," the boys would say, as they roughhoused in the playground. "Mrs. Chong will do a Bruce Lee on your ass. Then she'll turn around and *pow, pow* like Roberto Durán." Me and my girlfriends were more concerned with what Mrs. Chong had cooking in her pot. "Her kids are so lucky," Coco García said, salivating into her peanut butter sandwich. "They can have sweet and sour pork one night and *ropa vieja* the next." Kenya Moore added, "They could have won ton soup and black bean soup." Brenda Starr waved away all the comparisons with an impressive air of cool. "Face it," she said, crossing her legs and swinging the top one lazily, "her kids have got it made."

So, what was so special about a teacher from Long Island compared to a Cuban Chinese? Then Mrs. Newhouse went around the room and asked every kid what their father did for a living. When she got to me, I said, "Magician." Everyone in the class giggled. Hard of hearing or just not paying attention, she said, "Does your father play an instrument, dear?" I just shook my head. "No, Mrs. Newhouse," I said. "He's a ma-gi-cian." I made the word long and squeaky like "Long Island" so maybe she'd understand me better.

She smiled at me, a fake smile without teeth, then came over to my desk. She smelled of coffee and, on closer inspection, her red pantsuit had balls of lint along the thighs. She patted me on the head. "Here's an example of a very vivid imagination at work," she said. "I bet every little boy or girl wishes their father was a magician or a circus ringmaster or a flame thrower." She chuckled, as if she'd told a very funny joke; then she skipped me, moving on to the girl in the seat behind me. I didn't say another word the whole day. I just sat there, silent and furious.

The thing is I'd already come to school that day feeling bad. The night before my mother and father had had a huge fight because there was no money to buy me a new outfit for school, much less a pencil case or a small pair of plastic scissors or any of the school supplies on the list the counselor had given us. This, I was led to believe, was my father's fault.

Just the night before, my mother had been yelling about how my father was "no better than a child." Standing in the living room wearing a blue and green tie-dyed T-shirt and a pair of white jeans, she was beautiful, mad as she was. I thought she looked like a Charlie's Angel, a black Charlie's Angel. Her shoulder-length hair had been pressed to bone straightness and she wore it flipped back like Jayne Kennedy.

"Some sort of magician you are, Teddo," she screamed, ripping up pictures of my father's head shot. "Why don't you pull some motherfucking food out of your hat? Why don't you make some money appear, Magic Man?"

My father closed the paper he had been reading, then walked over to the stereo. "You're so small-minded," he said, clamping the bulky headset over his ears. "You've got such a fucking small mind. Can't you see that I'm trying to do something amazing with my life?"

My mother was on him in ten seconds, ripping two buttons off of his silk print shirt and pounding on his chest. "Amazing? You want to do something amazing?" she screamed. "Provide for your fucking child. Live up to your fucking responsibilities." He shrugged her off of him with one strong swoop of his arms. "This is a new shirt, man," he muttered to no one in particular.

My mother stumbled from my father's push but quickly got to her feet. She cut her eyes at my father, tossing him a long hard glare that would have been considered an invitation to rumble on any street corner in the city. But my father refused to take the bait, humming along to music only he could hear. "Come on, Angela," my mother said, leading me out of the living room. My hand felt small in her hand and in her anger, she clenched her long nails into my palm. I didn't care. She was my angel. My Charlie's Angel.

We were living in the South Bronx, in a basement apartment that had love beads and shag carpeting in every room. Even the bathroom was carpeted. As we walked back toward my tiny bedroom, I squeezed the carpet with my toes and willed myself not to cry. This was the first time I would not have a new dress for the first day of school. I understood the reason, but that didn't hold back the tears. There was no money. There was never any money. But it had never bothered me. Now I felt caught. For the first time, ever, I was drafted into the vicious no-money war my parents constantly battled. It felt terrible. Like playing a game of hot potato and having the cootie-contaminated object glued to your hands.

By the time we reached my room, I was quietly sobbing. I sat on the bed and my mother knelt in front of me. Her cocoa face glistened around the edges like a halo, where she'd combed her baby hair down with Vaseline. She pulled my face close to hers as if for a kiss and said, "I am so sorry. There's nothing I hate more than to see you go without. But I had no choice this month. Either I bought your clothes or paid the rent and I couldn't have us out on the street."

The notion of being out on the street was no idle threat. We'd lived in three apartments in as many years, and all around our Bronx neighborhood there was evidence of eviction sofas, like new, abandoned on the sidewalk, dining room tables left behind when somebody took all the chairs. Sometimes, after it rained, I saw family photographs and copies of birth certificates floating like paper sailboats in the street toward the gutter.

Mommy had grown up running from the bill collectors and the repo man. They would be in the middle of watching a favorite show—*Laugh In* or something silly—and the bell would ring and a guy would come in and take the TV. One day, she came home from school and found all of the contents of her apartment on the sidewalk and the neighbors making off with all of her stuff—her dolls, her clothes, even a bag of her barrettes. "Girls I knew," Mommy had said, her teeth clenched as if those stolen baby dolls had been real babies. "Girls who had been to my house, played with my toys, just took them. As if without four walls around them, our stuff was not our stuff. I never want you to go through something like that. Never."

Mommy told the story again as I cried my greedy new-dress tears, then she stood and opened my closet door. "It's a brand-new school, Angela," she said in a cheerleader's voice that I didn't believe. "Nobody's ever seen any of your clothes. Just make do for now, sweetie. First of the month, I'll buy you a new dress and new shoes."

I didn't want to hear it, and looked away at the poster on my wall of my namesake. Angela Davis' bright brown eyes were flashing and her lips were slightly open, but serious, as if she was about to say something powerful. I knew what Angela Davis would think of a little girl who cried for new clothes. I wiped my tears and hugged Mommy around the waist.

"Pick a dress," she said, kissing me on the forehead. "I'll iron it and it will look like new, I swear."

I stood up and reached for the outfit we both knew I'd choose. It was a pink peasant blouse with a pair of pink bell bottoms to match.

In the kitchen, Mommy gave me a purple notebook with stars and a new purple pen. "No book bag yet," she said. "But we'll get you one to match your coat." She looked outside and held her hand through the window—a human weather vane. "Thank God it's been warm 'cause you need a new coat, too."

I hadn't slept well the night before I'd met my new teacher, Mrs. Newhouse from Long Island. I'd been feeling nervous about the new school and on edge because my back-to-school clothes were really back-to-last-year clothes. I'd been feeling small and she made me feel smaller. So since she'd already said I was a liar, I went home and I told a lie.

Mommy was at work. Daddy was in the kitchen, making an omelet. It was three o'clock and he was still in his pajamas, which meant he didn't have a show, tonight, which meant there was no work.

"How was your first day at school, princess?" he asked in a sweet tone that told me he was sorry for fighting with Mommy the night before. When Daddy was feeling guilty, there was always sweet talk to spare. He'd be calling her Miss Black America and his dark-chocolate honey as soon as she got home. He'd offer to fix dinner and light candles and put on Teddy Pendergrass as soon as I went to bed. I knew the drill.

"It was terrible," I said, pouting for effect. "Not to mention, the teacher was talking about you."

"About me?" Daddy said, whipping around from the hot stove. "What did she say about me?"

For all his skillful hustling, Daddy was easier to play than a game of three-card monte. All you had to do was make him the star of the story—good or bad—and he got right involved.

"The teacher asked us what our fathers did for a living," I said, pausing dramatically. "And when I told her that my father was a magician, she rolled her eyes. She said, 'There's no such thing as a black magician.'"

"She said what?" Daddy growled ferociously. I had thought about pretending she'd said that there was no such thing as a nigger magician, but I figured that would be laying it on a bit thick. Always keep your con simple. Daddy had taught me that.

"She said she'd never heard of a black magician," I repeated. "Then she asked me if I hadn't meant musician and she asked me what instrument you played."

Daddy was livid. "Why we always got to sing and dance?" he fumed. Then he went off on a rant, barking like a mad dog. "It's not enough to be a talent like Bojangles. Got to sing 'Good Ship Lollypop' with Shirley Temple. You listen to me! It's not a 'good' ship unless white people are on it. Frank Sinatra and Dean Martin hanging out are just a couple of nice guys. Put a black man in with them and all of a sudden, it's the Rat Pack. Always got to be something negative with black people . . ."

"Daddy, the stove," I said, as the skillet began to smoke.

"In the cowboy films, the good guy wears white and the bad guy wears black," he continued.

"Daddy! Your omelet's burning."

He turned around and turned off the flame. "So because it's black, I'm not supposed to eat it?" he said with a grin, then sat down and ate every last burned bite.

The next day, Daddy walked me to school. Although it was eight o'clock in the morning, he was dressed in a black tuxedo, complete with top hat and tails. I felt slightly silly walking down the street with him. On each block, people peeked out of doorways and windows to stare. But I was more happy than embarrassed because I knew that my teacher was going to get it. Daddy was going to give her a tongue-lashing she'd never forget.

Which is exactly what he didn't do. After introducing himself to Mrs. Newhouse, Daddy said, "I understand that this is Career Day at school."

Mrs. Newhouse, dressed in a teal pantsuit identical to the one she'd worn the day before, went slightly green herself. "There's been a mistake, Mr. Brown. Today is not Career Day."

"It isn't?" Daddy said, shooting me a quizzical look. "That's what Angela told me." I was seated in the fifth seat of the third row and began silently willing myself and my chair to disappear.

"Well," Daddy said, cheerfully, "since I came all this way, would you mind terribly if I showed the kids some tricks?"

All the students began to clap. Three or four of the girls, the ones that I'd already designated as the snotty bunch, shot me winning smiles. They were sweet, "be my best friend/sign my slam book/make fortune-tellers with me" smiles and I ignored them, unsure that Daddy's spell would last past the minute he walked out the door.

"Actually, Mr. Brown, I'm afraid we don't have time for magic tricks," Mrs. Newhouse said, reaching out for a folder on her desk. "The Board of Ed has laid out a very strict lesson plan. Lots of learning to do, you know." She said this last sentence with a bit of a lilt, like a character in a musical.

Daddy reached his arm around Mrs. Newhouse's head, just past her jet-black modified beehive. "I won't argue with that," he said. "My great-granddaddy always told me that if you pour your wealth into your head, you will always be rich."

Mrs. Newhouse smiled her toothless smile and looked pointedly at the door. Daddy began to walk away, then turned around. "My dear Mrs. Newhouse," he said, in a faint British accent designed to flatter, "I need to use the payphone on my way out. A smart teacher like you, with a head full of knowledge, could probably spare some change." Then he pulled a quarter out of her ear and she gave a little gasp. The kids in class sat up on the edge of their seats. She'd asked Daddy to leave, she'd said there was no time for tricks, but he'd gone ahead and whipped a little something on her anyway.

Daddy lifted a large "Reading Is Fundamental" coffee cup off of Mrs. Newhouse's desk and held it up to her head. "You've poured so much knowledge, so much wealth, into your head, that you're a positive gold mine." He did the slot machine trick then, cranking Mrs. Newhouse's arm up and down as quarter after quarter fell out of her ear and into the cup.

The kids began to cheer and even Mrs. Newhouse let loose a giggle. "I have to say," she said, in a whispery tone that bordered on flirtatious, "that is really astounding. I think we can spare the time for one or two tricks more."

Daddy took out a large envelope, five notebook-size playing cards, and a piece of black photographic paper. He displayed each card slowly. On one card, there was a plus symbol; on another card, there was a square; on the third card, there was a circle; on the fourth card, there was a series of wavy lines, and on the last card, there was a star.

He turned his back to the class and asked Mrs. Newhouse to shuffle the cards. She did and handed the large cards back to Daddy, carefully with two hands as if she was afraid they might fall.

Daddy smiled at the class. "Since I'm taking up some of your important class time, I thought we'd do a review of basic mathematics."

He knelt down and placed three cards on the floor, then he asked, "Ladies and gentleman, how many cards on the floor?"

Everyone cried out, "Three!"

He stood up again. "That leaves how many cards in my hand?"

All the kids shouted out "Two!"

"Now what I'm about to show you moves out of the realm of math and into the realm of physics," Daddy continued. His smile, ever-present, glowed as if he was born to smile and was perfectly content at all times. I sat at my desk, remembering his fight with Mommy—the way he'd shrugged her off like a fly that bothered him. His face then had been so cold, so disgusted. *He is a million men*, I thought. *He sheds emotions like skin.*

"This, ladies and gentlemen, is what we call mind over matter," he said. Daddy knew that kids loved to be called "ladies and gentlemen." It made them feel grown-up and was just a little bit distracting and kept their mind off the mechanics of the trick. "I'm going to put these two cards face to face and put this magical black photographic paper between them. I'm going to place the whole thing in this envelope and then I want the lovely Mrs. Newhouse to take the envelope to the other side of the room."

Mrs. Newhouse took the envelope and practically skipped over to the little library in the back of the room.

"Now you won't believe what you're about to see," Daddy said. "A year from now, you may not even remember exactly what you saw. But I want you to remember this—mind over matter."

Daddy took off his long tuxedo coat and rolled up his sleeves. He closed his eyes and placed a finger on each temple. Then he began to hum. A few moments later, he announced, "I'm in harmony with those cards. It doesn't matter what they were when I put them in because I imprinted my will on that photographic paper. I have changed the cards!"

In a confident, almost slow-motion stroll, Daddy began to walk up and down the aisles between our desks. He looked each child in the face, pausing suspiciously, to gaze longer at certain kids. When he had made eye contact with every student in the room, including me, he asked, "How many of you believe that I can guess which two cards Mrs. Newhouse is holding in her hand?"

About half the kids held up their hands. "This is a tough crowd, Angela," Daddy said, winking at me. Then he asked again for a show of hands again.

He walked over to a boy named Charlie, the biggest kid in the room. Charlie had jet-black skin and a permanent scowl. He was the kind of kid that was genetically destined to be the class bully. "What's your name, son?" Daddy asked.

Charlie told him.

Daddy perched on the edge of Charlie's desk. "You don't believe I can guess those two cards," he said.

"Nope," Charlie answered.

"Well, how about I make you a deal?" Daddy purred. "I'm going to take a guess and if I'm wrong, I'll kill myself."

Everyone in the room, including Mrs. Newhouse, looked horrified. But Daddy wasn't finished. He stood up and, as he walked toward the front of

the classroom, he added, "However, if I kill myself, I'll do it by starvation."
He winked at Charlie. "I don't know if you'll want to wait around."

Everybody laughed. Mrs. Newhouse let out a sigh of relief. Then Daddy
pronounced, "You are holding the square and the wavy lines, Mrs. Newhouse."

And of course, she was. "House rules," as Daddy would say. The con
man always wins.

Daddy stayed until the lunch bell rang. When he took his final bow, the
entire class gave him a standing ovation.

In the cafeteria, I was surrounded by kids. Not just the ones in my class,
but fifth and sixth graders who'd heard about Daddy's performance. They
had a million questions, questions that just begged for me to lie some more.
For the first time, it looked like I might actually be popular—old clothes
and all. They wanted to know if I'd ever met Doug Henning. I said yes.
They wanted to know if we had a magic carpet at home. I said yes. They
wanted to know if we had a magic rabbit. I said yes. They asked if I knew
the secrets behind Daddy's tricks. "Of course," I said, feigning boredom.
The truth was I knew some of the devices—hidden compartments, rubber
thumbs big enough to squeeze handkerchiefs in, dummy hats and newspapers that were quickly swapped for the real thing. But I couldn't do magic—
not even a simple "pick a card, any card" deck trick.

What I wanted to tell them was it's more complicated than you think.
Sure, it helps to be a magician's daughter. I've got a few ins. But let's say your
mother is Patti LaBelle and you can carry a note. You still have to do more
than sing. You have to wear those crazy outfits and sport that fabulous hair.
You have to know how to dance and how to work an audience. You have to
know how to banter and how to wink and how to make a room hot when
everyone is just sitting there, staring, as frozen as a glass of ice cubes. You
have to be fearless and larger than life. Otherwise, you're just another church
mouse singing in the glee club or the Sunday choir. It's like that with magic,
I wanted to say. The tricks are the easy part. The things my father does that
make him amazing? That's what's magic.

Ghost Story

BY VICTOR D. LAVALLE

FROM *Slapboxing with Jesus*

Move anywhere, when you're from the Bronx, you're of the Bronx, it doesn't shed. The buildings are medium height: schools, factories, projects. It's not Manhattan, where everything's so tall you can't forget you're in a city; in the Bronx you can see the sky, it's not blotted out. The place isn't standing or on its back, the whole borough lies on its side. And when the wind goes through there, you can't kid yourself—there are voices.

I was at war and I was in love. Of both, the second was harder to hide, there was evidence. Like beside my bed, a three-liter bottle, almost full. I rolled from under my covers, spun off the cap, pulled down my pants, held myself to the hole and let go.

Besides me and the bottle, my room had a bed, some clothes hanging in the closet, books spread out across the floor. Somewhere in that pile of texts and manifestos were two papers I had to turn in if I ever wanted to be a college graduate.

Cocoa was in the next room, snoring and farting. I listened to him, all his sounds were music.

I finished, pulled up my sweatpants and closed the bottle; inside, the stuff was so clear you could hold it to one eye and read a message magnified on the other side. I religiously removed the label from this one like I had all the others, so when I put it at the bottom of the closet with them, in formation (two rows of three), I could check how they went from dark to lighter to this one, sheer as a pane of glass; each was like a revision—with the new incarnation you're getting closer and closer to that uncluttered truth you might be hunting privately. I would show them all to a woman I loved, one I could trust; that had been tried three times already—the two stupid ones had asked me to empty them and change my life, the smart one had dressed right then and walked out. This was my proof, their intolerance, that people hate the body. But me, I was in love.

Cocoa and I had grown up poor and I was the stupid one; I believed that's how we were supposed to stay. That's why, when I saw him on the train two months before, with his girl, Helena, her stomach all fat with his seed, I didn't leave him alone. I walked right over. I was at war, too, and needed the help.

She'd looked up before he did; the express cut corners and I fooled myself into thinking she was glad to see me. "Hey Sammy," she forced out. Cocoa was working, I was sure of that; she was rocking three new gold fronts on her bottom teeth.

I asked, "You going to be a mommy?"

Started telling me how many months along she was but I'd stopped listening; soon she wasn't talking. Her jewelry disappeared behind her closed mouth. Cocoa hugged me tight like when we were fourteen: me and him coming out of the crap church on the corner of 163rd, the one with neon-bright red bricks, the painted sign on the door, misspelling the most important word ("cherch"). It was when his mother died, quick, and we were leaving the ceremony, behind us the thirty more people who'd cared to come. It had been a nice day so fellas were hanging out in crews everywhere and despite them Cocoa hadn't been able to hide his crying like his father and uncles had. I put my hand on his shoulder, patted it hard like men do, but it wasn't enough. So I wrapped my arms around his neck and hugged, on the corner, like even his pops would never care: publicly. When Dorice walked by I didn't stop and she probably thought we looked gay; still, I didn't force him back and try to catch up to her. And Cocoa? He didn't push me away, he leaned closer. He hugged me like that when I saw him on the train, like there was a death nearby. He looked right at me.

"We need to chill again," I said.

The way Cocoa grinned, it was like I'd given him cash. He was small, but he had the kind of smile it takes two or three generations of good breeding to grow; the one descendants of the *Mayflower* had after four centuries of feeding themselves fruit I'd never get my lips around (the kind where fresh means just picked, not just brought out for display). It was a good smile that made people trust him, think he was going places. Helena touched his leg, but he brushed her back, saying, "I'm just getting his number."

I watched Helena's back curl like it would when the stomach got grander, the baby inside pushing out its little legs like it might kick a hole; as she sank I told Cocoa my number and he gave me his; he was living with Helena and her family, back in the Bronx.

"Wake up!" I yelled out to the living room.

There was a class today. Physics, I think, but me passing that now was like a dude trying to be monogamous—impossible. Cocoa hadn't missed a lecture or seminar all year, he'd bragged about it, so the last three days he'd been with me were only getting him in trouble with the mother-to-be. When she beeped him, every few hours, and he called back, she'd say she needed errands run, but her cousin Zulma was around, and her aunt; she was just on that ultrahorny pregnant-woman program and Cocoa knew. He would say, over the phone, "You know I can't sleep with you when you're pregnant, that would be wrong. I might give the baby a dent in its head." He laughed with me when he hung up, but while they were talking I said nothing; I listened from the kitchen to every syllable; if I'd had a pen and paper nearby I would have written it all down.

He stood in my doorway. He was slim as well as short but still seemed to take up all the space. Cocoa said, "You're messing me up. That stuff from last night is still bothering me. What did we drink?"

"I had a bugged dream," I muttered.

"I'd hate to hear it," Cocoa said. "I'm going to make some breakfast."

My hand, I placed it against the window to see how cold it was out. It wasn't a snowy winter. When I'd enrolled at City College it had been a big deal. I'd be getting my own place. My mother and sister were against it, but when you hit eighteen they call that adulthood and a lot more decisions are yours to make. Plus, you know how it is with boys in a family of women, they won't let go. When I'd first moved in, Mom and Karen were coming by once a week to check on me, but after two years of staying on top of things, schedules, they had no choice, they let me be.

Three nights ago, when Cocoa had come to hang out, I'd made him wait outside while I got things in place: threw my pillows and sheets back on my bed, plugged everything in. I kept up with news, they were doing renovations all over the Bronx: new buildings, the parks reseeded with grass and imported trees, you could almost pretend there wasn't a past.

After breakfast, for an hour, Cocoa and I took trains up and down the spines of Manhattan. Then we stood outside Washington Square Park, on the side farthest from NYU (Cocoa's school), staring at three women he thought he knew. I was shaking my head. "No, no. You don't know them. They're way too pretty to be talking to you."

He spat, "You criticize when you get them herpes sores off your lips."

I touched my chin. "They're only pimples."

"Then wash your face."

He'd been giving me advice since we were kids. He had thought that if he just told me how to be better I could be. Age ten was the first time for either of us that I acted up: When people whispering into telephones were talking about only me, a radio announcer was making personal threats "Someone out there, right now, is suffering and won't get relief until they're our ninety-eighth caller and gets these tickets to Bermuda!" And Cocoa grabbed me tight as I dialed and redialed the pay phone in front of our building, screaming for someone to lend me twenty cents.

Cocoa walked and I moved beside him; we entered the park. The day was a cold one so the place wasn't way too full like summers when you couldn't move ten feet without having to dodge some moron with a snake on his shoulders or a cipher of kids pretending they're freestyling lyrics they'd writ-

ten down and memorized months before. "I saw Evette the other day" I told
him.

He smiled. "What are you telling me that for? Anyway, she married
someone didn't she?"

"Well, you staring at them three girls, I thought I'd tell you about one
you actually got."

We had come to an NYU building and he told me to wait outside; he
was angry that I'd brought up this woman with him trying so hard to be
good; really, I don't know why I did. When I'd called him a few days earlier,
it had been because I knew I needed help, but once he was with me I
avoided the issue.

My hands in my coat pockets, they were full of those used tissues from
the flu in March. I had planned to keep them in a pillowcase under my bed
when I got better, but those were all filled with the hairs I clipped off and
saved, so it was September and I had never truly healed and my hands were
full of dried snot.

Maybe if he hadn't been doing so well, if his girl hadn't been so pretty, if
his grades weren't soaring, if he'd been unhealthy, anything, but I couldn't
confide in someone doing so much better than me. I wouldn't feel like I was
asking for help, more like charity. The man he was now, I couldn't sit down
with him and go through all the events in my day to figure out which thing
was damning me: that I woke up every day, alarmless, at seven-forty? that I
couldn't stand the taste of milk anymore? that I kept putting off a trip to the
supermarket and so the cupboards and fridge were empty? that I had two
pillowcases under my bed, one full of cut hair, the other full of old tissues?
They all made sense to me.

They all had reasons: 1) for two years I'd had nine A.M. classes so now my
body, even though I'd stopped attending, had found a pattern; 2) on campus two women had pulled me aside and shown me pamphlets about the
haphazard pasteurization process, pictures of what a cow's milk does to human lungs so that even just a commercial for cereal made my chest tighten;
3) I'd dated a woman who worked at the market two blocks away, had been
too open in explaining my collections to her one night, sat dejected and embarrassed as she dressed and walked out forever, so I couldn't go back in
there even if it was silly pride; there wasn't another grocery for blocks, when
I needed food I just bought something already made and I was mostly
drinking water now (to watch a cleansing process in myself) and you could
get that from a tap. And 4) it wasn't just my body, but The Body that I
loved. So where others saw clippings as waste and mucus as excess, all to be
collected and thrown away, spend no time on them, to me they were records
of the past, they were treasures. Just tossing them out was like burying a
corpse too quickly—rub your face against the cold skin, kiss the stony el-

bows, there is still majesty in that clay. People hate the body, especially those who praise the life of the mind. But even fingernails are miracles. Even odors. Everything of or in the body is a celebration of itself, even the worst is a holy prayer.

I found, as soon as he spoke, as I considered opening myself, I hated him again; I wanted to mention anything that would ruin his happiness. Like that, I brought up Evette and the night before it had been Wilma. Cocoa came out the building, pushing the glass door with power. Smiling.

"Your divorce come through?" I asked.

He stopped, composed himself back to pleasure. "Today, a little boy was born."

"Yours? I thought it wasn't for three or four more months." I was suddenly hopeful for the pain of something premature; I could talk to a man who was living through that kind of hurt.

"Not mine. Once a week I find out the name of a baby, a boy if I can, that was born. Newspaper, radio, Internet. This kid was born today, his father already posted pictures. Nine pounds seven ounces, man. Benjamin August something. He looked healthy. It's good luck."

I laughed. "I bet that kid wasn't born in the Bronx. If he was he'd have come out coughing." One fear of every South Bronx parent: asthma. It was enough to make Cocoa tap me one, hard, in the chest and I fell back onto a parked car. His child would be born in the Bronx, he didn't want to be reminded of the dangers. I put my fists out, up. I'd been planning for this, not with him, but with someone. Had been eating calcium tablets every day, fifteen of them (student loan refund checks are a blessing), and now my bones were hard like dictionaries.

He didn't hit anymore. It's what I wanted.

Do you remember the hospital? Not torturous (well, maybe one time), no beatings though; it wasn't even the drugs, try one word: boredom. You could move around but there was nothing to chase the mind, hardly even television if you weren't always good. Just the hours that were eons sitting on a couch, a row of you, ten or twenty, no books, magazines too simple for the mildly retarded and your active mind leaps further and further over an empty cosmos, as lonely as the satellites sent to find life in the universe. But in there, at least, was when I'd realized how they waged their war, my enemies: through sockets and plugs, through a current.

We balanced on a corner as cabs passed by in yellow brilliance. It was late morning. I noticed how much energy was on: Some streetlights never went off, people passing spoke on phones and the charged batteries glowed, radios came on and stayed on, computers were being run, every floor of every building. The taxi horns, engine-powered, began to sound like my name being called; I kept turning my head; the sounds bounced around inside my body, leafing through my bastard anatomy like I was a book of poems.

He spoke but the words were coming out of his mouth now all orange. I could see them, like the cones put out on the road at night to veer traffic away from a troubled spot. He said, "Look, let's not get craz, uh, let's not get agitated. I know someplace we could hang out. It'll be real good."

The NYU banners flapped with the wind, loud enough to sound like teeth cracking in your head. And how many times had I heard that noise! Like in the last month maybe five; whenever the remote control wasn't working or the phone bloopblopbleeped in my ear about no more Basic Service and I took each instrument between my teeth and bit down, trying to chew my anger out, that rage of mine which could take on such proportions.

Thought we'd catch the 4 to 149th and Grand Concourse—everybody out, everybody home. We could pass the murals of young men painted outside candy stores and supermarkets, where a thoughtful friend might have set out a new candle, where mourning seemed like a lifestyle. Instead we took the 6 and got out at 116th, walked blocks, then left, to Pleasant Avenue. My sister's home.

Cocoa saw me turn, flinch like someone had set off a car alarm in my ear, but then he put his arm on my shoulder and pushed hard, said, "Come on. Keep going." Cocoa kept pushing until we got upstairs, to the door, green, on it the numbers had been nailed in and the air had oxidized their faux-gold paint into that blackened color so familiar to buildings across our income level. He rang the bell. (Are they artificially powered?) The sound was so shrill I guessed they were part of the enemy army. Our first battle, twelve years before in the drab brown medical ward, had been so quick I'm sure they'd thought I'd forget. But I'd squirmed after they set those wires against my little forehead, so when they flipped the charge that one time, the lines slipped and burned both cheeks black; years later the spots were still there.

She opened the door. The whole place was going: television, microwave, coffeemaker, VCR. Karen was surprised to see me, but still, expecting it in some way. She was used to this.

I went to the bathroom but didn't shut the door. I filled my mouth with water and let it trickle out through my pursed lips, down into the toilet bowl so they'd think I was busy, held open the door some and my ears more:

Karen: "How did you end up with him?"

Cocoa: "I ran into Sammy a few weeks ago, gave him my number, then he wouldn't leave me alone."

Karen: "You think he's starting up?"

Cocoa: "I don't know what else. It's got to be. He hasn't done this nonsense in years. He calls me one morning and in an hour he's at my door, ringing the bell. I'm living with my girl's family, you know? He started kicking the door if I didn't answer. So I been with him three days."

Karen: "You should have called me or something."

Cocoa: "Called who? I wasn't even sure if you still lived here. I got lucky you and your man didn't get promoted or relocated. I called your mom but the number was disconnected."

Karen: "She needed to get away."

Cocoa: "Well, I know how she feels. You know I love that kid, but I can't keep this up. My son is about to drop in a few months. I'm trying to take care of this school thing. He's bugging, that's all I can say."

Karen: "You think you could help me out here, until Masai comes?"

Cocoa: "I can't take five more minutes. I'm sorry Karen, I am, but I can't be around him no more. I'm through."

I listened to him walk to the door, open and shut it quietly. That thing was a big metal one, if he'd just let it swing closed behind him it would have rattled and thundered, so my last thought of Cocoa was of him being delicate.

Washed my hands and crept out, pulled the door closed, and left the light on so she'd think I was still in there, and snuck into her bedroom. On the door was the family portrait everyone has from Sears. A big poster of my sister, her husband, and that baby of theirs. My niece. There was enough daylight coming in from outside that I didn't need the bulbs; besides, the light would have been like my rat-fink friend Cocoa, squealing to my sister about my goings-on.

There was a big bed in this big room, a crib in the corner, clothes in piles, just washed, on top of a long dresser. I walked to the crib and looked down at Kezia. She was wrapped up tightly, put to bed in a tiny green nightdress. Her diaper bulged and made noise when she moved. Dreaming little girl, she had dimples for laughing. I should have been able to make her smile even in her sleep.

From the hallway a slamming door, then, "Sammy? Samuel?" Karen kicked into the room like a S.W.A.T. team. I looked, but she didn't have a rifle. She flicked on the light and ran to me, but not concerned with me, looked down at Kezia and rolled her over, touched her face, pulled her up and onto Mommy's shoulder. The big light shook Kezia into crying and it was loud, torturous. I laughed because my sister had done some harm even though there was love in it.

"What are you . . . Is everything all right?"

I looked at her and said, "Of course. I was just looking at my niece."

"You might have woken her up."

"Seems like you did that just fine," I told her.

Kezia turned toward me and then looked to her crib, twisted and latched on to it, pulled at that because she wanted back in. Karen finally acquiesced and returned her. The tiny one watched me, remembering, remembering and broke out in a smile. You know why kids love me so much? Because all kids are very, very stupid.

"She'll never get to sleep now."

I thought Karen was wrong. I pointed. "Look at her eyes. She's still drowsy." Kezia was looking at me, intently. I started rocking from left to right on the balls of my feet and Kezia mimicked me. She held the crib's rail to keep her balance but when I leaned too far right she followed, tipped over on her side, huffed, grabbed the bars, and pulled herself back up to try again. She made a gurgle noise and I returned it, she went louder and I went louder, she screamed and I screamed; Karen flopped back against her married bed, holding her face, laughing.

My hands went around Kezia's middle, then I lifted her up as high as my arms would allow, brought her belly to my mouth and bit her there. She kicked her feet happily, caught me, two good shots right in the nose; that thing would be flaring up later. But she laughed and I did it again. I dropped her down two feet, quickly, like I'd lost my grip, and across her face came the look that precedes vomit, then a pause and like I knew it would, laughter.

Put her back in the crib and we returned to yelling, added movements with our hands and feet. Whenver I threw my palms in the air she did the same, lost her balance and fell backward; she lay there, rocking side to side so she could get some momentum for rising. I tickled her under the chin. We did it like this while Karen left the room and returned (repeat three times). Finally Kezia sat, watching me. I twirled in arms-open circles and she still had enough energy to smile, but not much else, and then she didn't have energy enough even for that and she watched me, silent, as she lay on her back, then Karen had to tap my shoulder and shush me because the kid was sleeping.

The lights were still on: Around the crib there were pictures taped up. Of our family and Masai's, all watching over; the picture of me rested closer to Kezia than all the rest, but in it I was only a boy. Looking at my crooked smile I felt detached from that child—like we could cannibalize his whole life and you still wouldn't have tasted me. Every memory would someday make the catalogue I kept in my room, eleven small green notebooks.

Me and Karen sat in the kitchen. She had been preparing dinner. I started making a plate. "Leave a lot for Masai. He'll be home from work soon."

I covered all the pots and poured myself some berry Kool-Aid. Karen's

Kool-Aid was the only thing I would drink besides water. After I gulped I told her, "You need more sugar."

She sucked her teeth. "Masai and me decided we should still have teeth when Kezia gets to be seven." Karen finished her rice. "You look awful," she said.

"Yeah, but I've always looked bad. You got the beauty and I got everything else."

She smacked me, gentle, across the chin. "I had my bachelor's before you had been left back for the first time. Have you thought about coming to stay with us?"

"I like where I'm at."

"You need to be around your family. You're acting stupid out there."

"Whatever. I shrugged. You don't know what I'm doing."

"I can see what you're not doing: washing, changing your clothes. Probably not going to class."

"Man," I said. "You don't understand subtlety. You've got to bring these things up cool, easy, otherwise you'll close all avenues of communication."

That's how long she paused, watching me. Then she went to the fridge, found a green plastic cup. She put it on the table, sat, sounded stern, "How about you take the medication mixed with something? You still like it with orange juice? I'll make it."

I looked at the cup, the white film on top, that clump and beneath it the actual Tropicana Original. There had been plenty at my apartment, taken regular for two years, on my own. But someday you want to rest. "How about you put some vodka in there?"

On top of the fridge Karen had left a Tupperware bowl of the boiled egg whites she'd been cutting up for her next day's meal. Even in the light blue bowl they seemed too bright. She wasn't kidding around. "Drink it. You told us you would. You were doing so well."

"It makes my head feel like rocks."

"But at least it keeps you thinking right. Just drink this cup. It'll be a new start. Come on."

See, but I was supposed to take that medicine twice a day, every day. She wanted me to drink this one glass and everything would go right but you can't dam a river with just one brick.

I said, "Karen, you can't stop the electric soldiers."

I was twenty-two years old and Karen was thirty. How long before it's just frustration in her, screaming to get out, wishing whatever was the pain would go away.

"Can you?" she asked.

Blissfully the goddamn fridge worked, I could hear its engine going, regular like a heartbeat, mumming along and I was so jealous. When I got up she draped herself across the table, spilling the juice and the orchids she had in a vase, the ones her husband had bought two days ago, purple like lips too long exposed to the cold.

It was lucky Masai was at work. I was much bigger than Karen and I could simply pluck her off my arm and leave, but if Masai had been there it would have gotten louder, the trouble in this kitchen would have been con-tagious, contaminating the living room, the bathroom, their bedroom. We would have been all over the place. But at some point, as I was tugging, she let go. She could fight harder, she had before. Her hands fell to her sides; she opened the door for me.

I had other people I could have seen, but I kept forgetting their addresses. I might have passed four or five out on Malcolm X Boulevard. Later, I walked by the mosque, the brothers in their suits and bow ties selling the *Final Call;* I wanted to buy one, help them out; walked over to a short one in a gold suit, he pushed me a paper like it would save my life. "Only a dollar."

"And what do I get?" I asked.

"You get the truth. All the news the white media won't show you."

I leaned close to him, he pulled back some. "You don't know that all this stuff is past tense?" I asked.

Now he looked away, to his boy at the other corner, in green, white shirt, black shoes, talking with two older women; each nodded and smiled, one brought out her glasses to read the headlines. "So you want to buy this or what?" My friend held it out again, the other twenty copies he pulled close to his chest. I could see on his face that his legs were tired.

But for what would I be buying that paper? Or if a Christian was selling Bibles? Name another religion, I had no use for any. I wanted to pull my man close, by the collar (for effect) and tell him I knew of a new god, who was collecting everything he saw around him and stashing it in his apart-ment on Amsterdam Avenue; who walked home from the 1 train stealing bouts of Spanish being spoken in front of stores and when he came home prodigiously copied them down; who stole the remnants of empty beer bot-tles that had been shattered into thirty-seven pieces, took the glass and placed it in his living room, in a jar, with the greens and browns of others— in the morning he sat there and watched the fragments, imagined what life had come along and done such destruction.

Instead I walked backward until I got to a corner, hugged myself tight against a phone booth with no phone in it as the people swam around me and ignored everything but the single-minded purposes of their lives. After an hour was up my brain sent signals to my feet: move.

I stood in front of my apartment again, had a paper to hand in. Go upstairs and slide it in an envelope, address it to the woman who led my seminar on black liberation movements. The one who lectured me only when I missed class and never remembered to mark it in her book. The one who had assured me that if I wrote it all down this mind would be soothed, salvaged. One Tuesday (Tues. & Thur. 9:00–10:45 A.M.) she had pulled me aside when lessons were over, confided, "These days, the most revolutionary thing you can be is articulate."

I had told her honestly, "I'm trying. I'm trying."

I touched the front door before opening it. I'd been struck by the fear that the building was on fire; a church and a mosque had been burned recently. In the secret hours of night they'd been turned to ash and in the daylight their destruction was like a screaming message to us all. Had the door been hot I would have run farther than I needed to, but it was cold so I walked in.

The elevator was still broken. I had ten stories to climb; my legs felt stiff and proud. I moved effortlessly until I reached the sixth floor and Helena stopped me. She was with her girls, they were coming down the stairs. As pregnant as she was I knew the climb couldn't have been easy, but the look on her face had nothing to do with exertion. It was all for me. "I was coming to talk to you Sammy," she said. Helena's cousin Zulma stood beside me; she was so big I felt boxed in.

"You should be out looking for your man," I told Helena.

Zulma looked like she wanted to leave, bored, but was there to get her cousin's back in case it was needed. If Helena had been alone I wouldn't have had any problem kicking her in the gut and running. When she'd rumbled to the bottom of the stairs I would have crawled down beside her and in her ear asked, "Now tell me, what does this feel like? Tell me every detail."

"Why you causing so much problems?" another of Helena's girls asked, but I didn't answer. Instead I told them one of my philosophies to live by. "I never tell a pretty woman I think she's pretty unless we're already holding hands."

Helena rubbed her face with frustration. "You need to leave Ramón alone. He's good when he's not around you." Her watch beeped, not loudly, but it echoed through the stairwell. Its face was glowing. Batteries gave it power.

"Have you been drafted too?" I asked Helena.

"Fuck this," Zulma muttered, then her elbow was in my chest.

As the five girls got all over different parts of me I swung wild. Caught Zulma in the mouth and the first drops of blood on my face were hers. They were yelling as I kicked out with both legs. Then I was burning everywhere and I knew without looking that the off-silver colors in my eyes were the

box cutters finding whole parts of me to separate. Fabric was tearing as they
removed swatches of my clothing so they could get nearer to my skin.
Zulma and Helena were at my face; neither of them smiled as they did the
cutting. They didn't seem angry. Their faces were so still.

I grabbed and reached for something, dipping my fingers in everything
spilling out of me. The colors were hard to make out in the bad light, but
the stuff was beautiful and thick, it pooled. The girls rose and ran; I listened
to five sets of sneakers move quickly down those stairs to the emergency
exit; the door swung out and stuck, there was the flood of an empty wind
up the staircase.

Clarity

BY DAVID WRIGHT

Because Darryl, at thirteen, was too young to work, his stepfather, Jack
Mitchell, found him odd jobs when he could. That way Darryl would
have his own pocket money, Jack Mitchell would explain; it would teach
him responsibility. One Wednesday in June, Jack Mitchell found work for
Darryl and his friend Two pulling weeds outside the new post office.

Jack Mitchell and the postmaster, Wiley Edwards, both held seats on the
Fitzgerald Town Council, and as fellow councilmen, they did each other fa-
vors. For Jack Mitchell, such amiability was a political move. For Darryl and
Two, though, his political jockeying meant twenty dollars, quick cash in
their pockets.

The new post office had been built on a dry, dusty lot on Mesquite
Street, just down the road from the county courthouse in downtown
Fitzgerald, Texas. Darryl and Two were to pull up the weeds and shrubs to
prepare the ground for sodding. It was mindless work, but the sun was demanding, and the roots had dug stubbornly into the rock-hard soil.
Whether the boys did the job in four hours or six or ten, the work was
worth twenty dollars each. After an hour and a half, they had finished more
than half the lot.

The boys had taken their T-shirts off, and the sun scorched their already
bronzed skins. Walking bent at the waist strained their lower backs, and the
mindlessness of the work wore on their minds. So they started singing.

"You know Chuck Berry?" Two asked.

"Yeah, I know Chuck Berry."

"My daddy's got a lot of Chuck Berry albums." Two straightened, stretching out his long back, then bent back to work. "He's got this song, 'School Days.' You know it?"

"How does it go?"

Two's head danced on his neck to the rhythm on the inside. He sang: "Up in the morning and off to schoo-ool . . ."

"Yeah," Darryl smiled, "I know it." His head started its own dance, like a camel's in stride, to the beat beating inside.

Two sang as they pulled: "Teacher be teaching the Golden Ru-ule."

Then Darryl: "Bell rings, time to go home,/ Grab some white boy's change and get 'long on."

They erupted with laughter as they clapped garden-gloved hands, steadily moving down the row.

Two continued: "Boy hollers, crying in his pla-ate . . . Slap 'im upside his head and don't be la-ate."

Then Darryl: "Cops, coming, so fast,/ They gonna get your black ass!"

But Darryl's palm-slapping laughter stopped when he didn't hear Two slap-laughing beside him. He glanced over and saw Two staring straight ahead, and then he saw what Two was staring at: a silver-suited pink balloon—Wiley Edwards—sucking a cigar and looming over them.

Wiley Edwards, his red face puckered around the protruding cigar, glared at the boys a long time. His belly surged over his belt and hung there, almost a separate, threatening entity. Darryl and Two straightened, a clump of pulled weeds in each hand.

"Yes, sir?" Darryl asked.

"You boys can go on home," Mr. Edwards said.

"Sir?"

Mr. Edwards pulled a wallet from his inner jacket pocket. "We didn't hire you boys to sing," he said. "We hired you to clear this lot." He gave each a ten-dollar bill. "Now, if y'all want to come out here and be disrespectful and play, well, y'all can just go on home." He turned. "You explain to Erskine why I sent you home." Then he waddled around the building and inside.

Darryl looked at the half-cleared lot, then at Two. "What was that about?" he asked.

"I don't know," Two said, "but I got me a ten-dollar bill, and I know what that's about. That's about seven dollars an hour."

"Jack Mitchell's going to kill me."

" 'Cause we got the ax?"

"Yeah."

"Can't do nothing about it," said Two. "We was working and white man told us to go on home."

"Still . . ."

"Can't do nothing about it," said Two.

Darryl put the bill in his pocket and followed Two onto Mesquite Street. They walked toward the Flats, where Two lived and where Jack Mitchell worked and would be waiting to drive Darryl home to Oakbrook Heights.

Two turned. "Hey, who's Erskine?"

They passed the Dairy Queen and crossed the street toward the bowling alley. "My stepdad," Darryl said. "Jack Mitchell."

"Erskine Jack Mitchell?" Two asked.

"Erskine Elie Mitchell," said Darryl. "They just call him Jack."

"Huh," Two said. "*Er-skine*, Ee-*lie*." Then he added, "Y'all Northern niggahs sure is some poetic folks."

"Must be a black thing then," said Darryl, "Bernard Ferdinando Lamar Waymans the second. What, couldn't your folks decide on a name?"

"Yeah," he said. "Two."

Two crossed the parking lot toward the Nite-Owl Lanes. "Let's go in here and spend some of this hard-earned cash."

"All right," said Darryl, but he was still preoccupied with how to explain getting fired to Erskine Elie Mitchell.

After getting change, they pumped quarters into video games. They played each other in a football game with such fury that their palms blistered.

"You see that pass!" Darryl said.

"I saw it." Two's team regrouped in a huddle on the screen while he selected one of the four defensive options. But his best option, it seemed, was to try to distract Darryl from his tactic. "So, what's your middle name?"

"I told you ten thousand times already," said Darryl, never looking up. "I don't have one."

"And I didn't believe you *then* neither."

"Well, it's true," he said. "I don't."

"You a lie."

"I don't."

"You know you a lie."

Darryl said, "What d'you want my middle name to be?"

Two stopped playing and looked across at Darryl. "Pharmaceuticals."

"All right. I'm Darryl Pharmaceuticals Young."

"Poetic," said Two.

"Just a black thing . . . Touchdown! D'you see that play?"

"Aw, man," Two said, "I wasn't even watching!"

"Well, quit squawking and play then . . ."

"You cheating Pharmaceuticals chump . . ."

"Go on, man," Darryl said, "it's your ball."

In no time they'd whittled their ten-dollar bills down to a dollar fifty (one seventy-five for Two), and they continued toward the Flats. As they walked along sidewalks like hot plates, the soles of their sneakers squooshing like sponges with each step, Darryl rehashed the morning in his head: they got to the post office on time, worked like beasts in that dusty heat, but still got fired. For laughing. They didn't do anything bad; if you can laugh while you work it makes the work go by better, that's all. Jack Mitchell would understand that. Of course, Darryl would leave out the part about the swear word.

"Two, man," he said, "we got fired for laughing."

"My daddy says white man don't like to see black folks laughing. Thinks they're laughing at him."

"Jack Mitchell'll understand that."

"Maybe so," said Two, "but you better start figuring how to make him understand your magic trick that made a ten-dollar bill turn into a buck seventy-five in change."

"Yeah." Darryl hadn't even considered that. And he only had one fifty left.

They walked on, searching silently for a solution. A Fightin' Pioneers poster taped in a shop window brought them to a halt. It announced the upcoming high-school football season, and on it was a picture of the quarterback, Hoodie Duncan, his arm cocked to throw a pass.

"Hoodie's my man," Darryl said,

"Hoodie's my main man," said Two. "Look it the arms on him." Two sat down suddenly on the curb and scrambled in his pockets. "Hang on a minute." He pulled out a fistful of rubber bands.

"What you got rubber bands for?" Darryl asked.

"I been wearing them," said Two. "Make me look strong."

"Huh?"

Two handed a wad of them to Darryl. "That's how folks can tell you're strong," he said, double-wrapping two around each wrist, then pumping his hands to inflate his forearms.

Darryl looked and mimicked Two's actions. "How's that?" he said.

"The veins be sticking out your forearms," Two said, inspecting his, then pumping his hands again. "That's how they know."

"Really?"

"Yeah. You look at Hoodie, or any of them tough brothers. They veins be winding like snakes all down they arms."

"That's true." Darryl remembered seeing Hoodie at the 7-Eleven once. Hoodie joked with the black attendant, signifying with his hands and holding his green and gold letter jacket in his first, and the veins of his arms seemed to jump off his skin. Darryl had been with his mom, who didn't see

Hoodie or the attendant or even Darryl, it seemed; their playfulness stopped, though, when Darryl and his mom entered, and their eyes followed her around the store as she busily searched one aisle then the next for the saltines she'd forgotten to buy at the A&P.

Darryl and Two resumed their walk, hands periodically pumping the air. Two said, "My daddy was a boxer and . . ."

"Really?"

"Yeah. In the army. A welterweight," Two explained. "So he could whoop upside some white boys' heads. He told me he used to beat on white boys' ass like there wasn't no tomorrow. Said it was the only way you could get at 'em in them days, with gloves on, in the ring. Otherwise, have the law and all kinds of white folks all after you."

"Yeah, they say it was like that." That Two's father, now just a mechanic for the town of Fitzgerald, had once been a recognized athlete put him in very high esteem in Darryl's eyes. He wished Jack Mitchell had been one. But Darryl couldn't imagine primping, bulbous Jack Mitchell in a letter jacket.

Jack Mitchell was the town's first and only black councilman. That meant something. When he married Darryl's mom and moved the family to Fitzgerald, they made up the town's first interracial couple, ever, and the only one still. Theirs was the only black family to live in Oakbrook Heights. But still, it wasn't the same thing.

Two said, "My daddy, when he was boxing, he said he'd walk around squeezing tennis balls. It helped his punch. He's still got all kinds of veins sticking out his arms."

"He's strong, huh?"

Two stopped and, face askew, stared Darryl down until Darryl stopped walking, too. "Let that niggah get a switch after your ass and ask me that again." Then he sauntered forward.

They cut through the Texaco onto Third Street. Walking between the pumps, Two stepped deliberately onto the slim rubber hose that ran out from the station. A bell clanged, but nobody stirred, so they continued walking.

Darryl said, "Your dad was a boxer."

"Yeah," said Two. "He was good."

When they arrived at the vacant lot that separated the back of Eastgate Mall from the Flats, Two inspected his forearms, then backpedaled away from Darryl into the shimmering, sun-scorched reeds, his arm cocked to throw a pass. "I'm Hoodie Duncan," he called, bouncing on the balls of his feet as if in the pocket. "You see him in that game against Dumas?"

"I saw the game with you, Two."

"Man, I ain't *never* seen nothing like that." Two scrambled left. "Hoodie

rolled left, and when the dude grabbed his right arm, he shook him"—
which Two did, mostly just jiggling his shoulder—"put the ball in his left
hand, and fired it downfield." Two mimed the motion. "Left-handed!"

"Hoodie's tough."

"Hell yeah, he's tough! You know he's tough. Just six niggahs on the
whole damn team? Shit, you know they ain't about to let n'an one of 'em
play quarterback unless he's two times as tough as every white boy on the
field." Two caught up to Darryl. "And Hoodie is. Being ambidextrous and
all."

"Ambi-*what*?"

"Ambidextrous," said Two. "Hoodie's ambidextrous. My daddy's ambidextrous, too. It means you can use your left hand just as good as your
right. Do whatever you want with either one."

Macadam turned to dirt in the Flats. Darryl and Two walked down the
dusty road toward the Three Jacks' Bar, where Jack Mitchell (the third Jack)
would be waiting. Darryl figured that Jack Mitchell had probably already
talked to Wiley Edwards, so he was in no rush to get there. Dragging along,
Darryl mimed a throwing motion with his left hand. It was awkward, had no
force.

Two, watching Darryl, cast his own left arm forward. "I'm ambidextrous,
too," he said.

"Sure you are."

"You know I am."

"Right."

"What you boys know?" they heard, and turned toward the porch from
where the sound was emitted.

It was Grandpa Thevenet. Two started onto the porch of the pea-green
house, and Darryl followed.

"Hey, Grandpa Thevenet," Two said.

"Hey," said Darryl.

Grandpa Thevenet, who was nobody's grandfather that either boy knew,
was magical. "Hey youself," he said to them.

Grandpa Thevenet had a piano-key smile and told stories that would
light up a place, wherever he happened to be. When Grandpa spoke, he
sounded like the French Canadians Darryl had seen in droves when Jack
Mitchell took the family to Disney World, but Grandpa Thevenet was from
Louisiana.

On his lap, between hands soft and strong and long like Sunday, rested
an accordion. Grandpa could do with his accordion what Hoodie Duncan
did with a football. "You boys tell me what you tink of dis song."

Some people called it zydeco. Grandpa Thevenet called it house-dance
music. The best music there is. Grandpa said he'd learned it as a boy in the

bayous in the twenties. He said his papa would play it on the violin on Saturday nights for the family and the neighbors. Folks sway-dancing and
laughing; the swamps would be charged on Saturday nights. Grandpa had
taken to the accordion and joined his papa in the music-making when he
was only eleven ("I wasn't not'ing but a son den") and could hardly handle
the accordion's bulk between his spindly arms. When his papa followed the
oil boom from the swamps of Louisiana to the plains of West Texas, they
brought the music along. For awhile, Beezville (which was what Grandpa
still called the Flats) had been plugged into the same current that had lit up
the bayous on Saturday nights. But he mostly played for himself now. And
very infrequently.

Two and Darryl, sitting Indian-style on the porch, clapped with the beat.
Grandpa smiled and swayed his head with the pumping accordion. The
smile seemed to be as much a part of his music as the instrument. It replaced the lyrics, which were few, and let the listeners know that no matter
what the words said, the people were together to have a good time.

"*Ma Claire est belle*," Grandpa sang:

> *Say, ma Claire, elle est belle.*
> *Mais les haricots n'sont pas salés*
> *Faut que je la renvoye chez elle.*

He threw back his head, loose sunshine-yellow shirt rustling with his
laughter. "Now, what you tink a dis song?" Grandpa asked, carefully laying
the accordion beside his chair.

"Tops," said Two.

"It was great," said Darryl.

"Ah, you like it."

"What do the words mean?" Darryl asked.

"Tey means: Ma girl Claire, she a beauty. But she no know how to make
my beans, so's I have to send her home."

The boys laughed.

"Naw," Grandpa laughed with them. "High-yalla gals just cain't *cook*," he
said, himself a shade only slightly darker than his shirt; and he laughed
some more. But then he stopped. "What's tat you got on your wrists?"

"Rubber bands," Two said, almost in a whisper and no longer looking at
Grandpa.

"Rubber bands?"

"Yeah."

"Boys, you take tose off now." He was no longer smiling. "You crazy? Cut
off te circulation to your hands." Grandpa Thevenet raised his own to ac-

centuate his point. His hands were beautiful: delicate but strong. They looked sculpted.

When Darryl unwound the bands, he noticed the bulge of veins on his forearms. On Two's, too. Like Hoodie Duncan.

He handed the rubber bands to Two, who was rising.

"We got to go, Grandpa Thevenet," Two said.

"Yeah." Darryl rose, too.

Two said, "Thanks for playing that music for us."

Grandpa Thevenet smiled again. Wide. "You boys don' be so scarce no more. Come by and see me some."

"OK," Two said.

"We will," said Darryl.

And they climbed down off the porch and into the dirt street.

The twins, Fredrick and Dedrick Horton, were walking in the other direction. Two scrawny boys who together might make one normal-sized teenager, they often acted as though, because they were one grade higher in school, they were superior to Darryl and Two. As they approached, Darryl noticed one or the other—Fredrick or Dedrick, he could never tell them apart—snickering and looking toward Two and him.

Two raised a pumped and protruding-vein-covered forearm and pointed at Fredrick and Dedrick. "Y'all see something funny?"

"Yeah," said Fredrick (or maybe it was Dedrick), "you two knot-headed nigros up there samboing like slave days with Grandpa Sambo hisself." The other's laugh (Dedrick's; or maybe it was Fredrick's) was equally derisive.

"If you see a knot-head nigro," Two said, "give him ten dollars." Two waited. "Uh-huh, that's just what I thought."

"If I had ten dollars, you the last niggah see the green on its back."

"You don't wanna be messing with me today, Fredrick . . ."

"I'm Dedrick."

"Don't care who you is," said Two. "You two big-lipped baboons look so much alike, it's like I'm talking to just one of you niggahs anyway. Just don't be messing with the kid. Not today."

"The kid?"

"Yeah," Two said, shaking his head *no* and raising his hands as if in disbelief. "Don't be missing with the kid. Or I'm a have to open me up a can of whoop-ass on you."

"Whoop-ass on who?"

Two looked around. "I don't see nobody else in this road."

Dedrick, leering, squared up on Two. "Well, *kid*, go ahead. Do it then . . ."

Darryl felt Grandpa Thevenet's stare on them and felt suddenly small.

He pulled back Two, who was now face-to-face with and mimicking Dedrick. "C'mon, Two. I've got to go. Jack Mitchell's waiting for me."

Dedrick turned on Darryl. "Well, go on and run after that tomming niggah then. Wasn't nobody talking to you. Oreo."

Darryl felt himself tighten, terror and rage racing through his body so strongly it turned his stomach. His legs felt weak. But he just stared at the other boy, who was now equally quiet.

Two stepped between Darryl and the twins, speaking excitedly. "Man, if I was you, Fredrick . . ."

"I'm Dedrick . . ."

"Don't care who you is, I'd quit that squawking and I'd be walking if I was you. My man Darryl wind up doing you just like I saw him do yo' momma the other day."

Dedrick surged at Two—"Don't be talking about my momma, niggah!"—but Fredrick reined his brother's charge. "Chill, Ded," said Fredrick. "Chill."

Grandpa Thevenet called from his pea-green porch, "Y'all boys cut t'at mess out 'fore I comes down t'ere and whups all ya's skinny tails myself."

Two, pulling Darryl by the shirt, shuffled backward, like an Ali dance step, wearing a victorious smile. Darryl still felt his throat choked up, his legs shaky; but Two, speaking with his hands, his body still dancing, delivered the knockout punch: "Yo, Dedrick. Yo, man . . ." When Dedrick finally calmed enough—leaning against his brother's restraining arm—to listen, Two sang: "I saw yo' momma at Burger King;/ Hit that bitch with a chicken wing!"

Dedrick swung wildly, but Darryl and Two were already laugh-shuffling up the road.

"Chill, Ded." Fredrick struggled to restrain his teary-eyed and flailing-armed twin. "Chill!"

"Yo, Fredrick," Darryl called over his shoulder. "She's your momma, too."

And Darryl and Two, hoofing it up the road, burst out laughing.

Their smiles died when they arrived at the gravel intersection where they would part. Two lived a few houses down the side street. The Three Jacks', cast in the shadows of trees, loomed quietly just a hundred yards up the road.

Looking toward the bar, Darryl said, "Jack Mitchell's going to kill me." Jack Mitchell didn't usually scold Darryl. Over dinner, driving his stepson to and from the Flats, he hardly even spoke. But this was different.

"Maybe they won't know," said Two, looking toward his house. "I'm a tell my daddy we got fired and white man didn't give us nothing."

But Jack Mitchell would know. He'd know how much they got, when they started and when they stopped, and he'd know what Darryl had said in the song. Jack Mitchell and Wiley Edwards and the other councilmen were buddies. In fact, had it been anybody *but* one of them, Jack Mitchell probably wouldn't say anything.

Two patted Darryl on the shoulder, moving past, and he smiled. "Oh well," he said, "can't die but once, and never be deader than that."

Darryl stood, looking down the road at the Three Jacks'. He could hear Two's quarters jingling in his pocket as he jogged toward his house. Then Darryl started walking to face Jack Mitchell. He steeled himself, his step steady and resolved, because he hadn't done anything wrong.

Pool balls' clacking clatter burst over the dusk of the Three Jacks' Bar and Lounge as Darryl entered. After his eyes adjusted to the lack of light, Darryl noticed the other two Jacks, Jack Pickering and Jack Johnston, playing cards at the bar. When he saw Darryl, Jack Pickering pointed over his shoulder. "Your daddy's waiting for you out back."

Marching through, Darryl thought: Jack Mitchell is *not* my daddy. Darryl called him *Dad* when addressing him directly, but otherwise he was always and only *Jack Mitchell*. A nice enough man; his mom's husband, his little sister's father; but not his own daddy. And it wasn't spite that made him feel this way. It was just the truth. So if Jack Mitchell was waiting out back to scold him, well, it disturbed Darryl; because Jack Mitchell was his elder, because he was an authority figure, it cowed Darryl—but it didn't haunt him, because it could involve no fall from grace. Jack Mitchell was not his daddy. Not like Mr. Waymans, the boxer, was to Two.

Jack Mitchell sat heavily in a too-small chair at the desk in the back office. He looked up when Darryl entered, stared, but said nothing.

Darryl stayed where he was, near the door. "Hey," he offered as greeting.

"What happened at the post office?"

"At the post office?" Darryl asked.

"You heard me fine."

Darryl shifted his weight. "Mr. Edwards sent us home," he said.

"Sent you home?" Jack Mitchell's eyes were working to meet Darryl's.

"Yes," Darryl said, looking from Jack Mitchell to his feet.

"Boy, you know better than playing around! . . ."

"We weren't playing around," Darryl said, looking back up. "We were working hard, but he heard us singing and told us to go home."

Jack Mitchell stopped. "Weren't playing around," he said. "But he told you to go home."

"Yes," Darryl said, eyes slipping down to his feet again.

"He told you to go home for a reason, I suppose?"

"For laughing, but we worked hard . . ."

"Boy, you know better than playing around! Laughing! White man sees you playing around and laughing, he thinks you're not working. He thinks you're clowning. Just another lazy niggah wanting a handout"—Jack Mitchell never used the word *nigger*; he said it was beneath him—"and now here *you* go, clowning and playing the fool and acting like a niggah. Is that what you want?" Jack Mitchell asked, and he stared at Darryl. Just stared.

Darryl didn't answer.

"You want to grow up to be nothing?"

He didn't answer. He stood by the door, looking down. When he looked up, Jack Mitchell had put his hat on his head and was rising, no longer even looking at Darryl, looking past him. "Let's go," he said, and he carried his bulk through the door and out of the office.

Darryl followed, a few feet behind, his face trained on the ground. He looked steadily down because he felt tears fighting their way up, and if he couldn't keep them in, he didn't want anybody to see.

"See you all tomorrow," he heard Jack Mitchell say.

The two other Jacks grumbled.

Outside, Darryl followed Jack Mitchell's round shadow to his Chrysler New Yorker. The tears were still there somewhere, but he felt that as long as Jack Mitchell didn't scold him anymore, he could keep them corralled on the inside.

Two would never cry like this. Two would go home and get his tail whipped for wasting his money and cry because of the pain, but never like this. Two would get sent to bed and wake up tomorrow and all would be forgotten, because Two was just a boy growing up, like Mr. Waymans had once been a boy growing up, and it was expected that a boy growing up get into trouble like this. "Spending all your money on games." He could hear Mr. Waymans say, the whip of the belt singing the chorus: "I sure ain't'bout to give you no more." But tomorrow all would be forgotten. Two would come out to play, Mr. Waymans staring on, his face quiet as a closed door, and all would be forgotten.

The inside of the car was too tight. Darryl was very close to Jack Mitchell and couldn't distance himself at all. Inside himself, though, was infinite space in all directions and nowhere anything to hold onto. Behind his eyes, Darryl was in midair, in free fall, and he didn't know when he would hit, nor where, nor how hard would be his landing. Behind his eyes, Darryl could see Grandpa Thevenet's Sambo song and Hoodie Duncan's wolfish leer and the twins' clowning scorn, black faces in blackface, with wide red lips and bug eyes, and laughing . . . These images, dancing in space behind his eyes, were all that Darryl could see. And inside he felt himself falling, falling, falling free.

My Mama, Your Mama

BY CONNIE PORTER

FROM *Imani All Mine*

been inside me to the place I ain't never wanted to know. That's what I was thinking to tell Bett-Bett when she asked me why I wasn't in school this past week. I say to her I been sick. Which is good enough for her to know about my business. I don't need her digging up some bone and passing it around. Last thing she need to know is the truth. That I missed school because of *him*.

I ain't saying his name. I ain't never, ever going to say it. I won't ever put it in my mouth. I don't even want it in my mind, because it's all connected to his face. And the day I seen his face in the cafeteria three weeks ago, I thought I was going to die right there, holding a tray of tacos and fruit cocktail. I seen him coming right at me from the snack line where you pay with money, not lunch tickets. He had a whole tray of fries and he ain't even see me. But I seen him and dropped my tray on the floor and run out the cafeteria. I ain't stop running until I got to the lavatory, even though this security guard started chasing me, screaming, Where you think you going? What you done did?

But he couldn't come in the lavatory. Wasn't nothing but these girls in there combing they heads and looking at theyselves in the mirror. I went in a stall and locked the door and I had to shit real bad. I usually can't go in a public place, but I couldn't hold it and I even sat down on the seat. Then this lady security guard come banging on the door of the stall I was in. Who in there? she ask.

I say, I'm sick. Can you just leave me alone? I ain't done nothing. I'm sick, is all.

She sick, I hear one them girls say. Hell, she smell like she dying. Then they laughed and I heard them leave. I was so embarrassed.

The security say, What you was running for? You know you ain't supposed to be running in the building.

And I'm thinking, Why she standing out there smelling my shit and asking me stupid questions? But I just say, I had to go.

She say, All right. I'll let you off this time. Next time you getting detention.

Then she left, too, and it was just me there with that boy name inside my head. With that boy name inside my mouth so nasty-tasting that I hocked and spit right on the floor. My knees was shaking like before. Like then.

That night. I wished Eboni was with me but she ain't even in school now. She having two twins and her doctor say she need to be home in bed. She already know they girls, and she done picked out names. Asia and Aisha. I wanted to cry but it seem like my tears is all dried up in me and they left some craziness behind like salt. I could taste it in my mouth when I spit.

All I could think to do was get out of school, and I went right straight to the nurse to get me a excuse. The nurse a white man here at Lincoln. Who ever heard of a man a nurse? He act like he ain't want to let me go home.

I'm sick, I say.

Is that so? he say. He was reading a book and snapping gum like a girl. Then he ask, What time does your soap opera come on, girl? One or two?

I say, Excuse me. I'm for real. It's my stomach. I got my period and I got some bad cramps. I done bled through three straight pads this morning.

He looked at me like he done heard that excuse a thousand times before and say, I don't care if you go home or not. It's no skin off my nose, hon.

Static. Static. Static. That's the thing be getting to me about school. Elementary school. Middle school. High school. Ain't no difference. It's all the time some teacher nem act like they know you. Act like they can shine a light inside your head and see what you thinking.

I ain't say nothing to that nurse. I let him think that my head was so empty that all I want to do was fill it watching some stupid-ass soaps about a bunch of skinny white women wearing expensive clothes and living in fancy houses even if they supposed to be poor and having a bunch of make-believe problems. Black women, too. They lives be just like the white women's. Fake. I got real problems. So I kept my mouth all shut up and got my excuse.

Then I got Imani from the nursery. She was sleeping, looking just like *me*. Even though I can't say I know what I really look like when I sleep, because I be sleeping and can't see myself. But it's got to be just like Imani. My eyes shut real tight like I'm studying on something. Like there be something in my dreams I especially want to see.

Mrs. Poole say babies dream. She say don't nobody know what they dream about. Sometime Imani be laughing in her sleep. If it's night, she be waking me up. I jump up thinking that girl wake. But she ain't, and I stand over her crib looking at her. I know Imani got to be dreaming about something. I be hoping it's me. Wishing there was a way I could climb down inside her dream and shine a light on me holding her in my arms. Seeing me rocking her in my arms strong like the branches of the tree outside my bedroom window. And her laughing because I'm rocking her higher and higher, past all the soft leaves and into the dark where the moon rising over us and she know she safe because I'm holding her and won't never ever let her fall.

When I was little, sometime I would wake up laughing. I never could remember exactly about what. I like to think it was Mama and me I was laughing about. That she was holding me with love all in her arms.

There wasn't no way I was going home that time of day. Mama would just have some more static for me, so I went over to Eboni. Miss Lovey wasn't there. Eboni was, and she wasn't even in bed like she was supposed to be. She was in the kitchen, making Buffalo wings. Her school tutor was already gone for the day. She ask me, Girl, what's the matter?

I was wondering if I looked so bad. If I looked so crazy. If that boy name was wrote right across my face. I say, I had to cut out early because I wasn't feeling good. Eboni know me real good. I know she could tell that wasn't all. But she say, Have lunch with me.

Imani was still sleep and I put her down in Eboni room and finished up making the chicken while Eboni sat down. I told her, You know you shouldn't even be on your feet.

Eboni say, Shoot, I'm hungry and I'm eating for three people.

I say, You should have wait until your mama come home. Miss Lovey a good cook.

Eboni say, She don't cook like I want. The doctor got me off salt and I ain't supposed to be eating fried foods. I done gained seventy-five pounds.

I ain't say nothing to Eboni about her weight. Because it wouldn't be nothing but the pot calling the kettle black. I'd already dumped almost a half block of some government butter in the skillet to melt over the wings. I got the hot sauce and had poured on a half of a big bottle, and Eboni say, Put on more.

You crazy, I say. They hot enough and that sauce full of salt.

She say, Then add some cayenne.

I put in a whole heap and Eboni took the plate of wings I fixed up for her with blue cheese and celery. She was eating them wings and slinging bones like she was starving. I sat there all quiet like, just watching the pile of empty bones grow on her plate.

She say, I know something really wrong with you if you ain't eating nothing. What happened at school?

I seen him, I say with my voice as flat as I could make it, trying to sound like I was feeling real normal and had some sense. Like the craziness ain't take me all over.

Who? Peanut? she ask.

I say, Not no Peanut. I don't care nothing about no Peanut. I seen *him.* You know who I mean. For a few seconds I think Eboni didn't know who I was talking about until she looked at me real hard in the face and I just know she seen that boy name wrote there.

Oooh, she say, sucking grease off her fingers. No, you ain't even seen *him.*

I did, I say. Right in the cafeteria. I guess he been there all the time. Ain't no way I would've ever come to Lincoln if I know that's where he go.

Eboni say, You should transfer. When I have the twins, I ain't coming back to Lincoln. I'm going to East. It's closer. Come with me.

Soon as Eboni say that, I got a pain right in my stomach like I needed to go to the bathroom again. I was thinking, How I'm going to tell Mama I want to switch schools? If I ain't want to after the shooting last month, ain't no way she was going to believe I want to do it now.

Lincoln ain't that kind of school where there be shootings and stabbings like it's a regular way of life. It ain't locked down like a prison and you got to be passing through metal detectors and getting patted down. Wasn't never even no shooting there until that day.

We was just being dismissed. I had got Imani from the nursery and had her in her stroller. We was in the main hall, where there was like two hundred to three hundred kids, when all these other kids come busting back in the main doors, running and screaming. They shooting. They shooting outside, they was screaming. And they kept on running right up the hall, pushing past people. Teachers. Kids. They even knocked down a security guard. Then all the kids already in the hall started running. I swear my heart wasn't even beating I was so scared. I thought they was going to run right over me and Imani. I snatched my baby out her stroller. Her leg got caught in the strap. I jerked her hard and got her loose just as I got smashed into some lockers. But I bounced off. I ain't have to think about where to go. The crowd carried me into the front office, where the principal and secretaries nem be. I got pushed behind the main desk where the secretaries was already on the floor. Everybody kept on pushing and screaming and I almost fell. Then I heard the principal, Mr. Diaz, yelling for us to all lay down. Get down, he say. Get down. Stay down!

I fell right where I was and landed on some girl who ain't say nothing. Then this boy landed right on top of me and Imani. And Imani started screaming. My baby, I say. You squashing my baby. Get off!

He was crying. Big old boy, too, with hair on his face. I wasn't crying. But I could feel my heart then going like crazy. Imani wasn't hurt. She was scared. Her eyes was all big like she want me to tell her what was going on. But I ain't know. I just held her tight to me.

Mr. Diaz jumped over the main desk like he was Superman or something. One of the secretaries was screaming, Mr. Diaz don't go out there. But he kept right on going. I could hear him in the halls telling kids to get down.

I ain't hear no gunshots. But all I could think was somebody was dead right outside the school and if I'd stepped out them doors a few minutes earlier it could've been me or Imani. Or whoever was shooting could run right on in the building and kill us where we was laying. I started shaking then. Thinking, Who would ever want to die like this? On some regular old schoolday. At some regular old school laying under a desk too scared to move. I wanted to go home.

Mr. Diaz come back in a few minutes and say for us all to return to homeroom. Don't go out the building until I say to. After the police come. Then he got on the intercom. Saying for everybody to stay calm and if they was hurt, to come to the nurse office.

I was still shaking when I left the office. The halls was packed and some kids was crying and others was laughing. These boys was saying that some dude got shot in the butt, that was all. They was laughing and other kids was laughing. Even some who was crying started laughing. Books and papers and backpacks everywhere. There was sneakers laying right where kids had run out of them. Half of the lockers open. I seen my stroller. It wasn't bad off. It was real dirty where it got stepped on, and one of the arms was bent, but I could still push it.

Me and Mama and Miss Odetta watched the news that night, and the shooting was on every channel. The boy was really only shot in the butt and they didn't keep him at the hospital. They say his wound was superficial. Mr. Diaz come on the news, looking all smooth. Like nothing happened. He say our school a good school and they ain't never had no problem like this. The boy that was shot didn't go to our school. It's outside agitators. All the while he saying this, some kids was jumping up and down in the background and making faces, laughing. Then they interviewed this girl and boy who say they seen a jeep. It started going slow and pulled up in front of a bus. Then *pow pow pow pow pow*. Like it's the Wild Wild West. That's all they seen, because they ran back inside. The newsman say it's a miracle nobody else got hurt or killed.

Miss Odetta say, They ain't going to catch nobody. You wait and see.

Mama say, Ain't this some shit? In front a school. They could've killed a bunch of kids. Them the kind of niggers don't care about nobody. I'm telling you. You ain't safe no goddamn place no more.

I say, They was probably all some drug dealers coming by our school messing things up.

Miss Odetta say, That ain't got to be true. Why it got to be about drugs? She pulled a cigarette out her bra and lighted it. Then she say, Shit. Niggers was getting shot before there ever was drug dealers.

Mama give me a look and smile behind Miss Odetta back. Me and her knew not to say nothing else. We know Miss Odetta just say that because of June Bug. Miss Odetta know we know that June Bug dealing. Miss Odetta the one act like what he do is all right. Living on the down low in her basement. You can't say nothing having to do with drugs without Miss Odetta throwing her two cent in. And what I really want to be doing when she do is throw her back a penny in change.

Mama say, They need to catch them and throw they asses under the jail.

Miss Odetta say, Don't hold your breath.

Mama asked if I want to go to another school. I told her I didn't. I got my daycare and everything all set up at Lincoln.

Mr. Diaz had a assembly the next day to tell us everything was safe. Even though I was thinking he can't stop some fool from shooting. I mean, damn, if he can do that, he need to come around my way. Because they still be shooting around here. If there's some shooting when me and Imani is up late, she don't look at me like she done the first time she heard it. Like she got a question. Seem like she done already figured out the answer.

So things just settled back down to regular at Lincoln. The only trouble was that mess girls keep going. There some jealous girls go to our school. A group of bitches who roam in packs. They don't like you if you pretty, so I don't have no problems with them. They don't even see me. They hunt girls like Coco. Two of them bitches beat Coco up in a lavatory. Ain't no way skinny little Coco stand a chance against no two girls. They ripped five extensions out her head right from the root. Tore her shirt and bra right off her. Scratched up her face. Coco say they told her she wasn't nothing. She wasn't shit. Coco ain't tell who it was. She too scared.

I know how she feel about not telling. Even though she know who them girls is. She got to see them every day. But she keep right on going like they ain't even there. With a secret. Ever since she was jumped, Coco carry a knife. Not no little one, neither. She showed it to me. It's a butcher knife like your mama keep in the kitchen drawer and be chopping on meat with. She have it right in her backpack inside one of her notebooks. She keep the pack half zipped so she can get to it easy.

He say he had a knife. That night. He ain't never show it to me. He say if he had to show it to me, he was going to have to use it on me. So he kept it like a secret.

When I was talking to Eboni that day after I seen him at school, I was thinking maybe that was what I need. A secret to keep me safe. Maybe I could sneak a knife out the house without Mama knowing, or go down to the Woolworth and buy one down in they basement. I'd be like Coco, have it where I could get to it easy. If he was to say something to me, he'd know all about it. I'd stab his ass right in the broad daylight in the cafeteria. But that was just that dried-up craziness in me. There ain't no way I could do something like that. Not having Imani. I don't know what she'd do if I was took from her or she was took from me.

Greasing on her chicken wings Eboni say to me, You should do like you should of done in the first place, Tasha. Tell your mama. I got me another pain in my stomach. I say, My mama ain't your mama. If Miss Lovey was my mama, I would've told her straight off. Eboni say, *My mother. Your mother. Live across the way. Fifteen. Sixteen. East Broadway.* It was a song we'd sing when we was picking sides for kickball. We'd be lining ourselves up so we could end up on the same side. Eboni knew I'd give her the next lines of the song. *Every night they have a fight and this is what they say. Icka Bicka Backa Soda Cracker. Out. Go. She.* We finished up together.

But I say to her, I'm for real, Eboni. You know I can't tell my mama. And don't you be even telling Miss Lovey. Eboni was sucking on a bone and making no promises to me.

When Imani woke up, I took her on home. It was still light out. Before I unlocked the front door, I stood on the porch and erased my face. I closed my eyes and wrote on it that I just come from another boring day of school, because I knew the first thing I would see was Mama sitting on the couch looking me dead in the mouth when I walked in. But she wasn't sitting there. The house ain't had no smell like some dinner had been cooking, neither. It smelled like perfume. I knew right then Mama was going out.

She done met some man I ain't even seen yet. He call sometime. All he say is can he speak to Earlene. Then she take the call up in her room. The thing is, he been calling for over a month and ain't never been to our house. Mama meet him off somewhere. That make me think he ain't got no car. Or she don't want me meeting him.

I went upstairs with Imani and peeked in Mama room. It was a mess. Her dresser top was covered with all kinds of makeup and brushes and sponges. Her shoes was all in a heap on the floor, and it looked like she throwed all her outfits across her bed. All it seem she decided on to wear was her nice bra and drawers. The kind men be liking. All black and made from lace.

Mama was sitting on the end of the bed with her face all made up, looking all pretty and soft, putting lotion on her legs. Her body all skinny like she ain't never had a baby. Even her stomach flat. It got only a few thin stretch marks that circle her belly button like the petals on a flower. They so tiny you can't hardly even see them. It's like I was in her but barely left no sign I was there.

She say, Come on in here, Tasha.

I could only get the door part open. I squeezed in with Imani on my hip.

Mama say, I was fenna to leave you a note. But you here now. I'm going out. There's a food stamp on the kitchen table if you want to go up to the Arabian store and get yourself something for dinner.

I ask, Where you going, Mama?

She say, Out. And smile like a girl going on a date. I don't know. Maybe she feel like a girl. Mama ain't nothing but thirty-two.

I ask, Well, when you coming back?

When I feel like it, Mama say. Girl, I'm grown. I know my way home. Why you in my business? Do I be in your business?

I say, Yeah, Mama, you do be.

And Mama laugh and snap the bottle of lotion shut. You damn straight I be in your business. Because I'm the mama and you the child. It's my job to know your business. Did you take your pill today, Tasha?

I say, I did. I always take it, Mama. You going out with Royster? I ask. Even though I know it ain't been him calling. Mama busted out laughing, and me too. Even Imani laughed like she knew who we was talking about.

Child, Mama say, I ain't even going out with the Jherri Curl King no more.

Mama was dating Royster before Imani was born. I never did like him. Royster old enough to be Mama daddy. He all the time had a plastic bag on his head that stuck to his bald spot in the middle. Mostly I ain't like him because he married. What Mama want with a married man, I don't know. Miss Odetta got her this married man Simpkin she been going out with ever since I can remember. He give Miss Odetta money. Maybe Mama thought Royster going to give her money. But he never gave her none I ever seen.

Mama got up from the bed and I sat down behind her with Imani. Imani started squirming and whining to get down. I ain't want to let her down in all that mess. She wasn't going to do nothing but put something in her mouth. These days she be putting all kinds of things in her mouth she find on the floor. I bounced her on my lap. Imani liked that.

Mama say, If you go up to the store, get some more bread. She was pulling on a pair of tight jeans.

I say, I don't think I'm going. I don't feel so good.

Mama put on a red blouse and left the top three buttons open. Then she come over to me, kicking shoes out the way. She put the back of her hand to my head. It was all cool, and I smelled her perfume sweet like some candy. I could see right down her shirt to her titties.

Mama say, You cool as a cucumber, girl.

I say, It's my stomach.

Mama say, Tasha, you just need to sit on the toilet. You probably constipated. Seem like you trying to get me to stay home with you tonight like you some baby.

I ain't say nothing. I looked at Imani. She got hold of Mama housedress and was chewing on a button. Mama went over to the mirror, brushing her hair. I did want Mama to stay home. But I ain't want to say it.

Mama say, Miss Odetta right next door if you need something. She was still looking in the mirror.

Imani need changing, I say. When I took the button out her mouth, she start crying, so I knew it was time for me to leave. I went to my room. Maybe I *was* being a baby. But I ain't want to see Mama go out. I turned my radio up all loud so I wouldn't have to hear the front door shut.

That evening I went on with the routine of feeding Imani and getting her ready for bed. When I put her in the tub, she kept on saying, Dada. Dada. She been saying that for a while now, but when she say it that night, it made me think of *him*. I washed off her tongue with the washcloth. Trying to wash that word right out her mouth. Don't you be saying that, I say. You say Mama. Mama.

Imani wasn't even stutting me. She kept right on saying Dada like she been saying. When I went to wipe out her mouth again, she grabbed hold of the rag and sucked on it like it was a bottle. My baby probably thought I was crazy. Which I ain't. I was just on my way.

She went right to sleep after I give her a bottle, so I ain't had no excuse for not doing homework. I left Imani in her crib, went on downstairs, and turned on the TV. I had a Latin test coming up on Friday. But I couldn't even keep my mind on my work. I wanted to talk to somebody. I thought about calling Eboni. But she had already told me what she thought I should do. So I picked up the phone and called Peanut. I ain't even let it ring one whole time before I hung up. I knew he ain't want me calling him.

Like the nut he is, Peanut done left Lincoln. He transferred to South Park High. We don't mess around no more. I don't know. I think he done changed. He act like he don't want to be with me now. Maybe he sick of doing it with me. If I call him, he act like I'm bothering him. He always got some excuse to get off the phone real quick. He tired. He on the other line. He doing homework. Like he do homework! He made the basketball team there. J.V. He say that keep him busy. But I know he ain't just getting busy with no basketball. I know he seeing another girl.

Coco the one brung me that bone. Her cousin go to South Park, too, and Coco say her cousin say Peanut be with this mixed girl. He be kissing her on the bus. It's not like I love him or nothing. I miss being with Peanut. Kissing him. I don't really miss doing it with him. He do it so fast. I always just wanted to get back to the kissing. I be dreaming about him sometime. That his long eyelashes is tickling my neck and I wake up laughing, and then be mad because it was only a dream.

It seem like after you been with somebody, after they done been all up inside you, that you could call them up. That you could say anything to them. Like, Hey, there's something that's bothering me. I don't want you to do nothing but listen to me talk. To let me get this boy name out my mind. To get his name out my mouth. Off my face. You think a person could do that. But I ain't even try it with Peanut. If I would've called him up and he had rushed me off the phone like I wasn't nothing to him. Like he was so great and I was just some stupid bitch he was throwing table scraps to by actually talking to me for two minutes on the phone. I would've gone all the way to crazy.

I ain't had nobody to talk to. I couldn't tell Mama about him. I couldn't tell her about that night. How stupid I was that night, the summer before Imani was born. Thinking he really liked me. As fat as I am. As black as I am. As much as my body look like it ain't never supposed to be loved by no boy. Touched by no boy. That's why I went from Skate-A-Rama with him instead of staying there like I should have. Because he say he liked me! I was smiling back too. Eboni wasn't there, because she was home on punishment. I wasn't skating much, because I'd rented a smaller size skate than what I really take. I was wearing a nine then, and I ain't want that big red number blazing out from the back of my skate, telling the world how big my feet was. So I got me a size seven. They was real cute on my feet while I was sitting down on a bench looking at them. He come up to me while I was sitting down judging my feet. He ain't even have on no skates. He ain't say nothing at first. Just sat there. I pretended like I was watching everybody skate so I could sneak a look at him. I can't say he looked fine to me. Because he didn't. He was big. Bigger than me and he had good hair. It wasn't no curl neither he was trying to fake up to look like good hair. His hair wasn't at all greasy, and he had it just long enough so you could see it had a natural curl to it. When I turned my head away, he say something to me. I ain't hear what he say because the music was so loud. So he slid up next to me and screamed loud in my ear his name. He ask me my name and I told him. The music was so loud, I couldn't hardly hear nothing he say. I did hear his name real clear and I heard him say he like me. We ended up going outside, because it was too loud to talk in there.

I turned in my skates and got my hand stamped so I could come back inside. You can't get no skates again, the lady behind the counter say. This session end in a half hour. You done for the night. I told her that was all right. Then I went out with him. Just to the parking lot, where we can talk, he say. There was some kids hanging out there. They was talking all loud. I wasn't stutting them. But he took hold of my hand and kept on walking. Where we going? I ask. Around the back, he say. Where it's more quieter. We can talk back there. You ain't scared of the dark, is you? No, I say. I ain't scared of no dark. And me, like a stupid stupid fool, walked right on with him. Like we was some couple just walking in love. I wasn't really thinking about no love with him. I was thinking about him saying, I like you, Tasha. Like he mean it. Like I was someone special to him. Like I was someone special to somebody even if it was a lie.

It was cool out even though it was August. Soon as we went around back, I could smell him. I don't know why I ain't smell him inside. But out in the dark quiet he smelled like smoke. Me and him went up this little hill into these trees and he took off his jacket for me to sit on. I don't even remember what we talked about, because we only talked a couple minutes. I know he never did say again that he liked me. I would've remembered that. He never said I was pretty or nothing before he kissed me right in the mouth. It wasn't like I never kissed a boy before. I did kiss this Puerto Rican boy two times around Eboni house and let him touch me outside my clothes. But when he was kissing me that night, I ain't like it. His mouth tasted real nasty. I tasted dirt before, when I was little, and his mouth tasted worse than dirt. I guess his mouth was like that from smoking. Like some nasty little animal had done crawled inside his mouth and built a nest.

All the while he steady kissing me and I'm steady trying not to breathe. Trying not to swallow so I wouldn't taste him while he was laying me back to the cold ground. I pulled my mouth away and say, Get on up off me. I don't know what you trying to do.

He say, What you want me to do. And he steady pushing me down harder. I could feel it then. His thing. It was pressing up inside my legs. All hard and mad inside his jeans. I tried to sit up. But he pressed his whole weight on me, squashing my titties so hard they hurt.

Hey, I screamed, leave me alone! Get up off of me! He put one of his big hands across my nose and mouth. I was screaming and kicking and trying to peel his hand off. But my screams wasn't doing no good. They was so tiny they never even escaped the trees. That's all I could hear, even though that boy talking to me real low with his face right in mine.

I don't know how many times he say, I got a knife. I got a knife. Before I heard it. But when I heard that, I stopped trying to scream. I stopped trying to fight.

Then he say, If I got to show it to you, I'm going to have to use it on you. Now shut up, you fat bitch, and take down your fucking pants. I had already shut up. He took his hand off my face and raised up off of me some. But I ain't move. So he pulled at my sweat pants. That's when I started helping him, because I was thinking he going to tear them, and how was I going to explain that to Mama?

It was the both of us that got them halfway down when he say for me to turn over and get on my knees. He raised up some more to let me turn over and I could see the lights of the Skate-A-Rama coming through the tops of the trees. When I turned over, he pushed my head down to the ground and

I couldn't see nothing no more. I ain't hear nothing until he pushed his naked self up against me and started doing it. And my hands grabbed for something to hold.

Hanging on to the grass, I swear I could hear them screams of mine quieter and quieter sinking into the ground. All the time I'm thinking, This ain't real. This got to be a dream. Not my dream. His dream. He done thought this all up in his mind. Had this all up in his mind. When I was thinking about him liking me, he was thinking about this. I'm all embarrassed with my butt all tooted up in the air and him sticking his thing in me harder and harder. Faster and faster. It seem like to me his thing was a knife. Mad with me. Cutting me. My insides was burning a little bit more. A little bit more. A little bit more. I couldn't stop my knees from shaking, and I was holding my breath in me to stop the pain.

He put his face right up next to mine and his breath come right in my ear. It was so strong I could taste it in my mouth. You know you like it, you stupid cunt, he say. Tell me you like it. Tell me to fuck you some more.

I ain't say nothing. He grabbed me by the hair. My breath come out in a moan.

He say, Yeah, that's right. That's right. He pushed my face back to the ground and got up off me. You can tell anybody you want, he say. I don't give a goddamn. Ain't nobody going to believe your dumb ass no way. He yanked his jacket up from under me. I heard him take off out them trees.

It was a while before I even moved. I don't know how long I stayed just like he left me, still burning inside. When I figured he was gone, really gone, I rolled over on my side and touched myself quick down there to see if I was bleeding. I was all wet. I ain't know if it was blood. The night was so dark, even with the yellow lights shining above me in the leaves. So I pulled my pants up and brushed myself off. My knees wouldn't stop shaking. But I got up. I ain't even went back in the Skate-A-Rama. I ain't even went back through the parking lot the way I came. I was shamed. I went around the other side and waited for the bus home. Spitting. Spitting. Spitting all the time I was waiting.

Mama was sitting on the couch when I got home. Watching TV with the lights out. She ain't even look up when I come in. It was a Friday night and she like to watch a cop show that come on. Mama say, Lock the door behind you. Which I did, and went right straight upstairs into the bathroom and pulled down my pants and panties. There wasn't no whole bunch of blood like I was expecting to see. Only a little spot, already turning dark like a old penny. That made me feel better. Like things wasn't so bad. Like I wasn't going to have to tell Mama about it because it was just a bad dream anyway.

I took me a shower and brushed my teeth with the water running all over me. I kept brushing them and brushing them, squirting out long white worms of toothpaste until my mouth tasted fresh and clean like mouths be on commercials. Like mint. Then I washed myself. I ain't even want to touch myself down there in my private parts. But I squatted down, with my knees still shaking, and washed off real gentle but real good two times. I wasn't burning like I was before.

When I laid down in bed that night, with the moon shining through the tree outside my window, with the moon shining down on me, I wanted to get up and go downstairs and tell Mama. I should have told her right then. I was so shamed. Even though my mouth was clean, seem like when I just thought of that boy, I got that nasty taste in my mouth again, and I wiped off my tongue with the back of my hand. I ain't want Mama to think it was me that was the nasty one. But I wanted her to come to me in my room that night because I was quiet. Because I had come in and gone straight upstairs. Which I never did. Showered without being told and got right into bed with no radio playing. No light on. No nothing. How come Mama ain't know that wasn't even me acting like that? What was she thinking about if she wasn't thinking about me? Royster, the Jherri Curl King?

When I was a little girl, if I was out of her sight and quiet for a minute, it seem like Mama would come to me. I would look up to see her face over me. Full and shining like the moon. Mama would watch me until she was satisfied I was all right and then she would slip away quiet. Quiet as the setting of the moon. I wouldn't even know she was gone until I looked up and seen she wasn't there.

I hid in the dark of my room that night like I was some little girl too shamed to tell on myself for doing something so stupid. Mama always been the one thinking I'm so smart. I'm so special. That I'm the one who has got a brain that's going to take me somewhere in my life. Maybe Mama think I got a brain that will take her somewhere too one day. Put her in a fine house. But that night I wasn't none of the things Mama say about me. I was what *he* say I was. All them nasty words he called me. Words Mama never would let me put in my mouth to say. *Fat bitch. Stupid cunt.* How I was going to open my mouth and say them words? Just thinking about them set me off crying. Not like I was crazy. I ain't make nam sound. And why ain't Mama come? She could've pushed the door to my room open and when the light of the hall fell on me she would've seen my face. Telling her what my two lips couldn't.

But Mama ain't come to me that night, and after then it was just easier to keep my mouth shut and let Mama think I was good and not nasty. So I opened up this place inside to leave everything he done and said to me. Not like it never happened. Because it did happen. But I found a place where I could close it off, and I really did think like some child, like some girl, like some fool, I wasn't never going to have to go inside it again.

After seeing *him* in the cafeteria, I knew that wasn't true. No matter how it looked to anybody, for the next two days after I seen him, I went back to that place. I was in it each night, curled up inside like some big old baby waiting to be born.

Instead of going to school, I went to Eboni's. Miss Lovey was home, looking after her state kids. She ain't say nothing to me about nothing when me and Imani went back in Eboni room and stayed until the tutor left. She ain't ask why I was there. I knew Eboni had told her. But I knew she wouldn't say nothing to my mama. Out in the kitchen, she made me one of her big meals. I could smell a chicken baking, greens boiling away with vinegar and hot pepper. Yams roasting with they sweet juice dripping in the stove. My stomach was making all kinds of noise just smelling how good that food was going to taste. But when it came time to eat it, I really ain't had no appetite.

I sat down with Eboni and Miss Lovey and them state kids in the kitchen. Miss Lovey made her and the oldest state kid a plate. He about three and he don't eat so much. His mama was on crack when she had him. Miss Lovey get WIC and food stamps. She be getting government cheese and butter, and he still so skinny he look like he could fall over if you blow on him. All he was eating was a teaspoon of food. Eboni, shoot, she was eating like food was going out of style at the end of the day. I ate me a plate just to be polite to Miss Lovey.

I went around Eboni house the next day, too, but on the third day Eboni wasn't there. Miss Lovey was all out of breath and sweating when she come to the door. She say, Come on in the kitchen. And I went. Miss Lovey was making grits and frying up some fish. She say, Eboni had her girls early this morning. I'm telling you, it was a easy labor. They were a minute apart. It seems like they were racing to get in the world. They're both healthy thank God and so pretty with good hair swirled around their heads. I say, Oooh, I want to go see her and the babies. Miss Lovey say, I'm sure Eboni wants to see you, too. You can leave Imani next door where I left the kids and we can go up to the hospital later. She made herself a plate and one for me.

I say, I ain't really hungry. I already ate.

Miss Lovey wasn't even stutting me. She opened up the stove and took out a pan of biscuits and put two on my plate. For a while she ain't say nothing. She ate. Sprinkling hot sauce on her fish. Slurping from a big cup of juice. Putting jelly and butter on her biscuits. I cracked open one of them hot biscuits and buttered and jellied it for Imani, who was sitting in her stroller whining because she knew there was food but wasn't none of it com-

ing to her mouth. I fed some to her and tasted it for myself. It was good. I
could tell it wasn't from no can popped open on the counter. Then I looked
up at Miss Lovey and stopped eating. She had that I-know-you-got-a-secret
look on her face. Right then I knew Eboni must have told.

You know, Miss Lovey say, I been meaning to talk to you.

I cut her right off. Not in a mean way. But I say, I know what you fenna
say, Miss Lovey.

Miss Lovey say, Is that so? If you know what I'm going to say, you need to
be on one of those psychic telephones making some money for yourself,
child.

I bust out laughing, even though I ain't want to.

Miss Lovey put one of her hands on top of one of mines. It was warm
and soft.

She say, Child, you have to go back to school. Shooting the hook won't
solve your problems.

I say, I know that, Miss Lovey.

She say, You don't act like it. I know you're scared of that boy who
raped you.

I looked down at the table. That was the first time that word been said.

Then Miss Lovey said it again. She say, I believe he did rape you.

I ain't say nothing. Miss Lovey reached over with her other hand and
started rubbing my back. Round and round in circles like you rub a baby
back to get them to sleep. Like I rub Imani. She say, It's all right to talk to
me about it.

I couldn't say nothing. I just found my hand that was on the table
squeezing her hand tight tight. Miss Lovey ain't ask me to say nothing else.
She moved up close to me and put my head down on her shoulder and kept
rubbing my back with her hand all warm. Pulling me back from inside myself. She was pulling me back every time she made a circle. Made a circle.
Made a circle. It was like she was looking for the place I was. Reaching
down inside that cold dark with her warm hand. Picking me up from that
ground. Pulling me out into the world where I opened my eyes into the soft
light.

It was a while before I lifted up my face. When Imani saw it she started
crying. Miss Lovey picked her up and put her on her lap to rock her. She fed
some grits to Imani right off her plate. Miss Lovey say, Go back to Lincoln
on Monday and see how you feel. If you want to get out, I'll help you.

I say, Only my mama can do that.

Miss Lovey say, I'll talk to your mother then.

I just shook my head.

Miss Lovey say, I won't tell her nothing you haven't. It's up to you to tell
her about the rape. She needs to hear that from your lips. But you need to

be in school. What kind of future can you make for this child with no education? I looked at my little greedy baby and she put out her arms to come to me and I took her in my arms. I was holding her all close feeling her heart beating up next to mines. Miss Lovey say for me not be worrying about going to another school. She say I would only have to cross that bridge if I come to it.

I made myself go back to Lincoln the next Monday. I was real nervous. About running into him. But I had so much schoolwork to catch up on, I spent most of my time with my mind on that. In the cafeteria I was looking for him and not looking for him, thinking maybe I wouldn't have to come to that bridge at all. It was the middle of the week before I seen him. Me and Coco was sitting together at lunch. I wasn't hardly eating. I was studying for a Latin test. When the bell rung we was rushing to take our trays up. That's when I seen him, just ahead of us at the dish room, putting his dirty tray on the belt. There I was at the bridge. I wasn't even thinking about crossing it. I wanted to jump off. Kids was pushing up behind me to take they trays back. My feet took on a mind of they own and ain't even move when he turned around to leave.

Coco stepped up right next to me and took my tray. What's wrong with you, Tasha? she asked. Making us late?

That boy looked up then. I got a pain in my stomach, thinking he heard my name. But he ain't even look at me. He was looking at Coco. Smiling at her. She sucked her teeth and rolled her eyes at him, and the smile he had on his face slid right off. He walked off without saying nothing.

I seen him the next day in the cafeteria, and he walked right on by me without noticing me. I knew I wasn't going to cross no bridge after all. I could feel it in my heart that he ain't know who I was. I was some girl with no name. I was some girl with no face. I was just some girl in a dream he ain't even remember.

FROM **Rails Under My Back**

BY JEFFREY RENARD ALLAN

Sunlight aroused Jesus from sleep. He pushed himself upright on the couch, and sat there, groggy, trying to clear his head against the growing hum of morning traffic.

Damn! His flesh luminous with heat. His feet cold. He looked down at them. No shoes. He could see No Face, fuzzy, cloudy, dim. No Face! he screamed.

No Face's black eye patch glowed like the barrel hole of a fired gun. I be dog. We fell asleep.

Nigga, what the fuck!

Some powerful shit. No Face's head hung suspended between his knees, a heavy balloon.

Every inch of Jesus's skin was alive, seeing, watching himself move in a dream. Bitch, what did you put in that weed? Jesus grabbed No Face by his collar and jerked him to his feet.

Nuthin. Somebody had stuck a red moon and a black moon in his face where the eyes should be. I told you I—

You can get hurt like that, seriously hurt. Hardly getting the words out, throat clogged with hate, each word anger-clotted.

But—

Jesus shoved him back on the couch. The sunlight scorched Jesus's socked-but-shoeless feet. Where my goddamn shoes? Once again he snatched No Face up from the couch.

No Face pointed. Red color began to bleed from his eye. He adjusted his black patch. Over there. By the couch. Jesus pushed No Face down like crumbs off of a table. Mamma musta put them over there while—

Jesus quickly shoved his warm shoes on his feet. I ain't never heard of no Buddha making nobody sleep like that. Pass out. He checked his pockets. Found everything in order. I mean, it's tomorrow already. I mean. He sat down on the couch.

The pipe on the coffee table had been cleaned of ashes.

I be dog.

Where'd you get that shit?

From Keylo. He musta gave me some of that crazy shit. Whacked. Nigga always be jokin around.

You lucky I don't . . . Jesus rested the words.

It's cool, No Face said. We're cool. Hey, you wanna watch some TV?

No.

We can watch some.

Bitch, do it look like I watch TV?

No Face studied the words, magnified them under the lens of his one eye. Well, what you wanna do?

Jesus felt a hole in his stomach, growing and spreading. His hands ran an orbit around his belly. Got anything to eat?

Sure.

He followed No Face to the refrigerator. Watched him open it. Almost threw up when he saw old cooking grease inside a mason jar, brown and gray like a rotting limb.

See anything you want? If you don't, we go down to Mamma Henry's house. She keep our meat in her freezer. And Mamma—

I know, Jesus said. I can't wait.

They took out some leftover meat loaf and ate it cold and fast, then drank milk, right from the gallon jug, sharing swigs until the plastic container was whistle-empty.

You can take a shower. No Face's anxious eye watched Jesus. I got some clothes you can wear. We go shoot some hoop.

Jesus looked at him. You lucky to be alive.

No Face directed his good eye somewhere else.

Real lucky.

Look. The eye returned. I got some of my own shit.

I don't wanna try no mo of yo shit. I mean—

You don't know me from Adam. I told you, that wasn't mine. Keylo gave me that. Look, I'll take you to my kitty so we can smoke us some real—

Nawl. I don't wanna smoke no mo.

Cool.

You lucky to be alive.

We can pick up some oysters.

What?

Oysters. Wit hot sauce.

That's what you like?

That's what I like.

Funny. Spokesman used to eat that.

Who?

Never mind. Jus somebody from back in the day. You don't know him.

So why—

It's cool. You can eat. I'll watch.

I ain't hungry. Let's shoot some hoop.

Some hoop?

Yeah, you know. No Face curved his wrist in a mock shot.

Well—

What's wrong? You don't want to?

I don't care. I'll whup yo ass in a game or two.

Follow me.

They squeezed through a narrow neck of doorway, then hurried to the elevator, which began to lower like a rusty bucket. The walls came rushing in and Jesus had to fight the urge to extend his arms in defense. The elevator opened into a dark vestibule. No Face miscalculated the height of the vestibule step and tripped out into the day. Jesus blinked forth upon the sky.

Hey, boys. Give you five dollars if you can tell me what kind of bird this is. The words emerged from pitch blackness, a dark niche cut deep in the building's brick. A face, then a body—blue overalls with dirty suspenders, parachute straps—pushed into the light, fist holding the groin. A janitor, Jesus thought. He's a janitor, cleaning up after this nigga trash. He saw Jesus looking at him. Flicked his tongue fast and dirty.

Damn, No Face said. You see that? He a stone-cold freak.

You can get hurt that way, old man, Jesus said.

The janitor cupped his hand over his ear. What? What you say?

Hurt.

And I can get hurt getting out of the bathtub, too.

Jesus turned up the heat in his eyes, red coals. The janitor winked at him. Dushan, the janitor said to No Face.

No Face did not answer.

Tell yo mamma I be up there to see her later.

Damn, Jesus said. You gon take that shit?

Aw, man, he can't sweat me. No Face waits a beat, watching Jesus.

Nigga, he talkin bout yo mamma.

You don't know me from Adam. He ain't nobody. That's Redtail.

Who?

Redtail.

What kind of name is that?

Well, his real name is Roscoe. Roscoe Lipton.

He yall janitor?

The superintendent.

A janitor.

Yeah.

Don't see how he can be nobody's janitor. Too fuckin ole. Nigga can hardly move.

Crazy too. Nigga be feedin rats and shit. Feedin em.

What?

Word.

Jesus shook his head.

I know. But guess what?

What?

He used to be a pilot.

What?

A pilot.

You mean an airplane?

Yeah.

Jesus tried to picture the old drunk in a cockpit. What he do, fly a bottle round his lips?

Nawl, in a war. Warplane. Flying Tiger. Hell from Heaven. He changed some enemies too.

That old drunk motherfucker?

Yeah.

He can't change his dirty draws.

He did.

Musta been a long time ago.

Yeah. Old nigga can't even hear.

I can tell that. *So that was why he did it, covered his deaf ear and cupped his good one.*

But he hear good nough to hear what he shouldn hear.

What?

He a transformer.

Jesus considered the possibility of this.

You do something, and he can't wait to snitch. Hey, he might even snitch on *you.*

Jesus looked at No Face.

Round here, he gotta watch his back. I almost changed that nigga a few times myself.

I bet. He walk like you. He talk like you. He yo daddy?

No Face watched—one red eye—Jesus hard for a stocktaking moment.

They began their journey. Above the river, a gull white-winged along a wave. A hang-tailed hound sat tough beside a garbage can until No Face roused it with a speeding stone. A ragtop speeded past, but slow enough for Jesus to be momentarily blinded by a flash of hand signals.

Trey Deuces, No Face said.

Right, Jesus said.

No Face took cautious steps crossing the street, as if fording a river. He walked, Jesus beside him, for several more blocks through a fog of belching cars, dragging his feet, tripping over his shadow, slow and purposeful, the blind motion of sleep. The morning increased, the wind rose, gusts of it shaking the branches, bringing a faint snow of spring petals, flake on sifting flake. Through rectangles of glass, Jesus saw men dipping their heads in coffee cups, sitting stiff with their beers or hiding their faces behind newspapers. He and No Face rounded the corner. The sun brightened in the distance, and Stonewall glittered white. Tall rockets of buildings, ready to blast off.

Damn, we walked that far? You ain't tell me we walkin to Stonewall?

Chill.

Nigga, you crazy.

You be aw ight.

A fenced-in basketball court loomed in the distance, thick shapes roving inside. Jetting along, Jesus and No Face found a stone bench and sat down to watch the game. Tongues circulated the circumference of the court. Homeys lined the fence, fingers poking through the chain-link holes, slurping Night Train and firing up missile-shaped joints. Floating heat. Sweat air. Grit that Jesus tasted in his cough.

Whirling colors, four men played the full-length of the court. Jesus took a good look. Two men in khaki pants and bare chests, and two in chests and blue jeans. Khaki One a tall (Jesus's height) man with a sharp-angled haircut like a double-headed ax (V from widow's peak to neckline). Bull-wide nose and thick worm lips. Wedges of muscle angling up from the waist and fanning out to a winged back. Big Popeye forearms. Dull white skin, as if faded from bleach. Whispered under his breath when he shot a free throw. Khaki Two a short nigga with carefully greased and patterned hair—a sculpture—and proud, bowed wishbone legs. He passed Khaki One the ball for a rim-ringing dunk. Serious hang time in the radiant haze. The opposing team took out the ball. Light-moving, the white man fell like an avalanche and smothered a shot. Drove the ball up the alley and around the other defender for the easy layup. Hoop, poles, and backboard cold-shuddered. The ball swirled around the rim before it flushed.

Good game.

Who got winners? Khaki Two curled up first one leg, then the other, checking his shoe soles. He pulled an old fighter pilot's helmet (World War I stick-winged biplane, Snoopy and the Red Baron) over his sculpted hair.

A scuffle flared up. No Face started for the court, Jesus followed him. Like a magnet, faces drew them in.

Keylo. No Face spoke to Khaki Two. Why you give me that whacked weed?

Give you? Bitch, I ain't give you shit. You paid me.

Jesus blinked. Focused. *Keylo?* So Khaki Two was Keylo, legend in the flesh. Word, drove an old red ambulance with a bed (stretcher?) in the back. His *ho buggy* he called it. Say he never changed the sheets.

Keylo approached, and Jesus imagined him choking No Face in the noose of his bowed legs. He smiled toothless, like a snake. Crunched his face, a single line of eyebrow above lidless rat eyes. Balled in a boxer's crouch. Rose on his toes with a dance in his body and pimp-slapped No Face upside the head.

Damn, Keylo. Why you always fuckin around?

Cause I want to. Keylo slapped No Face again. A storm of laughter convulsed the spectators.

Damn, Keylo. No Face's dreads rose like cobras. Quit.

Make me, bitch. Fists moving, Keylo circled No Face, dukes up, slow-moving like an old man. Circling, he fired slaps, loud as thunder in easy

rain, stinging blows which rocked No Face, hard, fast-pitched blows to the
soft mitt of his raised chin. No Face hung tough, refusing to go down.

Chill.

Laughter died down.

That's right. Chill.

Jesus searched for the voice's source. Khaki One. Sunlight streaked his
greased flesh, accentuating every vein. Chill, he said, voice feverish, cloggy
and hot, phlegm-filled as if from a cold.

Damn, Freeze.

Freeze. Freeze.

No Face alright, Freeze said. He hooked No Face's head under his elbow
and stroked the idiot's bowed head. No Face grinned, tongue fish-flopping
in his mouth. He alright. Freeze yanked down on No Face's head, then released it. No Face ballooned up to his normal height. Don't try to play him
like a bitch.

I was—

Freeze cut Keylo off with a sharp glance. Shoved him into No Face. Kiss
and make up.

What?

Kiss and make up. Freeze's biceps were round and solid, train wheels. Go
on. Kiss and make up.

Keylo searched the crowd, pleading eyes and mouth.

Freeze cut a grin. The crowd flew into stitches.

You see the look on his face?

Yeah.

Had that nigga goin'.

Yeah.

Thought he was serious.

Bout to piss his pants.

Shit.

No Face bobbed in place, grinning, cannibal teeth, appreciative, glad that
Freeze had made a fool of him. Freeze slapped him on the back. You did
good, he said. He looked at Jesus, and his eyes spoke recognition. Jesus was
sure of it. You did real good.

Thanks, No Face said.

Something inside told Jesus that Freeze's compliment went beyond the
battle with Keylo, addressed some secret subject.

Yo, Freeze.

The voice spun Freeze's head.

You had yo fun. A short dude spoke, coal-black face under a red baseball
cap, brim backward, manufacturer's tag dangling from the side like a tassel
on a graduate's mortarboard. You ready to do this?

Aw ight, Country Plus, Freeze said. If you hard.

I'm always hard.

So pick yo team.

Well you know I got my nigga here. Freeze nodded at Keylo. They slapped palms and locked fingers in some private ritual.

Huh, Country Plus said. So what else is new? Ain't yall married?

Freeze ignored the comment.

Give me MD 2020.

My nigga.

Cool, Freeze said. You can have him. Give me my man No Face. No Face swelled up with gratitude, chest out, lips inflated into a grin, one eye expanding expanding expanding, and he rose, tiptoes.

Thunderbird.

Damn, Freeze, Keylo said. You gon let this bitch play on our team?

Jesus breathed his first whiff of Keylo's gravedigger breath.

Give a nigga a chance, Freeze said. Even a bitch. He gave Keylo a quick hug.

Come on, Country Plus said. Choose another man.

Damn, who else? Freeze studied the crowd.

Pick him. No Face pointed to Jesus.

Freeze gave Jesus a fishy-eyed look. I want him.

That doofy-lookin' muddafudda, Keylo said. He and Jesus faced one another, eyes colliding.

And I'll take Mad Dog. Okay. We set.

Jesus pondered the faulty mathematics. *That's only four. Four players, not. . . .* No Face pulled Jesus into the huddle.

Yo, g, Freeze said. What's yo name?

Jesus.

Jesus?

Yeah.

Welcome, Jesus. I'm Freeze. Freeze extended his hand, and Jesus took it with his firmest grip.

Country Plus pulled a dime from his pocket and tossed it shimmering into the air. Call em.

Heads, Freeze said.

The coin fell to the surface of Country's skin. He slapped his palm over it.

See, Freeze said. You already lost.

What you call?

You know.

Country removed his palm. Heads.

See.

Country Plus stared into Freeze's face, the price tag dangling from his cap and jerking back and forth in the breeze like a hooked fish on a line. From this time forward, I will make you hear new things.

Whatever, Freeze said. You talk a good game. Let's see if you can play.

No Face unzipped his jacket and pulled it off, removed his T-shirt, and revealed his Mr. Universe torso.

Hey, Jesus, Freeze said. That's yo man. He pointed to Country Plus. Stick him.

Word, Jesus said. *Damn, how Freeze tryin to play me?* Jesus always played center, the tallest and strongest player on the court. And here Freeze was, playin him like a guard.

We skins, No Face said. Ain't you gon take off yo shirt?

Nawl.

Why not?

Nawl.

Yo shirt gon get all funky.

I'm aw ight.

Better take out yo earring.

Nawl.

Nigga yank it off.

Nawl.

No Face, Freeze said. Take out the ball.

No Face took out the ball. MD 2020 snatched his lazy entry pass and tossed an easy layup. Good steal. Country Plus congratulated his teammate, and his team—Thunderbird and Mad Dog—celebrated their first basket. No Face looked at Freeze with a drowning man's eyes (eye!), begging for mercy.

Country Plus threw Freeze the ball.

Wait a minute, Jesus said. It's their ball.

Wake up! Keylo said. You in South Lincoln. Red Hook rules. Stonewall rules. Stonewall rules.

Freeze took out the ball. Fired it to Keylo, who crouched low and ran it hard on his short, baby-thick legs. Country Plus's unit swooped down on him, a flock of small fast birds moving in streaks, sparrows in a room. Keylo froze in place. Fired the ball at Jesus, but Country Plus clawed it in midair, and in the spark of a moment swept Jesus aside like a swatted fly. Jesus gave chase with everything in his legs. Country Plus launched for the nest-high basket, his elbow catching Jesus in the throat.

Damn!

Don't sweat it, Freeze said. He took the ball out. Fired it in to Jesus. Jesus dribbled. Green-thumbed grass poked through the concrete and snatched at the ball. Tall weeds twisted around his legs. And puddles swamped him, quicksand. With each putting down of his heels, his whole body sank further into the court. Then Country Plus liberated the ball from his paralyzed fingers. Rode an invisible rainbow to the hoop. Reaming sight. The rim vibrated colors.

Freeze looked at Jesus. Took the ball out, fired it to Jesus. Jesus barely caught it. A large fish. It slipped from his hands back into the dark court waters. Country Plus clawed it up, bearlike. Lifted for the jump shot. Jesus jumped as hard and high as he could, springs in his toes. Fake. Country Plus had never left his feet. Now he took it casually to the hoop. Jesus landed back hard on the court, waves of hard concrete pulsing from his feet and through his body, mixing with waves of laughter circulating the court.

You see that muddafudda? Way up in the air.

Yeah. A real sucker.

Freeze took out the ball.

Wait, Jesus said. You take it in. The center is supposed to—

Freeze fired the ball hard into Jesus's defiant chest. Jesus watched him a moment, eyes working. He dribbled the ball up the court. Country Plus yanked it from his hands, a string on rolled twine. He dribbled, in front of him, behind his back, between his legs, while Jesus grabbed at the ball, again and again.

Damn, look at that mark nigga!

Gettin played like a bitch.

Country Plus blew past Jesus. Took it behind the backboard for the reverse lay-in.

In yo eye, punk.

Mark.

Trick.

Ranked and intense observers watched Jesus. No shifting, no craning among the still faces, the still eyes. Country Plus laughed in close, Jesus hearing himself, the laugh erupt from his own belly.

Be true to the game, Freeze said.

Jesus lowered his eyes. The ball went weightless in his hands, so he hugged it to prevent it from floating away. The leather skin peeled away to allow him to look directly into the ball's hollow inside, where shapes formed then started to move. Thick sweatbands pinch head and wrists. Sleeveless T-shirts loop skinny shoulders. Jogging shorts sag like oversized diapers. Layers of brightly colored socks curve like barber-pole stripes around thin calves. Converse All Stars, Pro-Keds, and leather Pumas scuff the court with rubber music. John, Lucifer, Spokesman, Dallas, and Ernie—the Funky Five Corners—geared up for battle. Chuckers doing chumps. John with his quick little hands, hands so fast they don't move when he passes the ball.

And Lucifer, mouth open, his tongue hangin in the air, some magical carpet lifting him above the ground, the court, the basket.

And you shoulda seen that nigga shout out when he jammed the ball. Served up a facial. He'd be like, Take that, you punk ass motherfucker!

Quiet Lucifer?

Yeah. Quiet Lucifer. I dawked that in yo face!

One-word Lucifer?

One-word Lucifer. How you like that motherfucker! Feel good? Taste good? That tongue just flappin. And those big hands shakin in yo face like he jus rolled seven. Yeah, he had some big hands, but they was slow. Lucifer wasn't no good at handling the ball. Dribblin. Catching a pass. Spokesman told John, Throw it at his face. He'll catch it then. It worked. Same way with everything: Spokesman had an answer. Standing there, watching from the sidelines, rubbing his belly like a crystal ball. Tryin to science the game. Geometrize plays for the Funky Five Corners. *This is a human behavioral laboratory. You know, white smocks and white rats. Test tubes and Bunsen burners. Ideas lead to buildings and bridges. I like to think about yall, us, the team, the Funky Five Corners, and visualize yall, us, the team, being better players through my schemes.* He measure the court with a slide rule and a triangle, then write some figures down on his notepad, sketch some pictures.

Damn, nigga. What you doin?

Always trying to science something.

You may be Einstein but you ain't no Jew. Still black. Science or no science.

One time he took these big-ass pliers and measured every nigga's head on the court. They let him, too, wanting to be part of the experiment, get written up. Spokesman. This other time he took this big magnet and poked it all around in the air and kept poking it. We jus shook our heads.

When he made his report he expected you to abide by it. He shook his head when you fumbled a pass. *A person your age and height normally covers three and a half feet with each step, so we must conclude that you shouldn't have taken more than ten paces. An unnecessary waste of energy.* Drew his lips tight with anger when you missed a layup. *Lucifer, be slow about obeying the laws of gravity.* And he was always placin bets. Oh, we can't lose. I got this all scienced out. John, if my right eye jump, we win money for sure. We won some money too. Serious money a coupla times. Lost some. Did we profit? Who can say? I guess it evened out.

Yall gon play or what?

A cool breeze wafted onto the stifling court, stirring up the stench of wine and weed. Jesus breathed through his hard-winded nostrils, unsure whether it was time to breathe in or breathe out. Everything was off, out of whack. *Just need some more time. Gotta learn how to fly again.* He was drowning in dark waters, in spinning lights. Blood on his tongue. He surveyed the players, searching for that one face which would sanction his plight. Freeze cracked his anxious knuckles. Keylo checked his shoe soles. No Face hard-breathed. Then the sun awakened, clean and clear.

I said yall gon play or what?

Jesus saw in precise detail thick, ropelike veins stretched lengthwise in skinny arms and hands. Saw a red sleeveless T-shirt and a red baseball cap, brim backward, the price tag dangling from it. Jesus saw him. Jesus knew him. Engaged sight the pulse of his color. Red, he would get back in the game. He would—yes he, he alone, not his team—make a run.

He fired the ball to No Face, who fired it to Freeze, who fired it to Keylo, who fired it back to Jesus. Jesus held the ball above him, squeezed in one hand. He brought it upcourt, dribbled three times, blip, blip, blip, then took it up the alley, body curved, elbows high. He faked the layup, drew back for the jumper, kicking his feet ballerina-like in midair. The ball arched from his fingertips. Sunk.

Country Plus grinned. I gave you that one, he said. Felt sorry for you. He took the ball in. Lifted off his toes for the jumper. Jesus caught the ball in the palm of his hand, midflight, fly to fly strip. Swatted the ball to Freeze, who lifted for the easy basket.

You got lucky on that one, Country Plus said. He looked Jesus flush in the face.

Guess so, Jesus said.

Mad Dog fired the ball to Country Plus. Country Plus crouched low in the dribble, challenging Jesus.

Pass the ball, Country.

Nigga, stop showin out.

Jesus punched the ball from between his legs, scooped it up, and arched it into the net.

Country looked at Jesus, anger and frustration concealed like fishhooks in his eyes.

Thunderbird inbounded the ball to Mad Dog, who bounced it in MD 2020's direction. Jesus hopped on the ball mid-air, squeexed it tight between his thighs, and rode it for a second or two like a bucking bull. Country Plus faced him, crouched, arms out, yellow sweat covering his forehead. Jesus bobbed and weaved, then broke for the basket, elbows working, tearing off a layer of Country's flesh. Jesus soared in solar heat—he could stay up in the air long as he wanted—gave niggas plenty time to count each tread mark on his rubber soles. He looked down on the basket miles below him, and re-leased the ball like a bomb.

Okay, okay. Don't get happy. Game ain't over.

Country Plus planted his feet, tent in a field. Wind, Jesus blew him flat.

Jumped for the shot. The ball hit the rim. Bounced. Once. Twice. Freeze snatched the rebound. The enemy unit trapped him within a wall of raised arms. Freeze fired the ball to No Face. Perfect pass. Except No Face was three seconds behind the ball.

Bitch, Freeze said.

Damn, you slow, Jesus said.

Bitch, Keylo said, you better stop fuckin up. Or I'll wrap my dick around yo head like a turban.

No playin bitch, Jesus said. Sweat dribbled down his nose, his mouth, his chin, every inch of his skin, every cell flooded with the energy of the game, the rhythm of his breathing. He studied his heart's double beat. Defense. That was the key. Offense through defense. Offense through defense. Fundamental. Time and distance. Count the pauses between bounces. Feel the game, deep down, somewhere behind the belly, near the lungs. Play as you breathe.

Country Plus rose like a wave for the basket, and Jesus chopped him down with one stroke.

Damn!

Jesus dunked and almost threw himself through the hoop. He landed on the court with easy footing, tiptoes, a ballerina.

That's game.

We won.

Country Plus lay flat and still on the concrete, like something you could stick a fork into. Mad Dog extended an aiding hand. MD 2020 and Thunderbird followed his lead, but Country Plus slapped their hands away, then raised himself warily, like someone trying to stand up on a rocking boat.

Next time, Country.

Next time.

Good game.

Yeah, Country said. Good game. He studied Jesus with nonforgetting, nonforgiving eyes. Good game. Catch yall later. He turned and led his unit from the court, parading his anger and his wound.

Jesus gave Freeze a high five, palms slapping. Slapped some skin with Keylo and No Face. Memory warm like sweat on his skin, of the Funky Five Corners—John, Lucifer, Spokesman, Ernie, Dallas—celebrating a victory.

You play a strong game, Freeze said. He greeted Jesus with a quick hug.

Yeah, Keylo said. He removed his pilot's cap, exposing a thick wave of greased hair, raised and stiff, a parrot's comb. He turned the cap upside down and dumped out a gallon of sweat. Liked the way you conned them mark niggas, actin like you couldn play at first. He fit the pilot's cap back snugly on his head.

You got it going on like a big fat hard-on.

Jesus said nothing. He wanted more game.

Straight up. Hard.

Ain't no man, woman, or beast can beat me, Jesus said, words warm with his heart's heat.

You got that right.

Word.

You the man.

Aw, Freeze, No Face said. You don't know him from Adam. This nigga can tell some stories.

Stories? What kinda stories?

Like—

Like the time he fucked yo mamma.

No Face looked at Freeze.

Keylo twisted off the metal cap on a cloudy, missile-shaped forty-ounce bottle of malt liquor. Threw his head back and gulped down the liquid, Adam's apple working. A big booty switched by. Some bitch got a big booty around here.

Keylo, Freeze said, you got no class.

Freeze, you know I'm a dog.

Yeah. Sniffin a bitch's ass.

No Face burped some laughs.

Tell one of them stories.

Later for that, Jesus said.

Nawl, tell one.

You really want to hear one?

Straight up.

Word.

All ears.

Awight. Why not? Once upon a time, this nigga went to this bitch's house. Her daddy come to the do. The nigga be like, I come to see your daughter Sally. The father let him in. Sally roll into the room.

Roll? Keylo hunkered down to listen.

Yeah, in a wheelchair. See, she ain't have no legs. Got nubs up to here. Jesus put the edges of his hands at the knees.

Damn. Head bent in listening.

Check it.

And she ain't have no arms. Nubs. Right here. Jesus put the edge of his hand at his elbow.

Shit.

What kind of bitch . . .

And she had this special wheelchair and all she had to do was throw her hips like this. Jesus demonstrated.

Oh, I see. One of them. Big-booty bitch.

Mad back.

Word.

Lumpin.

So the father say, Yall gon out in the backyard and talk. So the nigga and the crippled bitch go out. So he start kickin it to her. And she get hot, but she ain't never been fucked before. How you gon fuck a bitch with nubs? So the nigga see this clothesline stretched across the backyard. He gets an idea. He grabs two clothespins, then he takes the bitch out of the chair and pins one nub arm to the line, then pins the other nub arm to the line. He props an old wood barrel under her butt. Then he bump her from the back.

Damn!

Word!

Bumped that crippled bitch!

After he nut, he zip up his pants. Then he be like, See ya. Her father come out and find her three hours later. Pinned to the clothesline.

Laughter bounces around the court. Jesus is deep into it too, rejoicing from the gut.

And he left her like that?

Word.

Cold-blooded.

Hanging on the clothesline.

Word.

Heart.

But, nigga—Keylo shoved No Face's head back—that wasn't no joke.

You don't know me from Adam. I ain't said nothing bout no joke. I said a *lie.*

Bitch, stop lyin. Keylo stuck a big eyedropper into the forty and suctioned up liquid into the tube. When the dropper was full, he craned back his head, poked the dropper in his mouth, and squeezed liquid from the flooded ball at the dropper's end.

Funny story, Freeze said. He took Jesus's shoulders into the circle of his arm. Jesus saw that his own feet were no longer touching the ground. He bobbed in the air, bobbed in the circle of Freeze's sweat-warm arm. He could stay here, forever, and hang. Hang. Freeze released his shoulders. Anchorless now, Jesus concentrated, concentrated so as not to float away. Freeze walked a few steps, then turned to Jesus's trailing eyes. Keylo, he said, go to the sto fo me.

Damn, Freeze. I wanna check out another one of them jokes. Lies. Stories.

Me, too, No Face said.

Gon on, Jesus. Bust another one.

Yeah. Bust another one.

Stop repeatin' after me, bitch.

Keylo, go to the sto fo me. Buy me a . . . he nodded at Keylo's forty.

What about them stories?

Later for that.

Come on, Freeze.

Keylo.

Damn. Keylo tail-wagged off to the store—no, walking like an antelope, lifting hoof from knee.

And buy Jesus one, too.

No, thanks, Jesus said. I'm straight. He fluttered his feathers.

No Face, go with him. Make sure he don't get lost.

Aw, Freeze. But I wanna hear—

No Face.

Damn. Hey, Keylo, wait up. No Face trotted off. Jesus watched him grow smaller and disappear.

A pigeon skimmed the earth in flight, then headed toward the sky, and the sky breathed it in.

Freeze worked his arms through his T-shirt, and covered his bare chest and back. Pulled a pack of cigarettes from his back pants pocket. Shook the pack until one cigarette eased its length, extended, like a radio antenna. Want a square?

No, Jesus said. I quit smokin'.

Wish I could quit. Freeze pulled the antenna from the pack, tapped it against the back of his hand, then stuck it in his mouth. Using his thumbnail, he flamed a match. Where yo daddy?

What? Jesus said.

I said, where yo daddy?

My daddy? Jesus stood in a mass of tobacco smoke.

Yeah.

Jesus breathed in the silence. You don't know me.

Freeze watched the lit cigarette end. Where yo daddy?

Hey, you don't know me. Why you askin bout my daddy?

We got something to settle.

You must mean somebody else. He don't even know you.

He stole a bird from me.

Sound strikes what skin is meant to shield. Jesus wobbles. What?

He stole a bird from me.

A trapdoor shuts inside Jesus's chest. A bird?

Yes.

My daddy? Jesus fingers his chest, points to his heart.

Yeah. His name John, ain't it?

Nawl.

His name ain't John?

Yeah.

John ain't yo father?

Nawl.

Who yo father?

Jesus looked into the sky. Thinking: *I get it. No Face told you. Y'all running a game.* He laughed.

You think that's funny?

Jesus drank Freeze's milk-white eyes. No.

Ain't John yo father? John Jones?

Yeah, he my father. So, what up?

Like I said. Freeze took a drag on the cigarette. Exhaled through his nose, dragonlike. He stole a bird from me. Light lay in four colors on his face.

You serious?

Freeze said nothing.

Jesus shook his head. Fingered the words in his mind, measured them, searched for color and sense. When did he steal it?

Freeze smoked the square down to the butt. Does it matter? He crushed the butt under his heel.

John know you?

Know me good enough to steal from me. Know me good enough to steal from me then run off and hide like a lil bitch.

Jesus let truth move inside him, let himself move around inside it.

So now you know.

Yes.

And you believe?

Yes.

Good. So then you know. Know what I need you to do. So then you know that I need you to—

I know, Jesus said. I know.

You know?

I know. And I will.

You will?

Yes. Yes I will. Yes, I'll do it.

You can always choose—

Wait, Jesus said. He halted Freeze's words with his palms. Pushed them back. Wait. Feet carried him away. He didn't want to hear any more. No reason to. No reason, will, or desire. He walked, putting time and distance between himself and Freeze's request, command, mission. Maybe Freeze did know John. Maybe. And maybe John had stolen from him. No surprise there. John was a thief. Water-slick. Easy in, easy out. And John was forever desperate, light, seeking to add some weight to his pockets. But would he accept any color or shape of pay? *God marked every sparrow, Gracie said. Every sparrow.* Gravity, Jesus carried the thought inside. Raised it. High. Descended down the spit-mottled steps of the subway.

FROM **Dakota Grand**

BY KENJI JASPER

The water was a little too hot. But I liked it, especially the way it made her lips feel as they moved up and down on me. I wrapped my arm around her and pulled her close. We kissed time and time again with the water cascading down our faces. Then she stopped and stepped entirely out of the bathtup, dripping wet, and walked out of the bathroom. I followed. I knew what came next.

There was something about our cold wetness that was thrilling. Our nipples rose hard and thick as we playfully slipped and slid against each other. She moaned loudly as my tongue entered her, the sound bouncing off of the echo-creating bedroom walls.

We knew how to work each other. The water and sweat soaked into the matress as we scrambled across its surface. She climbed on top, tightening her walls, knowing what it did to me. Our orgasms collided, just before the alarm went off. We crashed to the mattress like lifeless dummies.

"We gotta start getting up earlier," she said, breathing heavily. She wiped herself off with the comforter and stood up at the foot of the bed. "I think I need two of these before I go to work. One just doesn't get me through the day anymore."

"If you worked from home like me you'd have all the time you need," I said, smiling and out of breath.

"But I can't fit a hundred computers into my room," she said as she passed the blanket back to me, damp. I grabbed the top sheet and pulled it off of the bed for my own wipedown.

"I've asked a million times already, but how come you make fifty thousand a year and live in a room in your uncle's house?"

"Because that's all I need," she said. "I send money to the DR for my parents and my little brother, pay my bills, do a little shopping, and help my uncle with his expenses."

"But he ain't broke. He owns a store."

"D, how many times do I have to tell you this?"

"Tell me what?"

"That I live my life the way I want to. Just be glad I'm keeping you in it."

"Well excuse me. But I'm sure your mornings wouldn't be as exciting without me."

"Hmmm. I guess you're right about that," she said with a grin before moving over and kissing me on the cheek.

"But I gotta run, baby." She jumped back up and climbed into the navy-blue business suit that was her favorite. Now all she needed were her shoes and jewelry, which she retrieved from the bathroom in record time.

"You know what today is?" I yelled into the bathroom.

"Yes I do, D."

"You gonna read it?"

"Yes I'm going to read it, D." With heels, earrings, and the twin silver bracelets she always wore, she was ready for her commute into downtown Brooklyn.

"You gonna miss me?" I asked.

"I always do," she said just before she kissed me on the cheek again and rushed towards the door. "But I'm five minutes late. I'm out—"

The door slammed shut behind her. I'd gotten used to her quick exits.

Winter had shifted to spring and everything was great. *Caution* was set to be published the following winter and I was even starting to get work from the real magazines. And the people over at *The Magazine* and places like *Gear* and *Maxim* were pretty good about getting me my checks on time. I was happy, and Carolina was the jewel in my crown.

It was the Day, the one I had been waiting for for nearly three months as my story on the artists formerly known as Arbor Day would finally reach a circulation of more than three million people. It had been a lifetime of edits and visits to the magazine office with Chad. He'd cut some of my best phrases, but it came with the territory. As long as I was getting a byline in his magazine, losing a few words here and there didn't matter.

A half hour later I was checking the weather on my new TV with my new and very illegal cable descrambler box. Two hundred channels for what I paid for basic cable. My book advance had made all the movie channels and pay-per-view absolutely free. The high was going to be 65 so I took my sky-blue Polo sweatshirt and a pair of matching jeans and laid them across the sofa.

The magazine had hit stands at 6 a.m., and though I could have gotten copies days before, I wanted to wait until it was in the hands of the people. I wanted to ride the train and see readers' eyes glued to the article. That kind of attention meant far more than the $5,000 paycheck I'd gotten for it.

The Day was going to be spent running around. I had to get my courtesy copies from *The Magazine,* run by Todd's office to drop off the first galleys of my novel to the production editor, and then go by *Maintain* to give Lamar a loan for a plane ticket he needed. He was flying to the "How Can I Be Down" convention in London and *Maintain* was too cheap to pay for him to go. And to round the day out I was supposed to have dinner with Carolina at the Joloff Restaurant back in the neighborhood since she was working late for the rest of the week and I probably wouldn't see her.

I flipped through the freshly delivered *Daily News* looking for positive current events but gave up just before I got to the sports section. I switched Thundarr the Barbarian on my 34-inch screen and listened to the bell in the church down the street. It signaled 10 a.m. I had to get moving.

On the train a bearded and wrinkled Jewish man shotgunned leaflets to apathetic commuters on his way through my car and towards the next. I took his offering and ran my eyes over the tiny faded print trying to find what it was he was selling. Even if it didn't cost I knew he was selling something. I looked down to see that his urgent message was a stack of stapled pages, Biblical prophecies that had supposedly come true during the second half of the twentieth century. The last page even contained prophecies specifically for the African-American community. I thought about reading it but folded it up and stuffed it in my bag, dooming the information to be lost forever.

The Magazine was on the twenty-sixth floor of a skyscraper near Rockefeller Center. It wasn't my usual part of town and I still got the building confused with the Fox News building further down Sixth Avenue. But the absense of Fox's midday lunch traffic near the entrance let me know that I was at the right place.

Upstairs, the lily-white receptionist once again mistook me for a messenger and pointed me towards the courier drop-off window. I told her I was there to see Chad and she motioned me to go in without a word. I made a left towards the editorial department, where they were already waiting for me.

"There he is, the man of the hour," Chad yelled across the entire section with the voice of a game show host. "This month's special cover man, Mr. Dakota Grand!"

Scattered applause rang throughout the office. Some people even stood up. There, on the edge of the room, it was good to be able to see the occasional dark face among the many white ones. But I still felt like the butt of a joke I didn't understand.

"What's goin' on?" I asked Chad as we shook hands stiffly.

"You're what's going on," he said with a sly grin. "Everybody around here is in love with your piece. Who knows? It might turn out to be some award-winning shit."

"Well I won't hold my breath on that one," I replied with a flash of teeth.

"No man, I'm serious. Rap artists maybe make a cover once a year but everyone agreed that your piece belonged there. Looks like you're in there, man."

"Well thanks," I replied, on the verge of blushing. But I wanted to make sure that I wasn't going to be a one-hit wonder. "I hope I can do somethin' else for y'all," I said humbly.

"Oh, you don't have to worry about that," he said as if he were speaking to a child. "We're already figuring out what to give you next."

Various members of the magazine staff approached and welcomed me like deacons do baptismal candidates. We shared words about lunch dates, meetings, and working on a contract basis. I had arrived. And I was ready to milk it for all that it was worth.

"So how did you start writing?" Claire asked before taking a sip from her Heineken an hour later. The editor in chief had invited me out to lunch at the Skylight Diner on Eighth Avenue. She looked like she was in her mid-thirties, a cross between Sharon Stone and Kathleen Turner. Her long blond hair was ponytailed behind her. Flanked by Chad on the left and Dan, the half Puerto Rican, half Asian managing editor, on the right, I felt like the final piece in a multiracial puzzle.

Claire told me that she had gotten her start in Atlanta as well, working as an assistant editor at *Atlanta Magazine.* It wasn't a hotbed for minority news and views but I had always liked the writing. Nevertheless it felt good to know that she knew a little about where I came from. Chad nodded along with her words like a TV reporter being filmed for reaction shots.

As they talked I looked around at the diner. The place had a '50s diner feel to it: neon signs in the windows, the old-school stools along the lunch counter, curving booths with circular tables in the middle. But we were '90s journalists personified: fresh haircuts, record-label T-shirts, jeans and khakis. Dan's cell phone came alive and he squirmed out of the booth towards the foyer to take the call. Lamar would have just yapped into the mouthpiece right in front of us.

"It's both a long and short story, Claire," I replied after a sip of water. "I wrote my first short story when I was nine. It was a class exercise but I really got into it. So I wrote more stories and then some poems. And it just grew like a plant. I published my first article in a local paper when I was twelve. The next thing I know I'm sitting here at a table with you."

"Twelve, huh? What was I doing at twelve?"

"I wasn't thinking about writing. I know that," Chad said.

"You definitely have it together," she replied. Dan casually returned to the table.

"I just can't wait to get back to work," I said after a brief period of silence. Once again I was met with nothing but smiles.

"Just scored a cover and he's already on to the next thing," Dan chimed in, as if he had been there all along. "It's good to see that you're hungry."

"That's the only way to be," I replied. Dan gave me a nod and grin of approval.

"Our editorial meeting is tomorrow so Chad will give you a call in the morning. We'll definitely have something else for you."

"But you gotta promise me something," Claire said with a warm smile.

"What?" I asked.

"Take today and enjoy your cover. Worry about your next piece tomorrow."

"I'll try," I said. "But I'm always thinkin' about tomorrow."

I shook each of their hands before departing, happy to put a line through another appointment on my schedule. I was also glad to be on my way to an office that had more color. On the street I lit a cigarette and fantasized about what assignment they would give me next. What would it take to move up in the ranks, to have them panting for the next big thing with my name on it?

I made a quick run into W. L. Pressman at 43rd and Sixth to leave the galleys for the production editor with the receptionist. I'd told Lamar I'd be there at three and I still had five minutes to be on time. Luckily *Maintain* was only a few blocks down Fashion Avenue. I knew that Lamar needed his money as soon as possible so I hopped into a cab just letting someone out and was on my way down to his building.

"Deez streets is madness," the Rastafarian cab driver yelled over the blaring boom of Burning Spear. I'd never ridden with a driver with such a loud system. I didn't think that cabbies were even supposed to play music at all. "You never know who you gonna bump into and what they want. You remember dat, ya-ear?"

"I hear you," I said, wondering if he was somehow talking about my life. The bass driven rhythm gave his words a strange importance. It also made the cab rattle. He cut a sharp left on 39th and then made a right on Lexington and we were there before I realized it.

"Wake up boy," the Rastaman yelled playfully as I snapped out of it. The cab was double-parked in front of the *Maintain* building. I handed him five singles.

"Wassup, D?" Fernando asked as I bypassed the visitors list and headed straight for the elevator. Fernando was the head of building security, a bulky Puerto Rican who had dreams of pro boxing when he wasn't keeping the building out of danger. I took him to lunch once back when I worked up in research because he'd spotted a FedEx guy about to deliver one of my packages to the wrong floor. Since then we were always cool and cordial.

Something touched me when I pushed the button for the elevator. It was cold and fluttery, a feeling and a voice that told me to turn away and go home. It told me that Lamar could get the money later. I toyed with complying and then I fully decided to do so. I would just run the dough by his apartment later, or come by when he was leaving at seven. But before I could turn towards the exit the center elevator's doors opened. It was too late.

Mirage stood three feet in front of me like Darth Vader 2000, two medium-sized soldiers beside and behind him. I noticed a copy of *The Magazine* held tightly in his fist.

"You!" he yelled as if I'd just murdered his best friend.

"Hey Mirage, what's goin' on?" I was too high on the day's events to see that his bloodshot eyes spelled anger all around.

He took two steps forward and answered with a fist that knocked me flat on the floor before I figured out what it was. I tried to get to my feet but his boys were already on me. As if on cue they grabbed both of my arms, pulled me to my feet, and held me there.

"What the fuck is this shit you wrote about me?" he asked before practically ramming his fist through my abdomen. I wanted to double over but they held me upright. I hoped Fernando was dialing for help, or arming himself with some kind of a weapon. But he'd probably just ducked down. There was no prize for him to win in that fight.

Mirage followed up with an uppercut. And after that the pain flooded in from everywhere. I had to do something. Rule number one back at home on Fair Street was that if you got jumped you had to at least get one good shot in before you went down. They had my arms but my left leg was in perfect alignment with his groin.

Mirage was doubled over on the ground in seconds. I shook one arm loose and hit the one to my right with the dreads and matching beard. That was when my highlight reel ended.

First and heels rained down in buckets. A bone snapped and pain flooded through my right arm. I heard other voices and took more blows as I curled into the fetal position. I closed my eyes and tried to get my mind somewhere else but I didn't make it. I couldn't black out either. Was I dying? Was my clock being punched at the ripe old age of twenty-two? Then, ever so slowly, it began to stop. The voices faded to an echo and finally it all dissolved into darkness. I wasn't happy anymore. I was never going to be happy again.

Love Jones

The Dinner Party

He called it our Great Escape. Since my love for Marc was absolute, I didn't ask any questions when my partner of more than a decade told me we were moving back to his hometown of Sugar Lick, Texas. There is a black-and-white sign when you enter town from the east that proclaims, WELCOME TO SUGAR LICK, CLASS AA STATE FOOTBALL CHAMPIONS 1982, POPULATION, 19,909. I guess the town's leaders would have to change the sign to 19,911.

I knew I would miss our Upper West Side apartment with its friendly neighbors, and its sweeping view of Central Park. I would also miss the smells I couldn't explain from street vendor's carts and the conversations I couldn't understand from people walking the streets of Manhattan. It would be hard not going to a Broadway play at the last minute just because we could.

The first couple of months in the small Texas town were wonderful. We moved into a three-story house a few miles from where Marc had attended elementary and high school. The ladies of the neighborhood brought home-made pies and tomatoes from their gardens and left them on our doorstep with notes welcoming us to the community. Oddly enough, we never met any of the neighbors, just waves from robe-wearing women as they picked up their morning newspapers from the porch.

Not much changed from our regular routine. Thanks to the Internet, I was able to continue my freelance writing assignments.

Marc would come home from his job as a stock broker and skim through the mail, take an evening run with our dog, Simba, and then return home and shower. He would put on his favorite Yale or Stanford sweatshirt with his boxers and then ask me about my day. I loved the fact that after all these years he was still genuinely concerned about me.

There was a lot to love about Sugar Lick; no traffic jams or noise into the wee hours of the morning. I didn't have to face the rejection of taxi drivers who didn't care if I was already late for an important meeting. I fell in love with the sweet smell of the air, crimson rays of sunset and stars that seemed to melt into the silver-edged sky.

Right before Christmas things changed quicker than a west Texas winter wind. I convinced Marc that the approaching holidays would be a chance to show our neighbors our gratitude for their kindness by hosting a dinner party.

I prepared a standing rib roast with miniature new potatoes, sauteed spinach with a touch of garlic, and baked a ham. I made a pitcher of Marc's favorite drink, apple martinis. I had my own special recipe using vodka, triple sec, and Pucker's sour apple. I would garnish it with a Granny Smith apple slice and add a dash of cinnamon.

The evening of the party Marc came home a couple of hours early. He had left his arm behind his back and he brushed his full lips teasingly against mine and then pulled away.

"Come here," I instructed as I pulled him toward me by his suit jacket and demanded he kiss me like he meant it.

"Sometimes my love for you is so strong it overwhelms me," I said softly.

"Me, too. Our guests should be here soon."

Four hours and two pitchers of martinis later, Marc and I sat alone in front of the quivering glow of candles that adorned the perfectly set dining table.

"Why do you think they didn't come?" I asked.

"Maybe we're not their kind of people," Marc said.

"This wouldn't have happened if we still lived in New York," I said, pouting.

"Now be honest. There were times in New York when we walked down the street holding hands and people looked at us strangely," Marc said.

"But we received more smiles of approval than disgusted frowns," I said.

"So do you want to move back to New York?"

I didn't answer. A part of me wanted to scream "Yes!" at the top of my lungs, but I realized how happy Marc had been since we moved. Besides, neither one of us were quitters. We'd faced far too many obstacles to allow a few rude people to alter the path we'd chosen.

Marc pulled me close to him and kissed me on my forehead. I was trying hard not to cry, so I held him tight, as though I was magically pulling the strength I needed from his body. When I finally released him I noticed the blinking green digits on the microwave clock.

It was almost midnight. We started to clear the table when the doorbell rang. Marc raced to the door as I drained the last drops from my glass.

Marc opened the door and there stood a small, wispy woman who was dressed in faux fur with matching hat. She was also carrying a stick with green-and-gold crepe paper strips.

"What can I do for you?" Marc asked as she walked in like she owned the place.

"Hey, babies. I'm Miz Clara. Patton is my married name, but my husband's been dead for years. I live down the road and I saw your lights were on so I wanted to stop by and thank you for your invitation and offer a little bit of advice. I mean, people wanted to run you two out of town when they got your lil' party invitations," she said as she took a seat on the sofa. Marc and I exchanged puzzled glances while Miz Clara removed her fur. She was wearing a green-and-gold sweatshirt with some wild looking animal on it and had on Kelly green corduroy pants.

"I know it's late but could I have a martini neat?"

"Sure," Marc said as he headed toward the kitchen. When Marc left the room, Miz Clara motioned for me to have a seat as she patted the empty space next to her.

"Now, Baby, I know y'all are different from folks around here but there are a few rules you must follow if you want to mingle in."

"What do you mean we're different."

"First of all, anyone with half a brain can see that. We might be country but we ain't stupid and we do have cable. We've seen folks like you."

"What rules?" I asked firmly.

"Well, this is Texas. More important, this is Sugar Lick. And nobody would throw a party on a Friday night this time of the year. Especially when the Sugar Lick Fightin' Panthers are playing the Salt Lick Bobcats for the State football Championship. It's been twenty years since we made it to the State finals and everybody in town was at the game. You two coulda stole the whole town tonight," she cackled as she hit her knee in delight.

"So, who won?" Marc asked as he walked into the living area with a tray of three martinis.

"Let me take a sip of my drink and then I'll tell you."

Marc and I exchanged quizzical glances with each other as Miz Clara finished her drink with two quick gulps. She looked at me and said, "I know his name 'cause he grew up around these parts, but honey, what's your name?"

Before I could tell her my name was Lisa, Clara shot off another question, "How long y'all been midgets?"

Meeting Frederick

BY JEWELL PARKER RHODES
FROM *Douglass's Women*

Late Spring ain't never sweet in Baltimore. Hot, slick. Sticky beyond dreaming.

I was twenty-eight, surviving as best I could. Had me a calico cat. *Lena.* I'd fan both her and me. Put ice chips in her milk. Ice on my head and wrists. May was as hot as July and there'd be no relief 'til November. Breezes didn't cool no sweat.

Legs itching against cotton. Arms damp, staining crinoline. Beads of water draining into my hair, down my cheek. Nights, just as bad. Laying in my shift, barely breathing, counting the tiniest stars I could see through the windo-top.

I felt drained. Hungry for more water. For something to fill me up.

I'd growed. I wasn't 'Lil' Bit' no more. Wasn't cute no more, either. Just short, round, dark; beyond lonely.

Mam say, "Beauty lives in the heart." But Mam was thirty miles away. Pa now dead, Mam had her own troubles living old. My trouble was forgetting the kind things she said, the words that made me feel special.

Now I was Anna, Housekeeper. Got servant's wages. Three dollars a month. Half sent to Mam. Got food, which I cooked. Milk for the cat. A room: clean but too small for a chair.

Eleven years. Working for the Baldwins. A good position. Nobody slapped me. Or cursed. Or expected me to bed them. But there wasn't much room for getting ahead. So I sewed and laundered on my off day. Thursdays. Anna, Seamstress. Wash woman. Carrying baskets to the docks.

Baltimore, great city then. Harbor for all kinds of goods and people. French and China silk. Spices. Rum. You need a gold cage for a bird? Baltimore. Sugar cane from Haiti? Bananas? Whale oil? All in Baltimore.

Irishmen, New Englanders, Virginia planters, Chinamen, British, Spanish, free colored men, they all passed through that harbor. And women—some dressed fine as queens, some barely dressed—waited for them. Waited for the men to slip them coins. Some folks went off in carriages; some went to the tavern; some got no farther than an alley.

Everybody mated, two by two.

Only new slaves—male and female—kept separate. Each had their own cage at the dock's east end. When I could, I slipped bread and meat to the women (some just children). On Sundays, men with great buckets splashed water at the slave holds. Great buckets to wash away the dirt and smell. Nothing washed away the heat. Except when my mistress ordered it, I kept clear of the docks on the Lord's Sabbath and Auction Days. Kept clear of seeing misery I couldn't fix.

Still. 1835. Baltimore, a great city.

Except for colored folks, everybody a bit rich. Got pennies to spare for colored gals to wash their shirts, pants, and privates. I worked for sailors stitching where a knife sliced, soaking tobacco stains and spit, cleaning where stew crusted on their sleeves and collars. I starched jackets for captains who brung tea, goblets, and Africans across the sea. Some I stitched gold braids for when they got promoted or won slaving treasure. But captains be the worse. Mean. They say your work not good. Insist you buy brand new shirt. After I lost my profit once, I never worked for any captain again.

This May that felt like late summer, I was working for Gardner's men. Carpenters with lots of money and no respect. Their clothes, more grease and sawdust than cotton. Mr. Gardner had a contract to build two man-of-war brigs for the Mexican government. They say July, if Gardner be done, he win big bonus. All the carpenters win bonuses, too. So everybody work hard—black and white—building those great ships.

I made my deliveries at dinner break. Men eating be generous. Less likely to complain: "This not clean enough." "This not ironed right." Foolishness. They complain to make me lower my price. Eating men don't talk much. Some even toss an extra penny.

I'd just finished giving William, the mast-maker, his clean clothes when I looked up and saw this young man standing at the unfinished bow, the ship still on stilts, looking out across the water. Not more than three feet away. He stood there, legs spaced, solid. Like nothing tip him over. No waves. No wind. He was pitched on the edge of the horizon. Boat beneath his feet. Orange-streaked sky above his head. Endless water fanning out the harbor. Seem like nothing move him from that space he choose to be. He could be a colored captain, watching, waiting for some change to happen. Some sign from the birds flying high. Some new streak of color in the sky. Some sweet odor of free.

His pants weren't fine. Brown burlap. His ankles and shins poke out. Shirt gone. His back was broad, rolling mountains. Copper-colored. Trails crisscrossed his back. I knew then he was a slave or ex-slave. No pattern to the marks. Just rawhide struck, hot and heavy. Enough to know someone had been very angry with him. Once. Twice. Maybe more.

I think I fell in love with his head. He look up, not down. Tilt of his head tell me he not beaten. Not yet. His hair curls in waves, almost touching his shoulders. Black strands lay on his neck. Made me want to reach out and feel. Made me wonder what it be like to bury my face in his hair. Would I smell the sea? Smell the oil they use to shine wood?

His hair made me think of Samson. God's strength upon him. Something else came up on me. Some wave of feeling I'd never felt. Made my feet unsteady. Made my heart race.

"Girl," Pete, the ironmaker call, "Hurry your nigger self here."

I scurried like a scared rabbit. So ashamed. This Samson man turned and saw me. Really saw. His eyes were golden, like light overflowing. I knew he saw me as a weak woman. Big. Too fat. Hurrying to this scum of a white man.

But I couldn't stop myself. Mam taught me, "Never irritate white folks. Do your work. Collect their money." But this one time I didn't want to scurry. I wanted to move slow, sashay my gown, and have this man I didn't know, think I was pretty. No. *Lovely*. I wanted to be lovely.

Twenty-eight and never had a man look at me with love. Never no passion. Desire. Mam taught me not to say those words. But I learned them as a woman. Learned them watching folks at the wharf. Learned them, too, listening to Miz Baldwin's friends—women promised to one man, yet mad about some other. They was mostly sorrowful. Passionate and sorrowful.

Mam said God made special feelings, especially for men and women. She and Pa felt them. I'd never felt one. Never 'til this man, this slave looked at me from the bow of an unfinished ship.

I hadn't enough backbone to tell this white man, "I'm coming. Don't hurry me." I scurried toward him and away from those light-filled eyes.

Head low, I got rid of all those clothes. Quick as possible. Out with the clean clothes, in with the dirty. Collect my money. Just move. Don't think about shame. The colored men were kind. Like they knew my sin. One tried to tell a joke. But it was no use. I hurried to leave that dock. Trembling. Not sure I'd ever come back. Ever hold my head high.

That evening I lay on my bed and cried. Cried 'cause I wasn't lovely. 'Cause this man would never love me. Cried 'cause he *couldn't* love me. Him being slave. I, being free. Him, young. I, old. Him, handsome. Me, ugly.

I cried and bit my pillow to keep from letting my screams out. I'd never have my own home. My own babies. I'd work my days 'til too old to work, 'til crippled and less than nothing, with no children, surviving on what little I'd set by.

Time makes the world fresh. Seven days, the world created. Seven days, my pain eased. Stopped feeling like a horse be sitting on my chest. Sabbath helped. I remembered the Lord loved me. And while I was singing "My Redeemer," I felt Mam just as if she was right beside me, taking my hand.

Got so I could see my reflection again and think I looked respectable.

Clear eyes. Thick lashes. Clear skin. I didn't have to worry about freckles like white women. But it was a sore fault not to have Mam's sweet smile or Pa's even nose.

Lilbeth got Mam's smile and four children. Even mean George, with his trim features, had a family of five. All told, I was aunt to twenty children. Two in the oven. Thinking about my family, I start thinking about this man. Handsomest man I've seen.

Between kneading bread, slicing yams, serving the Baldwin's food, I be thinking, *Why this man off by his self? Where his dinner pail? His food? Why this slave be at the shipyard? Why he not sitting with free coloreds? Where's his master?*

I think, *Charity. I can show him Christian charity.*

I keep thinking of his hair too. Light trapped in it. Him standing on the bow, looking like gold glowed about his head.

His daddy must be white. Most likely his daddy be his master. His Mam being white be rare. The grocer on Dinwidde Street had a daughter who visited with a free colored. Not even a slave. When her belly rose up, her folks whipped her awful. She lost the babe. The colored man ran to Canada.

I packed a dinner. Miz Baldwin wanted chicken and biscuits. So I cooked extras. Just a few. Then, I slipped in a piece of banana pie.

Charity was Jesus' blessing. I'd take that man supper.

I was so nervous. I wore my best dress. It was blue and I always felt small in it. Married women seemed small. Delicate and needful, like Miz Baldwin. If I didn't cook and clean for her, she'd fade away and die, resting on her ottoman.

My blue dress had little buttons down the front and back. Had lace at the wrists. Shouldn't have been wearing my best dress among those coarse men, among that sweat and dust. But I wanted that slave man to see me different.

The trip was all right. Passed out the white carpenters' clothes then went to the colored men. They ate off to the side. Gaines, a free colored, who trimmed sails acted shocked. "You almost pretty, Miz Anna." I nearly slapped him. Everybody would've seen me blush if I was less dark. I passed out the clean clothes. Collected new ones. William's pants had bloodstains from where a saw nicked his thigh. Everybody working too hard. Making mistakes. But now they was having dinner. I had passed out my clothes and if I was gonna meet this slave man, I had to do it now. Had to march myself to the ship edge and holler, "Good day."

I couldn't do it. Too nervous. I stood at the edge of the dry dock looking up. Looking up at this man looking out to sea on a ship on stilts, I started chuckling. Funny. Both of us weren't going nowhere.

He turned, looked down at me. His hand on the rail. He smiled. I did too. I said, "You eat?" His face twisted, puzzle-like. "You eat supper? You hungry?"

"No. I . . . I didn't eat. I am hungry."

My heart fell because he talked proper. Even so, I said, "Come down then." I lifted my smaller basket. "Else I'll feed this here to the gulls."

He smiled and it snatched my breath. He moved, fast yet smooth, down the bow steps, then ran to where it was safe to leap over the ship's rail. He, nimble, swift. He came upon me eager. Widest smile. His beauty nearly un-did me. I wonder whether Delilah felt this way when she first see Samson:

But he wasn't Samson. No Egypt black man. Seeing his features straight on, I could see more of the whiteness in him. But the drops of whiteness didn't matter. He still a slave. Such sadness undid me. My life was surely better than his. Not handsome, I knew I'd struggle to make a man love me. Pa said my darkness didn't matter but the world taught me it did. Even col-ored children called me "Afric."

But a handsome man—mixed black and white—might dream a better life. Might wish for genteel society. Hard to have Master be your father. Hard to see white brothers and sisters enjoy privileges not yours.

William catcall, "Better leave that slave alone. Ain't got the sense of a dog."

"Hush," I answered back. "Your sense got cut off with your baby finger."

"That's a fact," said Peter, the nail man.

The colored men laugh and I smile.

"It's true." This man's eyes were lit fierce. "I don't have a dog's sense." Then, his voice fell to a whisper. "A dog will stay where it's put. Or if it won't, a chain will hold him. I'm a man. I won't be held. Chained or un-chained."

I kept real still. I knew he was staring at me. Expecting some response. Maryland was a slave state. Words could get me whipped. But here was this man asking more of me. Asking me to agree that holding a man a slave was wrong. I inhaled, murmured low, "That's proper. Nobody has the right to hold a man."

He smiled sweetly at me.

"Or woman."

He tilt his head back and laugh. Then he held out his hand. "Frederick Bailey."

I forgot I was wearing my good dress and wiped my hand on my skirt. "Anna Murray."

"Anna," he say. My name sounded like a jewel. he clasped my palm good and solid and made me feel like I'd made a friend. Not just a good time friend but a forever friend.

And, just as quickly, the word "dangerous" flashed through my mind. "A dangerous friend." Don't know where those words come from. They just sprung up. As soon as they did, someone struck a bell and this heavy-set–looking man come between us.

"Boy. Hear that bell? Work needs doing. Go on. Get."

"He needs his dinner."

"Don't tell me what he needs," the man turned angrily, causing me to back step As I did, Frederick made a move forward. I held up my hand, not wanting to cause him trouble.

"No, sir," I said. "I understand. I just brung chicken. My Christian deed. It's still warm. You're welcome to some. I be trying to get my spirit right. Do a little something for my fellow man. But, next time, I'll come earlier, so I won't interfere with work. Would that be all right? I can bring you chicken too. My mistake this time."

This foreman looked at me. His eyes squinting as if figuring if I meant what I said. He had a big bushful of hair on his head and face. But his eyes seemed flat, weighing me cold as if we did or did not have a bargain. Then he smiled crooked, spoke tickled yet also mean.

"You sweet on him? Won't 'mount to much. Him a slave and all."

"I know," I said as Mr. Bailey said, "We're acquaintances."

I felt anger flood me at high tide. But all mixed up 'cause I wasn't sure I was upset at just the foreman. "Acquaintances" sounded cold. Yet that was us. Barely met. Barely knowing each other.

"I'm simply doing my Christian duty. Seem like his master would want him fed." I knew I was pushing too far.

"I'm his master as long as he's working for carpenters, learning how to build ships. Go on, now. Get."

"Good-bye, Mr. Bailey," I said, bowing neatly. Just like at a dance. Suddenly, I felt embarrassed.

"Good-bye, Miss Murray." He looked at me quizzing, like he don't understand me at all. Then, he bowed at the waist like he had all the time in the world.

"Boy. Come here, boy," somebody was already calling. Then, there was another cry from the opposite direction. "Boy. Over here. Brace this beam." The foreman was shoving Mr. Bailey along. I walked from the place real slow. I still held my baskets. One filled with old clothes. One filled with my best cooking.

I knew I'd return next Thursday. The sky was sheets of red, orange, yellow piled on top of one another. The clouds had turned slate gray. A storm be rolling in from the gulf, the Caribbean Sea. I felt happy and shy. Scared and nervous. My world was upside down.

How to be more than an acquaintance? How to get Mr. Bailey to think well of me? Few words exchanged on a year of Thursdays didn't add up to much. And even if it did—a free woman and a slave? Hah. Don't carry much future. I ain't so dumb I didn't know that.

But little things can add up to big. "Be special like you," Mam would always say. I just had to be patient. Take my chance when it comes.

That evening I looked for my cat. She come in late, purring. I turn my back and face the wall.

Thinking of Mr. Bailey, it be some time before I finally sleep.

Eva and Isaiah

BY VALERIE WILSON WESLEY
FROM *Ain't Nobody's Business*

WEDNESDAY, AUGUST 20

When all was said and done, Eva had to admit that any fool with two working eyes should have seen what was coming. It was bound to happen—and sooner rather than later, considering her state of mind. Yet it took her by surprise—just like everything else since that hot June night when Hutch had left. Isaiah Lonesome was more matter-of-fact about it.

"I knew the first time I saw you," he said. Although Isaiah reassured Eva that that first time was when he'd picked her up on the Garden State Parkway and *not* when Charley brought him home, and that his desperate search for a temporary home had nothing to do with where things ended up, Eva was still distressed by his words.

It all started out innocently enough, with a question about his music. Up until then, everything had gone as Eva had planned. So little seemed to have changed in her life, she hadn't even bothered to mention her new living arrangement to Charley or Steven. First of all, she was sure they would disapprove. Besides that, they were both preoccupied with living their own lives: Charlie with working and preparing for her October debut. Steven with Dana. Eva knew that one or the other was bound to stumble upon the truth at some point, and she'd do her explaining then. If she bothered to explain at all. Truth was, it felt good for once not to bother with what anyone—particularly her children—thought about her life. It made her feel free and completely independent.

As for her neighbors, they were neighborly enough to keep any questions they had about her new boarder to themselves. She spotted one or two giving Isaiah curious, appraising glances when he came home in the morning, but they were far too polite to ask her who he was or what he was doing there. Eva suspected that they assumed he was a college friend of Steven's, which was fine with her.

Things seemed to be going as Eva had planned. That first week they successfully avoided running into each other and that week established their pattern for the next two. Eva left at seven in the morning for the library just as Isaiah was coming home from the club in New York City. He left around seven at night, about an hour after she'd gotten home. She stayed in her room watching TV or he stayed in the guest room doing whatever he did until she was safely out of the house. When they ran into each other on the stairs or in the kitchen or garage, they would exchange a few pleasantries about the weather, the traffic or who would play in the World Series. He did all his laundry and made all of his calls from his apartment in Jersey City while his roommate and his new wife were at work. There were never dishes left in the sink or trash cans left unemptied. When Eva peeked into the guest room, she found that the bed was neatly made, the floor swept, and the guest towels in the small attached guest bathroom arranged on the towel rack in a tidy row. When she got home from work one Monday, she noticed that the lawn, which had begun to resemble hay, had been mowed and the newly repaired water sprinkler was shooting out rainbows of water. He paid two months' rent in cash when he moved in and always replaced any food that he took out of the refrigerator. There were times when Eva almost forgot he was there. But then she picked up his horn.

It happened on a Wednesday afternoon during the third week of his stay, almost two weeks before Labor Day. Because of a power outage at work, Eva's shift ended two hours early so she'd come home at three instead of six. She heard Isaiah's trumpet the minute she pulled into the driveway. The sound was so pure, she thought at first that it was a recording, but when he repeated the same phrase a dozen times with a new emphasis and a fresher line of sound each time, she realized he must be practicing. She opened the back door, pausing to hear the mellow tones that greeted her, and still holding her bag of groceries, was as lost in his music as she had been the first time she heard him.

He played scales, rapidly gliding through tones that were vaguely familiar, and then dashed off a riff. Transfixed, Eva sat down and listened as he settled into a sensuous, bluesy wail and then a haunting melody that made her feel wistful and melancholy. When he stopped playing, Eva anxiously waited for more. Then she put the milk in the refrigerator and headed to the sunroom, where he had been playing.

There were two entrances leading into the sunroom, which ran the length of the dining and living rooms, and as she stepped through one door he left through the other. Eva suspected that he'd heard her come in and was as anxious to avoid her as she was him. He'd left his trumpet, however, which lay in an open carrying case on a small side table.

The case was made of well-worn brown leather and lined in plush maroon velvet. The horn gleamed as if it were made of gold. Hesitating for a moment, Eva touched it with her fingertips, as if it posed some threat or would snap at her hand. Then she picked it up and examined it. It was heavier than she thought it would be, and she wondered how he could hold it as effortlessly as he did. As if in a trance, she put the instrument to her lips, curious about how it felt and where the sound came from, wondering what kind of skill it took to make music come from it like Isaiah did. For some odd reason, she expected it to be warm like skin.

"Why don't you try it?" Isaiah's deep voice coming from behind her startled her, and she nearly dropped the horn on the floor. She quickly placed it back in the case where it belonged and turned to face him, catching the scent of the lavender soap that she kept in the guest bathroom. She had bought the soap a year ago in Sag Harbor at a tiny perfume store that offered overpriced items for the "luxurious bath and bed" and had gone through her box in a month, showering and bathing with each bar until it was little more than a silver. Until this moment, she'd forgotten she had any more.

He was dressed in jeans and a royal blue cutoff T-shirt that showed off his smooth chestnut skin and his well-developed arms and shoulders. She noticed for the first time a jagged tattoo high up on his arm that encircled it like barbed wire. Eva hated tattoos but found herself staring at this one in fascination. His short black dreadlocks, which had curled up tightly from the moisture of his shower, still held tiny silver droplets of water, and one drop dripped down the side of his face like sweat. He wiped it away impatiently.

"Go ahead. Pick it up and try it."

"No. I don't think so."

"Go ahead."

Self-consciously, Eva brought the mouthpiece to her lips again, and cautiously blew through it.

"Did you blow?"

"Nothing happened."

"Try it again."

She blew again and a squawking sound, somewhere between a note and a grunt, came out. She handed the horn back to Isaiah.

"How do you do it?"

"It's all in the lips and the tongue and the way you work them." He took the horn and blew a few notes, followed it with a very fast riff and then something slow and moody. Captivated, Eva watched him, noticing how tenderly he held the instrument, almost as if it were alive.

"What were you playing earlier, before you went upstairs?"

"You could hear me?" He glanced at her sheepishly. "I hope it wasn't too loud. I don't want to freak out your neighbors."

"No. It's okay. Nobody has said anything. What was it?"

"Well, uh, you know, I compose sometimes. Play it, then write it down later. The music you heard? It was something I wrote. I'll write it down or something when I go back upstairs."

"Will you play it again?" Eva wasn't sure where that came from, asking him to play what he'd played, but she was curious, even though she knew how artists were about a work-in-progress and their hesitancy about sharing it until it was finished. She knew how she had been. She also noticed the shyness that had come into his eyes. "Well, you don't have to play it if you don't want to," she quickly added.

"No. That's okay." He picked up the horn and blew the notes he'd played before, but they were shrill and rushed. Eva wondered if she had trodden into a place she shouldn't have gone. "It sounds different every time I do it," he said, apologizing.

"Where does it come from?"

He looked puzzled as he put the horn down. "Where does what come from?"

"Turning a thought into sound. Where does it come from?" She had wondered about that from the first time she'd heard him play, from the moment he'd stepped away from the band and blown that solo that had taken her and everybody else prisoner. He had what she had lost, that was for sure. It didn't have a name, and she couldn't see, feel or touch it, but she could hear it when he picked up his horn, and she knew she had had it once, but she didn't know where or why it had gone.

His eyes questioned her. "I don't know where it comes from. I just blow."

"But how?"

He looked perplexed. "I don't know how. I just do it."

As if explaining, he picked up his trumpet and played something short filled with riffs and short blasts of sound. Then he smiled, shrugged and handed her the trumpet.

"Try it."

"You know I can't play like you."

"Just try it. Hold your lips like this." He pursed his lips together. Eva wondered if he was trying to change the subject, but she did what he said.

"Like this?"

"No." He pursed his lips again, demonstrating, and Eva tried it until hers came close. "Now you put it to your lips." Eva timidly took the horn and held it against her lips. "Now hold it this way," he said, pausing for a moment as he turned her body away from his. His arms encircled her body as he showed her how to grasp the horn, gently touching her underarms and gliding past her breasts as he held her in an embrace that wasn't quite an embrace. Eva stiffened, and then allowed her body to shift into his. She caught her breath. She liked the way he made her feel, so fragile and in an odd way protected. She could feel his body moving closer to hers, and his smell, blending subtly with that of the lavender, was inviting and dangerous. She drew back, aware suddenly that maybe she was enjoying this too much. But it was too late.

He nibbled very lightly on the back of her neck, his lips gently traveling upward to the base of her scalp, and then slowly and evenly back down again as far as they would go until they were cut off by the top of her collar. He stroked the curve of her neck and her chin and then gently caressed her breasts. Eva lost her breath and collapsed against him with a sigh. He took the horn from her hands, dropped it into the case, turned her toward him and kissed her fully and deeply, his tongue touching hers. Eva, completely aroused now by his touch and the surprise of it all, felt the rumble of sexual desire (which she hadn't felt in the better part of eight months) stir violently in the pit of her stomach. She pulled back.

"What's wrong?"

"I don't know!" She could hear the panic in her own voice.

He smiled that mischievous smile that she was never quite sure what to make of and nodded toward the stairs.

It was as if they did some Star Trek transport thing, it seemed to her when she thought about it later. She remembered being in the living room surprised that he was kissing her, and next thing she knew she was lying in his arms, completely nude in the guest bedroom. She couldn't remember negotiating the stairs or opening and closing the door to the room. She vaguely remembered seeing and entering it. The room was small and oblong with two windows, a hanging rhododendron and a ceiling fan, which whirred softly. But strangely enough, it was as if the room wasn't part of her house. Although she'd changed the linen before he came and had obviously bought it, she couldn't remember ever seeing it before. The whole room seemed unfamiliar, as if she were in the middle of some erotic dream and had never picked out the cream-colored wallpaper trimmed with blue cornflowers or the blue fake Persian rug of the glass IKEA vase filled with dried flowers that sat on the bureau. She didn't remember taking off her clothes or crawling next to him between the cool sheets. She remembered hearing the whir of the ceiling fan and thinking how good it felt against her naked skin, and how nice that it was on, but she didn't remember the time of day or whether it was dark or light or day or if she'd locked the front door.

His body was thinner than she had thought it would be, but muscular, and Eva was momentarily self-conscious about her own. But her desire for him quickly outweighed any embarrassment, and she realized she didn't give a damn one way or the other how she looked. When he'd pulled back the summer quilt, a cream-and-lace-covered number a friend had given her as a wedding gift, she felt a twinge of momentary guilt, but then realized she didn't give a damn about that either. She was too aroused to worry about anything but how good his smooth lean body felt next to hers. His obvious excitement was contagious, and she was over-powered by her need for him.

He opened her lips with his tongue again, kissing her fervently until she found herself with tongue in his mouth, wanting to touch and taste every part of him. His lips on her mouth and face, her eyelids, her neck, then all over her body, felt to her as if he were playing some long, sweet song. He followed the lines of her body with his hands, reading each piece of her with his fingertips and palms, as Eva touched, nuzzled, kissed every part of him that she could reach. He found new parts of her to touch or stroke—parts of her that she'd never known could be so quickly aroused—the small of her back, the tiny space between her breasts, the slender area near yet not touching her public hair, and finally gently teasing her clitoris with his tongue and bringing her to the edge of orgasm before he pulled away.

She wanted to devour him. She couldn't get enough of the salty taste of his neck on her tongue as it zipped down to his lips or the solid feel of his chest against the flat palm of her hand. Her fingertips slid over the muscles in his shoulders and upper arms. The ragged tattoo had fascinated her when she'd first spotted it and now she ran the bottom of her tongue down and across it, thrusting her face into his shoulders and arms, playing in the tight curly hair under his arms, around his belly button, and gliding down finally to slide his penis into her mouth as he buried his face into her stomach. And then finally, facing each other, pausing for a moment to gaze with stunned amazement into each other's eyes, as he thrust himself into her. Eva reached her first orgasm effortlessly, and then had a smaller, less intense one before he rolled onto his side, exhausted. And it was better the second time.

But the first thought that came to Eva's mind when they finally lay quiet and still beside each other was, *What have I done?* She tried to get up. Isaiah pulled her back down beside him.

"What's wrong?"

"Stop asking me that!"

"Tell me."

"When I figure it out, I'll tell you."

"You don't regret this, do you?" He had read her mind.

"I don't know yet." It was an honest answer.

"Then let's do it again," he said with his mischievous chuckle, and they did, more leisurely this time, as if getting to know each other again in a less frenzied, more intimate way.

When it was over, they slept for an hour. Eva awoke to Isaiah climbing out of bed. Fascinated, she watched him move around the room. She had known each crevice and crease of his body with her hands and mouth and now she studied him with her eyes, noticing how completely at ease he was with himself. He glanced up at her and smiled his strange amused smile.

"Come on, let's take a shower."

"Giye me a minute." Eva, her passion spent, was self-conscious again about the years between them, those little sags and wrinkles that would show up in the late afternoon sun that was streaming unfiltered through the window. *How could I have done something like this?* she wondered. Somewhere between the passion when they first hit the bed and the first time they made love, she had reminded him to use condoms, and she now said a prayer of thanks for *that* presence of mind. Nevertheless, she felt like an irresponsible fool.

When she heard him turn on the shower, she grabbed her clothes from the floor where she'd stripped them off and dashed out of the room and up the stairs to the safety of her bedroom. She closed her door, buried the impulse to lock it and jumped into her shower. When the water hit her body, she thought about Isaiah again and desire for him tore through her body with the sharpness of pain. She turned on the cold water, letting it drip down her back and breasts, opening her mouth to it, letting it run down her throat, tasting it the way she'd tasted him. Then she dried off with a rough towel, slipped into a caftan and went downstairs.

Isaiah was sitting at the kitchen table, fully dressed, sipping a Sprite. When Eva sat down on the opposite side of the table, he offered her the can. Avoiding his eyes, she took a swig and handed it back to him.

"So where did you go?"

"Back upstairs."

"Why?"

"I wanted to shower in my own bathroom."

"Oh." He shrugged. "I was thinking about what you asked me before," he said solemnly after a moment.

"What did I say?" *God knew what she'd screamed out.*

"About how I play my music. How I *create*. Don't you remember?"

Eva thought for a moment, and then nodded. *That* conversation certainly belonged to another age.

"Well . . ." He paused. "I start with a note. One note. And I'll blow until it's as perfect as I can get it, and then I go back and blow another, and another, until finally the whole thing is done. Nothing miraculous. Just one note at a time. That's the way I do it."

Neither of them said anything for a while after that. They just passed the Sprite can back and forth until it was empty. Then Isaiah glanced at his watch and said it was time to go to work, and he'd catch her later on that night. After he left, Eva sat at the table with her head in her hands and wondered what in the hell she'd gotten herself into.

FROM **Discretion**

BY ELIZABETH NUÑEZ

I took the train to Long Island. Marguerite picked me up at her station. I brought her red roses. I would bring her red roses the next time I saw her. One week later, when she was sure I knew she loved me, she asked me not to bring her red roses again.

"It makes me feel like a courtesan. Your mistress. I am more to you than a mistress."

We had been together again for just seven days and she knew that already.

But that first time when I brought her red roses, I had taken a risk for her that was more than the risk a man takes for a woman with whom he knows he would have only an affair, a temporary arrangement, sexual and nothing more.

I had had a meeting that afternoon with the U.N. ambassador from the United States. It was a meeting that my team had planned for weeks. We wanted a clear understanding of the extent of the U.S. commitment to the unconditional suffrage of all black people in South Africa. We were aware of the fears of the white world. We knew of the nightmares that terrorized even their waking hours: the specter of the masses of black people free at last. Liberated. *Armed.*

For decades white South Africa had unleashed indescribable cruelties upon its black fellow citizens—insufferable oppression, torture, humiliation. Now white South Africans were terrified. They knew that that kind of suffering demanded not simply justice, but revenge. This was not America. This was not England. Black people in South Africa were not in the minority. Only brute force, they believed, guns—weapons blacks could not afford—had been able to stop them from massacring their torturers. White South Africa was afraid to shut its eyes, afraid to sleep. What if the locks to the prisons where they had penned black people were removed? What if their passes were destroyed? The ones they had created to herd black people into slums, to rope them out of the areas where they had built their sprawling houses? Where their children played? They had let black people in, of course, to work in their kitchens, to dig their ditches, to empty their garbage, their refuse, but what if? *What if?*

We had met with the American ambassador as much to calm the nerves of white Americans, Europeans, white South Africans as to reassure ourselves that the West would not retreat from its position of outrage at the injustices that had been inflicted on black people in South Africa. I was prepared for this meeting. I had spent weeks rehearsing what I would say, anticipating objections, preparing rebuttals, and yet that afternoon, all I could think of was Marguerite, my mind unable to fix itself on anything else but her.

My teammates told me that I had looked at my watch three times. Brilliant strategy, they said. We let the Americans know that we were the ones running out of time. If they did not use their power immediately to force de Klerk into complying completely with our demands, we could not be responsible for what would happen in South Africa. We could not guarantee that white women would be safe. Who knows what could happen when the people get their hands on the white man's guns? On his money?

But it was not a strategy I had intended, and one man, the oldest on the team, suspected me. He was the brother of the president of my country. Bala Keye, my wife's uncle, a man I never liked, a man who never liked me. At the last minute my president had sent him to join the team.

"In case something happens to you, Oufoula. Like you're sick one day and we find ourselves in the unfortunate position where our country is not represented."

It was not an unusual arrangement for my president to make—to provide a contingency plan in case of an emergency. The only unusual part of it was that he had chosen his brother to be second in command on our team to the U.N.

Bala Keye was the youngest son of the president's father. He was a man with more ambition than talent and even less presence, and his brother knew it. Of the men who claimed they admired me but who I knew wished me misfortune, Bala Keye wished the worst for me.

I say he was the oldest man on the team, but not many years lay between us. Less than ten, enough that it seemed reasonable that he should be convinced that he had seniority over me and thus was entitled to more privileges than me, and yet sufficiently slight that he could consider me a peer, a contemporary, a competitor with whom he saw himself in contest for prizes he always lost. It was that precarious difference between our ages that was the cause of his resentment of me. That, and the fact that though the president was his brother, he had chosen me over him to be his first ambassador to Ghana.

Bala Keye carried this resentment like an albatross around his neck. Even when he laughed it was easy to mistake the quivers that ran through his body and the tears that rolled down his eyes as expressions of rage rather than joy. I did not know what caused the president to change his mind and send him on this mission to the U.N. Perhaps Bala Keye begged him and the president did not have the heart or the will to refuse him. The president was past seventy-five. There were many who said he was becoming soft, docile.

It was Bala Keye who pressed me to join the team for dinner that night. We were more certain than we had ever been of Mandela's release. My team wanted to celebrate. I said I was tired. I said I had a headache. The others were sympathetic. I had worked hard, they said. Harder than any of them. But Bala Keye was insistent.

It was five-thirty before I could get him to surrender. I was running out of the florist carrying the red roses I bought for Marguerite on my arm like a bridal bouquet when I saw him. Our eyes locked in one terrible moment before he turned away.

It was the gesture of an amateur diplomat, but he had put me on notice. He had an advantage over me, his eyes told me. He could trade on it whenever he wished.

I had made two mistakes that day, because of my desire for Marguerite. I, who had been known to be meticulous, a man whose appearance was that of a happy man, a contented family man. A man whose insouciance put the enemy at ease, who concealed his anger, his rage, his hatred, a man who did not wear his heart on his sleeve, who did not leave trails to the thoughts on his mind. Yet I had looked at my watch three times at a meeting with the U.N. ambassador from the United States. I had run like a lovesick puppy to the florist shop. I was seen cradling a bouquet of red roses on my arm rushing to the six o'clock train to Long Island. Rushing to Marguerite.

But these two were not the first mistakes I had made since I met Marguerite again. I had kissed her in the car on the corner of Thirty-eighth Street and Fifth Avenue. I had put my hand under her blouse and cupped her breasts. I had slid my fingers up her thighs and would have done more. Would have pressed her back against the car seat and made love to her there, in her car, had she not stopped me, had she not promised the weekend.

I would have done that though I was aware, though part of my brain was aware that I was in a car parked on the street in the middle of Manhattan.

That I could be seen. That in this city, in this country where fortunes are made by the humiliation of public figures, where a president can be brought down low, hauled into a court of senators, exposed before a nation for a single indiscretion, say, fondling the breasts of one of those willing sycophants intoxicated by the mere proximity to power, I could have tainted the reputation of my teammates, undermined the seriousness of our commitment to our mission, a mission that had consequences not only for the liberation of South Africa but for the liberation of all of Africa—the liberation from stereotypes that still persisted though Tarzan had been unmasked for what he was: a myth to quiet the white man's fears of the power of Africa.

Had I been asked to tell the principle that guided my life up to that moment, up through all the years to that moment, I would have said, as I believed then—as I believed that day when I tore up Catherine's letter, the letter that gave me Marguerite's phone number—one should not allow one's private affairs to affect one's public affairs. I had conducted my life according to this standard. I believed chaos would follow, confusion and disorder, if one's private life spilled into matters concerning one's public life.

But now disorder engulfed me. Yet I was not afraid, for chaos had not followed, nor confusion. Never before had I achieved such clarity of purpose. Never before had any decision of mine, any action I had taken, been so completely untainted by influence other than my personal desires, my personal needs. I knew what I was doing. I was choosing to do it, freely, of my own volition.

Up to that moment, for more than half a century, I had carefully compartmentalized my life. I had put the things that pleased me, the things that reassured me, in the front parts of my mind where I could see them, where I could retrieve them. The others—the things I did not like, the things I did not want to face, or could not—I had put in boxes and sealed them. I had stored them deep in the dark enclaves of my soul. And yet they had resurfaced. And yet always they had filtered through the reality I had orchestrated: the things I wanted to forget in the daylight—my mother's suicide, my father's indifference. Mulenga. Margarete, the dark fantasy I had created from Mulenga. Marguerite of flesh and blood. Marguerite, whom I loved, whom I lost. These memories filtered through my dreams, the lies I told as truths. They did not go away.

My mother must not have been afraid of the chaos I feared up to this moment. She must have found freedom when her passion for the man she loved spread over everything, engulfed everything, diminished everything—public expectations, public demands, her reputation, her place in her village community, her security, her future. The son she loved.

She must have been able to think her *own* thoughts then, feel her *own* feelings when the lines blurred, when the barriers came down between the things that ought to have mattered to her and the things that did. She loved me. She loved the man who slit his throat for love of her more than she loved me.

So it was that Marguerite mattered most to me now. At this moment. Not the American ambassador to the U.N., not Bala Keye, not the possibility that Bala Keye could blackmail me.

Marguerite's hair was up in a ponytail when she came to meet me, the way she had worn it the first time I saw her in New York. She had on a short black and tan plaid pants skirt, a white T-shirt, and a gray cardigan. She looked younger than she had seemed the night before. I felt old again, uneasy. I wished I had stopped to change my clothes, to take off my gray suit, my white monogrammed shirt, my drab blue striped tie—my old man's uniform—but Bala Keye, my nemesis, with his envious heart, had not allowed me. In seconds, though, my uneasiness dissipated. She was fifty years old. Women less than half her age had desired me. They considered me handsome. They knew I was a wealthy man, a man in a position of great power in my country. If I had not had affairs with them, it was not because I could not, but, rather, because I would not. It was because of my commitment to my family, my dedication to my work.

It was because of my love for Marguerite.

No woman who ever tempted me compared with Marguerite. No woman had been able to make me take the risk of losing my wife, my family, my position, my prestige—all I had.

Still, when Marguerite ran toward me, I broke out in a cold sweat. I was a man looking into a mirror of himself, terrified of the reflection there. A man who seemed to have no fear of what could await him, who did not care how his life could change now that he would have in reality the woman who had consumed his dreams for more than twenty-five years.

Once, passion had made me a prisoner in my room until a fantasy saved me. Once, passion had bereft me of a mother, caused her to take her life. I remembered all this as Marguerite approached me, but I could not turn back. That man in the mirror would keep on walking into that fire before me. Nothing I could say or do would deter him, not even the knowledge that the flames would devour him.

Marguerite reached up and kissed me passionately on my mouth. "I was surprised when you told me you were going to take the train," she said. She took the red roses from my hand as if I had given her a business card. I should have guessed then that the roses had not pleased her. "Where's your driver?"

"I take trains, too, you know."

"A man in your position?" She dug her fingers in my ribs and tickled me.

My tension broke. "Yes, a man in my position." I laughed with her. "But only for you."

"Well, I hope you don't mind driving in a beat-up old car."

I opened the car door for her. "So long as you're my driver," I said.

"And you go where I take you?"

Her smile and her question were the smile and the question of a woman of confidence, a woman who knew she could take me wherever she wanted and I would follow. The man in the mirror did not care. He would go with her willingly, anywhere.

Marguerite lived in a little house with white wood shingles, facing the Great South Bay in a small town on the South Shore of Long Island. She said it was the servants' quarters that was once connected to the dilapidated Victorian house that stood next to hers. It used to be the summer home of some rich Manhattanite, she told me, in the years before they discovered the Hamptons. She had gutted the interior and opened the roof with skylights. There were only three rooms in the house: a small bedroom, a kitchen that faced the street, and a large room in the back that opened to the sea. We had to walk through the kitchen to reach it.

"It's the secret of the South Shore." Marguerite stood next to me at the huge sliding glass door that extended from one end of the large room to the other.

The water surprised me. I would not have guessed it was there. We had driven through a residential area of tiny clapboard houses separated by squares of manicured lawn. The cars parked in the driveways and on the streets were domestic American cars, not the usual boxy foreign cars one associated with the rich, the people who could afford to live near the sea.

"Nobody guesses it either. A lot of streets here lead to the water—to the bay or the canal."

The water in front of us was still. Quiet. Two boats moved slowly across it. In the diaphanous twilight I could make out a dog and a man in one, two children and their parents in the other. "It seems so calm," I said.

"Because it's a bay, not the ocean."

"Does it ever flood?"

"Well, for one, we're built about eight feet above sea level. See the bulwark at the end of the lawn? And for the other, we're protected by that barrier reef in front of us." She pointed to a thin strip of land on the other side of the bay. "It protects us from the Atlantic, though sometimes the ocean breaks through, but not as far west as where we are. More to the east where the rich people have their houses."

"You don't seem to be doing too badly yourself," I said.

"I was lucky. The couple who bought the big house couldn't afford the servants' quarters. They needed the money, so they sold it to me at a bargain. It was a mess when I got it. It cost me more to fix it up than I paid for it. There are always banks that will lend money to someone with a full-time job."

She walked to the kitchen and I followed her.

"So you're still working full-time?"

"I'm tenured. You don't give that up. I teach at night. It still gives me time for my art in the day. Then I have the summers."

She opened a drawer under the kitchen counter and pulled out a tablecloth. "I put this on my drawing table and voilà," she said. "A dining room table."

It was the simple elegance of that ivory linen tablecloth accomplishing just what she wanted it to do that reminded me suddenly of Nerida. For the second time in two days I would find myself noticing how similar they were, and, perhaps, it was that thought more than anything else that calmed my anxieties finally.

There was no likeness, of course, in their physical appearance, but they had the same character—the same values, the same goals for the children. Now, as I could see, the same taste. Gone were the bright colors, the careless scattering of pillows I had found liberating in Marguerite's old apartment. But I was a different man now, with different needs. An older man. I wanted to gather in my nets. I wanted to hold on to the things I had. I wanted to bind to me the people I loved. The muted colors in my home suited me, reflected my mood. The colors in Marguerite's house were muted, too, the furniture sparse and neatly arranged. They pleased me.

Marguerite had folded her easel and stacked it against the wall to the side of the glass front door.

"When I work, I put it in the middle of the room under the skylight," she told me. "That way, I get the light from the sun above me and in back of me."

There was a wooden closet with large doors next to the easel. She told me she stored her tools there and her work. Apart from a striped gray and white couch that faced the bay, and her drawing table with two chairs that stood behind the couch, the only other furniture in the room was a matching pale gray armchair and a pine wood cocktail table on which she had placed a stack of large art books and an antique bronze metal jug filled with sunflowers.

I had noticed the sunflowers immediately when I entered the room. I knew she would not replace them with the roses I had given her. She had put my roses in a glass vase. After she set the table, she placed them on top of the linen tablecloth. They looked garish. Out of place. Vulgar. And yet I would bring her red roses two more times, until she stopped me. Until she told me that red roses were the flowers men brought to their mistresses—the peacock's plumage meant to announce to the peahen the peacock's readiness to straddle her: biology, the animal instinct, set irreversibly in motion.

"I'm not as colorful as I was before," she was saying to me now, as though she sensed my need for an explanation, some way to understand the change in her, to interpret the pale palette of colors before me.

"The sea tamed me. I couldn't compete. Only blend."

She said she kept her work in the closet to prevent it from being bleached by the sun. Most of it she took to her office. She had hung only one in the room. It was a large framed painting of bamboo trees. She had mounted it on the back wall, away from the windows on either side of the room.

"There was a pinkish carpet on the floor. At least I think pink was its original color, not red. Most of it had turned ivory, except in the places where I suppose there was furniture. I ripped it all out and sanded the floors. The wood turned out to be in good shape."

"It looks great," I said.

"I thought of staining it darker so it wouldn't look so raw."

"I like it," I said.

She smiled approvingly at me.

The furnishings in her bedroom were sparse, too, simple: a bed with a plain white spread, a pale green rug on the bare wood floor, a night table covered with a white cloth edged with white embroidery. On the table was a clay pot of purple African lilies and a silver reading lamp next to a stack of books. Opposite the bed, bookshelves, some buckling under the weight of too many books, lined the walls from ceiling to floor. There was no TV in the room. She kept it in the kitchen, she said. It distracted her when she cooked.

"Maybe I shouldn't be distracted." She laughed.

We sat down to eat. She had made poached salmon. It was a fish Nerida knew I loved. She had prepared it the way Nerida knew I enjoyed it.

"I can make this better, I promise you."

"Let me taste it," I said. I put some salmon on my fork and brought it to my mouth. "Perfect. It couldn't be better. Perfect." I touched her hand. "Like you, Marguerite. Like everything about you."

After dinner I searched the bookshelves in her bedroom looking for the books she once wanted me to read.

"Do you remember our quarrel over Achebe?"

She joined me. "*Things Fall Apart.*" She pulled it from the shelf.

"You were right, you know." I took it from her hand. "I was a callow fellow. I expected too much from Africa. I was too ready to blame Africa alone for its problems."

"I was also too young, too idealistic. I didn't want to believe that colonialism had done such damage. I didn't want to believe that it affected our minds, that it could distort our thinking. Fanon was right. Though the Europeans have gone, we still have to battle racism. The one we have internalized. Have you read him?"

I nodded. "A Martiniquan gave me a book of his."

"*Black Skin, White Masks*"?

"Yes, that's the one. But we should be easy on ourselves. We were both young, Marguerite. We didn't know better." I handed her back the Achebe novel.

"Do you still have the books I gave you?" She turned to put it on the shelf.

"They are in my bedroom," I said. "Opposite to my bed on my bookshelves. Like yours are." She was standing in front of me. I put my arms around her waist.

"Do you read them?"

"Sometimes," I said. "The times when I missed you."

She leaned her head against my chest. "Did you miss me?"

"There were times I missed you so much, I could not bear to have anyone around me."

She faced me and put her arms around my neck. "And did you dream of me?"

"More times than I would want to tell you."

She kissed my neck. "I want you to tell me," she whispered. "Tell me how many times you dreamed of me."

"There were nights I could not sleep, waking up from a dream about you."

She kissed my mouth. "For twenty-five years? You dreamed about me for twenty-five years?"

"Twenty-five years. I never forgot you."

She unbuttoned my shirt. "And what did you want to do when you dreamed about me?"

"I wanted to make love to you."

"Like we used to?"

She had taken off my shirt. My fingers were now under her T-shirt, unfastening her bra. She pulled her arms through her sleeves, and I lifted her T-shirt over her head.

"Did you ever dream of me?" I asked her.

"Many times."

"And did you want to make love to me?"

"Many times."

I slid off the band that held up her hair and kissed her behind her ears.

"Even when I was married," she said, "I dreamed of you."

I cannot blame what followed on these words she said to me. I cannot say that because she mentioned her marriage, I was reminded of mine, and because I was reminded of mine, my body refused me. For the truth was I had not forgotten my marriage. I was the son of a long line of men who had had many wives, a man who had come to Christianity after he had passed the age of myth. So Marguerite had often told me before.

So it must have been.

So it was that I felt no guilt when I kissed Marguerite, no guilt when I lay naked next to her. And so it had to be that when my body failed me, when it could not do what my heart, my soul, every fiber of my being desperately pleaded with it to do, I could not say it was because I was married, because Marguerite reminded me that I already had one wife.

"Did this ever happen to you before?"

I could hear the tremors in her voice.

I lay on top of her naked, impotent. "No," I said.

Tears gathered in the corners of her eyes. "It must be me. It must be me, then."

"No. No." I pulled her on top of me and hugged her. "It's not you. It's me."

"It's happened to me before," she said. "Harold . . ."

I put my finger to her lips. "It's not you. You are warm and beautiful and lovely."

"It happened with Harold," she said.

"I am not Harold."

"He said it was me."

"It's not you. How could it be you? Look at you. You're a sensual woman. Your skin is the color of the Sahara. Brown, warm, smooth. Not a blemish, not a mark. You smell like the desert. Like a flower in the desert."

"He said it was me," she repeated.

"Harold was a fool."

"He said I was hard to love."

"Harold was wrong."

"He said—"

"You are lovable, Marguerite. You are easy to love."

"Then why?"

"It happens to men, you know. More than we are willing to admit. I'm just nervous. Anxious. It's been too many years. Tomorrow," I said. "You'll see tomorrow. I'll be okay tomorrow."

I had told her the truth. I was anxious and nervous. But it had not happened to me before. Not in twenty-eight years of marriage to Nerida.

This was the fear every man lives with: the day he would lie on top of a beautiful woman and be betrayed by the body that had always served him.

And yet I did not think that this was happening to me—the impotence men of my age feared. I knew that the stories we told of our wives' declining libidos were a camouflage to mask our anxieties, our fear of losing our own sexuality, our potency. We sought reassurance from each other. We wanted to convince each other that the end had not come. And I did not think the end had come for me that night. I knew that when my heart had stopped racing, that when with each touch of Marguerite's hand on my body my toes would stop tingling, my spine would stop quivering, I would have control of my body again.

"Let's sleep," I said. "It's too much for one day. After so long."

After so long. Not only with Marguerite, but also with Nerida. But I did not tell her that. That it had been six months since Nerida had let me in her bed. I was overexcited, overstimulated. My desire for her too intense, my mind racing too fast for my body.

Yet I knew that when my body failed me, it was not only because anxiety had reduced me to jelly, not only because I had waited so long, wanted her for so long. Remnants of a hard-learned reticence had returned to plague me. When I lay naked, stretched out on top of her, trying in vain to make love to her, it came back to warn me: This thing I had taught myself to shun. I remembered the passion that took control of me with Mulenga, the passion that had driven me into my room in the mission school, a prisoner of my fantasies. The passion that drove me into my work when Marguerite ordered me to leave her apartment, the passion that sometimes made me a stranger in my house.

The passion that had cost my mother her life.

The passion that made the man who loved her put a razor to his throat.

"You are beautiful," I whispered to Marguerite. "Desirable. Too desirable."

She curled into my arms. "Tomorrow," she said. She kissed the hair on my chest. "I love you," she whispered.

Her words would make me sleep until morning, would make me forget. They allowed me to sleep without dreams that would wake me in a sweat. I had her with me now, the curves of her body locked into mine like the pieces of a puzzle. We were whole again. I was safe. The passion would not undo me.

In the morning I reached for her. The trembling under my skin had subsided, my blood ran warm again through my groin. We made love as we had before when we were young—with the same energy, the same intensity, the same passion. I remembered she liked my tongue in her navel. She remembered I liked hers in my ears. I remembered she loved when I kissed her neck. She remembered I loved when she licked my chest. When the moment came, she stretched out taut beneath me and pushed me away, shout-

ing the same words, "Get off. Get off." They had the same meaning. I
braced myself and held on to her until the moan that had begun in the back
of her throat rolled out to her lips, gathered force, and she screamed.
Screamed with the pleasure of it. Begged me not to stop, not to let go.
"Wait. Wait. Not yet. Not yet." And when I joined her, our voices became a
symphony of the past restored.

Afterward, she lay on her side next to me. My hand traveled across the
sand dunes of her body, the crest of her breasts, the slope down to her waist,
the incline up her hips. I kissed each inch I touched. I buried my face in the
basin that cradled her navel.

"I like this," I said. "I like this valley. I could lose myself in this valley."

She kissed the top of my head and turned my face upward to hers.

"And I love this," she said. She covered my eyes with her mouth, first one
eye, then the next, and she ran the tip of her tongue down the spread of my
nose and across my lips. "And I love this."

No one had ever kissed me like that. Not Nerida. No one. No one had
ever made me *feel* so worthy, so handsome. She said she loved my wide nose,
my thick lips, my nappy hair, my blue-black skin. I had a classical face, she
said. Like a piece of African art.

"Tell me," I asked her, grateful, wanting to give something back, "tell me
your secret. How do you stay so beautiful, so young?"

"I am beautiful and young because you think I am beautiful and young."

"No." I looked into her eyes. "I tell you this objectively. Without bias. A
man would have to be blind not to see how young you look, how beautiful."

"I'm short," she said. "Short people seem younger than they are."

"I know short people your age. They don't look as young as you."

"Ah," she said, "you mean menopausal women. You mean women who
can no longer have babies. Women whose wombs have dried up."

Discovered, I rubbed my chin across her hip to distract her.

"Ouch," she said. "That hurts."

"My stubble."

"I take a tiny little pink pill every morning." She would not let me off so
easily from the slip I had made—Ibrahim Musima's theories that had penetrated my defenses even as I rejected them.

"A what?"

"To keep me young."

"A pill?"

"The elixir of life for the menopausal woman. It keeps us vibrant. HRT.
Didn't you hear of it? Hormone replacement therapy. It gives us the estro-
gen we lose after menopause. It makes us young again, our breasts firm. It
makes our skin glow. It's bad for us."

"Bad?"

"Yes, bad." She turned on her back. "Some say it can cause breast cancer."

"Then why do you take it?"

"Vanity."

"If it's bad for you, throw it away."

"You see this skin you like?" Her fingers brushed her cheek. "It would be dry without it."

"I don't love your skin. I love you."

"All men say that, but we women know it's the image you love."

"Marguerite!" But as my tone of voice admonished her, my heart sank. What else did she know, my Marguerite?

"You can't imagine how terrible a woman feels when she sees the disappointment in a man's eyes that will inevitably be there, later if not sooner. Then she knows for certain that she is not who he has fantasized her to be." Her eyes grew dark.

She was speaking about men in general, but still she frightened me. She had come too close to a truth I had lived. But there could be no comparison between her and my fantasy. She was infinitely more beautiful, her character immeasurably more admirable.

"We are not talking about men and women, Marguerite," I said, and pulled her to me. "We are talking about you and me, and I, Oufoula, say to you, Marguerite, that I love you, not your skin."

She closed her eyes. "Let me get old, Oufoula."

She said it as if begging for something I would willfully withhold from her and, perplexed by this sudden change, the pleading evident in her eyes when she reopened them, I responded quickly, "We will get old together, Marguerite."

But that was not the answer she was looking for. "I don't want to have to make myself young to please you," she said.

"You don't have to. I love you the way you are. Because of who you are." I brushed my lips across her forehead.

"And will you still love the real me when my skin is wrinkled?"

"Oh, Marguerite."

I was about to add more protestations, swearing my love for her, when she sighed and pushed herself away from me. "We play your game," she said. Her lips curved downward, sadly.

"Game?"

"We wear the makeup, the fancy clothes. We diet. We let doctors cut us up. I take HRT. But thee is always someone younger, firmer, that TV gives men to dream about."

"Marguerite." I pulled her back to me. "I have no interest in someone younger. It is you I love."

"And will you still want me when I am dried up like a prune?"

"I will love you forever." I held her tightly to my chest. "When you are old, when you are gray . . ."

"Grayer."

"When you've lost your teeth. Forever."

She laughed, but she repeated the word after me. "Forever," she said.

We both believed that was true.

An Orange Line Train to Ballston

BY EDWARD P. JONES

The first time Marvella "Velle" Watkins saw the man with the dreadlocks, rain threatened and she just managed to get herself and her three children down into the subway before it began. The rain was waiting for them at the end of their trip. On the crowded Stadium-Armory subway platform, she held Avis, the baby, by the hand, lest the girl wander off, and Marvin, the oldest, stood on his mother's other side. Marvin was looking into the tunnel out of which the train would come. He held his bookbag under one arm and looked down at the lights that were flush with the floor and whose blinking would indicate the approach of the train.

"How do the lights know when the train is comin'?" he asked his mother. This was a new question. "I don't know," she said. "Avis, stop kicking like that." The girl continued to kick out at something imaginary in front of her and Marvella tugged at her arm until the girl stopped. "I guess," she said to Marvin, "that way down the line the moving train hits something on the tracks and that tells the lights ahead to start blinking."

Marvin seemed satisfied with the answer. He studied the lights and as he did they began to blink. The boy was nine. *My son the engineer*, his mother thought.

On the other side of Avis stood Marcus, her second son. Marvella noted out of the corner of her eye that he was yapping away, as usual, and at first Marvella thought he was talking to Avis or having another conversation with himself. "Everybody else is borin," he said to her the first time she asked why he talked to himself. He was now seven. Long before the train came into view, it sent ahead a roar, which always made Marvella look left and right to make certain her children were safe and close. And when she turned away from the coming train, she saw that Marcus had been talking to the man with the dreadlocks.

Marcus and Avis managed to find seats just in front of their mother, and she was surprised when the dreadlock man sat down beside her. Marvin found a seat on the aisle across from his siblings. Beside the boy was a woman as old as Marvella's mother, asleep, her head leaning against the window. For a few seconds Marvin looked at the old woman, then he opened his bookbag and took out a piece of paper.

The subway man running the train announced through the speakers in the ceiling that this was an orange line train to Ballston.

Marcus, after sitting for a few seconds or so, turned around and knelt in his seat, facing the man with the dreadlocks. Being so small, he hadn't been able to get a good look at the dreadlocks while he stood beside the man on the platform, but now he was closer and more or less head-to-head with the man and he planned to take advantage of the situation. I should tell him to turn around, his mother thought, but this might be one time when he's justified. Avis, a head or so shorter than Marcus, followed her brother's example and was staring at the man as well. A minute or so won't hurt, Marvella thought.

"Why you got your hair like that?" Marcus asked the man.

"You don't have no comb or nothin'?" Avis asked him. "My mama wouldn't do my hair like that." Avis was four and on any given day had a different answer about whether she liked the idea of going to school next year.

"Oh, yeah," the man said, "I got all the combs and brushes I need."

"Then why you do your hair like that?" Marcus said.

The train stopped and more people entered the car. The subway man told the new people what train they had entered.

The dreadlock man said, "It's nice like this. It makes me feel good to wear it like this."

"Oh," Marcus said.

"Oh," Avis said. Then she looked the man up and down and said, "Don't you want a haircut? My mama take my brothas to the barbashop. She can take you to the barbashop, too."

The man laughed. Marvella had been surprised that he did not have a West Indian accent. Each lock of his hair was at least a foot long and there were at least twenty locks with perhaps the roundness of a nickel. Around each lock, about an inch up from the end, there was a band, and each band was a different, dark color. The man smelled like the incense street vendors sold.

"No," the man said. "No barbershops for me. I like it like this."

The train stopped again. "Good mornin'. This is an orange line to Ball-ston," the subway man said.

Now there were people standing in the aisle and Marvella could not see Marvin.

"You look like a man I saw in a scary movie one time," Marcus said.

"Marcus, turn round!"

"It's okay," the dreadlock man said, and with one finger he momentarily touched Marvella's hand. "You like scary movies?" he said to Marcus.

"Yeah," the boy said. "But my mama don't let me watch 'em. Me and Marvin snuck and saw one at Granny's when she was sleepin'."

"They give you nightmares," the man said.

"Hey!" Marcus said, his eyes opening wide. "Thas what my granny said."

The train stopped again, and though it did not stop any more suddenly than before, Avis lost her balance and began to fall back. The man reached across and caught her arm, in a move that seemed almost as if it had been planned, as if he had known two stops or so back that the child would begin to fall at that moment. Marvella thought, *If I see him tomorrow, it will be a good sign.*

"Now see," she said. "Both of you turn around, and I mean it."

At the McPherson Square stop, Marvella and her children got off. Marcus and Avis told the man good-bye and he said that it was nice meeting them. It was raining when they came out of the subway. With the rain, it was hard going across Fourteenth Street and through Franklin Square Park to Thir-teenth Street. Marvella carried Avis in one arm and held the umbrella with the other hand. She had Marcus carry her pocketbook and he and Marvin shared an umbrella. Up the street from K on Thirteenth, they went through the wide alley leading to Thompson School on Twelfth Street, where she and Avis watched the boys run up the stairs and go inside. Her arms were tired and she put Avis down. She wrapped the strap of her pocketbook around her shoulder and held her daughter's hand as they made their way two blocks up Twelfth Street to Horizon House, where Marvella's mother lived. They took the elevator up to her mother's apartment, and in a minute or so Marvella was heading back down Twelfth Street to the C&P Tele-phone Company, where she was a service representative.

It was about eight-thirty in the morning. She saw her day as blocks of time. She entered the building at Twelfth and H, and the second block be-gan.

They did see the man with the dreadlocks the next day, the Friday before Washington's Birthday, but Marvella had forgotten that it was supposed to be a good sign. He sat across the aisle from the boys, and she and Avis shared the seat just in back of the one the boys were sharing. That morning, perhaps because of the holiday weekend, there were fewer people.

"You back, huh?" Marcus said to the man. "Still got the same hair, too."

"Yep, it's me," the man said. "How're you doing today?"

"Fine. No school tomorrow and we goin to the zoo if the weather good."

Avis, interested, leaned across her mother's lap. "You can't come to the zoo with us."

"Why not?" the man said.

" 'Cause my granny's comin' and she wants to give peanuts to the monkey-see, monkey-do."

"My granny always says there ain't no good men left in the world," Marcus said.

"Marcus . . ." his mother said.

"Well, if that's so," the man said, "it wouldn't be a good thing for the world."

Marcus hunched his shoulders, as if it didn't matter to him one way or another. "You goin to work?" Marcus said to the man.

"Yep," the man said.

"They let you come to work with your hair like that?" Marcus said.

"Marcus," his mother said.

The man said to her, "You have wonderful kids." She told him thank you. Then to Marcus, the man said, "Yeah, I go to work like this. They have to let me. They have no choice. I'm the best they have."

"If they don't let you come to work, you gon beat 'em up?" Marcus asked. Marvin had his head to the window, looking out into the darkness of the tunnel, his hands shading his eyes.

The train stopped and the subway woman announced that it was an Orange Line train to Ballston. Marvella and her children always got on at the Stadium-Armory stop in Southeast. It did not matter if they took the orange line, which ended at Ballston, or the blue line, which ended at National Airport, because both lines, traveling over the same tracks, went past their McPherson Square stop.

"No need to beat 'em up," the dreadlock man said. "You go to school?" he said to Avis.

"I ain't neva goin' to school," and she shook her head vigorously. "No way. No way. No way."

"I go," Marcus said. "It ain't bad." He leaned his head out into the aisle and moved it up and down as if he were watching a bouncing ball. When he looked back up at the man, he pointed at the hair and asked, "Whatcha call that kinda hair?"

"We call them dreadlocks."

"You sure you whatn't in that movie I saw? They had this man comin' out of the ground and everything. He was dead but he was still alive and no-body could kill him." He turned to his brother. "Marvin, don't he look like that man in that movie we saw at Granny's? You member?"

The train stopped again. Marvin turned from the window and consid-ered the man for a long time. The man smiled, but Marvin did not seem impressed with him or his hair and the boy did not return the smile. "You ask people too many questions," he said to his brother and turned back to the window.

My son the old man, his mother thought. The train had just passed the Smithsonian stop and, knowing that the trip was about to end, she found that she wanted the man to ask her something, anything, before they got off. She would have settled for something as inane as what was her sign, even though she hated such questions. And though she told the world that she did not believe in it all that much, she had nevertheless learned that she was not compatible with Capricorns and Libras. Her ex-husband was a Capricorn. If she had to guess, she would have said the man with the dread-locks was an Aries. But the last man she had slept with, three months ago, had been an Aries, a man she had met at a club she and her sister went to. The man at the club had been full of shit and she was glad that her children had never met him. "They call me Slide," the guy had introduced himself. "Short for Electric Slide."

It occurred to her as she and the children were crossing Franklin Square that the dreadlock man's finger touch the day before had been the first time a man had touched her—outside of handshakes with men at work—since the doofus she met at the club.

They did not see the man at all the next week, and she hated herself for hav-ing thought about him over the holiday weekend. Going home that Friday after not seeing him all that week, she began to think that maybe it had something to do with the fact that they had taken the Blue Line for at least three mornings that week. Maybe, she thought, he only went on the Orange Line.

The following week she managed to get the kids out the door and down to the subway platform at about the same time when she thought they had met the man the first week. On Monday and Tuesday she waited and looked about for him, then, because time was running out, she settled for a Blue Line.

"I thought you said it didn't matter if we took a Blue or an Orange Line," Marvin said after they were seated.

"Well, it doesn't matter," his mother said.

"Then why we wait while all those trains went by?"

My son the lawyer. "I don't know," she said. That was the only answer in life that ever seemed to shut him up.

"Hey, it's that man with the snake hair," Marcus said, spotting the man and waving to him. It was Wednesday and they were on the subway platform. The man came over and appeared genuinely glad to see them. She was happy to see him, but she was also upset that he had not been there on the other mornings. She had in her bag a slip of paper with her name and work and home telephone numbers in case he asked.

"Mornin'," the subway woman said after they entered the train. She sounded as if the last thing in the world she wanted to do was speak. "Orange Line . . . Ballston . . ."

"Where's Boston?" Avis asked the man, yawning. She was in her mother's lap and the man sat beside them. The boys were in the seat ahead of them, and again Marcus was kneeling facing them.

"It's Ballston," the man enunciated. "The end of the line. It's across the river. In a place called Virginia."

"A long way," the little girl said and yawned again. She closed her eyes and leaned back against her mother.

"Kinda. It depends," the man said.

"What's in the bag?" Marcus said to the man.

Avis's eyes popped open and she sat up straight. "What's in the bag?" she said.

"None of your business," Marvella said to both children. "And turn around in that seat, Marcus." The boy looked at the man as if for help from his mother's order. Marvin was writing a letter to his father. The movement of the subway took his words sloppily above and below the lines, but he did not seem to care.

"My lunch," the dreadlock man said. He opened the bag and took out an apple and held it before the girl. "What's that?" he asked her.

"A apple," Marcus said. "Anybody know that."

"He ast me," Avis said. "Mama, tell Marcus to stop."

"Thas all you got for lunch?" Marcus said. "Boy, you pretty cheap."

The man put the apple back. "No, I have a sandwich and a slice of cheese."

"I hate cheese," Avis said. "It taste nasty."

"Well, I love cheese," Marcus said. "I could eat it all day long."

They saw him again on Friday and he was wearing a tie without a coat, carrying the same type of lunch bag. Marvella carried the same slip of paper, but the man with the dreadlocks did nothing but banter with Marcus and Avis.

On Saturday morning, on the pretense that they would go exploring before their father picked the children up, she borrowed her nephew's car and
went driving about the neighborhood. She had grown up in Southeast, but
she had spent much of her married life in Northwest, where she and the
children had lived before they moved that summer to Southeast to share a
large house with her sister and her two children. By keeping the boys at
Thompson School in Northwest two blocks from her mother, she worried
less when the school day ended.

Turning on the car's engine, she realized how she must look—on a beautiful day, she was dragging her kids along to look for a man she did not
know, whom she could well come across strolling hand-in-hand with some
other woman, who would probably also be arrayed in dreadlocks. She drove
along an area bounded by Nineteenth Street, Potomac, Kentucky, and
North Carolina avenues, a very wide area that he would surely have to live
in if he got on the subway at Stadium-Armory. In case the children asked
what they were doing, she made up enough lies along the way for God to
send her straight to hell, but surprisingly, there was nothing said, except for
Marvin's comment that being so far from home, they might miss their father when he arrived. But, as if to punish her, God did not produce the
dreadlock man.

Over the next several weeks she saw the dreadlock man only four or five
times, and on most mornings she simply took whatever train came first. The
deeper they went into the year, the less she saw of him. But now and again,
she would wake with one of the kids screaming for this or that, and she
would take herself and them off to the subway determined to wait for him,
for an Orange Line train. When she did see him, she was glad that Marcus
and Avis engaged him in conversation and not once did she tell them to
turn around or stop bothering the man.

"How do the lights know to turn off when the train's gone?" Marvin
asked her one Thursday morning not long before Memorial Day. His father
had turned down the boy's request to live with him and his girlfriend across
the Maryland line in Capitol Heights. Marvella was surprised, and relieved,
that Marvin had let the matter drop the same day his father said no.

Marvella had been distracted and she asked him to repeat the question.

"None a your business," Avis said to Marvin.

"I wasn't even talkin' to you," Marvin said to his sister. "You want a fat
lip?"

"Alright, stop it. Both of you, and I mean it!"

Marvin asked her again.

She tried to think of something that would satisfy him. "I guess the last car of the train hits a switch that tells the lights it's gone and the lights turn themselves off."

The lights blinked, and a blue line train came without them getting on. Marvin wanted to know why and Marvella told him to be quiet, for a few people were staring at them. Marvin quieted after they got on the next train, an orange line. The subway was packed and at their stop they had to fight their way to the exit. "Hey! Hey!" Marcus hollered. "Lettus outta this joint!"

As they went up the first set of escalators at McPherson Square, Marvin began asking again why they had to all the time wait when the Blue train was like the Orange. Just in front of the farecard machines, Marvella put down Avis and grabbed Marvin by the arm. She pulled him along to a corner, away from the passing people. Marcus and Avis followed silently.

"I'm the boss around here, and you seem to be forgetting that," she said to him. He was utterly surprised and began to shake. "Who's the boss around here, you or me? Who? Who? Who's the mama in charge around here?"

His eyes filled with tears. "You are," he said, but not loud enough for her.

She did not like scenes like this, particularly around white people, who believed that nothing good ever happened between black people and their children, but she could not stop herself. "Who's the mama in charge around here, I said?" she kept asking the boy.

"You are," he said louder, crying. "You the mama. You the mama. You the mama in charge."

"Mama's the one in charge. Mama's the one in charge," Marcus chanted as they made their way across Franklin Square Park.

"Marcus, shut up!" his mother said just as Avis was about to take up the chant.

After that, she did not ever again see the man with the dreadlocks and she did not look for him anymore. But for some time, as she went about her days with their blocks of time, she would find herself comparing his hair with other dreadlocks she saw. By then the subway people had extended the orange line all the way to Vienna.

Lucielia Louise Turner

BY GLORIA NAYLOR

FROM *The Women of Brewster Place*

The sunlight was still watery as Ben trudged into Brewster Place, and the street had just begun to yawn and stretch itself. He eased himself onto his garbage can, which was pushed against the sagging brick wall that turned Brewster into a dead-end street. The metallic cold of the can's lid seeped into the bottom of his thin trousers. Sucking on a piece of breakfast sausage caught in his back teeth, he began to muse. Mighty cold, these spring mornings. The old days you could build a good trash fire in one of them barrels to keep warm. Well, don't want no summons now, and can't freeze to death. Yup, can't freeze to death.

His daily soliloquy completed, he reached into his coat pocket and pulled out a crumpled brown bag that contained his morning sun. The cheap red liquid moved slowly down his throat, providing immediate justification as the blood began to warm in his body. In the hazy light a lean dark figure began to make its way slowly up the block. It hesitated in front of the stoop at 316, but looking around and seeing Ben, it hurried over.

"Yo, Ben."

"Hey, Eugene, I thought that was you. Ain't seen ya 'round for a coupla days."

"Yeah." The young man put his hands in his pockets, frowned into the ground, and kicked the edge of Ben's can. "The funeral's today, ya know."

"Yeah."

"You going?" He looked up into Ben's face.

"Naw, I ain't got no clothes for them things. Can't abide 'em no way—too sad—it being a baby and all."

"Yeah. I was going myself, people expect it, ya know?"

"Yeah."

"But, man, the way Ciel's friends look at me and all—like I was filth or something. Hey, I even tried to go see Ciel in the hospital, heard she was freaked out and all."

"Yeah, she took it real bad."

"Yeah, well, damn, I took it bad. It was my kid, too, you know. But Mattie, that fat, black bitch, just standin' in the hospital hall sayin' to me—to me, now, 'Whatcha want?' Like I was a fuckin' germ or something. Man, I just turned and left. You gotta be treated with respect, ya know?"

"Yeah."

"I mean, I should be there today with my woman in the limo and all, sittin' up there, doin' it right. But how you gonna be a man with them ball-busters tellin' everybody it was my fault and I should be the one dead? Damn!"

"Yeah, a man's gotta be a man." Ben felt the need to wet his reply with another sip. "Have some?"

"Naw, I'm gonna be heading on—Ciel don't need me today. I bet that frig, Mattie, rides in the head limo, wearing the pants. Shit—let 'em." He looked up again. "Ya know?"

"Yup."

"Take it easy, Ben." He turned to go.

"You too, Eugene."

"Hey, you going?"

"Now."

"Me neither. Later."

"Later, Eugene."

Funny, Ben thought, *Eugene ain't stopped to chat like that for a long time— near on a year, yup, a good year.* He took another swallow to help him bring back the year-old conversation, but it didn't work; the second and third one didn't, either. But he did remember that it had been an early spring morning like this one, and Eugene had been wearing those same tight jeans. He had hestitated outside of 316 then, too. But that time he went in . . .

Lucielia had just run water into the tea kettle and was putting it on the burner when she heard the cylinder turn. He didn't have to knock on the door; his key still fit the lock. Her thin knuckles gripped the handle of the kettle, but she didn't turn around. She knew. The last eleven months of her life hung compressed in the air between the click of the lock and his "Yo, baby."

The vibrations from those words rode like parasites on the air waves and came rushing into her kitchen, smashing the compression into indistinguishable days and hours that swirled dizzily before her. It was all there: the frustration of being left alone, sick, with a month-old baby; her humiliation reflected in the caseworker's blue eyes for the unanswerable "You can find him to have it, but can't find him to take care of it" smile; the raw urges that crept, uninvited, between her thighs on countless nights; the eternal whys all meshed with the explainable hate and unexplainable love. They kept circling in such a confusing pattern before her that she couldn't seem to grab even one to answer him with. So there was nothing in Lucielia's face when she turned it toward Eugene, standing in her kitchen door holding a ridiculously pink Easter bunny, nothing but sheer relief . . .

"So he's back." Mattie sat at Lucielia's kitchen table, playing with Serena.

It was rare that Mattie ever spoke more than two sentences to anybody about anything. She didn't have to. She chose her words with the grinding precision of a diamond cutter's drill.

"You think I'm a fool, don't you?"

"I ain't said that."

"You didn't have to," Ciel snapped.

"Why you mad at me, Ciel? It's your life, honey."

"Oh, Mattie, you don't understand. He's really straightened up this time. He's got a new job on the docks that pays real good, and he was just so depressed before with the new baby and no work. You'll see. He's even gone out now to buy paint and stuff to fix up the apartment. And, and Serena needs a daddy."

"You ain't gotta convince me, Ciel."

No, she wasn't talking to Mattie, she was talking to herself. She was convincing herself it was the new job and the paint and Serena that let him back into her life. Yet, the real truth went beyond her scope of understanding. When she laid her head in the hollow of his neck there was a deep musky scent to his body that brought back the ghosts of the Tennessee soil of her childhood. It reached up and lined the inside of her nostrils so that she inhaled his presence almost every minute of her life. The feel of his sooty flesh penetrated the skin of her fingers and coursed through her blood and became one, somewhere, wherever it was, with her actual being. But how do you tell yourself, let alone this practical old woman who loves you, that he was back because of that. So you don't.

You get up and fix you both another cup of coffee, calm the fretting baby on your lap with her pacifier, and you pray silently—very silently—behind veiled eyes that the man will stay.

Ciel was trying to remember exactly when it had started to go wrong again. Her mind sought for the slender threads of a clue that she could trace back to—perhaps—something she had said or done. Her brow was set tightly in concentration as she folded towels and smoothed the wrinkles over and over, as if the answer lay concealed in the stubborn creases of the terry cloth.

The months since Eugene's return began to tick off slowly before her, and she examined each one to pinpoint when the nagging whispers of trouble had begun in her brain. The friction on the towels increased when she came to the month that she had gotten pregnant again, but it couldn't be that. Things were different now. She wasn't sick as she had been with Serena, he was still working—no, it wasn't the baby. *It's not the baby, it's not the baby*— the rhythm of those words sped up the motion of her hands, and she had almost yanked and folded and pressed them into a reality when, bewildered, she realized that she had run out of towels.

Ciel jumped when the front door slammed shut. She waited tensely for the metallic bang of his keys on the coffeetable and the blast of the stereo. Lately that was how Eugene announced his presence home. Ciel walked into the living room with the motion of a swimmer entering a cold lake.

"Eugene, you're home early, huh?"

"You see anybody else sittin' here?" He spoke without looking at her and rose to turn up the stereo.

He wants to pick a fight, she thought, confused and hurt. He knows Serena's taking her nap, and now I'm supposed to say, Eugene, the baby's asleep, please cut the music down. Then he's going to say, you mean a man can't even relax in his own home without being picked on? I'm not picking on you, but you're going to wake up the baby. Which is always supposed to lead to "You don't give a damn about me. Everybody's more important than me—that kid, your friends, everybody. I'm just chickenshit around here, huh?"

All this went through Ciel's head as she watched him leave the stereo and drop defiantly back down on the couch. Without saying a word, she turned and went into the bedroom. She looked down on the peaceful face of her daughter and softly caressed her small cheek. Her heart became full as she realized, this is the only thing I have ever loved without pain. She pulled the sheet gently over the tiny shoulders and firmly closed the door, protecting her from the music. She then went into the kitchen and began washing the rice for their dinner.

Eugene, seeing that he had been left alone, turned off the stereo and came and stood in the kitchen door.

"I lost my job today," he shot at her, as if she had been the cause.

The water was turning cloudy in the rice pot, and the force of the stream from the faucet caused scummy bubbles in rise to the surface. These broke and sprayed tiny starchy panicles onto the dirty surface. Each bubble that broke seemed to increase the volume of the dogged whispers she had been ignoring for the last few months. She poured the dirty water off the rice to destroy and silence them, then watched with a malicious joy as they disappeared down the drain.

"So now, how in the hell I'm gonna make it with no money huh? And another brat comin' here, huh?"

The second change of the water was slightly clearer, but the starch-speckled bubbles were still there, and this time there was no way to pretend deafness to their message. She had stood at that sink countless times before, washing rice and she knew the water was never going to be totally clear. She couldn't stand there forever—her fingers were getting cold, and the rest of the dinner had to be fixed, and Serena would be waking up soon and wanting attention. Feverishly she poured the water off and tried again.

"I'm fuckin' sick of never getting ahead. Babies and bills, that's all you good for."

The bubbles were almost transparent now, but when they broke they left light trails of starch on top of the water that curled around her fingers. She knew it would be useless to try again. Defeated, Ciel placed the wet pot on the burner, and the flames leaped up bright red and orange, turning the water droplets clinging on the outside into steam.

Turning to him, she silently acquiesced. "All right, Eugene, what do you want me to do?"

He wasn't going to let her off so easily. "Hey, baby, look, I don't care what you do. I just can't have all these hassles on me right now, ya know?"

"I'll get a job. I don't mind, but I've got no one to keep Serena, and you don't want Mattie watching her."

"Mattie—no way. That fat bitch'll turn the kid against me. She hates my ass, and you know it."

"No, she doesn't, Eugene." Ciel remembered throwing that at Mattie once. "You hate him, don't you?" "Naw, honey," and she had cupped both hands on Ciel's face. "Maybe I just loves you too much."

"I don't give a damn what you say—she ain't minding my kid."

"Well, look, after the baby comes, they can tie my tubes—I don't care." She swallowed hard to keep down the lie.

"And what the hell we gonna feed it when it gets here, huh—air? With two kids and you on my back, I ain't never gonna have nothin'." He came and grabbed her by the shoulders and was shouting into her face. "Nothin', do you hear me, nothin'!"

"Nothing to it, Mrs. Turner." The face over hers was as calm and antiseptic as the room she lay in. "Please, relax. I'm going to give you a local anesthetic and then perform a simple D&C, or what you'd call a scraping to clean out the uterus. Then you'll rest here for about an hour and be on your way. There won't even be much bleeding." The voice droned on in its practiced monologue, peppered with sterile kindness.

Ciel was not listening. It was important that she keep herself completely isolated from these surroundings. All the activities of the past week of her life were balled up and jammed on the right side of her brain, as if belonging to some other woman. And when she had endured this one last thing for her, she would push it up there, too, and then one day give it all to her—Ciel wanted no part of it.

The next few days Ciel found it difficult to connect herself up again with her own world. Everything seemed to have taken on new textures and colors. When she washed the dishes, the plates felt peculiar in her hands, and she was more conscious of their smoothness and the heat of the water. There was a disturbing split second between someone talking to her and the words penetrating sufficiently to elicits response. Her neighbors left her presence with slight frown of puzzlement, and Eugene could be heard mumbling "Moody bitch."

She became terribly possessive of Serena. She refused to leave her alone, even with Eugene. The little girl went everywhere with Ciel, toddling along on plump uncertain legs. When someone asked to hold or play with her, Ciel sat nearby, watching every move. She found herself walking into the bedroom several times when the child napped to see if she was still breathing. Each time she chided herself for this unreasonable foolishness, but within the next few minutes some strange force still drove her back.

Spring was slowly beginning to announce itself at Brewster Place. The arthritic cold was seeping out of the worn gray bricks, and the tenants with apartment windows facing the street were awakened by six-o'clock sunlight. The music no longer blasted inside of 3C, and Ciel grew strong with the peacefulness of her household. The playful laughter of her daughter, heard more often now, brought a sort of redemption with it.

"Isn't she marvelous, Mattie? You know she's even trying to make whole sentences. Come on, baby, talk for Auntie Mattie."

Serena, totally uninterested in living up to her mother's proud claims, was trying to tear a gold-toned button off the bosom of Mattie's dress.

"It's so cute. She even knows her father's name. She says, 'my Da da is Gene.' "

"Better teach her your name," Mattie said, while playing with the baby's hand. "She'll be using it more."

Ciel's mouth flew open to ask her what she meant by that, but she checked herself. It was useless to argue with Mattie. You could take her words however you wanted. The burden of their truth lay with you, not her.

Eugene came through the front door and stopped short when he saw Mattie. He avoided being around her as much as possible. She was always polite to him, but he sensed a silent condemnation behind even her most innocent words. He constantly felt the need to prove himself in front of her. These frustrations often took the form of unwarranted rudeness on his part.

Serena struggled out of Mattie's lap and went toward her father and tugged on his legs to be picked up. Ignoring the child and cutting short the greetings of the two women, he said coldly, "Ciel, I wanna talk to you."

Sensing trouble, Mattie rose to go. "Ciel, why don't you let me take Serena downstairs for a while? I got some ice cream for her."

"She can stay right here," Eugene broke in. "If she needs ice cream, I can buy it for her."

Hastening to soften his abruptness, Ciel said, "That's okay, Mattie, it's almost time for her nap. I'll bring her later—after dinner."

"Alright. Now you all keep good." Her voice was warm. "You too, Eugene," she called back from the front door.

The click of the lock restored his balance to him. "Why in the hell is she always up here?"

"You just had your chance—why didn't you ask her yourself? If you don't want her here, tell her to stay out," Ciel snapped back confidently, knowing he never would.

"Look, I ain't got time to argue with you about that old hag. I got big doings in the making, and I need you to help me pack." Without waiting for a response, he hurried into the bedroom and pulled his old leather suitcase from under the bed.

A tight, icy knot formed in the center of Ciel's stomach and began to melt rapidly, watering the blood in her legs so that they almost refused to support her weight. She pulled Serena back from following Eugene and sat her in the middle of the living room floor.

"Here, honey, play with the blocks for Mommy—she has to talk to Daddy." She piled a few plastic alphabet blocks in front of the child, and on her way out of the room, he glanced around quickly and removed the glass ashtrays of the coffee table and put them on a shelf over the stereo.

Then, taking a deep breath to calm her racing heart, she started toward the bedroom.

Serena loved the light colorful cubes and would some times sit for an entire half-hour, repeatedly stacking them up and kicking them over with her feet. The hollow sound of their falling fascinated her, and she would often bang two of them together to re-create the magical noise. She was sitting, contentedly engaged in this particular activity, when slow dark movement along the baseboard caught her eye.

A round black roach was making its way from behind the couch toward the kitchen. Serena threw one of her blocks at the insect, and, feeling the vibrations of the wall above it, the roach sped around the door into the kitchen. Finding a totally new game to amuse herself, Serena took off behind the insect with a block in each hand. Seeing her moving toy trying to bury itself under the linoleum by the garbage pail she threw another block, and the frantic roach now raced along the wall and found security in the electric wall socket under the kitchen table.

Angry at losing her plaything, she banged the block against the socket, attempting to get it to come back out. When that failed, she unsuccessfully tried to poke her chubby finger into the thin horizontal slit. Frustrated, tiring of the game, she sat under the table and realized she had found an entirely new place in the house to play. The shiny chrome of the table and chair legs drew her attention, and she experimented with the sound of the block against their smooth surfaces.

This would have entertained her until Ciel came, but the roach, thinking itself safe, ventured outside of the socket. Serena gave a cry of delight and attempted to catch her lost playmate, but it was too quick and darted back into the wall. She tried once again to poke her finger into the slit. Then a bright slender object, lying dropped and forgotten, came into her view. Picking up the fork, Serena finally managed to fit the thin flattened prongs into the electric socket.

Eugene was avoiding Ciel's eyes as he packed. "You know, baby, this is really a good deal after me bein' out of work for so long." He moved around her still figure to open the drawer that held his T-shirts and shorts. "And hell, Maine ain't far. Once I get settled on the docks up there, I'll be able to come home all the time."

"Why can't you take us with you?" She followed each of his movements with her eyes and saw herself being buried in the case under the growing pile of clothes.

" 'Cause I gotta check out what's happening before I drag you and the kid up there."

"I don't mind. We'll make do. I've learned to live on very little."

"No, it just won't work right now. I gotta see my way clear first."

"Eugene, please." She listened with growing horror to herself quietly begging.

"No, and that's it!" He flung his shoes into the suitcase.

"Well, how far is it? Where did you say you were going?" She moved toward the suitcase.

"I told ya—the docks in Newport."

"That's not in Maine. You said you were going to Maine."

"Well, I made a mistake."

"How could you know about a place so far up? Who got you the job?"

"A friend."

"Who?"

"None of your damned business!" His eyes were flashing with the anger of a caged animal. He slammed down the top of the suitcase and yanked it off the bed.

"You're lying, aren't you? You don't have a job, do your Do you?"

"Look, Ciel, believe whatever the fuck you want to. I gotta go." He tried to push past her.

She grabbed the handle of the case. "No, you can't go."

"Why?"

Her eyes widened slowly. She realized that to answer that would require that she uncurl that week of her life, pushed safely up into her head, when she had done all those terrible things for that other woman who had wanted an abortion. She and she alone would have to take responsibility for them now. He must understand what those actions had meant to her, but somehow, he had meant even more. She sought desperately for the right words, but it all came out as—

"Because I love you."

"Well, that ain't good enough."

Ciel had let the suitcase go before he jerked it away. She looked at Eugene, and the poison of reality began to spread through her body like gangrene. It drew his scent out of her nostrils and scraped the veil from her eyes, and he stood before her just as he really was—a tall, skinny black man with arrogance and selfishness twisting his mouth into a strange shape. And, she thought, I don't feel anything now. But soon, very soon, I will start to hate you. I promise—I will hate you. And I'll never forgive myself for not having done it sooner—soon enough to have saved my baby. Oh, dear God, my baby.

Eugene thought the tears that began to crowd into her eyes were for him. But she was allowing herself this one last luxury of brief mourning for the loss of something denied to her. It troubled her that she wasn't exactly what that something was, or which one of them was to blame for taking it away. Ciel began to feel the overpowering need to be near someone who loved her. I'll get Serena and we'll go visit Mattie now, she thought in a daze.

Then they heard the scream from the kitchen.

The church was small and dark. The air hung about them like a stale blanket. Ciel looked straight ahead, oblivious to the seats filling up behind her. She didn't feel the damp pressure of Mattie's heavy arm or the doubt that invaded the air over Eugene's absence. The plaintive Merciful Jesuses, lightly sprinkled with sobs, were lost on her ears. Her dry eyes were locked on the tiny pearl-gray casket, flanked with oversized arrangements of red-carnationed bleeding hearts and white-lilied eternal circles. The sagging chords that came loping out of the huge organ and mixed with the droning voice of the black-robed old man behind the coffin were also unable to penetrate her.

Ciel's whole universe existed in the seven feet of space between herself and her child's narrow coffin. There was not even room for this comforting God whose melodious virtues floated around her sphere, attempting to get in. Obviously, He had deserted or damned her, it didn't matter which. All Ciel knew was that her prayers had gone unheeded—that afternoon she had lifted her daughter's body off the kitchen floor, those blank days in the hospital, and now. So she was left to do what God had chosen not to.

People had mistaken it for shock when she refused to cry. They thought it some special sort of grief when she stopped eating and even drinking water unless forced to; her hair went uncombed and her body unbathed. But Ciel was not grieving for Serena. She was simply tired of hurting. And she was forced to slowly give up the life that God had refused to take from her.

After the funeral the well-meaning came to console and offer their dog-eared faith in the form of coconut cakes, potato pies, fried chicken, and tears. Ciel sat in the bed with her back resting against the headboard; her long thin fingers still as midnight frost on a frozen pond, lay on the covers. She acknowledged their kindnesses with nods of her head and slight lip movements, but no sound. It was as if her voice was too tired to make the journey from the diaphragm through the larynx to the mouth.

Her visitors' impotent words flew against the steel edge of her pain, bled slowly, and returned to die in the senders' throats. No one came too near. They stood around the door and the dressing table, or sat on the edges of the two worn chairs that needed upholstering, but they unconsciously pushed themselves back against the wall as if her hurt was contagious.

A neighbor woman entered in studied certainty and stood in the middle of the room. "Child, I know how you feel, but don't do this to yourself. I lost one, too. The Lord will . . ." And she choked, because the words were jammed down into her throat by the naked force of Ciel's eyes. Ciel had opened them fully now to look at the woman, but raw fires had eaten them worse than lifeless—worse than death. The woman saw in that mute appeal for silence the ragings of a personal hell flowing through Ciel's eyes. And just as she went to reach for the girl's hand, she stopped as if a muscle spasm had overtaken her body and, cowardly, shrank back. Reminiscences of old, dried-over pains were no consolation in the face of this. They had the effect of cold beads of water on a hot iron—they danced and fizzled up while the room stank from their steam.

Mattie stood in the doorway, and an involuntary shudder went through her when she saw Ciel's eyes. *Dear God*, she thought, *she's dying, and right in front of our faces.*

"Merciful Father, no!" she bellowed. There was no prayer, no bended knee or sackcloth supplication in those words, but a blasphemous fireball that shot forth and went smashing against the gates of heaven, raging and kicking, demanding to be heard.

"No! No! No!" Like a black Brahman cow, desperate to protect her young, she surged into the room, pushing the neighbor woman and the others out of her way. She approached the bed with her lips clamped shut in such force that the muscles in her jaw and the back of her neck began to ache.

She sat on the edge of the bed and enfolded the tissue-thin body in her huge ebony arms. And she rocked. Ciel's body was so hot it burned Mattie when she first touched her, but she held on and rocked. Back and forth, back and forth—she had Ciel so tightly she could feel her young breasts flatten against the buttons of her dress. The black mammoth gripped so firmly that the slightest increase of pressure would have cracked the girl's spine. But she rocked.

And somewhere from the bowels of her being came a moan from Ciel, so high at first it couldn't be heard by anyone there, but the yard dogs began an unholy howling. And Mattie rocked. And then, agonizingly slow, it broke its way through the parched lips in a spaghetti-thin column of air that could be faintly heard in the frozen room.

Ciel moaned. Mattie rocked. Propelled by the sound, Mattie rocked her out of that bed, out of that room, into a blue vastness just underneath the sun and above time. She rocked her over Aegean seas so clean they shone like crystal, so clear the fresh blood of sacrificed babies torn from their mother's arms and given to Neptune could be seen like pink froth on the water. She rocked her on and on, past Dachau, where soul-gutted Jewish mothers swept their children's entrails off laboratory floors. They flew past the spilled brains of Senegalese infants whose mothers had dashed them on the wooden sides of slave ships. And she rocked on.

She rocked her into her childhood and let her see murdered dreams. And she rocked her back, back the womb, to the nadir of her hurt, and they found it—a slight silver splinter, embedded just below the surface of the skin. And Mattie rocked and pulled—and the splinter gave way, but its roots were deep, gigantic, ragged, and they tore up flesh with bits of fat and muscle tissue clinging to them. They left a huge hole, which was already starting to pus over, but Mattie was satisfied. It would heal.

The bile that had formed a tight knot in Ciel's stomach began to rise and gagged her just as it passed her throat. Mattie put her hand over the girl's mouth and rushed her out the now-empty room to the toilet. Ciel retched yellowish-green phlegm, and she brought up white lumps of slime that hit the seat of the toilet and rolled off, splattering onto the tiles. After a while she heaved only air, but the body did not seem to want to stop. It was exorcising the evilness of pain.

Mattie cupped her hands under the faucet and motioned for Ciel to drink and clean her mouth. When the water left Ciel's mouth, it tasted as if she had been rinsing with a mild acid. Mattie drew a tub of hot water and undressed Ciel. She let the nightgown fall off the narrow shoulders, over the pitifully thin breasts and jutting hipbones. She slowly helped her into the water, and it was like a dried brown autumn leaf hitting the surface of a puddle.

And slowly she bathed her. She took the soap, and, using only her hands, she washed Ciel's hair and the back of her neck. She raised her arms and cleaned the armpits, soaping well the downy brown hair there. She let the soap slip between the girls breasts, and she washed each one separately, cupping it in her hands. She took each leg and even cleaned under the toenails. Making Ciel rise and kneel in the tub, she cleaned the crack in her behind, soaped her pubic hair, and gently washed the creases in her vagina—slowly, reverently, as if handling a newborn.

She took her from the tub and toweled her in the same manner she had been bathed—as if too much friction would break the skin tissue. All of this had been done without either woman saying a word. Ciel stood there, naked, and felt the cool air play against the clean surface of her skin. She had the sensation of fresh mint coursing through her pores. She closed her eyes and the fire was gone. Her tears no longer fried within her, killing her internal organs with their steam. So Ciel began to cry—there, naked, in the center of the bathroom floor.

Mattie emptied the tub and rinsed it. She led the still-naked Ciel to a chair in the bedroom. The tears were flowing so freely now Ciel couldn't see, and she allowed herself to be led as if blind. She sat on the chair and cried—head erect. Since she made no effort to wipe them away, the tears dripped down her chin and landed on her chest and rolled down to her stomach and onto her dark public hair. Ignoring Ciel, Mattie took away the crumpled linen and made the bed, stretching the sheets tight and fresh. She beat the pillows into a virgin plumpness and dressed them in white cases.

And Ciel sat. And cried. The unmolested tears had rolled down her parted thighs and were beginning to wet the chair. But they were cold and good. She put out her tongue and began to drink in their saltiness, feeding on them. The first tears were gone. Her thin shoulders began to quiver, and spasms circled her body as new tears came—this time, hot and stinging. And she sobbed, the first sound she'd made since the moaning.

Mattie took the edges of the dirty sheet she'd pulled off the bed and wiped the mucus that had been running out of Ciel's nose. She then led her freshly wet, glistening body, baptized now, to the bed. She covered her with one sheet and laid a towel across the pillow—it would help for a while.

And Ciel lay down and cried. But Mattie knew the tears would end. And she would sleep. And morning would come.

Fortune

BY R. ERICA DOYLE

Two doors down lives Fortune. She breathes in daybreak in black sarongs and flamboyant halter tops, orchids on her tongue. You watch her heave the gate open in the morning, trip-dance down the wooden steps to Morne Coco Road. The banana tree hides her for a moment, and your heart stops with her disappearance, starts again when her sandals clack on the street. The roosters crow before and behind her, hailing, "Fortune, ho ho, Fortune, ho ho." Her dougla hair, that curly mass of Africa and India making love, caresses her shoulders, bounces down her back, winds itself over the straps of her red handbag. She has bangles like a garden of silver on her full golden arms.

You stand in the doorway with your tea, now cold, sip it with a grimace. Fortune comes even with your hungry stance, two points converging, two pairs of cocoa eyes meeting, and then she is past you, throwing you a hard-won "Good morning Yvette!" over her shoulder. Her round buttocks describe circles under the cotton. "Fortune is a woman could walk and win' at the same time," Couteledge from down the road always said, "That what make them old hags tongue wag, can't stand no woman that age hard back and fete one time, no children no man to slow she down." The chickens in your front yard raise their heads from the dust they've been scouring for corn and insects to watch her. She is the sun rising over the hill, then setting below it, lost from your sight.

Something is pulling at the bottom of your short pants leg. You don't turn, know it is your little nephew, Selwyn, eighteen months old, awake and wanting breakfast. You wait. Two months now your sister, Dulce, send him from New York for you to raise. The child come walking, but ain't saying a word at first, only pointing and grabbing at things he want. To teach him you didn't answer those pulls, matched his silence with your own expectant stare, eyebrows raised into question marks, and smiling to show you not vexed, only waiting. Patience is one thing you always have. That and respect for few words. Finally he began to talk, say "Mek" for "Milk" and "Bah bah" for bottle or cup or ball or bath, and "Titi," his name for you, when he don't know the word at all. You pick things up for him then, showcase fruit, food, and toys like the game show white lady on Miss Flora television until he know what he wants.

"Titi?" says Selwyn, still pulling, but not too bad.

You turn, crouch down to meet his luminous gray eyes, smile. You open your arms and he falls in, laughing. "Good morning, Sello darling." His sweet still-baby smell of powder and coconut oil mix together, his fresh breath on your cheek.

"G'mah nah Titi," he replies.

"Good boy! You hungry?"

"Yesh, Titi!" He laughs at his own words, proud.

You stand and he runs into the house in front of you. You are always surprised at how quickly he covers distances with that chubby duckwalk he have. Not that there is far to go in the small house, it only have two rooms, but he speeds through like a windup toy, and into everything like a little monkey. When the stewardess handed him to you in Piarco airport, you called the woozy and fearful child "Paw Paw Boy" to make him smile, for he was dense and yellow as a papaya, with a shock of reddish hair to match the fruit's insides.

Selwyn climbs onto the seat you've stacked with newspapers to make him a high chair of sorts and fold his hands neatly on the table, ghost eyes shining.

"I have some roast bake for you this morning," you sing, holding up the iron skillet for him to see the bread round and solid within. "And some nice buljahl I make fresh fresh."

Selwyn giggles. His impossibly small teeth are like pearls between his pink lips. "Fwesh!"

"Yes, my dear." You place the bowl of codfish on the table next to the bake. "Uh-oh Sello—" you spread your hands wide in puzzlement. "One thing, one thing missing. What is it?" You place a finger on your forehead as if thinking, and his brow furrows to match. "Hmmm . . ."

"Jooch!" cries Selwyn.

"That's right my love, juice!" You take the plastic pitcher full of yellow juice from the narrow counter and put it on the table. "Now, what kind is it?"

"Mmm," says Sello, tapping his head with the palm of one tiny hand, "onch?"

"Good guess, but it's not orange. Try again."

"Magoh?"

"Mango is darker, love. Try again."

Selwyn thinks hard, then smiles and holds up one hand, fingers spread.

"Right, my dear! Five-finger fruit. But you can say 'star' if that's too too difficult. Can you say 'star'?"

"Shah."

"Very good. Now it's time to eat."

Selwyn claps his hands and sings one of his under-the-breath songs to himself, and you make him a small plate of bake and buljahl and pour some juice into his sippy cup, with its spout and two handles. You make some for yourself, and you both eat the salty fish and warm bread in silence.

After breakfast, you clear the table and Selwyn clambers down from his chair. He toddles through the curtain separating the second room from the parlor and kitchen, and goes to pull the sheets around on the bed you both share to "make it up." You rinse the plates in the sink, and put some water on to boil for his bath. This has become your routine, Fortune in the morning, breakfast with Sello, his bath, his toys and books, his nap, then wait for customers. He makes up the bed as the water boils and could probably do it for hours, until you call him. After his bath, you read to him from one of the books Dulce sent from America, and then sweep the kitchen while he plays in the bedroom with the puzzles and blocks Vilma just bring, also from Dulce. Books could be sent alone, but toys aren't likely to make it through customs "at all at all," Vilma had said, shaking her head in a long suck-teeth. "Is only thief they thiefing in that customs you hear? Thief the only custom them damn fools accustom."

After Sello clean and sweet and diapers change, playing quiet in the bedroom, you sweep the kitchen and parlor floor until the wood planks sing under the old straw broom. Out go the clouds of dust through the back door, which reminds you to feed the parrot, small and green in the big aluminum cage your cousin Panchita bring it in. "I know you care for it," she say to your sagging shoulders. "I found it on our mountain, I think the wing sore, and you know Mummy don't allow me to have no animal in the house." Panchita's mother was a woman from town who kept their Diego Martin home spotless and free of nonhuman life with a variety of pesticides she got from her shopping trips to Miami. Even the chameleons didn't escape her, though one had conveniently, and appropriately you thought, died in one of her fancy leather shoes. Even today you couldn't see the parrot without remembering the sight of Auntie Maxine bouncing around on one foot while holding the other, toe enmeshed with crushed lizard, and squealing. And so, like Rex, the black puppy, and Pepper, the old cat, the little fellow joined your crew of creatures needing someone to watch them.

You give the parrot some five-finger fruit and mango and some sunflower seeds. He whirls one black eye in your direction, still suspicious of your large brown figure. You run a hand through the short salt and pepper curls on your head and gesture toward the voluminous red-flowered shirt you are wearing, another gift from Dulce. Why she think you would wear a such a thing unless she give it, you don't know, but a gift is a gift. "See?" you tell the parrot. "I wearing my Sunday best only for you." The parrot is unimpressed, but hops down to peck at the seeds, twirling them on his black tongue to crack them just so. You sigh and go back into the house where Selwyn is waiting in the parlor.

"Chick? Chick?" he asks.

"Yes my dear, time to feed the chickens."

He runs ahead, out the front door, down the slanted wooden steps to the chicken coops on the side of the house, under the banana trees. His bare feet send up clouds of dusts in his wake. When they see him coming the chickens begin a soft clucking that sounds like the purr of a rainstorm. Selwyn gets the feed from the side of the coop and grabs it in his small fists, flailing his arms, opening his hands at just the right moment. The hens swirl around him kicking up dust and tickling him with their feathers until the rooster comes from behind the house and sends them cackling and scurrying. As he starts to eat, they converge again, and you watch the cloud of copper and black feathers, the flash of red combs and black eyes, the golden red-haired child throwing food in their midst, laughing in the mid-morning sun.

When the chickens are fed, Selwyn goes down for his nap. He climbs onto the bed flops down and watches as you push two pillows and some sofa cushions around him to make a small fortress. The first time he slept alone in the bed he'd fallen out three times before you realized that he just would not stay. You were amazed by that, that staying on the bed while sleeping was learned. To know where your surface edges were while unconscious, know boundaries in your dreams. So now you make this wall for him, so he'll be safe while you work. Sello snuggles down and watches until you back out through the curtain a finger on your lips to shush. When you check back before going out to the yard, his eyes are closed, thumb in his mouth with the index finger scratching the bridge of his nose gently.

Today's customers are regulars: Mam Flora, Couteledge, Auntie Meiling and Shireen. They all buy one, two, or three chickens for the week, and take them live in a basket, except for Miss Merle, Auntie Maxine's neighbor from Diego Martin, who comes down to Petit Valley in a shiny car she always call her "automobile." You send Cedrick, Miss Agnes' son from next door to fetch your cousin Ramon to wring the necks for her, as she too fancy to do it herself. While you wait for Ramon, Miss Merle stay in she car, playing classical music on the radio, to stimulate the brain she say. You stand quietly in the road near her, to be polite, though you don't like the way her beady eyes rove all over your cut-short pants and that flowered shirt Dulce send, with a look like you covered in cow shit or some such. She smile at you in a way those ladies do, when they about to slit your throat with they mako words, always in somebody business. Miss Merle and them can't stay silent in the presence of another human being, class notwithstanding, for very long.

"So, Boysie, tell me Flora girl Fortune home from America come back to Petit Valley to live?"

"Yes Mam, she living just there down the road."

"Oh ho, close close! All you must have a lot to talk about, America and thing."

You don't say anything. Fortune and you have not exchanged more than ten words since her return, but words and Fortune is something that don't mix. Fortune say, "Words ruin," and then take your hands in hers and that was that.

Miss Merle, seeing no reply forthcoming, continue. "Well, maybe not. I know your sister Dulce there in America making a very nice life for she self. Studying dentistry and everything. Is a a pity your poor mother bless her soul ain't live to see it. But all you doing real good. You have this little business take over from your father and Dulce in America going to be a doctor!" Well, dental assistant, but you don't bother to correct Miss Merle.

"But that Fortune." Miss Merle look both ways up and down the street and in she rearview mirror to make sure the coast is clear, before leaning out the window to meet your eyes with her own murky black ones. "Boyboy, tell me a true true reason she come back from America so fast. That reason she live in that house all alone, nobody come, nobody go, no man, no friend no *body*. You tell me Yvette, why is a woman look like that not have a man and no children to speak of? Taunting and tempting with she little shirts and breasts bouncing?" Beads of sweat form above Miss Merle's upper lip and spit flecks at the corners of her broken prune mouth. Then she sees Ramon and Cedrick approaching up the street and winds herself back into the car, breathing heavily.

"Tante, are you alright?" you ask, half amused, and a little worried for the state she's gotten herself into.

Staring straight ahead out the windshield, gripping the steering wheel, Miss Merle murmurs under her breath. "Obeah, I tell you, the girl is obeah woman or one ladiablesse, you mark my words Yvette, be careful with Dulce child!"

You lean into the car window and pat her shoulder, give her brown paper cheek a kiss. "Is alright Auntie, Devil Woman and thing, none of them happen here anymore. Don't worry about me and Sello." You hear the rhythmic squawking and the silence of Ramon catching the hens and killing them. He was always the fastest and the best at it of all his brothers. He brings the bodies in a basket out to the car.

"Thanks, cousin," you say as he puts them in the back seat.

"Eh eh!" exclaims Ramon to Miss Merle. "Auntie, what have you so frighten? Look like you see one jumbie!"

Miss Merle doesn't respond to his teasing except for one long suck-teeth. She puts her car into gear and drives off in a cloud of dust which leads Ramon to speculate on the rain that has been long in coming. You give him twenty dollars and he heads home, whistling.

Now it's past noon and too hot for business or money, but you add up the dollars in your head anyway. Forty-five dollars a chicken, you've made enough for today, anyone else would be extra. And besides, is almost time for Fortune to come home from her job at the market in town.

You close your eyes, feel the beads of sweat on your forehead, breathe the heat and tobacco from your own upper lip. The trees sway in the yard and on the hill across the road—cocoa, flamboyant, mango, jack fruit, and banana—just enough breeze to make a whisper of cool and force the leaves sing. From time to time a neighbor passes, or a cousin, on foot or in a wheezy car, and you wave them "Good afternoon."

Then here she comes, slightly slower of step than in the morning, eyes open not as wide, sandals still slap slapping the dusty road. On her head she balances a parcel must be brought from the market and a next one in the hand opposite the hand bag. She fills your horizon with her colors and packages.

You remember coming to her after midnight and leaving before dawn, the timeless embrace between. When she knelt above you, her hair was a net to catch the shadows, she coaxed out the light within you to bursting. The land and hollow of her, the slackness of her belly from the child she left in New York, the salt in the crevice of the backs of her knees, in the crow's feet near her eyes, released. Afterward, you slept lightly enough to hear Sello if he cried out, and, for those few hours, you listened to her breathe. Before roostercall, you slipped out her back door and behind Auntie Pricille's house to your own. Her jasmine smell enveloped you, you still tasted her on your lips.

As she draws even to your gate, she nods you a greeting, a hint of a smile beyond the tiredness at the corners of her eyes. *I will see you under the belt of Orion*, it says. *I will see you when the rooster is still. When the lily closes its eyes for the day, and the old women sleep upright in their easy chairs, hold me like milk in a river of stones. Wash me in stars, I will be your good Fortune.*

$100 and Nothing!

BY J. CALIFORNIA COOPER

Where we live is not a big town like some and not a little town like some, but somewhere in the middle, like a big little town. Things don't happen here very much like other places, but on the other hand, I guess they do. Just ever once in awhile, you really pay tention to what is going on around you. I seen something here really was something! Let me tell you!

Was a woman, friend of mind born here and her mama birthed her and gave her to the orphan house and left town. Her mama had a sister, but the sister had her own and didn't have time for no more mouths, she said. So the orphan home, a white one, had to keep her. They named her "Mary." Mary. Mary live there, well, "worked" there bout fifteen years, then they let her do outside work too and Mary saved her money and bought an acre of land just outside town for $5.00 and took to plantin it and growing things and when they were ready, she bring them into town and sell em. She made right smart a money too, cause soon as she could, she bought a little house over there at the end of the main street, long time ago, so it was cheap, and put up a little stall for her vegetables and added chickens and eggs and all fresh stuff, you know. Wasn't long fore she had a little store and added more things.

Now the mens took to hanging round her and things like that! She was a regular size woman, she had real short hair and little skinny bow legs, things like that, but she was real, real nice and a kind person . . . to everybody.

Anyway, pretty soon, one of them men with a mouth full of sugar and warm hands got to Mary. I always thought he had a mouth full of "gimme" and a hand full of "reach," but when I tried to tell her, she just said, with her sweet soft smile, "maybe you just don't know him, he alright." Anyway, they got married.

Now he worked at Mr. Charlie's bar as a go-for and a clean-up man. After they got married I thought he would be working with Mary, in the field and in the store, you know. But he said he wasn't no field man and that that store work was woman's work lessen he stand at the cash register. But you know the business wasn't that fast so wasn't nobody gonna be standing up in one spot all day doing nothing over that cigar box Mary used for a cash register.

Anyway, Mary must have loved him cause she liked to buy him things, things I knew that man never had; nice suits and shirts and shoes, socks and things like that. I was there once when she was so excited with a suit to give him and he just looked at it and flipped its edges and told her to "hang it up and I'll get to it when I can," said, "I wouldn'ta picked that one, but you can't help it if you got no eye for good things!" Can you magine!? That man hadn't had nothing!! I could see he was changing, done spit that sugar out!!

Well, Mary's business picked up more and more and everybody came to get her fresh foods. It was a clean little store and soon she had a cash register and counters and soda water and canned goods and oh, all kinds of stuff you see in the big stores. She fixed that house up, too, and doing alright!! But, she didn't smile so much anymore . . . always looking thoughtful and a little in pain inside her heart. I took to helping her round the store and I began to see why she had changed. HE had changed! Charles, her husband! He was like hell on wheels with a automatic transmission! She couldn't do nothing right! She was dumb! Called her store a hole in the wall! Called her house "junk!" Said wasn't none of that stuff "nothing."

But I notice with the prosperity he quit working for Mr. Charlie and got a car and rode around and walked around and played around! Just doing nothing! And when people go to telling Mary how smart she was and how good she doing and they glad she there, I heard him say at least a hundred times, "I could take $100 and nothing and have more than this in a year!!" Didn't like to see her happy and smiling! I think he was jealous, but he coulda been working right beside her! When he married her it was his business, too! I heard her tell him that and guess what he answered? "I don't need that hole in the wall with stuff sitting there drawing flies, I'll think of something of my own!" Lord, it's so many kinds of fools in the world you just can't keep up with them!!

I went home to lunch with Mary once and he got mad cause we woke him up as we was talking softly and eating. Lord, did he talk about Mary! Talked about her skinny legs and all under her clothes and her kinky hair. She tried to keep it up but she worked and sweat too hard, for him! She just dropped her head deeper down into her plate and I could see she had a hard time swallowing her food.

Then, she try to buy him something nice and he told her to give it to the Salvation Army cause he didn't want it and that he was going to give everything he had to the Salvation Army that she had picked cause it ain't what he liked! Ain't he something! Somebody trying to be good to you and you ain't got sense enough to understand kindness and love.

She cook good food for him, too, and he mess with it and throw it out saying he don't like her cooking, he feel like eating out! Now!

Just let me tell you! She want a baby. He say he don't want no nappy head, skinny, bow-leg baby and laughed at her.

She want to go out somewhere of a evening, he say he ain't going nowhere with the grocery bag woman!

I didn't mean to, but once I heard her ask him why he slept in the other bedroom stead of with her one night—she had three bedrooms—and he said he couldn't help it, sometime he rather sleep with a rock, a big boulder, than her. She came back in with tears in her eyes that day, but she never complain, not to me anyway and I was her best friend.

Anyway, Mary took to eatin to get fat on her legs and bout five or six months, she was fat! Bout 200 pounds but her legs was still small and skinny and bowed. He really went to talking bout her then, even in the store, front of other people. Called her the Hog! Said everybody else's Hog was a Cadillac but his was his wife! And laugh! He all the time laughing at her. They never laugh together, in front of me, anyway.

So, one day Mary say she going to take care some business for a few days and she went off alone. He say "Go head, do what she want to do." He don't care bout what she do! "Do whatever!" Just like that! Whatever! Whatever! Didn't finish it like other people do, like "Whatever you want to," just, "Whatever!" I guess he heard it somewhere and thought it was smart to say it like that. Well, when Mary come back, I coulda fell out cause she brought one of her cousins, who was a real looker; long hair, big busts, and big legs and a heart full of foolishness. Maybelline was her name and she worked in the store all day, I can't lie about that, she sure did help Mary, but where she got the strength, I don't know, cause she worked the men all night! In three or four months she had gone through all the legible men in town, some twice, and then all the married illegible ones, some of them twice too. She was a go-getter, that Maybelline. But, she did help Mary and Mary seemed to need more help cause she was doing poorly in her health. She was sighing, tired and achy all the time now.

But she still took care of her business, the paper work and all, you know. Once, I saw Charles come into the store and she needed him to sign a few things, if you please, and he took them papers and bragged to the fellas in the store that "See, I got to sign things around here to keep things goin." He didn't even read them, just waved his hand and signed them and handed them to Mary without even looking at her, like she was a secretary or something, and went on out and drove off with a big grin looking 50¢ worth of importance, to me anyway.

Well, Mary just kep getting worse off. I told her to see a doctor and she said she had in the big city and she had something they couldn't cure but she wish I wouldn't tell nobody, so I didn't. But I felt so bad for her I loved her. I knew whatever was killing her was started by a heavy sad heart, shaking hands, a sore spirit, hot tears, deep, heavy sighs, hurtful swallows and oh, you know, all them kinda things.

Soon she had to stay home in bed. Wasn't no long sickness though, I could see she was going fast. Near the end, one day I saw her out in her back yard picking up rocks and I knew the dear soul must be losing her mind also and I took her back in the house and tried to get her to let loose the rocks and throw them away, but she wouldn't let go. She was sick but she was strong in her hands, from all that work, I guess, she just held on to them, so I said, "Shit, you ain't never had too much you wanted to hold on to so hold the rocks if that what you want!" And she did.

Now, she asked Charles to take Maybelline back to the city to get the rest of Maybelline's things to move down there and Charles didn't mind at all cause I had seen him looking that Maybelline upways, downways, and both sideways and I could tell he liked what he saw and so could Maybelline cause she was always posing or prancing. Anyway, they went for a day, one night and back the next day. Before they went, I saw Charles sit on the side of Mary's bed and, first time I ever saw him do it, take her hand and hold it, then bend down and kiss her on the forehead. Musta been thinking bout what he was going to do to Maybelline while they was gone, but anyway, I'm glad he did do it. It brought tears to Mary's eyes. Then, they were gone and before they got back, Mary was gone.

I have to stop a minute cause everytime I think of that sweet woman . . .

She had told me what to do, the funeral and all, so I had taken care of some of those things and Mary was already gone to the funeral home and the funeral was the next day.

When they come home or back, whatever!, all they had to do was get ready to go to the parlor. I don't know when or nothing like that, but when Charles went to the closet to get something to wear, the closet was bare, except for a note: "Dear Charles," it say, "They gone to the Salvation Army just like you always say you want. Yours truly, Mary."

Now that man run all over trying to find some way to get them back but they was nice things and somebody had done bought them or either kept them, you know what I mean? Then, he rush over to the bank to get some money and found out his name wasn't on the account no more! The manager gave him a letter say: "Dear Charles, You told me so many times you don't need me or nothing that is mine. Not going to force you to do nothing you don't want to do! Always, Mary."

His name was replaced with Maybelline's so naturally he went to see her at the store. She say sure, and give him $50 and he say, "Come go with me and help me pick it out," and she say she ain't got time. So he told her take time. She say. "I got to take care this business and close the store for the funeral." He say, "I'll close the store, this ain't your business to worry about." She say, "This my store." He say, "Are you crazy?" She say, "I ain't crazy. I'm the boss!" He say, "I'm Mary's husband, what's here is mine!" She say,

"That's true, but this store ain't hers, it's mine! I bought it from her!" He say, "With what? You can't afford to buy no store as nice as this!" She say, "Mary lent me the money; it's all legal; lawyer and everything!" He say, "How you gon' pay her back? You got to pay me, bitch!" She say, "No . . . no . . . when Mary died, all debt clear." He say, "I'll see about that!" She say, "Here, here the lawyer's name and number." He snatched it and left. He musta found out she was right and it was legal cause I never heard no more about it.

Now everybody bringing food and all, the house was full, but I was among the last to go and when Charles got ready to go to bed he say he wasn't going to sleep in the room Mary died in and he went into the third bedroom. I heard him holler and went in there and the covers was pulled back and the bed was full of rocks . . . and a note say: "Dear Charles, Tried to get what you wanted, couldn't carry no boulder, honest. Yours, Mary." Me, I just left.

Next morning he opens the food cupboard and it was almost empty, but for a note and note say: "Dear Charles, here is 30 days supply of food. Waste that too. Yours, Mary." I'm telling you, his life was going upside down. He and Maybelline stayed in that house alone together and that old Charles musta had something going on that was alright cause pretty soon they were married. I knew he thought he was marrying that store again, but let me tell you, Maybelline was pretty and fleshy but she couldn't count and didn't like to pay bills or the workers on that little piece of land of Mary's and pretty soon she was broke and the store was closed cause nothing wasn't in there but some old brown dead lettuce and turned up carrots and empty soda bottles and tired squashy tomatoes didn't nobody want. Charles didn't have nothing but an almost empty house. They cussed and fought and she finally left saying she wasn't really his wife cause she didn't have no divorce from her last husbands! So there!

Now, that ought to be all but let me finish telling you this cause I got to go now and see bout my own life.

Exactly a year passed from the day Mary had passed and a white lady and a black lady came to Mary's house with some papers and I heard a lot of hollering and shouting after a bit and Charles was putting them out. They waved those papers and said they would be back . . . and they did, a week later, with the Sheriff. Seems like Mary had give Charles one year to live there in the house and then it was to go, all legally, to be a orphan home for black children.

Welllll, when everything was over, I saw him sitting outside in his car, kinda raggedy now, just sitting there looking at the house. I took a deep breath and went to my dresser and got out the envelope Mary had give me to give him one year from her death, at this time. I looked at it awhile thinking bout all that had happened and feeling kind of sorry for Charles till I remembered we hoe our own rows and what we plants there, we picks. So I went on out and handed him the envelope through the car window. He rolled me red eyes and a dirty look and opened the envelope and saw a one hundred dollar bill and . . . a note. He read it with a sad, sad look on his face. "Dear Charles, here is $100. Take all the nothing you want and in a year you'll have everything. Yours truly, your dead wife, Mary." Well, he just sat there a minute, staring at the money and the note, then started his car up and slowly drove away without so much as "good-by." Going somewhere to spend that money I guess, or just stop and stare off into space . . . Whatever!

Are You Experienced?

BY DANZY SENNA

Way back in 1969, there was this girl named Josephine, a Negro by race, but pale as butter, with straight black hair that fell to her waist. Everybody called her Jo.

She was married to a pretty boy named Charles, a failed musician, whom once upon a time she had loved something awful. Now she only needed him.

One cold week in December he decided Jo wasn't pretty enough, white enough, woman enough for him. He blew her week's earnings on the horses, and disappeared. Rumor had it that he had run off with a white chick named Barbara, which was certainly possible. White girls were always falling for him.

He left Jo without even a dollar for food or diapers for their three year old son, Diego.

She trembled with rage as she called the person she always called in moments like this: her best childhood friend, Carol Anne, who lived in the city.

"Girl," Carol Anne sighed when she'd finished her story, "You gone and married a bullshit artist. You need to leave his ass. You need to get your behind to the city, today."

"But what about the kid?" Jo said, sniffling, eyeing the boy where he sat banging blocks across the room.

"Leave him with Charlie's mother," Carol Anne said, without pause. "That's what grandma's are for. She'll spoil the child senseless and he won't notice anything's wrong. Give yourself a few days, Jo. I'll show you what you're missing. I'll show you a good time."

So Jo, whispering curses under her breath at her missing husband, did as her friend had told her. She packed a bag of clothes and diapers for Diego and brought him to his Grandma Louise on the other side of town. The old woman did not ask questions. She knew her son was no good. Jo told her she'd be gone a few days. Would the kid be okay with her? The old woman was happy to take him in. And he seemed content to sit in front of her black-and-white television, shoving cookies in his mouth. He did not pull his eyes away from the cartoon to say goodbye.

Jo left for New York that afternoon without man or child and, when the bus pulled away from the depot, she felt her rage transform into a giddy, girlish excitement, something she had not felt in a long, long time. She glimpsed her face in the window beside her and remembered that she was not bad looking. She said to her own reflection, "Two can play at this game."

Jo's girlfriend, Carol Anne, lived the life she had not chosen. Carol Anne was happily unmarried, childless, and worked designing costumes for rock musicians and Broadway musicals. She was a caramel colored girl with a light brown afro and the long muscular legs of a track star. The two women had grown up together in the nation's capital. They'd spent their teenage years plotting their escape from what they called "Boojie-dom." They considered themselves sisters—fellow conspirators in their escape from that high yellow prison.

They were both considered good looking, in a similar hinkety way. Lucky for them they had never had the same taste in men. No cause for conflict.

Carol Anne had loved white boys from the beginning. In their arms she could be anybody, a mystery girl with no past and no discernable future. While brothers could see right through her, with white boys she could affect accents, don costumes, rewrite history for herself—and never be called out on her lies. With this one she was the daughter of a Brazilian sailor. With that one she was the half-caste child of an Indian aristocrat and a Nigerian princess. With white boys, her life could be theatre. They encouraged her antics. Brothers, on the other hand, were always trying to make her behave.

Jo stuck closer to home. She had never much liked white boys. They had always seemed to her an alien species—their bodies could stand out in the dark. She had always had a preference for brothers. Not the uptight, Boojie boys she had grown up with, but men two shades darker than she, revolutionaries, who could teach her a thing or two about the world, the streets.

And so it had seemed strange that in the end she'd married a brother who wasn't dark at all. The moody and mysterious Charles Moore was paler than a brown paper bag. But what he lacked in melanin, he made up for with attitude. He was a jazz musician when she met him, with high ideas about how he was gonna conquer the world without ever trying. He was a first generation mulatto, the son of a brown-skinned housecleaner mother, and an anonymous white father. Jo had seen romance in his tragedy, splendor in his split roots.

Jo's family saw none of the allure. They had worked so hard to raise Jo up right, to send her to college, and at the end of the day, she had come home with this ragamuffin, bohemian, misfit bastard. Everything about him rubbed them wrong: the way he smoked those small brown cigarettes incessantly, cupped his mouth when he inhaled, the way he talked in a soft vague murmur about "the trouble with whitey." Jo's mother told her after dinner the night they met him: "Josephine, you can't trust them mixed bloods. They have too much anger, too much conflict running through their blood. Find yourself a good colored boy."

But Jo would hear none of it. She'd had enough of those over-bred puppy dogs her mother trotted out for her inspection—nice boys who were dry as toast at the end of the day.

When she'd told her mother she was marrying Charles, and dropping out of college to become a jazz singer, her mother seemed tired of fighting. She'd simply wrung her hands, looked heavenward, and said with a miserable smile: "Well at least he's got good hair. At least you'll make pretty babies."

In the early days of their union, Charles and Jo had been a team making music around the outskirts of the capital, and later in Boston at a small crowded jazz club on Tremont Street. But from the beginning it was clear: Jo's voice was better than Charles's playing. It wasn't that Charlie didn't have talent. He did, but it was talent without discipline. And he didn't shine the way Jo did on stage. The moment she took the stage, a hush would fall over the audience and her voice, smoky and androgynous, would fill the space with a remote yearning that could never be filled. Listening to her sing made one long for something indecipherable. Charles's horn, behind her, was just a background tune for her voice, nothing in itself. After a set, the boys and the girls would flock to the stage to compliment her. Charles would sit at the sidelines, rubbing a dirty cloth against his horn, glowering at his wife.

At first Jo had wanted to believe Charlies's failure was due to the alcohol or some inner torment that prevented him from being his best. She wanted to believe the reasons for his failure were complicated, traced back to his absent father and poverty-stricken youth.

But then one day, after a particularly bad show, it struck her: Charles was lazy. That was why he would never be great. He fancied himself a genius, and maybe he was, but he would never be more than mediocre. She had seen it so clearly she stopped breathing for a moment. Some people, she'd realized with a flash of lucidity, fall with a crash. Others, like Charlie, fall slowly, gently and slowly as a feather to their demise, so gradually they barely notice it happening. One day, they wake up, and they've hit the bottom. She thought, staring at her husband across the smoky nightclub air, that she would rather crash and burn any day of the week. There was nothing more horrifying to her than mediocrity. Nothing worse than a slow demise.

But she was loyal. She stuck by his side. Even when she had to stop singing, start working as a music teacher at a local public school to support them both and Charles had gotten a job as a cab driver (he said he wanted to feel he was moving somewhere, though he never got out of the car). Most nights, though, she came home to find him lying on the couch with a bottle of triple sec in one hand, a cigarette in the other. Sometimes, when he was sober and they would take the cab out and drive to the country, pretend they were really going on a trip. They would blast music, pass a joint between them, and giggle about the people they'd known in their club days, the wild things they'd seen.

But most of the time it wasn't like that. Most of the time they were fighting.

It didn't turn violent until after Diego was born.

The first time it happened she thought he'd lost control of his hand. She thought it had convulsed and ended up flying across her face. Holding her cheek she had stared at him silently as he turned away and shuffled back to the living room, muttering, "Shit," under his breath. The second time it happened was outside a club, where he'd just given his lousiest and last performance. Like before he'd back-handed her, but this time when she fell he gave her a swift kick in the belly for good measure.

It was evening when Jo arrived at Carol Anne's crumbling studio in the Bowery. Carol Anne gave her a big perfumey hug and told Jo to forget about the Failed Musician, to lighten up and smoke a joint. "Girl, we're goin *out* tonight. A party. New York style baby. I'm gonna show you how the other half live."

She did Jo's makeup, dressed her up in a rainbow mini dress that showed off her slight figure, and braided her hair so she looked like a Navajo princess. Jo missed her baby boy with a pain that gnawed at her stomach, but she did as Carol Anne told her, and tried to feel her freedom.

The two women shared a joint and reminisced about their girlhood in

D.C.—the clothes pins on their noses, the plaits in their hair—how far they'd wandered from all that. Linking arms, they'd leaned in towards one another against the icy wind, as they went out to meet the night.

As soon as they arrived at the party, in a tall doorman building overlooking Central Park, Jo felt out of place. The people there were in another league— dazzling and decadent, famous or at least pretending to be. She felt small and brown and dingy. As she stared at a blonde woman spinning circles in a sequined mini dress, she thought that she belonged at home, with her Failed Musician, and her little boy, Diego, who smelled of strawberry's behind his ears. But when she looked for Carol Anne, she was gone, swallowed up in the throngs, so Jo stood in a corner and anxiously sipped her champagne.

Later, somewhat tipsy, Jo wandered down the hall in search of a bathroom. Peeking in a door she saw a gaggle of white people surrounding one black man who sat like a king on a throne, his head tilted back and an expression that teetered between amusement and boredom. Jimi Hendrix. She recognized him immediately. She had listened to "Foxy Lady" fourteen times in a row one night. She had wanted to go to Woodstock, but the Failed Musician had said he didn't want to hang around with a bunch of filthy, greasy haired honkies who smelled like wet dogs.

The people who surrounded him looked like industry types, sycophants and handlers. They were talking to him excitedly, but he looked bored, smoking at tiny stub of his joint and tapping his foot impatiently. His heavy eyes caught hers at the door. He smiled, a strange, familiar smile, as if he had known her already, for years. The gaggle of white folks turned around and smiled at her as well, waved her toward them, as if they were offering her up to this sullen prince. She stepped inside the room and stood before him speechless. Everyone else was silent too, as if they were waiting for his verdict. His eyes roved up and down her slim yellow body, until, finally, he winked and said, "Hey sister. You lost?"

They slept together three times. Once that night, in the king sized water bed of the stranger who owned the apartment, and twice the next night, in his hotel suite at the Ritz. He said she reminded him of a world he had nearly forgotten. He traced his finger over her wide brown nipples and said she was a lovely little slip of a thing. She told him she was married to a Failed Musician who drank too much and sometimes slapped her upside her head. Naked beside him in the big sloshing bed, she showed him pictures of her little boy, Diego, and he admired the child, and said, giggling, he looked like a wet back. Before falling to sleep each night, she sang to Jimi with that smoky boy's voice of hers, and he told her, sleepily, that she had a voice that could make a grown man cry. On the third night, he asked her to come with him on the road. He told her he could make her a star. She only laughed, sadly, and told him it was too late for all that. She had a boy to go back to.

Then he was gone, and Jo was on a bus back home, where her husband had returned, tail between his legs, white girl discarded, ready to make peace. That first night back, she picked Diego up at his grandmother's house & the boy crawled all over her, kissing her face and pulling her hair, as if he were a hungry bird, and for a moment she was glad to be home.

The Failed Musician, strangely, did not suspect anything had gone on in his absence. He thought she had been pining for him at Carol Anne's apartment. Only later, much later, after her face had been smashed and put back together, would she utter the name of Jimi Hendrix.

Nine months passed, and Jo grew. When the Failed Musician slapped her, she didn't even think of her own face, but only of her belly, shielding this child. On a wet September night in 1970, the baby was born at Brigham and Women's Hospital. Jo had been to that hospital two other times during her pregnancy—once at four months, for spot bleeding, and once, at six months, for a broken nose. Now, on her third trip in nine months, she gave birth to a red faced, howling, slippery, squinty eyed little thing who she wanted to name Cheyenne, but whom her husband insisted on calling Mabel, after his great aunt.

The child was nothing like her brother. She did not like to be touched, for one thing. While Diego clung to his mother, begged to sleep beside her at night, the little girl wiggled and squirmed from both her mother's and father's touch, as if she had her eyes on some other destiny from the start. While Diego hid under the table, sobbing and begging, "Stop, stop," whenever the Failed Musician went after Jo with his fist, the little girl would just watch them, study them, solemnly, unblinking, in such a way that seemed to shame even the Failed Musician himself.

Jo noticed that this was how the girl watched everybody: her friends, her teachers, the whole world—from a distance, wide-eyed, unblinking, as if committing an image that would soon be gone.

Jo loved the little girl, but feared her gaze. Whenever the girl stared at her, Jo would see herself—painfully clear—the way she walked perpetually tilted to the side, as if warding off an invisible blow. Watching herself through that child's eyes she saw that she was doing what she had swore never to do: she was falling slowly, in an endless gentle descent toward a place where she could not recognize herself.

Over the years, she studied her daughter closely for signs of the dead musical genius, looked for the features that would prove her royal lineage. And sometimes, when Jo was drunk and bruised and angry, she would drag the girl down into the darkened living room and make her dance with her, sleepy, confused, to "Purple Haze," until the sun came up and the high wore down and the truth shone through the curtains—revealing the Failed Musician in her daughter's pale face.

Group Solo

BY SCOTT POULSON BRYANT

D ad?" asked my son James. "How should you tell someone you don't love them anymore?"

James is an actor. He's on an afternoon soap opera that airs after the game show which, ironically, just fired me from my job as host. His character, named Radcliffe, is a spy who speaks seven languages (none of which, I like to tease him, is Ebonics) and *Ebony* magazine says he is rumored to be one of the highest paid blacks on TV. This explains the luxurious expanse of his lower–Fifth Avenue apartment overlooking the entire southern tip of Manhattan on one end and the entire northern tip of Manhattan (and some of New Jersey) on the other end. His mother and I worked the Chitlin' Circuit for years before prime-time TV ever thought to call us; James went right from our house to Vassar to daytime drama and this elaborate spread. During his four years at Vassar, as a black boy in thrall to "art" and "acting" and "the classics," he was, I thought, completely, adolescently loathsome. But I loved him, as I love him now. Besides, I believe the long hours and aesthetic vulgarity of daytime television have humbled him. Which was clear to me when he said, "Dad, how should you tell someone you don't love them anymore?"

This was the first time James had ever brought up his love life to me. Other than the day he told us he was gay when he was eighteen years old, he's never talked about his romantic involvements. I said, "Your mother is the only woman I've ever loved and I never had to tell her that."

"But Mom—"

"What?"

"I just thought you and Mom had, uh, done things."

"We have," I told him, offering a smile. "With each other."

"Oh."

James is a good actor, but he is not a good liar. He is not good at hiding things; he is not good at keeping secrets. I've spent a lot of time at James' apartment since I was fired from the show, my way of still spending time in Manhattan instead of brooding in Long Island. I like the track lighting, glaring like spotlights, and the silk curtains draped over the windows like they're hiding a stage; the dazzling stereo set-up where I play my Motown hits at full blast, the wall of fame hung with magazine covers featuring James' handsome face. I love it here. But I haven't spent a lot of time with James, considering his long hours on the set. Now here we were talking, spending quality time together and he wanted to talk about how to end a relationship. My handsome son, who is not a good liar, was trying to tell me something.

"This isn't about you, is it?" I said to him. "You trying to tell me something?"

"Like what?"

"I don't know."

He flipped a page in the script he'd been studying. Finally he said, "You need to find a job, Dad." He shifted on the couch, pulling his bare feet up underneath his behind. "Everything flows from work. You used to tell me that, remember?"

James had been speaking to his mother. "You been talking to your mother?"

"You need to get a job, Dad."

That was two weeks ago. My name is Dennis Manning, but the woman who cuts my hair calls me Nissy, "short for Dennis, you know, like a nickname," she says, smacking orange-scented gum in my ear. "You know what I like, Nissy? You're kind of famous and you're the only guy who comes in here and asks specifically"—pronounced "pacifically"—"for me. I really like that." She talks the whole time she cuts my hair, offering long-winded tales of domestic life, about her pit bulls Kinky and Joe, and the constant loss of the remote control at the hands of Cyril, the three-year-old second cousin she baby-sits three nights a week. I don't know her age, but I assume she must be older than twenty-one, yet younger than twenty-five: She goes to a bar named The Misty Blue every weekend for dancing and drinking, and she refers to her boss Lyle (the quarterback to my tackle senior year of high school, Class of '64) as the Old Guy.

"Now that you ain't working, Nissy, you should come by the Misty Blue. You'd like it. You'd see all those guys from your high school days. They can *dance.*" She draws out the word dance until it actually seems to be dancing on the surface of her tongue. "You know what record I love? That old record by the Miracles. 'Tears of a Clown.' I bet you like that record. You should see the brothers getting down at the Misty Blue, man. I didn't think old guys would be able to get down like that, but *oh*"—and her voice goes up and up, as the razor buzzes closer to my right ear, drowning out her words, and I wonder if the glory of over-fifty carousers will some day cause me to become right-earless. But soon her voice softens and the razor subsides, and Jackie—that's her name—is extending a mirror behind me with one long-nailed hand and spinning the raised chair with the other, providing me with a multi-angled view of myself. She knows that I'll be satisfied—I'm the only guy that asks "pacifically" for her—but those are the rules and I follow them as I follow the ebb and flow of her outlandish stories, as I followed Lyle onto the field in those autumns long long ago. I pay Jackie, tipping her five, and she winks. "See you in ten days, Nissy," she's says, dropping the bills into the pocket of the billowy smock she wears. For a second I wonder what her body is like underneath that sheath of cotton speckled with the detritus of my graying temples. "Who's next?" she says, looking around the crowded shop. But there won't be a next, because the too-cool teenagers sprawled across the patent leather benches, flipping through the pages of sports magazines and inky tabloids, wait for Lyle, old-school football hero and style-cutter to the hip, high school elite. So, with no takers, Jackie just sweeps away the leftovers of my trim, picks up her own magazine—usually a car rag—and settles into one of the low-slung, beauty treatment chairs that tilt back toward a sink, and waits, I often wonder, through the ten days until I return.

"Come dance sometime," she says to me as I head out the door. "I'm gonna miss you dancing on TV." She's referring to *Group/Solo*, the game show I hosted for fifteen years, until last season, they, amid tabloid rumors of my forthcoming nervous breakdown (rumors that I only wanted to dance with the guests and had no interest in hosting the show), the new network regime—a green, ragtag assortment of twenty-eight-year olds who'd decided my style of hosting was, not "current" enough—put an old horse out of his low-rating 'ed misery. And I had no defense. The best part of the show did come at the end, when there'd be a group solo, in which I'd dance with the grand-prize winner. The house band would strike up some old standard and the winner and I would twirl away, as the credits rolled, past the gift displays and flashy game board. The new host, my youthful replacement who came to fame as a male cheerleader at USC, continues to dance, but he dances with younger contestants who swing and jack their taut, toned bodies into more current forms of social posturing. I couldn't do it. I wouldn't do it. I am not like Lyle, who thinks he hasn't aged, who has parlayed his years of experience and local celebrity into fashioning those young heads into visions of state-of-the-art black teenhood. Then again, growing old gracefully might work in the 'hood, but it has no place on TV.

After I leave the barbershop, I drive through the ragged remains of my hometown, down Water Street, the main drag, teeming with empty storefronts and devoid, it seems, of the life that existed there in my youth. I pass the old fabric store my father once owned, where the first publicity stills of Gail and me, the dancing couple, were taken years and years ago. (I still have the local newspaper clipping: "From Football Star to TV Star"). The "Black Astaire and Rogers" we were called, two hoofing black high school sweethcarts, drawn together by an obsession with dancing and great books. We tapped and tangoed our way across the nation's stages, through the Civil Rights movement and Black Power, through blaxploitation filcks and disco, dressed in the sequined and spangled two-pieces my mother sewed in my father's back room. After my father died the fabric store became a Jamaican roti house, then a bustling Chinese take-out joint people don't any more but they do go out to eat. Now it's just a hollow building, waiting for its next incarnation as a Latin grocery emporium. I drive past the curving line of workers and shoppers waiting for the first early-morning Water Street bus to carry them away from this listless relic of a town to more upscale places burgeoning with opportunity and some taste of liveliness. Then I'm on Exceptional Boulcvard, once the sight of a colorful and bouyant parade in my honor, heading toward the home—some say mansion—I have in the hills of the next town.

My wife's morning cab sits in the very center of the circular driveway. I pull in behind it and blow the horn. Gail comes out of the house, pauses on the steps to put envelopes in the mailbox, yells something back to Agatha, the maid, then comes over to the car. "Don't forget dinner tonight," she says. Her body and voice are here with me in Long Island, but her mind is already in the office in Manhattan, her heart somewhere I'll never guess. "Are you listening to me, Dennis? We're meeting James at seven. We *agreed* this should happen tonight, so have Agatha set the alarm so you'll be up by five." She smells of lilacs; her pearls tap against the half-raised car window as she leans to kiss me good-bye, turning her ear to me to avoid smudging her makeup. "Don't forget. You said you'd be there." Then she turns, tall and graceful on the edge of her heels, and gets into the cab, off to make the 9:15 am train. I watch the cab drive away, then head into the house, through the dark foyer swathed in the fragrance of Gail's lilac perfume, to the skylighted kitchen, where Agatha stands at the stove and moves bacon around a frying pan with a long-tined fork. The sizzle of the grease competing with the blare of the TV on the counter. Agatha smiles at me, as she often does these days, a little sadly it seems, like she knows that the war's over and she has to serve bacon and eggs to the lone casualty right on the site of battle.

"You're on again today," she says, with a hand on her hip and a nod toward the loud TV.

There I am, on the Game Show Network, a celebrity guest on *The $25,000 Pyramid*, sitting in the Winner's Circle, facing an anxious-looking, red-headed woman in a polka-dot dress. I'm leaning forward in my seat, yelling out a list of words to her, "groceries," I say, "dry cleaning," some "ums" and some "uhs," and then, in a burst of inspiration, I say, "a spare tire," and she shouts back at me "Things in a car trunk!" And I nod, and she jumps from her seat and we're hugging and Dick Clark (who never ever gets old; how old was he when we taped that?) comes over to the Winner's Circle and offers his congratulations. Cut to commercial.

"That was 1979," I tell Agatha.

"I know," she says. "You ripped that corduroy jacket right after you got home."

Cable TV, the funhouse mirror that talks back to retired TV performers like me, televising like some kind of cathode-ray Dorian Gray portrait brought to life. In the months since my firing I'd seen my younger self on *The Love Boat* (as the jewel thief cousin of Isaac the bartender), *Charlie's Angels* (as the prosecutor whose wife is seeing another man), on *Hollywood Squares* ("Which state is the Iditarod in?" I'm asked. "A frozen state," I reply, and the audience roars with laughter.) There I was on *Match Game* ("Freddie believed that the only way to make dogs like him better was to dress up as a BLANK." The contestant's answer was "A can of dog food." My answer, along with Richard Dawson and Brett Sommers, was "Fire Hydrant"). And there, between Patty Duke and John Astin and Mr. and Mrs. Phyllis Diller, were Gail and I together on *Tattletales* ("What's the one thing you hate most about your husband?" the wives were asked. Gail's answer: "The way Dennis snores." We got one hundred points for the Blue Section.) Who would have thought, I'd asked Gail one night—while we watched ourselves on a *Carol Burnett Show* rerun on the Comedy Channel—that Cable TV, this threat to the Big 3 Networks that had kept us in business, this wave of the media future, would actually become a clearinghouse for the old network shows it threatened to replace? She just shrugged her shoulders and said, "Can you please turn the channel? *Sex and the City's* about to come on."

I eat Agatha's bacon and eggs and drift up to bed to sleep until noon, to have one of the mean daytime dreams that I've been having lately.

My dream.

Picture this: a woman, my wife, honey-colored, just over fifty years old. She's wearing a tapered plaid skirt with a matching jacket, padded shoulders accentuating the cinched waist that she tends to diligently with daily sit-ups and diet pills. Her hair is swept up from her neck, poised there with a barrette that she'd covered herself the night before with the remaining scraps of her outfit's fabric. She likes everything to match. She stands in the center of a moving subway car, the A train swooshing downtown toward her son's Greenwich Village apartment, hanging onto the metal passenger bar so as not to tumble into the unsuspecting lap of the gentleman reading the *Post* seated directly beneath her. She wants a seat. She's tired from the daily PR grind of lunches and conferences and the metaphorical prostitution it entails, but no one offers her a seat—not the gentleman with the *Post*, not the teenager in hightops, nor the man she recognizes from the suite of offices next to her own expensive suite of office space. This lack of courtesy doesn't really bother her though; chivalry died, she told me once, with the interment of King Tut. She realizes (or rationalizes) that with her heels and her brown auburn-tinted hair and slightly tight-fitting suit hiding her age she could easily pass for thirty, thirty-five even. But sometimes she wishes she weren't so, so—a word doesn't even come to her. She wishes that the youthful zest that gets her extramarital affairs and whistles on the street could disappear the moment she appeared on the subway train. Because no one offers a young woman a seat. But this also refreshes her, catapults her into new reasons for striving harder . . . or so she says.

She likes everything to match. But, as she said to me, she and I don't match anymore.

Just after my dismissal from the game show, Gail (and I) had a party, a cocktail thing to which everyone came: television people glued to their Nokias like the tiny cell phones held the secret of life; vulgar young music business-types that Gail associates with at work, their boxer-clad asses gaping out of baggy jeans; nosy starstruck neighborhood boors bent on being impressed; and the new breed of nameless, free-drink–drinking wannabes looking to make names for themselves.

It really was Gail's party; no one wanted to talk about my recent departure from their professional entertainment ranks. While she waltzed around the house, floor to floor, guest to guest, I planted myself near the bar, chatting mainly with the nervous catering administrator who often interrupted our boundlessly empty conversation with snide orders to his celebrity-gazing staff. Gail glowed in these situations, and because she glowed, occasionally surrendering herself to the music and spinning like a bump-and-grind pixie, the house glowed, as did I, as best I could, feeling old and unwanted, but mainly just bored. (Gail doesn't dance with me at parties anymore. "I like to dance the way the kids dance," she says. "You want to get too close. I'm not in tap shoes anymore.") That night, she danced with our son, James, making a not unawkward fifty-four-year-old's stabs at the latest crazy dance steps, her head ajerk with the beat, her mouth wrapped around the lewd lyrics, and everywhere the house breathed her lilac odor echoed her laughter. It was the generous chortle of a young woman, reckless, massaged by the knowledge that her whole life lay before her like a road repaved solely for her to travel upon.

I wanted to see Jackie.

. . .

The energy emanating from the Misty Blue almost made up for the lack of life in my old hometown. The parking lot out front was thick with cars and people preparing to party. I could smell the tangy odor of marijuana to my left; could hear the drunken shouts of a thick-thighed woman in high heels and a short purple skirt coming from my right. I turned that way, and there was Jackie, holding up the woman, helping her toward her car.

"Is that you, Nissy?" She sped up her step, now dragging the woman along with her as she approached me. "Look at you, Nissy. Looking all cute." The drunk woman in her embrace looked up at me, as if the sight of me and my possible cuteness might snap her out of her daze. She seemed to recognize me for a second, but her buzz had a grip on her memory; it held it away from her and she couldn't grab it back. She gave up and let her head loll back on her shoulder.

"Be right back," Jackie said. She hurried the woman to a Taurus that was parked just ahead of my car and shoved her inside. Then she stood, pressed down the front of her own miniskirt and turned back to me, her face all bright eyes and smile.

At our table inside, Jackie pointed out some old-timers and updated me on their lives since I knew them in high school. She'd dated the sons of at least seven guys I'd known when I was younger than she is now.

"And one daughter," she said, with a grin illuminated by the vodka cocktails she sucked down. "But that was just an experiment," she added. "You know how it is, Nissy. You've seen the world."

"But I still live near here," I told her. "The world is overrated."

"I'll believe that when I see it." She took a sip of her drink, then shouted over the thump of the music, "Why aren't you home with your wife?"

"She's entertaining a houseful of people I don't like or know," I said.

"Maybe if you got to know them," Jackie said, "you'd like them."

"I'm too old for them," I said.

"But not too old for me?"

"Nope."

"Why not?"

I didn't know how to answer that at first. But I thought about her cutting my hair and I thought about her baby-sitting her second cousin and I looked at her dreadlocks and miniskirt against a background of old men with whisky glasses and smiles that had known what frowns felt like and cars that knew the lyrics to the songs that I loved and I said, "Because my wife will never forgive me."

She had started to sip again but paused, holding her glass before her, cutting me a look that could have shattered the cocktail glass she was holding. "You cheated on her?"

"Nope."

"Then what did you do to her?"

"I got old." My mind's eye was on Gail dancing at the party. "I got old *first.*"

"And that's unforgiveable?"

"She never thought that would happen," I said, suddenly warming to this conversation, warming to a theory I'd never spoken aloud and only rarely thought in any substantial way. "No," I said, and I took a long, deep gulp from the glass of wine that had been sitting there, untouched, in front of me. "No, that's not it. It's not that I got old. It's that I like it."

"You like being old," Jackie said.

"I love it," I told her. I wasn't exactly sure that I believed that last comment, but it felt good to say, so I said it again. "I love it and that's what my wife can't forgive."

"Wow," said Jackie.

"Wow, indeed," I said. "Let's have another round."

It was the first second round of many second rounds that I would share with Jackie, who became my best friend of sorts. We went to movies and basketball games. We shared ice cream at the Carvel on Water Street near my father's old fabric shop. We went to the amusement park in East Meadow where Jackie won me a teddy bear that looked, she said, like me when I came in for my haircut. One night, as we were driving back from a movie, a song called "I Think I'm Goin' Outta My Head" came on the radio and the falsetto tones of Little Anthony lifted me up inside. "I love this song," Jackie said. She grabbed my hand and yanked me out of the car and as drivers passed us, the radio turned to the highest volume, the headlights outlining our two-step, Jackie and I danced along Exceptional Boulevard.

Another evening, another party at our house, this time for our son, James, and his new contract. I invited Jackie.

She showed up in an apple-green dress and strappy high-heeled sandals, her dreadlocks piled high atop her beaming face. We talked for a while, I introduced her to Gail and some of the rappers Gail represented, then she swooped into the party, a whirl of green.

"She could be your daughter," Gail said.

"What are you talking about?" I said.

Gail just rolled her eyes at me and turned, melting back into the party.

Later I found Jackie on the dance floor and said, "Take a bow."

"What?"

"Follow me."

We went out onto the back patio. The stars were like tiny spotlights poking through the thick black fabric of the sky.

" 'Take a bow,' " I told Jackie, "is an old family saying. Whenever some-one was overreacting or overdramatizing or just cutting up, we'd say, "Okay, take a bow."

"Like, when a director says 'cut'?"

"Exactly," I said.

"The sky is beautiful, isn't it?"

"It is," I said. "My wife thinks you and I are having an affair."

"What?" Jackie's laugh was like a loud bark. "Should she be thinking that?"

"No," I said. "She shouldn't. But she wants to, I think. I think it would make me more interesting to her somehow."

"She's beautiful, your wife."

"Yes," I said. "She is."

"Have you told her that lately?"

"I haven't told her much of anything lately. We don't really talk to each other much."

"You need to tell her she's beautiful. Then she won't think you're jumping my bones."

"Maybe you're right," I said.

Jackie leaned onto the back of a patio chair. "I saw y'all on TV the other day."

"Who?"

"You and your wife and your little boy."

"He's not little anymore."

"I know that. Tell your wife that's the Manning I need to be having an af-fair with."

I had to laugh at that.

"I was watching this show about celebrities before they were celebrities and they showed an old TV show where you and your wife and your little boy were singing Christmas carols with some white lady."

I nodded. "Marlo Thomas," I said. "She had a Christmas special years ago. That was James' first public appearance."

"Y'all looked so happy," Jackie said. "Like a perfect little family."

"Yes," I said. "We did. We were."

"Which is why you need to go and tell that lady in there that she's beau-tiful. She wants somebody to tell her. Unless you waiting for one of those rappers to tell her." She pushed herself up from the chair and brushed off the back of her tiny apple-green dress. "That's all I got to say about that. Now I'm going back to the party. You coming?"

"I'm coming."

Toward the end of the evening, with twenty or so drunken dancers grip-ping each other in the center of the dance floor, Reuben Mays, James' agent, raised his gin into the air and began to recite Shakespeare, Lady Macbeth at Dunsinore, in garishly drunken tones. I picked up my own drink and looked around for Gail, who wasn't entwined with a partner on the floor. James, snuggled up to his latest flame, an Asian man he'd met in college, said he hadn't seen her. Mays was still warbling as I went down the three steps towards the kitchen. The last of the catering staff was struggling out with two huge bowls. Agatha stood, holding the back door for them, a stern territorial grimace tickling the edges of her lips.

"Good riddance," she said, slamming the door.

"I'm looking for Gail," I told her. Agatha seemed to ignore me. "Did you hear me, Agatha?"

"Upstairs."

I passed three people leaving as I fumbled my way up the stairs toward the bedrooms. In ours, on the bed, on the Mexican print James had given us last year, was Gail, in the arms of a tall, famous balladeer she represented. I watched them watch me before I turned and left the room.

I found Jackie downstairs in the foyer, draping herself in a big green poncho. Her sly eyes questioned me before she said a word.

"You tell her?"

"I told her," I said.

"See, man? That's all a woman wants to hear sometime. Just wanna know her man thinks she's the best-looking chick at the party." She pushed me playfully with her shoulder. "You seen the world. You know that. Now that you told her? You take your behind right on up those stairs and you *show* her she's the most beautiful woman at the party."

"Take a bow, Jackie."

"I know, I know. I'm leaving."

After everyone was gone, Gail said we didn't match anymore. "You're old and you're tired and you're bored, Dennis. You know what? I'm glad you caught me. You let yourself get kicked off the show because you refuse to change," she said. She pressed her lips together; fastened her gaze on some point directly above my head. "When we got married, I was still Little Miss Harlem, carrying around those silly blue ribbons from fashion shows, and tap-dancing behind you on the *Ed Sullivan Show*. You were doing your thing—"

"We were partners—"

"—now I'm doing mine and you just don't seem to be following. We don't match, Dennis. I'm going up and you're going down and I just can't accept that. I can't. I suggested you do a guest shot on James' soap. You turned that down. They wanted you—James wanted you—and you turned it down. I don't know what you want to do, Dennis. Sleep all day?" I didn't argue with her. Her speech sounded so rehearsed, I wanted to hear the climax and denouement.

"I guess," she said, as if on cue, "you're happy with your little barber who calls you nicknames."

"Jackie only cuts my hair. You know that Gail. We go to basketball games."

"I'm sure."

"Don't make your guilt into my guilt." I didn't know what else to say to her. So I said, "I love you Gail."

"It's not there anymore, Dennis. We just don't match."

How completely blissful it is to love a person who doesn't love you anymore. The drink flows; the possible onset of depression lifts you into a netherworld of fantastically ugly, bourbon-soaked reveries of revenge, and the lonesomeness created by betrayal seems to be a dangerous, inviting playground. Such thoughts occupy me as I search for a parking space along Ninth Street, passing young people and old who I believe to be happily entrenched in twosomes, untouched by the blemish of hidden romantic deeds done on the beds they shared with their partners. And, I say, as my son opens the door to his apartment, "How completely blissful it is to love a person who doesn't love you anymore."

I haven't been here since I started hanging out with Jackie. I haven't been here since James tried to warn me that his mother wanted to leave me.

"Mom's not here yet," he says, stepping aside, his head cocked to one side as I head over to the bar. "What did you say when I opened the door?"

"Never mind."

"Whatever. Nice haircut, Dad." There's something in his voice, if not his words, something sly and mean and haughty. But I can't be completely mad at his condescension, and for a moment I wonder if that's something Gail and I taught him. His eyes are blurry and I can smell vodka on his breath, though I'm not completely sure it's not my breath bouncing back off of him and ricocheting back to me.

We don't say much to each other as we wait for his mother to arrive. I look out the window, watching couples pass by. Soon I see Gail getting out of a sleek black Lincoln Town Car. My dream was incorrect. She hasn't taken the train, she's beaten the lack of chivalry, courtesy of one of the record companies that keep her in business.

James goes to the door when the bell rings. "Hey, Mom. Dad's already here."

"I'm starving," she says. "Where should we eat?" I can smell alcohol on Gail as well. It seems we all need to get drunk to spend any time together, just the three of us with no revelers to share in, to experience, the raging success of the Manning Family.

We go to the Front Row, a trendy little Italian boite on Sixth Avenue. James chats with an actress friend two tables away. Gail goes to the ladies room to fix her face. I sit at the table and smile back at the stares we get. When James and Gail join me at the table, we share a bottle of wine and small talk, like it's finger food to be picked over before the main dish arrives. All the while we are watched by patrons at other tables. One woman exclaims, "That's him, Jim," and runs over to our table, flinging a napkin down. "I love you, Radcliffe. You are my favorite. I swear." James signs his name on the napkin. "I swear," the woman yells to others as her husband escorts her out, "that boy is my absolute favorite."

We tell him as the waiter puts the clam sauce on the table between Gail and James. "I'm leaving your father," Gail says in careful, modulated tones, as if she's saying "I'm taking on a new client." But not for another man, she tells James. "Things are just different now." An astounding performance, this is. My son's performance is on par with his mother's. He stares at me as if he's seeing me for the first time, as if I'm someone he's only seen on TV who's come to life before him, just as people in the restaurant stare at him.

Gail says to James, "Your father has a crush on his barber."

And there it is. Her trump. I lost my job and now I'm cheating with my barber. I've given up my fame card and I'm dating a barber more than half my age.

"How old is he?" James asks.

At first I think James is asking about me.

I say, "Don't be absurd, Gail. She's James' age."

"My age?" James starts to laugh, loudly. He sets his wine glass on the table as he controls himself.

"And she has a nickname for him," Gail says, laughing now as well.

"A *nickname*?" James asks.

"She calls me Nissy," I tell him.

"Nissy?" he asks, as if he doesn't understand, as if spitting it out will lay the word on the table for us to decipher, like one of those extra-large family puzzles we used to do together on vacation.

"Short for Dennis," I say, smiling.

"Nissy?" James says it again. I notice that the sound of his laughter has grown louder as people at other tables turn to see what the celebrity is laughing at. "Oh, Dad." His words sound as if they're on display, as if this is some variety show and he's projecting to the balcony. I get it now. We're on stage. "Nissy? You let her call you Nissy?"

"I do," I tell him. "And she loves to dance." And suddenly I'm laughing as well, partner to my own abuse. Taking one for the family.

"You let Mom *divorce* you and you let your barber call you *Nissy*? Oh, Dad. Oh. Dad . . ."

Gail shakes with laughter, her hand on her stomach, the barrette bouncing as she moves forward and back. "*Nissy*," she repeats. "And she just *loves* to dance."

Soon, we're all at it, hitting the table for dramatic emphasis, inviting onlookers to share in our fun. "*Nissy*." I'm shouting now. "She calls me fucking Nissy."

"Oh, Dad . . ."

James looks wonderful in his denim shirt. His mother's almond-shaped eyes and my checkbones and chin combine to give his face a regal, dancing quality. But at that moment, the planes of his handsome face contorted in laughter, he has become a fine and heartbreaking mirror in which I can see all the gray hair that I no longer camouflage with black dye. I see the paunch and the wrinkles that lost me my job. I see the glassy eyes of a drinker whose wife considers him as good as dead. I see me, and realize that this dinner is a success because I feel overwhelmingly happy at the sight of all those flaws I haven't patched up. I feel like dancing.

And in my laughter, through the tears that I know are there, I try to imagine Dennis, a grown boy called Nissy, and Jackie, the unnamed costar in this family drama, dancing down Exceptional Boulevard. But here I am now in the middle of The Front Row, lifting my young almond-eyed son and pulling my youthful wife onto the table, breathing in the scenty hint of illacs, dancing a group solo to the strains of arch violins in the restaurant pavilion, then falling, to the floor, like a heavy brocade curtain, yes, indeed, falling.

Love

BY BERTICE BERRY

The sweet sounds of Maxwell played softly. I walked in the room and wanted to cry. I was tired, both physically and spiritually. Success is draining. Most folks looking at it from the outside can only see what they call glamour.

I made my way over to the CD player and pushed the volume button to the max. I don't drink, so I needed more Maxwell. The soulful sounds dulled the pain, at least for the moment.

I imagined myself in the younger man's audience, and noticed that even in my imagination, I was the oldest person in the room. For years my biological clock had been ticking, but because of my success and the use of new technology, it had been digital, so I couldn't hear it. But now, it was flashing midnight.

I watched the imaginary "other women" in my fantasy as they strolled about in anticipation that Maxwell would notice them. "Desperation is the world's worst perfume," I thought to myself. Maxwell entered the audience, and walked over to me. "Just a while longer baby," he sang for me alone. He moved in close enough to cause the other imaginary folks to disappear, and just as his wild mane of hair brushed across my eyelashes, the telephone rang.

"Peace," I said, not meaning it.

"Hey baby. What's that loud noise I hear? Are you having a party or something?" My mother's voice was as familiar to me as my own. I could read her like a book. I could tell that things were not good, because of the effort she was putting forth at sounding happy. "Hey Mom what's wrong?"

"What makes you think something's wrong? Maybe I'm just calling to say hi, or that I love you. Did you ever think of that?" she demanded.

"You're right, Mom," I offered. I knew better, but I dared not show it. My mother had a way of making me feel guilty for the things that happened to her as a child. She was even better with events after my birth.

To make matters worse, or better, depending on which side she stood on at that moment, my mother and I had what some might call a psychic bond. I could tell when things were going wrong with her, and she with me. The only difference was in how we received the message. For me it was just a feelling. Something like a shadow would cover my mood whenever my mother experienced pain or sadness. My mother received her intuitions in a much more dramatic fashion; the big toe on her left foot would throb. I don't know if she ever had these feelings for my other six brothers and sisters, and I never bothered to ask. I was too afraid she would share the graphic details of all the places on her body that ached or throbbed when one of her children was in need.

"Well, I might as well tell you, cause I know you, you'll find out sooner or later. Can't keep anything from you. I never have been able to from the time you could talk, and probably before that as far as I know. God only knows what you were thinking before you could talk. Cause you know you were born with a veil, a head full of hair and a couple of teeth . . ." My mother talked on and I allowed it. As she chattered away, I reduced the volume of my now dissipated imaginary boyfriend.

"What happened to the music?" My mother asked. "That was starting to sound good. Sort of like a young Al Green. Lord, me and your Aunt T, bless her soul, used to love some Al Green." My mind flashed back to the two of them at Aunt T's dinning room table. They would get as drunk as the proverbial skunk, and Al Green's voice would croon as loud as my music had earlier.

"Sing it to me Al, yes, yes, yes, yes. God knows that man knows how to make me feel." Aunt T and mom would listen to the same song over and over. "Love and Happiness" was their song.

"Make you wanna do right, make you wanna do wrong. God knows you know all bout that, girl," Aunt T would say. My cousin and I would laugh, not understanding the pain that sat around that table.

After years of my own struggles and loneliness I had learned a few things. "You there?" I heard my mother ask. "Lord chile, I hate these new phones. Don't ever work right. I told you I should have kept my phone with the rotary. Those were some good phones. But no, you want to bring me into the future. What for? Wasn't nothing wrong with my phone. I had that phone for bout twenty-five years. This new thing aint even a year old, and it already don't work. You there? hello?" "I'm here Mommy," I told her. "I was just listening."

"No you wasn't," she informed me. "You were daydreaming again, weren't you? Lord chile, you got some kind of imagination. I used to get all kinds of calls from your teachers. 'She won't pay attention, she has an over active imagination.' If it wasn't one thing, it was something else."

I'd heard all of this before, but if I said that, my mother would hang up. But not before telling me that I was sassing her, and that I thought I was too important to talk to my mother. And after all she had done for me and the other ungratefuls, as she often referred to us.

"Mom, I was daydreaming," I relinquished. "I just thinking about you and Aunt T. You two sure did love Al Green. You used to play the same songs over and over again." My mother laughed the way she always did right before she corrected me about something I thought I was sure of.

"We didn't love Al Green. True, we liked his voice, but it wasn't the man we played over and over again, it was what he was talking about. That man was a little too far on the funny side for me. But he could sing. Yes he could. I don't know what he's up to now. Every other day, he done found God, like God was lost or something. Anyway, I'm glad you think of Aunt T from time to time. That means you need some love in your life. Your Aunt T was the most loving woman God ever made, not counting me of course." She laughed her, now-you-know-I'm-lying laugh. "Aunt T could smile at vinegar and turn it into syrup. Never said a mean thing about nobody. If you cut her that woman would bleed love."

My mother got quiet and I knew that she was crying silently. Aunt T had done just that. Her husband of thirty years had been cheating on her from the moment they first married. One day when Aunt T got up the nerve to ask him about it, he turned crazy, as my mother called it. Uncle Charlie went into the kitchen, right past that dining room table where she and my mother had listened to AL Green, got the largest butcher knife he could find and stabbed her twenty-two times. Throughout her attack, Aunt T told Uncle Charlie that she still loved him, and there wasn't nothing that he could do about it. I try not to think of Aunt T.

"You keep on thinking about her," my mother said, confirming the connection between us. "She sure did love you, too. Besides," my mother said, sniffing, "When you think of her, you keeping her alive. She comes to you cause you need love. And before you try to get all intelligent on me, you need to go on and admit that I'm telling you the truth."

She was telling the truth, but I had no intention of admitting it.

By now, though, you know I didn't need to.

My mother dropped the subject just as easily as she had picked it up.

"Well," she said after what was for her a lengthy pause, "I should probably be asking you what's wrong. But that's not why I called. When you want to talk, you call me on your dime."

Her last comment was as absurd as most of the things that seemed to flow from her mouth. I had been paying most of my mother's bills for most of my adult life. My dime was her dime. But it never really needed to be said. I paid her bills along with my own, as if they were bills I had made. My mother was even more conscientious of my money than I was. If ever there were a need for more than the usual bills and the monthly amount that was deposited into her account, she would call. She never asked for money; she would simply talk in her, I-need-money-but-I'm-not-going-to-say-so tone.

"Life can be cruel. You know I don't like to bother you. God knows you got enough on your hands. Even without children, I know you got a lot on you." Whenever she did this, I wanted to use the line she had used on my siblings and me years before: "Signifying is worse than stealing, Mommy." I could hear myself say, but I never did. If I had, she would not be trying to have a conversation with me today. It was fine for me to think mad thoughts, but better not to say them.

"Well, as I was saying before you got me off on Aunt T, and Al Green, I called about your sister." I never had to ask which one. I had four sisters, one had passed, two were referred to by name, and the fourth was always called "your sister."

"What has Ophelia done now, Mommy?" I asked, waiting to hear about another crazy boyfriend, or some kind of money-making scheme she was trying to pull my mother into. "Well, you know she has always been a little on the selfish side."

When it came to Ophelia, my mother was the queen of understatement. Saying that Ophelia was a little selfish would be like saying Hitler was a little mean. Ophelia thought only of herself. She was the mother of three children, and they existed only for her pleasure.

As soon as I thought of the children, I knew why my mother was calling. "No Mom, don't tell me. She's pregnant again?" I asked expecting the worse.

"Alright, then I won't tell you," My mother said right before she hung up.

I called back immediately, knowing that I had better. Once when my mother did this, and I hadn't returned the call quickly, I was talked about for weeks. I knew this because my relatives all called to tell me how horrible I had been to my mother.

"Mom, what is she going to do?" I asked as if there hadn't been a break in the conversation.

"Well," my mother said slowly, "you know your sister. She gonna do what pleases her. Most likely that will be to have the baby. I don't know for sure, but I don't think that girl would ever think about having no abortion. I know you way more liberal than that, but well, you got your own life."

I had never discussed my false pregnancy with my mother. It happened during my marriage that lasted two years and too long. My now ex-husband decided that *we* didn't need children, because *I* was not ready for them. I agreed with him, but it was not until after we were divorced that I was glad that I had.

After the decision was made for me to have an abortion, we went to the doctor's office. Although my tests were all positive, nothing appeared on ultrasound, so I was told to come back in a month. When I did, I was informed that I had had a false pregnancy. My husband accused me of being so emotional, that I had caused a positive test.

I never told my mother, because she felt the same crazy dedication to my ex as she did for my sister.

Now, for the first time, I realized that she knew what I had been through. "Well baby", she said, "life is funny, what's taken away from us, is always given back."

Now I knew that she was talking about me and not my sister.

"What you saying, Mom?" I braced myself for the response.

What followed was a long statement that was disguised as a question.

"You think you can take your sister's children for a while? 'Cause if you don't, child protective services are gong to take them away. And you know that no matter how hard it was on me when you were coming up, ain't none of y'all got taken or sent away from me.

So I know you gonna do the right thing 'cause it's in you to do. Plus, if you been seeing Aunt T, well then you need love, and I know for a fact that the best way to get love is to give it."

I knew that there was no way out. My mother was right and I was too tired to object. The fact of the matter was I could use the distraction. My career as a media consultant was going very well. I owned my own company, and had enough smarter-than-me types to keep things running while I took care of whatever had to be done.

"When do I need to come, Mom?" I heard myself ask.

"How soon can you get here?"

The fifteen hour drive from Chicago to Norfolk Virginia did nothing to prepare me for the mess that would become my new life.

My sister's pregnancy had been kept from me long enough for her to give birth to a bright-eyed baby girl. She'd named her Nia, which means "purpose." I didn't know if my sister knew that when she chose the name, but someone, somewhere was watching out for this child, this purpose.

I spent exactly twenty-four hours in the state of Virginia. I would have left sooner, but I had to wait for family court to open. I had already talked to my friend Bernita, a lawyer and a real sister.

"It's fine for you to play Mary Poppins for a while, but don't be stupid," she told me. "Get legal custody of them brats so you can get them on your insurance and into good schools." I didn't know until later how necessary this advice would be.

When I first laid eyes on the four children, I realized how long it had been since I had last seen them. Robert, the oldest, was now eight. The last time I'd seen him was when he was four and raising everything but heaven. The twins were now five and the newborn really was one. All I could think of was the infamous Butterfly McQueen line, "I don't know nothing 'bout birthing no babies" and I didn't. They piled into my beautiful Mercedes and it was no longer the thing of pride it had once been. It was now a kidmobile. I strapped the infant into the car seat a friend had given me, only to find out after I returned it that I had her in the car backward.

Our first night back in Chicago is what days of therapy are for. I don't know how the children survived. I bundled Nia in an electric blanket hoping to keep her warm. When she ran a fever, I called another friend, who is a doctor, and asked for help. "Calm down and take her out of the blanket," she told me when I described the child's condition. "You are baking the child."

When I put Robert in the whirlpool tub, hoping to entertain him with the jets, I was the one in for the show. He opened all of my bath salts and gels, poured them into the water, and created a upstairs full of bubbles.

The twins were no less amusing. Sometime between getting Nia back to a normal tempurature and cleaning up Robert's mess, I got a call from the doorman who said that the children I had dragged in earlier were now going up and down the elevator without a stitch of clothing on. He informed me of this in his "you know we Black folks gotta stick together" tone. I thanked him for the lookout, found the boys and called the one woman that I swore I would not ask for advice: my mother.

"Hey, girl," she said, laughing. "Woooeee. You should be having a good time by now. The kids all in bed?" Since I was sure she could hear the screaming in the background, but this was her idea of torture.

"No, Mom. They are not in bed. They are right here making a mess of my once beautiful home." I don't know when I started to cry, but I could hear my mother saying something she must have heard in an old movie.

"Now, there, there," she said, trying to hold back the laughter.

"Mom, why are you laughing?" I was close to hysteria, which only made my mother laugh harder.

"Well, honey," she said in a tone that actually dripped with the stuff, "I'm laughing 'cause you getting a taste of what I went through, and what your sister has had to go through."

"Mom, with all due respect to you and my sister, I don't remember asking for children. I don't remember laying down to make any, and I don't remember anybody asking me what I wanted to do about my sister's mess. This thing was just handed to me. And it was you who did the handing."

My mother paused long enough for me to realize that I had gone too far. But she didn't say so.

"This is a hard thing that you have to do. But you are not alone. And I wasn't the one who handed this to you."

Now it was my turn to sit silently. The silence didn't last long. "Girl, this is from God. You've been chosen to bring up them kids. They are special. Just like you."

My mother hung up the phone and I never got the chance to ask her what she meant. She died that night in her sleep.

I didn't fully comprehend the things my mother said or did until after her passing. "You never miss the water 'til the well runs dry" was one of her favorite sayings. It's a hard thing to realize that after you lose it. It was not until I became a mother that I realized how much I needed her.

There's nothing like a black funeral. You see people that you haven't seen in years. The funeral always becomes more like a reunion of the living. My mother's funeral was packed to capacity. I learned afterward that there were people in the streets. This was no small thing for Ezion Mt. Carmel Baptist Church. It held five thousand people comfortably, so there had to be at least seven thousand crammed inside. I had no idea of my mother's popularity, or of her importance to the community.

She had fed, housed, and clothed half the neighborhood at some time or another. Now I could see where my money had been going. Folks told stories of her generosity and of her ability to see to their needs long before she even asked.

"Lord, your mother was a good woman. She knew more things than them psychic folks claimed to know," one woman told me through her tears.

"She came to me and said, 'Etta, that boy of yours is in big trouble, you get him out of town and he will get right, but he needs to get away from here fast.' Now, I kinda knew what she was talking about, cause my boy was always into something, but I didn't want to let on to nobody that I did. I told your mamma that I ain't have no way to get my boy nowhere, and she said that she had already took care of that. She handed me a ticket and some money and told me to see him to the bus station right away.

It was a good thing, too, cause that boy had got mixed up in some drug-dealing stuff. He wasn't selling, but his boys were and it turned out that they stole somebody's money. They all end up dead, but my boy is up North working and going to school at night. She saw all that in a dream. Believe me when I tell you this, there's lot's of folks 'round here who can see, 'cause that's the kind of place that this is, but most of them won't tell you nothing without charging you and they surely wouldn't be giving you nothing to get to your good fortune. Yes Lord, your mamma was a good woman, but you know that. I just wanted to let you know what she meant to me."

She hugged me and walked of smiling like she knew something that I wasn't privy to.

For days, I got letters and visitors telling of my mother's exploits. While it told me more of the woman she was, it didn't console me. I wanted my mother back. She had left me with a task that seemed to grow with her absence.

My sister didn't bother to come to the funeral. We didn't even know where she was. She just called to say that she wanted to make sure that we knew that mom's ring was supposed to go to her. "Would you like to talk to your children?" I asked her.

"No, I have to go," she said. "They'll be alright with you. Mom said so."

Then she was gone.

The children never saw there mother again, and I only saw her to identify her body. But that's a story for another time.

I'm just telling you this right now to let you know that my mother surely did know what she was talking about.

I needed love. But it didn't come in the form of a man, at least not at first.

Love for me came from the children I now call my tribe. Before them I had had no idea that love was something you show. I thought it was something that I could get. With them I learned that when you give it, you see it. It's not a feeling at all. My feelings had only led me down the road of loneliness.

I've learned something else, too. That by connecting with the thing you were made for, you open yourself to the gifts of the universe. Why am I telling you this? I think you already know.

FROM **Breathing Room**

BY PATRICIA ELAM

The café on Connecticut Avenue has dark walls covered with paintings by local artists. The metal tables and matching chairs have a quaint European look. Norma loves the way the windows are positioned so that sunlight has no choice but to lurch through them. The smell of ground coffee beans seems to leak from the wallpaper. Norma breathes it in like fresh air.

There are several customers eating, conversing, and reading the Sunday newspapers, more than Norma anticipated would be here this early. Some are part of a couple or a group, others are alone. A black woman with sagging cheeks and bosom sits on a stool by the window, reading the Bible. Norma watches as steam spirals up from the woman's mug and contemplates how striking a photograph the scene would make. *I'm seeing a man and he's white. No. I'm seeing somebody and he happens to be white.* She might shoot the photo standing behind and to the right, capturing the black woman unaware, with the light from the window nuzzled against the woman's face. If the woman was someplace more accessible, it would be a perfect shot for her zoom lens. She loves the intimacy a zoom provides. From quite a distance away, she can zero in without having to ask permission, without the subject posing and erasing the truth of the moment.

Norma has been standing near the doorway, where the chime sounds every time someone enters. She decides to hang her coat and uses the pay phone to leave Woody a message at his office. Several weeks ago, she impulsively looked up his home phone number and was both mesmerized and repelled at seeing it there. A reminder of his other life that she's not a part of. When his voice mail picks up now, she says, "It's Norma calling on Sunday. I know you're not there, just wanted to listen to your voice even if it's only a recording. Miss you." She knows he checks his messages on the weekends, anticipating hearing from her.

Norma selects a table against the wall to wait for Moxie. She sits and absently tucks her turtleneck into the waist of her pants. Looking up, she sees Moxie maneuvering toward the table. Her locks are wrapped with African fabric, and her cheeks appear rouged by the cold. Moxie shivers when she takes the seat across from Norma. "It's really chilly out there. Been here long?"

"Not long. A few minutes. It's more than chilly out," Norma says.

"Sorry I'm late. Fussing with Zadi." Moxie removes her coat and scarf and drapes them over the back of her chair.

"What now?"

"That girl makes me crazy sometimes. She doesn't get fired up enough about racial issues that come up at her school. Even though, mind you, I've exposed her since day one to cultural things. But she—I don't know why, just refuses to take a stand, so once again—I'll have to."

"I know how you agonize about her school, but you made a compromise with James, and you say you're satisfied with the academics. Think back— were you such an activist at her age? Sure she can't handle it without you getting involved?" Norma asks, cautiously. She scoots her chair closer to the table, allowing another patron to get by.

"Norma"—Moxie puts her hand up—"I don't even want to talk about it. You'll tell me you know what private school is like, meaning I don't; you'll side with Zadi and it'll just infuriate me again, so let's order." She turns in her seat and tries to read the posted menu. "What are you going to have?"

"Wait a minute. You just totally dismissed me in one sentence."

"Sorry. I get frustrated with that school on so many levels. I told you how I tried to organize a meeting of black parents, so we could check in with each other, compare notes on how the kids are doing. But I think only ten parents showed up out of the already paltry thirty-five or forty black families. Later I heard things like they thought it was going to be a gripe session or something divisive. From black people! Some of those folks act like they came to the school to get away from themselves. I swear—it's such a headache."

"I'm sure it's not easy for you," says Norma, opening her purse, somewhat annoyed. "But you have such strict standards." *Woody's a good man. He really is. He's white, but he's a good man.*

"Like what?" Moxie listens intently.

"Oh, come on. You know how you are. No one's ever black enough to suit you," Norma says with a smile. "If it was up to you, you would have me, Zadi, and your dad running around tied up in kente cloth all the time, celebrating Kwanzaa every other month." Norma laughs, pleased with her half-serious joke, and then busies herself, taking several dollars from her wallet. "I think I'm going to have a vanilla latte. What kind of tea do you want? I'll get yours."

" 'Tied up in kente cloth.' Norma, you're crazy." Moxie laughs, too. It's Norma's customary way of digging at her.

"You know what I'm saying is true, Moxie. You know it's your lifelong dream to someday be crowned Ms. African American."

Moxie waves her off. "Leave me alone." She squints at the sign displaying the coffee shop's offerings. Although she laughed, Moxie knows all too well what it's like to bear the brunt of a racial-Richter-scale judgment. She recalls feeling not black enough for some of the people at Zadi's African-centered preschool. Her gaze lingers on Norma's relaxed hair, cut in a bob with amber hair coloring to disguise the gray strands, a constant reminder of one of the differences they have silently agreed to sidestep for the sake of friendship.

"I was supposed to be ordering—What kind of tea do you want?" Norma asks. "Oh, I'll take that Gypsy Ginger Rose. Why'd they have to call it 'gypsy'? Why couldn't it be just plain 'ginger rose'? I mean, is that exoticism or racism?"

"See—you're the crazy one." Norma is still not as relaxed or ready as she had hoped. She leans forward and changes the subject. "So, Mox, it's a new year, any potential dates or mates on the horizon yet?"

Moxie clears her throat. "I told you. I'm not dealing with that. What— you don't believe me?"

"It was on your wish list *last* year."

"Yea, and where did it get me? Entanglements that stressed me out. I need to work on *me* before I can be involved with anyone. I'm tired of giving myself away to men and getting only half of them, or less, back in return. I don't even want them taking up space on my voice mail. I told the last guy I went out with to call me back after he'd had a year of therapy. He called and I said, 'Did you start therapy?' And he laughed, and said he didn't think I was serious. I was *very* serious. He had 'issues,' as Zadi would say. This year I'm concentrating solely on my family. Understand?" Moxie raises her eyebrows for emphasis.

"Yes, but remember Phillip, the guy from the Eastern Market Gallery we ran into before the holidays?" She can see that Moxie doesn't remember. "The halfway cute one who had his dog with him? He's asked me twice about you. If you want, I could arrange a little dinner, nothing fancy, grilled vegetables, lamb or chicken. Could be a nice hookup . . . never know."

"No thanks. I barely remember him, but unless he's the reincarnation of Gandhi, Martin, or Malcolm, I don't want a thing to do with him. What is with you and my father constantly trying to play matchmaker?"

Norma removes her sunglasses from her turtleneck collar and places them low on her nose. She looks over them at Moxie and speaks in a mock baritone. "I understand what you're saying, Sister Moxie. But I have a dream today. I have a dream, my sister, that you will walk into the sunset with an upstanding brother who is not only my reincarnation, but the others you mentioned, all rolled into one." They both laugh heartily, as Norma takes off the sunglasses.

"Norma. I'm serious, though," Moxie says, reaching across to touch Norma's arm. "This year I just want to be really happy with myself, by myself; I want to be closer to my dad and to Zadi; I want to make a difference in the lives of my clients. And of the utmost importance is keeping Zadi a virgin."

Norma puts her glasses back on her nose and deepens her voice once more. "I see, Sister Moxie. Let me understand, are you talking about for the rest of the girl's natural life?" They laugh again.

Moxie stops laughing, a little abruptly. "Well, at least until she's in college. I don't think that's too much to ask. Norma, I see so many parents knuckling under the pressure. They hand out condoms to their sons, take their daughters to get on the pill. To me, that's condoning it. And I'm not just being paranoid—I can tell Zadi's thinking about sowing her wild oats. Her body is blossoming like some damn springtime. She walks around with her boobs, bigger than mine, pushed out all the time and jiggling like Jell-O. Never mind that butt."

"Yeah. She's a brick house. So what? Are you jealous?" Norma's eyes brighten as she smiles impishly.

"I've had my brick-house moments," Moxie says, pushing her chest forward and placing her hands on her hips. "But she looks a bit too much like prime meat to me." She glances up at the menu again. "I thought you were going to order."

"Just don't go overboard with my girl, Moxie, please. Alright? Okay, I'm finally going to get the tea. Want anything else?"

Norma goes over to the counter while Moxie flips through the *New York Times* sections left at their table. Moxie looks up and notices a black man come in, locked in laughter with a tall red-haired white woman. His arm is hinged on her shoulder while she regards him as if he were the only person in the world. He glances around, Moxie thinks, to make sure all are taking note of their presence. She won't give him that satisfaction, though, and returns to perusing the newspaper. When Moxie looks up again, Norma is engaged in a conversation with a white woman who holds a small child's hand.

"You know so many white people," Moxie says to Norma when she returns carrying a tray with two steaming mugs on it.

"Oh, she's a parent from Miles' preschool," Norma says, ignoring the way Moxie's comment pricked through the surface. "I've run into her before. She's one of the few who recognize me outside of the center." Norma knows this statement will help put her back on track with Moxie. Moxie nods. Often when she encounters white people she knows through work or Zadi's school, they don't recognize her if the meeting takes place in a different context.

After Norma sits down, Moxie whispers, "Why does it feel worse when it's a brother?" She aims her eyes in the direction of the interracial couple.

Norma looks over her shoulder at the couple, then unwraps a muffin and puts a napkin in her lap. "Worse than what?"

"Worse than if it was a sister."

"Oh, no. Are we going to be subjected to your where-have-all-the-brothers-gone speech again? You know it doesn't bother me. If they're happy together, then so be it," Norma says, feeling slightly piqued. "What is it— you think he should be dating you instead?"

"No, thank you," Moxie says, blowing onto a spoonful of tea before bringing it to her lips. "I just wonder if he rejects *all* black women, and what his mama thinks about that."

"His mama! I don't believe you. For all we know, she's happy as a clam thinking about those light-skinned, straight-haired grandkids she's going to have." Norma glances at Moxie slyly, while she swallows a piece of her muffin.

"On the other hand, she might be the type who'd be devastated," Moxie says without smiling.

"Devastated? Don't you think that's a little strong?"

"Not really." Moxie frowns as she contemplates her statement. Norma says nothing, but shifts around in her seat. The black half of the interracial couple approaches Moxie's chair from behind, holding her scarf. "Excuse me, miss. Your scarf was on the floor."

Moxie turns and searches his face but receives only an empty smile. "Thanks," she says, as coldly as she can manage, wrapping the scarf around her neck. She watches him go back to the white girl. His narrow behind hardly moves beneath his leather bomber jacket.

"So, now did he redeem himself enough for you?" Norma says, leaning forward to playfully tug at Moxie's sweater.

"Just another lost brother." Moxie waves one hand, dismissively, and returns to her tea.

"That's not fair, Moxie. Remember, even your boy Malcolm X came to the conclusion that all white folks aren't devils."

Moxie adjusts her fabric hair wrap and peers at Norma. "And I never said they were. I just think it's important not to forget the history of who was the oppressor and who was the oppressed." She reaches across and tastes a piece of Norma's muffin. "Did I ever tell you what my old roommate used to call them?" she asks in an attempt to relax the conversation.

"Who? Brothers?"

"No, interracial couples."

"What?"

" 'IRCs.' " Moxie laughs. "Well, anyway, what's this big thing you want to talk to me about?"

Norma takes a sip of her latte, holding it in her mouth for a second before letting it slide down her throat. Moxie is the main one she has trusted with her secrets and feelings for more than ten years. *I'm having an affair with someone who's white.* "Moxie," Norma says slowly, not meeting Moxie's gaze, "I—I'm seeing somebody, a man I met." She can feel Moxie staring at her, but Moxie says nothing. "I put off telling you for a while because I know what you're going to say—that it's wrong. But you know I've been so unhappy for the past few years, and it's not like I haven't tried to work on my marriage." She gets it all out without taking a breath.

Moxie backs her seat away from the table. " 'Seeing somebody.' Does that translate into 'screwing somebody'?"

Norma nods.

"Well, I guess I don't have to say anything, since you already know what I'm going to say. Just hope you know what you're doing, that's all," Moxie says, feigning indifference. A bulky silence hangs between them.

Norma presses her fingers onto the leftover crumbs on her plate, then to her tongue. Moxie's words pierce the edges of her skin, making her feel nauseatingly warm and embarrassed, as if she were a scolded child. She looks at Moxie, and is not fooled. She sees the judgment shadowing her face. "It's not like I was out there looking for someone. This thing with Woody just happened." She covers her remaining crumbs with a napkin. "I told you because supposedly friends share things with each other."

Moxie drains the mug of tea. It's clear from Norma's unrelenting gaze that she longs for something Moxie can't give. Moxie looks away. She wishes she were somewhere else. Friendships change and grow over time, arching and aching along the way, but this one has been the sturdy monument that weathered anything. She thinks about the night she and Norma came into each other's life, how Norma's dormitory room, with Frankie Beverly crooning in the background, became her refuge. It disturbs her that, at this moment, she can think of absolutely nothing to say that won't be problematic.

Over the surrounding chatter, Norma notices that the coffee aroma seems even stronger than when she first entered. Moxie is drifting from her, and she fears she will be unable to reel her back in. "Things with Lawrence have been bad for a long time, and they're not getting better. You know this. I'm not justifying it, but Woody feels like a badly needed vacation. Maybe I am justifying it."

"What happened to working on your problems the way most married folk do?" Moxie lowers her voice when she realizes she's loud enough for others to hear. There is a long line of people at the counter. The black woman with the Bible, Norma's white friend and her child, and the interracial couple are gone, but they've been replaced. Almost every table is full.

"I've tried to work on my marriage for the past three years, but where has it gotten me?"

"Your marriage is made of gold compared to some of the ones I see and hear about. He's not beating your ass; he's not cussing you out; he's not trying to sell your children for drugs."

"Oh, come on. Moxie. You can cut the ghetto melodramas. James wasn't doing any of that to you either." Norma crosses her arms and holds her elbows, inching forward. "And you all split up."

"But I didn't start something else before the first thing was finished. And to this day I still have regrets, still wonder whether there wasn't something else I could have done to avoid divorce."

"My recollection, based on what you told me, is your situation boiled down to the suddenly-socially-conscious sista versus the money-instead-of-the-motherland material guy and never the twain could meet. Those weren't exactly insurmountable battered-wife, alcoholic-husband type issues." Norma's face is hot, tears threatening at the periphery of her eyes. She picks up her mug, but the latte is tepid and almost gone.

"You're missing my point, Norma. I'm saying yes, we had problems, but I wasn't sneaking around having an affair behind his back, smiling in his face at the same time. I spent my energy trying to salvage the marriage and then accepting when it couldn't be salvaged. I mean, how is this affair going to help you figure out your marriage? Have you thought about going back to counseling?"

Norma looks beyond Moxie for a moment, trying to collect her scattered feelings. "He wouldn't want to go. I wouldn't even ask him."

"No, I meant you."

"I don't know if I'm ready to listen to her questions and comments about me seeing Woody."

"Like you really don't want to hear mine." Moxie's tone softens. Some relief seeps through, loosening the conversation. "Norma, is it worth it? Is it that damn good?"

Norma rests her elbows on the table, hands under her chin. "Can't you just try for one minute to understand what I'm talking about? All this time I've been laying back, quietly tolerating Lawrence's indifferent lovemaking. Forgetting that I'm supposed to feel something, too. And no, it's not just about sex. Woody and I talk about our work, our children, our lives . . . Something I can't seem to do anymore with Lawrence."

"Well, I hope you think long and hard about what you're doing to your family. The more you continue, the more chances they have of finding out, Norma. With information like that, Lawrence could take Miles from you." A spiky-haired employee comes from behind the counter with a dishrag in his hand. He removes the tray and their empty cups and plates.

"Lawrence stopped letting me in on his feelings a long time ago." Norma sighs. "Maybe it doesn't sound like it, but I do care about Lawrence, Moxie. I never wanted us to end up like this. But I'm not in love the way I was, nose wide open, head all turned around like a broken Barbie doll. He blew it." An elderly man at the next table, with several medicine bottles lined up in front of him, leans over and asks to borrow the honey. Norma passes it to him. "Moxie, I feel like I'm stumbling around in the dark, trying to figure out my life, and here you come saying 'wrong move.' Makes me wish I hadn't told you. Can I please find out for myself whether it's the wrong move or not?"

"Sure," Moxie says. "Absolutely. You're right—this is your life. But don't you want to feel like you're doing your best? Isn't that what's supposed to happen as we get, supposedly, more mature and closer to dying? What about Miles? Have you thought about him?" Moxie refolds her napkin, so she doesn't have to look at Norma.

"Miles isn't even four years old yet—he doesn't know what's going on."

"You'd be surprised at what kids feel and remember."

"Oh, here we go. More expert advice from your probation-officer annals? I'm not Zadi, you know." Norma pushes her coffee cup to one side.

"Norma. I'm trying to help you see the whole picture. What you do affects everybody." Moxie presses at her temples out of habit. "I never told you this before, but I was in the pediatrician's office with my mother once, when I was around five or six. Dr. Luther, I think his name was, had already examined me, but we waited like two hours for him to finish with all the other patients, and then he gave us a ride home. Because it was raining, my mother said, and we had taken the bus there because she didn't like to drive in the rain. There was something about the way she and he talked and laughed together that struck me even at that young age. I remember he touched her shoulder when we got out of his car. I asked her if she liked him, and she said, 'Don't be silly.' But I never forgot how strange and a little scary it felt. Somehow I knew not to mention it to my father, even though she didn't tell me not to."

Norma stares at Moxie. "You never told me this."

"I haven't thought about it in a long time. I don't think she had an affair with him or anything, but I never forgot it."

"What happened when you went back to the doctor?"

"We switched pediatricians and never went to his office again. I thought about it several years later but didn't know how to verbalize what I wanted to ask. I never did mention it to my father because I didn't want to bring up something that would cause him more pain."

Norma nods and crosses her legs against the table. "The way your father talks about your mother, they must have really been in love, though. He makes it sound like they never even had arguments. My parents used to argue all the time, even though my father was in the service and away a lot; Irene and I were always afraid they were on the brink of divorce. But they stayed together, and now they seem very content."

Moxie takes her car keys from her purse and places them on the table. "It was different, I think, because, my mother was depressed so much of the time. She'd get mad at my father for little, absurd things, and he wouldn't react. I don't know how he did it," Moxie says. "Anyway, the point of my story is—Miles isn't too young to feel something, even though he might not be able to say what he's feeling."

They both know it's time to leave. Moxie removes her coat from the back of her chair. Norma stands and retrieves hers from the coatrack. Two white women weave their way purposefully toward the table Norma and Moxie are about to abandon. Moxie, irritated that the women can't even wait for them to move away, that white people always feel so entitled to everything, sits back down at the table and fumbles around in her purse, as if she's looking for something. This contrivance to hold up the two women embarrasses Norma, compelling her to tell them she and her friend are leaving, they're welcome to the table.

Outside the cafe, though, Norma embraces Moxie. Moxie hugs her back but is first to pull away. She stands still and watches Norma walk toward Dupont Circle. Partway down the street, Norma casts a brief glance over her shoulder at Moxie and waves vigorously. Moxie waves back, with less vigor.

Sunday, Jan. 10th
black jean skirt from Lerner
red & blk stretch top
black Banana Republic boots

Dear Sistergirl:
Spent the day doing homework and still didn't finish it all. When I took a break, Ma was watching Waiting to Exhale on TV tonight and laughing like crazy. I like the way Ma laughs when she's really happy and not stressed; it's like a wave that starts out small and gets bigger, and it makes you start laughing with her even when you don't know what she's laughing about. I asked her if I could watch the movie with her, and she said only if I had finished my homework. (I'm probably the only teenager in the world who isn't allowed to have a television in

their room.) The usual rule is no TV on school night. I reminded her that it was really still the weekend and that there's something I don't understand in math. I can get it done in study hall before class.

I saw Exhale *when it first came out. My favorite part is when Robin is waiting for Troy and he comes over all late and all high and she says, You leather-wearing-in-the-summertime blah blah blah. That shit is so funny. Lela Rochon's hair is off the hook in that movie. I wish I could have my hair like that or like Aaliyah's—all straight. I wonder if she wraps it, like Allegra says she does.*

Me and Ma sat under a comforter on the floor, and she made us popcorn. It was fun. I wasn't even bugging when she put her hands in my braids, which usually blows me. When it was over, Ma said her favorite part is the three of them dancing to TLC in Loretta Devine's house, drinking, and talking trash about men. She said it reminds her of when she and Norma were at Howard. They played old music and hand danced with each other once when they didn't have a date. I asked her if she used to drink and get high. She rocked me when she said, To tell you the truth, yes, which is why she hopes I never try it. She said even though at first she liked how she felt, later on she had bad experiences and kirked out and once even thought she was dying. She doesn't know about Norma cause Norma graduated way before her. Then she told me about a girl who drank so much she fell asleep on the toilet and they had to go in there and pull her panties back up and everything. That's so not mellow, like Janet says at the end of Free on the Velvet Rope *CD.*

Note: No call from Octavius.

Love

BY MAT JOHNSON
FROM *Drop*

Friday, I opened the door for her. This little woman, too proud to even look up at me past the rib she came to. She stood, beneath layers of white skies and before wet sidewalk, a vision. A face so black it was bold, cheeks a duo of sweeping circles beneath the soft rainbow of a head wrap that contained all the colors that could scream or cry for you.

"Is this the place?"

"Excuse me?"

"Is this the place that's supposed to be taking pictures of me?" she asked. She was so much smaller than I'd been expecting, but she had to be the dancer David hired: She was too pretty not to be getting paid for it.

"Please, please come in," I managed. I shouldn't even have been answering the door because by this time, besides clients growing and waiting for our attentions, Urgent had a secretary, too, a bony, Marlboro Light–smoking Brixton boy named Raz who should have been down here with this woman, saving me from my awkwardness. The shoot was scheduled for a half hour before, but models, David reminded, were always late. Taking in the smell of her: of violet water and hot sauce.

"Fionna Otubanjo?" She just walked by me and started heading upstairs; I couldn't tell if she'd nodded. Tiny, this one. The size of a girl but the shape and proportions of a woman, making the stairwell look cavernous as my eyes struggled to keep perspective.

After I took her coat, introduced her to the photographer, the stylist, and even Margaret, who was taking a rare intermission from her reading to make an appearance on the third floor, I showed Fionna to the bathroom that would be her dressing room for the day. Then I pulled David to a far and relatively secluded section of the floor.

"Cuz, she's gorgeous." Somebody in the room had to acknowledge this.

"Really? A bit of a head on a stick, I thought. A short stick at that. She looked bigger on her Z card. If you like, maybe later we'll go for a curry or something, you could ask her to tag along." David reached into the cereal box in his hand and threw a kernel into my mouth.

Golden Crowns, an old-brand cereal owned by one of several companies that realized Urgent knew how to implant hunger in even the most bloated, who understood that our work was the stuff people were starting to whisper about, the kind that would be bringing back industry awards in the year to come. Its box stood in the center of the white cove, ready for its picture to be taken, short and proud and belligerent with caloric prophecies. Golden Crowns, a combination of flour, water, high-fructose corn syrup, and yellow dye number 24, but also something so sweet it didn't need milk or morning.

"Alright, luv," David was bellowing at the emerged Fionna. "What we need you to do is just run, leap right over the box, right? Spread your legs open like scissors, give it as much as you can. We want to capture you directly above the Golden Crowns, almost as if they gave you the gift of flight."

"I can do that," Fionna said, looking at me, and wasn't it immediately clear that she could do much more? That she could hold your head in her lap, rub her little palms over your face and wipe away everything else besides the blackness behind closed eyes? That if there were arranged marriages I would have had David call her family immediately on my behalf, have stood behind him smiling and jumping up and down like a horny Masai?

The photographer's tin can lights sat on the floor, hung from erected scaffolding, rested on the ends of tables and chairs, all pointing in one direction, metallic ravens holding brilliant court. The heat almost solar in intensity, pulsing away from the illumination to the rest of the space beyond, the warm touch linking all those in the room together. And within the fire, one body moving. To watch her run, to see her leap. The determined start with bare feet slamming the floor and then the jump, the seizing of space with a ferocious kick, a smile that flashed gloriously as soon as the pivot foot left the ground. How could one so short fly so high? And all this along with a bowl of glued Golden Crowns in one hand and a spoon in the other. Running and leaping and landing. The toe and ball of one foot touched back down and the rest of the body followed, the flesh moving slightly past the limits of her bones for a moment until it bounced back into structure again. David walked behind me and snapped his fingers by my ear—"Pay attention to the work"—but how could anyone with her perspiring until the midnight fabric of her leotard became even darker beneath the neck and arms, her form becoming an essay on the possibilities of blackness, a diatribe about refusing the limitations of one word? I sat, leaned against David's desk with my shirt open, my sleeves rolled, watching. Witnessing the sweat drip away from her as she ran and explode around her when she landed, giving a shine to the floor. Steaming the windows to opaque rectangles, forcing me to sweat along with her, to feel my own oily wetness and susceptibility, until, in one particularly triumphant soar (spoon and bowl held by hunger), she landed in the puddle of sweat that she created, broke the spell, and bore a new one in a helpless painful cry.

"Oh, fucking hell!"

The first to reach her, I held Fionna's back as she held her ankle. "Are you okay?"

"No, it's not okay. I'm hurt!"

"Is it broken?"

"No. I don't know. I don't think so." Inspired by the urgency of the moment, I moved around Fionna and gently took her leg into my lap, touched her ankle with my famished fingertips, bent the joint slowly in my hands up until "Ow!" and slowly back down until "Oh!" and left "Ew!" and right "AY!" until "No, it's not broken" but damn, isn't it divine to hear you scream and imagine that the sound must be the same when pleasure motivates it?

After the food, after the drinks, after it was too late for a limping girl to ride all the way back to East London, I offered my place to her for the night. It was the perfect time to ask the question: I had finally reached that delicate plateau where I was drunk enough for bravery but not too smashed to pronounce the words. Fionna agreed that would be good, "Because I'm very tired." When I carried her from the cab into my apartment, the driver looked at me funny: Even he knew she was too pretty for a wreck like me to be holding. I managed to get out my keys and open the door without dropping her or her overstuffed duffel bag that weighed nearly as much as she did. What's in it?

"Just some of my clothes. Lately I've been staying with girlfriends while I hunt for a new bedsit. This is your place?" Fionna asked inside.

"Yeah. This is me."

"You live alone then? No roommates or anything? How much do you pay?"

"I don't know. David says he take it out of my salary."

"I've been looking for a new place for months, and I haven't seen one this nice. Not one that didn't cost a fortune." She made me feel unusually lucky.

I turned on every light in the house as I carried her upstairs to the living room, trying to destroy any shadow that might scare her. Trying also not to bang her bad ankle against a wall. The swelling had gone down in the hours since the sprain, assisted by a variety of towel-wrapped foodstuffs Margaret found for her, but it was still an ugly thing sitting above her foot.

"Were you robbed recently?" Fionna looked around like maybe she didn't want me to put her down in this place.

"No, is something wrong?"

"You don't have any furniture," she said, shocked, staring at my apartment with nothing more than its own dust and possibilities to fill it. "How long have you been living here?"

"About nine months. I bought a kitchen table and some chairs." Actually, Margaret had made that donation from her basement, along with some dishes, flatware, and pots and pans after the time she came by the house to offer me leftover spaghetti and had to watch me sit on the floor eating it with my hands.

"Do you like it here?" Fionna's was a new voice echoing around these walls.

"I love it. I'm not going back to America."

"I meant the flat. There's so much room, isn't there? You should really get some more furniture, right? Some carpets and such. Make a home. It could be really nice, once you get the proper things together. Then you could rent a room out or something. It's too big for one person." Fionna took the seat on the futon I offered to her. I turned on my clock radio hoping for something romantic; it was pathetic, that tinny, cheap, monotone sound. I slapped it off again and tried to smile.

"Have you thought of painting any of the rooms something besides white?" Fionna asked.

"I like the white walls, actually. It makes me feel kind of free, for some reason. No stimuli. It's like the color of silence. It's an old place: a bit more than a hundred years, I think. You should see what they used to paint the place. In some rooms, I've actually chipped at the paint a bit, with a knife, all the way down to the wood, to see all the layers the walls were covered in before. You know this room was actually pink once," I said, motioning around. "And light blue, too." What the hell was that? I was making things up and I still sounded like an idiot.

Fionna looked around. Her leg hung out of her dress; you could see the light cut a perfect line down whatever angle of it was closest to you. Her toes, poking out the front of her sandals, were long and beige on the bottom, as if she'd been walking through sweet pancake batter. On one toe was a golden ring, a strip of solid metal seizing a strip of delicate skin. If I took her foot in my hand and pulled that ring off slowly, she would be more naked than the mere lack of clothes could ever provide.

"Do you like it?" Fionna asked. "It's very expensive. I got it in the town of my father. In Nigeria. I could probably sell it here for enough for a car, if I wanted one." Keep talking. As long as we're talking I won't try to kiss you, and then things won't go wrong. There won't be that moment when you say "Please, no," and then that awkward time after I apologize when we're both sitting here, trying to act out the scene that mirrors this perfect time before anything stupid was done.

"I've always wanted to go to Africa. I actually got David to put some of my money aside, a bit each check, into a savings account, and that's the big thing I was planning. Fly down into Egypt, go into Côte d'Ivoire, then go by land the rest of the way into West Africa. Do you go back there a lot?"

"Sometimes. I go at Christmas sometimes, to see them. Christmas, there's parties, things to do. Our house, where I was born, is very big, very old. You would like it. It was the magistrate's, when it was still a colony. Tall ceilings, and so much wood. My whole family lives there. Maybe you could visit. We could have a good time there. I want to go to America someday."

"No, you don't."

Fionna fell asleep on the futon, halfway through an Alec Guinness flick on BBC2. Awake, I stared at her, petrified that if I fell asleep I would succumb to flatulence, or wake up with a viscous pool of my warm drool coating us both. So I just kept looking, scared she would wake up and catch me and then it would really be over. This wasn't like with Alex; it could not be as simple as reaching out to another sibling of solitude. Fionna was of another caste, the one stories were told about and pictures were taken of, so far above my own I was surprised she found me visible. I kept looking at her closed lids as the balls swam joyously beneath them. My ear resting on the mattress edge, listening to her breath.

Saturday, a lack of blinds combined with an eastern exposure meant that, as usual, I woke up at dawn blinded and sweating. Scared that she would awake and then leave me, I got dressed and went down to the supermarket to get some food, cook a breakfast so big that she couldn't move.

At Sainsbury's I resisted the urge to stand gawking at the incomprehensibly large selection of baked beans and pork products by jogging through the aisles, grabbing at staples. Back at my front door, I became sure Fionna had already vanished, that inside was a good-bye note with a smiley face but no phone number, but upstairs she was still lying there, pulling on her top sheet with the blind gluttony of the sleeping. Back down in the kitchen, I cooked in careful silence: Shoes off, movements slow and studied, I even turned down the heat on the potatoes when the grease started popping too loud. When I finished, I could hear her above me. A repetitive, scratching sound. Probably clawing her way out the living room window. But when I climbed the steps, the sound was coming from the bathroom. Fionna was in the tub. Crouched down on her knees, working on something. Her back to me, I saw her bare legs. The right ankle was so bloated it seemed to belong to another, much larger person.

'You don't clean the bath very often, do you? How can you take a bath in this?' Pushing all her weight into the brush in her hand, scratching at the stain I had confused for permanent.

'I take showers,' I offered, pointing at the hose that she'd disconnected from the nozzle.

'Well, I prefer baths,' Fionna said, and kept scrubbing. Taking away not just the dirt but the discoloration that hung beneath it. Elbow jerking frantically, purposeful, as if she never wanted to see it again.

Saturday night turned out to be Fionna's club night. Iceni, below Piccadilly: all jungle, free cocktails for the best dancers, ladies free before eleven, men a tenner at the door. I'd managed to keep her around all day (you want some lunch, a nap, have you seen this video, wow it's time for dinner) so I wasn't about to lose her to my hatred of nightclubs. Once her ankle was wrapped, I carried her on my back down to the mini-cab, and then, in the West End, through the streets and into the club to a table full of waving, pointedly attractive women the same size as herself. 'My American' was how I was introduced, to which the response was 'Oh, right!' with smiles and ungripping handshakes.

Everywhere fags smoldering, fags burnt out, snubbed, fags crushed and left to die at the bottoms of dark bottles. Bright fags with wet lipstick stains perpetually kissing their butts. And for all of the hunting for unspent packs and elaborate lighting rituals (which usually commenced as soon as a new man stopped by to pay his respects to their grouping), I seemed to be the only one who was actually smoking, who was actually pulling the dark cloud into me and letting it spill back, warming my nostrils and shielding me from this room. It was the perfect evening because this was the perfect arena for me to go David-less out into the world: concealed under an unyielding blanket of sound, obscured by a calculated mix of darkness and random, off-color lights. Snug within the mist of tobacco, sips of my pint-cured bursts of self-consciousness. Saved by music so loud that it made my social deficiencies irrelevant. I was actually succeeding. Everyone seemed very pleased with my presence, introducing me to strangers for no apparent reason. The other ladies bent forward to me with occasional questions or comments. Somehow they'd been given the impression I was from New York, so I endorsed this misconception with several unprovable lies that we would both forget the next morning. Fionna held tightly on to my arm as if we were lovers. And then, just when her hand was getting warm, an intro to a song came on that made everybody at the table's eyes inflate as they reached out to clasp one another's hands.

In the seconds it took for the beat to kick in, Fi's friends were gone, off to dancing. Foreplay was over. Fionna released my arm. Everyone was screaming on the floor, hands in the air, bouncing as it there was cash on the ceiling. I stood up to watch. Look at them, bumping, shaking, jerk, jounce. Fionna pulled herself up from her seat by grabbing my leg. Her head bobbed with them. On the floor, slightly below us, the crowd was spreading. These friends of hers could dance, and everyone in the room knew it. No partners: a flock of individuals, simultaneous soloists performing variations on the same work. The crowd grew still because watching them dance was more enjoyable than doing it themselves. I looked down at Fi to compliment them but her head had stopped nodding.

"Lift me."

Thank the Lord—time to leave. Riding this mood and with a little drink to blame any embarrassments on, I could make my move in the cab home. I grabbed Fi into my arms and started heading for the exit.

"Where are you going?"

Fionna pointed to a wall. "Over there," she said, her finger pointing toward the dance floor, that place everyone else in the room was staring at. I walked. Someone brushing past with two drink-filled hands banged Fionna's out-sticking foot and Fi screamed demonstratively, digging her nails into my arm as the guy cursed his spillage and kept going. "There. Over there." I was directed to a high table covered with flyers. "On top," I placed her rear at the table's edge. "No, on top." I lifted her higher till she had put her good foot down and was standing upon it, where everyone could see her. Immediately, knee bent and bad ankle behind her, arms reaching out to the air for balance, Fionna started dancing. "Chris, come on, come up and dance with me. No, come on, climb up. Now."

"I can't." I offered a grin as I yelled back to her. I really couldn't.

"Why?" Because if I got up there they would boo or laugh or throw rocks at my head. Because I wasn't made for the pedestal, I was unsuitable for display. No crowd would ever accept Chris Jones held up above them. Philly had already taught me that, and who knew me longer than it? Definitely not the graceful Fionna, who reached out to tug my hand while still doing her one-foot shuffle. I grasped hers just so she wouldn't stumble.

"I'll dance with you down here, so if you fall I can catch you," I told her, and she accepted that evasion, released me of the obligation of humiliating myself.

Look at the way she moves and imagine what she could do with two feet beneath her. Reluctantly fulfilling my promise, I began bobbing awkwardly below her, forwarding racial harmony by dispelling stereotypes of black grace with every pathetic jerk. But then the crowd took even that responsibility away from me. All around me, bodies stilling as they took her in. Little woman up above them moving like there was nothing you could put on her that she couldn't just shake off, radiating life so bright it might even burn your troubles, too. Whatever made us alive, whatever it was that made us more than functionally bags of blood, she had it and she was showing it to the room. A sliver of God vibrating there before us. And I knew everyone could see her the way I did because they were all trying to get a better glimpse, pushing me out of the way to do so. Knowing instinctively that I shouldn't even be there to witness this event, the crowd expelled me, shoved me shoulder by shoulder back to the dance floor, now emptied. Fionna kept going; I could make out from over their heads. I don't know if she knew I wasn't there anymore, but I knew she knew the crowd was. That they were yelling for more and she was feeding them.

I went back to the table we'd been sitting at, picked up a drink I was pretty sure was mine. The other seats were deserted, so I commandeered a dark pocket in the corner, against the wall. For the remaining hours, I sat and played shepherd to the jackets and lighters the dancers left behind. The club made snakebites and the waitress didn't care how many I ordered, as long as she could keep the change from the tenner each time. So by the time the music ended and the only sound was my ears buzzing, I felt prepared for the solitary night bus home. But, as I struggled to get up again, there was Fionna, hopping back from the light to greet me, tugging on my hand once more.

"Why you come back for me?" I managed.

"Because we need each other." Fionna giggled, hugging my waist tightly (or was she keeping a drunken man from falling down?). Propping me against a pillar and hopping back off again to call us a mini-cab out of there. Having the bouncer help me out to the car. Waking me up in Brixton by giving a pinch to my cheek and delivering the words "Christopher, we're home."

Sunday, my day-after embarrassment evaporated when Fionna walked into my bedroom, sheet wrapped around her, and said, "Chris, I have a bag of clothes already packed at my last bedsit that I've been meaning to retrieve. Maybe you could pick that up for me?" Immediately, fueled by hope, I was on the tube to Hornchurch, riding all the way out to the East London address she'd given me. The trip took as long as my last flight to Amsterdam, regardless of how close it looked on the Underground map. Maybe, if it was a large bag, she might stay the whole week.

The landlord was a big woman and a cop, dressed in a uniform when I got there. Her jacket was off and I could see her bra hugging her fiercely underneath the white shirt, her back looking as if it needed to be scratched. Smiling, I said I was here to pick up a bag for Fionna.

"Well, I'm sure you are, but first, let's see the money. Mind you, I told her that from before." There was an ATM a mile back by the tube station, so it didn't take me long to gather up the cash. When I got back the lady was standing at the door behind six suitcases, big enough to hide bodies and heavy enough to make me believe they did. I took a cab back to Brixton, paying the driver nearly forty bucks for the ride. From the car I walked to my door with three cases in each hand, letting the handles try to break my bones as the weight hammered my legs with each step.

At my front door, the odors—fried onions, sausage, hot pepper, and olive oil—all coming from my property. Inside, I stood at the kitchen door, luggage still in hand, looking at the place settings Fi had laid out on my table. "Try this." Grinning, she came toward me, one hand holding a spoon and the other guarding underneath it. She was wearing one of my T-shirts as if it was a dress; she'd even found one of my ties was a good belt for the outfit. My hands still caught inside handles, Fionna put the spoon's tip in my mouth and lifted it up so it could pour in. It was some kind of chili, I could taste the salt and the crushed tomatoes. When she pulled the spoon away, excess sauce dropped onto my bottom lip, sliding down to my chin. "Sorry," Fionna told me, and she reached forward and grabbed a dick that was already hard for her, pulling me down to her eye level. Slowly, with the end of her tongue, Fionna retraced the drip's path along my chin up to my bottom lip. When she reached it, Fi surrounded mine with both of her own, catching me in her teeth and sucking my flesh clean again. Oh, to put my hands on her, to hold her to me as hard as she was now biting, but at my sides my swollen hands were now stuck in the luggage handles, which made things even more difficult when Fionna started pulling me down to the linoleum. Her teeth released, and I wasted precious time trying to maintain contact with those lips before I realized that she really wanted my face to drift away.

"Talk to me," she demanded, and my words began pouring confessions of attraction, instant love and des—

"No. Talk to me black," African woman said to me, and neither one of us thought she meant Swahili, Yoruba, or Twi. Black. And not the black I coveted, not the one I was walking to. The other one. That was her price, the cost of this fantasy. Lady, do you know what you ask of me? Do you know what this payment says about my desire? Take it. So I gave that to her: released the ownership of my tongue to the sound it had been meant for. Oh, and wasn't that sound happy to be free again, eliminating prepositions and conjunctions with its loose grammar and curving my sentences into its drawl? Reveling in its parole and scheming for permanent freedom? Give ear to me, Fionna. Hear the voice of the life I want to smother. Listen to what the niggers on the corner have to say to you. Her fingers traced the moving lips that spoke to her until those same hands went to my neck and pushed my face lower, down to a place I wouldn't assume clearance. Lips to lips once more. "Keep talking," Fionna demanded as my tongue took on additional duties.

My hands still stuck in suitcase handles, my arms outstretched above me like a gull in flight, I continued to rap my ghetto garble. As Fionna's moaning grew, I spoke louder. Wet words wandered within her. Fionna's fingers slipped to the back of my head and stayed there.

Keys in my hand was the best part of the day because there it was, physically, in my hands: David's world, heavy and jagged and multiplicitous, held together by a ring attached to a black plastic duck. Everything he had was contained within its weight and I stood on the street alone with it, unprotected, unguarded.

I would find the brown, round-head key, slide it in the door, then walk up the stairs to the kitchen where I heard him yell, "Make us a cuppa" which meant pour the old water out of the electric kettle and add cold water for the new. Lay mustard on the white bread and cover that with cheddar and put it in the grill hung above the stove.

While water boiled and cheese melted and brown man spat and farted in the bathroom beyond; I read the newspaper that Margaret would place on the table after she left for work hours before (always the *Guardian* and always placed back in order, section within section, without crease or jam stain, just like new although she had surely read it over breakfast hours before). When the sounds of his shower had ended I went back to the kitchen and poured one inch of milk into a mug that held one gray tea bag, then laid the steaming water on top of it. David would appear, in long pajama bottoms and still no shirt but maybe a towel across his thick shoulders or on his head like a frustrated boxer. He would sit hunched over, a few feet from the table, so that his head was nearly level with it as he held his tea mug close to his mouth with both hands. Sipping was the only treble. For bass, he might moan.

When Red Rose had burnt away the encrusted syllables he might begin with explanations of the night before ("After you left, I really tied one on, got right pissed") or show me a souvenir of his travels ("See this sign? I pulled it off last night. Right off a stone wall with my hands, right? I was mad, pissed out of my head. I used to chat up this girl that lived on Thorncliffe, number seventy-four. Lovely, you should have seen her.") or passionately reveal his latest fascination ("Mushrooms are the fruit of the soil. It's like eating the earth when you eat them. That's what it is."). Then a walk to the third floor. David would get the messages from Raz, and we'd go down the blackboard in the center of the room, figure out the agenda and schedule whatever in-house or client meetings were needed.

But how long could that last? Particularly when the spritz of lager cans being opened marked the top of the hour better than Margaret's antique grandfather clock (the German one, with the thick oak sides, and the two brass pendulums)? Inevitably there came five-thirty, a time to pick up the downstairs before Margaret came home. A time to pull up empty and half-empty cans and the ashes of fags and spliff, for the list of chores to be executed while David hit the shower again, this time destined to arise with more clothes than his pajama bottoms. Was the work done? No, but as long as people were contacted, meetings were kept and deadlines were met, I could do all the work I needed to do that night, downstairs in my study, complete now with the drafting table, lamp, and file drawers that Fionna'd gotten me to buy, the only distraction being her calling me from upstairs to tell me when something good was on the telly ("Christopher, you'll like this one, come."). As long as David was there every morning, guiding me, massaging the clients, creating the designs, Urgent could keep going. David took care of the business, dealt with the people, I birthed the ideas. I was good at my job. I liked working. I liked working for him.

If the pre-Margaret chores were quick (get vitamin C, cod oil, and ginseng from Boots, renew the subscription to the *Voice*, mop kitchen floor) I could make my disappearance before six having taken care of things. If the chores took too long it was just "Do what you can do, I'll take over when she gets here. Wake me when you hear her keys in the door."

. . .

"Are you going to wipe his arse, too?" Fi asked me. I was late. Only a little, but she had been waiting for me down by the ticket machines in Brixton tube station and that short homeless brother with the busted lip and the lobotomy scar had yelled at her. We had opera tickets for the Royal Albert: I'd never gone and she was excited she was going to show me.

"You know it's not like that. He takes care of me also," I told her, going down the escalator.

"David takes care of himself."

"David pays my rent, he pays my bills, everything. He got me here. That's how he takes care of me. He's my boy. Without David I would have nothing." And without David, I would be nothing. Lady, you don't know it, but without him propping me up, you wouldn't even be standing next to me.

"That man will suck as long as you let him, and then when there's nothing more he will fly off like a bloated bat. By then you will be too weak to even swat him down." Fionna stared forward while she said this, as if she were watching this unfold. For a second she wasn't a beautiful woman, someone who looked just the way beauty was supposed to. For a moment Fionna was just a skinny little black girl, hair straightened, lipstick done, trying to look cute in a dress she had no hips to be wearing. She could be from Nicetown maybe, East Mount Airy or Ogontz.

"Fi, really, don't worry. David is cool. Just because he needs me doesn't mean he's using me."

"Chris, who am I? I'm the one who loves you, the one who will always be here for you. I am the woman holding your hand." Fionna's hand was a light thing, impossibly soft, even at the palm. The thin veins on top could barely be traced without looking. Later, when we got to the show, I held it during the entire performance, letting my hand explore hers as she led me through the sound.

The opera was a story about an old guy who married a young chick and then she cheated on him, and they all suffered, but that didn't matter; I was a Phillystine and didn't care about that silliness. What mattered was that we sat close enough that you could see the spittle shooting out of the actors' mouths, that the voices of these performers were so strong, their sense of the emotion so complete, that when they sang I could feel their sound upon me, vibrating the hairs in my nose, as loud as when you're waiting for the sub at Fairmont Avenue and the express roars by. What mattered was that here was a plain old Philly boy, costumed in a suit and actually enjoying the sounds of this world. The only one under these ornate ceilings who knew what malt liquor tasted like, what to do when someone starts shooting up a party or how to open a Krimpet without letting the icing stick to its plastic bag.

Antiquated Desires

BY CRIS BURKS

I was practical when I married Mr. Pete, or rather, I felt obligated to marry him.

Mr. Pete first broached the subject of marriage the summer of Alex's fourth year as we lazed in Mama's backyard on Loomis Avenue. It was too hot to do anything but sip lemonade and watch Alex play with Paris, Mama's cocker spaniel. Mr. Pete and Mama yakked about the good old days when my daddy was alive, and he and Mr. Pete ran the streets.

"Now, Helen, you know Alex never cheated," Mr. Pete assured Mama.

"Humph. Show me a man that doesn't cheat, and I'll show you a dead man," Mama said.

Mr. Pete laughed, low chuckles that sound sinister. The shrill of the phone disturbed our tranquillity.

"I'll get it." I rose, but Mama flagged me down.

"It's cranky old Pat," Mama said. "I told her I was coming over."

While Mama was in the house, Mr. Pete and I laughed at Alex and Paris's antics. Paris was so old that he limped as he tried to escape Alex's grasping hands.

"You know, I always wanted a son," Mr. Pete said.

"You and Miss Verna never had any children?" I knew the answer before I asked the question.

"No, Verna and I was married for almost forty years but she couldn't have children."

"Uhmm-hmm," I said. I was not good company for old folks like Mr. Pete and Mama. The past lived in their heads like old sitcoms, same stories told and retold. Their conversations revolved around things that happened, or should have happened, or shouldn't have happened.

"Here I am, seventy-three, and still wanting a child," Mr. Pete said. "A son from my blood."

"Well, Mr. Pete," I said brazenly, "you need a woman for that."

He looked at me and laughed. "Maybe you could be that woman? Ain't nobody in the world but me. The house is paid for. Got a few dollars saved, and there's my retirement annuity from the railroad. You'll get that forever."

"Mr. Pete, I'm only twenty-four!" I exclaimed. The last image I wanted in my head was that old man humping on top of me.

"Twenty-four with proof that you can give birth," he said. He nodded to Alex who chose that moment to look at us with an angelic face.

"Katie!" He shouted and ran toward us.

It was one of those storybook moments. He ran straight into my arms with Paris yelping at his heels. Mr. Pete chuckled, and I felt absolutely trapped. Just then Mama came out of the house, and I used her entrance to escape.

Mr. Pete was on a mission. He wanted a child. After that encounter, I saw him with a few of my high school classmates. The girls were always dressed to the nines with jewelry galore. Fine and dandy. I met James and married him. James and I got a divorce just when LaWanna Jordan, Regina's baby sister, announced her pregnancy by Mr. Pete. Her wedding plans were as grand as the plans for the royal wedding, fifteen bridesmaids, two flower girls, and a white limousine. Mama talked about the affair with distaste and disbelief.

"Can't believe Pete's letting some twenty-year-old child trick him into marriage. Everybody knows she ain't pregnant by him. Old goat! Thinks he gonna leave a string of children behind. Married to Verna for forty years and never a hint of a baby. Of course, he blames her. Go 'round saying she couldn't have any children, but the man cheated on her left and right. Where're the babies from all those affairs? And Verna? Heaven knows I loved that woman, but why she spent most of her life crying over that dog, I don't know."

"Woof-woof," Alex said from the floor. "Woof-woof."

"Stop that, boy!" Mama snapped.

He and I were watching our Thursday night television lineup, *Cosby, A Different World*, and anything else that NBC had to offer. Back then I spent Thursday evenings at Mama's house. Every other Saturday, I picked Alex up for a movie and dinner date. Sometimes he spent the night with me. Most of the time he didn't. I was in school at the time, trying to get my master's. It was so much easier for Alex to stay with Mama.

"You said he was a dog," Alex pushed his luck.

"You keep on, and you won't see another episode of *Cosby* this year," Mama warned.

I guess LaWanna would have married Mr. Pete and gone to Vegas for the honeymoon if she hadn't been spooked out of her plans. A week before the wedding, the story goes, LaWanna and Mr. Pete did a walk through his home. She wanted all of Verna's things gone, and planned to redo the house in soft lavender and blue, with sprinkles of yellow. On the second floor Mr. Pete walked past a closed door like it didn't exist. LaWanna insisted on going into that room.

"Pete, honey, I need to look in this room," she said.

"That there is gonna be the nursery," Mr. Pete said.

"Well, don't you think I should look inside and make some plans?" she asked.

Reluctantly he took out an old-fashioned skeleton key and unlocked the door. The room was large and bright. The cream wallpaper had teddy bears holding colorful balloons. There was a beautiful hand-carved oak crib against one wall. A wicker bassinet, draped with netting, stood against another wall. The bassinet and netting were yellowed with age. The third wall supported a changing station and small white dresser. A bamboo rocker sat by a window that overlooked the neighborhood. Scattered around the room were toys. GI Joes marched across the window sills. A Chatty Cathy doll and several Barbie dolls crawled across the lap of a huge panda bear. There were toys out of Burger King and McDonald's gift packs. A family of dead sea monkeys floated in a dirty fish tank. Winnie the Pooh rode a tricycle. Quick Draw McGraw sat on a bicycle. Fred Flintstone and Barney Rubble sat on a Big Wheel. A scale model Lionel train set, a go-cart, three racing tracks, and thousands of Matchbox cars ran around the room. There were Raggedy Ann and Andy, Winnie the Pooh, and Barney Rubble stuffed dolls. Posters of Mickey Mouse, Minnie Mouse, Underdog, and a rare one of the Little Rascals looked down from the wall. Model airplanes, ships, and a model of the U.S.S. *Enterprise* from Star Trek dangled from the ceiling on thin wires. There were smaller things like crayons, coloring books, bolo bats, jacks, marbles, a slinky, and a Rubik's cube. Mr. Pete had added to that collection of toys year after year.

Some said it was that rocker moving slowly back and forth that tipped the scale. Others swear that LaWanna heard Verna humming a lullaby. Still others testified that it was the ghost of Verna that made LaWanna back out that room until she hit the wall in the hallway. LaWanna swore that she felt something tap her on the shoulder. When she turned, Verna scowled down at her from a huge picture. I know that picture well. Verna was not happy that day. In that picture, her eyes were narrow, tight slits, her mouth, a wrinkled pucker. To this day, LaWanna swears Mama Verna whispered, *don't touch nothing here.* Anyway, LaWanna ran down the stairs, screaming at the top of her lungs, with Mr. Pete behind her calling:

"Girl, girl! What's the matter with you, girl?"

But Mr. Pete was old and LaWanna was fast. She was outside the house and running up Loomis Avenue before Mr. Pete could get to the first floor. LaWanna called the wedding off. She claimed she lost the baby in the flight. In less than a month, Mr. Pete was back to begging me to marry him. I married Mr. Pete for one reason only. He saved my son-brother's life.

I don't know about other cities, but in Chicago the children will get in the middle of the street and play ball—football, dodgeball, baseball, soccer. When cars came drivers would toot their horns and the kids would scatter.

The drivers never, ever rolled their cars over the children like a ball over bowling pins. The day Alex was mowed down, we sat on our stoops up and down the street watching the kids play dodgeball. An ice cream truck had passed, so almost everybody was munching on something. A few of the boys had wolfed down their treats and were back in the street. Alex, who was not allowed to play in the streets, was with them. He had a way of blending into a group of kids so Mama and I couldn't see him.

Along came a yellow Pontiac Firebird. It was a beauty. As it passed our house at top speed, I saw the red emblem on the back. Then I saw my child in its path.

I leaped up and screamed. I heard the screeching of tires. The car swerved. I heard the grind of metal against metal. I fainted. I regained consciousness as the ambulance wailed down our street. Mr. Pete kneeled by Alex. The Firebird had careened into a parked car but still managed to hit Alex on his side. Mr. Pete administered CPR. He breathed into Alex's mouth and pumped his tiny chest. Mama and all the other mamas were praying, "Dear Lord, oh, Jesus, save this child." By the time the ambulance made it way down our street, Alex was breathing. I vowed then to take CPR, which I later did.

Mr. Pete drove Mama to the hospital, while I rode in the ambulance. He handled the doctors because Mama and I were in shock. I was still in shock when he asked me to marry him. I was half-comatose with thoughts of losing my only son-brother. I said yeah and Mr. Pete didn't allow time for me to change my mind. He raced me from Mercy Hospital to city hall. We were married that day. Mama never spoke about that marriage.

By time Alex got out of the hospital and I realized my mistake, I was firmly ensconced in Mr. Pete's house. Verna never frowned at me or made any type of appearance. I thought, *Well hell, the man does think I'm pretty. He's nice, and he did say he would wait until I was comfortable being Mrs. Peter Smith, before we attempted to make his son.*

I reminded him of his promise to set up a trust fund for Alex's education and to change his will so I could get the house. I really didn't expect the old geezer to do it since Mama said a distant cousin of Verna's would inherit everything, but he did. One morning, he placed a manila envelope in my hands with all the appropriate paper work. What else could I do but keep my part of the bargain? I am a woman of my word.

On our official wedding night, bile sloshed in my stomach. Every time I looked at the old geezer, I shuddered. When I was a child, Mr. Pete wasn't bad looking but on our wedding night old age had twisted his good looks into a comedic nightmare. His pink lips were simply cups to hold saliva. His skin was thin, dry parchment with liver spots. He moved as if every bone in his body was on the verge of breaking. His soft curly hair had yellowed with age. His eyes were huge behind his triple thick eyeglasses.

I figured that Mr. Pete had one good go in him. He would hump me, roll over, and wait for the baby to grow in my stomach. I bought a black gown that surged so far down in the back that the crack of my butt gulped air.

A slit ran up the front and the bosom plunged down to my navel. I figured this would excite Mr. Pete so much that the whole sordid act would be over in, say, five minutes.

To guarantee the old geezer wouldn't have enough energy to last past a hit and a miss, I cooked a huge dinner; oxtails in speckled butter beans, candied yams, fried chicken, macaroni and cheese, fried okra, sliced tomatoes with mayonnaise, and a peach cobbler with so much butter and sugar in it that the crust glittered. Hell, that meal would have put the strongest man to sleep. I put on Isaac Hayes' *Hot Butter Soul* LP, and prayed that the man would be finished with my body before the long version of *Walk on By* was completed.

That night Mr. Pete started at my toes, licking and sucking them like candy, while his fingers played my satin hips like a fine harp. He nibbled my calves while he massaged my ankles and I felt the first stirring, the first quivering of excitement. He nibbled up my body to my navel. His tongue darted in and circled slowly, almost ticklishly. An ancient core of lust burned inside my stomach. Did it matter that his body was as wrinkled as an old cotton sheet? No. When he took one of my nipples into his mouth and rolled his tongue around it, I heard myself groan from some hot orange place where desire controlled my mind and body. I clawed the bed and pulled the sheets as my hips rose. By the time that old man released my hardened, wet nipple from his mouth, I was begging him for more. I hated him for that. I tell you, I despised him. I did not want to want him, but there I was writhing on his bed underneath the watchful eyes of Verna, writhing and saying "*please*" like some young girl who didn't know any better. And Mr. Pete, was a master, he nursed at my breasts softly. Notice I said nursed, not lick'd or nibbled, but nursed one after the other. Long before we consummated our marriage, I had orgasms. I had many mini-orgasms. When he finally entered me, I could only scream as flashes of light, intensely bright, filled my sight. Little did I know that was only a mid-size orgasm under his masterful hands. I thought it was a major thing, but Mr. Pete I took me on one roller coaster ride after another. At one point, I thought my heart would explode. He moved slowly, like honey coming out of a jar, like he had a lifetime to consummate our marriage. There was no rush, no hurry. Whenever I thought the old geezer was at the point of orgasm, he would stop, just stop and breathe. Obviously, he intended to go on forever. By the time the man finally ejaculated—no, wrong word—unloaded all that was in him, I was weak and angry. I curled away from him, ashamed of my body's betrayal. His hand rested on my belly. Lying in the darkened bedroom, I wanted to scream. I had married a man who expected a baby and who had the stamina to work diligently toward that goal.

When Mr. Pete died a couple of months later, I had the house and his retirement, and Alex had what was in his bank account in a nifty little trust fund, but I was not pregnant. After Mr. Pete's funeral, I donated the toys (except a few collectible items) to LaRabida Children's Research Hospital. I gave all the furniture away to Goodwill Industries. I painted the house and rented it to the Gordons, a couple with life. I moved to the North Side, far away from Englewood. Folks looked at that house on Loomis and thought *If that old goat hadn't tried to make a baby he would have lived much longer.* But, if that old goat had lived any longer, he would have worn my young body out.

FROM **Rest for the Weary**

BY ARTHUR FLOWERS

I am Flowers of the Delta Clan Flowers and the line of O. Killens. This tale I tell as told to me. Once upon a time there was an angel. And a conjureman. *Walk with me Lord Legba.*

Horns, whistles and noisemakers erupt through the thin walls of the hotel. Outside the snug cocoon of their room New Orleans parties in the New Year. She leans over him, silvered hair a translucent curtain around their heads. He is acutely conscious of the points where her body lies warm against his. "What happens" she says, when the dream dies.

He looks up at her, waiting for a reprieve. The lamp behind her backlights the silvered curtain that shelters them. He clears his throat. Dreams never die he says, what are you trying to tell me, baby?

It's over the says, you've got to leave in the morning.

There is a finality he has not heard before. This time he thinks, this time she is going to make it stick. Six, seven months hes been fired six, seven times. But always before the dream brought her back. His hand slowly strokes the flaring curve of her hip. Perhaps this is the last time he'll handle her. The first time they've made love without watching the clock. The first time shes slept in his arms.

They had come to New Orleans for New Year's 2000. She had told him she was going down to visit her parents and he had asked if he could come down for a New Year's Eve dinner with her. I'll leave right away he said, just take you to dinner he said. She said she would have a hotel room for when she needed a break from her parents. He could stay over if he wanted to. A couple of nights if you want. I probably wont stay there with you though.

She works in the little neighborhood library at the mouth of the park, on the corner of Riverside and Person. Both library and neighborhood named after Riverside Park, about a mile or so of thickly wooded Mississippi River bluff in deep South Memphis. He lives in the park itself, and alongside the river, in a little house on the bluff sitting treetop tall on stilts dug deep in delta mud. Neighborhood folk call it a treehouse but it only looks that way, a tight little box of a house, old gray wood as weathered as the trees that surround it and barely visible in the bright months of sanctuary. The good folk of Riverside quick to point out late night lights glowing deep in the Park to folks from less blessed Memphis neighborhoods. See there they say, where the lights are? Thats where the hoodooman stay they say. In a house on stilts. So he can see.

He tells stories, delta classics on the college circuit, festivals, community dothingees, it's a living. Late forties dreadman, thick and bearded and built to take punishment, a bluegummed twoheaded man with hooded eyes and a face of carved wood that showed only what he wanted it to. Met her at the library, where he likes to nest among the fruits of solitary labors. She is the reference desk librarian and it just so happens that from his favorite chair (back to the wall and facing the door, a child of the 60s) she be in his line of sight. Interesting woman, a classic beauty, long and lean, with an unruly mane of prematurely silvered dreads. They nod, exchange pleasantries, have lunch occasionally. She is, he soon realizes, a strange and fascinating woman, an iconoclastic sort within whom he detects the complicated soul of an artist.

They had been on nodding terms for years when lunches were inaugurated by a fortuitous encounter at the Hole in the Wall, the local juke eatery across from the library and next to the Riverside Baptist Church. Angel, she told him. Angel, he said. Hard name to carry he said. My parents thought very highly of me she said. And when she laughed at herself she threw her head off to the side in a manner that struck him like revelation.

Perhaps that's why one day he blurted out, surprising himself, Angel, I realize youre a married woman, but I would like to court you.

She watched him fidget, intrigued since the first time they met with the power she has over him. (You drooled she told him.)

Highjohn I'm very flattered but you know Im a married woman and I hope you can respect that is what he expected. Instead she looked at him with this stricken look. I'm sorry he babbled, I hope I haven't upset you, I just . . . No, no, she said, you haven't upset me . . . I am married, though.

I know, he murmured, head tucked down into his shoulders, I just had to say it you know. I'll . . . uh . . . see you later. But as he turned away she brushes his beard with the palm of her hand. You didn't upset me, she said.

All night long conjureman feeling the angelsbrush of her palm. And the goodfolk of Riverside, heavier in ash'e than most, toss and turn in their sleep cause the conjureman howling at the midnight moon.

The next morning an e-mail saying she wanted to talk. They arrange to meet at the Hole. The old ease gone. Eyes that fidget and flicker. I cant be what you want me to be, she said. But I didnt get any sleep last night thinking about what you said. You can't . . . court me . . . like, that . . . I have a husband you know. But we can continue to be friends. To have lunch like we have. If you're comfortable with that.

Very. Thankful, even. What on earth could he have been thinking of? That evening he e-mailed an apology. She replied that it wasnt necessary. Says she wants to finish the conversation when he got a chance.

They took to walking in the park during her lunch breaks, solemnized by the wooded calm. He found himself telling her things he himself didn't understand. Told her he wanted to save the race. Take the trick off the souls of blackfolk, Said I am Legba Child. Told her the park was a holy ground. A hole in the wall.

Said Brer Rabbit and his crew lived there. Said they wary of humanfolk but sometimes late at night I settle back and close my eyes and act like Im sleeping and soon enough old Brer Rabbit come peeping in the door and when he see me sleeping like that he call the rest of them in and they commence to partying. Brer Bear pull out; bluesharp Rabbit play; Sister Coon play, she guitar bigger than she; Brer and Sister Fox commence to kicking up their heels, and sometimes I get in the spirit and I forget myself and I open my eyes and the music stop and they all hide away till I close my eyes again.

She showed him dreams she has long carried in secret places. A story she once wrote, a nightblack African goddess born of stars and thunder. Kinda corny, I know, she said, I've never shown it to anybody. He listens with all his power to a wildweed childhood wandering the storytale streets of New Orleans when she should have been in school. Stories about her oldschool New Orleans family, funny ways and all, the second masters, the damned doctorate, ABD, if she can squeeze the time. Told him about late-night archaeology classes at the University of Memphis, the summer digs on the Harriet Tubman Home in Auburn, the Tubman birthplace in Maryland. An extraordinary woman, she said, deltasun leaping off the river and igniting her eyes. Most people only know of her slaverytime and Civil War exploits.

But in her last years she built a home for homeless exslaves. She never quit struggling. She speaks to me.

The first time he kissed her was in the park. Spring probably, pollen so thick you could taste it. They were standing high on the bluff and she was entirely too close. She turned to say something, their eyes meet and flicked away bruised. Before he realized it he was leaning in to kiss her. Caught himself. May I kiss you? he said. She nodded most imperceptibly. Then he kissed her and his world lurched spun shouted and spoke in tongues while he savored her lips, her tongue. Lost in the grace of Oshun. *And I will be worthy of this blessing Oshun, I am forevermore your devoted fool.* He opened his eyes, looked at her face up against his, put his hand on her neck to feel the warmth of her skin, the heartbeat under his finger. She drew back suddenly and pushed at his chest. No, she said, I shouldn't. He stepped back and she dropped her head into her hands. (Something moved in me, in my body and I knew it was a dangerous thing we were doing. I knew it then.) He stood there frozen. Never wanted to cause her grief. Sorry he mumbled and backed up to the edge of the bluff. Not your fault, she said, I need to get back. Sure, he said. They crossed the bridge over the expressway that separated the park from the city without speaking, much too aware of boundaries broken and fingers unlinked only upon crossing.

The second time was better than the first. This time he held her in his arms. This time she let him. But it was the first time they made love that the earth shifted under his feet. An easy peace wrapped their souls in a little warm blanket.

Then she fired him. For Legba is a jealous loa and does not care to share. I was going to tell you it was over, she said, pulling away and sitting on the edge of the bed, body still sleek with sweat. Sure, he said, no problem. she would be back he thought and when she came back she better have a better attitude. He was still cool when he watched her drive off. Then he got to thinking. *What if she didn't. Come back.* Classic alpha, the conjureman tend to command games. But could he take that chance with this one. *What if she didn't. Come back.*

Evening come and the conjureman walking the 'hood like he do, de village witch doctor keeping he finger on the pulse, the patterns unbroken the harmonies clean, his invisible thing, I see but am not seen. Some folk, heavy with the ash'e, see him just fine, but most just feel the passing breeze of hoodooman walking. But this time he distracted by the very things that generally please him. Families sitting comfortable on wraparound porches, greeting folk and watching the day fall. Light glowing through windows as the sky darkens. Couples walking hand in hand with that coordinated rhythm. This time the conjureman retreats early into the leafy darkness.

Acutely conscious of being damn near fifty and living in the park like a kid playing games.

Conjureman sitting on a driftwood throne and handling he roots in he hand. *Throw shift frown.* Not a good time for unclear signs. *Throw shift.* Or perhaps it is just that he does not like what he see. Conjureman dont care for distraction. The faint brush of Fa like spiderwebs on the face. *Throw Shift. Frown.* He observes the habitual urge to slip back into his fortress, comfortable enough and answerable to nobody. When they were just flirting it was one thing but now that they have been intimate it is entirely another. Already he can feel significance lingering about the edges. The intoxicating scent of a power greater than his own.

Surely just the overwrought passion of new love. The trees are greener afterall, the air fresher, his faded dreams once again bright and shiny things. He has been here before. *No, not here,* says the power.

To win her I would change the world.

He called. Cleared his throat and asked her to lunch. Said he wanted to talk. If that's alright with you. Okay, she said. Okay.

In the park and on the bluff. The park was deeply quiet and they can barely sense the city around them. The jagged treeline of Arkansas. I tried to be cool, he said, when you said what you said yesterday. I should have fallen on my knees and begged you to reconsider.

I wrote you she said. Wrote you a letter. I dont want to stop. What we doing.

He was glad he had come to her first. I am such a bohemian, he said. Thats not necessarily a bad thing, she said. You have no idea, he said.

If I were to go with you, what kind of life would we live.

He decides then that he will hoodoo her, bind her to him with a web of lovemagic. He commence to spinning dreams. Magical, he said. Whatever you want, he said. And he found himself caught up suddenly in the spell of his own dream. With all my power I will serve you, he said. I will tell stories of you that will be a beacon light unto the generations. Stories of my love for you. I will immortalize you, he said.

The letter was there when he got home. She really cared for him, it said. She cared for him and she cared for her husband and she was confused, she said, two men she cared for in her life, two fires, one for my husband and a growing one for you. Not contacting him would be hard, she said. I do love you, she said.

She canceled New Orleans twice. Twice she relented. The day he was supposed to leave he didnt answer the phone for fear she would tell him not to come. Didn't know what to expect until she met him in the lobby of a classic Quarters hotel on Quarles, the Vila something or other, intimate, faintly decadent, a little elevator pushing them together and forcing a hug, a quickish peck.

An equally classic room with thick brocaded walls and lace covered windowdoors. They were just above the oldworld rooftops of the Quarter and a rainy drizzly day shrouded the crenelated roofs surrounding them. They sat on a wroughtiron balcony drinking champagne with bread, fruits and cheeses and only occasionally came inside to make candlelit love on the big brass bed.

God, this is good. Spooned up behind her and fitted in all particulars. God I want you, he says, into her ear. So does my husband, she says, he wants me, too. Well what do you want, he says. She turned and went into his chest. I want you, she says, so soft he more felt than heard it, my warrior, my fearless warrior. His heart swells and his power glows hot like a burning sun. And when he comes in her he is claiming her. Thats what he tells himself, convinces himself. Murmurs in her ear as she comes on him and he in her, Do you want me to be faithful to you baby, do you.

Oh yes, she moaned, oh yes baby yes.

But it was walking the little streets of the Quarter, weaving through festive New Year's crowds of tourists and natives in beads, sequins, and feathers, that he is happiest, holding her hand and being a couple. I'm going to drop all my women, he talk her, all my negotiations. I'm going to tell them all I'm in love with you.

I can't ask you to do that she says. I can't be that to you.

That's why I asked when I did.

They wander into Congo Square and the milling New Year's Eve crowds are left behind in the Quarter proper. The Square is quiet and fittingly somber with thick willows draped over it like dignified sentinels. The enslaved used to come here to do their sacred dances, she told him, you can still feel the history here. They are sitting beneath a sprawling elder. It is a comfortable moment. Until she says, if I do leave my husband, it doesn't mean I will get married again.

He ignores the heart beating in his chest and asks why not.

Why would I, she says, fingering beads she has accumulated. Been there done that.

He blinks. Pulls off a silver mask. Maintains cool. He knows she resents her husband. Sees marriage as an unescapable trap. I dont read books written by men she once told him. She rarely speaks about her marriage but the conjureman always listening. Dude got oldschool ways. She had to wait till he left the country to sneaklearn how to drive. But Highjohn ain't much better. Always been the boss. Assume any woman he with to adjust herself to him. His work. His way. But to be with her he has had to adjust himself to her rhythms and it has been a revelation. He been thinking optimal scenario: Angel leaves husband Angel marries him they live happy ever after. But no. He will be dancing forever. Her husband has forgotten the steps and no longer hears the music. Most likely never did. De conjureman he open she armored heart with massive doses of unconditional affection.

If I were to come with you, you won't always love me like this.

There is nothing I would not do to keep you happy. Nothing I would not be.

Both sincerity and intensity speak to her and they spend the night wrapped in the passionate moment. Lying face to face in a moment of acute satisfaction, he says, I am jealous of him. Of your husband.

In a twenty-year marriage, she says, there's not a lot of sex left.

Well that's good, he thinks, but not what he's jealous of. It's the rest he wants. I'm jealous of him snuggling up with you before you go to bed. Wiping your brow when you fevered. That burn you got taking that apple pie out of the oven. Hurried breakfast before rushing out to your jobs.

I'm the only one rushing out. He takes a deep breath. Well he said, is he going to get a job. Or are you going to keep supporting him. No, he's not she said. I'm going to keep working. He pushes it. That's okay with you? No, it's not, she said, I want a chance, too. She turns her back to him and his fingers trace the knobs of her spine like a blind man finding his way. You aren't a gardener, she said, but it's like two plants and over the years their roots are twisted up together and one is suffering but if you try to break up the roots you might destroy them both.

You deserve more than that, he finally gets out. Fucking pimp.

She shifts, sits up. My husband is a good man. And you dont know him. You dont know what it is about him that keeps me with him. In his own way my husband is good to me.

If he is that good to you, he thinks, *you wouldn't be here with me.* But what he says is I'm sorry. I knew what I was doing when I said it. I know you did she said and turns on the bedside lamp. Thats when she leaned over him. Asked what happens when the dream dies. Told him he had to leave.

Cool. Since I have known her I have been braced to be fired. Okay baby, he said, New Year rising up wild around them. I will officially quit chasing you. This time I will make it stick. Can you, she asked. Can you quit.

When he got back to Memphis he disappeared into the leafy sanctuary of the park.

A letter finds him. Postmarked New Orleans. He sitting on the landing of steps that run up the side of house. There is a hurricane building in the Gulf and Memphis is braced for the fringe. It is the deep breath quiet before a delta storm and dont nothing move, not a leaf not a wind, and the world waiting still like a mountain's heart. He put he roots down he open he letter. She thinks they should just be friends. Says she doesn't think hes ready for a real commitment. Real life. Real world. Says she is not a real woman to him. Say she wont be no mans fancy. Says he has control issues. Too fond of headgames. And finally, she says, I am committed to somebody else and am unable to give you the love and attention you need. Can you, she asks. Can you really quit.

Well. At least I'm a free man again. The old Highjohn that I know and love. Tired of being a beggar anyway. A fucking supplicant. I don't need her. I am free of her spell.

Then the delta wind come moaning and around him trees bow low and sing homage. Windsong whistling in great gusts through the trees shift he roots ever so faintly and lift he dreads in a whipping halo. Branches brush against the walls of his aerie in aboral symphony, and the sky opens wide and the rains they come. Stormbringer raises his head to the cooling spray.

Conjureman can't help but be amused. Thought he would bring so much magic down into her life she would never consider leaving him and instead brought the magic into his own. Called himself hoodooing and got hoodooed.

He handle he roots, he begin he story. One that will make the world as he wants it to be. One in which he dreams come true and he soul be saved. One that would be rest for the weary.

FROM **Church Folk**

BY MICHELE ANDREA BOWEN

After a week of emotionally charged revival preaching, Theophilus was too spent to race straight back to the arms—and the demands—of his Memphis congregation. He was tired and hungry, and he needed some time alone. So he was glad to see 32 West off of Highway 55, the exit for Charleston, Mississippi, where he knew of a place to stay, Neese's Boarding House for Negroes. He had also heard about a place there, Pompey's Rib Joint, which had the best rib tip sandwiches around—not to mention being known for hosting some of the best blues artists in the region.

It was in Charleston, a tiny Delta town thirty minutes west of Oxford, that the Lord's second and most important life-changing miracle for Theophilus occurred. It was his second miracle, the one he prayed for deep in his heart, not even aware of how intensely God was listening to him and not aware that the Lord loved him so much—He really did know the exact number of hairs on his head.

He drove to the "Smoky" section of the town and found the Negro boarding house. As he walked in, he took care not to let anyone sitting in the living room area catch a glimpse of his robe. His workday was over and he didn't want to have to explain if he happened to run into someone from the boarding house over at Pompey's. He felt a little twinge of guilt about going to Pompey's after preaching a revival, but he shrugged it off by telling himself that Pompey's was probably the best place he could go to have some peace. The last thing folks at Pompey's would be looking for was a preacher to tell their troubles to.

His room was simple, immaculate, and comfortable. The high double bed looked inviting with its starched white linens, and yellow and white cotton patch quilt. There was a large gray, yellow, and white rag rug in the middle of the worn but freshly waxed beige linoleum floor, and crisp white cotton curtains at the one window facing the bed across the room. There were even fresh daisies in a plain white pitcher with a yellow satin ribbon tied around it sitting on an embroidered linen runner on the dresser.

Theophilus put his things on the bed and unzipped his garment bag to get some fresh clothes. He had no intention of showing up at Pompey's in the navy chalk-striped suit, white shirt, and blue, black, and white tie he was now wearing. He selected a pair of silvery gray slacks and a pale gray silk knit sports shirt with silver buttons down the front, and matching pearl gray silk socks. He got his bathrobe, toiletry bag, fresh underwear, and left the room in search of towels and the bathroom so that he could take a quick bath and shave.

Thirty minutes later, he pulled into a dirt parking lot across the road from Pompey's Rib Joint. The smell of succulent ribs and the light from the hot pink neon sign that blinked POMPEY'S RIB JOINT—BEST RIBS IN THE DELTA led a straight path in the black night to the old brick building sitting off to itself on the other side of the road. Inside, where there was a rough wood floor, light purple walls, and unfinished wood tables and chairs, was packed. As soon as he walked in, Theophilus saw that the only seats left were at the bar.

He pressed his way over to the bar and put his hand on a stool just as a short, round woman wearing an orange print dress and holding a big white pocketbook on her arm was about to sit on it. He had begun to apologize when she spotted some friends and gave him the seat. Mouthing thanks, he squeezed through the narrow space and a thin, light-skinned man with freckles and a broad smile moved his stool to make more room for him. He lifted his shot glass in a neighborly fashion when Theophilus nodded a quick "thank you" and settled his large, muscular frame on the shaky barstool.

He got more comfortable and started looking around the room, unintentionally making eye contact with two women who were dressed in identical lime green chiffon dresses. One of the women ran her tongue over the top of her lip and blew him a quick kiss when she was certain her man wasn't watching her. He nodded at her, taking great care not to get caught by her man. It was one of those no-win situations. If he ignored that red-bone woman with "good" hair, chances are she would get mad at him and say something about him man. If he were too friendly with her, then her man, a wiry fellow with a process and dressed in a red suit, would get insulted and probably be inclined to fight. And the one thing he knew about little wiry-built men was that they were easily insulted, mean, and carried a serious weapon.

Theophilus was relieved when the waitress finally came to take his order, making it possible for him to have a decent reason to stop the eye contact with that woman and her friend. But it took him aback when she walked up to him and right into the space between his legs as she rubbed his knee and whispered in his ear, "What you think you be wantin' tonight, baby?"

All he could do was smile at first. He was fully aware that he should know better than to respond to such outrageous flirtation. But the man in him, the part that loved getting attention from good-looking women, couldn't stand to let her get the best of him. He just had to give her back as good as he got. So Theophilus sat back on his stool and smiled, looking her up and down, admiring how good she looked with her sepia-colored skin in that skimpy black satin dress she was wearing. He stroked his chin and said, in a voice that sounded to her like midnight on a clear summer evening, "I don't need much, sweetheart. Just a tall glass of iced tea with a few sprigs of mint leaves and a rundown of what you have to eat. And make sure it is something succulent for a hungry man like me."

She grinned at Theophilus, moved closer to him and spoke into his ear, this time allowing her lips to brush the tip of his earlobe, sending a rush of warmth across his neck and shoulders.

"We has a rib tip sandwich special tonight. And baby, them ribs so good till they will make you want to do something real bad and nasty, if you know what I mean."

Theophilus gave her a sultry smile to let her know that he knew exactly what she meant. Then he winked at her and said, "So, tell me, sweetheart. What's on this sandwich that makes it so good it'll make me want to do something nassty?"

She felt a little quiver in her thighs and had to take a few deep breaths before she said, "Them tips is just good, baby. They soaked in hot, homemade barbecue sauce, with potato salad on top, and Wonder Bread."

He smiled at her again. "I'm gonna trust you and take one of those sandwiches. But, sweetheart, if the sauce is real hot, bring me some ice water along with my order. I think I'll need more than a glass of tea to cool me down with a sandwich like that."

She leaned on him one more time, a big smile spreading across her face. She inhaled the scent of his cologne some more before saying in the sexiest voice she could, "I'll bring your tea real fast and then go get your order settled."

Theophilus smiled to himself as he watched the waitress walk away, deliberately giving him an eyeful of her fat, fine behind just swinging and swaying all for him. He thought to himself, "Boy, get yourself together, carrying on like that. Just a few hours ago you were all down on your knees at church and glad to be there, too. Shame on you, Reverend Simmons."

The waitress brought his tea just as the band performing tonight, Big Johnnie Mae Carter and the Fabulous Revues, finished setting up on stage. The Fabulous Revues was a good-size band—bass player, lead guitarist, tenor saxophone player, trumpet player, pianist, and drummer. These men, who were anywhere from the ages of thirty to fifty, looked good in crisp black pants with razor-sharp creases, light-purple silk shirts, shiny black Stacy Adams shoes, and slick black straw hats cocked on the side of their heads. When everybody was in place, the drummer raised his drumsticks high in the air, brought them down hard on the first beat, and Pompey's Rib Joint got to jumping.

Big Johnnie Mae Carter, a tall, husky, square-shaped woman with big breasts and a headful of coarse bleached-blond hair piled high on top, was in rare form tonight. Decked out in a long light-purple evening gown with slits up to the knee on each side and rhinestones glittering in her ears, she strutted her stuff to the funky Delta blues rhythms of her band, from the front door of Pompey's all the way up and on to the stage. Then she finally stepped up to the microphone, throwing back her shoulders and whipped out the words of the song:

"If you was a bee baby, I'd turn myself into the sweetest flower.

"And if you was the rain, Daddy, and me the Mississippi? I'd flood this old Delta 'cause I couldn't keep all of your sweet lovin' all to myself.

"And if you just happened to be the devil. Then, Lawd, Lawd, Lawdy, just help me please.

" 'Cause see, I'd be tryin' to up and sell my soul just to make sure you kept on lovin' up on me.

"I said, Lawd, Lawd, Lawdy, Help, Help, Help me please.

" 'Cause I know I'd be doing so wrong just to keep you lovin' up on me."

Big Johnnie Mae looked like she was feeling that music from head to toe as she stretched out her arms, snapped her jeweled fingers, and moved her hips from side to side. As the lead guitarist stepped forward to pick out his solo, she shifted aside, still dancing, rolling her hips in a sinuous way, and finally shimmying on down to the stage floor. The guitarist looked down at Big Johnnie Mae and smiled. She, in turn, smiled back up at him, pulled that dress up to her knees and rolled her hips some more. All the other musicians stopped playing and just let the lead guitar, accompanied by Big Johnnie Mae's dancing, carry the song.

Now Big Johnnie Mae began to weave her way back up, all the while crooning around the melody, stretching to her full height in front of the microphone. Then the band rose up behind her full and strong, as she reached for a note that sounded like it had started way down deep in the basement and came on upstairs to blow the roof off the joint.

A man sitting only a couple of feet from the stage jumped up and shouted, "Damn, baby. You sho' 'nough is hot tonight! Lawd! What I wouldn't give to be that there micro-ro-phone you holdin' on to right now."

The freckle-facedman leaned over toward Theophilus and said, "Now, that Negro don't have no sense. 'Cause the way she was movin' down on that flo', any fool would know he need to turn hisself into some wood."

Theophilus could only smile at this observation and raise his tea. He stopped short of nodding his head in agreement. He wasn't so sure he wanted to "turn hisself into some wood." because he wasn't so sure he was man enough to hold all of the woman that was Big Johnnie Mae Carter. Theophilus thought that perhaps he could be the sound system that carried her voice to the ears of her listeners. He sipped his tea and nodded his head at that thought. It would be nothing short of a religious experience to feel her voice coursing through his body and on out to the eager audience. He sipped on his tea some more, bobbing his head to the beat of the next song. The tea felt good, too—cooling him down at the same time that Big Johnnie Mae and the Fabulous Revues were warming up his soul and making him feel almost as good as he had felt at church.

Just as Big Johnnie Mae ended this last song and started up on one with a calmer rhythm, a different woman came toward Theophilus with a plate of food in one hand and a big glass of ice water, a napkin, and silverware in the other.

"You the man who ordered the rib tip sandwich and glass of ice water?" she asked.

He said, "Ummm-hmmm."

She pushed the food out toward him.

"Here, this is yours and you owe me buck twenty-five."

Theophilus took the plate, silverware, and glass of water from her and put them on the bar. He reached back to get his empty tea glass off the bar and then fumbled in his pocket for some money.

Watching him, the woman had to agree with the waitress, who was now stuck helping the bartender fix drinks, that the man in the "silver gray outfit" was sure enough a "big and pretty chocolate man." She tried to steal a better look at his face without his noticing it. She knew that you didn't look at the men coming in here too hard unless you wanted to send them a message you hoped they wanted to answer.

Then he smiled at her, handing over the money while looking her over so thoroughly until she wished she had worn her large cook's apron. It covered a lot of her body but she hated bringing customers their food in that barbecue- and grease-splattered thing. But at least that grimy coverage would have slowed down the speed with which this man's eyes took in her body. She was standing there in a shirt and Bermuda shorts, so her only defense was to narrow her already slanted eyes and give him a nasty look. He wouldn't be the first man to get this look. But he *was* the first one who made her wonder if she had looked at him just a little too mean when she walked back to the kitchen.

Theophilus shrugged off the glare that little woman had given him and turned toward the bar to eat his food. The sandwich was so thick and juicy he had to eat it with a fork. The tips were tender and dripping in some of the best barbecue sauce he had tasted in a long time. And there was a generous helping of potato salad spread evenly on each slice of bread. The waitress hadn't lied about this sandwich. It did taste good enough to make you "want to do something real bad and nasty."

As he ate, Theophilus found his mind fixed on the image of that mean-acting little woman. She sure was a fine little thing, with that dark honey–colored skin, thick reddish brown hair held in place with a light blue headband, heart-shaped face, full lips, and those sexy slanted, light brown eyes cutting him in two when he stared at her too hard. And she looked cute in those baby blue Bermuda shorts with her petite, hourglass figure and her backside swinging her own natural, uncontrived rhythm when she walked away from him.

Umph, umph, umph, he thought to himself. If that girl didn't have some big pretty legs, I don't know who did.

Just then the waitress came switching back to him to ask if he needed anything else from her. Figuring she was offering more than just another glass of tea, he thought that he had better add a little extra sugar to his smile before he asked a question he knew she wouldn't want to answer.

"Who brought me my food, sweetheart?"

She looked confused and said, "Something wrong with your food?"

"No. I just want to know who was the woman who brought me my food.

She didn't look like she was a waitress. And judging from the way she just walked off with my money after I paid her, she didn't act like one, either. I mean, look at you. You're standing here all sweet-like, making sure I'm alright."

"She wasn't nasty-actin' was she?" the waitress asked. She knew Essie Lane was good for giving these men that old nasty, slit-eyed look of hers.

"No, sweetheart, nothing like that. I just want you to tell me who she was."

"That was Essie Lane. She the cook on duty tonight."

"Well, I have to thank a woman who can cook some rib tips like that. Where is she?"

The waitress didn't look too happy about Theophilus wanting to talk to Essie but she said, "She back in the kitchen," and pointed him in that direction.

"Thank you, sweetheart," he said as he gave her a sexy wink and put some money in her hand.

She put her smile back on her face and said, "I just knowed you was the kind of man who really knows what to do with a woman," as Theophilus got up and headed back to the kitchen.

Sighing with regret, she looked down at her tip. The five-dollar bill she was holding in her hand stretched her smile into a big wide grin. Five dollars was a huge tip for a waitress working at Pompey's Rib Joint.

When Theophilus walked into that hot kitchen, Essie was drinking some ice water and stirring a big pot of collard greens. Sensing someone watching her, she turned around, hoping it wasn't that old drunk who kept waving a dollar bill at her every time she came out on the floor. When she saw that it was the good-looking man in silver-gray, she was kind of relieved but also wondering why he was standing in the doorway looking at her like that. Ready to run him out of the kitchen if need be, she put a hand on her hip and looked him dead in the eye.

"What do you want?" she asked.

Theophilus wasn't surprised by the attitude in her voice. At the gut level he knew she was one of those good women who didn't allow for foolishness from a man. And as nasty as she sounded, he liked her voice. It was the kind of voice that could move swiftly from giving a command one dare not disobey, to girlish laughter, to a deep, throaty sigh. The desire to hear that sigh nestled itself quietly and comfortably in the most private, yet-to-be awakened region of his heart.

"I said, what do you want?"

He wanted to smile at her but didn't want to be chased out of this kitchen before he had a chance to meet her. So he decided to put on his "receiving line" face, which seemed to carry him a long way with most folks he greeted after Sunday morning service. He held that look in place as he tried to think of something to say that would match his disarming expression. The best he could come up with was, "Sister, that food was so good, I just had to come back here and humble myself before the chef," with what he truly hoped had a good dose of the preacher in his voice.

He knew better than to say what he was really thinking, which was *Baby, you so fine, you make me want to say things that can only be whispered in your ear.*

Essie just looked at him and said, "The chef, huh?" with a frown on her face. "You are talking about a 'chef' in a country place like Pompey's Rib Joint? You must think you in New York City. But you ain't. And since you ain't, get out of my kitchen right now, before somebody gets hurt." She edged over to a small table with a big meat cleaver on it.

Theophilus saw her reach for the meat cleaver and backed away, saying, "Hey, wait a minute, baby," before he could catch himself right.

Looking at him like he was out of his mind, Essie said, "Negro, I know you ain't calling me no baby."

Theophilus moved toward her gingerly, trying to placate her. "Look, girl, I didn't mean you any harm. Your food was good and I just wanted to see you—"

"Wanted to see me? For what? If my food was so good, why didn't your cheap self send me a note about my good food, along with a tip?"

Theophilus didn't even try to defend himself on that one, realizing he had been too distracted to tip her. She was looking at him real hard, meat cleaver firm in her grip.

He tried another tack, extending his hand and saying, "My name is Theophilus—"

"I believe I know your name, Reverend. I thought you looked familiar when I brought you your food. Ain't you that revival preacher who was in Jackson this week?"

Before Theophilus could answer her, she said, "You sure are. And now you back up this way spending up their offering money and thinking you can talk up some little juke joint cook. Man, sometimes you preachers can truly act as bad as the worst street Negroes." She blew a puff of air out of her mouth in disgust, adding, "And I'd be surprised if you ain't a married man to boot."

Theophilus was embarrassed at the mess he had made in his effort to meet this woman. And now he had to convince her that he didn't see her as some "little juke joint cook." But the way she was holding that meat cleaver made him think real carefully before he opened his mouth again.

"I realize that I haven't made much of an impression on you this

evening," he began. "But you have to believe me when I say that I didn't
come back here to be disrespectful. I just wanted to meet you. You should
call Reverend Murcheson James over at Mount Nebo Gospel United
Church and ask him about me. Maybe a good word or two from him will
make you feel comfortable enough to see me again."

"Reverend James is my pastor. I'm a member of Mount Nebo."

Theophilus felt like shouting. This woman went to Mount Nebo? Now
he knew the Lord was truly on his side. He smiled at her as he said, "You
should also know that I'm a single man, all by myself, just hoping to find a
good woman."

Essie rolled her eyes at him. "All by yourself? I've never seen a preacher all
by himself without a whole bunch of women to choose from. For some reason, women just seem to love preachers. I don't know why."

Theophilus decided to ignore that last comment and said, "Yes, there
sure are a lot of women who love preachers and would be glad for one to
choose them. But I just told you that I'm looking for a good one."

"And you gonna find her in Pompey's Rib Joint?"

"I'm talking to a good woman right now, right?" Theophilus said, standing over Essie, looking down at her, daring her to differ with him.

Essie knew she was a good woman, one who worked real hard to see that
everybody at Pompey's knew it, too. To be sure, good-looking Negro men
had crossed her path on many an evening at work. But they all made the fatal error of missing the point—that Essie Lee Lane was not only fine-
looking with big sexy legs, she was a woman of fine character who knew she
deserved better than what they always wanted to offer her.

"You haven't answered my question."

"What question?"

"I asked you if you were a good woman and you've been standing there
staring at me."

Now it was Essie's turn to be embarrassed. She hadn't realized that she
was staring at him.

"So, I'm talking to a good woman in the kitchen of one the hottest juke
joints in the Delta. Am I not?"

Essie struggled, trying to compose just the right answer to that question.
The way he looked her over, head to toe, was jumbling up her thoughts. She
frowned. "Why you looking at me like you got X-ray vision? You know that
ain't right for no man and especially one claiming to be a preacher."

Theophilus checked his gaze, traveling down to get a fully lighted view of
those legs. He wondered if her legs would feel as soft and satiny to his hands
as they looked. But he wasn't about to apologize because he couldn't keep
his eyes off her. "You know something, Miss—"

"Essie Lee. Essie Lee Lane."

"You know something, Miss Essie Lee Lane. I don't have X-ray vision. Truly I don't. But to be perfectly honest, at times like these I sure wish I did." He gave her a smile that started at his eyes and traveled leisurely down to his mouth.

Essie felt flushed looking at him smiling at her like that. Here was a man—a preacher, in fact—who told her he wished he had X-ray vision and gave her a look that said volumes about how he would use this gift if he were so blessed with it. She had always been skeptical of ministers—felt that too many of them didn't practice what they preached and had big-headed notions about themselves. But for some reason, she felt differently about this man, which was disturbing, the more she thought about it.

"What's the matter with you, Miss Essie Lee Lane? You got a thought you don't like?"

Essie couldn't believe he could see through her like that and said, "Nothing wrong, just thinking."

"Just thinking, huh?" Theophilus said with a warm smile that didn't have a trace of freshness in it. "I bet you're thinking you kind of like me and might just let me see you again, right?"

Essie sighed, trying not to let him see that he was getting all up under her skin. She would rather die than so much as breathe a "yes" in his direction.

"Yes, I bet you're still thinking about me, isn't that right, Miss Essie Lane? And it's bothering you that you want to see this preacher just one more time."

Essie just looked at him as if to say, "Don't flatter yourself." She said, "I ain't troubled about nothing that has anything to do with you. Just because you can see me again—nothing about it that needs extra thought to it. All you'll be doing is what you asked to do, seeing me again."

"Well, well, well, God is truly good. I think nothing short of an act of God would convince Miss Essie Lane to let me—X-ray vision and all—see her again."

Essie blew air out of her mouth and rolled her eyes as if to say "please." She said, "I think no harm could come from you visiting me."

Theophilus guessed correctly that this was about as close to a yes as he was going to get. But with a soft laugh in his voice, he pressed, "So, you're telling me that I can see you again, huh? Is that what you are saying, Miss Essie Lane?"

The slight smile on her lips made him feel certain that he was getting next to her, if only a little.

"Maybe I could see you tomorrow afternoon," he said. "If it's okay with you, I can stop by your house after my visit with Reverend James."

"Yes. Yes," she replied. "You can come by my house tomorrow and eat lunch with me."

His heart swelled with hope.

"With me, my mama, and my Uncle Booker," she continued. "That way you'll know without a doubt that there ain't no good times to be had down here with this little small-town Mississippi girl. Way I figure it, once you're certain about that point, you probably won't want to see me again anyway."

The expression on his face changed. Gone was the heat and in its place was a look she didn't know what to make of. Was it hurt?

He said, "Essie, please know that the only time I am really looking to have, is *more of it* with you. And the only thing I want from you is for you to tell me how to find your house tomorrow."

I I

Theophilus settled his bill at Rose Neese's Boarding House for Negroes and went to visit with Rev. James. He spoke of the revival with warmth and feeling, thanking his mentor for the role he had surely played in getting him the chance to serve as the guest preacher there. But Reverend James couldn't help but notice how the excitement in his voice rose when Theophilus spoke of meeting that fine young woman from his congregation, Essie Lee Lane. He approved of Essie inviting Theophilus to lunch with her mother, Lee Allie, and her Uncle Booker, both of whom he knew well. Being a kind, patient, and extremely observant man, he could see how hard Theophilus was working to stay focused on any topic other than Essie. So he decided to cut their visit short. He knew better than to compete for the attention of a young man whose mind kept straying to his upcoming lunch with a young lady like Essie Lane.

Much as he loved Rev. James, Theophilus was relieved to be dismissed, for it had taken everything in him not to hop up from his seat and run out to find the Lane house. When he walked up on the small porch and knocked on the screen door, a woman he just knew had to be Essie's mother came and unhooked the latch. She was a nutmeg-colored woman, with thick brown hair that was twisted into an attractive French roll. She bore a strong resemblance to Essie but didn't have her slanted, golden brown eyes. Theophilus did notice, in the most respectful way, of course, that she had Essie's figure and legs.

Lee Allie Lane had been just as anxious for this Rev. Simmons to get to her house as he was to come there. Essie didn't bother with any of the men who came to Pompey's, and she had never shown the slightest interest in a man who was a preacher. So when Essie told her that she invited a minister she met in the kitchen of Pompey's to lunch, Lee Allie was about to bust open with curiosity. There was something mighty special about Rev. Simmons if Essie was allowing him to come to the house, let alone asking him over to eat.

As soon as Lee Allie answered the door, she knew why Essie couldn't resist seeing this preacher again. He was a six-foot-three, coffee-with-no-cream-colored man, with close-cut, coarse black hair framing a handsome face, and dark brown eyes, draped with long, thick black lashes under well-shaped eyebrows. He had a slender nose that flared at the nostrils, well-defined cheekbones, and deep dimples on each side of his face. His full, richly colored lips were accentuated by the well-groomed mustache that stopped right at the corners of his mouth. And from what she could see of him, Lee Allie had the distinct impression that his navy suit, with his starched white shirt and blue, maroon, and silver paisley print tie, hid strong brown arms, a neat waist, long, nicely shaped legs, and one of those backsides that only a Negro man had—it was a backside that made you thank the Lord for making you a Negro woman.

"You must be Reverend Simmons," she said, opening the screen door and waving for him to come in. As he stepped into the house, the comforting scent of fresh-baked rolls went straight up his nose. The pretty room he entered was simple, cozy, and warm, with a soft yellow on the walls, off white sheers at the windows, and plants scattered around, spilling over their bright red, blue, and purple pots. The soft mint green sofa made you want to stretch out on it and read the paper, and the pale blue chair with the matching ottoman was the kind that had "Sunday nap" written all over it. After admiring the room, he extended his hand to Essie's mother.

"Theophilus Simmons from Greater Hope Gospel United Church in Memphis. Your pastor, Reverend James, has known me for years and is my mentor."

Lee Allie gave his hand a firm shake and said, "It is a pleasure to meet you, Reverend Simmons. I am Essie Lee's mother, Mrs. Lee Allie Lane. When she told me and my brother, Booker, that you wanted to come by this afternoon, we both wanted to get a good look at a man who likes to preach and listen to Big Johnnie Mae all in one workin' day."

She motioned for him to sit down in the blue chair and hollered down the hall.

"Booker, come on in the living room, the Reverend just got here and you need to come meet him."

Essie's Uncle Booker walked into the living room finishing a roll and wiped his hands on his pants leg before giving Theophilus a firm, "don't take no mess off a nobody" handshake and motioning for him to sit down. He looked a lot like his sister in the face and had her coloring. But where she was small, he was stocky and of medium height.

Lee Allie said, "Essie Lee not here yet. Had to go by the store to pick up a few things. She'll be back right shortly, though. Give you, me, and Booker a chance to get acquainted. You pastoring Greater Hope in Memphis? That's a pretty good-size church for a young pastor like you, Reverend Simmons. How many folks at your church now?"

Theophilus shifted around in the chair and got as comfortable as possible, feeling like he was gearing himself up to face the Inquisition.

"Greater Hope has about 365 members," he said. "I have been there just about a year. And I won't lie to you—pastoring that church has been one of the most difficult challenges I've ever had to face. I've learned a lot. But I stay on my knees, Mrs. Lane, stay on my knees."

Lee Allie opened her mouth again, but before she got a chance to ask Theophilus more about his pastoring, Uncle Booker jumped in.

"Now, Reverend, what I want to know is how you come to preach and swing at Pompey's at the same time? I don't go on about all this thou-cain't-do-anything-if-you-want-to-serve-the-Lord foolishness, but I do think you need to tell me something. This ain't no church business visit. I'll bet some money you sweet on Essie Lee. Am I right, Reverend?"

Theophilus didn't know what to say or even how to say it if he did know. Essie's uncle looked like he could whip his tail if he had a mind to do so.

Uncle Booker, who had been leaning against the front door, now sat down on the couch across from where Theophilus was sitting. Staring intently at Theophilus, as if to look through him, he said, "Don't you sit there searching for no answers to what I just said. You tell me the truth. Because if you hand me some cockamamie preacher double talk, I'll know it. I'm used to church folk."

"Booker! Reverend Simmons is a minister," Lee Allie said.

"Lee Allie, don't you go and start getting all upset with me. This here preacher went up in Pompey's last night, ordered something to eat, looked my baby-girl niece over, and then came over here the very next day to get a better look at her. Now, he must like the girl to do all of that."

Uncle Booker looked at Theophilus real hard. "Now, son, you have some likin' for my niece, don't you, Reverend?"

"Yes, sir. I saw your niece and wanted to meet her."

"And you liked what you saw, right?"

"Yes, sir. Your niece is a very striking woman."

"Mess. That's just some funky mess, boy. Essie Lee got next to you and you darn well know it. Striking woman, my black behind. Just what you up to, preacher?"

Theophilus respected Uncle Booker's right to look after his niece but he didn't appreciate being treated like some jive-acting, jackleg preacher. He figured he'd better let these people know right now what he was about. He sat up straight in the chair and looked directly at Uncle Booker.

"Mr.—"

"Webb. My last name's Webb."

"Mr. Webb, you're right to think I'm not your regular kind of preacher. Truth is, sometimes I go to places like Pompey's to eat some good food and relax a little without being troubled with church business. You know, I do like being able to talk to folks about more than church. And I like being treated like a regular man instead of always being treated like 'the Pastor.'

"And, sir, when I saw your niece last night, she gave me the impression that she was a good, solid woman. And if you don't mind my being so bold, she is a fine-looking woman, too—so fine in fact, that she held my attention for the rest of the night. So, I came by here today to let her know I was interested in getting to know her. And I knew I needed to meet her family so she'd know I wasn't after her for all the wrong reasons."

This response seemed a little bold to Uncle Booker, who didn't answer but sat weighing what Theophilus had said. Finally he extended his hand. "Son, I'm glad to know that you ain't one of those preachers who so intent on making sure everybody know just how saintly and pure they are. I like that. Lets me know you know you just a man and not some fool who think he got the only connection to the Lord."

Theophilus grabbed Uncle Booker's hand and sighed out loud with relief.

"Mr. Webb, I understand that you need to know what I'm all about. I'm not perfect but I was raised right."

They were interrupted by the sound of Essie pulling at the screen door. She didn't know why her mother waited until the last minute to send her out for kosher dill pickles, big green olives, pickled okra, jalapeño peppers, and potato chips to go with lunch. She thought they had enough to eat, with the fresh-baked turkey stuffed in large, homemade rolls, fresh garden tomatoes, butter lettuce and cucumber salad, and homemade custard ice cream with lemon-flavored tea cakes. But Lee Allie had insisted that these things would make lunch so much better. Essie hoped Theophilus didn't think she was rude for not being there when he arrived.

Theophilus stood up, trying hard to control the big grin stretching across his face when Essie walked into the house.

"Afternoon, Reverend. Hope you haven't been waiting too long."

"No, I haven't been here long."

Lee Allie looked back and forth between the two of them, took the bag of groceries from Essie, handed it to Booker, and said, "Reverend Simmons was telling us a little about his church in Memphis." She turned to Theophilus and asked, "Reverend, how big is your choir? Most solid congregations have good choirs."

Theophilus sat back down. "Mrs. Lane, we have a little over thirty people in our choir, a pianist and organist. One of the first things I did as the new pastor was to appoint a new choir director. Seems like the old one didn't want to sing what the congregation wanted to hear. Lot of folks at Greater Hope love hard-core gospel and they have said that service is so much better now that the choir is rocking the church with some good music. I know I enjoy listening to the choir more now than when I first came as the pastor."

While Theophilus was talking to Lee Allie, he could not stop himself from stealing looks at Essie, who was leaning against the doorway leading to the hall. She was wearing red pants, a red and white horizontal-striped, short-sleeved knit top, and red sneakers. Although the pants showed off her figure well, he sure wished he could have caught another good look at those big legs before he went back to Memphis.

Later, as Essie and Lee Allie sat in the kitchen, shelling snap beans for supper, Lee Allie said, "Essie, I don't know why you didn't hold more conversation with the Reverend. The whole time he was here, you held up that wall, just sizing him up like you was looking for something wrong with him."

"Mama, I didn't have to look for something to be wrong with him. Whole time he was here, he ran his eyes all over me, head to toe, when he thought nobody was looking."

"Essie Lee, he was looking at you so hard because he likes you, girl. And I hate to tell you this, baby, but a man gone look at you like that when he likes what he sees. Even a good man gone look, baby. He cain't help it 'cause he a man. And the Reverend young, too. So he really gone be looking before he can catch himself. What is he, about twenty-eight or so?"

"Twenty-nine. The revival program said he was twenty-nine."

"Well, like I just said, at twenty-nine, he still young enough for his nature to spill out over his home training when he think nobody's lookin'. And remember, even Booker had a good impression of him. I think the Reverend is a decent man. He sure 'nough a good-lookin' one, too. So the next time he comes, you be sure to give him a chance to talk to you."

"Mama, what makes you think he coming back anytime soon?"

"Because I invited him to be our church's guest preacher for Missions Day," Lee Allie said with a smile on her face. "I called Reverend James and my missionary group. Reverend James said that Reverand Simmons was a fine preacher and that he would come at a price we could afford. So now you'll have a chance to see him again."

Essie rolled her eyes, not wanting her mother to know she was happy that Lee Allie had engineered a reason for Theophilus to return to Charleston.

"Girl, why you rolling your eyes like that? You the one who invited him over here in the first place. Besides, you need to meet somebody and leave Charleston. 'Cause you don't need to stay here."

"Mama, I'm not that crazy about preachers. They can be some worrisome men and wear on your nerves something terrible when you are around them. Some of them can be so greedy—buying big cars, always wanting folk to cook them a whole bunch of food, and then will sit there and practically eat up everything in sight. Remember the last guest preacher who came to Mount Nebo? Ate all of the best pieces of ribs and he didn't even offer Rev. James the last piece. Just snatched it out of the pan and gobbled it up."

Lee Allie interrupted her. "That preacher was greedy, all right, but the problem was that we shouldn't have let Mother Harold convince us to invite him in the first place. Several people knew something about him and didn't care much for his ways. But we just sat back and let Mother Harold have her way again. Should have known better. 'Cause we all knew from the get-go that she wanted him to come just so she could look him over for Saphronia. Lord, if that woman don't wear out my patience looking for some preacher to marry her old stuck-up grandbaby."

She shook her head a few times just thinking about the preacher and Mother Harold.

"But Mama—" Essie began.

"But Mama nothing, Essie Lee. Every preacher ain't like that and you doggone well know that fact is the truth. Reverend James is a good man who loves God and takes his pastoring seriously. And you think Reverend Simmons is okay, too. Otherwise, you sure were some fool to let him come over here to see you. You know, Essie Lee, some preachers really do want to do right."

"And you think Theophilus is a man that wants to do right?"

"Umm-hmm. I think *Theophilus*, as you seem to be callin' him now, wants to do right," Lee Allie answered with emphasis on his name.

Essie looked embarrassed. She didn't want her mama reading any more into this situation than she knew she already had. She said, "Well, he'll just have to convince me he is all that you saying he is."

Lee Allie gave Essie a "look" and dismissed that foolishness with a wave of her hand.

BY THOMAS GLAVE

—But Lou—, he say's—

—No.

—But can't you just say it—or—

—I said, No.

—But even if I—

—Stop begging, Ricky. What did I tell you? See, now—

—Don't you want it?

—That ain't the point, now. Get dressed!

—Why don't you . . .

—What?

—make me . . .

—Boy . . . see, now—

—Uh, huh?

—You better quit playing games and get dressed! What you *doing?*

—Proposing.

—Yeah, to the wrong one, says that other. Who is Lou Jay. Easing himself up on the bed. Thinking, mama just changed these damn sheets yesterday and now in the late-morning heat they were already sticking to the sweat on his back. Thinking, the bedroom was all right enough—was home. Thinking, the postcards and pictures of Miami and New York and whatnot made it more . . . the way they liked it. Had liked it. Him and Ricky. Thinking: *Uh-huh,* 'cause the boy had been in there often enough (only one who had been)—thinking, *Uh-huh,* best friend, searching for the word to describe him, my, my—my *what?* And now that the mama and daddy were out for a while Miss Ricky was actually going to *try it:* going to try to go on and be his hardheaded self as usual and show out like a fool even with everything getting set to happen on schedule tomorrow. But, see—

—I wish Renee would catch your ass in here like this.—Looking straight over at Ricky kneeling on the floor beside the bed.

—That stupid—don't talk about that now. Don't even get me started.

—Yeah, uh-hmm. That stupid—listen to me, talking just as nasty as you! Well, she gone be your wife in a day. Less than a day.

—So? We could still—

—What did I say, fool? No.

—Why not?

—'Cause I said so, that's why not. You need to listen for once, stead of being so damn—

—Hardheaded. I know.

—Well, then.

—You sound like Daddy.

—He got some sense.

—He ain't got nothing. You know he's forcing me!

—He needs to. Somebody needs to.

—I'm seventeen, Lou Jay!

—You *eight*een.

—I *will* be. What he got to go on and try to force me to get married for?

—'Cause he want him some grandkids.

—He got eleven already. I got brothers, Lou Jay!

—Six.

—And no sisters, neither.

—But you his baby. His baa-by Ricky.

—Shit, Ricky said. One long syllable the color of the snarl that formed it.

—Tell that to the preacher, he said.

—Well, baby, you better go on out and get you a nice sweet fancy ring.

—I'ma smack you down in a second, bitch. I swear.

—You be acting too grown sometimes any old way. Get up off your knees, Ricky.

—What you talking about grown for, trying to act like you so grown, giving out orders? You ain't but two months older than me, baby. I could stay on my knees if I want to. You want to know what Daddy said?

—About what? The wedding? Everybody far way as Decatur already knows. That's all folks do round here is talk, okay? But ain't nobody saying nothing to your daddy's face, that's all. They could shame you *and* me if they wanted to.

—I ain't studying all that. And you—

—You need to.

—You want to know what Daddy said?

—Told you I already knew.

—Don't be acting all grand, Miss Girl, 'cause you don't know all this. He got his gun!

—What? For what?

—You know what. Fittin to shoot off my ass if I don't marry little Renee. And you know he could shoot good. He learned me. And I learned you, Lou Jay. My baby.—Reaching over to squeeze the other man's naked thigh, then moving his hand slightly above and to the center of it. Their skins, together, all of a glow in the thickening heat.

—You'll always be my baby, Lou Jay. You know that.

—Ricky—

—Since we was thirteen we been playing *on.* I got you now, Lou. You got me. I don't never want nobody but you. We got us something! You think I could let you go for some little piece of—

—All right, now. We ain't got no time for all that sweet talk—stop, boy, that tickles!—with some man, your daddy no less, putting a gun all up in your face. No, uh-uh. I ain't having it. Didn't I ask you to stop?

—Aw, girl, you love what my hands do. Anyway, Daddy ain't only got his gun up in my face. He got it aimed all up in my behind, too.

—*Um*-hmm. 'Cause he know what's been all up *in* there.

Laughter, until they choke. But already he is looking. Ricky, having laughed, stilled, now looking. Thinking how hard, how very very hard it is not to focus, fixate, his eyes on Lou Jay. How hard not to see, looking, just how *pretty*. How fine and all that, he thinks. How hard not to carry to dreams and private thrusts the big old shoulders and pretty lips and nipples, after his very own lips have traversed the skin . . . the shoulders and nipples all hard now hard-hard yet soft, like the eyes, beneath the shirt . . . when he wore a shirt. Hard not to think, Yeah, 'cause I could just take him right now, couldn't I, and do *all* a that and more. I could (uh huh, do all of it, that and *that*) get him all relaxed (the calm-down part) and whisper back behind his neck about the house they'd buy someday (or, no: *I* will buy. *I* will. For him. Ricky-for-Lou Jay. Uh-huh) in Decatur or maybe . . . that one. The one they'd fix up nice with a front yard just like everybody else's and some back land too just like everybody else's so they could live someplace far away from all those others, those others with guns and bullet eyes, those others like his own daddy. Far away from the eyes, from the Now-what-y'all-got-into-some-nasty-shit-no-doubt pressed lips and hands on hips. Far from the sucked teeth and curling sneers. Someplace where the two of them, him-and-Lou Jay, could just settle and say, All right, now. Because this here is Lou Jay's and Ricky's house and we been up in it together going on how long now? so don't y'all ignorant motherfuckers even *try* no fierce shit up in here. Uh-huh. The ones with the guns (Daddy) who could never know how it felt when that part of him that was on Lou Jay, right there, slow and silky out in the fields at night sometimes or right here in Lou Jay's room, like when after his mama and daddy are asleep and it's just him and me and is that your hand, Lou? I can't hardly tell no more. It all feels like soft sand, smooth reeds, watergrass. Hot silk. All water. *My face in the sand, in the soft soft reeds.* Enough to know for now. Better not to know yet about (though he knows already) the curling snakes on the shore, the blue things that, in murky rivers, curl about ankles, drag them down to drown. Enough to know, for now, what their hotsilkiest dreams tell them:

that they are here, alive, and that, right here, on this hot morning beneath the pecans and the sizzling live oaks, all snakes are in their holes, all blue things uneasily at rest. Here, where, whatever else might be known or feared, each can be certain, remembering warm sand and siltyslim reeds, that the other will always be his and his. Lucky, he thinks, or something. And I'ma make sure we stay lucky. But says:

—I swear, Lou, it's like we was living in—

—You need to tell me what Daddy Malcolm said. You ain't tell me everything.—Reaching over to the bedside table for a cigarette.

—Well—

—Go on.

—All right. He *said*—get this, now, this's Daddy—he said, "Boy, if you don't marry Renee I'll blow your head off myself. You *will* marry her," he said. Sounding all white. Daddy!

—Lord Jesus. He got to know about me.—Blowing out a thick smoke stream.

—He do. What you think? He *been* knowing. Why the hell else you think he been pushing me all up in Renee's face?— Looking out into the June sunlight. Turning his face to the day and noticing how the air is free, humid; how bugs are chattering between birdsong.

—I don't want to marry that girl, Lou.

—Why you so sure she want to marry *you?* She must have something to say. It ain't like you the only one out here seen her. And no matter what folks say I don't think she stupid. We know Renee.

—Well, she don't know nothing about us.

—She don't know nothing about us cause we ain't never done nothing in her face and we watched that anyway. Daddy Malcolm, now, that's a different story. He always did look at me funny. I ain't messing with that.

—Evil, you mean. You got that right. He thinks you switch. Plus you ain't never had no girlfriend.

—Ain't never wanted none.

—You should've, Lou Jay. You coulda saved us a whole lotta trouble that way. Maybe Daddy wouldn't be breathing all down my neck now if you did.

Lou Jay smoked for a while in silence, then turned his face to the freedom of the day and the birds singing and the trees looking so peaceful, quiet, beneath the bright wheeling sun.

—Can't nobody make me to nothing I don't want to, Ricky. Not even Daddy Malcolm.—Not quite believing his own words, but they sounded brave.—Anyway, answer my question. Why you so sure she want to marry—

—She do. Lou Jay, she *do.* You know Renee always liked me! Anyway her mama said she better and Renee ain't gone hardly go against her mama.

—She can't—she can't do nothing to get rid—

—Hell, no, Lou Jay! What you saying? If she even opened up her mouth to say something like that Miss Gaines would kill her with the switch before she could even say jump up. And Daddy—I don't even want think about what Daddy would do. Besides, we ain't got all that kinda money. I don't even know where we could get one. We ain't never known nobody who did that.

—Far as we know.

—Far enough.

—Goddamn! Her mama, your daddy . . . — Falling silent once more. Turning his eyes down to Ricky's hands at rest between them on the sheet.

—I just don't see that y'all got much choice now. You know Daddy Malcolm ain't playing. I think he *would* rather see you dead. He don't want him no sissy son no matter what. And Renee gone have you a kid. You gone be a daddy.—Pausing. Those eyes raised again to Ricky's face.

—How could y'all do that? Practically right in my face.

—Lou Jay—

—You wasn't even thinking about us when you did that, Ricky. You wasn't thinking about Renee, neither. No you wasn't. And all this time you and me been making plans and whatnot. Talking shit. And now you gone come back *in* my face telling me you *love* me and how we gone do so *much*.

—Baby—

—I shoulda—I . . . that was just stupid, that's all. Don't look at me all innocent! Y'all was wrong. *You* was wrong—I can't really say too much against Renee. And I know you know y'all was wrong.—Pausing once more. Taking in the tender curve of the neck, eyelashes.

—I know you know, Rick.

—But I told you—

—You just wanted to see what it felt like? It ain't all that different. I coulda told you that.

—No, you couldn't.

—Well, maybe not.—Sucking on the cigarette.—But that don't change nothing. And now you gone have you a wife *and* a kid. I'll be damned. Ain't that something!

—Don't take the Lord's name—

—I didn't.—Smoking some more. Frowning.

—Lou Jay.

—What?

—You don't understand . . .

—What . . . what don't I under*stand?* Tell me! Since you got all the answers.

—Just . . . damn, Lou Jay! She don't mean nothing to me. She ain't—she ain't shit.

—I told you to get your hands off me. Oh, so now she ain't shit, huh? That's nice. Real nice, baby. You the one, I tell you.

—What you mean?

—She our friend, you dumb mother—Jesus! We all growed up together, you and me and Miss Girl, fool! That oughta mean something. Like more than just she ain't shit. I got to say I feel kinda sorry for her, laying up in bed with somebody she don't even know don't want her ass cept for what she got tween her legs.—Still watching Ricky, of course still watching him. Feeling the sadness rising up in him again, in that place, like the peepers' dying sundown calls: there, right at the edge of the shore, where most of the time he feels, deep inside, only Ricky. Then gathering all of it, the dusk and the shore, as they rise out of him, hover between them, joined by that lonely something else of lowered eyes, as Ricky moves closer to him on the bed. Putting first one hand, then another, on those big old shoulders. As Lou Jay rests his cheek on one of the hands. Closes his eyes.

—You know what the worse part is, Lou?

—What?

—It's like now—now I feel like—

—Yeah?

—Like I hate her. Renee.—Whispered.

—Like—like I ain't never hate nobody in my life—not no girl, and—
The eyes, opened.

—I know, I know. Don't look at me like that, Lou Jay! You know what—

—What you saying?

—I—I don't know. I don't know why cept I know I been laying up in bed at night thinking about how much I—
Lou Jay looking at him.

— . . . how I hate that girl now, Lou. Can't even stand to look in her face no more. That—
Lou Jay looking at him.

—Don't look at me like that, Lou Jay! I can't—

—I guess you want me to say something.

—I can't—

—What you going on hating her for? *She* ain't done nothing to you. Last time I heard takes two to make a baby. And she settin up in that house knowing she gone have you a kid and her mama looking at her all cross-eyed and you settin up here talking about some you hate her. What you doing hating folks?

—You don't like her neither.

—I don't like what y'all did but I don't hate nobody. I hope.

—She so proud, walking around telling everybody, "Yup, we getting married!" Just yesterday she was up the road telling folks, "He so fine, wait til y'all see him in his wedding suit."

—Well, you are.—Very quietly. *But I swear to God I won't never tell you that too many times,* he thinks, *'cause you just too hardheaded for words.*

—Uh-huh. But just watch me wear some tennis shoes to the church.

The other silent.

—Why can't we go away, Lou? Up to New York—even Atlanta! What I'ma do, married to some—

—What you did the night you got you a baby.

—Lou Jay—

—You do what you got to do. Like I'm going on to college. U.A.'s waiting.

—You really gone do that, Lou? Go on and leave me here with her and Daddy?

—You left me.

—I didn't! Listen, Lou. Listen to me. Whyn't you leave Alabama for school so we could go away? I could work.

—And get Daddy Malcolm up on my ass to come on and shoot me dead. Uh-*uh.* No, thank you.

—Coward.

—No. See, now, listen. Try I don't want your mess all up in my business, fucking with my shit again. Try that.

—Oh, bitch—

—No, baby, no. We ain't gone have that, now. Didn't I tell you how long ago now to go on and get dressed? You gone stick around here all day, when you getting married in—what is it now—twenty-two hours? Besides, Mama and Daddy'll be back in a few.

—Where they went to?

—Probably out with your daddy, looking for your ass. You need to go on home.

—They know what we was doing last night?

—When did we ever tell em? Do they *know.* Do they *know.*— The disgust in his face and voice cruel enough to slash cane. Hiding from the slash or seeking to conjure the face of the water and the reeds, Ricky put his own face in his hands.

—So I'm just gone ruin my life, and you ain't gone do shit to help.— From between fingers.

—Help you ruin your life? You don't need no help. Gimme one a your cigarettes.

—I ain't got but two left. You don't even care, do you? Bitch?

—Excuse me? Ain't nobody your bitch up in here. I got to buy me some.

—I said, you don't even *care*, do you?

—I heard you. What you expect? You want me to drop dead?

—Whyn't you try? Ricky said, but the laughter returned. Later, Lou Jay would remember that just then he had noticed neither the glimmer in Ricky's eye nor its presaging the speed that followed as, with the barest shifting of a thigh, Ricky leaped onto Lou Jay's chest and farted loudly and squarely on the most sacred spot, just below the neck. A way of possessing it, the victor knows; the surest way of leaving behind his most private smell where before only the mouth and skin had been. Then feeling the strong hands attempting to push him off, but the feeling of those fingers about his hips once more, even in protest, nothing compared to the victim's grimace and the victor's delight.

—Now see if I give a fuck about some Renee, Ricky said, purring—for, like many, the foul gifts of his own innards entranced him.

—Well, thank you, you nasty—

—Aw, you love it, honey.

—Take your hand off me.

—Lou—

—Come *on.*

Ricky moving lower over him, then closer.

—Let's just run away.— Whispered.

—Aw, shit. Here we go again. I swear—

—You could cook. Make me chicken in dressing. Pear preserves and biscuits. In our own house. You could cook, Lou Jay.

—I know I can.— The beautiful smile at last emerging in full.—Did I or did I not ask you for a cigarette?

A reach over to the table, a cigarette pulled from the pack. Lit, then placed, ever so gently, into that mouth.

—See, Lou, I could light your cigarettes for you.

—Uh-huh.

—We could get married.

—Boys don't *get* married. To each other.

—You need to look at the news, girl. Boys be marrying each other up in Oregon—

—I ain't moving to no Oregon. And if it's boys marrying each other, you know it's white boys.

—Or in California where it don't matter. Where don't nobody know nobody.

—Fuck that bullshit. U.A. U.A. You got it? September, now!

—Why you acting like—damn, hold still, boy! Can't I even get me a kiss? What you scrunching up your mouth all stupid for?

—You got your kisses from Miss Renee.

—Lou Jay—goddamn!—I told you—

—Speak the truth and shame the devil. Now! Tell your Daddy I said that.

Ricky silent. Watching those lips move over the cigarette.

—It ain't even like that, Lou.—Very quietly.—You know I just—

—It's time for you to go. Now I ain't—

—I'm serious. You think I'm playing?

—I'ma say one more time—

—Just one kiss, baby. Please? Then I'll go on. Please? Open up.

This is *one hardheaded fool,* the other thinks, the kind that sooner or later—

—Don't you love me, Lou Jay?

A look at those eyes, asking; a look away. And now Lou Jay, lying on his back, feeling what's on the way, doesn't have to say anything, not a word or even a tune, because it's all there—yes, right there beneath the watcher's curling lashes that match his own, there in the neck's curve, where the veins are exposed, where the look is hot silk, *where you can't even hardly stop it cause you are.*

—What you doing, Rick?—But all at once his voice is all water.

—Get up offa me, he says, but how the silt of the smooth river glides, glides across his moving sand.

—You can't say nothing now, Ricky says, sucking air where there is none.

—Get your hand out from all up under me, Lou Jay whispers, but how the waters have already parted, a circle of ripples pushing gently where the weeds are thickest.

—Ain't nobody gone be back for a while, neither, Ricky says, wetting his face where it is warm.

—See if I marry that girl.—Straining the weeds, the soft grasses, through his teeth.

You will if your daddy makes you, Lou Jay thinks, running his fingers up and down, up and down a single blade.

The bugs, still conversing. The jaybirds, over the water, darting. Everywhere blue, black to blue, blueblue.

Renee will be there soon. Lou Jay, remembering. But moving now faster against the weeds, pushing more deeply into the sand, up to his buckling knees, until the entire river, its source and moan, rises and swells, swells and flows, wetting his sand, soaking his weeds. Filling every space of that warmth in his open throat.

—A beautiful dress,—she was saying. The three of them walking out along the Stone Bridge Road that led down the long hill to the Creek Meadow valley just outside of town. And she *was* pretty, Lou Jay had to admit—the type who surprised you with that devil in her that came out when you least expected it. And when you most expected it because it didn't. The Gaines' least favorite girl, folks in town said, who from the looks of things spent half her time daydreaming and should have been quicker than she apparently was considering she was Elvira Gaines' girl, since you could see Elvira had known quick enough to get Renee off her hands and into Ricky's, whose daddy owned not only twenty acres here in town but fifty more too up around Decatur *and* his own house and business and had those seven boys, six of whom had already come close to doing the same. Nice girl, everybody said, but looked simple sometimes, too, like them Birthwright brothers up on the hill who fooled away the day playing with cats and whatnot—the kind who ought to see things she needed to and didn't, things that sure enough, please, Jesus! didn't bear mentioning. But then others said no, not simple just innocent—who wouldn't be, by force or His holy reckoning, raised under Elvira's switch? A few to whom almost nobody listened said naw, that girl was *deep* if you just looked. And—who knows?—maybe with that fury (the source of which they'd quickly forgotten or had never known) that in ever-shifting forms still took nightly and daily aim against them even as they slept, and which now firmly in their grip propelled them to devote the meaner, smaller parts of themselves to caring too much about some things, like the image of two boys pressing hands to each other's bellies in the slow velvet dance of a kiss—maybe with that same fury that moved them to cut their eyes and storm over policemen's bullets and marauding church fires in their midst, they'd never bothered to look very deeply into the most quiet part of that girl's eyes—or not far, anyway, beyond so many guesses as to the eventual worth of that girl and her kind as sweet fast pieces. Her gaze darker, deeper than ever today. Skin shining in the heat, hair permed and tied back in just that way that made so many of the other boys in town think nothing of going right up in her face to whoo-zop a little of the Bird they hadn't known they'd owned, za-bazz out some of the 'Trane they'd not suspected still seared in their veins, and say Miss Renee, hey, hey! All right, girl. 'Cause, well, uh huh. So, why don't you. And. Not that she couldn't handle them, Lou Jay thought. And Daddy Malcolm too had welcomed her into the Malcolms' with wide-open arms (a little too open, some said) because he'd always loved her anyway (a little too much, some also said)—like the daughter I ain't got, he'd said more than six times, and loved her even more these days, some folks murmured, now that she was marrying his baby son. Everybody swears Miss Renee got herself a man, Lou Jay thought, but I had him first, y'all, in places y'all couldn't even *dream* of. Shocked at how much it scratched at his heart to think of them having a baby together—what was a little baby, after all? But scratched even more to think of it now because they'd all been friends and he wanted them all still to be so long as he could just have Ricky and they could get far away from here and everybody and get that house, something, someday. Away. And none of it fair to her neither, he thought. She hadn't never hurt nobody, not once. But even harder now for him to like her when he almost wanted to. When the wedding was getting closer and they all were together here talking about (but what? please, Jesus) her wedding dress. Ricky! he cried out silently, what we gone do, Rick? Distant field noises coming drowsily across to them in the mid-afternoon heat. Lou Jay's parents having returned from visiting somebody's sick wife, and Renee come looking for Ricky (where else but at his best friend's? Boys would be just like that, getting married and couldn't care less about tomorrow). The Stone Bridge Road walk had seemed to suit all but the soon-groom. He would fidget, the other two thought, and be his sillyass self, but why looking evermore like he wanted to kill somebody?

—What's wrong with you, Ricky? What you looking at Lou Jay all evil for?

—Nothing.—Skipping stones in front of his shoes on the road.

—I ain't paying him no mind.

—Go on ahead of us, Lou Jay. Me and Ricky got to talk about something for a minute. In *private.*—Raising her eyebrows at Lou Jay and jerking her head toward the road ahead of them. The two young men exchanged startled looks.

—Anything you got to say to me Lou Jay could hear, Renee. I don't know what you got to say that could be so—

—Let me go on, y'all, Lou Jay said quickly. Moving ahead.—I'll wait for y'all on up some.—He was already gone by the time Ricky opened his mouth to protest, then turned back to face Renee standing in the road; her face grave, upturned to the source of light. The light in her eyes not golden, the face not smiling.

—Well, what?

Her eyes, looking at him.

—Well?

—What you taking that tone with me for, Ricky? You acting like somebody did something evil to you. What's wrong with you?

—Just tell me what you got to say, Renee. It's hot out here.

And there's so much he don't even know, she thinks. That he won't ever know.

—Well . . . —A pause.

—Yes?

—I just . . . I just wanted to say I hope everything's gone go all right tomorrow—

—What you mean, go right?

—Just what I said.—Pausing once more. Continuing:

—I mean I hope you show up on time like Daddy Malcolm said you would and don't come in the church looking all evil like you looking now. Mama and Daddy gone be settin' right up in front with your mama and Daddy Malcolm and we don't need to have no kinda fuss. Mama picked out my dress and Daddy Malcolm paid for it, so that's that. I guess you know all that anyway. I know you're nervous, but I'm nervous, too. You acting like you the only one. But don't forget—I'm the one's having the baby!

—Girl, you don't even . . .

—Listen! This ain't no joke, Ricky. You think I ain't scared too with a baby coming? I ain't never had no baby. I ain't even so sure I want one, to tell you the truth. I don't know. But we gone have one and that's why we getting married.—Stopping then to look at him with those eyes suddenly filled with dark birds in rapid flight through a country he'd never known— or had never wanted to know.

—Renee—

—You listen to me, Ricky. I got a lot to say and I don't know if I'm gone be able to say it straight out like this again.—Her feet planted squarely on the road's dry, hard, sun-baked earth. Looking almost as if she will rise into that other country from which her own voice seems to be coming, thinking. But this can't be me talking like this, not to him, not to nobody, who ever gave me the—? *Or did I always*—? But maybe too scary, right now, even to think. Rising into the sky might be easier than continuing to speak, continuing to look at him burning at her that way as the brids race through her eyes, their wings' beating her own secret desire to soar with them, so secret even she is unaware of it, *how could such a soaring ever take place?* she does not quite think but senses. Senses that the question itself is rarely, if ever, permitted, at least (but why?) to her; that the freedom to dream in a language of wings, if that is what freedom is, to fly, the sort of freedom her almost-but-not-quite dreams intone—such freedom truly must be a journey, must lead to grace. Petite, pretty girl on a country road. Hair tied back, lips parted to speak or to fly and so much, so much now and always, an entire world and beyond in her eyes. Now speaking from that place where she continues to stand, knowing that it is in fact her own voice she hears, her own words and the wings between them, as the words' weight and her feet so planted continue to pull her down into another vital yet hidden part of herself—a small, reaching figure outlined and illumined in the merciless sun.

—It's like I been thinking . . . —Her voice almost gentle.—You said one time—only one time, Ricky, that you loved me. But I know just like I got two eyes in my head that you ain't been showing me that side much lately.

Daddy Malcolm's been real nice to me like always. Why can't you act right? You got the same face like your daddy but you don't act nothing like him.

—Renee . . .

—I ain't finished. Just listen. You got to understand something, Ricky. I don't want nobody in this town talking about you and me and our business. One thing I can't stand is a bunch of *nosy*— . . . The vehemence in her voice halting him.

—Renee—

—No. No. Let me tell you. Already somebody come up to Mama saying something about how it must be hard to have a fast girl in the house and how still waters run deep and all a that. Mama picked up the switch so fast I ain't even know what hit me. She said she ain't raised no fast girl for folks to laugh at and I know I don't want nobody laughing at me or you neither. So I'm just saying we gone have this baby and live right and since you gone be a daddy I hope you know we ain't gone have time for you to be running all over town with Lou Jay like y'all ain't got nothing better to do.

—Renee, lemme tell you something . . .

—Hold on, Ricky. Whyn't you listen for a minute? I'm just saying we could all still be friends and whatnot but he *is* going off to college and you and me gone have to get jobs and work, you hear? Cause I ain't about to put this baby off on Mama so she could take up the switch on me again and tell me something about how it's time I acted grown. We can all still have fun and get together but we—we gone have to be *responsible*. That's what Mama been telling me all along and I think she right.

The birds fluttering, settling. A new fear creeping into the spaces between their wings.

—I ain't gone feel that switch no more, Ricky.— A small, quiet voice.

—Renee—

—I ain't, Ricky. And, see, I'm not my mama, neither. I'm me. You know? I mean, *me*. And *me*, I mean me and you, *we* ain't gone use no switch on this baby. No, we not.

Opening his mouth to speak but the sweep of those birds stopping him.

—Don't say nothing to me while you still looking all evil, Ricky. Just come on.— As she turns and walks up the road, shoulders a little lower than before, he doesn't see the falling birds beginning to die in her eyes. As he follows with that slow dull heat that begins in his ears and continues on creeping down into what still feels like his neck. When they catch up, Lou Jay will look back at him, see that new (but what is it?) searing out of his eyes, and turn quickly to her. Will put his almost-burly arm through her fine-boned one and say:

—What about that dress, girl?— Pulling her forward.— What was you saying?

—Y'all got to see it. It's got satin—wait'll y'all see it!—satin ruffles. And—

—It's bad luck to see it til I marry you.— Gazing off toward some white houses on one of the surrounding hills.

—Well, excuse me, you ain't gone see me *in* it til tomorrow. Didn't I already say—

—Don't pay him no mind, Renee.— Shooting Ricky a Don't you start no mess out here! look. Behind Renee's back, Ricky grabbing his own crotch. Flicking Lou Jay the finger.

—You gone act right today or what, Ricky?— Over her shoulder, walking on.

—I got a headache.— Renee missing the kick he aimed just then at Lou Jay's behind.

—Well, don't talk then.

—Go on, Renee.— Smiling so that only Ricky can see.

Smiling, the other thinks. But not smiling that day when I asked you why, Daddy. Why, and you saying 'Cause that's what you gone do, boy. Nothing else. I know you know why so don't be asking. You man enough to put a baby in her, you gone be man enough to marry her. You *will* marry her.

But I don't want to, Daddy. I—I can't. I don't—

Why *can't* you? Why don't you *want* to? Boy, don't be telling me nothing that's gone make me kill you up in here.

Would y'all quit that fussing and come on.

Mama. Mama, talk to Daddy.

What you want me to say, baby?

Quit crying, now! Quit crying!—you little asslicking sissy-ass. I wouldn't even call you my own. You think I don't know? You my own and you done shamed me. Shamed me!

Daddy, don't hit me! Don't—

I'll kill you.

But didn't say all that. Even though he did hit me we ain't said all that. But we should've. We should've so I coulda known sooner he did hate me. You. You hate me and him. But I just want him. And I don't give a fuck cause we gone get the hell outa here anyway no matter what and buy us a piece of something someplace no matter what 'cause it don't matter what you say you ain't never gone make me marry no girl, Daddy. You could kill me if you want to. You could try. You could just try.

And she told her mama but ain't told her daddy she got a baby in her. Didn't mind telling my daddy but she ain't told her own. Maybe I could blackmail her. I got less than a day.

But now he sees the car coming down the road toward them. Raising dust clouds, an air-wake in the bright distance. The enveloping heat, disturbed, breaking into shimmers. The dust after a moment circling back on itself, settling on the thick grass, on the leaves of the heavy dark pecan trees along the road.

—That's Daddy Malcolm's car, Rick.—Lou Jay, seeming prepared to run.

—Not his daddy—my father-in-law, Renee corrected him.

—Not yet.—Ricky threw a stone over her head.

—Since when y'all got a station wagon?—Lou Jay looking from Ricky to her.

—Since you know when.

—Maybe he could buy us one.—The snort from behind her that followed her words not reaching her ears.

The car pulling up to them. Ricky's father, sticking his head out.

—Well, what we got here? Three pretty rats.

—Sir.—Lou Jay, not looking.

—Daddy Malcolm.—Renee, moving closer.

—You—to Ricky—you ain't got nothing to say to your daddy, boy?

Something just beneath the surface of his father's face swiftly urged the bloodsnarl trembling in Ricky's throat to a mumble that, in the wavering heat, passed well enough for respect.

—*Sir.*

—Uh huh. And so now where you all walking to?

—No place.—Her voice low as she cast a brief glance at Ricky.—You know we got rehearsal in a little bit. You coming, Daddy Malcolm?

—Church be too hot for rehearsal now.

—We know. Later on this afternoon, we going.

The gray or heavy thing beneath Mr. Malcolm's face softened into a smile before he glanced back at Lou Jay.—That sounds better. Just call me when. I got to bring the preacher.—Sharpening his gaze on Lou Jay.—And you, boy—

—Sir?

—Guess you must be fittin to go off to U.A.—Moving something on his lap.

—Yes, sir.

—You won't be coming back too much, then—this summer's the last we gone see of you. You'll be so *busy.*

—Maybe.

—Ain't no maybe about it.— Pulling up into view a long, shiny rifle he'd been holding out of their sight on his lap.

—Ain't she good-looking?— A smile.—I'm fittin' to get me some hunting.—Patting the rifle fondly, looking from Lou Jay to his son, smiling at their unsmiles.

—I could knock off something *big* with this.

—You could shoot us something.— Moving closer to the smiling face until Ricky's hand reached out for, tightened around, hers.

—Honey, I'd shoot anything for you, looking so pretty. We know why, boys, don't we?

Dust, heavy things, silence. A memory of birds, rivers, blue things. The two young men unsmiling, wordless.

—Got to say, Lou boy, nice to see you talking so sweet with a girl—even my son's fiancee. Ricky!

—What?— Slow steps forward from where he'd been pulling leaves off a few bushes on the other side of the road. Lou Jay and Renee walking farther down the road to stand in the shade.

—Don't you *what* me.

His son silent.

—Come closer, boy.

His father's eyes, burning into him.

The older man looking straight into his son's eyes to say:

—I know you member what we talked about.

—Daddy—

—Seven sons,— his father continues, a sudden bitterness hardening that deep voice,—seven sons and my baby son gone leave us tomorrow to take him a wife. Thank you, Jesus! he shouts, shattering the stillness beneath the trees. Looking about as if expecting Christ to come down off the cross, then driving that hot gaze toward his son. Only then does Ricky see the face that had stormed, kissed, wept over, sang to and cajoled him through the years in that house they lived in up on the hill change in that very second into something utterly destroyed, like the face of a person in flames—a face all at once of hideous suffering. Melting, shifting, a face of pure rage and something else, unspeakable: what in that moment the witness knows has been familiar to him all his life, throughout every cold space back of communal keening, visions of dark birds in someone else's eyes, beneath blue things lurking in rivers and deep within his own frightened silences—a face offering no escape for itself or anyone. In that collapsed minute he sees in the face too much like his own every twisted face that once torched barns and left fiery crosses in their place, faces that have stalked his dreams; then the face of every corn-whiskey peckerwood coon hunter; then all the faces before his time and of it, that above jeers and fire had strung up heavy women and ripped out their insides, to crush beneath the heel the dreaded commingled issue so desired and despised. *Daddy*. Backing away in horror from the face as he feels himself drawn with a greater fearful yearning than ever before for who and what he is sure, this time, are behind it—the strange human power or just the pain, in the body of a man or a lurching, broke-spirited god. And then in that other very old language which possesses no words but only the power of harsh vision and the brute killing force of pain—a kick to the stomach, a sharp knife to the groin—he knows that the terrible something inside himself that burns what he feels for her, for *her*—maybe just something like hate itself, looking for an easy place to settle and spit—forms part of this face, corners its edges; as he knows too where sensation blows cold and fierce enough to slay everything that all faces of this face were devised long ago, in three (or two, or four, or eight hundred) closed moments of the most deadly cunning, silence. Sensing all at once a weakening in his knees that feels as though—yes, as though it's accusing him of something. Backing away still further from the face. But it continues to speak.

—You mind you tell Satan to get behind you, boy,— it hisses, —for the rest of your days on Earth. You hear?

The faces staring at each other in the heat.

Then the older face is gone. Become Daddy Malcolm again, same as before.

—Lou Jay! Renee!— Mr. Malcolm, shouting. —Y'all come on over here now.

The two of them running over, sweat-faced. Lou Jay not looking at Ricky.

—I know y'all gone get to the church on time. Mind, now.

With one sharp movement, Ricky turned away to face Renee. And she ain't even nowhere near ugly, he thought, I wish I could say I did like girl-pussy.

—I got to tell you something.— Looking her straight in the face.

His father raising the gun. Lou Jay's eyes opening wide.

—What, Ricky?— The birds gone from her eyes, now reflecting back only the stone certainties of the future.

Daddy Malcolm's gun pointed directly at his son's back. A click from the trigger.

Ricky turning. Gazing at his father.

—You really would, wouldn't you.

The face emerges once more, but by the time the skin has finished its shifting and melting the scream strangled in Ricky's throat has risen up into his head, to remain there.

—He would what?— Only Ricky's body preventing her from seeing where the gun is aimed.

—I would love to see my son get married tomorrow. Y'all know Ricky's my baby son. Seven boys, six married, tomorrow the last one. And it's gone happen, too. So nice to see young people loving each other, living a normal life. Lou Jay!

—Sir?— Lou Jay's voice thick through the clustered reeds in his chest. In that moment looking exactly like what he had never been known to be in that town: completely stupid.

—We will miss you, boy.— The gun lowered. The look on Ricky's face unchanged. Renee looking off into the distance with what none of them can yet know—a memory of dark birds from another country dying at her feet. Nice-looking girl, the older man reflects, and a shame, only seventeen in two months, she coulda saved it for a real man.

—Yes, sir. Thank you.— Backing away as the car slowly begins to move off. As it runs right over where he'd been standing.

—I'll be with your mama and daddy for a while, Renee. Y'all don't forget—later at the church.

—We won't! she screams, but the car has gone. —What's wrong, Ricky?

No answer. Trembling in spite of the intense heat, he turns to Lou Jay, says:

—You coming?

Lou Jay also shaking. Hands stuck in pockets. The shoulders stiff.

—Nope. I need to get back. I got things to—

—Wait a minute. Am I gone see you after the wedding?

—You gone see him later, Ricky! What you—

—Don't say nothing, Renee, fore we get into a fuss. Am I gone see you after?

—Ricky, your daddy—you saw—

—I asked you something.

—Well, sure, you gone see me. I live here, don't I?

—That's right.— Her voice still low. —And Lou Jay, if you—

—Renee, shut up.— I'll knock you down in a second, he thinks, but only Lou Jay can see how she is staring now at the face none of them had ever glimpsed in the man who must soon be her husband.

—I asked you, am I gone see you? I mean *see* you.—Hands folded into tight purple fists.

—Ricky—

—I got to see you, Lou Jay! You don't know—

—Ricky, now—

—Tell me!

—I got to go, y'all. I'll see y'all in the church.

—Lou Jay!

—Bye.

—Lou!

—Bye, Ricky.—Walking off quickly up the road in the direction from which they'd all walked earlier. The air becoming cooler as he mounted the hill—and strange, he would think later, because there wasn't hardly no shade up there, after all.

Feeling Ricky's stare burning into him all the way up the hill, until he rounded the curve near the higher meadow that bordered the farm-fields where there should have been a gentle breeze and wasn't. Recalling the horrible burn, like the feeling, he'd received only once in his young life, when he'd put the wrong finger at the wrong time into a beaker of hydrochloric acid in high school biology lab. The finger hadn't ever been the same, not really. One of the fingers he would need to write postcards from Birmingham, like those pasted on his bedroom wall, if he could find them on that campus seen only once. But Birmingham was far enough away . . .

When, just as he finished rounding the curve, he heard the screams far below and behind him, he ran all the way back to the part of the road where there was a view right down the steep slope into the Meadow valley. He saw Renee. Down in the dirt on the side of the road. And saw Ricky, pulling her hair and kicking her all around, especially in her stomach. Saw her bleeding, spitting up blood. Saw how she tried to get up, and how Ricky punched her hard, right in the mouth, then kicked her in the side of her head. Again. And again. Even from that distance, perhaps because of the day's still heat, the sounds seemed audible for miles. Soft, wet noises. Thinking, before his mind began to scream along with Renee, that to some people there was no better proof of love than that.

—Ricky! he screamed, running as fast as he could down the hill,—Ricky, stop! You want your daddy to kill me? You fittin' to get you and me killed! I got to go to college! You gone kill your own child, Ricky! You gone be a daddy! That's Renee you beating on! We all friends! Ricky! You hear me? You can't go beating up on no girl like that! Stop that now fore you kill Renee!—Then feeling his heart chugging up inside him in the way of the heart attack that had been predicted for him before he reached forty, just like his daddy. But still he couldn't stop, not even when one dark bird and then another and then still another flew out of nowhere right into his face and he fell flat on his behind in the road, tumbling over and over on those sharp little stones until he raised himself in the dust to see the blood and dirt on his hands and forearms as he tasted it in his mouth and felt it warm and sticky and dirt-smeared all over his face. Thinking that it was, yes, Mama, like he couldn't even taste or feel Ricky in that private place inside him anymore, *Then take me now, Lord,* or the water and the reeds, *and wash me, Jesus,* or the sand and the soft soft grasses, *and O shall come on a cloud descending,* but could only sense that big new bitter taste, *that* one, inside every part of him that he knew he shared with the one who knew it all and had been all up inside it and back around, cause *thou art the light, cause I ain't never wanted nobody else not nobody but you,* cause *I feel a fire in me, Lord, when I see you riding up this way, but O your daddy learned you good and you ain't know til now how good did you,* he thought, flying: knowing that it was that terror and all before it back to the time of the holy rider and his blazing flight unto the fiery angels and their swords and light that were lifting him now, exploding in sharp fragments inside him as he ran and felt the sun and the sweat on his back and the familiar blood on his face, as just then and for the rest of his descent a million dark birds released from dreams charged blindly up into the sky turned a deeper red with the heat of the day, as each eye of that face came out to look at them and score into them the curling marks once recognized in blistered skin—right there, where the prophets spoke in flaming tongues, the flier knew, and where the first words of their lasting flame were always, before anything anyone could call truth or love, just plain old hurting sorrow.

Black and Boo

BY MICHAEL KAYODE

Sandwiched between undulating and chaotic vehemence to his left, stiff machismo to his right and the swirl of voices off of the TV screen Black sat his mind churning.

Sergio was the vehemence. He'd an attitude all day, refusing to share with anyone what was bothering him. He was funny like that sometimes, just let it things burn him up until a channel for release came along, like a tarantula still and observant waiting for the perfect prey. He'd spent the better part of the day wiping stains off of his brand new red and white Jordan's with his hand. A long plain white shirt exposed the contours of his gangly frame and blue jean shorts stopped at the base of his calf. They hung over three pairs of fresh slouch socks.

The stiff machismo was Sam. Sam was a twenty-two-year-old neighborhood dude. He was dark skinned and wore a plain black baseball cap over his closely tapered fade. He rarely smiled or showed any emotion for that matter. He always acted like he was being watched. Although his movements were sudden and mechanical, his hands always stayed in a defined position. Either one was clenched in a fist and sat in the palm of the other or it stroked his chin hairs as he supported his elbow in his palm.

Dink was the 4th member of the gang He & Dink had known each other for a long time but they just started hanging tough in the last couple of months.

They were passing around a blunt, which Dink had taken into the kitchen with him. Although it was very hot outside, the temperature was cool in Dink's three-bedroom apartment at the bottom of Maryland Avenue. His building sat in a lowland about one hundred feet away from Langston Hughes golf course. Under the dim ceiling lights the television provided most of the rooms' illumination, as well as serving as the center of attention. The group had gravitated towards the black, hard plastic, twenty-five-inch monitor that was rounded on the corners, behaving like giant gnats with the TV as an equally large porch light. It sat like a monument to procrastination under a thick cloud of marijuana and boat smoke.

Earlier in the day they smoked a blunt of boat: mint leaves wet down with embalming fluid. Sitting sat around the kitchen table, the sun casting a bright rectangular ray on the flowery table cloth, Dink had asked Black if he'd ever smoked boat.

Black had looked across the table at the stony expression on Sam's face and unflinchingly told Dink a bold faced lie which he'd instantly regretted. He wasn't a liar. He might lie to his mother to avoid chastisement, but he didn't lie to his friends. Well, there was that one time a couple of years back before he lost his virginity when he told them he'd had sex. This time he'd concluded it had either been an attempt to impress Sam or to have one up on Sergio. Sergio However, knew he hadn't smoked boat, unless he'd done so in the two weeks since their conversation where he said that he hadn't.

Regardless, Black had wrinkled his face and disdainfully spat, "Yeah man, come on," his voice morphing from his usual bass laden tone to a high pitched whine as he spoke.

Dink had looked in Black's eyes, inhaled what seemed like all of the oxygen in the room and said, "Aiight," then heavily exhaled.

He'd then exchanged a meaningful eye contact with Sam, who he sometimes referred to as Sam-Sam, and continued rolling the blunt. Sergio, facing the wall with his fingers interlocked and his forearms resting on the corner of the table, he nodded his head in a rhythmical motion to the sound of Tupac's "Come with Me." During the brief silence that followed Dink's statement, he'd restlessly squirmed in his seat, his feet unconsciously shifting towards the front door.

"I know you smoked boat before," Dink had blurted as he looked at Sergio.

He was licking the blunt and his head was bowed so his eyeballs rolled to the top of his sockets. Sergio looked straight at Dink.

"Yeah, young. Why don't you hurry up and light that shit," said Sergio.

This was his way. To recklessly attack a situation when he felt threatened or challenged. Dink heeded his words and lit the blunt, then passed it across the table to Sergio, breaking the rotation. The rotation was the rule that the blunt was to travel either clockwise or counter clockwise. Sergio placed it in the small opening between his lips and vacuumed in the smoke, then immediately coughed the smoke back out stirring up riotous laughter amongst the group. Black' made sure his laugh was the softest. In fact he smiled more than laughed. Surprisingly Sergio didn't try to save face, just gathered himself as the laughter simmered down to chuckles and took another pull. This time it was a baby pull. Still the fumes irritated his throat. He caught his cough in his mouth but his body jerked as a cause of it. This was also funny to the guys. He looked like a young Dizzy Gillespie.

Black also knew that if he inhaled deeply he would cough, because he occasionally coughed when smoking good weed. Taking the blunt, he asked it into an simply soda can to his right while he devised a way to make it appear that he wasn't the novice Sergio revealed himself to be. Then He inhaled the smoke into his mouth but used his tongue to cut off the channel to his esophagus. After swallowing the smoke like a sip of fluid he hastily expelled it through his nostrils. Then ashed it again, giving himself time to absorb the dry chemically saturated taste. It didn't taste like weed. It tasted like wrapping your lips around the exhaust pipes of a Metro bus as it pulled away from the curb. He put the blunt in his mouth and cautiously inhaled at an even slower rate. The entire time he kept his eyes fixed on the cherry. Once it flared up and burned the blunt he stopped, then opened his eyes wide as he held the smoke in the pit of his mouth before blowing it out like a kiss. He passed the blunt across the table to Sam. The movement made his head feel woozy. His arm felt like it was moving in slow motion. Tupac sounded like he was defending him as he berated his enemies with verbal taunts. He sat back flushed with the feeling of accomplishment. Mission accomplished, he thought they laughed when Sergio smoked but didn't when I did.

Now, hours later, he was close to sleep, but just as he was about to doze off he was awakened by Boo's whiney voice. His eyes met hers as soon as they opened. She was smiling and standing over him with her left hand on her hip. He could tell she'd been getting some sun because her skin was a nice dark, smooth syrupy color. Her hair was tied in a ponytail with a black rubber band She was looking very sexy in some skin tight sky blue jeans that hugged her from black belt with square silver ornaments to ankles. She wore an equally tight tank top tucked into her jeans. Her round breasts poking out created an erotic fervor in Black's heart. The tank top was so tight it revealed the contours of her bra from the shoulder straps to the lining. Her nipples pointed straight at him.

"One of y'all gotta walk with me to take Shontay home," she demanded.

Shontay hovered near the door. She wore some tight black jeans and a red shirt with a leather coat. She was a honey-complexioned girl with short frizzy hair, sodden with gel. Because she had a little weight on her she stood with her back to the wall hiding her wide butt. Black figured Boo befriended the girl because she wouldn't compete with her for any boys.

Black looked around. Sergio was seated to the left of Black eyeing Boo hungrily.

"I'll go wit y'all," Sergio offered enthusiastically.

"Nah, you aiight, you was watching the movie," said Boo. "Go head and watch your movie. Come on, Black, go with us. You ain't doin' nothin'," she whined as she gently kicked his foot.

"Go 'head, young," exclaimed Black as he kicked her back. Every time he and Boo where in each other's presence they bickered like first graders trying to hide the fact that they liked one another.

I mean she cute and all but she too silly. She definitely gettin' phat, I'll give her that, but I don't wanna fuck wit her. I'll find a reason not to fuck with her. Sometimes it's because she's Dink's peoples, then because she too fuckin' annoyin'. Both my brother and Dink be tellin' me I should go head and fuck her. It's like when somethin' be real easy I don't be wantin' to do it. I don't know, that's just me. I like hard shit. If nobody think I can do it, then that's what I'm a do. With her, if I give her what she want all she gonna do is want more and more. She asked me for a dollar one day and I slipped up and gave it to her. Now every time she sees me she ask me for a dollar. I don't hardly got it like that. Now if I don't go walk wif her to her friends house then she gonna try to make me feel bad. She good at makin' somethin' out of nothin'. She'll probably come back sayin' some strange man looked at her funny or some nigga grabbed her just to make me feel bad. Then she gonna hype it up like I'm being mean to her. For real, for real that's why I ain't got no time for her cause she too hype.

"Come on, Black, you not gonna do that for me?" moaned Boo.

When she got desperate her neck limply tilted to the side, her eyebrows arched inward and her lips poked out Black looked at Sam, then Sergio and let out a loud sigh. Boo reached down, grabbed his left arm and tugged on it. Black let his body go limp to provide the maximum resistance. He was only sixteen but at 5′ 11″, 186 pounds he was solid. Boo was grimacing her body in a tug of war stance as she pulled on his arm. Still he barely budged. Dink reentered the room & their eyes met and they simultaneously shook their heads.

"Please, Black", whined Boo in a phony innocent tone.

"Leave my company alone Boo," Dink said jokingly.

The only reason Dink was still standing was because he anticipated sitting on the cushion soon to be vacated by Black. He injected his comment with the intention of stirring things up. He knew how to manipulate Boo and vice versa. He'd been doing it all his life.

Boo turned to Dink while still tugging on Black's arm and said, "Ill, mind your business Dink. Ain't nobody worried about you."

"Aiight, aiight. Let me go first," reluctantly said Black.

"Nah, 'cause if I let go of your arm. All you gonna do is sit right back down," said Boo.

"No, I ain't," said Black.

"What's the difference? If you goin', you might as well get up now," said Boo.

Black knew Boo had no shame and she would go to any lengths to have her way. He began wondering whether his resistance was even worth it. After all, she had successfully disturbed his frame of mind.

"For real, let me go, young," Black shouted in a tone that made Boo's heart skip a beat.

"You comin', right?" said Boo.

Black responded with a stone-faced glare. Boo released his arm warily. Black nestled his rear end deep into the cushion and straightened his pants out with his hands. Then he gestured for Boo to move out of the way by waving his right hand to left, horizontally to the ground. Sergio covered his mouth with his left hand and chuckled. Dink shook his head. Black felt relieved when he heard the laughter. He didn't want to show any signs of succumbing to Boo even though he was. Boo's eyes tensed as if she'd been bitterly betrayed.

"Fuck you Black", said Boo.

As she marched toward the door all eyes, including Dink's, were on her butt cheeks as they swung back and forth. Her butt wasn't big—the cheeks were about the size of volleyballs—it was just right and she had great legs to go with it. In those tight jeans she was almost irresistible to the average man.

Black sighed heavily. Then slowly rose from the couch and walked behind her. Boo felt his presence. Turning her head to the side she gave him an over the shoulder evil eye. Black heard a chorus of "Aws," "Suckers" and various other jibes as he walked out the door behind the two girls.

The sun was setting in front of them as they walked up the hill toward Shontay's house. It left its heat behind as a parting gift. The sky was a three layered mesh of dark blue at the top, sky blue in the middle and fiery orange at the bottom. The evening crawled with life. The streetlights had just come on, voices of children and adults filled the air and sirens sounded faintly in the distance. Cars drove past blasting an assortment of urban tunes. Kids rolled by on bikes. Bands of children darted in the streets and through the courtyards between the buildings. There were small groups of teenage boys on almost every corner and in front of most buildings. Groups of females paced up and down the sidewalks wearing revealing, bright-colored clothes.

Boo was making a concerted effort to ignore Black. She walked along the wire fences with Shontay between them, milking the moment for all it was worth. Black could tell she wanted a formal apology from him for embarrassing her, but Black's take on the situation was that she had embarrassed herself.

Black began to lag a few feet behind wondering why he was walking with them. Boo peeked at him out of the corner of her eye. She didn't think he saw it, but he did. Then she steadily chirped in Shontay's ear about boys who liked her, and how she didn't know what to do. Many thoughts enter Black's mind. The dominating one was of Boo's ass. As much as he tried to look away, his eyes kept finding their way back. Passion invaded his body. He fought it off valiantly with thoughts of old experiences and images of other girls he viewed on the avenue.

His mind and body were in agreement that they wanted to have sex with Boo, but his spirit was still undecided. He could already envision having to talk on the phone with her every day or come over to visit her. And he didn't want to dog her because as much as she pissed him off, he genuinely liked her. Boo didn't have a boyfriend and in an unexplainable way he thought she was waiting for him. He was sure that if he came on to her she would melt like butter in a bowl of cream of wheat. He was confident that she would get hooked on the sex. He'd seen other guy's dicks in porno movies and in the showers at school. From this he'd concluded he had a bigger-than-average penis.

"Ill, why you walking back there?" Boo asked.

"Y'all talkin'. I ain't wanna interrupt. I thought you was mad at me or somethin'."

"Why? 'Cause you was showin' off for your friends?" said Boo. "I wasn't mad at you. You was just gettin' on my damn nerves."

"Psst. Man, I'm sorry," Black said in a staged somber tone. "I ain't know you thought I was showing off. Ill, what I'ma show off for them for, come on now. I was just smacked. For real for real."

"Nah, that's alright. You ain't gotta apologize. I know how you go now," said Boo.

"Whatever, young," said Black. "Go head."

They came to a busy intersection at the bottom of the hill, a divider marking the middle of the street. Cars zoomed past in six different directions. Buses moaned as they stopped and then started again. Across the street was another apartment complex. To the left and behind them was a shopping plaza. To the right was an imposing apartment building and a convenience store on an island. The signs lit up the night.

Standing at the corner they waited for the light to turn red or or for a break in the traffic, whichever came first. Black took a couple of steps into the street then stepped back on to the curb as a minivan rolled over the spot he'd just been standing in. Finally the light turned red and a caravan of cars came to a halt behind each other. They drift wove their wall through the thicket of vehicles, over the divider, and sprinted across the other side of the street as cars from the crossing streets turned onto the road. Boo gripped the back of Black's shirt, screaming jovially while Shontay waddled behind.

They hit the corner and walked down an eerily dark, desolate street. There were no streetlights. Fans and air conditioners hummed ominously. Large oak trees exploded out of plots on the sidewalk, their leaves twice as abundant on this street side because they naturally sought the illumination of the sun. The apartment buildings blocked the sun and on the left side of the street tall row houses did the same. The bases of some of the trees were as wide as twelve feet around. Mushroomed at the top they looked like green and brown pom-poms. Other than the lights that shone through the blinds of the windows of the apartment buildings and houses. it looked like the residents of the block had been tipped off about an impending apocalypse.

They passed an alleyway that led behind the apartment complex. It took them three seconds to pass yet Black still saw a sight he'd never seen before. Time stood still as he beheld a dingy mutt with a brown coat and a black snout cornering a woolly gray cat against a fence and a power line pole. The cat's eyes glowed as he defended his ground. The dog prodded the cat with its nose, exposing surprisingly sharp teeth. The cat rested on three legs holding the front right one up like a tired boxer trying to conserve energy by doing everything with one arm. He let out a savage meow. The dog viciously barked back. Then the cat retracted his paw and violently swung it across the face of the dog. Blood trickled down the dog's face as he staggered backward, flustered and deeply lacerated. The cat ran through an opening in the fence.

I'm glad Dink ain't here. If he would've seen that, trust me he would've been like "Man I wish I had my pistol with me. I'm bout to let y'all walk home by y'all selves." Or he would probably get real cold and be looking at everybody funny. That's my nigga but he be lunchin' sometimes. I be wit him on that shit sometimes but then he'll come up with some crazy shit that'll make you be like "What the fuck is you smokin?"

"Daaaaaaamn," said Black.

"What?" said Boo.

"Nothin'," said Black after he paused. "I just seen some vicious shit."

As they approached the corner they noticed a group of five boys huddled in front of a house near the middle of the next block laughing loudly and acting out. They were a rag-tag looking bunch. Black took notice of them. He knew how the boys around his neighborhood treated strangers.

"Oh shit that's Lonté and them," said Boo as she turned her head down and to the side. "I thought he was locked up."

Lonté was a tall, lanky, dark-skinned juvenile, the color of a coffee bean. His eyes were narrow and his jaw protruded from his face like it was swollen. His posture was arrogantly thuggish. He wore a long white T-shirt with some jean shorts. The shorts were cuffed and came to his kneecaps.

"He got out two weeks ago, He just ain't been comin' around here 'cause he was in a group home," said Shontay.

"Damn, damn, damn," said Boo. "He play too much. I don't feel like bein' bothered right now. He probably still think we go together."

Black remained quiet as they slowly shortened the distance between themselves and the group. He thought about the possibilities that lay ahead. He conjured up an image of the boy saying something to him or about him and how he would react. He developed tunnel vision down a road called "worst possibilities."

Boo grabbed him by his biceps and said, "Pretend you my boyfriend." When he didn't immediately respond she followed up with, "Aiight. Aiight."

Black's uneasiness grew exponentially as they approached the group. Most of the boys were already staring at them with looks meant to freeze them stiff, even as they calmed down their raucous interaction. None of them could've been over twenty years old. Black's heartbeat rose wildly. He tried to check it by holding his breath, but it didn't do any good. He thought Boo could hear it because she was draped on him. He kept his face expressionless. Boo plastered a smile on her face as they encountered the group standing directly in their path.

"Shontay," said one of the boys.

"What's up, Man?" replied Shontay.

The boy ran up beside her and said, "Hold up."

She stopped and faced the boy as he talked. It was her old boyfriend, the one who hooked Boo up with Lonté. Black and Boo stood several feet behind her on the edge of the sidewalk under a tree. Their position was awkward. Standing like Siamese twins between the four boys to their left and Shontay and Man to the right. Boo had the side of her head embedded in Black's shoulder. She made sure her butt wasn't facing the boys. All of them gazed lustily at her but one stare was particularly piercing. Lonté leaned against the rail of a fence with his arms crossed. He had a maniacal gaze and appeared to be holding something back. Black just wanted Shontay to stop talking so they could move on.

"Ohh, you can't speak, Boo," said Lonté'.

"Hi Lonté," said Boo in a shy, sullen tone. "Where you been at?"

"I was locked up. Remember?" Lonté' said gruffly. "Who is that?" Black knew it was on. He wasn't gonna get out of here without trouble. Even if he bitched out he would have to fight. He knew the jealous ex-boyfriend routine.

"This my friend," said Boo as she squeezed hard on the inside of Blacks biceps.

"I thought I said you can't have no friends," said Lonté.

"Lonté', stop playin' with me. Why don't you carry your ass back around where you came from?" Boo spat out the words with a defiance that surprised Black.

"You don't want me to do that," said Lonté' and the boys laughed like it was an inside joke.

"Whatever," said Boo.

"Why? You tryin' to go wif me?" Lonté' asked amid a chorus of laughter.

Shontay and Man had walked down a bit and were involved in a serious conversation about the future of their relationship. For her, getting back together. For him, having sex tonight.

"Ill. Nah. Don't no body wanna go nowhere with you," Boo said, still squeezing Black's arm.

"So what you sayin, I can't still hit it?" Lonté' asked.

Boo stormed off, pulling Black. When they got to where Shontay was standing Boo interrupted their conversation saying, "Come on Shontay, Lonté' getting' on my nerves. Oooh."

"Why don't you just go home?" Shontay said, turning to look at her house which was a few yards down the street, "Call me as soon as you get in the house."

Boo pouted, then she turned and they walked up the street toward the boys. Black felt like a death row inmate waiting for his number to be called. The group parted, letting them pass through.

"Come here, Boo," Lonté' said hopefully.

"No," said Boo. "Leave me alone."

Lonté' pushed off the fence with his butt and followed them. They felt as well as heard his black Nikes scraping the ground. Boo simultaneously rolled her eyes, took a deep breath, and looked at Black. Black looked at her and exhaled while shaking his head. They kept walking. Black was tense but he wasn't scared. His adrenaline pumped, causing him to inadvertently ball his fist. The sounds of Lonté's sneakers scratching the concrete got faster as he shifted into a jog. When he got close enough he reached out, grabbed Boo's arm, and pulled her to a stop. She let out a yelp that sliced through the calm night air. She was holding on to Black so tightly, she pulled him back.

"Don't fake for cuss," said Lonté.

"Leave my girl alone, young," said Black, staring stoically into Lonté's lazy eyes.

He couldn't believe these words "my girl" had rolled off his lips. An incident was about to kick off and it was all because he was supposedly Boo's boyfriend. The idea was almost funny.

"What? Oh you fakin' cuz," exclaimed Lonté in a high-pitched voice as he pulled up his britches and braced himself. "What's up then. How you wanna carry it?"

"Fakin', you the one tryin' to put your hands on my girl," said Black.

"That's my girl, cuz," said Lonté. "But fuck all that, how you wanna carry it. It's whatever," and he spread his arms like bird wings.

His boys began walking up on the scene. Their postures were aggressive. Boo stood to the side and observed the fracas with an awed expression.

"Whatever, man," said Black as he turned his head to the side exposing his profile.

"Oh, it's whatever than," said Lonté as he stepped closer to Black.

He breathed hot air into Black's face. Black remembered how his friend CJ always told him to have his back in the streets no matter who or what it was. And how he advised him to throw the first punch at all times. He also told him gangstas don't start fight; they end them.

"Man, if you don't get the fuck out of my face, cuz," Black barked, high off the thought of his brother's words.

"What? Man I'm 'bout to break this nigga jaw if he don't stop fakin'," said Lonté as his boys hovered close by.

"Oh, y'all gonna jump me. That's fucked up," said Black in an attempt to buy some time while he mustered up the fortitude to swing on Lonté.

"Nah, nigga I'm a bang your bitch ass out myself," said Lonté.

Black turned his head quickly to look at Boo. She had a blank look on her face that he'd never seen in the fifteen years they'd known each other. Turning his face back around to meet Lonté's eyes, Black cocked back his arm and threw a wild haymaker, picturing every dude who he let slide with some slick-ass comment or nasty look. By the time it connected with Lonté's lower jaw it was a virtual club. The punch shattered Lonté's jaw bone and caused him to bite down, chipping teeth in the process. He staggered backward, dazed and disoriented. Black was bent over on his left leg like a pitcher falling off the mound just after he releases a pitch.

Man and Shontay ran up on the scene as Boo grabbed his wrist.

"All that fakin' and got slam knocked out," said Man. "Aye, cuz,' you better roll out young."

Boo started up the street pulling him. Black was hype so he resisted her.

"Come on, Black. Let's just leave. Come on," said Boo.

Lonté' had begun to get some wits about him and mumble in a low tone, "I'ma kill you motherfucka."

Then he mumbled, "Go get my gun young . . . it's in the bushes."

Black relented and began to briskly walk down the street. Then they started jogging. Boo leading him like he didn't know the way, both of them looking back every couple of steps. They saw a boy run into the yard while the rest of them tried to pick Lonté' up. They heard loud threats and taunts. As they got closer to the bright lights of the avenue Black felt like a slave coming up on the Mason Dixon line.

When they entered Boo's building Black slammed the door and leaned against the wall to catch his breath. The lighting was dim because one of the lightbulbs had blown out. Names were written with markers, spray paint, lighters, anything you could across the walls.

Before he could reflect on what had just taken place Boo fell into him and leaned back. Her soft butt fit into his crotch like a piece of a jigsaw puzzle. His chest heaved out when hers dipped in, creating a grinding sensation. The smooth glazed bricks felt frigid against his sweaty back. After a moment of contemplation, he put his arms around Boo's waist and rested his chin on her shoulder. Her heartbeat immediately began to return to normal. She delicately caressed his forearms with her sweaty palms. His penis grew as she pressed against it.

What he felt was more than a crush. It was like a warm sensation in the core of his body. The only catch was that it was Boo who was causing it. Not that he wanted to change anything. He just was in disbelief at how quickly it got to this point. An hour ago she was getting on his nerves. Now they stood there silently in each other's arms like they'd been together forever.

"I'm scared," whispered Boo. "What if he comes around here? He knows where I live."

Black's heart skipped a beat and he was sure Boo felt it. Nevertheless he kept his cool veneer.

"If he wanna get his niggas. I got niggas. My niggas is right in there," said Black as he nodded his head toward the apartment. "Sheed, you know how Dink go, he down for whatever. And my brother, come on now, and Sergio psst."

"I know. That's what I'm talking about. I don't want you to get involved in none that bullshit. That's not you, Black," said Boo.

Her comment brought Black down to Earth. He wondered how it would be to shoot someone. He wondered if he could go through with squeezing the trigger and actually kill someone. He hadn't thought he had it in him to punch Lonté' and look what happened.

"So what you tryin' to say?" said Black as he raised his chin from her shoulder.

"Don't be like that, Black," said Boo. "I'm just worried about you. I can't believe I'm here in your arms. I mean this is like a dream come true. You don't know how much I like you and how long I liked you. Like even when we was little I liked you."

"For real?"

"Oh come on, Black. Don't play dumb with me. I know you."

"Nah, I guess I knew you liked . . ."

"I love you, Black. You don't know how many times I wanted to tell you, but I never did."

Boo turned around to face him. Black stood up, put his arms around her waist and gripped her butt. She played with the wrinkles in his shirt and rubbed his chest with her palms. Her face was so angelic now. Although cute she had always appeared upset or annoyed. In this moment she took had a brand new loveliness. He was afraid to make eye contact with her because he felt his feelings would grow even more. They could hear the voices coming from her apartment, mainly Sergio's.

"I don't like him," said Boo as Sergio's voice echoed against the walls.

"Go 'head, young," said Black as he cocked his head back and rolled his eyes.

"I'm serious," said Boo as she slapped him lightly on his chest. "I don't like the way you act around him. You ain't . . . real. It's like you don't want him to think you," said Boo.

"Look, just let it go man. You blowin' me," said Black.

Boo apologized, sort of, and gave him a warm hug. She rested the side of her head on his chest and gazed at the door. A door upstairs opened, then slammed. They both held their breaths and their grips on each other instinctively loosened, taking on the personas of guilty children about to be discovered by their parents in the midst of mischief. Loud footsteps thumped each stair with the force of a plummeting bowling ball. They tensed up and their grips relaxed even more. But it was just Artise, a preadolescent who lived in next door. He went by in a

"We should go in," said Black.

"Nohhhh," whined Boo. "I want to be alone with you."

"Psst," said Black.

"You know what? I'm a fuck you up, Black," said Boo.

"I'm just sayin' we could be alone up there," said Black.

"Ill, I don't want all them niggas in my business," said Boo frowning.

"What you think—I want them in my business so they can playa hate? Come on, now," said Black. "I'ma chill wit them for a minute, until they leave then I'm a come in there with you."

"Nohhh, that's too long for us to be apart," whined Boo. "The way I feel right now, it's like I can't explain it. I just don't want you to leave my . . . presence."

She looked up into his eyes with an expression that could've corrupted a monk. He clutched her close to him and plotted on kissing her. She felt so soft and tender, but he just felt weird. It was like he knew things would never be the same if he kissed her. He knew it was going to happen that night. He was just stalling it out.

Incognito

Rossonian Days

BY WILLIAM HENRY LEWIS

—FOR ERNEST HOLLIMAN, EARL MCADAMS,
AND EVERY OTHER MUSICIAN NOBODY HEARD.

Anyone who's ever blown knows you gotta feel it to say it; only a few really ever know the Truth and then play it.

—JOHN HENDRICKS

The memory of things gone is important to the jazz musician. Things like the old folks singing in the moonlight in the backyard on a hot night . . .

—DUKE ELLINGTON

Listen. This happens for just a moment. The car is headed north, to Denver. That's where the gig is. The band is from Kansas City. West by south, through Pueblo, and every dirty-snow mile of Route 87 stretching north by west. This kind of traveling never takes the short way. More road than anybody wants. Not much else to see. The fields will be gray for months. Land slips from the road, rolls in swells of rye and hay across the plain to the Front Range.

The car is long and the wheels are wide. Front grille stout, like America itself. The car is a Lincoln, rides like horsehair across bass-strings.

Nothing is small time here. No two-tone paint job. All black. Six coats of pure gloss. Shine for days. Tinted glass. Chrome nothing more than nuance. More power switches than anybody will ever use: E-Z drive *power* steering. *Power* windows. *Power* locks. *Power* antenna. *Power* seats. What don't got *power*, the car don't *need.* The whole deal, chrome trim sidewalls to suicide doors, holds more class than most will get from getting in. You don't drive it. You *ride* it. The Lincoln Continental four-door convertible: chariot for the rebirth of the cool.

Inside, everybody's got room without anybody's last nerve being worked over. The bass is strapped to the roof; horns and drums packed like china; clothes for tonight rest on instrument cases. The worries ride up front, steaming the windows.

· · ·

Call back to memories less rich but more grand, like Milt Hinton snapshots that didn't make print: Ellington, asleep in a cashmere topcoat, fedora brim angled across his the bridge of his nose, head at rest on Strayhorn's shoulder. Missouri is outside. They glide through the dusk of the Midwest, "Lush Life" drifting on A.M., *night coming on.*

In another image—maybe Ohio this time—Duke at work, writing in the small spot of a car lamp. Harry Carney sawing logs, shoulder to Duke's shoulder. Too many road gigs were cats filling a car like the last boxcar headed North: Sweet Pea, Monster, Snooky, all the rest, blessings on the stand, but all the same, smelly-sock brothers filling space where, if the Duke is on, a "Black and Tan Fantasy" is always birthing. Not all of his rides smooth, but you know the elders always wander the hard way first.

Call back to days of try. Edward Kennedy Ellington: Duke before there was Wayne, regent of a tight backseat, sounds making themselves on pages under dim light, no hambone room. Outside, it was always night, dark in the heartland, where brothers wasn't safe after dark. You ain't been blue 'til you had that "Mood Indigo." Ride a million miles through Columbus, Des Moines, Perioa, Tulsa, Vidor, Lincoln, just to enter the Cotton Club through the front door . . . Hambone, hambone, where you been?

Somebody before now played this road—someone heard by some, or maybe never whispered—so drive this Lincoln like holding the family photographs, and when it rolls in, brother, stride right.

It is some time after the turn of the year: Say it's 1965, or a year later, maybe years ealier. There's no stick to this moment, but it will echo. Don't need a year to know this story is old. The trip has been made by many: like making good time in a '31 Hudson from Baton Rouge to Chi-town. Been in moments like this, riding with hay discs strapped to the slatboards of a flatbed International Harvester, bound for Macon. Been up to and down from Ft. Worth for a summer of Saturday nights. Skylark was the ride in those days. Chickory, pork chops, grits, a skillet of cornbread cooling in the pantry every morning. In and out of icehouses of all sorts, sometimes even those for WHITES ONLY. Been asked back to and booed out of every juke joint on the Chit'lin Circuit, Southern route that splits cats who are *down* from those who ain't, and *if you miss the A train, you have missed the quickest way to Harlem.*

No matter the year, it is winter. The plains are a hard, gray-brown bed nobody wants. For long breaths the road is lost in angry wind and tired snow, and the only thing that keeps the car on track is the tenor player at the wheel, working through Moody's "Tin Tin Deo," Afro-Latino jam, up from beneath the underdog's fatback jawbone. A downbeat, thick like *adobado* sauce to go with that *arroz con pollo*; the band chanting . . . *oh, tin*

tin deo . . . and now the conga is in it . . . *oh, tin tin deo* . . . cowbell, crisp like momma's catfish . . . *oh, tin tin deo, oh, tin tin deo* . . . a four-four swing gone East Harlem *bebop*, the rhythm something you know, but the rattle is new: stick on a can, good groove under the Lexington Avenue local, 104th Street.

Long after the tune leaves his humming, the tenor thinks he still hears it . . . *oh, tin tin deo* . . . on his last breath, from the backseat, deep in some-body's chest, or fifty miles back. Wind keeps rhythm. White sky stained gray like old bone. The fields empty. More snow coming. Bourbon is passed from backseat to front, and somebody says if there's a God out in all of that, he best be blowin' for us. Then all is quiet.

Not much to say once you hear the call. A body has been waiting a long time for that call, through the passage of centuries, through all the rent party nights and ten-cent coffee hours. Time was when days were three shifts: some of one spent sleeping and practicing, most of two spent work-ing or looking for work. Word spreads down the Sante Fe line, an ad cut from the *Kansas City Call*, letter from a cousin in Pueblo, an auntie in the parlor with the phone pressed to the radio: a "jazz-endorsed" P.S.A. from WVBA, the disc jockey calling out from far away, late night, low and steady, like a talking drum across the bend of the savannah's horizon:

> *Are there any musicians left out there? Here's this from the Rossonian Auditorium, Denver's best kept secret: Management would like to remind you there's always a stage for great talent at the Rossonian. Maybe you have got a talent that we would want to showcase. Perhaps you're the next swinging sensation, ready to strike it big back East. Go East, young man, but swing in the West! Give us a call—Albion-6867—tell us your name and address, and let us know what your talent is: horn, piano, vocals? Have you got a band? Call soon, Albion-6867, or write us, Management, The Rossonian Auditorium, 2640 Welton, Denver, Colorado. Tell us what you can do . . .*

Many places are right for moments like this, but the moments are fewer than the places. Where it's at is now: the band, the car, the road, and where all three will stop. So Kansas City is gone. The gig is at The Rossonian. In Denver. On Five Points. Where Welton meets Washington. Come night, the people are there, roasting ribs and frying catfish, domino games in front rooms, Cadillacs angled to the curbs like Crisscrafts. Five Points, where it has been and is. It's not Beale Street or Eighteenth and Vine, but it wants to be.

The Saturday night local headliner is bound to pack it tighter than the mickeys allow anyplace else. Nobody has a care, except for showing up and showing out their hard-earned, store-bought clothes, ones that won't do Sunday morning, but do it right on Saturday night. Can't roll up to that scene in some small-money ride. Nobody will take the scene for serious. These days, cats are pulling out their best jive; everybody who's nobody is hustlin'. *Everybody can blow a horn son, but what can **you** do*? So drive the Points in the soft-top Lincoln, Continental *convertible*, shag top shiny in a stingy man's winter. Drive up in some sorry vehicle, that's what folks re-member.

They remember Andy Kirk and Mary Lou Williams—*When you hear the saxes ride, what's the thing that makes them glide? It's the lady who swings the band!* Basie and Jimmy Rushing. They remember Charlie Parker. But Bird didn't need no car to break out of K.C. Mary and Andy floated in style through the West with the Twelve Clouds of Joy. And elders are quick to say *ain't nobody worth a damn come out of Missouri since the thirties . . .*

But it is 1960, give or take some years back or forward and the arrange-ment of players doesn't matter—a piano man, tenor and trumpet players, drums, double-bass man, maybe a trombone, maybe a singer—no one knows their name.

It doesn't matter, but everything matters: Bebop has died, straight ahead Jazz is dying. The small traveling band ain't long for this road. Long Playing records play the hits, what's popular spinning on records for less than any five-piece group driving state to state. They not gonna like you out West because you Sonny Rollins, son, they gonna like you cause they heard your record was on the tops of the Billboard and Downbeat lists. Or maybe you got an angle: Dave Brubeck and Chet Baker blowin blues like the Brothers but their blues ain't about paying the bills. Only a few will rise off the highways and land on wax.

Make that no never mind. *This* car is headed for a gig. There are high-ways full of these long, black cars, carrying the best jazz nobody's ever heard. To hear it *live*: another breakdown chorus, Basie swinging "April in Paris"—*"one more time . . ."* a third reprise, volta, groove, call it what you want, it swings just the same—*"jus' one more, once . . ."*

Music from the marrow. At clubs a rung above juke joint; velvet-draped lounge or speakeasy; intimate auditorium, backlit in blue. No need for a name, just a love for Blues, a four-four swing tapping your toe, *hit that jive, jack, put it your pocket 'til I get back. The show*: standards spill like laughter, one into the next; the piano man is running through "Twinkletoes"; the tenor is just sitting down; the trumpet man sips on his sour mash and picks lint from his sleeve; the drum player's got a new suit: Ivy League cut, iridescent green rust shimmers when his brushes ease across the snare, left stick teasing the cymbal like a pastor's blessing. Late night makes early morning, the glow of early morning shows through the skylight, stars like embers through the wireglass. A third set beginning, lights low, dim footers set brown skin glowing. Folks look younger than they ever have or ever will.

> *Play on, Brother, play on, it don't matter that tomorrow is a workday, or a Sunday, or another sack o' woe day, play on, because right now, everything is right.*

No record or radio catches that. But it's hits that are selling now, not that *better-get-it-in-your-soul* music, all its mothers and fathers sold off to new owners. It's the sixties. Just forty years gone since they lynched 617 in three months. Red Summer's strange fruit rots slowly in our gut. We get silent. We learn the ulcers we bear. Or we forget. But you know the Emmitt Till Blues. Where's your singing now? Just a whistle get you dead.

> *This is a voice stowed in the Middle Passage. Call looking for Response. After the chain and yoke, there were weeks of dark quiet, the wash of sea water against the ship's bow. Inside, a song of rot breathing head to foot, row over row. This was a voice that sang Benin, Ibo, Fang, Hausa. This is a voice that learned Georgia, Louisiana, Tennessee, South Carolina, all the Dixon below Mason. This is a voice that learned cotton, tobacco, and sugarcane. This is a voice that almost unlearned itself.*
>
> *No more drums, no elders' words. They beat you if you speak out or refuse the labor. They hunt you when you run. They listen for the bell welded around your neck, smell you out with hounds when you run from the noose. Not much music in hose-spray or last snap of rope, jolt of cord and spine; that razor quick like fire and fierce between the legs. No voice in that night.*

But Coltrane preaches "Alabama," so listen: People been hanging from trees; elders gone North and West and back again; Harlem, Detroit, Chicago, burned, Northern lights when they told you only Mississippi was burning. And who sang the Oklahoma Blues? Tulsa, 1921: that fire fierce but silenced. No news carried that. That's our Death, people: no story, no wire, no radio, no voice, no ear, no report, no Call and Response to know that people out here are living and dying. Nobody to sing their Blues. Nobody to hear it wail.

> *Listen. You got to listen: Trane's Blues. Four girls, baptized with bombs. Bessie Smith a story we forgot. The ghost-whistle of Emmitt Till*

cups the street corner of every young black man's dreams. People going broke on Northern city Blues, and their voice, only thing they ever owned for sure, sold for the price of a record.

Soon enough, they don't want to hear no "Strange Fruit." Sing us "Body and Soul," Billie, they cheer. Smile and sweat through "Body and Soul" for the money thing. Soon enough, change chimes in Brothers' pants pockets as they easy-step the sunny side of Lenox Avenue; Billie Holiday all but gone, another echo in the alley.

The road and the soundless miles are for the singers and players, heard and unheard. They all want the voice, they travel. Once they've heard the voice it will never leave them alone. They travel. Most will never hear it, but they travel. This is the road jazzfolk play. Have played. Been playing. Been played by. Will play for.

I let a song go out of my heart
it was the sweetest melody
I know I lost heaven,
'cause you were the song.

Before King's English. Before the Word, there was story, in song and wail, drumbeat, hambone, and sand shoe, the hot breath of mothers birthing field-to-factory-generations. Thick and light, the sound moved as the people did, on to East St. Louis, on to South Detroit and Cleveland, to Chi-town, where brothers blew that hard, Midway-city, get-ol-man-Hawk-out-my-draws bop.

On North and East, to Philly, and, of course, The City, The Village, 52nd Street, and 125th street, Harlem, Mecca at Lenox Ave, nothing small in Small's Paradise, where anybody on the move was moving. On out west-ward: Austin, Lincoln, Denver, K.C.—all the gigs before, in between, and after—all the way out to the Pacific, that high-tone, low-key, California-here-we-come land of give up the gravy.

Just one night, one good jam in Denver—tear up the Rossonian—and the skate to the West Coast was smooth.

After that, return to the South slow and easy, like nobody's ancestors ever left it. A stroll on Beale. Cakewalk down Rampart.

After that, leave it, freer than any freedom train headed North.

After that, to The City. The road will lead to The City.

After that, only Ancestors and Elders know . . .

. . .

Some kind of way, this trip will be made. There are so many cities, all too far from Kansas City, but the trip will be made. Phone rings, the gig is on. Denver. The Rossonian, Down in Five Points. The Rossonian: two sets, one night, a hundred heads, fivespot to get in, two drinks to stay, a quarter take of the door. Fill the place, management is happy, band is happy, and like that, the Rudy Van Gelder is the Call from Englewood Cliffs, just across the Hudson, where the studio is still buzzing from when Miles Davis Quintet was the Word.

So the trip will be made: Three days, two nights. Head out Route 24 after a half-day's shift, roll past Topeka, already lit in the winter early dusk of the Plains, pass through Kandorado as the blue bowl of late night pours its last stars across the West; make Pueblo for the late set at the Blossom Heath. Two encores milk gas money for the trip— *nice work if you can get it.* Sleep off late night's drunk until just before new day's dark, then a biscuit, coffee, corn liquor, junk, or smack. Here comes Denver. The Rossonian: oasis in Jazz Nowhere on the way to Jazz Somewhere. Someday soon, stompin' at the Savoy.

And after the gig is swung, tired or no, never mind hangover, no time for a strung-out morning, the Lincoln will make fast back to Kansas City, the small low-money gigs, the stormy Monday job, the life that always expects the empty-handed return.

So the phone rings, for the bassist, the drummer, the singer, the piano man; maybe a vibraphone player, but maybe they ain't ready for the vibes out in the Mile High, not yet, and this ain't the time for testing new waters.

The phone rings for the hornplayers, the sax, trumpet, trombone, whichever horns, any of them are waiting for that phone to ring. Everybody wants that *taste* like what Canonball and Nat got on the grill out in California. Monk fixing on which suit coat to wear—dark or light—while the car is running and the photographer is waiting. Ain't we all been waiting for *that* phone to ring? Cannonball Adderley filling seats like it was summer Bible school. Mercy, mercy, mercy. Dizzy blowing that horn easy as waxing the Cadillac: L.A. smooth, beret, goatee, horn rims, and herringbone. Ivy League cut suit, fresh bed, dry martini, *salt peanuts, salt peanuts.*

> *Go get some. Don't bring no soft sound. There are few chances, one or two big moments. Many misses. The young cats, they got good at hitting the target, notes all dressed up and in line, so on top of technique the soul got blowed out. They miss. Those brothers will rattle some walls with a few records but, come five years, those cats are quiet, waiting on that phone. They missed.*
>
> *The phone didn't have to ring for Satchmo, who never missed. Not Charlie, who was blessed with more jam than he could jive. Not Bessie,*

who was hit enough to bring it back black and blue—beautiful like that until she couldn't bring no more. Not Prez or Johnnie, who didn't know what slow was. Not Billie, who didn't know what "no" was, and gave her soul to encores and needles. Not Ella, who never knew an off note. Not Milt, who gave Bag's Groove to the grooveless. Not Chet, who gave to music and no one else. Not Nina, who got more sugar in her bowl, her well-deep voice the middle of whatever best and worst day anybody ever lived through. Not even Clifford, who lived through one car wreck only to be taken in another before he was twenty-seven. Not even thirty yet, and he needed no phone to ring. He already swung with strings, just like Charlie Parker.

The phone rings for the rooftop and boiler room players. The Brother scales on his lunch hour. Down by the riverside. With mute when it's late. A bus ride hum. Not yet twenty, but a lifetime waiting on that phone. Sometimes, it rings. They pick it up. They say yes. They travel.

The bag is packed, shirt's been pressed for weeks, instrument oiled, shoes shined—chamois across alligator pumps, matchstick to clean each wingtip hole. The savings is cracked—quarters and singles from days of pinching for days of playing. The landlord is dodged. Never mind the bills. The bossman is conned: . . . *you see, I just gotta see my Auntie Berthene, up over in Denver, else she likely to up and die fore this time next week.*

And somebody will always be left behind. A woman, a man, maybe large-eyed children, but somebody's left on the porch in the day's first light. They wonder what makes this time the time when it's the *Big Time*? What makes it different from the last big time? St. Louis: gone for three days. Or Memphis: gone for a week, and come back with half the world dragged out in between. Somebody will be left. Somebody is always left. But nobody will remember after the record deal is signed, and the reel-to-reel is playing back "If I Were a Bell," take two. Gin gimlets all around. Someone will tell the story about Ben Webster trying out the tenor when the piano had no luck in it for him. "In a Mellow Tone," from that day on. It will feel like that, your story will be told down the ages. When that new sound comes everyone will know the name on the album, bookings sticking at Birdland, Leonard Feather calling for a *Downbeat* feature, and nobody will never, ever, be left alone again. Whoever it is that's left behind, that's the promise left on their lips as night air makes their embrace stiff.

Inside the Lincoln it's quiet-cool. Nobody looks at anyone else. Snow's still coming. The sax player drives the car quietly now, changes and progressions silent secrets to an inner hum of his head. The drum player is almost asleep, slumped against the passenger window as he syncopates fingertaps between the hushed beats of passing fenceposts. The trumpet player works a soft-scat to the high C he's never hit. The piano man has blank paper at the ready. The singer low-moans spirituals that got her through the ten-hour days of working somebody else's clothes against a washboard. *Joshua fit the battle of Jericho* . . .

The bassist rubs a match stick, pushing it to spark, pulling back before the rasp springs to fire. The car is full with the quiet of knowing. Some kind of way, they know some sound is going to roll up the highway and reclaim the song-breath of blackfolk.

*This voice **something** like some **thing** drifting in the summer air of childhood days, caught and lost in sun-glare. It's wind lingering in the branches of the boabab just before rain covers the savannah. An Elder whispering. A mother's sigh carried on the wind, the rasp of callused hands across burlap bags when the cotton is high. It's Biloxi crickets, never seen but heard, in want of wet and hot, loud for days even in winter, through the cold, hard bright of day, out here, on the winter-bare spine of the Rockies—miles of dry and nothing—where crickets echo only in imagining.*

The tight air waits for any sound, and when the bass player strikes his match, everyone is startled. Wait for it: brass stopper and snare skin, bass string strained, sevenths and discordant ninths sustained on the high registers of the ivories. *I let a song go out of my heart.* Nothing is captured: not time, rushing past the Lincoln, come and gone, down the road fast, like it's the car—not the passing of seconds or minutes—pushing the hours; not this vast rust-out bowl of land spilling from the Rockies; not the wail of prairie birdsong, ringing like something forgotten, impossible in March, not here, not now, not this road.

I let a song go out of my heart
believe me, darlin, when I say
I won't know sweet music,
until you return someday

The music of open air is waiting. The Blues has done its sliding, the be-bop's been straight and never narrow, and still here's that yearning, like the song were so many grapes to be plucked, and rolled around in the mouth like a lover's tongue. Driving from gig to gig, all fixed life loses itself for want of that fresh new groove. Everyone wants the sound we haven't heard yet. Since we were children we wanted that song to fit in somewhere between the first jumble of quarter-note and half-rest and the last few miles before the gig; measure after measure of notes. And that sound is taunting, take me in.

... child, take me in, roll me in your mouth, under your hands; pull me from blank space and empty air and make me beautiful: love me. Begin the Beguine. I am a Love Supreme. I am the song you've always wanted, so love me.

It is hours before the Rossonian. Night has already covered Missouri. The wind and snow are dropping off, and it's near dusk in Colorado. Sun so low it lays sideways into the frost on the windows. The Rockies are all but gone, last light like a wick on Pike's Peak.

There is no company but the crackle of prairie air across radio waves and a worry of what Denver holds in store: an old town, maybe a new night; fresh start, worn body; *maybe* a different crowd or the same women in different dresses, the men in their one good suit. Another night of promises never spoken. To the body: *please, no more, no more up and down the road and in and out of the blues;* to the people: *tonight, on this one night, we truly are glad to be here;* to whoever was left last night, *you know I'm working all this for you, baby;* to the nameless body at the end of this night, *you know I'm working all this for you, baby;* to the bottle, *you know I'm working all this for you;* to the smack, the junk, the horse, the krik-krak monkey, five-and-dime-sho'-nuff-right-on-time feeling, *you know I'm working all this for you;* the horn, the strings, to the drums, those piano keys, and the run that's coming tonight, it's gonna be tonight, it's *gotta* be tonight, because it needed to be tonight for the past five years, *you know I'm working all this for you.*

It takes the heart all day to find its beat for the big night. Soon as the gear is packed out of the Colorado Springs club—even though there's a night to be had in the Springs—the hands start twitching with want for the next night. Where's that song? Waiting on a song to come: For all of the sound in the world, Colorado Springs the night before the Rossonian is a world of too much quiet. Soon it will be provin' time. Hands, be still.

Heart, be loud.

Denver will rise out of the plain. The road will soon pull the band down Colorado Boulevard, past homes where maids and yardmen work toward tonight. "Begin the Beguine."

The streets will rush toward Five Points, a turn into the alley, the rise of stairs to stage door from the cobblestones. An open door, and a taste of Rossonian air. Breathe once, let out the long road coming. Wait a moment. No breathing, in or out. The quiet room. Step to the empty stand.

Imagine walls lit from the floor. Imagine arched alcoves vaulting into a dome the color of any night full of lovers. Night in Tunisia. Imagine calls of the ancients, taking their rest above the balcony. Hear the drums, the voices. Somewhere voices call across grasslands. Imagine a room with doors all directions, not just North. Now inhale, take in the thick, dark air of from here to who knows what's next.

In one of those long-mile hours they wondered, Why this *long trip? Why have we gone all this way to have so little? We have come this far, through many beginnings and endings, and rebirths, to this: No more to show than we did before we began. We been down this road, but what of this long life and no voice?*

We wonder as we wander, and maybe we make it big at the end of this moment we've been driving to. If we don't make it, we'll steal away until we do, and if we do, we'll be playing for the money and the name, but someday, somewhere down this road, or the road to L.A. or the road to New York, somebody's going to say boy, you got to use the back door; boy, smile that big-lip grin for the camera; boy, you real lucky to get even ten percent of the take at the door . . .

Then we remember why the call and response dies a bit each day. When that happens, will we look out to the flat, barren horizon, still voiceless like now, still driving to that next chance and cry, what craziness brought us here?

But anybody who's played up and down these roads will tell you that something touched sent them flowing, somebody spoke to them, dipped them in call and response.

It could have been Basie, or Big Joe Turner, shouting the Blues down Vine Street, *Kansas City Blues* swung in a low key, *Black and Tan Fantasy*, or havin' it bad and that ain't being good, but it didn't have to be. The sound that says *play me* came before mouth to mouthpiece or stick to high-hat.

It was Momma singing "Get Away Jordan" in the backyard or it was a frontroom evening full of her momma's stories.

It was Daddy's comin' home whistle and Sunday-stroll scrape of wingtips on porch steps.

It was the late-night laughter of an uncle back home from Up South, on the road, looking for one night's meal and one good year of work.

It was a grade school teacher, short on smiles, long on the blackboard screech and scratch sharp through the chalk haze and radiator knock.

It was the wind-heavy sigh before summer storms.

The early-evening call of the icee-man in mid-July, a joyful echo gone too soon after childhood.

A reverend at an all-Sunday service full of Tennessee heat. Every spiritual almost forgotten. Every low bellow. Each high wail of every elder come and gone.

It was somebody testifyin'. Like a whole tentful of folks bearing witness in the middle of some South Carolina field.

Getting ready to take the stand, one of these musicians will tingle with a remembrance of childhood and fantasy afternoons. And of long Sundays. The Rossonian audience will remember Sundays, too. Right then, before the blowing begins, something mighty spiritual will happen. *Come Sunday.* Whether it's song or sermon, or both being the same, the people will come from the offices, the factories, the markets, and the fields, where song and sermon were born. All will remember how that reverend had it together: everybody's story in one Sunday afternoon.

And that remembrance feels like taking the stand.

It will be hot like the August of '23, only elders speak of that. The congregation has waited all day for the sermon. Men's Sunday-white collars ringed with sweat; talcum women, dust above their bosoms gone in that first hour, when the organist broke into "Old Landmark."

Children have dozed, stirred, and fallen off again to the heat of high summer. Tithe plate's been passed around enough so that everybody's given, even the one deacon who's passed more plates than he ever helped fill. The choir's turned itself out, rising from "In the Upper Room" to "He Saved My Soul," and now, after the sun has pushed its dust-heavy beams from the back of the church to the front, they are tired. Everybody's tired. Been tired since before last Sunday. Since before the church was built, burnt, and rebuilt. Before runaway prayer-meetings. Before men came with Bible and whip. Been tired.

The Rossonian audience will be waiting. The band will soon be giving in to that next moment of happening. It's like that for the reverend, too, and as he steps to the stand, afternoon sun angles through the transoms, shafts of light burning on his lectern like a signal fire. He walks with the step of wise griot women. His brow is furrowed, his blood is quick. He smiles at young ones and nods to the elders. And then starts in with *my brothers and sisters, we come too far to stop singin now . . .*

This is when stories mix: traveling band from far away taking the stand, hard working people stepping out to be graced with music, and the air of that room, many times graced itself. This could be Zion Baptist or the Minton, back in Kansas City. There's something to be heard. The Word will be played. This is the language many know but few can speak.

. . . a Love Supreme, a Love Supreme, a Love Supreme, a Love Supreme, a Love Supreme, a Love Supreme, a Love Supreme, a Love Supreme . . .

Soon it will be time for you to take the stand. Time's come to blow, that's the real time, when the lights lose their glare, faces in the crowd spring from smoke-dark into the footlights; the band is in the groove, *sho' nuff*, but they sound mono while the jam that's buzzing in your head is all *stereo*. Hi-fi. Good-to-the-wood, down-to-the-wax groove. And you heard it from way off, like back into the bridge of the second song in the first set, when *Cherokee* was busted out like anybody who's somebody from Kansas City would swing it.

From way off, you wanted that groove, you heard the jam coming, like before anybody took the stand, before the Lincoln pulled to Rossonian stage door, open like any drumming circle in a Congo square, sanctuary from all roads long and tired, from the long way North and the width of the Midwest.

By the time you feel it, the jam has been at work from way back, *music back to your momma*, when hand slap and down beat filled Southern evenings, drums or weary blues cotton-picking song, rising into the heatfaded poplar and pollen heavy pine that divided plantations; still further, on the slow spine of the Blue Ridge or rippling above turtle wake in some South Carolina swamp, where many had run and few masters were greedy enough to follow. Back then and there, you might have heard drums and song drifting from the swamps and thickets, places unlivable, but more livable than living chained with iron, with the bloody knuckle from cotton husk, with a new God and *His* words, with a hard-handed owner called silence.

To get here from there remember the songs of elders now gone. Take Duke's hand through the *Money Jungle*. *Steal Away, steal away*, follow Harriet Tubman from the swamp, from prayer meetings, from memories of taballo and kalimba chime, follow Sojourner Truth on the railroad that runs only North and West, catch the train, it's Underground, it's straight ahead, the A train, Coltrane's Blue Train, it's the only train, *follow the drinking gourd, follow the drinking gourd.*

And from there to here came the groove that fills your head. A sound coming like the answer that knows it needs no reason to be, no story is needed, no event, no particular year. Just the knowledge call that somebody may be out there, just beyond where you begin to hear your song drift past hearing, out to where there's a brother or a sister in the audience, down the block, in the next state, on that next plantation plot; maybe nobody you love, but somebody who came from where your people came from, and with just an utterance there may be an answer back, like any *right-on, praise-the-lord-pass-the-peas, I-heard-that, call-and-response*, because out there, they know that yes,

This voice comes from somebody, and it tells the story of who I am, who my people are, day-by-day, and no matter joy or the weary blues, I will lift my sound to the evening air—across tired miles, across rivers I've known, across the

*sea I never knew could bring so much dark to light, across the bones of my eld-
ers—because I know that somebody out there will hear it, nod their head, answer back, knowing the same pain, the same Middle Passage, many other
passages from then to now, and can know a great many things, but only need
know that this is a voice, it is blowing to the world, it is bold, it is strong, it
knows no yoke, no money, no god, but knows a way. It is my language. It is the
story. It pushes against the hard morning of yet another day, and it is mine. It is
mine.*

Helter Skelter

BY MARITA GOLDEN

"Miss me?" You issue the blunt question that is also a command each
time you see the boy. He nods his head, moving it up and down, up
and down. Too fast. Automatic. Like a tic or a reflex. Does he really miss
you? It's a simple question. Juwan's response makes you feel like shit.
Though it's the end of October, there's still only a hint of fall but Bunny's
made him wear a thick parka, a turtleneck sweater and corduroy pants.
Strapped into the passenger side front seat, the safety belt holding him in
place, the boy is staring at you, deep eyes aglow with an innocence you wonder if you ever knew.

There's no escape from the wide, round brown eyes, the lashes thick and
lush as fur. No escape once the boy turns those eyes on you. You study the
shapely head and the frail, almost feminine face that lives behind a veil of
something secret and unreachable to you. As if at any moment, with the
slightest pressure, the boy will break. Ten years old and no sign yet of the
gritty toughness he should have by now. After all he is your son.

You have picked him up at school as a weekday surprise. You wanted it to
be just you and the boy. He has broken your heart. But who and what
hasn't? You don't know how you are breathing, how you stand, wake up or
sleep, swimming as you do every moment through the wreckage you have
wrought. Trying to resist the pull of the undertow.

He is a quiet boy. This always unnerves you. Infects you with a guilt that
is old and punishing and all-purpose. Last weekend you skipped seeing the
kids. The undertow got you. Dragged you, no sucked you into a murderous

whirlpool. Ate your black ass for breakfast. Lunch. Dinner. You stayed in the house all weekend. At the kitchen table. Smoking. Cleaning your guns.

On the way to the movies, Juwan asks if he can turn to another radio station. You've got it on smooth jazz. When he asks this, you remember the radio fights in this car with Bunny ("God, I hate that jazz muzak, it's like a drug"). She always wants to listen to people talking, talking, on NPR, and the kids, begging you to turn to a station that plays hip hop or rap. "Sure," you tell the boy, the sound of those jovial arguments a snarled tape on fast forward behind a locked door in your mind. On those rare Saturday or Sundays, you were all driving together, you solved the sparring by giving everybody ten minutes on their station of choice. The girls sitting in the backseat, their high-pitched, quivering voices singing along with Aaliyah:

Rock the boat
Rock the boat
Work the middle
Work the middle
Change Positions
Change Positions

snapping their fingers, twisting and squirming in their seats imitating the now-dead singer's video moves.

DMX blasts through the speakers and the song—profane, apocalyptic, thunderous—is the beat of everything you feel inside. But beside you Juwan is moving his head to the sounds so you let it go. Let it slide.

When the song ends and the commercials come on Juwan asks, "You feel better, Dad? Mom said last week you were sick."

"Yeah, I'm better now," you lie. The lie opens you up and you ask about the twins. Juwan squinches up his face, takes a deep breath and then launches into a catalogue of the girls' recent offenses and punishments. You don't like this about the boy, the way he savors being a tattle tale. Roslyn was caught playing with matches in the basement.

Mom told her no video games and no T.V. But she could still do gymnastics because of the competition next week. She couldn't let down the team. And she made her apologize to Gramma for almost burning the house down.

Juwan is rarely punished. You wonder if he has any imagination at all. You've seen their sibling rivalry. You know kids are cruel, mean little bastards but "Burn down the house," you yell, almost side swiping a car at the thought.

Juwan purses his lips, eyes gleaming with a hard, mischievous glow. "Some magazines caught fire. Roslyn threw a lit match on them to see what would happen. That's when Roseanne ran upstairs and Mom came down and stomped on the fire and put it out."

He likes to make things up. Always exaggerating. You can hardly trust anything he tells you. It would be okay if he just lied in those stories he writes. That's what storytelling is, a pack of lies. His teacher, Miss Harley, had him transferred to the Gifted and Talented program in part because of his essays and poems and stories. But he's got to learn that you don't lie all the time. And you just told him you were feeling fine.

At the mall you park close to the theater. It's a new mall, built like a small town with brick sidewalks and old-fashioned streetlights and a nostalgic atmosphere to make it easier for you to open your wallet. At Juwan's insistence, you stop at the bookstore. He rushes through the doors straight back to the children's section, that's designed like an indoor playground. You stand in the front of the store, trying to catch your breath. It's one of the chains where they sell coffee, cookies, cards, cups, CD's, calendars, why not condoms too you wonder? It's like a cathedral, and you recall how big churches convince you they got nothing to do with God and how the Smithsonian, the times you went there with Bunny and the kids, made you hate *culture*, made you glad that you watch the *X-Files* and had seen *A Few Good Men* sixteen times.

You wander to the back of the store and find Juwan and he's got an armful of books. He's just like you in this. If you come into a store, you already know what you want. You find it and get the hell out. He's holding books about dinosaurs and two Harry Potter books and one called *Bud, Not Buddy*. You'll have to use your plastic.

"Pleeeeeze?" he whines.

You're proud that he reads, that he's an honor roll, Gifted and Talented kid. But you also know that nobody likes a kid who's too smart. Because books send another message too. *You think you're better. Too good to shoot some hoops with us. Too good to hang out.* You heard Bunny tell him one day, "Books are bridges to people and experiences. You're never lonely with a book." You'd wanted to tell Juwan books can also be walls and to ask him, "What's in those books anyway? What are you hiding from?"

But you leave the store carrying a bag full of books. You walk across the street to the theater. The movie is *Shrek*. It's slick, animated, and rated PG, but the inside jokes and smart humor are for you. Although he downed a Coke and shared a tub of buttered popcorn with you, as you leave the theater Juwan announces, "I'm hungry." It is now dusk and will soon be dark. It's a school night. Bunny will raise hell, you getting him back so late. But he's your kid and he wants to go to McDonald's. As a cop you ate so much of that crap you should own stock in the company, so you take him instead to TGI Friday's, a few steps from the theater. And over dinner as he munches his fries and wolfs down the cheeseburger, Juwan tells you he's thinking about being an animator when he grows up, so he can make movies like *Shrek*. He wants to work for Disney and already knows how much money animators make, how many hours the cartoonists spent drawing the figures in the film.

As you walk to the car he reaches for your hand. This time you do not falter in your touch, grateful for the way the boy's palm in yours steadies you, even for just a moment.

Parked in front of your mother-in-law's house, where your wife and children now live, he asks, "Daddy, can you come inside? Can you stay?" He is sliding his hands up and down the seat belt.

"Juwan, you know I can't stay."

Your words inspire that sad-eyed, near-tears, stricken look that you hate. But this time it's a show of love, you're sure. Not like when you force him to go outside and play with the other boys in the neighborhood. Boys who had stopped coming to knock on the door to ask for Juwan because he's always in his room, his head stuck in a book or drawing (not even playing video games like the other boys, like his sisters even).

"I can't come in, but you'll be coming home soon." You hear the arch, almost sinister trembling in your voice. You're sure he hears it, too.

But he asks hopefully, a smile shattering the solemnity of only a moment ago. "To stay?"

"To stay." Just saying the words, assuring the boy of what you fear is a lie, melts a measure of the disdain gnawing at you. After all, you and the boy want the same thing. For them to come home.

"Your mom and me just gotta work some things out." You feel suddenly generous and pull out your wallet and press a five dollar bill in his hand. "This is just for you. Put it in your bank."

"My bank's at home."

"Well put it wherever you keep your stuff here. Okay?"

"Okay." Juwan releases the safety belt, lifts his parka, and stuffs the bill into the pocket of his pants.

"Now, go tell your mom to come out. I want to talk to her." The words sound like a court order, like a summons, although they spring, in fact, from the hungry soil of your need for Bunny, for him, for the girls.

"Okay," the boy says, reaching to open the door, then hesitating as the eyes look again at you and ask, as they always do, for more than you can give.

You playfully punch him on the jaw and say, "I'll call you tomorrow." You watch him walk away from the car to the house, wondering if you will call him tomorrow, what you will say.

Once the front door is open you hear Juwan's excited, pleading voice.

Bunny stares at you through the glass top of the storm door and nods. Then she closes the door. She'll probably make you wait like last time. Ten fucking minutes before she came to the car. Her mother, Elmira, had told you *she'd* prefer if you waited for the children outside.

"I don't have much," she'd told you, blocking your entry that day, "but I want to keep it. I don't want anything to get started in my house." Like you can't be trusted in the same room with your own wife and kids. Like you're dangerous. You only ever hit Bunny that one time. One time because everything was falling apart. Everything still is. Elmira, short, stout, her hands on her wide hips as she looked up at you contemptuously. Her graying hair is nappy, uncombed, shooting out all over her head. She reminds you of a pit bull, always looking for trouble. And Bunny letting her talk to you that way.

"What do you want, Carson?"

You hadn't even heard Bunny approach the car. You turn on the ceiling light. She's leaning through the open window on the passenger side, her long auburn hair grazing her arms. Her arms and hair are inside the car, filling it with the fragrance of Dove soap, hair conditioner, and Jergens lotion. You aren't like some men. You even know what size bra (36D) and panties (6), and shoes (8 ½) she wears. You know everything you are sure, about your wife. The car is thick with her smell, the scent of a woman who has had your babies and whose love is the only thing you want in this world or the next. Her arms and her hair are inside the car. But she keeps her face outside. You look at her hands. She's still wearing her wedding ring. Your wedding ring. A dark deep brownish-red color stains her lips and her skin glows like she's just had a facial or maybe great sex.

"You look good," you say slowly, seeing in her gaze that you look like shit. You haven't slept a full night since she left. And you feel like you've always felt, even in the uniform, even with the badge and the night stick, like a too-short, freckle-faced, sandy-haired red-bone runt. You don't know how *you* ended up with *her.*

"What is it, Carson? What do you want?"

"I wanna talk."

Bunny rolls her eyes, looks away, staring back at the house, pursing her lips as though your request, simple, humble even, is causing her pain. You follow her glance back to the house and see the porch lights on. Until this moment you had not realized how dark it is. Not until your wife asks, "What is it Carson? What do you want?" do you realize that night has fallen and you feel it close and smothering.

"Come on, get in."

"*Now* you wanna talk."

"Yeah, *now* I wanna talk." You keep the words forceful but strong, tap down the rage you feel. *Begging your own wife to talk to you. Bunny, like everybody else, against you. On the other side. Standing there looking at you like you're some jive nigguh on the corner trying to rap to her.* You remind her, "I still got rights."

Bunny opens the door and slides into the car. She sits where only moments before Juwan sat staring at you. You openly appraise her, the black wool turtleneck sweater and the tight jeans, the big hoop earrings. You've been apart thirty-eight days, and every time you see her she looks better. Rested. She's even shed some of the weight she'd gained years ago with the twins. *Thirty-eight days. Nine hundred and twelve hours. Fifty-four thousand seven hundred and twenty minutes.* Bunny squirms beneath your gaze, and looks at her hands, looks anywhere but at you.

"If you'd come back . . ." You lean closer to her, all the smells mingling, enveloping you in a cocoon of hope and longing, and she slides away from you, closer to the door. *Bitch.*

"Carson we've been there."

"Well, let's go there again." You lean in closer, just to fuck with her. Your lips almost touch. You want to kiss her. You *could* kiss her. *You're still my wife.*

"Why you freaking? Acting like I'm gonna hurt you. Like you don't even want me to touch you, huh? I mean, look at this. You take my kids. Leave me at the worst possible time. I'm getting sued. I got lawyer's fees."

Hearing your voice, everything you've just said, how the words careen and pile up, how they ring with the sound of ruin. You decide to back off.

"Carson, I'd been thinking about leaving for a long time."

"I quit the force. Isn't that what you wanted? Isn't it what you've always wanted?" You ask her this gently. A peace offering.

"Once I thought it might make a difference. I thought that might save us. I thought I couldn't get close to you because you were always wearing your uniform. Even when you weren't in it. But after what happened, I saw it wasn't the uniform. It was you." She's looking at you as she says this and now you wish she'd look at her hands. You offer peace. She wants war.

"Carson, just give us some time," she says, reaching to touch you. You want to feel her hands on you. Even if she just touches your jacket. You're sure you'll feel her fingers through the cloth. You miss her that bad. But instead this time *you* pull away.

"I don't have time. Not anymore," you say, shaking your head, quick, fast, with everything inside you. Like Juwan. "I can't live like this. Visiting my kids on the weekends. My own wife not wanting me to get close to her."

"Carson—"

"Standing by while you get involved with some other man." The accusation slithers through your lips as you look at Bunny out of the corner of your eye. You look at her and you are not moving, not breathing. So you can catch the flinch, the giveaway expression she'll try to hide.

"You know there's no one else."

"Do I?"

"Carson, it's only been a month."

"It's been five weeks," you correct her, stung by the "only," when you've felt each day like an eternity.

"We've needed some time apart for a while."

"Maybe you've needed to be away from me. But I've never needed to be away from you."

Bunny looks at you skeptically and you see all your sins in her gaze. "I haven't been perfect. I know that—"

"Don't say anymore, Carson, please."

"Maybe you can live without me. I can't live without you." There you said it. You've been whipped since you first laid eyes on her. You're pushing too hard. You feel her pulling away again. Not her body this time, but her feelings. *Stop. Stop. Back off. She's still your wife.*

But you can't stop. "I want you and the kids back. I'm not gonna let you screw me like the department did, stringing me along for months, making me think I had a chance and then kicking me off the force, telling me to re-sign or I'd be fired. What kind of choice is that? Like I'm a murderer. Like what happened to me couldn't have happened to one of them in a second. In a split second. Bunny, I want to know by the end of the week if you're coming back. Fuck this trial-separation crap. This isn't anything I want to try on for size."

These are the words that have filled you head with a wayward clamoring. And yet, you say them quietly. Quietly. You don't want to frighten her. You want her back.

"Bunny, whatever it's gonna be, tell me."

"I will, Carson," she whispers.

"I still want the kids this weekend."

"I'll bring them over on Friday, after school."

She squeezes your hand, which is tight and red-knuckled, gripping the steering wheel. You don't touch her, because if you do, touching her hand, her arm or her face won't be enough. You'll want everything. And you don't want to scare her. Not when what you're feeling for her and about every-thing is scaring *you.*

"I'll have the girls call you tonight." The words sound like a salve, but they are salt eating into your wounds. *I should be grateful.*

"Alright."

"Good-bye." With that word, she's out of the car.

You watch her walk toward the house. If she looks back, even with a glance tossed over her shoulder like looking at an object she no longer needs. Even if she turns to look quickly, hoping you won't see, no matter. *Just look back.* But Bunny walks away from you with long, defiant strides. Like she's crossing the Sahara. Climbing Everest. Treading a path she's charted in her mind, alone, without you. Her arms are folded in front of her. Sealing her tight. Against you. She doesn't look back. The front door closes behind her and stares at you like the smug, grim face of the entrance to a vault.

Fifteen minutes later, you're cruising the streets of your old beat. Martin Luther King, Jr., Boulevard is a wide, four-lane stretch of road that's always busy. Every major city you've visited in America has got a street named for King and it's always the main drag of the ghetto. Even when you weren't in your squad car patrolling the area, the hyper, unpredictable energy of this commercial zone clung to you like sweat. Although it's been eight months since you were last on duty, driving these streets that you will never patrol again, you still have the eyes of a cop. Suspicious, probing, curious, you had to know the street and be prepared for anything, all the time. They didn't ask much of you being a cop, just the damn near impossible.

There are the fast-food places, Popeyes, KFC, McDonald's, Wendy's, the liquor stores, like outposts, one every third intersection, the car washes, and the pawn shop housed in an old laundromat, the words PAWN SHOP large in garish green and yellow neon, crowning the building. Until this moment you've never wondered why cops called the stretch of territory you'd been sworn to protect against crime and mayhem a beat. But that's what the streets did to you. The length and breadth of this section of Cartersville is veiled in a permanent gloom. Cops call it "Dodge City."

If you were still on the force, you'd have started your shift at four o'clock, savoring the early near-quiet first hour before the traffic accidents, speeders and red-light runners took over. Then when people got home, got settled, and the domestic disturbances flared like summer brush fires. People couldn't wait to get home, but then soon as they open the front door, they lose it. Two brothers argue over who controls the T.V. remote control. One lands in the hospital, the other in jail. A woman locks her boyfriend out of the apartment and throws his clothes out the window into the parking lot. You're called to mediate. Kids spray paint store windows. Complaints of barking dogs. A couple that's lived together three years argues, the woman accuses the man of rape, then recants the story an hour later. You collar three fourteen-year-olds selling weed in the unlocked basement of an elementary school. A father suspects his son of stealing his money to buy drugs and wants you to evict him from the house.

You pull into a gas station and get out to fill up. The gas station mini-mart is crowded. You walk over to the coffee stand and pour a decaf into a large Styrofoam cup. Tear open two packs of sugar, stir, snap the top on and get in line. It's almost nine o'clock. You stand behind a burly, gray-haired taxi driver who pulled in moments before you. The line for lottery tickets at the second cash register is long and you recall having seen something on the news about the state lottery. Was it fifty, sixty, eighty million dollars? The people in line haven't got a prayer and they seem to know it, standing solemn, cheerless, quiet as penitents clutching crinkled bills in their hands, staring into space, or deep in thought, worrying about bills, wondering what they'll do if they win. The odds against them are criminal. *And even if they won, nothing would change,* you think. *Nothing that matters, anyway.*

The Pakistani who owns the station smiles at you in recognition. "Sergeant Blake," he says, the words clipped and heavily accented, the voice flush with a respect for you that you have never heard in an American voice. He's got large, droopy dark eyes and a thin angular face that tells you nothing of his age. He reaches for the dollar and quarter for the coffee. But when you tell him "Twenty on number seven," he nods and waves a brown hand, his skin darker than yours, saying, "Have a good night."

Since you arrested the men who robbed him and his son a two years ago, he's insisted on giving you a free fill-up when you come in. They burst through the door of the mini-mart two minutes before closing, pistol-whipped the son, blinding him in one eye, then tied father and son up and locked them in the back storage room. All for $387.50. Two nights later you caught the two at the end of a high-speed chase that lasted half an hour and involved six squad cars. They were driving away from the third station they'd held up in an hour and a half. It took a year for the case to come to trial. They got five years. After the arrest, Mohammed Musharraf's wife brought a banquet of Pakistani dishes to the station one night as a show of thanks. Standing in the station house Musharraf kept shaking your hand, and saying "Anything, anything, I can do for you just tell me." He knows what happened. Knows you're not on the force anymore, but calls you "Sergeant" anyway. You let him.

Outside you put the nozzle in the tank and fill up. In the distance, atop a rise that is part of the Belle Manor apartment complex, you see a group of boys shooting hoops on a tiny patch of cement court. It's a Monday night. You've seen those boys shooting hoops in the snow. In the rain. A mural of Tupac, sloe-eyed and watchful, hovers over the boys' shoulders.

You've made one hundred and fifty arrests in twelve years, and "Dodge City" still overflows with drugs. It's a wasteland. You're not a sergeant. You're a garbage collector. (You will always think like a cop. It will always be present tense for you.) The still neat but weathered bungalows that line the streets adjacent to King Boulevard are home to some of the first blacks who moved out to Cartersville from D.C. Some of their kids are dealers. Some of *them* are buyers.

To the drug dealers, you're the interloper, the intruder, hassling them on their turf. Their hatred of you rubs off on the kids, turning them into urban Robin Hoods. Even the hardworking adults who don't hate you, don't trust you either. They never look you straight in the eye, scream brutality if you look ready to touch them, but never tell you you've done a good job when you throw the dealers in jail.

You stopped seeing their faces years ago. But there are some faces you can still see. Some you always will. The seven people you've shot at, or wounded. *The young man I killed.*

You politely dismiss the orange-hatted elderly who actually think that a group of sixty- or seventy-year-olds sitting on a corner, or patrolling with flashlights, decreases crime. (The smartest dealers simply put out the word not to touch the old people because of the heat it will bring down on them). And to the middle-aged couples who make dozens of calls, to complain about the weekend night drag racing along the boulevard (thirty or forty cars that scatter as soon as you drive up and then regroup once you leave), you keep your advice simple: "Move." Your old beat. You beat. And got beat. Leaning on your trunk, watching the familiar scene the thudding, taut wires of your heart activate your hands that reach reflexively for the gun in the holster at your side that no longer is there. That pulse kept you sharp. Kept you on top. Kept you alive.

Bunny accusing you of "wearing your uniform all the time." What are you supposed to do? You carry a gun everywhere. You sleep with a gun. Not in your hands but in your head. You're a cop twenty four/seven. *A cop* banging your wife or girlfriend, your mistress, or a quick piece of surprise "bonus pussy" you lucked up on. *A cop* singing hymns in church on Sunday morning. A cop sitting in a restaurant with your family, eyes scanning the place (you can't help it; it's automatic), hoping, *Please nobody go crazy in here and start acting a fool.* But just in case, you got your revolver strapped to your ankle. *A cop* stumbling out of some bar in plainclothes, head tight, but not quite wasted, coming upon a burglary. The sight instantly clears you and as you pull out your revolver a fellow officer, *in uniform* arrives, and you're yelling, "I'm on the job. I'm on the job," thrusting your shield into the darkness.

Cars fill the parking lot of the liquor store across the street like the lot at nearby Fed Ex Field on a home-game Sunday. In that same lot with only a month on the force, you were called to break up a fight. Young. Inexperienced. Scared of fucking up. Making a bad arrest. Adrenaline pumping you up, pushing you, making you feel crazy, invincible and yeah, you're still scared. Right off the bat you violate rule number one. Wait for backup. But you want to prove yourself. And surely you can handle this. There's a crowd but they're just watching the two men go at it. A big, burly Incredible Hulk mutha and a wiry, short guy who's bloody, but won't stop fighting. You radio for backup. But you don't wait. Can't wait. Hell, the guy could get killed. So you jump out of the car and swing into the crowd. Your night stick breaks when you slam it on the back of the bruiser, who turns around, not even flinching at the sight of you in uniform, shouting into your radio for backup. He doesn't even stop in his tracks. You try to body slam him, but it's like scaling a mountain. You're on the ground and the monster is astride you, choking you. The crowd's voices are a lurid, wild, jeering chant. Some are rooting for you. Some are shouting "Kick the cop's ass." Straining to remove the mutha's greasy huge hands from your neck, you hear your radio slide, cold and slick, across the parking lot into the crowd. The bastard starts banging your head against the cement. Once. Twice. Pain numbs and reverberates, blasts across your temples, and for a moment you can't see. Then two men from the crowd jump in, wrestle the guy off you just as two police cruisers arrive. The lights and the sirens, loud, disorienting, disperses the crowd. You suffer a concussion. That's not the only ass-whipping you get. You've been shot in the arm at the scene of a bank robbery, suffered whiplash when your cruiser crashed into another patrol car chasing a stolen SUV. But you gave as good as you got. Got even. Got even and then some.

You top off the tank and pull out of the station. You're driving. Headed nowhere. You just don't want to go home. No longer are you guardian of these streets. Driving you feel like a nomad. One with no destination.

It's 1988 when you join the force. Your first partner is a white guy named Deek Rehnquist. He's been on the force twenty years and is a go-along to get-along granny goose. He figures he ain't been shot yet so he's not putting his ass anywhere near the line of fire. But you joined the force to make a difference, to catch the bad guys, to see some action And this *fuck* is your partner. You have missed the worst of the eighties crack wars, but there's still plenty to do. Deek talks about the early eighties like it was Korea, or Vietnam. "Hell, sometimes we'd take fifteen, sixteen service calls a shift," he tells you, shaking his head and letting out a long, smooth whistle of disbelief at the memory. "We were patrolling all the hell holes. The crack dens, the open-air markets. And for all that work, we got the minimum mandatory sentences, it was just a revolving door." You realize quick that a partner is like another wife. On Bunny's birthday, yours and the kids, on Christmas, on your wedding anniversary, you're with Deek. Your shift is 95 percent boredom, 5 percent terror. Half your shift is just talking, talking to your partner, as you cruise the beat, keeping your eyes on the street and everybody *on the street.*

Deek grew up in the county like you, but out in Crofton, where his old man was the sheriff. He talks guns and hockey, deer hunting, and how great a President Ronald Reagan was. On bad days Deek grumbles about his seventeen-year-old granddaughter getting pregnant by a "colored" boy at her high school and deciding to keep the baby and what the hell is the family supposed to do? You remind him that you're not Oprah and that nobody says "colored" anymore.

"I'm not a racist. I want you to know that, Carson," he tells you as you pull into the lot of a 7 Eleven to get your third cup of coffee of the shift. Deek's got a slow, country, long-legged gait, and the beginnings of a paunch. His buzz crew cut shows more of his scalp than ought to be legal. "My daddy hired the first colored deputy in Crofton and took heat for it, too."

"Am I sposed to say thank you?"

"I just want you to know I ain't no redneck."

Deek may not be a redneck, but you know that he's scared shitless of black perps. When you pick up a young Blood, you can smell Deek's fear. How quick he is to pull his gun, how he goes overboard with the black suspects even when they offer little resistance. You're the rookie, so you don't say anything. You go along to get along. Like Deek. Your beat samples a bit of the whole county—the just-made-it middle-class white section, the boogie-black haven called Heaven's Gate, and the streets of Dodge City. You see Deek put on the kid gloves, or just ignore shit in *his* neighborhood. But you don't say a word. Back then you can't imagine that one day they'll all just be perps to you.

After a while you start listening to Deek and he's got all sorts of stories about the department, the chief, the politics of the department, who's getting promoted, who's not. And all of it you need to know. He's not interested in you much at all and that suits you fine. You can't imagine yourself telling Deek about Bunny. But what galls you is that Deek's lazy. You damn near have to twist his arm to get him to stop for a traffic violation or to park in a strategic spot in a crime-ridden area to make a point, or some arrests. He wants to drive and talk the whole shift.

Then one afternoon the day after Easter Monday, two dealers erupt into a shoot-out over a drug deal gone bad along one of the quietest, loveliest streets nearly hidden in the backside of Dodge City. A twelve-year-old girl riding her bike is killed, caught in the crossfire. Within an hour the department knows who they're looking for. There's an APB out and everybody is working overtime, questioning witnesses and cruising, looking for the suspect.

You and Deek have been given a description of the shooter and his car. It's seven o'clock and you can't believe it when you and Deek pass a Popeyes and you spot the car and the suspect. He's leaning against the hood of the car, laughing and talking trash. You wonder if he's laughing about the girl he killed earlier that day. As you and Deek pull into the parking lot he breaks into a run. Deek radios for back up and you bolt out of the car and chase him. He runs behind the stores to the back of the mall. You're running faster than you knew you could. You hear Deek behind you. Not close enough. And you also hear another squad car, its siren closing in. The suspect trips and falls in front of a trash Dumpster. On the ground, he's holding his ankle, squealing like a pig in pain. Your flashlight speckles the darkness with light that lands on his face and you figure he's maybe sixteen at the most. His dark-skinned, childish face is mangled, twisted by belligerence and rage. He wears a bandanna tied around his head like he's a Blood or a Crip. Deek finally catches up and is all over the kid, searching him and cuffing him, raising from the ground with a gun and a palm full of tiny cellophane packets of crack.

You hear more footsteps and you turn to see Vincent Proctor nearing you. He's a light-skinned blue-veined *brother*. You thought he was white when you first saw him. Even in the darkness you see the tiny pencil-thin mustache, the small eyes that are as hard as metal flints. Some cops love him. Some cops hate his guts. You don't know why. To your eyes Vincent Proctor walks like a man who's got everything he needs—*with him, on him. All the time.* He's a kick-ass who prefers the uniform to undercover and who saved the life of another cop trapped in a burning car and another with a gun pointed at his head in a hostage situation. On the ground, the kid is yelling about the cuffs being too tight and his ankle being broken.

"Nigga, if you don't shut up I'll give you a real reason to scream," Proctor tells him.

"Fuck you muthafucka," the kid shouts.

"This ain't no rap video you stupid-ass," Proctor yells as he begins kicking the kid in the head, the ribs, in the groin, in the back, his thick muscular arms outstretched almost as if he is balancing himself or performing a dance movement with each kick. You can't believe how loud is the sound of Proctor's shoes against the kid's clothing and his flesh. The kid's moans strangle the chilly April air. Deek is holding the gun and the crack, watching Proctor, his eyes huge and still.

"Fuck *you* muthafucka," Proctor taunts. A dim halogen bulb hangs from the roof of the back of the pizza parlor above the trash Dumpster. And so you see everything. The boy's face, blood soaked and unrecognizable, Proctor's foot on the kid's stomach as though to hold him in place. The hands cuffed in front of him. Proctor, his pencil-thin mustache the only color on his ghost-white face, and his presence making you feel smaller and the moment bigger than anything you've been a part of before. You hear Proctor asking "Blake, you want a piece a this?"

The kid's moans sicken you. But Proctor is watching and if any questions are asked, it's three men and one story. You've known that since the first day. The first kick is half-hearted, the second and the third, you just close your eyes so you don't see the kid. The fourth and fifth, it's like you're a machine. And then you feel Proctor's hand on your shoulder. You know it's Proctor, not Deek, and he's saying, "I think he's got the point." You open your eyes and Proctor winks at you and you know the lesson is through. You and Proctor and Deek haul the kid off the ground and lead him out of the alley. You've left something back there on the ground where the kid had lain beneath the light, something mixed in with the trash and dirt overflowing from the Dumpster. Walking out of the alley into the rows of police cruisers that had blocked off the alley, that night isn't the last night you don't look back to see what it is.

Here

BY AUDREY PETTY

There's no way to not pass The Pita Hut and the men who come early to wait. Today, it makes me laugh, the way they lose language at the sight of live women. From thirty feet, they begin preparing. Shifting like ants, their circle opens in formation. They slouch at attention—narrowed eyes, mouths panted open. But Deanna says what she knows and hates is that they'd never look at one of their own women like that. And she's right. And I'm mad before I know it, fumbling to do something I mean: stop and stare, spit and curse, scream the world out of place. They are still looking when I turn back for their eyes. Aproned fools. I can live without their fucking hummus. Deanna catches me before I keep going. "Slow down, girl. We're here."

The air in the cooler dries the sweat to my face. I watch my biceps settle under the weight of trays of poached salmon, going up and up and up the bruised stairs to the narrow kitchen in the back of the store. Deanna sighs over coffee, eyes closed and rubbing her brows like she's reading her mind, thumb and forefinger meeting, parting at the bridge of her nose. She leans into the steam before closing the cambro. "That's all I need," she says.

We'll let Howard be the man and heave all this coffee up and out. He'll be running late and have some Howard stories to make laughter, even once the mosquitoes hum hungry into us, and folks start getting wine-rowdy. I gather my braids in a knot and change into white shirt and apron.

We are traying asparagus when Ben walks in without footsteps, complaining that the cake won't be ours. "This is a corner man and wife have chosen to cut." He smirks and winks at no one in particular. Sometimes, I get tired of puns. "It's coming from Leona's," he adds. Leona uses mix and bright, heavy frosting. With a cake like that, these won't be big tippers. Ben sets down the folder with a half smile and heads out, grabbing the van keys and mumbling about booze and ice.

And so we wait. The food's unpacked. Howard's stocked the bar. Deanna's folded napkins, set out china and candles on all the tables, inside and outside. She twists in a stuffed chair in the sitting room, reading *Incidents in the Life of a Slave Girl.* If she leaves it visible, it will make someone nervous. Deanna acts like she doesn't know this. Howard and Allison lean and bend, uncorking fat bottles of vino verde. The harpist is carting around, looking for the spot to play without an amp. Summer heat has filled this big old house. The ice will not last the night. The florist came too soon.

The bride's sister introduces herself as the bride's sister. Tracy. I see the resemblance. Severe cheekbones. Orphan Annie hair. She asks me if I am who I am. It happens like this. "Yes, I'm in charge," I tell her. "Yes, we're ready for the guests." I glance sideways to remind Deanna not to set any tablecloths on fire. Tracy should be going by now, but she remains in place, smiling a sniffing smile. I turn back to the house to make myself useful.

We eat while we can, while the house creaks, while the tent is full of quiet people, all except the man up front, talking with his hands. Bride and groom kiss, and the applause sounds like rain from this distance. I roll up my sleeves and straighten my collar. It's time go outside and disappear.

"Scallops wrapped in bacon . . . Scallops wrapped in bacon." "Scallops wrapped in bacon?" "Scallops wrapped in bacon."

Some say "here" for me to stop. Others "please." Most wait silently, glancing to be understood.

I cut more lemons for ice water and look forward to the scent they will leave on my palms. Deanna edges past, her tray full with toothpicks, balled napkins, the shards of a plate. She dumps them and Handiwipes her hands and neck. There's not much left to size up in the fridge. Deanna moves in closer, bending and humming. She smiles at the last tray of stuffed mushrooms.

"Notice the brother out there?"

"Hard to miss." I saw him on my way past the bar. Howard was opening his bottle of beer. Pale-green linen suit. Looked a little like my cousin Ray. Broad-chested and peacefully serious.

"Tell you now, he's the kind that looks away. We remind him."

"Black bean spirals? . . . Black bean spirals? . . . Black bean spirals . . . Black bean spirals?"

Guests are spread across the lawn. They buzz in polite circles, happy with their beverages. Some open as I approach. Reaching for a spiral, a man with a handlebar mustache talks about the films of Kieslowski. "Genius of our lifetime," he declares. The circle waits for him to chew. I look ahead to the next, waiting for the silence of full hands.

It is time to relieve Howard and Allison at the bar. They're grateful and a bit sluggish. Howard is hungover today, quieter than he really is. "Take fifteen," I tell them. "Rest. Standing in one place can make a person tired." Finally still, I realize the day is almost over. I will serve women impatient for wine. I will serve children who rattle their cups for Coca-Cola. I will serve beer to men who really want eye contact. But for now, I am alone in this corner of the porch, my face cupped in my lemoned palms, my elbows cooling where ice has melted. I watch the horizon dusking ripe and remember the darkness of that one Kieslowski film—the scene, that scene, when Veronika collapses.

Veronika is blushing and singing, losing her heart as her voice swells and thickens. And when she falls, the camera sees the sky of that concert hall ten different ways before the noise of her body meeting the stage and the leap and zoom overhead in a brief, straight line—before someone finally holds her wrist, limp as a promised fish.

Tracy's sister approaches. Her dress has a righteous train. She beams. "Call me Liz," she insists, holding herself. They are finished with pictures.

"Come in," I tell her. "Come in for the buffet."

Deanna's pouring out the last of the fruit salad. "Old boy on the harp is just sad." She laughs to herself and tops the platter with mint. "Out there playing the theme from 'Cheers.' And trying to get funky before . . . Lionel Richie, Bee Gees, somebody." I haven't heard the harpist for hours. I want to remember that song from the movie.

I carry full bags of trash to the big metal cans outside, empty and sour from all this happiness. Only hours to go. Back in the kitchen, I soap my hands and forearms and rinse them with fast, warm water.

There are those sighs and gasps and someone flashing a camera when I wheel out the cake. Deanna will follow with the engraved knife. I watch for darting children and feel my breath caught and my arms stiffening a tremble.

I rinse and stack things that can already be put away. The groom thinks I can help him.

"What was in that fucking chicken?" he asks, slamming his Pilsen, rubbing the top of his neck through his bowtie.

"Excuse me, sir?" He moves closer until I can see that his mouth is a bit greasy and his face is strange—red, expectant. The door is still snapping behind him in short, frantic arcs.

"One of you girls drop a fingernail in my food?"

"Excuse me?"

"Listen. I swallowed something wrong." His voice breaks like a child's and his stare begins to twitch.

I dry my hands, considering. "The chicken was garnished with rosemary," I say. He stops and leans forward, his knee bent and atop the folded stepladder. "You swallowed a sprig, maybe."

I hold his gaze until he starts looking past me, over my shoulder, clearing his throat over and over, jerking his head, becoming the bird he has eaten.

Something soft to chew may help make him right again. I pull the final baguette from the tote and turn to find him draining the beer from his glass. I will not cut my hand slicing for this groom. I take my time and hand him three rounds.

"Thank you," he confesses.

Veronika never sings in the film. She lives sadly in Paris, waiting until things begin to happen.

People with children have already left. It is beginning, the last hour of this party. The tent is empty now, all but for an armful of plates and bottles. A few guests come to tell me that the food was exquisite. Someone is howling near the bar.

Somebody's momma is always wearing sequins at their child's wedding. This one reaches to touch my hair before she even speaks. I hold the empties close to my chest and I wonder. "Aaah"—her fingers work their way up and down a braid—"beautiful. Feels like rope." I wonder who she thinks I am. She wants to know does it take long.

There are others who wait for my answer. "Like Whoopi Goldberg," some old man says. I feel myself smile and I don't know why. "Six, seven hours," I say. Someone else's hand is reaching. I remember his freckles from the bar and I back away before something gets broken. "Can you wash it?" he wants to know. "I'll get more napkins," I explain, moving swiftly to leave the bottles with Howard at the bar, regathering my hair on my way through the parlor.

Before I reach the kitchen, I find them glowing on the bureau in the corner of the sitting room, bound with a broad white sash. I gather them and head out back, past the trash cans, to the small barn that holds crates for china, boxes for linen, things I cannot see. I settle underneath the light hanging high from the beam, studying these strange, strange flowers. I do not know the name for them, but I am drawn in by their blush, their velvet purple centers, by the way they show their seeds. I imagine the island they should come from, lush and distant, my own twin there, waiting for that tug so that something might begin. I touch their warm waxy skin and close my eyes. Outside, another car starts and slows away, and there's that harp music, somewhere farther, finally beautiful. I take my time and pull each petal free.

Summer Comes Later

BY ROBERT FLEMING

Looking out the car window, he saw the red oasis city of Marrakech in the distance, toward the dark outline of the mountains. Ahead three men in ragged djellabas herded a flock of sheep along the road. The truck in front of him weaved wildly back and forth, then jerked to a sudden stop before the sea of unruly wool. The abrupt halt of his ancient Saab sent the entire backseat cargo sailing in the humid air, down into a jumble on the floor, his camera equipment, thermos, pair of battered suitcases, and rumpled bag of figs and dates.

He recognized that he was in exile, away from New York. Fleeing from America. Historically, he was not the first writer in his late thirties to seek a place of solace other than home, the troubled land of his birth, to recover and heal. Baldwin did it. Hemingway did it. In fact, many of his countrymen did it. Still, none of his pals understood why he would walk away from a good-paying job on a newspaper to catch his breath. But he was a refugee of the wounded heart and tarnished romance. He'd had his moment of glory, his day in the sun, his fifteen minutes of fame, and then it'd been all downhill. Like so many baby boomers, he was feeling the aggression of the hungry, skilled young black reporters, half his age, who were not scarred by the memories of Jim Crow and determined to make their mark in the business. He saw them ruthlessly pushing forward throughout the industry, breaking through on every level, more comfortable with whites and the corporate world than he ever could be. This was what he was up against. This was what his wife never understood. In her mind, he had never achieved his potential; he had failed their dream.

His moment under the media sun's glistening rays had come when he'd interviewed Yasir Arafat in the early 1980s in a small pock-marked building in Beirut, Lebanon. A car, full of the man's private staff, all armed, had picked him up at his hotel and driven him blindfolded into the Arab quarter. He'd been guided, staggering, into a room, where the blinders were removed and the short, bearded man sat before him at a long table with a large Palestinian flag mounted on the wall behind him: The first thing he'd noticed about Arafat was his drab–green military fatigues and the large holstered gun on his hip.

"It is the will of Allah that I lead my people back to their homeland, that I overcome the Jewish invaders," Arafat had said, staring at him as if he were an alien being. "This struggle will not be won overnight. It will take years, maybe generations, to come, but it will come. Before it is over, there will be much war waged in the name of peace, many will die, but it will come."

When he'd tried to question the PLO leader about the so-called Islamic menance to peace, Moslem extremists, the wild card of Arabian oil, and the interference of the West in the battle for a homeland, Arafat reminded him of the sacking of the Holy Temple of Jerusalem by the Romans in A.D. 70, the calling for a Jewish state of Palestine by Theodor Herzl in 1887, the dominance of the British during the late 1930s, the 1947 Partition, the first war by the Arabs against the Jews shortly thereafter, and the annexing of the West Bank by Jordan and the Gaza by Egypt. Without a doubt, it was a history lesson rendered slowly and expertly by the tiny man with the penetrating dark eyes.

"You must know how we feel to be forced from one place to another, nomads, never at home anywhere," Arafat said through clenched teeth. "Your people endured it as slaves so it must not be a strange feeling for you to understand."

Every foreign reporter he knew had warned him how shrewd and perceptive Arafat could be, possessing skills that often misled journalists into underestimating him, much to their chagrin. But he would not be fooled. He researched the leader from his early days as a founder of the Al Fatah, the guerilla army formed to fight the Israelis in 1959, to his post in the fledgling PLO in the mid 1960, and finally to his ascension to PLO chairman in 1969. When the PLO was kicked out of Jordan in 1970, Arafat and the boys moved to Beirut.

"Why aren't you writing this down?" Arafat asked him, motioning to one of his aides.

"Well, this is pretty much background," he'd replied, holding his pad up. "I'm waiting for your response to my questions about any movement to the peace process."

Arafat picked up the telephone and spoke quietly into it. While the leader talked, one of his most trusted men tried to place his chief in context, speaking softly about his exploits in battle, the speeches, and the botched assassination attempts. He was indeed a survivor.

"Someone must pay the cost of peace, take it on, and not be afraid to die," Arafat continued after the phone call ended. "I'm not popular with anyone. The guns are pointed at my head from every direction. Let me ask you this. Do you think the Americans will ever accept us as they do the Jews?"

The two men talked for almost three hours nonstop and the result was a series of articles *ARAFAT SPEAKS!* that brought him praise and book offers back in the West. That was then. That was before the days of the Great Drought.

Now he was back in the region, following up leads about fundamentalist hardliners, terrorist cells, threats to American embassies, and the changing winds of the Islamic Jihad. On the road to Marrakech, he understood that his nerves were frayed at the edges, unraveling swiftly, and nothing could prevent him from doing something stupid.

Tempers flared in the white glare of the noonday sun. He watched the men in the truck descend on the Berber herders, arms waving, shouting in harsh Arabic for the herders to clear a path. Fierce and proud, the Berbers took their time, moving at a slow regal pace, casually guiding the animals to the road's narrow shoulders with well-aimed pokes of their sticks. Behind him, others grew impatient, filling the air with sharp curses, guttural threats and the angry barks of their car horns.

Sitting behind the steering wheel of his aging car, wrapped in the stifling Moroccan heat his mind went back to his beloved ex-wife Janet, her satiny voice in his head mixing in seamless unison with the cacophony of mayhem outside. The tape played on, spilling brine onto his internal wounds, triggering that bone-deep ache, the bitter regret of his failed marriage.

Finally, the traffic moved, winding up the road toward the city. Woozy from the long drive from Tangiers, he tried to remember his first trip to Morocco in the 1970s, when he stayed at the El Monsour in Casablanca, the Rebat Hilton and the grand old Momounia in Marrakech. He was a kid then, in his early twenties. His father gave him the trip after reading Paul Bowles' novel, *The Sheltering Sky*, with Port and Kit trying to jump-start their dull lives with an ill-fated trip to the desert: the vast, merciless Sahara. His father, ever the academic with his literature class at Columbia, stood with him in the air terminal, going through his checklist of essentials for international travel. First, travel light. Second, buy your medicines such as aspirin, cold medications, and toiletries before leaving the States. Third, and most important, keep your traveler's checks, credit cards and cash on your person in an inside jacket pocket, not in your carry-on luggage or other suitcases. Fourth, lock up your valuables in the hotel safe. Don't leave them unprotected in your hotel room. All good advice. Being well-traveled, the old man knew what he was talking about.

This time in Marrakech, he stayed in a small hotel not far from the city's Holiday Inn, which featured adequately sized rooms with telephone and old Philco televisions harking back to the glory days of Milton Berle and Sid Caesar. After checking in, he sat on the queen-sized beds, thinking of taking a stroll down near Hotel Layesh where there was always action and a questionable clientele. Kif peddlers. Quick-fingered thieves. Burned out torch singers. Forsaken women on carnal display, outside of the protection of the Qur'an. Dangerous at night, it was also not particularly safe to stroll down there in daylight.

The telephone rang. It was Dr. Mrabet, a great friend of his father and his old Columbia professor in Middle Eastern literature and philosophy. Word was he possessed a connection to several terrorist groups in the region, some of them violent and extreme.

"William, welcome to Marrakech," the doctor said. "So what are your plans?"

"Following up a story on the Al Kufir, a band of hardcore extremists who have had their hands in much of the terrorist attacks in Israel, Egypt, Jordan, Yemen, Pakistan, India and Afghanistan," he answered. "I'm waiting for a contact, someone to get me inside."

"Maybe that's a story you should leave alone," the doctor replied. "One you should step away from. Come around and see me. We'll talk about old times."

"Why do you say I should leave it alone?"

"Because there are some things you should not bother. Walk away and go home. These people are fundamentalists devoted to the Islamic Jihad and I don't think they're anyone you might want to aggravate. You're an American. They hate Americans. I say leave it alone and go home."

"I can't," he said. "I've got to take a chance. I need this one."

The doctor switched gears. "Why aren't you married, good looking man like you?"

"Our marriage didn't take," I said. "My wife stopped loving me. I came here to get my head on straight. To heal. And to win a Pulitzer by doing the first inside story on Al Kufir. I can't leave until I do that."

"Do you know what I'm hearing, William?" The doctor's voice had a bite to it.

"What?"

"There is talk around the city that you're not just a journalist, that you are something else. A spy, a CIA operative. Believe me, if you go digging for your story in the wrong quarters, you will be killed. These are very serious, dedicated people. The streets are not safe. There have been shootings, bombings, kidnappings of foreigners, and other things. General unrest. The police and army are everywhere. Be careful, please.

The spy comment struck a nerve. "So that's what they say. Well, I am what I say I am."

The doctor laughed low in his throat. "Tell that to the men who follow you about. My son, your every move is being watched. If you stay here, you're a marked man. Enough about this story. We'll talk more when I see you."

"I look forward to that," he replied.

"Insha'allah, worry not because Allah makes all things right," the doctor said. "He is merciful, compassionate and fair. If you are meant to get this story, it will be so and nothing can stop it from happening. If it is the will of Allah. Worry not, my son. What is meant cannot be stopped."

The phone went silent. After the call, William reviewed his notes, checked the addresses from his sources, and fell asleep on the bed. It was just a matter of time.

Now at dusk, he remained holed up awaiting word if the righteous would welcome him, an infidel, into the world. While he waited he watched a nude couple through the window on the side of the hotel. He could see everything. The woman knew how to work her magic. Her Arab lover did his part as well, letting her straddle him on the bed, kissing and licking the soft brown skin of his broad chest around and near his erect nipples. At times, she indulged in her love play as if her life depended on the heat of her passion. But there were moments when the fervent kisses, frenzied caresses, and demented wails bordered on fake, like something out of a well re-hearsed strip show, a practiced lie nevertheless. She rode him hard and strong, the man's hairy hands worrying her moist sex underneath the cloth while her fingers encircled his neck. When his nature had been sufficiently aroused and his sap was high, he applied his tongue to the tender skin near her navel and down in the curly cleft between her legs. Her screams of joy echoed in the air to mix with the occasional murmur of gunfire. Her Arab lover then tilted the amber glow of the lamp as he moved to re-enter her, so the watcher could see his thin, craggy face. Once the brown man plunged into her again, he never took his eyes off the stranger across the alley until she trembled violently once or twice underneath him, her sweaty legs locked tightly around his gleaming buttocks. The Arab man knew the dark Ameri-can was watching them.

Watching them brought it all back. Janet and the days before the crack-up. He felt utterly alone now, cut off from the world, from all tenderness, love or redemption. Despair, terror, and gloom landed against his chest like a series of cruel, vicious slaps.

"Sweetheart," Janet, his wife said the night before she left him.

"What, baby?"

"William, tell me you'll never leave me. Tell me you love me."

She was toying with him. The marriage was already dead. He never answered her, mumbled something under his breath and rolled away from her, angered that she'd even asked that of him.

When his editor called two hours later from New York, his eyes were swollen from crying. His voice was thick with tears and the words stuck in his throat. None of it was lost on the white man who had hired him when no one else would, especially on a big time city daily.

"How's the story coming?" his editor asked, his tone cheery.

"It's a waiting game but I expect something to break any day now. I've put some feelers out and the fish are circling. I expect a nibble soon."

"Bill, we believe in you. But we can't foot the bill for you to take a vacation. We expect results. Find the rag heads you need to talk to and get this thing over with. And don't take any unnecessary chances."

"Yeah, you bet," he said, then hung up. Outside, police sirens sounded in an annoying chorus.

If it is the will of Allah. What is meant cannot be stopped. If it is the will of Allah.

He looked out of the window toward the hotel across the street, hoping for a distraction from the room where the young Arab couple met every day. But the shade was down and there was nothing to see. Not a damn thing to watch. Killing time, he sprawled on the bed, completely nude, smoking cigarette after cigarette. As the ashtrays filled and the black telephone on the nightstand near his bed remained silent, he became more and more anxious. Then his mind wandered back a few years to when he covered a rash of terrorist bombings in Tangiers, committed by a new splinter group determined to shake up the status quo.

Once in Tangiers, he saw a woman, dressed in rather risqué Western clothes, being shunned by other Arabs walking along one of the city's narrow side streets. Her head and eyebrows were shaved, much like the French woman collaborators of the Nazis, who were marched through cobbled Parisenne streets after the Second World War. The unforgiving crowd parted for her, this vessel of condemned female flesh, like the stacked waters of the Red Sea under the power of Moses' blessed staff. As he'd neared the scarlet woman, he'd seen alarm and fear in her dark eyes and in the contorted expressions of the others as they went out of their way to move around her, avoiding all contact. His companion, Abu Omar, a writer from a local Arab newspaper, had cautioned him to steer clear of her as well. No talking or touching.

The woman's beauty was in her modern attitude, her courage to be bold, at least that was what he told himself. To her, he was just another American infidel. As she passed him her gaze changed from fear to a sharp look of disdain, and she marched past with her head held arrogantly aloft. Each of her proud steps sounded a brutal note of contempt for both him and the crowd.

Eventually, the memories of the woman and Tangiers dissolved into another fit of worry and self-loathing. He was not a weak man but lately all of his feelings were right at the surface. He cried again, the same stale tears. As he reached for a tissue, the telephone rang. The game was on. A man speaking thick Arabic mentioned Al Kubir, his Islamic Jihad story, the doctor's revered name, and said for him to be at the marketplace, at Djemaa El Fna tomorrow at two. The caller concluded with a threat that if he were not there, there would not be a second chance. They would not contact him again. Dr. Mrabet's words came back to him with a fury: *If it is the will of Allah.*

After hanging up, he sat on the windowsill and smoked a cigarette, watching the soldiers man a barricade down the street from his hotel. Twice he'd tried to go to the open-air market on the edge of the square not four blocks away, but soldiers, carrying machine guns, had turned him back. They told him that it was not safe to be on the streets, to return home because a group of rowdies were shooting at anyone dumb enough to be out walking on the cobbled roads. Which was not true. Something else was going on in the city. Angry, he defied them this day to make a short jog across the road to a turbaned merchant, who sold him a bag of nectarines, mangoes, figs, raisins, and a bottle of fermented palm wine.

Upon his return, the man at the desk told him that he had two international calls while he was out. One from a woman with a husky voice, sounded like a man with a bad head cold and the other from a man with high-pitched nasal voice who asked if he was still alive and whether the hotel had been strafed by bullets during the afternoon ruckus. Neither person left a number to call back. He went upstairs and turned on the radio to listen to the evening program of foreign chatter and music. That night, there was no show across the alleyway, although he did see the woman leave the building dressed in traditional garb with veil with a man in European clothes carrying two gift-wrapped boxes. They drove off in a small dark sedan, which had a jagged line of bullet holes in the door on its passenger side and a shattered rear window.

With the coming of dawn, he could see how dark and dismal the morning would be. It was not long before a strong wind whipped down the narrow corridors of the town, accompanied by forks of lightning and sheets of driving rain. Still, he heard the sound of military helicopters circling overhead, searching the streets for any odd activity. After breakfast, he decided to go for a walk to see what was happening in the town. To hell with the authorities. Maybe his press pass would carry some weight this time. Soldiers, tanks, and jeeps with mounted machine guns were parked on every corner and checkpoints were set up at all of the key points of the areas where the trouble had broke out for the past four nights. Twice he was stopped by police, questioned, and checked for identification. The fact that he was an American journalist brought scowls from the armed military men, but little else happened and he was allowed to go on his way.

Still, none of it was cool. He looked at his watch. He was screwed. It was well after three. If it wasn't for bad luck, he wouldn't have any luck at all.

The Bulging Bag

BY UNOMA N. AZUAH

The harsh Lagos sun came down on the motley crowd of traders, civil servants, market women, mad people, children, hawkers, and beggars. Presently, a rickety bus called a *molue* appeared, quaking and shuddering in an attempt to stop. People jumped out, others in the same manner jumped in. When the bus eventually came to a stop, the press of people from the inside and the outside created a temporary dam. Seeing this, the driver adroitly jerked the bus a few meters forward; the dam burst, spilling its contents.

Mr. Akpan broke into a run, panting toward the moving *molue*. He had almost missed the bus while selling some tablets to his customers. There was no sitting space in the bus when he hopped in, so he stood holding on to a rail above him. Six baskets of chickens were on top of the *molue* supported by four rails. His raised hand sent the chickens flapping their wings in an attempt to fly out. Their eyes were bright as they croaked, lifting each of their legs, theirs claws clutched.

Mr. Akpan looked down, as they began to calm. His eyes rested on a crying baby. His mother was coaxing him to stop, making a clicking sound with her tongue, shaking her lips, but he yelled the more only pausing to lick his running nose. His mother sucked the mucus, and spat it out of the window. The baby gasped in relief but continued crying. His mother pulled out her left breast and thrust it into his mouth. He stopped crying. Behind the woman, a middle-aged man was snoring, his head swinging to and fro. The woman sitting next to him sighed incessantly because once in a while, his swinging head rested on her shoulder, but only shook him awake when a trail of slimy saliva crept down his faded coat. The coat was green with different buttons and threads. The button in the middle of the coat had slipped off, the buttonhole too big for it. The collar of the coat was patched with a red piece of cloth. Waking, he mumbled an apology opened his bloodshot eyes. And he wiped the saliva with a brown handkerchief. His hands were swollen, his fingers coarse. His nails were long and dirty. He had deep grooves of wrinkles on his brow, and a few gray hairs were sprinkled on his head. When he coughed, his whole body shook.

The *molue* swayed. In a bid to make himself comfortable, Akpan stepped on a woman's foot.

"Aaih!" the woman cried with a grimace, soothing her foot. "Craze man, you no dey see, abi . . ."

"Sorry, madam, na mistake," Mr. Akpan pleaded.

"Which kin mistake!" she spat out. "You no get eye for face? You fit mistake for other people leg, no bi ma own, a beg!" she concluded.

Mr. Akpan had hardly heaved a sigh of relief when close to him, another woman yelled out to a chic, well-dressed lady.

"Sidon well now, abi you tin say na your boyfriend car you dey . . ."

All heads turned toward them, but the lady ignored her.

"If you won do sisi, you no for enter *molue*," continued the woman.

Mr. Akpan recognized the offender as one of his customers.

"Oh, Rose, na you, wetin happen?"

Rose, who couldn't repress herself anymore, blurted out, "Can you imagine, the bus swerved and we went along with it. I was only trying to adjust myself when she yelled out like the market woman she is!"

Some market women gave a murmur of protest. One boldly spoke up in her Yoruba accent, "Oko ri, sisi eko, you no bi market woman, you bi Miss Nigeria!"

"So you even sabi blow gramma," insisted the first woman. "I bin think say you dey deaf and dumb, nonsense!"

Mr. Akpan gave Rose a sign to keep calm, and that ended the quarrel.

"Who took my wallet? Who took my wallet?!" a voice rang out. It was a young man sitting behind the driver. "It was here in my pocket!" he screamed, springing up from his seat and stretching his hands in appeal. When nobody responded, he insisted on searching everybody on the bus.

He scrambled up to his neighbor, who stared hard and said, "If you search me finish an you no see anything, I go so beat you ehh, your people go prepare ya funeral service today!"

The young man looked closely at the man. He had a red piece of cloth tied round his head. His eyes were deep in their sockets. Lumps of pimples concentrated on his cheeks. His lips were swollen and he had gaps in his upper teeth. His red shirt, which had no buttons, exposed a hairy chest. He was wearing a dirty pair of jeans and rubber slippers. His feet were clumpy with dust. The young man's eyes settled on his muscles. He changed his mind and sat down with clenched fists, tears glittering in his eyes.

"Ye ye, man!" his neighbor breathed down at him, then sat down.

Eventually, feeling at ease, Mr. Akpan cleared his throat and announced, "Ladies and gentlemen, I have something very important here. Content Super Tablets, manufactured by W and C Pharmaceutical Industries, Limited, for headache, fever, pain, dysentery, and for any other bodily discomfort. Content Super Tablet go kill am one time. If you buy dis medicine, and no show, arrest me anywhere you see me. Obuda na ma town. I come Lagos for 1977, follow my mates begin business, I start with cleaning, no work. I enter for iron melting no way, I begin sell newspaper, sell newspaper tire, enter for iron bending, so tay all my fingers bend finish." He displayed his crooked fingers and people roared in laughter. Some started for his tablets, mostly traders and market women. A few did so in appreciation of his sense of humor.

"How much . . . ?" asked one of the buyers.

"Na one naira fifty kobo, but take am for one naira," Mr. Akpan answered.

He did not finish his story and did not see the need to, since he had sold out most of the tablets. This invented story had proved most effective for the past six months, and it cost him only fifty *kobo* for each bus trip.

He waited for what seemed an age for people to leave the bus, so that he could have a little privacy to count his money. There were just a handful of people. He looked around and smiled to himself, then noticed a promisingly bulging bag at an obscure corner of the bus. He fought with the urge to go see its contents and the urge to wait; he did not want anyone to see the supposed treasure. He decided to remain in the bus till it became empty.

"Na here we de stop for fifty kobo, if we pass here na one naira you go pay oh!" announced the conductor.

"Na small thing . . ." two hefty men replied from behind. "We pass one naira!"

Mr. Akpan left his seat and sat near the bag with a feigned air of ownership. It was when the two men moved toward him that he realized he shared a common interest with them. An idea struck him. He did not stop to think, but grabbed the bag, threw it out of the window, and followed suit through the door. The men went after him. Seeing his hopeless state, he ran toward a policeman standing by.

"Na wetin?" the policeman asked.

"See dem, dem be tifs, na from molue dem begin follow me, make dem carry my property!" panted Mr. Akpan.

"Na lie!" said one of the men who had caught up with him. A stifled odor of cigarette and beer oozed out of his mouth. The policeman took a step backward to avoid the reek from both men.

"We jus lev dis bag, dey talk to driver, wen dis hungry man grab am begin run . . ." he said.

"God na my witness!" Mr. Akpan shouted. He went down on his knees, took some dust and licked it. "I swear na me get the bag!" And he pointed his finger to the sky. The policeman gave the suspicious-looking men a stern stare.

"Wetin de inside?" the policeman asked the men.

"Na some moni with small clothe!" they answered.

"You, wetin dey am?" referring to Akpan.

"Na-na . . . moni wey I pack from bank," he fumbled.

The policeman took the bag from Mr. Akpan and began to unwrap it. Plantin leaves fell out.

"Yes! Dis na di leaves wey I take wrap am!" Mr. Akpan interrupted.

The policeman continued unwrapping, His hands froze as a human head bounced out of the bag. He recovered in time to grab Mr. Akpan, who was about to escape. The two men took to their heels.

FROM **Sap Rising**

BY CHRISTINE LINCOLN

"LIKE DOVE WINGS"

I remember when she come back home, carryin' her blues in a faded pink blanket, edges frayed. I was the first to see her. Half stumblin' down the road. In the darkness. My own restlessness makin' it so I couldn't sleep. Even from where I sat, I could see a bone-weariness all over that poor child, the way her arms held on to that baby only because they been used to doin' so. I thought about how we all be holdin' on, even if what we holdin' on to is a whole lot of nuthin'. How we go through life pretendin' to be full up on emptiness.

I used to believe the only thing worse than leaving this place was having to come back in need. But life has a way of making your worst fears greater than the point it brings you to, until nothing else matters except putting

one foot in front of the other, in front of the other, in order to find your way
back home. Even still, I come back to Grandville at night, a shame that is
not my own keeping me from treading the street in broad daylight and under the eyes of those who once created the me I used to be.

She wouldn't come out for the first three months she was home. Didn't want
nobody to know about a baby with no father and a young girl whose dreams
amounted to a faded blanket and a half-mile trek back down a dust-covered
road. But I knew. Just like I'd known she would leave in the first place.
Could tell she was the runnin' kind.

When she finally decided to show herself, it was at church, of all places.
That baby on her hip. Struttin' down the aisle to the pew her sister, Loretta,
usually took every Sunday. The sight of Ebbie, her citified self, caused a heat
to rise in the already warm room. Womenfolk fanned themselves, ashamed
for a girl who didn't have sense enough to be ashamed of herself.

As soon as I knocked on the door, as soon as Loretta answered, I knew what
I was in for. Her eyes, tight at the corners, accusing, greeted me in silence.
When she helped me into a chair so I could rest my feet, and took Pontella
from my arms, it was with an unforgiving face. And if my own sister, my
flesh and blood, could look at me as if she didn't know who or what I was, I
could only imagine how the rest of the town folks must feel about me.

So I stayed close to the house. Never left except at night, when Pontella
was down for the evening and the only thing looking at me as if I had some
explaining to do was the frogs and crickets, creatures whose world I had disturbed when they thought they were free to sing.

She ain't come back to church after that first time, though we see her around
town every now and again. Time passes, and I can't explain it, but I find myself lookin' for her. Thinkin' about her, wonderin'. While Dorothy, Irma,
and Zeta chitter like a bunch of squirrels, gossipin', I stare off into the distance, tryin' to wrap my mind around what this woman was and not what
they say she is. They say she some kind of a witch. Say they men been actin'
real funny ever since she come back. Folks arguin' more'n usual. The
chirrun carryin' on like they don't have a lick a sense. And it's been near
'bout a whole year and ain't nobody got pregnant. Whispers say she done
somethin' to dry up our wombs. Done stole our seed.

I can't go back to that place. The way everyone's eyes read my life from the
rips in my clothes and the baby who slept in my arms. It was as if they all
thought they knew everything they needed to know about a woman like

me. And when the coldness filmed each gaze and hardened every familiar face, I knew I would never find in them what it was I needed.

Funny, but me sitting in church, in the house of the Lord, was just like that woman in the Bible, the adulteress, and every single one of those God-fearing church folk were ready with stones. Except Jesus didn't come and gather me up. He didn't shield me with his body or stoop down and write something in the dirt at my feet. I knew that if I were to continue to go there, all I would do was keep them from taking the planks out of their own eyes, because they'd be so busy tending to the stick in mine.

Yesterday the weather broke. There is a hint of prefrost in the wind, causin' my cheeks to redden when I'm outdoors too long. Folks will be stayin' in more. Ebbie, too. Though she ain't out much anyways. Gone are the days of watermelon chillin' in the icy creek until one of the men strikes it against a rock to split it open. The sweet flesh explodin' on the tongue.

But the hog'll be delivered soon, and it'll be slaughterin' time. A season for killin'. It will come innocent, unawares of its fate. Squealin' in its pen in the back of Mr. Kenton's truck. And after a few days, Leonard will slit its throat from ear to ear. String it up by its back legs to drain the blood. It will become cuts of meat: a ham shank, slabs of bacon, its bladder a balloon to be tossed about. And me and Leonard will feed on it all winter long, forgettin' the day it come to us in the back of Kenton's truck. Whole.

Fall comes quickly, bringing with it cool days and even cooler nights. I watch as the earth and the things of the earth prepare to bed down for winter, hoping that I, too, will be able to settle in. Like Pontella has done. How she runs from room to room like they all belong to her. The way she tastes and touches everything that catches her eye and that's just within her reach, as if by feasting on balls of dust that scurry across the floor and dead spiders hidden in corners, she'll become one with this world.

For a squirrel, say, or a two-year-old without memory, finding a place in the world is an easy thing to do. But for one who has never known her place, a woman's place, it is nearly impossible. So I stumble through green kitchen, into white bedroom, and back through blue parlor, trying to catch sight of something—anything—that resembles me, just to keep from falling away.

Somethin's been pullin' me from sleep almost every night lately. We got the Indian summer and the nights are warm, even though the leaves have already started to change in their eagerness for somethin' different. I go to sit on the back porch, my mama's shawl wrapped tight around me like arms tryin' to hold me together, and even there I feel the pull to go down to the Pinder place, just to see if she's still there. Just to get a look at her.

Everybody sittin' around talkin' about her like she a dog, when all she did was what half of us have wanted to do at one time or another but was too damned sorry or scared to try. Too busy worryin' about what everybody else'd think. But nobody'd admit it. Then they'd have to say that maybe somethin' was wrong with all of us, too. Instead, me and the others make like Ebbie's the one need fixin'. At least that's what we say out loud.

If not for my baby girl and the night, I would die here. Each day I play with Pontella little games I've made up. I contort my face into silly pictures that make even me giggle. Or chase her around the yard until we both fall exhausted, laughing, on beds of grass. The smell of her skin and hair after I have given her a bath, me nibbling at the layers of pudge on her legs and arms, around her neck—I drown in the scent of all that innocence. But that's what keeps me during the day.

At night I creep outside to sit beneath the moonlit sky. It's there I get what I couldn't get in church that Sunday. At those moments I know I still belong to this world, this universe. Just like the trees and the earth and the stars. I find something out here that even Pontella can't give me. Out here I don't have to be a child's mother, Loretta's sister, or that Pinder girl who ran away. Out here, with God looking down on me, where their shame can't follow me, I'm just like His other creations. Only I'm a tree whose roots have pulled free, a sunflower that no longer follows the movements of the sun.

And when I couldn't stand it no longer, I went down there. To the Pinder place. I saw her sittin' in the backyard under a cluster of trees a little ways from the house. She held her face to the moon like she was at church. I wanted to go over to her and hold her like I would a child, amazed by how small she looked under the largeness of the sooty sky. I expected her to be six foot tall by now. Like she should have grown from all the signifyin'. How big we had been makin' her with our words. In our own minds. But she was small. I wondered how we all must look when we got to stand alone. How I must look on the other side of the road, hidden in darkness.

I saw that woman Leonard married standing across the street, watching me. At first I was angry. I figured she must have heard I was the one he'd once loved, though we loved in secret. A woman knows. She can always tell when there has been another, can feel the presence of another like a shadow that hovers just out of reach, blocking out the fullness of the sun, causing a chill that goes down to the bones. And then I felt sorry for her: the one who comes to see the one who loved a man she can never know. A man who strolled among whispering trees and still dreamed dreams. As if by seeing me she might somehow discover what it is she wants to see in him.

Before I could call up enough sense to stop myself, I ran down the road and over to where I knew she'd be. My mouth opened and the words spilled out of me like one of those angry rains. They was hard and fast, the words that spewed from me:

Who you think you is comin' back here like you some movie Star? With no shame whatsoever. How dare you? And now our chirrun actin' up. Our husbands. Stealin' our seeds, makin' it so all we can talk about or think about is Miss Ebbie Pinder, hauntin' me so's I can't even sleep at night—why you have to come back here remindin' us of what we done tried so hard to forget?

When I was done, I fell to my knees in the grass beside her, my chest heavin', too empty to cry. My words had been the tears, and the prayers, my mournin' song, and in the tellin', they had become hers, too.

When I looked up, she was already standing over me as if she wanted to strike me. Her hands were clenched in fists so tight they shook. Even in the moonlight, her eyes looked like pools of glittering black glass. I sat, too stunned to move, while her words fell over me and pierced my skin in accusation, until I realized she wasn't talking about me at all. Then I watched as her words became snow that tumbled from her trembling lips onto the grass and dissolved into the earth, feeding the rich brown soil while the air between us grew heavy with pain and loneliness and fear. When she was done, all I could do was lay my hand on her bowed head and whisper over and over, "I know, I know."

Now we meet almost every night, meander through the orchards in silence. Or sit and talk. Mostly we talk, comment on how two women so different could be so much alike, inside where eyes don't go. How one could leave this place, the other one stay put. And we realize the reasons were the same: fear. One afraid she would turn out like everyone else, the other scared to death she wouldn't.

We share secrets denied us in our youths. The truth about who we are. The stuff no one wanted us to know. We share the story about the women called maniacs. Women who lived a long time ago. They were just country women, really, who got tired of cookin' and cleanin', takin' care of the husband and chirrun. Got tired of everybody else usin' up what was supposed to be their lives. So they met in the woods one night and had this dance. When the men found out, they got angry and tried to put an end to their women's foolishness. But they couldn't. The women rebelled. Started gatherin' every night. Before long the men started callin' the women crazy, and started treatin' them like they was, until the women began to believe it.

Why is it when a man wants to be free, he's just being a man, but when a woman wants to live life from the position of the birds, the first thing folks say is that she's crazy?

That's what we ask ourselves.

We shake our heads as if unsure of the answer. But we know. It's because they know what'll happen if we ever really do get free. They scared.

Ebbie say God must be a woman. That we was made in Her image, though she whispers it like she's afraid He may hear her talkin' about Him thataway. I tell her she's blasphemin'. Ebbie say she been blasphemed against all her life. That I been blasphemed against, too. Just because we womenfolk. She asked me to think over how many times someone spoke to me, to my womanness, with irreverence. Me. A sacred bein' like them stars, only Ebbie say more so 'cause I was fashioned in God's likeness. And me not ever knowin' it. I laugh at her, but that night when I creep back home and let myself in the screen door, real quiet so's not to wake Leonard, somethin' deep down in my belly tingles at the idea of God with Her nappy hair, coffee-and-cream skin, and lips thick as plums. Lookin' like me.

Ruthie craves a child of her own the same way I once ached to leave Grandville. So I tell her about when I was pregnant with Pontella, when she first fluttered. And the women who already had children—how they told me it would feel like I had a belly full of butterflies. Only it wasn't like that at all. I'd felt butterflies before; they came with the fear.

This was something else. More like dove wings, bringing me peace for the first time in my life. And for a while I thought I was having a bird, until I saw the coal-black coils of hair peeking out from between my thighs. When the midwife turned Pontella's head in order to sweep her mouth, seeing her face, that ancient face, I realized for the first time that a whole being had lived in me. The awe made it so I could barely breathe or move.

I could hardly hear the midwife telling me to push one more time, the shoulders. And me taking the deepest breath I could, so deep my chest burned, hunching my back and pushing with all of my might. I felt in my soul more than in my body the ripping, like the ripping of the veil. Shaking, I fell backward onto the bed, my eyes rolled up into my head. It was like I'd fallen into the bluest of oceans, sinking, sinking into the warm, rushing waters of life. I had fallen into myself. I had become the world, my womb the center of the universe. I had become one with God, one who knew what it meant to be creator. Life-giver.

That's how I know God is a woman.

· · ·

Ebbie gives me permission. That's all, permission. Like someone sayin' it's all right to just be. And whatever all I was meant to be in the first place. Before they told me that girls couldn't chew gum or climb trees or wear jeans. That a woman's value counted on how well she fed her husband and children and the way she kept up her home. Before they told me a girlchild was what you wanted only after findin' out you couldn't have anythin' at all. I believed 'em, every one of those baldfaced lies. And them some powerful lies, too, anytime they can talk a person out of bein' what God made her to be. Talk a person right out of her soul. But Ebbie come along and tell me the truth of the matter. Truth always burn away anything that ain't like it.

Selfishly, I tell Ebbie that I could go on like this forever. As soon as I say it, I see somethin' in her eyes shrink from my words. At that moment, I know it's only a matter of time before she leaves again. I tell her how it gets harder for me to fit myself into a life that someone else created for me. Never understood that it wasn't even supposed to be thataway. And when I leave her, I'm scared and angry all at the same time. Scared to think of what I have to go back to if she ever leaves me, angry at the ones who made it so.

Tired of bein' treated like a fall hog.

Ruthie comes to me after two days, her eyes hidden, black ice cupped by purple moons. I look at her bruised face with both anger and guilt. Someone else's desecration making me feel responsible, and her ashamed of her womanhood, her vulnerability. She says Leonard beat her because she refused to cook and clean. I don't tell her he beat her because she stopped making him believe that he was the only reason she ever existed at all. Like the husbands of the maniacs, he knows that the young girl he married is already a memory.

When we go to leave the orchards that night, a chill invading the air, disturbing the illusion given by our Indian summer, I know I have to go. For a brief moment it's been enough to know that someone else is as I am. To find myself in someone else. So I won't have to feel so very alone. But I'm the one who made it that way, forcing my own nature on her and maybe even on Pontella if I were to stay.

I say it's getting too cold for us to meet. I promise I'll see her in the spring. I hold her close, inhale the nutty scent of wet earth from her hair, holding back the pain of unshed tears in my chest, knowing it will be the last time. Winter will come and I will settle in with the child I created, make memories of my own.

Ruthie talks about forever as if there really is such a thing. When even our future is already our past. But for a time our souls met, and danced, and soared. We were able to live like the maniacs, and we were comforted by that knowledge.

It's not until spring I learn Ebbie has left me and Pontella. Left before I could tell her she gave me back my seed. Now I walk through my life like one who goes by a familiar place that has been torn to rubble, one who can't quite remember what once stood.

I feel the months slide by and I watch my skin stretch taut over the swell of promise. I could almost pretend like this never happened at all, except for the movement in my belly, like dove wings, remindin' me of my nights with Ebbie and what it felt like to be really free, pullin' me from Leonard's side each night. I sleep beneath maples cast in shadows, lettin' tears fall warm and without excuse. Folks talk so, but to Leonard's face they tell him it's my bein' pregnant. That I'll return to normal once I have the baby. While every night I lie on a bed of grass-covered earth, fall into a sleep filled with dreams more real than this world, where I am a fish the color of rainbows, a bird that soars to the depths of the ocean. They say when a woman is full with life, she dreams strange dreams.

Fire: An Origin Tale

BY FAITH ADIELE

I'm nearly sixteen years old before I learn the true story of my birth. It is the spring of 1979, fifteen months before snowcapped Mount Saint Helens will wake up a few hundred miles away and create a new country; seventeen years after my teenage mother lay down on the floor of her father's house and contemplated suicide. I can picture her in 1962 with her apple cheeks and light brown ponytail, lying flat against the gray carpet, looking too brunette to be Scandinavian and much younger than her nineteen years. She might have been wearing a sleeveless blue cotton smock, the patch pockets stuffed with half-used tissues, and a mannish pair of black glasses. Those droopy blue eyes of hers, so deceptively sleepy, would have been wide open for once. Seventeen years later, except the short bowl haircut swirled with cowlicks, she looks exactly the same.

Time has stopped in the living room of our tiny house. It's as if my mother's silence, has cast a spell that descends over us like the ash when

Mount Saint Helens erupts, turning cars and flowerbeds silver. We will have to wear surgical masks outside, just like at the Annual Portland Rose Festival to the south, thousands of spectators and beauty queens waving to each other from behind white paper cones. But for now, my mother contemplates the ceiling, and the cats on the roof fall asleep, whiskered chins upturned in the shade of the honeysuckle vine.

Bound by the spill of her silence, no one on Gregory Avenue moves. Next door, Mr. Graham turns to stone in the midst of his prized hybrid teas and floribunda. Across the street, Tommy the Plumber stalls, tattoos motionless in the hairy forests of his arms and legs and chest. At the end of the street, the boys on the high school wrestling team—state champions for three years straight—slump, drooling, onto gym mats, while next door at my mother's junior high, three kids smoking joints topple over on the football field.

The entire town of Sunnyside, Washington—where according to the Chamber of Commerce, the sun shines 360 days a year—holds its breath. At the feedlot near the sign welcoming visitors to SUNNYSIDE—HOME OF AS-TRONANT BONNIE DUNBAR, the milk-faced Herefords and polled Angus stand vacant-eyed and slack-jawed, just like when the volcano blows. In the tiny business district, the Rotarians and Kiwanis and Elks and Eagles stop singing in mid-song; the neon warrior on the awning of the Safari Lounge watches his spear and shield blink and fizzle out; and the Golden Pheasant Chinese restaurant actually closes.

The blond kids up on Harrison Hill drift in their blue swimming pools, while Mexican workers doze on ladders in the sooty fruit orchards, their burlap bags slipping to the ground. Nothing much was happening to start with at the big Catholic and Mormon and Episcopalian and Methodist and Baptist and Presbyterian churches, but in the tiny new churches that are continually forming and separating at any time of day—so many that Sunnyside is in the *Guinness Book of World Records*—the congregations begin to snore in their folding chairs.

This hush, while I wait for my mother to call the true tale of my origins up from hibernation, carries out of town, past Old Doc Querin's big animal practice, past the huge Dutch dairies with their tin-roofed barns, past fields strung high and beaded with hops. It wafts along the restricted road to the Hanford Nuclear Reservation, which did the plutonium finishing for the bombs dropped on Hiroshima and Nagasaki, and where people say that strange, new insects breed in the chalky limestone. It floats by the Moore farm with its collapsing barn and twelve kids, the Kludas farm with its narrow lambing shed and single giant son, and my grandparents' farm wedged in between. For once the woodpecker attacking their trees is quiet, enjoying the bright pink blossoms on the thorny Hawthorn, the heart-shaped leaves of the Catalpa, the drooping Weeping Willow. The silence winds along the irrigation ditch to the asparagus fields at the tiny airport, the same fields where my mother walked barefoot in 1962, the soil damp between her toes, and considered killing herself and her unborn child.

"I need the form that shows you have custody of me," I repeat, in case my mother didn't hear me. A permission slip for a study program in Mexico rests on the sofa cushion between us.

A few minutes ago, when I announced that the study program required the signatures of both parents—unless one can prove sole custody—my mother grunted, setting the spell. Now her eyes contemplate the ceiling, blue specks beneath a field of gently waving cowlicks.

I wait. It is 1979, my sophomore year of high school, the moment for which I have been raised. From our monthly United Nations Day dinners where my mother and I dress in makeshift *rebosas* and saris and dashikis and make optimistic stabs at crêpes and *piroshki* and *kimchee* from the Time Life international cookbooks series, to the home curriculum she designs for me from her college anthropology textbooks, to our mispronounced mutterings over the *kinara* ("*Umoja* means 'unity' . . .") and the *Haggadah* ("We were slaves of Pharaoh . . .") and the *shahāda* ("There is no god but God . . ."), my mother has been preparing me for this. It is to be my first trip out of North America—the escape from Sunnyside she never quite managed herself. The only thing standing in the way is my father's signature.

"I'll get the custody agreement." I offer, holding out a pen. Program enrollment to Mexico is on a first come–first served basis. "Where is it?"

Anything having to do with my father, who lives overseas, is a bit of a mystery. He and my mother divorced when I was still a baby, and in time she returned to her hometown and he to his. His photograph—a college man with close-cropped curls, thick glasses matching hers, and a green wool overcoat—hangs above my bed. Occasionally I write to him, and his affectionate replies drag themselves in months later. I know what he looks like and I know his handwriting. I know that he loves me very much. I just can't remember ever having seen him.

If I think about this, I'm a bit bewildered. I believe that, no matter how young I was when he left, I should remember my father. At least the sharp bouquet of Lux soap, the scratch of green wool against my cheek, the rich bass of his full-throated laugh, the lush Rs of his accent. He is, after all, the only one in the family like me. The only one who is black.

Being black matters. It was the reason for the trouble. Though my mother's story is sparse, always the same information presented in the exact same words, she has always been forthcoming about the trouble. For years I've watched her bee-stung lips twist into tight shapes as she describes how

my grandfather demanded that she stop seeing my father, a Nigerian graduate student. How, when she refused, he forced her to transfer to another college hundreds of miles away.

It was 1961, a moment of firsts. My father was the first in his family to
come to the West; my mother was the first in her family of Scandinavian
immigrants to go to college. "I was wild about it," she confesses, eyes gleaming. "All those books—I thought I had died and gone to heaven!" Her freshman year she met my father, and they became the first interracial couple on
campus. This among ten thousand college students.

After my mother was sent away, my parents met in secret and were married at the Seattle courthouse one Saturday. "I wore a pale green princess-
style dress with matching jacket like Jackie Kennedy might have
worn—only much cheaper," she says, smile firmly in place, "and your
grandfather immediately disowned me." Without his support, she was
forced to drop out of college and banned from ever going home or seeing
her mother and brother.

The newlyweds were broke. The apartment swelled with international
students who were also broke and who stopped by for dinners of vegetable
curry and groundnut stew. I remember being poor—a chalky taste like
scorched kidney beans—and I remember the stew, my mother's wooden
spoon swirling peanut butter into tomato sauce—a vivid, oily spiral of red
and brown. I remember murmured discussions about Cuba and Vietnam
lasting late into the night, backed by Bob Dylan's whine or smooth African
Highlife on the hi-fi. I remember the scent of vanilla drifting from the coffee table and the squish of warm wax between my fingertips as I caught candle drips before being chased off to bed. I don't remember my father.

After politics, my parents' great loves were movies and dancing. I know
little else. But if we are riding the bus and pass a former hangout of theirs,
or if I come across a photograph of one of their friends, my mother dusts off
a memory and presents it to me. "Your poppie used to like this place," she
might say, or "That girl was dating a West African too, and once we double-
dated." She chooses these anecdotes carefully, sparingly, as if we are still
poor.

I was born at Saint Elizabeth's Hospital in Spokane, Washington, in
1963. I don't know why Spokane, which is hundreds of miles from Seattle. I
do know that my mother enjoyed being pregnant: sleepy, swollen, with a
ready-made excuse to spend entire days reading. I can see her seventeen
years ago, propped against the sofa bed of their tiny apartment, stacks of
history textbooks and news magazines and dime-store mysteries covering
every inch of the linoleum.

"Tell me again what the nurses said when they saw me for the first time,"
I demand.

She laughs, dog-earing a page of *The Guerrilla—And How to Fight Him* and settling my head in her lap. On this last point she is always eloquent. The nurses had never seen a mixed baby before, she recounts, slim fingers working my curls. "They fussed over you for days. Everyone did. For years strangers stopped us in the street and gave you presents—pieces of candy, shiny dimes—old men who looked like they had nothing to give."

Despite the sun shining from my face, my parents divorced soon after, and my father returned to West Africa. We haven't seen him since.

Before we could afford to buy the Norse legends and African folktales that peopled my childhood, my mother wrote stories set in mythic African lands and illustrated them with her own watercolor paintings of wise queens and beautiful warrior princesses in pastel tunics. Every morning and evening she read aloud to me, creating different voices for each character. Sometimes, if she was tired from teaching, she lost a voice, and I would bolt upright, protesting. "*That's* not the right voice!"

"No?" she would say, blinking rapidly as she does when she's trying to think. "Was it higher?" She would try again. "*Dear Prince Amalu—*"

My eyes would widen in horror.

"Lower? Ahem, *Dear Prince—*"

"*No!*" I'd wail, hands trembling like leaves.

"Okay, pause for a minute." She would lean forward and enact her usual ritual—a sip of tepid water masquerading as tea, a quick blow of her nose, the unwrapping of a half-sucked cough drop, and the popping it into her mouth.

Throughout all this, I would squirm. How could she take so long? How could she have forgotten this character who'd been living with us for days?

"Okay, let's see." She'd clear her throat and begin anew.

Not until she recaptured the correct voice—or invented a new one close enough to placate me—could I resume my curl in her lap, accept the narrative. Her own tale, however, she delivered in a detached, matter-of-fact tone.

"Who was at your wedding?" I'd ask periodically, hungry for the details of my origins. Some of my father's African classmates? What about her college roommate, the one who borrowed her nicest outfit, a sophisticated black cocktail dress with tiny buttons, and never returned it, despite my mother's increasingly bitter letters?

"Oh, no one really," she'd answer, glancing up from *Report from a Chinese Village.* "Just a pal of your poppie's and his girlfriend. I can't even remember their names."

I don't understand it. For years she labored to create the definitive family history, spending hours hunched over an old manual typewriter, clacking out family names and places and dates. She drew floor plans of childhood houses she remembered her mother and aunt describing. She pored over albums and scrapbooks and boxes of photographs. As with her anecdotes about my father, she was reductionist, a perfectionist. She chose photographs the same way she chose her memories—only the most representative and best preserved. History in her hands was finite. I wonder why major family events like my grandparents' wedding got a single photograph in the album. Did she have only one, or was it her rigid aesthetic taste?

The spring of 1979, the year before Mount Saint Helens decides to wake from her 123-year slumber, the self my mother has kept dormant these seventeen years creeps out of the past. The last time the mountain blew was 1857, the same year the U.S. Supreme Court decided that blacks were not citizens. And like the pressure now building beneath our feet, the Dred Scott case weakened the fault line between the Northern abolitionists and Southern slaveholders, four years later exploding into civil war.

Mount Saint Helens' very first outburst was the stuff of legends, an origin tale that also pitted brother against brother. According to the Klickitat, who call her *Tah-one-lat-cha* ("Fire Mountain"), and the Puyallup, who call her *Loowitlatka* or *Loowit* ("Lady of Fire"), and the Yakima, our local tribe, the mountain was a lovely, white-clad maiden with whom both sons of the Creator fell in love. They battled each other for her, causing the sun to darken and the earth to tremble. As they hurled molten rock back and forth, entire forests and villages disappeared in flames. Angered, the Creator turned one son into Mount Adams, the other into Mount Hood, and Loowit into the symmetrically beautiful Mount Saint Helens, perennially encased in ice and snow.

For three months in 1980, prior to the eruption, the ground beneath her will tremble—ten thousand quakes in seven weeks. A crater will yawn in her mouth, growing at a rate of six feet per day. Though geologists and biologists recognize the signs, they will ignore them. When at last Loowit succumbs to the pressure, the avalanche preceding the blast will splash water 850 feet high, temperatures will reach 1,000 degrees, and 500 million cubic yards of rock will be released in one of the largest volcanic explosions in North American history. The entire mountaintop will slide into the Toutle River Valley.

Two hundred miles away in Sunnyside, we will sit openmouthed before the television, watching thick white smoke curdle like brain matter against a blackened crater. We will hear the stunned cries of journalists and rescue workers. "It doesn't even look like the same country!" someone shouts into a radio. "I can't find any landmarks. It doesn't look like anyplace I've ever been before."

The Lady of Fire will forge an entirely new country. Before the explosion, Sunnyside is so dry that when it rains, school closes. When Loowit blows, the largest landslide in recorded history will level 230 square miles of forest in three minutes, wiping out entire populations of elk, deer, bear, and coyote. Glistening Spirit Lake, where my cousin Heidi and I crest through snow thaw, will become a bowl of mud, as will the Columbia River, going from a depth of forty feet to thirteen and stranding four dozen freighters in the process. The silvery ash will drift in a fifteen-mile-high column all the way here to southeast Washington. By noon, ash will be falling in Idaho. In two weeks, it will circle the globe. After that, rain in Sunnyside becomes normal and school is never canceled.

The spring before our geography irrevocably changes, my mother breaks the spell that holds us to the living room sofa. "Well," she says, rubbing her temple with the same hand that now holds the permission slip to Mexico, "can you keep a secret?" She half-grins.

I bite the insides of my mouth to keep from smiling back. This must be big, bigger even than my first trip abroad. I nod, as chill as mountain runoff. "Sure."

"Well . . ." she begins, tilting her head to the side and looking a bit like me when caught rifling her drawers for old photographs and letters. "I can't prove sole custody because"—she pauses—"your father and I were never divorced." She gives me an amused, expectant look.

After a minute I ask, "What do you mean—did Dad die?" Even as I say it, I suspect it can't be the explanation. My father writes to me, after all. And though I haven't heard from him in five years, as we learned following his three-year silence during the Nigerian civil war, as we will learn a mere three weeks after Loowit blows when horsetail rushes and fireweed pop up through the still-smoldering ash, followed by a scurry of pocket gophers and ground squirrels, rebirth is always possible.

My mother shakes her head, and unbidden, The Question arises from childhood memory, where it dozes fitful, ever near. I can feel it rumble through my stomach, force its way into my head as clearly as if I am on the playground, surrounded by a crowd of children who have just seen my mother's white skin for the first time and won't stop asking. "Is that your real mom?"

"Uh-huh" is my reply, rushing to head off the inevitable barrage of questions. I shut down my mind and chant my answer like a nursery rhyme: "My father is black. He's darker than me. My mother is white. Black and white together make brown." I present my arm for inspection. "See?"

Sometimes the scowls relax, the play resumes. There is frequently one who doubts. "Nuh-*uh*," he or she insists, balled hands against Toughskin-clad hips, as if this were high noon at the O.K. Kiddie Corral. "She can't be your real mom." Pale eyes squint through potential holes in my story. Then, the drawled challenge: "Where's your *real* mom?"

Suddenly it's *The Big Country*, and I'm Gregory Peck, Eastern navy captain turned rancher, raised to reason. I flail, repeating my claim to my mother, tender-footed and at a loss out here in the Western territories. Only a grown-up can save me. But when they arrive, it's often clear that the parents have no more idea than their offspring how I could possibly be my mother's child. Herding my challenger away, they glance back over their shoulders, as if the question of my origins is somehow unspeakable.

When I'm lucky, my mother herself appears, cowlicks crackling and baby cheeks aflame as she marches, all five-feet-two of her, up to full-grown men and jeering teenagers. "Do you have something to say to my daughter?" she roars, loud as any natural phenomenon. She stands on tiptoe and jabs a finger in their faces. They could be big as Burl Ives, Gregory Peck's *Big Country* nemesis, or belligerent as Chuck Conners, his rotten son; she doesn't care.

Kids "too young to know any better" get hugged. "Hey, hey," she says, kneeling on the asphalt, dimpled arms firmly encircling her captive. "What's going on here?"

By now Gregory Peck and Chuck Conners are both wailing, snot streaking our faces. Through my tears I watch her pink cheeks, her mouth working close to the kid's ear. I never hear what she says, other than her prerelease signal—"Okay?"—more statement than query.

The stranger's son or daughter nods, Toughskins tensed to flee and yet surely relieved, too, to have the unexplainable explained by someone so certain of right and wrong.

At times even I wonder about my origins. For all her efforts to create our definitive history, there are no photographs of my parents' wedding in the family album, none of my mother pregnant, and none of me as a newborn. There is a lone snapshot of me taken before the age of seven months: a blurry infant in light blue, teetering on a bed I do not recognize. I see little resemblance to the buttery-colored baby my mother claimed I had been, the newborn whose sloping forehead and masses of wavy hair looked "just like a Mayan or Egyptian princess." Whenever I demand proof of this previous incarnation, she explains wistfully that they could not afford a camera. By the time they got one, my forehead had rounded out and my hair tightened into curls. But that was fine, too, according to her.

Back rigid against the sofa, I now unfurl The Question onto my tongue. Though I am nearly sixteen, it drags in my throat. "So . . . I'm adopted?"

My mother whips her head from side to side. "No, no, no. I'm just saying that your poppie and I were never married." A faint smile lurks around the corners of her mouth.

Not married! My best friend Cheryl will undoubtedly add this to her list of why my mother and I are going to Everlasting Hellfire—first being my refusal to accept Jesus as my personal savior and second my inability to get my mother to vote Republican. I can see her now asking her youth group to take a break from playing rock records backward in the church basement in attempt to detect messages from Satan, so that they can spend an afternoon praying for my bastard soul.

I grin, mildly titillated by my parents' unconventionality. Here at last are the romance and drama of my origins. I sit back, eager to hear the rest.

My mother explains that the last time she saw my father was June 1962, his final secret visit to Seattle, during which they broke up. A few months later, she discovered she was pregnant. They made some gestures toward reconciliation, but my father was on his way to the East Coast for his doctorate and they soon realized it wouldn't work.

When my grandfather found out, he was furious, insisting that my mother get an abortion. She refused. *That* was the real reason he disowned her. The reason she had dropped to the living room floor after wandering barefoot in the asparagus fields. The reason I had been born in Spokane.

My mother cocks a brow and takes me by surprise: "That's where the home for unwed mothers was." She winces a bit, waits.

The home for unwed mothers? In a good origin tale, miraculous babes are found beneath garden leaves, nestled on riverbanks, even in the womb of a she-wolf, rarely in state-run institutions reeking of cabbage and shame. My mouth drops, and it occurs to me that she is making this whole thing sound easier than it was. This version may be more truthful, but it's still a story. Perhaps my mother's decision to have a mixed-race child alone was not a carefree slap in the face of convention after all. Perhaps—I try this idea on for the first time—she was not in control of her fate.

The image of my self-sufficient mother being hustled out of town in the middle of the night to give birth at some secret institution hundreds of miles from home is so foreign that I feel my mind withering. My scope of my questions shrinks to meet it. "How did you get pregnant?"

She confesses that she had been intentionally careless. "I think I knew we were breaking up," she confides, "and subconsciously I wanted a baby."

"What about Saint Elizabeth's?" Was Saint Elizabeth's a lie? And what of the nurses who vied to hold me, who had never seen such well-defined features in a newborn, such heavily lashed eyes, such a full rosebud mouth? Who had really been there as I took my first breath?

My mother assures me that both the nurses and Saint Elizabeth's were real. The only difference is that I had been born in the home's maternity ward. Saint Elizabeth's Hospital sent nurses and doctors to the home to oversee the deliveries. Together the two institutions collaborated on a procedure of secrecy. Saint Elizabeth's staff signed my birth certificate and registered my arrival with the hospital so that no record of my true birthplace would exist.

I hear this, and the mother I believe I know slips out of focus. I squint at her, as I might have squinted at myself on the playground, had I advanced such a tale. "What about your wedding outfit?" I have such a vivid image of the pale green suit and corsage that I've constructed a photograph of my mother the bride—pouty mouth, slim hand in a white glove, lacy sprig of baby's breath against a soft lapel. My father as groom is the same bespecta-cled graduate student who stares out from my bedroom wall. I imagine sep-arate portraits hanging over my bed, almost touching in their cheap gilt frames. Until now I had not noticed never imagining my parents together in the same scene.

She laughs and tugs the loose curls at the back of my neck. Yes, the green suit was a real suit, a detail recalled from one of my father's visits.

My mother then teaches me how to lie: "It's always best to stay as close to the truth as possible," she says, as if she has not just spent sixteen years drilling the importance of honesty into me. I have been trained to return ex-tra change to the penny, to raise my hand to confess wrongdoing, to resist the pressure of peers and authority figures alike.

She grimaces and gives her head a rueful shake. "I'm not a very good liar," she confesses. "I have such a poor memory."

I will later discover that my mother's poor memory spans most of my parents' break-up and the entire duration of her pregnancy. This is partly because her family kept her hidden like an insane aunt in the attic. No ver-bal or photographic record exists of her experience. Her recollection is a se-ries of brief vignettes, fading into a broader, cloudy background like the constant rotation of a camera lens seeking focus.

And what she does remember is difficult to verify. "If you keep telling the same lies over and over," she warns me, "after a while you forget the truth."

My mother does not remember telling her parents she was pregnant. "But I remember roaming barefoot at dusk through the asparagus fields and contemplating suicide. Your grandfather was threatening to toss me into the street if I didn't get an abortion, and of course I didn't have any money of my own and neither did your poppie. He was the eldest of eleven and had been supporting himself on meager teaching fellowships for years." It was at this point that my nineteen-year-old mother fell to the floor of her father's house and resolved not to get up until she had decided once and for all what to do.

In 1979 as we sit on the sofa together, she gazes out the picture window at the spellbound landscape and recalls one of the few images that has stayed with her: a yellow farmhouse in a knot of trees, uncharacteristically empty. Her parents and brother had gone to town. My mother, who has always pre-ferred solitude to companionship, had extended her arms and muddy feet as if making snow angels. The textured gray carpet had felt solid beneath her, the design swirling between her fingers. She'd stared up at the ceiling with its glitter flecks and reminded herself that she could be just as stubborn as her father.

She was lying on the floor of white, rural, Christian, soon-to-be-middle-class, pre–*Roe v. Wade* America. "And I had four options: illegal abortion, marriage, adoption, or death." She did not want a backstreet abortion and she did not want to marry my father. She rolled on her side, feeling the scratch of the carpet against her cheek.

Now her voice is light. "That left two options: have the baby and give it up for adoption, or kill us both."

Adoption wouldn't solve the problem of being destitute and having to drop out of college. Besides, in some secret recess of her mind she wished she could somehow keep the baby. "I worried, who would adopt a mixed-race baby?"

That left suicide.

Even at sixteen I know that my mother is not the kind of woman who considers suicide. For sixteen years she has been fierce, hugging tolerance into strangers' intolerant children, creating pastel-clad African queens to talk to me. Besides, there are simply too many books to read.

What nearly toppled my mother as she teetered on the edge of suicide was the fact that she wouldn't be able to finish college. College. The collective dream of her immigrant, just-leaving-working-class family—the collective dream of her entire dusty town, really. Her escape from life on the farm, from the *World's Record for Most Churches Per Capita, Small Town Division*, from 360 days of sun. Her release from a country where fathers packed their daughters away for life or married them off to sweaty farmboys at the end of a shotgun or paid strangers to fish around inside them with a rusting coat hanger.

As soon as my mother hefted death in one hand and thunked its round-ness with her knuckle, everything fell into place. "It was all so simple." She shrugs, the mother I know returned to join us on the sofa. "The situation was not about suicide or shame or having no options. Money was the only thing holding me back from what I truly wanted—from college, from keeping the baby." Money and her father, wielding it like a weapon against her. "Money, nothing more."

And so she set herself free. "Let him disown me, I thought," she says, flipping her hands palms up. The ground as she got up off the floor of her father's house was solid beneath her feet. She would act without her father, without a husband, without anyone's approval. "I decided to have the baby, you."

Her voice drops, tender as a spring seedling. And it hits me, the message in my name. Despite fighting with my father and the entire town of Sunnyside over their staunch Christianity, despite claiming not to know why she chose the name—regardless of what she can or cannot remember—the evidence is there. It is the photograph she couldn't afford upon my arrival, the decision she made from her four options, the gift she prayed for—Faith.

There was, as to be expected, much more to the tale of my origins that my mother would reveal when I was older. The story of whom she called and what happened in the home. Still later would be the stories I had to uncover for myself. The rest of my name and what happened to my father. Who knows how much I would have been able to comprehend, had she been able to recall it, that spring day in 1979? I was sixteen, my primary concern getting to Mexico.

As if sensing this, my mother takes her arms from around me and offers to write a letter explaining that she is a single mother and have it notarized. I can give it, on the condition of secrecy, to the tour leader.

I frown. This is degrading. Why lie? Why give power to some unknown tour leader of undetermined discretion?

My mother turns to me. There will be no youth group praying for our souls in the church basement. "I confided in you," she stresses, "because you're old enough to know the truth, but you have to swear not to tell a soul; I could lose my job."

I protest. "C'mon, this is 1979. You've been teaching forever. No one cares."

"This is still Sunnyside," she replies. The town she had grown up in and tried to escape, then been cast out of. The town to which she eventually returned to raise me. A dip in the earth that resists each new decade with the fervor of the recently converted. A Christian holdout on the edge of the desert soon to be covered in 600,000 tons of volcanic ash. A mere forty-five minutes after the Lady of Fire blows, the sky will become black as night, and though it is only nine-thirty in the morning, all over Sunnyside, streetlights will sputter into light.

I have heard my mother's friends in the living room. I know that one teacher lost his job for lingering too long in the high school parking lot with a woman who was not his wife. Another found himself jailed after admitting his sexual orientation. Careers have been lost on more suspicion.

And so I inherit my mother's secret, continuing what is—though I do not know it then—a time-honored tradition among the women of our family. Neither of us has any way of knowing that this secret I force down my throat will turn out to be as bruising as the chunks of pumice that rain down from Loowit. My mother is mistaken—I am not old enough to know the truth. At least, not old enough to carry it, like my heavy, unpronounceable African name, out into the world alone.

Like any good creation myth, the true tale of my origins is deceptive. Upon first telling, it seems harmless enough. The major themes endure: My parents cared for each other and loved me; my mother managed alone. The only differences, I tell myself, are simple matters of legality and geography—the absence of a marriage certificate, a birth at a forgotten address across town. But beneath the thin crust of the earth we think we know, the new world shifts and steams.

Tan Son Nhut Airport, Ho Chi Minh City, 1997

BY GENARO KY LY SMITH
FROM *The Land South of the Clouds*

To some extent I can understand their suspicions. Long before we boarded the plane in Los Angeles, Uncle Ngo told me this would happen. It's not every day that they see a Vietnamese man with an African American man in Ho Chi Minh City. Alone, he'd be fine. They could easily buy Uncle Ngo's story: He wants to return home, to see relatives he hasn't seen since leaving in 1972. In my case they might I'm a Vietnam vet making a personal journey to heal emotional wounds, except that I'm only twenty-eight.

So, when they asked me in English the nature of my visit, I told them the truth: I was here to see my mother. They became quiet, turning to one another with opened mouths. Then they both studied my passport. The woman looked up and pursed her lips to speak. I knew she wanted to say, "No. Really?" Instead she raised the passport up to her face and frowned into the black and white photo, at the name Long-Vanh Nguyen printed next to it. All the information was correct: place of birth (Nha Trang), date of birth (6/17/68), citizenship (U.S.); the name was distinctly Vietnamese, as was the long neck with the vulnerable Adam's apple, the large mouth. Everything checked out except the dark skin and the short, neatly cropped hairstyle worn by African Americans nowadays. They didn't match with everything else.

Uncle Ngo and I are now in a room with a picture of a gaunt-looking Ho Chi Minh hanging on the wall, his white goatee covering the buttoned collar of his shirt. Standing side by side Uncle Ngo and I watch as the customs officers slide and wriggle their hands inside tight-fitting latex gloves, snap them against their wrists, then pull neatly folded shirts and jeans from our suitcases one by one, and shake them free of their perfect creases. Their hands plunge inside the pockets, front and back, and when they are through with each article of clothing, they pile them on the table. The woman opens my jar of Noxzema and sniffs it. Scrunching up her nose, she holds it out to us and asks, "Cái gī đây?"

"Để rửa mặt," Uncle Ngo says, making a circular motion with his hands in front of his face. He turns to me and asks, "Better than soap, huh?"

"Ah, yes. It cleans the pores." I clear my throat.

The woman stares at my face as if to see how well it has worked on my complexion. They peer inside the jar, frowning at the white substance. Replacing the cap, she sets the jar to the side.

I want to look behind me and count the number of officers standing in front of the closed door. At times I hear them opening and closing the door, and only when they come and go can I hear other people walking about, dragging their luggage behind them, and a woman speaking over the intercom in a language I never learned. But I am afraid to turn my head. However many there are, I can feel them staring at the back of my head, and my neck burns from their constant gaze. Sweat forms on my forehead, and I wish they'd turn on the fan. There are no windows in the room.

I watch Uncle Ngo from out of the corners of my eyes. He's standing still, and I do the same, leaving my arms at my side and staring straight ahead, but my arms tremble. The way the officers go through our things with such intense concentration on their brows convinces me they'll find something I overlooked. Maybe something in my Noxzema doesn't smell right. Perhaps the ammonium level is too high by Vietnamese standards. And part of me wishes they were crooked enough to plant an ounce of coke or dried-up buds in my suitcase. Anything to keep me from that moment I drive into Nha Trang and see my mother for the first time in the seventeen years since she left Los Angeles.

When I got the phone call several weeks ago, I hadn't expected it to be Mother. How could I? I hadn't thought she had been dead these past seventeen years, but when I hadn't heard from her once, I'd simply accepted the fact that I had no mother, dead or alive. But there was her voice at the other end just as I remembered it from my childhood, stern and absent of feelings. And I thought, *How can she speak that way? After so much time?*

But I was only able to say "Mother." I'm not sure if I stammered, or if my voice echoed in the receiver within the walls of white noise caused by long distances.

That was all I could say, over and over, before Uncle Ngo took the phone out of my hand. I stood beside him and listened as he spoke to her in Vietnamese, his voice low. I could not understand a word. All I heard were the rise and fall of syllables, mere sounds. Then he hung up, and we stared at each other without saying a word.

The customs officer continue to go through our things quietly. When the man uncaps a tube of Crest toothpaste and squeezes enough of it to cover the tip of his finger, Uncle Ngo lets out a low grunt. The woman shakes the can of Gillette shaving cream and presses the tab until her hand cups foam. Holding it up to her nose, she sniffs before wiping her hand on the table. The male officer tears open a box of Irish Spring soap. With a switchblade he pares layers off the way one would a fruit.

I reach inside my shirt pocket, take out my pack of Marlboros, and jerk one free with a quick flick of the wrist. Before I even have a chance to put it in my mouth, the woman says, snapping each syllable, "Dep di. Cam hut tuoc."

I raise both hands, and hear the officers stirring behind me, but I don't look back. The man hurries from around the table and snatches the pack out of my one hand and my cigarette from the other. Uncle Ngo reaches inside his denim pocket and produces his pack of cigarettes.

"Nó chì lā thuòc lá thôi. Coi. See." Uncle Ngo holds his pack out to the officer but doesn't look at him.

The inspector snaps the cigarette at the filter, sniffs it, and rubs one end between two fingers so that the tobacco spills onto the floor. Again, Uncle Ngo shows the officer his pack of cigarettes, talking at the same time. The officer nods his head, walks back behind the table, and sets my pack down.

"Đây," Uncle Ngo gives me a cigarette from his pack. "You take mine." He fishes inside his pocket for his Zippo lighter; at the same time he flips the lid open, it lights; a trick I can't do.

I puff until the cigarette catches, then I take a drag, holding it in for a moment before exhaling. The officers go back to inspecting our luggage. Uncle Ngo lights up a cigarette. After my third drag I start to feel dizzy, so I hold the cigarette between my fingers and stare at it, thinking how lucky Uncle Ngo is that he gets to keep his pack. But I can only stare at my cigarette for so long.

Our suitcases lie wide open and empty. The officers feel around the edges, smooth the palms of their hands against the lining. Ho Chi Minh sits high on the wall, staring over our heads toward the back. I continue to smoke despite how it makes me feel.

Then the male officer does something that makes me gasp. He stoops down to pick up a rectangular box and sets it on the table. I turn to Uncle Ngo then, but he only smokes his cigarette. Opening his switchblade, the officer cuts the string that holds it all together, then slices the box right down the middle, parting the seams and corners where I've taped it.

He pockets the switchblade, opens the flaps, and together, he and the female officer bring out the *ao dais*, long-sleeved satin gowns, and the black pantaloons that go with them. They turn them over with their gloved hands, smooth their palms over the length of the dresses, rub the material between their fingers, fondle the hem. The woman even holds one up against her body, checking the length. Thus, as though remembering who she is and what her duties are, she catches herself and looks at me, bringing the *ao dai* away from her body.

"They're my mother's. She left them behind."

She merely blinks her eyes several times before folding the *ao dai* in half and setting it on top of everything else. The man takes out two bundles of letters bound by rubber bands. He inspects the cover of one of them reading the addresses in the center and lefthand corner. He sets them aside and proceeds to the manila envelope. He digs his hand inside and extracts Polaroids of me and Mother and Dad. The man says something that I take to mean *look* because the woman leans in and together they gaze at each photo, frowning for long moments, most likely dissecting Mother and Dad to see their features in me. After they are through, he puts them back in the envelope. Catching sight of one he missed, he takes it out. It is an eight-by-ten photograph, the only big one in the set. He raises it to his face, and his eyes widen.

"Ba Nguyen," I say. "My grandfather."

The man looks up at me and he says something to the woman. She nods her head and frowns, and it's as if the darkness of my skin has turned pale for them, and my hair became straight and gray. And I want them to say it, admit how much I look like my grandfather despite my dark skin and hair, admit that I am one of you. But the man simply replaces the photo in the envelope and closes the flap.

Stepping away from the table, the officers yank the latex gloves off their hands. They speak to Uncle Ngo, and he nods his head eagerly. He tosses his cigarette on the floor and crushes it with the heel of his shoe. I let mine burn between my fingers.

"Come on Long-Vanh." Uncle Ngo waves me forward as he walks up to the table.

Uncle Ngo picks up a pair of jeans and begins to fold them. I set what's left of my cigarette at the edge of the table and sort through the pile. Both officers are speaking to Uncle Ngo. He nods his head at times, says "um-hm" as he folds the sleeves of his shirts behind their backs before doubling them at the torsos. Still, they continue to speak, and like Uncle Ngo, I don't look up at them. One of them, the male officer, extends his hand out and Uncle Ngo drops a pair of boxers onto the table to shake it. He pumps it several times while exchanging words. He even smiles. When Uncle Ngo lets go of his hand, the woman extends hers and he shakes it. The officers come from around the table with the box and leave the room.

"What's happening? Where are they going with Mother's things?" I whisper.

"Later," Uncle Ngo says. "Just fold clothes."

We continue to untangle long shirt sleeves from around pant legs.

"What next?" I ask.

Uncle Ngo lights his cigarette, snaps shut the Zippo, takes a long drag, and exhales before he sits back into the bench.

"They keep our passports, your Mother's *ao dais*, the letters, pho-to-graphs. For two days . . . maybe three. For now, we stay here."

"Here in the airport?" I point at the floor.

"No. Here. Ho Chi Minh City. We stay. Besides, we cannot go an-ee-where without passport," he says slowly, enunciating each syllable so that he's not misunderstood.

I rub my hands together and look about the airport. Our luggage is be-side us. In a room that looks like a warehouse, people stand behind a queue with slips of papers in their hands, the same slip they gave me to claim the items they are holding for further inspection. Officers stand on the other side and shelved behind them are the people's luggage. Other officers re-trieve luggage from off the shelves and hand them it to people.

Often, the officers point at the luggage they hand the patrons, insisting that it is theirs. And it's funny. It's funny because even though they've spent so much time packing their belongings into suitcases, once the suitcases have been taken from them, they forget which is theirs despite differences in color, size, and weight. Confused, they are doubtful that they've been handed the right suitcase until they think to check the tags.

After they get their luggage, the people make their way past Uncle Ngo and me, and every one of them stares. I nod my head, even give a slight wave of my hand, but they don't return a greeting of any kind. They just continue parading past us, some even bumping into the person in front of them. One man is videotaping as he walks along, and he turns his Cam-corder in our direction, giving commentary. He, along with everyone else, makes his way to the far end of the lobby to where guards stand with hol-stered firearms. Behind them, men, women, and children wait. Most of them hold up signs with names written on them, and I recognize some of the names: Phuong, Lop, Thanh, Huang. And although I know Mother is not here to meet us, I search each card, expecting to find my name on one of them. But I don't see Long-Vanh, and even if she were here, I wonder if Mother will look the same or if the only way I'll recognize her will be by see-ing a sign bearing my name in the hands of a woman I don't know.

Between Black and White

BY NICOLE BAILEY-WILLIAMS

In my father's dreams, there is no color, only varying shades of black. And the blackness haunts him. So, in every waking moment, he runs to whiteness.

That's how he met my mother.

She seemed everything he was not. She was everything he desired. Her skin, like cream, contrasted his coal color. Her hair, like corn silk, was silent as his raged. Her voice, like tiny bells, tinkled; his boomed. She was everything the women of his past were not, and he wanted to possess her. But, like the child who cradles a wounded bird too tightly, he crushed her. Almost. In the split second it took him to reposition his hands to get a tighter hold, she saw the crack of light from the outside world and rushed toward it. Leaving him. Leaving me. And I'm not enough for him.

My memories of them together come in like waves, and like the waves, they threaten to drown me. But I gasp and struggle through, remembering that always there is a surface, and with the surface comes air, and in the air, I'll be okay.

THE EQUATION

We had lived in Mt. Airy from the time I was born. The cozy community was far enough from what my father called "North Philly Nigga Shit" and close enough to chic Chestnut Hill for it to feel like a real home. Mt. Airy was a cauldron of cultures, bubbling and stewing until they became one. One common way of speaking. One common style of dress. One common way of thinking. My father believed that Mt. Airy was the place where he and my mother would live as one forever. And they did, we did, for a time.

I REMEMBER

I remember my first day of school. My mother stood at the corner bus stop, waving to me. She looked like an angel, only she was crying. I never thought that angels cried, but when I looked at my mother's face, I knew that God's helpers shed tears from time to time.

I remember that until I started school, I lived in racial oblivion. I was just another shade in my community, just another shade in my family. I just was. Then I boarded the school bus heading toward Rush Elementary School in Chestnut Hill.

I remember marching toward the bus bravely like a big girl, knowing that my mother was watching me. I wanted her to be proud, so I raised my chin like I had seen actors do before showdowns. I didn't know, I couldn't know, that that one act, the slight lifting of the chin, would define people's reactions to me forever. Forever. Forever different. Forever an outsider. Forever alone.

I remember that the ride to school was uneventful, yet my mind raced with anticipation. Questions about cubby holes and mid-morning snacks raced through my head as I stared out the window. So fast and furious were my thoughts that I didn't notice the furtive looks cast my way or the fingers pointing at me. It was better that I didn't or else I, like a crab being removed from the bushel, would have sensed the impending death of my innocent spirit.

I remember approaching the morning with optimism. Sitting at my desk, I folded my hands just like my mother taught me. Every now and then I would catch some of the girls looking at me. Sometimes it was a brown girl who would grin shyly if I caught her eye. Other times, it was a tan girl who would stare unsmiling, trying to decipher the puzzle that was me.

I remember lingering longer than necessary in the cubbyhole room, trying to see if anyone would invite me to play with them. After I removed my jump rope, I repacked and zipped my book bag. One of the brown girls sidled up to me.

I remember the envy in her eyes as she eyed my two honey-colored ponytails before saying, "You've got pretty hair."

I remember another brown girl tapping her foot impatiently. Half disgusted, half hateful, she snorted, "Come on, Tiffany."

Then Tiffany left, and I remember walking outside last and alone while everyone else formed Noah's Ark–like pairs ahead of me. It was an early representation of what would define the rest of my life.

THE NEXT DAY

Hope swirled in my head the next day when I awoke. *Things will be different*, I had assured myself before drifting into sleep.

The wait at the bus stop was the same. But how much different could that possibly be? All the kids were waiting with their parents. The ride on the bus was the same. But how much different could that be? It's a short ride from Mt. Airy to Chestnut Hill, and besides, the bus can get a little noisy with all those gears shifting and all. The first part of the school day was the same. But how different could that be? It's wrong to talk in class despite the fact that other kids managed to sneak in jokes and share some secrets. Their names got written on the board, but I got a star for good conduct. The walk to the cubby hole room was the same. Then I got nervous. Suppose everything was the same, and I ended up with that same lonesome feeling.

Then a change. A little girl, who looked all golden and fair like my mother, approached me.

"Hi," she said.

"Hi," I returned shyly.

"Do you want to play with us?" she asked, gesturing toward a small group of tan girls.

I smiled and nodded my head. Gathering my rope, I fell in step beside her.

"I asked my mom if it would be okay to play with you," she said innocently. "I told her that you're almost my color, just a little darker. You aren't nearly as dirty as those other girls, so you must be one of us."

My mouth fell open, partly from shock, partly from my desire to tell her that the brown is not dirt. It's not like mud.

Before I could say anything, she continued. "Besides, Heather said that she saw your mom, and she's one of us. I told my mom, and she said that at least you're half good, so you can play with us."

Her words did not immediately register in my head, but my heart felt them. Then my stomach quivered as if epic memories of burning bodies and burning crosses resurfaced into my consciousness. I ran to the bathroom to throw up the vestiges of Emmett Till and the four little girls. My teacher ran after me.

I was spared from recess that day. Looking out the window of the nurse's office, I watched as the other kids naturally fell into groups together. Tan girls. Brown girls. Brown boys. Tan boys. As I watched, the tans became white and the browns became black. And I fell somewhere in between black and white.

EVERY DAY

Every day my mother waited for me at the bus stop. Her eyes anxious, her mouth ready to smile. Her aura was light, heavenly. She seemed so happy, I didn't want to crush her with stories of my colored confusion. So I lied.

Every day I filled her ears with tales of my popularity and acceptance. I told her that so many girls wanted to play with me at recess that I had to choose. I told her that girls always wanted to share their snacks with me, and that was why I wasn't really hungry at dinner. I told her that one of my classmates invited me to her birthday party this Saturday, but because we were going to Baltimore, I declined. I told her that one of the black girls, though it was brown girls for her virgin ears, brushed my hair at recess every day, telling me that it was the most beautiful hair she'd ever seen.

And I learned that mothers and white people were gullible enough to be fooled by a good story and a smile.

AND THEY SAID

Into the bathroom, the black girls came.
"Hi, Shana," one said, sneering my name.
"Shana, we don't like you. You think you're cute."
"Don't look surprised, honey, we've got proof."
"Remember the bus rides all those years in the past?"
"You were too good to speak on the bus and in class."
"You always looked down your nose at us."
"I didn't say anything, didn't want to cause a fuss."
"But, you zebra bitch, your cozy days are through."
"We'll make these school days a living hell for you."
With those final words came a slap across my face.
And they taught me that among them I had no place.

ALMOST EVERYDAY

The fingers. They pinch.
The mouths. They spit.
The feet. They kick.
The hands. They hit.
The fists. The punch.
The teeth. They crunch.
The hands. They shove.
The mouths. They munch.
The feet. They smoosh.
The hands. They push.
The shoes. The squoosh.
The doors. They smush.

And they almost never leave a mark.

THE WORDS

I tried to tell, but the words got stuck in my throat. And when they were dislodged, they came out all wrong.

The three of us were sitting in the sunroom. Dad, Mom, and me. Black.

white, and between. I was eight years old, but my soul felt so much older. I was weary from years of uncried tears.

I looked from mother to father, noting all of their differences. Her softness, his hardness. Her pleasantness, his sternness. Her hope, his anger. Her optimism, his pessimism. I decided to shoot straight down the middle, making my words plain.

"I don't like my school," I said, then held my breath.

My mother looked up from her book. My father didn't look up at all.

"Honey, why not?" she asked, her light voice incompatible with the heaviness in my heart.

I inhaled deeply though clenched teeth, gathering strength before saying, "Nobody likes me."

"Of course, they do. They're always sharing their snacks with you and inviting you places."

Before I could fix my lips around the words, the dam broke, and my face was flooded with three years of uncried tears.

My mother rushed over to me, scooping me into her arms, holding me so close that between my snot and her sweater, I felt that I would suffocate.

I heard my father's voice demand, "Is somebody messing with you?"

"Shh," my mother snapped. "Girls don't cry only if someone is hitting them. You should know that by now."

"Well, why is she crying?"

"I don't know," she said, rocking me. "She probably had a bad day."

I heard my father mumble something. Then I heard his heavy feet walk across the sunroom and go into the house. Then my ears were filled with my mother's humming while my heart was still filled with grief.

FALLING DOWN

We were at Miles Park for a picnic on Memorial Day. I remember it like it was yesterday because it marked the onset of a series of changes in my life. I should have known that the picnic was just the beginning of imminent change because things always happen in threes.

Mom, determined to bring us closer as a family, had packed a picnic basket of delectable delicacies. Shrimp salad on fat, crusty bagels from Rosensweig's deli. Corn and tomato salsa to cover gourmet chicken burritos from Don Pepe's. Sweet Potato French Fries and Surprise Iced Tea from Sugarene's Soul Food Spot.

Dad had laid out the blanket and was beginning a game of solitaire while Mom had pulled out her latest Danielle Steel fantasy read. I pulled out my jump rope and attempted to jump rope on a flat patch of grass.

Conversation was sparse in our household, and I was used to it, but sometimes under my father's watchful, wordless stare I grew uncomfortable. It seemed that in his watching, he was waiting. Waiting. Ever waiting for me to make a mistake. Mess up. And when I did, he would pounce.

"Watch what you're doing!" "You're making a mess!" "Look at yourself! You're such a slob." "Damn it! Can't you do anything right?"

So I tried to be perfect. Maybe in my perfection, I thought, I could gain his acceptance. That Memorial Day, I gained more that acceptance. I gained his love. At least temporarily.

Tired of jumping rope, I went to explore the "Kiddie Community." There were mini-houses like sheds, complete with flower boxes and benches. Uninterested in the frilly girl's stuff inside, I peered up to the roof. There boys walked their big-stepped walk, happy and free. The sun beat down on their faces, and under its warm glare, their colors melted into one. They were all golden brown in its rays. I wanted to be up there. In the sun. In with the others. Like the others.

So I climbed up and up like Jack and the Beanstalk until I reached the top. It wasn't that high, only about seven feet, but on top, I felt like the queen of the world. I tried to do the big-stepped walk, claiming every inch between my feet, on top of the roof, in the world. I wanted to be big, complete, perfect, but in my quest for perfection, I stumbled, and I, like Icarus, came crashing to the earth. The sun, my betrayer, beat down on me.

From outside of my body, I watched my father spring into action. He scooped me up, carrying me to the car. Alone, just the two of us, he charged down Germantown Pike, racing for my life. Through stoplights he sped, pressing his shirt under my chin, trying to stop the bleeding. There in the car, through the fear, through the worry, through the pain, I saw that the way to his heart was through danger. As long as my physical needs were met, he didn't worry. Yet if I were in harm's way, he would save me.

THING TWO OF THREE

I turned nine that summer, and I had my first real birthday party, complete with decorations and a cake. My dad had broken his rule about staying out of North Philly. He had bitten the bullet and gone to Denise's Delicacies for my cake.

"They have the best cakes in the city," my mother had whined. My father's jaw had been tight as he clenched his teeth and looked at me. I scratched my chin, and I could see guilt dance in his eyes before he snapped at me.

"Leave your face alone!"

Mumbling, he collected his keys and headed back to the place from which he hailed, the place he grew to despise.

"Mommy, why does he hate going to North Philly?" I questioned after hearing his car pull away.

She sighed and wiped her hands on her apron, wondering what to say and how to say it.

"Your dad had a hard childhood," she began, wondering where to tread and what to reveal.

My innocent eyes compelled her to continue speaking.

"I don't really know how to explain it, because I'm not sure if I understand it myself. He just got tired of poverty and despair."

"But if there's a good bakery there, and other good businesses are there, can it be all that bad?"

"I don't know, honey. But he hates everything that reminds him of there, and he loves anything that's different," she said.

Then I heard her sniffle before her head went down. She wept silently while fingering her wedding band.

That afternoon, my mother's family poured into our home to celebrate my birthday. My mom dished up the cake while my dad served drinks. He kept his glass filled, and every time he got the chance, he refilled the glass of my mom's younger sister. She smiled appreciatively and soon she began giggling whenever he approached. Soon, the two of them disappeared. Together.

THING THREE OF THREE

My mother was gone. She left us at the end of the summer. Just walked away, leaving a note for my father in her stead.

James,

I should have known. I should have known that you could never love me when you hate yourself. I thought I could help heal you. Lift you up. Lead you to love, but you never even lit the path.

Know that I don't hate you. I don't hate my sister. I don't hate any of the others. I don't hate my child. Please make sure she knows that. I just need to preserve myself since no one else will.

I love you. Tell Shana that I love her with all of my heart, but I have to go. Please love her, James. Let her know that the skin she's in is not a curse. Make her know that she has a place between black and white.

Elizabeth

He folded up her letter and put it in a drawer. He never mentioned her again.

THE LENS

I fell in love with the lens when I was fifteen. In that stage of swirling emotions, I dug the way I could manipulate the lens and create flatness. Flatness
of emotion and energy. Yet if I wished, I could also capture frenzy and excitement. The camera and the lens became my means of control. Despite
the circumstances surrounding me, despite the drama, I could create peace.
Thinking of it still gives me a rush, and in my egomaniacal moments, I
imagine, just for a split second, what it's like to be God.

Around my high school, I came to be known as something of a beatnik,
what with my weed-smoking and endless supply of black clothes. I was the
Herb Ritz of Girls' High. I *was* the Photography Club and the Art Club. I
didn't like taking pictures for the newspaper or the yearbook because the
shots were always so staged.

"Here's Becky, the president of Rotary Interact. Smile, Becky."
Click.
"Here's Yolanda, captain of the basketball team. Yolanda, hold up that bas-
ketball for us and say cheese."
Click.

Even the ones that were supposed to be candid were fake.

"See the Key Club as they box up the donations from this year's Christmas
Drive. Aren't they magnanimous?"
Click.

All people have an image they want to convey, a way they want to be
seen. Then, there's the truth. That's what I try to capture on film. The truth.
But truth is fleeting. Yet still I try.

HIM

I've always tried to freeze people in the moment their raw purity is exposed.
Those moments just come to me. I can't create them. So I must wait. That's
what I was doing the first time I saw him.

He raced into my peripheral vision as I sat on a bench on Thirteenth
Street in the heart of Temple University's campus. Leaning my back against
the table, my camera resting on my stomach, I felt his heat before I saw him.
I fumbled for my camera, my breath catching in my chest as I watched the
northbound specimen in admiration. His white tank top revealed his glowing golden skin. His tight shoulders led to arms etched with muscles. His
torso was lean; his stomach, flat. His behind was tight and high, and his
legs, ripped with muscles, carried him quickly as he sprinted away.

Something stayed with me long after he was gone. Though his face looked relaxed, his hands were drawn into tight fists, telling me that his heart was torn. I wanted to get inside of that torn heart, to mend it from the inside out.

ONE O'CLOCK

I determined that with his runner's discipline, he was a creature of habit. That habit would lead him back to Thirteenth Street where he would run north like his ancestors had probably done generations before. He would pass briefly through my life again at one o'clock. I sat ready, like a cheetah waiting to pounce, camera poised to capture his naked edge.

Again I felt his heat before I saw him. I wondered what it was about him that made me sense his presence. It was like I was a heat-seeking missile, and he was my target, only that analogy made me feel too predatory. Whatever it was, whatever I called it, it drew me toward him, and I hoped that the camera's eye could catch and preserve it until I could catch him.

I lifted the camera to my eye and pointed it in his direction, moving slowly to match his pace as he approached.

Click.
Calm.
Click.
Ease.
Click.
Despair.
Click.
Peace.
Click.
Pleasure.
Click.
Pain.
Click.
Happiness.
Click.
A nod and a smile at me.
Click.
Got him.

ONCE MORE

The next day was Friday, and I wanted to see him once more before the weekend claimed him. Camera in hand, I headed toward my usual spot after my eleven-thirty African American Lit Class ended. Gladfelter Hall on

Twelfth Street was the only place on campus where I didn't feel quite so different. It housed the African American Studies Department and, from the moment I stepped off the elevator onto the eighth floor, I felt at home. Only my own home was not this warm. Anyway, leaving Gladfelter felt like leaving a cocoon, but it was okay. I could feel a similar heat radiate from him. I knew that I would feel it even more once I was actually able to get next to him.

As I walked up Montgomery toward Thirteenth, something felt different. I felt the heat, but I knew I shouldn't have felt it so soon. I checked my watch. Twelve forty-five. He was early. What was he doing down here?

I slowed my pace and scanned the street looking for him. I spotted him on the other side of the street, also approaching Thirteenth. He waved at me as he passed. I waved back, hoping that his feet and heart would guide him to me. Instead, once he reached Thirteenth, he turned left and headed south.

And I was left with my camera in hand, heart on my sleeve, wondering why.

RUNNING

"So where do you go when you run?" I asked, looking into his eyes.

"It depends on my mood," he said, staring boldly back.

"Explain."

He looked down for a second, as if gathering strength. "I run north on Thirteenth Street when I'm trying to remember—"

"Remember what?" I asked interrupting.

"When I'm trying to remember my roots and where I've been."

"And you run south on Thirteenth when . . ."

"I run south when I'm trying to forget."

"What are you trying to forget, Lionel?" I asked, looking directly into his eyes. Waiting.

"Shana, I believe in being completely honest, but I'm not ready to tell you that yet. Okay?"

"Okay."

We spent the rest of the afternoon lounging on Kelly Drive, where I took pictures of boats passing along the Schuykill River. As his hand came to rest on my thigh, I felt his heat combine with my own, and the result for me was almost orgasmic.

Hincty

BY KAREN BATES

FROM *The Chosen People*

James Simpson Lee Hastings, Jr. was a chunk of the nineteenth century that had been vomited into the lap of the twenty-first. Simp Hastings; as he'd been known since his days at an East Coast boarding school, had been a moderately competent Boston accountant who had put himself on the mainstream media map by becoming the social arbiter of modern Negro society. His gossipy history of same, *Chosen People*, had briefly been on the *New York Times* bestseller list. Since then, Hastings had all but quit his day job to make the circuit, describing to innocent and unknowing white people Who Counts—and Who Doesn't—in black communities across the country.

The West Coast swing of a speaking tour had landed him here in Los Angeles, at Ashanti Books, one of the country's biggest and best black bookstores. I'd dropped down to see, firsthand, what all the fuss had been about, and perhaps to get column out of it.

My name is Alex Powell, and I am a journalist. I write a column for *The Los Angeles Standard* that runs in the Metro section on Thursdays and Sundays, and I'm always looking for good ideas.

This, however, might not have been one of them. Simp Hastings' book had been the cause of considerable ire in several sectors of black communities across the country. Although many of the upper-crust black folks about whom Simp had chosen to write had resolutely refused to talk to him "If we keep quiet," one Philadelphia doyenne had sniffed, "perhaps he'll just go away . . ." A few had cooperated and, augmented by a raft of eager wannabes, given him interviews. As a result, *Chosen People* spent several hundred pages chronicling the "I gots" of a certain kind of black person, and listing the Right Clubs and Organizations to which strivers should strive to belong.

Some of the Negro Old Guard thought Simp suspect as well as traitorous. "Really," grumbled one Chicago doctor; "who is he, anyway? I've never heard of him. My children have never heard of him." A Charleston socialite from a family that had been living in that city for over 150 years simply sighed and said (to one of my aunts), "The bad part is, they get it wrong and we—myself included, I'm sorry to say—don't speak up and correct them when they do."

Black activists who'd struggled for decades to minimize class differences among us in the interest of developing a more progressive agenda that would benefit all of us were furious. They felt that Simp was ripping the scab off old hurts covering touchy issues such as skin color, hair texture, and the keenness of one's features. They bitterly mocked his now-trademark inquiry to every new acquaintance: "Do I know your people?"

So here I was, at 7 P.M. on a rainy Monday night, crowded into a standing-room-only group of people who'd come to be given The Word from J.S.L. Hastings, Jr., as he was listed on the book's cover.

The room seemed to be about equally divided between business-suited professionals and afrocentrically-dressed people in cowrie-tipped dreadlocks and clothes from the Motherland. The room quieted as Hastings stepped to the podium.

"Good evening," he began.

His voice was high-pitched and boyish, like Mike Tyson's. But unlike Tyson's Bronx accent, Simpson's was a carefully-aped Locust Valley Lockjaw, a nasal, almost whiny voice, kind of like millionaire Thurston Howell III's had been, on *Gilligan's Island.*

And instead of the onetime heavyweight champ's massive body, James Simpson Lee Hastings, Jr., was tiny, elfin. His skin was a deep, unattractive yellow—almost orange—as if he'd just gotten over a severe case of jaundice. His hair crunched in poorly suppressed waves all about his head. There was less of his chin than there should have been, proportionately speaking, and his nose stuck out of his flat-cheeked face like Pinocchio's.

Hastings did possess two saving graces, however: He had a magnificent set of teeth—white, even and natural—and beautiful eyes that I'd seen change color from bright green to gold to light brown, depending on what he was wearing.

Tonight they were greenish, and fairly snapping with excitement. And maybe just a little malice. Hastings shot his cuffs, straightened his tie, took a drink from the glass of flat mineral water that had been carefully placed at his elbow, and smiled out at the assembled.

"Good evening," he cooed to his audience, again.

"Good evening," the audience dutifully responded.

"Whassup?" yelled some wag from the back.

When the laughter subsided, Simp Hastings continued.

"What's up, indeed? That's why we're here tonight, isn't it?—to discuss what *is* up with the depiction of black people in this country. For too long, the only images of us have been of happy slaves, buffoons, or criminals. Today when the media writes about 'real black life,' it's always welfare mothers with eight children and no daddy, gangbangers, and crack addicts."

There were murmurs of assent from some in the audience.

"Well, I'm sure those people do exist—I know they do—but those people are not my people. *My* people get up and go to work every day, and they are successful at what they do . . ."

"Uh-hum," a fiftyish lady in a burgundy tweed suit murmured, nodding in assent.

"*My* people live in lovely homes, with original art on the walls and inherited silver in their sideboard drawers . . ."

Two women my mother's age nudged each other as if to say "Finally!" while a young woman with expensively monogrammed everythings—purse, tote bag, shoes, and earrings—waved her hand, revival-style, in the air and said "Tell it!"

"*My* people have been summering with other people like them, in the same places for decades . . ."

"Hincty muthafucka," snorted a man near me, shaking his head in disgust.

"*My* people are not ashamed to have servants, and they know what to do with them . . ."

Uncertain looks all around.

"In short, my people have not been discussed by mainstream America, which has no idea we exist. Which is why I wrote *Chosen People*. I want America to know that we are here. I want us to take our rightful place in American society. I want people with money and taste and breeding to stop hiding these assets and to be proud of them. We *should* be proud: We are special. We are different. We are *chosen*. And now is our time to shine."

The room broke into vigorous applause from the people who felt strongly as Simp did. Others kept their hands in their pockets, frowning. Some people shook their heads, as if they couldn't believe what they were hearing. And about four folks simply got up and left.

During all this, a white magazine journalist for the local monthly was scribbling furiously into his notebook. Clearly he'd never met or heard from anyone like JSL Hastings, Jr., and was fascinated.

"Now, I could go on for hours," Hastings chuckled. "My fiancée—who some of you out here may know; she has an M.D. and a J.D. from Yale and she's a medical correspondent for the *Today* show—Dr. Sheila Howe?—says I go on all the time. But I'll stop, because I'm sure you have questions, and I'd love to hear them. And answer them."

So saying, he drank some more water, and looked over the rim of his glass at the audience. You could hear chairs squeaking as people shifted.

"Come on, don't be shy! What's on your mind?—Tell me!"

A tall, thin woman rose slowly. She was elegantly dressed, all in beige, with a cream-colored cashmere shawl draped gracefully around her shoulders.

"What I'd like to know, Mr. Hastings, is this: Why?"

He blinked.

"I beg your pardon?"

"Why bring all this up now? We've gone through so much as a people, this is such a hurtful subject for many in our community. Why do you insist on raising it?"

Her voice was well modulated and confident. She was probably in her late sixties. Her gold bracelets jingled softly as she sat again.

"Well, Mrs . . . ?"

"Elton, Grace Elton."

"Oh my God—I cannot believe I'm talking to you, finally!" Simp squeaked. "Does anybody here not know who this is?"

Many people looked at him as if saying "Duh—of course we do." A few people shrugged, confused. They didn't remain unenlightened for long.

"This is the wife of Dr. Howard Elton, one of the premiere civil rights activists in this city. Dr. Elton's father established the first black hospital in Los Angeles. You may be too young to remember any of this—I am, too, actually, but I did my homework: The hospital Dr. Elton senior started is now Los Angeles Municipal Children's Hospital."

Gasps of recognition.

"You're *exactly* who I wanted to write about in this book!" Simp Hastings chided the woman old enough to be his mother. "You should have let me interview you!"

Mrs. Elton rose again, and looked squarely at him.

"I had no interest in being in your book, Mr. Simpson. Like my late husband, I feel strongly that if we are to move forward as a people, we have to concentrate on what binds us together, not focus on what could tear us apart. This book never should have been written. Or perhaps it *should* have been written—by someone else. I have no quarrel with a book that outlines the achievements of successful blacks, but this is not that book. This is merely a . . . a *shopping list* of things to have and to get, and a wretched catalogue of the worst snobberies and sillinesses some of our people insist on displaying. So I have become a Chosen Person: I have *chosen* to remove myself from any association with it at all. I wish some of the people who had decided otherwise had had second thoughts. And I pity you, Mr. Hastings. You have completely missed the boat on what being black means in this day and age.

"I'm sorry," Grace Elton turned and apologized to those around her; "I'm becoming a little emotional. I wish you all a good evening."

And, wrapping her shawl more closely around her, the chic Mrs. Elton picked up her purse and left to thundering applause.

Simp Hastings wasn't fazed in the least.

"Well," he said, only a smidge huffily, "*some* people are still in denial alled as he walked out into the misty night air. "I'll be right

a huge trunk or he was having trouble finding the books, be-
minutes, Simp Hastings hadn't returned.

's out having a smoke," someone suggested.

g a call on his cell phone."

the bookstore owner, "he can't see. Those rental cars are noto-
ing off as many of the essentials as possible. I'll bring him a

k in forty-five seconds, looking ashen.

olice—now!" he snapped to his startled cashier.

us left in the store looked up.

g bad has happened," the bookstore owner said tersely. "No-
de."

ant, of course, that everyone immediately did.

started screaming at once. I pushed her aside to look, and
't.

the ground, promised books in his outstretched hand, was
n Lee Hastings, Jr., wearing an ear to ear grin.

k.

ti or To Hell

BY ALEXS D. PATE

od on the bow of the *Starry Eye* as it hit the breakwater. He felt
standing there. If it would have borne his weight, he'd have
very tip of the bowsprit. If he could, he'd stand there with his
s large brown chest with its thick nest of kinky coils the only
m the salt spray, and ride the rolling power of the water below
from this place, even sliding along the tranquil waters of this
he could feel the gentle bucking and bobbing of the ship as
ed port.

to touch dry land. Much had happened since he'd last stepped
nd he had the booty to prove it. And although his crew was

about their station in life. Such a pity. Sh‹
clude. Other questions?"

It went on for about a half hour, with v‹
he included So-and-So but not Thus-and-
clude more cities in the Midwest? Would
of "the best sororities and fraternities? Wh
had these organizations for years . . ." W
consultant to a Movie of the Week abo
vanished black summer resorts?

After the questions, Simp Hastings si
Some people bought loads—one for the
people bought them for their children
about us."

Toward the end, a big, burly brother v
came up to the signing table, leaned forv

"We should be beyond this shit by
holding us back. You need to rethin‹
brother."

The menace in his voice was unmista‹

"I'll be sure to do that," Simp said b‹
of the store.

"What's with him?" wondered Logo‹
signed.

"E-N-V-Y," Simp said, looking at
slipped the books into a stylish tote wit‹

Hastings had promised a brief interv‹
and the white guy from the city maga‹
the last person to receive a signed copy.

Unfortunately for the remaining f‹
Simp had sold seventy-five in thirty mi‹

"Oh no!" one disappointed custome‹
my mother for her birthday."

"We're getting another shipment in‹
her.

"My mother's birthday is *tomorrow,*‹
The owner retreated to the cash
"last-minute Negroes who think the‹
when their mama's birthday is the sam‹

Disappointed Customer rolled her‹

"Know what? I think I have a few e‹
"Let me go out and look, and if I do,

"Oh, would you? Thank you! Do I‹

"Yes,"‹
back."

Either he‹
cause afte‹
"Mayb‹
"Or m‹
"Or," ‹
rious for‹
flashlight.

He was‹
"Call t‹
The fe‹
"Somet‹
body go o‹
Which‹
Logo L‹
wished I h‹
There,‹
James Sim‹
On his ‹

To Ha‹

A rrow s‹
power‹
stood on th‹
shirt open, ‹
protection f‹
him. But ev‹
Tortuga Bay‹
they approac‹

He was read‹
foot ashore,

tense, he knew they were also satisfied that their adventures had returned a profit. Brethren of the coast, they were. Scallywags all. Arrow didn't like the word "pirate," and refused to let that word be used in his presence. But regardless of what he called them, he knew what they were. They were out for themselves.

Luckly, Arrow also knew who *he* was. If you made a mistake and crossed his path in free and open waters, then you'd better have a very fast ship or an army hidden in your hull. He straightened his crisscrossed leather sashes so that they intersected at the center of his chest, just below the cut in the neck of his shirt. Affixed on these sashes was a collection of razor-sharp throwing knives. Twenty in all. And no one could throw knives as quickly and accurately as Arrow. That was how he'd gotten his name. He threw knives with an archer's skill. But faster. So fast that he could pepper a group of ten or twelve men with those darts in an eye's blink. So fast that men who witnessed his skill often turned on their heels. In shipboard fights, when he joined boarding parties, he could stand in one place and cause the ruin of a third of a small ship's company. Arrow would also carry and use his firearm, but by the time he got to his pistol, there would already be a handful of dead men lying about. He was the Black Arrow. A knife throwing terror who now sailed on his fastest ship yet, the *Starry Eye*.

Arrow turned aft and headed amidships, ordering sails dropped and the anchor readied. Their journey was over. His strong voice danced about the decks, over the trouble he could feel brewing. Yes, they had come into some fortune and the crew was happy about that. But last night after they'd divided up the booty and each man received his share, and before the rum keg was opened, Arrow had announced his plans to sail to St. Domingo after a short stay in Tortuga. He knew they were uneasy about it, given the rumors about the revolution that was coming there.

But there had been no way to have a deliberation about that then. Everyone had been too excited to be sailing into the port the next morning. They were almost giddy as the shares were divided. That spontaneous ceremony had graduated into a carnage of rum, petty fights, and loud singing. Now even he felt a little light-headed in the midday sun. He was ready for a good meal, some drink, and a standing bed. And he would present no strong argument to the first pretty woman who offered to join him there.

His loins stirred with a force only a woman could tame. He looked forward to the surrender his body was determined to make.

. . .

As with the end of every voyage he'd taken, there was a natural sadness that overtook the ship when the next port was sighted. Yes, everyone wanted to hit shore. Everyone wanted the same things, and most of those things were found on land. To the seaman dreams exist on land. The only reason to be engaged in the business of piracy was to get money so that life on land was better. Well, that wasn't entirely true. There were some, whom Arrow knew, who loved the sea more than anyone or anything else. On land, these men were hopeless drunks or beat-down husbands. But once the ship was under way they became crackerjack shipmates. Foisting and heaving and battling at the slightest need. But that wasn't what had driven Arrow to the sea, wasn't what had pushed him to the ostensible command of his crew of sixty-seven men. Oh, he loved the sea. He did. But it was a lucky thing that he loved it. He was there because it was the only place in the entire world where he actually was free.

No, he didn't just feel free, he was really free on his ship with his men. He'd once been a slave. A man of bondage. He shuddered whenever he remembered it. For nearly twenty years he'd been nothing more than a thinking work animal. But providence had intervened. Or more accurately, it was the meeting of providence and preparation. Arrow, then known as Luke Dunly, had, under the tuteladge of an uncle on the same plantation, developed a skill in knife throwing. He practiced every minute he could behind the outer ring of slave quarters. He'd knifed up the back of so many shacks people took to pleading with him to practice farther out in the woods. And then, one night as he was sneaking back to the men's quarters, three of his friends had dashed past him. He'd called to them, but they hadn't even turned around. So he'd taken off after them. After about twenty strides, one named Jingo had stopped and faced Arrow.

"Boy, get back."

"Where y'all goin'?"

"We'se gonna freedom." With that Jingo had turned and taken off again. Arrow had just stood there listening as their footfalls disappeared into the woods. And then he'd heard new footsteps and realized he would be taken for a runaway. And just as this thought had formed in his head, he'd seen Breathin' Heavy, the overseer's bloodhound, come galloping down the path. He'd instinctively brought Breathin' Heavy down with one of the two knives he had in his hand. And then he too had taken flight along the same route as those who'd gone before. The point where preparation and providence came together.

That was a bit more than five years ago. How things had changed. He'd found his way to the sea. They said it was the water that had brought him

here. Maybe water could take him away. And it had, in a way. He now knew
that Africa was on the other side of the world and he wasn't sure that's where
he wanted to go. He had six Africans in his crew. Pulled them from a slave
ship on a previous voyage and offered them a place. He always offered black
men a choice. They could join him or they could try to make their own way.
Most chose to be let go, not realizing that on this side of the world, when a
white man wanted a black man he almost just had to claim him. He never
saw or at least recognized any of those he set free. But ten had stayed with
him. Four of them had died, two in battle, two from sickness.

Fortune had brought him to the Caribbean and now the Caribbean was
his fortune. He plied it like the best of his ilk.

There was no feeling like being out on the high seas, trying to command
movement when the sea itself had such a great will. An overwhelming will.
No maps and all the instinct in the world could not save you from an angry
sea bent on your destruction.

And he'd not sailed them in peace. Far from it. Arrow and his crew had
taken two ships on this voyage. The last being the ship he was now putting
into port, the *Starry Eye*. When he'd ousted its English captain, a Mister
Downs, he'd asked politely if the good captain minded if he rechristened
her. And of course Downs, seeing clearly that he was at a large disadvantage
joyfully assented.

"Yes, yes . . ." He spat, trying to smile docilely, "Please sir, if I may insist.
Name her as you will."

At which moment, Arrow graciously swept his upper body forward, bowing at the waist, uncovering his hat in the manner of the fine European gentlemen he'd had the great pleasure of knowing. And he'd known them all.
From royalty to the lowest Jack Tar he knew them. He'd been a slave to one.
And now he was teaching them the wrongs of their ways. They could no
longer keep him down. Not the Black Arrow.

Arrow leaned close to the puffy face of Captain Downs, "I see by ya
clothes that you be a gentleman, sir. And by your manner, of which I do ap-
prove, sir, I would love to accommodate your request for leniency, sir." They
were in Down's quarters. Arrow, Downs and Dirty Bill who was Arrow's
quartermaster and de facto, the ship's mediator and dispenser of justice.
Dirty Bill was completely loyal to Arrow, seeing as how it was him who'd
saved his life more than once and who'd taken him on in the first place. But,
as was usual when Arrow was present, Dirty Bill stood back, calmly, watching.

"I truly would like to see a fine gentleman like yo'self to be free to strut
about with those fine clothes and all the things you dearly love. I truly
would. But you see, I must . . . you see," Arrow stopped abruptly and
turned his back on Downs. He walked toward Dirty Bill, whose sun

burned, muscled face in the shadows looked demon-like to Arrow. His eyes, dark from the previous night's celebration, stared blankly ahead of him. Not really looking at Arrow. He knew what was about to happen. He knew Arrow had no choice. Poor Captain Downs was to meet his destiny in the form of the Main's most notorious colored pirate captain. Arrow could no more let the good Captain live than throw his gold in the drink.

With a sudden swoosh, Arrow whirled around, in the same motion unloosing one of his blades and still, even to Dirty Bill—who'd seen this same motion so many times he'd could never account for them all—in the very same movement of torso and arms sent that same blade into Down's heart. The man slumped immediately. Arrow continued his turn until he was again facing Dirty Bill. "You see, sir, I must increase the fear of me. I must make it legendary or I will not be respected. I did not ask for this life and its needs. I truly did not. Tell him Bill. Tell him that if this world were different, I'd be different too. Isn't that true Bill?"

"Aye, Cap'n." Dirty Bill stood perfectly still.

"But, forgive the immodesty, sir. I am the Black Arrow, and in this world of legendary thieves and brigands of all sorts, fakers mostly, men of limited skill whose reputations seem so great in the pubs when I goes to 'em and hear about all these exploits and how many ships they takes and all this fancy talk, I figured I had to follow suit if you know what I mean to say. But," Arrow tuned now to the dead captain, "I want to thank you for your clothes which I will take good care of and especially those boots you got on. Yes. Well, Bill, get Mobley and Frenchie to clean this place up. We got permission to rename this lady." And with that he walked by Dirty Bill and went above decks to survey the loot.

And now he was returning to a port in which his safe passage and accommodation were all but assured. The gold and jewels the ship carried, even after the split, along with bolts of materials and other sundry items, would be more than enough to grease the palms of various officials and provide for a little relaxation before they took to the seas again. Besides there were four other ships of questionable registry already sitting in the harbor. Tortuga looked to be busy with the brethren of the sea.

The crew had decided before the drinking started on the previous night to take two long boats into port, leaving behind a skeleton crew for protection. It was also decided that Arrow would be in the first boat so as to make the appropriate arrangements. They'd not been to Tortuga in nearly a half year. And on the Spanish Main, officials changed with the whim of queens and kings thousands of miles away.

Arrow changed into an outfit he'd picked from Captain Downs' locker. His pants were a tough but smooth broadcloth, dyed dark blue. His shirt was a dingy white made from the same material. It, as were most of the shirts Arrow favored, opened two inches above his navel and flared out to its rather long collars. Over this he flung his knife belts. As he strode briskly past his men in Captain Downs' scuffed, but still quite fine leather boots, Arrow felt a feeling he knew well. He was in fact, the captain. These were his men. Men who he'd fought alongside, ate and drank with and, in moments when someone had to say what to do, commanded. He knew that some of them resented his leadership, but Dirty Bill kept them honest and there had been only a few minor purges. Besides no man aboard the *Starry Eye* was willing, in his right mind, to go against the Black Arrow.

As he passed through the crew on his way to the ladder to climb down into the boat, he felt strong, prideful. His knives gleamed and showed all of the effort Frenchie had put into the their polish. He was greeted with the rising energy of a sea crazy crew an hour away from the beach.

"Ayyyyyy," Dockson called. "Look at the captain, here. Decked out he is. Tryin to get there 'fore we do, eh Cap'n? Wants 'em all for hisself, he does, dressed like that."

"You'll have your turn, Dockson," Arrow said smiling. Dockson was a tall muscular man, English and mean. Dirty Bill had often reminded Arrow that Dockson might one day prove a threat. But today, Dockson's salt-worn face showed levity. Arrow smiled back. "And if I remember correctly you already have a 'lady' waitin for you. And if I can say it plainly in front of your mates, here, she was a mighty powerful little somethin'." Laughter began to bubble around them.

"Aye, Cap'n you've made your point."

"I thought I might, Dockson, for you're much more the scoundrel everywhere but here. And since I go ashore before you do, if I were you, I'd keep my trap shut and go in peace when your turn comes." That was Arrow at his best. And his men appreciated it. He could give as good as he got.

"Now you dregs," Arrow went on, now in full voice, "We've come a full circle. And we've got the profits of it in our belts. But do not let land lull you to sleep. We will not grow root here." Arrow craned his neck to see to the back of the group. "How long will it take you to drink up this here loot, Bracken? How long?"

Everyone turned to look at Bracken, an Irishman who could drink a stone to sand. He was propped against a storage locker, barely able to stand after last night's binge. "Well Captain, after I settles a few previously made notes I won't have enough to make it to more than two-three months. At least best I can gather with my head spinnin' the way it is."

Arrow laughed. "Hear that, mates? Three months. We all know that if we stay here that long, you'll be dead, Bracken. And we won't have that will we?" There were shouts of agreement. "No, we will be under weigh in a fortnight. So, stay out of jail. Try to keep from getting married. And keep your legs seaworthy because before you know it we'll be fightin' the swells."

The crew cheered its agreement and the first boat was loaded and disembarked.

Four hours later, Arrow was seated in the shadows of a rum house, stomach full, head spinning, picking at his nails with one of his knives. But he was only half focused on his fingers, his gaze kept cutting across the hazy room. From one group of sailors playing cards, to the games of other sailors, to the women who bounced about like buoys in a storm—from one man to the next—to the sullen loners, like himself who were content to drink themselves into empty moments of empty mindlessness. It was odd how they could come ashore in the afternoon and by night have steadied their legs well enough to feel some semblance of normalcy. It was also strange the way the crews of the various ships knew each other, had fought with or in some instances against each other, and yet there was a sense of family between them. Although most were European—Frenchmen, Englishmen, Dutchmen, Norse—there were a smattering of runaways, Indians, Caribs, Africans, even a few Asians jammed into the tavern. And they understood at least one thing that bound them all together. They knew that each one of them depended on the seas and the weakness of the Spanish or the arrogance of the British merchants for their livelihood.

"Cap'n." It was Dirty Bill suddenly standing off to Arrow's side. He waited there, asking with his body for permission to sit.

Barely turning his head toward him, Arrow nodded his assent. "How goes it, Bill? Where were ye?" Arrow was a self-educated man. Most of his book learning came from one slave or another who'd had the courage to defy the law and teach him. He knew how to read and did when he could find something to read. And even more significantly he could write. Not many of his mates could claim that. But when he spoke, you wouldn't necessarily figure he'd grown up on a southern plantation. More likely you'd think he'd been an urchin in the streets near the docks of London. Arrow had learned early among the pirates, that the more like them he talked, the better they treated him.

"The Flyin' Fish. There's more of our men there than here. Cap'n Flagg's crew is there besides. Much merriment over there. More women and ah . . . a looser sort than here."

"Ah." Arrow could imagine the bacchanal that was probably in progress. He hoped that he'd be able to reassemble his crew when the time came. "Nothin like one of our heathens loose in the world with his pockets full of gold. Nothin's safe, Bill. Not a farthing or a silk slip."

"Aye, that's for sure." He paused, Arrow could feel him trying to decide whether or not to say something. And then, before Arrow could command him to do so, Dirty Bill continued. "Ah . . . Cap'n, there's some men that's a little worried about what you said last night before we got our shares. . . . about going to St. Domingo to help those nig . . . ah. . . . to . . . well . . . just about going there."

Arrow was motionless. He'd known when he'd told them of his intentions there might be disagreement. He held his rigid pose for a bit, then leaned his chair back against the wall. Most of what it meant to be captain of a pirate ship was the ability to keep the crew together. They did nearly everything by majority decision. He was captain when there was a battle. He was captain when it came time to chose leeward or windward approach or when it came to the decision to spare someone's life or not. But for the decisions concerning the actual business of the ship, everyone wanted to have their say. It was his chore to listen and make his case. The proof that he had their ears and their hearts was in the fact that they always agreed to do what he wanted. Now he wanted to go to Haiti to help the black people there in their fight for freedom. He wanted to go because he could see the beginning of the end of slavery there. There, in Santo Domingo, was a powerful force just coming together under the leadership of Jean Jacques Desalines. There were stories floating about that black sailors were making their way there, especially runaways, because a liberated Haiti would probably provide legal relief from slavery.

"So, they's worried are they?" Arrow asked finally.

"We are white men, Cap'n. What in the world we want to go there for? We're out for the loot. If we wanted to fight for the sake of fightin' we'd have stayed in Her Majesty's Royal Navy, prison though it is. No we come out for ourselves. For the gold and the chance to get some fortune in this paradise."

Arrow looked up at him. "Sit down, Bill." He watched the hulking man as he labored into the chair. "Now you know I'd cut off my arms for my men. You know that."

"I do, Cap'n. I know that. But . . ."

"And I ain't white, Bill."

"Aye, that's a fact."

"But I am the captain, unless something's happened I don't know about."

"No Cap'n, you still Captain."

"That's good Bill. That's real good. Because when we weigh anchor I'm bound for Haiti."

"But Cap'n, it's just gonna make . . ."

"Worried? Scared?"

"Not scared, Cap'n. Not scared. We ain't scared of nothin'. It's just . . . well . . . as you said, you as sure as God is black and they don't hold that against you because you served our former captain well and you've shown your true colors to us on many occasions. But that don't make us blind.

These islands is full of blacks. You the only one I ever met on the open water.

"You know yourself, Bill, that there are many black pilots."

"Port pilots, yes, but ship captains?" He sucked his teeth. "I been all over
the Caribbean and I ain't never seen no other black man but you at the helm
of a ship."

"Well, seein' as how I have this great distinction, Bill, as your captain I
order you to tell me what the devil this is all about."

"You see, Cap'n, up to now, the fact that you're a . . . ah . . . black wasn't
a concern. You did good by us and you're one of the best sailors I know.
Able. Very able. But now, you're askin' us to give comfort to those niggers in
Haiti and that don't sit well." He paused again, relieved to have said it. "It
don't sit well at all. Where's the profit in that?"

"When we took the *Drury*, loaded with slaves, and I say let them go or let
them join us . . ."

"We ain't slavers, Cap'n. We didn't want nothin' to do with that. That
was fine by us. Let 'em go. Some white man would kill or claim them, anyway. That's just the way the world is. That's not our business. We're"—again
he paused, searching for a word when he knew all the time what he had to
say—"we're pirates."

"Mind you." Arrow put an edge in voice.

"But we *are*, Cap'n. I know you don't like that word, but that's what we
are. We're pirates, not mercenaries. Besides our fellow brothers are starting
to laugh at us. There were two fights over at the Flyin' Fish before I left."

"Laughing? Why?"

"They say we're being led by a monkey. 'Captain Monkey' they called
you, and the one who said it paid dearly. But the laughter was still there."

"I see." Arrow sighed. "And the crew is affected by this talk?"

"Aye."

"Bill, that ship out there is mine. Those men are mine. You," he righted
his chair and now leaned into Dirty Bill's face, "You are mine." Their eyes
locked. In Bill's he saw, for the first time a fear. At first he wasn't sure what
the fear was, but as he stared into those eyes, Arrow could feel the meaning.
Dirty Bill was afraid that they were approaching a parting of the way. And
then the fear loosened and Dirty Bill smiled.

"I am Cap'n Arrow. I am yours for the time. And I don't want that to
change."

Arrow slowly brought his strong right arm up to Dirty Bill's neck, his
charcoal fingers encircling the thick throated man. "I can squeeze the life
right out of your empty head." Dirty Bill tried to say something, but Arrow,
swiftly brought his other hand up and put in it in front of Dirty Bill's
mouth. "You needn't utter one more word, Bill. Not one more or you won't

ever say momma. Or Jesus or anything. I have not killed and plundered this small world, nor served our fine Captain Threatcher 'til his untimely death with every breath I had to be bullied by you or any man. White or whatever. Now, I love you Bill, like a brother. And I will die for you. But I demand the same. Or I'll kill you right here. Right now. Do we see eye to eye?"

Dirty Bill, trying to keep from gasping, nodded his head. Arrow loosened his grip. "I weren't talkin mutiny Cap'n. I am yours . . ."

At that moment a crowd of men burst through the doors bringing, it seemed, a thundercloud of noise and tension with them. It was then that Arrow realized that many in the room had been watching him and Bill the entire time. They'd seen his black hands around Bill's white throat. But before he could fully consider the meaning in all this, Dockson stood before him with many of his crew and some sundry others crowding up behind.

"Cap'n, we ain't interested in goin to Haiti. That's not our fight."

Arrow leaned back again. He waited a moment and then asked very softly, "Am I your captain?"

Dockson was taken off guard. The talk at the Flyin' Fish had pumped him and he'd forgotten who Arrow really was. "Yes, you are my captain. But we . . ."

"Don't want to follow a nigger? Do you mean to say that you will not be led by a nigger? A black man?"

"No! Cap'n . . . I mean yes. . . . I ahhh . . . I . . . We have followed you this far. But . . ."

"This Captain Monkey has gotten too far ahead of himself, taking us into the grip of more monkeys who have forgotten their place? Is this what you mean to say?"

Dockson had broken out in a profuse sweat. He looked around. The red faces behind him flashed all manner of expressions. Some, obviously up for the fight. Some, in full retreat. Seeing this unhinged Dockson even more. He fell silent.

"Monkey talk." Someone in the back shouted. "It ain't right. No white man should take that from that animal." All eyes went in that direction. Standing at the bar were four from the notorious pirate Captain Flagg's crew. To the side of them, maybe ten more of their crew.

"This is private crew business," Dockson shouted to him.

"Aye. I'd believe you if I didn't see a monkey at the helm." Dockson moved in the man's direction. Arrow remained motionless. Dirty Bill stood. It was as if a bell had rung, immediately cutlasses were openly displayed.

"You owe me an apology, brother," Dockson said approaching the man.

"There will be none, my brother. You have lost my respect and someone must put these things aright." He advanced on Dockson. Their steel clashed. Everyone around them located their closest adversary and prepared their defense or offense as the case warranted.

In truth there were two Arrows. One was the Black Arrow, who in a moment or two would kill two men in an instant. The other was the man who was filled with dismay. His struggles were meaningless in a world where other men had to fight for his own right to be a man. And yet, that was precisely why he was bound for Haiti. To fight for other men to be free. At this moment he even loved Dockson. But he was also intensely sad. This was his fight. It was about him. Simply because he was.

Dockson and his opponent had only touched cutlass a few times before Arrow stood and, let fly three knives, felling two of the original four men, including the one who was about to take advantage of Dockson's slow reflexes. They stumbled once and hit the floor. The third knife lodged in another man's thigh. Everyone stopped and looked at Arrow.

"If I had known a name like Captain Monkey, would excite you so I might have taken such a name. Especially if it caused you to fear me. For fear me you should. But, alas, I was limited by my experience. I could only contrive this name, Arrow. So I am Captain Arrow, and if you are lucky and will live to tell of what you've seen and you may say to the lucky hearer of your tale that you once saw the Black Arrow stick this man or that. And that then you saw him sail off under the black flag that is his true color. Off into the horizon with his crew of men who will take no quarter and who will do to their advantage without regard to this primate's heritage."

And with that he walked slowly toward the door, his men forming a wall at his back. "To hell with this," he shouted, "To Haiti or to hell!"

Mirror Image

BY AMY DU BOIS BARNETT

Six stops. White people got on, then black, some Latinos, a sprinkling of Asians—in the six stops between Brooklyn and Manhattan, the racial composition of my subway train changed six times. Every morning for the past five years, I'd watched this underground metamorphosis, feeling something of a traitor when I got off the train with all the white people at the first stop in Manhattan—Wall Street.

Men with hair slicked stiff and wet-looking from too much gel, in dark suits and ties with tiny symbols of power printed hundreds of times on them, jostled against one another. Expensive silk scarves were knotted at the necks of the few suited women, most of whom looked very driven and very tired. I emerged from the station with them and entered the sweep of people pushed along the financial district's ancient narrow streets. A clear division of power was visible; the men, *Wall Street Journals* tucked under arms weighted by leather briefcases, strode down the sidewalks, cleaving paths through the gaggles of female secretaries wearing floral dresses, white panty-hose, and sneakers, gossiping and delaying the beginning of another dreary day. There were almost no black men to be seen, even fewer black women.

I was one of the suited women. I tied silk scarves at my neck, pulled my hair back into a neat bun to expose dainty gold hoops, wore nude pantyhose and business suits in neutral colors, skirts no more than two inches above my knee. Briefcase, trench coat, New York *Times*—I blended in.

My mother taught me how important this is—the art of blending in. I would watch her getting dressed in the morning in designer suits, silk blouses, gold brooches, pearl earrings. In this outfit she would cease to be my mother, instead becoming the Radcliffe B.A., President and CEO of Rose Advertising. It was only when she came home, kicked off the heels, changed into some pants, and put on some old jazz record that she became more accessible. From college on, Mom was always one of a few, the only, or the first black woman; she told me that it wasn't as if no one noticed her, but she'd simply figured out how to dress, speak, and carry herself as if there could be no doubt as to whether or not she actually belonged. I never questioned her—never thought about the consequences of blending in—because she made it seem as if I had no choice.

During my senior year of college, Mom tried her best to convince me to join her at Rose Advertising after I graduated. "It'll be the greatest opportunity in the world. It's your birthright," she insisted. After several months of fruitless visits to the career services office, I almost agreed. But the thought of returning to St. Louis made me keep trying, until I finally convinced a large commercial bank that four years of last minute papers and barely-studied-for exams qualified me to be a research coordinator in their corporate finance division. Eventually Mom agreed that I'd actually found a good job on my own and bought me five suits, ten shirts, three pairs of shoes, and a jewelry box full of appropriately conservative necklaces, earrings, and pins. I added a few of my own touches over the years but never strayed from the basics, and every morning I put on a well-cut, tastefully accessorized suit of armor. At night I came home, took down my hair, turned on the stereo and felt like me again. No one at the office ever saw my toenails painted black, my pierced navel, the circular tattoo in the small of my back depicting the sun in six stages of eclipse.

. . .

I arrived at work over half an hour late, soaked with sweat and flustered. After trotting through the streets to the bank, I paused for breath at the massive doors to my building before pushing them open to feel the initial sting of frigid air. The lobby was quiet—9:07am—everyone was already at their desks. I hurried to the Media and Communications department on the 38th floor, furtively walked to my cubicle, and turned on my computer so its dark screen wouldn't betray the fact that I'd just arrived. No such luck. Marie, the only other black senior analyst on the floor, emerged from the ladies room.

"Linda's been looking for you," she said, leaning against my desk. I could smell the strong perfume she had on and hoped it would wear off as the day progressed. Marie reached up, adjusted the scarf tied securely under her chin and ran a hand over her short, careful hair. As usual, not a strand was out of place.

"You know what she wanted?" I asked.

"No idea," Marie bent forward to examine what files I was opening on my hard drive. "I had to tell her that I hadn't seen you all morning."

"Thanks Marie." She must have loved that, I thought as she shrugged and sauntered off. I'd been promoted to senior analyst a few months before her and she'd decided that it was because I'd made sure to befriend the right people, which was only one of the reasons she didn't like me.

I walked down the long hallway, wondering what had convinced the decorator to use only shades of gray: ash-colored carpeting, pearl and taupe cubicles, steel accents. Under the long rows of fluorescent lights humming along the ceiling, the large space looked cold and stony as a mausoleum. On the right, the row of glass-enclosed offices was full, the vice presidents on their phones, bent over their desks or staring at their computers. I'd never caught any of them procrastinating—reading a magazine, staring out of the window. On the left, the secretaries all had coffee on their desks and were talking loudly to one another. As I passed they called out, "What's doing, Dana?" "Cheer up, hump day's the worst." "Hot as shit outside, eh?" "How's that fine man of yours?"

In her glass office, Linda was on the phone but she waved me in and ended her conversation. Her skin was even more sun-tanned than usual, probably from another evening at the tanning salon, and her hair was a brassier shade of blond. She seemed to spend a lot of time and money on her appearance—exercising every day, constantly changing her hairstyle, buying new clothing—but this only accentuated the coarseness of her features, her large pores, her thick, short limbs. She cocked her head and frowned as if reading my mind. I smiled brightly to dispel any doubt that I was thinking anything that wasn't work-related.

"I missed you this morning," she said, now smiling but with slightly raised eyebrows.

"Train trouble."

"Oh that's right. You come in from Brooklyn." To Linda Whitelaw, Brooklyn was too far from the Upper East Side to be considered a part of New York City even though I'd explained to her that my commute rarely took longer than 20 minutes. "Anyway," Linda went on, "I just wanted to check on the Southstar report."

"I'll have it to you before lunch," I said.

"Excellent, Dana. Very good, then." She dismissed me with a wave of her manicured hand.

Back at my desk I flipped the page on my desk calendar to August 28th and, as I had the past three days, made a small red X on the page to indicate the heat wave. Then I picked up a blue pen and wrote 44, then a green 289, and a black 1548. I was often asked what the color coding was but refused to tell. Not that it would have been particularly interesting to anyone other than myself, but it was private, to protect from strangers who would have thought me odd for choosing to make a careful and deliberate record of the weather, days until my birthday, days until my mother's birthday, and days since she died. Why would anyone understand why the calendar was such a minefield for me? The beginning of the year was horrible because the holidays in November and December, which I spent by myself or with somebody else's family, depressed me well into January. Valentine's Day was usually anti-climactic. Then I'd get a respite of a few months until Mother's Day in May. The summer would crawl by, my mother's birthday and the anniversary of her death having started it off in June. A few months until my birthday at the beginning of October, then the holidays would start all over again. I'd simply given in to this cycle and written in the painful events as official holidays.

I slowly turned the pages of the calendar to June 3rd. Four years ago on this date I went to my mother's funeral in St. Louis, and this was the last time I'd seen the house that I'd lived in from kindergarten through high school—first with my mother and father, then Mom alone, and finally Mom and Gerald. After the funeral I'd flown back to New York and tried to forget what I'd left behind. Now I had thirteen years of belongings to sort out and I couldn't put it off any longer. I bought a plane ticket to St. Louis for that weekend, then called Gerald and left a message on his answering machine. "Hi, it's Dana. Sorry about yesterday. I can't ever seem to be normal talking about Mom. I'm coming in Friday night but I'll just take a cab from the airport."

Just before lunch I gave Linda my credit report, which she handed back with only a few minor changes to my five year projections. The figures were a little too low and she complained that I was always too harsh with my future predictions. "Even for a bank there's no need to be quite this severe. Although I applaud your research," she told me.

Linda had a point; I was absolutely thorough and I cut no slack, even for longtime clients. I picked over annual reports looking for signs of deception. I studied *Moody's* and *Value Line* analyses for any perceivable weaknesses. I looked for potential causes of industry fluctuation, indicators that the company could lose competitive advantage, character flaws in the principal officers. I was relentless; this was the most enjoyable part of my job. I'm a Libra, the balancer, which, when you look at life away from the office, makes sense. But when I did a credit report, I felt my astrological sign was a fluke, an accident of my having been born two weeks late. I was meant to be a Virgo, the analyzer, and if not for my pre-natal stubbornness, my desire to stay put inside my mother's safe womb, I would have been.

It had taken me all afternoon to spread the balance sheet and income statement numbers again and I'd just given Linda the new projections when Will called me. "We still on?" he asked.

"Yup. I'm psyched to try this place."

"So you still want Vietnamese?" he asked.

I sighed, "I said I was psyched."

"You have been known to change your mind lately."

"What are you talking about?"

"Remember last Thursday? We left the first bar because the crowd was too conservative, the next because the people were too young, and the last because you saw that woman you hated from college."

"That was different. We're just talking about dinner, here. Besides, it was fun."

"That night was supposed to be just drinks. And Leo and Maya didn't seem to like schlepping all over the City."

"That's my word. You're copying again."

"As long as we don't get to the restaurant and have you decide you feel like pizza."

"Okay, fine. But Will, you always talk like me. Schlep sounds so weird coming out of your mouth." I could hear him light a cigarette, exhale with a faint whistle. "And you smoke every time we talk on the phone," I said.

"Now that bugs you too?" I could hear him blowing more smoke although I could tell he'd turned his head away from the phone to do it.

"So what time?" Will continued, ignoring my lack of response.

"Seven, out front."

"Cool."

I replaced the phone and reached a hand up to press my fingers against my rigid neck muscles, closed my eyes for a moment when the phone rang again. I figured it was Will since he'd often call me back immediately after I'd hung up the phone, saying, "Hey, Dana. Forgot to mention . . . ," and proceeded to tell me something that definitely could have waited.

I picked up.

"Dana. Sean. Guess what?"

It was exciting, still exciting, to hear his voice. "How could I, Sean. I never know what you're going to say these days," I said carefully.

"Oh come on. You underestimate yourself, as usual."

"Underestimate?" I asked incredulously.

"No matter. Anyway I had to call you with the big news."

"All right. What is it?"

"Okay, so Pace came by this morning. Pace, you recall, is the Director of Research."

"I recall."

"Okay, so Pace came by to give me my quarterly review. And then he offered me the plum spot of vice president."

"Which you readily accepted. Congratulations."

"Declined. Know why?" he asked.

"I'm sure this is going to be good," I said, but was not at all surprised when Sean proceeded to tell me he'd be joining a venture capital firm specializing in telecommunications companies. I used to wonder why research didn't bore him more since he was such a risk-taker.

"You're going to love playing with fire every day," I told him.

"That's one way of looking at venture capital. I prefer to think of it as bringing a young company to life. Helping it through its infancy."

"Infancy? God, you sound like a proud parent. Why didn't you think of this before?"

"Oh, but I did. I had it all planned."

"And I thought you hated to plan."

"That was before." He seemed unsure of what to say next.

"You mean before your recent maturation," I said before he could continue. "The whole, 'But Dana, I'm truly ready to be an adult, now' thing." There was a long pause during which I realized I should get off the phone before the conversation descended into the usual recriminatory bullshit. "Look, I should go. Linda's been on me lately."

"I know you must be getting a kick out of this, but I'm really quite serious, about everything," Sean said before I could hang up.

"Just tell me why I should believe you?" I asked.

"There's no good reason," he sighed. "You have no good reason to trust me. You've already expressed that."

I could hear the frustration in his voice, but I didn't care. "What did you expect?" I asked. "For me to drop everything and get back together with you just because you say you're ready to be an adult? Because you think you're ready to commit to me?"

"Just admit it. You still love me," he said. "You know we belong together."

I wished I could tell him, 'No. No, I don't,' and mean it enough so that he'd believe me and leave me alone. But I couldn't. Instead, I asked, "Whatever happened to Maureen?"

"I told you, already. That was just a temporary, meaningless thing."

"And you think I'm permanent?"

"Yes."

I gave a short laugh, more of a nervous snort, "I just wonder what would happen if I called your bluff."

"Then we'd go ring shopping this weekend."

I caught my breath, immediately hoping he didn't hear. When Sean and I were together I'd fantasized about him on bended knee, ring box in hand.

"I can't talk about this now," I whispered. "I've got a bunch of work to do before I meet Will for dinner."

"I won't keep you, then," he said quickly. "Have fun with Will."

"Hey, congratulations on the new job."

"Thanks," Sean said and hung up.

He'd sounded so annoyed I almost regretted letting him go on that note. His calls had been regular enough over the past few months that I'd come to expect them—maybe even depend on them—even though by the end of almost every conversation I'd been pissed off, more angry than I'd felt since we'd broken up. After the shock of Sean's betrayal had worn off, I'd found myself reluctantly missing him. I would have even taken him back if he'd groveled just a little bit; I wouldn't have wanted to, but I'd have been helpless in the face of whatever meager remorse he offered. When it became obvious that he wasn't going to come back on his knees, I'd been furious; nothing had ever made me feel so strongly, not even my mother's death. Then, after a long while, I'd felt nothing; that's when I'd thought I was over him, totally safe. Will and I had met just as my anger was fading into numbness and I'd credited him with that final transition. Now that Sean was affecting me so deeply again, I didn't know what to think.

As usual, Will and I met on the street in front of the bank. I loved to see him through the throng of wrinkled suits, sneakered women, and tired faces. Will was always dressed in black. It was his trademark, the monochromatic uniform of downtown chic. Once I'd bought him some bright shirts to wear under a black sweater or jacket—lime, indigo, orange—and he hated them, although he never told me. To be truthful, he was right. Any departure from black—except the occasional brown or charcoal gray—

made him look oddly childish; in those loud shirts he'd seemed vulnerable and needy, but in dark colors will looked vaguely gangsterish, someone to be taken seriously—an appearance I liked because it allowed me to pretend there was real toughness in his personality. The bright shirts gradually slunk and slouched to the back of his closet.

I'd met Will a year and a half before in a wine tasting class which he, the lunch chef at a well-known Midtown restaurant, was taking so he'd be able to contribute ideas to the wine list. I had enrolled in the class looking for a new adventure, something I hadn't yet tried, and against the crowd of white faces and white button-down shirts, Will seemed to be just what I'd come for. He was wearing jeans, heavy boots and a T-shirt—all black, of course, and in the class of thirty, we were the only black people. My mother taught me that if I was somewhere where there were only a few other black folks and you happen to run across one, always be friendly. So, I'd smiled at him—not too hard to do since he was really attractive. Seeing that he wasn't going to make the first move, I introduced myself.

Naturally, Will remembered everything we were taught in that class. I, meanwhile, could no longer recall the difference between Pouilly-Fumé and Pouilly-Fuissé, any of the wine-making regions of Germany, even the major red and white grape varieties.

During the first few months we hung out he bought me elaborate meals in places where his restaurant colleagues would have the waiters would bring us free appetizers and desserts; he knew romantic spots I'd never been to like the Cloisters and the roof garden at the Met; he lit my cigarettes before his own and tagged along to all my favorite clubs and bars, ordering martinis and looking elegant in his black turtleneck and slacks. And I fell in love, fast. Only later did I discover that he wore black not because of some rebellious desire to look dangerous, but because it was the easiest way to appear "cool," and that what I had mistaken for fearlessness and strength was actually steadfastness and competence.

Will never could reconcile the contradictions in his life: his Daddy's-a-doctor-Mommy's-a-lawyer strict upbringing with his spectator's fascination with downtown culture; his Ivy League education with his desire to work with his hands, to knead bread and massage spices onto chicken and de-bone salmon for a living; his black heritage with his mostly white neighborhood, schools, and profession. His hands shook slightly when he met new people and he followed me around when we were in a crowd; he was afraid to challenge himself and refused to pursue opening his own restaurant; he would try his best to avoid any kind of confrontation; and he hated to be alone, would do anything to avoid the emotional demands of silence. I knew I shouldn't judge him so harshly for having become diffident and quiet. It was just hard to comprehend why he seemed to shrink smaller and smaller the larger his world became, why his experiences didn't make him more insightful and diplomatic, confident in most situations instead of unsure.

One hand in his pocket, the other dangling a cigarette, shoulders sloping forward, Will waited—on time, as usual. I stood in the lobby and looked at him—his back facing me, his delicate features and smooth redbrown skin only visible when he glanced sidelong at the doors. I watched him flick the cigarette into the street, straighten the silver buckle on his belt, affect boredom. He projected confidence to the casual onlooker, and seeing this from a distance made him attractive to me. I walked out into Will's arms and breathed in his familiar smell of smoke and cinnamon gum.

The Vietnamese restaurant was nearly empty and the noise we made bursting through the door—laughing, the paper bag that held the wine crinkling, my heels clacking on the cheap linoleum floor—filled the spare room. We ordered a huge dinner of steamed rice crepes with chicken and shrimp, hot and sour seafood broth, green papaya salad with grilled beef, and red curried prawns in coconut milk; Will wanted to sample different dishes because he was looking for one more spice to enliven a coulis he meant to serve over striped bass.

"I checked out some restaurants on Atlantic Avenue because I thought I'd go North African. You know, use some harissa. But that whole thing's been played out," he said, dipping a spoon into the Banh Hoi sauce. "I was also thinking maybe thyme—so classic it's unexpected. Right? But then lemongrass or basil and lime could be interesting. Nice and light."

I watched him, saying nothing, having nothing to say. I'd never been that particular about food. I'd inherited my mother's long limbs, but not her curves; instead, I got my father's fast metabolism along with his terrible eating habits: scrambled eggs and bacon for breakfast and a hamburger and fries for dinner one day, no breakfast and cereal for dinner the next. Mom would try to get me to eat better, but I always fell back on my old habits. It wouldn't matter how much I ate, I always looked the same—limber from dance class, but way too gangling with no butt or breasts at all, earning me the nickname "firepole" from the none-too-sympathetic boys in my school. Since Mom died I cared even less about food, eating only when I had to, and then efficiently, with little passion.

"Good idea," I said.

"Or something totally different," He kept on, oblivious to my disinterest. "Blacken it or maybe pan-fried with garlic mashed potatoes?"

"I don't understand this whole comfort food trend." I took up my knife and fork, cut a piece of broccoli in half. "I mean, why go out for mashed potatoes?"

"People want to feel at home everywhere. Part of the whole cocooning thing."

"Well, that's exactly how I do not want to feel."

"Maybe if you ate more." Will gestured at my plate; he'd served me and the beef and prawn were piled dangerously high atop a mountain of rice. "You're so skinny."

"You never complained about my body before."

"And I never would. I just want to feed you."

"Because you're a chef."

"Maybe." He paused, wiped his hands then touched my knee under the table. "Spend this weekend at home with me?"

I'd forgotten to tell him about St. Louis, or maybe was avoiding talking about it. "My stepfather called yesterday at the crack of dawn to say he was selling the house and could I please come and get my things," I told him. "I'm leaving Friday."

"Why didn't you tell me before?"

"I meant to."

"You always say that, and you still don't tell me stuff."

"Whatever, Will." His mannerisms—the constant little shrugs, the way most of his statements ended in questions, the way he jiggled his right foot—suddenly began to get on my nerves. Irrationally, I knew, I was angry. I could always feel myself being impatient and unreasonable with Will, but usually couldn't stop the comments from slipping from my mouth like noxious wisps of smoke. "Look, I'm just a little pissed off that I have to deal with this right now."

"Okay, but don't take it out on me."

"Well, don't make everything about you."

Will shrugged again. "You're right," he said.

"I guess, I just can't believe it. I still have a key to that house."

"It has been four years since your Mom died," he said, ripping the tail off a prawn and taking a bite.

"And?" I asked drawing out the word and raising my eyebrow—a warning sign that he should have recognized.

"Why shouldn't he sell it?"

I rolled my eyes and leaned forward to whisper, "Is it so hard to understand that I don't want strangers to live in the house I grew up in?"

Will shrank back a little in his seat. "Nobody wants random people in their childhood bedrooms, but it's not like you ever go back, or have very much with you from St. Louis, for that matter," he said.

"That doesn't mean I never want to again."

"Maybe Gerald doesn't know that. Anyway, don't you think he has a right to move on?"

"A right to move on? Are you saying that he has a right to sell my mother's shit and move to Rio with the money?" I couldn't coax the hardness out of my voice.

"I only meant that Gerald might not be able to get on with his life living there. Why read everything you don't want to hear into what I say?"

"Because you sound just like Gerald."

"I'm on your side, Dana." Will waited for me to say something. "I'll go with you," he offered.

"What do you mean?"

"To St. Louis."

"No," I said quickly and regretted my tactlessness. Will ran a hand over the top of his short hair in the direction that he'd trained it to lie against his head—back to front. There was always a part at the top of his head separating the hair he brushed toward his neck from the hair he brushed forward. Thinking of that vulnerable line of pale scalp, of Will in the morning brushing his half inch of hair flatter and flatter, I couldn't be mad any longer; I was only irritated, and very tired.

"I'm going to be rushing around packing and there'd be nothing for you to do. I'll be fine." I reached for his hand. His skin was soft, his palm vaguely moist, and I curled my fingers through his. Will couldn't come with me. His very presence—solidity and calm fortified by his large stable family, happily married parents, a brother and two sisters and too many cousins, grandparents, and aunts and uncles to name—would be enough to remind me that I was in my childhood home with no blood relatives, packing my things to take away and never return.

"I'm sorry," I said after a minute. "You know how I get when I talk about this."

"No, actually. No, I don't." Will withdrew his hand and called for our check.

The heat settled heavy over the City. Still, I wanted to be outside for awhile. I left Will at a subway station and began to walk west through Chinatown. The twisted streets were filled with shops, open and crowded despite the late hour, and busy restaurants whose names promised "Golden Life" and "Prosperity" or, at the very least, "Lovely Food." I walked by stooped women carrying three and four orange plastic bags of groceries, teenage girls with shy faces and too much eye makeup, and groups of boys wearing black leather jackets and combat boots, until I emerged from Chinatown's convoluted center. The streets widened. Yellow lines on the sidewalk demarcated truck loading areas on both sides of the street as people, shops, and tenements buildings gave way to warehouses and long-closed industrial supply stores secured by locked metal gates. I was at the edge of TriBeCa, about to turn south toward the subway on Chambers Street, when I stopped at a street corner. I felt totally alone, not lonely so much as isolated, and decided that I wasn't quite ready to go back to Brooklyn.

I made a right instead of a left and ended up at the bar of a Mexican restaurant on Franklin Street with a pack of Camels and a margarita sitting in front of me. Some guy two stools down lit my first cigarette. He was no more than twenty years old and looked exhausted and underfed. His hands twitched as he held up the match and I could see his dark-ringed eyes blinking too fast, the pupils only pinpoints. I swung away from him to face the dining room. It's 11:00 on a Wednesday, I thought, I ought to be in bed, covers up over my head. At the same time I was glad not to be waiting in a hot subway station for a train that would take me back to my dark apartment.

The dining room was half full, the tables holding mostly empty plates and glasses, the diners lingering over one last drink; I wanted to go sit at one of the tables, to blend in with the crowd of people who obviously did not set their alarms for 6:30am every weekday morning. Then across the room a guy wearing a business suit held up a martini in a toast to his dinner companion who I couldn't see from my stool. A sturdy-looking man with wavy auburn hair, ruddy cheeks, a blunt nose, and broad shoulders. Sean. He'd never ordered a martini in the two years that he and I were together, but it looked like Sean. Though I hadn't seen him in over a year, my stomach clenched and I finished my margarita in one gulp. I reminded myself, almost murmuring aloud, that it was different now—he'd been calling me for the past few months, had even called me today. He wanted me.

I stood up and, pretending to look for the ladies room, wove around the tables toward the man. I drew close and saw the person he was with—a Japanese woman with blond highlights unevenly striating her dark hair like veins of fat in a porterhouse. She glanced up at me as I approached, wary at first, but I must have looked too nervous to be threatening and she let out a soft condescending laugh. Then the man looked over and I opened my mouth to say, "Sean, hi! What a coincidence," when I realized that it wasn't him. I registered the difference first in his mouth—it was too thin with mean little wrinkles at the corners; the man's skin wasn't healthy red but martini-flushed; his eyes were green instead of hazel; flesh gathered under his chin and filled out his midsection. I stopped, twisted my head to the left and right as if trying to find something, then turned toward the restrooms. Locked in a stall, heart pounding with adrenaline and embarrassment, I waited long minutes until I had the courage to pass through the dining room to the street and hail a taxi to Brooklyn.

FROM **What You Owe Me**

BY BEBE MOORE CAMPBELL

The Braddock Hotel was the rich old uncle of downtown Los Angeles. I'd never seen anything as grand in Inez, where the largest hotel was only three stories high and always needed a new coat of paint. Braddock was nearly fifty years old and took up half a city block; the entire front was beige marble, and the entrance was two huge glass doors. Inside there were fifteen floors and a gigantic ballroom. The lobby was grand, with two huge crystal chandeliers, exactly like the one that was in the ballroom. The walls were the color of cream and the carpet was a swirl of soft rose and green. Plush sofas, comfortable armchairs, and carved tables sitting on a soft rug—it was like a magazine picture. The guest rooms were spacious and furnished even more luxuriously than the lobby. Mostly businessmen came to Braddock, and the place got its share of conventions, too.

It was not far from the Hollywood Freeway. I was used to one-lane highways and dirt roads, but LA had the Hollywood and the Pasadena freeways, and more were being built every day, connecting different parts of the city and even the suburbs, which I'd only heard about. From the upper floors in Braddock I could look out the windows and watch cars that seemed to fly along the asphalt ribbon that was divided into three lanes. I'd never seen so many automobiles in my life, and the sight of them, the thrumming sound they made, excited me and made me imagine going places far away from brooms and mops.

By the time she'd been working at Braddock for a year, we all were used to Gilda's quiet ways. Mr. Weinstock put Gilda and me on the same shift. Some days we worked from five o'clock in the morning until two or three in the afternoon. Early morning was the time we washed the linens and towels and folded everything. We mopped the grand hotel lobby, polished all the marble and glass. Sometimes when I was giving her the ammonia our hands would touch. She had soft hands, and I wondered how long they would stay nice.

Thanksgiving rolled around again. The maids weren't looking forward to the holidays, at least not *working* them. There were always lots of parties and formal affairs at Braddock during this time. People would get plenty liquored up, and drunk people are not the most fastidious. This was the time of year we had to wipe up vomit and urine that didn't make it to the toilet bowl. And then, too, even though Los Angeles didn't have a real winter like the ones in Texas that could turn your skin the kind of gray colored folks call ashy, people still caught colds. A lot of the maids would stay out sick, and then Mr. Weinstock would put us on double shift. By Christmas we'd be too worn out to enjoy our own festivities. But what else was new?

The first weekend in December, Gilda and I both got put on midday and late shift, which meant we had to come in at one and we didn't go home until after midnight. You wouldn't think that there would be that much to do late at night but that's when Mr. Weinstock wanted us to wash windows, clean the mezzanine bathrooms, and change the big Chinese vases of flowers that were always in the lobby. It took two people to carry those vases. And he liked to have some maids on hand when there were big parties in the hotel. People would stay in bed all day and then go out at night, and when they came back they expected clean rooms.

That Saturday night around ten o'clock, Mr. Weinstock told us to go up to the sixth floor. Guests had just left, and two rooms needed to be made up. When we got there, the floor seemed deserted, except for Brewster, who did repairs. He was carrying his toolbox, standing in front of the service elevator when we got off. He smiled politely when he saw us, especially at Gilda. "How are you girls doing tonight?"

"Fine," we both said.

We chatted with him for a few minutes before we made our way down the hall.

I worked on one room and Gilda cleaned the other. They were only about three doors apart. Maybe because I trained Gilda, she and I had similar timing, and we'd end up at the carts together. That's where we were when the man came in holding the boy by the hand.

We both smelled evil at the same moment. The first thing that hit me was that the man was white and the boy, who must have been about seven or eight, was Mexican. He was a scrawny little kid, not dressed for the chilly weather. He was wearing shorts and an undershirt, and he had on sandals. His little legs and arms were dirty. The man was drunk, and the boy looked scared, the kind of scared that means he has to go along with the show because of the money that's waiting when the curtain comes down. I'd seen that fear before at Braddock, in the eyes of young hookers with old johns who stumbled down the hall beside them. I'd never seen that expression on a child's face, and to tell you the truth, I didn't want to look.

They went into the room between the ones we'd just made up. When the door closed, my eyes met Gilda's. She whispered, "He is a bad man." When she said the words her body started shaking, and she had to wipe away the moisture that started popping out on her forehead.

I knew he was a bad man but he was a bad *white* man, and he was a guest. I thought about calling Mr. Weinstock, but Ole Sweat and Farts wouldn't do anything to help a Mexican street kid if it meant offending a paying customer. I considered contacting the police, but then I'd have to give my name, take them to the room, and by that time the damage would be done. And if Mr. Weinstock found out, I could forget about my job, and my candy store.

Gilda walked right to the room. We could hear the boy crying, soft, pitiful sounds. I knocked on the door and said, "Is everything all right in there?" I tried to sound stern, like a teacher, which is what I would have been if my daddy had had money for college.

Before he could answer, Gilda had pulled out her key and opened the door. "Girrrrrl," I said, and put my hand on her shoulder to hold her back. But she shook it off and walked in, and I followed her.

The room smelled like sour milk. The little boy was naked, lying on the bed facedown. The man was on top of him with his pants and shorts around his ankles. He jumped up. His penis was hard and red. His cheeks looked slapped. "What the hell are you doing in here?" he said. "Get out, the both of you."

"You stop hurting that boy," Gilda said.

"Get the hell outta here." He turned back to the child.

Gilda pulled something shiny out of her sweater pocket. When I saw it was a knife, I opened my mouth and couldn't close it, but not a sound came out. The next thing I knew she was stabbing the man in his ass.

He jumped up and grabbed himself, wiping off the blood and staring at Gilda as though he couldn't believe what he was seeing. Truth be told, I was looking at her the same way.

"Get out! Get out! Get out!" She was screaming, waving the knife. He started coming toward Gilda. I grabbed the table lamp and held it like I was going to bash his head in. He stopped when he saw me do that, then he started backing up toward the door, pulling up his pants. Crazy Gilda kept coming toward him, waving the knife so close to him that I was afraid he was going to take it away from her and I would have to hit him upside his head. But he kept backing up. She got right up on him and then her voice went down real low. She said, "You go tell. See what happens to you tonight. I have the key."

"Fucking bitch," he said, and with his next breath he turned to me. "Nigger." Then he fled out the door.

After he left, Gilda went over to the little boy. He was still crying and whimpering something in Spanish. We took him in the bathroom, gave him a bath and washed his hair. Gilda dried him off and took a small bottle from her sweater pocket, poured something white and creamy in her palms, and started rubbing him all over with it. Then we helped him get dressed. He didn't say anything, but he wasn't crying anymore.

We took him down the back stairwell that led to the street. Outside the air was biting. Gilda took off her sweater and put it on the child, and we each gave him a dollar. Then we watched as he walked back to wherever he came from.

"Damn, girl," I said when we were riding up on the service elevator. I kept looking at her, trying to see what I couldn't see.

We were back in Our Room when I noticed the numbers on Gilda's arm, little blue tattooed numbers, a brand. Then I figured things out, but not all of it. Even on this side of the fence, there are some things I'll never understand.

We were sitting on the broken-down sofa. There was some church music playing in the background. Gilda started talking. Gilda loved gospel music and all kinds of hymns. The first time I played the Five Blind Boys for her, she started crying. On this night, The Mighty Clouds of Joy were singing a real slow song. I can't remember the name of it but the lyrics seemed to meld into her story. She told me how the Germans rounded up her family and put them in the death camps and how everybody she loved—her mother, father, brother, aunts, uncles, grandparents—had been killed. Her father's brother had settled in America before the war. When she was liberated she came to Los Angeles, because he and his wife lived here with their children. Four people were her only remaining relatives. It was her uncle who got her the job. Mr. Weinstock's brother owned the apartment building where they lived.

Her crying started as a tiny, weak noise, like a newborn might make. Came from way down inside her somewhere and then kept rising and getting deeper. I pulled her into my chest and held her, rubbed her back a little, told her not to be afraid, that everything was all right now. I spoke the words as soon as they came to my mind. "You need to take those numbers off your arm."

She sat up, looked at me, then cried a little bit more. She said, "I have no one, no one, no one," the words an echo that kept turning on itself.

"You do have someone," I said. "You have *you*. And you have what's *in* you. That's how you survived, girl."

Gilda didn't say anything for a long time. Then she looked at me and said, "Will you take me to get it done?"

I took her to the dentist first. The way I figured, the sooner she started smiling, the better for her. I asked her if she knew of any dentists in her neighborhood but she looked troubled and told me that we couldn't go there. So, one day after work, I took her to a colored dentist over on Central Avenue. He seemed surprised to see the two of us together, but that was just in his eyes. He didn't say anything. She had to go back a couple of times but he cleaned her teeth, got all the brown off, and when she smiled that first time, she looked pretty, not like Lana Turner or Liz Taylor, or any of the movie stars or models. She had her own special kind of frizzy-haired beauty, which wasn't even American, at least not yet.

We went to a tattoo parlor not too far from the dentist and the owner examined the numbers under a magnifying glass, and then patted her arm the same kind of way my daddy used to when I fell down or was crying. He told her that whatever he could do for her would leave a scar. Gilda hesitated, then she said, "Go ahead." I guess she figured that the numbers were the worst scar. He used needles and some kind of acid. Gilda was moaning a little bit the entire time he was working on her. She grabbed my hand while he was doing it, and she liked to squeezed me to death.

Riding the bus on our way back from the tattoo place, I told her about Inez. Gilda said it was another kind of death camp, that the poison gas came out in spurts, not enough to kill the body, just the soul. She had a lot of questions for me. She wanted to know why colored people couldn't go certain places, why our hair wasn't as long as white people's, why our voices sounded different from theirs. I didn't have all the answers but I did my best.

"They are envious of you," she told me.

"Who?"

"The white people."

"Why?"

"Because you have the most beautiful skin. White people sit in the sun to try to get your color. Your features, your lips and nose, are warm. You make wonderful music. And your spirit is powerful. They try to crush your spirit, but they can't."

We never heard from the man Gilda stabbed, and she and I never mentioned him. I found myself looking whenever I saw a group of Mexicans, but I didn't see the little boy again either. Gilda and I seemed to be together a lot more after what happened. When we had lunch at the same time, we ate side by side. Sometimes at the end of our break, she'd pull out a book and start reading. She still studied from the English manual, but she read other things as well. Her books were about history and science, and she liked novels, too. Often she'd read a portion to me and get me so interested in the story that when she finished, I'd pick it up. A couple of times, Fern would ask me what I was reading, and I'd share it with her.

Gilda told me that she had been attending college when the war broke out. "I studied literature," she said, and there was sadness in her voice.

I hadn't ever had enough time to read just for the pure pleasure of it, but that's one hobby I acquired from Gilda. As I read, I became aware of mistakes that I was making when I spoke, and I began to improve, little by little. In a way, I started sounding like Thomasine, who Tuney had broken up with, thank God.

The other maids noticed the new way I was speaking. One time when I finished saying something, Winnie said, "La-di-da," and looked toward Hattie, who was muttering under her breath that I was trying to be white. She knew better than to say it to my face. But those "la-di-das" put an alley between the other women and me. Gilda and I were walking down the main boulevard together.

Will Not Be Televised

BY JEWELLE GOMEZ

I slammed through the elegantly carved wood door of the hotel's Mayflower Bar like government forces were on my trail and flung myself onto a bar stool at the far corner of an extravagant expanse of mahogany. I knew this shit would happen. CL Leonard still has radar, after all these years. Why is it that the last man in the world you want to see is always the first one in your path? I pretended not to be hiding from an ex-boyfriend as I turned away from two twenty-something white guys in expensive lawyer suits who were trying not to notice my dramatic entrance. How could I still be so annoyed with a man I haven't said more than ten words to in thirty years?

See! I knew I didn't need to come to some damn reunion. Who wants yesterday sitting up in your face? With my luck Sheila would be next. And the only thing worse than an "ex" you can't stand is your slightly testy, former roommate carrying a thirty-year grudge about a burning stick of patchouli incense accidentally falling on her favorite Marvin Gaye album or some other ancient madness.

I knew that couldn't be the only reason Sheila and I lost contact after graduation, but I was hanging onto to it like a life raft. Inseparable for four years, we practically invented student unrest together on our mostly white Boston campus. Churning out the black weekly paper, *Off the Pig*, and turning the ever popular sit-in into an art form were a major part of our curriculum. Those old days may not all have been good but they changed how we saw the world and how the world saw us. Everything I feel about activism today started right there in our dorm room where we waded through the most effective methods for reporting Nelson Mandela's imprisonment and figured out whether to invite The Last Poets or Tina Turner to campus first.

I volunteer at the Bethany AIDS hospice and attend community board meetings today just because I can remember the tears and the rage in Sheila's eyes when we read about the Black students shot at Jackson State. All those late night political conversations made us promise each other to always follow our motto: "Don't just mourn—do something."

There had to be a monumental reason Sheila was angry with me. Was it something I said about Baldy after they got married? Did I not send them birthday cards regularly after graduation? Had I gotten so involved in my marriage that I put our friendship too far at the back of the stove? Half the cells that store my memory are on an accelerating path to oblivion so how am I supposed to know? And I've always been too chicken to contact her and find out.

Call me the sensitive child of divorced parents, call me a menopausal wuss but deliberately putting myself in the down draft of one of Sheila's notorious icy breezes was not my idea of a good time. I only needed to be given the cold shoulder once—which I was when I bumped into her the afternoon I was photographing a conference in Washington fifteen years ago.

I peered back at the door to be sure CL hadn't followed, then ordered a glass of Merlot to forget the chill. I took the first sip to wash the thought of him and Sheila out of my mind. It went down so smoothly I closed my eyes, cut their images loose and let them drift away. I didn't even wave good-bye.

I glanced behind the bar at my face reflected in the highly polished mirror, which was the size of a small town skating rink. The burnt orange silk and linen jacket I'd finally settled on was just right for my oak-brown skin and dark eyes. I'd recently cut my dreadlocks to shoulder length and was pleased with the effect. The roundness of my face, no longer a surprise to me, was actually appealing. As my favorite aunt Henrietta says: a few extra pounds never hurt anyone. So what was it about CL's attentions, be it 1971 or 2001, that set me off? Maybe it was as simple as I wasn't interested and he always chose to ignore my signals. I was going to have to brush up on my rejection skills in order to get through this weekend.

Insistent beads of perspiration decorated my forehead and I blotted them with the skimpy little napkin they always set out with drinks as if you were going to leave a water ring on their grandmother's table. I wasn't sure if my rising heat was the effect of the wine, of running into CL, or one of those predictable hormonal flushes, but I took another sip and leaned back. I closed my eyes again to really push the image of CL away. What replaced it were pictures just as old as my relationship with him.

The moment that sealed the sisterhood between Sheila and me unfurled in my mind and I could almost feel the breeze on my face. A tingle of panic had crawled across my skin as my brain registered that the view from the fourth floor of the administration building might as well have been from the forti-eth. Clutching the window frame, I gulped for air as the Temptations song, "I Can't Get Next to You," played in my head. I stretched dangerously out the window. Still the banner remained out of my reach. I looked to see if campus security had shown up yet. No sign of the cops, but Tank was below, waving down the "Say Brother" news van that was pulling into the quadrangle. At least that part of Sheila's plan was going right. "Don't look down!" Sheila called from the fifth-floor window where she held the top end of the red, black and green banner. Her voice caught me and the dizziness cleared. Swinging my gaze back up toward the symbol of Black Power flapping in the breeze, I did my version of a prayer.

"Shit!"

If I screwed this up just because I'd skipped all those physical education classes I wouldn't have to worry about being expelled for staging a building takeover. I'd die of embarrassment first. I dropped my olive-drab jacket be-hind me onto the floor of the office and dug my toes practically through my Frye boots into my perch—the top of the air conditioning unit just inside the window—as I stretched out again. "Shit" became my mantra as I pushed my fingers higher, climbing the gray brick wall like Spiderman.

How could this part foul up? Our group had negotiated the support of other progressive student caucuses. We'd gotten ourselves into the adminis-tration building with enough food for a week and managed to chain all the exits and get word to the press. Our allies, consisting of Edie, the Jewish girl who lived across the hall from me and Sheila in the dorm, and her boyfriend in from Brandeis for the weekend, were distracting campus police over by the parking lot. Tank was getting our leaflets into the hands of anybody who passed. Now, if I could just get the damn banner!

I still didn't hear any sirens. Good sign. I exhaled, shoved myself against the window frame like it was the last man I'd ever have, and reached out one more time. The red, black and green banner waved just beyond my finger-tips. I looked up at Sheila terrified I'd mess up and our occupation of the ad-min building would go down the tubes. Her eyes were glistening with fear and excitement. Her look told me I could do it.

Pretend it's George Wallace's neck, I thought. Grab it! Damn, if only I had those fake nails like Blanche, I'd have . . . Got it!

"Right on!!!" I exclaimed.

Then I realized someone was standing beside me at the bar; I was almost too embarrassed to open my eyes. I peeked through one, prepared to put my boxing gloves back on if it was CL, I was relieved to see Tank grinning down at me.

"Sisters should never drink alone especially when it makes 'em talk to themselves!"

I slid off the stool, my embarrassment and surprised squelched by my genuine joy at seeing him. A lot of folks, back in the day, used to think Tank was an agent but I'd never believed it. He threw his arms open and we stood in the big loud embrace of people who've known each other's youth.

"Roxie Page! Hey, hey, hey," he kept saying through his laughter like a suave Fat Albert. In fact he kind of looked like Bill Cosby, if the Coz had been a defensive tackle.

"God, you look great," I said, meaning it.

"Look who's talking."

"I knew I'd be seeing you all but it's still a shock."

"Hey, sister we survived, what more to say."

He still had a broad, appealing smile. A little thicker than he'd been when we graduated in '71, his dark skin was heightened by silver that gleamed sexily at the temples of his close cut hair. With every ball player in the big time favoring the menacing Mr. Clean look today, Tank's tightly napped hair was a welcome sight. His tailored jacket and sharply creased slacks, neither of which were wrinkled, told me he certainly hadn't just gotten off a plane.

"So when'd you get in?" I asked.

"This morning. I wanted to walk around a little. I saw Jerome, 'course he got in yesterday, and what's her name . . . Sarah . . . used to play cards all night? She's helping him organize this shindig."

"Did I just hear you say 'shindig' " I laughed.

"Wait 'til I catch you in one, my sister!"

"Black is power," I said and raised my glass.

"Black is power," Tank answered repeating the name of our old student group.

We both laughed and shook our heads thinking about Jerome. It was a wonder we'd all gotten as far is the hotel with him pulling the reunion together.

Whenever he'd attempted to organize anything for the BIPs it was fraught with complications. His last screw up negotiating with the administration was why I ended up dangling from the fourth floor ledge of McMillan Hall before we occupied the building for three days. I wondered what we would wind up doing this time.

I listened as Tank talked about his job with a radio station in Atlanta and his divorce. He showed me pictures of his not so young kids and talked like a man who knew more about them than just their names and where they worked.

I did a quick reality check to make sure I wasn't feeling regret that I'd decided not to have children. With all the traveling Dennis and I did when we got together it just wasn't a good idea. We'd built an amazing photographic archive, keeping track of faces and issues that were quickly fading from the news. For me, little could compete with the triumph of a subtle shot of the young Amiri Baraka holding a group of students mesmerized with his poems or capturing Nikki Giovanni's fire in my flash.

Besides I firmly believe in Zero Population Growth, so it didn't seem like a total sacrifice. I did a photo shoot for an article on Black adoptions about seven years back and the idea had begun to appeal to me, then Dennis got sick. But the notion kept swirling around inside, popping to the surface every once and a while, especially in situations like this.

I oohed and aahed dutifully at each of Tank's snapshots but kept thinking how odd it was that I was talking to the guy people thought was an FBI agent. I really liked Tank, he was like his nickname—solid. He'd played football, how could he have been an agent? I wondered shaking my head.

"I know, hard to believe, isn't it. Man, sometimes I thought I'd get my head—or my nuts—knocked off on that field and never have any kids."

"Why were you playing?"

"For the cash, of course. You guys got the brain money, I got the brawn money. I had to work a couple of years after high school to save up, my coach kept pushing me even then. He's the one who wangled me the scholarship."

My picture of Tank began to shift. I didn't know why I hadn't known any of this already.

"Once I got in I was going to get that piece of paper if it took forever. Which it almost did. But, god, do I hate football!"

"You're kidding!"

"Nope. I did some coaching in the pee wee league when my boy was young, that's as close to a field as they could ever get me. Now, I catch some basketball on TV, the girls' teams are great. But football? That got me through here and that's it."

I looked at Tank's mammoth shoulders, firm against the elegance of his suit, and started laughing, "Yeah, I can see all that muscle's gone to fat."

"A gym is a beautiful thing, ain't it?"

"I really expected you to go on to a professional team or something," I said, still finding this new picture of Tank hard to get into focus.

"Never happen!" Tanks laugh boomed again. "You know why I couldn't do that whole occupation thing with you guys? You know, get locked up in admin and all? I was afraid I'd get kicked off the team—lose my scholarship," he said his voice still colored with regret after all those years.

I was surprised. Of the many reasons we used to toss around about Tank not joining us in the building I couldn't believe not one of us thought it could be about money.

"I felt really bad, like I was letting you all down. But damn if it wasn't the best thing I ever did," he said. When I looked puzzled he went on.

"Hanging out with the news crews in the quad was how I figured out I wanted to maybe pursue broadcasting. You know, I was digging on how they did everything and then seeing it on TV that night. They were so scared you were going to blow up the building, and kind of hoping you would at the same time. It was weird," Tank said shaking his head.

"But I dug being the liaison between you all, and seeing how they figured out what to say about us. I was hooked by the second day."

Tank looked almost shy at that moment and it reminded me of how young we'd been at the time. Even if he was a year or two older than most of us he would have still been a kid.

"We didn't feel like you were letting us down, Tank. In fact you were probably the only thing I could see from the window when I was hanging on for my life trying to grab that damn banner!"

"Sister, lemme tell you. I thought I was gonna have to retrieve your butt when you came tumbling down!"

"Yeah right. You were just waiting to see if Sheila would drop out the sky into your arms!" I said laughing and squeezing Tank's biceps. Sheila had been the campus' Black beauty queen, at least half the brothers had been waiting for her to fall into their arms.

"Now that would have been a hell of a save." Tank grinned as he savored the thought of Sheila, the girl every guy dreamed about.

"Hey, she coming?"

I shrugged, honestly having no idea. "Have you heard anything from her?" I asked trying not to let my unsettled feelings seep through.

"I can't believe y'all haven't talked! What's up with that?" Tank was genuinely puzzled. He peered at me unable to conceal his confusion.

"Uh, nothing. You know how time slips through your fingers."

"Umph," Tank muttered unconvinced. "I saw her picture in *Ebony* when she made partner in that law firm, out there in San Francisco, I think."

"Yeah, I saw that. Great, huh?"

I sipped my wine. Tank shredded the damp napkin.

"You know," he started, "I heard—"

He was interrupted by a generalized squeal of delight at the entrance to the lounge. Then Tank's barrel-chested: "Hey, hey, hey" put an end to whatever news he was about to pass on. I turned knowing it had to be Blanche.

Nobody ever squealed in quite the same way. Omigod, she's doing the matron thing!

Her sandy brown Afro was now confined to a tight upsweep, her mascara and blush were Essence Magazine perfect. The regulation fatigue pants and Malcolm X T-shirt were replaced by the unmistakably fluid elegance of a Tamotsu suit that had to cost $700 if it cost a dime. No longer size 12—more like an 18—but she was still a squiggler. Something about the way she walked and talked gave the impression that all her parts were moving at once. And guys still loved it.

She was lost in Tank's massive arms and somehow managed not to wrinkle her suit, smudge her makeup or stop moving. When she turned to me her engine lowered to idle but she was still a wonder of biodynamics.

"Girrrrl . . ." Blanche said in her high pitched voice, dragging out the word as if she were just up from Charleston and was still charming the dorm floor. "Look at youuuu!"

I found myself enveloped in her scented embrace; no longer Arabian musk, it was more like something from the ground floor at Macy's. In that moment I flashed on how much she used to irritate me. It usually took about twenty minutes of her girlish, high-pitched enthusiasm before I wanted to tie her to a chair and stick a cork in her mouth. I tried to do some multiplication in my head: I hadn't seen her since graduation, let's see—thirty years times twenty minutes—how long before I would have to restrain myself?

"Come on, let's get comfortable," Tank said, taking Blanche's arm and dragging us both away from the bar to a grouping of banquettes and cocktail tables. I smiled, remembering when Tank's barely concealed desire to drag Blanche off used to be a running joke. She'd usually been too busy with one out of town Don Juan or another to be bothered.

"Any other Angelas coming?" he asked.

"Hell, don't start on that." Blanche said

The look of alarm on her face was not far from her expression in the cafeteria when she'd told us about being detained by the police because someone thought she looked like Angela Davis. Other than her Afro and lighter brown skin she didn't remotely resemble Angela, whose picture was plastered all over post offices and newspapers, but the differences hadn't registered with white cops eager to see themselves on the evening news after catching America's most wanted Black radical. The same thing happened that year to Ernestine and Aisha, who didn't look much like each other or Angela either.

"That mess almost lost me my first big job."

"Oh come on," I said.

"No really!" When I finally got an interview at Della Robbia, I'd been struggling to get into advertising forever. Then I had to fill out this form and when I got to where it asked if I'd ever been arrested I froze. I mean really, like paralytic."

Tank and I erupted into laughter.

"Who the hell was going to think being mistaken for an FBI fugitive was amusing?"

"So what'd you do?" I asked trying to keep sarcasm out of my voice. I couldn't imagine Ernestine or Aisha in such a quandary.

"What any good revolutionary does when pinned down by the man—I lied."

Tank's laugh again filled the room. It was obvious he was still susceptible to her charms.

"Technically it wasn't an arrest," I said dryly. I don't know why, but I felt like we were being disloyal to Angela. "You didn't even stay overnight."

"Sitting in a job interview in a corner office on Madison Avenue, literally on Madison Avenue . . . in New York City . . . didn't seem like the time to discuss subtle legal philosophy, my sister."

I had to smile even though her condescending tone usually got on my last nerve.

"Hey, I'm going to order some grumbles," Tank interrupted, still running interference between folks when it looked like some kind of disagreement was on the horizon. "Any requests?"

"Grumbles? Tank I haven't heard that word since—"

"Now don't you start, too. You want food or not."

"Yeah," Blanche and I answered together like we were cheerleaders, which we'd never been. He went off to the bar to put in a request for a selection of appetizers.

"You still in advertising?" I asked.

"Yeah, it's a living," Blanche said with the lowest level of enthusiasm I'd ever heard in her voice. "My ex-husband has a small firm and I manage his office."

"Ex?"

"Believe me it was cheaper to stay working there than try to get anything out of him!"

I was surprised to hear the edge of disappointment in Blanche's voice.

"Business is going great," Blanche said re-igniting her spark, as if she needed to refute my thoughts. "We keep a steady flow of work going. I can't complain."

From the cut of her suit it looked like she really was doing fine despite the unusual arrangement, but clearly there was something missing.

"You still doing photography?"

"Oh yeah."

"You know, I have seen your pictures." Blanche rolled her eyes upward and seemed to search her perfectly colored coif for a memory: "Once, in the *Times*, I think. I couldn't believe it!"

Why the hell not! I was just about to spit out when Tank came back with another BIP in tow.

"Edwin!" Blanche squealed and leaped up from her seat as if she were relieved we weren't going to talk about our professions any more. He'd always been the quietest Black man I ever met, and when he said hello it sounded like he hadn't changed much. You still had to lean in to hear what he said; but now the manner had a subtle authority. The fullness in his face was new and the oversized leather FUBU jacket almost concealed his extra pounds.

"Brother man, it's like old times," Tank said.

"I hope not," Edwin shot back as he clasped Tank's hand in the multiple grips of the Black Power handshake that went on for four minutes.

I hadn't seen Edwin in years, but we had spoken on the phone a while back when I gave him permission to use some of our photos for a PBS documentary he was directing. Even though he'd filled out, Edwin's tightly coiled energy gave the impression he was wiry.

"The last time I saw you two together Tank was beating your ass in a game of bid whist and you were chugging on a bottle of Creme White Concord!" I said.

"Still cracking wise Miss Roxie." Edwin's grin widened further as he hugged me. The waiter arrived with a couple of bottles of New York State champagne and glasses.

"At least we don't drink screw top wine anymore," Edwin dropped into a chair as we widened the circle.

"Righton!" Blanche said, deliberately enunciating like a Black Vanna White. I could see the young, white waiter working hard not to smile as he was popping the cork.

"I loved the last piece you produced for . . . was it "Lehrer News Hour"?" Tank said.

"Oh yeah, Edwin, that really was good," I said, remembering I'd seen it too.

"It was deep," Tank said solemnly.

"What, what?" Blanche asked, wriggling in her seat.

There's something that happens around people's eyes when they don't want you to see inside. Edwin masked his discomfort almost completely. "It was a documentary about people who're mixed race."

"Mixed . . . ?" Blanche didn't squeal. Her voice, perplexed, dropped down to her ample chest. There are always some details that get lost in memory.

"You know, like Tiger Woods," I said, trying not to sound like I was talking to an adolescent.

"Like me," Edwin added.

I could see Blanche reassessing Edwin's medium brown skin tones and lightly waved hair, searching to remember if she knew this information already. He'd always been a gung ho nationalist, yet avoided the harshest "hate whitey" rhetoric. He was one of only a few BIPs who'd been on the losing side with me when the controversy broke about changing the name of our newspaper from *Off the Pig* to *Black Times*.

"Basically I got a chance to look at the larger idea of what it means to be Black in the U.S. and not rely on some constructed mythology of race or cultural purity that we all know is . . . well just myth."

"Go, brother, I hear you." Tank's enthusiasm seemed sincere. Did that weigh in on the side of agent or not?

"That may be the last you hear of me," Edwin said shaking his head wearily. "The way money is drying up now, if your name ain't Burns, don't even think about getting funds for a documentary these days."

"Well . . ." Tank intoned as if he were in the amen corner.

"His stuff is good." Edwin jumped back in, not wanting to sound like he was bad-mouthing another filmmaker. "But I can name you three other black guys who've been trying for the past twenty years to rustle up money for films on blacks in baseball and in jazz."

There was silence while we each sipped champagne and wondered how depressed we'd make ourselves before the reunion really got going.

"Speaking of white devils," Blanche said after a moment, tickled with herself. "You know who's coming tomorrow, don't you?"

It didn't take much thought for us to say simultaneously: "Jackson Wright." He overused that epithet so much by the time we graduated, he'd worked everybody's nerves, including the one brother who was aspiring to be FOI for *The* Nation.

Blanche led the laughter this time. If I wasn't mistaken, it looked like Blanche's sparkle was spreading itself in Tank's direction very specifically.

"Man!" Edwin said in disgust. "That guy . . ." His voice trailed off and each of us remembered Jackson Wright's way of dealing with people who disagreed with him: nail them to the wall for not being "Black enough." Unfortunately, since he's an award-winning poet and our most famous alum to date, Jackson was booked to be the featured speaker at the Saturday-night program.

No matter what the poem, he eventually had to break into an egotistical rant that skewered some Black person he judged to be betraying Blackness, or a white person who was betraying him. His tongue was so sharp it should have been registered as a weapon. Wright is brilliant, I'll give him that, but . . .

"They need to put some of those contestants from one of those survivor TV shows in a room with Wright and see who lasts to win the million!" Edwin said, breaking into my thoughts. "Did you check him out on that BET talk show awhile back?"

We all shook our heads together slowly, as if we were synchronized swimmers.

"You really missed a scene. He went on and on about white feminists ruining his career. I think that was when he was filing a class-action suit against the National Organization of Women."

"Oh stop!" I exploded.

"The host was egging him on like Wright was the second coming, I kid you not."

"Talk about ecology . . . what a waste of air!" Blanche sucked her teeth.

"He should have been spending the time pushing for some more money from the networks or public TV for Black producers or something. But not this guy." The anger was ripe in Edwin's words.

"That was during the 'Me' decade, wasn't it?" I asked rhetorically, knowing that whenever Jackson Wright turned up it was the "Me" decade. Seeing all the optimism that had fueled us reduced to careerism, midlife crises, and BMWs made me a little nauseous. But unless there's a national emergency, I was resigned to enduring the Saturday-night program.

"Jackson did have a tendency to go a little overboard," Tank said in his most conciliatory tone.

"You know," Blanche said, the pitch rising in her voice along with the sparkle in her eye as she tried to keep a straight face, "they're having a separate reunion this weekend . . ." Her pause were perfectly timed, then she went on: "All the young white girls Jackson slept with when he was head of Afro House . . . over at Harvard Stadium!"

The laughter burst from us as if we were still huddled together in the student lounge. It almost scared away the waiter who was now delivering a tray of appetizers.

"There was some serious jungle fever going on all around, brothers, so don't be laughing too hard at Mr. Wright," Blanche said knowingly. "Don't get me started naming names!"

There were a couple of coughs, then genuine laughter again. Blanche had put us back in sync while we settled into the familiar act of eating together. I almost expected Otis to pop up beside the table with French fries he'd smuggled out of the hot food line.

"Hey, has anyone heard from Otis?" I wondered out loud.

"Otis?" Blanche wrinkled her forehead.

"Otis, right. He used to work in the cafeteria." Edwin was digging through his memory. "He wasn't registered though, was he?"

"Naw," Tank said, chewing on a Buffalo chicken wing and still looking elegant.

"He was in some kind of probation program . . . got him the job in the school cafeteria. That brother tightened up the Black table every day!"

"He was trying to get his life together. I remember now," Blanche said.

"You never went to Wally's with me and Sheila?" I asked, recalling the name of a local bar we used to sneak off to.

"That pit?" Edwin said with enough middle-class disdain to make the Dean of Students proud.

"Hey! Wally's wasn't as bad as some buckets of blood I went to back in Chicago. Otis was a great dancer."

As the memory flooded in, I realized how disappointed I was that no one had heard from him. I'd thought about Otis every once in a while over the years. In addition to an incredible smile and smooth dance moves, he'd been a stalwart supporter of the BIPs. He must have been the same age as we were, but he had the edge of someone who knew things about the world he wished he didn't.

Me and Tank and some of the others had come from neighborhoods not too different from the South End where Otis lived. It was literally on the other side of the railroad tracks from the university; undercapitalized and forgotten by the politicians, except when the police were sent in. Then the Movement had stepped in instead.

"Affirmative Action babies," they call us now, which rankles my nerves. There was nothing babyish about clawing my way out of the cycle of street shootings and pregnancies in my 'hood. And certainly nothing babyfied about trying to survive on a white campus where teachers and students looked at us like we were space aliens. That was before space aliens got their own TV shows.

I'd spent my freshman year mystified by academic topics no high school teacher had ever bothered to mention. And being humiliated by financial aid administrators who acted like they were giving me money out of their own little piggy banks. If they treated Black students that bad I couldn't imagine what working in the cafeteria had been like for Otis.

"Earth to Roxie." Blanche snapped me back to the table. "What're you sucking your teeth about, girl?"

"The dim-wits trashing Affirmative Action, so don't get me started."

"Oh, there she go!" Tank teased.

"How the hell did we end up in this mess?" I asked without the tiniest hope of an answer.

"Girl, when I saw what they put Anita Hill through on TV I knew it was the end of civilization as we know it." The tinkle in Blanche's voice was greatly subdued.

"And that's only the stuff they let us see," Edwin said.

"You just got to keep pushing," Tank said, as if trying to convince himself. "There is good stuff happening out there."

"Nothing to make the evening news, my brother," Edwin said.

"Maybe we better not be counting on the evening news," Tank responded from a serious place deep in his chest.

"People are too busy shopping on the Web for revolution now," Blanche spouted, the disillusion I'd heard earlier returning to her voice.

I know I'm something of a ranter, which is how I ended up coming to this reunion thing, so I decided to keep my mouth shut. The plushly carpeted room around us soaked up the disappointment that was spilling out of our reminiscences.

It was hard to believe we were sitting here, only a few blocks from the campus where we'd spent four years determined to change the world. I almost felt like I was the same person I was back in the day. I didn't care any less now about people being hungry or not learning to read or making drugs their religion. Maybe I was a little slower, but still I worked forty- and fifty-hour weeks leaping in front of other news photographers and setting up impossible shooting angles. Hanging out the fourth-floor window of McMillan Hall had paid off.

Tank looked like he could still take on the first string of anybody's opposing team, and was much smarter than I remembered. Even Blanche still had the spirit when she didn't try to flirt too much. I'm not one who believes you have to be young and poor to be hungry for action and change. But something was missing. And the comfort of the hotel bar was starting to feel like a trap.

"Anybody mind if I take a few shots while we're hanging?" I pulled my favorite little Leica from the Le Sportsac bag I carried everywhere, relieved to stand and get some energy going.

"Roxie!" Blanche protested as she grabbed her Fendi purse up from the floor and reapplied her lipstick. "Don't be snapping me with my mouth full."

"Blanche, would I do that to you?"

"Yes." Her pinky went up as she dropped her purse back to the floor, hoisted a small square of something from the tray of snacks, and popped it into her perfectly painted mouth.

"Did you work on the slide show for tomorrow?" Edwin asked, excited.

"I sent in some of the shots we had from the demo." Oops, there was that "we" again. I went on quickly: "But I think the "Say Brother" folks from WGBH had a bunch of material. You all sent pictures in, too, right?"

"Yeah, but you're the professional." Tank smiled at me.

"Not then I wasn't," I said. I snapped Tank just as he turned his high beams on Blanche.

"Roxie, I never sent a card or anything, but I was sorry to hear about Dennis passing," Edwin said it in that soft voice of his. His awkward sincerity was soothing, not the hard slap I'd been afraid I'd feel when I first heard Dennis' name out loud. These had been my best friends when Dennis and I met. Our occupation of McMillan Hall provided the chance for Dennis's first professional breakthrough. The pictures he'd taken in those three days documented a serious leap in the significance of Black student activism and in the relationship between us. These were the friends who'd nurtured both events. I looked at Edwin directly, not through the camera lens and smiled. I was afraid to try to say thanks out loud. It doesn't look good for folks from Chicago to cry.

"Those shots he took when y'all were locked up inside McMillan Hall were kickin' it!" Tank said.

"I still have that one he sent me, I'm sleeping under that desk, remember?" Blanche said wistfully.

I nodded and slipped back behind the camera appreciative that they felt good about Dennis. At the same time I tried to fight the feeling that Dennis was the celebrity and I was just the girl who married him. I used to really identify with Yoko Ono when she hooked up with John Lennon and the other Beatle boys got set on ragging her. Fortunately I was never going to try singing rock and roll.

"I don't suppose you got a sympathy card from CL?" Blanche said slyly after a moment.

"No, I don't suppose I did."

"Oh, don't look so grim, girl. I was just teasing. After 30 years who cares about Charles Leonard?"

"Charles Leonard would be first on that list," I said. Blanche almost fell out of her chair laughing. The sound of it made my anxiety ease up. I'd been so busy remembering the things about Blanche that got on my nerves I'd forgotten how many laughs we always had together.

"I don't know why you sisters were so hard on CL," Edwin said.

"You don't know what?" Blanche's voice raised only slightly, but small strands of hair threatened to explode from her do. I returned to my camera. I'd done my battling just getting myself past him in the lobby, I wasn't about to break down CL to these guys.

"He had his nose stuck in the air a little but, damn, he was always down with us," Tank tried to keep the conversation light.

"Charles 'CL' Leonard made Mike Tyson look like the Image Award winner at the NAACP."

"Aw, come on . . . let's . . ." Edwin was startled by the anger in Blanche's voice.

"Let's what? Okay, how 'bout let's each of you tell me how many times you slapped your girlfriends upside their heads?"

The guys were silent and I was too, except for the click of my shutter. Despite the statistics, it was impossible for me to conjure up a picture of either Tank or Edwin doing something like that.

"Okay," Blanche said letting up. "But I didn't see none of you rushing in to school that brother on keeping his hands in his pockets."

"That was all rumors, Blanche," Edwin said.

"Maybe to you all, if you didn't want to see the facts."

Tank looked disturbed and, for once, had no words of defense.

'Go girl!' I was thinking but I figured we didn't need to have this conversation in the hotel bar. "You know folks, CL's actually here. I saw him earlier. So, uh . . ."

We each looked up at the door as if our parents might catch us swearing. Then we returned to our champagne, everyone in an uneasy silence. I sipped from my glass remembering CL's girlfriend after me, a freshman. She'd arrived at a BIPs meeting more than once with more makeup on than was required for cranking out a newsletter. The guys never noticed and I know I never said anything. I guess nobody wanted to see what was really up. Fortunately for CL, he and I weren't dating long enough for me to find out.

"So, do you have an archive, your own, I mean?" Edwin asked, carefully guiding us back to comfortable ground.

"Oh yeah! We . . . I've got every demo ever staged, that was our specialty for a while." I chewed the inside of my lip, wondering when I'd be comfortable with the singularity of the word. Even though there had been time enough for me to be used to being on my own I'd been resisting it way too long. I might as well start here and now. "I have a major collection I'm thinking of donating to some HBC sometime."

"Right on!" Tank said raising his glass of champagne.

"You should do a book," Edwin said, his eyes twinkling with enthusiasm.

At that moment I wondered if it were possible that some of my friends back home in Chicago had somehow gotten in touch with the BIPs and bribed them to read their lines. One or another of them was always driving me crazy with ideas of photo books I should do: Black Male Professionals, Black Women Professionals, Young Black Athletes, Old Black Athletes. I could never figure out where the hell people got these ideas.

"Yeah! A book on us. It's just the right time." Suddenly Blanche was a publishing consultant.

"Blanche got something, Roxie. Listen to the woman." Edwin sat up in his chair as if he were seeing the cover right then and there.

Whenever the idea of my doing a book came up I felt a ripple of fear pulse through my body as if a police siren was wailing outside my door. I knew I should do it. Time was passing and who better to document the awakening of the 1960s than a photographer? And now, before our eyesight gets so bad we can't see the pictures. I took some deep breaths trying to keep the ripple from turning into a tidal wave.

"Hey, I saw that spread you did on Curtis at his marketing company a couple of years ago. In Ebony, right?" Tank leapt in for the save.

"Didn't he look great?"

"So that's what he's up to?" Edwin asked.

"Public relations. In Connecticut," Blanche answered. "We did a job with him a couple of years ago! Is he coming?"

"Maybe. He e-mailed me a month or so back." I was happy to have a new topic.

"I can't believe he's still around." Edwin said with a tightness in his voice that was puzzling. I wondered what's that all about, then I got it.

"Of course, he's still around," I said. "Curtis is just gay, not terminal."

"I know, I know . . . but that last year was hard on him. Then AIDS and everything."

"Let's be clear, the year wasn't hard on Curtis, it was CL and Jackson Wright that were hard on him." Blanche was in rare form, reminding me of another reason I couldn't stand my ex and Mr. Afro House.

"Yeah, that was the only thing they could ever agree on," Tank said glumly.

"Egotistical shits," I said with a shudder.

"I don't know what the big deal was," Edwin said. "Long as Curtis kept his johnson in his pants around me, what'd I care?"

"I don't think most folks felt that casual about him, Edwin," I said flashing on the disaster our last BIPs party had turned into, at least for Curtis. When his folks came to graduation he told them that the black eye and cracked rib were from a car accident.

"And just because Curtis is gay doesn't mean he's got to die with HIV." I tried to keep my voice level but memory was making it hard. After four years of sister this and As Salaam Alaikum that, I was still livid at how shallow brotherhood could be. I assumed Edwin would have a deeper perspective, working in film and all.

"Well, like I said, I'm just glad to hear he's . . . you know . . . doing okay." Edwin's discomfort hung around him bigger than his jacket.

"You know what's her name," Blanched waggled her hand in the air trying to pull down a name. ". . . what's her name? You know, she got the one part in "West Side Story" they bothered to give to somebody colored. Uh . . . uh . . . you know . . . really tall, hazel eyes? She was on our floor, but down the other end."

"Always wore that huge green shawl!" The image began to resolve in my head. "She used to bring a big box of chocolate chip cookies back from break!"

"Yeah!" Tanks deep voice boomed. Food would be the thing to jog his memory.

"She's gay, too," Blanche said as she took a sip of her champagne.

"You're kidding?" Shock rang in Edwin's voice.

"Uh huh. I ran into her at a conference. She works in advertising too; more television than print. It was an industry thing, in Denver a while back. She was there, with her significant other. Good looking girl, from St. Croix I think."

I was surprised Blanche was so casual but clearly she was not having the problem with it Edwin was. He just kept asking her if she was kidding.

"I'm telling you I met the woman!" Blanche reiterated impatiently. "She's a nurse or something."

"Damn!" Edwin said.

"Don't be a drip, Edwin." Blanche was clearly getting to the end of her tolerance. As I watched her through the lens the set in the lines of her face wiped out all of the giggle and squiggle. I could see where Blanche was maybe deeper than her affect suggested.

"No point getting tense." Tank poured more champagne in Edwin's glass. "I did a program a year or so back, just for the locals, you know. Atlanta has quite a gay community," Tank continued shyly. "If statistics are right we're due to have at least 7 more gay people show this weekend, my brother."

Edwin slugged the champagne down like that would make everything clearer.

Well, we were certainly striking out with the contemporary issues. I know men can't talk about sex unless they're in the middle of having it but Edwin was about to blow our high. I figured I'd take the lull in conversation as a cue to make my exit. I searched in my bag for money to put on the table.

Then Tank looked up and did his best imitation of an Isaac Hayes riff. All talking stopped. "Ooh Miss Hot Buttered Soul herself!!!"

"That's Ms. Hot Buttered Soul," Sheila Mills Baldwin said as she grabbed a chair from one of the other tables, moving across the room like the Black campus queen she'd been. Sheila was tall and slender, one of those people who always looked elegant, even in the days of combat fatigues. Her lilac silk pants suit complimented her smooth dark skin; a close ring of curls had replaced the intricate weave of braided rows. The hands that had sown together our red black and green banner were now manicured to perfection. The smile lines at the corners of her eyes only gave her character. She looked like not a day had passed, or at least no more than a week.

My honest response was pure joy and then I felt bad that our friendship had lapsed. Hadn't friendship been at the heart of all the work we'd done? Did I let it go too easily?

I snapped a picture of Sheila just as she eased into the circle we'd formed and tossed her large matching lilac leather Coach bag onto the floor. Her smile was luminous as the voices of the other's swirled around her in greeting. Her perfume mixed with Blanche's and Tanks after shave, filling the air around me so I couldn't think. Tank and Blanche disentangled themselves from embracing Sheila while Edwin held her chair for her.

I stood, put my Leica back in my bag and was uncertain which direction to turn. Through a lens it's easy to put everything into focus. It only took a slight turn of the wrist and the picture was clear and clean. Too bad real life wasn't so easy. When she sat down Sheila fixed me with an impassive stare that dared me to leave.

Yeah, this was going to be one long weekend. Shit!

Fear of Floating

BY BRYAN GIBSON

"Conversation enriches the understanding, but solitude is the school of genius. . . ."

—EDWARD GIBBON, *The Decline and Fall of The Roman Empire*

I will say to you this: *Melancholy,* that wretched cousin to Sorrow, is, without a doubt, a parasite of the soul that devours its host until spirit and body are inspired to divide. For those of you who consider this hyperbole, I would argue that you have never truly known *blue, gray,* or *black*—colors of the river through which flows despair . . . And since this condition (your ignorance) means that you are among a privileged few, I shall, despite envy, so

that you might at once become familiar with the sentiments I profess, bring
to you this adventure, in which is contained the horrors of the spectrum.

FEAR OF FLOATING
(VARIATIONS ON A THEME BY CERVANTES)

To whom this may concern (specifically, to the good and fair people of
Promenade management):

In this complex I have lived twenty-one years; I am, therefore, espe-
cially knowledgeable concerning the history of this dwelling, more so than
yourselves, who have worked here for way less than half that time. Need-
less to say, I am aware of the recent tumult our establishment has suffered,
for I, too, have endured its fall.

As I am mostly confined to my apartment (due to a debilitating ill-
ness), I seldom venture beyond the security of my front door; however, on
one such occasion, having exited the first-level entranceway, I was accosted
by three youths who, I believe, also live in this complex (and as a result of
Section-8[1])—youths who, because of their previous environment no doubt,
still find it necessary to behave like the inhabitants of a zoo, the place from
which they were rescued by our wretched benefactors, the city.

Understand: I am not writing to bemoan my molestation, but to pro-
claim—both for myself and for my fellow cooperators (men and women
who lead exemplary lives, and have done so without interruption)—that
further desecration of our homes must not, and will not, go unpunished;
for if it does, if the usurpers are continued to be allowed here, then, like
Rome before us, which foolishly permitted to sully their regions the bar-
barian Goths, our dwelling, as did the empire, will most certainly perish.
And so to prevent this, I have gathered here a few suggestions which
should, if followed strictly, aid in the dismissal of the pillaging few:

*(1) **Our enemies**: Unlike most, I believe, absolutely, in Swift's con-*
tention that man is an unreasonable brute who sometimes, on occasion,
behaves reasonably. From this we must conclude there is but one way to
deal with our foes: to treat them not as thinkers (higher man) but as actors
(lower man), who know nothing of discretion, modesty, or subtlety—for
all these require thought, which, as you know, they can perform only on
occasion. A speedy justice must be exacted; families of the villains expelled;
and announcements—many announcements—discharged to responsible
officials, warning them that the Promenade is not a haven for the hap-
lessly low, nor a shelter for the neglected multiudes, *by this I mean, sav-*

---

[1]Author's note: *Section-8*, as referenced here, is a federally subsidized program which allo-
cates funds for public and private housing, provided that a fixed number of apartments be
set aside for the poor and indigent.

ages, *who, because of ill birth, have risen no further than the lowest rungs of life.*

*(2) **Our allies**: Living here for many years I have come to know my neighbors; though personal contact has been scarce (due to my condition), I have, nevertheless, learned that most are industrious employees, diligent pupils, loving parents, and caring friends; and, because of this, I no doubt believe they would gladly sacrifice a few dollars to maintain our tranquillity. This suggests the obvious: Rally the legions, secure the boundaries, display the purple (and the pride therefrom), and at once move against the uncivilized, who will know, and for all time, the Promenade is not a place for them.*

*(3) **Our benefactors**: Being that we are here and they are not, it shouldn't be too difficult to understand their apathy regarding our decay; for our triumph or fall affects them not in the least. And so we alone must wield the sword, inflict the wound, shed the blood; for if we delay, or, even worse, fail to act at all, then I fear the Promenade will be lost to the vulgar and the plain, as occurred on the final days of a once great empire.*

Sincerely,
A Concerned Citizen

This was the epistle sent to the uninformed, by a man who feared that he would someday fly away.

Imagine your life this way: Each day, and so each month and year, alone, afraid, consumed by a thought—that Gravity, a phantom whose cause is to maintain the heavens (and the creatures within), was a monster, lurking perpetually, and preparing for your doom![2]—And though this life may seem a ridiculous one, and remote, you should know that not too long before this day lived a man whose curse it was to live it. His name was *****, and as was revealed in his letter, he suffered an illness which kept him mostly from the world.

In his pockets he carried stones; on his wrists and ankles the heaviest weights; and against his skin layers of dense fabric that, while indoors, kept him safe from the sky and stratosphere; for he was terrified of gravity, that it would one day disappear, pushing him above the clouds, into space, and towards the fires of a star. How he came to be this way no one knows, and I, the author, can only dabble in conjecture, so my opinion will stay where it belongs, in a dark and quiet place.

To continue then: In his home he stayed; and in that space was born a child named *Loneliness*, whom he spoke to often, but never for as long as he

---

[2]For those readers who are, at bottom, inquisitive, I believe the condition is referred to as *Barophobia: Fear of Gravity.*

would have liked. While isolated he read and studied, and in the shadows he listened to Chopin, whose genius moved him to record these words:

> *Let us talk of Chopin—specifically, Sonata No. 3, in B minor:*
> *There are very few artists who endeavor to achieve the impossible, and in this magnificent work the master does just that; for here, within precise and immaculate keystrokes, Chopin does something I once thought unattainable: he actually makes beauty . . . palatable.*

One day, when courage had come to move him so, *****, for reasons of necessity, escaped his home to be amongst his fellow men, who, though free of his psychosis, were still just as disturbed; for not moments from the doorway, just seconds from the home, ***** was harassed and beaten; and though in his pockets were the weapons of hard stones, he dared not touch them, for of floating.

Soon after this assault was written the letter previously disclosed, which contained both genius and contempt, but left anonymous the penman's name; but few who read it were unclear of the work's composer: for many had seen his mugging, and had quickly spread the news of its having occurred, and to everyone *but* the authorities, who would have done their best to do nothing, I'm sure. Be that as it may, having read *****'s epistle, many were so moved by his sapience, so impressed by his profundity, that, shortly after its publication, knowing who he was and where he lived (for such is the ability of gossips)—I say, shortly after this, envelopes began to appear beneath *****'s door, cluttering the foyer, containing requests for the inhabitant's wisdom.

At first he left them to gather dust, feeling no need ot entertain his attackers, whom he mistakenly believed were responsible for the parcels; but eventually, overtime, curiosity provoked him to open one, then all of the correspondence; and though some were unintelligible pros written by lowborn scoundrels—neighbors who hadn't liked being called *savages*—most were concise, well-written appeals for prudence that was uniquely his own. And so, moved that he had touched so many, and elated that his acumen could aid his fellow man, ***** acquiesced, and responded to his neighbors. Of the letters he chose these, which most concerned him:

> *Dear Sir—*
> *I am seventeen, nearing my eighteenth year, and am with child. I am desperate for your words. I do not want to kill my baby, but I do not want to kill my future either (for all will be lost if the child is born). My question to you is this: Being that I am only in my third week of pregnancy, and since the thing inside me as yet resembles a boy or girl, or anything close to these, if I*

choose to abort, would it in fact be killing? For so early is my condition can whatever is inside me truly, and accurately, be called human?

Most sincerely,
A Troubled Soul

And to this he answered:

To Troubled Soul—

Your concerns are dear, and your circumstance dire; but do not transform concern into sophistry. The question you are asking is a simple one: When is a baby a baby?—and I shall respond in this way (for doing so will guarantee your understanding me): When making a cake, one, usually, follows a recipe containing a list of ingredients—flour, sugar, vanilla, eggs, etc.—and none of these, before they are combined, can be said to be a cake, only a maniac would dispute this. Moreover, all of these components, and whatever else it requires to make a cake, if gathered together, side by side, but remain unmixed, are nothing but parts, parts which may, possibly, become a greater whole—nothing more. However, when these ingredients are combined—either sufficiently or haphazardly—even in this primordial, gelatinous state (for how else does one describe batter), I say, what you will have is cake; for no other purpose are these ingredients combined, for no other utility would they serve; and indeed, no matter how you choose to bake it, when or where, trapped in tin foil or dispersed in a muffin pan—what you will have, once put into the oven and baked, I repeat, what you will have is cake—maybe malformed, possibly burnt and crispy, but, nevertheless, cake. And what makes reality even more potent than my analogy is this: one could argue (and their are some who will, I'm sure) that only in the oven does baking begin, and it is ultimately through this process that a cake is truly born. And, for reasons of amusement, let us say I agree with this (and do so alacritously, because in their argument is found the greatest truth): Would you not, then, concede that our baby, our cake—whether he be angel or devil food, lightly sweetened or saccharine laced—begins baking as soon as sperm punctures egg?[3] and that in his mother is found the most glorous oven ever designed by Nature?

Troubled Soul, I burden you with my pros only to belabor this point: that you not diminish the act you are considering, which, because it so violently impacts your life, and more so than anyone else now capable of opinion—because of this, you, and you alone, must decide your embryo's

---

[3]And will do so always, unless sperm or egg is defective.

fate, and then live, and perhaps suffer, with the choice you've made.—I
hope that I've been helpful.

Sincerely,
A Concernced Citizen

The second note was as follows:

To Occupant:
  I observed your letter as it was printed in the Promenade, *and was so*
impressed by your correspondence that I was moved to send you this note,
which has taken me forever to compose.
  I am a husband and a parent, and love dearly my wife and daughter;
but yesterday (a few days before your receiving this), I cheated—at least, I
think I did; for never did my genitals touch another's, which means, in
the literal sense, there was no sex; and if there was no sex, then, I believe,
as does my favorite President, I did nothing wrong, for what is mere pet-
ting but harmless play? Indeed, I go to sleep at night free from guilt be-
cause I know—as you do, I'm sure—that nothing I did can be interpreted
as cheating. Still, I would very much like your opinion on the matter.

Thank you,
Friend of the President

Which inspired this response:

Dear Friend:
  Being that I, like you, am a man, and therefore know well your de-
sires, I can truly empathize with your position; for we are sadly, loathsome
creatures driven towards monsters more loathsome than ourselves. Be that
as it may, what you are suggesting is ridiculous, and for this reason: A
man sticks his tongue in your wife's ear—how do you feel? He then puts
his pinkie on each of her butt-cheeks (which she allows free from guilt, for
what is mere petting but harmless play?)—again, how do you feel? And
then, simply because it thrills him to do so, he places a toe between her
breasts—once more, how do you feel? . . . My point is simply this: Inti-
mate contact of any kind, with someone—anyone!—beyond your signifi-
cant other is cheating, and wherever the placement of genitalia; I'm sure
your anger, given life by my merely proposing such debauches, is proof
enough that I speak true. Admit to this now, and, maybe, possibly, I'll re-
move my toe from between your wife's tits.

Sincerely,
A Concerned Citizen

The third correspondence went this way:

To a wise and knowledgeable fellow:
 Please answer this (for your doing so, quickly and promptly, will at once alleviate a tremendous load which threatens, daily, my bones and extremities): What's the deal with the Fed?[4] *and moreover, its chairman, Alan Greenspan? I ask this because over the past year Fortune has blessed me, and I have, aided by her keen advice, acquired lots of things—money, car, clothes, women—and enjoy each immensely; however, I am quite fearful of the* Joker *at the bank, whose tinkering promises to deprive me of all these.—What say you?*

         Impatient for your reply,
         A Restless Neighbor

Which was answered thusly:

To Restless Neighbor:
 Being that I am a simple man, I am uncertain how to respond to your note; of its parts, the first is too vague, but the second, however, is a matter I myself have contemplated often, and can best answer thusly: A man in his car is on a road headed for "Prosperity"; every mile takes him closer to where he wants to be, and each mile seems (and is) smoother than the one before it, making his ride a joyous one; but for fear of an accident which has yet to occur, caused by an oil-spill he has yet to see, the man slows then stops his motion, allowing the car no progress beyond its passing through time (which cannot be altered by deceleration). So afraid is he of the "might" and the "maybe" that the traveler doesn't dare go further, even reversing the car so to move away from impending doom, which, of course, he has only imagined. Eventually, over time, when he determines it safe to continue, the car, for whatever reason, stalls, though ultimately progresses, but only after much coaxing from its driver. Still, when it does go the vehicle moves much slower than before, and its handling isn't nearly as steady: the road has changed, as has the car, for on this journey time is the only constant; and so the driver, for lack of speed, finds "Prosperity" to be much farther away.
 On Alan Greenspan I say to you this: When traveling, no matter the distance or destination, one should, one must*, have courage—and Greenspan lacks this.*
 Having written thusly, I trust my anecdote was readily understood; for you are, it seems, a very shrewd man; one does not amass the sums you have on simple good fortune. Still, beyond your query, there is a more rele-

[4]Federal Reserve Board.

vant question before us, one which, upon my asking, should help alleviate your fear concerning Greenspan's actions: Why does having "things" matter to you?—and what are you without them? I ask the latter because: when a man is himself nothing, he requires additions to make him whole, i.e., money, car, clothes, women—anything that might bring to him greater visibility—by this I mean, relevance. Ponder this, answer this, and learn from that result; for only then will you have something which, it appears, Fortune has yet to grant you . . . peace.

Sincerely,
A Concerned Citizen

The fourth:

Kind Sir—
My boyfriend and I argue incessantly, and always about the same thing: My clothes. Being that I am young, beautiful, and shapely—and will be none of these forever—I feel it is both my right and duty to display to the world my magnificence; for is not beauty meant to be shared, adored, and admired?—Am I not doing, by wearing clothes that reveal to lesser eyes my glory—I say, am I not doing only what is right?

Without shame,
Venus

Which inspired this:

Dear Venus—
I agree: Beauty is a thing that should be shared and admired; nevertheless, you got to have class with that ass.

The fifth:

To whomever is capable of answering this:
My dilemma is a desperate one; for it deals with the heart, a broken heart, and one belonging to me.
Three years ago I broke up with my dearest love, a woman whom I cherished more than anything or anyone, in this world or the one beyond it. Nevertheless, despite my affection, I, using faithful logic, one day determined that this woman—this angel!—though fulfilling all my emotional and sexual needs, was my lesser intellectually, and could never placate that part of me which requires more than simple hugs and kisses. Still, as I have said, it has been three years since my leaving, and my soul screams for her, as it did when we were lovers. Because of this I cannot sustain a rela-

tionship beyond a few months, so long is the shadow she casts, so black is my heart, which dies form lack of sun, its peddles . . . wilting. and so I have chosen to remain alone (for circumstance will not permit our reuniting). I hate being this way, but what am I to do? I ask you: Will I ever love again?

> *With reverence,*
> *Anteros*

And to this he responded:

Anteros:
  Know this: The question is not will you ever love again? but will you ever stop loving? For it is only when you no longer love this girl will you be free to love another.

> *Sincerely,*
> *A Concerned Citizen*

The Sixth:

To you who would quell my sorrow; at least, to you who would try—
  On the 15th of May was born my only child—the sweetest melody, the loveliest portrait, the finest poem has yet to be which could describe to you the boy, who was from God, who was . . . mine.—On the 18th of May, three days' following his eleventh year, was born my gravest sorrow, my darkest day . . . it was then . . . when Ian was no more.
  I write to you now not for pity but for relief; it has been four years since Ian's departure, and my tears come just as quickly as the day when first he left. I cannot eat or sleep, and every child I pass—boy or girl—reminds me of him. Even now I cry . . . even not I see his face. I ask you: When shall there be sleep? When shall there be peace? When shall I not know pain? . . .

> *Somberly,*
> *Less*

And this way he replied:

My dearest Less—
  There are no words . . . only these: A child is an extension of the soul, the soul of its progenitor, the parent; and as the child grows, becomes strong, robust—the parent, the entity from whence he came, becomes . . . less; for that is the order of things: The parent (prima causa) sacrifices for the child his self, his soul, until resources are depleted, until nothing is left, and the parent is no more; not even Cronos could alter this.

However, if the effect *(the child) perishes before the* affect *(the parent), the soul is disturbed; for its growth, its extension, is lost, thus disturbing the order of things, thus disturbing* order.

But these words only illustrate why *you are hurting, and explain nothing about your future mending, which, sadly, I have no knowlege of. Be that as it may, know that your sorrow now extends to me; for I too shall bare your burden, as if Ian were the child to whom my soul would someday pass. And so, Less, with me you are more.—*

Most Sincerely,
A Concerned Citizen

The seventh (and final):

To him:
*—**Happiness** is something I will never know, not will it ever know me.*
*—**No greater pain** have I ever known than that which comes from reflection.*
*—**The worst thing**, however, is that at 27 the best is over, and now I must face the rest of my days knowing no future as grand as childhood.*
*—**And she can give to me nothing!**—not the love I want, nor the acceptance I require.*
*—**When I die**, I don't want Heaven; give me the universe!*
*—**There is no hate** more potent than mine for life—for my own or anyone else's.*
*—**Today** I began carrying a hammer in my gym bag; and as I carried it (the bag in which the hammer rested), I dreamt that every woman was a nail.*
*—**There are moments** on this earth when nothing matters: not the pleasant breeze of summer, nor the calming warmth of my lover's arms. It was during one such moment that I decided to leave this place for another, in search of solitude and better days.*
*—**What ought to be** . . . will.*

Frankly,
Me

And the response:

To Me (and to the heart of the matter):
You no doubt suffer from depression; I too suffer from this, which comes and goes and comes again—indeed, there is rarely a day when I don't fear its arrival, never a moment when I don't look for it to appear.

*The following is a passage from when last depression touched me; I hope
my thoughts are helpful.*

BLUE TO BLACK

The mind—by this I mean, that part of us resting just beneath the conscious, far beyond the reach of man or machine—the mind, I say, never lies;
and it is for this reason that mortals suffer depression: for while the conscious can be tricked into believing falsities, the subconscious (the mind) is
impervious to our fairy tales, which we create to make life less severe.

Beyond its inability to hide from truth, the mind (the subconscious) is
perpetual, that is, it never stops its work—thinking, constructing, destroying, conjoining ideas without rest, and doing so for no other cause than the
fulfillment of its purpose, which is *discovery!* —and it discovers no matter
how harsh or unpleasant the result, no matter our feelings; for what is emotion to the mind, which knows only reason.

Again: The mind is a device for absorbing truth, and the knowledge it
consumes is redirected by us, to be altered and obscured; to the conscious
goes the tainted truth, and to the subconscious goes the pure—and our ability to access the latter's information is determined by innate predispositions;
for example: The dim have almost no entranceway into the mind, and, because of this, have its contents infected by the conscious, which almost always spoils its fruits. The smart, however, who are intellectually inclined
(though only somewhat), have greater access to the mind, but are unable to
do this freely and are often confused by the gifts of the subconcious, and so
stumble around using mostly intuition, like the dumb, just not as feebly. It
is only those blessed with genius who, at so high a perch, have the best view
and thus passage into the mind, and, as a result, can both easily access and
comprehend its treasures; for genius has the ability to tap into the subconscious and bring the idea to the fore, the pure idea, the uncut idea, one not
diluted by commonness. This is why, more often than not, the genius, being
surrounded by us who are mostly deaf and blind, the genius, I say, is rarely
understood, for he is speaking to those who cannot possibly see or hear him.

(DEPRESSION: HOW THE MIND SUPPLIES IT FUEL)

As we previously noted, the mind is composed of two parts—the conscious
and the subconscious—and both have a significant purpose: the subconscious, to discern the truth; the conscious, to mainly protect us from it—indeed, most would be unable to function if the truth of their world were
revealed. For example: How could the poor bare their lives if, suddenly, they

understood that most, despite their efforts, will remain impoverished until death? And how could the ugly, the homely, the wretchedly offensive—how could they endure a second knowing what the subconscious knows, that no matter how many pretty clothes they purchase, or pretty people they befriend, no matter how much money they acquire to be spent on pretty things, no matter these, they will *always* be ugly? And so the conscious, to protect them from harshest truth, keeps reality at bay and supplies each with hope, the most effective hallucinogen.

However, sometimes the conscious is overwhelmed; for some have existence so miserable that all truth cannot be kept behind the veil—this, of course, ultimately leads to depression, a state in which the world (your world) beomes all too clear.

(THE VOICE OF REASON: HOW IT WHISPERS UNTIL WE ARE DEAF)

Once the subconscious begins to crack, to break, then eventually, to burst, a sudden stream of awareness makes its way into our thoughts, and we are, understandably, overwhelmed. In order to function, the conscious, newly burdened, creates for itself a helper (a hindrance), which manifests itself in a voice we soon come to hear. At first the voice is quite reasonable (afterall, it was created to help us); however, over time, as reality makes itself know (for now it bares no masks, and we are entirely exposed), the voice becomes *too* honest, and guides us towards escape, by this I mean, suicide, which was an option previously unrealized before reason made it known.

To extend beyond this point: The spirit is separate from the mind—moreover, the spirit is separate from the body, the world, the universe, and is free to explore all things. The spirit, unlike the mind, has no stake in our being, that is, it exists beyond us, despite us, and will do so long after we are gone.

(ON THE SPIRIT'S SELF-INTERESTED DESIGN, AND HOW WE SUFFER FROM IT)

The spirit, however liberated from the body, is, nevertheless, trapped; for as long as there is a body, and with it a mind, it (the spirit, the soul) is deprived of omniscience, which occurs because of us, who are but anchors of the soul. And so, the spirit has as its design a complete and total separation from its jailer, man, which it accomplishes upon his death; and since the spirit is impatient, it hastens our end by twisting logic and altering reason, which happily assures us that, to be free of torment, death is the only way.—

These are just a few of my notes on the subject; I do not wish to burden
you with more, which would, because of volume, bring you to the floor.—
Keep healthy, by strengthening your mind: suffer books, endure sym-
phonies, so that, like me, you will be able to resist the voice which so often
calls our name.

Sincerely,
Me Too

Having ended with these words, ***** named and sealed each envelope,
then slid all beneath his door, unconcerned if any reached their destinations,
for his mind was consumed by other things. The correspondence had taken
its toll; the notes, each of them (but especially the latter two), had freed
emotions which had, he thought, long been restrained, held down, and put
to rest; but before him now was Sorrow, Anger, Grief, and Despair, who had
come for conversation.

Chopin played, beautifully, and as the notes descended, so too did the
listener, whose mood grew dark, whose pleasantness faded into shadow; for
suddenly, before him was the truth, uncut and pure: he was pathetic, he was
alone, he was afraid . . . of gravity.

Slowly, cautiously, he began removing from his pockets all that they contained, and, moving for the window, felt his body rising from the floor, his
soul smiling from the heavens (for soon it would be free). Shortly after,
***** was no more; and though he had long believed it to be his enemy, on
this day, Gravity was his friend.

FROM **The Queen of Harlem**

BY BRIAN KEITH JACKSON

Yo. Yo wassup?" *asks a young man, planting himself in front of me. Though*
the temperature hardly warrants it, he's already wearing his new black
parka, with fur trimming the hood. The coat is his business suit, different from
the one I wear but a business suit nonetheless. "You cool?" *That is all he says,*
and I fully understand the nature of the weather report.

I smile, somewhat tempted by the offer, but I pass with a simple lift of the
hands. The moment does find me cool, so the young man, with a swagger and a

sway, pushes off on his way. He doesn't take it personally; in his business, and in mine, a no is a yes, an offer away.

"*Great day, huh?*" *says a guy walking by with a briefcase.*

"*Yeah,*" *I say.* "*Can't complain.*"

"*I hear ya. Have a good one.*"

"*You too.*"

Autumn has alwyas been my favorite season. It's when time turns back on it-self, if only for an hour.

Spring forward. Fall back.

I sit on the stoop of the town house, checking out the refurbished Marcus Garvey Park, which has been renamed Mount Morris. The leaves, going through their changes, sway with the breeze in the air as though Billie Holiday is singing "Autumn in New York."

I cherish the moment because I haven't been back to this street, haven't been back to New York, in four years. But here I sit where it all began.

A group of kids on the sidewalk across the street are double-Dutching, maybe hoping to one day take the crown back from the Japanese team. They are scream-ing with delight and the sting of the frayed extension cord they use goes unno-ticed. They are used to its touch.

I bob my head to the sound of the cord slapping the concrete; my dreads swing to its cadence, almost as though my turn is coming up. Watching the kids, I'm loving their natural high.

An old woman tosses bread crumbs for the pigeons, and their velvet coos at-tract a swarm and they settle on the sidewalk at her feet. All the pigeons look alike to me, but I'm certain the old woman can spot a few of her favorites, her "babies"; perhaps the ones that most resemble doves. The pigeons begin to scurry as a car passes, but the little girls across the street double-Dutching never miss a beat.

"*Mr. Randolph?*"

"*Yes,*" *I say, standing, closing my journal.*

"*Diane Turner,*" *she says, sticking out her hand.* "*So nice to meet you. Sorry I'm tardy, but this area is booming and I've had to show four other town houses today. Of course, this one is the prize.*"

"*That's fine. I was having a great time just sitting here checking things out.*"

"*Yes. The neighborhood has changed drastically in the last several years. This town house is a jewel.*" *I suspect she knows what time it is, but she takes a look at her watch.* "*I actually have another client coming to see it in an hour. Shall we?*" *Diane Turner walks up the steps. I follow.*

"*Didn't that park used to be called Marcus Garvey?*" *I ask.*

"*Yes. Well, actually it was Mount Morris Park first, then it was renamed Marcus Garvey Park in 1973, but due to the current changes in the area they thought it would be best to again call it Mount Morris. Full circle, wouldn't you say?"*

"Yes. It seems so. Malcolm X Boulevard hasn't been renamed, has it?" She smiles but gives no answer.

"After you," says Diane Turner, opening the door. "As you can see, fabulous." She places her hand behind her ear. "Just listen. You hear that? That's the sound of history."

Though the place has been renovated it's still as familiar to me as a childhood scar.

"I see you've brought a notebook," says Diane Turner, glancing at my old journal. She looks like a fancy black doll in her tangerine designer suit and matching suede shoes. A black and gold silk scarf covers her neck, and her lips are painted into a permanent smile. "That's wise. It's amazing how much people forget."

"Yes. It's just something to refer to."

"You said you're new in town?

"Somewhat. But I like the area."

"I'm sure you'll enjoy New York. Harlem is definitely the place to be. It's as the kids say, 'All that.' You'll find this town house to be a worthy investment. The best space for the buck. It's all in the details."

"You've got that right."

"I don't normally advertise, but I used to be the only broker handling properties up here. White brokers wouldn't touch it with a gloved hand when it was just shit. Anyone can appreciate the harvest, but few have seen the seeds I've sown. We do what we can. I'm sure as a young brother, and a lawyer no less, you understand."

"Yes," I say, catching her eye. "I think I do."

A cell phone rings and I reach inside my jacket pocket. "Oh, that's me," she says, taking her black alligator purse off her shoulder, digging inside. "This will only take a sec." Then into the phone, "Diane Turner . . . Hello, dahling. How are you? . . . Yes . . . Well, we do what we can . . . Um huh . . . Well, I'm showing another house at the moment . . . Yes, of course. Hold on." Diane Turner covers the phone, then whispers to me like telling a friend a secret, "Listen, hon, a couple interested in a property around the corner—mind you, not nearly as fabulous as this—is waiting for me. They want to take another look. Do you mind if I just—"

"No, please. Feel free to go. I'll just make myself at home."

"Clever. Clever," she says, slapping me on the arm playfully. "I feel good about this. I think it's going to work out for you here." Diane Turner winks at me. "I have another appointment to show the house in an hour, but I'll try to be back before then. I think this deal around the corner is about to come together. A lovely couple, they. Did you say you were married?"

"No," I say. "I'm not."

"Well, FYI, a great many gay people have moved into the neighborhood. Follow the gays, I say. They really are the best people. Just fabulous. Give gays a ghetto and they'll fix it right up . . . Not that I'm implying you're gay, but if you were, just know, it certainly wouldn't be held against you."

I open my mouth to speak, but Diane Turner with a hold-that-thought gesture returns to her phone call. "Hello. Yes, I'll be right there . . . Nonononono, don't be silly. Anything for you . . . I'm just around the corner. I had a feeling you would want to take another look."

Yes, another look. but for me it was more than that.

I'd been staying at Jim's East Village apartment for two weeks, but as we sat in his favorite bar on East Fourth Street downing dollar drafts, the air was let out of the keg.

"Listen, Mason, it's been cool having you crash, but if you wanna keep kicking it in New York you're gonna need to find your own place."

Jim was your average hipster whose claim to fame was that he was the first white guy, that he knew, to have dreadlocks. All summer I had been twisting my hair, trying to attach myself to something associated with black heritage.

I know. I've been looking," I said. "I've checked the ads every day."

"Fuck the ads," said Jim, holding up his empty mug to the tattooed bartender. "Just tell everybody you meet that you're looking. It's the only way. That's how I found my place."

The "place" was a railroad flat. At least that's what they're called in New York. In the South it's called a shotgun house. But at that moment it was more than I had.

I'd crossed out all the possible ads but one remained:

HOUSEMATE WANTED
TO SHARE TOWN HOUSE
450/month. Rarely home
No. 20 W. 120th St.
Appt. 4–4:15, 15 October

I'd circled it as a lark. Sure, I was going to go to Harlem, at some point, to check it out, but I'd never really considered living there.

"Please be sure to take all of your belongings when leaving the train. And be mindful of your wallets, for the hand in your pocket may not be your own." Voice over the intercom of the 6 train, tunneling through Manhattan's East Side.

I got out of the subway at 125th Street, and the rush of color, fabric as well as skin, filled me like a Jamaican patty. The air was different, alive. Incense filled my nose, and the different languages and accents felt good in my ears.

Harlem.

"Dreads?" said the West African woman, stepping up to me. "You want dreads? Twist?"

"No, thank you," I said with a smile as I walked on, avoiding the rolling tumbleweeds of hair that hadn't made it onto someone's head.

"Yo. Yo, playa. Wassup?" said a voice. I turned around as he stood on a stoop. His three friends stayed on the steps, sipping forties and sporting their latest bubble coats. "You a-ight? You need something?"

"Nah, man. I'm cool. Thanks," I said, stopping, hoping to strike up a conversation. Bond with the brothers.

" 'I'm cool. Thanks,' " he said, not at all trying to cover his mocking tone. His friends started laughing like Richard Pryor was doing a show. "Yeah, I see. You one of them uppity niggas. Probably get your shit delivered. Look at this motherfucker," he said, turning back to the peanut gallery. "He look like one of them niggas they always have in an ad, peeping out from behind the white boys. Like he don't care they got his ass stuck in the back. 'Just so happy to be here, massa.' Black boy blending."

I smiled, trying to brush off the situation. *That* I was used to, but not this.

"Your name's probably Theo. You a Huxtable?"

"Nah, man. It's not like that," I said, trying to change my voice, deepen it. "My name's Mason."

" 'No. My name's Mason.' "

"Malik," said one of the guys on the stoop. I glanced over at the guy, happy for the interruption. "Give the brother a break."

"Brother? This nigga ain't no brother. You ain't from up here, are you?" asked Malik. I wanted to just walk away but I didn't want to turn my back on him.

"No," I said. "But I'm checking out a place, though."

" 'I'm checking . . .' Nigga, you better head on back downtown. Harlem ain't for you. You too soft." He pushed me hard in the chest and I stumbled back. I couldn't smile anymore. At the end of the street I could see a cop car turning the corner and rolling our way.

"Malik," said one of his friends. "Chill, man. Damn."

"I'm just fucking with this li'l nigga." Malik looked me up and down, then starting laughing. He reached out his hand and I shook it, feeling the calluses on his palm as he slid his hand from mine and headed back to the stoop.

The cop car stopped but the policemen didn't get out, fully aware that their presence was more than enough. "How's it going, fellas?"

"It's all good," said Malik. "Just keeping it real, ain't that right, Theo?"

He changed my name so easily; he saw me as Theo, and as far as he was concerned, that's who I was: a black TV character from the eighties, living in a brownstone, successful parents, beautiful sisters, no troubles in the world. Theo Huxtable, easy as that. "Fine, Officer," I said, using this as an excuse to start walking away. I felt Malik's eyes on me, but I just walked on, hands jammed in my pockets, a slight ache in my chest.

I thought of going back to the ads, back downtown, back to something familiar, but I wasn't going to let one incident stop me. Still a man, in Harlem, I marched on.

My steps weren't as strong as they were before running into Malik and they became even more strained when I turned the corner off of Fifth Avenue onto 120th Street. Standing outside of the town house was a mostly white crowd, all looking attentive, ready to claim the space. I stopped for a moment, nervously twisting my hair; dreading rejection.

Black hair is hard work.

As I stood there it was like Malik had left his friends on the stoop and was standing in front of me, forty in hand, then spitting in my face, "Black boy blending." I crossed the street and went into Marcus Garvey Park. I took off the sweater I'd gotten in Ireland and stuffed it in my backpack. I pulled out my shirt and T-shirt and let the tails hang. There was no way to hide my loafers so I took off my belt and pushed my khakis down as far as they could go without falling off.

The park was hardly a telephone booth and Superman I wasn't, but with a slow swagger I walked toward the group standing outside of the town house like I belonged in the neighborhood and they were mere loiterers. "Wassup?" A few people nodded their heads but didn't say anything. I made my way to the back of the crowd, hoping that being set off from the rest would draw attention to me, praying that on this trip a whale in the distance is more alluring than those circling the boat.

We didn't have to wait long. At four o'clock the front doors of the town house opened. A woman stepped out and my body straightened and I shifted my weight from foot to foot to try to get a better look.

She closed the door and walked down the steps, leisurely as though an aria was ending, the cadenza on its way. She had on a fitted black sweater, a gray ankle-length skirt with a slit up the side, and tied around her shoulders was a light blue cardigan. Her hair was high on her head, as though pulling up her neck, where a strand of pearls pulled it all together.

"Women," she said, looking over our heads. She said it like it was the only word worth saying. "You may leave."

My penis had helped me survive the first cut of the apartment hunt bris and I was thankful for it.

"I gather you boys are here to see me," said the woman, a gleam in her eyes. Her voice was intimate and soothing. Chocolate mocha ice cream. A few men started to leave. I guess it wasn't their cup of black oolong, but I felt like honey ready to melt into the mix. Stir it up.

"You and you," then pointing with eyes only, way in the back toward me, "and you. The rest of you, thank you." She did this with ease, no exuberance, no explanation. It was like I'd called on God and he'd put me on hold, but at least Mahalia Jackson was singing while I waited. I pulled up my sagging pants as I made my way up to the front, stoked to be one of the Yous. I could feel the eyes on me and I loved it. *Who da man? Who da man? How ya like me now?*

"Hello," she said as we stood in the entryway. "I'm Carmen England."

"Richard Downing," said one of the guys, wearing a designer pin-striped suit and spit-shined shoes. He'd gone all out and I started to worry.

"Nice to meet you," said Carmen, then looking at the other guy.

"Scott Franklin," he said. His dark hair was cut short in the back and the sides, but he'd left it full on top. He had huge dimples and couldn't seem to stop smiling.

"A pleasure," said Carmen, then she looked at me. "And you?"

"Ma-Malik," I said, tugging on my pants, slightly slouching, giving aloof. "Malik Randolph."

I instantly felt alive. I didn't care that it wasn't my name, but just saying it made me feel powerful. Assertive. Assured. Just the name alone made me feel as though I could walk down the streets of Harlem without scorn or ridicule; bubble coat on my back, forty-ounce in my hand. If I wasn't going to get the place, it wasn't going to be because I was blending.

"Wassup?" I said, extending my hand to her.

Carmen arched her eyebrow, then said, "Never extend your hand to a lady unless she offers hers first."

I dropped my hand back to my side and started rubbing it against my pant leg, hoping that would salve the sting before it began to swell.

"Sorry."

"Don't be. It's nice to meet you, Mamalik."

"What? Uh, oh," I said, "It's just Malik."

"That's very seventies. Power to the people."

"You know," I said, trying to compete with Scott's smile. "Gotta keep it real."

· · ·

My twists and the way I was wearing my clothes would have made my mother have a fit and it would have even made those at Johnny's Barbershop, an institution in Layton, Louisiana, pause. Though appointments weren't taken at Johnny's, people would line up for hours before the shop opened to be one of the first to take a number.

Clovis was the most skilled barber and always cut my hair. If you wanted any style, Clovis was your man. But he never got to try them fully on my nonthreatening fade.

There was always lively conversation going on, but once the soap operas started, all attention went to the television on top of the "pop" machine. These men were as avid about their "stories" as any woman and were loyal to the CBS lineup. They would talk about when Nikki was a stripper before marrying Victor or when Mrs. Chancler had her first facelift, long before she met Rex, or they'd talk about Billy and his drinking problem. They'd shake their heads at the woes of the television rich.

But whenever I'd walk into the shop they'd want to know what was up with the "Randolph boy." I don't think many of them knew my first name, but they knew, or knew of, my father and I was his son.

One day I was getting a haircut because I was going to Baton Rouge to represent Layton in the Louisiana State Spelling Bee. I'd told Clovis and he made a point to share the news. As usual, the old men sitting in the chairs that lined the wall, beneath the coat hooks and old posters of old hairdos sure to come back, were encouraging.

Clovis finished my cut, put the stinging green rubbing alcohol around the hairline and brushed me down with talc powder. He removed the barber's cloth and I stepped down from the chair, but before I could start to leave, Joe motioned me over.

Blue-eyed Joe was a fixture in the shop. He'd take the lunch orders and phone them in to Marianne's, the soul food joint a few doors down. He also swept up the different textures of hair that had fallen around the base of the chairs, all becoming one.

Black hair is hard work.

The bluish haze coating his left eye was how he got his name. No one knew if he could see out of it and no one ever asked. Mr. Joe never said more than he had to.

He patted the fold-out chair next to him. I sat, but he didn't look at me. He kept looking at the action in the pool hall in the back of the shop.

"Don't ever smile too big when thangs going good for you," said Joe. "We's proud of you here, hear?"

"Yes, sir, Mr. Joe."

"Just know, ever'body in that world out there ain't gonna be like that.

Some people, Colored or other, ain't never gonna want to see no black man looking too happy. Godspeed."

Joe turned away from the pool hall and looked up to the television set. As I opened my mouth he put his hand up to stop me.

As the World Turns was starting.

Carmen showed us the room available for rent. It was small, right across from the kitchen and under the stairs, but a window looked onto the garden. I knew I could work with it.

We followed her back down the hall and into "the parlor." I looked around, taking it all in. The gilt mirror over the mahogany fireplace, the wainscoting, the decanters on the drinks cabinet, the ceiling cornices, the Oriental rugs and the pocket doors that closed off another room. The smell of the old didn't bother me.

She eased down onto the edge of a chair and motioned for us to take a seat. Richard headed for the chair to her right.

"Not in that chair, dear heart," she said. "It may not appear so, but the arm is loose and I can't be bothered to have it mended. I broke it when I was a child. When fine things begin to fall apart, only then do they reveal their true essence. Trust." Richard made his way over and joined us on the sofa.

"So. What is it that you boys do," she said, and after a brief pause, "for a living?"

I listened, getting nervous, as they spoke. Scott was a model, Richard a lawyer. Carmen focused on them with debutante attention and it took everything I had not to start twisting my hair. When they finished she looked at me.

"I don't have a job." I found myself thinking, *Oh, now you wanna tell the truth.* I could feel the sweat huddling in my armpits, ready to fall like rain from a dark cloud on a New Orleans afternoon. "Yet."

Carmen laughed and the other two guys relaxed in their seats, all of us certain that I'd blown my chance.

"I just got to the city a couple of weeks ago," I said, forgetting that I was trying to be cool, trying to be down, trying to turn this dead end into a cul-de-sac. "But you know, I have some leads and I do have enough for the deposit and the first month's rent. As soon as I find a crib I'll focus on the job, but you need shelter." Then against my better judgment I mumbled, "It's hard on a brother out there."

Carmen looked at me for a moment like she was a doctor examining an X ray, trying to see if there was something she missed, seeing if I'd break. "Well then, it's evident to me that you're in need of the place more than these two gentlemen."

"Yes," I said. Victory mine.

"And an excellent winner to boot," said Carmen. I sunk into the sofa. I knew this outburst would make her change her mind. But she smiled and said, "I like that. Modesty is a learned affectation, wouldn't you say?"

Relief.

Carmen got up from her chair and the two guys stood, knowing they had to keep looking.

"It was nice of you to come," she said, like a host at the end of a party. She touched each of them on the back and walked them to the entryway. "You're both fine young men and I'm certain neither of you will have any difficulty finding a place."

I heard the front door close. The sound of the lock made me wonder what I'd gotten myself into. I sat waiting for her to come back into the room, but she didn't. She walked down the hall like she'd forgotten I was there. I wasn't sure what I should do, but I got up and quietly walked to the door and looked down the hall. I didn't see her.

"Ms. England," I said, like being alone in a dark empty house and asking if anyone is there. "Ms. England."

I heard a noise behind me and I jumped. "Please. Call me Carmen," she said, sliding open the pocket doors that separated the parlor from the dining room. She had a bottle of champagne and two flutes. "I suppose we're housemates, which is cause for champers."

"Sounds good," I said, walking back to the sofa. I sat then stood, trying to figure out which was best. I decided to stand. She opened the bottle and when the cork flew off she screamed like it was New Year's Eve, then poured for two. She walked toward me until she was just a few inches away and handed me a flute. "Cheers."

"Cheers," I said, focusing on the flute like it held a magic potion.

She took her finger and placed it under my chin, then lifted my head. "You should always look in the eyes of the person you're toasting. If you can't have a connection with the person with whom you're toasting, then you really shouldn't toast."

"Oh, I'm sorry." I was nervous, certain I was doing everything wrong and would soon be back on the hunt.

"Don't be." She moved in a little closer. "Let's try it again. To us," she said.

"To us."

She took her first sip and this time I held her gaze for as long as I could. The champagne had warmed in my mouth before I was able to swallow. I moved away and walked back over to the sofa and sat down. She walked around the room as though looking at everything for the first time. Her champagne flute swung in her hand like a pendulum and I was ready to be hypnotized. I watched every move: the gleam of leg peeping out of the slit of her skirt; the red of her painted toes peeking out of her shoes; the way her tennis bracelet slid down her forearm when she raised the flute to her mouth; the lipstick kiss on the rim. I watched and she didn't seem to mind.

She picked up the champagne bottle from the mantel, refilled her glass, then walked over to me and topped off mine. I watched as the bubbles reached the top of the glass but refused to fall over. She put the bottle on the coffee table. I could see my mother coming over and picking it up. *That's why we have coasters.* I took a swallow of the champagne, trying to shake the image of my mother out of my mind. Carmen walked back to her chair and finally sat. She leaned back and crossed her legs, letting her arms rest on the chair's. I sat back on the sofa, more for support than comfort. I was trying to think of something to say, but I didn't have to.

"I don't have staff here, but you should know that I do have a cleaning lady, Rosita, who comes in once a week. The way she acts, one would think she owns the place. I make every effort to see that I'm not home when she arrives." Carmen took a deep breath, and when she released it, she said, "This maison de ville has been in my family since Harlem was chic, lost its chic, then became chic again, and that's a damn long time. Uptown real estate is becoming popular and people are starting to pay cute money for properties. 'Gentrification.' Such a nice-sounding word. Much better than 'Take your shit and get.' "

I started to relax; the champagne didn't hurt. "You know," I said, "I didn't think I had a shot at the place."

"Really. You were my favorite from the beginning."

I perked up a bit. "Why's that?" I asked, reeling out the line for an ego pat.

"Just a hunch. I can't quite put a finger on it, but I saw something familiar in you."

"Gotta keep it real."

"Yes. I believe you mentioned that."

"And one hand does wash the other," I said, pulling out the race card.

"Indeed. But two hands wash the face." That almost knocked me through the sofa, but I took it and slowly eased back. "But if you must know—" She stopped then said, "What's your name again?"

There it was. I'd forgotten that little detail. My grip tightened around the champagne flute. I thought of coming clean, telling her the truth. But I was in and I wanted to savor it. Wanted to live in Harlem. Wanted to experience her. I ran my hand over my twists and those words came back to me: *Black boy blending.*

"Malik. Malik Randolph."

"Yes, Malik. Right. You see, the model was definitely eye candy and would have been a nice bauble on my arm, yet white boys that age can be gorgeous one day and ass-ugly the next. So a proper five-to-ten-year scan is always necessary. Trust."

I felt drunk, but not just from the "champers." She downed the rest of her flute, then held it out toward me. I picked up the bottle, walked over and refilled her glass.

"You're too kind," she said, touching my forearm. I felt the hairs rise under my shirt. I walked back to the sofa and put the bottle on the coaster, then I moved it, trying to stay in the moment, remain cool, appear at ease. If she didn't mind a water stain, why should I?

"As for the lawyer," she said. "He's probably just out of school. Columbia, perhaps, which means he's nothing more than a well-dressed gofer. He's definitely from a good Northeastern family because the firm he mentioned rarely lets outsiders roast marshmallows at their fire.

"In a few years he will have moved up in the firm, and as this is a rather small town, I will more than likely run across him again, socially. He'll pretend to forget his experience here today, but will be a good little soldier and play nice, realizing that I may prove helpful in the future. And even if he's engaged to some poor girl who will have done more than just put in her time for his grandmother's ring, he'll still want to fuck me."

I laughed. I had to. I'd always found something sexy about a woman who could say "fuck" without hesitation, claiming it, owning it.

"You are a sweetie," she said, getting up and walking over to the sofa. She sat down. I was about to move over, but I caught myself and eased back into the cushions, opening my legs wide and placing my arm along its top like I imagined Malik would do. *Just chilling.*

"You're a Southerner, aren't you?"

"Yeah," I said. "I'm from—"

"Wait. Let me guess." She placed her index finger behind her ear as if trying to pick up the radio waves of my accent. "Mississippi!" Her answer wasn't presented as a question so I was more than happy to let her be right. Why not? If I could be Malik, I could be from Mississippi. It was a sister state.

"Good ear."

"Never question a woman's skills," she said with a self-assured glow. "Southerners are so respectful and well behaved. Everyone knows their place. Lovely."

My mood suddenly turned and I began to feel uncomfortable. I felt defensive, but I forced a smile. My life had been built on staying in my place, not rocking the boat. But I wasn't in the South. I was in New York, in Harlem, in a house with Carmen, trying to change the subject, trying to change.

"Thanks for the hookup," I said. "I really needed a place and you don't have to worry about the rent."

"I'm not worried about that. I bet you're a hard little worker bee. We like that," she said. She put her hand lightly on my leg and I flinched. She smiled. "I think it'll work out wonderfully."

Carmen again held up her empty glass and I picked up the champagne bottle and refilled it. The last drop went to her.

"Move in when you like. The key is on the hook near the door," she said, standing. "Be a dear and let yourself out. It's time for my nap."

She walked out of the room and started up the stairs. I sat there for a while longer, almost like I was waiting for permission to get up, be dismissed, waiting for direction from Carmen England.

My Girl Mona

BY CRYSTAL WILKINSON

He's short and bald, round like a black snowman but handsome. He's my head doctor, the third psychiatrist I've seen this year. The doctor leans back in his soft green leather chair and brings the tips of his fingers together like he's wise. He's not the smiley type. He nods and that's my cue to start talking.

Mona is forty-three and still got the kind of body that makes brothers act a fool, I say.

I look at Doctor like, *You know what I'm saying?* Doctor clears his throat.

We was sitting in that little diner off US-150 catching up like we do once a month, I tell him. I was sipping my 7-Up trying not to think about how much better Mona looks than me. More kids, more husbands, but she still looks like she did in junior high. Dark skin, perky titties, a waist that curves in tight then fans out into hourglass hips for miles.

The doctor says I'm having panic attacks, I tell Mona, and I go through the rigmarole of symptoms: heart flutters, dizzy spells, the sweats, an odd feeling of otherworldliness. When I say *otherworldliness*, Mona looks at me like she's being held hostage, but I keep talking. She takes a toke off her third cigarette, which takes away from her good looks. I've heard brothers say that about her, you know, wrinkling up their noses like smoking a cancer stick sends Mona from fine to ugly that quick.

You know what I mean? I say to Doctor not as a real question but just to be saying it. He just nods like he knows.

The waitress, who is so skinny her collarbones show through her tight-knit blouse, freshens Mona's coffee with a trembling hand like the pot is full of rocks. She looks at Mona with an eyebrow raised. Mona with all her flash is a fish out of water in Stanford now.

Mona's always been a part of my life, I say to Doctor. I still see us as little girls sometimes even now when we get together. Doesn't seem that long ago when we played down by the old creamery or recited our memorized verses in unison in front of God and everybody in the church, but it's been almost thirty years now. I was the everyday girl—not bony, not fat, not dark, not light—the girl who carried her opinions in her neck. Right here, I say to him and press my fingers into the center of my throat, a big old knot.

You were in training for panic attacks even then, Doctor says.

Doctor, she was something, I say. Mona was the one who could draw every eye across a room.

Back when everybody was trying to have that perfect Angela Davis fro, Mona opted for the Farrah Fawcett look even before it caught on. She had long hair for a dark sister—down past her shoulders. Mona was always trying to shellac her skin with lightener, but I loved her walnut-hull brown. She was the first black girl in Stanford to be prom queen. Mona was always first. The first to get her period, the first to sprout butt and tits, the first to "do it." If Doctor had been a light-skinned brother or a white man, he would have turned red.

The summer I turned fourteen, Junior, my husband to this day, was the one boy we could tolerate. He was the kind of boy who was all-boy but could hang out with the girls without grabbing his private place. He wasn't like all them other nappy-heads who played kick ball under the streetlight. The girls would sit on the curb in our halter-tops and hot pants, trading pullout posters from *Right On!* magazine—swapping Ricky Sylvers for Michael Jackson and listening to the Ohio Players on Mona's eight track. When the game was over, the boys turned their attention to us. We all stayed out until our mamas called us home. Or until the mosquitoes started biting so hard that we all would run home itching, whelps rising up all over our little hot bodies.

That year it seemed like me and Mona spent every day of our lives wondering what it would be like to be kissed by a boy. We watched our mamas' stories on TV and read the dirty parts of every romance book we could find. We wondered what "doing it" really was, even though neither of us wanted the label that came with the girls who let boys touch. But we already knew there were girls like Jeanette Stokes, who actually went into one of the un-locked cars parked along the streeet and let a boy untie her top so he could see her breasts. And she let one of the boys she really liked finger her in the dark. The ironic thing about it though was that even through all that, Jeanette Stokes was still a virgin when we graduated from high school but Mona wasn't.

Doctor catches me remembering, staring off into empty space that makes up my yesterdays and then I come on back.

Through the smoke cloud, Mona strokes her red acrylic nails, extends them out like crawdad claws to pick up her knife and cuts her chicken sandwich, I continue telling Doctor. She clears her throat and fidgets with the collar of her blouse, then smoothes invisible wrinkles from her skirt. I know she can't wait for me to hush, but I keep on talking like my life depends on it.

Imagine that, I tell her. Hell, I've never had anything like this before. Junior had to take me to the emergency room the first time it happened. I thought I was having a heart attack. I've always been healthy. No, never had anything like this before. Not when cancer took Grandmamma or when they fired me up at the factory. They said it was a permanent layoff. Not even when Junior messed around on me with that white woman.

That bit of juice gets Mona's attention and I stop talking for just a second before I start back up, timing it just right, making sure it's not long enough for her to jump in.

Oh, I guess shit happens, I say. Guess I'm getting older. Right at that moment, as always, I'm trying to figure out on my own exactly why Mona's been my girl all these years.

And why do you think that is? Doctor asks me, leaning forward like he's getting close to an answer.

Don't know, I say to him, It's a long story.

So I can see that I am making Mona nervous, I continue telling him. I'm waiting for Mona to chime in with a friend's concern or at least to tell me how sorry she is to hear about my nervous condition but she don't. I'm waiting to hear, *What are you going to do? Is there anything I can do? Can they give you something for it?* But her mascara-rimmed eyes are meddling with the people eating in the booths around us. Flirting with Mr. Taylor, who's stuffing a hamburger in his mouth, mustard running down his chin. Nodding hello to Callie Sumner, who owns the restaurant. We went to high school with Callie. She saunters by with a large orange tray filled with hamburgers and fries held high above her head, her flabby arms flopping in her own wind.

I guess we are all getting old. Getting fat. Mona's not even listening to me. When she looks back in my direction, I switch subjects and tell her about Junior's teaching job up at the middle school. He is one of the first black teachers in the county.

Did you know that, Doctor?

No, I didn't that's interesting.

I tell her about Daddy's trip to the hospital with appendicitis. I finish by telling her about my daughter, Shauna, getting caught shoplifting in Lexington.

She's just driving us crazy, I say. We had to go up there and get a hotel for two days to get it all straightened out.

But all of these are things Mona probably already knows from the newspaper or the grapevine. Nobody's business is sacred in a small town.

I can see that I've got Doctor's full attention. He's looking at me starry-eyed like a boy listening to a tall tale.

By the end of that summer all of us girls had at least been kissed, I tell him. Even Candy Patton, the quietest and most religious among us, prayed for seven straight days not to go to hell because she let Peanut rub her ass. It's all right, they're married now.

I should have said *hind end* in front of Doctor but I didn't. I was comfortable, like we were old friends.

Somehow we had willed the girlness out of our bodies, I say. Instead of playing hide-and-go-seek, or hopscotch, or Chinese jump rope, or watching the boys play kick ball, in the shadows against somebody's daddy's Plymouth or Nova, we paired up with the boys and kissed. We turned our heads to the side, puckered and kept our lips shut tight so the boys could keep their germs to themselves.

I can't help but to start laughing.

Anything else? Doctor says to me crossing his expensive britches legs and adjusting his self, wide in the chair, where I can see the folds of his crotch and not cracking a smile.

What do you remember most about this? Tell me everything, Doctor says and reaches over and squeezes my wrist like that's a comfort. And it sure nuff is.

Me and Mona named ourselves the kissing experts after seeing my brother, Kiki, and his girlfriend, Ina, on the couch, I say. We crouched outside the doorway of the living room, a place my mother never let us go into. The living room that was always ten times cleaner than the rest of the house, where the antiques and the good coffee table and the glass-topped lamp stood. The centerpiece was the white couch, still covered in plastic, that Daddy bought for Mama one year with the income-tax money. That living room was the show-off room only reserved for company, especially out-of-town company. It was the one thing my country mother had that rivaled anything belonging to the relatives who would ease back home from Cincinnati driving their new Cadillacs or Bonnevilles.

Kiki met Ina up at the Lexington Mall and drove his green Impala up to see her every weekend. When he brought her home to meet us, Mama told me and Mona to stay out from underfoot and let Kiki have his privacy. But me and Mona were looking through a crack in the door to the living room when Kiki and Ina kissed so much, their tongues going in and out of each others' mouths, that they looked hungry, like two starved people feasting on Christmas dinner. Me and Mona looked at each other horrified at first, but we were also looking when Kiki's hand rubbed all over Ina like mad and disappeared under her green paisley culottes. We took notes in our diaries and secured our secrets with the turn of the little gold diary keys we wore around our necks.

Now we know how it works, Mona says in a whisper, clutching her diary to her chest, her eyes fluttering up toward the ceiling like a prayer had been answered. I nodded, yes, without speaking a word. Stunned. Never knowing my brother, who I deemed Big Nasty for not lifting the seat on the toilet, the one who denied me his barbecue potato chips or candy sticks, the brother who tried to coax me into washing his funky laundry, was capable of making a girl moan and smile the way Ina did.

Later that day, Kiki walked hand-in-hand with Ina all over Stanford. Ina with her fashion-model looks and in-style clothes and Kiki with his football-player muscles were a sight to see. Everybody saw them walking down Water to Maxwell Street on their way to Carter's Grocery for ice cream, their perfect eight-inch Afros side by side like two black moons.

While they were gone, me and Mona pilfered Ina's purse and claimed her Satin Dreams lip gloss for our own. We shared it as a token of our sexual orientation. In secret we slathered it on our lips and tried to cut our eyes and walk with our hips rocking the way Ina did. We even talked Kiki into driving us to the Lexington Mall one weekend so we could buy ourselves some wooden high-heeled shoes just like the ones that Ina wore with her hip hugger blue jeans. Up until the time Kiki and Ina broke up, me and Mona would stare at her and follow her around when she was in town, hoping to get hold of some of her twenty-year-old womanly secrets.

I laugh and Doctor smiles, then catches himself and takes the smile back quick. I guess he thinks he's not being professional. I'm wishing he would just come off this for a minute and just be the black man that a sister girl needs to share her problems with and not *the doctor*.

So anyway, I sat to Doctor. I know Mona's been waiting for the conversation to open up one fraction so she can come in full force and fill it to the brim with her, so I ask her how she's doing.

Well, she says, running her fingers through her hair, then patting it down in the front and pursing her lips together to refresh her lipstick, I'm doing fine. No drama, she says.

But of course that was just warm-up talk; with Mona there's always drama. Soon Mona is smiling and gesturing wildly across the table. I listen as she sifts through child support and alimony, great sex and the kids like she's prom queen again—fake smiling so wide her unsightly dark gums show. It's an unflattering look and I catch myself relishing in the snickers that Mona doesn't notice coming from two lanky brown girls who are drinking milkshakes across from us. Look at that old lady trying to be hip, is what I'm sure they're saying. Well maybe "hip" is not the word they use these days.

Mona doesn't seem like she's from Stanford at all anymore. She has swallowed her small-town twang and is speaking in some generic tone that doesn't even say Lexington. I wonder how she could have moved only fifty-miles north of here and be such an outlander. Her clothes are young—a bright blue blouse with enough opened buttons to show a peek of the black bra underneath, a tight black skirt that I can see only the beginnings of above the table, her legs are crossed and one of her white girlish platform shoes is bobbing up and down into the aisle while she talks.

Doctor, Mona outgrew me in high school. I just looked up one day and she was a younger version of our mamas and I was still a girl. It wasn't her body so much, which had blossomed in junior high, but something else. She was suddenly able to gold a gaze with a man without giggling or looking away. I first saw her use it on my brother, Kiki, who was twenty-five at the time.

I stop talking.

Continue, Doctor says. Interesting, he says like I'm a bug under a microscope. And so I keep on with my story like I have to.

Mona stayed over one Saturday night our junior year, I continue enjoying Doctor's full attention. We had planned to stay up all night, cornrow each other's hair and try on new makeup, but Mona spent the whole night sitting in my bed, straddle-legged in her baby doll pajamas, trying to hold my brother's attention as he walked by the room. She told me she had to use the bathroom, but soon I heard her in Kiki's room.

Get out of here girl, I heard Kiki say through the walls.

But soon their voices were lowered and I could hear the familiar squeaking of the bed and the grunts and snorts that Kiki made when he would sneak girls over. I expected silence from Mona. Thought she'd try to protect me from knowing, but the moaning sounds she made were so loud that I feared that my parents would come to investigate.

Later, I heard water running in the bathroom, but Mona still brought the smell of sex with her into my bedroom.

Y'all out of toilet paper, she said, never saying a word about screwing my brother.

I stared at her and rolled my eyes.

What? She said.

What you think? I said.

Didn't nothing happen, she said. But I knew she was lying.

After that I think Mona hoped Kiki would prance her around like he had Ina, but when Mona was around, Kiki would sull up and find a reason to rev up his Impala and be gone. I could tell she was hurt by it all, but she never let on. Even as close as me and Mona were, there were a million miles between us.

Keep going, Doctor says prodding out my lifetime.

A short time after that, we went to the skating rink in Danville. I watched Mona skate right over to Junior and rub his chest. Under the black lights and the strobe flashing with the music playing a slow song, Junior looked as helpless as I felt when Mona kissed him full on the lips. Junior, who was supposed to be my boyfriend, followed her around for weeks, lingering at my locker, talking to me, but waiting on Mona to come by. It was clear that Mona really didn't want Junior, that he was being used for target practice and looking back, I want to think that she didn't mean me any harm. That she was just testing herself, trying to grab back something lost. Junior tells me to this day that it was nothing.

I married you didn't I, he says. Leave the past in the past.

When he messed around on me, I barely gave him a chance to apologize before I took him back.

Doctor says I should have expressed my feelings.

Later that night when Junior holds me in his arms I will get tickled about that. If I had expressed my feelings, Junior would still have a skillet mark on his head.

What you laughing at? Junior will ask me and I will say, Nothing.

Ever wish you married Mona? I ask him sometimes.

Woman, he says back, we were teenagers ain't you ever gonna give up on that?

Then he kisses me and we make love. But even then with him on top of me I am less assured. Feel like I'm a second place trophy.

I slow down my story to make sure Doctor is still following me.

So when Mona says, *Darling, I have a blessed life,* like she's the Gabor sister from *Green Acres* or some other made-for-TV white woman, my heart pounds out of my chest and sweat pours down my back. My chest is closing in and I'm shaking like a leaf. I am sure that any moment somebody in the restaurant will notice my predicament and holler for Callie to call the life squad. I'm waiting for that shift of time when Mona leaves her own world for just a second and notices that I'm in trouble. But nobody notices. All the eyes in the place are darting towards Mona. I don't say a world and just ride that one out.

Good! Doctor says, louder than I think he means too. You have to teach yourself to do that, to speak to your rational self and as you say, ride it out.

Mona's voice dims to the humming the deep freezer makes when I'm ironing clothes in the basement.

I'm not dying. I'm not dying, I say to myself over and over. It's just another spell. It's just another spell.

In a matter of minutes that seem to draw out for a lifetime, everything leaves then becomes clear again.

In the parking lot, after we've parted, Mona turns, waves to me and hollers, *See you next time. I'll let you know about the wedding,* she says and winks.

There is no *I hope you feel better* or *let me know how you're doing.* I wave back and watch her heels clicking across the asphalt toward her Volvo.

I couldn't say anything I had on my mind to say, I tell Doctor. I feel tears rising up in my neck.

I see, Doctor says, knocking his posed fingers against his forehead. You did well though, he says, I think you are getting better. You are gaining control. And you look so good today, he adds, well rested.

But I know he's thinking I'm screwed up in the head. He's a brother too, which makes it worse. There is so much more I want to say. So much more I want to know. I want to ask him if he's married, and if he is would he cheat on his wife. I am wondering if he would find Mona attractive. I want to ask him if he's hungry. If he wants to go get a bite to eat just to talk some more. I want to bury my head into his shoulder and just cry but I can't, I've already told him too much. In a few minutes he will write me a prescription, shake my hand, and schedule me another appointment. But before that moment he gives me a smile. A genuine smile that I snuggle in and feel clear down to my toes. And I am waiting with hope for what comes next.

About the Contributors

FAITH ADIELE has received the Dorothy & Granville Hicks Residency in Literature from the Yaddo Corporation, as well as fellowships from the MacDowell Colony, Virginia Center for the Creative Arts, the Ragdale Foundation, and the Banff Centre for the Arts. Additional honors include the first Willard R. Espy Award in Nonfiction and the PEN New England Emerging Writer Award. Faith divides her time between Minneapolis, Minnesota, and Iowa City, Iowa, where she is currently enrolled in The Writers Workshop and the Nonfiction Writing Program at the University of Iowa. She is at work on a memoir.

JEFFERY RENARD ALLEN is the author of the novel *Rails Under My Back* and *Harbors and Spirits* and received his Ph.D. in English from the University of Illinois in Chicago.

UNOMA N. AZUAH received the Hellman/Hammett grant for her writings on women's issues as well as the 2000 Leonard Trawick creative writing award from the English Department at Cleveland State University, where she got her MA in English. Ms. Azuah served as the secretary of the Association of Nigerian Authors (ANA Lagos), and as the publicity secretary of Women Writers of Nigeria (WRITA).

NICOLE BAILEY-WILLIAMS is also the author of *A Little Piece of Sky*, a novel that spent two months in the #1 bestselling position for coming-of-age novels on Amazon.com. In addition to being an English teacher with the Ewing Township Board of Education, she is a freelance writer and co-host of *The Literary Review*, a book review show which airs on WDAS (1480 AM). She writes for national publications like *Publishers Weekly*, *Black Issues Book Review*, and *QBR (Quarterly Black Review)*, and she was a contributing writer in the *Notable Black American Men* reference book. She currently resides in Mercer County, New Jersey, with her husband, Gregory.

STEVEN BARNES, the author of fifteen novels including *Lion's Blood* and as many teleplays, has been nominated for both the Hugo and Cable

Ace awards. Mr. Barnes lives in Washington with his wife, author Tananarive Due, and his daughter.

AMY DUBOIS BARNETT is editor-in-chief of *Honey* magazine and an award-winning journalist. Previously, Barnett spent two years at *Essence* magazine, where she oversaw five sections: Food, Home, Entertaining, Travel, and Parenting. She also top-edited the magazine's fashion stories and edited features. Prior to that, Barnett was Fashion and Beauty Features Editor at *Essence* magazine. She is the recipient of the Hurston/Wright Foundation Award for fiction writing and is currently working on a novel.

KAREN GRIGSBY BATES is the author of *Plain Brown Wrapper* (an Alex Powell Novel) and coauthor of *Basic Black: Home Training for Modern Times.* She is also a contributing columnist for the op-ed pages of the *Los Angeles Times,* has written for *Vogue,* the *New York Times, Quarterly Black Review of Books, Essence, Emerge,* and other publications. She is a correspondent on National Public Radio's "The Tavis Smiley Show" and her commentaries frequently appear on NPR's "All Things Considered."

BERTICE BERRY, Ph.D., is an inspirational speaker, sociologist, and former standup comedian. She is the author of four works of nonfiction and the novels *Redemption Song, The Haunting of Hip-Hop,* and *Jim and Louella's Homemade Heart-Fix Remedy.* She lives in San Diego, California.

MICHELE ANDREA BOWEN, the author of *Church Folk,* graduated from the University of North Carolina at Chapel Hill with master's degrees in both history and public health. She lives in North Carolina.

CONNIE BRISCOE is the author of *P.G. County, Sisters & Lovers, Big Girls Don't Cry,* and *A Long Way from Home.* She is the former managing editor of the *American Annals of the Deaf* at Gallaudet University and has been hearing-impaired for most of her adult life. She lives in Ellicott City, Maryland.

LORI BRYANT-WOOLRIDGE, the author of the novel *Read Between the Lies,* is a veteran of the television broadcasting business. She spent seven years at ABC and has worked at PBS and Black Entertainment Television. She has won an Emmy Award for Individual Achievement in Writing.

CRIS BURKS earned her MFA in creative writing at Columbia College in Chicago, where she taught fiction writing for several years. Her poetry and short stories have appeared in several literary publications, including

Shooting Star Review and *Short Fiction by Women*. She lives in Sacramento, California, and is the author of *SilkyDreamGirl.*

BEBE MOORE CAMPBELL is the author of three acclaimed novels: *Your Blues Ain't Like Mine,* which won an NAACP Image Award for Literature, *What You Owe Me,* and the New York *Times* bestsellers *Brothers and Sisters* and *Singing in the Comeback Choir.* She lives in Los Angeles.

LORENE CARY is the author of *Black Ice,* a memoir, and the novels *Pride* and *The Price of a Child.* She teaches writing at the University of Pennsylvania and lives in Philadelphia with her husband and two children.

VERONICA CHAMBERS, a former editor at the New York *Times Magazine* is the author of the memoir *Mama's Girl.* Currently, Veronica is a cultural writer for *Newsweek.* She is a frequent contributor to both the New York *Times Book Review* and the Los Angeles *Times Book Review,* and author of a book about filmmaker John Singleton, *Poetic Justice: Filmmaking in South Central.* She is also the author of two children's books, *Amistad Rising: The Battle for Freedom* and *Marisol and Magdalena.* She is in the early stages of other fiction projects.

MAXINE CLAIR is the author of the novel *October Suite* and *Rattlebone,* a collection of short stories, which won the *Chicago Tribune's* Heartland Prize for fiction, among other awards. She is also a Guggenheim Fellow.

PEARL CLEAGE is the author of the novels *I Wish I Had a Red Dress* and *What Looks Like Crazy on an Ordinary Day* as well as *Mad at Miles: A Black Woman's Guide to Truth* and *Deals with the Devil and Other Reasons to Riot.* She is an accomplished playwright and a cofounder of the literary magazine *Catalyst.* Ms. Cleage lives in Atlanta with her husband.

J. CALIFORNIA COOPER is the author of *The Future Has a Past* and five other collections of short stories, including *Homemade Love,* winner of the 1989 American Book Award, and the novels *The Wake of the Wind, Family,* and *In Search of Satisfaction.* She lives in northern California.

DANA CRUM is a journalist amd poet who lives in Harlem where he graduated with an MFA. Crum has built an impressive résumé as a freelance writer. Since getting his first big break in the urban magazine *The Source,* Crum has successfully made a name for himself in both commercial and underground syndication.

EDWIDGE DANTICAT is the author of *After the Dance* and two novels, *The Farming of Bones* and *Breath, Eyes, Memory*. *Krik? Krak!*, her collection of stories, was nominated for a National Book Award. Critical acclaim and awards for her first novel, *Breath, Eyes, Memory*, included a Granta Regional Award for the Best Young American Novelists, a Pushcart Prize, and fiction awards from *Essence* and *Seventeen* magazines.

R. ERICA DOYLE's fiction has appeared in *Blithe House Quarterly*. She has published poems and articles in *Callalloo, Ms., Best American Poetry 2001*, and *Black Issues Book Review*, among other venues.

TANANARIVE DUE is the author of the novels *The Living Blood, The Black Rose, My Soul to Keep*, and *The Between. Freedom in the Family*, a book written with her mother, Patricia Stephens Due, will be published in 2003. Tananarive Due has a BS in journalism from Northwestern University and an MA in English literature from the University of Leeds, England, where she specialized in Nigerian literature as a Rotary Foundation Scholar.

DAVID ANTHONY DURHAM is the author of *Gabriel's Story* and *A Walk Through Darkness*. He was born in New York City and spent his formative years in Trinidad, his parents' homeland. He received a BA and MFA from the University of Maryland and won the Zora Neale Hurston/Richard Wright Fiction Award in 1992. Durham, along with his wife and children, divides his time between Scotland and the United States.

PATRICIA ELAM is the author of *Breathing Room*. Her fiction and nonfiction have been published in the Washington *Post, Essence, Emerge, Newsday*, and in anthologies such as *Fathers' Songs* and *New Stories from the South*. A winner of the O. Henry Award, she has been a commentator for National Public Radio, NBC News, CNN, and the BBC. She lives in Washington, D.C.

PERCIVAL EVERETT is a professor of English at the University of Southern California and the author of fourteen books, including *Glyph, Frenzy, Watershed*, and *Suder*. He lives in Los Angeles.

ROBERT FLEMING, a former award-winning reporter at the *New York Daily News*, is the author of *The Wisdom Of The Elders, The African American Writer's Handbook, Havoc After Dark: Tales of Terror*, and the editor of *After Hours: A Collection of Erotic Writing by Black Men*. His poetry, essays, and fiction have appeared in numerous periodicals and books, such as

Brotherman, UpSouth, Sacred Fire, Brown Sugar, and *Dark Matter.* He lives in New York City.

ARTHUR FLOWERS is the author of two novels, *De Mojo Blues* and *Another Good Loving Blues.* He is a cofounder of the New Renaissance Writers Guild.

THOMAS GLAVE is the author of *Whose Song? And Other Stories.* Voted a "Writer on the Verge" in June 2000's the *Village Voice Literary Supplement,* he has won many writing awards, among them the prestigious O. Henry Prize. He is only the second gay black writer, after James Baldwin, to claim that honor. A 1993 honors graduate of Bowdoin College and a graduate of Brown University, he traveled as a Fulbright Scholar in 1998–99 to Jamaica, where he studied Jamaican historiography and Jamaican-Caribbean intellectual and literary traditions. Glave has been published and praised in many prestigious literary journals and his work has appeared in various anthologies. Born in the Bronx, New York, and raised there and in Kingston, Jamaica. He is assistant professor of English at the State University of New York, Binghamton.

MARITA GOLDEN is the author of nine works of fiction and nonfiction, including her memoir, *Migrations of the Heart,* and the bestselling books *Long Distance Life* and *Saving Our Sons.* Her most recent novel is *The Edge of Heaven.* Marita Golden serves as president of The Hurston/Wright Foundation.

JEWELLE GOMEZ is an activist, teacher, arts administrator, and literary critic. A transplanted Bostonian, she has lived in New York for twenty years, most recently in Brooklyn. She is the author of *The Gilda Stories.*

E. LYNN HARRIS is a former IBM computer sales executive and a graduate of the University of Arkansas at Fayetteville. He is the author of eight previous novels: *A Love of My Own, Any Way the Wind Blows, Not a Day Goes By, Abide with Me, If This World Were Mine, This Too Shall Pass, Just As I Am,* and *Invisible Life.* In 1996 and 2002 *Just As I Am* and *Any Way the Wind Blows* were named Novel of the Year by the Blackboard African American Bestsellers, Inc. *If This World Were Mine* won the James Baldwin Award for Literary Excellence. In 2000 and 2001 Harris was named one of the fifty-five "Most Intriguing African Americans" by *Ebony* and inducted into the Arkansas Black Hall of Fame. In 2002, Harris was included in *Savoy* magazine's "100 Leaders and Heroes in Black America." Harris divides his time between New York City and Atlanta, Georgia.

DAVID HAYNES is the author of a number of books including *All American Dream Dolls*, *Somebody Else's Mama*, and *Right By My Side*, which was a winner in the 1992 Minnesota Voices Project and was selected by the American Library Association as one of 1994's best books for young adults. Two of Haynes's stories have been recorded for the National Public Radio series *Selected Shorts*. In 1996 Haynes was named by *Granta* magazine as one of the best young American novelists. Haynes is at work on his next novel, *The Majordomo's Daughter*.

RAVI HOWARD is a graduate of the MFA Creative Writing Program at the University of Virginia in Charlottesville. A native of Montgomery, Alabama, Ravi's winning story *Like Trees, Walking* was inspired by the 1981 lynching of Michael Donald by the Ku Klux Klan. Howard is at work on the novel *Like Trees Walking*.

BRIAN KEITH JACKSON is the author of *The Queen of Harlem*, *Walking Through Mirrors*, and *The View from Here*. Jackson has received fellowships from Art Matters, the Jerome Foundation, and the Millay Colony for the Arts. *The View from Here* won the American Library Association Literary Award for First Fiction from the Black Caucus of America. Jackson lives in Harlem.

MITCHELL JACKSON is a native or Portland, Oregon. He received a BS in Speech Communications and an MA in creative writing from Portland State University. Jackson, is a former associate producer for two network affiliates in Portland.

SANDRA JACKSON-OPOKU is the author of *Hot Johnny* and *The River Where Blood Is Born*, which won the Black Caucus of the American Library Association Award for Fiction in 1998. Jackson-Opoku has received several honors and awards, including a National Endowment for the Arts Fellowship and two Gwendolyn Brooks Poet Laureate Awards.

KENJI JASPER is the author of the novels *Dakota Grand* and *Dark*. His work has appeared in *Vibe*, *Essence*, *The Source*, and other publications. A native of Washington, D.C., and a graduate of Morehouse College, he now lives in Brooklyn.

YOLANDA JOE is the author of the novels *This Just In*, *Bebe's By Golly Wow*, *He Say*, *She Say*, and *Falling Leaves of Ivy*. She also writes mysteries under the name Ardella Garland. Joe is a native of Chicago and received her

MS from the Columbia School of Journalism in New York. After returning to Chicago, she began working in news radio for CBS, then switched to television news and worked as a writer/producer for a decade before beginning a full-time writing career.

MAT JOHNSON is the author of *Drop*. He was a recipient of the Thomas J. Watson Fellowship, and received his MFA from Columbia University. He now lives in Harlem, where he's working on and setting his second novel.

R.M. JOHNSON is the author of the novels *Father Found* and *The Harris Men*. He lives in Chicago.

EDWARD P. JONES's debut collection of short stories, *Lost in the City: Stories* was nominated for the National Book Award in 1992 and won the PEN/Hemingway Foundation Award for best first fiction.

TAYARI JONES is the author of the novel *Leaving Atlanta*. She is a native of Atlanta, Georgia.

AGYMAH KAMAU is the author of *Flickering Shadows* and *Pictures of a Dying Man*. He is originally from Barbados.

MICHAEL KAYODE lives in Washington, D.C., where he is at work on a novel.

VICTOR D. LAVALLE is the author of *Slapboxing with Jesus*, a collection of stories, and the novel *The Ecstatic*. He graduated from Cornell University with a degree in English and received his MFA in Fiction from Columbia University. He has been a fellow at the Fine Arts Work Center in Provincetown, Massachusetts. Currently he is at work on his first novel.

HELEN ELAINE LEE is the author of the novels *Water Marked* and *The Serpent's Gift*. She teaches in the Program in Writing and Humanistic Studies at MIT. Educated at Harvard College and Harvard Law School, Lee won rave reviews and a BCALA First Novel Award for *The Serpent's Gift*. She lives in the Boston area.

WILLIAM HENRY LEWIS is the author of a collection of stories, *In the Arms of Our Elders*, and his work has appeared in numerous publications, including *The Best American Short Stories 1996*.

CHRISTINE LINCOLN is the author of *Sap Rising*. Lincoln was born and raised in Baltimore. At age thirty-four, she graduated from Washington College and was awarded the school's Sophie Kerr Prize, an event that was covered by the New York *Times* and the Washington *Post*.

BERNICE L. MCFADDEN was born, raised, and currently lives in Brooklyn, New York. In 1997, Ms. McFadden quit her job and dedicated seven months to rewriting the novel that would become *Sugar*. McFadden is the author of three novels, the national bestsellers *Sugar* and *The Warmest December*, and *This Bitter Earth*. The trade paperback edition of *The Warmest December* was published in January 2002.

TERRY MCMILLAN is the author of *Mama, Disappearing Acts*, and the bestsellers *Waiting to Exhale, How Stella Got Her Groove Back*, and *A Day Late and a Dollar Short*. She is also the editor of the groundbreaking anthology *Breaking Ice*.

WALTER MOSLEY is the author of the acclaimed Easy Rawlins series, *Blue Light*, and *RL's Dream*, and two collections of stories featuring the character Socrates Fortlow: *Always Outnumbered, Always Outgunned*, for which he received the Anisfield-Wold Award, and *Walkin' the Dog*. He was born in Los Angeles and lives in New York.

ANIKA NAILAH is the author of *Free: And Other Stories*. Nailah is the director of Books of Hope, a program that encourages young people to write and self-publish their own books. Her stories have appeared in several African American newspapers, including *Reunion* and *Flare*. She lives in Massachusetts.

GLORIA NAYLOR is the author of *The Women of Brewster Place, Linden Hills, Mama Day*, and *Bailey's Cafe*.

ELIZABETH NUNEZ is the author of four novels, including *Discretion* and *Bruised Hibiscus*, winner of an American Book Award. She lives in Amityville, New York. A new novel, *Grace*, will be published in 2003.

GWENDOLYN M. PARKER is the author of *The Passing* and *These Same Long Bones*. She lives in Connecticut.

ALEXS D. PATE's work has appeared in the Washington *Post, Utne Reader*, and *Artpaper*. He is the author of the novels *West of Rehobeth, The Multicultiboho Sideshow, Sideshow, Losing Absalom*, and *Finding Makeba*.

AUDREY PETTY teaches at Knox College in Galesburg, Illinois, where she is completing her first novel. Her work has appeared in *Callaloo, Painted Bride Quarterly,* and *Crab Orchard Review.*

CONNIE PORTER is the author of *Imani All Mine.* She has taught English and creative writing at Emerson College in Massachusetts and at Southern Illinois University at Carbondale. Porter's *Addy* books for young readers have sold more than three million copies. Named a regional winner in *Granta's* Best Young American Novelists contest for her first novel, *All-Bright Court,* she lives in Virginia.

SCOTT POULSON BRYANT was one of the founding editors of the hip-hop magazine *Vibe.* His writing has appeared in *Rolling Stone,* the *Village Voice,* the New York *Times, The Source, Essence,* and *Spin* magazine. He divides his time between New York and Miami.

NANCY RAWLES is a novelist and playwright who grew up in Los Angeles and began her career as a professional writer in Chicago. Her first novel, *Love Like Gumbo,* was awarded the 1998 American Book Award and Washington State's Governor's Writers Award, and her plays have been produced in Chicago, San Francisco, Minneapolis, St. Louis, Los Angeles, and Seattle. She lives and teaches creative writing in Seattle. Her next novel, *Crawfish Dreams,* will be published in 2003.

JEWELL PARKER RHODES is the author of the novels *Voodoo Dreams* and *Magic City* and has received a National Endowment for the Arts award in fiction and a Yaddo Creative Writing Residency. Rhodes is also a professor of creative writing and American literature at Arizona State University. She lives in Scottsdale, Arizona. She is also the author of *The African American Guide to Nonfiction* and *Free Within Ourselves: Fiction Lessons for Black Authors.*

NELLY ROSARIO is the author of *Song of the Water Saints.* She earned a bachelor's degree in engineering from MIT and an MFA in fiction from Columbia University. She has received numerous awards, including a 1999 Barbara Deming Memorial Fund Fellowship, the Bronx Writers' Center Van Lier Literary Fellowship for 1999–2000, two National Arts Club Writing Fellowships, the 1997 Hurston/Wright Award in Fiction, and most recently she has been chosen as a "Writer on the Verge" by the *Village Voice Literary Supplement* for 2001. Rosario is published in the anthology *Becoming American* (Hyperion, 2000). She now lives in Brooklyn, New York, with her daughter Olivia.

DANZY SENNA is the author of *Caucasia*. She holds an MFA in creative writing from the University of California, Irvine, where she received several creative writing awards. She lives in New York City.

GENARO KY LY SMITH of Lake Charles, Louisiana, won the ninth annual Hurston/Wright Award for his novel excerpt *Land South of the Clouds*. Smith is a student at McNeese State University.

DAWN TURNER TRICE is the author of *Only Twice I've Wished for Heaven* and *An Eighth of August*. She writes for the Chicago *Tribune* and NPR's "Morning Edition." She lives outside Chicago with her husband.

VALERIE WILSON WESLEY is the author of the nationally bestselling Tamara Hayle mystery series, which includes *When Death Comes Stealing, Devil's Gonna Get Him, Where Evil Sleeps, No Hiding Place,* and *Easier to Kill*. Her mysteries are also published in Germany, France, Poland, and the UK. Her fiction and nonfiction have appeared in *Essence, Ms.*, the New York *Times*, and numerous other publications. She was the recipient of the 2000 Black Caucus of the American Library Association Literary Award for *Ain't Nobody's Business If I Do*. Ms. Wesley has two daughters and is married to noted screenwriter and playwright Richard Wesley.

JOHN EDGAR WIDEMAN is the author of a number of books including *Brothers and Keepers, Philadelphia Fire, Sent for You Yesterday, Hoop Roots Fever,* and *The Hiding Place*. His work has been widely anthologized.

CRYSTAL WILKINSON is the 2002 recipient of the Chaffin Award for Appalachian Literature and a member of a Lexington-based writing collective, The Affrilachian Poets. She has presented workshops and readings throughout the country, including the Sixth International Conference on the Short Story in English at the University of Iowa and the African American Women Writers Conference at the University of the District of Columbia. She is the author of two books, *Blackberries, Blackberries* (July 2000), and *Water Street* (September 2002), both published by Toby Press. Wilkinson is currently Writer in Residence at Eastern Kentucky University.

DAVID WRIGHT is the author of *Fire on the Beach: Recovering the Lost Story of Richard Etheridge and the Pea Island Life Savers*. His fiction has appeared in *Sixty-Four, Southern Review, Painted Bride Quarterly,* and *African American Review*. He has published essays on Malcolm X and Martin Luther King, Ernest Hemingway, James Baldwin, and the teaching of literacy. His television feature, *The Pea Island Story*, won a Salute to Excellence

First Prize from the National Association of Black Journalists. He has received an NEH Fellowship, a Paul Cuffe Fellowship, and the Zora Neale Hurston/Richard Wright Award.

SHAY YOUNGBLOOD is the Georgia-born author of the novels *Black Girl in Paris* and *Soul Kiss* and a collection of short fiction, *The Big Mama Stories.* Her plays, *Amazing Grace, Shakin' the Mess Outta Misery,* and *Talking Bones* (Dramatic Publishing Company), have been widely produced. Her other plays include *Black Power Barbie* and *Communism Killed My Dog.* An Edward Albee honoree, and the recipient of numerous grants and awards, including a Pushcart Prize for fiction, a Lorraine Hansberry Playwriting Award, several NAACP Theater Awards, and an Astraea Writers' Award for fiction, Ms. Youngblood graduated from Clark-Atlanta University and received her MFA in Creative Writing from Brown University. She has worked as a Peace Corps volunteer in the eastern Caribbean, as an au pair, artist's model, and poet's helper in Paris, and as a creative writing instructor in a Rhode Island women's prison. She is a member of the Writers' Guild of America and the Dramatists' and Authors' Guild. She lives in New York City.

Credits

Grateful acknowledgment is made to the following for permission to reprint the stories in this volume:

"The Dew Breaker," by Edwidge Danticat, reprinted by permission from the author; from *RL's Dream,* by Walter Mosley, copyright © 1995 by Walter Mosley, all rights reserved; "The Boy-Fish" by David Anthony Durham, reprinted by permission from the author; "The Way I See It," from *A Day Late and a Dollar Short,* by Terry McMillan, reprinted by permission from the author; from *Pride,* by Lorene Cary, reprinted by permission from the author; "Mourning Glo," by Lori Bryant-Woolridge, reprinted by permission from the author; from *These Same Long Bones* by Gwendolyn Parker, reprinted by permission from the author; "Your Child Can Be a Model!" by David Haynes, © 2001 David Haynes; from *Song of the Water Saints,* by Nelly Rosario, copyright © 2002 by Nelly Rosario, used by permission of Pantheon Books, a division of Random House, Inc.; "Miss Prissy and the Penitentiary," by Yolanda Joe, reprinted by permission from the author; "Luminous Days," by Mitchell Jackson, reprinted by permission from the author; from *Only Twice I've Wished for Heaven,* by Dawn Turner Trice, reprinted by permission from the author; "Sonny-Boy," from *Pictures of a Dying Man,* by Agymah Kamau, reprinted by permission from the author; from *Water Marked,* by Helen Elaine Lee, reprinted by permission from the author; from *October Suite* by Maxine Clair, copyright © 2001 by Maxine Clair, used by permission of Random House, Inc.; "Like Trees, Walking," by Ravi Howard, reprinted by permission from the author; "Weight," by John Edgar Wideman, reprinted by permission from the author; from *P. G. County,* by Connie Briscoe, reprinted by permission from the author; "My Heavenly Father," by Dana Crum, copyright © 2000 by Dana Crum, "My Heavenly Father" originally appeared in *64 Magazine* and is reprinted here by permission of *64 Magazine* and the author; "Lion's Blood," by Steven Barnes, copyright © 2002 by Steven Barnes; "The Knowing," by Tananarive Due, © 2002 by Tananarive Due; "Luscious," from *Loving Donovan,* by Bernice L. McFadden, reprinted by permission from the author; from *Crawfish Dreams* by Nancy Rawles, reprinted by permission from the author; "Press and Curl," by Tayari Jones, reprinted by permission from the author (this story inspired the novel *Leaving Atlanta,* Warner Books, 2002); "I Don't Know Nothin' 'Bout Birthin' No Babies," from *The River Where Blood Is Born,"* by Sandra Jackson-Opoku, reprinted by permission from the author; "Draggin' the Dog," by Anika Nailah, © 2002 Anika Nailah; "Museum Guide," from *Black Girl in Paris,* by Shay Youngblood, Copyright © 2000 by Shay Youngblood, used by permission of Riverhead Books, a division of Penguin Putnam, Inc., and by permission from the Sandra Dijkstra Literary Agency; "School," from *Miss Black America,* by Veronica Chambers, reprinted by permission from the author; "Ghost Story," from *Slapboxing with Jesus,* by Victor D. LaValle, reprinted by permission from the author; "Clarity," by David Wright, reprinted by permission from the author; "My Mama, Your Mama," from *Imani All Mine,* by Connie Porter, reprinted by permission from the author; from *Rails Under My Back,* by Jeffery Renard Allen, reprinted by permission from the author; "Meeting Frederick," from *Douglas's Women,* published by Pocket Books, a division of Simon & Schuster, 2002, reprinted by permission from the author; "Eva and Isaiah," from *Ain't Nobody's Business If I Do,* by Valerie Wilson Wesley, published by Avon/HarperCollins, 1999, reprinted by permission from the author; "An Orange Line Train to Ballston," by Edward P. Jones, reprinted by permission from the author; "Lucielia Louise Turner," from *The Women of Brewster Place,* by Gloria Naylor, reprinted by permission from the author; "Fortune," by R. Erica Doyle, reprinted by permission from the author ("Fortune" first appeared in *Voices Rising: An Anthology of Black Lesbian, Gay, Bisexual, and Transgender Writing*); "Are You Experienced?" by Danzy Senna, reprinted by permission from the author; "Love," by Bertice Berry, reprinted by permission from the author; from *Breathing Room,* by Patricia Elam, Pocket Books 2001 publication, reprinted by permission from the author; "Love," excerpted from *Drop* by Mat Johnson © 2002, reprinted with permission from Bloomsbury Publishing; "Antiquated Desires," by Cris Burks, reprinted by permission from the author; excerpt from the novel *Rest for the Weary* by Arthur Flowers, reprinted by permission of Ellen Levine Literary Agency, Inc., copyright © Arthur Flowers; "Black and Boo," by Michael Kayode, reprinted by permission from the author; "Here," by Audrey Petty, reprinted by permission from the author; "Summer Comes Later," by Robert Fleming, reprinted by permission from the author; "The Bulging Bag," by Unoma N. Azuah, reprinted by permission from the author; from *Sap Rising,* by Christine Lincoln, © 2001 by Christine Lincoln; "Fire: An Origin Tale," by Faith Adiele, reprinted by permission from the author; "Tan Son Nhut Aiport, Ho Chi Minh City, 1997," from *The Land South of the Clouds,* by Genaro Ky Ly Smith, reprinted by permission from the author; "Between Black and White," by Nicole Bailey-Williams, reprinted by permission from the author; "Hincty," from *The*